38. Beta from a simple linear regression

$$\beta = \frac{\left(T \times \sum_{i=1}^{N} X_i Y_i\right) - \left(\sum_{i=1}^{N} Y_i \times \sum_{i=1}^{N} X_i\right)}{\left(T \times \sum_{i=1}^{N} X_i^2\right) - \left(\sum_{i=1}^{N} X_i\right)}$$

39. Alpha from a simple linear regression

$$\alpha = \frac{\sum_{i=1}^{N} Y_i}{T} - \frac{\beta \times \sum_{i=1}^{N} X_i}{T}$$

40. Standard deviation of the random error term from a simple linear regression

$$\sigma_e = \left[\frac{\sum_{i=1}^{N} Y_i^2 - \left(\alpha \times \sum_{i=1}^{N} Y_i\right) - \left(\beta \times \sum_{i=1}^{N} X_i Y_i\right)}{T - 2}\right]^{1/2}$$

41. Standard error of beta from a simple linear regression

$$\sigma_\beta = \frac{\sigma_e}{\left[\sum_{i=1}^{N} X_i^2 - \frac{\left(\sum_{i=1}^{N} X_i\right)^2}{T}\right]^{1/2}}$$

42. Standard error of alpha from a simple linear regression

$$\sigma_\alpha = \frac{\sigma_e}{\left[T - \frac{\left(\sum_{i=1}^{N} X_i\right)^2}{\sum_{i=1}^{N} X_i^2}\right]^{1/2}}$$

43. Correlation coefficient

$$\rho = \frac{\left(T \times \sum_{i=1}^{N} X_i Y_i\right) - \left(\sum_{i=1}^{N} Y_i \times \sum_{i=1}^{N} X_i\right)}{\left\langle\left[\left(T \times \sum_{i=1}^{N} Y_i^2\right) - \left(\sum_{i=1}^{N} Y_i\right)^2\right] \times \left[\left(T \times \sum_{i=1}^{N} X_i^2\right) - \left(\sum_{i=1}^{N} X_i\right)^2\right]\right\rangle^{1/2}}$$

44. Beta of the firm

$$\beta_{firm} = \beta_{debt}\left[\frac{(1-\tau)D}{V_u}\right] + \beta_{equity}\left(\frac{E}{V_u}\right)$$

45. Beta of the firm's equity

$$\beta_{equity} = \beta_{firm} + (\beta_{firm} - \beta_{debt})\left(\frac{D}{E}\right)(1 - \tau)$$

46. Adjusted historical beta

$$\beta_a = a + b\beta_h$$

47. Capitalization-of-income method of valuation

$$V = \sum_{t=1}^{\infty} \frac{C_t}{(1+k)^e}$$

48. Zero-growth DDM

$$V = \frac{D_1}{k}$$

49. Constant-growth DDM

$$V = \frac{D_1}{k - g}$$

50. Multiple-growth DDM

$$V = \left[\sum_{t=1}^{T} \frac{D_t}{(1+k)^t}\right] + \left[\frac{D_{T+1}}{(k-g)(1+k)^T}\right]$$

51. "Normal" price-earnings ratio with constant growth

$$\frac{V}{E_0} = p\left(\frac{1 + r(1-p)}{k - r(1-p)}\right)$$

52. Lintner dividend payout model

$$D_t = ap^\star E_t + (1-a)D_{t-1}$$

53. Annual earnings as a random walk

$$E_t = E_{r-1} + \varepsilon_t$$

54. Quarterly earnings as an autoprogressive process

$$QE_t = QE_{t-4} + a(QE_{t-1} - QE_{t-5}) + b + e_t$$

55. Intrinsic value of puts and calls

$$IV_C = MAX(0, P_S - E)$$
$$IV_P = MAX(0, E - P_S)$$

56. Put call parity

$$P_P + P_S = P_C + \frac{E}{e^{RT}}$$

57. Black-Scholes formula for the fair value of a call option

$$V_C = N(d_1)P_S - \frac{E}{e^{RT}} N(d_2)$$

$$d_1 = \frac{\ln\left(\frac{P_S}{E}\right) + (R + 5\sigma^2)T}{\sigma\sqrt{T}}$$

$$d_2 = \frac{\ln\left(\frac{P_S}{E}\right) + (R - 5\sigma^2)T}{\sigma\sqrt{T}} = d_1 - \sigma\sqrt{T}$$

58. Black-Scholes formula for the fair value of a put option

$$P_P = \left(\frac{E}{e^{RT}}\right)N(-d_2) - P_S N(-d_1)$$

59. Fair value of a futures contract

$$P_f = P_S + I - B + C$$

60. Fair value of an index futures contract

$$P_f = P_S + RP_S - yP_S$$

61. Investment company's net asset value

$$NAV_r = \frac{MVA_t - LIAB_t}{NSO_t}$$

62. Return on an investment company's shares

$$r_t = \frac{(NAV_t - NAV_{t-1}) + I_t + G_t}{NAV_{t-1}}$$

63. Risk tolerance (as implied by a choice of a portfolio)

$$\tau = \frac{2(r_C - r_f)\sigma_S^2}{(r_S - r_f)^2}$$

64. Certainty equivalent return

$$u_i = r_p - \left(\frac{1}{\tau}\right)\sigma_p^2$$

65. Ex post alpha

$$\alpha_p = ar_p - ar_{bp}$$

66. Ex post alpha based on the CAPM

$$\alpha_p = ar_p - [ar_f + (ar_M - ar_f)\beta_p]$$

67. Ex post characteristic line

$$r_p - r_f = \alpha_p + \beta_p(r_M - r_f)$$

68. Reward-to-volatility ratio (Treynor ratio)

$$RVOL_p = \frac{ar_p - ar_f}{\beta_p}$$

69. Sharpe ratio

$$SR_p = \frac{ar_p - ar_f}{\sigma_p}$$

70. M²

$$M_p^2 = ar_f + \left(\frac{ar_p - ar_f}{\sigma_p}\right)\sigma_M$$

71. Ex post characteristic curve

$$r_p - r_f = a + b(r_M - r_f) + c[(r_M - r_f)^2]$$

72. Ex post characteristic lines

$$r_p - r_f = a + b(r_M - r_f) + c[D(r_M - r_f)]$$
where: $D = 0$ if $r_M > r_f$
$$D = -1 \text{ if } r_M < r_f$$

73. Return on a foreign investment

$$r_F = r_d + r_c + r_d r_c$$

74. Standard deviation of a foreign investment

$$\sigma_F = (\sigma_d^2 + \sigma_c^2 + 2\rho_{dc}\sigma_d\sigma_c)^{1/2}$$

Take the Canadian Investment Challenge

sponsored by

GREEN LINE
CANADA'S DISCOUNT BROKER

University & College Division

- Manage a $500,000 simulated portfolio in real-time
- Win Cash Prizes
- 20%-25% Discount when you register with your access code
- Experience Bay Street.....First Hand

Imagine being given half a million dollars to experience the world of investing while assuming absolutely no risk. Now consider the valuable experience you'll gain from buying and selling and purchasing on margin - all at current market prices. Experience the excitement of Bay Street in the Green Line Investment Challenge, the nation's most realistic stock market simulation. Form a team, or do it individually.

Playing the Green Line Investment Challenge is easy. We'll give you all the resources you'll need to make your experience a hit. By the end of the Green Line Challenge you'll be able to walk, talk and act like you work on Bay Street. Who knows? You may even win your share of the thousands of dollars in prizes and even get your picture in a national newspaper. This semester don't just read about it – experience it.

FREE Trial offer for Professors:

The Green Line Investment Challenge provides all the resources professors need to easily and effectively implement the program into their classrooms:

- Free Professor Portfolio
- Classroom Reports (including ROI, # of trades, types of trades, etc.)
- Ability to view students' accounts
- Toll-Free Professor Support Line
- Professor Chat Room

For More Information:

Challenges are offered each semester. For information, please call The Investment Challenge at **1-800-487-3862** or visit the website at **<www.ichallenge.net/phcanada>**

Your Discount Student Access Code is: | EE6E-S8M-8A0 | This access code is good for one time use only! Register with this Serial Number and save 20%-25%. Register online at **<www.ichallenge.net/phcanada>** or call **1-800-487-3862.**

How Does It Work?

The Green Line Challenge mimics the daily operations of a real brokerage firm. With a $500,000 fictional brokerage account, you get to experience the markets just like the professionals. Implement your best investment strategy by buying and selling equities and options listed on all the major exchanges (TSE, ME, VSE, ASE, NYSE, NASDAQ, AMEX, CBOE, PSE, and PHLX). In addition, you can try your hand at purchasing on margin and short selling. The Challenge is so realistic, it even incorporates commission schedules, dividends and stock splits. Trades can be placed online, via the Green Line Investment Challenge Website at <www.ichallenge.net/phcanada>, or by fax, answering machine or through our live brokers using the toll-free number 1-800-487-3862. For maximum authenticity, every trade is placed using real-time prices (i.e. no delay).

If Investing Intimidates You...Don't Worry.

The Green Line Investment Challenge's staff of brokers are there to answer all your questions by phone or e-mail. They can guide you through the basics of buying a stock to even the most sophisticated option trades. Whatever your needs or questions, our staff is there to help.

The Right Account For You

WebTrader Account

- Exclusive Internet trading
- Online Investment Manual
- Online Newsletters
- Online stock research info
- Full e-mail support

TradersEdge Account

- All WebTrader features plus:
- Access to live brokers
- Biweekly mailed newsletters
- Biweekly mailed account statements

National Competition

Compete against university and college students from across the country for a chance to win thousands of dollars in prizes.

- Prizes for top performers
- Weekly prizes
- Recognition in a national newspaper
- Special prizes and rankings for Investment Clubs

Your Résumé's Weapon

The Green Line Investment Challenge provides the kind of hands-on experience that looks great on a résumé and makes an excellent topic of conversation in interviews. Whether you're thinking of a career in the financial services industry or just wanting to learn more about the stock market, participating in the Green Line Investment Challenge will be a valuable asset.

<www.ichallenge.net/phcanada>

Register Today

Call 1-800-487-3862, or register online at <www.ichallenge.net/phcanada>

- **Save 25% off WebTrade Account**
- **Save 20% off TradersEdge Account**

GREEN LINE
CANADA'S DISCOUNT BROKER

TD

INVESTMENTS

THIRD CANADIAN EDITION

William F. Sharpe
Stanford University

Gordon J. Alexander
University of Minnesota

Jeffery V. Bailey
Dayton Hudson Corporation

David J. Fowler
York University

Dale L. Domian
University of Saskatchewan

PRENTICE HALL CANADA
SCARBOROUGH, ONTARIO

Canadian Cataloguing in Publication Data

Main entry under title:

Investments
3rd Canadian ed.
Includes index.

ISBN 0-13-011445-6

1. Investments - Canada. 2. Investment analysis. I. Sharpe, William F.

HG4521.S43 2000   332.6'0971   C99-930529-8

© 2000, 1997, 1993 Prentice-Hall Canada Inc., Scarborough, Ontario
Pearson Education

Prentice-Hall, Inc., Upper Saddle River, New Jersey
Prentice-Hall International (UK) Limited, London
Prentice-Hall of Australia, Pty. Limited, Sydney
Prentice-Hall Hispanoamericana, S.A., Mexico City
Prentice-Hall of India Private Limited, New Delhi
Prentice-Hall of Japan, Inc., Tokyo
Simon & Schuster Southeast Asia Private Limited, Singapore
Editora Prentice-Hall do Brasil, Ltda., Rio de Janeiro

ISBN 0-13-011445-6

Vice President and Editorial Director: Patrick Ferrier
Senior Acquisitions Editor: Dave Ward
Marketing Manager: Don Thompson
Copy Editor: Shirley Corriveau
Senior Developmental Editor: Lesley Mann
Production Editor: Mary Ann McCutcheon
Production Coordinator: Deborah Starks
Cover Design: Sarah Battersby
Cover Image: Wataru Yanagida/photonica
Page Layout: Pronk&Associates

Original U.S. Edition published by Prentice Hall, Inc.
Upper Saddle River, New Jersey 07458
Copyright © 1999, 1995

1 2 3 4 5   04 03 02 01 00

Printed and bound in Canada

Visit the Prentice Hall Canada Web site! Send us your comments, browse our catalogues, and more at **www.phcanada.com**. Or reach us through e-mail at **phcinfo_pubcanada@prenhall.com**.

Every reasonable effort has been made to obtain permissions for all articles and data used in this edition. If errors or omissions have occurred, they will be corrected in future editions provided written notification has been received by the publisher.

To Kathy
WFS

To my mother and in memory of my father
GJA

To Stephen and Megan
JVB

To Lesley
DJF

To Susan
DLD

Brief Contents

Contents

Preface to the Third Canadian Edition

Investment management once seemed a simple process. Well-heeled investors would hold portfolios composed, for the most part, of shares and bonds of blue chip industrial companies, as well as government bonds, and bills. The choices available to less well-off investors were much more limited, confined primarily to bank savings accounts and Canada Savings Bonds. If the investment environment can be thought of as an ice cream parlour, then the customers of past decades were offered only chocolate and vanilla.

Mirroring the diversity of modern society, the investment ice cream parlour now makes available a myriad of flavours to the investing public. Investors face a dizzying array of choices. The stocks and bonds of large companies and the debt securities of the Government of Canada remain the predominant favourites. However, to mention only a few additional choices, investors can now own the shares of small companies, the shares and bonds of companies headquartered from London to Auckland, high-yield bonds, mortgage-backed securities, floating rate notes, swaps, puts, calls, and futures contracts. The list is seemingly endless, and it continues to grow. Furthermore, the ability to purchase these securities has become both less expensive and more convenient with the advent of advanced communications and computer networks, along with the proliferating market for mutual funds that has developed to serve large and small investors alike.

The difficulty of writing a textbook on investing has increased as the investment environment has become more complex. Virtually all types of securities, be they traditional or of recent origin, merit at least some discussion. The challenge to us as textbook writers, therefore, is daunting. We must enumerate and describe the various securities and markets in a clear and concise manner that accurately blends theory and practice. However, with the rapid evolution that the investment industry is undergoing, we must also present a discussion of new investment management techniques. Preventing the textbook from reaching encyclopedic proportions thus becomes a difficult project in itself.

The subject matter for this edition of *Investments* has evolved considerably since 1978 when the first US edition was published. For example, since 1992 when the first Canadian edition appeared, international investing has expanded rapidly, securities such as swaps and mortgage derivatives have become increasingly popular, and investors have placed much more emphasis on investment styles. Our task has been to keep *Investments* fresh and stimulating and to continue to offer students and instructors the most thorough survey of the investment environment available. We believe that we have accomplished these objectives and hope that you agree.

We designed *Investments*, Third Canadian Edition for advanced undergraduate and graduate students. In doing so, we assumed that these students have been exposed to basic economics, accounting, statistics, and algebra. Furthermore, it is our belief that serious students of investments should receive a balanced presentation of theoretical and practical information without being burdened by excessive detail. A textbook that focuses solely on institutional features leaves students unable to appreciate the subtle and important issues faced by investment professionals.

In preparing the Third Canadian Edition we have followed the same guiding principles that were used in adapting the earlier editions—descriptions of US institutional arrangements are replaced by relevant Canadian material and the results of US empirical studies are augmented by the corresponding Canadian results where these are available.

As any textbook author will attest, a previous work can always be improved—even one that has been in existence as long as this one. Over the years we have received many helpful suggestions from instructors and reviewers regarding ways in which we can make *Investments* better. In each new edition we have tried to enhance the book's breadth and presentation style. In this edition, we have made numerous improvements from the previous edition. Of particular note are:

- **Updated coverage of material.** Where appropriate, we have updated the text to keep students abreast of the latest developments in investments. More specifically, we have revised tables and graphs and added discussions in order to incorporate current information and recent academic research.
- **Changes affecting stock exchanges in Canada and worldwide.** The advent of computerized trading systems has changed the way in which securities are traded and eliminated the need for a traditional trading floor. The effect of these changes on Canadian exchanges, particularly the Toronto Stock Exchange, is examined.
- **A new chapter on efficient markets.** We have added an entire chapter devoted to discussing the notion of market efficiency that underlies much of current investment thinking.
- **Statistical concepts appendix.** We have added to Chapter 6 an appendix that explains certain basic statistical concepts that are fundamental to understanding the quantitative side of investing.
- **A description of Canadian mutual fund evaluation services.** The spectacular growth of the mutual fund industry has brought with it a demand, by investors, for easily understood information that will allow them to evaluate the performance of mutual funds. The information provided by two companies that have responded to this demand is described.
- **Coverage of financial analysis expanded and revised.** The discussion of financial analysis has been notably expanded and now includes a real-life corporate example.
- **New "Institutional Issues."** Students typically want to know how the concepts presented in the text are applied in the real world. In each chapter we have updated and in some cases added more of the Institutional Issues features that offer discussions concerning issues that face large institutional investors, such as pension funds and mutual funds.
- **Additional end-of-chapter problems and CFA examination questions.** These have been added to give students a better opportunity to learn the material and prepare for the CFA examinations.
- **Additional annotated references.** For those students who are interested in further study of subjects presented in the text, we have updated our extensive set of references organized by topic at the end of each chapter.

An expanded list of references of particular relevance to Canadian students is included.

We are particularly proud of the "Institutional Issues" features in each chapter. Many are specifically written for *Investments*; they are designed to give students a sense of how various investment issues and techniques are applied by practitioners. For example, the Chapter 2 features discuss how institutional investors create market neutral portfolios utilizing short selling and introduce readers to hedge funds. One of the Chapter 23 features considers how pension funds go about structuring groups of money managers to achieve specific investment objectives while one of the Chapter 25 features describes the controversial issue of whether or not to hedge the currency risk of an international portfolio. Furthermore, Ann Guenther Sherman of the Hong Kong University of Science and Technology has written two "Institutional Issues" features that deal with investing in the People's Republic of China, which we view as the ultimate emerging market—particularly now that Hong Kong is part of the PRC. In several chapters, the "Institutional Issues" section includes readings from the financial press covering topics of special interest to Canadian investors. In summary, we believe that the "Institutional Issues" features will provide both interesting reading for the students and a stimulating source of classroom discussion material.

Instructor supplements have been carefully reviewed and revised for the Third Canadian Edition. The supplements package includes:

Instructor's Manual with Solutions: Carefully revised by Dale Domian, Canadian co-author of the text, the IM includes detailed solutions to all end-of-chapter problems plus course outlines designed to accommodate a variety of teaching approaches and course emphases. ISBN 0–13–013220–9

Test Item File: The Test Item File has been updated by Dr. Eben Otuteye of the University of New Brunswick. It includes multiple choice and true/false questions, with correct answers, page references, level of difficulty, and special flagging of CFA examination questions. ISBN 0–13–013232–2

PH Test Manager: Prentice Hall's Windows-based computerized test program offers a comprehensive suite of tools for testing and assessment, allowing instructors to create, print, and distribute tests in print or online. Comprehensive online help files, a guided tour, and complete written documentation are provided. ISBN 0–13–013233–0

The *Canadian Investment Review* has continued to provide a lively forum for the presentation of work by Canadian researchers—academics and practitioners alike—and is as interesting and thought provoking as ever. We hope it continues to prosper.

A number of people have assisted us in the preparation of the Third Canadian Edition. We would like to acknowledge their assistance along with that of those who helped with earlier editions. Our thanks go to our colleagues at the Finance Area of the Schulich School of Business, York University—Elizabeth Maynes, Moshe Milevsky, Eli Prisman, Gordon Roberts, and Chris Robinson; and the Finance Area of the College of Commerce, University of Saskatchewan—Adham Chehab, Said Elfakhani, Moon Lee, Prem Mathew, and George Tannous. We would also like to thank Sebouh Aintablian, Phil Anisman, Bernard Augustin, Andy Aziz, Tim Baikie, Sandra Bell, Rob Bell, Carl Bellé, Pierre Brodeur, Jamie Carlsen, Marcus Dancer, Marc Desrosiers, Cindy Ferguson, Suzanne Firth, John Friedlan, Larry Gould, Roy Hill, Susan Jenah Wolberg, Vijay Jog, John Kaszel, Daniel Kelly, Don Lato, Knut Larsen, Willie Mackenzie, Fionulla Martin, Brett Matthews, Melanie Moore, Micajah Pickett, Teng Qiang, Olga Raudoja, Steve Rive, Wendy Rudd, Dawn Scott, Will Snelgrove, Carl Searle, Mark Taugher, Charles Wakefield, Mary Webb, Shawn Wilcox, Dino Mastroiani, and Patrick McDonagh.

Finally, we thank the following reviewers for their detailed and perceptive comments: Steve Beveridge, University of Alberta;

Alex Faseruk, Memorial University;

Eldon Gardner, University of Lethbridge;

Lew Johnson, Queen's University;

Moon Lee, University of Saskatchewan; and

Corey Wentzell, Vice President-Learning Development, Canadian Securities Institute

We have learned much by writing this book and hope that you will learn much by reading it. Although we have done our best to eliminate errors from the book, experience tells us that perfection is unattainable. Thus we encourage those students and instructors with constructive comments to send them to us at either **domian@commerce.usask.ca** or **edit_phch@prenhall.com**

David J. Fowler
Dale L. Domian
William F. Sharpe
Gordon J. Alexander
Jeffery V. Bailey

For the Third Canadian Edition of *Investments* I have been very grateful for the able collaboration of Dale Domian from the University of Saskatchewan, who will be solely responsible for future editions. As always the task of preparing this edition has been eased by the pleasant relationship with the editorial staff at Prentice Hall (Canada) Inc.

David Fowler

About the Authors

William F. Sharpe

William F. Sharpe is presently the STANCO 25 Professor of Finance at Stanford University, and is also Chairman of the Board of Financial Engines, Incorporated, a firm that provides electronic investment advice for individual retirement savings. He has published articles in a number of professional journals, including *Management Science, Journal of Business, Journal of Finance, Journal of Financial Economics, Journal of Financial and Quantitative Analysis,, Journal of Portfolio Management,* and the *Financial Analysts Journal.* Dr. Sharpe is past president of the American Finance Association, and in 1990 received the Nobel prize in Economic Sciences. He received his Ph.D., M.A., and B.A. in Economics from the University of California, Los Angeles.

Gordon J. Alexander

Gordon J. Alexander is presently Professor of Finance at the University of Minnesota, having recently completed a two-year stint working in the Office of Economic Analysis at the Securities and Exchange Commission. Dr. Alexander has published articles in *Financial Management, Journal of Banking and Finance, Journal of Finance, Journal of Financial Economics, Journal of Financial and Quantitative Analysis,* and *Journal of Portfolio Management..* He received his Ph.D. in Finance, M.A. in Mathematics, and M.B.A. from The University of Michigan, and his B.S. in Business Administration from the State University of New York at Buffalo.

Jeffery V. Bailey

Jeffery V. Bailey is Director of Benefits Finance at Dayton Hudson Corporation. Previously he was a Principal at the pension fund consulting firm of Richards & Tierney, Inc. Before that he was the Assistant Executive Director of the Minnesota State Board of Investment. Mr. Bailey has published articles in the *Financial Analysts Journal* and the *Journal of Portfolio Management..* He has contributed articles to several practitioner handbooks and has co-authored a monograph published by the Research Foundation of the Institute of Chartered Financial Analysts. Mr. Bailey received his B.A. from Oakland University and his M.A. in Economics and his M.B.A. in Finance from the University of Minnesota. He is a Chartered Financial Analyst.

David J. Fowler

David J. Fowler is Associate Professor Emeritus at the Schulich School of Business at York University in Toronto. Dr. Fowler has published two books, *The Drug Industry: A Case Study in Foreign Control* and *Endowed Charitable Foundations in Canada: A Study of Spending and Investment Strategies Under Revenue Canada Regulations,* as well as numerous articles in professional publications such as *Journal of Business Finance and Accounting, Journal of Finance, Journal of Financial Economics,* and *Journal of Financial Research.* Dr. Fowler received his B.Sc (Eng) from the Imperial College of Science & Technology at the University of London, and his M.B.A. and Ph.D. at the University of Toronto.

Dale L. Domian

Dale L. Domian is Professor of Finance in the College of Commerce at the University of Saskatchewan. Dr. Domian has published articles in academic and professional journals including *Financial Management, Financial Review, Financial Services Review, Journal of International Financial Management and Accounting, Journal of Money, Credit, and Banking, Journal of Portfolio Management, Quarterly Review of Economics and finance,* and *Review of Financial Economics.* An avid investor for the past 30 years, he currently owns shares in more than 100 Canadian corporations. Dr. Domian received his B.A. in Economics, Mathematics, and Music from the University of Wisconsin, and his Ph.D. in Finance and Economics at the University of Minnesota.

Introduction

Canadian Pacific
www.cpr.ca

Toronto Stock Exchange
www.tse.com

T his book is about investing in marketable securities. Accordingly, it focuses on the investment environment and process. The **investment environment** encompasses the kinds of marketable securities that exist and where and how they are bought and sold. The **investment process** is concerned with how an investor should proceed in making decisions about marketable securities in which to invest, how extensive the investments should be, and when the investments should be made. Before discussing the investment environment and process in more detail, the term **investment** will be described.

Investment, in its broadest sense, means the sacrifice of current dollars for future dollars. Two different attributes are generally involved: time and risk. The sacrifice takes place in the present and is certain. The reward comes later, if at all, and the magnitude is generally uncertain. In some cases time predominates (for example, government bonds). In other cases risk is the dominant attribute (for example, call options on common shares). In yet others, both time and risk are important (for example, shares of common stock).

A distinction is often made between investment and **savings**. Savings is defined as foregone consumption; investment is restricted to "real" investment of the sort that increases national output in the future. Although this definition is useful in other contexts, it is not especially helpful here. The distinction between real and financial investments, however, is important.

Real investments generally involve some kind of tangible asset, such as land, machinery, or factories. **Financial investments** involve contracts written on pieces of paper, such as shares and bonds. The financing of an apartment house provides a good example. Apartments are sufficiently tangible ("bricks and mortar") to be considered real investments. Where are the resources required to pay for the land and the construction of the apartments obtained? Some may come from direct investment—for example, a wealthy doctor who wants to build an apartment house may use some of her money to finance the project. The rest of the resources may be provided by a mortgage. In essence, someone loans the doctor money, with repayment promised in fixed amounts on a specified schedule over many years. In the typical case the "someone" is not a person, but an institution acting as a financial intermediary. Thus, the doctor has made a real investment in the apartment house, and the institution has made a financial investment in the doctor.

As a second example, consider what happens when Canadian Pacific (CP) finds itself in need of money to pay for plant construction. This real investment may be financed by the sale of new common shares in the **primary market** for securities. The common shares themselves represent a financial investment to the purchasers, who may subsequently trade these shares in the **secondary market**—for example, on the Toronto Stock Exchange

Real Investment An investment involving some kind of tangible asset, such as land, equipment, or buildings.

Financial Investments An investment in financial assets.

(TSE). Although transactions in the secondary market do not generate money for CP, the fact that such a market exists makes the common stock more attractive and thus facilitates real investment. Investors would pay less for new common shares of common stock if there were no way to sell them quickly and inexpensively.

These examples have introduced the three main elements of the investment environment—securities (also known as financial investments or financial assets), security markets (also known as financial markets), and **financial intermediaries** (also known as financial institutions). They are discussed in more detail next.

The Investment Environment

▶ Securities

Financial Institution (Financial Intermediary) An organization that issues financial claims against itself and uses the proceeds of the issuance primarily to purchase financial assets issued by corporations, government entities, and other financial intermediaries.

Primary Security Market The market in which securities are sold at the time of their initial issuance.

Secondary Security Market The market in which securities are traded that have been issued at some previous point in time.

When someone borrows money from a pawnbroker, he must leave some item of value as security. Failure to repay the loan (plus interest) means that the pawnbroker can sell the pawned item to recover the amount of the loan (plus interest) and perhaps make a profit. The terms of the agreement are recorded via pawn tickets. When a university student borrows money to buy a car, the lender usually holds formal title to the car until the loan is repaid. In the event of default, the lender can repossess the car and attempt to sell it to recover his costs. In this case the official certificate of title, issued by the province, serves as the security for the loan. When someone borrows money for a vacation, she may simply sign a piece of paper promising repayment with interest. The loan is unsecured in the sense that there is no collateral, meaning no specific asset has been promised to the lender in the event of default. In such a situation, the lender would have to take the borrower to court to try to recover the amount of the loan. Only a piece of paper, called a promissory note, stands as evidence of such a loan.

When a firm borrows money, it may or may not offer collateral. For example, some loans may be secured (backed) by specific assets (buildings, equipment, and so on). Such loans are registered as mortgage bonds, which indicate the terms of repayment and the particular assets pledged to the lender in the event of default. However, it is much more common for a corporation simply to pledge all its assets, perhaps with some provision for the manner in which the division will take place in the event of default. Such a promise is known as a debenture bond.

Finally, a firm may promise a right to share in the firm's profits in return for an investor's funds. Nothing is pledged, and no irrevocable promises are made. The firm simply pays whatever its directors deem reasonable from time to time. However, to protect against serious malfeasance, the investor is given the right to participate in the determination of who will be members of the board of directors. Her property right is represented by a share of common stock, which can be sold to someone else who will then be able to exercise that right. The holder of common shares is said to be an *owner* of the corporation and can, in theory, exercise control over its operation through the board of directors.

In general, only a piece of paper represents the investor's rights to certain prospects or property and the conditions under which she may exercise those rights. This piece of paper, serving as evidence of property rights, is called a *security.* A security, with all its rights and conditions, may be transferred to another investor. Thus, everything from a pawn ticket to a share of CP common stock is a security. Hereafter the term **security** will be used to refer to *a legal representation of the right to receive prospective future benefits under stated conditions.* One of the objectives of security analysis is to identify mispriced securities by determining their prospective future benefits, the conditions under which they will be received, and the likelihood of their occurring.

Security A legal representation of the right to receive prospective future benefits under stated conditions.

By and large the focus here is on securities that may be easily and efficiently transferred from one owner to another. Thus, the concern is with common shares and bonds rather than with pawn tickets, although much of the material in this book applies to all three types of instruments.

Figure 1.1 and Table 1.1 show the year-by-year results obtained from investing in four types of securities over the 48-year period from 1950 through 1997. In each case the percentage change in a hypothetical investor's wealth from the beginning to the end of the year is shown. This amount, known as the **rate of return** (or simply the *return*), is calculated as follows:

$$\text{Return} = \frac{\text{End-of-period wealth} - \text{Beginning-of-period wealth}}{\text{Beginning-of-period wealth}} \tag{1.1}$$

In calculating the return on a security, it is assumed that the investor purchases one unit (for example, one bond or one share of common stock) of the security at the beginning of the period. The cost of this investment is the amount entered in the denominator of equation (1.1). The value in the numerator is the answer to a simple question—how much better (or worse) off is the investor at the end of the period?

For example, assume that Widget Corporation's common stock was selling for $40 per share at the beginning of the year and for $45 at the end of the year and paid dividends of $3 per share during the year. The return on Widget for the year would then be calculated as [($45 + $3) − $40]/$40 = .20, or 20%.[1]

Treasury Bills

The first type of security listed in Figure 1.1 involves loaning money on a short-term basis (three months to one year) to the Canadian Government. Such a loan carries little (if any) risk that payment will not be made as promised. Moreover, while the rate of return varies from period to period, at the beginning of any single period it is known with certainty. The return on these investments, known as Treasury bills, ranged from a high of 19.09% per year (in 1981) to a low of 0.51% per year (in 1950), with an average value of 6.50% during the entire 48-year period.

Long-Term Bonds

The second and third types of securities shown in Figure 1.1 are bonds and also involve loaning money. Each type of bond represents a long-term commitment on the part of the issuer (that is, the borrower) to the investor (that is, the lender). This commitment is to make cash payments each year (the coupon payment) up to some point in time (the maturity date), when a single final cash payment (the principal) will also be made. The prices at which these bonds can be bought and sold prior to maturity vary from time to time. Thus, while coupon payments are easily predicted, the end-of-period selling price of the security before maturity is uncertain at the beginning of the period, thereby making the return difficult to predict in advance.

The second type of security (Government of Canada bonds, also known as long Canada bonds) involves loans with a maturity of 10 years or more to the Canadian Government. The third type of security (industrial bonds, otherwise known as corporate bonds), involves long-term loans to Canadian industrial corporations. This data series is based on a small sample of bonds that are not controlled as to maturity.

Finance Canada
www.fin.gc.ca

---

[1]Generally, any cash received during the period is treated as if it were received at the end of the period. However, this assumption typically results in an understatement of the actual return. For example, if the dividends on Widget were received at midyear, the investor could have put them in a bank savings account and earned, for example, 4% interest for the rest of the year. This interest then would have amounted to $.04 \times \$3.00 = \$.12$, resulting in the annual return being equal to [($45 + $3 + $.12) − $40]/$40 = .203, or 20.3%.

Figure 1.1 Annual returns, 1950–1997.

(a) Canadian Treasury Bill Returns

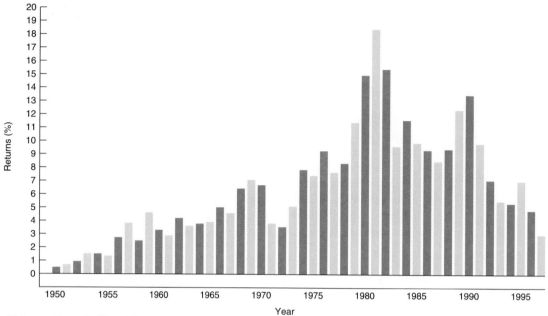

(b) Long Canada Bond Returns

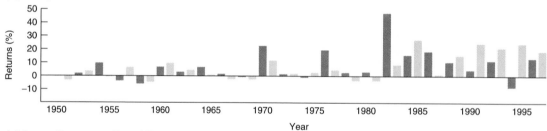

(c) Long Corporate Bond Returns

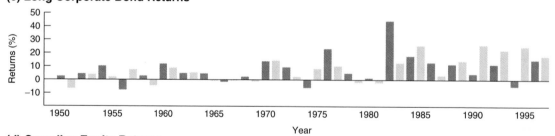

(d) Canadian Equity Returns

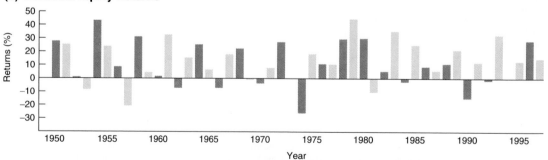

Table 1.1 Annual Returns: Equities, Bonds, Treasury Bills and Changes in the Consumer Price Index (CPI), 1950–1997.

			Total Returns		
Year	Treasury Bills	Long Canada Bonds	Long Corporate Bonds	Equities	CPI
1950	0.51	−0.11	2.68	27.91	6.10
1951	0.71	−3.01	−6.44	25.50	10.73
1952	0.95	2.05	4.49	1.17	−1.73
1953	1.54	3.76	3.99	−8.28	0.00
1954	1.53	9.78	10.34	43.61	0.35
1955	1.36	−0.43	2.18	24.11	0.35
1956	2.75	−3.54	−7.58	8.81	3.15
1957	3.83	6.60	7.58	−20.58	2.03
1958	2.51	−5.82	2.99	31.25	2.66
1959	4.62	−4.44	−4.28	4.59	1.29
1960	3.31	6.88	11.94	1.78	1.28
1961	2.89	9.75	8.91	32.75	0.32
1962	4.22	3.16	4.95	−7.09	1.57
1963	3.63	4.59	5.38	15.60	1.86
1964	3.79	6.74	4.71	25.43	1.82
1965	3.92	1.04	−0.58	6.68	2.98
1966	5.03	1.72	−1.53	−7.07	3.48
1967	4.59	−2.27	−0.34	18.09	4.20
1968	6.44	−0.62	2.43	22.45	4.03
1969	7.09	−2.36	−1.04	−0.81	4.65
1970	6.70	22.70	13.97	−3.57	1.48
1971	3.81	11.79	14.48	8.01	4.87
1972	3.55	1.59	9.51	27.38	5.10
1973	5.11	1.96	2.40	0.27	9.27
1974	7.85	−0.98	−5.86	−25.93	12.32
1975	7.41	2.74	8.35	18.48	9.53
1976	9.27	19.65	23.32	11.02	5.91
1977	7.66	4.68	10.34	10.76	9.46
1978	8.34	2.76	5.00	29.66	8.36
1979	11.41	−3.30	−1.77	44.77	9.80
1980	14.97	3.23	1.41	30.13	11.19
1981	18.41	−3.26	−1.96	−10.25	12.10
1982	15.42	47.39	44.33	5.54	9.26
1983	9.62	8.58	12.75	35.49	4.55
1984	11.59	15.85	17.87	−2.39	3.76
1985	9.88	27.24	25.74	25.07	4.35

Table 1.1   (Continued)

Total Returns

Year	Treasury Bills	Long Canada Bonds	Long Corporate Bonds	Equities	CPI
1986	9.33	18.60	13.05	8.95	4.17
1987	8.48	1.26	3.37	5.88	4.15
1988	9.41	10.65	11.77	11.08	3.96
1989	12.36	15.39	14.13	21.37	5.17
1990	13.48	4.64	4.53	−14.80	5.00
1991	9.83	24.52	26.16	12.02	3.78
1992	7.08	11.58	11.61	−1.43	2.14
1993	5.51	21.12	22.25	32.55	1.70
1994	5.35	−8.14	−4.79	−0.18	0.23
1995	7.01	24.36	24.86	12.92	1.90
1996	4.82	13.34	14.93	28.35	2.24
1997	3.00	18.69	17.71	14.98	0.73
Mean	6.50	7.34	8.13	12.13	4.33
Std. Dev.	4.13	10.72	10.22	16.36	3.52

SOURCE: Reprinted, with permission, from James E. Hatch and Robert W. White, *Canadian Stocks, Bonds, Bills, and Inflation: 1950–1987*, Copyright 1988, The Research Foundation of The Institute of Chartered Financial Analysts, Charlottesville, VA.; Melanie Moore, *ScotiaMcLeod's Handbook of Canadian Debt Market Indices: 1947–1997* (Toronto: ScotiaMcLeod Inc., 1998).

These two kinds of bonds had their highest annual return in 1982, reaching 47.39% for government bonds and 44.33% for industrial bonds. The lowest annual return for each, however, was reached in different years. For government bonds, the lowest return occurred in 1958 (−5.82%) whereas for industrial bonds the minimum was reached in 1956 (−7.58%). Thus, whereas the second and third types of securities have considerable variability, on average they provide somewhat larger returns than Treasury bills.

Common Shares

The fourth and final type of security is common shares, which represent a commitment on the part of a corporation to pay periodically whatever its board of directors deems appropriate as a cash dividend. Although the amount of cash dividends to be paid in a year is subject to some uncertainty, it is relatively predictable. However, the amount for which a share can be bought or sold varies considerably, making the annual return highly unpredictable. Figure 1.1 shows the return from a portfolio of shares that approximately replicates the TSE 300 Composite Index from 1950 to 1997. Returns ranged from an exciting 44.77% in 1979 to a depressing −25.93% in 1974 and averaged 12.13% per year over the entire period. Such investments can provide substantial returns, which are larger, on average, than the returns provided by corporate bonds. However, these returns also have substantial variability, being more volatile than those of either type of long-term bond.

Risk, Return, and Diversification

Table 1.1 provides year-by-year returns for the four types of securities shown in Figure 1.1. The table also includes the annual percentage change in the Consumer Price Index (CPI) as an indicator of changes in the cost of living. Average annual returns are shown at the bottom of the table. Below these values are the values of the standard deviations of annual returns, which serve as measures of the variability of the returns on the respective securities.[2] Table 1.2 compares the rates of return on comparable securities in Canada and the US over the period 1950 to 1996. This table shows that average rates of return and standard deviations of returns in the two countries were quite similar, which should not be surprising given the degree to which Canada's economy is related to that of the US. Table 1.3 provides average annual returns and standard deviations for securities from the United States, Japan, Germany, and the United Kingdom during the period from 1970 to 1996.

The historical record revealed in Figure 1.1, Table 1.1, Table 1.2, and Table 1.3 illustrates a general principle: *When sensible investment strategies are compared with one another, risk and return tend to go together.* That is, securities that have higher average returns tend to have greater amounts of risk.

It is important to note that historical variability is not necessarily an indication of prospective risk. The former deals with the record over some past period; the latter has to do with uncertainty about the future. The pattern of returns on Treasury bills provides one example. Although the values have varied from period to period, in any given period the amount to be earned is known in advance and is thus riskless. On the other hand, the annual return on a common share is very difficult to predict. For such an investment, past variability may provide a fairly good measure of the uncertainty surrounding the future return.[3]

Table 1.2	A Comparison of Average Returns on Stocks, Bonds, Treasury Bills, and Changes in the CPI in Canada and the US, 1950–1996.			
	Canada		US	
	Return	Standard Deviation	Return	Standard Deviation
Treasury bills	6.57%	4.15%	5.20%	3.03%
Long-term government bonds	7.09	10.70	6.03	10.81
Long corporate bonds	7.93	10.23	6.49	10.34
Equities	12.06	16.53	14.02	16.76
Changes in the CPI	4.40	3.52	4.18	3.16

SOURCE: Derived from Table 1.1 above and Table 1.1 in W. F. Sharpe, G. J. Alexander, and J.V. Bailey, *Investments* (Englewood Cliffs, NJ: Prentice Hall, Inc., 1998).

To see how difficult it is to predict common share returns, cover the portion on Table 1.1 from 1965 on and then try to guess the return in 1965. Having done this, uncover the value for 1965 and try to guess the return for 1966. Proceed in this manner a year at a time, keeping track of your overall predictive accuracy. Unless you are very clever or very lucky, you will conclude that the past pattern of share returns provides little help in predicting next year's return. It will be seen that this apparent randomness in security returns is a characteristic of an **efficient market**—that is, a market where security prices reflect information immediately.

Is one of these four types of securities obviously the best? No. To oversimplify, the right security or combination of securities depends on the investor's situation and preferences for returns relative to his distaste for risk. There may be "right" or "wrong" securities for a particular person or purpose. But it would be surprising, however, to find a security that is clearly wrong for everyone and every purpose. Such situations are simply not present in an

Efficient Market A market for securities in which every security's price equals its investment value at all times, implying that a set of information is fully and immediately reflected in market prices.

---

[2]Standard deviation was calculated as being equal to the square root of $\sum_{t=1}^{48}(r_t - \bar{r})^2/47$, where r_t is the return for year t ($t = 1$ corresponds to 1950, $t = 2$ to 1951, and so on) and $\bar{r}$ is the average return over the 48-year period. A larger standard deviation means a greater amount of dispersion in the 48 returns and, as discussed in Chapter 6, indicates more risk.

[3]Studies have found that (1) shares have not become more volatile recently and that (2) shares have tended to be more volatile during recessions (particularly during the Great Depression of 1929 to 1939).

efficient market. Figure 1.2 illustrates the tradeoffs involved between risk and return. Note that the types of securities with higher historical returns also have had higher levels of risks, suggesting that no type of security dominates any other by having both higher return and lower risk. Also shown in the figure under "Portfolio" is the risk-return performance of a portfolio that at the beginning of each year was reconfigured to have one-half of its funds invested in corporate bonds and the other half in common shares. Careful examination reveals that the portfolio's average return equals one-half of the average return of corporate bonds and one-half the average returns of common shares. However, the risk of the portfolio is less than half the risk of corporate bonds plus half the risk of common shares. This illustrates a fundamental principle of diversification: when securities are combined into a portfolio, the resulting portfolio will have a lower level of risk than a simple average of the risks of the securities. Intuitively, this is because when some securities are doing poorly, others are doing well, and vice-versa, thereby lowering the portfolio's volatility.

Table 1.3	Summary Statistics for US, Japanese, German, and UK Securities, 1970–1996.							
	Average Return*				Standard Deviation			
	US	Japan	Germany	UK	US	Japan	Germany	UK
Short-term interest rates	6.93%	5.95%	6.35%	10.69%	2.71%	3.21%	2.39%	3.10%
Government bonds	9.88	7.34	8.05	11.96	12.18	5.15	5.23	12.82
Common stocks	13.47	13.32	10.59	18.45	16.14	29.25	25.62	33.02
Inflation	5.52	4.48	3.65	8.43	3.26	5.13	2.05	5.73

*Foreign returns are calculated in local currencies. Foreign stock returns include dividend income adjusted for the tax rate applicable to US investors. Government bonds include maturities greater than one year.

SOURCE: US financial market data adapted from *Stocks, Bonds, Bills, and Inflation 1997 Yearbook* (Chicago: Ibbotson Associates, 1997). All rights reserved. Foreign financial market data provided by Brinson Partners, Morgan Stanley Capital International, International Financial Statistics, and DRI/McGraw-Hill.

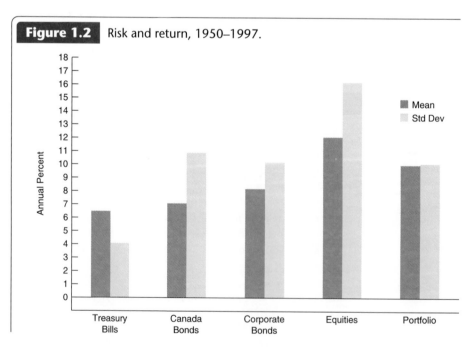

Figure 1.2 Risk and return, 1950–1997.

Security Markets

Security Market A mechanism designed to facilitate the exchange of financial assets by bringing buyers and sellers of securities together.

Security markets exist in order to bring together buyers and sellers of securities, meaning they are mechanisms that exist in order to facilitate the exchange of financial assets. There are many ways in which they can be categorized. One way has already been mentioned—primary and secondary financial markets. Here the key distinction was whether or not the securities were being offered for sale by the issuer. Interestingly, the primary market itself can be subdivided into seasoned and unseasoned new issues. A seasoned new issue refers to the offering of an additional amount of an already existing security, whereas an unseasoned new issue involves the initial offering of a security to the public. Unseasoned new issues are often referred to as *initial public offerings,* or *ipo's.*

Money Markets Financial markets in which financial assets with a term-to-maturity of typically one year or less are traded.

Another way of distinguishing security markets involves the life span of financial assets. **Money markets** typically involve financial assets that have a maturity of one year or less, whereas **capital markets** typically involve financial assets that have a maturity greater than one year. Thus, Treasury bills are traded in a money market, and long-term bonds are traded in a capital market.

Capital Markets Financial markets in which financial assets with a term-to-maturity of typically more than one year are traded.

Financial Intermediaries

Financial intermediaries, also known as financial institutions, are organizations that issue financial claims against themselves (meaning that they sell financial assets representing claims on themselves in return for cash) and use the proceeds from these issues to purchase primarily the financial assets of others. Financial claims simply represent the right-hand side of the balance sheet for any organization; the key distinction between financial intermediaries and other types of organizations involves the items on the left-hand side of the balance sheet.

For example, a chartered bank issues financial claims against itself in the form of debt (for example, chequing and savings accounts) and equity, but then again so does a typical manufacturing firm. However, looking at the assets held by a chartered bank reveals that most of the bank's money is invested in loans to individuals and corporations as well as in government securities such as Treasury bills, whereas the typical manufacturing firm has its money invested mostly in land, buildings, machinery, and inventory. Thus, the bank has invested primarily in financial assets, whereas the manufacturing firm has invested primarily in real assets. Accordingly, banks are classified as financial intermediaries and manufacturing firms are not. Other types of Canadian financial intermediaries include trust companies, caisse populaires, credit unions, life insurance companies, mutual funds, and pension funds.

Financial intermediaries provide an indirect method for corporations to acquire funds. As illustrated in Figure 1.3(a), corporations can obtain funds directly from the general public by the use of the primary market, as mentioned earlier. Alternatively, they can obtain funds indirectly from the general public by using financial intermediaries, as shown in Figure 1.3(b). Here the corporation gives a security to the intermediary in return for funds. In turn, the intermediary acquires funds by allowing the general public to maintain investments such as chequing and savings accounts.

The Investment Process

As previously mentioned, the investment process describes how an investor should decide which marketable securities to invest in, how extensive the investment should be, and when the investment should be made. A five-step procedure for making these decisions forms the basis of the investment process:

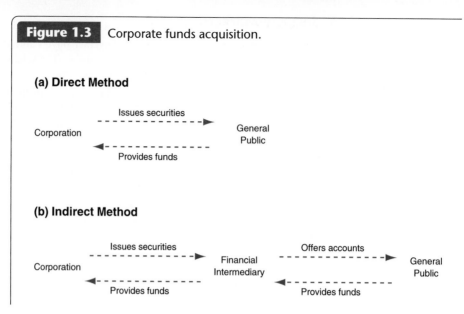

Figure 1.3 Corporate funds acquisition.

(a) Direct Method

Corporation
- - - Issues securities - - -→ General Public
←- - - Provides funds - - -

(b) Indirect Method

Corporation
- - - Issues securities - - -→ Financial Intermediary
←- - - Provides funds - - -
- - - Offers accounts - - -→ General Public
←- - - Provides funds - - -

1. Set investment objectives and policy.

2. Perform security analysis.

3. Construct a portfolio.

4. Revise the portfolio.

5. Evaluate the performance of the portfolio.

◗ Investment Policy

Investment Policy A component of the investment process that involves determining an investor's objectives and amount of the funds available to invest.

The first step, setting **investment policy**, involves determining the investor's objectives and the amount of his investable wealth. Since there is a positive relationship between risk and return for sensible investment strategies, it is not appropriate for an investor to say that his objective is to "make a lot of money." What is appropriate for an investor in this situation is to state that the objective is to attempt to make a lot of money while recognizing there is some chance that large losses may be incurred. Investment objectives should be stated in terms of both risk and return.

This step in the investment process concludes with identification of the potential categories of financial assets for consideration in the ultimate portfolio. This identification will be based on, among other things, the investment objectives, amount of investable wealth, and tax status of the investor. For example, as shall be seen later, it does not usually make sense for individual investors in high tax brackets to purchase preferred shares or for tax-exempt investors (such as pension funds) to invest in securities that provide significant tax deferral opportunities.

Investment policy guides an investor's plan. The old adage, "If you don't know where you're going, any road will do," aptly applies to investing. Whether an investor is an individual or represents an institution, without a clear sense of why investments are being made and how long-run goals are to be achieved, she is likely to pursue inefficient approaches that lead to unsatisfactory results. An investor needs a plan that directs her efforts. Such a plan is guided by *investment policy.*

Investment policy is a combination of philosophy and planning. It expresses the investor's attitudes toward a number of important investment management issues such as, "Why am I investing in the first place?" or "To what extent am I willing to accept the possibility of large losses?" The answer to these questions will vary among investors depending on their financial circumstances and temperaments.

Investment policy is also a form of long-range strategic planning. It delineates the investor's specific goals and how the investor expects those goals to be realized. In this sense, investment policy comprises the set of guidelines and procedures that direct the long-term management of the investor's assets.

Essentially, any relatively permanent set of procedures that guide the management of a plan's assets fall under the rubric of investment policy. Nevertheless, a comprehensive investment policy should address a group of issues that includes (but is not restricted to):

- **Mission statement**. A description of long-run financial goals. For example, an individual's focus might be on saving for a child's university education. A pension fund might therefore have as its purpose the accumulation of sufficient assets to fund promised benefits.
- **Risk tolerance**. The amount of risk that an investor is willing to bear in pursuit of his investment mission(s). An elderly retiree may have a relatively low risk tolerance. Conversely, a well-funded pension fund with a young workforce may have a relatively high risk tolerance.
- **Investment objectives.** The specific investment results that will indicate when the investment program has been successful. For example, an investor's common shares portfolio might be expected to perform at least as well as a broad stock market index over a multi-year period.
- **Policy asset mix.** The investor's long-run allocation to broad asset classes, such as shares and bonds. This choice is by far the most important decision that the investor makes and should be consistent with the investor's mission, risk tolerance, and investment objectives.
- **Active management.** The extent to which the investor attempts to "beat" the market by hiring investment management firms that analyze and select individual securities or groups of securities expected to exceed the performance of specified benchmarks.

A critical part of any investment policy involves the prepatation of a written Investment Policy Statement (IPS). An IPS summarizes the investor's key investment policy decisions and explains the rationale for each decision. The level of IPS detail will vary among investors. Institutional investors, who typically have more complex investment programs, should generally prepare more detailed statements than individual investors. Nevertheless, an IPS serves the same role for all investors: it enforces logical, disciplined investment decision making and it limits the temptation to make counterproductive changes to an investment program durig periods of market stress.

Security Analysis

The second step of the investment process, performing **security analysis**, involves examining a number of individual securities (or groups of securities) within the broad categories of financial assets previously identified. The principal objectives of security analysis are to identify the expected return and risk characteristics of different securities; to identify securities that fit an investor's tax and liquidity needs and to identify mispriced securities. There are many approaches to security analysis. However, most of these approaches fall into one of two classifications. The first classification is known as **technical analysis** (performed by technicians or technical analysts). The second is known as **fundamental analysis** (performed by fundamentalists or fundamental analysts). In discussing these two approaches to security analysis, the primary focus is on common shares. The analysis of other financial assets is discussed later.

In its simplest form, technical analysis involves the study of historical stock market prices in an attempt to predict future price movements for the common share of a particular firm. Initially, past prices are examined in order to identify recurring trends or patterns in price movements. Then, more recent share prices are analyzed in order to identify emerging trends or patterns that are similar to past ones. This matching of emerging trends

Security Analyst An individual who analyzes financial assets in order to determine the investment characteristics of those assets and to identify mispricings among those assets.

Technical Analysis A form of security analysis that attempts to forecast the movement in the prices of securities based primarily on historical price and volume trends in those securities.

Fundamental Analysis A form of security analysis that seeks to determine the intrinsic value of securities based on underlying economic factors. These intrinsic values are compared to current market prices to estimate current levels of mispricing.

or patterns with past ones is done in the belief that these trends or patterns repeat themselves. Thus, by identifying an emerging trend or pattern, the analyst expects to be able to predict future price movements for that particular stock.

Fundamental analysis starts with the assumption that the "true" (or "intrinsic") value of any financial asset is equal to the present value of all cash flows that the owner of the asset expects to receive. Accordingly, the fundamental stock analyst will attempt to forecast the timing and size of these cash flows and then will convert them to their equivalent present value by using an appropriate discount rate. More specifically, the analyst must attempt to forecast the stream of dividends that a particular share will provide in the future, which is equivalent to forecasting the firm's earnings per share and payout ratios. The discount rate must then be estimated. Once the true value of the common share of a particular firm has been determined, it is compared to the current market price of the common share in order to see if the share is fairly priced or not. Shares that have a true value less than their current market price are known as overvalued or overpriced shares, whereas those that have a true value greater than their current market price are known as undervalued or underpriced shares. The magnitude of the difference between the true value and current market price is also important information, since the strength of the analyst's conviction that a given share is mispriced will depend, in part, on this difference. Fundamental analysts believe that notable cases of mispricing will be corrected by the market in the future, meaning that prices of undervalued shares will show unusual appreciation and prices of overvalued shares will show unusual depreciation.

Portfolio Constructon

Portfolio Construction
A component of the investment process that involves identifying which assets to invest in and determining the proportion of funds to invest in each of the assets.

The third step of the investment process, **portfolio construction**, involves identifying those specific assets in which to invest as well as determining the proportions of the investor's wealth to put in each one. Here the issues of selectivity, timing, and diversification need to be addressed by the investor. **Selectivity**, also known as microforecasting, refers to security analysis and thus focuses on forecasting price movements of individual securities. **Timing**, also known as macroforecasting, involves the forecasting of price movements of common stocks in general relative to fixed-income securities, such as corporate bonds. **Diversification** involves constructing the investor's portfolio so as to minimize risk, subject to certain restrictions.

Selectivity An aspect of security analysis that entails forecasting the price movements of individual securities.

Timing An aspect of security analysis that entails forecasting the price movements of asset classes relative to one another.

Diversification The process of adding securities to a portfolio in order to reduce the portfolio's unique risk and, thereby, the portfolio's total risk.

Portfolio Revision

Portfolio Revision
A component of the investment process, involving periodically repeating the processes of setting investment policy, conducting security analysis, and constructing a portfolio.

The fourth step of the investment process, **portfolio revision**, concerns the periodic repetition of the previous three steps. That is, over time the investor may change her investment objectives, which, in turn, means that the currently held portfolio may no longer be optimal. Instead, perhaps a new portfolio should be formed by selling some securities currently held and purchasing new ones. Another motivation for revising a given portfolio is that over time the prices of securities change, so that some securities initially considered unattractive may become attractive and others that were attractive may no longer be so. Thus, the investor may want to add the former to her portfolio while simultaneously deleting the latter. Such a decision will depend upon, among other things, the size of the transactions costs incurred in making these changes as well as the magnitude of the perceived improvement in the investment outlook for the revised portfolio.

Portfolio Performance Evaluation

Portfolio Performance Evaluation A component of the investment process involving periodic analysis of how a portfolio performed in terms of both returns earned and risk incurred.

The fifth step of the investment process, **portfolio performance evaluation**, involves periodically determining how the portfolio performed in terms of not only the return earned, but also the risk experienced by the investor. Thus, appropriate measures of return and risk as well as relevant standards (or benchmarks) are needed.

Institutional Investors

The past 30 years have witnessed a concentration of financial power in the hands of relatively few organizations collectively known as *institutional investors*. The economic and social consequences of this consolidation have been enormous. Because this book is about investing, we will discuss not only the basic concepts, but also how they are applied by, and apply to, these immensely influential organizations.

The term *institutional investors* is used nebulously by practitioners. In a very broad sense, institutional investors are simply financial intermediaries of any type. This definition sets them apart from *retail investors,* who are individuals owning portfolios for which they are the direct beneficiaries.

At times, however, practitioners refer to institutional investors in a narrower context. For example, when discussing the consequences of increased institutional investor participation in the common stock market, the focus is primarily on pension funds, mutual funds, insurance companies, and non-pension-fund money invested by bank trust departments. These organizations, in aggregate, own a large fraction of the outstanding market value of Canadian corporations.

Unquestionably, the most dynamic institutional investors today are pension funds and mutual funds. Pension funds are a relatively recent phenomenon. Over the past 40 years, participation in pension funds has mushroomed, with approximately 40% of the working population enrolled in some type of pension plan today.

Until recently, most pension funds were invested conservatively in bonds and common shares. Since that time these organizations have become the driving force behind many investment industry innovations. They have moved into international stocks and bonds, derivative securities, and various "alternative equity" investments, such as oil and gas, venture capital, and timberland. Furthermore, they have popularized a variety of investment management techniques, such as passive management and market timing.

In terms of sheer growth, mutual funds have been even more impressive than pension funds. As late as 1990, many investors viewed mutual funds skeptically as speculative investments. The industry still suffered a hangover from the collapse of many equity funds in the 1973–1974 recession. Today the mood has changed dramatically.

The financial deregulation of the 1980s led to an explosion of mutual fund products. Mutual fund sponsors expanded their offerings in terms of both types of assets and investment styles. Whereas previously most mutual funds concentrated on investments in Canadian stocks, investors can now own mutual funds investing in foreign stocks, Canadian and foreign bonds, Canadians and foreign short-term fixed-income securities, options, futures, and real estate. Funds may emphasize value or growth shares, mortgage or Canada bonds, passive or active management. The variations are seemingly endless and continue to grow. Where once *The Globe and Mail* could list mutual fund data on half a page, it now devotes over a page and a half to daily mutual fund activity.

Willie Sutton remarked that he robbed banks because "that's where the money is." Institutional investors command attention because they are now "where the money is," with most of it invested in common stocks and corporate and government bonds. Recently, pension funds (and RRSP holders) were allowed to raise their foreign holdings from 10% to 20% of the portfolio value. This opened up new investment avenues for portfolio investors. By comparison, as the importance of retail investors has declined, the traditional investment services provided to individuals have been reduced in number and increased in price.

The growth in institutional investor portfolios has had a bearing on many of the financial instruments and investment management techniques discussed in this text. Consider the following examples:

Security Markets. Institutional investors now dominate security trading. They control over 50% of the daily trading on the Toronto Stock Exchange (TSE). Furthermore, 20 years ago few TSE trades involved share amounts over 5000. Today trades of that magnitude are commonplace. The growth in large common stock trades has threatened to overwhelm the traditional trading systems. In response new mechanisms have been created, such as computerized trading and the formation of block trading specialists (see Chapter 3).

Corporate Control. As a consequence of their size, institutional investors collectively own a significant interest in many large publicly traded corporations. Only in the last 10 years have institutional investors made a concerted effort to exercise their influence on corporations, but that effort had already had a noticeable impact. Numerous corporate boards have been altered and businesses restructured in response to pressure from institutional investors (see Chapter 16).

Futures. Institutional investors have largely avoided commodity futures. However, their involvement with financial futures (which were not even traded 20 years ago) has helped generate additional dollar trading volume in common stock index futures (see Chapter 20).

Investment Management. Institutional investors have demanded new types of investment management techniques. For example, by allocating large sums to passive management, they single-handedly created a new industry (see Chapter 23).

Portfolio Performance Evaluation. Institutional investors have placed considerable emphasis on understanding how well their investments have performed and identifying the sources of those results.

This emphasis has led to the development of sophisticated portfolio monitoring and performance analysis systems (see Chapter 24).

Quantitative Techniques. Institutional investors have pioneered the application of quantitative security valuation techniques, such as dividend discount models (see Chapter 17). They have explicitly sought to maintain adequate portfolio diversification and to control systematic and unsystematic risk using complex risk models (see Chapters 7, 10, and 23).

Fixed-Income Securities. In large part because of the diverse needs of institutional investors, bond trading firms have created an array of complex fixed-income securities. Mortgage-backed securities (MBSs), real return bonds, and floating-rate notes are but a few examples (see Chapter 13).

Given current demographic trends, the growth in assets controlled by institutional investors seems unlikely to abate. For example, as "baby boomers" reach their peak saving years (ages 40–60) over the next two decades, purchases of mutual fund shares and contributions to pension funds will continue to rise. Consequently, the influence of institutional investors on security markets can be expected to increase further in the years ahead.

Investments as a Career

In one way or another, investments affect virtually everyone. Investments both reflect and influence the health of the economy. Direct contact with investing may be as simple as participation in an employer's retirement plan. Or it may involve investing personal assets in mutual funds or individual securities.

Opportunities exist for those interested in making investments a career. As shown in Table 1.4 employment in the industry has continued to keep pace with the overall economy. In 1996, roughly 1 out of every 28 nonagricultural workers dealt with investments, broadly defined. As the Canadian population ages, one can expect savings rates to rise and demand for investment services to continue to grow.

Within the investment industry, there exists a wide range of career options. Using the outline of the investment industry shown in Table 1.4 as a starting point, those options are briefly discussed next.

Banks and other deposit-accepting intermediaries are the largest sector in terms of employment. The banking sector provides such traditional services as collecting deposits, providing access to deposited funds through cheque writing, and lending. Banks also provide custodial services to institutional investors and trust services to individuals. In this latter capacity, banks employ security analysts and portfolio managers to invest their clients' funds in the stock, bond, and money markets. In recent years, banks have moved aggres-

Table 1.4	Number of Employees: Finance and Insurance Industries 1971–1996.				
	Number of Employees (thousands)				
Employer	1971	1981	1986	1991	1996
Deposit accepting intermediaries	133.3	261.4	272.3	322.3	288.3
Consumer and business financing	17.3	20.3	14.2	21.5	19.9
Investment intermediaries	20.3	21.6	26.1	26.8	36.7
Insurance industries	70.8	104.6	124.6	177.4	136.0
Other financial intermediaries	14.3	22.6	27.6	28.8	41.2
Total	256.0	430.5	464.8	576.9	522.1
Employees in this industry as a percent of total employees in nonagricultural industries	2.97%	3.57%	3.56%	3.99%	3.52%

SOURCE: Statistics Canada, *Census of Population* (Ottawa, ON), various years.

sively to offer investment services such as discount brokerage, mutual funds, and investment banking. Legal limitations on banks involvement in the investment industry have largely been dismantled. Chartered banks have become major participants in many financial services from which they were exluded in the past. Investment-related employment at banks is increasing significantly.

Insurance industries, including both life and property and casualty insurers, is the second largest sector. Insurance companies invest funds generated by the premiums paid on insurance product. The insurance companies' combined investment portfolios are worth billions of dollars and are invested across a variety of asset types. The insurance industry employs hundreds of security analysts and portfolio managers to invest these funds.

The fastest growing sector of the industry is the other financial intermediaries segment that includes security brokers and dealers, mortgage brokers, and security and commodity exchanges. The brokerage sector facilitates investors' purchases and sales of securities by providing investment advice, execution and processing of trades, recordkeeping, and market making. Brokerage firms also provide investment banking to corporations and governmental organizations as well as portfolio management for institutions and individuals. These firms also trade for their own accounts in the domestic and foreign capital markets. Although it is the most lucrative and high-profile sector of the investment industry, the brokerage business is very cyclical and employment takes wide swings in tandem with the profitability of the business.

Another high-growth area is the investment intermediary sector that includes portfolio investment intermediaries, mortgage companies, and trusteed pension funds. The extraordinary growth of mutual fund investments and retirement savings plans over the past five years accounts for most of the growth in this sector, although pension funds are also an important contributor to employment growth. Some of the decline in employment in the insurance sector can be attributed to the fact that many life insurance companies have "spun off" their investment management departments into separate and independent subsidiaries that provide services to both the parent company and outside clients.

The smallest sector is the consumer and business financing segment that predominantly consists of consumer loan, sales finance, credit card, and financial leasing companies. This is not a high-growth area given the aging population that emphasizes saving for retirement rathet than borrowing for immediate consumption.

What type of training can best prepare one for a career in investments? There is no rigid formula. Most current entrants to the industry have received undergraduate degrees (although not necessarily in business) and many have earned or plan to soon acquire MBA degrees. Succesful completion of the Canadian Securities Course offered by the Canadian Securities Institute is almost a prerequisite for entry into the industry. The Chartered Financial Analyst Certification (see Chapter 22) has become an increasingly common requirement for advancement in the investment industry.

Despite these common denominators, the backgrounds of successful investors are quite varied, ranging form art history to nuclear physics. Investing requires a blend of verbal, writing, mathematical, and cognitive skills. In the last 25 years the investment industry has become more "quantitative" and highly computer-oriented. However, the need for "qualitative" skills (particularly intuition, insight, and initiative) remains critical.

Globalization

The "globalization" of the investment business has become a recurring theme in recent years. The US and Canadian economies are now much more integrated with the rest of the world than they were several decades ago. Similarly, these financial markets are now more sensitive to events abroad than was previously the case. The growth in foreign security markets has significantly increased international opportunities for North American investors.

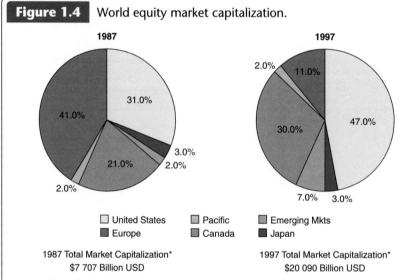

Figure 1.4 World equity market capitalization.

1987 Total Market Capitalization*
$7 707 Billion USD

1997 Total Market Capitalization*
$20 090 Billion USD

Canada's market only makes up 2% of the total world market. Invest in world markets for further diversification and risk reduction with potential for higher returns.

* Estimated

SOURCE: Morgan Stanley Capital International, *All Country World Index*, reprinted in special advertising supplement by Canada Trust in *Saturday Night*, October 1998.

Figure 1.4 compares the distribution of total market value of common stock markets around the world in 1987 and 1997. Most striking is the tremendous growth in the market value of common shares worldwide. Since 1987, the total value of the world's major equity markets has grown from less than $8 trillion to over $20 trillion, a growth of 130% over the 10-year period. The following are the three largest areas of expansion: the emerging markets that increased from $0.174 to $1.41 trillion, a growth of 700%; the US market that increased from $2.70 to $9.44 trillion, a growth of 250%; and the European markets that increased from $1.83 to $2.83 trillion, a growth of 230%. These growth areas were counterbalanced by a remarkable decline in the Japanese equity market from $3.57 to $2.21 trillion, a shrinkage of 38%. The growth of Canadian and Pacific equity markets kept pace with the world average, thereby maintaining a market share of 2% and 3% respectively. The current financial crisis in the Pacific countries and Russia and the lagging Japanese economy suggests that, for the next few years, growth in equity markets will be confined to North America and Europe.

Summary

1. Because this book is about investing, it focuses on the investment environment and the investment process.
2. An investment involves the sacrifice of current dollars for future dollars.
3. Investments may be made in real assets or in financial assets (securities) through either primary markets or secondary markets.
4. The primary task of security analysis is to identify mispriced securities by determining the prospective future benefits of owning those securities, the conditions under which those benefits will be received, and the likelihood of such conditions.
5. The rate of return on an investment measures the percentage change in the investor's wealth due to owning the investment.
6. Studies of the historical rates of return on various types of securities demonstrate that common shares produce relatively high but variable returns. Bonds generate lower returns with less variability. Treasury bills provide the lowest returns with the least variability.
7. In an efficient market, security prices reflect information immediately. Security analysis will not enable investors to earn abnormally high returns.
8. Security markets exist to bring together buyers and sellers of securities.
9. Financial intermediaries (financial institutions) are organizations that issue financial claims against themselves and use the proceeds to purchase primarily the financial assets of others.
10. The investment process describes how an investor makes decisions about what securities to invest in, how extensive these investments should be, and when they should be made.
11. The investment process involves five steps: set an investment policy, perform a security analysis, construct a portfolio, revise the portfolio, and evaluate the portfolio performance.
12. Although the investment industry is of modest importance relative to total employment figures, it has a profound impact on everyone's life.

QUESTIONS AND PROBLEMS

1. Why do secondary security markets not generate capital for the issuers of securities traded in those markets?
2. Following the overthrow of communist regimes in Eastern Europe, many of the fledgling democracies placed the development of security markets near the top of their economic agendas. Why do you think that they did so?
3. Colfax Glassworks stock currently sells for $36 per share. One year ago the stock sold for $33. The company recently paid a $3 per share dividend. What was the rate of return for an investor in Colfax stock over the year?
4. At the beginning of the year, Ray Fisher decided to take $50 000 in savings out of the bank and invest it in a portfolio of shares and bonds; $20 000 was placed into common shares and $30 000 into corporate bonds. A year later, Ray's share and bond holdings were worth $25 000 and $23 000, respectively. During the year $1000 in cash dividends was received on the shares, and $3000 in coupon payments was received on the bonds. (The share and bond income was not reinvested in Ray's portfolio.)

a. What was the return on Ray's share portfolio during the year?

b. What was the return on Ray's bond portfolio during the year?

c. What was the return on Ray's total portfolio during the year?

5. Explain why the rate of return on an investment represents the investor's relative increase in wealth from that investment.

6. Why are Treasury bills considered to be a risk-free investment? In what way do investors bear risk when they own Treasury bills?

7. Why are corporate bonds riskier than Canadian government bonds?

8. The following table shows the annual returns on a portfolio of small shares during the 20-year period from 1976 to 1995. What is the average return and standard deviation of this portfolio? How do they compare with the 1976–1995 average return and standard deviation of the common stock portfolio whose annual returns are shown in Table 1.1?

1976:	57.38%	1981:	13.88%	1986:	6.85%	1991:	44.63%
1977:	25.38%	1982:	28.01%	1987:	−9.30%	1992:	23.35%
1978:	23.46%	1983:	39.67%	1988:	22.87%	1993:	−20.98%
1979:	43.46%	1984:	−6.67%	1989:	10.18%	1994:	−3.11%
1980:	39.88%	1985:	24.66%	1990:	−21.56%	1995:	34.46%

9. Does it seem reasonable that higher-return securities historically have exhibited higher risk? Why?

10. Give an example, outside of the financial markets, in which you commonly face a tradeoff between risk and return.

11. Examining Table 1.1, you can find many years in which Treasury bills produced greater returns than common stocks. How can you reconcile this fact with the statements made in the text, citing a positive relationship between risk and return?

12. Calculate the average annual return on common shares, government bonds, and Treasury bills during the four decades from the 1950s through the 1980s. Which period was clearly the "decade of the financial asset"?

13. Why might it be reasonable to believe that including securities issued in foreign countries will improve the risk-reward performance of your portfolio?

14. Describe how life insurance companies, mutual funds, and pension plans each act as financial intermediaries.

15. What are the five steps to the investment process? What is the importance of each step to the entire process?

16. Why does it not make sense to establish an investment objective of "making a lot of money"?

17. Financial advisors often contend that elderly people should invest their portfolios more conservatively than younger people. Should a conservative investment policy for an elderly person call for owning no common shares? Discuss the reasons for your answer.

18. What factors might an individual investor take into account in determining his investment policy?

19. Distinguish between technical and fundamental security analysis.

CFA EXAM QUESTIONS

20. Donovan believes that the Board should emphasize the fundamental long-term considerations related to investment for BI's plan and de-emphasize the short-term performance aspects. Recognizing that a well-structured investment policy is an essential element in investing, Donovan requests your help in drafting such a document.

a. Discuss why the investment time horizon is of particular importance when setting investment policy for a corporate pension plan.

b. Briefly explain the importance of specifying each of the following when constructing an effective pension investment policy:

(i) an appropriate risk tolerance

    (ii) appropriate asset-mix guidelines

    (iii) the benchmarks to be used for measuring progress toward plan objectives

21. Ambrose Green, 63, is a retired engineer and a client of Clayton Asset Management Associates ("Associates"). His accumulated savings are invested in Diversified Global Fund ("the Fund"), an in-house investment vehicle with multiple portfolio managers through which Associates manage nearly all client assets on a pooled basis. Dividend and capital gain distributions have produced an annual average return to Green of about 8% on his $900 000 original investment in the Fund, made six years ago. The $1 000 000 current value of his Fund interest represents virtually all of Green's net worth.

    Green is a widower whose daughter is a single parent living with her young son. While not an extravagant person, Green's spending has exceeded his after-tax income by a considerable margin since his retirement. As a result, his non-Fund financial resources have steadily diminished and now amount to $10 000. Green does not have retirement income from a private pension plan, but does receive taxable government benefits of $1000 per month. His marginal tax rate is 40%. He lives comfortably in a rented apartment, travels extensively, and makes frequent cash gifts to his daughter and grandson, to whom he wants to leave an estate of at least $1 000 000.

    Green realizes that he needs more income to maintain his lifestyle. He also believes his assets should provide an after-tax cash flow sufficient to meet his present $80 000 annual spending needs, which he is unwilling to reduce. He is uncertain as to how to proceed and has engaged you, a CFA Charterholder with an independent advisory practice, to counsel him.

    Your first task is to review Green's investment policy statement.

Ambrose Green's Investment Policy Statement

Objectives

- I need a maximum return that includes an income element large enough to meet my spending needs, so about a 10% total return is required.
- I want low risk, to minimize the possibility of large losses and preserve the value of my assets for eventual use by my daughter and grandson.

Constraints

- With my spending needs averaging about $80 000 per year and only $10 000 of cash remaining, I will probably have to sell something soon.
- I am in good health and my noncancellable health insurance will cover my future medical expenses.

1. Identify and briefly discuss four key constraints present in Green's situation not adequately treated in his investment policy statement.
2. Based on your assessment of his situation and the information presented in the introduction, create and justify appropriate return and risk objectives for Green.

KEY TERMS

investment environment (p. 1)

investment process (p. 1)

investment (p. 1)

savings (p. 1)

real investment (p. 1)

financial investment (p. 1)

primary market (p. 1)

secondary market (p. 1)

security (p. 2)

rate of return (p. 3)

efficient market (p. 7)

security market (p. 9)

money market (p. 9)

capital market (p. 9)

investment policy (p. 10)

security analysis (p. 11)

technical analysis (p. 11)
fundamental analysis (p. 11)
portfolio construction (p. 12)
selectivity (p. 12)

diversification (p. 12)
portfolio revision (p. 12)
portfolio performance evaluation (p. 12)
timing (p. 12)

REFERENCES

1. The following provide a perspective on Canadian security returns and Canadian holdings of financial assets:

   James E. Hatch and Robert W. White, *Canadian Stocks, Bonds, Bills, and Inflation: 1950–1987* (Charlottesville, VA: The Research Foundation of The Institute of Chartered Financial Analysts, 1988).

   Melanie Moore, *ScotiaMcLeod's Handbook of Canadian Debt Market Indices: 1947–1997* (Toronto: ScotiaMcLeod Inc., 1998). ScotiaMcLeod also publishes a monthly bulletin entitled *Debt Market Indices*.

2. A major source of historical returns on US security markets is contained in either one of the two following publications:

   Roger G. Ibbotson and Rex A. Sinquefield, *Stocks, Bonds, Bills, and Inflation: The Past and the Future* (Charlottesville, VA: Financial Analysts Research Foundation, 1983). Note that the Financial Analysts Research Foundation has since been renamed the Research Foundation of the ICFA. It can be contacted by calling (804) 980-3647.

   Stocks, Bonds, Bills, and Inflation 1997 Yearbook (Chicago: Ibbotson Associates, 1997). This annual yearbook of monthly and annual data can be purchased by calling (312) 616-1620.

3. Additional historical data on US common share returns can be found in:

   Jack W. Wilson and Charles P. Jones, "A Comparison of Annual Common Stock Returns: 1871–1925 and 1926–85," *Journal of Business* 60, no. 2 (April 1987): 239–258.

   Jeremy J. Siegel, *Stocks for the Long Run: A Guide to Selecting Markets for Long-Term Growth*, (Homewood, IL: Irwin, 1994).

   Charles P. Jones and Jack W. Wilson, "Probabilities Associated with Common Stock Returns," *Journal of Portfolio Management* 22, no. 1 (Fall 1995): 21–32.

4. The historical relative returns of US stocks versus bonds are studied in:

   Jeremy J. Siegel, "The Equity Premium: Stock and Bond Returns Since 1802," *Financial Analysts Journal* 48, no. 1 (January–February 1992): 28–38.

   Peter L. Bernstein, "What Rate of Return Can You Reasonably Expect... or What Can the Long Run Tell Us about the Short Run?" *Financial Analysts Journal* 53, no. 2 (March–April 1997): 20–28.

   Roger G. Ibbotson and Laurence B. Siegel, "The World Bond Market: Market Values, Yields, and Returns," *Journal of Fixed Income* 1, no. 1 (June 1991): 90–99.

5. Comparable Japanese data for a more limited time period are presented in:

   Yasushi Hamao, "A Standard Data Base for the Analysis of Japanese Security Markets," *Journal of Business* 64, no. 1 (January 1991): 87–102.

6. Historical data on global market returns are presented in:

Roger G. Ibbotson and Laurence B. Siegel, "The World Bond Market: Market Values, Yields, and Returns," *Journal of Fixed Income* 1, no. 1 (June 1991): 90–99.

Jack W. Wilson and Charles P. Jones, "Long-Term Returns and Risk for Bonds," *Journal of Portfolio Management* 23, no. 3. (Spring 1997): 9–14.

7. The volatility of common stocks is examined in:

G. William Schwert, "Why Does Stock Market Volatility Change Over Time?" *Journal of Finance* 44, no. 5 (December 1989): 1115–1153.

Peter Fortune, "An Assessment of Financial Market Volatility: Bills, Bonds, and Stocks," *New England Economic Review* (November–December 1989): 13–28.

8. For a discussion and analysis of US common stock indices, see:

G. William Schwert, "Indexes of US Stock Prices from 1802 to 1987," *Journal of Business* 63, no. 3 (July 1990): 399–426.

9. For a discussion of using historical capital markets return data in making portfolio decisions, see:

Maria Crawford Scott, "Planning Assumptions: Will the Real Long-Term Return Please Stand Up?" *AAII Journal* 19, no. 10 (November 1997): 10–12.

10. Investment policy is discussed in:

Charles D. Ellis, *Investment Policy* (Homewood, IL: Dow Jones-Irwin, 1985)

Keith D. Ambachtsheer, *Pension Funds and the Bottom Line: Managing the Corporate Pension Fund as a Financial Business* (Homewood, IL: Dow Jones-Irwin, 1986).

Keith D. Ambachtsheer, "Pension Fund Asset Allocation: In Defense of the 60/40 Equity/Debt Asset Mix, *Financial Analysts Journal* 43, no. 5 (September–October 1987): 14–24.

Wayne H. Wagner, "The Many Dimensions of Risk," *Journal of Portfolio Management* 15, no. 2 (Winter 1988): 35–39.

Jeffery V. Bailey, "Investment Policy: The Missing Link," in Frank J. Fabozzi (ed.), *Pension Fund Management* (Chicago: Probus, 1990), p. 11–26.

Editorial Board, "Investment Policy Statement," *Financial Analysts Journal* 46, no. 5 (September–October 1990): 14–15.

Walter R. Good and Douglas A. Love, "Reactions to the Pension Investment Policy Statement," *Financial Analysts Journal* 47, no. 2 (March–April 1991): 7–10.

CHAPTER 2

Buying and Selling Securities

Broker An agent, or middleman, who facilitates the buying and selling of securities for investors.

Account Executive or **Registered Representative** A representative of a brokerage firm whose primary responsibility is servicing the accounts of individual investors.

Regional Brokerage Firm An organization offering brokerage services that specializes in trading the securities of companies located in a particular region of the country.

Discount Broker An organization that offers a limited range of brokerage services and charges fees substantially below those of brokerage firms that provide a full range of services.

Commission The fee an investor pays to a brokerage firm for services rendered in the trading of securities.

When a security is sold, many people are likely to be involved. Although it is possible for two investors to trade with each other directly, the usual transaction employs the services provided by brokers, dealers, and markets.

A **broker** acts as an agent for an investor and is compensated via commission. Many individual investors deal with brokers in large retail houses—firms with many offices that are connected by private wires with their own headquarters and, through the headquarters, with major markets. The people in these brokerage firms with prime responsibility for individual investors are termed **account executives**, or **registered representatives**.

Institutional investors, such as chartered banks, pension funds, and other financial institutions, deal with these large retail brokerage firms typically through separate divisions that handle their specific trading needs. Institutional investors also conduct business with smaller *boutiques* that maintain one or two offices and specialize in institutional business.

Two other types of brokerage firms are **regional brokerage firms** and **discount brokers**. The former concentrate on transactions within a geographic area, meaning the securities being traded have a special following in that area of the country. This may be because the issuers of the securities are located in that area. Discount brokers provide "bare-bones" services at low cost, meaning they provide fewer services than do *full-service brokerage firms* such as CIBC Wood Gundy or RBC Dominion Securities. Investors who simply want to have their orders executed and do not seek investment advice can save a substantial fraction of the commission by using a discount broker. Lately a special type of discount broker has emerged who accepts, executes, and confirms orders electronically over the Internet for even lower comissions than those of generic discount brokers.

An account executive's compensation is typically determined in large part by the **commissions** paid by his or her customers—an amount that is directly related to the amount of turnover (that is, trading) in an investor's account. This provides some temptation to recommend frequent changes in investors' holdings. Furthermore, since the commission rates on various types of investments differ, there is some temptation to recommend changes in those types of investments with the highest rates. In the long run, however, account executives who encourage excessive turnover (or "churning") will often lose customers and may even be subjected to lawsuits.[1] Nonetheless, such behaviour may be advantageous for them in the short run.

---

[1] For more on churning, see Seth C. Anderson, Sue L. Visscher, and Donald A. Winslow, "Guidelines for Detecting Churning in an Account," *AAII Journal* 11, no. 9 (October 1989): 12–14.

It is a simple matter to open an account with a brokerage firm: simply appear at (or call) the local office. A registered representative is assigned to you and helps you to fill out a *New Client Application Form.*[2] After this form has been signed, everything else can be done by mail or telephone. Transactions are posted to your account as they are to a bank account. For example, you can deposit money, purchase securities using money from the account, and add the proceeds from security sales to the account. Brokers exist (and charge fees) to make security transactions as simple as possible. All that the investor has to do is to provide the broker with what is referred to here as **order specifications**.

Order Specifications The investor's instructions to a broker regarding the particular characteristics of a trading order, including the name of the security's issuing firm, whether to buy or sell, order size, maximum time the order is to be outstanding, and the type of order to be used.

In discussing order specifications, it will be assumed that the investor's order involves common shares. In this situation the investor must specify

1. the name of the firm
2. whether the order is to buy or sell shares
3. the size of the order
4. how long the order is to be outstanding
5. what type of order is to be used

The last three specifications are discussed next in more detail.

Order Size

Board Lot The standard unit of trading, generally 100 shares.

In buying or selling common shares, the investor places an order involving either a **board lot**, an **odd lot**, or both. The size of a board lot on Canadian stock exchanges varies with the price of the stock, as shown in Table 2.1. Any order less than a board lot is referred to as an odd lot. Orders that are for more than 100 shares but are not multiples of 100 are viewed as a mixture of board and odd lots. Thus an order for 259 shares is viewed as an order for two board lots and an odd lot of 59 shares.

Odd Lot An amount of stock, less than a board lot, generally from 1 to 99 shares.

Time Limit

Day Order A trading order that the broker will attempt to fill only during the day in which it was entered.

The investor must specify a time limit on his or her order, meaning the time within which the broker should attempt to fill the order. For **day orders**, the broker will attempt to fill the order only during the day in which it was entered. If the order is not filled by the end of the trading session, it expires. If a time limit is not specified by the investor, the broker will treat an order as a day order. **Good through orders** are valid for a specified number of days and automatically expire if they have not been executed by the expiry date.

Good Through Order An order to buy or sell that is good for a specified length of time and automatically cancelled if it has not been filled by the end of the period.

Table 2.1   Trading Lot Sizes at Four Canadian Exchanges.

| | Board Lot | | |
Share Price	ME/TSE	ASE	VSE
under $0.10	1 000	1 000	1 000
at $0.10 to $0.99	500	500	500
at $1.00 to $100.00	100	100	100
over $100.00	100	100	100

SOURCE: The Canadian Securities Course (Toronto: Canadian Securities Institute, 1992).

---

[2]For more information on opening an account see *The Canadian Securities Course* (Toronto, November 1997), ch. 12, p. 8.

Good-Till-Cancelled Order or **Open Order** A trading order that remains in effect until it is either filled or cancelled by the investor.

All or None Order An order that states the minimum number of shares, bought or sold, that the client will accept. The trader must execute the number of shares specified before the client will accept the fill.

Open orders, also known as **good-till-cancelled**, or **GTC**, **orders**, remain in effect until they are either filled or cancelled by the investor. However, during the time period before the order has been filled, the broker may periodically ask the investor to confirm the order. **All or none orders**, or **AON**, require the trader to execute the total number of shares specified before it will be accepted. Such an order must specify the minimum number of shares required. **Any part order** is the opposite of an AON in that the client will accept all shares offered in odd lots or broken lots up to the full number in the order.

Discretionary orders allow the broker to set the specifications for the order. The broker may have virtually complete discretion, in which case he decides on all the order specifications, or limited discretion, in which case he decides only on the price and timing of the order.

Types of Orders

Any Part Order An order that is the opposite of an AON in that the client will accept all shares offered in odd lots or broken lots up to the full number in the order.

Discretionary Order A trading order that permits the broker to set the specifications for the order.

Market Order A trading order that instructs the broker to buy or sell a security immediately at the best obtainable price.

Limit Order A trading order that specifies a limit price at which the broker is to execute the order. The trade will be executed only if the broker can meet or better the limit price.

Limit Price The price specified when a limit order is placed with a broker, defining the maximum purchase price or minimum selling price at which the order can be executed.

There are a number of types of orders that investors can place with their broker. By far the most common types are market and limit orders. Although used to a lesser degree, stop and stop limit orders can also be used. Lastly, there are a variety of special types of orders that are rarely used; readers interested in them should contact their broker.

At the Market Orders

The most common type of order is the **at the market order** or simply **market order**. Orders that do not specify a price are treated as market orders. Here the broker is instructed to buy or sell a stated number of shares immediately. In this situation the broker is obliged to act on a "best-efforts" basis to get the best possible price (as low as possible for a purchase order, as high as possible for a sell order) at the time the order is placed. Consequently, when placing a market order the investor can be fairly certain that the order will be executed, but is uncertain of the price. However, there is generally fairly good information available beforehand concerning the likely price at which such an order will be executed. Not surprisingly, market orders are day orders.

Limit Orders

A second type of order is a **limit order**. Here, a **limit price** is specified by the investor when the order is placed with the broker. If the order is to purchase shares, then the broker is to execute the order only at a price that is less than or equal to the limit price. If the order is to sell shares, then the broker is to execute the order only at a price that is greater than or equal to the limit price. Thus, for limit orders to purchase shares the investor specifies a ceiling on the price, and for limit orders to sell shares the investor specifies a floor on the price. In contrast to a market order, an investor using a limit order may not be certain that the order will be executed. Hence, there is a tradeoff between these two types of orders—immediacy of execution at an uncertain price versus uncertain execution within a bounded price range.

For example, assume that the common stock of the ABC Corporation is currently selling for $25 a share. An investor placing a limit order to sell 100 shares of ABC with a limit price of $30 per share and a time limit of one day is not likely to have her order executed, since this price is significantly above the current price of $25. Only if today's price becomes much more favourable (meaning in this case that the stock price rises by at least $5 per share) will the limit order be executed.

Stop Orders

Stop-Loss Order A trading order that specifies a stop price. If the security's price reaches or passes the stop price, then a market order is created.

Stop-Buy Order In a buy order, the stop price must be above the market price at the time the order is placed.

Stop Price The price specified by an investor when a stop order or a stop limit order is placed that defines the price at which the market order or limit order for the security is to become effective.

Cash Account An account maintained by an investor with a brokerage firm in which deposits (cash and the proceeds from security sales) must fully cover withdrawals (cash and the costs of security purchases).

Two special kinds of orders are **stop-loss orders** and **stop-buy orders**. For a **stop order** the investor must specify what is known as a **stop price**. If it is a sell order, the stop price must be below the market price at the time the order is placed; conversely, if it is a buy order, the stop price must be above the market price at the time the order is placed. If someone else later trades the stock at a price that reaches or passes the stop price, then the stop order becomes, in effect, a market order. Hence, a stop order can be viewed as a conditional market order.

Continuing with the ABC Corporation example, a stop-loss order at $20 would not be executed until a trade involving others had taken place at a price of $20 or lower. Conversely, a stop-buy order at $30 would not be executed until a trade involving others had taken place at a price of $30 or more. If the price did not fall to $20, then the stop-loss order would not be executed. Similarly, if the price did not rise to $30, the stop-buy order would not be executed. In contrast, a limit order to sell at $20 or a limit order to buy at $30 would be executed immediately, since the current market price is $25.

One potential use of stop orders is to "lock in" paper profits. For example, assume an investor had purchased ABC stock at $10 per share two years ago, and thus has paper profits of $25 − $10 = $15 per share. Entering a stop-loss order at $20 per share means that the investor will be sure of making roughly $20 − $10 = $10 per share if the stock falls in price to $20 or less. If, instead of falling, the stock price rises, then the investor's stop-loss order is ignored and her paper profits increase in size. Thus, the stop-loss order will provide the investor with a degree of profit protection.[3]

One of the dangers of stop orders is that the actual price at which the order is executed may be some distance from the stop price. This can occur if the stock price moves very rapidly in a given direction. For example, ABC may have an industrial accident that results in a spate of lawsuits and causes the stock price to fall very rapidly to $12 per share. In this situation a stop-loss order at $20 may be executed at $16, for example, instead of near the stop price of $20.

Margin Accounts

Margin Account An account maintained by an investor with a brokerage firm in which securities may be purchased by borrowing a portion of the purchase price from the brokerage firm, or may be sold short by borrowing the securities from the brokerage firm.

Street Name An arrangement between an investor and a brokerage firm where the investor maintains an account in which the investor's securities are registered in the name of the brokerage firm.

A **cash account** with a brokerage firm is like a regular chequing account: deposits (cash and the proceeds from selling securities) must cover withdrawals (cash and the costs of purchasing securities). A **margin account** is like a chequing account that has overdraft privileges: Within limits, if more money is needed than is in the account, a loan is automatically made by the broker.[4]

When opening a margin account with a brokerage firm, an investor must sign a *Margin Account Agreement Form.* This agreement grants the brokerage firm the right to pledge the investor's securities as collateral for bank loans, provided the securities were purchased using a margin account. Most brokerage firms also expect investors to allow them to lend their securities to others who wish to "sell them short," procedures that are described later in this chapter.

In order to facilitate either the pledging or lending of securities, brokerage firms request that securities purchased through a margin account be held in **street name**.[5] This means

---

[3]Stop-buy orders can be used to lock in paper profits for what are known as short sales, which are discussed later in this chapter.

[4]There are other types of accounts; it should be noted that an investor may have more than one type of account with a brokerage firm.

[5]Investors with cash accounts may voluntarily elect to have their securities held in street name. Reasons offered for doing so include reduced risk of theft and improved recordkeeping (typically the brokerage firm will send monthly statements detailing the investor's holdings).

Tokyo Stock Exchange
www.tse.or.jp

that the owner of the security, as far as the original issuer is concerned, is the brokerage firm—that is, the registered owner is the brokerage firm. As a result, in the case of common shares the issuer will send all dividends, annual reports, and voting rights to the brokerage firm, not to the investor. However, the brokerage firm will act merely as a conduit in this situation and simply forward these items to the investor.[6] Accordingly, holding a security in street name will not result in the investor being treated in a substantively different manner from holding the security in his own name.[7]

With a margin account, an investor may undertake certain types of transactions that are not allowed with a cash account. These transactions are known as margin purchases and short sales, which are discussed next.

Margin Purchases

Margin The proportion of the value of a security that must be provided by the investor who uses credit to buy the security.

With a cash account, an investor who purchases a security must pay the entire cost of the purchase with cash. However, with a margin account the investor must come up with cash for only a percentage of the cost (referred to as **margin**) and can borrow the rest from the broker.[8] The amount borrowed from the broker as a result of such a **margin purchase** is referred to as the investor's **debit balance** (also known as **loan value**). The interest charged on loans advanced by a broker for a margin purchase is usually calculated by adding a service charge (for example, 2%) to the broker's chartered bank's **prime rate**. In turn, the prime rate is the rate paid by the broker to the chartered bank that loaned the broker the cash that ultimately went to the investor to pay for part of the purchase.

Margin Purchase The purchase of securities financed by borrowing a portion of the purchase price from a brokerage firm.

Debit Balance The dollar amount borrowed from a broker as the result of a margin purchase.

For example, the bank may loan money to the broker at a rate of 6% and then the broker may loan this money to the investor at a rate of 8%. Note that the prime rate (6% in this example) can change over time and with it the interest rate that investors are charged.

The securities purchased by the investor serve as collateral on the loan made by the broker. In turn, the broker uses these securities as collateral on the loan made by the bank. Thus, the broker is, in a sense, acting as a go-between in the lending process, facilitating a loan from the bank to the investor.

Prime Rate The interest rate charged by the chartered banks on loans to their customers with the highest credit rating.

Minimum Margin Requirement

Minimum Margin Requirement The minimum proportion of the value of a security that must be provided by the investor who buys on margin or short sells.

The minimum percentage of the purchase price that must come from the investor's own funds is known as the **minimum margin requirement**. The minimum margin requirements are established jointly by the stock exchanges and determine the maximum loan that may be extended for long positions in securities (excluding bonds and debentures) listed on any recognized exchange in Canada, the US, the Tokyo Stock Exchange First Section, or on the stock list of the Stock Exchange in London, England. Individual brokerage firms, however, are allowed to require margins higher than the minimum. Hypothetically, therefore, the industry could set a minimum margin of 50% and your broker could require 60%.

---

[6]It is possible that the investor will not receive the voting rights if the stock has been loaned to a short seller. This is discussed later in the chapter.

[7]An investor whose securities are held in street name may be concerned about what happens if the brokerage firm goes bankrupt. If this were to happen, the Canadian Investor Protection Fund (CIPF), an industry sponsored contingency fund that insures investors' accounts against brokerage firm insolvency, would step in and cover the investors' losses up to $250 000.

Settlement Date The date after a security has been traded, on which the buyer must deliver cash to the seller and the seller must deliver the security to the buyer.

[8]With either a cash or a margin account, the investor who purchases stock has up to three business days after an order is executed to provide the broker with the necessary cash. Accordingly, the third business day after execution is known as the **settlement date.** A shorter time period is allowed for bonds, bills, or options. For margin purchases, the loan value of certain other securities can be used instead of cash as a down payment, in which case these securities must be provided by the settlement date. Sellers of securities must also provide their brokers with their securities by the settlement date. If requested, an investor may be able to get an extension to the settlement date.

On Listed Securities Selling at:	Minimum Margin Requirements[a]
Option eligible securities[b]	30% of market
$2.00 and over	50% of market
$1.75 to $1.99	60% of market
$1.50 to $1.74	80% of market
under $1.50	100% of market

Table 2.2 Minimum Margin Requirements on Long Positions in Listed Equities.

[a]These rates apply to the initial transaction. If the share price falls, the investor provides additional margin and the broker's loan is reduced.

[b]*Option Eligible Securities* (OES), are those that meet the eligibility criteria as underlying securities for either Canadian or US exchange-traded options. Also included are securities convertible into OES and preferred shares of companies whose equity qualifies.

SOURCE: The Canadian Securities Course (Toronto: Canadian Securities Institute, 1997).

Table 2.2 shows the minimum margin requirements, which vary with the share price.[9] In general investors are advised to avoid the practice of margining close to the prevailing price limits (i.e., maintaining a minimum amount of margin in the account) in order to provide some protection against having to respond to a margin call following a minor adverse price change.[10]

Consider, as an example, an investor who purchases on margin 100 shares of Widget Corporation for $50 per share. With a margin requirement of, say, 60%, the investor must pay the broker $.6 \times 100$ shares $\times$ $50 per share = $3000. The remainder of the purchase price, $(1 - .6) \times 100$ shares $\times$ $50 per share = $2000, is funded by a loan from the broker to the investor.[11]

These Widget shares can then be said to have a collateral value of $2000, which is the amount of the loan. Note that the sum of the margin in the account and the collateral value is equal to $5000. This relationship must be maintained for the whole time that the investor holds Widget shares in her margin account.

Actual versus Required Margin

The required margin that the investor must maintain in his account varies as the price of the shares changes and is calculated or **marked to market** daily. The required margin is then compared with the actual cash in the account to determine whether there is a surplus or a deficit in the account. Suppose that the price of Widget shares falls to $40 per share. The collateral value of the shares then falls to $1600. The investor then receives a **margin call** from the broker requesting the addition of $400 to the account to eliminate the deficit.

This can be done by either depositing cash or securities into the account, or selling some securities currently held in the account and using the proceeds to pay off part of the

Marked to Market The process of calculating, on a daily basis, the actual margin in an investor's account. Equivalently, the daily process of adjusting the equity in an investor's account to reflect the daily changes in the market value of the account's assets and liabilities.

Margin Call A demand upon an investor by a brokerage firm to increase the equity in the investor's margin account. The margin call is initiated when the investor's actual margin falls below the margin requirement.

[9]Margin requirements for the purchase of most debt securities are significantly lower than those for equities and vary according to the quality of the issue and its time to maturity.

[10]The procedures followed in the US involve slightly more structure. *Initial margin requirements* established by the Federal Reserve Board must be met at the time of the original transaction. Subsequently, the investor must keep the actual margin in the account at or above the *maintenance margin,* which is lower than the initial margin. Maintenance margin levels are established by the exchanges and may be raised by the brokers.

[11]Generally, at the end of each month the interest on the loan will be calculated and added to the amount of the loan appearing on the right-hand side of the investor's balance sheet. For ease of exposition, this fact is ignored in the examples given here.

loan.[12] If the investor does not act (or cannot be reached), then in accordance with the terms of the margin agreement, the broker will sell securities from the account to increase the actual margin to (at least) the minimum margin requirement.

If, instead of falling, the share price rises, then the investor can take part of the increase out of the account in the form of cash, since the actual margin in the account will have risen above the minimum margin requirement.[13] Suppose that the share price increases to $60 per share, then the collateral value of the shares increases to $2400 and the required margin falls to $5000 − $2400 = $2600. As the actual cash in the account is $3000, the investor may withdraw the surplus of $400 from the account.

Table 2.3	**Potential Market Account Conditions and Actions for a Margin Purchaser.**		
Share price	$ 40	$ 50	$ 60
Market value	4 000	5 000	6 000
Collateral value	1 600	2 000	2 400
Required margin	3 400	3 000	2 600
Actual cash in account	3 000	3 000	3 000
Surplus/(deficit)	(400)	0	400
Possible action	1. Add cash or securities. 2. Sell Widget shares to pay off part of loan.	1. Do nothing.	1. Do nothing. 2. Withdraw surplus cash.

Table 2.3 summarizes the state of the investor's margin account under each of the three conditions described above.

Rate of Return

Financial Leverage The use of debt to fund a portion of an investment.

The use of margin purchases allows the investor to engage in **financial leverage**. That is, by using debt to fund part of the purchase price, the investor can increase the expected rate of return of the investment. However, there is a mitigating factor in the use of margin, and that is the effect on the risk of the investment.

Consider Widget again. If the investor believes the stock will rise by $15 per share over the next year, the expected rate of return on the cash purchase of 100 shares of Widget will be ($15 × 100 shares)/($50 × 100 shares) = 30%, assuming that no cash dividends are paid and the purchase price is $50 per share. A margin purchase, where the interest rate on margin loans is 8% and the minimum margin requirement is 60%, on the other hand, would have an expected return of [($15 × 100 shares) − (.8 × $2000)]/$3000 = ($1500 − $160)/$3000 = 44.7%. Thus, the investor has increased the expected rate of return from 30% to 44.7% by the use of margin.

What will happen, however, to the rate of return if the stock falls by $10 per share? In this case the investor who made a cash purchase will have a rate of return equal to (−$10 × 100 shares)/($50 × 100 shares) = −20%. The margin purchaser, on the other hand, will have a rate of return equal to [(−$10 × 100) − (.8 × $2000)]/$3000 = (−$1000 − $160)/$3000 = −38.7%. Thus, the margin purchaser will experience a much larger loss than the cash purchaser for a given dollar decline in the price of the stock.

---

[12]The broker may ask the investor immediately (in some cases within the settlement period, but usually sooner) to bring the actual margin up to a level corresponding to the minimum margin requirement or to one that is even higher.

[13]Alternatively, the cash could be used as part of the minimum margin requirement on an additional margin purchase by the investor. In fact, if it was large enough, it could be used to meet the entire requirement.

Margin purchases are usually made in the expectation that the stock price will rise in the near future, meaning that the investor thinks the stock's current price is too low. If an investor thinks that a given stock is not too low but too high, then the investor may engage in what is known as a short sale, which is discussed next.

Short Sales

An old investor's adage is to "buy low, sell high." Most investors hope to do just that by buying securities first and selling them later.[14] However, with a **short sale** this process is reversed: the investor sells a security first and buys it back later. In this case the old adage about investors aspirations might be reworded to "sell high, buy low."

Short sales are accomplished by borrowing share certificates for use in the initial trade and then repaying the loan with certificates obtained in a later trade. Note that the loan here involves certificates, not dollars and cents (although it is true that the certificates at any point in time have a certain monetary value). This means the borrower must repay the lender by returning certificates, not dollars and cents (although it is true that an equivalent monetary value, determined on the date the loan is repaid, can be remitted instead). It also means that there are no interest payments to be made by the borrower.

Rules Governing Short Sales

Any order for a short sale must be identified as such. The exchanges in Canada have ruled that short sales may not be made when the market price for the security is falling. This allows investors with long positions to liquidate before short sellers can profit in a declining market. The precise rule on the TSE is that a short sale must not be made on the Exchange below the price of the last sale of a board lot. This implies that a short sale may be effected on an **uptick** (for a price higher than that of the previous trade).[15]

Within three business days after a short sale has been made, the short-seller's broker must borrow and deliver the appropriate securities to the purchaser. The borrowed securities may come from the inventory of securities owned by the brokerage firm itself or from the inventory of another brokerage firm. However, they are more likely to come from either the inventory of securities held in street name by the brokerage firm for investors that have margin accounts with the firm or from the holdings of institutional investors (such as a pension fund that is willing to lend its securities). The life of the loan is indefinite, meaning there is no time limit on it.[16] If the lender wants to sell the securities, then the short seller will not have to repay the loan providing that the brokerage firm can borrow shares elsewhere, thereby transferring the loan from one source to another. If, however, the brokerage firm cannot find a place to borrow the shares, then the short seller will have to repay the loan immediately. Interestingly, the identities of the borrower and lender are known only to the brokerage firm—that is, the lender does not know who the borrower is and the borrower does not know who the lender is.

---

[14]After purchasing a security, an investor is said to have established a *long position* in the security.

[15]The tick rule is not applicable in the over-the-counter (OTC also known as the CDN) market, suggesting that short selling can be done at any time in that market providing that the required shares can be borrowed. (The CDN market is discussed in a later section of this chapter.)

[16]The Toronto Stock Exchange publishes a semimonthly list of the **short interest** in its securities (short interest refers to the number of shares of a given company that have been sold short where, as of a given date, the loan remains outstanding).

An Example

An example of a short sale is indicated in Figure 2.1. At the start of the day, Mr. Leung owns 100 shares of the XYZ Company, which are being held for him in street name by Brock, Inc., his broker. During this particular day, Ms. Smith places an order with her broker at Brock to short sell 100 shares of XYZ (Mr. Leung believes the price of XYZ stock is going to rise in the near future, whereas Ms. Smith believes it is going to fall). In this situation, Brock takes the 100 shares of XYZ that they are holding in street name for Mr. Leung and sells them for Ms. Smith to some other investor, in this case Mr. Jones. At this point XYZ will receive notice that the ownership of 100 shares of its stock has changed hands, going from Brock (remember that Mr. Leung held his shares in street name) to Mr. Jones. At some later date, Ms. Smith will tell her broker at Brock to purchase 100 shares of XYZ (perhaps from a Ms. Poole) and use these shares to pay off her debt to Mr. Leung. At this point, XYZ will receive another notice that the ownership of 100 shares has changed hands, going from Ms. Poole to Brock, restoring Brock to their original position.

Cash Dividends

What happens when XYZ declares and subsequently pays a cash dividend to its shareholders? *Before the short sale*, Brock would receive a cheque for cash dividends on 100 shares of stock. After depositing this cheque in their own account at a bank, Brock would write a cheque for an identical amount and give it to Mr. Leung. Thus, neither Brock or Mr. Leung has been made worse off by having his shares held in street name. *After the short sale*, XYZ will see that the owner of those 100 shares is not Brock any more but is now Mr. Jones. Thus, XYZ will now mail the dividend cheque to Mr. Jones, not Brock. However, Mr. Leung will still be expecting his dividend cheque from Brock. Indeed, if there was a risk that he would not receive it, he would not have agreed to have his securities held in street name. Brock would like to mail him a cheque for the same amount of dividends that Mr. Jones received from XYZ—that is, for the amount of dividends Mr. Leung would have received from XYZ had he held his shares in his own name. If Brock does this, then they will be losing an amount of cash equal to the amount of the dividends paid. In order to prevent themselves from experiencing this loss, they make Ms. Smith, the short seller, give them a cheque for an equivalent amount.

Consider all the parties involved in the short sale now. Mr. Leung is content, since he has received his dividend cheque from his broker. Brock is content, since their net cash outflow is still zero, just as it was before the short sale. Mr. Jones is content, since he received his dividend cheque directly from XYZ. What about Ms. Smith? She should not be upset with having to reimburse Brock for the dividend cheque given by them to Mr. Leung, since the price of XYZ's common stock can be expected to fall, on the ex-dividend day, by an amount roughly equal to the amount of the cash dividend, thereby reducing the dollar value of her loan from Brock by an equivalent amount.

Financial Reports and Voting Rights

What about annual reports and voting rights? Before the short sale, these were sent to Brock, who then forwarded them to Mr. Leung. After the short sale, Brock no longer receive them, so what happens? Annual reports are easily procured by brokerage firms free of charge, so Brock probably got copies of them from XYZ and mailed a copy to Mr. Leung. However, voting rights are different. These are limited to the registered shareholders (in this case, Mr. Jones) and cannot be replicated in the manner of cash dividends by Ms. Smith, the short seller. Thus, when voting rights are issued, the brokerage firm (Brock, Inc.) will try to find voting rights to give to Mr. Leung (perhaps Brock owns shares or manages a portfolio that owns shares of XYZ and will give these voting rights to Mr. Leung). Unless he is insistent, however, there is a chance he will not get his voting rights once his shares have been borrowed and used in a short sale. In all other matters, he will be treated just as if he were holding the shares of XYZ in his own name.

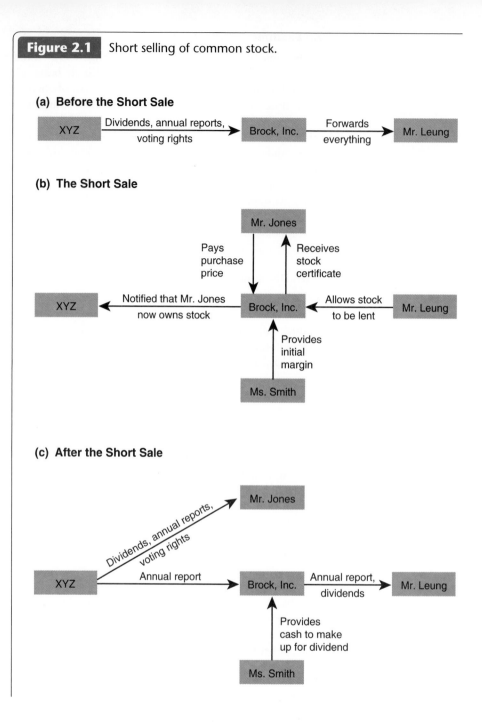

Figure 2.1 Short selling of common stock.

(a) Before the Short Sale

XYZ — Dividends, annual reports, voting rights → Brock, Inc. — Forwards everything → Mr. Leung

(b) The Short Sale

Mr. Jones

Pays purchase price ↓

Receives stock certificate ↑

XYZ ← Notified that Mr. Jones now owns stock — Brock, Inc. ← Allows stock to be lent — Mr. Leung

Provides initial margin ↑

Ms. Smith

(c) After the Short Sale

Mr. Jones

Dividends, annual reports, voting rights ↗

XYZ — Annual report → Brock, Inc. — Annual report, dividends → Mr. Leung

Provides cash to make up for dividend ↑

Ms. Smith

Margin Requirements

As previously mentioned, a short sale involves a loan. Thus, there is a risk that the borrower (in the example, Ms. Smith) will not repay the loan. In this situation the broker would be left without the 100 shares that the short seller, Ms. Smith, owes him. Either the brokerage firm, Brock, is going to lose money or else the lender, Mr. Leung, is going to lose money. To prevent this from happening, the cash proceeds from the short sale, paid by Mr. Jones, are not given to the short seller, Ms. Smith. Instead, they are held in her account with Brock until she repays her loan. Unfortunately this will not assure the brokerage firm that the loan will be repaid.

In the example, assume the 100 shares of XYZ were sold at a price of $100 per share. In this case, the proceeds from the short sale of $10 000 are held in Ms. Smith's account, but she is prohibited from withdrawing it until the loan is repaid. Now imagine that at some date after the short sale, XYZ stock rises by $20 per share. In this situation, Ms. Smith owes Brock 100 shares of XYZ with a current market value of 100 shares × $120 per share = $12 000 but has only $10 000 in her account. If she skips town, Brock will have collateral of $10 000 (in cash), but a loan of $12 000, resulting in a loss of $2000. However, Brock can use margin requirements to protect itself from experiencing losses from short sellers who do not repay their loans. In this example, Ms. Smith must not only leave the short-sale proceeds with her broker, but she must also give her broker sufficient funds to raise the margin in her account to the prescribed minimum. Assuming that the minimum margin is 160%, she must give her broker .6 × $10 000 = $6000 cash.

Table 2.4	Minimum Margin Requirements on Short Positions in Listed Equities.

On Listed Securities Selling at:	Minimum Margin Requirement[a]
Option eligible securities[b]	130% of market
$2.00 and over	150% of market
$1.50 to $1.99	$3.00 per share
$0.25 to $1.49	200% of market
under $0.25	100% of market plus $0.25 per share

[a]These rates apply to the initial transaction. If the share price increases, the investor provides additional margin.
[b]*Option Eligible Securities* (OES) are those that meet the eligibility criteria as underlying securities for either Canadian or US exchange-traded options. Also included are securities convertible into OES and preferred shares of companies whose equity qualifies.

SOURCE: *The Canadian Securities Course* (Toronto: Canadian Securities Institute, 1997).

Table 2.4 shows the minimum prescribed margin requirements for short sales in Canada.

The price of XYZ stock would have to rise above $160 per share in order for Brock to be in jeopardy of not being repaid. Thus, the minimum margin provides the brokerage firm with a certain degree of protection. However, this protection is not complete, since it is not unheard of for stocks to rise in value by more than 60%. It is vigilance that protects the brokerage firm from losing money in such situations. As soon as the share price rises the broker must issue a margin call in order to maintain the required margin in the account. In this example, if the share price rises to $130 per share then the margin required will be $13 000 × 1.6 = $20 800, but there is only $16 000 in the account and she will receive a margin call. Just as in margin calls on margin purchases, she will be asked to put up more margin, meaning she will be asked to add cash or securities to her account.

If, instead of rising, the share price falls, then the short seller can take a bit more than the drop in the price out of the account in the form of cash, since in this case the actual balance has risen above the minimum balance required.[17]

---

[17]Alternatively, the short seller could short sell a second security and not have to put up all (or perhaps any) of the minimum balance requirement.

Table 2.5 Potential Market Account Conditions and Actions for a Short Seller.

Share price	$ 130	$ 100	$ 70
Market value	13 000	10 000	7 000
Required margin	20 800	16 000	11 200
Actual cash in account	16 000	16 000	16 000
Surplus/(deficit)	(4 800)	0	4 800
Possible action	1. Add cash or securities. 2. Buy back shares to pay off part of loan.	1. Do nothing.	1. Do nothing. 2. Withdraw surplus cash.

Table 2.5 summarizes the state of the investor's margin account in a short position for different share prices.

What happens to the cash in the short seller's account? When the short position is covered, cash is withdrawn from the account by the broker to purchase the securities required to return the shares borrowed. Any cash remaining in the account can be withdrawn by the investor.

Before the loan is repaid, however, the cash in the account is treated as two separate and distinct amounts—the proceeds from the short sale and the funds contributed by the investor. In the first case, the brokerage firm usually keeps the cash proceeds and can invest the funds to earn interest. The short seller receives no interest and the lender of the securities receives no compensation. The brokerage firm then makes money not only from the commission paid by the short seller, but also on the interest earned on the cash proceeds from the short sale. In an increasing number of sales, however, the securities may be lent only on the payment of a premium by the short seller; therefore, the short seller not only foregoes interest on the cash proceeds, but must also pay a fee for the use of the shares borrowed. In the second case, the short seller may earn income on her contribution to the margin account by depositing interest-bearing securities, such as Treasury bills, in lieu of cash for the margin requirements.

Rate of Return

The use of short selling results in opposite rates of return to the investor than would be earned if the shares were purchased on margin (assuming that initial margin for the short sale is met by depositing cash and that the short loan is "flat," and ignoring interest on the margin loan). Hence, short sales also involve the use of financial leverage.

Consider XYZ shares once again, which Ms. Smith short sold at a price of $100 per share. If she later repays the short loan when the shares are selling for $75 per share and just after XYZ has paid a $1 per share cash dividend, then her rate of return would be equal to ($100 − $75 − $1)/(.6 × $100) = $24/$60 = 40%. In contrast, note that the return for someone who had purchased the shares of XYZ on margin would be equal to ($75 + $1 − $100)/(.6 × $100) = −$24/$60 = −40%, whereas the rate of return for someone who had purchased the shares without using margin would be equal to ($75 + $1 − $100)/$100 = −$24/$100 = −24%.

However, if Mrs. Smith has incorrectly predicted the future price movement of XYZ and it goes up to $120 per share just after paying as $1 per share cash dividend, then her rate of return would be equal to ($100 − $120 − $1)/(.6 × $100) = −$21/$60 = −35%. Conversely, if the shares had been purchased on margin, her rate of return would have been equal to ($120 + $1 − $100)/(.6 × $100) = $21/$60 = 35%. Without margin, the rate of return on the shares would be equal to ($120 + $1 − $100)/$100 = $21/$100 = 21%.

What happens to these rate of return calculations if interest is earned on both the initial margin and the short proceeds? It increases the rate of return to the short seller.

Market Neutral Strategies

Institutional investors have traditionally viewed management of common share portfolios as a one-sided problem: buy underpriced shares that are likely to appreciate in value relative to an established benchmark. However, that perspective is rapidly changing as these investors explore investment techniques that involve purchases *and* short sales of stocks so as to systematically control portfolio risk and profit from insights into mispriced securities. These techniques are collectively known as "market neutral" strategies.

The logic underlying market neutral strategies is simple. If on average all securities are fairly priced, then mispricing must be a zero-sum game—underpriced securities must be accompanied by overpriced securities. Therefore if an investor can discover mispriced securities, why should she restrict herself to buying the underpriced securities? Why not profit by short selling the overpriced securities as well?

The basic process of implementing market neutral strategies is similarly straightforward. The investor holds a portfolio consisting of three investments: short-term risk-free securities (for example, 90-day Treasury bills), long positions in shares, and short positions in shares. The market value of each investment is the same. Furthermore, the long and short share positions have equal exposures to common causes of stock market variability. (See Chapter 10 for a discussion of factors affecting share returns.) The resulting portfolio, therefore, is fully hedged against any type of stock market movement.

Why should this hedged portfolio be of interest? After all, it should earn only the risk-free return. The answer lies with the share selection skills of the market neutral investor. If the investor possesses valuable knowledge of mispriced securities, then she will purchase underpriced shares whose unique circumstances will cause them to increase in value relative to the market. Conversely, she will short sell overpriced shares whose unique circumstances will cause them to decrease in value relative to the market. The net result is that the investor benefits from her ability to identify mispriced stocks, without exposure to the vagaries of the stock market.

As a simple example, consider an investor who begins the year with $100 in cash. The investor uses the cash to purchase $100 of stocks. At the same time the investor short sells $100 of stocks. These purchases and short sales have been carefully designed to exhibit no net exposure to any industry or other factor influencing stock market returns. (For example, the investor might form long-short pairs within industries—buy $5 of GM stock and short sell $5 of Ford stock.) At the beginning of the year the investor's portfolio appears as follows:

Long	Short	Cash	Total
$100	−$100	$100	$100

Assume that the investor selects wisely and the long portfolio is worth $110 at year-end, for a 10% return. (By comparison, the stock market's return was 8%.) Furthermore, the short portfolio also has risen in value (but not by as much as the long portfolio or the stock market) to $105 (a 5% return), and the cash holdings have earned $2 in interest (a 2% return). At year-end the investor's portfolio appears as follows:

Long	Short	Cash	Total
$110	−$105	$102	$107

This investor has earned $7 on a $100 portfolio, or a 7% return, without assuming any market risk. The only risk the investor has taken lies in her ability to identify mispriced shares. The return from adroit share selection is known as "alpha" (see Chapter 24). In fact, the market neutral investor earns a "double alpha" by gaining from insights into both underpriced and overpriced shares.

Of course, the real world, with its unaccommodating nature, makes the implementation of market neutral strategies much more complex than our simple example implies. Consider the following steps that the market neutral investor must follow:

1. **Establish a margin account**. As the text describes, short selling must be conducted in a margin account. Thus, the investor must select a broker to hold the stocks and cash involved in the market neutral strategy.
2. **Make long and short transactions simultaneously**. Long positions must always equal short positions, or the portfolio may be exposed to

unintended risks. The Toronto Stock Exchange's uptick rule (see page 30) and the limited availability of appropriate stocks for short selling complicates this task.

3. **Maintain collateral with the broker**. The stocks from the long positions and cash from the short sales must be deposited with the broker.

4. **Reimburse for dividends paid and substitute for recalled borrowed stocks**. The investor must compensate the stock lender for any dividends paid on the borrowed stocks. Also, if the borrowed securities are sold by the lender and cannot be replaced, the investor must find appropriate substitutes.

5. **Continuously monitor portfolio positions**. Security price movements will affect the long-short balance in the portfolio. Only careful daily monitoring can prevent the portfolio from moving away from a market neutral stance.

Institutional investors pay special attention to selecting a broker for their market neutral strategies. They invariably choose large, established brokers with impeccable credit ratings. These brokers have the best access to securities for short sales, either through their street name holdings or through security lending networks. Institutional investors also consider the interest income rebates provided by the brokers. Unlike small investors, who typically receive no interest on their short sale proceeds, institutional investors can negotiate to receive anywhere from 75% to 90% of the income earned by the broker on the short sale proceeds.

Any investment organization can implement market neutral strategies. However, investors using quantitative investment processes (for example, dividend discount models—see Chapter 17) are the primary purveyors of this approach. Their processes typically rank a large number of stocks from highly attractive to unattractive—a step necessary to develop a diversified collection of long and short opportunities. Moreover, these investors' portfolio construction methods usually are very structured, thus facilitating the intricate design and maintenance of offsetting long and short positions.

Some institutional investors extend the market-neutral strategies and "equitize" the cash held in their portfolios—that is, they purchase common stock futures contracts (see Chapter 20), effectively creating stock market exposure equal to the value of their cash holdings. Their portfolio returns then become the return on the stock market plus the returns produced by their insights into attractive long and short stocks.

This "equitization" technique opens up a vast range of investment strategies that permit the market-neutral investor to "transport" her skills to other markets (see Chapter 20). For example, consider a pension fund with a policy requiring investment of a portion of its assets in fixed-income securities. It could simply buy a portfolio of bonds to satisfy the policy guidelines. However, suppose that the pension fund had access to skillful market neutral stock managers. The pension fund could use those managers' investment talents, while at the same time purchasing Treasury bond futures contracts to give it the required fixed-income market exposure. Thus the pension fund's investment policy is satisfied and, if the market neutral managers are successful, then the pension fund profits from their skill as well. In essence, the pension fund has "transported" the market neutral stock managers' skills to the bond market.

Market neutral strategies offer no guarantee of success, as they rely on the stock selection abilities of the investor. A poor investor can generate substantial transaction costs (see Chapter 3), while adding no "alpha" to the portfolio. Moreover, if the offsetting long-short positions are constructed inaccurately, the portfolio could experience unpleasant surprises.

Despite these caveats, market neutral strategies represent an intriguing combination of portfolio risk control and security selection. These strategies have been employed on a large scale for only a few years. Nevertheless they are rapidly making their influence felt as institutional investors examine the very essence of how value is added to their portfolios through active management.

Consider the example where XYZ fell to \$75, and assume that the short seller earned 5% on the initial margin deposit and 4% on the short proceeds. In this case the return to the short seller would be equal to $\$100 - \$75 - \$1 + (.05 \times .6 \times \$100) + (.04 \times \$100) / (.6 \times \$100) = \$31/\$60 = 51.7\%$, which is notably higher than the 40% previously calculated. Hence, financial leverage is even more effective when interest is paid to the short seller.

Securities Lending

Securities Lending The process of making available securities owned by one investor to another investor in the form of a loan. The borrower provides collateral to the lender to secure the loan and pays the lender a fee.

In the example of Ms. Smith's short sale, Brock Inc. used Mr. Leung's shares of XYZ Company held in street name to facilitate the transaction. In some situations, a broker will not hold a security that a client wishes to sell short in its street name inventory. In that case, another method to obtain securities for short selling is through **securities lending**. Three parties usually participate in a securities lending transaction: the lender, the lender's agent, and the borrower. Lenders usually are institutional investors, such as pension or endowment funds, who hold a large inventory of securities in the normal course of their investing activities. The lender's agent is usually a bank who acts as a custodian and recordkeeper for the lender. Finally, the borrower is a broker who may be borrowing securities on behalf of clients.

Figure 2.2 Securities lending process.

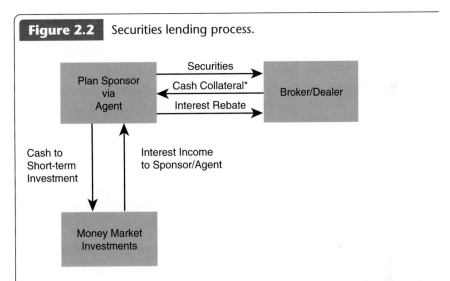

*Non-cash collateral (for example, bank letters of credit or government securities) may be used. In that case, the borrower pays a fee to the lender in lieu of the lender investing cash.

Figure 2.2 displays the steps involved in securities lending. The lender, through its agent, makes available the desired securities to the borrower. The borrower, in turn, provides collateral for the loan, usually in the form of cash. The amount of collateral equals between 102% to 105% of the borrowed securities' market values and is adjusted daily based on changes in these securities' values. The lender's agent invests the collateral in short-term fixed-income investments and rebates a portion of the interest earnings to the borrower. The retained portion represents securities lending income, which is shared by the lender and its agent. The percentage split of the rebated and retained portions depends on the supply and demand for the borrowed securities.

Legal ownership of borrowed securities passes to the borrower during a loan's life, although the lender continues to receive all dividend or interest income from the borrower. A loan usually has no maturity date, although occasionally a fixed period of time such as a month may be attached to the loan agreement. In an open-ended loan, the lender has the right to cancel the loan and demand return of the borrowed securities at any time. In that case the lender's agent will search among its other clients' security holdings to find an identical security. If the agent is unsuccessful, the borrower must return the security to the lender.

Aggregation

An investor with a margin account may purchase several different securities on margin or may short sell several different securities. Alternatively, she may purchase some on margin and short sell others. The determination of whether an account is under or overmargined depends on the total activity in the account. For example, if one stock is undermargined and another is overmargined, then the overmargined stock can be used to offset the undermargined stock, provided it is overmargined to a sufficiently large degree. How these multiple transactions are aggregated in one account in order to see the state of the account on any given day is shown next.

Multiple Margin Purchases

In the case of multiple margin purchases, aggregation is straightforward. The investor's surplus/(deficit) in the account is determined by recalculating the market value of all the stocks held using current market prices. Here the current market price of any particular security usually means the price at which the last trade was made in the market involving that security on the previous day.

Multiple Short Sales

In a similar manner, the surplus/(deficit) in the margin account of an investor who has short sold more than one stock can be determined. The minimum margin requirement for each individual share is calculated, aggregated, and compared with the total cash in the account.

Simultaneous Margin Purchases and Short Sales

The situation where the investor has purchased some stocks, perhaps on margin, and has short sold others is more complicated than either of the situations just described. The simplest way to proceed is to consider the surplus/(deficit) in the long and short positions separately and then aggregate. This can best be illustrated with an example.

Consider an investor who short sells 100 shares of ABC on August 1 at $50 per share and purchases 100 shares of XYZ on margin at $100 per share on August 15 when ABC shares are still selling at $50 per share. The margin requirement for both transactions is 60%. On August 31, ABC shares are selling for $40 per share and XYZ for $80 per share.

On August 1 the investor's short sale account will be credited with $5000 representing the proceeds of the short sale and, in addition she will have to add $5000 × 0.6 = $3000 cash to her margin account for a total credit balance of $8000. On August 15 there is no change required on account of the short sale because the price of ABC remains at $50 per share. The total value of the purchace of XYZ shares is $10 000 and, given the 60% margin requirement, the investor must add $6000 to her margin account and is given a margin loan of $4000 by her broker. The collateral value of the XYZ shares, therefore, is $4000. On August 31 when her accounts are marked to the market the ABC shares are now worth $4000 so the margin requirement is now $4000 × 1.6 = $6400, but there is $8000 in the account or a surplus of $1600. The drop in the price of XYZ shares, however, has reduced the collateral value of these shares from $4000 to $8000 × 0.4 = $3200, therefore, the minimum margin requirement is now $10 000 − $3200 = $6800 or a deficit of $800. The net effect is that the investor can withdraw $1600 − $800 = $800 from her margin account on August 31 as a result of the two price changes.

Table 2.6 shows a summary of the investor's account on both August 15 and August 31.

Table 2.6 Summary of the Aggregate Margin Account for an Investor with Both Long and Short Positions.

A. August 15

Margin Account	Short Position	Long Position	Aggregate
Share price	$ 40	$ 100	$ –
Market value	5 000	10 000	–
Collateral value	–	4 000	–
Minimum margin	8 000	6 000	14 000
Cash in account	8 000	6 000	14 000
Surplus/(deficit)	0	0	0

B. August 31

Margin Account	Short Position	Long Position	Aggregate
Share price	$ 50	$ 80	$ –
Market value	4 000	8 000	–
Collateral value	–	3 200	–
Minimum margin	6 400	6 800	13 200
Cash in account	8 000	6 000	14 000
Surplus/(deficit)	1 600	(800)	800

In practice, the investor would probably not withdraw the funds because the accounts are marked to market daily and, in volatile markets particularly, the margin requirements can fluctuate considerably. The $800 surplus then acts as a cushion against any adverse movements in the prices of the securities to avoid frequent margin calls.

INSTITUTIONAL ISSUES

Hedge Funds

Hedge funds are a US phenomenon that captured the attention of institutional investors and the financial press in the 1990s. During the extended bull market for financial assets, these organizations became synonymous with an aggressive, freewheeling investment style that produced some extraordinary successes and some spectacular failures.

Years ago, the classic hedge fund focused on buying and selling short stocks and bonds issued in US markets. The term "hedge" came from the fact that much of the market exposure associated with owning stocks and bonds was offset by the corresponding short positions. These hedge funds were designed to make money regardless of the direction of the overall market, although in practice that objective was not always achieved. Leverage (that is, borrowed funds) was often used, but primarily to obtain the margin needed to sell short. Hedge funds were few in number and participation was limited almost entirely to high net worth individuals.

Today, although hedge funds still use a combination of long and short positions, much else has changed, and generally these changes have been toward a more aggressive posture. Hedge funds now invest in a broad spectrum of securities around the globe, ranging from traditional stocks and bonds to options, futures, currencies, and commodities. Leverage is used to bolster profits by increasing the assets available for investment, in some cases by up to 20 to 30 times. The clientele has also changed as has the number of funds available. Institutional investors now constitute the largest source of new monies entering hedge funds. It is estimated that over $100 billion is now invested in over 3000 hedge funds.

A new breed of hedge fund manager has also emerged. Where before hedge funds attempted to profit largely from pricing discrepancies between individual securities, many hedge funds now seek to identify mispricings among whole asset classes. These "macro" hedge funds may take large bets that US interest rates are going to fall or that the German Deutschemark is going to rise relative to the British pound. When correct, these macro bets can generate enormous returns for the funds, but they also run the risk of sizeable losses. Macro hedge funds have been blamed for roiling the international financial markets with their aggressive speculation.

Hedge funds are usually organized as private partnerships. They avoid government regulation in one of two ways. Either they limit the number of partners to no more than 100 and do not promote their funds to the investing public or they require investing individuals to own at least $5 million in financial assets and institutions to have more than $25 million under management. Consequently, they are not required to disclose performance results, expenses, or portfolio composition as are registered investment companies (see Chapter 21). Nor are they restricted in terms of diversification, allowing them to hold more concentrated portfolios than can investment companies.

Performance (unadjusted for risk) has always been the name of the game for hedge funds. Hedge fund clients expect their managers to produce positive double-digit returns, regardless of the market environment. As one would expect in a highly efficient market (see Chapter 4), few hedge funds are able to satisfy such lofty return expectations. Still, while comprehensive performance data is hard to come by, informally at least, returns of up to 120% in a good year and consistent annual returns of over 20% have been reported for successful funds. Unfortunately, "survivor bias" contaminates what aggregate performance data is available on hedge

funds. That is, poorly performing funds simply close up shop and their returns are expunged from consultants' databases, giving the impression of better overall performance than actually occurred.

Although some hedge funds pursue conservative, tightly risk-controlled strategies, in general, hedge fund investing is a very risky proposition. Macro hedge funds in particular have produced highly variable results. Many such funds lost billions in 1994 betting that US interest rates would fall and that the Japanese yen would decline relative to the US dollar. The most infamous hedge fund collapse occurred in 1994 at a $600 million fund run by Askin Capital Management. In that debacle, investors (including several large, sophisticated institutions) saw their holdings wiped out through the failure of a highly leveraged, mortgage derivatives strategy. More recently (September 1998) the near collapse and bailout of the $4.6 billion *Long Term Capital Management LP* hedge fund by several commercial banks sent shock waves through world capital markets.

The lack of information about hedge funds' portfolios and performance results makes it difficult for investors to monitor their risks and evaluate results. Appropriate benchmarks (see Chapter 24) for most hedge funds are difficult to construct. Investors typically have very little understanding of how their hedge fund holdings fit with their other investments in a total portfolio context.

The unregulated nature of hedge funds and their increasing size has begun to draw the attention of regulators. Central banks, in particular, have become concerned about the impact of hedge funds on the stability of international financial markets. In the United States, as hedge funds have become more daring in their solicitations of potential clients, the Securities and Exchange Commission has started to question just how much leeway hedge funds should be allowed in promoting themselves. Whether hedge funds can continue to escape government supervision in the years ahead is problematic.

Still interested in investing in a hedge fund? Be sure to have substantial assets on hand. Initial investments are typically $500 000 and up. Fees range between 1% and 2% of assets under management, and the fund's general partners typically keep 20% of all fund profits. (Note, however, that the general partners do not similarly share in losses. Thus the incentive system is heavily skewed toward aggressive risk taking.) Withdrawals are usually restricted. Investors may have to commit funds for months or even years and afterward may be limited to quarterly or semiannual redemptions.

Despite these risks and limitations, institutional investors and high net-worth individuals continue to pour money into hedge funds of various types. The lure of high returns is always tantalizing. Successful hedge fund managers, both past and present, are the stuff of Wall Street legend, including Michael Steinhardt, Julian Robertson, and George Soros, among others. Hedge funds provide an interesting study of the techniques of aggressive investment managers, a perspective one cannot usually find in more traditionally managed equity funds.

Summary

1. Investors typically buy or sell securities through brokers who are compensated for their services with commissions.
2. When transacting in a security, investors must specify the following: the security's name; buy or sell; order size; time limit; and type of order.
3. The three standard types of orders are market, limit, and stop.
4. Investors may purchase securities with cash or may borrow from brokerage firms to buy securities on margin.
5. Investors must make down payments on their margin purchases, maintain minimum actual margin levels in their margin accounts, and pay interest on margin loans.
6. If an investor's actual margin falls below the minimum required, the investor's account is undermargined. The investor will receive a margin call and must increase the actual margin level in the account.
7. Buying on margin results in financial leverage, thereby magnifying (positively or negatively) the impact of a security's return on the investor's wealth.
8. Short sales involve the sale of securities that are not owned, but rather are borrowed by the sellers. The borrowed securities must ultimately be purchased in the market and returned to the lenders.
9. A short seller must deposit the proceeds of the short sale and the required margin with his broker. The short seller must also maintain a minimum actual margin level in his margin account or face a margin call.
10. For investors who purchase on margin or short sell several securities, the determination of whether an account is undermargined or overmargined depends on the aggregated activity in their accounts.

QUESTIONS AND PROBLEMS

1. Describe the conflict of interest that typically exists in the investment advisory relationship between a brokerage firm and its clients.
2. How many board lots and what odd lot size are in an order for 511 shares?

3. Discuss the advantages and disadvantages to the investor of the following:
   a. Market order
   b. Limit order
   c. Stop order
4. Why are margin account securities held in street name?
5. Lucille Killefer purchases on margin 200 shares of Landfall Corporation stock at $75 per share. The margin requirement is 55%. Prepare Lucille's balance sheet for this investment at the time of purchase.
6. Buck Ewing opened a margin account at a local brokerage firm. Buck's initial investment was to purchase 200 shares of Woodbury Corporation on margin at $40 per share. Buck borrowed $3000 from a broker to complete the purchase.
   a. At the time of the purchase, what was the actual margin in Buck's account?
   b. If Woodbury stock subsequently rises in price to $60 per share, what is the actual margin in Buck's account?
   c. If Woodbury stock subsequently falls in price to $35 per share, what is the actual margin in Buck's account?
7. Sam Arnovich buys on margin 1000 shares of Rockford Systems stock at $60 per share. The margin requirement is 50%, but Sam only uses 75% margin. If the Rockford stock falls to $50, will Sam receive a margin call?
8. Avalon Company's stock is currently selling for $15 per share. The margin requirement is 60%. Charles Anson buys 100 shares of Avalon stock on 75% margin. To what price must the stock fall for Charles to receive a margin call?
9. Liz Arlington has deposited $15 000 in a margin account with a brokerage firm. If the margin requirement is 50%, what is the maximum dollar amount of stock that Liz can purchase on margin?
10. Penny Bailey bought on margin 500 shares of South Beloit Inc. at $35 per share. The margin requirement is 45% and the annual interest on margin loans is 12%. Over the next year the price of the stock rises to $40. What is Penny's return on investment?
11. Calculate Buck Ewing's rate of return in parts (b) and (c) Problem 6 under the assumption that the margin loan was outstanding for one year and carried an interest rate of 10%, and that the prices of $60 and $35 were observed after one year during which the firm did not pay any cash dividends.
12. Ed Delahanty purchased 500 shares of Niagara Corporation stock on margin at the beginning of the year for $30 per share. The margin requirement was 55%. Ed paid 13% interest on the margin loan and never faced a margin call. Niagara paid dividends of $1 per share during the year.
    a. At the end of the year, if Ed sold the Niagara stock for $40 per share, what would Ed's rate of return be for the year?
    b. At the end of the year, if Ed sold the Niagara stock for $20 per share, what would Ed's rate of return be for the year?
    c. Calculate your answers to parts (a) and (b) assuming that Ed made the Niagara stock purchase for cash instead of on margin.
13. Individual investors are sometimes contacted by their brokers and told that they have "unused buying power" in their brokerage accounts. What do the brokers mean by this statement?
14. Beatrice Bancroft short sells 500 shares of Rockdale Manufacturing at $25 per share. The margin requirement is 50%. Prepare Beatrice's balance sheet as of the time of the transaction.
15. Through a margin account, Cindy Cummings short sells 200 shares of Madison Inc. stock for $50 per share. The margin requirement is 45%.
    a. If Madison stock subsequently rises to $58 per share, what is the actual margin in Cindy's account?

b. If Madison stock subsequently falls to $42 per share, what is the actual margin in Cindy's account?

16. Daniel Benoit short sells 500 shares of Naperville Products at $45 per share. The margin requirement is 55%, but Daniel provides 70% margin at the time of purchase. If Naperville stock rises to $50, will Daniel receive a margin call?

17. Sun Prairie Foods stock currently sells for $50 per share. The margin requirement is 50%. If Willie Keeler short sells 300 shares of Sun Prairie stock and provides 60% margin, to what price can the stock rise before Willie receives a margin call?

18. Eddie Gaedel is an inveterate short seller. Is it true that Eddie's potential losses are infinite? Why? Conversely, is it true that the maximum return that Eddie can earn on his investment is 100%? Why?

19. The stock of DeForest Inc. sold at the beginning of the year for $70 per share. At that time David Barclay short sold 1000 shares of the stock. The margin requirement was 50%. DeForest stock has risen to $75 at year-end, and David faced no margin calls in the interim. Further, the stock paid a $2 dividend at year-end. What was David's return on this investment?

20. Calculate Cindy Cummings' rate of return in parts (a) and (b) of Problem 15, assuming that the short loan was flat, but the margin deposit earned interest at a rate of 8%, and that the prices of $58 and $42 were observed after one year during which the firm did not pay any dividends.

21. What aspects of short selling do brokerage houses typically find to be especially profitable?

22. Peter Barnhart purchases 100 shares of Batavia Lumber Company stock on margin at $50 per share. Simultaneously, Peter short sells 200 shares of Geneva Shelter stock at $20 per share. With an initial margin requirement of 60%:
    a. What is the initial equity (in dollars) in Peter's account?
    b. If Batavia and Geneva rise to $55 and $22 per share, respectively, what is Peter's equity position (in dollars)?

23. On May 1, Ivy Olson sold short 100 shares of Lac Minerals stock at $25 per share and bought on margin 200 shares of St. Louis Park Company stock for $40 per share. The initial margin requirement was 50%. On June 30, Lac stock sold for $36 per share and St. Louis Park stock sold for $45 per share.
    a. Prepare a balance sheet showing the aggregate financial position on Ivy's margin account as of June 30.
    b. Determine whether Ivy's account is subject to a margin call on June 30.

KEY TERMS

broker (p. 23)
account executive (p. 23)
registered representative (p. 23)
regional brokerage firm (p. 23)
discount broker (p. 23)
commission (p. 23)
New Client Application Form (p. 24)
order specifications (p. 24)
board lot (p. 24)
odd lot (p. 24
day order (p. 24)
good through order (p. 24)
open order (p. 25)

good-till-cancelled order (p. 25)
all or none order (p. 25)
any part order (p. 25)
discretionary order (p. 25)
market order (p. 25)
limit order (p. 25)
limit price (p. 25)
stop-loss order (p. 26)
stop-buy order (p. 26)
stop price (p. 26)
cash account (p. 26)
margin account (p. 26)
street name (p. 26)

margin (p. 27)
margin purchase (p. 27)
debit balance or loan value (p. 27)
prime rate (p. 27)
minimum margin requirement (p. 27)
settlement date (p. 27)
marked to market (p. 28)

margin call (p. 28)
financial leverage (p. 29)
short sale (p. 30)
uptick (p. 30)
short interest (p. 30)
securities lending (p. 37)

REFERENCES

1. For a discussion of the mechanics of purchasing and selling securities, along with margin purchasing and short selling, see:

   How to Invest in Canadian Securities (Toronto: Canadian Securities Institute, 1994).

   The Canadian Securities Course (Toronto: Canadian Securities Institute, 1997).

   James J. Angel, "An Investor's Guide to Placing Stock Orders," *AAII Journal* 15, no. 4 (April 1993): 7–10.

   J. Randall Woolridge and Amy Dickinson, "Short Selling and Common Stock Prices." *Financial Analysts Jounal* 50, no. 1 (January–February 1994): 20–28.

2. An interesting discussion of margin requirements and their impact on market volatility is contained in:

   David A. Hsieh and Merton H. Miller, "Margin Requirements and Market Volatility," *Journal of Finance* 45, no. 1 (March 1990): 3–29.

3. A recent study that examines levels and changes in short interest is:

   Averil Brent, Dale Morse, and E. Kay Stice, "Short Interest: Explanations and Tests," *Journal of Financial and Quantitative Analysis* 25, no. 2 (June 1990): 273–289.

4. Market neutral investment strategies are discussed in:

   Bruce I. Jacobs and Kenneth L. Levy, "Long/Short Equity Investing," *Journal of Portfolio Management* 20, no. 1 (Fall 1993): 52–63.

   Richard O. Michaud, "Are Long-Short Equity Strategies Superior?" *Financial Analysts Journal* 49, no. 6 (November–December 1993): 44–49.

   Bruce I. Jacobs and Kenneth N. Levy, "More on Long-Short Strategies," *Financial Analysts Journal* 51, no. 2 (March–April 1995): 88–90.

   Jess Lederman and Robert A. Klein (eds.), *Market Neutral* (Chicago: Richard D. Irwin, 1996).

   Bruce I. Jacobs and Kenneth N. Levy, "20 Myths about Long-Short," *Financial Analysts Journal* 52, no. 5 (September–October 1996): 81–85.

   John S. Brush, "Comparisons and Combinations of Long and Long/Short Strategies," *Financial Analysts Journal* 53, no. 3 (May–June 1997): 81–89.

5. For a thorough description of the basic security lending concepts and mechanics, see:

   Paul C. Lipson, Bradley K. Sabel, and Frank Keane, "Securities Lending, Part 1: Basic Transactions and Participants," *Journal of Commercial Bank Lending* XX, no. 2 (February 1990): 4–18.

Paul C. Lipson, Bradley K. Sabel, and Frank Keane, "Securities Lending, Part 2: Basic Transactions and Participants," *Journal of Commercial Bank Lending* XX, no. 3 (March 1990): 18–31.

6. For a Canadian perspective see:

S. Elfakhani. "Short Sellers Aren't Always Right," *Canadian Investment Review* X, no. 4 (Winter 1997–98): 9–16.

Security Markets

A security market can be defined as a mechanism for bringing together buyers and sellers of financial assets in order to facilitate trading. One of its main functions is "price discovery,"—that is, to cause prices to reflect currently available information. The quicker this is done, the more efficiently financial markets will see that capital is allocated to its most productive opportunities, thereby leading to greater improvement in public welfare. **Secondary security markets** involve the trading of financial assets that were issued at some previous point in time. This chapter is devoted to such markets, while Chapter 16 discusses the initial issuance of securities in the **primary security market**.

Secondary Security Market The market in which securities are traded that have been issued at some previous point in time.

Call and Continuous Markets

Call Markets

In **call markets**, trading is allowed only at certain specified times. In such a market, when a security is "called," those individuals who are interested in either buying or selling it are physically brought together.[1]

Then there may be an explicit auction in which prices are called out until the quantity demanded is as close as possible to the quantity supplied. Alternatively, orders may be left with a clerk, and periodically an official of the exchange sets a price that allows the maximum number of shares from the previously accumulated orders to be traded.

Continuous Markets

In **continuous markets**, trades may occur at any time. Although only investors are needed for such a market to operate, it generally would not be very effective without intermediaries also being present. In a continuous market without intermediaries, an investor who wants to buy or sell a security quickly might have to either spend a great deal of money searching for a good offer or run the risk of accepting a poor one. Because orders from investors arrive more or less randomly, prices in such a market would vary considerably, depending on the flow of buy orders relative to the flow of sell orders. However, anyone willing to take temporary positions in securities could potentially make a profit by ironing out these transitory variations in supply and demand. This is the role of intermediaries

Primary Security Market The market in which securities are sold at the time of their initial issuance.

Call Market A security market in which trading is allowed only at certain specified times. At those times, persons interested in trading a particular security are physically brought together and a market clearing price is established.

Continuous Market A security market in which trades may occur at any time during business hours.

---

[1]Enough time is allowed to elapse between calls (for example, an hour or more) so that a substantial number of orders to buy and sell will accumulate by the time of the next call.

known as dealers (also known as market-makers) and specialists. In the pursuit of personal gain, they generally reduce fluctuations in security prices that are unrelated to changes in value and, in doing so, provide **liquidity** for investors. Here, liquidity refers to the ability of investors to convert securities into cash at a price that is similar to the price of the previous trade, assuming no new information has arrived since the previous trade.

Security markets for common shares (as well as certain other securities) in Canada typically involve dealers. This chapter provides a detailed description of how these markets function and the role played by the dealers. Although the focus is on markets for common shares, many of the features of such markets are applicable to the markets for other types of financial assets (such as bonds). **Organized exchanges**, which are central physical locations where trading is done under a set of rules and regulations, are discussed first. Examples of such exchanges for common shares are the New York Stock Exchange, the Toronto Stock Exchange, the Montreal Exchange, and various regional exchanges.

The New York Stock Exchange

The New York Exchange (NYSE) is the world's largest continuous auction market and is the model for most North American exchanges. It is important, therefore, to have an understanding of the way in which the NYSE functions. Of particular interest to Canadians is the fact that there are 74 Canadian companies whose shares are traded on both the TSE and the NYSE and, therefore, must conform to the rules of both.

New York Stock Exchange

The NYSE is a corporation that has 1366 full members. It has a charter and a set of rules and regulations that govern its operation and the activities of its members. A board of 26 directors that is elected by the membership supervises the exchange. Of the directors, 12 are members and 12 are not; the latter are known as "public directors." The remaining two directors are full-time employees: a chair who also functions as the chief executive officer and a vice-chair who also functions as president.

In order to become a member, a **seat** (comparable to a membership card) must be purchased from a current member. By holding a seat, the member has the privilege of being able to execute trades using the facilities provided by the exchange. Since most trades of common shares, in both dollar size and number of shares, take place on the NYSE, this privilege is valuable.[2]

Not surprisingly, many brokerage firms are members, meaning that either an officer (if the brokerage firm is a corporation) or a general partner (if the brokerage firm is a partnership) or an employee of the firm is a member. Indeed, many brokerage firms have more than one member. A brokerage firm with one or more NYSE memberships is often referred to as a **member firm**.

A stock that is available for trading on the NYSE is known as a **listed security**. In order for a company's stock to be listed, the company must apply to the NYSE. The initial application is usually informal and confidential. If approved, the company then makes a formal application that is announced publicly. Given an earlier approval on the informal application, approval at this stage is almost certain. The general criteria used by the NYSE in approving an application are

---

[2]During 1996, trading volume on the NYSE averaged, on a daily basis, 412.0 million shares, worth nearly $7 billion. The American Stock Exchange, the second largest US organized exchange, had comparable daily values of less than one-tenth these amounts.

- the degree of national interest in the company;
- its relative position and stability in the industry; and
- whether it is engaged in an expanding industry, with prospects of at least maintaining its relative position.[3]

Companies that are approved for listing must agree to pay a nominal annual fee and provide certain information to the public. After listing, if trading interest in a company's stock declines substantially, the NYSE may decide to **delist** the company, meaning that its stock is no longer available for trading on the exchange. Delisting also occurs when a listed company is acquired by another company or is merged into another company, since the originally listed company no longer exists in such situations. A company may also voluntarily ask to have its stock delisted even though it is still eligible for listing. Companies may apply for listing on more than one exchange; therefore, the NYSE has some companies listed on it that are also listed on either other US exchanges or on foreign exchanges. Typically, those companies that are listed on other US exchanges are US companies and those listed on foreign exchanges are foreign companies.

Trading Halts and Circuitbreakers

While delisting refers to the permanent suspension of exchange trading for a particular firm's shares, occasionally the need arises for a **trading halt**, which is a temporary suspension of trading in a firm's shares. Trading halts typically are issued by the NYSE when trading in a stock is roiled due to rumours or a recent news announcement (such as a rumour of a takeover attempt or an announcement of unexpected low quarterly earnings). The opening of trading can be delayed for similar reasons or if a large imbalance of orders has accumulated since the previous close.

The NYSE also has the ability to temporarily halt trading simultaneously in all its listed stocks (or a large number of them). This is done automatically by the use of **circuitbreakers** when circumstances indicate that there is a need to reduce market volatility and promote investor confidence. Under Rule 80A, whenever the Dow Jones Industrial Average moves 50 or more points from the previous day's close, all subsequent index arbitrage orders (a form of program trading discussed in Chapter 20) involving the 500 stocks in the Standard & Poor's 500 Stock Index are subject to a tick test. (Both of these widely quoted indices are discussed in Chapter 24.) The NYSE defines an index arbitrage order as an order simultaneously involving at least 15 stocks with an aggregate market value of at least $1 million. The tick test means that in a down market, the sell orders can only be executed on either a plus tick (for a price higher than that of the previous trade) or a zero-plus tick (for a price equal to that of the previous trade, but higher than that of the last trade at a different price). In an up market, the buy orders can only be executed on either a minus tick (for a price lower than that of the previous trade) or a zero-minus tick (for a price equal to that of the previous trade, but lower than that of the previous trade).

Under Rule 80B, as revised in December 1997, if the Dow Jones Industrial Average declines 350 points in a day before 3 p.m., the NYSE shuts down for one-half hour (if the 350-point decline occurs after 3 p.m., then the market is not shut down). If the market continues to decline after it reopens so that its aggregate decline that day is at least 550 points, then the market closes for an hour, unless the 550-point decline occurs after 2 p.m., in which case the market closes for only one-half hour. If the 550-point decline occurs after 3 p.m., the NYSE shuts down for the rest of the day.

A 50-point move in the Dow Jones Industrial average implies less than a 1% change in its value. As a result, Rule 80A is frequently triggered. Whether the rule actually reduces market volatility, as its originators intended, is open to considerable debate. The much

Delisting The process of removing a security's eligibility for trading on an organized security exchange.

Trading Halt A temporary suspension in the trading of a security on an organized exchange.

Circuitbreakers
Established by the New York Stock Exchange, a set of upper and lower limits on the market price movements as measured by the Dow Jones Industrial Average. Depending on the magnitude of the price change, breaking through those limits, particularly on the downside, results initially in restrictions on program trading and ultimately in closing the exchange. The Toronto Stock Exchange follows the NYSE's lead in invoking circuitbreakers.

Dow Jones & Company
www.dowjones.com

---

[3] *Fact Book 1997 Data*, New York Stock Exchange, 1997, p. 37.

larger intraday price decline implied by Rule 80B has occurred only once since the rule's inception. On October 27, 1997, the Dow plunged 554.25 points (7.2%), triggering first the one-half hour shutdown and quickly thereafter the one hour shutdown. Because the last trading halt took place at 3:30 p.m., the NYSE closed for the rest of the day. The next day the Dow rose 337 points. Critics claimed the existence of the circuitbreakers actually destabilized the market. They argued that after the first trading halt, investors rushed to submit sell orders to beat the anticipated next shutdown, thereby accelerating the market's decline. Many market participants have called for elimination or substantial restructuring of the circuitbreakers.

New York Stock Exchange Members

Members in the NYSE fall into one of four categories, depending on the type of trading activity in which they engage. These categories are commission brokers, floor brokers, floor traders, and specialists. Of the 1366 members of the NYSE, roughly 700 are commission brokers, 400 are specialists, 225 are floor brokers, and 41 are floor traders. The trading activities of members in these categories are as follows:

1. **Commission brokers.** These members take orders that customers have placed with their respective brokerage firms and see to it that those orders are executed on the exchange. The brokerage firms that they work for are paid commissions by the customers for their services.
2. **Floor brokers,** also known as two-dollar brokers. These members assist commission brokers when there are too many orders flowing into the market for the commission brokers to handle alone. For their assistance, they receive part of the commission paid by the customer. (Sometimes both floor brokers, as defined here, and commission brokers are lumped together and called floor brokers.)
3. **Floor traders.** These members trade solely for themselves and are prohibited by exchange rules from handling public orders. They hope to make money by taking advantage of perceived trading imbalances that result in temporary mispricings, thereby allowing them to "buy low and sell high." These members are also known as registered competitive market-makers, competitive traders, or registered traders.
4. **Specialists.** These members perform two roles. First, any limit order that the commission broker cannot execute immediately because the current market price is not at or better than the specified limit price will be left with the specialist for possible execution in the future. If this order is subsequently executed, the specialist is paid part of the commission. The specialist keeps these orders in what is known as the **limit order book** (or specialist's book). Stop and stop limit orders are also left with the specialist, who then enters them in the same book. In this capacity the specialist is acting as a broker (that is, agent) for the customer's broker and can be thought of as a "broker's broker."

Second, the specialist acts as a **dealer** in certain stocks (in particular, for the same stocks in which she acts as a broker). This means that the specialist buys and sells certain stocks for her own account and is allowed to earn a profit in doing so. However, in acting as a dealer, the specialist is required by the NYSE to maintain a "fair and orderly market" in those stocks in which she is registered as a specialist. Thus the NYSE expects the specialist to buy or sell shares from her own account when there is a temporary imbalance between the number of buy and sell orders. (In doing so, specialists are allowed to short sell their assigned stocks, but still must abide by the plus-tick rule.) Even though the NYSE monitors the trading activities of the specialists, this requirement is so ill-defined that it is difficult, if not impossible, to enforce.

As might be inferred from the preceding discussion, specialists are at the centre of the trading activity on the NYSE. Each stock that is listed on the NYSE currently

Limit Order Book (Alternatively, **Electronic Book**.) The records kept by the exchange identifying the limit, stop, and stop limit orders that brokers have entered for execution in a particular security. On the TSE the information in the Electronic Book is available to all participants.

Dealer A person who trades in financial assets for his or her own account and maintains an inventory of particular securities. The dealer buys for and sells from this inventory, profiting from the difference in the buying and selling prices.

has one specialist assigned to it.[4] (In a few instances in the past, two or more specialists were assigned to the same stock.) There are over 2000 common stocks listed on the NYSE and only about 400 specialists. This suggests that each specialist is assigned more than one stock, and indeed this is the case.

All orders involving a given stock must be taken physically or electronically to a **trading post,** a spot on the floor of the NYSE where the specialist for that stock stands at all times during the hours the NYSE is open.[5] It is here that an order is either executed or left with the specialist.

Placing a Market Order

The operation of the New York Stock Exchange is best described by an example. Mr. B asks his broker for the current price of General Motors shares. The broker punches a few buttons on a PC-like quotation machine and finds that the current **bid** and **asked prices** on the NYSE are as favourable as the prices available on any other market, being equal to $61 and $61\frac{1}{4}$, respectively. In addition, the quotation machine indicates that these bid and asked prices are good for orders of at least 100 and 500 shares, respectively. This means that the NYSE specialist is willing to buy at least 100 shares of GM at a price of $61 (the bid price) and is willing to sell at least 500 shares of GM at $61\frac{1}{4}$ (the asked price).[6] After being given this information, Mr. B instructs his broker to "buy 300 at market," meaning that he wishes to place a market order with his broker for 300 shares of GM. At this point the broker transmits the order to his firm's New York headquarters, where the order is subsequently relayed to the brokerage firm's "booth" on the side of the exchange floor. Upon receiving the order, the firm's commission broker goes to the trading post for GM.

The existence of a standing order to buy at $61 means that no lower price need be accepted, and the existence of a standing order to sell at $61\frac{1}{4}$ means that no higher price need be paid. This leaves only the spread between the two prices for possible negotiation. If Mr. B is lucky, another broker (for example, one with a market order to sell 300 shares for Ms. S) will "take" the order at a price "between the quotes," here at $61\frac{1}{8}$, resulting in "price improvement." (This happens often, as about one-third of the volume in NYSE-listed stocks is traded between the bid and asked quotes.) Information will be exchanged between the two brokers and the sale made. Figure 3.1 illustrates the procedure used to fill Mr. B's order.

If the gap between the quoted bid and asked prices is wide enough, an auction may occur among various commission brokers, with sales made at one or more prices between the specialist's quoted values. This auction is known as a **double** (or two-way) **auction,** since both buyers and sellers are participating in the bidding process.

---

[4]The assignment is made by the board of directors and also includes any preferred stock or warrants that the company has listed on the exchange. At the end of 1996 there were 2907 companies listed in the NYSE, with 3285 stock issues being traded, meaning that there were over 300 different issues of preferred stock being traded in the NYSE. There were also 116 warrants on these companies' stock that were traded. Bonds are also listed on the NYSE, but are traded in an entirely different manner that does not involve the use of specialists. At the end of 1996 there were 563 companies that had 2064 issues of bonds listed on the NYSE.

[5]The NYSE is currently open from 9:30 a.m. until 4 p.m. However, the NYSE often considers extending its hours of operations in order to overlap with the London and Tokyo stock markets. The NYSE does allow certain computerized trading to take place after close in Crossing Session I (4:15 p.m. to 5:00 p.m.) and each trade in Crossing Session II must involve a "basket" of at least 15 NYSE-listed stocks and an aggregate price of $15 million (prices are set for the baskets, not individual stocks).

[6]These quotations may represent either orders for the specialist's own account or public orders. It should be noted that these quotations may not be the "best" ones, since under certain circumstances specialists are not required to display them on the screens of quotation machines. However, such "hidden orders" would appear in the limit order book and would be revealed on the exchange floor. As a matter of NYSE policy, only the specialist is allowed to see the contents of the limit order book. However, in 1991 the NYSE began to allow the specialists to disclose some information about buying and selling interest to others on the floor.

Trading Post The physical location on the floor of an organized exchange where a market-maker in a particular stock is located and where all orders involving the stock may be taken for execution.

Bid Price The price at which a market-maker is willing to purchase a specified quantity of a particular security.

Asked Price The price at which a market-maker is willing to sell a specified quantity of a particular security.

General Motors
www.gm.com

Double Auction Bidding among both buyers and sellers for a security that may occur when the market-maker's bid-ask spread is large enough to permit sales at one or more prices within the spread.

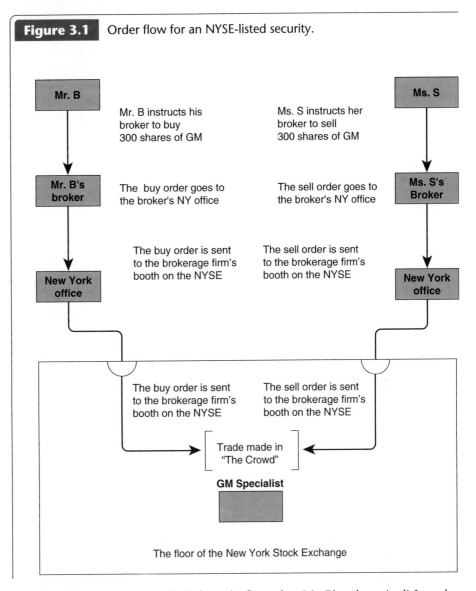

Figure 3.1 Order flow for an NYSE-listed security.

Mr. B

Mr. B instructs his broker to buy 300 shares of GM

Ms. S instructs her broker to sell 300 shares of GM

Ms. S

Mr. B's broker

The buy order goes to the broker's NY office

The sell order goes to the broker's NY office

Ms. S's Broker

The buy order is sent to the brokerage firm's booth on the NYSE

The sell order is sent to the brokerage firm's booth on the NYSE

New York office

New York office

The buy order is sent to the brokerage firm's booth on the NYSE

The sell order is sent to the brokerage firm's booth on the NYSE

Trade made in "The Crowd"

GM Specialist

The floor of the New York Stock Exchange

What if no response came forth from the floor when Mr. B's order arrived? In such a case the specialist would "take the other side," selling 300 shares to Mr. B's broker at a price of $61\frac{1}{4}$ per share. The actual seller might be the specialist or another investor whose limit order is being executed by the specialist. Sometimes the specialist will "stop" the order, meaning that the order will not be immediately filled, but that the specialist will guarantee that a price that is no worse than her quote will be obtained for the investor before the day is over. Often such orders are later filled at prices that are better than the quotes that were posted at the time the order was initially received. It is also possible that the specialist will take the other side at $61\frac{1}{8}$ for strategic reasons even though the quote is $61\frac{1}{4}$. (Sometimes a specialist wants an order to be recorded at a specific price at a given time; for example, a trade at $61\frac{1}{8}$ would make it subsequently easier to execute a short order under the up-tick rule than if the trade were executed at $61\frac{1}{4}$.)

If the bid-ask spread on a stock is no larger than the standard unit in which prices are quoted (typically $\frac{1}{16}$ of a point, or 6.25 cents, on the NYSE), market orders are generally executed directly by the specialist at the prevailing quote. This is because there is little room for price improvement. In the previous example, if the specialist had quoted bid and asked prices of \$61 and $\$61\frac{1}{16}$, then there is little incentive for Mr. B's commission broker to try to obtain a better price for the purchase order than $\$61\frac{1}{16}$, since any seller could obtain a price of \$61 from the specialist. That is, to entice someone other than the specialist to sell GM to Mr. B, his commission broker would have to offer a better price than \$61, since this is the price the seller could obtain from the specialist. Given that the next highest price is $\$61\frac{1}{16}$, and that the specialist is willing to sell at that price, Mr. B's commission broker will typically deal with the specialist at the specialist's bid quote rather than with the "crowd."

Major Markets in Canada

The Toronto Stock Exchange

The Toronto Stock Exchange (TSE) is a provincially incorporated not-for-profit organization that (as of December 1997) had 100 members. It has a charter and a set of by-laws governing its operation and the activities of its members. A 13-person board of governors elected by the membership supervises the exchange. Eight of the governors are members and four are not members; the latter are known as **public governors** (two are from institutional investors and two from outside the industry). The president and chief executive officer is the remaining governor.

Public Governor The governors of the TSE who are not associated with the brokerage industry.

A recent report by the Board of Governors of the TSE recommends wide-ranging changes not only to its trading operations, but also to its corporate structure. The most radical recommendation is that it should become a for-profit business with the member-seatholders becoming shareholders.[7]

Interlisted Securities Companies listed on more than one exchange either within Canada or abroad.

The procedures for becoming a member by purchasing a seat are very similar to those described for the NYSE, as are the listing and delisting requirements[8] and procedures[9] Trading halts follow similar rules and the TSE does not have a separate circuitbreaker system, but follows the NYSE when they invoke theirs.

Companies may apply for listing on more than one exchange either within Canada or abroad and these are known as **interlisted securities.** In the case of Canadian stocks that are interlisted in the US, it is usual for these securities to trade directly on both the Canadian and US exchanges (commonly the NYSE or NASDAQ).

NASDAQ
www.nasdaq.com

Computer-Assisted Trading System (CATS) A computer system for trading stocks on the Toronto Stock Exchange that involves a computer file containing a publicly accessible limit order book.

Trading on the Toronto Stock Exchange

The TSE closed its trading floor in Toronto on April 27, 1997, and transferred the trading of all shares to the **Computer Assisted Trading System (CATS)**, which had been in use for certain listings since 1977.[10] Following this change, all orders were entered and processed electronically, thereby eliminating all floor traders. Members are now allowed to have trading representatives who must be approved by the Investment Dealers Association and also trained in the use of the exchange's access devices to allow them to trade shares on CATS. Trading representatives fall into two categories depending on type of trading activity in which they engage.

---

[7]See the *Toronto Stock Exchange: A Blueprint for Success,* a report prepared by the Board of Governors, released October 8, 1998.

[8]For further details see a current issue of the TSE publication *Listing Requirements*.

[9]In the case of initial public offerings it is usual for these to be underwritten by an investment dealer and to trade initially in the OTC market. Only after a satisfactory trading record has been established will the exchange agree to list the shares.

[10]One of the other changes that is taking place at the TSE is the replacement of CATS with an improved trading system known as TOREX.

Order (or Desk) Trader
A floor trader who may only trade client orders on the floor of an exchange.

Registered Trader A floor trader who may execute both client and the firm's orders on the floor of an exchange.

Minimum Guaranteed Fill (MGF) The number of shares a designated market-maker stands ready to buy or sell in order to execute an order with no other counterparty.

1. **Order (or desk) traders**. These representatives take orders that the public has placed with brokerage firms and see to it that they are executed on the exchange; the brokerage firms that they work for are paid commissions by the customers for their services. They are precluded from trading for their employer's account, but are permitted to trade for their personal account provided that their orders are entered in the same way as the public's.
2. **Registered traders**. These representatives are allowed to handle customer's orders and also to trade on their firm's behalf. In the latter case they generally share in any trading profits that may be realized. A special subgroup of these traders are known as registered traders responsible for a stock, generally referred to as market-makers (MM).

The MM is required to maintain an orderly market for his or her securities of responsibility. This includes establishing an opening price that (as far as possible) clears all outstanding orders, maintaining posted bid and offer (ask) quotations,[11] maintaining a **minimum guaranteed fill (MGF)** size, assisting other traders in executing orders, and ensuring fair and orderly trading. The principal function of the MM is to provide liquidity to the market. To this end, the MM is required to fill any public (not institutional) order whose size is equal to or smaller than the MGF for which there is no counterparty. In order to accomplish this the MM is expected to maintain an inventory (either long or short) of the shares for which he or she is responsible and may alter the bid-ask spread at any time so as to adjust the size of this inventory.[12]

Like the specialist on the NYSE, who performs a similar function, the MM is a monopolist as there is only one market-maker for each MM company. In addition, a given MM may handle several listings with any accompanying rights and warrants, but not necessarily preferred shares issued by the same company. In order to become a MM, a registered trader applies to the TSE and, following a satisfactory review by a selection committee, is allocated the requested listing. Shares listed on the TSE, however, fall into two categories, Tier A and Tier B, depending on their trading frequency. Table 3.1 shows the distribution of shares listed on the TSE by different categories as of June 1998.

The table shows that the liquidity of Tier B shares is obviously a cause for some concern. From an MM's point of view, Tier A shares are much more desirable than Tier B shares. As a result, it is sometimes difficult to find dealers willing to make a market in the latter shares. In such cases, MMs with Tier A shares assume responsibility for Tier B shares that cannot be allocated by the selection committee. Nonetheless, there are Tier B2 shares with no MM that trade with no MGF.

The minimum required MGF for all Tier B shares with an MM is two board lots plus an odd lot. The required MGF for listings with a board size of 100 shares, then, is 299 shares. The maximum MGF for Tier A listings is 15 board lots plus an odd lot or 1599 shares for a listing with a board lot size of 100 shares.

---

[11]The *bid-ask spread* is the difference between the ask and the bid prices. The following minimum quotation spreads (between bid and offer prices) that are the same as the minimum trading increments are permitted on the TSE:

Price per Share	Minimum Spread
Under $0.495	$0.005
$0.50 and under $5.00	$0.01
Over $5.00	$0.05

SOURCE: The Toronto Stock Exchange.

[12]The MM must enter an order (either buy or sell) to effect a change in either the level or size of the bid-ask spread.

Table 3.1	Listed Shares Categorized by Trading Frequency.	
Tier	Average Number of Trades Daily[a]	Number of Listings
A1	>144	67
A2	51–143	113
A3	25–50	145
B1	12–24	236
B2	<12	1286

[a]Calculated over a six-month period.

Placing a Market Order

At the time of writing, trading procedures on the Toronto Stock Exchange are in a state of flux in that CATS is being phased out and replaced by the TOREX System in the near future, which will bring some minor changes to the trading procedure; the basics will, however, remain the same. The current procedure can best be described using a specific example. Today Mr. B in Sudbury calls his broker (or consults his computer) to obtain a quotation on ABC shares. His broker informs him that the current bid and ask prices on the TSE are 12.10 and 12.20 respectively, 1600 shares traded yesterday, the closing price was 12.00, the opening price was 12.10 and the last trade was executed at 12.10. The broker also adds that the MGF for this listing is 599. After digesting this information Mr. B instructs his broker to "buy 300 at market," meaning that he is placing a market order for 300 shares of ABC.

The broker in Sudbury transmits the order to his firm's headquarters in Toronto where it is relayed to the firm's desk trader who enters it into CATS. This is a fully automated system where all orders are executed immediately at either the current bid or ask price. As this is a buy order it will be executed at a price of 12.20 by the MM, as the order size is less than the MGF and the confirmation is sent immediately to the brokerage firm for transmission to the client.[13] Figure 3.2 shows schematically the procedure used to fill Mr. B's order. It should be noted thet there is no auction possible under this system so there is no price improvement as there is on the NYSE. The decimal trading increments used on the TSE, however, are narrower than the fractional increments used in New York so there is less room for price improvement even if it were possible.

Placing a Limit Order

So far, the discussion has been concerned with what would happen to a market order that was placed by Mr. B. What if Ms. C had placed a limit order instead of a market order? There are two situations that can occur with a limit order. First, the limit price may be within the bid and ask prices of the MM. Second, the limit price may be outside these prices. In the first situation, when the MM is quoting prices of 49 and 49.10, assume Ms. C has placed a limit order with her broker to buy 300 shares of DEF at a price of 49.05 or better. When this order is entered, it is possible that it will be executed by the order trader for the limit price of 49.05, since there may be a market order to take the other side of the transaction. After all, anyone with a sell order can transact with the MM at the price of 49. To these people, the limit price of 49.05 looks more attractive, since it represents a higher selling price to them. Thus, they would prefer to do business with Ms. C's order trader rather than with the MM.

---

[13]Odd-lot orders are handled in the same way as board lots with no price premium or discount. The brokerage firm, however, will charge higher transaction costs for handling such an order.

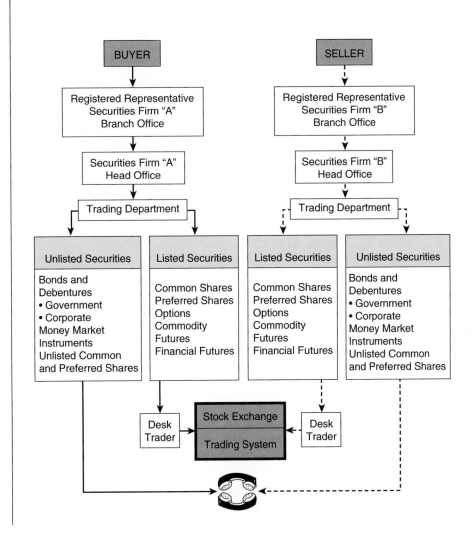

Figure 3.2 Order flow for a typical securities transaction on the OTC market and on the TSE.

In the second situation, assume Ms. C has placed a limit order to buy 300 shares of DEF with a limit price of 48. When this order is entered, the order trader will not even attempt to fill it, since the limit price is outside the MM's current bid and offer prices. That is, since anyone with a sell order can deal with the MM at a price of 49, there is no chance that anyone will want to sell to Ms. C for the limit price of 48. Thus, the order will be given to the MM to be entered in the limit order book for possible execution in the future. Limit orders in the book are executed in order of price. For example, all purchase orders with limit prices of 48.50 will be executed (if at all) before Ms. C's order is executed. If there are several limit orders in the book at the same price, they are executed in order of arrival (that is, first in, first out).

It may not be possible to fill an entire order at a single price. For example, a broker with a market order to buy 500 shares might obtain 300 shares at 49.05 and have to pay 49.10 for the remaining 200. Similarly, a limit order to buy 500 shares at 49.05 or better might result in the purchase of 300 shares at 49.05 and the entry of a limit order in the limit order book for the other 200 shares.

Limit orders entered on CATS are queued according to price and arrival time within each price level and will trade when their price matches the other side of the market.

It is clear that the limit order book contains valuable information as it shows the available supply and demand for shares at different prices. On the NYSE, the market-maker or *specialist* has sole access to this information, which can be profitably used to the specialist's advantage. The TSE differs significantly in this respect in that all information is electronically displayed and available to investors. Figure 3.3 shows an example of the information displayed in the Electronic Book. A market order that exceeds the MGF is handled by CATS according to the following allocation rule that relies on data contained in the Electronic Book:

Incoming tradeable orders are allocated among members' limit orders in the book at the bid or ask price in the following sequence:

to book orders belonging to the same member (i.e. "crosses");

to book orders with established priority to the extent of the priority size (priority is given to book orders that better the market);

equally to each member with orders at the bid or ask to a maximum of 2000 shares;

pro-rata among members based on the total number of shares that each member has booked at the bid or ask:

When shares are distributed to members, client orders will be filled before non-client orders. (Information provided by the TSE.)

Large Orders

Block A large order (usually 10 000 shares or more) to buy or sell a security.

Exceptionally large orders are generally defined as orders involving 10 000 or more shares or a value exceeding $100 000 (whichever is less) and are known as **blocks**. Typically, these orders are placed by institutional customers and may be handled in a variety of ways. One way of handling a block order is to take it directly to the MM and negotiate a price for it. However, if the block is large enough, it is quite likely that the MM will lower the bid price (for sell orders) or raise the asked price (for buy orders) by a substantial amount or will not

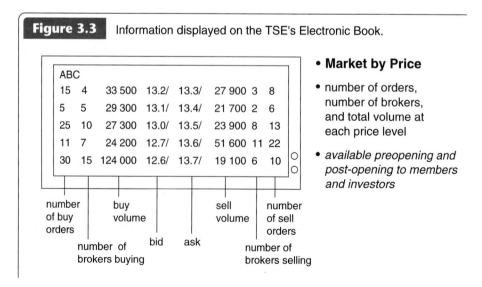

Figure 3.3   Information displayed on the TSE's Electronic Book.

• **Market by Price**

• number of orders, number of brokers, and total volume at each price level

• *available preopening and post-opening to members and investors* be interested in the offer. This will occur because of the risks involved: taking the order will probably cause the MM's inventory of the shares to exceed the acceptable long or short position.[14]

Certain investment dealers specialize in handling block trades. Since they are well-known, they are in a position to arrange counter-trades among their customers. These blocks are then crossed on the floor of the exchange at the prevailing market price without involving the MM or anyone else. Alternatively, the investment dealer may take on the block as a principal and either retain the block in inventory or attempt to distribute it in the market. In such a case the dealer pays a net price that is fractionally below the market. Under TSE rules the maximum spread allowable is specified and is designed to reflect the risks involved.[15] These trades are referred to as taking place in the *upstairs market*.

For example, suppose the CN Pension Fund informs an investment dealer that it wishes to sell 20 000 shares of Imperial Oil (IMO). The dealer then finds three institutional investors that want to buy, say, 5000 shares apiece; the dealer decides that it too will buy 5000 shares of IMO stock from CN. Noting that the buyers have said that they would be willing to pay $70 per share, the block house subsequently informs CN that it will buy the 20 000 shares for $69.75 each, less a commission of $8000. Assuming that CN accepts the deal, the dealer now becomes the owner of the shares but must first cross them on the TSE, since the dealer is a member of the exchange. After the cross, the dealer gives 5000 shares to each of the institutional buyers in exchange for $350 000 (5000 shares × $70 per share) and hopes that the remaining 5000 shares that it now owns can be sold in the near future at a favourable price. Needless to say, the possibility of not being able to sell them at a favourable price is one of the risks involved in being such a dealer. At this point the MM may decide that he would like to participate by buying 5000 of these shares.

Liquidity on the Toronto Stock Exchange[16]

Liquidity represents the ability to trade a substantial number of shares in a short time period without creating a significant adverse price movement. The existence of a substantial number of limit orders in the Electronic Book is one of the key factors in maintaining liquidity.

Share ownership by institutional investors in Canada has increased from approximately 50% to an estimated 80% of total equity capitalization between 1983 and 1998. The trading needs of institutional investors differ significantly from those of retail investors. The former look for anonymity and confidentiality in their trading to avoid "tipping their hand" before entering a block trade, thereby avoiding an adverse price movement. Retail investors are more concerned about liquidity and the "fairness of the market."

In order to preserve anonymity institutional traders resort increasingly to the upstairs market to avoid exposing their trades to the public in the Electronic Book. It is noteworthy that total trading volume has increased 300% between 1989 and 1998, but the size of the order book has remained unchanged. It is ironic that successful upstairs trading relies on information contained in the Electronic Book to establish the basis for a negotiated price, yet the practice itself curtails the effectiveness of the book. The trend towards upstairs trading, therefore, threatens the credibility of the price discovery process and reduces market liquidity, especially for retail investors.

---

[14]One alternative for the institution that is thinking of placing the block order is to sequentially place many small orders. However, institutions generally do not want to do this, since it means that their block order will not be executed with due speed.

[15]Currently the maximum spread is limited to 0.25.

[16]The material in this section draws heavily on *The Toronto Stock Exchange: A Blueprint for Success,* prepared by the Board of Governors. For more information on Alternative Trading Systems see E. Kirzner, "PETS and Other Liquidity Pools—What's Next? *Canadian Investment Review* XI, no. 1 (Spring 1998).

CN Rail
www.cn.ca

Imperial Oil
www.imperialoil.ca

Another serious competitive threat to traditional organized exchanges is Alternative Trading Systems (ATS) or Proprietary Electronic Trading Systems (PETS). These are privately operated computerized systems that match buy and sell orders and provide post-execution information. ATSs offer institutional investors with anonymous trading, reduced transactions costs, and linkages to many exchanges. ATSs have flourished in the United States with over 50 companies offering electronic trading. It is estimated that 20% of OTC (NASDAQ) and 4% of NYSE volume is transacted via ATSs. The development of ATSs in Canada is currently restricted by securities regulations but this is expected to change. The recommendations in the October 1998 by the Governors are specifically designed to address the threats to the TSE posed by ATSs.

Alberta Stock Exchange
www.alberta.net

INSTITUTIONAL ISSUES

Exchanges Must Face Reality

By Matthew Ingram

The Alberta Stock Exchange is to be congratulated for kick-starting a discussion among the western exchanges about setting up a "virtual" electronic stock market, but let's be clear about one thing: This is being dictated by necessity, and unless the ASE and the rest put away their traditional bickering, they run the risk of sliding into irrelevance.

Alberta Stock Exchange president Tom Cumming said last week that he plans to talk to his member firms and to the Vancouver and Winnipeg stock exchanges about a co-operative effort to create a single electronic market for junior and speculative companies. The three exchanges would act as a front end for this market, but there would be a single trading system.

This idea is so sensible and timely that it will probably never happen. It also requires an unprecedented level of co-operation among the western stock exchanges, and when it comes to co-operation, the three don't exactly have a killer track record. Some kind of joint venture or merger between Alberta and Vancouver—or even Alberta and Winnipeg—has been suggested several times in the past, but the idea has run aground every time.

This on-and-off debate about stock exchange mergers is similar to the long-running debate over the securities idea of a single national regulator. A streamlined Canadian regulatory system was first proposed in the 1960s and has surfaced periodically as a national issue, only to founder on the shoals of the country's provincial and regional differences.

Alberta Securities Commission head Bill Hess was one of the first to promote the idea of a virtual securities regulatory system as a way around some of the interprovincial bickering, since electronics systems isn't really based anywhere. The national association of securities regulators took up the idea, and it is on its way to becoming a reality.

In a similar way, a virtual electronic exchange tying together the three western stock exchanges could be a way around the interprovincial ego clashes that have kept Alberta and Vancouver from ever really considering a merger, even though there is ample reason to suspect that such an arrangement would be beneficial for the clients of both exchanges.

The reason for the stiff-arming on both sides isn't too hard to pinpoint: Until recently the VSE was significantly larger than the ASE, and it probably has a hard time seeing its neighbour as an equal. Alberta, meanwhile has grown dramatically in the past 10 years—much of that growth coming at Vancouver's expense and yet is still consumed, to some extent, by the desire to beat Vancouver rather than collaborate with it.

That said, all that either exchange has to do is read its industry's own newsletter and the evidence is there: Markets everywhere are merging in part because of the threat of electronic trading. The American Stock Exchange has agreed to merge with the NASDAQ Stock Market and the Philadelphia exchange has said it is considering doing the same.

NASDAQ, meanwhile—which has itself taken much of the trading action from the New York Stock Exchange—is in talks with exchanges in Germany, Hong Kong, and several other countries about creating a single electronic market that would be open to listings from any country.

Like the Alberta exchange, NASDAQ is doing this partly out of necessity, since a good deal of activity has been taken away from NASDAQ by electronic exchanges such as Instinet. The Pacific Exchange and the Chicago Board Options Exchange are also merging, even as an electronic options market is being set up by the founder of on-line brokerage firm E*Trade.

Andrew Klein, a former Wall Street securities lawyer, has set up a prototype for a virtual stock exchange through his company, Wit Capital, and only recently discovered that he would have some competition from a proposed electronic market being developed by E*Trade and Compaq Computer that has asked for approval from the U.S. Securities and Exchange Commission.

In Canada, the threat of electronic trading systems such as that developed by Versus Technologies (which runs E*Trade Canada) was recognized more than four years ago by then-head of the Ontario Securities Commission, Ed Waitzer. But little has been done to deal with the issue, partly because the country's largest exchange, the Toronto Stock Exchange, has been paralyzed until relatively recently by severe technological turmoil and infighting.

Now, having belatedly come to its senses and realized that a stock market is already more of an idea than it is an actual place or thing, even the TSE is talking (theoretically) about allowing anyone with a computer to have access to its virtual trading floor.

Alberta, for its part, got a glimpse of an unpleasant future when securities regulators came across something called the World Stock Exchange, which turned out to be a couple of guys in Edmonton with a computer server based offshore, on which they are trying to construct their own virtual stock exchange serving Alberta companies looking to go public.

It seems absurd, but what does a stock market really consist of? Computers shuffling and matching trades by approved buyers and sellers. That's just not that complicated, and if the Alberta and Vancouver and Winnipeg exchanges don't hoist that idea on board soon, they will be doomed to watch the action pass them by—and it won't be a pretty sight.

Readers can reach *Matthew Ingram by fax* at (403)*244-9809 or by* E-mail at *mingram@g*lobeandmail.ca

SOURCE: Printed with permission of *The Globe and Mail* (November 17, 1998)

Compaq Computer
www.compaq.com

Versus Technology
www.versustech.com

Vancouver Stock Exchange
www.vse.ca

Winnipeg Stock Exchange
www.wse.ca

Regional Exchange An organized exchange that specializes in trading the securities of companies located in a particular region of the country.

• **Other Exchanges**

Table 3.2 shows the total trading volume of securities listed on each of the active stock exchanges in Canada in 1996 and 1997. The Toronto Stock Exchange dominates the list. Second in importance is the Montreal Exchange (ME), which shares the listing of many companies with the TSE and also lists a number of significant Quebec-based companies exclusively. The Vancouver Stock Exchange has specialized in junior and more speculative issues. The Alberta and Winnipeg stock exchanges are termed **regional exchanges** since, historically, each served as the sole location for trading securities primarily of interest to investors in its region. The trading volume on these regional exchanges is quite small, being comparable to that of the over-the-counter (OTC) market.

These other stock exchanges use procedures similar to those of the Toronto Stock Exchange. The role of the market-maker and the extent of automation differ, but the approach is basically the same.

Options exchanges and futures exchanges utilize some procedures that differ significantly from those employed by stock exchanges. Futures exchanges often have daily price

Table 3.2 Trading Volumes on Canadian Stock Exchanges.

(a) Trading Volume, 1996 to 1997

	Shares, 1996	Percent	Shares, 1997	Percent
TSE	22 341	57.7%	25 670	62.6%
ME	4 302	10.5	4 321	10.5
VSE	8 322	22.5	7 116	17.3
ASE	4 102	9.3	3 929	9.6
WE	neg.	*	4	*
Total	39 068	100.0	41 041	100.0

*Less than 1 percent

(b) Trading Value, 1996 to 1997

	Shares, 1996	Percent	Shares, 1997	Percent
TSE	301 299	81.6%	423 170	85.0%
ME	50 167	13.6	61 912	12.4
VSE	12 004	3.2	8 670	1.7
ASE	5 971	1.6	3 871	0.8
WE	neg.	*	36	*
Total	369 441	100.0	497 658	100.0

*Less than 1 percent

SOURCE: Toronto Stock Exchange.

limits instead of having specialists with directions to maintain fair and orderly markets. In Canadian options trading the market-maker is referred to as a specialist, and is charged with responsibility for the book of limit orders and with the maintenance of an orderly market.

The Over-the-Counter Market

In the early days, banks acted as the primary dealers for stocks and bonds, and investors literally bought and sold securities over the counter at the banks. Transactions are more impersonal now, but the designation remains in use for transactions that are not executed on an organized exchange but, instead, involve the use of a dealer. Most bonds are sold over the counter, as are the securities of small (and some not-so-small) unlisted and foreign companies.

The over-the-counter market for stocks in Canada is still relatively primitive. In 1986, the Ontario Securities Commission established the *Canadian Over-the-Counter Automated Trading System* (COATS). This provides quotations and trading data for unlisted securities trading in Ontario. In March 1991, the **Canadian Dealing Network Inc.** (CDN), a subsidiary of the TSE, assumed responsibility for the operation and market regulation of COATS. This is now called the CDN System and provides two kinds of market information: current market bid and offer prices provided by approved market-makers and statistics for the previous trading day (volume, opening, high, low, and closing sale prices, or closing bid and ask quotations, and net changes for the day).

The CDN System is a quotation system and not a trading system. Actual transactions are made via direct negotiation between broker and dealer.[17] The price paid by a customer buying shares is likely to be higher than the amount paid by the broker to procure the

Canadian Dealing Network Inc. A subsidiary of the TSE, which assumed responsibility for the operation and market regulation of COATS.

Canadian Dealing Network
www.tse.com

---

[17]Generally the order will be a market order, since there is no limit order book in the over-the-counter market. Limit orders will be handled (if at all) in an informal manner by the broker, who will periodically check to see if the order can be executed without violating the limit price; stop and stop limit orders are not allowed in the OTC market. 100% margin is required on all OTC transactions.

Table 3.3	Size of a Board Lot on the CDN System.	
Price Range		Number of Shares
< $0.10		1000
$0.10 to $0.99		500
$1.00 to $99.875		100
$100 to $199.875		10
$200 or more		1

Markup The difference in prices between what an investor pays and what the investor's broker pays for a security purchased in the over-the-counter market.

Markdown The difference in prices between what an investor's broker receives and what the investor receives for a security sold in the over-the-counter market.

shares (the difference is known as a **markup**). When selling shares, the customer receives a price less than that received by the broker (here the difference is known as a **markdown**). In rare instances the customer may also be charged a commission. The size of these markups and markdowns is expected to be "reasonable" and should reflect the riskless nature of the agency transaction.

Dealers apply to CDN Inc. to become market-makers in CDN securities in the System. They are provided with terminals with which to enter bid and asked prices for the shares of any stock in which they "make a market." Such dealers must be prepared to execute trades for at least one normal trading unit (board lot) at the prices quoted. Table 3.3 shows the size of a board lot that depends on the security's price. As soon as a bid or asked price is entered for a security, it is placed in a central computer file and may be seen by other subscribers (including other dealers) on their own terminals. When new quotations are entered, they replace the dealer's former prices. Market-makers are required to provide uninterrupted bid and ask quotations from 9:30 a.m. to 5:00 p.m. on every day that the CDN System is open for business. There may be more than one market-maker for any given security.

To have quotations displayed on the CDN System, a security must have at least one registered market-maker (that is, one dealer), the firm must meet the OSC reporting requirements, and the application to quote must be approved by the board of directors of CDN Inc. Other securities that do not meet these requirements simply have their trading statistics reported daily. Currently there are about 500 securities that have quotations displayed. Brokers with orders to buy or sell securities for which there are no quotations use less formal communication networks to obtain "best execution" for their clients.

Foreign Markets

After New York the two largest stock markets in the world by market capitalization are in London and Tokyo. These stock markets each have different rules and operating procedures that offer some interesting contrasts.

London

In October 1986 the "Big Bang" introduced several major reforms to the London Stock Exchange. Fixed brokerage commissions were eliminated, membership was opened up to corporations, and foreign firms were allowed to purchase existing member firms. Furthermore, an automated dealer quotation system similar to NASDAQ was introduced. This system, known as SEAQ (Stock Exchange Automated Quotations), involves competing market-makers whose quotes are displayed over a computer network. Small orders can be executed by using SAEF (SEAQ Automated Execution Facility), which functions like NASDAQ's SOES; large orders are handled over the telephone. Limit orders are not handled centrally, but instead are handled by individual brokers or dealers who note when prices have moved sufficiently that they can be executed.

The London Stock Exchange's reforms have proven highly successful. The exchange has attracted trading in many non-UK stocks, thereby enhancing its status as the dominant

London Stock Exchange
www.londonstockex.co.uk

European stock market. Even the US stock markets have felt the competition. In an attempt to recapture some of the lost trading in US securities from the London Stock Exchange, the NASD received approval from the SEC for a computer system like NAS-DAQ, which involves trading of many of the stocks listed on either the NYSE, AMEX, or NASDAQ/NMS. This system, known as **NASDAQ International**, opens for trading six hours before the NYSE, which corresponds to the opening time of the London Stock Exchange, and closes a half-hour before the NYSE opens.

Tokyo

Similar to the London Stock Exchange, the Tokyo Stock Exchange has recently experienced major reforms. CORES (Computer-assisted Order Routing and Execution System), a computer system for trading all but the 150 most active securities, was introduced in 1982. Then in 1986 the exchange began to admit foreign firms as members, and in 1990 FORES (Floor Order Routing and Execution System) was introduced as a computer system to facilitate trading in the most active stocks.

Interestingly, the system of trading both the most active and the relatively less active securities is quite different from any system found in either the United States or the United Kingdom. It is centred on members known as *saitori* who act, in a sense, as auctioneers in that they are neither dealers nor specialists. Instead they are intermediaries who accept orders from member firms and are not allowed to trade in any stocks for their own account.

At the openings of the exchange (because the exchange is open from 9 a.m. to 11 a.m. and 12:30 p.m. to 3 p.m., there are two openings per day) the *saitori* members follow a method called *itayose,* which operates like a call market in that the *saitori* seeks to set a single price so that the amount of trading is maximized (subject to certain constraints). This involves constructing supply and demand schedules for the market and limit orders that have been received, and noting where the two schedules intersect. (An example of how this is done is described and illustrated in Chapter 4.) After the opening of the exchange, the *saitori* follows a method known as *zaraba,* where orders are processed continually as they are received—that is, market orders are offset against previously unfilled limit orders. New limit orders are filled, if possible, against previously unfilled limit orders. If these new limit orders cannot be filled, then they are entered in the limit order book for possible future execution. Unlike the limit order book on the NYSE, the limit order book in Tokyo is available for inspection by member firms. Furthermore, unlike the NYSE, the Tokyo Stock Exchange prohibits trading at prices outside a given range based on the previous day's closing price. Hence there can be situations where trading in a stock ceases until the next day (when the price range is readjusted) unless two parties decide to trade within the current range.

Information-Motivated and Liquidity-Motivated Traders

Perhaps the single major concern of a dealer is the adverse consequences she experiences as a result of buying or selling from an informed trader. When such a trader approaches a dealer, the dealer cannot tell whether the trader knows something about the stock that she does not know. That is, the dealer cannot tell whether the trader has an information advantage. However, the dealer understands that if the trader is informed, then it is likely that any information will soon be disseminated, that is, good news for the stock if the informed trader bought it, and is bad news if the informed trader sold it. For example, assume that the bid-ask quotes for Widget are $20–$21 and an informed trader (remember that at this point the dealer does not know whether the trader is informed) arrives and sells 1000 shares to the dealer at $20. Typically, a negative piece of information about the company will be released shortly thereafter that will cause the dealer to lower her quotes to, say, $18–$19. Thus, the dealer has just bought 1000 shares for $20, but now is offering and likely will sell them for $19, a potential loss of $1000. (In this example it is also assumed that the dealer cannot quote an asked price of $20 since there are other dealers that would undercut her at that price.) Conversely, if an informed trader arrives and buys 1000 shares at $21, typically there will be a positive piece of information announced shortly thereafter that will cause the dealer to raise her quotes to, say, $22–$23, resulting in an opportunity loss of $1000. In both of these cases, the dealer has been "picked off" by informed traders, losing money in the process.

So how does the dealer earn a profit? By transacting with uninformed traders, since their trades are not consistently followed by news of any particular type. After an uninformed trader buys 1000 shares when the quotes are $20–$21, it is equally possible that good or bad information (if any) about the stock will be subsequently released. The dealer, on average, will not be adversely affected by transacting with an uninformed trader. Consequently, the dealer will set a spread so that her expected losses from dealing with informed traders equals her expected gains from dealing with uninformed traders. In the language of financial economists, the dealer copes with this *adverse selection problem* by setting a spread so that the losses from trading with *information-motivated traders* is offset by the gains from trading with *liquidity-motivated traders* (so called because they either have excess cash to invest in stocks or else need cash and hence sell stocks to raise it).[18]

To see just how the spread is set, imagine the dealer believes there is a 40% probability that Widget stock is worth $10 and a 60% probability that it is worth $20. Hence, its expected value is $(.4 \times \$10) + (.6 \times \$20) = \$16$. Furthermore, 10% of all traders are information motivated in that they know what the stock is worth (they know whether it is worth $10 or $20), while the remaining 90% are not information motivated. The dealer must set his or her asked price A at a level so expected losses equal expected gains:

$$.1 \times .6 \times (\$20 - A) = .9 \times .5 \times (A - \$16)$$

or

$$A = \$16.47$$

The left-hand side of this equation shows that there is a 10% chance of an information-motivated trader arriving, and a 60% chance that he will buy. Since the loss on the trade with such an investor is $20 − A$, the expected loss with an asked price of $16.47 is $1 \times .6 \times (\$20 - \$16.47) = \$.21$. On the right-hand side, there is a 90% chance of a liquidity-motivated trader showing up, and a 50% chance that he will buy; since the gain on the trade with such an investor is $A − \$16$, the expected gain with an ask price of $16.47 is $.9 \times .5 \times (\$16.47 - \$16) = \$.21$. Thus, the $.21 expected loss from selling to an information-motivated trader is exactly offset by the $.21 expected gain from selling to a liquidity-motivated trader when the asked price is set at $16.47.

Similarly, the bid price B is set so that the expected losses from selling to the information-motivated investor equals the expected gains from selling to the liquidity motivated trader:

$$.1 \times .4 \times (B - \$10) = .9 \times .5 \times (\$16 - B)$$

or

$$B = \$15.51$$

---

[18]A similar classification of traders that has often been used by financial economists involves (1) informed speculative traders who possess both public and private information, (2) uninformed speculative traders who possess just public information, and (3) noise traders whose trades are not based on information. Hence the first two types can be viewed as information-motivated traders, the third as liquidity-motivated traders. See Sanford J. Grossman and Joseph E. Stiglitz, "On the Impossibility of Informationally Efficient Markets," *American Economic Review* 70, no. 3 (June 1980): 393–408.

Thus, the spread is $16.47–$15.51, or $.96. If it is wider, the dealer will not get any business due to competition from other dealers (or will get business on just one side—either buying a lot of shares or selling a lot of shares). If it is narrower, then the dealer will likely go out of business due to too many losses from transacting with information-motivated traders.[19] While this model does not explicitly provide for the dealer making a profit, that feature is easily accommodated by simply expanding the $.96 spread by an amount sufficient for the dealer to cover costs and earn a reasonable profit on her investment in inventory. However, competition among dealers will continue to limit the size of the spread and hence profits.

One feature of this model is that the larger the proportion of informed traders, the larger the spread. For example, in the above example, if that proportion is 20% instead of 10%, then the asked and bid prices will be $16.92 and $15.00, respectively, for a spread of $1.92 instead of $.96. Intuitively, this makes sense because there is now a greater likelihood of the dealer being "picked off" by an informed trader.

Clearing Procedures

BCE Inc.
www.bce.ca

Most securities are sold the standard way, which requires delivery of certificates within the settlement period (three business days). On rare occasions, a sale may be made as a cash transaction, requiring delivery the same day, or the seller may be given the choice of any delivery day within a specified period (typically, no more than 60 days). On other occasions, such as new issues, extensions to the settlement period are granted.

It would be extremely inefficient if every security transaction had to end with a physical transfer of share certificates from the seller to the buyer. A brokerage firm might sell 500 shares of BCE Inc. stock for one client, Mr. S, and later that day buy 500 shares for Ms. B, another client. Mr. S's 500 shares could be delivered to his buyer, and Ms. B's shares could be obtained by accepting delivery from her seller. However, it would be much easier to transfer Mr. S's shares to Ms. B and instruct Ms. B's seller to deliver 500 shares directly to Mr. S's buyer. This would be especially helpful if the brokerage firm's clients, Mr. S and Ms. B, held their securities in street name. Then, the 500 shares they traded would not have to be physically moved and their ownership would not have to be changed on the books of BCE.

Clearing Corporations

The process can be facilitated even more by a *clearing corporation*, the owners of which are brokerage firms, banks, and other financial institutions. Records of transactions made by members during a day are sent there. At the end of the day, both sides of the trades are verified for consistency; then all transactions are netted out. Each member receives a list of the net amounts of securities to be delivered or received along with the net amount of money to be paid or collected. Every day, each member settles with the clearing corporation instead of with various other firms.

In Canada there is one clearing corporation, the Canadian Depository for Securities Limited (CDS), to handle trades made on all the exchanges and in the OTC market. Nonparticipating financial institutions may use CDS services as clients of direct participants. Some banks belong simply to facilitate delivery of securities that, for example, may serve as collateral for secured demand loans.

---

[19]There are a number of implicit assumptions associated with this model that have not been spelled out here. The interested reader is directed to Lawrence R. Glosten and Paul R. Milgrom, "Bid, Ask, and Transaction Prices in a Specialist Market with Heterogeneously Informed Traders," *Journal of Financial Economics* 14, no. 1 (March 1985): 71–100.

By holding securities in street name and using clearing corporations, brokers can reduce the costs of transfer operations. But even more can be done with book based systems—certificates can be immobilized almost completely. The CDS accomplishes this by maintaining computerized records of the securities "owned" by its member firms (brokers, banks, and so on). Members' share certificates are credited to their accounts at the CDS, but the certificates are transferred to the CDS on the books of the issuing corporation and remain registered in its name unless a member subsequently withdraws them. Whenever possible, one member will "deliver" securities to another by initiating a simple bookkeeping entry in which one account is credited and the other debited for the shares involved. Dividends paid on securities held by the CDS are simply credited to members' accounts based on their holdings and may be subsequently withdrawn in cash.

Insurance

Canadian Investor Protection Fund (CIPF)
An industry maintained fund that insures investors' accounts against loss due to the failure of a brokerage firm.

When a brokerage firm fails, its clients may discover for the first time that securities and cash balances in their accounts are no longer physically available. This could lead to erosion of investor confidence; therefore, the Toronto, Montreal, Vancouver, and Alberta Stock Exchanges, the Toronto Futures Exchange, and the Investment Dealers Association of Canada have jointly established the **Canadian Investor Protection Fund (CIPF)** to protect the investing public against losses due to the financial failure of a member of one of the sponsoring organizations. When an investor becomes a customer of a member of any one of the sponsors, that customer's accounts are covered by the CIPF. Each account is insured up to a stated amount ($250 000 per account in 1997).[20] The cost of the insurance is borne by the member firms through regular annual fees and periodic special assessments. Should this be insufficient to settle all claims, the CIPF can borrow through a line of credit provided by two Canadian chartered banks.

In addition to providing investor insurance the CIPF also undertakes the following oversight activities as part of its role in monitoring the self-regulatory system:

1. the examination of monthly, quarterly, and annual reports from member firms to assist in detecting problems so that prompt action can be taken;
2. periodic surprise visits to the offices of member firms (at least once per year) to ensure full compliance with the CIPF's national standards;
3. at least one unadvertised financial questionnaire annually;
4. an annual audit and report by a public accounting firm;
5. ensuring that customers' fully paid securities and excess margin securities are segregated promptly from all other securities held by the member and reported appropriately in their records;
6. establishing that member firms meet the capital and liquidity standards established by the CIPF; and
7. enacting the appropriate penalties and sanctions against member firms in violation of the Self-Regulatory Organization's standards.

---

[20]A given client may have more than one type of account and may, therefore, be able to claim more than the limit shown.

Commisions

Fixed Commissions

Until 1975, the New York Stock Exchange required its member brokers to charge fixed minimum commissions for stocks, with no "rebates, returns, discounts or allowances in 'any shape or manner,' direct or indirect."[21] Fixed commissions were also charged on the TSE and remained in force until 1983.

In the era of fixed commissions, brokerage firms did not compete with one another over commissions. However, those brokerage firms that belonged to the Toronto Stock Exchange competed with one another in a different manner—namely, by offering a panoply of ancillary services to customers. Large institutions were provided with security analysis, performance measurement services and the like in return for **soft dollars**—brokerage commissions ostensibly paid for having a brokerage firm execute their trades and indirectly designated as payment for services rendered. The US experience indicates that for every $3 in commissions received on large trades, brokerage firms were willing to spend up to approximately $2 to provide ancillary services to the customers. Thus, it follows that it cost brokerage firms roughly $1 per $3 of commission received just to execute a large trade for a customer. Apparently, up to two-thirds of the fixed commission rate ($2 out of $3) on such large orders was pure (marginal) profit.

The existence of fixed commissions has been attributed to the natural monopoly arising from economies of scale in bringing together many people (either physically or via modern communication technology) to trade with one another. The potential profits from such a monopoly are limited by the advantages it confers. The increasing institutionalization of security holdings and progress in communications and computer technology have diminished the advantages associated with a centralized physical exchange. Thus, the removal of legal protection for this particular type of price fixing may only have been another example of a response to technological change.

Competitive Commissions

The system of fixed commissions in the US was finally terminated by the Securities Act Amendments of 1975 (but only after repeated challenges by the NYSE). Since May 1, 1975 (known in the trade as **May Day**), brokers have been free to set commissions at any desired rate or to negotiate with customers concerning the fees charged for particular trades. The former procedure is more commonly employed in "retail" trades executed for small investors, whereas the latter is used more often when handling large trades involving institutional investors and others.

Prior to May Day, commission rates in Canada were generally higher than those in the US. Following the introduction of negotiated rates in the US, trading in interlisted securities tended to migrate to US exchanges where transaction costs were lower. This forced Canadian dealers to match US commission rates on large trades in order to protect their business. On April 1, 1983, Canada moved to negotiated commission rates.[22] After April 1983, rates for large trades in Canada fell substantially. So did those charged for small trades by firms offering only bare-bones brokerage services. On the other hand, broad-line firms that provided extensive services to small investors for no additional fee continued to charge commissions similar to those specified in the earlier fixed schedules. In succeeding years, as costs have risen, charges for smaller transactions have increased, whereas those for large trades have not.

---

[21] See Wilford J. Eiteman, Charles A. Dice, and David K. Eiteman, *The Stock Market* (New York: McGraw-Hill, 1969), p. 138.

[22] Even before this date commissions were negotiable for trades in excess of $500 000.

Soft Dollars Brokerage commissions ostensibly paid for having a brokerage firm execute a trade and indirectly designated, in part, as payment for non-trade-related services rendered.

May Day The date (May 1, 1975) that the New York Stock Exchange ended its fixed-commission rate requirement and permitted member firms to negotiate commission rates with customers.

Increased competition among brokerage firms has resulted in a wide range of alternatives for investors. Following April 1983, some firms *unbundled*, meaning they priced their services separately from their pricing of order execution. Other firms *went discount* meaning they dropped almost all ancillary services and cut commissions accordingly. Still others bundled new services into comprehensive packages. Some of these approaches have not stood the test of time, but just as mail-order firms, discount houses, department stores, and expensive boutiques coexist in retail trade, many different combinations are viable in the brokerage industry.

Transaction Costs

▸ The Bid-Ask Spread

Bid-Ask Spread The difference between the price that a market-maker is willing to pay for a security and the price at which the market-maker is willing to sell the same security.

Commission costs are only a portion of the total cost associated with buying or selling a security. Consider a "round-trip" transaction, in which shares are purchased and then sold during a period in which no new information causes investors collectively to reassess the value of the shares (more concretely, the bid and asked prices quoted by dealers do not change). The shares will typically be purchased at the dealers' asked price and sold at the bid price, which is lower. The **bid-ask spread** thus constitutes a portion of the round-trip transaction costs.

According to one study covering US markets, the spread between the bid and asked prices for a typical stock is approximately $.30 per share for the securities of large, actively traded companies. This amounts to less than 1% of the price per share for most stocks of this type—a reasonably small amount to pay for the ability to buy or sell in a hurry. However, not all securities enjoy this type of liquidity. Shares of smaller firms tend to sell at lower prices but at similar bid-ask spreads. As a result, the percentage transaction cost is considerably larger.

Spreads are inversely related to the amount of trading activity in a stock. That is, stocks with more trading activity (or trading volume) tend to have lower spreads.[23] The inverse relationship between the amount of trading activity (or market value) and spread size can be explained once it is recognized that the spread is the dealer's compensation for providing investors with liquidity. The smaller the amount of trading, the less frequently the dealer will capture the spread (by buying at the bid and selling at the asked). Hence the dealer will need a wider spread in order to generate a level of compensation commensurate with more frequently traded securities.

The majority of the stocks traded on the TSE fall into the lower market capitalization ranges of the NYSE. Therefore, it is likely that transaction costs are generally higher in Canada than in the US. This conclusion is borne out by a study conducted by Tinic and West in the early 1970s in which they compared bid-ask spreads on TSE listed stocks with those on the NYSE and the OTC.[24] Even after controlling for daily trading volume,

---

[23]Roger D. Huang and Hans R. Stoll, *Major World Equity Markets: Current Structure and Prospects for Change*, Monograph Series in Finance and Economics 1991–93, New York University Salomon Center, New York, 1991, p. 11.

[24]Seha M. Tinic and Richard R. West, "Marketability of Common Stocks in Canada and the USA: A Comparison of Agent Versus Dealer Dominated Markets," *Journal of Finance* 29, no. 3 (June 1974): 729–746. Schulman presents evidence that spreads in December 1988 on the TSE 35 stocks were, on average, higher than on the NYSE, as shown below:

	Bid/Ask Spread	
	TSE 35	*NYSE*
High	1.80%	1.31%
Median	0.65	0.38
Low	0.22	0.08

SOURCE: E. Schulman, "The 'Global Village' Securities Market: Will Canada be a Participant… or a Bystander?" *Canadian Investment Review* II, no. 2 (Fall 1989): 61–66. For a difference of opinion on the significance of the spread differential, see K. Cachia and E. Schulman, "Comparison of Bid-Offer Spreads on NYSE and TSE: Comment and Response," *Canadian Investment Review* III, no. 1 (Spring 1990): 31.

Soft Dollars

Suppose that you have decided to build a new home. As your first step you hire a general contractor to oversee the different construction phases. The general contractor, in turn, hires various subcontractors to lay the foundation, frame the house, install wiring, and so on.

You can compensate the general contractor in large part based on the charges billed by the subcontractors. Now assume that the general contractor allowed the subcontractors to charge more than the true costs of their services. The difference between the billed costs and the true costs was then rebated to the general contractor in the form of payments for goods and services only indirectly related to the general contractor's work on your home, such as accounting services or transportation vehicles.

Presumably you would find such an arrangement objectionable. After all, fairness dictates that the general contractor's charges to you include only the actual cost of the subcontractor's labour and materials. The general contractor should pay for accounting services directly out of its own pocket. The efficiency and equity of such an arrangement seems unquestionable, except perhaps in the investment management business, where each year institutional investors pay hundreds of millions of "soft" dollars to brokerage firms in a situation analogous to our hypothetical home-building example.

Soft dollars are brokerage commissions paid by institutional investors in excess of amounts required to compensate brokers for simply executing trades. As the text describes, soft dollars had their origin in the fixed commission rates imposed by exchanges in years past. Large institutional investors paid the same commission rates as small retail investors, despite the obvious economies of scale present in carrying out large trades as opposed to small trades.

Brokerage firms competed with one another, not by lowering commission rates, but by rebating a portion of the commissions to large investors. These brokerage firms did so by offering a plethora of "free" services to the investors. These services typically involved various types of investment research, although on occasion they included such ethically questionable items as airline tickets and lodging for trips abroad.

After the deregulation of commission rates it was widely assumed that soft dollars would disappear. Investors would pay brokers only for executing their trades in the most cost-effective manner. Other services, such as investment research, would be purchased directly from the supplying firms. This decoupling of payments for trade execution from other services is known as "unbundling."

Surprisingly, the soft dollar industry, despite some initial rough going following deregulation, did not wither away. In fact, it flourished. Investment research continued to be paid for out of commissions.

One factor affecting the use of soft dollars was the general trend of institutional investors towards hiring external investment managers to invest their assets. These managers, in a loose sense, act as the general contractor referred to earlier. The managers have discretion over the allocation of their clients' commissions. They are permitted (and, in fact, have a strong incentive) to use soft dollars to pay for various forms of investment research. That research primarily includes fundamental company analyses, data on expected earnings, and economic forecasts. It also includes computer software and hardware, performance measurement, and educational services. By using soft dollars to pay for such research, the costs are effectively shifted to the managers' clients, rather than paid for by the managers themselves.

Establishing the size of the soft dollar industry is difficult, but it is large and lucrative enough to support a number of brokerage firms devoted solely to supplying third-party research services to investors in exchange for soft dollars. These brokerage firms make arrangements with providers of investment research to funnel payments for services rendered to investment managers in exchange for having the managers execute trades through the brokerage firms.

In the investment industry, prices for research services are often quoted on two levels: hard (straight cash payment) or soft (price in commission dollars). The ratio of the two prices implies a conversion rate. Although this conversion rate is negotiable, an approximate figure is two commission dollars paid to receive one dollar in services.

The stated rationale behind managers' use of soft dollars is that their clients benefit from the research services purchased. Presumably, in the absence of soft dollars, managers would raise their fees to enable them to purchase the necessary research directly, yet maintain their current profit margins. However, managers are not required to provide their clients with a detailed accounting of their soft-dollar use.

Thus, it is difficult for clients to assess whether their commission dollars are being wisely allocated by their managers. One is hard-pressed to imagine how clients are better off under a system of unidentified, implicit fees than they would be if commission payments were completely unbundled.

Why don't institutional clients insist that soft-dollar use be prohibited or at least be fully divulged?

Inertia and ignorance appear to be two explanations. Another reason is that many institutional investors have themselves become beneficiaries of soft dollars. They use soft dollars by directing their managers to purchase various services for their immediate benefit. (Soft dollars generated in this manner are sometimes called "directed commissions.") For example, a corporate pension fund staff may use their managers' soft dollars to purchase performance measurement services that the corporate budget would not normally allow.

Over the years, soft dollars have been criticized as being inefficient and ripe for abuse. Calls for prohibition of soft dollars have occasionally been heard. However, the soft-dollar industry is powerful and to date has been able to ward off any substantive changes.

---

average stock price, price volatility, trading frequency, and the number of markets in which the security is listed (but not market capitalization), they found that bid-ask spreads on the TSE are larger than those on either of the US markets. They concluded that the price of liquidity was higher on the TSE and the marketability of TSE-listed stocks was inferior. They attributed this inferior performance to the lack of a well-developed dealer market in Canada. Whereas the specialist on the NYSE and the dealers on the OTC were committed to filling board lot orders, and thereby maintaining an active and continuous market, the registered traders on the TSE were only required to provide bid and offer quotations and to fill odd-lot orders (at a premium or a discount). Both the market-making function on the TSE and the capitalization of member firms have changed significantly, however, in the past 20 years, so these conclusions require updating and confirmation.

▶ Price Impact

Price Impact The effect on the price of a security resulting from a trade in that security. Price impact is the result of several factors: size of the trade, demand for immediate liquidity, and presumed information of the individual or organization placing the order.

Brokerage commissions and bid-ask spreads represent transaction costs for small orders (typically 100 shares). For larger orders, the possibility of **price impacts** must be considered. Consider purchase orders. Due to the law of supply and demand, the larger the size of the order, the more likely the investor's purchase price will be higher. Furthermore, the more rapidly the order is to be completed and the more knowledgeable the individual or organization placing the order, the higher is the purchase price charged by the dealer.

Table 3.4 offers a profile of trading activity conducted by a sample of institutional investors over the 12-month period ending June 30, 1996. The table presents information encompassing 1.3 million trades on both the NYSE and the NASDAQ/NMS markets. Stocks traded are divided into three groups based on their market capitalization, which equals the market value of the firm's outstanding equity (that is, its share price times the number of shares outstanding). For example, large capitalization stocks are classified as those with market capitalizations greater than 10 billion dollars. The table also segments the trades themselves into three groups based on the number of shares involved in the transactions. For example, large trades are classified as those involving over 50 000 shares.

Table 3.4 Price Impact Analysis, 12 Months Ending June 30, 1996.

New York Stock Exchange Trades

	Size	Percent of Total	Avg. Price Impact $	Avg. Commission $	Avg. Market Capitalization $ (Billions)	Avg. Traded Shares	Percent of Daily Volume	Avg. Price/ share $
Large market Capitalization	+$10 billion	28%	$ .10 (.17%)	$.045	$34.4	24 000	15%	$75
Mid market Capitalization	$1–$10 billion	51	.09 (.25%)	.046	4.4	24 000	32	35
Small market Capitalization	Less than $1 billion	21	.07 (.36%)	.044	0.6	17 000	54	19
Small trades	0–10 000 shares	63	.04 (.10%)	.040	15.2	2 000	4	41
Medium trades	10–50 000 shares	26	.055 (.14%)	.044	13.6	23 000	14	39
Large trades	+50 000 shares	11	.105 (.27%)	.046	18.7	133 000	34	39

NASDAQ/NMS Trades

	Size	Percent of Total	Avg. Price Impact $	Avg. Commission $	Avg. Market Capitalization $ (Billions)	Traded Shares	Daily Volume	Price/ share $
Large market Capitalization	+$10 billion	7%	$ .17 (.35%)	n.a	$34.5	38 000	11%	$48
Mid market Capitalization	$1–$10 billion	32	.19 (.52%)	n.a	3.4	28 000	24	37
Small market Capitalization	Less than $1 billion	61	.16 (.80%)	n.a	0.5	17 000	48	20
Small trades	0–10 000 shares	58	.06 (.23%)	n.a	5.5	3 000	13	28
Medium trades	10–50 000 shares	32	.125 (.43%)	n.a	4.6	22 000	23	29
Large trades	+50 000 shares	10	.22 (.68%)	n.a	11.1	128 000	33	32

SOURCE: Plexus Group, 1997. All rights reserved.

Table 3.4 indicates that the commissions charged on NYSE trades are relatively similar regardless of the stocks' market capitalizations. However, because average price per share tends to be inversely related to market capitalization, commissions, stated as a percentage of the dollar value of a trade, increase as market capitalization declines. Further, the smaller is the market capitalization of a traded stock, the greater is the price impact of the trade. Similarly, the larger is the trade in terms of shares traded, the greater is the price impact.

Figure 3.4 provides estimates of the average cost of institutional trading. All three sources of costs are included: brokerage commisssions, bid-ask spreads, and price impacts. The figure refers to the total cost of a "round trip" for purchase followed by a sale. It illustrates the round trip cost for stocks with varying market capitalizations and varying trade size expressed relative to the daily volume of trading carried out in that stock on a typical day. Transaction costs increase as both market capitalization declines and as the proportion of a day's trading volume consumed by the trade rises. There is no reason to believe that the situation is any different in Canada, although the overall cost may be higher.

Figure 3.4

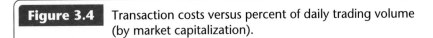

Figure 3.4 Transaction costs versus percent of daily trading volume (by market capitalization).

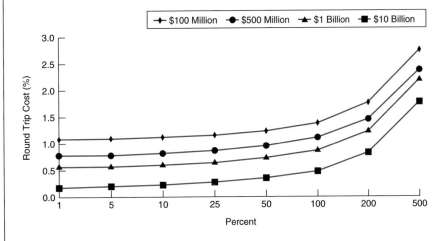

Regulation of Security Markets

Ontario Securities Commission (OSC) A provincial agency that regulates the issuance of securities in the primary market and the trading of securities in the secondary market.

Self-Regulation A method of governmental regulation where the rules and standards of conduct in security markets are set by firms that operate in these markets, subject to the oversight of various governmental agencies such as the OSC.

Securities regulation in Canada is a provincial responsibility. The first such legislation was enacted in Manitoba in 1912. Other provinces followed suit and for a considerable period legislation in this country resembled a patchwork quilt. Interprovincial cooperation has increased significantly following recognition of the fact that the Canadian market is national and increasingly becoming international in scope. In 1965, the *Report of the Attorney-General's Committee on Securities Legislation in Canada* (the Kimber Report) recommended significant revisions to Ontario's securities laws modelled on the US Securities Act of 1933 (sometimes called the truth-in-securities law) and the Securities Exchange Act of 1934. The resulting *Ontario Securities Act, 1966* requires registration of new issues, disclosure of relevant information by the issuer, and prohibits misrepresentation and fraud in security sales. It also covers secondary markets by requiring national exchanges, brokers, and dealers to be registered, as well as those who counsel or advise investors and specifying reporting requirements for insider trades. Many of these provisions have been included in securities legislation enacted by other provinces. Subsequent amendments to the Ontario Securities Act have included the extension of corporate reporting requirements and the introduction of regulations governing takeover bids. An example of interprovincial cooperation in this area is the adoption of a number of national policies by all the securities commissions in the country. In this way uniformity of regulation across the country has increased.

The organization of the **Ontario Securities Commission (OSC)** is typical of most provincial commissions. There are ten commissioners consisting of a chair, two vice-chairs and seven members, plus a director who oversees day-to-day operations. Other commissions vary as to the number of members appointed by the provincial governments. The OSC differs from the securities commissions in other provinces in having a larger enforcement branch and a department dealing with derivative securities.

Securities legislation relies heavily on the principle of **self-regulation**. The securities commissions in general delegate part of their authority over trading practices for listed securities to the organized exchanges within their jurisdiction and maintain a watching brief over their activities. Trading in over-the-counter securities has been delegated to the Canadian Dealing Network Inc. (CDN) and the Investment Dealers Association (IDA).

Canadian stocks interlisted on US exchanges fall under the joint jurisdiction of the appropriate provincial body and the US Securities and Exchange Commission (SEC). The SEC imposes more stringent reporting requirements and more extensive information disclosure in prospectuses than is generally required in Canada. On the other hand, the SEC has less strict takeover rules than the OSC; therefore, interlisting may provide a way of avoiding some types of regulatory constraint. In recent years there has been increased cooperation between the SEC and the larger provincial securities commissions in such matters as insider trading, improper trading activity, fraud, and incomplete disclosure.

Summary

1. Security markets facilitate the trading of securities by providing a means of bringing buyers and sellers of financial assets together.
2. In Canada, common stocks are traded primarily on organized security exchanges or in the over-the-counter market.
3. Organized security exchanges provide central locations where trading is done under a set of rules and regulations.
4. The primary organized security exchange in Canada is the Toronto Stock Exchange. Various regional exchanges also operate.
5. Trading on organized security exchanges is conducted only by members who transact in a special group of securities.
6. Exchange members fall into one of two categories, depending on the type of trading activity in which they engage. Those categories are order traders and registered traders.
7. Market-makers (MM) are charged with maintaining an orderly market in their assigned stocks. In this capacity they perform two roles. They maintain a limit order book for unexecuted trades, and they act as a dealer, trading in their stocks for their own accounts.
8. In the over-the-counter (OTC) market individuals act as dealers in a manner similar to MMs. However, unlike MMs, OTC dealers face competition from other dealers.
9. Most of the trading in the OTC market is done through a computerized system known as the Canadian Dealer Network (CDN).
10. Trading in listed securities may not take place outside the various exchanges.
11. Foreign security markets each have their own particular operating procedures, rules, and customs.
12. Dealers typically make money trading with liquidity-motivated traders and lose money trading with adept information-motivated traders. A dealer must set a bid-ask spread that attracts sufficient revenue from the former group, but avoids excessive losses to the latter.
13. Clearinghouses facilitate the transfer of securities and cash between buyers and sellers. Most Canadian security transactions are now cleared electronically.
14. The Canadian Investor Protection Fund (CIPF) is an industry organized agency that insures the accounts of clients of all brokers and members of exchanges against loss due to a brokerage firm's failure.
15. Following deregulation, commissions have been negotiated between brokerage firms and their larger clients. In a competitive environment, commission rates typically vary inversely with the size of the order.
16. Transaction costs are a function of the stock's bid-ask spread, the price impact of the trade, and the commission.

17. The most prominent security market regulator is the Ontario Securities Commission (OSC), a provincial agency directed by ten commissioners. Regulation of the Canadian security markets involves both federal and provincial laws.

18. The OSC has delegated to the TSE, the CDN, and the IDA the power to control trading practices through a system of self-regulation.

QUESTIONS AND PROBLEMS

1. Virtually all secondary trading of securities take place in continuous markets as opposed to call markets. What aspects of continuous markets causes them to dominate call markets?

2. Circuitbreakers were first instituted after the market crash of October 1987. Some observers argue that the rapid increase in the stock market's value since 1987 has diminished whatever value the rules may originally have possessed. Why?

3. Differentiate between the role of a MM on the TSE and the role of a dealer on the CDN system.

4. Give several reasons why a corporation might desire to have its stock listed on the TSE.

5. Describe the functions of order traders and registered traders.

6. Pigeon Falls Fertilizer Company is listed on the TSE. George Hartnett, the MM handling Pigeon Falls stock, is currently bidding 35.30 and asking 35.40. What would be the likely outcomes of the following trading orders?

   a. Through a broker, Eva Rooney places a market order to buy 100 shares of Pigeon Falls stock.

   b. Through a broker, Eva places a limit order to sell 100 shares of Pigeon Falls stock at 36.

   c. Through a broker, Eva places a limit order to buy 100 shares of Pigeon Falls stock at 35.35. Another order comes in to sell 100 shares of Pigeon Falls stock at 35.35.

7. The limit order screen for International Enterprises appears as follows:

Limit-Sell		Limit-Buy	
Price	Shares	Price	Shares
$30.250	200	$29.750	100
30.375	500	29.000	100
30.500	300	28.500	200
30.875	800	27.125	100
31.000	200	26.875	200

The last trade in the stock took place at $30.

   a. If a market order to sell 200 shares arrives, what will happen?

   b. If another market order to sell 100 shares arrives just moments later, what will happen?

8. Because MMs such as Chuck Goodwin are charged with maintaining a "fair and orderly" market, at times they will be required to sell when others are buying and buy when others are selling. How can Chuck earn a profit when required to act in such a manner?

9. Why is the CDN so important to the success of the OTC market?

10. When the TSE moved to decimal pricing with prices moving in $.05 increments, was there greater opportunity for price improvement over current pricing system? Explain.

11. Using the model described in the text, calculate the appropriate bid-ask spread for a dealer making a market in a security under the conditions that 15% of all traders are information-motivated, there is a 30% chance that the stock is worth $30 per share, and a 70% chance that it is worth $50 per share.

12. How might a dealer attempt to discern whether a trader is information motivated?

13. The NYSE has strongly opposed the creation of alternative market trading structures such as off-exchange crossing systems. The NYSE claims that these alternative structures undermine its ability to offer "best execution" to all investors. Discuss the merits of the NYSE's contention.

14. Why was the deregulation of commissions such an important event for the TSE?

15. What is the purpose of CIPF insurance? Under what conditions might CIPF insurance be expected to be effective? Under what conditions might it fail to accomplish its objectives?

16. After deregulation, why did commission rates fall so sharply for large investors, but decline so little (or even increase) for small investors?

17. Transaction costs can be thought of as being derived from three sources. Identify and describe those sources.

18. Why does the price impact of a trade seem to be directly related to the size of the trade?

19. What functions does a clearinghouse perform?

KEY TERMS

security market (p. 46)
secondary security market (p. 46)
primary security market (p. 46)
call market (p. 46)
continuous market (p. 46)
liquidity (p. 47)
organized exchange (p. 47)
seat (p. 47)
member firm (p. 47)
listed security (p. 47)
delist (p. 48)
trading halt (p. 48)
circuitbreakers (p. 48)
limit order book (p. 49)
dealer (p. 49)
trading post (p. 50)
bid price (p. 50)
asked price (p. 50)
double auction (p. 50)
public governor (p. 52)
interlisted securities (p. 52)

Computer Assisted Trading System (CATS) (p. 52)
order (or desk) trader (p. 53)
registered trader (p. 53)
registered trader responsible for a stock (p. 53)
minimum guaranteed fill (MGF) (p. 53)
blocks (p. 56)
regional exchange (p. 59)
Canadian Dealing Network Inc. (CDN) (p. 60)
markup (p. 61)
markdown (p. 61)
NASDAQ International (p. 62)
Canadian Investor Protection Fund (CIPF) (p. 65)
soft dollars (p. 66)
May Day (p. 66)
bid-ask spread (p. 67)
price impacts (p. 69)
Ontario Securities Commission (OSC) (p. 71)
self-regulation (p. 71)

REFERENCES

1. A good reference source for Canadian stock markets is:

The Canadian Securities Course (Toronto: The Canadian Securities Institute, 1997).

2. Other valuable sources are the following fact books, with Web sites, which are updated annually:

New York Stock Exchange, *Fact Book: 1997 Data.* . . 1998; www.nyse.com

American Stock Exchange, *American Stock Exchange 1997 Fact Book*, 1998; www.amex.com

National Association of Security Dealers, *The NASDAQ Stock Market 1997 Fact Book & Company Directory,* 1997; www.nasd.com or wwwnasdaq.com or www.nasdr.com

London Stock Exchange, *Stock Exchange Official Yearbook;* www.londonstockex.co.ul

Toronto Stock Exchange, *Annual Report and Fact Book, 1997;* www.tse.com

Tokyo Stock Exchange, *Tokyo Stock Exchange 1997 Fact Book*; www.tse.or.jp/eindex.html

Readers should also consider the Securities and Exchange Commission's Web site: www.sec.gov

3. For a description of various stock markets, see:

Guiseppe Tullio and Giorgio P. Szego, eds., "Equity Markets—An International Comparison: Part A," *Journal of Banking and Finance* 13, nos. 4–5 (September 1989): 479–782.

Guiseppe Tullio and Giorgio P. Szego, eds., "Equity Markets—An International Comparison: Part B," *Journal of Banking and Finance* 14, nos. 2–3 (August 1990): 231–672.

Roger D. Huang and Hans R. Stoll, *Major World Equity Markets: Current Structure and Prospects for Change*, Monograph Series in Finance and Economics 1991–1993, New York University Salomon Center, New York, 1991.

Roger D. Huang and Hans R. Stoll, "The Design of Trading Systems: Lessons from Abroad," *Financial Analysts Journal* 48, no. 5 (September–October 1992): 49–54.

Bruce N. Lehman and David M. Modest, "Trading and Liquidity on the Tokyo Stock Exchange: A Bird's Eye View," *Journal of Finance* 49, no. 3 (July 1994) 951–984.

Alexandros Benos and Michael Crouhy, "Changes in the Structure and Dynamics of European Securities Markets," *Financial Analysts Journal* 52, no. 3 (May–June 1996) 37–50.

4. Other useful sources for information on market microstructure are:

James L. Hamilton, "Off-Board Trading of NYSE-Listed Stocks: The Effects of Deregulation and the National Market System," *Journal of Finance* 42, no. 5 (December 1987): 1331–1345.

Ian Domowitz, "The Mechanics of Automated Execution System," *Journal of Financial Intermediation* 1, no. 2 (June 1990): 167–194.

Lawrence E. Harris, *Liquidity, Trading Rules, and Electronic Trading Systems*, Monograph Series in Finance and Economics 1990–1994, New York University Salomon Center, New York, 1990.

Peter A. Abken, "Globalization of Stock, Futures, and Options Markets," *Federal Reserve Bank of Atlanta Economic Review* 76, no. 4 (July–August 1991): 1–22.

Joel Hasbrouck, George Sofianos, and Deborah Sosebee, "New York Stock Exchange Systems and Procedures," NYSE Working Paper 93–01, 1993.

5. For a discussion of the effects of listing and delisting on a firm's stock, see:

Gary C. Sanger and John J. McConnell, "Stock Exchange Listings, Firm Value, and Security Market Efficiency: The Impact of NASDAQ," *Journal of Financial and Quantitative Analysis* 21, no. 1 (March 1986): 1–25.

John J. McConnell and Gary C. Sanger, "The Puzzle in Post-Listing Common Stock Returns," *Journal of Finance* 42, no. 1 (March 1987): 119–140.

Gary C. Sanger and James D. Peterson, "An Empirical Analysis of Common Stock Delistings," *Journal of Financial and Quantitative Analysis* 25, no. 2 (June 1990): 261–272.

6. Empirical studies that examine the costs of trading include:

Harold Demsetz, "The Cost of Transacting," *Quarterly Journal of Economics* 82, no. 1 (February 1968): 33–53.

Walter Bagehot, "The Only Game in Town," *Financial Analysts Journal* 27, no. 2 (March–April 1971): 12–14, 22.

Larry J. Cuneo and Wayne H. Wagner, "Reducing the Cost of Stock Trading," *Financial Analysts Journal* 31, no. 6 (November–December 1975): 35–44.

Gilbert Beebower and William Priest, "The Tricks of the Trade," *Journal of Portfolio Management* 6, no. 2 (Winter 1980): 36–42.

Jack L. Treynor, "What Does It Take to Win the Trading Game?" *Financial Analysts Journal* 37, no. 1 (January/February 1981): 55–60.

Thomas F. Loeb, "Trading Cost: The Critical Link Between Investment Information and Results," *Financial Analysts Journal* 39, no. 3 (May–June 1983): 39–44.

Wayne H Mikkelson and M. Megan Partch, "Stock Price Effects and Costs of Secondary Distributions," *Journal of Financial Economics* 15, no. 2 (June 1985): 165–194.

Robert W. Holthausen, Richard W. Leftwich, and David Mayers, "The Effect of Large Block Transactions on Security Prices," *Journal of Financial Economics* 19, no. 2 (December 1987): 1237–1267.

Stephen A. Berkowitz, Dennis E. Logue, and Eugene E. Noser, Jr., "The Total Cost of Transactions on the NYSE," *Journal of Finance* 43, no. 1 (March 1988): 97–112.

André F. Perold, "The Implementation Shortfall: Paper Versus Reality," *Journal of Portfolio Management* 14, no. 3 (Spring 1988): 4–9.

Lawrence R. Glosten and Lawrence E. Harris, "Estimating the Components of the Bid/Ask Spread," *Journal of Financial Economics* 21, no. 1 (May 1988): 123–142.

Joel Hasbrouck, "Trades, Quotes, Inventories, and Information," *Journal of Financial Economics* 22, no. 2 (December 1988): 229–252.

Hans R. Stoll, "Inferring the Components of the Bid-Ask Spread: Theory and Empirical Tests," *Journal of Finance* 44, no. 1 (March 1989): 115–134.

Robert W. Holthausen, Richard W. Leftwich, and David Mayers, "Large-Block Transactions, the Speed of Response, and Temporary and Permanent Stock-Price Effects," *Journal of Financial Economics* 26, no. 1 (July 1990): 71–95.

F. Douglas Foster and S. Viswanathan, "Variations in Trading Volume, Return Volatility, and Trading Costs: Evidence on Recent Price Formation Models," *Journal of Finance* 48, no. 1 (March 1993): 187–211.

Hans R. Stoll, "Equity Trading Costs In-The-Large," *Journal of Portfolio Management* 19, no. 4 (Summer 1993): 41–50.

Joel Hasbrouck and George Sofianos, "The Trades of Market-Makers: An Empirical Analysis of NYSE Specialists," *Journal of Finance* 48, no. 5 (December 1993): 1565–1593.

Ananth Madhavan and Seymour Smidt, "An Analysis of Changes in Specialist Inventories and Quotations" *Journal of Finance* 48, no. 5 (December 1993): 1595–1628.

Mitchell A. Petersen and David Fialkowski, "Posted Versus Effective Spreads: Good Prices or Bad Quotes?" *Journal of Financial Economics* 35, no. 3 (June 1994): 269–292.

Jack L. Treynor, "The Invisible Costs of Trading," *Journal of Portfolio Management* 22, no. 1 (Fall 1995): 71–78.

7. For a comparison of trading costs on NASDAQ and the NYSE, see:

Roger D. Huang and Hans R. Stoll, "Competitive Trading of NYSE Listed Stocks: Measurement and Interpretation of Trading Costs," *Financial Markets, Institutions & Instruments* 5, no. 2 (1996).

Roger D. Huang and Hans R. Stoll, "Dealer Versus Auction Markets: A Paired Comparison of Execution Costs on NASDAQ and NYSE," *Journal of Financial Economics* 41, no. 3 (July 1996): 313–357.

Michele LaPlante and Chris J. Muscarella, "Do Institutions Receive Comparable Execution in the NYSE and NASDAQ Markets? A Transaction Study of Block Trades," *Journal of Financial Economics* 45, no. 1 (July 1997): 97–134.

8. For a historical essay on the development of American capital markets, which includes a significant discussion of regulation, see:

George David Smith and Richard Sylla, "The Transformation of Financial Capitalism: An Essay on the History of American Capital Markets," *Financial Markets, Institutions & Instruments* 2, no. 2 (1993).

9. For more on the adverse selection problem that dealers face in setting spreads, see:

Lawrence R. Glosten and Paul R. Milgrom, "Bid, Ask, and Transaction Prices in a Specialist Market with Heterogeneously Informed Traders," *Journal of Financial Economics* 14, no. 1 (March 1985): 71–100.

Albert S. Kyle, "Continuous Auctions and Insider Trading, " *Econometrica* 53, no. 6 (November 1985): 1315–1335.

Murugappa Krishnan, "An Equivalence Between the Kyle (1985) and the Glosten-Milgrom (1985) Models," *Economic Letters* 40, (1992): 333–338.

Steven V. Mann, "How Do Security Dealers Protect Themselves from Traders with Private Information: A Pedagogical Note," *Financial Practice and Education* 5, no. 1 (Spring–Summer 1995): 38–44.

Michael J. Brennan and Avanidhar Subrahmanyam, "Investment Analysis and Price Formation in Securities Markets," *Journal of Financial Economics* 38, no. 3 (July 1995): 361–381.

10. Articles on soft dollars include:

Keith P. Ambachtsheer, "The Soft Dollar Question: What is the Answer?" *Financial Analysts Journal* 49, no. 1 (January–February 1993): 8–10.

Marshall E. Blume, "Soft Dollars and the Brokerage Industry," *Financial Analysts Journal* 49, no. 2 (March–April 1993): 36–44.

Miles Livingston and Edward S. O'Neal, "Mutual Fund Brokerage Commissions," *Journal of Financial Research* 19, no. 2 (Summer 1996): 273–292.

11. For a Canadian perspective on the topics covered in this chapter, see:

Jeffrey G. McIntosh and Ronald J. Daniels, "Capital Markets and the Law: The Peculiar Case of Canada," *Canadian Investment Review* III, no. 2 (Fall 1990).

K. P. Ambachtsheer, "Soft Dollars: The $60 Million Question," *Canadian Investment Review* V, no. 2 (Winter 1992).

R. Daniels, "How 'Broke' is the System of Securities Regulation?" *Canadian Investment Review* V, no. 1 (Spring 1992).

L. A. Sauvé, "L'Ecart Vendeur-Acheteur et L'Information boursière à Toronto," *Finéco* 2, no. 2 (2e semestre 1992).

M. Robinson and R. White, "Sizing Up the Block Trading Market," *Canadian Investment Review* VII, no. 2 (Summer 1994).

R. Cheung, L. Kryzanowski, and H. Z. Lang, "Decimalization's Winners and Losers," *Canadian Investment Review* IX, no. 4 (Winter 1996–1997).

E. Kirzner, "PETS and Other Liquidity Pools—What Next?" *Canadian Investment Review* XI, no. 1 (Spring 1998).

D. Cyr, "Intra- and Inter-Day Behaviour of Canadian Stock Market Indices," *Proceedings,* Administrative Sciences Association of Canada Conference, Montreal, June 1996.

Usha Mittoo, "The Bad News Bearers," *Canadian Investment Review* IX, no. 3 (Fall 1996).

Usha Mittoo, "The Winners and Losers of Listing in the U.S.," *Canadian Investment Review* XI, no. 3 (Fall 1996).

J. J. Wolverton, "Dirty Little Secrets?" *Canadian Investment Review* IX, no. 3 (Fall 1996).

Efficient Markets, Investment Value, and Market Price

Payments provided by securities may differ in size, timing, and riskiness. Thus, a security analyst must estimate the size of such payments along with when, and under what conditions, these payments will be received. This typically requires detailed analysis of the firm involved, the industry (or industries) in which the firm operates, and the economy (either regionally, nationally, or internationally) as a whole.

Once such estimates have been made, the overall investment value of the security must be determined. This generally requires conversion of uncertain future values to certain present values. The current prices of other securities can often be utilized in this process. If it is possible to obtain a similar set of payments in some other way, the market price of doing so provides a benchmark for the investment value of the security being analyzed, because an investor would neither want to pay more than this for the security nor to sell it for less. In some cases, however, equivalent alternatives may not exist, or the mere act of buying or selling the security in question in the quantities being considered might affect the price substantially. Under these conditions, the preferences of the investor may have to be utilized explicitly in the process of estimating the security's investment value.

Later chapters discuss in detail the manner in which estimated future payments can be used to determine investment value. Methods for estimating the payments and finding equivalent alternatives will be discussed after the characteristics of the securities have been introduced. In this chapter, some general principles of investment value and how it is related to market prices in an efficient market are presented, leaving valuation methodology for specific types of securities for later.

Demand and Supply Schedules

Royal Bank
www.royalbank.com

Although there are over 300 million shares of the Royal Bank of Canada common stock outstanding, on a typical day less than 1 million shares will be traded. What determines the prices at which such trades take place? A simple (and correct) answer is demand and supply. A more fundamental (and also correct) answer is investors' estimates of the Royal Bank's future earnings and dividends, since such estimates greatly influence demand and supply. Before dealing with such influences, it is useful to examine the role of demand and supply in the determination of security prices.

As shown in the previous chapter, securities are traded by many people in many different ways. Although the forces that determine prices are similar in all markets, they are slightly more obvious in markets using periodic "calls." One such market corresponds to the *itayose* method of price determination that is used by the *saitori* at the twice-a-day openings of the Tokyo Stock Exchange, as discussed in Chapter 3.

Demand-to-Buy Schedule

At a designated time, all brokers holding orders to buy or sell shares of a given stock for customers gather at a specified location on the floor of the exchange. Some of the orders are market orders. For example, Mr. A may have instructed his broker to buy 100 shares of Minolta at the lowest possible price, whatever it is. His personal **demand-to-buy schedule** at that time is shown in Figure 4.1(a): he wishes to buy 100 shares no matter what the price. Although this schedule captures the contractual nature of Mr. A's market order at a specific point in time, Mr. A undoubtedly has a good idea that his ultimate purchase price will be near the price for which orders were executed just before he placed his order. Thus, his true demand schedule might be sloping downwards from the upper-left portion to the lower-right portion of the graph. This is shown by the dashed line in the figure. It indicates his desire to buy more shares if the price is lower. However, to simplify his own tasks as well as his broker's tasks, he has estimated that the price for which his order will ultimately be executed will be in the range at which he would choose to hold 100 shares. In the example shown here, this price is 945 yen per share.

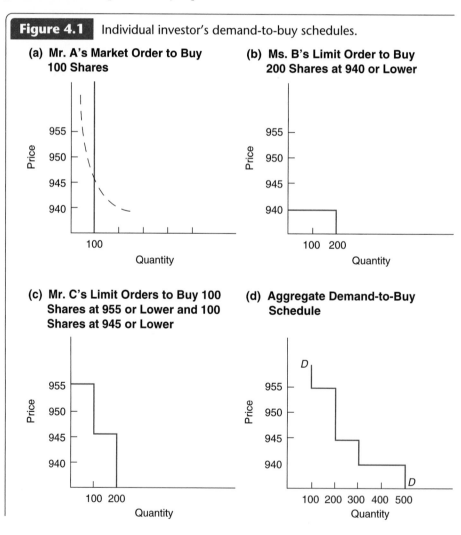

Figure 4.1 Individual investor's demand-to-buy schedules.

(a) Mr. A's Market Order to Buy 100 Shares

(b) Ms. B's Limit Order to Buy 200 Shares at 940 or Lower

(c) Mr. C's Limit Orders to Buy 100 Shares at 955 or Lower and 100 Shares at 945 or Lower

(d) Aggregate Demand-to-Buy Schedule

Other customers may place limit orders with their brokers. Thus, Ms. B may have instructed her broker to buy 200 shares of Minolta at the lowest possible price if and only if that price is less than or equal to 940 yen per share. Her demand schedule is shown in Figure 4.1(b).

Some customers may give their broker two or more orders for the same security. Thus, Mr. C may wish to buy 100 shares of Minolta at a price of 955 or less, plus an additional 100 shares if the price is at or below 945. To do this, Mr. C places a limit order for 100 shares at 955 and a second limit order for 100 shares at 945. Figure 4.1(c) portrays his demand schedule.

If one could look at all the brokers' books and aggregate all the orders to buy Minolta (both market and limit orders), it would be possible to determine how many shares would be bought at every possible price. Assuming that only Mr. A, Ms. B, and Mr. C have placed buy orders, the resulting aggregate demand-to-buy schedule would look like line *DD* in Figure 4.1(d). Note that at lower prices more shares would be demanded.

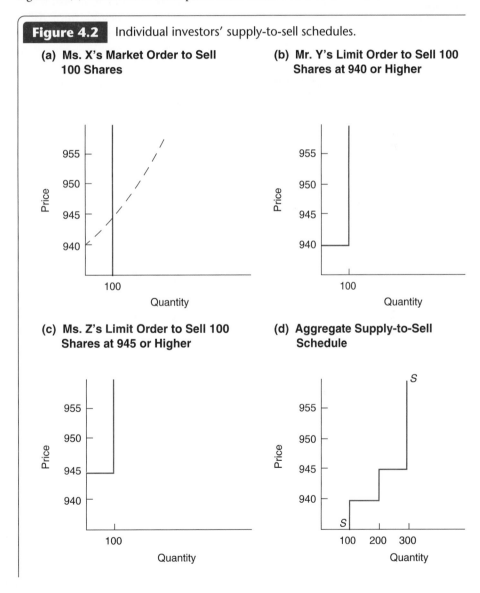

Figure 4.2 Individual investors' supply-to-sell schedules.

(a) **Ms. X's Market Order to Sell 100 Shares**

(b) **Mr. Y's Limit Order to Sell 100 Shares at 940 or Higher**

(c) **Ms. Z's Limit Order to Sell 100 Shares at 945 or Higher**

(d) **Aggregate Supply-to-Sell Schedule**

Supply-to-Sell Schedule

Supply-to-Sell Schedule
A description of the quantities of a security that an investor is prepared to sell at alternative prices.

Brokers will also hold market orders to sell shares of Minolta. For example, Ms. X may have placed a market order to sell 100 shares of Minolta at the highest possible price. Figure 4.2(a) displays her **supply-to-sell schedule**. As with market orders to buy, customers generally place such orders on the supposition that the actual price will be in the range in which their true desire would be to sell the stated number of shares. Thus, Ms. X's actual supply schedule might appear more like the dashed line in Figure 4.2(a), indicating her willingness to sell more shares at higher prices.

Customers may also place limit orders to sell shares of Minolta. For example, Mr. Y may have placed a limit order to sell 100 shares at a price of 940 or higher, and Ms. Z may have placed a limit order to sell 100 shares at a price of 945 or higher. Panels (b) and (c) of Figure 4.2 illustrate these two supply-to-sell schedules.

Similar to buy orders, if one could look at all the brokers' books and aggregate all the orders to sell Minolta (both market and limit orders), it would be possible to determine how many shares would be sold at every possible price. Assuming that only Ms. X, Mr. Y, and Ms. Z have placed sell orders, the resulting aggregate supply-to-sell schedule would look like line *SS* in Figure 4.2(d). Note that at higher prices more shares would be supplied.

Minolta
www.minolta.com

Figure 4.3   Determining a security's price by the interaction of the demand-to-buy and supply-to-sell schedules.

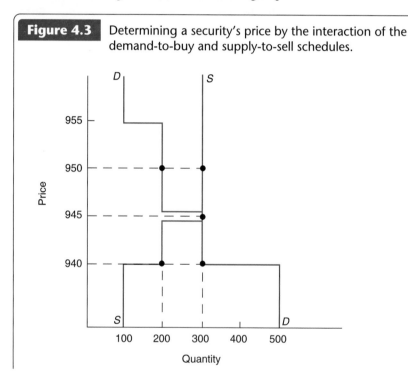

Interaction of the Schedules

The aggregate demand and supply schedules are shown on one graph in Figure 4.3. In general, no one would have enough information to draw the actual schedules. However, this in no way diminishes the usefulness of the schedules as representations of the underlying forces that are interacting to determine the market-clearing price of Minolta.

What actually happens when all the brokers gather together with their order books in hand? A clerk of the exchange "calls out" a price—for example, 940 yen per share. The brokers then try to complete transactions with one another at that price. Those with orders to buy at that price signify the number of shares they wish to buy. Those with orders to sell do likewise. Some deals will be tentatively made, but as Figure 4.3 shows, more shares will be demanded at 940 than will be supplied. In particular, 300 shares will be demanded, but only 200 shares will be supplied. When trading is completed (meaning all possible tentative deals have been made), there will be a number of brokers calling "buy," but nobody will stand ready to sell to them. The price of 940 is too low.

Seeing this, the clerk will cry out a different price—for example, 950. As the previous trades are all cancelled at this point, the brokers will consult their order books once again and signify the extent to which they are willing to buy or sell shares at this new price. In this case, as Figure 4.3 shows, when trading is completed, there will be a number of brokers calling "sell," but nobody will stand ready to buy from them. In particular, 300 shares will be supplied, but there will be a demand for only 200 shares. The price of 950 is too high.

Undaunted, the clerk will try again, and again, if necessary. Only when there are relatively few unsatisfied brokers will the price (and the associated tentative deals) be declared final. As Figure 4.3 shows, 945 is such a price. At 945, customers collectively wish to sell 300 shares. Furthermore, there is a collective demand for 300 shares at this price. Thus, quantity demanded equals quantity supplied. The price is "just right."

Elasticity of the Demand-to-Buy Schedule

How elastic (that is, flat) will be the aggregate demand-to-buy schedule for a security? The answer depends in part on the extent to which the security is regarded as "unique." Securities are considered more unique when they have few close substitutes. Securities are considered less unique when they have more close substitutes. This means that the aggregate demand-to-buy schedule will be more elastic (that is, more flat) for less unique securities. Equivalently, the less unique a security is, the greater will be the increase in the quantity demanded for a given fall in price. This is because these shares will produce a smaller increase in the typical portfolio's risk when substituted for other shares. At one extreme, other securities are viewed as perfect substitutes for the one being analyzed. In this case the security's demand-to-buy schedule will be horizontal, or perfectly elastic. At the other extreme where there are no substitutes, the security has an almost vertical (or almost perfectly inelastic) demand schedule.

Shifts of the Demand-to-Buy and Supply-to-Sell Schedules

If one investor becomes more optimistic about the prospects for a security while another investor becomes more pessimistic about the same security, they may very likely trade with one another with no effect on the aggregate demand-to-buy and supply-to-sell schedules. In this situation there will be no change in the market price for the security. However, if more investors become optimistic rather than pessimistic, the demand-to-buy schedule will shift to the right (for example, to $D'D'$ in Figure 4.4) and the supply-to-sell schedule will shift to the left (for example, to $S'S'$ in Figure 4.4), causing an increase in price (to P'). Correspondingly, if more investors become pessimistic rather than optimistic, the demand-to-buy schedule will shift to the left and the supply-to-sell schedule will shift to the right causing a decrease in price.

A factor that complicates an analysis of this type is the tendency for some investors to regard sudden and substantial price changes in a security as indicators of changes in the future prospects of the issuer. In the absence of further information, an investor may interpret such a change as an indication that "someone knows something that I don't know." While exploring the situation, the investor may at least temporarily revise her own assessment of the issuer's prospects and, in doing so, may alter her demand-to-buy or supply-to-sell schedule. For this reason, few investors place limit orders at prices substantially different from the current price, for fear that such orders would be executed only if the security's prospects changed significantly. If such a large price change actually occurred, it would imply the need for a careful reevaluation of the security before buying or selling shares.

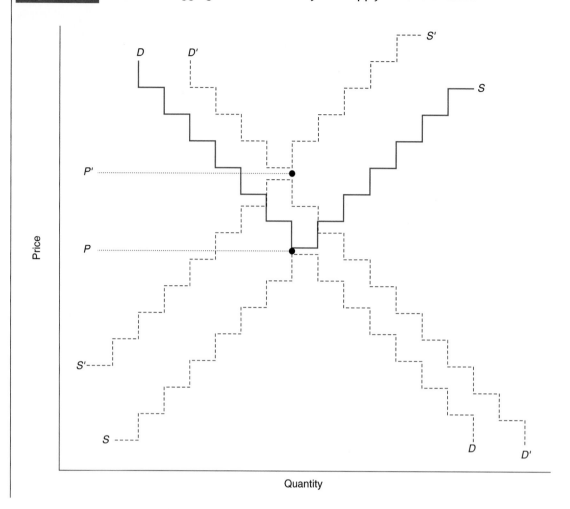

Figure 4.4 Shifts in the aggregate demand-to-buy and supply-to-sell schedules.

Price

Quantity

Summary

Trading procedures employed in security markets vary from auction markets to dealer markets and from call markets to continuous markets. However, the similarities are more important than the differences. In Canada, for example, market-makers at the Toronto Stock Exchange and dealers in the over-the-counter market provide some of the functions of the *saitori* at the Tokyo Stock Exchange, and trades can take place at any time. Nevertheless, the basic principles of security price determination still apply. In general, market price equates quantity demanded with quantity supplied.

Market Efficiency

Allocationally Efficient Market A market for securities in which those firms with the most promising investment opportunities have access to the needed funds.

The topic of market efficiency has been and is likely to continue to be a matter of intense debate in the investment community. In order to understand and participate in this debate, it is important to understand just what is meant by market efficiency. First of all, most financial economists would agree that it is desirable to see that capital is channelled to the place where it will do the most good. That is, a reasonable goal of government policy is to encourage the establishment of **allocationally efficient markets** in which those firms with the most promising investment opportunities have access to the needed funds. However,

The Arizona Stock Exchange: A Better Mousetrap

So you think that supply and demand curves are merely esoteric figments of ivory-tower thinking. Perhaps a valid concept, you say, but they cannot possibly be of any practical use in establishing security prices. Well, do not tell that to AZX Inc. Since early 1991 that organization (or its predecessor, Wunsch Auction Systems, Inc.) has been conducting regular security auctions among institutional investors for a broad list of common stocks. Market clearing prices in those auctions are determined by the explicit interaction of the investors' supply and demand preferences.

Step back for a moment and recall how prices are set on organized security exchanges or the OTC market (see Chapter 3). Dealers (whether specialists or OTC dealers) "make markets" in particular securities—that is, acting as intermediaries, they buy and sell from other investors for their own accounts. The dealers quote prices (bid-asked) to sellers and buyers on a continuous basis. They adjust prices as they sense supply and demand building and ebbing. It is the competitive efforts of these intermediaries that determine security prices.

AZX has developed a market mechanism quite different from that of the conventional dealer markets. AZX calls this mechanism the Arizona Stock Exchange, although it bears no resemblance to any existing stock exchange. (The name derives from financial support provided to AZX by the state of Arizona.) The concept behind the Arizona Stock Exchange is simple. Auctions are scheduled on a regular basis. (Originally an auction was held once a day at 5 p.m. EST, after the New York Stock Exchange closes. More recently, a second auction was added at 9:15 a.m. for NASDAQ National Market system issues and an additional morning auction is being planned.) Prior to a scheduled auction, investors submit orders electronically to buy or sell specified quantities of a security at specified prices (essentially limit orders—see Chapter 2).

At the time of the auction, the orders of all participating investors are aggregated by computer—that is, the computer calculates supply and demand curves for each security being auctioned. The intersection of these curves determines the market clearing price for a security. At that price the maximum number of shares of stock will be exchanged. (All buy orders above and all sell orders below the equilibrium price are matched, whereas orders at the equilibrium price are matched on a time priority basis.)

Investors are able to access the auction order information (in graphic or tabular form) up to the time of the auction through an open limit order book. As opposed to a specialist's proprietary closed limit order book, the Arizona Stock Exchange permits investors to examine the current supply and demand for a stock. This allows investors to raise their bid prices (or lower their asked prices) to adjust to the current market conditions. In order to prevent manipulative behaviour, withdrawn orders incur a penalty charge.

The Arizona Stock Exchange possesses some intriguing advantages over traditional dealer markets:

1. It is simple and fair. All investors have access to the same auction information, and all investors trade at the same price.
2. Investors have direct access to the market. This feature removes the inherent conflicts of interest present in dealer markets.
3. Investors' orders are anonymous. Orders and trade executions are handled by computer.
4. It matches "natural" buyers and sellers (those with an explicit desire to transact), thereby perhaps establishing more robust and stable prices.
5. Transaction costs are low (about 1¢ per share versus 10¢ to 20¢ per share in dealer markets).

This last point warrants elaboration. Traditional dealer markets are continuous—trading can occur at any time during the trading day. Continuous trading mechanisms are expensive and require dealers because the "other side" of a trade is not always immediately available. Dealers provide liquidity to investors who wish to transact immediately. With more frequent large trades having been made by institutional investors in the last decade, the ability of dealer markets to provide continuous liquidity has been severely tested. The market crash of October 1987 was an extreme, but not singular, example.

Many (and perhaps most) institutional investors do not require immediate liquidity. They can wait several hours to trade, particularly if by waiting their transaction costs are reduced significantly. In lieu of the continuous intervention of the dealer, the Arizona Stock Exchange substitutes a periodic call to market. Without the expensive overhead of the dealer, the Arizona Stock Exchange can afford to match buyers and sellers at a small fraction of the cost of the dealer market.

What are the disadvantages of the Arizona Stock Exchange? Conceptually, there are none to investors who do not require immediate liquidity. However, if you throw a party and no one comes, the party is a failure no matter how elaborate the preparations. Likewise, to be successful, AZX must attract enough institutional investors to generate sufficient liquidity and to contribute to the "discovery" of market prices. Consequently, AZX must overcome investor inertia and ignorance. As with any fledgling trading mechanism, the Arizona Stock Exchange faces a catch-22: institutional investors want to see large trading volumes before they will participate, but those large volumes can occur only if institutional investors participate.

An operation like the Arizona Stock Exchange would not be permitted in Canada, where all trades must pass through an organized exchange. However, the process is very similar to the opening procedures on the TSE. In the morning all the trades that have accumulated overnight are analyzed by computer and an opening price is established that ensures that the maximum number of shares will be exchanged at the opening bell.

To date traders have not beaten a path to AZX's door. Currently 20 to 25 institutional investors use the system on any given day, and daily trading volume runs several hundred thousand shares. While these figures pale in comparison to the activity on the New York Stock Exchange, participating investors and trading volumes have been growing over the last few years. Regardless of whether or not the Arizona Stock Exchange succeeds in its present form, the concept of an electronic call to market is likely to gain increasing attention in the years ahead.

Externally Efficient Market A market for securities in which information is quickly and widely disseminated, thereby allowing each security's price to adjust in an unbiased manner to new information so that it reflects investment value.

Internally Efficient Market A market for securities in which brokers and dealers compete fairly so that the cost of transacting is low and the speed of transacting is high.

in order for markets to be allocationally efficient, they need to be both internally and externally efficient. In an **externally efficient market**, information is quickly and widely disseminated, thereby allowing each security's price to adjust rapidly in an unbiased manner to new information so that it reflects investment value (a term that will be discussed shortly). In comparison, an **internally efficient market** is one where brokers and dealers compete fairly so that the cost of transacting is low and the speed of transacting is high. While external market efficiency has been the subject of much research since the 1960s, internal market efficiency has only recently become a popular area of research.[1] Indeed, government regulators have adopted polices aimed at improving the internal efficiency of markets, primarily by setting rules and regulations that affect the design and operations of security markets. Nevertheless, from now on the term "market efficiency" will denote external market efficiency, since this is the subject that has generated the most interest among practitioners and academics.

The Efficient Market Model

Arizona Stock Exchange
www.azx.com

Imagine a world in which (1) all investors have costless access to currently available information about the future; (2) all investors are capable analysts; and (3) all investors pay close

---

[1]A burgeoning field of research in finance is known as market microstructure, which involves the study of internal market efficiency.

Investment Value The present value of a security's future prospects as estimated by well-informed market participants.

Efficient Market A market for securities in which every security's price equals its investment value at all times, implying that a set of information is fully and immediately reflected in market prices.

Weak-Form Market Efficiency A level of market efficiency in which all previous security price data is fully and immediately reflected in current security prices.

Semistrong-Form Market Efficiency A level of market efficiency in which all relevant publicly available information is fully and immediately reflected in security prices.

Strong-Form Market Efficiency A level of market efficiency in which all relevant information, both public and private, is fully and immediately reflected in security prices.

attention to market prices and adjust their holdings appropriately.[2] In such a market, a security's price will be a good estimate of its **investment value**, where investment value is the present value of the security's future prospects as estimated by well-informed and skilled analysts who use the information that is currently at hand. (Investment value is often referred to as the security's "fair" or "intrinsic" value.) That is, an **efficient market**, defined as one in which every security's price equals its investment value at all times, will exist.

In an efficient market, a set of information is fully and immediately reflected in market prices. But what information? A popular definition, offered by Fama, is the following:[3]

Form of Efficiency	Set of Information Reflected in Security Prices
Weak	Previous prices of securities
Semistrong	All publicly available information
Strong	All information, both public and private

This leads to an equivalent definition of an efficient market as follows:

A market is efficient with respect to a particular set of information if it is impossible to make abnormal profits (other than by chance) by using this set of information to formulate buying and selling decisions.

That is, in an efficient market investors should expect to make only normal profits by earning a normal rate of return on their investments. For example, a market would be described as being **weak-form efficient** if it is impossible to make abnormal profits (other than by chance) by using past prices to formulate buying and selling decisions. Similarly, a market would be described as being **semistrong-form efficient** if it is impossible to make abnormal profits (other than by chance) by using publicly available information to formulate buying and selling decisions. Lastly, a market would be described as being **strong-form efficient** if it is impossible to make abnormal profits (other than by chance) by using any information whatsoever to make buying and selling decisions. Typically, when people refer to efficient markets, they really mean semistrong-form efficient markets, since Canada and the US have strict laws about the use of insider information (a form of private information) to formulate buying and selling decisions. Hence, it is interesting to investigate whether markets are semistrong-form efficient since that involves the set of publicly available information that analysts are restricted to using in preparing their recommendations.

Why have the above statements included the qualifying phrase "other than by chance" in the definition of an efficient market? Simply because some people, for example, may invest on the basis of patterns in past prices and end up making an extraordinarily high return. However, in an efficient market this outcome would have had nothing to do with the investor's use of past price information. Instead, it would have been merely due to luck, just as someone who wins a lottery after using a method for picking a number does not necessarily have a successful method for picking winning lottery numbers.

---

[2]Actually, not all investors need to meet these three conditions in order for security prices to equal their investment values. Instead, what is needed is for marginal investors to meet these conditions, since their trades would correct the mispricing that would occur in their absence.

[3]Eugene F. Fama, "Efficient Capital Markets: A Review of Theory and Empirical Work," *Journal of Finance* 25, no. 5 (May 1970): 383–417.

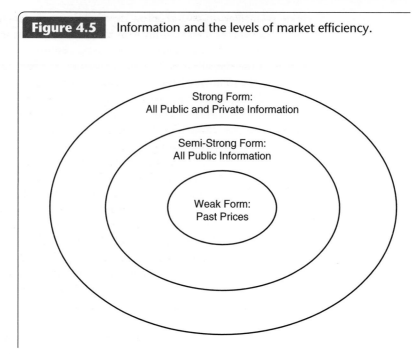

Figure 4.5 Information and the levels of market efficiency.

Strong Form:
All Public and Private Information

Semi-Strong Form:
All Public Information

Weak Form:
Past Prices

Figure 4.5 illustrates these three forms of efficiency. Note how in moving from weak to semistrong to strong-form efficiency, the set of information expands. Thus, if markets are strong-form efficient, then they are also semistrong and weak-form efficient. Similarly, if markets are semistrong-form efficient, then they are also weak-form efficient.

Fama's Formulation of the Efficient Market Model

Fama presented a general notation describing how investors generate price expectations for securities. That is:

$$E(p_{j,\,t+1}/\varPhi_t) = [1 + E(r_{j,\,t+1}/\varPhi_t)]p_n \tag{4.1}$$

where:

E = expected value operator
$p_{j,\,t+1}$ = price of security j at time $t + 1$
$\varPhi_t$ = the set of information available to investors at time t

so $E(p_{j,\,t+1}/\varPhi_t)$ denotes the expected end-of-period price on security j, given the information available at the beginning of the period. Continuing, the term $[1 + E(r_{j,\,t+1}/\varPhi_t]$ denotes the expected return over the forthcoming time period on securities having the same amount of risk as security j, given the information available at the beginning of the period. Lastly, $p_{j,t}$ denotes the price of security j at the beginning of the period. Thus, Equation (4.1) states that the expected price for any security at the end of the period $(t + 1)$ is based the security's expected normal (or equilibrium) rate of return during that period. In turn, the expected rate of return is determined by (or is conditional on) the information set available at the start of the period, $\varPhi_t$. Investors are assumed to make full and accurate use of this available information set. That is, they do not ignore or misinterpret this information in setting their return projections for the coming period.

What is contained in the available information set $\varPhi_t$? The answer depends on the particular form of market efficiency being considered. In the case of weak-form efficiency, the information set includes past price data. In the case of semistrong-form efficiency, the information set includes all publicly available information relevant to establishing security values, including the weak-form information set. This information would include published financial data about companies, government data about the state of the economy, earnings estimates disseminated by companies and securities analysts, and so on. Finally, in the case of strong-form efficiency, the information set includes all relevant valuation data, including information known only to corporate insiders, such as the planned corporate takeovers and extraordinary positive or negative future earnings announcements.

If markets are efficient, then investors cannot earn abnormal profits trading on the available information set Φ_t other than by chance. Again employing Fama's notation, the level of over or undervaluation of a security is defined as:

$$x_{j,\,t+1} = p_{j,\,t+1} - E(p_{j,\,t+1}/\Phi_t) \tag{4.2}$$

where $x_{j,\,t+1}$ indicates the extent to which the actual price for security j at the end of the period differs from the price expected by investors based on the information available at the beginning of the period. As a result, in an efficient market it must be true that:

$$E(x_{j,\,t+1}/\Phi_t) = 0 \tag{4.3}$$

That is, there will be no expected under or overvaluation of securities based on the available information set. That information is always impounded in security prices.

▣ Security Price Changes as a Random Walk

What happens when *new* information arrives that changes the information set Φ_t, such as an announcement that a company's earnings have just experienced a significant and unexpected decline? In an efficient market, investors will incorporate any new information immediately and fully in security prices. New information is just that: new, meaning a surprise. (Anything that is not a surprise is predictable and should have been anticipated before the fact.) Since happy surprises are about as likely as unhappy ones, price changes in an efficient market are about as likely to be positive as negative. While a security's price might be expected to move upwards by an amount that provides a reasonable return on capital (when considered in conjunction with dividend payments), anything above or below this would, in such a market, be unpredictable.

In a perfectly efficient market, price changes are random.[4] This does not mean that prices are irrational. On the contrary, prices are quite rational. Since information arrives randomly, changes in prices that occur as a consequence of that information will appear to be random, sometimes being positive and sometimes being negative. However, these price changes are simply the consequence of investors reassessing a security's prospects and adjusting their buying and selling appropriately. Hence the price changes are random but rational.

As mentioned earlier, in an efficient market a security's price will be a good estimate of its investment value, where investment value is the present value of the security's future prospects as estimated by well-informed and capable analysts. In a well-developed and free

Random Walk In general, a situation in which changes in the value of a random variable are independent and identically distributed. When applied to common shares, it refers to a situation in which security price changes are independent and identically distributed, meaning that the size of a security's price change from one period to the next can be viewed as being determined by the spin of a roulette wheel.

Random Walk with Drift A situation in which security prices follow a random walk, except that those prices are expected to rise over time.

Submartingale Process A process in which a stock's expected price in period $t + 1$, given the information available at time t, is greater than the stock's price at time t.

---

[4]Some people assert that daily stock prices follow a **random walk**, meaning that stock price changes (say, from one day to the next) are independently and identically distributed. That is, the price change from day t to day $t + 1$ is not influenced by the price change from day $t - 1$ to day t; and the size of the price change from one day to the next can be viewed as being determined by the spin of a roulette wheel (with the same roulette wheel being used every day). Statistically, in a random walk, $P_t = P_{t-1} + e_t$ where e_t is a random error term whose expected outcome is zero but whose actual outcome is like the spin of a roulette wheel. A more reasonable characterization is to describe daily stock prices as following a **random walk with drift**, where $P_t = P_{t-1} + d + e_t$ where d is a small positive number, since stock prices have shown a tendency over time to go up. However, since it can be reasonably argued that the random error term e_t is not independent and identically distributed over time (that is, evidence suggests that the same roulette wheel is not used every period), the most accurate characterization of stock prices is to say they follow a **submartingale process**. This simply means that a stock's expected price in period $t + 1$, given the information that is available at time t, is greater than the stock's price at time t.

market, major disparities between price and investment value will be noted by alert analysts who will seek to take advantage of their discoveries. Securities priced below investment value (known as underpriced or undervalued securities) will be purchased, creating pressure for price increases due to the increased demand to buy. Securities priced above investment value (known as overpriced or overvalued securities) will be sold, creating pressure for price decreases due to the increased supply to sell. As investors seek to take advantage of opportunities created by temporary inefficiencies, they will cause the inefficiencies to be reduced, denying the less alert and the less informed a chance to obtain large abnormal profits. As a consequence of the efforts of such highly alert investors, at any time a security's price can be assumed to equal the security's investment value, implying that security mispricing will not exist.

Observations about Perfectly Efficient Markets

There are a number of interesting observations that can be made about perfectly efficient markets.

1. **Investors will make a fair return on their investment but no more.** This means that looking for mispriced securities with either technical analysis (where analysts examine the past price behaviour of securities) or fundamental analysis (where analysts examine earnings and dividend forecasts) will not prove to be fruitful activities. Investing money on the basis of either type of analysis will not generate abnormal returns (other than for those few investors who turn out to be lucky).

2. **Markets will be efficient only if enough investors believe that they are not efficient.** The reason for this seeming paradox is straightforward—it is the actions of investors who carefully analyze securities that make prices reflect investment values. However, if everyone believed that markets are perfectly efficient, then everyone would realize that nothing is to be gained by searching for undervalued securities, and hence nobody would bother to analyze securities. Consequently, security prices would not react instantaneously to the release of information, but instead would respond more slowly. Thus, in a classic catch-22 situation, markets would become inefficient if investors believe that they are efficient, yet they are efficient because investors believe them to be inefficient.

3. **Publicly known investment strategies cannot generate abnormal returns.** If somebody has a strategy that generated abnormal returns in the past and subsequently divulges it to the public (for example, by publishing a book or article about it), then the usefulness of the strategy will be destroyed. The strategy, whatever it is based on, must provide some means to identify mispriced securities. The reason that it will not work after it is made public is that a number of investors will try to capitalize on it, and in doing so will force prices to equal investment values the moment the strategy indicates a security is mispriced. The action of investors following the strategy will eliminate its effectiveness at identifying mispriced securities.

4. **Some investors will display impressive performance records.** However, this is merely due to chance (despite their assertions to the contrary). Think of a simple model where half the time the stock market has an annual return greater than Treasury bills (an "up" market) and the other half of the time its return is less than T-bills (a "down" market). With many investors attempting to forecast whether the stock market will be up or down each year and acting accordingly, in an efficient market about half the investors will be right in any given year, and half will be wrong. The next year, half of those that were right the first year will be right the second year too. Thus, $\frac{1}{2} \times \frac{1}{2} = \frac{1}{4}$ of all the investors will have been right both years. Continuing for a third year, about half of the surviving investors will be right then, so that in total $\frac{1}{2} \times \frac{1}{2} \times \frac{1}{2} = \frac{1}{8}$ of all the investors can show that they were right all three years. Thus, it can be seen that $(\frac{1}{2})^T$ investors

will be correct every year over a span of T years. Hence if $T = 6$, then $\frac{1}{64}$ of the investors will have been correct all six years, but this is only because they were lucky, not skillful. Consequently, it is misleading to listen to anecdotal evidence about the success of certain investors. Indeed, it would mean that any fees paid to obtain advice from such investors would be wasted.

5. **Professional investors should fare no better in picking securities than ordinary investors.** This is because prices always reflect investment value, and hence the search for mispriced securities is futile. Consequently, professional investors do not have an edge on ordinary investors when it comes to identifying mispriced securities and generating abnormally high returns.

6. **Past performance is not an indicator of future performance.** Investors who have done well in the past are no more likely to do better in the future than investors that have done poorly in the past. This is because those who have done well in the past have been merely lucky, while those who have done poorly have merely had a streak of misfortune. Since past luck and misfortune do not have a tendency to repeat themselves, historical performance records are useless in predicting future performance records. (Of course, if the reason for the poor performance was due to incurring high operating expenses, then poor performers are more likely to remain poor performers.)

Observations about Perfectly Efficient Markets with Transactions Costs

The efficient market model discussed earlier assumed that investors had free access to all information relevant to setting security prices. In reality, it is expensive to collect and process such information. Furthermore, investors cannot adjust their portfolios in response to new information without incurring transaction costs. How does the existence of these costs affect the efficient market model? Grossman and Stiglitz considered this issue and arrived at two important conclusions.[5]

1. **In a world where it costs money to analyze securities,** analysts will be able to identify mispriced securities. However, their gain from doing so will be exactly offset by the increased costs (perhaps associated with the money needed to procure data and analytical software) that they incur. Hence, their gross returns will indicate that they have made abnormal returns, but their net returns will show that they have earned a fair return and nothing more. Of course, they can earn less than a fair return in such an environment due to the failure to properly use the data. For example, by rapidly buying and selling securities, they may generate large transactions costs that would more than offset the value of their superior security analysis.

2. **Investors will do just as well using a passive investment strategy where they simply buy the securities in a particular index and hold onto those investments.** Such a strategy will minimize transaction costs and can be expected to do as well as any professionally managed portfolio that actively seeks out mispriced securities and incurs costs in doing so. Indeed, such a strategy can be expected to outperform any professionally managed portfolio that incurs unnecessary transactions costs (by, for example, trading too often). Note that the gross returns of professionally managed portfolios will exceed those of passively managed portfolios having similar investment objectives, but that both kinds of portfolios can be expected to have similar net returns.

---

[5] Sanford J. Grossman and Joseph E. Stiglitz, "On the Impossibility of Informationally Efficient Markets," *American Economic Review* 70 (June 1980): 393–408.

The Active Versus Passive Debate

The issue of market efficiency has clear and important ramifications for the investment management industry. At stake are billions of dollars in investment management fees, professional reputations, and, some would argue, even the efficient functioning of our capital markets.

Greater market efficiency implies a lower probability that an investor will be able to consistently identify mispriced securities. Consequently, the more efficient is a securities market, the lower is the expected payoff to investors who buy and sell securities in search of abnormally high returns. In fact, when research and transaction costs are factored into the analysis, greater market efficiency increases the chances that investors "actively" managing their portfolios will underperform a simple technique of holding a portfolio that resembles the composition of the entire market. Institutional investors have responded to evidence of significant efficiency in Canadian and US share and bond markets by increasingly pursuing an investment approach referred to as *passive management*. As the text describes, passive management involves a long-term, buy-and-hold approach to investing. The investor selects an appropriate target and buys a portfolio designed to closely track the performance of that target. Once the portfolio is purchased, little additional trading occurs, beyond reinvestment of income or minor rebalancings necessary to accurately track the target. Because the selected target is usually (although not necessarily) a broad, diversified market index (for example, the TSE 300 for domestic common shares) passive management (see Chapter 23) is commonly referred to as "indexation," and the passive portfolios are called "index funds."

Active management involves a systematic effort to exceed the performance of a selected target. A wide array of active management investment approaches exist, far too many to summarize in this space. Nevertheless, all active management entails the search for mispriced securities, or mispriced groups of securities. Accurately identifying and adroitly purchasing or selling these mispriced securities provides the active investor with the potential to outperform the passive investor.

Passive management is a relative newcomer to the investment industry. Prior to the mid 1960s, it was axiomatic that investors should search for mispriced stocks. Some investment strategies had passive overtones, such as buying "solid, blue-chip" companies for the "long term." Nevertheless, even these strategies implied an attempt to outperform some nebulously specified market target. The concepts of broad diversification and passive management were, for practical purposes, nonexistent.

Attitudes changed in the 1960s with the popularization of Markowitz's portfolio selection concepts (see Chapter 7), the introduction of the efficient market hypothesis (see this chapter), the emphasis on "the market portfolio" derived from the Capital Asset Pricing Model (see Chapter 9), and various academic studies proclaiming the futility of active management. Many investors, especially large institutional investors, began to question the wisdom of actively managing all of their assets. The first common stock index fund was introduced in the US in 1971. By the end of the decade, roughly $100 million was being invested in index funds. Today, hundreds of billions of dollars are invested in domestic and international stock and bond index funds. Even individual investors have become enamoured of index funds. Passively managed portfolios are some of the fastest growing products offered by many large mutual fund organizations.

Proponents of active management argue that capital markets are inefficient enough to justify the search for mispriced securities. They may disagree on the degree of the markets' inefficiencies. Technical analysts (see Chapter 22), for example, tend to view markets as dominated by emotionally driven and predictable investors, thereby creating numerous profit opportunities for the creative and disciplined investor. Conversely, managers who use highly quantitative investment tools often view profit opportunities as smaller and less persistent. Nevertheless, all active managers possess a fundamental belief in the existence of consistently exploitable security mispricings. As evidence they frequently point to the stellar track records of certain successful managers and various studies identifying market inefficiencies (see the appendix to Chapter 16 that discusses empirical regularities).

Some active management proponents also introduce into the active-passive debate what amounts to a moralistic appeal. They contend that investors virtually have an obligation to seek out mispriced securities, because their actions help remove these mispricings and thereby lead to a more efficient allocation of capital. Moreover, some proponents derisively contend that passive management implies settling for mediocre, or average, performance.

Proponents of passive management do not deny that exploitable profit opportunities exist or that some managers have established impressive performance results. Rather, they contend that the capital markets are efficient enough to prevent all but a few with inside information from consistently being able to earn abnormal profits. They claim that examples of past successes are more likely the result of luck rather than skill. If 1000 people flip a coin 10 times, the odds are that one of the will flip all heads. In the investment industry, this person is crowned a brilliant money manager.

Passive management proponents also argue that the expected returns from active management are actually less than those for passive management. The fees charged by active managers are typically much higher than those levied by passive managers. (The difference averages anywhere from 0.30% to 1.00% of the managers' assets under management.) Further, passively managed portfolios usually experience very small transaction costs, whereas, depending on the amount of trading involved, active management transaction costs can be quite high. Thus, it is argued that passive managers will outperform active managers because of cost differences. Passive management thus entails settling for superior, as opposed to mediocre, results.

The active-passive debate will never be totally resolved. The random "noise" inherent in investment performance tends to drown out any systematic evidence of investment management skill on the part of active managers. Subjective issues therefore dominate the discussion, and as a result neither side can convince the other of the correctness of its viewpoint.

Despite the rapid growth in passively managed assets, most domestic and international stock and bond portfolios remain actively managed. Many large institutional investors, such as pension funds, have taken a middle ground on the matter, hiring both passive and active managers. In a crude way, this strategy may be a reasonable response to the unresolved active-passive debate. Clearly, all assets cannot be passively managed—who would be left to maintain security prices at "fair" value levels? On the other hand, it may not take many skillful active managers to ensure an adequate level of market efficiency. Further, the evidence is overwhelming that managers with above-average investment skills are in a minority of the group currently offering their services to investors.

Testing for Market Efficiency

Having described how prices are determined in a perfectly efficient market, it is useful to take a moment to consider how to conduct tests to determine if markets actually are perfectly efficient, reasonably efficient, or not efficient at all. There are a multitude of methodologies, but three stand out. They involve conducting event studies, looking for patterns in security prices, and examining the investment performance of professional money managers.

First, *event studies* can be carried out to see just how fast security prices actually react to the release of information. Is it rapid or slow? Are the returns after the announcement date abnormally high or low or are they simply normal? Note that the answer to this question requires a definition of a "normal return" for a given security. Typically this is done by the use of some equilibrium-based asset pricing model, two of which will be discussed in Chapters 9 and 11. An improperly specified asset pricing model can invalidate a test of market efficiency. Thus, tests of this nature are really joint tests, as they simultaneously

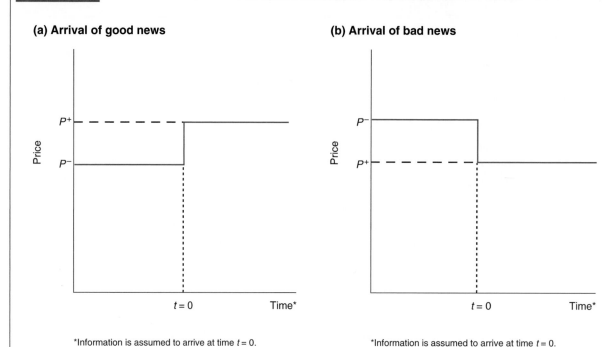

(a) Arrival of good news

(b) Arrival of bad news

*Information is assumed to arrive at time $t = 0$.

*Information is assumed to arrive at time $t = 0$.

involve tests of the asset pricing model's validity and of market efficiency. A finding that prices react slowly to information might be due to markets being inefficient, or it might be due to the use of an improper asset pricing model, or it might be due to both.

As an example of an event study, consider what happens in a perfectly efficient market when information is released. When it arrives in the marketplace, prices will react instantaneously to this information and, in doing so, will immediately move to their new investment values. Figure 4.6 has two panels that show what happens in such a market when good news and bad news arrives, respectively. Note how in both cases the horizontal axis is a time line, while the vertical axis is the security's price so that the figure reflects the security's price over time. At time 0 ($t = 0$), information is released about the firm. Observe how shortly beforehand the security's price was at a price P^-. With the arrival of the information the price immediately moves to its new equilibrium level of P^+, where it stays until some additional piece of information arrives. (To be more precise, the vertical axis would represent the security's abnormal return, which in an efficient market would be zero until $t = 0$, when it would briefly be either significantly positive (in the case of good news) or significantly negative (in the case of bad news). Afterwards it would return to zero. For simplicity, prices are used instead of returns, since over a short time period surrounding $t = 0$ the results are essentially the same.

Figure 4.7 displays two situations that cannot occur with regularity in an efficient market when good news arrives (a similar situation, while not illustrated here, cannot occur when bad news arrives). In panel (a) the security reacts slowly to the information so that it does not reach its equilibrium price P^+ until $t = 1$. This cannot occur regularly in an efficient market, as analysts will realize after $t = 0$ but before $t = 1$ that the security is not priced fairly, and hence will rush to buy it. Consequently, they will force the security to reach its equilibrium price before $t = 1$. Indeed, they will force the security to reach its equilibrium price moments after the information is released at $t = 0$.

In panel (b) the security's price overreacts to the information, and then slowly settles down to its equilibrium value. Again, this cannot occur with regularity in an efficient mar-

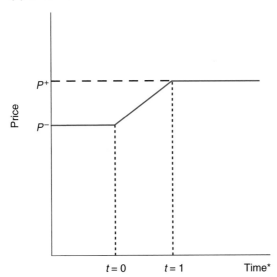

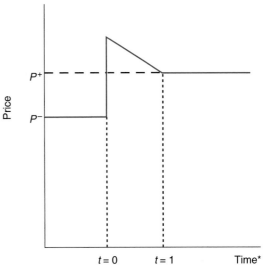

(a) Slow Reaction of Stock Price to Information

(b) Overreaction of Stock Price to Information

*Information is assumed to arrive at time $t = 0$.

*Information is assumed to arrive at time $t = 0$.

ket. Analysts will realize that the security is selling above its fair value, and will proceed to sell it if they own it or to short sell it if they do not own it. As a consequence of their actions, they will prevent its price from rising above its equilibrium value, P^+, after the information is released.

Many event studies have been made about the reaction of security prices, particularly stock prices, to the release of information, such as news (usually referred to as "announcements") pertaining to earnings and dividends, share repurchase programs, stock splits and dividends, stock and bond sales, stock listings, bond rating changes, mergers and acquisitions, and divestitures. Indeed, this area of academic research has become a virtual growth industry.

A second method to test for market efficiency is to investigate whether there are any patterns in security price movements attributable to something other than what one would expect. Securities can be expected to provide a rate of return over a given time period in accordance with an asset pricing model. Such a model asserts that a security's expected rate of return is equal to a risk-free rate of return plus a "risk premium" whose magnitude is based on the riskiness of the security. Hence, if the risk-free rate and risk premium are both unchanging over time, then securities with high average returns in the past can be expected to have high returns in the future. However, the risk premium, for example, may be changing over time, making it difficult to see if there are patterns in security prices. Indeed, any tests that are conducted to test for the existence of price patterns are once again joint tests of both market efficiency and of the asset pricing model that is used to estimate the risk premiums on securities.

In recent years, a large number of these patterns have been identified and labelled as "market anomalies." For example, one of the most prominent market anomalies is the January effect. Security returns appear to be abnormally high in the month of January. Other months show no similar type returns. This pattern has a long and consistent track record and no convincing explanations have been proposed. (The January effect and other market anomalies are discussed in Chapter 16.)

The third approach is to examine the investment record of professional investors. Are more of them able to earn abnormally high rates of return than one would expect in a perfectly efficient market? Are more of them able to consistently earn abnormally high returns period after period than one would expect in an efficient market? Again, problems are encountered in conducting such tests, since they require the determination of abnormal returns which, in turn, requires the determination of just what are "normal returns." Because normal returns can only be determined by assuming that a particular asset pricing model is applicable, all such tests are joint tests of market efficiency and an asset pricing model.

Summary of Market Efficiency Test Results

Many tests have been conducted over the years examining the degree to which security markets are efficient. Rather than laboriously review the results of those tests at this point, the most prominent studies are discussed in later chapters where the specific investment activities associated with the studies are considered. However, a few comments about the general conclusions drawn from those studies are appropriate here.

Weak-Form Tests

Early tests of weak-form market efficiency failed to find any evidence that abnormal profits could be earned trading on information related to past prices. That is, knowing how security prices had moved in the past could not be translated into accurate predictions of future security prices. These tests generally concluded that technical analysis, which relies on forecasting security prices based on past prices, was ineffective. More recent studies, however, have indicated that investors may overreact to certain types of information, driving security prices temporarily away from their investment values. As a result, it may be possible to earn abnormal profits buying securities that have been "oversold" and selling securities whose prices have been bid up excessively. (It should be pointed out, however, that these observations are contentious, and have not been universally accepted.)

Semistrong-Form Tests

Tests of semistrong-form market efficiency have been mixed. Most event studies have failed to demonstrate sufficiently large inefficiencies to overcome transaction costs. However, various market "anomalies" have been discovered whereby securities with certain characteristics or during certain time periods appear to produce abnormally high returns. For example, common stocks in January have been shown to offer returns much higher than those earned in the other 11 months of the year.

Strong-Form Tests

One would expect that investors with access to private information would have an advantage over investors who trade only on publicly available information. In general, corporate insiders and stock exchange specialists, who have information not readily available to the investing public, have been shown to be able to earn abnormally high profits. Less clear is the ability of security analysts to produce such profits. At times, these analysts have direct access to private information and in a sense they also "manufacture" their own private information through their research efforts. Some studies have indicated that certain analysts can discern mispriced securities, but whether it is due to ability or chance is an open issue.

Summary of Efficient Markets

Tests of market efficiency demonstrate that Canadian and US security markets are highly efficient, rapidly impounding relevant information about investment values into security prices quickly and accurately. Investors cannot easily expect to earn abnormal profits trading on publicly available information, particularly once the costs of research and transactions are considered. Nevertheless, numerous pockets of unexplained abnormal returns have been identified, guaranteeing that the debate over the degree of market efficiency will continue.

Summary

1. The forces of supply and demand interact to determine a security's market price.
2. An investor's demand-to-buy schedule indicates the quantity of a security that the investor wishes to purchase at various prices.
3. An investor's supply-to-sell schedule indicates the quantity of a security that the investor wishes to sell at various prices.
4. The demand and supply schedules for individual investors can be aggregated to create aggregate demand and supply schedules for a security.
5. The intersection of the aggregate demand and supply schedules determines the market clearing price of a security. At that price the quantity traded is maximized.
6. The market price of a security can be thought of as representing a consensus opinion about the future prospects for the security.
7. An allocationally efficient market is one in which firms with the most promising investment opportunities have access to needed funds.
8. Markets must be both internally and externally efficient in order to have allocationally efficient markets. In an externally efficient market, information is quickly and widely disseminated, thereby allowing each security's price to adjust rapidly in an unbiased manner to new information so it reflects investment value. In an internally efficient market, brokers and dealers compete fairly so that the cost of transacting is low and the speed of transacting is high.
9. A security's investment value is the present value of the security's future prospects, as estimated by well-informed and capable analysts, and can be thought of as the security's fair or intrinsic value.
10. In an efficient market a security's market price will fully reflect all available information relevant to the security's value at that time.
11. The concept of market efficiency can be expressed in three forms: weak, semistrong, and strong.
12. The three forms of market efficiency make different assumptions about the set of information reflected in security prices.
13. Tests of market efficiency are really joint tests about whether or not markets are efficient and whether or not security prices are set according to a specific asset pricing model.

1. What is the difference between call security markets and continuous security markets?

2. Using an aggregate demand-to-hold schedule and associated demand-to-buy or supply-to-sell schedules, explain and illustrate the effect of the following events on the equilibrium price and quantity traded of Fairchild Corporation's stock.
   a. Fairchild officials announce that next year's earnings are expected to be significantly higher than analysts had previously forecast.
   b. A wealthy shareholder initiates a large secondary offering of Fairchild stock.
   c. Another company, quite similar to Fairchild in all respects except for being privately held, decides to offer its outstanding shares for sale to the public.

3. Is it true that in the short run the supply schedule for a security is perfectly inelastic, whereas the demand-to-hold schedule is typically elastic? Explain.

4. Short sellers do not receive the proceeds from their short sales, must put up initial margin, and often do not receive interest on these sums held by their brokers. How does this affect the aggregate demand-to-hold schedules for securities?

5. Ian Begley is pondering the statement, "The pattern of security price behaviour might appear the same whether markets were efficient or security prices bore no relationship whatsoever to investment value." Explain the meaning of this statement to Ian.

6. We all know that investors have widely diverse opinions about the future course of the economy and earnings forecasts for various industries and companies. How then is it possible for all these investors to arrive at an equilibrium price for any particular security?

7. Distinguish between the three forms of market efficiency.

8. Does the fact that a market exhibits weak-form efficiency necessarily imply that it is also strong-form efficient? How about the converse statement? Explain.

9. Consider the following types of information. If this information is immediately and fully reflected in security prices, what form of market efficiency is implied?
   a. A company's recent quarterly earnings announcement.
   b. Historical bond yields.
   c. Deliberations of a company's board of directors concerning a possible merger with another company.
   d. Limit orders.
   e. A brokerage firm's published research report on a particular company.
   f. Movements in the TSE 300 Composite Index as plotted in *The Financial Post*.

10. Would you expect that fundamental security analysis makes security markets more efficient? Why?

11. Would you expect that TSE market-makers should be able to earn an abnormal profit in a semistrong efficient market? Why?

12. Is it true that in a perfectly efficient market no investor would consistently be able to earn a profit?

13. Although security markets may not be perfectly efficient, what is the rationale for expecting them to be highly efficient?

14. When a corporation announces its earnings for a period, the volume of transactions in its stock may increase, but frequently that increase is not associated with significant moves in the price of its stock. How can this be explained?

15. What are the implications of the three forms of market efficiency for technical and fundamental analysis (discussed in Chapter 1)?

16. The years 1986 and 1987 will probably be long remembered for the insider trading scandals that were exposed in the United States.
    a. Is successful insider trading consistent with the three forms of market efficiency? Explain.
    b. Play the role of devil's advocate and present a case outline the benefits to financial markets of insider trading.

17. The text states that tests for market efficiency involving an asset pricing model are really joint tests. What is meant by that statement?

18. In perfectly efficient markets with transaction costs, why should analysts be able to find mispriced securities?

19. When investment managers present their historical performance records to potential and existing customers, market regulators require the managers to qualify those records with the comment that "past performance is no guarantee of future performance." In a perfectly efficient market, why would such an admonition be particularly appropriate?

CFA Exam Questions

20. Discuss the role of a portfolio manager in a perfectly efficient market.

21. Fairfax asks for information concerning the benefits of active portfolio management. She is particularly interested in the question of whether or not active managers can be expected to consistently exploit inefficiencies in the capital markets to produce above-average returns without assuming higher risk.

    The semistrong form of the Efficient Markets Hypothesis (EMH) asserts that all publicly available information is rapidly and correctly reflected in securities prices. This implies that investors cannot expect to drive above-average profits from purchases made after the information has become public because security prices already reflect the information's full effects.

    a. i. Identify and explain two examples of empirical evidence that tend to support the EMH implication stated above.
       ii. Identify and explain two examples of empirical evidence that tend to refute the EMH implication stated above.
    b. Discuss two reasons why an investor might choose an active manager even if the markets were, in fact, semistrong-form efficient.

KEY TERMS

demand-to-buy schedule (p. 80)
supply-to-sell schedule (p. 81)
allocationally efficient market (p. 84)
externally efficient market (p. 86)
internally efficient market (p. 86)
investment value (p. 87)
efficient market (p. 87)

weak-form efficiency (p. 87)
semistrong-form efficiency (p. 87)
strong-form efficiency (p. 87)
random walk (p. 89)
random walk with drift (p. 89)
submartingale process (p. 89)

REFERENCES

1. A discussion and examination of the demand curves for stocks is contained in:

   Andrei Shleifer, "Do Demand Curves Slope Down?" *Journal of Finance* 41, no. 3 (July 1986): 579–590.

Lawrence Harris and Eitan Gurel, "Price and Volume Effects Associated with Changes in the S&P 500: New Evidence for the Existence of Price Pressures," *Journal of Finance* 41, no. 4 (September 1986): 815–829.

Stephen W. Pruitt and K. C. John Wei, "Institutional Ownership and Changes in the S&P 500," *Journal of Finance* 44, no. 2 (June 1989): 509–513.

2. For articles presenting arguments that securities are "overpriced" due to short sale restrictions, see:

Edward M. Miller, "Risk, Uncertainty, and Divergence of Opinion," *Journal of Finance* 32, no. 4 (September 1977): 1151–1168.

Douglas W. Diamond and Robert E. Verrecchia, "Constraints on Short-Selling and Asset Price Adjustment to Private Information," *Journal of Financial Economics* 18, no. 2 (June 1987): 277–311.

3. Allocational, external, and internal market efficiency are discussed in:

Richard R. West, "Two Kinds of Market Efficiency," *Financial Analysts Journal* 31, no. 6 (November–December 1975): 30–34.

4. Many people believe that the following articles are the seminal pieces on efficient markets:

Paul Samuelson, "Proof That Properly Anticipated Prices Fluctuate Randomly," *Industrial Management Review* 6 (1965): 41–49.

Harry V. Roberts, "Stock Market 'Patterns' and Financial Analysis: Methodological Suggestions," *Journal of Finance* 14, no. 1 (March 1959): 1–10.

Eugene F. Fama, "Efficient Capital Markets: A Review of Theory and Empirical Work," *Journal of Finance* 25, no. 5 (May 1970): 383–417.

Eugene F. Fama, "Efficient Capital Markets: II," *Journal of Finance* 46, no. 5 (December 1991): 1575–1617.

5. For an extensive discussion of efficient markets and related evidence, see:

George Foster, *Financial Statement Analysis* (Englewood Cliffs, NJ: Prentice Hall, 1986), Chapters 9 and 11.

Stephen F. LeRoy, "Capital Market Efficiency: An Update," *Federal Reserve Bank of San Francisco Economic Review*, no. 2 (Spring 1990): 29–40. A more detailed version of this paper can be found in: Stephen F. LeRoy, "Efficient Capital Markets and Martingales," *Journal of Economic Literature* 27, no. 4 (December 1989): 1583–1621.

Peter Fortune, "Stock Market Efficiency: An Autopsy?" *New England Economic Review* (March–April 1991): 17–40.

Richard A. Brealey and Stewart C. Myers, *Principles of Corporate Finance* (New York: McGraw-Hill, 1991), Chapter 13.

Stephen A. Ross, Randolph W. Westerfield, and Jeffrey F. Jaffe, *Corporate Finance* (Homewood, IL: Richard D. Irwin, 1993), Chapter 13.

6. Interesting overviews of efficient market concepts are presented in:

Robert Ferguson, "An Efficient Stock Market? Ridiculous!" *Journal of Portfolio Management* 9, no. 4 (Summer 1983): 31–38.

Bob L. Boldt and Harold L. Arbit, "Efficient Markets and the Professional Investor," *Financial Analysts Journal* 40, no. 4 (July–August 1984): 22–34.

Fischer Black, "Noise," *Journal of Finance* 41, no. 3 (July 1986): 529–543.

Keith C. Brown, W. V. Harlow, and Seha M. Tinic, "How Rational Investors Deal with Uncertainty (Or, Reports of the Death of Efficient Markets Theory Are Greatly Exaggerated)," *Journal of Applied Corporate Finance* 2, no. 3 (Fall 1989): 45–58.

Ray Ball, "The Theory of Stock Market Efficiency: Accomplishments and Limitations," *Journal of Applied Corporate Finance* 8, no. 1 (Spring 1995): 4–17.

7. For a Canadian perspective on this chapter, see:

Steve Forester, "Canadian Market Anomalies," *Canadian Investment Review* XI, no. 2 (Summer 1998): 61–62.

The Valuation of Riskless Securities

$\mathbf{A}$ useful first step in understanding security valuation is to consider those fixed-income securities that are certain of making their promised payments in full and on time. The obvious candidates are the securities representing the debt of the Canadian government. Since the government can print money whenever it chooses, the promised payments for such securities are virtually certain to be made on schedule. However, there is a degree of uncertainty as to the purchasing power of the promised payments. While Government of Canada bonds may be riskless in terms of their nominal payments, they may be quite risky in terms of their real (or inflation-adjusted) payments. This issue will be discussed further in Chapter 12.

Despite this concern with inflation risk, it will be assumed hereafter that there are fixed-income securities whose nominal and real payments are certain. Specifically, to the extent that inflation exists, it will be assumed that its magnitude can be accurately predicted. Such an assumption makes it possible to focus on the impact of time on security valuation. Having accomplished this, the influence of other attributes on security valuation can be considered.

Yield-to-Maturity

Interest rates are associated with investments and investments differ in longevity. Therefore, there are many interest rates, not just one. Furthermore, there are many ways that interest rates can be calculated. One such method results in an interest rate that is known as the yield-to-maturity; another results in an interest rate known as the spot rate, which is discussed in the next section.

In describing yields-to-maturity and spot rates, we will assume that three hypothetical riskless securities that are free from default risk (meaning that investors have no doubts about being paid fully and on time) are available. By considering these securities, the impact of differing degrees of default risk on yields-to-maturity and spot rates has been removed. These three securities are referred to as bonds A, B, and C. Bond A matures in one year, at which time the investor will receive $1000. Similarly, bond B matures in two years, at which time the investor will receive $1000. Bond C is a coupon bond that pays the investor $50 one year from now and matures two years from now, paying the investor $1050 at that time. The prices at which these bonds are currently being sold in the market are:

Bond A (the one-year pure-discount bond): $934.58
Bond B (the two-year pure-discount bond): $857.34
Bond C (the two-year coupon bond): $946.93

Yield-to-Maturity For a
particular fixed-income
security, the single interest
rate (with interest
compounded at some
specified interval) that, if
paid by a bank on the
amount invested in the
security, would enable the
investor to obtain all the
payments made by that
security. Equivalently, the
discount rate that equates
the present value of future
cash flows from the security
to the current market price
of the security.

The **yield-to-maturity** on any fixed-income security is the single interest rate (with interest compounded at some specified interval) that, if paid by a bank on the amount invested, would enable the investor to obtain all the payments made by the security in question. It is a simple matter to determine the yield-to-maturity on the one-year security, bond A. Since an investment of $934.58 will pay $1000 one year later, the yield-to-maturity on this bond is the rate r_A that a bank would have to pay on a deposit of $934.58 in order for the account to have a balance of $1000 after one year. Thus, the yield-to-maturity on bond A is the rate r_A that is the solution to the following equation:

$$(1 + r_A) \times \$934.58 = \$1000 \tag{5.1}$$

which is 7%.

In the case of bond B, assuming annual compounding at a rate r_B, an account with $857.34 invested initially (the cost of B) would grow to $(1 + r_B) \times \$857.34$ in one year. Leaving this total intact, the account would grow to $(1 + r_B) \times [(1 + r_B) \times \$857.34]$ by the end of the second year. The yield-to-maturity is the rate r_B that makes this amount equal to $1000. In other words, the yield-to-maturity on bond B is the rate r_B that is the solution to the following equation:

$$(1 + r_B) \times [(1 + r_B) \times \$857.34] = \$1000 \tag{5.2}$$

which is 8%.

For bond C, consider investing $946.93 in an account. At the end of one year, the account would grow in value to $(1 + r_C) \times \$946.93$. Then the investor would remove $50, leaving a balance of $[(1 + r_C) \times \$946.94] - \$50$. At the end of the second year this balance would have grown to an amount equal to $(1 + r_C) \times \{[(1 + r_C) \times \$946.93] - \$50\}$. The yield-to-maturity on bond C is the rate r_C that makes this amount equal to $1050:

$$(1 + r_C) \times \{[(1 + r_C) \times \$946.93] - \$50\} = \$1050 \tag{5.3}$$

which is 7.975%.

Equivalently, yield-to-maturity is the discount rate that makes the present value of the promised future cash flows equal to the current market price of the bond.[1] When viewed in this manner, yield-to-maturity is analogous to internal rate of return, a concept used for making capital budgeting decisions that is often described in corporate finance textbooks. This can be seen for bond A by dividing both sides of equation (5.1) by $(1 + r_A)$, resulting in:

$$\$934.58 = \frac{\$1000}{(1 + r_A)} \tag{5.4}$$

Similarly, for bond B both sides of equation (5.2) can be divided by $(1 + r_B)^2$, resulting in:

$$\$857.34 = \frac{\$1000}{(1 + r_B)^2} \tag{5.5}$$

whereas for bond C both sides of equation (5.3) can be divided by $(1 + r_C)^2$:

$$\$946.93 - \frac{\$50}{(1 + r_C)} = \frac{\$1050}{(1 + r_C)^2}$$

or

$$\$946.93 = \frac{\$50}{(1 + r_C)} + \frac{\$1050}{(1 + r_C)^2} \tag{5.6}$$

Since equations (5.4), (5.5), and (5.6) are equivalent to equations (5.1), (5.2), and (5.3), respectively, the solutions must be the same as before, with $r_A = 7\%$, $r_B = 8\%$, and $r_C = 7.975\%$.

---

[1] This calculation assumes that the bond will not be called prior to maturity. If it is assumed that the bond will be called as soon as possible, then the discount rate that makes the present value of the corresponding cash flows equal to the current market price of the bond is known as the bond's *yield-to-call.*

For coupon-bearing bonds, the procedure for determining yield-to-maturity involves trial and error. In the case of bond C, a discount rate of 10% could be tried initially, resulting in a value of $913.22 for the right-hand side of equation (5.6), a value that is too low. This indicates that the number in the denominator is too high, so a lower discount rate, such as 6%, is used next. In this case, the value on the right-hand side is $981.67, which is too high and indicates that 6% is too low. This means the solution is between 6% and 10%, and the search could continue until the answer, 7.975%, is found.

Fortunately, computers are good at trial-and-error calculations. One can describe a very complex series of cash flows to a computer and get an answer concerning yield-to-maturity in short order. In fact, some hand-held calculators come with built-in programs to find yield-to-maturity, where one simply enters the number of days to maturity, the annual coupon payments, and the current market price and then presses the key that indicates yield-to-maturity; then in a few seconds the answer appears.

Yield-to-maturity is the most commonly used measure of a bond's "interest rate," or "return." It can be computed for any bond and it facilitates comparisons among different investments. However, it has some serious drawbacks. In order to understand these drawbacks, the concept of spot rates will be introduced.

Spot Rates

A **spot rate** is measured at a given time as the yield-to-maturity on a pure-discount security and can be thought of as the interest rate associated with a spot contract. Such a contract, when signed, involves the immediate loaning of money from one party to another. The loan, along with interest, is to be repaid in its entirety at a specific time in the future. The interest rate that is specified in the contract is the spot rate.

Bonds A and B in the previous example were pure-discount securities, meaning an investor who purchased either one would expect to receive only one cash payment from the issuer. Accordingly, in this example the one-year spot rate is 7% and the two-year spot rate is 8%. In general, the t-year spot rate, s_t, is the solution to the following equation:

$$P_t = \frac{M_t}{(1 + s_t)^t} \tag{5.7}$$

where P_t is the current market price of a pure-discount bond that matures in t years and has a maturity value of M_t. For example, the values of P_t and M_t for bond B would be $857.34 and $1000, respectively, with $t = 2$.

Spot rates can also be determined in another manner if only coupon-bearing bonds are available for longer maturities. Generally the one-year spot rate (s_1) will be known, since there frequently will be a one-year pure-discount Treasury bill available for making this calculation. However, it may be that no two-year pure-discount security exists. Instead, only a two-year coupon-bearing bond may be available for investment, having a current market price of P_2, a maturity value of M_2, and a coupon payment one year from now equal to C_1. In this situation, the two-year spot rate (s_2) is the solution to the following equation:

$$P_2 = \frac{C_1}{(1 + s_1)^1} + \frac{M_2}{(1 + s_2)^2} \tag{5.8}$$

For example, assume that only bonds A and C exist. In this situation it is known that the one-year spot rate, s_1, is 7%. Now, equation (5.8) can be used to determine the two-year spot rate, s_2, where $P_2 = \$946.93$, $C_1 = \$50$, and $M_2 = \$1050$:

$$\$946.93 = \frac{\$50}{(1 + .07)^1} + \frac{\$1050}{(1 + s_2)^2}$$

The solution to this equation is $s_2 = .08 = 8\%$. Thus, the two-year spot rate is determined to be the same in this example regardless of whether it is determined directly by analyzing pure-discount bond B or indirectly by analyzing coupon-bearing bond C in conjunction with bond A. Although this will not always be the case, often the differences are insignificant.

Discount Factors

Discount Factor The present value of one dollar to be received from a security in a specified number of years.

Market Discount Function The set of discount factors on all default-free bonds across the spectrum of terms-to-maturity.

Discounting The process of calculating the present value of a given stream of cash flows.

Having determined a set of spot rates, it is a straightforward matter to determine the corresponding set of **discount factors**. A discount factor, d_t, is equivalent to the present value of $1 to be received t years in the future from a government security and is equal to:

$$d_t = \frac{1}{(1 + s_t)^t} \qquad (5.9)$$

The set of these factors is sometimes referred to as the **market discount function** that changes from day to day as spot rates change. In the example, $d_1 = 1/(1 + .07)^1 = .9346$ and $d_2 = 1/(1 + .08)^2 = .8573$.

Once the market discount function has been determined, it is fairly straightforward to find the present value of any default-free security. Let C_t denote the cash payment to be made to the investor at year t on the security being evaluated. The multiplication of C_t by d_t is termed **discounting**: converting the given future value into an equivalent present value. The latter is equivalent in the sense that P present dollars can be converted into C_t dollars in year t via available investment instruments, given the currently prevailing spot rates. An investment paying C_t dollars in year t with certainty should sell for $P = d_t C_t$ dollars today. If it sells for more, it is overpriced; if it sells for less, it is underpriced. These statements rest solely on comparisons with equivalent opportunities in the marketplace. Valuation of default-free investments thus requires no assessment of individual preferences, only careful analysis of available opportunities in the marketplace.

The simplest and, in a sense, most fundamental characterization of the structure of the market for default-free bonds is given by the current set of discount factors, referred to earlier as the market discount function. With this set of factors, it is a simple matter to evaluate a default-free bond that provides more than one payment, for it is, in effect, a package of bonds, each of which provides only one payment. Each amount is simply multiplied by the appropriate discount factor, and the resultant present values are summed.

For example, assume that the government is preparing to offer for sale a two-year coupon-bearing security that will pay $70 in one year and $1070 in two years. What is a fair price for such a security? It is simply the present value of $70 and $1070. This can be determined by multiplying $70 and $1070 by the one-year and two-year discount factors, respectively. Doing so results in ($70 × .9346) + ($1070 × .8573), which equals $982.73.

No matter how complex the pattern of payments, this procedure can be used to determine the value of any default-free bond of this type. The general formula for the bond's present value (PV) is:

$$PV = \sum_{t=1}^{n} d_t C_t \qquad (5.10)$$

where the bond has promised cash payments C_t for each year t through year n.

At this point, it has been shown how spot rates and, in turn, discount factors can be calculated. However, no link between different spot rates (or different discount factors) has been established. For example, it has yet to be shown how the one-year spot rate of 7% is related to the two-year spot rate of 8%. The concept of forward rates makes the link.

Forward Rates

In the example, the one-year spot rate was determined to be 7%. This means that the market has determined that the present value of $1 to be paid by the government in one year is $1/1.07, or $.9346. That is, the relevant discount rate for converting a cash flow one year from now to its present value is 7%. Since it was also noted that the two-year spot rate was 8%, the present value of $1 to be paid by the government in two years is $1/1.08^2$, or $.8573.

An alternative view of $1 to be paid in two years is that it can be discounted in two steps. The first step determines its equivalent one-year value. That is, $1 to be received in two years is equivalent to $1/(1 + f_{1,2})$ to be received in one year. The second step determines the present value of this equivalent one-year amount by discounting it at the one-year spot rate of 7%. Thus, its current value is

$$\frac{\$1/(1 + f_{1,2})}{(1 + .07)}$$

However, this value must be equal to $.8573, since it was mentioned earlier that, according to the two-year spot rate, $.8573 is the present value of $1 to be paid in two years. That is,

$$\frac{\$1/(1 + f_{1,2})}{(1 + .07)} = \$.8573 \tag{5.11}$$

which has a solution for $f_{1,2}$ of 9.01%.

Forward Rate The interest rate that links the current spot interest rate over one holding period to the current spot interest rate over a long holding period. Equivalently, the interest rate agreed to at a point in time where the loan will be made at a future date.

The discount rate $f_{1,2}$ is known as the **forward rate** from year 1 to year 2. That is, it is the discount rate for determining the equivalent value of a dollar one year from now if it is to be received two years from now. In the example, $1 to be received two years from now is equivalent in value to $1/1.0901 = $.9174$ to be received one year from now (in turn, note that the present value of $.9174 is $.9174/1.07 = $.8573$).

Symbolically, the link between the one-year spot rate, two-year spot rate, and one-year forward rate is:

$$\frac{\$1/(1 + f_{1,2})}{(1 + s_1)} = \frac{\$1}{(1 + s_2)^2} \tag{5.12}$$

which can be rewritten as:

$$(1 + f_{1,2}) = \frac{(1 + s_2)^2}{(1 + s_1)} \tag{5.13}$$

or

$$(1 + s_1)(1 + f_{1,2}) = (1 + s_2)(1 + s_2) \tag{5.14}$$

More generally, for year $t - 1$ and year t spot rates, the link to the forward rate between years $t - 1$ and t is:

$$(1 + f_{t-1,t}) = \frac{(1 + s_t)^t}{(1 + s_{t-1})^{t-1}} \tag{5.15}$$

or

$$(1 + s_{t-1})^{t-1} \times (1 + f_{t-1,t}) = (1 + s_t)^t \tag{5.16}$$

Figure 5.1 on page 109 illustrates this by referring to the example and generalizing from it.

There is another interpretation that can be given to forward rates. Consider a contract made now, in which money will be loaned a year from now and paid back two years from now. Such a contract is known as a **forward contract**; the interest rate on the one-year loan that is specified in it (note that the interest will be paid when the loan matures in two years) is known as the forward rate.

Forward Contract A contract that involves the delivery of some specific asset by a seller to a buyer at an agreed-upon future date.

Almost Risk-free Securities

Risk-free securities play a central role in modern financial theory, providing the baseline against which to evaluate risky investment alternatives. It is perhaps surprising, therefore, that no risk-free financial asset has historically been available to Canadian and US investors. Recent developments in both countries' government bond markets, however, have brought that deficiency to an end.

A riskless security provides an investor with a guaranteed (certain) return over the investor's time horizon. As the investor is ultimately interested in the purchasing power of his investments, the riskless security's return should be certain, not just on a nominal, but on a real (or inflation-adjusted) basis.

As the text notes, although government securities have zero risk of default, even they have not traditionally provided riskless real returns. Their principal and interest payments are not adjusted for inflation over the securities' lives. As a result, unexpected inflation may produce real returns quite different from those expected at the time the securities were purchased.

However, assume for the moment that inflation remains low and fairly predictable, so that we can effectively ignore inflation risk. Will government securities provide investors with riskless returns? The answer is generally "no."

An investor's time horizon usually will not coincide with the life of a particular security. If that time horizon is longer than the security's life, then the investor must purchase another security when the first security matures. If interest rates have changed in the interim, the investor will earn a different return than he originally anticipated. (This risk is known as reinvestment-rate risk—see Chapter 8.)

If the government security's life exceeds the investor's time horizon, then the investor will have to sell the security before it matures. If interest rates change prior to the sale, the price of the security will change, thereby causing the investor to earn a different return from the one originally anticipated. (This risk is known as interest-rate or price risk—see Chapter 8.)

Even if the security's life matches the investor's time horizon, it generally will not provide a riskless return. With the exception of Treasury bills and stripped bonds, all government securities make periodic interest payments (see Chapter 13), which the investor must reinvest. If interest rates change over the security's life, then the investor's reinvestment rate will change, causing the investor's return to differ from that originally anticipated at the time of the security's purchase.

Clearly, what investors need are default-free securities that make only one payment (which includes principal and all interest) when those securities mature. Investors could then select a security whose life matched their investment time horizons. These securities would be truly riskless, at least on a nominal basis.

A fixed-income security that makes only one payment at maturity is called a zero-coupon bond. Until the 1980s, however, zero-coupon government bonds did not exist, except for Treasury bills (which have a maximum maturity of one year). However, a coupon-bearing government security can be viewed as a *portfolio* of zero-coupon bonds, with each interest payment, as well as the principal, considered a separate bond. In 1982, several brokerage firms came to a novel realization: a government security's payments could be segregated and sold piecemeal through a process known as coupon stripping.

For example, brokerage firm XYZ purchases a newly issued 20-year government bond and deposits the bond with a custodian bank. Assuming semi-annual interest payments, XYZ creates 41 separate zero-coupon bonds (40 interest payments plus one principal repayment). Naturally, XYZ can create larger zero-coupon bonds by buying and depositing more securities of the same issue. These zero-coupon bonds, in turn, are sold to investors (for a fee, of course). As the government makes its required payments on the bond, the custodian bank remits the payments to the zero-coupon bondholders of the appropriate maturity and effectively retires that particular bond. The process continues until all interest and principal payments have been made and all of the zero-coupon bonds associated with this bond have been extinguished.

US brokerage firms have issued zero-coupon bonds based on Treasury securities under a number of exotic names, such as LIONs (Lehman Investment Opportunity Notes), TIGRs (Merrill Lynch's Treasury Investment Growth Receipts), and CATs (Salomon Brothers' Certificates of Accrual on Treasury Securities). Not surprisingly, these securities have become known in the trade as "animals."

Brokerage firms and investors benefit from coupon stripping. The brokerage firms found that the sum of the parts was worth more than the whole, as the zero-coupon bonds could be sold to investors at a higher combined price than could the source government security. Investors benefited from the creation of a liquid market in riskless securities.

In 1985, the US Treasury introduced a program called STRIPS (Separate Trading of Registered Interest and Principal Securities). This program allows purchasers of certain interest-bearing Treasury securities to keep whatever cash payments they want and to sell the rest. The stripped bonds are "held" in the Federal Reserve System's computer (called the *book entry system*), and payments on the bonds are made electronically. Any financial institution that is registered on the Federal Reserve System's computer may participate in the STRIPS program. Brokerage firms soon found that it was much less expensive to create zero-coupon bonds through STRIPS than to use bank custody accounts. They subsequently switched virtually all of their activity to that program.

The introduction of stripped bonds still did not solve the inflation risk problem faced by investors seeking a truly risk-free security. Finally, in 1991 the Government of Canada offered the first Canadian securities whose principal and interest payments were indexed to inflation, Real Return Bonds. The US followed with inflation-indexed bonds in 1997, joining Australia, Israel, New Zealand, Sweden, and the United Kingdom in issuing debt that is indexed to the rate of inflation.

To date, the Government of Canada has issued only two maturities, December 2021 and December 2026. The principal amounts of these "indexed" bonds are adjusted based on the cumulative change in the Consumer Price Index (CPI) since issuance of the bonds. A 4.25% fixed rate of interest, determined at the time of the bonds' issuance, is paid on the adjusted principal, thereby producing inflation-adjusted interest payments as well. Coupon stripping is allowed so that investors can purchase zero-coupon inflation-protected bonds—apparently the real McCoy of risk-free securities.

Only a nitpicker would note some flaws in this arrangement. First, the bonds' issuer (the Canadian government) controls the definition and calculation of the CPI. In light of concerns over whether the CPI accurately measures inflation, there is some risk that the government might change the index in ways detrimental to real return bondholders (although the government could adjust the bond terms to compensate for such an adverse change). Further, for taxable investors, the adjustments to the bonds' principal values immediately become taxable income, reducing the inflation protection provided by the bonds. Despite these complications, it appears that the government has finally introduced a security that can truly claim the title of (almost) "risk-free."

It is important to distinguish this rate from the rate for one-year loans that will prevail for deals made a year from now (the spot rate at that time). A forward rate applies to contracts made now but relating to a period "forward" in time. By the nature of the contract, the terms are certain now, even though the actual transaction will occur later. If instead one were to wait until next year and sign a contract to borrow money in the spot market at that time, the terms might turn out to be better or worse than today's forward rate, since the future spot rate is not perfectly predictable.

In the example, the marketplace has priced these securities such that a representative investor making a two-year loan to the government would demand an interest rate equal to the two-year spot rate, 8%. Equivalently, the investor would be willing simultaneously to (1) make a one-year loan to the government at an interest rate equal to the one-year spot rate, 7%, and (2) sign a forward contract with the government to loan the government

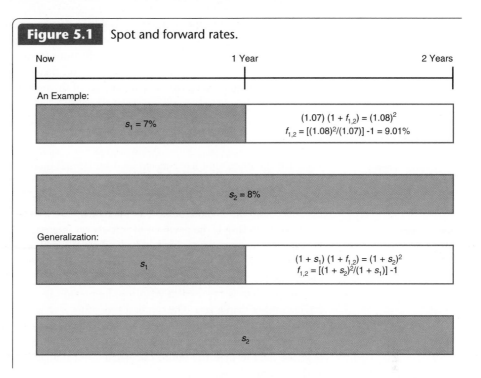

Figure 5.1 Spot and forward rates.

Now   1 Year   2 Years

An Example:

$s_1 = 7\%$

$(1.07)(1 + f_{1,2}) = (1.08)^2$
$f_{1,2} = [(1.08)^2/(1.07)] - 1 = 9.01\%$

$s_2 = 8\%$

Generalization:

s_1

$(1 + s_1)(1 + f_{1,2}) = (1 + s_2)^2$
$f_{1,2} = [(1 + s_2)^2/(1 + s_1)] - 1$

s_2

money one year from now, being repaid two years from now, where the interest rate to be paid is the forward rate, 9.01%.

When viewed in this manner, forward contracts are implicit. However, forward contracts are sometimes made explicitly. For example, a contractor might obtain a commitment from a bank for a one-year construction loan a year hence at a fixed rate of interest. Financial futures markets (discussed in Chapter 20) provide standardized forward contracts of this type. For example, in April one could contract to pay $984.70 in September to purchase a 91-day Treasury bill that would pay $1000 in December.

Forward Rates and Discount Factors

In equation (5.9) it was shown that a discount factor for t years could be calculated by adding 1 to the spot rate for t years, raising this sum to the power t, and then taking the reciprocal of the result. For example, it was shown that the two-year discount factor associated with the two-year spot rate of 8% was equal to $1/(1 + .08)^2 = .8573$.

Equation (5.14) suggests an equivalent method for calculating discount factors. In the case of the two-year factor, this method involves multiplying the one-year spot rate by the forward rate and taking the reciprocal of the result:

$$d_2 = \frac{1}{(1 + s_1) \times (1 + f_{1,2})} \tag{5.17}$$

which in the example is

$$d_2 = \frac{1}{(1 + .07) \times (1 + .0901)} = .8573$$

More generally, the discount factor for year t that is shown in equation (5.9) can be restated as follows:

$$d_t = \frac{1}{(1 + s_{t-1})^{t-1} \times (1 + f_{t-1,t})} \tag{5.18}$$

Thus, given a set of spot rates, it is possible to determine the market discount function in either of two ways, both of which will provide the same figures. First, the spot rates can be used in equation (5.9) to arrive at a set of discount factors. Alternatively, the spot rates can be used to determine a set of forward rates and then the spot rates and forward rates can be used in equation (5.18) to arrive at a set of discount factors.

Compounding

Compounding The payment of interest on interest.

Thus far, the discussion has concentrated on annual interest rates by assuming that cash flows are compounded (or discounted) annually. This is often appropriate, but for more precise calculations a shorter period may be more desirable. Moreover, some lenders explicitly compound funds more often than once each year.

Compounding is the payment of interest on interest. At the end of each compounding interval, interest is computed and added to principal. This sum becomes the principal on which interest is computed at the end of the next interval. The process continues until the end of the final compounding interval is reached.

No problem is involved in adapting the previously stated formulas to compounding intervals other than a year. The simplest procedure is to count in units of the chosen interval. For example, yield-to-maturity can be calculated using any chosen compounding interval. If payment of P dollars now will result in the receipt of F dollars 10 years from now, the yield-to-maturity can be calculated using annual compounding by finding a value r_a that satisfies the equation

$$P(1 + r_a)^{10} = F \tag{5.19}$$

since F will be received 10 annual periods from now. The result, r_a, is expressed as an annual rate with annual compounding.

Alternatively, yield-to-maturity can be calculated using semiannual compounding by finding a value r_s that satisfies the equation

$$P(1 + r_s)^{20} = F \tag{5.20}$$

since F will be received 20 semiannual periods from now. The result, r_s, is expressed as a semiannual rate with semiannual compounding. It can be doubled to give an annual rate with semiannual compounding; alternatively, the annual rate with annual compounding can be computed for a given value of r_s by using the following equation:

$$1 + r_a = (1 + r_s)^2 \tag{5.21}$$

For example, consider an investment costing $2315.97 that will pay $5000 10 years later. Applying equations (5.19) and (5.20) to this security results in

$$\$2315.97(1 + r_a)^{10} = \$5000$$

and

$$\$2315.97(1 + r_s)^{20} = \$5000$$

respectively, where the solutions are $r_a = 8\%$ and $r_s = 3.923\%$. Thus, this security can be described as having an annual rate with annual compounding of 8%, a semiannual rate with semiannual compounding of 3.923%, and an annual rate with semiannual compounding of $2 \times 3.923\% = 7.846\%$.[2]

To reduce the confusion caused by the many different methods that can be used to express interest rates, the US federal truth-in-lending law requires every lender to compute

---

[2]Note how, using equation (5.21), $r_a = (1.03923)^2 - 1 = 8\%$, a solution that is the same as the one provided by equation (5.19).

Annual Percentage Rate (APR) With respect to a loan, the APR is the yield-to-maturity of the loan computed using the most frequent time between payments as the compounding interval.

and disclose the **annual percentage rate (APR)** implied by the terms of a loan. This is simply the yield-to-maturity, computed using the most frequent time between payments on the loan as the compounding interval. Although some complications arise when payments are required at irregular intervals, the use of APRs clearly simplifies the task of comparing lenders' terms. Canadian consumers could benefit from some standardization of reported interest rates.

Semiannual compounding is commonly used to determine the yield-to-maturity for bonds, since coupon payments are usually made twice a year. Most preprogrammed calculators and computers use this approach.

The Bank Discount Method

Bank Discount Method A method of calculating the interest rate on a fixed-income security that uses the principal of the security as the security's cost.

Despite the US truth-in-lending law, other methods are still used to determine interest rates. One time-honoured procedure for reporting interest rates is the **bank discount method.** If someone "borrows" $100 from a bank, to be repaid a year later, the bank will discount the interest of, for instance, 8% and give the borrower $92. According to the bank discount method, this is an interest rate of 8%. The borrower only receives $92, for which she must pay $8 in interest after one year. The "true" interest rate (APR) must be based on the money the borrower actually gets to use. In this case, the rate is 8.70%, since $8/$92 = .0870.

It is a simple matter to convert an interest rate quoted on the bank discount method to a true interest rate. If the bank discount rate is BDR, then the true rate is simply $BDR/(1 - BDR)$. Substituting the figures from the previous example into this expression gives $.08/(1 - .08) = 8.70\%$, thereby demonstrating that the bank discount rate of 8% understates the true cost of borrowing by .7% in this example.

Yield Curves

At any time, fixed income securities will be priced approximately in accord with the existing set of spot rates and their associated discount factors. Although there have been times when all the spot rates were roughly equal in size, generally they have different values. Often the one-year spot rate is less than the two-year spot rate, which in turn is less than the three-year spot rate, and so on (that is, s_t increases as t increases). At other times, the one-year spot rate is greater than the two-year spot rate, which in turn is greater than the three-year spot rate, and so on (that is, s_t decreases as t increases). It is wise for the security analyst to know which case currently prevails, as this is a useful starting point in valuing fixed-income securities.

Unfortunately, this is easier said than done. Only government bonds are clearly free from default risk. However, the features of such bonds may differ from issue to issue. Despite these problems, a summary of the approximate relationship between yields-to-maturity on Government of Canada securities of various terms-to-maturity is presented in the form of a graph illustrating the current yield curve.

Yield Curve A visual representation of the term structure of interest rates.

Term Structure The set of yields-to-maturity across bonds that possess different terms-to-maturity, but are similar with respect to other attributes.

A yield curve is a graph that shows the yields-to-maturity (on the vertical axis) for government securities of various maturities (on the horizontal axis) as of a particular date. Figure 5.2 provides an example that shows the relationship that existed on August 31, 1998. The curve estimates the current **term structure** of interest rates, and it changes daily as prices (and, hence, yields-to-maturity) change. Current yield curves can be obtained from investment dealers and investment counsellors (for a fee). Many institutional

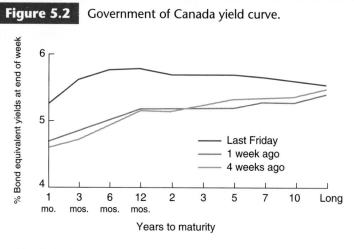

Figure 5.2 Government of Canada yield curve.

% Bond equivalent yields at end of week

Years to maturity

Last Friday
1 week ago
4 weeks ago

SOURCE: Royal Bank of Canada. Published in *The Globe and Mail: Report on Business,* August 31, 1998.

investors produce their own on a regular basis. Figure 5.3 shows some of the commonly observed shapes for the yield curve that have been recorded in the past.[3]

Generally, the relationship between yields and maturities is less than perfect. That is, not all the securities lie exactly on the yield curve. This is largely due to the fact that the yield-to-maturity on a coupon-bearing security is not clearly linked to the set of spot rates currently in existence. Since the set of spot rates is a fundamental determinant of the price of any government security, there is no reason to expect yields to lie exactly on the curve. Indeed, a more meaningful graph would be one where spot rates are measured on the vertical axis instead of yields-to-maturity. With this in mind, two interesting questions to ponder are: why are the spot rates of different magnitudes? And why do the differences in these rates change over time, where sometimes long-term spot rates are greater than short-term spot rates and sometimes the opposite occurs? Attempts to answer such questions can be found in various term structure theories.

Term Structure Theories

Four theories have been generally used to explain the term structure of interest rates. The focus of the discussion is on the term structure of spot rates, since it is these rates and not yields-to-maturity that are critically important in determining the price of any government security.

● The Unbiased Expectations Theory

Unbiased Expectations Theory An explanation of the term structure of interest rates. It holds that a forward rate represents the average opinion of the expected future spot rate for the time period in question.

The **unbiased expectations theory** (also known as the pure expectations theory) holds that the forward rate represents the average opinion of the expected future spot rate for the period in question. Thus, a set of spot rates that is rising can be explained by arguing that the marketplace (that is, the general opinion of investors) believes that spot rates will rise

---

[3]Occasionally, the yield curve will be "humped," where it rises for a short while and then declines, perhaps leveling off for intermediate to long-term maturities. For more on yield curves and term structure, see Carol Lancaster and Jerry L. Stevens, "Debt Term Structures: Beyond Yield to Maturity Assumptions." *Financial Practice and Education* 5, no 2 (Fall–Winter 1995) 125–137.

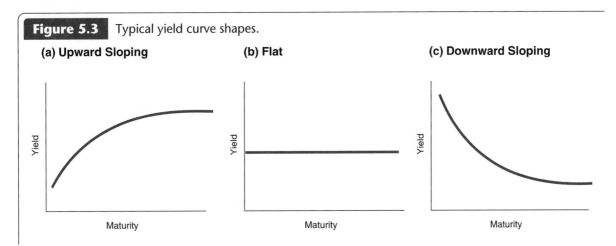

Figure 5.3 Typical yield curve shapes.

(a) Upward Sloping

Yield

Maturity

(b) Flat

Yield

Maturity

(c) Downward Sloping

Yield

Maturity

in the future. Conversely, a set of decreasing spot rates is explained by arguing that the marketplace expects spot rates to fall in the future.[4]

Upward Sloping Yield Curves

In order to understand this theory more fully, consider the earlier example where the one-year spot rate was 7% and the two-year spot rate was 8%. The basic question is, why are these two spot rates different? Equivalently, why is the term structure upward sloping?

Consider an investor with $1 to invest for two years (for ease of exposition, it will be assumed that any amount of money can be invested at the prevailing spot rates). This investor could follow a *maturity strategy*, investing the money now for the full two years at the two-year spot rate of 8%. With this strategy, at the end of two years the dollar will have grown in value to $1(1.08)(1.08) = $1.1664. Alternatively, the investor could invest the dollar now for one year at the one-year spot rate of 7%, so that the investor knows that one year from now he will have $1(1.07) = $1.07 to reinvest for one more year.

Although the investor does not know what the one-year spot rate will be one year from now, he has an *expectation* about what it will be (this expected future spot rate will hereafter be denoted by $es_{1,2}$). If the investor thinks it will be 10%, then his $1 has an expected value two years from now of $1(1.07)(1.10) = $1.177. In this case, the investor would choose a *rollover strategy*, meaning the investor would choose to invest in a one-year security at 7% rather than in the two-year security, since he would expect to have more money at the end of two years by doing so (note that $1.177 > $1.1664).

However, an expected future spot rate of 10% cannot represent the general view in the marketplace. If it did, people would not be willing to invest money at the two-year spot rate, since a higher return would be expected from investing money at the one-year rate and using the rollover strategy. Thus, the two-year spot rate would quickly rise, since the supply of funds for two-year loans at 8% would be less than the demand. Conversely, the supply of funds for one year at 7% would be more than the demand, causing the one-year rate to fall quickly. Thus, a one-year spot rate of 7%, a two-year spot rate of 8%, and an expected future spot rate of 10% cannot represent an equilibrium situation.

---

[4]Recently a "modern" expectations theory has been developed that is economically more logical than the "unbiased" expectations theory. However, it provides approximately the same empirical implications and explanations of the term structure as those given by the unbiased expectations theory. Thus, given the similarities between the two theories, only the unbiased expectations theory is presented here.

What if the expected future spot rate is 6% instead of 10%? In this case, according to the rollover strategy, the investor would expect \$1 to be worth \$1(1.07)(1.06) = \$1.1342 at the end of two years. Since this is less than the value the dollar will have if the maturity strategy is followed (\$1.1342 < \$1.1664), the investor would choose the maturity strategy. Again, however, an expected future spot rate of 6% cannot represent the general view in the marketplace because if it did, people would not be willing to invest money at the one-year spot rate.

Earlier, it was shown that the forward rate in this example was 9.01%. What if the expected future spot rate was of this magnitude? At the end of two years the value of \$1 with the rollover strategy would be \$1(1.07)(1.0901) = \$1.1664, the same as the value of \$1 with the maturity strategy. In this case, equilibrium would exist in the marketplace because the general view would be that both strategies have the same expected return. Accordingly, investors with a two-year holding period would not have an incentive to choose one strategy over the other.

Note that an investor with a one-year holding period could follow a maturity strategy by investing \$1 in the one-year security and receiving \$1.07 after one year. Alternatively, a *naive strategy* could be followed, where a two-year security could be purchased now and sold after one year. If so, the expected selling price would be \$1.1664/1.0901 = \$1.07, for a return of 7% [the security would have a maturity value of \$1.1664 = \$1(1.08)(1.08), but since the spot rate is expected to be 9.01% in a year, its expected selling price is just the discounted value of its maturity value]. Since the maturity and naive strategies have the same expected return, investors with a one-year holding period would not have an incentive to choose one strategy over the other.

Thus, the unbiased expectations theory asserts that the expected future spot rate is equal in magnitude to the forward rate. In the example, the current one-year spot rate is 7% and, according to this theory, the general opinion is that it will rise to a rate of 9.01% in one year. It is this expected rise in the one-year spot rate that is the reason behind the upward-sloping term structure when the two-year spot rate (8%) is greater than the one-year spot rate (7%).

Equilibrium

In equation format, the unbiased expectations theory states that the expected future spot rate is equal to the forward rate:

$$es_{1,2} = f_{1,2} \qquad (5.22)$$

Thus, equation (5.14) can be restated with $es_{1,2}$ substituted for $f_{1,2}$, as follows:

$$(1 + s_2)(1 + s_2) = (1 + s_1)(1 + es_{1,2}) \qquad (5.23)$$

which can be conveniently interpreted to mean that the expected return from a maturity strategy must equal the expected return on a rollover strategy.[5]

The previous example dealt with an upward-sloping term structure, where the longer the term, the higher the spot rate. It is a straightforward matter to deal with a downward-sloping term structure, where the longer the term, the lower the spot rate. While the explanation for an upward-sloping term structure was that investors expect spot rates to rise in the future, the reason for the downward-sloping curve is that investors expect spot rates to fall in the future.

---

[5]Equation (5.22) can be expressed more generally as $es_{t-1,t} = f_{t-1,t}$. Thus, using equation (5.16), the unbiased expectations theory states that, in general, $(1 + s_t)^t = (1 + s_{t-1})^{t-1} \times (1 + es_{t-1,t})$.

Changing Spot Rates and Inflation

An interesting follow-up question is, why do investors expect spot rates to change, either by rising or falling, in the future? A possible answer to this question can be found by noting that the spot rates that are observed in the marketplace are nominal rates. That is, they are a reflection of the underlying real rate and the expected inflation rate.[6] If either (or both) of these rates is expected to change in the future, then the spot rate will be expected to change.

For example, assume a constant real rate of 3%. Since the current one-year spot rate is 7%, this means that the general opinion in the marketplace is that the expected rate of inflation over the next year is approximately 4% (the nominal rate is approximately equal to the sum of the real rate and expected inflation rate). Now, according to the unbiased expectations theory, the expected future spot rate is 9.01%, an increase of 2.01% from the current one-year spot rate of 7%. The spot rate is expected to rise by 2.01% because the inflation rate is expected to rise by 2.01%. That is, the expected inflation rate over the next 12 months is approximately 4%, and over the following 12 months it is expected to be higher, at approximately 6.01%.

To recapitulate, the two-year spot rate (8%) is greater than the one-year spot rate (7%) because investors expect the future one-year spot rate to be greater than the current one-year spot rate. They expect it to be greater because of an anticipated rise in the expected rate of inflation, from approximately 4% to approximately 6.01%.

In general, when current economic conditions make short-term spot rates abnormally high (owing, say, to a relatively high current rate of inflation), according to the unbiased expectations theory, the term structure should be downward sloping. This is because inflation would be expected to abate in the future. Conversely, when current conditions make short-term rates abnormally low (owing say, to a relatively low current rate of inflation), the term structure should be upward sloping, since inflation would be expected to rise in the future. Examination of historical term structures suggests that this is what has actually happened, since the structure has been upward sloping in periods of lower interest rates and downward sloping in periods of higher interest rates.

However, examining historical term structures uncovers a problem. In particular, with this theory it is logical to expect that over time there will be roughly as many occurrences of upward sloping term structures as downward sloping term structures. In reality, upward sloping structures tend to be more frequent. The liquidity preference theory provides an explanation for this observation.

◗ The Liquidity Preference Theory

Liquidity Preference Theory An explanation of the term structure of interest rates. It holds that the term structure is a result of the preference of investors for short-term securities. Investors can only be induced to hold longer-term securities if they expect to receive a higher return.

The **liquidity preference theory** (also known as the liquidity premium theory) starts with the notion that investors are primarily interested in purchasing short-term securities. That is, even though some investors may have longer holding periods, there is a tendency for them to prefer short-term securities. This is because these investors realize that they may need their funds earlier than anticipated and recognize that they face less "price risk" (that is, interest-rate risk) if they invest in shorter-term securities.

Price Risk

For example, an investor with a two-year holding period would tend to prefer the rollover strategy, since she would be certain of having a given amount of cash at the end of one year, when it may be needed. If a maturity strategy had been followed, then the investor would have to sell the two-year security after one year if cash was needed. However, it is not

---

[6]See Chapter 12 for a discussion of the nature of the relationship between nominal rates, real rates, and expected inflation rates.

known now what price the investor would get if she were to sell the two-year security in one year. Thus, there is an extra element of risk associated with the maturity strategy that is absent from the rollover strategy.[7]

The upshot is that investors with a two-year holding period will not choose the maturity strategy if it has the same expected return as the rollover strategy, since it is riskier. The only way investors will follow the maturity strategy and buy the two-year security is if its expected return is higher. That is, borrowers are going to have to pay the investors a risk premium in the form of a greater expected return in order to get them to purchase two-year securities.

Will borrowers be inclined to pay such a premium when issuing two-year securities? Yes, they will be so inclined. First, frequent refinancing may be costly in terms of registration, advertising, paperwork, and so on. These costs can be lessened by issuing relatively long-term securities. Second, some borrowers will realize that relatively long-term bonds are a less risky source of funds than relatively short-term bonds, since they will not have to be as concerned about the possibility of refinancing in the future at higher interest rates. Thus, borrowers may be willing to pay more (via higher expected interest costs) for relatively long-term funds.

In the example, the one-year spot rate was 7% and the two-year spot rate was 8%. As mentioned earlier, according to the liquidity preference theory, the only way investors will agree to follow a maturity strategy is if the expected return from doing so is higher than the expected return from following the rollover strategy. This means that the expected future spot rate must be something *less* than the forward rate of 9.01%—perhaps it is 8.6%. If so, then the value of a $1 investment in two years is expected to be $1(1.07)(1.086) = 1.1620, if the rollover strategy is followed. Since the value of a $1 investment with the maturity strategy is $1(1.08)(1.08) = 1.1664, it can be seen that the rollover strategy has a lower expected return for the two-year period, which can be attributed to its smaller degree of price risk.[8]

Liquidity Premium

The difference between the forward rate and the expected future spot rate is known as the **liquidity premium**.[8] It is the extra return given investors in order to entice them to purchase the more risky two-year security. In the example, it is equal to $9.01\% - 8.6\% = .41\%$. More generally,

$$f_{1,2} = es_{1,2} + L_{1,2} \tag{5.24}$$

where $L_{1,2}$ is the liquidity premium for the period commencing one year from now and ending two years from now.[9]

How does the liquidity preference theory explain the slope of the term structure? In order to answer this question, note that with the rollover strategy, the expected value of a dollar at the end of two years is $\$1(1 + s_1)(1 + es_{1,2})$. Alternatively, with the maturity strategy the expected value of a dollar at the end of two years is $\$1(1 + s_2)(1 + s_2)$. As mentioned earlier, according to the liquidity preference theory there is more risk with the

Liquidity Premium The expected incremental return of longer-term securities over shorter-term securities that compensates investors for the greater interest rate risk entailed in holding longer-term securities.

---

[7]Unfortunately, this risk is often referred to as *liquidity risk*, when it more appropriately should be called *price risk*, since it is the price volatility associated with longer-term securities that is of concern to investors. Partially offsetting this price risk is a risk that is present in the rollover strategy and absent from the maturity strategy—namely, the risk associated with having an uncertain reinvestment rate at the end of the first year when the rollover strategy is chosen. The liquidity preference theory assumes that this risk is of relatively little concern to investors.

[8]Sometimes the difference is referred to as the *term premium*. See Bradford Cornell, "Measuring the Term Premium: An Empirical Note," *Journal of Economics and Business* 42, no. 1 (February 1990): 89–92.

[9]It should be noted that while the forward rate can be determined, neither the expected future spot rate nor the liquidity premium can be observed. All that can be done is to estimate their respective values.

maturity strategy, which in turn means that it must have a higher expected return. That is, the following inequality must hold:

$$\$1(1 + s_2)(1 + s_2) > \$1(1 + s_1)(1 + es_{1,2}) \tag{5.25}$$

or

$$(1 + s_2)(1 + s_2) > (1 + s_1)(1 + es_{1,2}) \tag{5.26}$$

This inequality is the key to understanding how the liquidity preference theory explains the term structure.[10]

Downward-sloping Yield Curves

Consider the downward-sloping case first, where $s_1 > s_2$. The preceding inequality will hold in this situation only if the expected future spot rate $(es_{1,2})$ is substantially smaller than the current one-year spot rate (s_1).[11] Thus, a downward sloping term structure will be observed only when the marketplace believes that interest rates are going to decline substantially.

As an example, assume that the one-year spot rate (s_1) is 7% and the two-year spot rate (s_2) is 6%. Since 7% is greater than 6%, this is a situation where the term structure is downward sloping. Now, according to the previously given inequality,

$$(1 + .06)(1 + .06) > (1 + .07)(1 + es_{1,2})$$

which can hold only if the expected future spot rate $(es_{1,2})$ is substantially less than 7%. Given the one-year and two-year spot rates, the forward rate $(f_{1,2})$ is equal to 5.01%. Assuming the liquidity premium $(L_{1,2})$ is .41%, then according to equation (5.24), $es_{1,2}$ must be 5.01% − .41% = 4.6%. Thus, the term structure is downward sloping because the current one-year spot rate of 7% is expected to decline to 4.6% in the future.

In comparison, the unbiased expectations theory would also explain the term structure by saying that the reason it was downward sloping was because the one-year spot rate was expected to decline in the future. However, the unbiased expectations theory would expect the spot rate to decline only to 5.01%, not 4.6%.

Flat Yield Curves

Consider next the case of a flat term structure, where $s_1 = s_2$. The preceding inequality will hold in this situation only if $es_{1,2}$ is less than s_1. Thus, a flat term structure will occur only when the marketplace expects interest rates are going to decline. Indeed, if $s_1 = s_2 = 7\%$ and $L_{1,2} = .41\%$, then $f_{1,2} = 7\%$ and, according to equation (5.24), the expected future spot rate is 7% − .41% = 6.59%, a decline from the current one-year spot rate of 7%. This is in contrast to the unbiased expectations theory, where a flat term structure would be interpreted to mean that the marketplace expected interest rates to remain at the same level.

---

[10]Equation (5.24) can be expressed more generally as $f_{t-1,t} = es_{t-1,t} + L_{t-1,t}$. Thus, using equation (5.14), the liquidity preference theory states that

$$(1 + s_t)^t = (1 + s_{t-1})^{t-1} \times (1 + es_{t-1,t} + L_{t-1,t})$$

Since $L_{t-1,t} > 0$, it follows that, in general,

$$(1 + s_t)^t > (1 + s_{t-1})^{t-1} \times (1 + es_{t-1,t})$$

[11]If $es_{1,2}$ were equal to or greater than s_1, then the inequality would not hold in the correct direction, since it was assumed that $s_1 > s_2$.

Upward-sloping Yield Curves

The last case of an upward-sloping yield curve is one where $s_1 < s_2$. If it is slightly upward sloping, this can be consistent with an expectation that interest rates are going to decline in the future. For example, if $s_1 = 7\%$ and $s_2 = 7.1\%$, then the forward rate is 7.2%. In turn, if the liquidity premium is .41%, then the expected future spot rate is 6.79% = 7.2% − .41%, a decline from the current one-year spot rate of 7%. Thus, the reason for the slight upward slope to the term structure is that the marketplace expects only a slight decline in the spot rate. In contrast, the unbiased expectations theory would argue that the reason for the slight upward slope was the expectation of a slight increase in the spot rate.

If the term structure is more steeply sloped, then it is more likely that the marketplace expects interest rates to rise in the future. For example, if $s_1 = 7\%$ and $s_2 = 7.3\%$, then the forward rate is 7.6%. Continuing to assume a liquidity premium of .41%, equation (5.24) indicates that the marketplace expects the one-year spot rate to rise from 7% to 7.6% − .41% = 7.19%. The unbiased expectations theory would also explain this steep slope by saying that the spot rate was expected to rise in the future, but by a larger amount. In particular, the unbiased expectations theory would state that the spot rate was expected to rise to 7.6%, not 7.19%.

In summary, with the liquidity preference theory, downward-sloping term structures are indicative of an expected decline in the spot rate, whereas upward-sloping term structures may indicate either an expected rise or an expected decline, depending on how steep the slope is. Generally, the steeper the slope, the more likely it is that the marketplace expects spot rates to rise. If roughly half the time investors expect spot rates will rise and half the time investors expect spot rates will decline, then the liquidity preference theory suggests that there should be more occurrences of upward-sloping term structures than downward-sloping ones. As mentioned earlier, this is indeed what has happened.

The Market Segmentation Theory

Market Segmentation Theory An explanation of the term structure of interest rates. It holds that various investors and borrowers are restricted by law, preference, or custom to certain maturity ranges. Spot rates in each market segment are determined by supply and demand conditions there.

Preferred Habitat Theory An explanation of the term structure of interest rates. Similar to the market segmentation theory, it holds that various investors and borrowers have segments of the market in which they prefer to operate. However, these investors are assumed to be willing to leave their desired maturity segments if there are significant differences in yields between the various segments.

A third explanation for the determination of the term structure rests on the assumption that there is market segmentation: various investors and borrowers are asserted to be restricted by law, preference, or custom to certain maturities. Perhaps there is a market for short-term securities, another for intermediate-term securities, and a third for long-term securities. According to the **market segmentation theory,** spot rates are determined by supply and demand conditions in each market. Furthermore, in its most restrictive form, this theory suggests that investors and borrowers will not leave their market and enter a different one even when the current rates indicate that there is a substantially higher expected return available by making such a move.

With this theory, an upward-sloping term structure exists when the intersection of the supply and demand curves for shorter-term funds is at a lower interest rate than the intersection for longer-term funds. Conversely, a downward-sloping term structure would exist when the intersection for shorter-term funds was at a higher interest rate than the intersection for longer-term funds.

The Preferred Habitat Theory

A more moderate and realistic version of the market segmentation theory is the **preferred habitat theory.** According to this theory, investors and borrowers have segments of the market in which they prefer to operate, similar to the market segmentation theory. However, they are willing to leave their desired maturity segments if there are significant differences in yields between the various segments. These yield differences are determined by the supply and demand for funds within the segments.

As a result, like the liquidity preference theory, the term structure under the preferred habitat theory reflects both expectations of future spot rates and a risk premium. Unlike the liquidity preference theory, though, the risk premium according to the preferred habitat theory does not necessarily rise directly with maturity. Instead, it is a function of the extra yield required to induce borrowers and investors to shift out of their preferred habitats. The risk premium may, therefore, be positive or negative in the various segments.

Empirical Evidence for the Theories

Empirical evidence based on US data provides some insight into the determinants of the term structure, but it is difficult to assess the relative importance of these four theories with a high degree of precision.

The market segmentation theory receives relatively slight empirical validation. This is understandable, given that the theory will not hold if there are some investors and borrowers who are flexible enough to be willing to move into whatever segment has the highest expected return. By their actions, these investors and borrowers will give the term structure a continuity that is linked to expectations of future interest rates.

There does appear to be some evidence that the term structure conveys information about expected future spot rates, as hypothesized by the unbiased expectations, preferred habitat, and liquidity preference theories. However, the evidence tends to favour the latter theory, since liquidity premiums also appear to exist.[12] In particular, there appear to be liquidity premiums of increasing size associated with US Treasury securities of up to roughly one year in maturity. However, there do not appear to be any additional premiums beyond one-year maturities. That is, investors seem to demand a premium in order to get them to purchase a one-year security instead of, say, a one-month security. However, no additional premiums are needed in order to get them to purchase two-year securities (even though the two-year security has more price risk than a one-year security).

Two tests of term structure theories show that Canadian data are consistent with the unbiased expectations plus liquidity preference theories in the intermediate maturity range, but the possibility that some market segmentation exists in the long end of the market cannot be rejected.[13]

In summary, it appears that expectations about future spot rates are important determinants of the term structure. Liquidity premiums appear to exist, but do not increase in size beyond roughly a year, meaning that investment strategies involving securities with maturities of one year or more will have roughly the same expected return.

Examining the term structure of interest rates is important for determining the current set of spot rates, which can be used as a basis for valuing any fixed-income security. Such an examination is also important because it provides some information about what the marketplace expects regarding the level of future interest rates.

---

[12]The empirical evidence is not without dispute. Fama has argued that the evidence is inconsistent with both the unbiased expectations and liquidity preference theories, but McCulloch refutes Fama's findings and argues in favour of the latter theory. See Eugene F. Fama, "Term Premiums in Bond Returns," *Journal of Financial Economics* 13, no. 4 (December 1984): 529–546 and J. Huston McCulloch, "The Monotonicity of the Term Premium: A Closer Look," *Journal of Financial Economics* 18, no. 1 (March 1987): 185–192 and "An Estimate of the Liquidity Premium," *Journal of Political Economy* 83, no. 1 (February 1975): 95–119. McCulloch's findings are supported by Matthew Richardson, Paul Richardson, and Tom Smith in "The Monotonicity of the Term Premium: Another Look," *Journal of Financial Economics* 31, no. 1 (February 1992): 97–105.

[13]J. S. McCallum, "The Expected Holding Period Return, Uncertainty and the Term Structure of Interest Rates," *Journal of Finance* 30, no. 2 (May 1975): 307–323, and Maureen E. Howe and John S. McCallum, "The Term Structure of Interest Rates in Canada: The Empirical Evidence," *Journal of Business Administration* 12, no. 1 (Fall 1980): 137–146.

Expected Holding-Period Return

Calculating Holding-period Return

Yield-to-maturity calculations do not take into account any changes in the market value of a security prior to maturity. This might be interpreted as implying that the owner has no interest in selling the instrument prior to maturity, no matter what happens to its price or her situation. The calculation also fails to treat intermediate payments in a fully satisfactory way. If the owner does not wish to spend interest payments, she might choose to buy more of these securities. But the number that can be bought at any time depends on the price at that time, and yield-to-maturity calculations fail to take this into account.

While few dispute the value of yield-to-maturity as at least an indicator of a bond's overall return, it should be recognized as no more than this. For some purposes other measures may prove more useful. Moreover, for other types of securities there is no maturity. Common shares provide the most important example.

Holding-period Return
The rate of return on an investment over a given holding period.

A measure that can be used for any investment is **holding-period return**. The idea is to specify a holding period of major interest, and then assume that any payments received during the period are reinvested. Although assumptions may differ from case to case, the usual procedure assumes that any payment received from a security (for example, a dividend from a share, a coupon payment from a bond) is used to purchase more units of that security at the then current market price. Using this procedure, the performance of a security can be measured by comparing the value obtained in this manner at the end of the holding period with the value at the beginning. This **value-relative** can be converted to a holding-period return by subtracting 1 from it:[14]

Value-relative The holding-period return for a security, plus one.

$$r_{hp} = \frac{\text{value at the end of the holding period}}{\text{value at the beginning of the holding period}} - 1$$

Holding-period return can be converted to an equivalent return per period. Allowing for the effect of compounding, the appropriate procedure would be to find the value that satisfies the relationship

$$(1 + r_g)^N = 1 + r_{hp}$$

or

$$r_g = \left(N\sqrt{1 + r_{hp}} \right) - 1$$

where:

N = the number of periods in the holding period

r_{hp} = the holding-period return

r_g = the equivalent return per period, compounded every period

Suppose that a stock sold for $46 per share at the beginning of one year, paid dividends of $1.50 during that year, sold for $50 at the end of the year, paid dividends of $2 during the next year, and sold for $56 at the end of that year. What was the return over the two-year holding period?

To simplify the calculations, assume that all dividend payments are received at year-end. Then the $1.50 received during the first year could have bought $1.50/$50, or .03, shares of the stock at the end of the first year. In practice, of course, this would be feasible only if the money were pooled with other funds similarly invested[15]—for example, in a

Price-relative The price of a security in one period divided by the price of that same security in a previous period.

---

[14]The term **price-relative** refers to the ratio of a security's price on a given day to its price on some previous day. Hence, it is the same as the value-relative if there are no cash flows associated with the security between the two days.

[15]It is possible to buy fractions of a company's shares through a *Dividend Reinvestment Plan*.

mutual fund (for example, the dividends from 100 shares could have been used to buy three additional shares). In any event, for each share originally held, the investor would have obtained $1.03 \times \$2$, or \$2.06, in dividends in the second year, and have had shares with a value of $1.03 \times \$56$, or \$57.68, at the end of the second year. The ending value would thus have been $\$57.68 + \$2.06$, giving a value-relative of

$$\frac{\$59.74}{\$46.00} = 1.2987$$

The holding-period return was thus 29.87% per two years. This is equivalent to $\sqrt{1.2987} - 1 = .1396$, or 13.96% per year.

An alternative method of computation treats the overall value-relative as the product of value-relatives for the individual periods. For example, if V_0 is the value at the beginning, V_1 the value at the end of the first year, and V_2 the value at the end of the second year:

$$\frac{V_2}{V_0} = \frac{V_2}{V_1} \times \frac{V_1}{V_0}$$

Moreover, there is no need to carry the expansion in number of shares from period to period, since the factor (1.03 in the example) will simply cancel out in the subsequent periods' value-relatives. Each period can be analyzed in isolation, an appropriate value-relative calculated, and the set of such value-relatives multiplied together.

In our example, during the first year, ownership of shares with an initial value of \$46 led to shares and cash with a value of $\$50 + \$1.50$ at the end of the year. Thus,

$$\frac{V_1}{V_0} = \frac{\$51.50}{\$46.00} = 1.1196$$

During the second year, ownership of shares with an initial value of \$50 led to shares and cash with a value of $\$56 + \$2$ at year-end. Thus,

$$\frac{V_2}{V_1} = \frac{\$58}{\$50} = 1.16$$

The two-year holding-period value-relative was therefore

$$1.1196 \times 1.16 = 1.2987$$

which is exactly equal to the value obtained earlier.

The value-relative for each period can be viewed as 1 plus the return for that period. Thus the return on the stock being analyzed was 11.96% in the first year and 16% in the second. The holding-period value-relative is the product of 1 plus each return. If N periods are involved,

$$\frac{V_N}{V_0} = (1 + r_1)(1 + r_2) \cdots (1 + r_N)$$

To convert the result to a holding-period return stated as an amount per period, with compounding, one can take the *geometric mean* of the periodic returns:

$$1 + r_g = \sqrt[N]{(1 + r_1)(1 + r_2) \cdots (1 + r_N)}$$

More sophisticated calculations may be employed within this overall framework. Each dividend payment can be used to purchase shares immediately upon receipt, or, alternatively, allowed to earn interest in a savings account until year-end. Brokerage and other costs associated with reinvestment of dividends can also be taken into account, although the magnitude of such costs will undoubtedly depend on the overall size of the holdings in question. The appropriate degree of complexity will, as always, be a function of the use for which the values are obtained.

Unhappily, the most appropriate holding period is often at least as uncertain as the return over any given holding period. Neither an investor's situation nor her preferences can usually be predicted with certainty. Moreover, from a strategic view, an investment manager would like to hold a given security only as long as it outperforms available alternatives. Attempts to identify such periods in advance are seldom completely successful, but managers quite naturally continue to try to discover them. Holding-period return, like yield-to-maturity, provides a useful device for simplifying the complex reality of investment analysis. While no panacea, it allows an analyst to focus on the most relevant horizon in a given instance and offers a good measure of performance over such a period.

Summary

1. In order to understand how bonds are valued in the marketplace, it is convenient to examine initially those fixed-income securities that are free from default risk—namely, government securities.
2. The yield-to-maturity of a security is the discount rate that makes the present value of the security's promised future cash flows equal to the current market price of the security.
3. The spot rate is the yield-to-maturity on a pure discount security.
4. Once spot rates (each one associated with a different maturity) have been calculated, they can be used, for example, to value coupon-bearing government securities.
5. A forward rate is the interest rate, established today, that will be paid on money to be borrowed at some specific time in the future, and to be repaid at an even more distant time in the future.
6. The payment of interest on interest is known as compounding.
7. Increasing the number of compounding intervals within a year will increase the effective annual interest rate.
8. A yield curve shows the relationship between yield-to-maturity and term-to-maturity for government securities. This relationship is also known as the term structure of interest rates.
9. Four theories have generally been used to explain the term structure of interest rates: the unbiased expectations theory, the liquidity preference theory, the market segmentation theory, and the preferred habitat theory.
10. The unbiased expectations theory states that forward rates represent the consensus opinion about what spot rates will be in the future.
11. The liquidity preference theory states that forward rates overstate the consensus opinion about future spot rates by an amount necessary to compensate investors for holding longer-maturity securities.
12. The market segmentation theory states that different spot rates have different values because of the interaction of supply and demand for funds in markets that are separated from each other by maturity.
13. The preferred habitat theory states that different spot rates occur because investors and borrowers at times must be induced to leave their preferred maturity segments (or habitats).
14. Evidence tends to favour the liquidity preference theory, at least over maturities up to roughly one year.
15. A security's holding-period return compares the expected value of all of the security's cash flows from the current date until a given future date (with those cash flows reinvested at an assumed interest rate), relative to the current market price of the security.

1. Consider two bonds, each with a $1000 face value and each with three years remaining to maturity.
   a. The first bond is a pure-discount bond that currently sells for $816.30. What is its yield-to-maturity?
   b. The second bond currently sells for $949.37 and makes annual coupon payments at a rate of 7% (that is, it pays $70 in interest per year). The first interest payment is due one year from today. What is this bond's yield-to-maturity?
2. Camp Douglas Dirigibles has a bond outstanding with four years to maturity, a face value of $1000, and an annual coupon payment of $100. What is the price of the Camp Douglas bond if its yield-to-maturity is 12%? If its yield-to-maturity is 8%?
3. The concept of yield-to-maturity is based on two crucial assumptions. What are those assumptions? What will happen to the bondholder's return if those assumptions are violated?
4. Patsy Dougherty bought a $1000-face-value bond with a 9% annual coupon and three years to maturity that makes its first interest payment one year from today. Patsy bought the bond for $975.13.
   a. What is the bond's yield-to-maturity?
   b. If Patsy is able to invest the bond's cash flows at only 7%, what is Patsy's actual annual compounded return on the bond investment, assuming that it is held to maturity? (Hint: Think in terms of the cash flows paid to Patsy, the bond's purchase price, and the term of the investment.)
5. Consider three pure-discount bonds with maturities of one, two, and three years and prices of $930.23, $923.79, and $919.54, respectively. Each bond has a $1000 face value. Based on this information, what are the one-year, two-year, and three-year spot rates?
6. What are the discount factors associated with three-year, four-year, and five-year $1000-face-value pure-discount bonds that sell for $810.60, $730.96, and $649.93, respectively?
7. Distinguish between spot rates and forward rates.
8. Given the following spot rates for various periods of time from today, calculate forward rates from years one to two, two to three, and three to four.

Years from Today	Spot Rate
1	5.0%
2	5.5
3	6.5
4	7.0

9. Given the following forward rates, calculate the one-, two-, three-, and four-year spot rates.

Forward Time Period	Forward Rate
$f_{0,1}$	10.0%
$f_{1,2}$	9.5
$f_{2,3}$	9.0
$f_{3,4}$	8.5

10. Assume that the current one-year spot rate is 6% and the forward rates for one year hence and two years hence are, respectively:

$$f_{1,2} = 9\%$$
$$f_{2,3} = 10\%$$

What should be the market price of an 8% coupon bond, with a $1000 face value, maturing three years from today? The first interest payment is due one year from today. Interest is payable annually.

11. Assume that the government has issued three bonds. The first, which pays $1000 one year from today, is now selling for $909.09. The second, which pays $100 one year from today and $1100 one year later, is now selling for $991.81. The third, which pays $100 one year from today, $100 one year later, and $1100 one year after that, is now selling for $997.18.
    a. What are the current discount factors for dollars paid one, two, and three years from today?
    b. What are the forward rates?
    c. Helen Wagner, a friend, offers to pay you $500 one year from today, $600 two years from today, and $700 three years from today in return for a loan today. Assuming that Helen will not default on the loan, how much should you be willing to loan?

12. La Banque Nationale offers a passbook savings account that pays interest at a stated annual rate of 6%. Calculate the effective annual interest rate paid by La Banque Nationale if it compounds interest:
    a. Semiannually
    b. Daily (365 days in a year)

13. Marty MacDonald is considering placing $30 000 in a three-year, default-free fixed-income investment that promises to provide interest at the rate of 8% during the first year, 10% in the second year, and 12% in the third year. Coupon payments can be reinvested at the rate in effect for the following year.
    a. Assuming annual compounding and repayment of principal at the end of the third year, to what value is Marty's investment expected to grow after three years?
    b. Recalculate your answer to part (a) assuming semiannual compounding.

14. A finance company offers you a loan of $8000 for two years. Interest on the loan of $1500 is subtracted from the loan proceeds immediately.
    a. What is the bank discount rate on this loan?
    b. What is the annual percentage rate (APR) on this loan?

15. Using *The Globe and Mail* as a data source, turn to the table entitled "Canada Bonds." Find the yield-to-maturity for government securities maturing in approximately one month, three months, one year, five years, ten years, and twenty years. With this information, construct the yield curve as of the paper's publication date.

16. Is it true that an observed downward-sloping yield curve is inconsistent with the liquidity preference theory of the term structure of interest rates? Explain.

17. Assume that the current structure of forward interest rates is upward sloping. Which will have a lower yield-to-maturity:
    a. A 15-year pure-discount bond or a 10-year pure-discount bond?
    b. A 10-year 5% coupon bond or a 10-year 6% pure-discount bond?

18. How would your answers to question 17 change if the forward interest rate structure were downward sloping?

19. Four theories explaining the term structure of interest rates are described in this chapter. Which theory do you believe best explains the relationship between spot rates and term-to-maturity? Provide supporting arguments for your answer.

20. Assume that the current spot rates are as follows:

Years from Today	Spot Rate
1 year	8%
2 years	9
3 years	10

If the unbiased expectations theory holds, what should be the yields-to-maturity on one- and two-year pure-discount bonds one year from today?

21. The one-year spot rate is 9% while the two-year spot rate is 7%. If the one-year spot rate expected in one year is 4.5%, according to the liquidity preference theory, what must be the one-year liquidity premium commencing one year from now?

22. If an investment returns 7% per year, how long does it take for the investment's value to double?

23. Paul Perritt purchased 100 shares of Waunakee Inc. and held the stock for four years. Paul's holding period returns over these four years were:

Year	Return
1	+20%
2	+30%
3	+50%
4	−90%

a. What was the value-relative of Paul's investment over the four-year period?

b. What was Paul's geometric mean return for the four-year period?

24. Assume that you own a bond that you purchased three years ago for $10 300. The bond has made three annual interest payments of $700 to you, the last of which was just paid. At the end of year 1 the bond sold for $10 100. At the end of year 2, it sold for $9900. The bond now sells for $9500. Assuming that you could have reinvested your interest outcome in fractional portions of the bond, what was your holding period return over the three-year period?

CFA Exam Questions

25. The following are the average yields of US Treasury bonds at two different points in time.

Term to Maturity	Yield-to-Maturity	
	January 15, 19XX	May 15, 19XX
1 year	7.25%	8.05%
2 years	7.50	7.90
3 years	7.90	7.70
10 years	8.30	7.45
15 years	8.45	7.30
20 years	8.55	7.20
25 years	8.60	7.10

a. Assuming a pure expectations hypothesis, define a forward rate. Describe how you would calculate the forward rate for a three-year US Treasury bond two years from May 15, 19XX, using the actual term structure above.

b. Discuss how each of the three major term structure hypotheses could explain the January 15, 19XX, term structure shown above.

c. Discuss what happened to the term structure over the time period and the effect of this change on the US Treasury bonds of two and ten years.

d. Assume that you invest solely on the basis of yield spreads, and in January 19XX acted upon the expectation that the yield spread between one-year and twenty five-year US Treasuries would return to a more typical spread of 170 basis points. Explain what you would have done on January 15, 19XX, and describe what happened between January 15, 19XX, and May 15, 19XX.

26. a. Calculate the two-year spot rate implied by the US Treasury yield curve data given below. Assume that interest is paid annually for purposes of this calculation. Show all calculations.

Years to Maturity	Current Coupon Yield-to-Maturity	Spot Rate
1	7.5%	7.5%
2	8.0	—

b. Explain why a spot rate curve can be derived entirely from the current coupon (yield-to-maturity) yield curve.

c. Given a US Treasury one-year spot rate of 9.0% and a US Treasury two-year spot rate of 9.5%, calculate the implied one-year forward rate for the two-year US Treasury security with one year remaining to maturity. Explain why a one-year forward rate of 9.6% would not be expected to prevail in a market given these spot rates.

d. Describe one practical application of the spot rate concept and one practical application of the forward rate concept.

KEY TERMS

yield-to-maturity (p. 103)
spot rate (p. 104)
discount factors (p. 105)
market discount function (p. 105)
discounting (p. 105)
forward rate (p. 106)
forward contract (p. 106)
compounding (p. 110)
annual percentage rate (APR) (p. 111)
bank discount method (p. 111)

yield curve (p. 111)
term structure (p. 111)
unbiased expectations theory (p. 112)
liquidity preference theory (p. 115)
liquidity premium (p. 116)
market segmentation theory (p. 118)
preferred habitat theory (p. 118)
holding-period return (p. 120)
value-relative (p. 120)
price-relative (p. 120)

REFERENCES

1. Many of the fundamental concepts having to do with bonds are discussed in:

Homer Sidney and Martin L. Leibowitz, *Inside the Yield Book: New Tools for Bond Market Strategy* (Englewood Cliffs, NJ: Prentice Hall, 1972).

Marcia Stigum, *The Money Market* (Homewood, IL: Business One Irwin, 3rd ed., 1990).

Frank J. Fabozzi, ed., *The Handbook of Fixed-Income Securities* (Howewood, IL: Irwin Professional Publishing, 5th ed., 1997).

2. A discussion of the zero-coupon government bond market is presented in:

Deborah W. Gregory and Miles Livingston, "Development of the Market for US Treasury STRIPS," *Financial Analysts Journal* 48, no. 2 (March–April 1992): 68–74.

3. A brief overview of the term structure of interest rates is contained in:

Mark Kritzman, "...About the Term Structure of Interest Rates," *Financial Analysts Journal* 19, no. 4 (July–August 1993): 14–18.

4. For a thorough review of term structure theories and the associated empirical evidence, see:

John H. Wood and Norma L. Wood, *Financial Markets* (San Diego, CA: Harcourt Brace Jovanovich, 1985), Chapter 19.

Peter A. Abken, "Innovations in Modeling the Term Structure of Interest Rates," Federal Reserve Bank of Atlanta, *Economic Review* 75, no. 4 (July–August 1990): 2–27.

Steven Russell, "Understanding the Term Structure of Interest Rates: The Expectations Theory," Federal Reserve Bank of St. Louis, *Review* 74, no. 4 (July–August 1992): 36–50.

Frederic S. Mishkin, *Financial Markets, Institutions, and Money* (New York: HarperCollins, 1995), Chapter 6.

Frank J. Fabozzi, Franco Modigliani, and Michael G. Ferri, *Foundation of Financial Markets and Institutions* (Upper Saddle River, NJ: Prentice Hall, 1998), Chapter 12.

James C. Van Horne, *Financial Market Rates and Flows* (Upper Saddle River, NJ: Prentice Hall, 1998), Chapter 6.

5. For an intriguing tax-based explanation of why the yield curve has usually been upward sloping see:

Richard Roll, "After-Tax Investment Results from Long-Term vs. Short-Term Discount Coupon Bonds," *Financial Analysts Journal* 40, no. 1 (January–February 1984): 43–54.

Ricardo J. Rodriguez, "Investment Horizon, Taxes and Maturity Choice for Discount Coupon Bonds," *Financial Analysts Journal* 44, no. 5 (September–October 1988): 67–69.

6. For a discussion of problems in the measurement of the yield curve, see

J. Huston McCulloch, "Measuring the Term Structure of Interest Rates," *Journal of Business* 44, no. 1 (January 1971): 19–31.

———, "The Tax Adjusted Yield Curve," *Journal of Finance* 30, no. 3 (June 1975): 811–830.

7. For a Canadian perspective on the topics covered in this chapter, see:

Steven Dobson, "The Term Structure of Interest Rates and the Maturity Composition of the Government Debt: The Canadian Case," *Canadian Journal of Economics* (August 1973).

Clarence L. Barber and John S. McCallum, "The Term Structure of Interest Rates and the Maturity Composition of the Government Debt," *Canadian Journal of Economics* (November 1975).

James E. Pesando, "The Impact of the Conversion Loan on the Term Structure of Interest Rates in Canada: Some Additional Evidence," *Canadian Journal of Economics* (May 1975).

Soo-Bin Park, "Spot and Forward Rates in the Canadian Treasury Bill Market," *Journal of Financial Economics* 10, no. 1 (March 1982): 107–114.

G. Lan et E. Otuteye, "L'Evolution des Taux courants et à Terme Sur le Marché de Bons de Trésor (Canada, 1962–1991), *Finéco* 4, no. 1 (1er semestre 1994).

CHAPTER 6

The Portfolio Selection Problem

Holding Period The length of time over which an investor is assumed to invest a given sum of money.

Most securities available for investment have uncertain outcomes and are thus risky. The basic problem facing each investor is to determine what particular risky securities to own. Because a portfolio is a collection of securities, this problem is equivalent to the investor selecting his optimal portfolio from a set of possible portfolios. Hence it is often referred to as the *portfolio selection problem.* One solution to this problem was put forth in 1952 by Harry M. Markowitz, when he published a landmark paper that is generally viewed as the origin of the *modern portfolio theory* approach to investing. Markowitz's approach begins by assuming that an investor has a given sum of money to invest at the present time. This money will be invested for a particular length of time, known as the investor's **holding period**. At the end of the holding period, the investor will sell the securities that were purchased at the beginning of the period and then either spend the proceeds on consumption or reinvest the proceeds in various securities (or do some of both). Thus, Markowitz's approach can be viewed as a single-period approach, where the beginning of the period is denoted by $t = 0$ and the end of the period is denoted by $t = 1$. At $t = 0$, the investor must make a decision about what particular securities to purchase and hold until $t = 1$.[1]

Expected Return The return on a security (or portfolio) over a holding period that an investor anticipates receiving.

In making this decision at $t = 0$, the investor should recognize that security returns (and thus portfolio returns) over the forthcoming holding period are unknown. Nevertheless, the investor could estimate the **expected** (or mean) **returns** on the various securities under consideration and then invest in the one with the highest expected return. (Methods for estimating expected returns are discussed in Chapter 17.) Markowitz notes that this would generally be an unwise decision because the typical investor, although wanting "returns to be high," also wants "returns to be as certain as possible." This means that the investor, in seeking to both maximize expected return and minimize uncertainty (that is, **risk**), has two conflicting objectives that must be balanced against each other when making the purchase decision at $t = 0$. The Markowitz approach to how the investor should go about making this decision gives full consideration to both of these objectives.

Risk The uncertainty associated with the end-of-period value of an investment in an asset or portfolio of assets.

One interesting consequence of having these two conflicting objectives is that the investor should diversify by purchasing not just one security but several. The ensuing discussion of Markowitz's approach to investing begins by defining more specifically what is meant by initial and terminal wealth.

---

[1]Markowitz recognized that investing is generally a multiperiod activity, where at the end of each period, part of the investor's wealth is consumed and part is reinvested. Nevertheless, his one-period approach is optimal under a variety of reasonable circumstances. See Edwin J. Elton and Martin J. Gruber, *Finance as a Dynamic Process* (Englewood Cliffs, NJ: Prentice Hall, 1975), particularly Chapter 5.

Initial and Terminal Wealth

In equation (1.1) of Chapter 1 it was noted that the one-period rate of return on a security could be calculated as

$$\text{Return} = \frac{\text{end-of-period wealth} - \text{beginning-of-period wealth}}{\text{beginning-of-period wealth}} \tag{1.1}$$

where beginning-of-period wealth is the purchase price of one unit of the security at $t = 0$ (for example, one share of a firm's common stock), and end-of-period wealth is the market value of the unit at $t = 1$, along with the value of any cash (and cash equivalents) paid to the owner of the security between $t = 0$ and $t = 1$.

Determining the Rate of Return on a Portfolio

Because a portfolio is a collection of securities, its return r_p can be calculated in a similar manner:

$$r_p = \frac{W_1 - W_0}{W_0} \tag{6.1}$$

Here W_0 denotes the aggregate purchase price at $t = 0$ of the securities contained in the portfolio. W_1 denotes the aggregate market value of these securities at $t = 1$ as well as the aggregate cash (and cash equivalents) received between $t = 0$ and $t = 1$ from owning these securities. Equation (6.1) can be manipulated algebraically, resulting in

$$W_0(1 + r_p) = W_1 \tag{6.2}$$

From equation (6.2) it can be seen that **initial wealth** (as W_0 is sometimes called), when multiplied by 1 plus the rate of return on the portfolio, is equal to **terminal wealth** (as W_1 is sometimes called).

Earlier, it was noted that the investor must make a decision on which portfolio to purchase at $t = 0$. In doing so, the investor does not know what the value of W_1 will be for most of the various alternative portfolios under consideration, since the investor does not know what the rate of return will be for most of these portfolios.[2] Thus, according to Markowitz, the investor should view the rate of return associated with any one of these portfolios to be what is known in statistics as a **random variable**. Such variables can be "described" by their *moments*, two of which are **expected** (or mean) **value** and **standard deviation**.[3]

Markowitz asserts that investors should base their decisions solely on expected returns and standard deviations. That is, the investor should estimate the expected return and standard deviation of each portfolio and then choose the "best" one based on the relative magnitudes of these two parameters. The intuition behind this is actually quite straightforward. Expected return can be viewed as a measure of the potential reward associated with any portfolio, and standard deviation can be viewed as a measure of the risk associated with any

Initial Wealth The value of an investor's portfolio at the beginning of a holding period.

Terminal Wealth The value of an investor's portfolio at the end of a holding period. Equivalently, the investor's initial wealth multiplied by one plus the rate of return earned on the investor's portfolio over the holding period.

Random Variable A variable that takes on alternative values according to chance.

Expected Value A measure of central tendency of the probability distribution of a random variable that equals the weighted average of all possible outcomes using their probabilities as weights.

Standard Deviation A measure of the dispersion of possible outcomes around the expected outcome of a random variable.

Variance The squared value of the standard deviation.

---

[2]One portfolio that would not have an uncertain rate of return would involve the investor putting all of his or her initial wealth in a government security that matures at $t = 1$. Alternatively, the investor's initial wealth could be put into a term deposit at a bank. However, for almost all other portfolios the rate of return would be uncertain.

[3]A random variable's expected value is, in a sense, its "average" value. Thus, the expected value for the return of a portfolio can be thought of as its expected, or average, return. The standard deviation of a random variable is a measure of the dispersion (or "spread") of possible values the random variable can take on. Accordingly, the standard deviation of a portfolio is a measure of the dispersion of possible returns that could be earned on the portfolio. Sometimes **variance** is used as a measure of the dispersion instead of standard deviation. However, because variance is simply the squared value of the standard deviation of the random variable, this distinction is not of importance here. These concepts are discussed in more detail in Appendix A.

portfolio. Thus, once each portfolio has been examined in terms of its potential rewards and risks, the investor is in a position to identify the one portfolio that appears most desirable to him.

An Example

Consider the two alternative portfolios A and B, shown in Table 6.1. Portfolio A has an expected annual return of 8% and portfolio B has an expected annual return of 12%. Assuming the investor has initial wealth of $100 000 and a one-year holding period, this means that the expected levels of terminal wealth associated with A and B are $108 000 and $112 000, respectively. It would appear, then, that B is the more desirable portfolio. However, A and B have annual standard deviations of 10% and 20%, respectively. Table 6.1 shows that this means there is a 2% chance that the investor will end up with terminal wealth of $70 000 or less if he purchases B, whereas there is virtually no chance that the investor's terminal wealth will be less than $70 000 if he purchases A. Similarly, B has a 5% chance of being worth less than $80 000, whereas A again has no chance. Continuing, B has a 14% chance of being worth less than $90 000, whereas A has only a 4% chance. Going on, B has a 27% chance of being worth less than $100 000, whereas A has only a 21% chance. Since the investor has initial wealth of $100 000, this last observation means there is a greater probability of having a negative return if B (27%) is purchased instead of A (21%). Overall, it can be seen from Table 6.1 that A is less risky than B, meaning that on this dimension A would be more desirable. The ultimate decision about whether to purchase A or B will depend on this particular investor's attitude towards risk and return, as will be shown next.

Table 6.1 A Comparison of Terminal Wealth Levels for Two Hypothetical Portfolios.

Level of Terminal Wealth	Percent Chance of Being Below This Level of Terminal Wealth	
	Portfolio A[a]	Portfolio B[b]
$ 70 000	0%	2%
80 000	0	5
90 000	4	14
100 000	21	27
110 000	57	46
120 000	88	66
130 000	99	82

[a] The expected return and standard deviation of A are 8% and 10%, respectively.
[b] The expected return and standard deviation of B are 12% and 20%, respectively.
Initial wealth is assumed to be $100 000 and both portfolios are assumed to have normally distributed returns.

Nonsatiation and Risk Aversion

Nonsatiation

Nonsatiation A condition whereby investors are assumed to always prefer higher levels of terminal wealth to lower levels of terminal wealth.

Two assumptions are implicit in this discussion of the portfolio selection problem. First, it is assumed that investors, when given a choice between two otherwise identical portfolios, will choose the one with the higher level of expected return. More fundamentally, an assumption of **nonsatiation** is made in utilizing the Markowitz approach, meaning that investors are assumed always to prefer higher levels of terminal wealth to lower levels of terminal wealth. This is because higher levels of terminal wealth allow the investor to spend more on consumption at $t = 1$ (or in the more distant future). Thus, given two portfolios with the same standard deviation, the investor will choose the portfolio with the higher expected return.

However, it is not quite so obvious what the investor will do when having to choose between two portfolios with the same level of expected return but different levels of standard deviation, such as A and F. This is where the second assumption enters the discussion.

Risk Aversion

Risk-averse Investor An investor who prefers an investment with less risk over one with more risk, assuming that both investments offer the same expected return.

Generally, it is assumed that investors are **risk-averse**, which means that the investor will choose the portfolio with the smaller standard deviation, A.[4] What does it mean to say that an investor is risk-averse? It means that the investor, when given the choice, will not want to take *fair gambles*, where a fair gamble is defined to be one that has an expected payoff of zero. For example, imagine flipping a coin where heads means you win \$5 and tails means you lose \$5. Since the coin has a 50–50 chance of being heads or tails, the expected payoff is $(.5 \times \$5) + (.5 \times -\$5) = \$0$. Accordingly, the risk-averse investor will choose to avoid this gamble. To understand why, the concept of investor utility must be introduced.

Utility

Utility The relative enjoyment or satisfaction that a person derives from economic activity such as work, consumption, or investment.

Economists use the term **utility** to quantify the relative enjoyment or satisfaction that people derive from economic activity such as work, consumption, or investment. Satisfying activities generate positive utility while dissatisfying activities produce negative utility (or disutility). Because tastes (or preferences) differ among individuals, one person may experience more utility from a particular activity than another person. Nevertheless, people are presumed to be rational and allocate their resources (such as time and money) in ways that maximize their own utilities. The Markowitz portfolio selection problem can be viewed as an effort to maximize the expected utility associated with the investor's terminal wealth.

Marginal Utility

The exact relationship between utility and wealth is called the investor's *utility of wealth function*. Under the assumption of nonsatiation, all investors prefer more wealth to less wealth. (Money is indeed assumed to buy happiness.) Every extra dollar of wealth enhances an investor's utility. But by how much?

Marginal Utility The extra utility that a person derives from engaging in an extra unit of economic activity.

Each investor has a unique utility of wealth function. As a result, each investor may derive a different increment of utility from an extra dollar of wealth. That is, the **marginal utility** of wealth may differ among investors. Further, that marginal utility may depend on the level of wealth that the investor possesses prior to receiving the extra dollar. (A rich investor may value an extra dollar of wealth less than a poor investor.)

A common assumption is that investors experience diminishing marginal utility of wealth. Each extra dollar of wealth always provides positive additional utility, but the added utility produced by each extra dollar becomes successively smaller. Figure 6.1(a) illustrates the utility of wealth function of an investor with diminishing marginal utility. Higher levels of wealth (read off the horizontal axis) produce higher levels of utility (read off the vertical axis). The assumption of nonsatiation requires that the utility of wealth function is always positively sloped no matter what the level of wealth. However, this utility of wealth

---

[4]Investors who are risk-seeking would choose F, whereas investors who are risk-neutral would find A and F to be equally desirable. Appendix B to this chapter discusses both risk-neutral and risk-seeking investors.

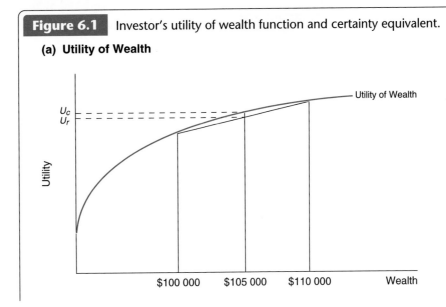

Figure 6.1 Investor's utility of wealth function and certainty equivalent.

(a) Utility of Wealth

function is concave—that is, it is bowed downward. As wealth increases, the corresponding increase in utility becomes smaller.

An investor with diminishing marginal utility is necessarily risk-averse. As discussed previously, a risk-averse investor is unwilling to accept a fair bet. The utility of wealth function can now be used to explain that preference.

Smith has been offered the choice of two investments. One is to invest $100 000 and earn a certain return of 5%. The expected terminal wealth of this investment is $105 000. The alternative investment also requires an outlay of $100 000. It has a 50% probability of returning a $10 000 gain (a 10% return) and a 50% probability of returning only the original investment (a 0% return). The expected terminal wealth of the risky investment is the same as that of the certain investment: $.5 \times \$100\ 000 + .5 \times \$110\ 000 = \$105\ 000$ or a 5% expected return. Which investment will Smith prefer?

The answer is shown in Figure 6.1(a). The utility associated with the certain investment is found by moving up from the terminal wealth axis at $105 000 to the utility of wealth function and then moving across to the utility axis. The utility of the certain investment is identified as U_c. The expected utility of the risky investment is found by connecting the utility of the upper and lower possible outcomes on the investment ($100 000 and $110 000) with a straight line and then moving up from the expected terminal wealth of the investment ($105 000) on the terminal wealth axis to that line and then moving across to the utility axis. The expected utility of the risky investment is labelled U_r. Note that since U_c is greater than U_r, Smith will choose the certain investment.[5] This conclusion can be generalized for any pair of certain and risky investments with the same expected terminal wealth: a risk-averse investor will derive greater satisfaction by selecting the certain investment over the risky investment.

The reasoning for this preference is straightforward. A risk-averse investor displays diminishing marginal utility of wealth. Thus the negative utility (or disutility) associated with a one dollar (or $5000) loss is more than the positive utility of earning one dollar (or

---

[5]Equivalently, in order to determine U_r, one could calculate the utility of $100 000 and the utility of $110 000, and then take a weighted average of them where the weights correspond to the posibilities of the outcomes occurring, which in this case is .5 for each of them. That is, the expected utility U_r of the risky investment is equal to $[.5 \times U(\$100\ 000)] + [.5 \times U(\$110\ 000)]$.

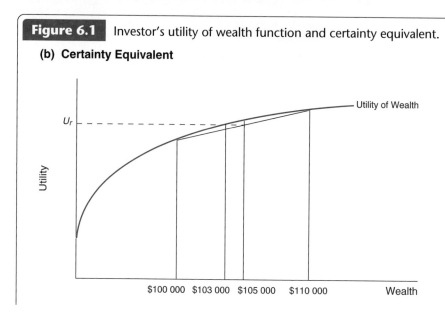

Figure 6.1 Investor's utility of wealth function and certainty equivalent.

(b) Certainty Equivalent

Utility of Wealth

U_r

Utility

$100 000 $103 000 $105 000 $110 000   Wealth

$5000). That is, at any point along a concave utility of wealth function, if one moves one dollar (or $5000) to the right the corresponding increase in utility is smaller than the decline in utility if one were to move one dollar (or $5000) to the left.

Certainty Equivalents and Risk Premiums

Figure 6.1(b) introduces two additional concepts. Again, Smith is given the chance to enter into the same risky investment as described in the previous example. Moving horizontally from the utility axis at the expected utility of the risky investment to the utility of wealth function and then moving down to the terminal wealth axis indicates the **certainty equivalent** wealth associated with the risky investment. In this case that wealth is $103 000. This is the amount of terminal wealth that, if offered with certainty, would provide the same amount of expected utility as the risky investment. Smith will be indifferent between a $100 000 investment that offers a terminal wealth of $103 000 with certainty (a 3% certain return) or this risky investment with an expected terminal wealth of $105 000 (a 5% risky return). Further, the additional $2000 in expected terminal wealth (or additional 2% in expected return) offered by the risky investment over the certain investment is termed a **risk premium**: it is the expected increase in terminal wealth (or expected return) over the certain investment required to compensate the investor for the risk incurred. For a risky investment with a given expected terminal wealth, more risk-averse investors will have lower certainty equivalents and commensurately higher risk premiums than will less risk-averse investors.

Risk-averse investors are willing to forgo some expected terminal wealth (that is, accept lower expected returns) in exchange for less risk. Thus various combinations of expected terminal wealth (or expected returns) and risk will produce the same level of expected utility for an investor. This leads to the concept of indifference curves, which are discussed next.

Certainty Equivalent Return For a particular risky investment, the return on a risk-free investment that makes the investor indifferent between the risky and risk-free investments.

Risk Premium The expected increase in terminal wealth (or expected return) over the certain investment required to compensate the investor for the risk incurred.

Indifference Curves

Indifference Curve All combinations of portfolios, considered in terms of expected returns and risk, that provide an investor with an equal amount of satisfaction.

An **indifference curve** represents a set of risk and expected return combinations that provide an investor with the same amount of utility. The investor is said to be indifferent between any of the risk-expected return combinations on the same indifference curve. Because indifference curves indicate an investor's preferences for risk and return, they can be drawn on a two-dimensional figure where the horizontal axis indicates risk as measured by standard deviation (denoted σ_p) and the vertical axis indicates reward as measured by expected return (denoted $\bar{r}_p$).

Figure 6.2 illustrates a "map" of indifference curves that a hypothetical investor might possess. Each curved line indicates one indifference curve for the investor and represents all combinations of portfolios that provide the investor with a given level of utility. For example, the investor with the indifference curves in Figure 6.1 would find portfolios A and B (the same two portfolios that were shown in Table 6.1) equally desirable, even though they have different standard deviations, because they both lie on the same indifference curve, I_2. Portfolio B has a higher standard deviation (20%) than portfolio A (10%) and is therefore less desirable on that dimension. However, exactly offsetting this loss in desirability is the gain in desirability provided by the higher expected return of B (12%) relative to A (8%).

Because all portfolios that lie on a given indifference curve are equally desirable to the investor, by implication *indifference curves cannot intersect*. To see that this is so, consider two curves that do intersect such as those that are shown in Figure 6.3. Here the point of intersection is represented by X. Remember that all the portfolios on I_1 are equally desirable. This means thay are all as desirable as X, since X is on I_1. Similarly, all the portfolios on I_2 are equally desirable and are as desirable as X, since X is also on I_2. Given X is on both indifference curves, all the portfolios on I_1 must be as desirable as those on I_2. But this presents a contradiction, since I_1 and I_2 are two curves that are supposed to represent different levels of desirability. Thus in order for there to be no contradiction, these curves cannot intersect.

Figure 6.2 Map of indifference curves for a risk-averse investor.

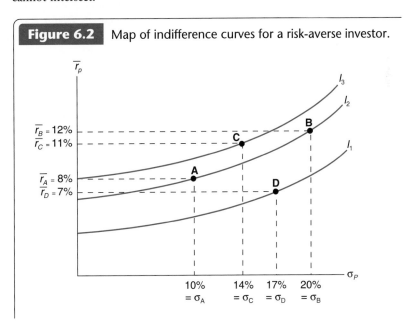

Although the investor represented in Figure 6.2 would find portfolios A and B equally desirable, she would find portfolio C, with an expected return of 11% and a standard deviation of 14%, preferable to both of them. This is because portfolio C happens to be on an

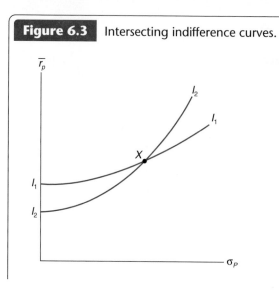

Figure 6.3 Intersecting indifference curves.

indifference curve, I_3, that is located to the "northwest" of I_2. Now C has a sufficiently larger expected return relative to A to more than offset its higher standard deviation and, on balance, make it more desirable than A. Equivalently, C has a sufficiently smaller standard deviation than B to more than offset its smaller expected return and, on balance, make it more desirable than B. This leads to the second important feature of indifference curves: *a risk-averse investor will find any portfolio that is lying on an indifference curve that is "further northwest" to be more desirable (that is, provide greater utility) than any portfolio lying on an indifference curve that is "not as far northwest."*

Lastly, it should be noted that *an investor has an infinite number of indifference curves.* This simply implies that whenever there are two indifference curves that have been plotted on a graph, it is possible to plot a third indifference curve that lies between them. As can be seen in Figure 6.4, given indifference curves I_1 and I_3, it is possible to graph a third curve, I^*, lying between them. It also implies that another indifference curve can be plotted above I_2 and yet another below I_1.

How does an investor determine what her indifference curves look like? After all, each investor has a map of indifference curves that, while having the previously noted features, is nevertheless unique to that individual. One method, as will be shown in Chapter 23, involves presenting the investor with a set of hypothetical portfolios, along with their expected returns and standard deviations.[6] Then she would be asked to choose the most desirable one. Given the choice that is made, the shape and location of the investor's indifference curves can be estimated. This is because it is presumed that the investor would have acted as if she had explicit knowledge of her own indifference curves in making this choice, even though those indifference curves would not have been directly referenced.

In summary, every investor has an indifference map representing his or her preferences for expected returns and standard deviations.[7] This means that the investor should deter-

---

[6]For an alternative procedure, see Ralph O. Swalm, "Utility Theory: Insights into Risk Taking," *Harvard Business Review* 44, no. 6 (November–December 1966): 123–136. Also see footnote 5.

[7]At some point the reader may wonder why an investor's preferences are based only on expected returns and standard deviations. For example, it may seem logical that the investor's preferences should be based on expected returns, standard deviations, and the probability that a portfolio will lose money. The assertion that an investor's preferences are not based on anything other than the expected returns and standard deviations follows some specific assumptions coupled with *utility theory.* See Gordon J. Alexander and Jack Clark Francis, *Portfolio Analysis* (Englewood Cliffs, NJ: Prentice Hall, 1986), particularly Chapters 2 and 3, for more details. It should be noted that there is some dispute about the validity of using utility theory to describe people's behaviour. Those holding the opposing viewpoint are often referred to as behaviourists. For a discussion of their views, see the entire second part of the October 1986 issue of the *Journal of Business* and the *Institutional Issues: Behavioural Finance* in the chapter.

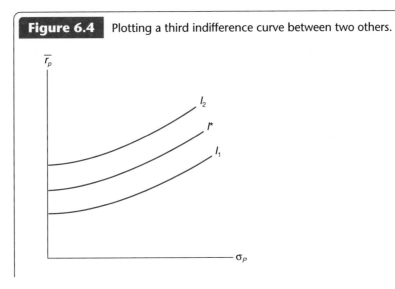

Figure 6.4 Plotting a third indifference curve between two others.

mine the expected return and standard deviation for each potential portfolio, plot them on a graph such as Figure 6.2, and then select the one portfolio that lies on the indifference curve that is "furthest northwest." As shown in this example, from the set of the four potential portfolios—A, B, C, and D—the investor should select C.

The two assumptions of nonsatiation and risk-aversion cause indifference curves to be positively sloped and convex.[8] Although it is assumed that all investors are risk-averse, it is not assumed that they have identical degrees of risk aversion. Some investors may be highly risk-averse, whereas others may be only slightly so. This means that different investors will have different maps of indifference curves. Panels (a), (b), and (c) of Figure 6.5 display maps for investors who are highly risk-averse, moderately risk-averse, and slightly risk-averse, respectively. As can be seen in these figures, a more risk-averse investor has more steeply sloped indifference curves.

Calculating Expected Returns and Standard Deviations for Portfolios

The previous section introduced the portfolio selection problem that every investor faces. It also introduced the investment approach of Harry Markowitz as a method of solving that problem. With this approach, an investor should evaluate alternative portfolios on the basis of their expected returns and standard deviations by using indifference curves. In the case of a risk-averse investor, the portfolio with the indifference curve that is "furthest northwest" would be the one selected for investment.

However, certain questions have been left unanswered. In particular, how does the investor calculate the expected return and standard deviation for a portfolio?

---

[8]Convexity of indifference curves means that their slopes increase when moving from left to right along any particular one. That is, they bend upward. The underlying reason for convexity is found in utility theory; see footnote 7.

Figure 6.5 Indifference curves for different types of risk-averse investors.

(a) Highly Risk-Averse Investor

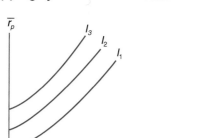

(b) Moderately Risk-Averse Investor

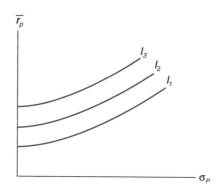

(c) Slightly Risk-Averse Investor

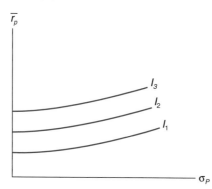

INSTITUTIONAL ISSUES

Behavioural Finance

The bedrock on which theories of risky security valuation rest is the presumed existence of rational investors who respond in a predictable manner to the opportunities for gain and the risks of loss. As the text discusses, these investors are assumed to assess potential investments on the basis of expected returns and standard deviations that are derived from estimates of the investments' probability distributions of returns. Furthermore, the investors' estimates are assumed to exhibit no systematic biases relative to the "true" probability distributions. That is, investors do not consistently make mistakes in one direction or another when examining potential investments.

If such assumptions of rationality make sense for individual investors, then we might reasonably believe that they apply even more appropriately to institutional investors. After all, institutional investors bring to bear extensive analytical resources on the investment management problem. Moreover, the decision-making structures of institutional investors—such as hierarchies of personnel, committees, and performance reviews—are all designed to promote consistent and rational investment choices.

The view of investors as objective decision makers has traditionally gone unchallenged in the academic world. While many professional investors have argued that investing is dominated by the emotions of fear and greed, their opinions have been dismissed by academics as anecdotal and self-serving. More recently, however, a school of thought has developed among certain academics that argues that investors may not deal with risky choices in a totally rational manner. This line of reasoning is based on a branch of psychology known as *cognitive psychology*, which studies the capacity of human beings for perception and judgment.

Applied to the study of economic decision making, and investments in particular, cognitive psychology draws some intriguing conclusions. Most fundamentally, people do not appear to be consistent in how they treat economically equivalent choices if the choices are presented in significantly different contexts. These differences are referred to as *framing effects*. Two prominent cognitive psychology researchers, Daniel Kahneman and Amos Tversky, cite a simple example of framing effects.*

Suppose that you are walking to a play carrying a ticket that cost $100. On reaching the theatre you discover that you have lost your ticket. Would you pay another $100 for a ticket at the door? Now suppose that you were planning to buy the ticket at the door. On arriving you find that you have lost $100 on the way. Would you still buy a ticket?

The economic consequences of these two situations are identical. You have lost $100 and now must decide whether to spend another $100. Interestingly, however, most people buy a ticket in the second case, but not in the first. People therefore appear to "frame" the choices differently. They treat the loss of cash differently from the loss of a ticket.

In terms of investing, these framing effects have been suggested to cause deviations from rational decision making. For example, it appears that people react differently to situations involving the prospects for large gains as opposed to large losses. That is, investors are assumed to choose a more risky investment over a less risky one only if the expected return of the more risky investment is greater than that of the less risky investment. (This trait is known as risk aversion, as mentioned earlier in the chapter.) Indeed, this assumption seems to hold well for situations involving large gains. For example, consider a situation where you have invested in a start-up company and have a 90% chance of receiving $1 million

and a 10% chance of receiving nothing. Therefore, the expected payoff is $(.9 \times \$1 \text{ million}) + (.1 \times \$0) = \$900\ 000$. If somebody offered to buy you out for $850 000, most likely you would accept the offer, since it has nearly the same expected payoff but much less risk. That is, you would be exhibiting risk-averse behaviour.

Now, however, consider a situation involving large losses. Suppose that you had invested in another start-up company. Things are going poorly, and if nothing changes there is a 90% chance of losing $1 million, but a 10% chance that things might work out well enough to not lose (or gain) anything. In this case, the expected loss is $(.9 \times -\$1 \text{ million}) + (.1 \times \$0) = \$900\ 000$.

Another investor offers to take over the company if you pay him or her $850,000—a certain $850,000 loss. Most people would reject the offer and choose to remain with the risky option even though it has a lower expected value (−$900,000 versus −$850,000). Thus in a situation involving large expected losses, people do not seem to exhibit risk-averse behaviour—a framing effect.

People also seem to overestimate the probability of unlikely events occurring and underestimate the probability of moderately likely events occurring. These traits may explain the popularity of lotteries but may also have direct ramifications for the pricing of investments when the chances of success are low—such as bonds and stocks of bankrupt companies, start-up companies, and options whose strike prices are far above the underlying securities' prices.

Framing effects may also be involved in the observed tendency of investors to overreact to good and bad news. That is, some studies suggest that investors bid up the prices of companies reporting unexpectedly good earnings beyond the amount fairly warranted by the improved earnings. The converse seems to occur for companies reporting unexpectedly poor earnings.

Are the observations of cognitive psychologists relevant to the study of financial markets? Do these framing effects produce market anomalies that produce exploitable investment opportunities or even undermine commonly accepted theories of security valuation? Or are these framing effects merely interesting stories whose impacts are overwhelmed by the sophistication and profit motive of avaricious investors? Certainly, investors as a whole are far from irrational, for large and persistent disparities between "fair" values and market values are difficult to find. Nevertheless, the behavioural observations of cognitive psychologists are likely to provide a better understanding of how investors make decisions and help to explain certain apparent market inefficiencies. Indeed, it has opened up a whole new field known as *behavioural finance*.

---

* Daniel Kahneman and Amos Tversky, "The Psychology of Preferences," *Scientific American* (January 1982).

Expected Returns

With the Markowitz approach to investing, the focus of the investor is on terminal (or end-of-period) wealth, W_1. That is, in deciding which portfolio to purchase with his initial (or beginning-of-period) wealth, W_0, the investor should focus on the effect the various portfolios have on W_1. This effect can be measured by the expected return and standard deviation of each portfolio.

As mentioned previously, a portfolio is a collection of securities. Thus, it seems logical that the expected return and standard deviation of a portfolio should depend on the expected return and standard deviation of each security contained in the portfolio. It also seems logical that the amount invested in each security should be important. Indeed, this is the case.

In order to show how the expected return of a portfolio depends on both the expected return of the individual securities and the amount invested in these securities, consider the three-security portfolio shown in Table 6.2(a). Assume that the investor has a one-year holding period and that for this period he has estimated the expected returns on Able, Baker, and Charlie stock to be 16.2%, 24.6%, and 22.8%, respectively. This is equivalent to stating that the investor has estimated the expected end-of-period per-share values of these three stocks to be, respectively, $46.48 [since ($46.48 − $40)/$40 = 16.2%], $43.61 [since ($43.61 − $35)/$35 = 24.6%], and $76.14 [since ($76.14 − $62)/$62 = 22.8%].[9] Furthermore, assume that this investor has initial wealth of $17 200.

Using End-of-Period Values

The expected return on this portfolio can be calculated in several ways, all of which give the same answer. Consider the method shown in Table 6.2(b). This method involves calculating the expected end-of-period value of the portfolio and then using the formula for calculating rate of return shown in Chapter 1. That is, first the initial portfolio value (W_0) is subtracted from the expected end-of-period value of the portfolio (W_1), and then this difference is divided by the initial portfolio value (W_0), the result of which is the portfolio's expected return. Although the example shown in Table 6.2(b) involves three securities, the procedure can be generalized to any number of securities.

Using Security Expected Returns

An alternative method for calculating the expected return on this portfolio is shown in Table 6.2(c). This procedure involves calculating the expected return of a portfolio as the

---

[9]The figures given for the expected end-of-period values include both the expected prices and the expected dividends for the period. For example, Able has an expected end-of-period value of $46.48, which could consist of a hypothetical expected cash dividend of $2 and share price of $44.48. These expected returns and values are estimated by use of security analysis, which will be discussed in Chapter 17.

weighted average of the expected returns of its component securities. The relative market values of the securities in the portfolio are used as weights. In symbols, the general rule for calculating the expected return of a portfolio consisting of N securities is

$$\bar{r}_p = \sum_{i=1}^{N} X_i \bar{r}_i \tag{6.3a}$$

$$= X_1 \bar{r}_1 + X_2 \bar{r}_2 + \cdots + X_N \bar{r}_N \tag{6.3b}$$

where:

$\bar{r}_p$ = the expected return of the portfolio
X_i = the proportion of the portfolio's initial value invested in security i
$\bar{r}_i$ = the expected return of security i
N = the number of securities in the portfolio[10]

Table 6.2 Calculating the Expected Return for a Portfolio.

(a) Security and Portfolio Values.

Security Name	Number of Shares in Portfolio (1)	Initial Market Price per Share (2)	Total Investment (3) = (1 × 2)	Proportion of Initial Market Value of Portfolio (4) = (3)/W₀
Able Co.	100	$40	$4000	$4000/$17 200 = .2325
Baker Co.	200	35	7000	7000/ 17 200 = .4070
Charlie Co.	100	62	6200	6200/ 17 200 = .3605
				Sum of proportions = 1.0000

(b) Calculating the Expected Return for a Portfolio Using End-of-Period Value.

Security Name	Number of Shares in Portfolio (1)	Expected End-of-Period Value per Share (2)	Aggregate Expected End-of-Period Value (3) = (1) × (2)
Able Co.	100	$46.48	$46.48 × 100 = $4 648
Baker Co.	200	43.61	43.61 × 200 = 8 722
Charlie Co.	100	76.14	76.14 × 100 = 7 614

Expected end-of-period value of portfolio = $\overline{W}_1$ = $20 984

Portfolio expected return = $\bar{r}_p = \dfrac{\$20\ 984 - \$17\ 200}{\$17\ 200} = 22.00\%$

(c) Calculating the Expected Return for a Portfolio Using Security Expected Returns.

Security Name	Proportion of Initial Market Value of Portfolio (1)	Security Expected Returns (2)	Contribution to Portfolio Expected Return (3) = (1) × (2)
Able Co.	.2325	16.2%	.2325 × 16.2% = .77%
Baker Co.	.4070	24.6	.4070 × 24.6 = 10.01
Charlie Co.	.3605	22.8	.3605 × 22.8 = 8.22

Portfolio expected return = $\bar{r}_p$ = 22.00%

---

[10]Security weights in a portfolio can be either positive (indicating a long position) or negative (indicating a short position). However, due to margin requirements, an investor does not have direct access to the proceeds of a short sale

(continued on pg. 142)

Expected Return Vector
A column of numbers that corresponds to the expected returns for a set of securities.

Thus, an **expected return vector** can be used to calculate the expected return for any portfolio formed from the N securities. This vector consists of one column of numbers, where the entry in row i contains the expected return of security i. In the previous example, the expected return vector was estimated by the investor to be

$$\begin{matrix} \text{Row 1} \\ \text{Row 2} \\ \text{Row 3} \end{matrix} \begin{bmatrix} 16.2\% \\ 24.6\% \\ 22.8\% \end{bmatrix}$$

where the entries in rows 1, 2, and 3 denote the expected returns for securities 1, 2, and 3, respectively.

Because a portfolio's expected return is a weighted average of the expected returns of its securities, the contribution of each security to the portfolio's expected return depends on its expected return and its proportionate share of the initial portfolio's market value. Nothing else is relevant. It follows from equation (6.3a) that an investor who simply wants the greatest possible expected return should hold one security: the one he considers to have the greatest expected return. Very few investors do this, and very few investment advisors would counsel such an extreme policy. Instead, investors should diversify, meaning that their portfolios should include more than one security. This is because diversification can reduce risk, as measured by the standard deviation.

◗ Standard Deviations

A useful measure of risk should somehow take into account both the probabilities of various possible "bad" outcomes and their associated magnitudes. Instead of measuring the probability of a number of different possible outcomes, the measure of risk should somehow estimate the extent to which the actual outcome is likely to diverge from the expected outcome. Standard deviation is a measure that does this, since it is an estimate of the likely divergence of an *actual* return from an *expected* return.

It may seem that any single measure of risk would provide at best a very crude summary of the "bad" possibilities. But in the more common situation where a portfolio's prospects are being assessed, standard deviation may prove to be a very good measure of the degree of uncertainty. The clearest example arises when the **probability distribution** for a portfolio's returns can be approximated by the familiar bell-shaped curve known as a **normal distribution**. This is often considered a plausible assumption for analyzing returns on diversified portfolios when the holding period being studied is relatively short (say a quarter or less).

Probability Distribution
A model describing the relative frequency of possible values that a random variable can assume.

Normal (Probability) Distribution A symmetrical bell-shaped probability distribution, completely described by its mean and standard deviation.

A question with standard deviation as a measure of risk is, why count "happy" surprises (those above the expected return) at all in a measure of risk? Why not just consider the deviations *below* the expected return? Measures that do so have merit. However, the results will be the same if the probability distribution is symmetric, as is the normal distribution. Why? Because the left side of a symmetric distribution is a mirror image of the right side. Thus, a list of portfolios ordered on the basis of "downside risk" will not differ from one ordered on the basis of standard deviation if returns are normally distributed.[11]

---

[10](see Chapter 2). As a result, the return on a stock sold short is not the opposite of the return on a stock held in a long position. This implies that a negative sign cannot simply be inserted into equation (6.3a) to indicate a short position without adjusting the security's expected return for the effects of the short-selling margin requirements.

[11]If returns are not normally distributed, the use of standard deviation can still be justified in an approximate sense provided there are small probabilities of extremely high and low returns. See H. Levy and H. M. Markowitz, "Approximating Expected Utility by a Function of Mean and Variance," *American Economic Review* 69, no. 3 (June 1979): 308–317; and Yoram Kroll, Haim Levy, and Harry M. Markowitz, "Mean-Variance versus Direct Utility Maximization," *Journal of Finance* 39, no. 1 (March 1984): 47–61. Some researchers have argued that the best model for a stock's returns is a mixture of normal distributions; for a discussion and references, see Richard Roll, "R^2," *Journal of Finance* 43, no. 3 (July 1988): 541–566, particularly footnote 11 on p. 561.

Formula for Standard Deviation

Now just how is the standard deviation of a portfolio calculated? For the three-security portfolio consisting of Able, Baker, and Charlie, the formula is:

$$\sigma_p = \left[\sum_{i=1}^{3} \sum_{j=1}^{3} X_i X_j \sigma_{ij} \right]^{1/2} \tag{6.4}$$

where σ_{ij} denotes the **covariance** of the returns between security i and security j.

Covariance

Covariance A statistical measure of the relationship between two random variables. It measures the extent of mutual variation between two random variables.

Covariance is a statistical measure of the relationship between two random variables. That is, it is a measure of how two random variables such as the returns on securities i and j "move together." A positive value for covariance indicates that the securities' returns tend to go together—for example, a better-than-expected return for one is likely to occur along with a better-than-expected return for the other. A negative covariance indicates a tendency for the returns to offset one another—for example, a better-than-expected return for one security is likely to occur along with a worse-than-expected return for the other. A relatively small or zero value for the covariance indicates that there is little or no relationship between the returns for the two securities.

Correlation

Closely related to covariance is the statistical measure known as correlation. In fact, the covariance between two random variables is equal to the correlation between the two random variables times the product of their standard deviations:

$$\sigma_{ij} = \rho_{ij} \sigma_i \sigma_j \tag{6.5}$$

Correlation Coefficient A statistical measure similar to covariance, in that it measures the degree of mutual variation between two random variables. The correlation coefficient rescales covariance to facilitate comparison among pairs of random variables. The correlation coefficient is bounded by the values −1 and +1.

where ρ_{ij} (the Greek letter rho) denotes the **correlation coefficient** between the return on security i and the return on security j. The correlation coefficient rescales the covariance to facilitate comparison with corresponding values for other pairs of random variables.

Correlation coefficients always lie between −1 and +1. A value of −1 represents perfect negative correlation, and a value of +1 represents perfect positive correlation. Most cases lie between these two extreme values.

Figure 6.6(a) presents a scatter diagram for the returns on hypothetical securities A and B when the correlation between these two securities is perfectly positive. Note how all the points lie precisely on a straight upward-sloping line. This means that when one of the two securities has a relatively high return, then so will the other. Similarly, when one of the two securities has a relatively low return, then so will the other.

Alternatively, the returns on the two securities will have a perfectly negative correlation when the scatter diagram indicates that the points lie precisely on a straight downward-sloping line, as shown in Figure 6.6(b). In such a case the returns on the two securities can be seen to move opposite each other. That is, when one security has a relatively high return, then the other will have a relatively low return.

A case of special importance arises when the scatter diagram of security returns shows a dispersion that cannot be represented even approximately by an upward-sloping or down-ward-sloping line. In such an instance, the returns are uncorrelated, meaning the correlation coefficient is zero. Figure 6.6(c) provides an example. In this situation, when one security has a relatively high return, then the other can have either a relatively high, low, or average return.

Double Summation

Given an understanding of covariance and correlation, it is important to understand how the double summation indicated in equation (6.4) is performed. Although there are many ways of performing double summation, all of which lead to the same answer, one way is

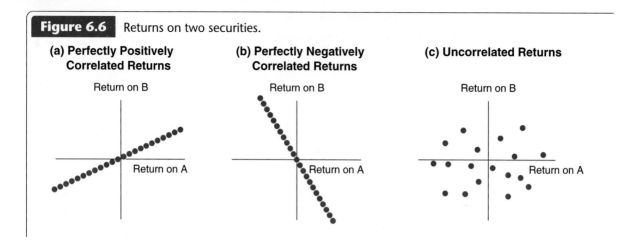

Figure 6.6 Returns on two securities.

(a) Perfectly Positively Correlated Returns

Return on B

Return on A

(b) Perfectly Negatively Correlated Returns

Return on B

Return on A

(c) Uncorrelated Returns

Return on B

Return on A

perhaps more intuitive than the others. It starts with the first summation and sets i at its initial value of 1. Then the second summation is performed for j going from 1 to 3. At this point, i in the first summation is increased by 1, so that now $i = 2$. Again the second summation is performed by letting j go from 1 to 3, except that now $i = 2$.

Continuing, i in the first summation is again increased by 1, so that $i = 3$. Then the second summation is again performed by letting j go from 1 to 3. At this point, note that i and j are each at their upper limits of 3. This means it is time to stop, as the double summation has been finished. This process can be shown algebraically as follows:

$$\sigma_p = \left[\sum_{j=1}^{3} X_1 X_j \sigma_{1j} + \sum_{j=1}^{3} X_2 X_j \sigma_{2j} + \sum_{j=1}^{3} X_3 X_j \sigma_{3j} \right]^{1/2} \tag{6.6a}$$

$$= [X_1 X_1 \sigma_{11} + X_1 X_2 \sigma_{12} + X_1 X_3 \sigma_{13}$$
$$+ X_2 X_1 \sigma_{21} + X_2 X_2 \sigma_{22} + X_2 X_3 \sigma_{23}$$
$$+ X_3 X_1 \sigma_{31} + X_3 X_2 \sigma_{32} + X_3 X_3 \sigma_{33}]^{1/2} \tag{6.6b}$$

Each term in the double sum involves the product of the weights for two securities, X_i and X_j, and the covariance between these two securities. Note how there are nine terms to be added together in order to calculate the standard deviation of a portfolio consisting of three securities. It is no coincidence that the number of terms to be added together (9) equals the number of securities squared (3^2).

In general, calculating the standard deviation for a portfolio consisting of N securities involves performing the double sum indicated in equation (6.4) over N securities, thereby involving the addition of N^2 terms:

$$\sigma_p = \left[\sum_{i=1}^{N} \sum_{j=1}^{N} X_i X_j \sigma_{ij} \right]^{1/2} \tag{6.7}$$

An interesting feature of the double sum occurs when the subscripts i and j refer to the same security. In equation (6.6) this occurs in the first ($X_1 X_1 \sigma_{11}$), fifth ($X_2 X_2 \sigma_{22}$), and ninth ($X_3 X_3 \sigma_{33}$) terms. What does it mean to have the subscripts for covariance refer to the same security? For example, consider security one (Able) so that $i = j = 1$. Since σ_{11} denotes the covariance of security 1 (Able) with security 1 (Able), equation (6.5) indicates that

$$\sigma_{11} = \rho_{11} \sigma_1 \sigma_1 \tag{6.8}$$

Now the correlation of any security with itself, in this case ρ_{11}, can be shown to be equal to +1.[12] This means that equation (6.8) reduces to

$$\sigma_{11} = +1 \times \sigma_1 \times \sigma_1$$
$$= \sigma_1^2 \tag{6.9}$$

which is just the standard deviation of security one squared, known as the variance of security one. Thus, the double sum involves both variance and covariance terms.

Variance-covariance Matrix

As an example, consider the following **variance-covariance matrix** for the stocks of Able, Baker, and Charlie:

$$
\begin{array}{c}
\\
\text{Row 1} \\
\text{Row 2} \\
\text{Row 3}
\end{array}
\begin{array}{ccc}
\text{Column 1} & \text{Column 2} & \text{Column 3} \\
\left[\begin{array}{ccc}
146 & 187 & 145 \\
187 & 854 & 104 \\
145 & 104 & 289
\end{array}\right]
\end{array}
$$

The entry in cell (i, j) denotes the covariance between security i and security j. For example, the entry in $(1, 3)$ denotes the covariance between the first and third securities, which in this case is 145. Also, the entry in cell (i, i) denotes the variance of security i. For example, the variance of security 2 appears in cell $(2, 2)$, and is equal to 854. Using this variance-covariance matrix along with the formula given in equation (6.6b), the standard deviation of any portfolio that consists of investments in Able, Baker, and Charlie can now be computed.

For example, consider the portfolio given in Table 6.2 that had proportions $X_1 = .2325$, $X_2 = .4070$, and $X_3 = .3605$:

$$
\begin{aligned}
\sigma_p = [&X_1 X_1 \sigma_{11} + X_1 X_2 \sigma_{12} + X_1 X_3 \sigma_{13} \\
&+ X_2 X_1 \sigma_{21} + X_2 X_2 \sigma_{22} + X_2 X_3 \sigma_{23} \\
&+ X_3 X_1 \sigma_{31} + X_3 X_2 \sigma_{32} + X_3 X_3 \sigma_{33}]^{1/2} \\
= [&(.2325 \times .2325 \times 146) + (.2325 \times .4070 \times 187) + (.2325 \times .3605 \times 145) \\
&+ (.4070 \times .2325 \times 187) + (.4070 \times .4070 \times 854) + (.4070 \times .3605 \times 104) \\
&+ (.3605 \times .2325 \times 145) + (.3605 \times .4070 \times 104) + (.3605 \times .3605 \times 289)]^{1/2} \\
= [&277.13]^{1/2} \\
= &16.65\%
\end{aligned}
$$

Several interesting features about variance-covariance matrices deserve mention. First, such matrices are square, meaning that the number of columns equals the number of rows and that the total number of cells for N securities equals N^2.

Second, the variances of the securities appear on the diagonal of the matrix, which are the cells that lie on a line going from the upper left-hand corner to the lower right-hand corner of the matrix. In the previous example, the variance of security 1 (146) appears in row 1 of column 1. Similarly, the variances of securities 2 and 3 appear in row 2 of column 2 (854) and row 3 of column 3 (289), respectively.

Third, the matrix is symmetric, meaning the number appearing in row i of column j also appears in row j of column i. That is, the elements in the cells above the diagonal also appear in the corresponding cells below the diagonal. In the previous example, note that the element in row 1 of column 2, 187, also appears in row 2 of column 1. Similarly, 145

---

[12]Remember that correlation refers to how two random variables move together. If the two random variables are the same, then they must move exactly together with each other. This can be visualized by graphing the values of the same random variable on both the X-axis and Y-axis. In such a graph, all points would lie on a straight $45°$ line passing through the origin, thereby implying a correlation of +1.

Alternative Risk Measures

Virtually all investment textbooks (this one being no exception) define a portfolio's investment risk to be its volatility of returns, measured by the standard deviation (or, equivalently, the variance) of the portfolio's return distribution. This definition's pedagogical dominance reflects the practice of academics and, to a lesser extent, those investment professionals steeped in quantitative portfolio management techniques.

Yet ask the average person on the street to define investment risk, and she will invariably refer to the chances of something "bad" happening. To suggest to this person that risk also has some association with the possible occurrence of good outcomes will almost certainly draw a disbelieving look.

If, on the surface, the textbook definition of risk appears to have only an indirect relationship with an intuitive sense of risk, why has this "risk as standard deviation" definition so thoroughly dominated investment research? Further, why have alternative risk measures that directly address the likelihood of experiencing undesirable outcomes not been more widely considered and applied?

The straightforward answer to the first question is that standard deviation is computationally easier to work with than any alternative. Proofs and applications of various risk-return investment principles are typically simpler to derive using standard deviation as the measure of risk. For example, Harry Markowitz originally suggested a risk measure involving only negative outcomes when he developed his pioneering work on efficient sets (see Chapters 6 to 8). He rejected that approach in favour of standard deviation in order to simplify the calculations.

As our average person on the street intuitively understands, the biggest problem with standard deviation is that it "discriminates" against investments with volatility on the "upside." As the text describes, we assume that investors dislike risk. Therefore, if we define risk to incorporate both good and bad results, then our risk-reward evaluation of potential investments penalizes investments that might give us positive surprises just as we penalize those investments for the possibility of giving us negative surprises.

All of this concern is moot if investment returns are symmetrically distributed, particularly in the form of a normal distribution (or "bell-shaped" curve). In that case, the chances of a positive outcome a certain distance away from the centre of the distribution are just as great as the chances of a negative outcome an equal distance in the opposite direction. The fact that results above the expected value are included with those below the expected value becomes irrelevant. The standard deviation accurately summarizes the "bad" part of an investment's return distribution.

However, what if investment returns are not normally distributed? For example, we have good reason to believe that common stock returns do not conform to this pattern. Consider that common stock investors face limited liability (see Chapter 16)—the most that they can lose is their original investment. Further, the potential upside gains on their investments are unlimited. Finally, most common stock returns are expected to fall near the market average. What we have just described is a "right-skewed" distribution rather than a normal distribution. Standard deviation insufficiently characterizes the risk of a right-skewed security, ignoring the fact that most of the security's volatility is on the "good" side of the security's expected return.

Interestingly, a simple mathematical transformation can often convert a right-skewed distribution to a normal distribution. If we add 1.0 to a security's return and then compute the natural logarithm of this value, the resulting transformed return distribution may appear to be normally distributed. Consequently, researchers are often concerned with whether security returns are "lognormally" distributed rather than normally distributed. Although the empirical evidence is open to debate, most observers consider lognormality to adequately characterize common stock returns.

Unfortunately, the returns on certain types of securities are neither normally nor lognormally distributed. The most obvious are options (see Chapter 19). For example, a call option allows the owner, for a price, to participate in positive returns on an underlying asset, but avoid the asset's negative returns. Essentially, a call option truncates the underlying asset's return distribution at the point where losses begin. The investor then owns only the "good" or right side of the return distribution. The returns on a call option are definitely not normally distributed.

Moreover, some securities have options embedded in them. For example, callable bonds (see Chapter 14) allow issuers to redeem them at the issuer's discretion. They do so only if interest rates move in their favour. Home mortgages in the US (which are often packaged and sold in pass-through securities—see Chapter 13) have similar prepayment features. Therefore, their returns are also not normally distributed.

If we wish to explicitly focus only on the likelihood of undesirable investment results in defining and measuring risk, what alternatives are available? The simplest answer is called *shortfall probability*. It measures the chances that a security's return will fall short of the expected return. Essentially, it is the proportion of the probability distribution lying to the left of the expected return.

More complex downside risk measures are provided by a family of statistics known as *lower partial moments*, or LPMs. For example, *mean shortfall* measures the average deviation of a security's returns below the expected return. Mean shortfall is more useful than shortfall probability because it takes into account the distance of each downside return from the expected return. That is, shortfall probability tells us only how likely it is that a security's return may fall below the expected return. Mean shortfall

tells us how far below the expected return that shortfall is likely to be.

Semivariance is analogous to variance, but only those potential returns below the expected return are used in its calculation. As semivariance is the average squared deviation below the expected return, it penalizes securities with relatively large potential shortfalls.

Applied to securities with non-normal (and non-lognormal) return distributions, these downside risk measures are not only more intuitively appealing but are more flexible in their application than the traditional risk measures. Standard deviation is measured from the mean of the return distribution. However, an investor may want to evaluate investments using some other value as a target, such as the return on a market index or an absolute number such as 0%. Downside risk measures can accommodate these preferences.

However, downside risk measures have their own problems. In particular, they ignore the nature of an investment's possible outcomes above the target return. An alternative to using downside risk measures is to directly bring skewness into the evaluation of an investment. That is, we might assume that investors analyze potential investments not only on the basis of their expected returns and standard deviations, but also on their amount of right-skewness. In essence, risk becomes multidimensional; it includes both standard deviation and skewness. If two investments have the same expected return and standard deviation, the most right-skewed investment would be preferred.

No one risk measure can be expected to function well in all circumstances. Standard deviation has proved effective in the majority of the situations encountered by practitioners. In those cases where it is inadequate, alternatives must be considered not only in light of how well they describe the return distribution, but also in terms of the complexity that they add to the analysis.

appears in both row 1 of column 3 and row 3 of column 1, and 104 appears in both row 2 of column 3 and row 3 of column 2. The reason for this feature is quite simple—the covariance between two securities does not depend on the order in which the two securities are specified. This means that, for example, the covariance between the first and second securities is the same as the covariance between the second and first securities.[13]

Summary

1. The Markowitz approach to portfolio selection assumes that investors seek both maximum expected return for a given level of risk and minimum uncertainty (risk) for a given level of expected return.
2. Expected return serves as the measure of potential reward associated with a portfolio. Standard deviation is viewed as the measure of a portfolio's risk.
3. The relationship between an investor's utility (satisfaction) and wealth is described by the investor's utility of wealth function. The assumption of nonsatiation requires the utility of wealth function to be upward sloping.
4. Risk-averse investors will have diminishing marginal utility. Each extra unit of wealth provides the risk-averse investor with additional, but increasingly smaller, amounts of utility.
5. An indifference curve represents the various combinations of risk and return that the investor finds equally desirable.
6. Risk-averse investors are assumed to consider any portfolio lying on an indifference curve "further to the northwest" more desirable than any portfolio lying on an indifference curve that is "not as far northwest."
7. The assumptions of investor nonsatiation and risk aversion cause indifference curves to be positively sloped and convex.
8. The expected return on a portfolio is a weighted average of the expected returns of its component securities, with the relative portfolio proportions of the component securities serving as weights.
9. Covariance and correlation measure the extent to which two random variables "move together."
10. The standard deviation of a portfolio depends on the standard deviations and proportions of the component securities as well as their covariances with one another.

APPENDIX A

CHARACTERISTICS OF PROBABILITY DISTRIBUTIONS

Chapter 6 introduced the concepts of expected return and risk for a portfolio of securities. That discussion presumes that the reader has some familiarity with probability distributions and the measures of central tendency and dispersion. This appendix is designed to provide a brief overview of these and other statistical concepts. Additional information can be obtained by consulting an introductory statistics textbook.

---

[13]For any variance-covariance matrix there is an implied correlation matrix that can be determined by using the data in the variance-covariance matrix and equation (6.5). Specifically, this equation can be used to show that the correlation between any two securities i and j is equal to $\sigma_{ij}/\sigma_i\sigma_j$. The values of σ_{ij}, σ_i, and σ_j can be obtained from the variance-covariance matrix. For example $\rho_{12} = 187/(\sqrt{146} \times \sqrt{854}) = .53$.

Probability Distributions

A probability distribution describes the possible values that a random variable might take on and the associated probabilities of those values occurring. A discrete probability distribution displays a finite number of possible values that the random variable might assume. For example, in a classroom the possible amounts of money that students might have in their pockets would constitute a discrete probability distribution, as the smallest unit of currency that any student might hold is $.01. A continuous probability distribution, on the other hand, contains an infinite number of values for the random variable. For example, the distribution of temperatures that might occur during the day is described by a continuous probability distribution, as one can always divide temperature into smaller and smaller fractions of a degree.

Table 6.3 presents information regarding the probability distribution for Alpha Company's common stock returns, where there are assumed to be seven different "states of nature," or simply, "states" [column (1)]. In this example, Alpha stock can produce seven different returns [column (2)], depending on the state that occurs. The probability of each return occurring is also shown in the table [column (3)]. Note that the sum of the probabilities is 1.0—there is a 100% chance that one of these returns will occur. The probability distribution of Alpha's stock returns is graphed in Figure 6.7. Typically distributions such as this one are estimated (in reality, distributions of economic variables are almost never known) by using either past data or intuition or both.

A probability distribution is characterized by a number of measures. Two of the most important such characteristics relate to the central tendency and dispersion of the probability distribution. They are discussed next.

Central Tendency

Median The outcome of a random variable where there is an equal probability of observing a value greater or less than it.

Mode The outcome of a random variable that has the highest probability of occurring.

The centre of a probability distribution is measured by several statistics. The **median** is the middle outcome of the distribution when the possible values of the random variable are arranged according to size. The **mode** is the most likely value. Finally, the expected value (or mean) is the weighted average value of the distribution, where all possible values are weighted by their respective probabilities of occurrence.

Inspecting Table 6.3, the median and the mode of Alpha Company stock both can quickly be identified as 5%. The expected value (or mean) is less obvious. It is calculated

Table 6.3

(1)	(2)	(3)	(4)	(5)	(6)	(7)
				Deviation from		
	Possible	Return		Expected	Squared	
State	Return	Probability	(2) x (3)	Return	Deviation	(3) x (6)
1	−10%	.07	−.7%	−15.0%	225	15.8
2	−5	.10	−.5	−10.0	100	10.0
3	0	.18	0	−5.0	25	4.5
4	5	.30	1.5	0.0	0	0.0
5	10	.18	1.8	5.0	25	4.5
6	15	.10	1.5	10.0	100	10.0
7	20	.07	1.4	15.0	225	15.8
		Expected Return	= 5.0%		Variance =	$60.6\%^2$

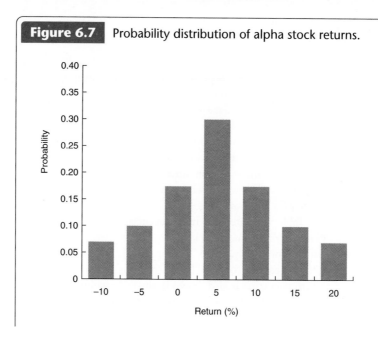

Figure 6.7 Probability distribution of alpha stock returns.

as the sum of the products of each of the possible values times their associated probabilities. That is:

$$EV = \sum_{i=1}^{N} p_i X_i$$

where:

$x_i = i^{\text{th}}$ possible value for the random variable

p_i = probability of the ith value occurring

N = number of possible values that the random variable might take on (that is, the number of states)

In the case of Alpha Company, the expected return on its stock is found by multiplying each possible return by its associated probability [column (4)]. The expected return for Alpha stock is:

$$\bar{r}_{\text{Alpha}} = \sum_{i=1}^{7} p_i r_i$$

Table 6.3 displays the results of this calculation, with the expected return on Alpha's stock equal to 5%. (Note that the equality of the median, mode, and expected value is a feature of a random variable having a normal distribution.)

Dispersion

The dispersion of possible values around the expected value is measured by the variance (and equivalently, the standard deviation) of the probability distribution. The probability distributions of two random variables can have the same expected value, yet one can have a much smaller variance (or standard deviation) than the other. This means that the values of the less dispersed random variable are less likely to stray from the expected value of its probability distribution than are those of the random variable with the higher variance (or standard deviation).

The variance of a random variable is calculated as the weighted average of the squared deviations from the expected value of the random variable. The weights assigned to those deviations are the probabilities of the particular values occurring. That is:

$$\sigma^2 = \sum_{i=1}^{N} p_i(X_i - EV)$$

In the case of Alpha Company's stock, its variance of returns is found by solving:

$$\sigma_{\text{Alpha}}^2 = \sum_{i=1}^{7} p_i(r_i - \bar{r}_{\text{Alpha}})^2$$

The results of that calculation are shown in columns (5) to (7) of Table 6.3. The expected return of 5% is subtracted from each of the seven possible Alpha returns [column (5)]. The resulting value is squared [column (6)] and multiplied by the probability of that particular return occurring [column (7)]. Finally, the sum of the squared deviations is computed to arrive at a variance of 60.6%².

The variance is calculated in units that are similar to those used to calculate the expected value of the random variable. However, because the variance is an average squared deviation, these units are squared. Conceptually, this causes some difficulty for users attempting to interpret variance, as the units of "return squared" or "percent return squared" are not readily understood by most people. The standard deviation overcomes this problem by simply taking the square root of the variance, thus producing a statistic expressed in the same units as the expected value. That is:

$$\sigma = \sqrt{\sum_{i=1}^{N} p_i(X_i - EV)^2}$$

Taking the square root of the variance of returns for Alpha Company gives:

$$\sigma_{\text{Alpha}} = \sqrt{\sigma_{\text{Alpha}}}$$
$$= \sqrt{(60.6\%)^2} = 7.8\%$$

Note how the units of measurement are "percent," just like the units used to measure Alpha's expected return.

Comovement

Covariance measures the tendency for two random variables to move together (covary). Instead of referring to the probability distribution for a single random variable, covariance considers the joint probability distribution of two random variables. That is, in a given state both random variables assume particular values. The joint probability distribution describes what those pairs of values are for each possible state and the probabilities of those outcomes occurring. Covariance is found by computing the weighted average of the product of the deviations of two random variables from their respective expected values. The weights assigned to these joint deviations are the probabilities of the two random variables taking on their associated joint values. That is:

$$\sigma_{xy} = \sum_{i=1}^{N} p_i(X_i - EV_X)(Y_i - EV_Y)$$

In the case of variance, the ith outcome referred to the value the random variable takes on when the ith state occurs. In the case of covariance, the ith outcome refers to the values that both random variables X and Y take on when the ith state occurs.

Continuing with the example of Alpha Company, consider now a second company's stock, that of Omega Company. Table 6.4 shows that corresponding to each of the seven possible returns on Alpha stock [column (2)], Omega stock has its own corresponding return [column (3)]. As an exercise, the reader can calculate the expected returns and standard deviation of returns for Omega Company, which are respectively, 11.8% and 5.9%. Computing the deviations of both Alpha and Omega's returns from their expected values for each of the seven possible outcomes [columns (5) and (6)], taking the product of those two deviations for each possible outcome [column (7)], multiplying the product by the probability of the outcome occurring [column (8)], and finally summing across all seven states gives the covariance between Alpha and Omega stock. That is, the covariance of Alpha and Omega's returns equals:

$$\sigma_{Alpha,\,Omega} = \sum_{i=1}^{7} p_i(r_{Alpha} - \bar{r}_{Alpha})(r_{Omega} - \bar{r}_{Omega})$$

which, as shown in the table, equals $-41.5\%^2$. Note that the units of measurement here are "percent return squared," just like the units used to measure variance are.

Once the covariance of Alpha's and Omega's returns have been calculated, it is a simple matter to compute the correlation between their returns. In general, this calculation is given by:

$$\rho_{xy} = \frac{\sigma_{xy}}{\sigma_x \sigma_y}$$

In the case of Alpha and Omega, the correlation is calculated to be

$$\rho_{Alpha,\,Omega} = \frac{-41.5}{7.8 \times 5.9} = -.90$$

APPENDIX B

RISK-NEUTRAL AND RISK-SEEKING INVESTORS

Earlier, it was mentioned that the Markowitz approach assumes that investors are risk-averse. Although this is a reasonable assumption to make, it is not necessary to do so. Alternatively, it can be assumed that investors are either risk-neutral or risk-seeking.

Risk-seeking Investor An investor who prefers an investment with more risk over one with less risk, assuming that both investments offer the same expected return.

Consider the **risk-seeking investor** first. This investor, when faced with a fair gamble, will want to take the gamble. Furthermore, larger gambles are more desirable than smaller gambles. This is because the utility (or "pleasure") derived from winning is greater than the disutility (or "displeasure") derived from losing. Because there is an equal chance of winning and losing, on balance the risk-seeking investor will want to take the gamble. What this means is that when faced with two portfolios that have the same expected return, this type of investor will choose the one with the higher standard deviation. Such investors have utility functions that are upward sloping and convex.

For example, in choosing between two portfolios with the same expected return, but different standard deviations, the risk-seeking investor will choose the portfolio with the higher standard deviation. This suggests that the risk-seeking investor will have negatively sloped indifference curves.[14] In addition, risk-seeking investors will prefer to be on the

---

[14]It can also be shown that for a risk-seeking investor, these indifference curves will be concave, meaning that their slopes decrease when moving from left to right along any particular one. The underlying rationale for concavity lies in utility theory; see footnote 7.

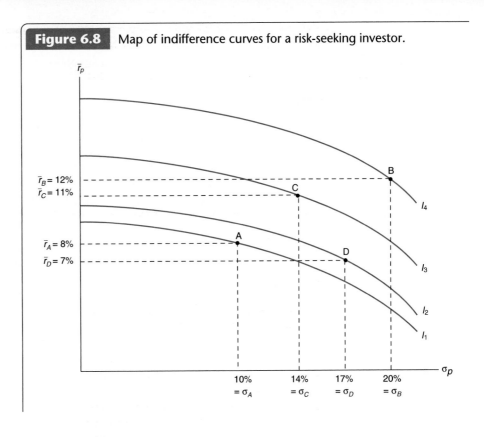

Figure 6.8 Map of indifference curves for a risk-seeking investor.

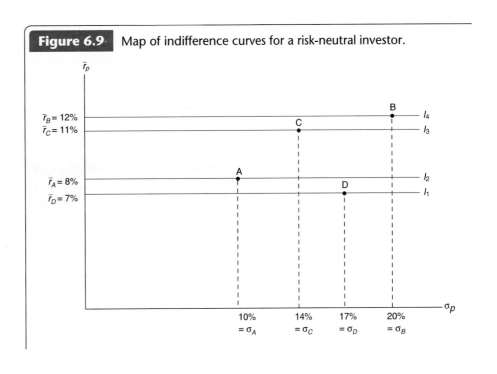

Figure 6.9 Map of indifference curves for a risk-neutral investor.

indifference curve that is "furthest northeast." Figure 6.8 illustrates a map of the indifference curves for a hypothetical risk-seeking investor. As shown in the figure, when choosing between A, B, C, and D (the same four portfolios shown in Figure 6.1), this investor will choose B.

Table 6.4

(1) State	(2) Alpha Possible Return	(3) Omega Possible Return	(4) Outcome Probability	(5) Alpha Deviations	(6) Omega Deviation	(7) (5) x (6) Deviation Products	(8) (4) x (7)
1	−10%	25%	.07%	−15.0%	13.3%	−199.5	−14.0
2	−5	15	.10	−10.0	3.3	−33.0	−3.3
3	0	18	.18	−5.0	6.3	−31.5	−5.7
4	5	10	.30	0.0	−1.8	0.0	0.0
5	10	7	.18	5.0	−4.8	−24.0	−4.3
6	15	10	.10	10.0	−1.8	−18.0	−1.8
7	20	0	.07	15.0	−11.8	−177.0	−12.4
	Expected Return = 5.0%	Expected Return = 11.8%					Covariance = −41.5%^{2}

Risk-neutral Investor An investor who has no preference between investments with varying levels of risk, assuming that the investments offer the same expected return.

The risk-neutral case lies between the risk-seeking and risk-averse cases. While the risk-averse investor does not want to take fair gambles and the risk-seeking investor does want to take such gambles, the risk-neutral investor does not care whether or not the gamble is taken. This means that risk, or more specifically, standard deviation, is unimportant to the risk-neutral investor in evaluating portfolios. Accordingly, the indifference curves for such investors are horizontal lines as shown in Figure 6.9. These investors prefer to be on the indifference curve that is "furthest north." When faced with the choice of A, B, C, and D, such an investor will choose B, because it has the highest expected return. Such investors have utility functions that are upward sloping and straight.

Whereas investors can be either risk-seeking or risk-neutral, there is evidence to suggest that they are more accurately characterized as being, in general, risk-averse. One piece of evidence is the observation that equities have historically had higher average returns than bonds, suggesting that investors have had to be induced with higher rewards in order to get them to make riskier purchases.

QUESTIONS AND PROBLEMS

1. Why must it be the case that an investor with diminishing marginal utility of wealth is risk-averse?
2. Listed below are a number of portfolios and expected returns, standard deviations, and the amount of satisfaction (measured in utils) these portfolios provide Art Vaughn. Given this information, graph Art's identifiable indifference curves.

Portfolio	Expected Return	Standard Deviation	Utility
1	5%	0%	10 utils
2	6	10	10
3	9	20	10
4	14	30	10
5	10	0	20
6	11	10	20
7	14	20	20
8	19	30	20
9	15	0	30
10	16	10	30
11	19	20	30
12	24	30	30

3. Why are the indifference curves of typical investors assumed to slope upward to the right?

4. What does a set of convex indifference curves imply about an investor's tradeoff between risk and return as the amount of risk varies?

5. Why are typical investors assumed to prefer portfolios on indifference curves lying to the "northwest"?

6. What is meant by the statement that "risk-averse investors exhibit diminishing marginal utility of income"? Why does diminishing marginal utility cause an investor to refuse to accept a "fair bet"?

7. Explain why an investor's indifference curves cannot intersect.

8. Why are the indifference curves of more risk-averse investors more steeply sloped than those of investors with less risk aversion?

9. Consider the following two sets of indifference curves for investors Helen Wilson and Kathy Culver. Determine whether Helen or Kathy:

   a. Is more risk-averse.
   b. Prefers investment A to investment B.
   c. Prefers investment C to investment D.

   Explain the reasons for your answers.

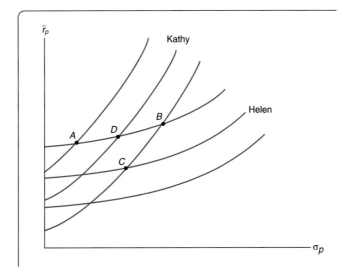

10. Consider four stocks with the following expected returns and standard deviations:

Stock	Expected Return	Standard Deviation
A	15%	12%
B	13	8
C	14	7
D	16	11

Are any of these stocks preferred over another by a risk-averse investor?

11. Do you agree with the assumptions of nonsatiation and risk aversion? Make a case for or against these assumptions.

12. At the beginning of the year, Chris Bradley owned four securities in the following amounts and with the following current and expected end-of-year prices:

Security	Share Amount	Current Price	Expected Year-End Price
A	100	$50	$60
B	200	35	40
C	50	25	50
D	100	100	110

What is the expected return on Chris's portfolio for the year?

13. Given the following information about four stocks comprising a portfolio, calculate each stock's expected return. Then, using these individual security's expected returns, calculate the portfolio's expected return.

Stock	Initial Investment Value	Expected End-of-Period Investment Value	Proportion of Portfolio Initial Market Value
A	$ 500	$ 700	19.2%
B	200	300	7.7
C	1000	1000	38.5
D	900	1500	34.6

14. Alice Procino has been considering an investment in Oakdale Merchandising. Alice has estimated the following probability distribution of returns for Oakdale stock:

Return	Probability
−10%	.10
0	.25
10	.40
20	.20
30	.05

Based on Alice's estimates, calculate the expected return and standard deviation of Oakdale stock.

15. The expected returns and standard deviations of stocks A and B are:

Stock	Expected Return	Standard Deviation
A	13%	10%
B	5	18

Max McQuarry buys $20 000 of stock A and sells short $10 000 of stock B, using all of the proceeds to buy more of stock A. The correlation between the two securities is .25. What are the expected return and standard deviation of Max's portfolio?

16. Both the covariance and the correlation coefficient measure the extent to which the returns on securities move together. What is the relationship between the two statistical measures? Why is the correlation coefficient a more convenient measure?

17. Give an example of two common stocks that you would expect to exhibit a relatively low correlation. Then give an example of two that would have a relatively high correlation.

18. Nancy Brock has estimated the following joint probability distribution of returns for investments in the stock of Lakeland Halfway Homes and Afton Brewery:

Lakeland	Afton	Probability
−10%	15%	.15
5	10	.20
10	5	.30
20	0	.35

Based on Nancy's estimates, calculate the covariance and correlation coefficient between the two investments.

19. Calculate the correlation matrix that corresponds to the variance-covariance matrix given in the test for Able, Baker, and Charlie.

20. Given the following variance-covariance matrix for three securities, as well as the percentage of the portfolio that each security comprises, calculate the portfolio's standard deviation.

	Security A	Security B	Security C
Security A	459	−211	112
Security B	−211	312	215
Security C	112	215	179
	$X_A = .50$	$X_B = .30$	$X_C = .20$

21. Ruth Bressler owns three stocks and has estimated the following joint probability distribution of returns:

Outcome	Stock A	Stock B	Stock C	Probability
1	−10	10	0	.30
2	0	10	10	.20
3	10	5	15	.30
4	20	−10	5	.20

Calculate the portfolio's expected return and standard deviation if Ruth invests 20% in stock A, 50% in stock B, and 30% in stock C. Assume that each security's return is completely uncorrelated with the returns of the other securities.

22. If a portfolio's expected return is equal to the weighted average of the expected returns of the component securities, why is a portfolio's risk not generally equal to the weighted average of the component securities' standard deviations?

23. When is the standard deviation of a portfolio equal to the weighted average of the standard deviation of the component securities? Show this mathematically for a two-security portfolio. (Hint: Some algebra is necessary to solve this problem. Remember that $\sigma_{ij} = \rho_{ij}\sigma_i\sigma_j$. Try different values of ρ_{ij}.)

24. Consider two securities, A and B, with expected returns of 15% and 20%, respectively, and standard deviations of 30% and 40%, respectively. Calculate the standard deviation of a portfolio weighted equally between the two securities if their correlation is:
   a. 0.9
   b. 0.0
   c. −0.9

25. Listed here are estimates of the standard deviations and correlations coefficients for three stocks.

| | Standard | Correlation with Stock: | | |
Stock	Deviation	A	B	C
A	12%	1.00	−1.00	0.20
B	15	−1.00	1.00	−0.20
C	10	0.20	−0.20	1.00

   a. If a portfolio is composed of 20% of stock A and 80% of stock C, what is the portfolio's standard deviation?
   b. If a portfolio is composed of 40% of stock A, 20% of stock B, and 40% of stock C, what is the portfolio's standard deviation?
   c. If you were asked to design a portfolio using stocks A and B, what percentage investment in each stock would produce a zero standard deviation? [Hint: Some algebra is necessary to solve this problem. Remember that $X_B = (1 - X_A)$.]

26. (Appendix Question) Calculate the expected return, mode, and median for a stock having the following probability distribution:

Return	Probability of Occurrence
−40%	.03
−10	.07
0	.30
+15	.10
+30	.05
+40	.20
+50	.25

27. (Appendix Question) Bob Schmitz has estimated the following probability distribution of next year's dividend payments for Mauston Inc.'s stock. According to Bob, what is the standard deviation of Mauston's dividend?

Dividend	Probability
$1.90	.05
1.95	.15
2.00	.30
2.05	.30
2.10	.15
2.15	.05

28. (Appendix Question) Given the following joint probability distribution of returns for Securities A and B, calculate the covariance between the two securities:

State	Security A	Security B	Probability
1	10%	20%	.10
2	12	25	.25
3	8	33	.35
4	14	27	.20
5	19	22	.10

29. (Appendix Question) Using the data given in Tables 6.3 and 6.4, calculate the correlation coefficient between the returns on Alpha and Omega stock.

KEY TERMS

holding period (p. 129)
expected return (p. 129)
risk (p. 129)
initial wealth (p. 130)
terminal wealth (p. 130)
random variable (p. 130)
expected value (p. 130)
standard deviation (p. 130)
variance (p. 130)
nonsatiation (p. 131)
risk-averse investor (p. 132)
utility (p. 132)
marginal utility (p. 132)

certainty equivalent (p. 134)
risk premium (p. 134)
indifference curve (p. 135)
expected return vector (p. 142)
probability distribution (p. 142)
normal distribution (p. 142)
covariance (p. 143)
correlation coefficient (p. 143)
variance-covariance matrix (p. 145)
median (p. 149)
mode (p. 149)
risk-seeking investor (p. 152)
risk-neutral investor (p. 154)

REFERENCES

1. The seminal work developing the mean-variance model is credited to Harry Markowitz, co-winner of the 1990 Nobel prize in economics, who developed his ideas in a paper and later in a book:

Harry M. Markowitz, "Portfolio Selection," *Journal of Finance* 7, no. 1 (March 1952): 77–91.

Harry M. Markowitz, *Portfolio Selection: Efficient Diversification of Investments* (New York: John Wiley, 1959). A reprint of this book that also contains some new material is available form Basil Blackwell, in Cambridge, MA; its copyright date is 1991.

2. While utility theory can be traced back to the work of Daniel Bernoulli in the early part of the eighteenth century, the modern notion of utility theory was developed in:

John von Neumann and Oskar Morgenstern, *Theory of Games and Economic Behavior* (New York: John Wiley, 1944).

Kenneth J. Arrow, *Essays in the Theory of Risk-Bearing* (Chicago: Markham, 1971).

3. Significant other work in utility theory is reviewed in:

Paul J. H. Schoemaker, "The Expected Utility Model: Its Variants, Purposes, Evidence and Limitations," *Journal of Economic Literature* 20, no. 2 (June 1982): 529–563.

4. For an introduction to uncertainty and utility theory, see:

Mark Kritzman, "...About Uncertainty," *Financial Analysts Journal* 47, no. 2 (March–April 1991): 17–21.

Mark Kritzman, "...About Utility," *Financial Analysts Journal* 48, no. 3 (May–June 1992): 17–20.

5. For a description of various alternative measures of risk, see:

Mark Kritzman, "...About Higher Moments," *Financial Analysts Journal* 50, no. 5 (September–October 1994): 10–17.

Leslie A. Balzer, "Measuring Investment Risk: A Review," *Journal of Investing* 4, no. 3 (Fall 1995): 5–16.

Frank A. Sortino and Hal J. Forsey, "On the Use and Misuse of Downside Risk," *Journal of Portfolio Management* 22, no. 2 (Winter 1996): 35–43.

Robert A. Olsen, "Investment Risk: The Experts' Perspective," *Financial Analysts Journal* 53, no. 2 (March–April 1997): 62–66.

CHAPTER 7

Portfolio Analysis

The previous chapter introduced the portfolio selection problem that every investor faces. It also introduced the investment approach of Harry Markowitz as a method of solving that problem. With this approach, an investor should evaluate alternative portfolios on the basis of their expected returns and standard deviations by using indifference curves. In the case of a risk-averse investor, the portfolio with the indifference curve that is the "furthest northwest" would be the one selected for investment.

However, the previous chapter left certain questions unanswered. In particular, how can Markowitz's approach be used once it is recognized that there are an infinite number of portfolios available for investment? What happens when the investor considers investing in a set of securities, one of which is riskless? What happens when the investor is allowed to buy securities on margin? This chapter and the next one will provide the answers to these questions, beginning with the first one.

The Efficient Set Theorem

As mentioned earlier, an infinite number of portfolios can be formed from a set of N securities. Consider the situation with Able, Baker, and Charlie companies where N is equal to 3. The investor could purchase just shares of Able or just shares of Baker. Alternatively, the investor could purchase a combination of shares of Able and Baker. For example, the investor could put 50% of his money in each company, or 25% in one company and 75% in the other, or 33% in one and 67% in the other, or any percent (between 0% and 100%) in one company with the rest going into the other company. Without even considering investing in Charlie, there are already an infinite number of possible portfolios in which to invest.[1]

Does the investor need to evaluate all these portfolios? Fortunately, the answer to this question is no. The key to why the investor needs to look at only a subset of the available portfolios lies in the **efficient set theorem**, which states that:

Efficient Set Theorem
The proposition that investors will choose their portfolios only from the set of efficient portfolios.

---

[1] This can be seen by noting that there are an infinite number of points on the real number line between 0 and 100. If these numbers are thought of as representing the percentage of the investor's funds going into shares of Able, with 100 minus this number going into Baker, it can be seen that there are an infinite number of portfolios that could be formed from just two different securities. In making this assertion, however, it has been assumed that an investor can buy a fraction of a share if he so desires. For example, the investor can buy not only one or two or three shares of Able but also 1.1 or 1.01 or 1.001 shares.

An investor will choose his optimal portfolio from the set of portfolios that:
1. Offer maximum expected return for varying levels of risk, and
2. Offer minimum risk for varying levels of expected return.

The set of portfolios meeting these two conditions is known as the **efficient set**, or *efficient frontier*.

The Feasible Set

Figure 7.1 provides an illustration of the location of the **feasible set**, also known as the *opportunity set*, from which the efficient set can be located. The feasible set simply represents the set of all portfolios that could be formed from a group of N securities. That is, all possible portfolios that could be formed from the N securities lie either on or within the boundary of the feasible set (the points denoted by G, E, S, and H in the figure are examples of such portfolios). In general, this set will have an umbrella-type shape similar to the one shown by the figure. Depending on the particular securities involved, it may be more to the right or left, higher or lower, or fatter or skinnier than indicated here. The point is that its shape will, except in perverse circumstances, look similar to what appears here.

The Efficient Set Theorem Applied to the Feasible Set

The efficient set can now be located by applying the efficient set theorem to this feasible set. First, the set of portfolios that meet the first condition of the efficient set theorem must be identified. Looking at Figure 7.1, there is no portfolio offering less risk than that of portfolio E. This is because if a vertical line were drawn through E, there would be no point in the feasible set to the left of the line. Also, there is no portfolio offering more risk than that of portfolio H. This is because if a vertical line were drawn through H, there would be no point in the feasible set to the right of the line. Thus, the set of portfolios offering maximum expected return for varying levels of risk is the set of portfolios lying on the "northern" boundary of the feasible set between points E and H.

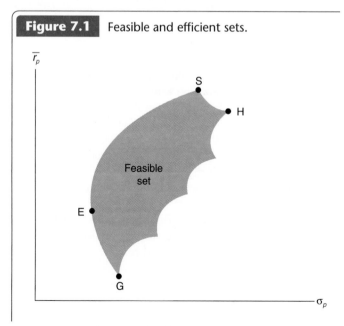

Figure 7.1 Feasible and efficient sets.

Considering the second condition next, there is no portfolio offering an expected return greater than portfolio S, since no point in the feasible set lies above a horizontal line going through S. Similarly, there is no portfolio offering a lower expected return than portfolio G, since no point in the feasible set lies below a horizontal line going through G. Thus, the set of portfolios offering minimum risk for varying levels of expected return is the set of portfolios lying on the "western" boundary of the feasible set between points G and S.

Remembering that both conditions have to be met in order to identify the efficient set, it can be seen that only those portfolios lying on the "northwest" boundary between points E and S do so. Accordingly, these portfolios form the efficient set, and it is from this set of **efficient portfolios** that the investor will find his optimal one.[2] All the other feasible portfolios are **inefficient** and can be safely ignored.

Selection of the Optimal Portfolio

How will the investor select an **optimal portfolio**? As shown in Figure 7.2, the investor should plot her indifference curves on the same figure as the efficient set and then choose the portfolio that is on the indifference curve that is furthest northwest. This portfolio will correspond to the point where an indifference curve is just tangent to the efficient set. As can be seen in the figure, this is portfolio O* on indifference curve I_2. Although the investor would prefer a portfolio on I_3, no such portfolio exists, and so wanting to be on this indifference curve is just wishful thinking. In regard to I_1, there are several portfolios that the investor could choose (for example, O). However, the figure shows that portfolio O* dominates these portfolios, since it is on an indifference curve that is further northwest. Figure 7.3 shows how the highly risk-averse investor will choose a portfolio close to E. Figure 7.4 shows that the slightly risk-averse investor will choose a portfolio close to S.[3]

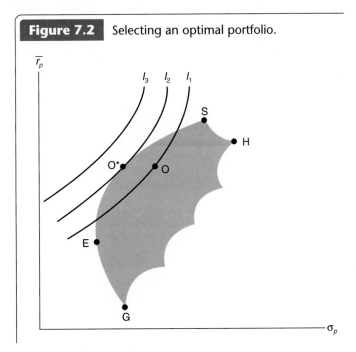

Figure 7.2 Selecting an optimal portfolio.

Upon reflection, the efficient set theorem is quite rational. In Chapter 6, it was shown that the investor should select the portfolio that puts her on the indifference curve furthest northwest. The efficient set theorem, stating that the investor need not be concerned

---

[2]In order to determine the compositions of the portfolios on the efficient set, the investor must solve a quadratic programming problem. See Markowitz's book entitled *Portfolio Selection* (cited at the end of the chapter), particularly pp. 176–185.

[3]The risk-neutral investor will choose portfolio S, whereas the risk-seeking investor will choose either S or H.

The Trouble with Optimizers

Suppose that the captain of a modern luxury liner chose not to use the ship's state-of-the-art navigational system (a system that employs computers to triangulate off geostationary-orbiting satellites, thereby estimating the ship's position accurately to within a few feet). Instead, suppose that the captain chose to rely on the old-fashioned method of navigating by the stars, an antiquated method fraught with problems and imprecision. Most people would view the captain's choice as, at best, eccentric and, at worst, highly dangerous.

When it comes to constructing portfolios, many investment managers make a choice analogous to that of the ship's captain. They reject computer-based portfolio construction methods in favour of traditional approaches. Are their decisions as foolhardy as the captain's? Or is there a method to their apparent madness?

As this chapter discusses, the concepts of the efficient set and the investor's optimal portfolio are central to modern investment theory. But how can investors actually go about estimating the efficient set and selecting their optimal portfolios? Harry Markowitz first described the solution in the early 1950s. Using a mathematical technique called *quadratic programming*, investors can process expected returns, standard deviations, and covariances to calculate the efficient set (see Appendix A to this chapter). Given an estimate of their indifference curves (as reflected in their individual risk tolerances—see Chapter 23), they can then select a portfolio from the efficient set.

Simple, right? Certainly not in the 1950s. Given the data-processing facilities available to investors at that time, calculating the efficient set for even a few hundred securities was essentially impossible. However, with the advent of low-cost, high-speed computers in the 1980s and the development of sophisticated risk models (see Chapter 10), an efficient set can be created for thousands of securities in a matter of minutes. The necessary computer hardware and software are available to virtually every institutional investor at a relatively low cost. In fact, the process has become so commonplace that it has acquired its own terminology. Using a computer to identify the efficient set and select an optimal portfolio is colloquially known as using an "optimizer." Portfolios are "optimized" and investors are said to apply "optimization techniques."

Despite the technology's widespread availability, relatively few investment managers actually use an optimizer to build portfolios. Instead, they rely for the most part on a series of qualitative rules and judgments.

Why do investment managers resist applying optimization techniques to portfolio building? Ignorance is not the answer. Most investment managers are well aware of Markowitz's portfolio selection concepts and the available technology, having graduated from business schools where these ideas are discussed in detail. Instead, the resistance derives from two sources: territorial concerns and implementation inadequacies.

From a territorial perspective, many investment managers are simply not comfortable with a quantitative approach to investing. Their decision-making emphasizes intuition and complex subjective judgments. The application of optimization techniques to portfolio construction imposes a very systematic and formal decision-making structure. Security analysts must become responsible for generating quantifiable expected return and risk forecasts. Portfolio managers must implement the decisions of a computer. As a result, the optimizer destroys the "artistry and grace" of investment management.

Further, with the introduction of an optimizer, a new breed of investment professional gains influence—the quantitative analyst (derisively called a "quant")—who coordinates the collection and application of risk and return estimates. Authority gained by quantitative analysts diminishes the influence of the traditional security analysts and portfolio managers, much to their consternation.

From the implementation perspective, serious problems have arisen with optimizers in practice. In particular, they tend to produce counterintuitive, uninvestable portfolios. This situation is not so much a problem with optimizers as it is the fault of the human operators supplying inputs to the optimizers. Here the GIGO (garbage in, garbage out) paradigm rules.

By their design, optimizers are attracted to securities with high expected returns, low standard deviations, and low covariances with other securities. Often this information is derived from historical databases covering thousands of securities. Unless the risk and return data are carefully checked, errors (for example, understating a security's standard deviation) can easily lead the optimizer to recommend purchases of securities for erroneous reasons. Even if the data are "clean," extreme historical values for some securities may lead the optimizer astray.

Unless programmed to take transaction costs into account, optimizers also display a nasty habit of generating high turnover and recommending investments in illiquid securities. *High turnover* refers to significant changes in portfolio composition from one period to the next. High turnover can result in unacceptably large transaction costs (see Chapter 3), thereby hindering portfolio performance. *Liquidity* refers to the ability to actually buy the securities selected by the optimizer. Selected securities may possess desirable risk-return characteristics but may not trade in sufficient volume to permit institutional investors to purchase them without incurring sizeable transaction costs.

Solutions to these implementation problems do exist, ranging from checking data carefully to placing constraints on maximum turnover or minimum liquidity. In the end, however, nothing can substitute for skillful judgmental forecasts of security returns and risks, balanced by properly applied notions of market equilibrium.

Territorial and implementation problems have given investment managers convenient reasons to avoid optimizers and stick to traditional portfolio construction methods. Nevertheless, the outlook for quantitative portfolio construction techniques is actually quite bright. The increasing efficiency of capital markets has forced institutional investment managers to process more information about more securities more rapidly than ever before. In response, they have generally increased their use of quantitative investment tools. While most do not directly integrate optimizers into their portfolio construction procedures, virtually all have become more sensitive to the objective of creating diversified portfolios that display the highest levels of expected return at acceptable levels of risk.

with portfolios that do not lie on the northwest boundary of the feasible set, is a logical consequence.

Indifference curves for the risk-averse investor were shown to be positively sloped and

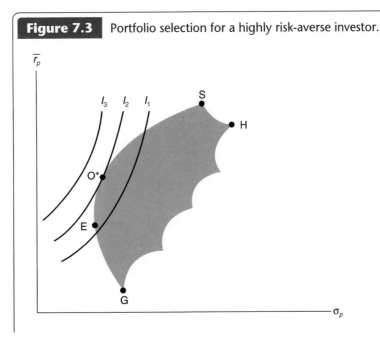

Figure 7.3   Portfolio selection for a highly risk-averse investor.

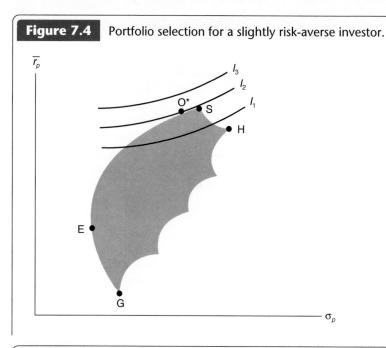

Figure 7.4 Portfolio selection for a slightly risk-averse investor.

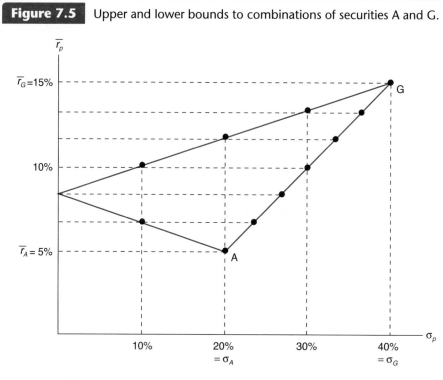

Figure 7.5 Upper and lower bounds to combinations of securities A and G.

convex in Chapter 6. Now it will be shown that the efficient set is generally concave, meaning that if a straight line is drawn between any two points on the efficient set, the straight line will lie below the efficient set. This feature of the efficient set is important because it means that there will be only one tangency point between the investor's indifference curves and the efficient set.

Concavity of the Efficient Set

In order to see why the efficient set is concave, consider the following two-security example. Security 1, the Ark Shipping Company, has an estimated expected return of 5% and standard deviation of 20%. Security 2, the Gold Jewelry Company, has an estimated expected return of 15% and standard deviation of 40%. Their respective locations are indicated by the letters A and G in Figure 7.5.

Bounds on the Location of Portfolios

Now consider all possible portfolios that an investor could purchase by combining these two securities. Let X_1 denote the proportion of the investor's funds invested in Ark Shipping and $X_2 = 1 - X_1$ denote the proportion invested in Gold Jewelry. Thus, if the investor purchased just Ark Shipping, then $X_1 = 1$ and $X_2 = 0$. Alternatively, if the investor purchased just Gold Jewelry, then $X_1 = 0$ and $X_2 = 1$. A combination of .17 in Ark Shipping and .83 in Gold Jewelry is also possible, as are respective combinations of .33 and .67, and .50 and .50. Although there are many other possibilities, only the following seven portfolios will be considered:

	Portfolio A	Portfolio B	Portfolio C	Portfolio D	Portfolio E	Portfolio F	Portfolio G
X_1	1.00	.83	.67	.50	.33	.17	.00
X_2	.00	.17	.33	.50	.67	.83	1.00

In order to consider these seven portfolios for possible investment, their expected returns and standard deviations must be calculated. All the necessary information to calculate the expected returns for these portfolios is at hand. In doing so, equation (6.3a) must be utilized:

$$\bar{r}_p = \sum_{i=1}^{N} X_i \bar{r}_i$$

$$= \sum_{i=1}^{2} X_i \bar{r}_i \qquad (6.3a)$$

$$= X_1 \bar{r}_1 + X_2 \bar{r}_2$$

$$= (X_1 \times 5\%) + (X_2 \times 15\%)$$

For portfolios A and G, this calculation is trivial, since the investor is purchasing shares of just one company. Thus, their expected returns are 5% and 15%, respectively. For portfolios B, C, D, E, and F, the expected returns are, respectively,

$$\bar{r}_B = (.83 \times 5\%) + (.17 \times 15\%)$$
$$= 6.70\%$$
$$\bar{r}_C = (.67 \times 5\%) + (.33 \times 15\%)$$
$$= 8.30\%$$
$$\bar{r}_D = (.50 \times 5\%) + (.50 \times 15\%)$$
$$= 10\%$$
$$\bar{r}_E = (.33 \times 5\%) + (.67 \times 15\%)$$
$$= 11.70\%$$
$$\bar{r}_F = (.17 \times 5\%) + (.83 \times 15\%)$$
$$= 13.30\%$$

In calculating the standard deviation of these seven portfolios, equation (6.7) is used:

$$\sigma_p = \left[\sum_{i=1}^{N} \sum_{j=1}^{N} X_i X_j \sigma_{ij} \right]^{1/2}$$

$$= \left[\sum_{i=1}^{2} \sum_{j=1}^{2} X_i X_j \sigma_{ij} \right]^{1/2} \qquad (6.7)$$

$$= [X_1 X_1 \sigma_{11} + X_1 X_2 \sigma_{12} + X_2 X_1 \sigma_{21} + X_2 X_2 \sigma_{22}]^{1/2}$$

$$= [X_1^2 \sigma_1^2 + X_2^2 \sigma_2^2 + 2 X_1 X_2 \sigma_{12}]^{1/2}$$

$$= [(X_1^2 \times 20\%^2) + (X_2^2 \times 40\%^2) + 2 X_1 X_2 \sigma_{12}]^{1/2}$$

For portfolios A and G, this calculation is trivial, since the investor is purchasing shares of just one company. Thus, their standard deviations are just 20% and 40%, respectively.

For portfolios B, C, D, E, and F, application of equation (6.7) indicates that the standard deviations depend on the magnitude of the covariance between the two securities. As shown in equation (6.5), this covariance term is equal to the correlation between the two securities multiplied by the product of their standard deviations:

$$\sigma_{12} = \rho_{12} \times \sigma_1 \times \sigma_2 \qquad (6.5)$$

$$= \rho_{12} \times 20\% \times 40\%$$

$$= 800 \rho_{12}$$

This means that the standard deviation of any portfolio consisting of Ark Shipping and Gold Jewelry can be expressed as

$$\sigma_p = [(X_1^2 \times 20\%^2) + (X_2^2 \times 40\%^2) + (2 X_1 X_2 \times 800 \rho_{12})]^{1/2} \qquad (7.1)$$

$$= [400 X_1^2 + 1600 X_2^2 + 1600 X_1 X_2 \rho_{12}]^{1/2}$$

Consider portfolio D first. The standard deviation of this portfolio will be somewhere between 10% and 30%, the exact value depending upon the size of the correlation coefficient. How were these bounds of 10% and 30% determined? First, note that for portfolio D, equation (7.1) reduces to

$$\sigma_D = [(400 \times .25) + (1600 \times .25) + (1600 \times .5 \times .5 \times \rho_{12})]^{1/2} \qquad (7.2)$$

$$= [500 + 400 \rho_{12}]^{1/2}$$

Inspection of equation (7.2) indicates that σ_D will be at a minimum when the correlation coefficient, ρ_{12}, is at a minimum. Now, remembering that the minimum value for any correlation coefficient is −1, it can be seen that the lower bound on σ_D is

$$\sigma_D = [500 + (400 \times -1)]^{1/2}$$

$$= [500 - 400]^{1/2}$$

$$= [100]^{1/2}$$

$$= 10\%$$

Similarly, inspection of equation (7.2) indicates that σ_D will be at a maximum when the correlation coefficient is at a maximum, which is +1. Thus, the upper bound on σ_D is

$$\sigma_D = [500 + (400 \times 1)]^{1/2}$$

$$= (500 + 400)^{1/2}$$

$$= (900)^{1/2}$$

$$= 30\%$$

In general, it can be seen from equation (7.1) that for any given set of weights X_1 and X_2, the lower and upper bounds will occur when the correlations between the two securities are −1 and +1, respectively. Applying the same analysis to the other portfolios reveals that their lower and upper bounds are as follows:

Portfolio	Standard Deviation of Portfolio	
	Lower Bound	Upper Bound
A	20%	20.00%
B	10	23.33
C	0	26.67
D	10	30.00
E	20	33.33
F	30	36.67
G	40	40.00

These values are shown in Figure 7.5.

Interestingly, the upper bounds all lie on a straight line connecting points A and G. This means that any portfolio consisting of these two securities cannot have a standard deviation that plots to the right of a straight line connecting the two securities. Instead, the standard deviation must lie on or to the left of the straight line. This observation suggests a motivation for diversifying a portfolio. Namely, *diversification generally leads to risk reduction*, since the standard deviation of a portfolio will generally be less than a weighted average of the standard deviations of the securities in the portfolio.

Also interesting is the observation that the lower bounds all lie on one of two line segments that go from point A to a point on the vertical axis corresponding to 8.30% and then to point G. This means that any portfolio consisting of these two securities cannot have a standard deviation that plots to the left of either of these two line segments. For example, portfolio B must lie on the horizontal line going through the vertical axis at 6.70% but bounded between the values of 10% and 23.33%.

▶ Actual Location of the Portfolios

In sum, any portfolio consisting of these two securities will lie within the triangle shown in Figure 7.5, with its actual location depending on the magnitude of the correlation coefficient between the two securities.

What if the correlation were zero? In this case, equation (7.1) reduces to

$$\sigma_p = [(400X_1^2) + (1600X_2^2) + (1600X_1X_2 \times 0)]^{1/2}$$
$$= [400X_1^2 + 1600X_2^2]^{1/2}$$

Applying the appropriate weights for X_1 and X_2, the standard deviation for portfolios B, C, D, E, and F can therefore be calculated as follows:

$$\sigma_B = [(400 \times .83^2) + (1600 \times .17^2)]^{1/2}$$
$$= 17.94\%$$
$$\sigma_C = [(400 \times .67^2) + (1600 \times .33^2)]^{1/2}$$
$$= 18.81\%$$
$$\sigma_D = [(400 \times .50^2) + (1600 \times .50^2)]^{1/2}$$
$$= 22.36\%$$
$$\sigma_E = [(400 \times .33^2) + (1600 \times .67^2)]^{1/2}$$
$$= 27.60\%$$
$$\sigma_F = [(400 \times .17^2) + (1600 \times .83^2)]^{1/2}$$
$$= 33.37\%$$

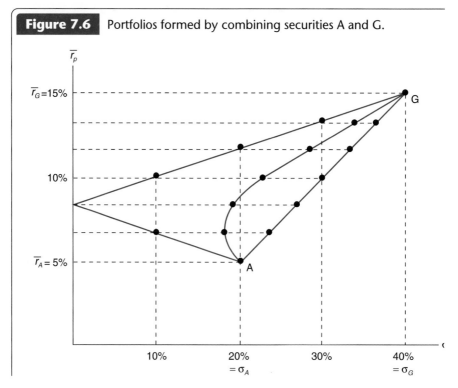

Figure 7.6 Portfolios formed by combining securities A and G.

Figure 7.6 indicates the location of these portfolios along with the upper and lower bounds that were shown in Figure 7.5. As can be seen, these portfolios—as well as all other possible portfolios consisting of Ark Shipping and Gold Jewelry—lie on a line that is curved or bowed to the left. Although not shown here, if the correlation were less than zero, the line would curve more to the left. If the correlation were greater than zero, it would not curve quite as much to the left. The important point of this figure is that as long as the correlation is less than +1 and greater than −1, the line representing the set of portfolios consisting of various combinations of the two securities will have some degree of curvature to the left. Furthermore, the northwest portion will be concave.

Similar analysis can be applied to a situation where there are more than two securities under consideration. When this is done, as long as the correlations are less than +1 and greater than −1, the northwest portion must be concave, just as it is in the two-security example.[4] Thus, in general, the efficient set will be concave.[5]

The Market Model

Suppose that the return on a common stock over a given time period (say, a month) is related to the return over the same period that is earned on a market index such as the widely cited TSE 300.[6] That is, if the market has gone up then it is likely that the stock has gone up, and if the market has gone down then it is likely that the stock has gone down. One way to capture this relationship is with the **market model**:

Market Model A simple linear model that expresses the relationship between the return on a security and the return on a market index.

---

[4]This "curvature property" can also be used to explain why the right-hand side of the feasible set has the umbrella shape noted in Figure 7.2. A more rigorous demonstration of concavity is contained in Appendix A.

[5]For a demonstration of why there cannot be a convex region on the efficient set, see Gordon J. Alexander and Jack Clark Francis, *Portfolio Analysis*, (Englewood Cliffs, NJ: Prentice Hall, 1986): 50–55.

[6]This is an example of a single-factor model where the factor is the return on a market index (see Chapter 10 for more on factor models; see Chapters 24 and 25 for more on market indices). The model is actually more generally

(continues on page 171)

$$r_i = \alpha_{iI} + \beta_{iI}r_I + \epsilon_{iI} \qquad (7.3)$$

where:

r_i = return on security i for some given period

r_I = return on market index I for the same period

α_{iI} = intercept term

β_{iI} = slope term

ϵ_{iI} = random error term

Assuming that the slope term β_{iI} is positive, equation (7.3) indicates that the higher the return on the market index, the higher the return on the security is likely to be. (Note that the expected value of the random error term is zero.)

Consider stock A, for example, which has α_{iI} = 2% and β_{iI} = 1.2. This means that the market model for stock A is

$$r_A = 2\% + 1.2r_I + \epsilon_{AI} \qquad (7.4)$$

so that if the market index has a return of 10%, the return on the security is expected to be 2% + (1.2 × 10%) = 14%. Similarly, if the market index's return is −5%, then the return on security A is expected to be 2% + (1.2 × −5%) = −4%.

Random Error Terms

Random Error Term The difference between the actual value of a random variable and the predicted value based on some model.

The term ϵ_{iI}, known as the **random error term** in equation (7.3), simply shows that the market model does not explain security returns perfectly. That is, when the market index goes up by 10% or down by 5%, the return on security A is not going to be exactly 14% or −4%, respectively. The difference between what the return actually is and what it is expected to be, given the return on the market index, is attributed to the effect of the random error term. Hence, if the security's return were 9% instead of 14%, the 5% difference would be attributed to the random error term (that is, ϵ_{AI} = −5%; this will be illustrated shortly in Figure 7.9). Similarly, if the security return were −2% instead of −4%, the 2% difference would be attributed to the random error term (that is, ϵ_{AI} = +2%).

The random error term for a security is a random variable with an expected value of zero and a standard deviation denoted by $\sigma_{\epsilon i}$.[7] It can be thought of as the outcome that will occur when a special kind of roulette wheel is spun. One feature of such a random error term is that its expected outcome is zero.

For example, security A may be thought of as having a random error term corresponding to a roulette wheel with integer values on it that range from −10% to +10%, with the values evenly spaced.[8] This means that there are 21 possible outcomes, each of which has an equal probability of occurring. Given the range of numbers, it also means that the expected outcome of the random error term is zero:

$$[-10 \times \tfrac{1}{21}] + [-9 \times \tfrac{1}{21}] + \cdots + [9 \times \tfrac{1}{21}] + [10 \times \tfrac{1}{21}] = 0$$

---

[6]than indicated here in that the return need not be on a market index. It can be on any variable that is believed to have a major influence on individual stock returns, such as the predicted rate of increase in industrial production or gross domestic product.

[7]To be technically correct, the standard deviation of the random error term should be denoted $\sigma_{\epsilon iI}$, because it is measured relative to market index I. The subscript I is not shown here for ease of exposition.

[8]Since the range refers to the possible outcomes and the spacing refers to the probabilities of the various outcomes occurring, it can be seen that the roulette wheel is just a convenient way of referring to the random error term's probability distribution. Typically, it is assumed that the random error term has a normal probability distribution.

The Active Manager Portfolio Selection Problem

The classic formulation of the portfolio selection problem depicts an investor who must choose a portfolio on the efficient set that exhibits the optimal combination of expected return and standard deviation, given the investor's risk-return preferences. In practice, however, this description inadequately characterizes the situation faced by most organizations that manage money for institutional investors. We want to consider how the portfolio selection problem can be modified to fit the concerns of institutional investors.

Certain types of institutional investors, such as pension and endowment funds (whom we will call the "clients"), typically hire outside firms (whom we will call the "managers") as agents to invest their assets. These managers usually specialize in a particular asset class, such as common stocks or fixed-income securities. The clients establish performance benchmarks for their managers. These benchmarks may be market indices (such as the TSE 300) or specialized benchmarks that reflect specific investment styles (such as small-capitalization growth stocks).

The clients hire some managers to simply match the performance of the benchmarks. These managers are called *passive managers* (see Chapter 23). The clients hire other managers to exceed the returns produced by the benchmarks. These managers are called *active managers.*

In the case of passive managers, the portfolio selection problem is trivial. They simply buy and hold the securities that constitute their assigned benchmarks. Their portfolios are called *index funds.* Passive managers need not refer to the efficient set or risk-return preferences. Those issues must be dealt with by their clients. (Whether the benchmarks chosen by the clients are efficient is a separate, although important, subject that we will not address here.)

Active managers face a much more difficult task. They must create portfolios that produce returns exceeding the returns on their assigned benchmarks in sufficient magnitude and with enough consistency to satisfy their clients.

The greatest obstacle confronting active managers is their lack of omniscience. Even the most capable of them make numerous errors in their security selections. Despite fables about managers who outperform the market's return every year by 10 percentage points, common stock managers who exceed their benchmarks' returns (after all fees and expenses) by 1–2 percentage points per annum are considered exceptional performers. Managers lacking skill (with skill defined in this case as the ability to accurately forecast security returns) will lose to their benchmarks as their fees and trading costs diminish their returns.

We refer to the returns that active managers earn above those of their benchmarks as *active returns.* For example, a manager whose portfolio and benchmark generate returns of 7% and 4%, respectively, has earned a 3% active return (7% − 4%). The expected active return for highly skillful managers exceeds that of less talented managers. Nonetheless, in any given period, through sheer chance, the less capable manager's active return may exceed that of the highly skillful manager.

Because the results of active managers' investment decisions are uncertain, their returns relative to their benchmarks exhibit variability over time. We refer to the standard deviation of active return as *active risk.*

Active managers (at least those with some investment forecasting ability) can increase their expected active returns by taking on more active risk. Suppose that Manager X forecasts that Noranda stock will earn a return above that of the benchmark. Noranda constitutes 2% of the benchmark. Manager X could "bet" on Noranda by holding a portfolio with a 4% position in Noranda stock. The difference between the actual portfolio's position in Noranda and the benchmark's position (4% − 2% = +2%) we call an *active position.* If Noranda does perform well, Manager X's active return will be enhanced by the positive active position in Noranda. However, if Noranda performs poorly, then Manager X's active return will be diminished. The larger Manager X's active position is in Noranda, the greater is her expected active return. However, the larger also is Manager X's active risk.

Active risk (and, hence, expected active return) can be eliminated by owning every benchmark security at weights matching those of the same securities in the benchmark. Passive managers follow this approach. Active managers assume active risk when they deviate in their portfolio holdings relative to their benchmarks. Rational and skillful active managers will take on active risk only with the expectation of earning a positive active return.

The outline of the portfolio selection problem for an active manager now becomes clear. The manager is not concerned with the tradeoff between portfolio expected return and standard deviation. Rather, the manager chooses between higher expected active return and lower active risk.

This process requires that we make an assumption about the manager's ability to forecast security returns. With that information, we can construct a manager's "efficient set" (based on expected active return and active risk) that exhibits the highest combination of expected active return per unit of active risk and the lowest active risk per unit of expected active return. Managers with greater skill will have

efficient sets that lie further to the northwest than managers with less skill.

Indifference curves, analogous to those applied in the classical portfolio selection problem, indicate various combinations of active return and active risk that the manager finds equally desirable. The steepness of these indifference curves reflects the manager's degree of risk aversion, which is directly related to the manager's assessment of how his clients will respond to various investment outcomes.

The manager's optimal combination of active return and risk is that point on the efficient set that is tangent to one of the indifference curves. We can view this point as the manager's desired level of aggressiveness in implementing his security return forecasts. Managers (and clients) with higher risk aversion will choose portfolios with lower levels of active risk. Conversely, managers (and clients) with lower risk aversion will choose portfolios with higher levels of active risk.

Noranda
www.noranda.com

As can be seen, this calculation involves multiplying each outcome by its probability of occurring and then summing up the resulting products. The standard deviation of this random error term can now be shown to be equal to 6.06%:

$$[(-10 - 0)^2 \times \frac{1}{21}] + [(-9 - 0)^2 \times \frac{1}{21}] + \cdots$$
$$+ [(9 - 0)^2 \times \frac{1}{21}] + [(10 - 0)^2 \times \frac{1}{21}]^{1/2} = 6.06\%$$

This calculation involves subtracting the expected outcome from each possible outcome, then squaring each one of these differences, multiplying each square by the probability of the corresponding outcome occurring, adding the products, and finally taking the square root of the resulting sum.[9]

Figure 7.7 illustrates the roulette wheel corresponding to this random error term. In general, securities will have random error terms whose corresponding roulette wheels have different ranges and different forms of uneven spacing. Although all will have an expected value of zero, they will typically have different standard deviations. For example, security B may have a random error term whose expected value and standard deviation are equal to 0 and 4.76%, respectively.[10]

---

[9]Appendix A of Chapter 6 discusses several basic statistical concepts, including expected value (or outcome) and standard deviation.

[10]This would be the case if security B had a random error term whose roulette wheel had integers from −9% to +9% on it, but the spacing for each integer between −5% and +5% was twice as large as the spacing for each integer from −9% to −6% and +6% to +9%. This means that the probability of any specific integer between −5% and +5% occurring is equal to $^2/_{30}$, whereas the probability of any specific integer from −9% to −6% and +6% to +9% occurring is equal to $^1/_{30}$.

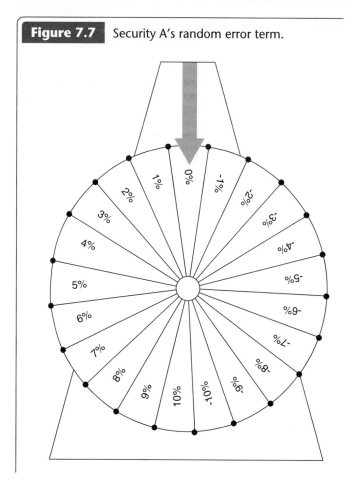

Figure 7.7 Security A's random error term.

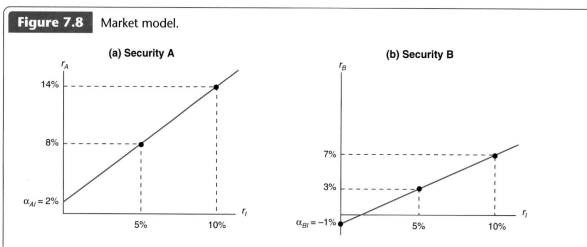

Figure 7.8 Market model.

(a) Security A

r_A

14%

8%

$\alpha_{AI} = 2\%$

5% 10% r_I

(b) Security B

r_B

7%

3%

$\alpha_{BI} = -1\%$

5% 10% r_I

Graphical Representation of the Market Model

The solid line in panel (a) of Figure 7.8 provides a graph of the market model for security A. This line corresponds to equation (7.4), but without the random error term. Accordingly, the line that is graphed for security A is

$$r_A = 2\% + 1.2r_I \tag{7.5}$$

Here, the vertical axis measures the return on the particular security (r_A) whereas the horizontal axis measures the return on the market index (r_I). The line goes through the point on the vertical axis corresponding to the value of α_{AI}, which in this case is 2%. In addition, the line has a slope equal to β_{AI}, or 1.2.

Panel (b) of Figure 7.8 presents the graph of the market model for security B. The line can be expressed as the following equation:

$$r_B = -1\% + .8r_I \tag{7.6}$$

This line goes through the point on the vertical axis corresponding to the value of α_{BI}, which in this case is −1%. Note that its slope is equal to β_{BI} or .8.

● Beta

At this point it can be seen that the slope in a security's market model measures the sensitivity of the security's returns to the market index's returns. Both lines in Figure 7.8 have positive slopes, indicating that the higher the returns of the market index, the higher the returns of the two securities. However, the two securities have different slopes, indicating that they have different sensitivities to the returns of the market index. Specifically, A has a higher slope than B, indicating that the returns of A are more sensitive than the returns of B to the returns of the market index.

For example, assume that the market index's expected return is 5%. If the market index subsequently has an actual return of 10%, it will have returned 5% more than expected. Panel (a) of Figure 7.8 shows that security A should have a return that is 6% (14% − 8%) greater than initially expected. Similarly, panel (b) shows that security B should have a return that is 4% (7% − 3%) greater than initially expected. The reason for the 2% (6% − 4%) difference is that security A has a higher slope than security B—that is, A is more sensitive than B to returns on the market index.

The slope term in the market model is often referred to as **beta**, and is equal to

$$\beta_{iI} = \sigma_{iI}/\sigma_I^2 \tag{7.7}$$

where σ_{iI} denotes the covariance of the returns on stock i and the market index, and σ_I^2 denotes the variance of returns on the market index. A stock that has a return that mirrors the return on the market index will have a beta equal to one (and an intercept of zero, resulting in a market model that is $r_i = r_1 + \epsilon_{iI}$). Hence stocks with betas greater than one (such as A) are more volatile than the market index and are known as **aggressive stocks**. In contrast, stocks with betas less than one (such as B) are less volatile than the market index and are known as **defensive stocks**.[11]

● Actual Returns

The random error term suggests that for a given return on the market index, the actual return on a security will usually lie off its market model line.[12] If the actual returns on securities A and B turn out to be 9% and 11%, respectively, and the market index's actual return turns out to be 10%, then the actual return on A and B could be viewed as having the following three components:

Beta A relative measure of the sensitivity of an asset's return to changes in the return on the market portfolio. Mathematically, the beta coefficient of a security is the security's covariance with the market portfolio divided by the variance of the market portfolio.

Aggresive Stocks Stocks that have betas greater than 1.

Defensive Stocks Stocks that have betas less than 1.

---

[11]How beta is estimated will be addressed in Chapter 16.

[12]If the random error term takes on a value of zero, then the security will lie *on* the line. However, the probability of this occurring is very small for most securities.

	Security A	Security B
Intercept	2%	−1%
Actual return on the market index × beta	12% = 10% × 1.2	8% = 10% × .8
Random error outcome	−5% = 9% − (2% + 12%)	4% = 11% − (−1% + 8%)
Actual return	9%	11%

In this case, the roulette wheels for A and B can be thought of as having been spun, resulting in values (that is, random error outcomes) of −5% for A and +4% for B. These values can be viewed as being equal to the vertical distance by which each security's actual return ended up being off its market model line, as shown in Figure 7.9.

Figure 7.9 Market model and actual returns.

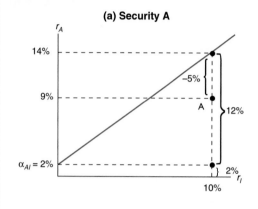

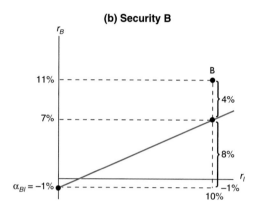

Diversification

Market Risk A part of a security's total risk that is related to moves in the market portfolio and, hence, cannot be diversified away.

According to the market model, the total risk of any security i, measured by its variance and denoted σ_i^2, consists of two parts: (1) **market** (or systematic) **risk**; and (2) **unique** (or unsystematic) **risk**. That is, σ_i^2 equals the following:

$$\sigma_i^2 = \beta_{iI}^2 \sigma_I^2 + \sigma_{\epsilon i}^2 \tag{7.8}$$

where σ_I^2 denotes the variance of returns on the market index. Thus $\beta_{iI}^2 \sigma_I^2$ denotes the market risk of security i, and $\sigma_{\epsilon i}^2$ denotes the unique risk of security i as measured by the variance of the random error term, ϵ_{iI}, appearing in equation (7.3).

Unique Risk That part of a security's total risk that is not related to moves in the market portfolio and, hence, can be diversified away.

● **Portfolio Total Risk**

When the return on every risky *security* in a portfolio is related to the return on the market index as specified by the market model, what can be said about the total risk of the *portfolio*? If the proportion of funds invested in security i for a given portfolio p is denoted X_i, then the return on this portfolio will be

$$r_p = \sum_{i=1}^{N} X_i r_i \tag{7.9}$$

Substituting the right-hand side of equation (7.3) for r_i in equation (7.9) results in the following market model for the portfolio:

$$r_p = \sum_{i=1}^{N} X_i(\alpha_{iI} + \beta_{iI}r_I + \epsilon_{iI})$$

$$= \sum_{i=1}^{N} X_i\alpha_{iI} + \left(\sum_{i=1}^{N} X_i\beta_{iI}\right) r_I + \sum_{i=1}^{N} X_i\epsilon_{iI}$$

$$= \alpha_{pI} + \beta_{pI}r_I + \epsilon_{pI} \tag{7.10a}$$

where:

$$\alpha_{pI} = \sum_{i=1}^{N} X_i\alpha_{iI} \tag{7.10b}$$

$$\beta_{pI} = \sum_{i=1}^{N} X_i\beta_{iI} \tag{7.10c}$$

$$\epsilon_{pI} = \sum_{i=1}^{N} X_i\epsilon_{iI} \tag{7.10d}$$

In equations (7.10b) and (7.10c), the portfolio's vertical intercept (α_{pI}) and beta (β_{pI}) are shown to be weighted averages of the intercepts and betas of the securities, respectively, using their relative proportions in the portfolio as weights. Similarly, in equation (7.10d), the portfolio's random error term (ϵ_{pI}) is a weighted average of the random error terms of the securities, again using the relative proportions in the portfolio as weights. Thus, the portfolio's market model is a straightforward extension of the market model for individual securities given in equation (7.3).[13]

From equation (7.10a), it follows that the total risk of a portfolio, measured by the variance of the portfolio's returns and denoted σ_p^2, will be

$$\sigma_p^2 = \beta_{pI}^2\sigma_I^2 + \sigma_{\epsilon p}^2 \tag{7.11a}$$

where:

$$\beta_{pI}^2 = \left[\sum_{i=1}^{N} X_i\beta_{iI}\right]^2 \tag{7.11b}$$

and, assuming the random error components of security returns are uncorrelated:[14]

$$\sigma_{\epsilon p}^2 = \sum_{i=1}^{N} X_i^2\sigma_{\epsilon i}^2 \tag{7.11c}$$

Equation (7.11a) shows that the total risk of any portfolio can be viewed as having two components, similar to the two components of the total risk of an individual security. These components are again referred to as market risk ($\beta_{pI}^2\sigma_I^2$) and unique risk ($\sigma_{\epsilon p}^2$).

Diversification The process of adding securities to a portfolio in order to reduce the portfolio's unique risk and, thereby, the portfolio's total risk.

Next, it will be shown that increased **diversification** can lead to the reduction of a portfolio's total risk. This occurs due to a reduction in the size of the portfolio's unique risk while the portfolio's market risk remains approximately the same size.

Portfolio Market Risk

Generally, the more diversified a portfolio (that is, the larger the number of securities in the portfolio), the smaller will be each proportion X_i. This will not cause β_{pI} either to decrease or to increase significantly unless a deliberate attempt is made to do so by adding either

---

[13]Appendix B shows how the market model can be used to estimate expected returns, variances, and covariances for the securities in the feasible set; with these estimates in hand, the efficient set can subsequently be determined. See footnote 2.

[14]The assumption of noncorrelated random error components is an approximation. The market-weighted sum of all the residuals must be zero. Therefore, on average, the residuals must have a slight negative correlation. However, the average correlation is so small that it can safely be assumed to equal zero.

relatively low or high beta securities, respectively, to the portfolio. That is, because a portfolio's beta is an average of the betas of its securities, there is no reason to suspect that increasing the amount of diversification will cause the portfolio beta, and thus the market risk of the portfolio, to change in a particular direction. Accordingly, diversification leads to *averaging* of market risk.

This makes sense because when prospects for the economy turn sour (or rosy), most securities will fall (or rise) in price. Regardless of the amount of diversification, portfolio returns will always be susceptible to such marketwide influences.

Portfolio Unique Risk

The situation is entirely different for unique risk. In a portfolio, some securities will go up as a result of unexpected good news specific to the company that issued the securities (such as an unexpected approval of a patent). Other securities will go down as a result of unexpected company-specific bad news (such as an industrial accident). Looking forward, approximately as many companies can be expected to have good news as bad news, leading to little anticipated net impact on the return of a "well-diversified" portfolio. This means that the more diversified a portfolio becomes, the smaller will be its unique risk and, in turn, its total risk.

This can be quantified precisely if the random error components of security returns are assumed to be uncorrelated, as was done when equation (7.11c) was written. Consider the following situation. If the amount invested in each security is equal, then the proportion X_i will equal $1/N$, and the level of unique risk, as shown in equation (7.11c), will be equal to

$$\sigma_{\epsilon p}^2 = \sum_{i=1}^{N} \left[\frac{1}{N} \right]^2 \sigma_{\epsilon i}^2 \tag{7.12a}$$

$$= \frac{1}{N} \left[\frac{\sigma_{\epsilon 1}^2 + \sigma_{\epsilon 2}^2 + \ldots \sigma_{\epsilon N}^2}{N} \right] \tag{7.12b}$$

The value inside the square brackets in equation (7.12b) is simply the average unique risk of the component securities. But the portfolio's unique risk is only one-Nth as large as this, since the term $1/N$ appears outside the square brackets. Now, as the portfolio becomes more diversified, the number of securities in it (that is, N) becomes larger. In turn, this means that $1/N$ becomes smaller, resulting in the portfolio having less unique risk.[15] That is, diversification can substantially *reduce* unique risk.

Roughly speaking, a portfolio that has 30 or more randomly selected securities in it will have a relatively small amount of unique risk. This means that its total risk will be only slightly greater than the amount of market risk that is present. Thus, such portfolios are "well diversified." Figure 7.10 illustrates how diversification results in the reduction of unique risk but the averaging of market risk.

An Example

Consider the two securities, A and B, that were referred to earlier. These two securities had betas of 1.2 and .8, respectively; the standard deviations of their random error terms were, respectively, 6.06% and 4.76%. Thus, given that $\sigma_{\epsilon A} = 6.06\%$ and $\sigma_{\epsilon B} = 4.76\%$, it follows that $\sigma_{\epsilon A}^2 = 6.06^2 = 37$ and $\sigma_{\epsilon B}^2 = 4.76^2 = 23$. Now assume that the standard deviation of the market index, σ_I, is 8%, which implies that the variance of the market index is

---

[15]Actually, all that is necessary for this reduction in unique risk to occur is for the maximum amount invested in any one security to decrease continually as N increases.

Figure 7.10   Risk and diversification.

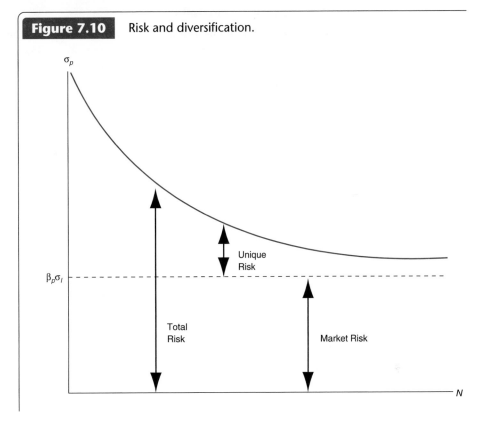

$8^2 = 64$. Using equation (7.8), this means that the variances of securities A and B are as follows:

$$\sigma_A^2 = (1.2^2 \times 64) + 37$$
$$= 129$$
$$\sigma_B^2 = (.8^2 \times 64) + 23$$
$$= 64$$

A Two-security Portfolio

Consider combining securities A and B into a portfolio, with an equal amount of the investor's money going into each security. That is, consider a portfolio that has $X_A = .5 = X_B = .5$. Since $\beta_{AI} = 1.2$ and $\beta_{BI} = .8$, the beta of this portfolio can be calculated using equation (7.10c):

$$\beta_{pI} = (.5 \times 1.2) + (.5 \times .8)$$
$$= 1.0$$

Using equation (7.11c), the variance of the portfolio's random error term, $\sigma_{\epsilon p}^2$, equals

$$\sigma_{\epsilon p}^2 = (.5^2 \times 37) + (.5^2 \times 23)$$
$$= 15$$

From equation (7.11a), it can be seen that this portfolio will have the following variance:

$$\sigma_p^2 = (1.0^2 \times 64) + 15$$
$$= 79$$

This represents the total risk of the two-security portfolio.

A Three-security Portfolio

Consider what would happen if a third security (C) was combined with the other two to form a three-security portfolio having $X_A = X_B = X_C = .33$. This third security has a beta of 1.0 and a random error term whose standard deviation ($\sigma_{\epsilon c}$) is 5.50%. Thus the variance of the random error term is $\sigma_{\epsilon c}^2 = 5.5^2 = 30$, and the security's variance is

$$\sigma_c^2 = (1.0^2 \times 64) + 30$$
$$= 94$$

First of all, note that the three-security portfolio has the same amount of market risk as the two-security portfolio, because both portfolios have a beta of 1.0:

$$\beta_{pI} = (.33 \times 1.2) + (.33 \times .8) + (.33 \times 1.0)$$
$$= 1.0$$

Thus, increased diversification has not led to a change in the level of market risk. Instead it has led to an averaging of market risk.

Using equation (7.11c), the variance of the portfolio's random error term equals

$$\sigma_{\epsilon p}^2 = (.33 \times 37) + (.33 \times 23) + (.33 \times 30)$$
$$= 10$$

Note that the variance of this three-security portfolio's random error term is less than the variance of the two-security portfolio's random error term (that is, $10 < 15$). Thus, in this example, increased diversification has indeed reduced unique risk.

From equation (7.11a), it can be seen that this three-security portfolio will have the following variance:

$$\sigma_p^2 = (1.0^2 \times 64) + 10$$
$$= 74$$

This represents the total risk of the portfolio and is less than the total risk of the two-security portfolio ($74 < 79$). Thus, increased diversification has led to a reduction in total risk.

Random Diversification

The process of creating diversification in a portfolio by randomly selecting securities without regard to the standard deviations and correlations of the securities.

Efficient Diversification

The process of creating diversification in a portfolio by selecting securities in a manner that explicitly considers the standard deviations and correlations of the securities.

Random Versus Efficient Diversification

Equation (7.12b) demonstrates how adding randomly selected securities, and combining them in equal proportions, reduces a portfolio's unique risk. That analysis explicitly assumes that the random error components of the securities' returns are uncorrelated. In more general terms, this **random diversification** implicitly assumes that an investor has no knowledge of the standard deviations and correlations of the available securities. This contrasts with the Markowitz approach to portfolio construction. Using estimates of securities' risks allows an investor to make maximum use of the diversification potential of a group of securities, as is reflected in the efficient set by explicitly considering their standard deviations and correlations. Diversifying a portfolio in this way is referred to as **efficient diversification**.

Summary

1. The efficient set contains those portfolios that offer both maximum expected return for varying levels of risk and minimum risk for varying levels of expected return.
2. Investors are assumed to select their optimal portfolios from among the portfolios lying on the efficient set.
3. An investor's optimal portfolio is located at the tangency point between the investor's indifference curves and the efficient set.

4. The proposition that the efficient set is concave follows from the definition of portfolio standard deviation and the existence of assets whose returns are not perfectly positively or perfectly negatively correlated.

5. Diversification usually leads to risk reduction, because the standard deviation of a portfolio generally will be less than a weighted average of the standard deviations of the component securities.

6. The relationship between the return on a security and the return on a market index is known as the market model.

7. The market index's return does not completely explain the return on a security. The unexplained elements are captured by the random error term of the market model.

8. The slope in a security's market model measures the sensitivity of the security's return to the market index's return. The slope term is known as the security's beta.

9. According to the market model, the total risk of a security consists of market risk and unique risk.

10. A portfolio's vertical intercept, beta, and random error term are weighted averages of the component securities' intercepts, betas, and random error terms, respectively, with the securities' relative proportions in the portfolio serving as weights.

11. Diversification leads to an averaging of market risk.

12. Diversification can substantially reduce unique risk.

APPENDIX A

THE MARKOWITZ MODEL

Determining the Composition and Location of the Efficient Set

Previously, it was noted that there are an infinite number of possible portfolios available to the investor, but that the investor needs to be concerned with only those portfolios that are on the efficient set. However, Markowitz's efficient set is a curved line, which means that there are an infinite number of points along it. This, in turn, means that there are an infinite number of efficient portfolios! How can Markowitz's approach be used if an investor needs to identify the composition of each one of an infinite number of portfolios? Fortunately, there is no need to despair. Markowitz saw this potential problem and, in a major contribution, presented a method for solving it.[16] It involves the use of a quadratic programming algorithm known as the *critical-line method*.

Although the algorithm is beyond the scope of this book, it is important to recognize what it does. To begin with, the investor must estimate the expected return vector and variance-covariance matrix. For example, consider the three-security example presented earlier in the chapter.[17] The expected return vector, denoted by *ER*, and the variance-covariance matrix, denoted by *VC*, are estimated to be

$$ER = \begin{bmatrix} 16.2 \\ 24.6 \\ 22.8 \end{bmatrix} \qquad VC = \begin{bmatrix} 146 & 187 & 145 \\ 187 & 854 & 104 \\ 145 & 104 & 289 \end{bmatrix}$$

The algorithm then identifies a number of *corner portfolios* that are associated with these securities and completely describe the efficient set. A corner portfolio is an efficient

---

[16]See Harry Markowitz, "The Optimization of a Quadratic Function Subject to Linear Constraints," *Naval Research Logistics Quarterly* 3, nos. 1–2 (March–June 1956): 111–133.

[17]This example is based on one from Markowitz's book entitled *Portfolio Selection* (New Haven, CT: Yale UP, 1959): 176–185.

portfolio with the following property: any combination of two adjacent corner portfolios will result in a portfolio that lies on the efficient set between the two corner portfolios. Just what this means is illustrated in the example.

The algorithm begins by identifying the portfolio with the highest expected return. This portfolio corresponds to point S in Figure 7.1 and is an efficient portfolio. It is composed of just one security—the security with the highest expected return.[18] That is, if the investor wanted to purchase that portfolio, all she would have to do is to purchase shares of the company whose stock had the highest expected return. Any other portfolio would have a lower expected return, since at least part of the investor's funds would be placed in shares of other companies that have an expected return lower than S.

In the example, the company whose shares have the highest expected return is the second one, Baker Company. The corresponding efficient portfolio is the first of several corner portfolios that the algorithm will identify. Its composition is given by the following weight vector, denoted by $X(1)$:

$$X(1) = \begin{bmatrix} .00 \\ 1.00 \\ .00 \end{bmatrix}$$

Its expected return and standard deviation correspond to the expected return and standard deviation of Baker, which are equal to 24.6% and $(854)^{1/2} = 29.22\%$ respectively. In Figure 7.11, this corner portfolio is denoted by $C(1)$.

The algorithm then identifies the second corner portfolio. This portfolio is on the efficient set below the first corner portfolio and has a composition given by the following weight vector, denoted by $X(2)$:

$$X(2) = \begin{bmatrix} .00 \\ .22 \\ .78 \end{bmatrix}$$

That is, the second corner portfolio is a portfolio where the investor puts 22% of her funds into Baker common stock and the remainder, 78%, into Charlie common stock. Applying these weights to equations (6.3a) and (6.7), the expected return and standard deviation of this corner portfolio can be calculated; they are equal to 23.20% and 15.90%, respectively. In Figure 7.11, this corner portfolio is denoted by $C(2)$.

What is important about the first and second corner portfolios is that they are *adjacent* efficient portfolios, and any efficient portfolio lying on the efficient set between them has a composition that is just a combination of their compositions. For example, the efficient portfolio lying halfway between them has the following composition:

$$[.5 \times X(1)] + [.5 \times X(2)] = .5 \times \begin{bmatrix} .00 \\ 1.00 \\ .00 \end{bmatrix} + .5 \times \begin{bmatrix} .00 \\ .22 \\ .78 \end{bmatrix} = \begin{bmatrix} .00 \\ .61 \\ .39 \end{bmatrix}$$

That is, the portfolio has weights of .61 in Baker stock and .39 in Charlie stock. Using equations (7.3a) and (7.7), the expected return and standard deviation of this portfolio turn out to be 23.9% and 20.28%, respectively.

Having identified the second corner portfolio, the algorithm then identifies the third one. Its composition is

$$X(3) = \begin{bmatrix} .84 \\ .00 \\ .16 \end{bmatrix}$$

---

[18]If two or more securities have the same highest return, then one can be given a slightly higher expected return to break the tie.

The weights can now be used to calculate the expected return and standard deviation of this portfolio, which are 17.26% and 12.22%, respectively. As was noted for the previous two corner portfolios, this corner portfolio is an efficient portfolio and is denoted by $C(3)$ in Figure 7.11.

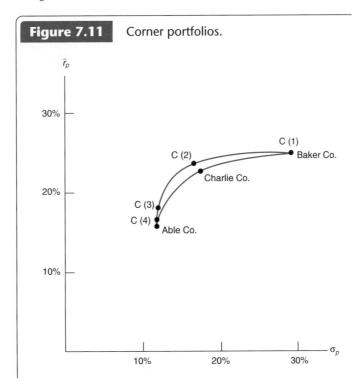

Figure 7.11 Corner portfolios.

Since they are adjacent, combinations of the second and third corner portfolios result in efficient portfolios that lie on the efficient set between them. For example, if the investor puts 33% of her money in the second corner portfolio and 67% in the third corner portfolio, then the resulting efficient portfolio has the following composition:

$$[.33 \times X(2)] + [.67 \times X(3)] = .33 \times \begin{bmatrix} .00 \\ .22 \\ .78 \end{bmatrix} + .67 \times \begin{bmatrix} .84 \\ .00 \\ .16 \end{bmatrix} = \begin{bmatrix} .56 \\ .07 \\ .37 \end{bmatrix}$$

Using equations (6.3a) and (6.7), this portfolio can be shown to have an expected return of 19.10% and a standard deviation of 12.88%.

Earlier it was mentioned that only combinations of *adjacent* corner portfolios will be efficient. This means that portfolios formed by combining *nonadjacent* corner portfolios will not lie on the efficient set. For example, the first and third corner portfolios are nonadjacent, which means that any portfolio formed by combining them will not be efficient. For example, if the investor put 50% of her funds in the first corner portfolio and 50% in the third corner portfolio, the resulting portfolio would have the following composition:

$$[.5 \times X(1)] + [.5 \times X(3)] = .5 \times \begin{bmatrix} .00 \\ 1.00 \\ .00 \end{bmatrix} + .5 \times \begin{bmatrix} .84 \\ .00 \\ .16 \end{bmatrix} = \begin{bmatrix} .42 \\ .50 \\ .08 \end{bmatrix}$$

With these weights, the expected return and standard deviation of this portfolio can be shown to be equal to 20.93% and 18.38%, respectively. However, this is an inefficient portfolio. Since its expected return (20.93%) lies between the expected return of the second (23.20%) and third (17.26%) corner portfolios, by combining these two adjacent corner portfolios the investor will be able to form an efficient portfolio that has the same expected return but lower standard deviation.[19]

Table 7.1   Corner Portfolios for a Three-Security Example.

	Weights			Corner Portfolio	
Corner Portfolio	Able Co.	Baker Co.	Charlie Co.	Expected Return	Standard Deviation
C (1)	.00	1.00	.00	24.60%	29.22%
C (2)	.00	.22	.78	23.20	15.90
C (3)	.84	.00	.16	17.26	12.22
C (4)	.99	.00	.01	16.27	12.08

Continuing, the algorithm now identifies the composition of the fourth corner portfolio:

$$X(4) = \begin{bmatrix} .99 \\ .00 \\ .01 \end{bmatrix}$$

Its expected return and standard deviation can be calculated to be 16.27% and 12.08%, respectively. Having identified this portfolio as the one corresponding to point E in Figure 7.1 [and $C(4)$ in Figure 7.11], meaning that it is the portfolio that has the least standard deviation of all feasible portfolios, the algorithm stops. The four corner portfolios, summarized in Table 7.1, completely describe the efficient set associated with the shares of Able, Baker, and Charlie.

It is a simple matter for the computer, using its capability for graphics, to draw the graph of the efficient set. Perhaps it will find the composition, and in turn the expected return and standard deviation, for each of 20 efficient portfolios that are evenly spaced between the first and second corner portfolios. Then it will "connect the dots," tracing a straight line between each of the 20 successive portfolios. This will give the graph the appearance of a curved line, as shown in Figure 7.11, since these portfolios are located close to each other.

Proceeding in a similar fashion, 20 efficient portfolios between the second and third corner portfolios will be located and the corresponding segment of the efficient set traced. Then the same procedure will be followed for the region between the third and fourth corner portfolios, at which point the graph has been completely drawn.

Determining the Composition of the Optimal Portfolio

Once the location and composition of Markowitz's efficient set have been determined, the composition of the investor's optimal portfolio can be determined. This portfolio, indicated by O^* in Figure 7.2, corresponds to the tangency point between the efficient set and one of the investor's indifference curves. The procedure for determining its composition starts by the investor noting graphically the level of its expected return. That is, from the graph the investor can note where O^* is located and then calibrate its expected return simply by

---

[19]In this example, the efficient portfolio having an expected return of 20.93% can be determined by solving the following equation for Y: $(23.20\% \times Y) + [17.26\% \times (1 - Y)] = 20.93\%$. Because this is a linear equation with one unknown, it can easily be solved. The solution, $Y = .62$, indicates that by putting .62 of her funds in the second corner portfolio and .38 $(1.00 - .62)$ in the third corner portfolio, the investor will have an efficient portfolio with the same expected return but lower standard deviation (specifically, 14.09%) than the portfolio involving a 50-50 combination of the first and third corner portfolios.

using a ruler and extending a line from it to the vertical axis (with computers, more precise ways exist for doing this—see Appendix B to Chapter 8 for one method).

Having done so, the investor can now identify the two corner portfolios with expected returns "surrounding" this level. That is, the investor can identify the corner portfolio with the expected return nearest to but greater than this level (the surrounding corner portfolio that is above O^*) and the corner portfolio with the expected return nearest to but less than this level (the surrounding corner portfolio that is below O^*).

If the expected return of the optimal portfolio is denoted by $\bar{r}^*$ and the expected returns of these two surrounding portfolios are denoted by $\bar{r}^a$ and $\bar{r}^b$, respectively, then the composition of the optimal portfolio can be determined by solving the following equation for Y:

$$\bar{r}^* = (\bar{r}^a \times Y) + [\bar{r}^b \times (1 - Y)] \tag{7.13}$$

The optimal portfolio will consist of a proportion Y of the "above" surrounding corner portfolio and a proposition $1 - Y$ of the "below" surrounding corner portfolio.

In the example, if the optimal portfolio had an expected return of 20%, then it can be noted that the second and third corner portfolios are the above and below surrounding corner portfolios, since they have expected returns of 23.20% and 17.26%, respectively. Equation (7.13) thus looks like this:

$$20\% = (23.20\% \times Y) + [17.26\% \times (1 - Y)]$$

Solving this equation for Y results in $Y = .46$, meaning that the optimal portfolio consists of a proportion of .46 in the second corner portfolio and .54 in the third corner portfolio. In terms of the amount of investment in the securities of Able, Baker, and Charlie companies, this translates to

$$[.46 \times X(2)] + [.54 \times X(3)] = .46 \times \begin{bmatrix} .00 \\ .22 \\ .78 \end{bmatrix} + .54 \times \begin{bmatrix} .84 \\ .00 \\ .16 \end{bmatrix} = \begin{bmatrix} .45 \\ .10 \\ .45 \end{bmatrix}$$

Thus, the investor should put 45%, 10%, and 45% of her funds in shares of Able, Baker, and Charlie, respectively.

More generally, if the weight vectors of the above and below surrounding corner portfolios are denoted by X^a and X^b, respectively, then the weights for the individual securities comprising the optimal portfolio will be equal to $(Y \times X^a) + [(1 - Y) \times X^b]$.

APPENDIX B

DETERMINING THE INPUTS NEEDED FOR LOCATING THE EFFICIENT SET

In order to construct the efficient set, the investor must estimate the expected returns of all the securities under consideration, as well as all of the variances and covariances. Subsequently, the optimal portfolio can be identified by noting where one of the investor's indifference curves is tangent to the efficient set, as shown in Figure 7.2.

Considerable effort is needed to construct this efficient set. First, the expected return for each security must be estimated. Given that there are N risky securities, this means that N parameters must be estimated. Second, the variance for each one of these securities must be estimated. Again, because there are N risky securities, this means that another N parameters must be estimated. Third, the covariance between each pair of risky securities must be estimated. There are $(N^2 - N)/2$ of these parameters to be estimated.[20]

This means that the total number of parameters that need to be estimated is equal to $(N^2 + 3N)/2$, determined as follows:

Expected returns	N
Variances	N
Covariances	$(N^2 - N)/2$
Total	$(N^2 + 3N)/2$

For example, if there were 100 risky securities under consideration, then $[100^2 + (3 \times 100)]/2 = 5150$ parameters would need to be estimated, consisting of 100 expected returns, 100 variances, and 4950 covariances. These parameters can be estimated one by one, a task that will be quite time-consuming, if not impossible. Fortunately, alternatives exist, including one that is based on the market model.[21]

With the market model approach, the expected return on the market index must be estimated initially. Then, the vertical intercept and beta for each security must be estimated. At this point, $(1 + 2N)$ parameters have been estimated (1 for $\bar{r}_I$; $2N$ for the vertical intercept; and beta for each of the N risky securities). In turn, these figures can be used to estimate the expected return for each security using equation (7.3), restated as follows:

$$\bar{r}_i = \alpha_{iI} + \beta_{iI}\bar{r}_I \tag{7.14}$$

Earlier, the expected return on the market index was estimated to be 5%. Given these figures, the expected return for security A was estimated to be 8%, because the vertical intercept and beta of this security were estimated to be 2% and 1.2, respectively:

$$\bar{r}_A = 2\% + (5\% \times 1.2)$$
$$= 8\%$$

Similarly, the expected return for security B was estimated to be 3%, because its vertical intercept and beta were estimated to be −1% and .8, respectively:

$$\bar{r}_B = -1\% + (5\% \times .8)$$
$$= 3\%$$

Using the market model approach, the variance of any security i can be estimated by multiplying the squared value of the security's beta by the variance of the market index and then adding the variance of the random error term to the product. The equation for doing this was given earlier:

$$\sigma_i^2 = \beta_{iI}^2\sigma_I^2 + \sigma_{\epsilon i}^2 \tag{7.8}$$

---

[20]This number was arrived at in the following manner. The variance-covariance matrix has N rows and N columns, meaning that there are N^2 cells in it whose corresponding parameters need to be estimated. The cells on the diagonal contain the N variances mentioned earlier, leaving $(N^2 - N)$ covariances to be estimated. Because the variance-covariance matrix is symmetric, only those covariances below the diagonal need to be estimated (this is because they also appear in corresponding locations above the diagonal), leaving a total of $(N^2 - N)/2$ parameters to be estimated.

[21]The market model approach is an approximate one (as are all the other alternatives) because it makes a number of simplifying assumptions. For example, this approach assumes that the random error terms for any two securities are uncorrelated [an assumption that was needed in deriving equation (7.11c) and later in (7.15)]. This means that the outcome from a spin of the roulette wheel for one security (such as Mobil) has no bearing on the outcome from a spin of the roulette wheel for any other security (such as Exxon). It has been argued that this is not true for securities within certain industries. See Benjamin F. King, "Market and Industry Factors in Stock Price Behavior," *Journal of Business* 39, no. 1 (January 1966): 139–170; and James L. Farrell, Jr., "Analyzing Covariation of Returns to Determine Homogeneous Stock Groupings," *Journal of Business* 47, no. 2 (April 1974): 186–207.

where σ_I^2 denotes the variance of the market index and $\sigma_{\epsilon i}^2$ denotes the variance of the random error term for security i.

Assuming that the variance on the market index is 49, the respective variances of securities A and B can be estimated as follows:

$$\sigma_A^2 = (1.2^2 \times 49) + 6.06^2$$
$$= 107.28$$
$$\sigma_B^2 = (.8^2 \times 49) + 4.76^2$$
$$= 54.02$$

This means that the standard deviations of these securities are estimated to be equal to $10.36\% = \sqrt{107.28}$ and $7.35\% = \sqrt{54.02}$, respectively.

Lastly, the covariance between any two securities i and j can be estimated by the product of the three numbers: the beta of security i, the beta of security j, and the variance of the market index. That is, the following formula can be used:

$$\sigma_{ij} = \beta_{iI}\beta_{jI}\sigma_I^2 \tag{7.15}$$

Thus, for securities A and B, the estimated covariance would be

$$\sigma_{A,B} = 1.2 \times .8 \times 49$$
$$= 47.04$$

In summary, if the market model approach is used to estimate expected returns, variances, and covariances, then the following parameters must first be estimated:

For the market index:
Expected return ($\bar{r}_I$)	1
Variance (σ_I^2)	1

For each security:
Vertical intercept (α_{iI})	N
Beta (β_{iI})	N
Variance of random error term ($\sigma_{\epsilon I}^2$)	N
Total	$3N + 2$

Thus, for 100 risky securities $(3 \times 100) + 2 = 302$ parameters need to be estimated when the market model approach is used to determine the efficient set and tangency portfolio. Once these 302 parameters have been estimated, then it is a simple matter to use equations (7.14), (7.8), and (7.15) to estimate the expected returns, variances, and covariances for the risky securities. Alternatively, the expected returns, variances, and covariances could be estimated one by one as noted earlier, in which case 5150 parameters would need to be estimated. As can be seen with this example, the market model approach results in a notable reduction in the number of parameters that need to be estimated.

After the expected returns, variances, and covariances have been estimated, a computer can be given these values. Then, using a "quadratic programming algorithm," the computer can proceed to identify the efficient set. At this juncture, the investor's optimal portfolio can be determined by finding the point at which one of the indifference curves is tangent to the efficient set.

QUESTIONS AND PROBLEMS

1. Why would you expect individual securities to generally lie in the "eastern" portion of the feasible set, whereas only portfolios would lie in the "northwestern" portion?
2. Explain why most investors prefer to hold a diversified portfolio of securities as opposed to placing all of their wealth in a single asset. Use an illustration of the feasible and efficient sets to explain your answer.

3. Why would you expect most Canadian common stocks to have positive covariances? Give an example of two stocks that you would expect to have a very high positive covariance. Give an example of two stocks that you would expect to have a very low positive (or even negative) covariance.

4. Discuss why the concepts of covariance and diversification are closely related.

5. Maya Haas is a portfolio manager. On average, the expected returns on all securities that Maya is researching are positive. Under what conditions might Maya be willing to purchase a security with a negative expected return?

6. In terms of the Markowitz model, explain, using words and graphs, how an investor goes about identifying his or her optimal portfolio. What specific information does an investor need to identify this portfolio?

7. David Brinker owns a portfolio of two securities with the following expected returns, standard deviations, and weights:

Security	Expected Return	Standard Deviation	Weight
A	10%	20%	.35
B	15	25	.65

For varying levels of correlation between the two securities, what is the maximum portfolio standard deviation? What is the minimum?

8. Briefly explain why the efficient set must be concave.

9. Lee Kim owns a portfolio whose market model is expressed as:

$$r_p = 1.5\% + 0.90r_I + \epsilon_{pI}$$

If the expected return on the market index is 12%, what is the expected return on Lee's portfolio?

10. How is beta derived from a security's market model? Why are high beta securities termed "aggressive"? Why are low beta securities termed "defensive"?

11. In the following table you are presented with 10 years of return data for the stock of Glenwood City Properties and for a market index. Plot the returns of Glenwood City and the market index on a graph, with the market index's returns on the horizontal axis and Glenwood City's returns on the vertical axis. Draw your best guess of the market model through these points. From this graph only, compute an estimate of the beta of Glenwood City stock.

Year	Glenwood City	Market Index
1	8.1%	8.0%
2	3.0	0.0
3	5.3	14.9
4	1.0	5.0
5	–3.1	–4.1
6	–3.0	–8.9
7	5.0	10.1
8	3.2	5.0
9	1.2	1.5
10	1.3	2.4

12. Consider the stocks of two companies, Woodville Mink Farms and New Richmond Furriers.
    a. If you are told that the slope of Woodville's market model is 1.20 and that the slope of New Richmond's market model is 1.00, which stock is likely to be more risky in a portfolio context? Why?

b. If you are now also told that the standard deviation of the random error term for Woodville stock is 10.0%, whereas it is 21.5% for New Richmond stock, does your answer change? Explain.

13. The market model specifies a very simple relationship between a security's return and the return on the market index. Discuss some "real world" complexities that might diminish the predictive power of the market model.

14. Two portfolios, one invested in electric utilities and the other in gold mining companies, have the same beta of 0.60. Why would a security analyst be interested to know that the gold portfolio has a much larger standard deviation of the random error term (unique risk) than the utility portfolio?

15. Lyndon Station Ltd. stock has a beta of 1.20. Over five years, the following returns were produced by Lyndon stock and a market index. Assuming a market model intercept term of 0%, calculate the standard deviation of the market model random error term over this period.

Year	Lyndon Return	Market Index
1	17.2%	14.0%
2	−3.1	−3.0
3	13.3	10.0
4	28.5	25.0
5	9.8	8.0

16. Why does diversification lead to a reduction in unique risk, but not in market risk? Explain both intuitively and mathematically.

17. Stephan Picovich owns a portfolio composed of three securities with the following characteristics:

Security	Beta	Standard Deviation Random Error Term	Proportion
A	1.20	5%	.30
B	1.05	8	.50
C	0.90	2	.20

If the standard deviation of the market index is 18%, what is the total risk of Stephan's portfolio?

18. Consider two portfolios, one composed of four securities and the other of ten securities. All the securities have a beta of one and unique risk of 30%. Each portfolio distributes weight equally among its component securities. If the standard deviation of the market index is 20%, calculate the total risk of both portfolios.

19. (Appendix Question) What is a corner portfolio? Why are corner portfolios important for identifying the composition of the efficient set?

20. (Appendix Question) Why is the market model approach a simpler technique than the original Markowitz approach for constructing the efficient set?

21. (Appendix Question) If the variance of the market index is 490 and the covariance between securities A and B is 470, what is the beta of security B, knowing that security A's beta is 1.20?

22. (Appendix Question) How many parameters must be estimated to analyze the risk-return profile of a 50-stock portfolio using (a) the original Markowitz approach and (b) the market model approach?

CFA EXAM QUESTION

23. Explain the concepts of specific risk, systematic risk, variance, standard deviation, and beta as they relate to investment management.

KEY TERMS

efficient set theorem (p. 161)
efficient set (p. 162)
feasible set (p. 162)
efficient portfolio (p. 163)
inefficient portfolio (p. 163)
optimal portfolio (p. 163)
market model (p. 170)
random error term (p. 171)

beta (p. 175)
aggressive stock (p. 175)
defensive stock (p. 175)
market risk (p. 176)
unique risk (p. 176)
diversification (p. 177)
random diversification (p. 180)
efficient diversification (p. 180)

REFERENCES

1. As mentioned at the end of Chapter 6, the seminal work developing the mean-variance model is credited to Harry Markowitz, who presented his ideas in a paper and later in a book:

   Harry M. Markowitz, "Portfolio Selection," *Journal of Finance* 7, no. 1 (March 1952): 77–91.

   Harry M. Markowitz, *Portfolio Selection: Efficient Diversification of Investments* (New York: John Wiley, 1959). (A reprint of this book that also contains some new material is available from Basil Blackwell, in Cambridge, MA; its copyright date is 1991.)

2. The technique used for determining the location of the efficient set, along with the composition of the "corner portfolios" that lie on it, was developed in:

   Harry M. Markowitz, "The Optimization of a Quadratic Function Subject to Linear Constraints," *Naval Research Logistics Quarterly* 3, nos. 1–2 (March–June 1956): 111–133.

3. The market model, initially mentioned by Markowitz in a footnote on p. 100 of his book, was developed in:

   William F. Sharpe, "A Simplified Model for Portfolio Analysis," *Management Science* 9, no. 2 (January 1963): 277–293.

4. An extensive discussion of the market model can be found in Chapters 3 and 4 of:

   Eugene F. Fama, *Foundations of Finance* (New York: Basic Books, 1976).

5. For discussions of how diversification reduces market risk, see:

   Paul A. Samuelson, "Risk and Uncertainty: A Fallacy of Large Numbers," *Scientia* 98, (1963).

   John L. Evans and Stephen H. Archer, "Diversification and the Reduction of Dispersion: An Empirical Analysis," *Journal of Finance* 23, no. 5 (December 1968): 761–767.

   W. H. Wagner and S. C. Lau, "The Effect of Diversification on Risk," *Financial Analysts Journal* 27, no. 6 (November–December 1971): 48–53.

   Meir Statman, "How Many Stocks Make a Diversified Portfolio?" *Journal of Financial and Quantitative Analysis* 22, no. 3 (September 1987): 353–363.

   Gerald D. Newbould and Percy S. Poon, "The Minimum Number of Stocks Needed for Diversification," *Financial Practice and Education* 3, no. 2 (Fall 1993): 85–87.

6. A discussion of some statistical problems that are encountered in partitioning total risk is contained in:

Bert Stine and Dwayne Key, "Reconciling Degrees of Freedom When Partitioning Risk: A Teaching Note," *Journal of Financial Education* 19 (Fall 1990): 19–22.

7. Some of the statistical problems encountered in using optimization techniques to manage portfolios (specifically, the problem of how to cope with *estimation risk*) are discussed in:

J. D. Jobson and Bob Korkie, "Putting Markowitz Theory to Work," *Journal of Portfolio Management* 7, no. 4 (Summer 1981): 70–74.

Gordon J. Alexander and Jack Clark Francis, *Portfolio Analysis* (Englewood Cliffs, NJ: Prentice Hall, 1986), Chapter 6.

Peter A. Frost and James E. Savarino, "Portfolio Size and Estimation Risk," *Journal of Portfolio Management* 12, no. 4 (Summer 1986): 60–64.

Peter A. Frost and James E. Savarino, "For Better Performance: Constrain Portfolio Weights," *Journal of Portfolio Management* 15, no. 1 (Fall 1988): 29–34.

Richard O. Michaud, "The Markowitz Optimization Enigma: Is 'Optimized' Optimal?" *Financial Analysts Journal* 45, no. 1 (January–February 1989): 31–42.

Philippe Jorion, "Portfolio Optimization in Practice," *Financial Analysts Journal* 48, no. 1 (January–February 1992): 68–74.

Vijay K. Chopra and William T. Ziemba, "The Effects of Errors in Means, Variances, and Covariances on Optimal Portfolio Choice," *Journal of Portfolio Management* 19, no. 2 (Winter 1993): 6–11.

Kenneth L. Fisher and Meir Statman. "The Mean-Variance-Optimization Puzzle: Security Portfolios and Food Portfolios," *Financial Analysts Journal* 53, no. 4 (July–August 1997): 41–50.

8. The active manager portfolio selection problem is addressed in:

Richard C. Grinold, "The Fundamental Law of Active Management," *Journal of Portfolio Management* 16, no. 4 (Summer 1989): 30–37.

Richard Roll, "A Mean/Variance Analysis of Tracking Error," *Journal of Portfolio Management* 19, no. 4 (Summer 1989): 13–22.

George Chow, "Portfolio Selection Based on Return, Risk, and Relative Performance," *Financial Analysts Journal* 51 no. 2 (March–April 1995): 54–60.

9. For a Canadian perspective on the topics covered in this chapter, see:

B. Korkie and H. Turtle, "The Canadian Investment Opportunity Set, 1967–1993," *Canadian Journal of Administrative Sciences* 15, no. 3 (September 1998): 213–229.

CHAPTER 8

Risk-free Lending and Borrowing

The previous two chapters focused on how an investor should go about determining what portfolio to select for investment. With Markowitz's approach, the investor is assumed to have a certain amount of initial wealth (W_0) to invest for a given holding period. Of all the portfolios that are available, the optimal one is shown to correspond to the point where one of the investor's indifference curves is tangent to the efficient set. At the end of the holding period, the investor's initial wealth will have either increased or decreased depending on the portfolio's rate of return. The resulting end-of-period wealth (W_1) can then be either completely reinvested, completely spent on consumption, or partially reinvested and partially consumed.

The Markowitz approach assumes that the assets considered for investment are individually risky—that is, each one of the N risky assets has an uncertain return over the investor's holding period. Because none of the assets has a perfectly negative correlation with any other asset, all the portfolios also have uncertain returns over the investor's holding period and thus are risky. Furthermore, the investor is not allowed to use borrowed money along with her initial wealth to purchase a portfolio of assets. This means that the investor is not allowed to use financial leverage, or margin.

In this chapter, the Markowitz approach to investing is expanded by first allowing the investor to consider investing not only in risky assets but also in a risk-free asset. This means there will now be N assets available for purchase, consisting of $N - 1$ risky assets and one risk-free asset. Second, the investor is allowed to borrow money but has to pay a given rate of interest on the loan. The next section considers the effect of adding a risk-free asset to the set of risky assets.

Defining the Risk-free Asset

Risk-free Asset An asset whose return over a given holding period is certain and known at the beginning of the holding period.

What exactly is a **risk-free asset** in the context of Markowitz's approach? As this approach involves investing for a single holding period, it means that the return on the risk-free asset is certain. That is, if the investor purchases this asset at the beginning of the holding period, then she knows exactly what the value of the asset will be at the end of the holding period. Since there is no uncertainty about the terminal value of the risk-free asset, the standard deviation of the risk-free asset is, by definition, zero.

In turn, this means that the covariance between the rate of return on the risk-free asset and the rate of return on any risky asset is zero. This is so because the covariance between the returns on any two assets i and j is equal to the product of the correlation coefficient between the assets and the standard deviations of the two assets: $\sigma_{ij} = \rho_{ij}\sigma_i\sigma_j$. Given that $\sigma_i = 0$, if i is the risk-free asset, it follows that $\sigma_{ij} = 0$.

As a risk-free asset has, by definition, a certain return, this type of asset must be some kind of fixed-income security with no possibility of default. Since all corporate securities have some chance of default, the risk-free asset cannot be issued by a corporation. Instead, it must be a security issued by the federal government. However, not just any security issued by the Canadian government qualifies as a risk-free asset.

Consider an investor with a three-month holding period who purchases a long Canada Bond maturing in 20 years. Such a security is risky, since the investor does not know what this security will be worth at the end of her holding period. That is, interest rates very likely will have changed in an unpredictable manner during the investor's holding period, meaning that the market price of the security will have changed in an unpredictable manner. Since the presence of such **interest-rate risk** makes the value of the bond uncertain, it cannot qualify as a risk-free asset. Indeed, no government bond with a maturity date greater than the investor's holding period can qualify as a risk-free asset.

Next, consider a bond that matures before the end of the investor's holding period, such as a 30-day Treasury bill in the case of an investor with the three-month holding period. In this situation, the investor does not know at the beginning of the holding period what interest rates will be in 30 days. This means that the investor does not know the interest rate at which the proceeds from the maturing Treasury bill can be reinvested (that is, "rolled over") for the remainder of the holding period. The presence of such **reinvestment-rate risk** in all government securities of shorter maturity than the investor's holding period means that these securities do not qualify as a risk-free asset.

This leaves only one type of government security to qualify as a risk-free asset—one with a maturity that matches the length of the investor's holding period. For example, the investor with a three-month holding period would find that a Treasury bill with a three-month maturity date had a riskless return. Since this security matures at the end of the investor's holding period, it provides the investor with an amount of money at the end of the holding period that is known for certain at the beginning of the holding period when an investment decision has to be made.[1]

Investing in the risk-free asset is often referred to as **risk-free lending**, since such an investment involves the purchase of Treasury bills, and thus involves a loan by the investor to the federal government.

Interest-rate Risk The uncertainty in the return on a fixed-income security caused by unanticipated fluctuations in the value of the asset due to changes in interest rates.

Reinvestment-rate Risk The uncertainty in the return on a fixed-income asset caused by unanticipated changes in the interest rate at which cash flows from the asset can be reinvested.

Risk-free Lending The act of investing in a risk-free asset.

Allowing for Risk-free Lending

With the introduction of a risk-free asset, the investor is now able to put part of his money in this asset and the remainder in any of the risky portfolios that are in Markowitz's feasible set. Adding these new opportunities expands the feasible set significantly and, more important, changes the location of part of Markowitz's efficient set. The nature of these changes needs to be analyzed, since investors are concerned with selecting a portfolio from the efficient set. In doing so, consideration is given initially to determining the expected return and standard deviation for a portfolio that consists of combining an investment in the risk-free asset with an investment in a single risky security.

---

[1] To be truly risk-free, the security must not provide the investor with any coupon payments during the holding period. Instead, it must provide the investor with only one cash inflow, and that inflow must occur at the end of the investor's holding period. Any intervening coupon payments would subject the investor to reinvestment-rate risk, since he would not know the rate at which the coupon payments could be invested for the remainder of the holding period. It should also be noted that the discussion has focused on an asset that is risk-free in nominal terms, since the presence of inflation means that virtually all government securities are risky in real terms. These points are explored further in the Institutional Issues section of Chapter 5.

Investing in Both the Risk-free Asset and a Risky Asset

In Chapter 6, the companies of Able, Baker, and Charlie were assumed to have expected returns, variances, and covariances as indicated in the following expected return vector and variance-covariance matrix:

$$ER = \begin{bmatrix} 16.2 \\ 24.6 \\ 22.8 \end{bmatrix} \quad VC = \begin{bmatrix} 146 & 187 & 145 \\ 187 & 854 & 104 \\ 145 & 104 & 289 \end{bmatrix}$$

Defining the risk-free asset as security number 4, consider all portfolios that involve investing in just the common shares of Able and the risk-free asset. Let X_1 denote the proportion of the investor's funds invested in Able, and $X_4 = 1 - X_1$ denote the proportion invested in the risk-free asset. If the investor put all her money in the risk-free asset, then $X_1 = 0$ and $X_4 = 1$. Alternatively, the investor could put all her money in just Able, in which case $X_1 = 1$ and $X_4 = 0$. A combination of .25 in Able and .75 in the risk-free asset is also possible, as are respective combinations of .50 and .50, and .75 and .25. Although there are other possibilities, the focus here will be on these five portfolios:

	Portfolio A	Portfolio B	Portfolio C	Portfolio D	Portfolio E
X_1	.00	.25	.50	.75	1.00
X_4	1.00	.75	.50	.25	.00

Assuming that the risk-free asset has a rate of return (often denoted by r_f) of 4%, all the necessary information for calculating the expected returns and standard deviations for these five portfolios is at hand. Equation (6.3a) can be used to calculate the expected returns for these portfolios:

$$\bar{r}_p = \sum_{i=1}^{N} X_i \bar{r}_i \qquad (6.3a)$$

$$= \sum_{i=1}^{4} X_i \bar{r}_i$$

Now, portfolios A, B, C, D, and E do not involve investing in the second and third securities (that is, Baker and Charlie companies), meaning that $X_2 = 0$ and $X_3 = 0$ in these portfolios. Thus, the previous equation reduces to

$$\bar{r}_p = X_1 \bar{r}_1 + X_4 r_4$$
$$= (X_1 \times 16.2\%) + (X_4 \times 4\%)$$

where the risk-free rate is now denoted r_4.

For portfolios A and E this calculation is trivial, since all the investor's funds are being placed in just one security. Thus, their expected returns are just 4% and 16.2%, respectively. For portfolios B, C, and D, the expected returns are, respectively,

$$\bar{r}_B = (.25 \times 16.2\%) + (.75 \times 4\%)$$
$$= 7.05\%$$
$$\bar{r}_C = (.50 \times 16.2\%) + (.50 \times 4\%)$$
$$= 10.10\%$$
$$\bar{r}_D = (.75 \times 16.2\%) + (.25 \times 4\%)$$
$$= 13.15\%$$

The standard deviations of portfolios A and E are simply the standard deviations of the risk-free asset and Able, respectively. Thus, $\sigma_A = 0.00\%$ and $\sigma_E = 12.08\%$. In calculating the standard deviations of portfolios B, C, and D, equation (6.7) must be used:

$$\sigma_p = \left[\sum_{i=1}^{N} \sum_{j=1}^{N} X_i X_j \sigma_{ij} \right]^{1/2} \qquad (6.7)$$

$$= \left[\sum_{i=1}^{4} \sum_{j=1}^{4} X_i X_j \sigma_{ij} \right]^{1/2}$$

Remembering that $X_2 = 0$ and $X_3 = 0$ in these portfolios, this equation reduces to

$$\sigma_p = [X_1 X_1 \sigma_{11} + X_1 X_4 \sigma_{14} + X_4 X_1 \sigma_{41} + X_4 X_4 \sigma_{44}]^{1/2}$$

$$= [X_1^2 \sigma_1^2 + X_4^2 \sigma_4^2 + 2 X_1 X_4 \sigma_{14}]^{1/2}$$

This equation can be reduced even further, since security 4 is the risk-free security that, by definition, has $\sigma_4 = 0$ and $\sigma_{14} = 0$. Accordingly, it reduces to

$$\sigma_p = [X_1^2 \sigma_1^2]^{1/2}$$

$$= [X_1^2 \times 146]^{1/2}$$

$$= X_1 \times 12.08\%$$

Thus, the standard deviations of portfolios B, C, and D are

$$\sigma_B = .25 \times 12.08\%$$

$$= 3.02\%$$

$$\sigma_C = .50 \times 12.08\%$$

$$= 6.04\%$$

$$\sigma_D = .75 \times 12.08\%$$

$$= 9.06\%$$

In summary, the five portfolios have the following expected returns and standard deviations:

Portfolio	X_1	X_4	Expected Return	Standard Deviation
A	.00	1.00	4.00%	0.00%
B	.25	.75	7.05	3.02
C	.50	.50	10.10	6.04
D	.75	.25	13.15	9.06
E	1.00	.00	16.20	12.08

These portfolios are plotted in Figure 8.1. In this figure, it can be seen that the portfolios lie on a straight line connecting the points representing the location of the risk-free asset and Able. Although only five particular combinations of the risk-free asset and Able have been examined here, it can be shown that any combination of the risk-free asset and Able will lie somewhere on the straight line connecting them; the exact location will depend on the relative proportions invested in each asset. Furthermore, this observation can be generalized to combinations of the risk-free asset and any risky asset. That is, any portfolio that consists of a combination of the risk-free asset and a risky asset will have an expected return and standard deviation such that it plots on a straight line connecting them.

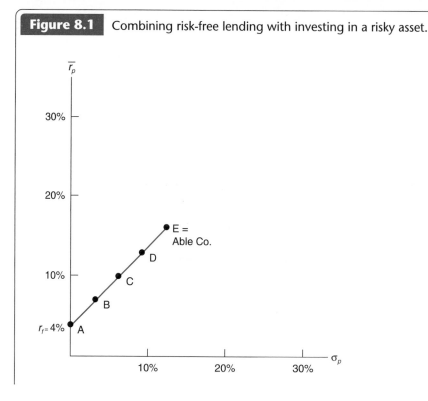

Figure 8.1 Combining risk-free lending with investing in a risky asset.

Investing in Both the Risk-free Asset and a Risky Portfolio

Next, consider what happens when a portfolio consisting of more than just one risky security is combined with the risk-free asset. For example, consider the risky portfolio that consists of Able and Charlie in proportions of .80 and .20, respectively. Its expected return (denoted by $\bar{r}_{PAC}$) and standard deviation (denoted by σ_{PAC}) are equal to

$$\bar{r}_{PAC} = (.80 \times 16.2\%) + (.20 \times 22.8\%)$$
$$= 17.52\%$$
$$\sigma_{PAC} = [(.80 \times .80 \times 146) + (.20 \times .20 \times 289) + (2 \times .80 \times .20 \times 145)]^{1/2}$$
$$= 12.30\%$$

Any portfolio that consists of an investment in both *PAC* and the risk-free asset will have an expected return and standard deviation that can be calculated in a manner identical to that previously shown for combinations of an individual asset and the risk-free asset. A portfolio that has the proportion X_{PAC} invested in the portfolio *PAC*, and the proportion $X_4 = 1 - X_{PAC}$ in the risk-free asset will have an expected return and standard deviation that are equal to, respectively,

$$\bar{r}_p = (X_{PAC} \times 17.52\%) + (X_4 \times 4\%)$$
$$\sigma_p = X_{PAC} \times 12.30\%$$

For example, consider investing in a portfolio that consists of *PAC* and the risk-free asset in proportions of .25 and .75, respectively.[2] This portfolio will have an expected return of

---

[2]Note that investing the proportion .25 in portfolio *PAC* is equivalent to investing the proportion .20(.25 × .80) in Able and the proportion .05(.25 × .20) in Charlie.

$$\bar{r}_p = (.25 \times 17.52\%) + (.75 \times 4\%)$$
$$= 7.38\%$$

and a standard deviation of

$$\sigma_p = (.25 \times 12.30\%)$$
$$= 3.08\%$$

Figure 8.2 shows that this portfolio lies on a straight line connecting the risk-free asset and *PAC*. Its exact location is indicated by the point *P* on this line. Other portfolios consisting of various combinations of *PAC* and the risk-free asset will also lie on this line, with their exact locations depending on the relative proportions invested in *PAC* and the risk-free asset. For example, a portfolio that involves investing a proportion of .50 in the risk-free asset and a proportion of .50 in *PAC* lies on this line exactly halfway between the two end points.

In summary, combining the risk-free asset with any risky portfolio can be viewed as being no different from combining the risk-free asset with an individual risky security. In both cases, the resulting portfolio has an expected return and standard deviation such that it lies on a straight line connecting the two endpoints.

The Effect of Risk-free Lending on the Efficient Set

As mentioned earlier, the feasible set is changed significantly as a result of the introduction of risk-free lending. Figure 8.3 shows how it changes the feasible set for the example at hand. Here, all risky assets and portfolios, not just Able and *PAC*, are considered in all possible combinations with the risk-free asset. In particular, note that there are two boundaries that are straight lines emanating from the risk-free asset. The bottom line connects the risk-free asset with Baker. Thus, it represents portfolios formed by combining Baker and the risk-free asset.

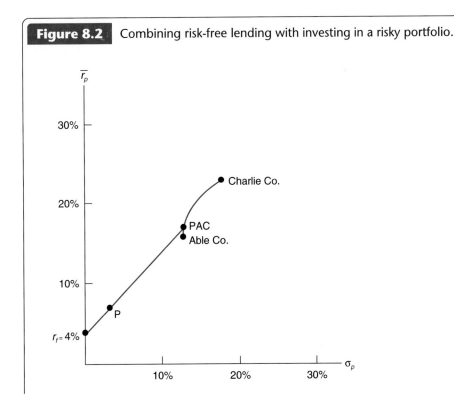

Figure 8.2 Combining risk-free lending with investing in a risky portfolio.

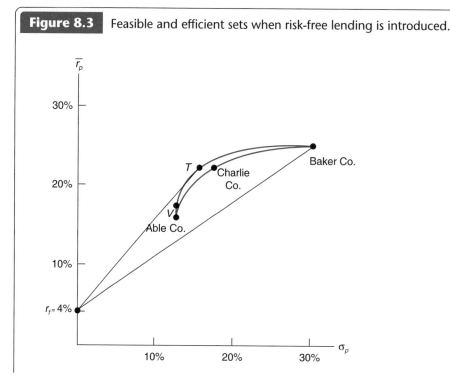

Figure 8.3 Feasible and efficient sets when risk-free lending is introduced.

The other straight line emanating from the risk-free asset represents combinations of the risk-free asset and a particular risky portfolio on the efficient set of the Markowitz model. It is a line that is just tangent to the efficient set of the Markowitz model, with the tangency point being denoted by T. This tangency point represents a risky portfolio consisting of Able, Baker, and Charlie in proportions equal to, respectively, .12, .19, and .69. Substituting these proportions into equations (6.3a) and (6.7) indicates that the expected return and standard deviation of T are 22.4% and 15.2%, respectively.

Although other risky efficient portfolios from the Markowitz model can also be combined with the risk-free asset, portfolio T deserves special attention because there is no other portfolio consisting purely of risky assets that, when connected by a straight line to the risk-free asset, lies northwest of it. In other words, of all the lines that can be drawn emanating from the risk-free asset and connecting with either a risky asset or a risky portfolio, none has a greater slope than the line that goes to T.

This is important, since part of the efficient set of the Markowitz model is dominated by this line. In particular, the portfolios on the Markowitz model efficient set going from the minimum risk portfolio, denoted by V, to T are no longer efficient when a risk-free asset is made available for investment. Instead, the efficient set now consists of a straight-line segment and a curved segment. The straight-line segment is the straight line going from the risk-free asset to T and thus consists of portfolios made up of various combinations of the risk-free asset and T. The curved segment consists of those portfolios to the northeast of T on the Markowitz model efficient set.

The Effect of Risk-free Lending on Portfolio Selection

Figure 8.4 shows how an investor would go about selecting an optimal efficient portfolio when there is a risk-free asset available for investment in addition to a number of risky assets. If the investor's indifference curves look like those shown in panel (a), then the

Figure 8.4 Portfolio selection with risk-free lending.

(a) An Optimal Portfolio that Involves Risk-free Lending

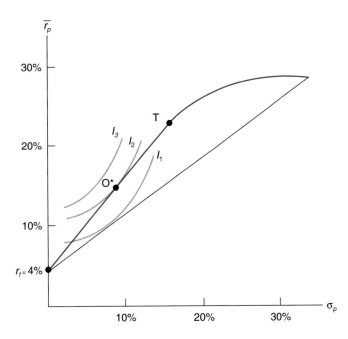

(b) An Optimal Portfolio that Involves Only Risky Assets

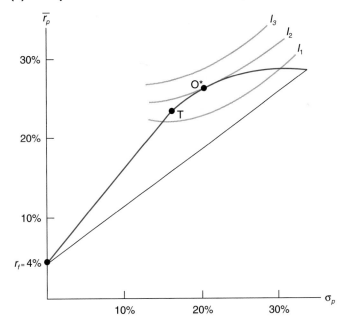

investor's optimal portfolio O* will involve investing part of his initial wealth in the risk-free asset and the rest in T, because O* lies on the straight-line segment of the efficient set.[3] Alternatively, if the investor is less risk-averse and has indifference curves that look like those shown in part (b), then the investor's optimal portfolio O* will not involve any risk-free investing because O* lies on the curved segment of the efficient set that lies to the northeast of T.

Allowing for Risk-free Borrowing

The analysis presented in the previous section can be expanded by allowing the investor to borrow money. This means that the investor is no longer restricted to his initial wealth when it comes time to decide how much money to invest in risky assets.[4] However, if the investor borrows money, then interest must be paid on the loan. Since the interest rate is known and there is no uncertainty about repaying the loan, this is often referred to as **risk-free borrowing**.

It will be assumed that the rate of interest charged on the loan is equal to the rate of interest that could be earned from investing in the risk-free asset.[5] Using the earlier example, this means that the investor not only has the opportunity to invest in a risk-free asset that earns a rate of return of 4%, but also may borrow money, for which the investor must pay a rate of interest equal to 4%.

Earlier, the proportion invested in the risk-free asset was denoted by X_4, and this proportion was constrained to be a nonnegative number between 0 and 1. Now, with the opportunity to borrow at the same rate, X_4 will no longer be so constrained. In the earlier example, the investor had initial wealth of $17 200. If the investor borrows money, then he will have in excess of $17 200 to invest in the risky securities of Able, Baker, and Charlie.

For example, if the investor borrows $4300, then he will have a total of $17 200 + $4300 = $21 500 to invest in these securities. In this situation, X_4 can be viewed as being equal to $-$4300/$17 200 = -.25$. However, the sum of the proportions must still equal 1. This means that if the investor has borrowed money, the sum of the proportions invested in risky assets would be greater than 1. For example, borrowing $4300 and investing $21 500 in Able means that the proportion in Able, X_1, is $21 500/$17 200 = 1.25$. Note how in this case $X_1 + X_4 = 1.25 + (-.25) = 1$.

Borrowing and Investing in a Risky Security

In order to evaluate the effect that the introduction of risk-free borrowing has on the efficient set, the example presented in the previous section will be expanded. In particular, consider portfolios F, G, H, and I, where the investor borrows a proportion of his initial wealth equal to .25, .50, .75, and 1.00, respectively. In all four portfolios, the investor will invest all the borrowed funds as well as his own funds in Able. Thus, the proportions for these portfolios can be summarized as follows:

---

[3]A more risk-averse investor (meaning an investor whose indifference curves have greater slopes) would choose an optimal portfolio that is closer to the risk-free asset on the line that connects the risk-free asset to T. Ultimately, if the investor is infinitely risk-averse, the optimal portfolio will consist of an investment in just the risk-free asset.

[4]Allowing for borrowing can be viewed as giving the investor the opportunity to engage in margin purchases if he so desires. That is, with borrowing the investor is allowed to use financial leverage.

[5]Appendix A discusses what happens to the efficient set when the investor is able to borrow, but at a rate that is greater than the rate that can be earned by investing in the risk-free asset.

	Portfolio F	Portfolio G	Portfolio H	Portfolio I
X_1	1.25	1.50	1.75	2.00
X_4	-.25	-.50	-.75	-1.00

The expected returns of these portfolios are calculated in the same manner as was shown in the previous section. Equation (6.3a) is still used:

$$\bar{r}_p = \sum_{i=1}^{N} X_i \bar{r}_i$$

$$= \sum_{i=1}^{4} X_i \bar{r}_i \tag{6.3a}$$

$$= X_1 \bar{r}_1 + X_4 r_4$$

$$= (X_1 \times 16.2\%) + (X_4 \times 4\%)$$

Thus, portfolios F, G, H, and I have the following expected returns:

$$\bar{r}_F = (1.25 \times 16.2\%) + (-.25 \times 4\%)$$
$$= 19.25\%$$
$$\bar{r}_G = (1.50 \times 16.2\%) + (-.50 \times 4\%)$$
$$= 22.30\%$$
$$\bar{r}_H = (1.75 \times 16.2\%) + (-.75 \times 4\%)$$
$$= 25.35\%$$
$$\bar{r}_I = (2.00 \times 16.2\%) + (-1.00 \times 4\%)$$
$$= 28.40\%$$

Similarly, the standard deviations of these portfolios are calculated by using equation (6.7), as in the previous section:

$$\sigma_p = \left[\sum_{i=1}^{N} \sum_{j=1}^{N} X_i X_j \sigma_{ij} \right]^{1/2}$$

$$= \left[\sum_{i=1}^{4} \sum_{j=1}^{4} X_i X_j \sigma_{ij} \right]^{1/2} \tag{6.7}$$

which was shown to reduce to

$$\sigma_p = X_1 \times 12.08\%$$

Thus, the standard deviations of the four portfolios are

$$\sigma_F = 1.25 \times 12.08\%$$
$$= 15.10\%$$
$$\sigma_G = 1.50 \times 12.08\%$$
$$= 18.12\%$$
$$\sigma_H = 1.75 \times 12.08\%$$
$$= 21.14\%$$
$$\sigma_I = 2.00 \times 12.08\%$$
$$= 24.16\%$$

In summary, these four portfolios, as well as the five portfolios that involve risk-free lending, have the following expected returns and standard deviations:

Portfolio	X_1	X_4	Expected Return	Standard Deviation
A	.00	1.00	4.00%	0.00%
B	.25	.75	7.05	3.02
C	.50	.50	10.10	6.04
D	.75	.25	13.15	9.06
E	1.00	.00	16.20	12.08
F	1.25	−.25	19.25	15.10
G	1.50	−.50	22.30	18.12
H	1.75	−.75	25.35	21.14
I	2.00	−1.00	28.40	24.16

In Figure 8.5, it can be seen that the four portfolios that involve risk-free borrowing (F, G, H, and I) all lie in the same straight line that goes through the five portfolios that involve risk-free lending (A, B, C, D, and E). Furthermore, the larger the amount of borrowing, the further out on the line the portfolio lies (equivalently, the smaller the value of X_4, the further out on the line the portfolio lies).

Although only four particular combinations of borrowing and investing in Able have been examined here, it can be shown that any combination of borrowing and investing in Able will lie somewhere on this line, with the exact location depending on the amount borrowed. Furthermore, this observation can be generalized to combinations of risk-free borrowing and an investment in any particular risky asset. This means that borrowing at the risk-free rate and investing all the borrowed money plus the investor's own money in a risky

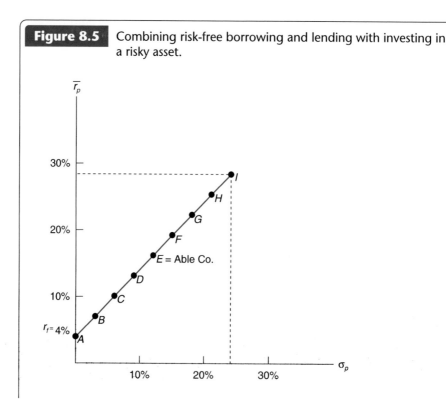

Figure 8.5 Combining risk-free borrowing and lending with investing in a risky asset.

asset results in a portfolio that has an expected return and standard deviation that lies on the extension of the straight line connecting the risk-free rate and the risky asset.

Borrowing and Investing in a Risky Portfolio

Next, consider what happens when a portfolio of more than one risky asset is purchased with both the investor's own funds and borrowed funds. Earlier it was shown that the portfolio having proportions invested in Able and Charlie equal to .80 and .20, respectively, had an expected return of 17.52% and a standard deviation of 12.30%. This portfolio was referred to as PAC. Any portfolio that involves borrowing money at the risk-free rate and then investing these funds and the investor's own funds in PAC will have an expected return and standard deviation that can be calculated in a manner identical to the one previously shown when borrowing was incurred and Able was purchased. A portfolio that involves borrowing the proportion X_4 and investing these funds and all the investor's own funds in PAC will have an expected return and standard deviation that are equal to, respectively,

$$\bar{r}_p = (X_{PAC} \times 17.52\%) + (X_4 \times 4\%)$$
$$\sigma_p = X_{PAC} \times 12.30\%$$

For example, consider borrowing an amount of money equal to 25% of the investor's initial wealth and then investing all the investor's own funds plus these borrowed funds in PAC. Thus, $X_{PAC} = 1 - X_4 = 1 - (-.25) = 1.25$.[6] This portfolio will have an expected return of

$$\bar{r}_p = (1.25 \times 17.52\%) + (-.25 \times 4\%)$$
$$= 20.90\%$$

and a standard deviation of

$$\sigma_p = (1.25 \times 12.30\%)$$
$$= 15.38\%$$

In Figure 8.6, it can be seen that this portfolio (denoted by P) lies on the extension of the line that connects the risk-free rate with PAC. Other portfolios consisting of PAC and borrowing at the risk-free rate will also lie on this extension, with their exact locations depending on the amount borrowed. Thus, borrowing in order to purchase a risky portfolio is no different from borrowing in order to purchase an individual risky asset. In both cases, the resulting portfolio lies on an extension of the line connecting the risk-free rate with the risky investment.

Allowing for Both Risk-free Lending and Risk-free Borrowing

The Effect of Risk-free Lending and Borrowing on the Efficient Set

Figure 8.7 shows how the feasible set is changed when both risk-free lending and borrowing at the risk-free rate are allowed. Here, all risky assets and portfolios, not just Able and PAC, are considered. The feasible set is the entire area between the two lines emanating from the risk-free rate that go through the location of Baker and the portfolio denoted by

---

[6]Note that investing the proportion 1.25 in portfolio PAC is equivalent to investing the proportion 100 (1.25 × .80) in Able and the proportion .25 (1.25 × .20) in Charlie.

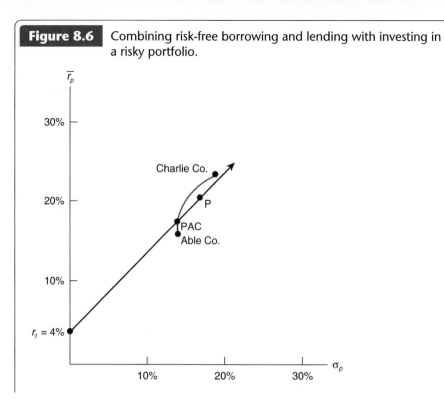

Figure 8.6 Combining risk-free borrowing and lending with investing in a risky portfolio.

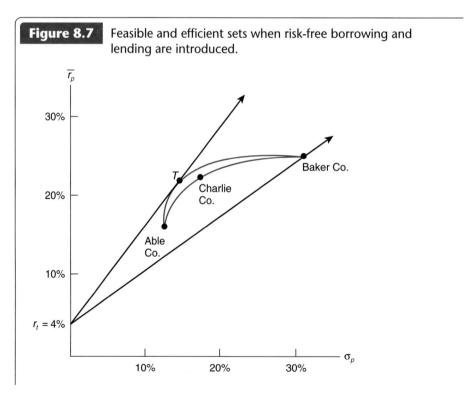

Figure 8.7 Feasible and efficient sets when risk-free borrowing and lending are introduced.

The Cost of Short-term Borrowing

The extension of the Markowitz model to incorporate borrowing and lending assumes that investors can borrow or lend at the risk-free rate. Certainly, every investor has the opportunity to lend at the risk-free rate by simply purchasing government securities with maturities corresponding to the length of her investment holding period.

Borrowing at the risk-free rate is another matter. In reality, only one entity has the option to borrow at the risk-free rate: the Canadian government. Other investors, be they individuals or institutional investors, must borrow at interest rates exceeding those paid by the government.

Just what level of interest rates do investors pay to borrow? To provide some perspective on this issue, we briefly survey some of the interest rates available in the market for short-term financial assets, known as the *money market*.

The standard of comparison for all money market interest rates is the rate paid on short-term Canadian securities called Treasury bills (see Chapter 1). The return on Treasury bills is completely certain over the short term because the federal government will never default on its obligations. It always has the option to print money or raise taxes to pay off its debts.

Other borrowers, no matter how strong their current financial position, run at least some risk of defaulting on their short-term debts. Largely due to this fact, virtually all nongovernment borrowers must pay interest rates exceeding those paid by the federal government. The difference between what the government pays to borrow money and what other borrowers pay is known as the *spread*. How large is the spread for nongovernment borrowers?

Large, financially strong corporations usually borrow in the money market through an instrument known as *commercial paper*. Commercial paper represents the negotiable, short-term unsecured promissory notes of finance, industrial, utility, insurance, and bank holding companies. On May 26, 1999, three-month commercial paper interest rates were 4.82%, a spread of .35 percentage points over three-month Treasury bills.

Corporations without the size and financial strength to borrow in the commercial paper market must obtain their short-term financing from banks. The interest rate officially quoted by banks on short-term unsecured loans to their best customers is known as the *prime rate*. The prime rate is not always an accurate measure of short-term borrowing costs, as banks often discount from it on loans to their financially strong borrowers. Financially weaker clients, on the other hand, may be charged a premium above the prime rate. On May 26, 1999, the prime rate was 6.25%, a 1.78 percentage point spread over three-month Treasury bills.

Banks also borrow in the money market in large quantities at wholesale rates. Although these borrowings are unsecured and not insured under federal deposit insurance, the strong financial standing of the chartered banks means that they pay little more than the government for these borrowings. The Bank of Canada rate is an indication of the maximum rate the banks would have to pay. On May 26, 1999, the Bank of Canada rate was 4.75%, indicating that banks would have to pay a maximum spread of .28 percentage points over three-month Treasury bills.

If you as an individual investor wish to finance your investment in securities, you typically purchase them on margin from your broker. The same holds true for institutional investors. In such transactions the broker actually borrows money elsewhere in the money market (usually drawing down a line of credit at a bank and pledging securities as collateral). The interest rate paid by the broker is known as *call money* (see Chapter 3). Brokers use either the prime rate or the call money rate to determine the interest rate charged their margin purchase customers, adding a markup of typically 1% to 2%. Larger investors can usually negotiate more favourable borrowing terms than smaller investors.

On May 26, 1999, the call money rate was 4.59%. By comparison, the three-month Treasury bill rate was 4.47%. The call money spread, therefore, was .12 percentage points. Assuming a 1 percentage point markup over the call money rate, margin investors could expect to pay about 1.12 percentage points over the Treasury bill rate. The same markup over the prime rate would be 2.75 percentage points above Treasury bills.

From this brief money market survey, it is apparent that the Treasury bill rate is relevant to investor borrowing only as a base of comparison. Investors actually have to pay more, sometimes much more, to borrow in the money market, but then, of course, such borrowing is not considered risk-free, at least by the lenders.

Figure 8.8 Portfolio selection with risk-free borrowing and lending.

(a) An Optimal Portfolio that Involves Risk-free Lending

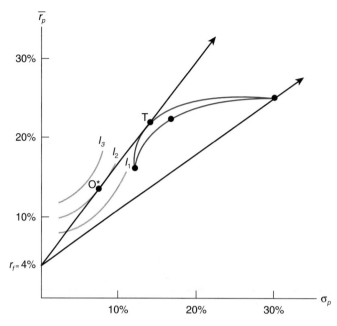

(b) An Optimal Portfolio that Involves Risk–free Borrowing

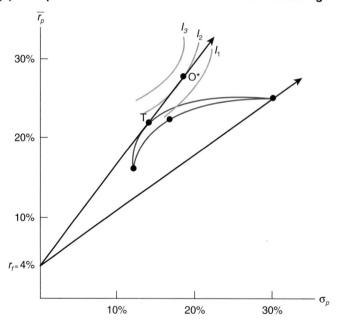

T. These two lines extend indefinitely to the right if it is assumed that there is no limit to the amount of borrowing that the investor can incur.

The straight line that goes through the portfolio T is of special importance, since it represents the efficient set. That is, it represents the set of portfolios that offer the investor the best opportunities, since it represents the set of feasible portfolios lying furthest northwest. Portfolio T, as was mentioned earlier, consists of investments in Able, Baker, and Charlie in proportions of .12, .19, and .69, respectively.[7]

As before, the line going through T is just tangent to the Markowitz model efficient set. None of the portfolios, except for T, that were on the Markowitz model efficient set are efficient when risk-free lending and borrowing are introduced. Every portfolio (except T) that lies on the Markowitz model efficient set is dominated by a portfolio on this straight line having the same standard deviation along with a higher expected return.

The Effect of Risk-free Lending and Borrowing on Portfolio Selection

Given the opportunity to either lend or borrow at the risk-free rate, an investor would identify the optimal portfolio by plotting her indifference curves on the graph and noting where one of them is tangent to the linear efficient set.[8] Figure 8.8 (on page 206) shows two alternative situations. If the investor's indifference curves look like the ones in panel (a), then the investor's optimal portfolio O* will consist of an investment in the risk-free asset as well as in T. Alternatively, if the investor is less risk-averse and has indifference curves that look like those in panel (b), then the investor's optimal portfolio O* will consist of borrowing at the risk-free rate and investing these funds as well as her own funds in T.[9]

Summary

1. The return on a risk-free asset is certain. The risk-free asset's standard deviation is zero, as is its covariance with other assets.
2. In extending the Markowitz feasible set to include risk-free lending, investors are assumed to allocate their funds among a risk-free asset and a portfolio of risky assets.
3. With risk-free lending, the efficient set becomes a straight line from the risk-free rate to a point tangent to the curved Markowitz efficient set, in addition to the portion of the Markowitz efficient set that lies northeast of this tangency point.
4. Introducing risk-free borrowing permits an investor to engage in leverage. The investor may use all of his money, plus money borrowed at the risk-free rate, to purchase a portfolio of risky assets.
5. With risk-free lending and borrowing, the efficient set becomes a straight line from the risk-free rate through a point tangent to the curved Markowitz efficient set.
6. With risk-free lending and borrowing, the efficient set consists of combinations of a single risky portfolio and various proportions of risk-free lending or borrowing.

---

[7]The composition of the tangency portfolio T can be found by use of commonly available mathematical algorithms. On a historical note, an early simple approach to determining the composition of T that did not require the identification of corner portfolios was presented in Edwin J. Elton, Martin J. Gruber, and Manfred D. Padberg, "Simple Criteria for Optimal Portfolio Selection," *Journal of Finance* 31 no. 5 (December 1976): 1341–1357.

[8]Appendix B illustrates how the composition of the investor's optimal portfolio O* is determined.

[9]The less risk-averse the investor is, the smaller the proportion in the risk-free rate (X_f) and the larger the proportion in $T(X_T)$.

7. The investor's optimal portfolio is determined by plotting his indifference curves against the efficient set.
8. The investor's optimal portfolio will include an investment in the risky portfolio and borrowing or lending at the risk-free rate.
9. Investors with higher levels of risk aversion will engage in less borrowing (or more lending) than investors with less risk aversion.

APPENDIX A

ALLOWING FOR DIFFERENT BORROWING AND LENDING RATES

In this chapter it was assumed that the investor could borrow funds at the same rate that could be earned on an investment in the risk-free asset. As a result, the feasible set became the area bounded by two straight lines emanating from the risk-free rate. The upper line represented the efficient set and had one portfolio in common with the curved efficient set of the Markowitz model. This portfolio was located where the straight line from the risk-free rate was tangent to the curved efficient set. But what happens if the investor can only borrow at a rate that is greater than the rate earned by an investment in the risk-free asset? The rate on the risk-free asset will be denoted r_{fL}, where L indicates lending (because, as mentioned earlier, an investment in the risk-free asset is equivalent to lending money to the government). The rate at which the investor can borrow money will be denoted r_{fB} and is of a magnitude such that $r_{fB} > r_{fL}$.

One way to understand the effect on the efficient set of assuming that these two rates are different is as follows. First, consider what the efficient set would look like if risk-free borrowing and lending were possible at the same rate, r_{fL}. The resulting efficient set would be the straight line shown in Figure 8.9 that goes through the points r_{fL} and T_L.

Second, consider what the efficient set would look like if risk-free borrowing and lending were possible at the higher rate, r_{fB}. The resulting efficient set would be the straight line shown in Figure 8.9 through the points r_{fB} and T_B. Note that the portfolio T_B lies on

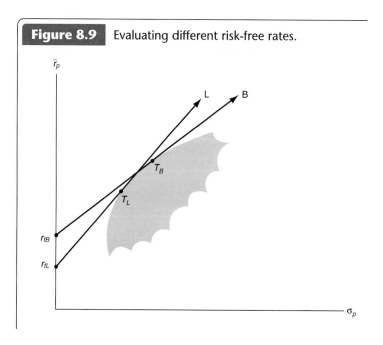

Figure 8.9 Evaluating different risk-free rates.

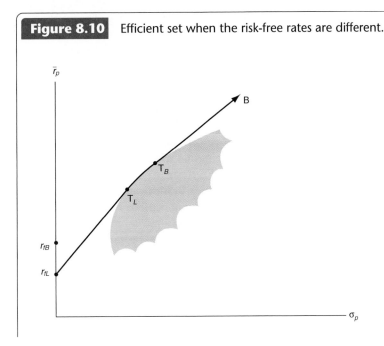

Figure 8.10 Efficient set when the risk-free rates are different.

Markowitz's efficient set above the portfolio T_L because it corresponds to a tangency point associated with a higher risk-free rate.

Third, as the investor cannot borrow at r_{fL}, that part of the line emanating from r_{fL} that extends to the right of T_L is not available to the investor and can thus be removed from consideration.

Fourth, as the investor cannot lend at the risk-free rate r_{fB}, that part of the line emanating from r_{fB} and going through T_B but lying to the left of T_B is not available to the investor and can thus be removed from consideration. The northwest boundary of what remains, shown in Figure 8.10, is the resulting efficient set.

This efficient set consists of three distinct but connected segments. The first segment is the straight line going from r_{fL} to T_L that represents various amounts of risk-free lending combined with investing in the portfolio of risky assets denoted T_L. The second segment is the curved line going from T_L to T_B that represents various risky portfolios that were also on Markowitz's curved efficient set. The third segment is the straight line extending outward from T_B that represents various amounts of borrowing combined with an investment in the risky portfolio denoted T_B.

The optimal portfolio for an investor will be, as before, the portfolio that corresponds to the point where an indifference curve is tangent to the efficient set. Depending on the investor's indifference curves, this tangency point could be on any one of the three segments that comprise the efficient set.

APPENDIX B

Determining the Composition of the Investor's Optimal Portfolio O*

Once the investor has identified the straight line efficient set by locating the tangency portfolio T, he can move on to determine the composition of his optimal portfolio. This portfolio, denoted O* in Figure 8.8, corresponds to the tangency point between the efficient set and one of the investor's indifference curves. It will be a combination of the tangency portfolio and risk-free borrowing or lending. The question is, what is that combination?

One procedure for determining the composition of the optimal portfolio assumes that the investor's indifference curves are of the following general form:

$$S = \bar{r} - a\sigma^2 \qquad (8.1)$$

where $\bar{r}$ and σ^2 denote the expected return and variance of a particular portfolio, respectively.[10] The term S is a constant that indicates the level of utility associated with an indifference curve.[11] Various combinations of expected return and standard deviation can provide the investor with the same utility. Higher values of S correspond to indifference curves that are further northwest. Lastly, the term a is a positive constant that indicates the investor's degree of risk aversion, where larger values indicate greater degrees of risk aversion.[12] (Note that when $a = 0$, the investor is risk neutral since the amount of satisfaction a given portfolio provides is not dependent upon its riskiness, which is measured by σ^2. In the limit when $a = \infty$, the investor is completely risk-averse and will not invest in any asset that has risk.) The investor's optimal portfolio O* will provide a level of utility given by:

$$S = \bar{r}^* - a\sigma^{*2} \qquad (8.2)$$

where $\bar{r}^*$ and σ^* denote the optimal portfolio's expected return and standard deviation, respectively.

Next, remember that the expected return of the investor's optimal portfolio is a weighted average of the risk-free rate, r_f, and the expected return of the tangency portfolio T, $\bar{r}_T$:

$$\bar{r}^* = (\bar{r}_T \times Y) + [r_f \times (1 - Y)] \qquad (8.3)$$

where Y is the proportion invested in the tangency portfolio and thus $(1 - Y)$ is the proportion invested in the risk-free rate. Furthermore, the standard deviation of this portfolio is simply:

$$\sigma^* = Y\sigma_T \qquad (8.4)$$

since the standard deviation of the risk-free rate is zero. Inserting the right-hand sides of equations (8.3) and (8.4) into the appropriate places in equation (8.2) results in:

$$S^* = (\bar{r}_T \times Y) + [r_f \times (1 - Y)] - aY^2\sigma_T^2 \qquad (8.5)$$

which indicates that the utility that an investor will get from his optimal portfolio will depend on the proportions invested in T and r_f.

In order to determine the optimal values for these proportions, a bit of differential calculus in needed. In particular, the value of Y is sought that maximizes the value of S^* in equation (8.5). This can be determined by taking the derivative of S^* with respect to Y in equation (8.5) and setting the result equal to zero:

$$\bar{r}_T - r_f - 2aY\sigma_T^2 = 0 \qquad (8.6a)$$

which can be solved for Y:

$$Y = \frac{(\bar{r}_T \times Y)}{2aY\sigma_T^2} \qquad (8.6b)$$

Remembering that the term a is positive, this means that a greater difference between the expected return on the tangency portfolio and the risk-free rate will cause the investor to

---

[10]Equation (8.1) is linear in form because the variance (σ^2) of the portfolio is used instead of the standard deviation (σ). If standard deviation were used, then equation (8.1) would be expressed in the more commonly recognized form of a parabola that opens upward.

[11]The concept of investor utility is discussed in Chapter 6.

[12]Risk aversion is discussed further in the appendix to Chapter 23.

purchase more of the tangency portfolio and less of the risk-free rate, an intuitively pleasing result. A similar result will also occur when either the investor is less risk averse (meaning the term a is smaller) or the standard deviation of the tangency portfolio is smaller, which also squares with our intuition.

As an example, consider again the situation illustrated in Figure 8.8a where the tangency portfolio associated with Able, Baker, and Charlie companies had an expected return of 22.4% and a standard deviation of 15.2%, given the risk-free rate was 4%. Assuming the risk aversion coefficient for the investor was $a = 7.96$, equation (8.6b) indicates that:

$$Y = \frac{.224 - .04}{(2 \times 7.96 \times .152^2)}$$
$$= .50$$

Thus, the investor will allocate his investable wealth so as to use 50% of it to purchase the tangency portfolio. In terms of the amount of investment in Able, Baker, and Charlie companies, this translates to:

$$[.50 \times X(T)] = .50 \times \begin{bmatrix} .12 \\ .19 \\ .69 \end{bmatrix} = \begin{bmatrix} .060 \\ .095 \\ .345 \end{bmatrix}$$

Thus the investor should invest an amount of money that is equal to 6%, 9.5%, and 34.5% of his initial wealth in shares of Able, Baker, and Charlie, respectively. Furthermore, 50% of the investor's initial wealth should be used to buy the riskfree asset.

Alternatively, consider the example displayed in Figure 8.8b where the investor is less risk averse, having $a = 3.19$. In this situation, equation (8.6b) indicates that:

$$Y = \frac{.224 - .04}{(2 \times 3.19 \times .152^2)}$$
$$= 1.25$$

Thus, the less risk-averse investor will allocate his investable wealth so as to use 125% of it to purchase the tangency portfolio, with the extra 25% coming from borrowing at the risk-free rate. In terms of the amount of investment in the securities of Able, Baker, and Charlie companies, this decision translates to:

$$[1.25 \times X(T)] = 1.25 \times \begin{bmatrix} .12 \\ .19 \\ .69 \end{bmatrix} = \begin{bmatrix} .150 \\ .238 \\ .862 \end{bmatrix}$$

Thus the less risk-averse investor should invest an amount of money that is equal to 15%, 24%, and 86% of his or her initial wealth in shares of Able, Baker, and Charlie, respectively.

QUESTIONS AND PROBLEMS

1. Why is a pure discount government security (that is, one that does not make coupon payments, pays interest at maturity, and hence sells at a discount from par) with no risk of default still risky to an investor whose holding period does not coincide with the maturity date of the security?
2. Distinguish between reinvestment-rate risk and interest-rate risk.
3. The covariance between a risk-free asset and a risky asset is zero. Explain why this is the case and demonstrate it mathematically.
4. Lindsay Brown owns a risky portfolio with a 15% expected return. The risk-free return is 5%. What is the expected return on Lindsay's total portfolio if Lindsay invests the following proportions in the risky portfolio and the remainder in the risk-free asset?
   a. 120%

b. 90%

c. 75%

5. Consider a risky portfolio with an expected return of 18%. With a risk-free return of 5%, how could you create a portfolio with a 24% expected return?

6. Harriet Baker owns a risky portfolio with a 20% standard deviation. If Harriet invests the following proportions in the risk-free asset and the remainder in the risky portfolio, what is the standard deviation of Harriet's total portfolio?

   a. −30%

   b. 10%

   c. 30%

7. Oswald Burns's portfolio is composed of an investment in a risky portfolio (with a 12% expected return and a 25% standard deviation) and a risk-free asset (with a 7% return). If Oswald's total portfolio has a 20% standard deviation, what is its expected return?

8. Vivian Chao argues that buying a risky portfolio with risk-free borrowing is equivalent to a purchase of the risky portfolio on margin. Patsy Cahill contends that such an investment can be viewed as selling the risk-free asset short and using the proceeds to invest in the risky portfolio. Who is correct? Explain.

9. How does the efficient set change when risk-free borrowing and lending are introduced into the Markowitz model? Explain with words and graphs.

10. Why does the efficient set with the Markowitz model extended to include risk-free borrowing and lending have only one point in common with the efficient set of the Markowitz model without risk-free borrowing and lending? Why are the other points on the "old" efficient set no longer desirable? Explain with words and graphs.

11. Based on the assumptions developed in this chapter, is it true that all investors will hold the same risky portfolio? Explain.

12. How does the feasible set change when risk-free borrowing and lending are introduced into the Markowitz model? Explain with words and graphs.

13. With the Markowitz model extended to include risk-free borrowing and lending, draw the indifference curves, efficient set, and optimal portfolio for an investor with high risk aversion and an investor with low risk aversion.

14. Given the following expected return vector and variance-covariance matrix for three assets:

$$ER = \begin{bmatrix} 10.1 \\ 7.8 \\ 5.0 \end{bmatrix} \qquad VC = \begin{bmatrix} 210 & 60 & 0 \\ 60 & 90 & 0 \\ 0 & 0 & 0 \end{bmatrix}$$

    and given the fact that Peter Traynor's risky portfolio is split 50–50 between the two risky assets:

    a. Which security of the three must be the risk-free asset? Why?

    b. Calculate the expected return and standard deviation of Peter's portfolio.

    c. If the risk-free asset makes up 25% of Peter's total portfolio, what is the portfolio's expected return and standard deviation?

15. What does the efficient set look like if risk-free borrowing is permitted but no lending is allowed? Explain with words and graphs.

16. What will be the effect on total portfolio expected return and risk if you borrow money at the risk-free rate and invest in the optimal risky portfolio?

17. Suppose that your level of risk aversion decreased as you grew richer. In a world of risk-free borrowing and lending, how would your optimal portfolio change? Would the types of risky securities you hold change? Explain with words and graphs.

18. (Appendix Question) How does the efficient set change when the condition of borrowing and lending at the same risk-free rate is changed to borrowing at a rate greater than the rate at which risk-free lending can be conducted? Explain with words and graphs.

19. (Appendix Question) Richard Gerken owns a tangency portfolio composed of four securities held in the following proportions:

$$X(T) = \begin{bmatrix} .18 \\ .30 \\ .24 \\ .28 \end{bmatrix}$$

The risk-free rate is 4%. The expected return and standard deviation of the tangency portfolio are, respectively, 12% and 18%. What is the composition of Richard's optimal portfolio if Richard has a risk-aversion coefficient of 2.47?

KEY TERMS

risk-free asset (p. 192)
interest-rate risk (p. 193)
reinvestment-rate risk (p. 193)

risk-free lending (p. 193)
risk-free borrowing (p. 200)

REFERENCES

1. Credit for extending Markowitz's model to include risk-free lending and borrowing belongs to:

James Tobin, "Liquidity Preference as Behavior Towards Risk," *Review of Economic Studies* 26, no. 1 (February 1958): 65–86.

James Tobin, "The Theory of Portfolio Selection," in *The Theory of Interest Rates*, ed. F. H. Hahn and F. P. R. Brechling (London: Macmillan and Co., 1965).

2. For a discussion of various mean-variance models that involve different sets of assumptions regarding risk-free lending and borrowing, margin purchasing, and short selling, see:

Eugene F. Fama, *Foundations of Finance* (New York: Basic Books, 1976), Chapters 7 and 8.

Gordon J. Alexander and Jack Clark Francis, *Portfolio Analysis* (Englewood Cliffs, NJ: Prentice Hall, 1986), Chapter 4.

3. For a discussion of how to determine the composition of portfolios on the efficient set under a variety of different assumptions, see:

Edwin J. Elton, Martin J. Gruber, and Manfred D. Padberg, "Simple Criteria for Optimal Portfolio Selection," *Journal of Finance* 31, no. 5 (December 1976): 1341–1357.

Gordon J. Alexander, "Short Selling and Efficient Sets," *Journal of Finance* 48, no. 4 (September 1993): 1497–1506.

Edwin J. Elton and Martin J. Gruber, *Modern Portfolio Theory and Investment Analysis* (New York: John Wiley, 1995), Chapters 6 and 9.

CHAPTER 9

The Capital Asset Pricing Model

C hapters 6, 7, and 8 presented a method for identifying an investor's optimal portfolio. With this method, the investor needs to estimate the expected returns and variances for all securities under consideration. Furthermore, all the covariances among these
securities need to be estimated and the risk-free rate needs to be determined. Once this is
done, the investor can find out the composition of the tangency portfolio as well as its
expected return and standard deviation. At this juncture the investor can identify the optimal portfolio by noting where one of her indifference curves touch but do not intersect the
efficient set. This portfolio will involve investing in the tangency portfolio, along with a
certain amount of either risk-free borrowing or lending, since the efficient set is linear (that
is, a straight line).

Such an approach to investing can be viewed as an exercise in **normative economics**,
where investors are told what they should do. Thus, the approach is prescriptive in nature.
In this chapter we enter the realm of **positive economics**, and provide a descriptive model
of how assets are priced. The model assumes, among other things, that all investors use the
approach to investing given in Chapters 6, 7, and 8. The major implication of the model
is that the expected return of an asset will be related to a measure of risk for the asset that
is known as beta. The exact manner in which expected return and beta are related is specified by the **Capital Asset Pricing Model (CAPM)**.

Since many current practices in the investment industry are based on various extensions and modifications of the CAPM, a sound understanding of the original version is
important. Accordingly, this chapter presents the original version of the CAPM.[1]

Normative Economics A
form of economic analysis
that is prescriptive in nature,
dealing with what "ought to
be."

Positive Economics A
form of economic analysis
that is descriptive in nature,
dealing with "what is."

**Capital Asset Pricing
Model (CAPM)** An
equilibrium model of asset
pricing that states that the
expected return on a
security is a positive linear
function of the security's
sensitivity to changes in the
market portfolio's return.

Assumptions

In order to see how assets are priced, a model (that is, a theory) must be constructed. This
requires simplification, in that the model builder must abstract from the full complexity of
the situation and focus only on the most important elements. The way this is achieved is
by making certain assumptions about the environment. These assumptions need to be simplistic in order to provide the degree of abstraction that allows for some success in building the model. The *reasonableness* of the assumptions (or lack thereof) is of little concern.
Instead, the test of a model is in its ability to help the user understand and predict the pro-

---

[1]Some extended versions of the CAPM are discussed in Appendix A.

cess being modeled. As Milton Friedman, recipient of the 1976 Nobel Memorial Prize in Economics, has stated in a famous essay:

> [T]he relevant question to ask about the "assumptions" of a theory is not whether they are descriptively "realistic," for they never are, but whether they are sufficiently good approximations for the purpose in hand. And this question can be answered only by seeing whether the theory works, which means whether it yields sufficiently accurate predictions.[2]

Some of the assumptions that underlie the CAPM also underlie the normative approach to investing that was described in previous chapters. These assumptions are as follows:

1. Investors evaluate portfolios by looking at the expected returns and standard deviations of the portfolios over a one-period horizon.
2. Investors are never satiated, so when given a choice between two otherwise identical portfolios, they will choose the one with the higher expected return.
3. Investors are risk-averse, so when given a choice between two otherwise identical portfolios, they will choose the one with the lower standard deviation.
4. Individual assets are infinitely divisible, meaning that an investor can buy a fraction of a share if he so desires.
5. There is a risk-free rate at which an investor may either lend (that is, invest) or borrow money.
6. Taxes and transaction costs are irrelevant.

To these assumptions the following are added:

7. All investors have the same one-period horizon.
8. The risk-free rate is the same for all investors.
9. Information is freely and instantly available to all investors.
10. Investors have **homogeneous expectations**, meaning that they have the same perceptions in regard to the expected returns, standard deviations, and covariances of securities.

As can be seen by examining these assumptions, the CAPM reduces the situation to an extreme case. Everyone has the same information and agrees about the future prospects for securities. Implicitly, this means that investors analyze and process information in the same way. The markets for securities are **perfect**, meaning there are no *frictions* to impede investing; potential impediments such as finite divisibility, taxes, transaction costs, and different risk-free borrowing and lending rates have been assumed away. This allows the focus to be changed from how an individual should invest to what would happen to security prices if everyone invested in a similar manner. By examining the collective behaviour of all investors in the marketplace, we can describe the nature of the resulting equilibrium relationship between each security's risk and return.

Homogeneous Expectations A situation in which all investors possess the same perceptions with regard to the expected returns, standard deviations, and covariances of securities.

Perfect Markets Security markets in which no impediments to investing exist. These impediments include such things as finite divisibility of securities, taxes, transactions costs, and costly information.

The Capital Market Line

The Separation Theorem

What are the implications of these 10 assumptions? First, investors would analyze securities and determine the composition of the tangency portfolio. In doing so, *everyone would obtain the same tangency portfolio.* This is not surprising, since there is complete agreement among investors on the estimates of the securities' expected returns, variances, and covariances as well as on the size of the risk-free rate. This also means that the linear efficient set

---

[2]Milton Friedman, *Essays in the Theory of Positive Economics* (Chicago: The University of Chicago Press, 1953), p. 15.

(described in Chapter 8) is the same for all investors because it simply involves combinations of the agreed-upon tangency portfolio and risk-free rate.

As all investors face the same efficient set, the only reason they will choose different portfolios is because they have different indifference curves. Thus, different investors will choose different portfolios from the same efficient set because they have different preferences toward risk and return. For example, as was shown in Figure 8.8, the investor in panel (a) will choose a different portfolio from the investor in panel (b). Note, however that although the chosen portfolios will be different, *each investor will choose the same combination of risky securities*, denoted by T in Figure 8.8. That is, each investor would spread his funds among risky securities in the same relative proportions, adding risk-free borrowing or lending in order to achieve a personally preferred overall combination of risk and return. This feature of the CAPM is often referred to as the **separation theorem**:

> The optimal combination of risky assets for an investor can be determined without any knowledge about the investor's preferences towards risk and return.

In other words, the determination of the optimal combination of risky assets can be made separately from the determination of the shape of an investor's indifference curves.

The reasoning behind the separation theorem involves a property of the linear efficient set that was introduced in Chapter 8. There, it was shown that all portfolios located on the linear efficient set involved an investment in a tangency portfolio combined with varying degrees of risk-free borrowing or lending. With the CAPM, each person faces the same linear efficient set, meaning that each person will be investing in the same tangency portfolio (combined with a certain amount of either risk-free borrowing or lending that depends upon that person's indifference curves). It therefore follows that the risky portion of each person's portfolio will be the same.

In the example from Chapter 8, three securities were considered, corresponding to the shares of Able, Baker, and Charlie companies. With a risk-free rate of return of 4%, the tangency portfolio T was shown to consist of investments in Able, Baker, and Charlie in proportions equal to .12, .19, and .69, respectively. If the 10 assumptions of the CAPM are made, then the investor shown in panel (a) of Figure 8.8 would invest approximately half of her money in the risk-free asset and the remainder in T. The investor shown in panel (b), on the other hand, would borrow an amount of money equal to approximately one-quater of the value of her initial wealth and proceed to invest these borrowed funds as well as her own funds in T.[3] Thus, the proportions invested in the three stocks for the investors of panels (a) and (b) would equal[4]

$$(.5) \times \begin{bmatrix} .12 \\ 19 \\ .69 \end{bmatrix} = \begin{bmatrix} .060 \\ .095 \\ .345 \end{bmatrix} \quad \text{for the investor in panel (a)}$$

$$(1.25) \times \begin{bmatrix} .12 \\ .19 \\ .69 \end{bmatrix} = \begin{bmatrix} .150 \\ .238 \\ .862 \end{bmatrix} \quad \text{for the investor in panel (b)}$$

While the proportions to be invested in each of these three risky securities for the panel (a) investor (.060, .095, .345) can be seen to be different in size from those invested for the

---

[3]If the investor had initial wealth of $40 000, this means that she would borrow $10 000 and then invest $50 000 ($40 000 + $10 000) in T.

[4]Note that the proportions in these three stocks sum to .5 for the panel (a) investor and 1.25 for the panel (b) investor. Since the respective proportions for the risk-free rate are .5 and −.25, the aggregate proportions for the stocks and risk-free rate sum to 1.0 for each investor. See Appendix B to Chapter 8.

panel (b) investor (.150, .238, .862), note that the relative proportions are the same, being equal to .12, .19, and .69, respectively.

The Market Portfolio

Another important feature of the CAPM is that, in equilibrium, each security must have a non-zero proportion in the composition of the tangency portfolio.[5] That is, no security could, in equilibrium, have a proportion in T that was zero. The reasoning behind this feature lies in the previously mentioned separation theorem, in which it was asserted that the risky portion of every investor's portfolio would be independent of the investor's risk-return preferences. The justification for the theorem was that the risky portion of each investor's portfolio would simply be an investment in the tangency portfolio. If every investor is purchasing T and T does not involve an investment in each security, then nobody is investing in those securities with zero proportions in T. This means that the prices of these zero-proportion securities must *fall*, thereby causing the expected returns of these securities to *rise* until the resulting tangency portfolio has a non-zero proportion associated with them.

In the previous example, Charlie had a current price of $62 and an expected end-of-period price of $76.14. This meant that the expected return for Charlie was ($76.14 − $62)/$62 = 22.8%. Now imagine that the current price of Charlie is $72, not $62, meaning that its expected return is ($76.14 − $72)/$72 = 5.8%. If this were the case, the tangency portfolio associated with a risk-free rate of 4% would involve just Able and Baker in proportions of .90 and .10, respectively.[6] As Charlie has a proportion of zero, nobody would want to hold shares of Charlie. Consequently, orders to sell would be received in substantial quantities, with virtually no offsetting orders to buy being received. As a result, Charlie's price would fall. However, as Charlie's price falls, its expected return would rise, since the same end-of-period price of $76.14 is forecast for Charlie as before and it would now cost less to buy one share. Eventually, as the price falls, investors would change their minds and want to buy shares of Charlie. Ultimately, at a price of $62, investors will want to hold shares of Charlie so that, in aggregate, the number of shares demanded will equal the number of shares outstanding. Thus, in equilibrium, Charlie will have a non-zero proportion in the tangency portfolio.

Another interesting situation could also arise. What if each investor concludes that the tangency portfolio should involve a proportionate investment in the stock of Baker equal to .40, but at the current price of Baker there are not enough shares outstanding to meet the demand? In this situation orders to buy Baker will flood in, and brokers will raise the price in search of sellers. This will cause the expected return of Baker to fall, making it less attractive and thereby reducing its proportion in the tangency portfolio to a level where the number of shares demanded equals the number of shares outstanding.

Ultimately, everything will balance out. When all the price adjusting stops, the market will have been brought into equilibrium. First, each investor will want to hold a certain amount of each risky security. Second, the current market price of each security will be at a level where the number of shares that are demanded equals the number of shares that are outstanding.[7] Third, the risk-free rate will be at a level where the total amount of money borrowed equals the total amount of money lent. As a result, the proportions of the tan-

---

[5] Securities that have zero net amounts outstanding will not appear in the tangency portfolio. Options and futures, discussed in Chapters 19 and 20, are examples of such securities.

[6] Although the expected return of Charlie has been changed, all the variances and covariances as well as the expected returns for Able and Baker are assumed to have the same values that were given in Chapter 6, 7, and 8. The singular change in the expected return of Charlie alters not only the composition of the tangency portfolio but, more generally, the location and shape of the efficient set.

[7] In this situation the market for the security is said to have *cleared.*

gency portfolio will correspond to the proportions of what is known as the **market portfolio**, defined as follows:

> The market portfolio is a portfolio consisting of an investment in all securities where the proportion to be invested in each security corresponds to its relative market value. The relative market value of a security is simply equal to the aggregate market value of the security divided by the sum of the aggregate market values of all securities.[8]

The reason the market portfolio plays a central role in the CAPM is because the efficient set consists of an investment in the market portfolio, coupled with a desired amount of either risk-free borrowing or risk-free lending. Thus, it is common practice to refer to the tangency portfolio as the market portfolio and to denote it as M instead of T. In theory, M consists of not only common stocks but also other kinds of investments such as bonds, preferred shares, and real estate. However, in practice some people restrict M to just common stocks—a procedure that may give inappropriate results in some applications.

The Efficient Set

In the world of the CAPM, it is a simple matter to determine the relationship between risk and return for efficient portfolios. Figure 9.1 portrays it graphically. Point M represents the market portfolio and r_f represents the risk-free rate of return. Efficient portfolios plot along the line starting at r_f and going through M and consist of alternative combinations of risk and return obtainable by combining the market portfolio with risk-free borrowing or lending. This linear efficient set of the CAPM is known as the **Capital Market Line** (CML). All portfolios other than those employing the market portfolio and risk-free borrowing or lending would lie below the CML, although some might plot very close to it.

The slope of the CML is equal to the difference between expected return of the market portfolio and that of the riskless security, $\bar{r}_M - r_f$, divided by the difference in their risks, $\sigma_M - 0$, or $(\bar{r}_M - r_f)/\sigma_M$.[9] Because the vertical intercept of the CML is r_f, the straight line characterizing the CML has the following equation:

$$\bar{r}_p = r_f + \left[\frac{\bar{r}_M - r_f}{\sigma_M} \right] \sigma_p \tag{9.1}$$

where $\bar{r}_p$ and σ_p refer to the expected return and standard deviation of an efficient portfolio.[10]

In the previous example, the market portfolio associated with a risk-free rate of 4% consisted of Able, Baker, and Charlie in the proportions of .12, .19, and .69, respectively. It was shown in Chapter 8 that the expected return and standard deviation for a portfolio with these proportions was 22.4% and 15.2%, respectively. Therefore, the equation for the resulting CML is

$$\bar{r}_p = 4 + \left[\frac{22.4 - 4}{15.2} \right] \sigma_p$$
$$= 4 + 1.21\sigma_p$$

---

[8]The aggregate market value for the common stock of a company is equal to the current market price of one share times the number of shares outstanding.

[9]The slope of a straight line can be determined if the location of two points on the line are known. It is determined by rise over run, meaning it is determined by dividing the vertical distance between the two points by the horizontal distance between the two points. In the case of the CML, two points are known, corresponding to the risk-free rate and the market portfolio, so its slope can be determined in this manner.

[10]The equation of a straight line is of the form $y = a + bx$, where a is the vertical intercept and b is the slope. Since the vertical intercept and slope of the CML are known, its equation can be written as shown here by making the appropriate substitutions for a and b.

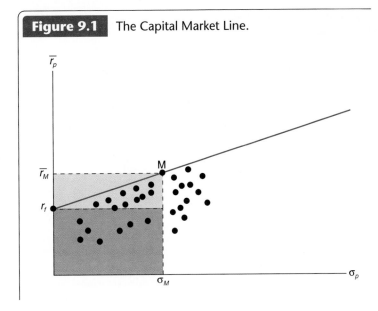

Figure 9.1 The Capital Market Line.

Equilibrium in the security market can be characterized by two key numbers. The first is the vertical intercept of the CML (that is, the risk-free rate), which is often referred to as the *reward for waiting*. The second is the slope of the CML, which is often referred to as the *reward per unit of risk borne*. In essence, the security market provides a place where time and risk can be traded, with their prices determined by the forces of supply and demand. Thus, the intercept and slope of the CML can be thought of as the "price of time" and the "price of risk," respectively. In the example, they are equal to 4% and 1.21, respectively.

The Security Market Line

◉ Implications for Individual Risky Assets

The CML represents the equilibrium relationship between the expected return and standard deviation for efficient portfolios. Individual risky securities will always plot below the line, since a single risky security, when held by itself, is an inefficient portfolio. The CAPM does not imply any particular relationship between the expected return and the standard deviation (that is, total risk) of an individual security. To say more about the expected return of an individual security, deeper analysis is necessary.

In Chapter 6 the following equation was given for calculating the standard deviation of any portfolio:

$$\sigma_p = \left[\sum_{i=1}^{N} \sum_{j=1}^{N} X_i X_j \sigma_{ij} \right]^{1/2} \tag{6.7}$$

where X_i and X_j denoted the proportions invested in securities i and j, respectively, and σ_{ij} denoted the covariance of returns between securities i and j. Now consider using this equation to calculate the standard deviation of the market portfolio:

$$\sigma_M = \left[\sum_{i=1}^{N} \sum_{j=1}^{N} X_{iM} X_{jM} \sigma_{ij} \right]^{1/2} \tag{9.2}$$

The Elusive Market Portfolio

The market portfolio holds a special place in modern investment theory and practice. It is central to the CAPM, which assumes that the market portfolio lies on the efficient set and that all investors hold the market portfolio in combination with a desired amount of risk-free borrowing and lending. Furthermore, the market portfolio represents the ultimate in diversification. Consequently, passive investors (or index fund managers—see Chapter 23), who do not *bet* on the performance of particular securities but rather desire broad diversification, seek to hold the market portfolio. The market portfolio also serves as a universal performance evaluation standard. Investment managers and their clients often compare the manager's results against the returns on the market portfolio.

Despite its widespread application, the market portfolio is surprisingly ill-defined. In theory, the composition of the market portfolio is simple: all assets are weighted in proportion to their respective market values. In reality, actually identifying the *true* market portfolio (or even a close approximation) is beyond the capability of any individual or organization.

Consider how we might go about specifying the market portfolio. The process would involve two steps: enumerating the assets to be included and calculating the market values of those assets.

First, we must list the various types of assets that constitute the market portfolio. These days we should think globally by considering assets held by investors both here at home and in foreign countries. Of course we want to include all securities representing the assets of businesses. Therefore, we should include common stocks, preferred stocks, and corporate bonds. In that vein we should also consider the value of proprietorships and partnerships. How about government debt? This should be considered if the debt is backed by real assets such as buildings. (Due to deficit spending, much of the government's debt is actually backed by future taxes and thus does not represent current wealth—a technical matter often overlooked.) We should also include real estate, cash holdings, monetary metals (primarily gold), and art. But we have not finished yet. We should also include consumer durable assets, such as autos, furniture, and major appliances. Last, but certainly not least, we should include the largest asset of all, the training and education in which people have invested vast sums, called *human capital*.

Simply listing the composition of the market portfolio is a complex undertaking. Measuring its value is even more problematic. Given the sophistication of Canadian capital markets, the values of domestic publicly traded assets are relatively easy to collect. (We should be careful, however, to avoid double-counting—for example, when one corporation owns part of another corporation.) Data availability in foreign markets varies from country to country. In some markets, such as those in the United Kingdom and Japan, security data collection systems are very sophisticated. In other markets, such as those in Third World countries, comprehensive security valuation data are difficult to acquire.

A similar situation exists with respect to non-publicly traded asset values. In some countries, the government attempts to make accurate estimates of a myriad of asset values from real estate to consumer durable goods. In other countries, little or no effort is made to compile these data.

Finally, with respect to estimating the value of human capital—well, good luck.

The difficulties involved in determining the composition and value of the true market portfolio have led to the use of market portfolio proxies. In dealing with common stocks, for example, most researchers and practitioners arbitrarily define the market portfolio to be a broad stock market index, such as the TSE 300.

What are the ramifications of not knowing the market portfolio's true composition? From a theoretical perspective, the potential problems are significant. In two controversial articles (*Journal of Financial Economics*, May 1977, and *Journal of Finance*, September 1978), Richard Roll argued that the ambiguity of the market portfolio leaves the CAPM untestable. He contended that only if one knows the true market portfolio can one test whether it actually lies on the efficient set. Considering that the CAPM linear relationship between expected return and beta depends on the efficiency of the market portfolio, Roll's argument should not be taken lightly. Furthermore, Roll argues that the practice of using proxies for the market portfolio is loaded with problems. Different proxies, even if their returns are highly correlated, could lead to different beta estimates for the same security. Roll's arguments, it should be noted, were strongly contested by prominent CAPM defenders.

From a practical perspective, investors have generally been willing to overlook the market portfolio's ambiguity. Passive managers typically segment the market into various asset classes, such as stocks and bonds. They then define somewhat arbitrarily a market portfolio for each of those asset classes and construct portfolios to track the performance of the respective asset class market portfolios. Similarly, active managers frequently refer to a designated market portfolio when they devise their investment strategies. Performance evaluators employ market proxies in their CAPM-risk-adjusted return calculations (see Chapter 24).

where X_{iM} and X_{jM} denote the proportions invested in securities i and j in the market portfolio, respectively. It can be shown that another way to write equation (9.2) is as follows:

$$\sigma_M = \left[X_{1M} \sum_{j=1}^{N} X_{jM}\sigma_{1j} + X_{2M} \sum_{j=1}^{N} X_{jM}\sigma_{2j} + X_{3M} \sum_{j=1}^{N} X_{jM}\sigma_{3j} \right.$$
$$\left. + \cdots + X_{NM} \sum_{j=1}^{N} X_{jM}\sigma_{Nj} \right]^{1/2} \quad (9.3)$$

At this point a property of covariance can be used: the covariance of security i with the market portfolio (σ_{iM}) can be expressed as

$$\sum_{j=1}^{N} X_{jM}\sigma_{ij} = \sigma_{iM} \quad (9.4)$$

This property, as applied to each one of the N risky securities in the market portfolio, results in the following:

$$\sigma_M = [X_{1M}\sigma_{1M} + X_{2M}\sigma_{2M} + X_{3M}\sigma_{3M} + \cdots + X_{NM}\sigma_{NM}]^{1/2} \quad (9.5)$$

where σ_{1M} denotes the covariance of security 1 with the market portfolio, σ_{2M} denotes the covariance of security 2 with the market portfolio, and so on. Thus, the standard deviation of the market portfolio is equal to the square root of a weighted average of the covariances of all the securities within it, where the weights are equal to the proportions of the respective securities in the market portfolio.

At this juncture an important point can be observed. Under the CAPM each investor holds the market portfolio and is concerned with its standard deviation, since that will influence the magnitude of his investment in the market portfolio. The contribution of each security to the standard deviation of the market portfolio can be seen in equation (9.5) to depend on the size of its covariance with the market portfolio. Accordingly, each investor will note that *the relevant measure of risk for a security is its covariance with the market portfolio*, σ_{iM}. This means that securities with larger values of σ_{iM} will be viewed by investors as contributing more to the risk of the market portfolio. It also means that securities with larger standard deviations should not be viewed as necessarily adding more risk to the market portfolio than those securities with smaller standard deviations.[11]

From this analysis it follows that securities with larger values for σ_{iM} will have to provide proportionately larger expected returns in order for investors to be interested in purchasing them. To understand why, consider what would happen if such securities did not provide investors with proportionately larger levels of expected return: they would contribute to the risk of the market portfolio without contributing proportionately to the expected return of the market portfolio. This means that deleting such securities from the market portfolio would cause the expected return of the market portfolio, relative to its standard deviation, to rise. Since investors would view this as a favourable change, the market portfolio would no longer be the optimal risky portfolio to hold. Thus, security prices would be out of equilibrium.

The exact form of the equilibrium relationship between risk and return can be written as follows:

$$\bar{r}_i = r_f + \left[\frac{\bar{r}_M - r_f}{\sigma_M^2} \right] \sigma_{iM} \tag{9.6}$$

As can be seen in part (a) of Figure 9.2, equation (9.6) represents a line having a vertical intercept of r_f and a slope of $[(\bar{r}_M - r_f)/\sigma_M^2]$. Since the slope is positive, the equation indicates that securities with larger covariances (σ_{iM}) will be priced so as to have larger expected returns ($\bar{r}_i$). This relationship between covariance and expected return is known as the **Security Market Line** (SML).[12]

Interestingly, a risky security with $\sigma_{iM} = 0$ will have an expected return equal to the rate on the risk-free security, r_f. Intuitively, the reason for this is that the risky security, just like the risk-free security, does not contribute to the risk of the market portfolio. This is so even though the risky security has a positive standard deviation, whereas the risk-free security has a standard deviation of zero.

Security Market Line
Derived from the CAPM, a linear relationship between the expected returns on securities and the risk of those securities, with risk expressed as the security's beta (or equivalently, the security's covariance with the market portfolio).

Figure 9.2 The Security Market Line.

(a) Covariance Version

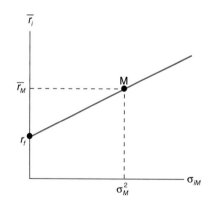

(b) Beta Version

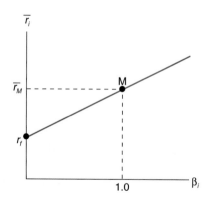

---

[11]More precisely, σ_{iM} is the relevant measure of a security's risk because $\partial\sigma_M/\partial X_{iM} = \sigma_{iM}/2\sigma_M$. That is, a marginal change in the weight in security i will result in a marginal change in the variance of the market portfolio that is a linear function of the security's covariance with the market portfolio. Accordingly, the relevant measure of the security's risk is its covariance, σ_{iM}.

[12]A more rigorous derivation of the SML is provided in Appendix B.

It is even possible for some risky securities (meaning securities with positive standard deviations) to have expected returns less than the risk-free rate. According to the CAPM, this will occur if $\sigma_{iM} < 0$, thereby indicating that they contribute a negative amount of risk to the market portfolio (meaning that they cause the risk of the market portfolio to be lower than it would be if less money were invested in them).

Also of interest is the observation that a risky security with $\sigma_{iM} = \sigma_M^2$ will have an expected return equal to the expected return on the market portfolio, $\bar{r}_M$. This is because such a security contributes an average amount of risk to the market portfolio.

Another way of expressing the SML is as follows:

$$\bar{r}_i = r_f + (\bar{r}_M - r_f)\beta_i \tag{9.7}$$

where the term β_i is defined as

$$\beta_i = \frac{\sigma_{iM}}{\sigma_M^2} \tag{9.8}$$

Beta Coefficient
(Alternatively, **Market Beta**.) A relative measure of the sensitivity of an asset's return to changes in the return on the market portfolio. Mathematically, the beta coefficient of a security is the security's covariance with the market portfolio divided by the variance of the market portfolio.

The term β_i is known as the **beta coefficient** (or simply the beta) for security i, and is an alternative way of representing the covariance risk of a security. Equation (9.7) is a different version of the SML, as can be seen in panel (b) of Figure 9.2. While having the same intercept as the earlier version shown in equation (9.6), r_f, it has a different slope. The slope of this version is $\bar{r}_M - r_f$, whereas the slope of the earlier version was $(\bar{r}_M - r_f)/\sigma_M^2$.

One property of beta is that *the beta of a portfolio is simply a weighted average of the betas of its component securities, where the proportions invested in the securities are the respective weights.* That is, the beta of a portfolio can be calculated as

$$\beta_p = \sum_{i=1}^{N} X_i \beta_i \tag{9.9}$$

Earlier it was shown that the expected return of a portfolio is a weighted average of the expected returns of its component securities, where the proportions invested in the securities are the weights. This means that since every security plots on the SML, so will every portfolio. More broadly:

> Not only every security but also every portfolio must plot on an upward-sloping straight line in a diagram with expected return on the vertical axis and beta on the horizontal axis.

This means that efficient portfolios plot on both the CML and the SML, whereas inefficient portfolios plot only on the SML.

Also of interest is that the SML must go through the point representing the market portfolio itself. Its beta is 1, and its expected return is $\bar{r}_M$, so its coordinates are $(1, \bar{r}_M)$. Since risk-free securities have beta values of 0, the SML will also go through a point with an expected return of r_f and with coordinates of $(0, r_f)$. This means that the SML will have a vertical intercept equal to r_f and a slope equal to the vertical distance between these two points, $\bar{r}_M - r_f$, divided by the horizontal distance between these two points, $1 - 0$, or $(\bar{r}_M - r_f)/(1 - 0) = \bar{r}_M - r_f$. Thus, these two points suffice to fix the location of the SML, indicating the *appropriate* expected returns for securities and portfolios with different beta values.

The equilibrium relationship shown by the SML comes to exist through the combined effects of investors' adjustments in holdings and the resulting pressures on security prices (as shown in Chapter 4). Given a set of security prices, investors calculate expected returns and covariances and then determine their optimal portfolios. If the number of shares of a security collectively desired differs from the number available, there will be upward or downward pressure on its price. Given a new set of prices, investors will reassess their desire for the various securities. The process will continue until the number of shares collectively desired for each security equals the number available.

For the individual investor, security prices and prospects are fixed, whereas the quantities held can be altered. For the market as a whole, however, these quantities are fixed (at least in the short run) and prices are variable. As in any competitive market, equilibrium requires the adjustment of each security's price until there is consistency between the quantity desired and the quantity available.

It may seem logical to examine historical returns on securities in order to determine whether or not they have been priced in equilibrium, as suggested by the CAPM. However, the issue of whether or not such testing of the CAPM can be done in a meaningful manner is controversial. For at least some purposes, affirmative test results may not be necessary in order to make practical use of the CAPM.

▶ An Example

In the example that was used earlier, Able, Baker, and Charlie were shown to form the market portfolio in proportions equal to .12, .19, and .69, respectively. Given these proportions, the market portfolio had an expected return of 22.4% and a standard deviation of 15.2%. The risk-free rate in the example was 4%. Thus, for this example, the SML as indicated in equation (9.6) is

$$\bar{r}_i = r_f + \left[\frac{\bar{r}_M - r_f}{\sigma_M^2} \right] \sigma_{iM} \tag{9.6}$$

$$= 4 + \left[\frac{22.4 - 4}{(15.2)^2} \right] \sigma_{iM}$$

$$= 4 + .08\sigma_{iM} \tag{9.10}$$

The following expected return vector and variance-covariance matrix were used in the examples shown in Chapters 6, 7, and 8, and are also used here

$$ER = \begin{bmatrix} 16.2 \\ 24.6 \\ 22.8 \end{bmatrix} \quad VC = \begin{bmatrix} 146 & 187 & 145 \\ 187 & 854 & 104 \\ 145 & 104 & 289 \end{bmatrix}$$

The covariances of each security with the market portfolio can be calculated by using equation (9.4). More specifically, the covariances for the market portfolio for Able, Baker, and Charlie are equal to

$$\sigma_{1M} = \sum_{j=1}^{3} X_{jM}\sigma_{1j}$$

$$= (.12 \times 146) + (.19 \times 187) + (.69 \times 145)$$

$$= 153$$

$$\sigma_{2M} = \sum_{j=1}^{3} X_{jM}\sigma_{2j}$$

$$= (.12 \times 187) + (.19 \times 854) + (.69 \times 104)$$

$$= 257$$

$$\sigma_{3M} = \sum_{j=1}^{3} X_{jM}\sigma_{3j}$$

$$= (.12 \times 145) + (.19 \times 104) + (.69 \times 289)$$

$$= 236$$

Note how the SML as given in equation (9.10) states that the expected return for Able should be equal to $4 + (.08 \times 153) = 16.2\%$. Similarly, the expected return for Baker should be $4 + (.08 \times 257) = 24.6\%$ and the expected return for Charlie should be $4 + (.08 \times 236) = 22.8\%$. Each one of these expected returns corresponds to the respective value given in the expected return vector.

Alternatively, equation (9.8) can be used to calculate the betas for the three companies. More specifically, the betas for Able, Baker, and Charlie are equal to

$$\beta_1 = \frac{\sigma_{1M}}{\sigma_M^2}$$
$$= \frac{153}{(15.2)^2}$$
$$= .66$$
$$\beta_2 = \frac{\sigma_{2M}}{\sigma_M^2}$$
$$= \frac{257}{(15.2)^2}$$
$$= 1.11$$
$$\beta_3 = \frac{\sigma_{3M}}{\sigma_M^2}$$
$$= \frac{236}{(15.2)^2}$$
$$= 1.02$$

Now, equation (9.7) indicated that the SML could be expressed in a form where the measure of risk for an asset was its beta. For the example under consideration, this reduces to

$$\bar{r}_i = r_f + (\bar{r}_M - r_f)\beta_i$$
$$= 4 + (22.4 - 4)\beta_i \qquad (9.11)$$
$$= 4 + 18.4\beta_i$$

Note how the SML as given in this equation states that the expected return for Able should be equal to $4 + (18.4 \times .66) = 16.2\%$. Similarly, the expected return for Baker should be $4 + (18.4 \times 1.11) = 24.6\%$ and the expected return for Charlie should be $4 + (18.4 \times 1.02) = 22.8\%$. Each one of these expected returns corresponds to the respective value given in the expected return vector.

It is important to realize that if any other portfolio is assumed to be the market portfolio, meaning that if any set of proportions other than .12, .19, and .69 is used, then such an equilibrium relationship between expected returns and betas (or covariances) will not hold. Consider a hypothetical market portfolio with equal proportions (that is, .333) invested in Able, Baker, and Charlie. Since this portfolio has an expected return of 21.2% and a standard deviation of 15.5%, the hypothetical SML would be as follows:

$$\bar{r}_i = r_f + \left[\frac{\bar{r}_M - r_f}{\sigma_M^2} \right] \sigma_{iM}$$
$$= 4 + \left[\frac{21.2 - 4}{(15.5)^2} \right] \sigma_{iM}$$
$$= 4 + .07\sigma_{iM}$$

Able has a covariance with this portfolio of

$$\sigma_{1M} = \sum_{j=1}^{3} X_{jM}\sigma_{1j}$$
$$= (.333 \times 146) + (.333 \times 187) + (.333 \times 145)$$
$$= 159$$

which means that Able's expected return according to the hypothetical SML should be equal to $4 + (.07 \times 159) = 15.1\%$. However, since this does not correspond to the 16.2%

figure that appears in the expected return vector, a portfolio with equal proportions invested in Able, Baker, and Charlie cannot be the market portfolio.[13]

The Market Model

Chapter 7 introduced the market model, where the return on a common stock was assumed to be related to the return on a market index in the following manner:

$$r_i = \alpha_{iI} + \beta_{iI} r_I + \epsilon_{iI} \tag{7.3}$$

where:

r_i = return on security i for some given period

r_I = return on market index for the same period

α_{iI} = intercept term

β_{iI} = slope term

ϵ_{iI} = random error term

It is natural to think about the relationship between the market model and the Capital Asset Pricing Model. After all, both models have a slope term called "beta" in them, and both models somehow involve the market. However, there are two significant differences between the models.

First, the market model is a *factor model*, or to be more specific, a single-factor model where the factor is a market index. Unlike the CAPM, however, it is not an equilibrium model that describes how prices are set for securities.

Second, the market model uses a *market index* such as the TSE 300, whereas the CAPM involves the *market portfolio*. The market portfolio is a collection of all the securities in the marketplace, whereas a market index is in fact based on a sample of the market broadly construed (for example, 300 in the case of the TSE 300). Therefore, conceptually the beta of a stock based on the market model, β_{iI}, differs from the beta of the stock according to the CAPM, β_i. This is because the market model beta is measured relative to a market index while the CAPM beta is measured relative to the market portfolio. In practice, however, the composition of the market portfolio is not precisely known, so a market index is used. Thus, while conceptually different, betas determined with the use of a market index are treated as if they were determined with the use of the market portfolio. That is, β_{iI} is used as an estimate of β_i.

In the example, only three securities were in existence—the common stocks of Able, Baker, and Charlie. Subsequent analysis indicated that the CAPM market portfolio consisted of these stock in the proportions of .12, .19, and .69, respectively. It is against this portfolio that the betas of the securities should be measured. However, in practice they are likely to be measured against a market index (for example, one that is based on just the stocks of Able and Charlie in proportions of .20 and .80, respectively).

Standard & Poor's
www.stockinfo.
standardpoor.com

Market Indices

One widely known US index is Standard & Poor's 500 Stock Price Index (generally referred to as the S&P 500), a value-weighted average of the market prices of 500 large stocks.

[13]Baker and Charlie have covariances of 382 and 179, respectively, which means that their expected returns should be equal to $4 + (.07 \times 382) = 30.74\%$ and $4 + (.07 \times 179) = 16.53\%$. However, these figures do not correspond to the respective figures (24.6% and 22.8%) appearing in the expected return vector, indicating there are discrepancies for all three securities. While this example has used the covariance version of the SML, the analysis is similar for the beta version of SML shown in equation (9.7).

Complete coverage of the stocks listed on the New York Stock Exchange is provided by the NYSE Composite Index, which is like the S&P 500 in that it is a value-weighted index of share prices but is broader in that it considers more stocks. The American Stock Exchange computes a similar index for the stocks it lists, and the National Association of Security Dealers provides a value-weighted index of the prices of over-the-counter stocks traded on the NASDAQ system. The Russell 3000 and the Wilshire 5000 are the most comprehensive indices of common stock prices that are published regularly in the United States and are thus closer than the others to representing the overall performance of American common stocks.[14]

In Canada there are three widely quoted indices—the TSE 300 Composite, the Toronto 35, and the TSE 100—based on TSE-traded securities. The first is a broadly based index of 300 of the more representative stocks listed on the exchange. It is a unique value-weighted index in that the weights are based on the total number of shares outstanding minus the number of shares in any control blocks. The weights therefore, are representative of the trading float. Thirty-five of Canada's larger publicly listed companies make up the Toronto 35 Index, which was developed primarily for the trading of derivative securities. This is a modified value-weighted index: although the weights are based on the number of shares outstanding, no one stock is permitted to represent more than 10% of the index. The Toronto 35 is also designed to track the TSE 300. Therefore, all industry groups except real estate and construction are included. The TSE 100 includes the Toronto 35 firms plus another 65 companies. The composition of these indices is altered periodically to reflect changing economic conditions and fluctuating company fortunes.

Without question the most widely quoted market index is the Dow Jones Industrial Average (DJIA). Although based on the performance of only 30 stocks listed on the New York Stock Exchange and utilizing a less satisfactory averaging procedure, the DJIA provides at least a fair idea of what is happening to stock values.[15]

Market and Non-market Risk

In Chapter 7 it was shown that the total risk of security σ_i^2 could be partitioned into two components as follows:

$$\sigma_i^2 = \beta_{iI}^2 \sigma_I^2 + \sigma_{\epsilon i}^2 \tag{7.8}$$

where the components are:

$$\beta_{iI}^2 \sigma_I^2 = \text{market risk, and}$$
$$\sigma_{\epsilon i}^2 = \text{unique risk}$$

Because beta, or covariance, is the relevant measure of risk for a security according to the CAPM, it is only appropriate to explore its relationship to the total risk of the security. It turns out that the relationship is identical to that given in equation (7.8) *except that the market portfolio is involved instead of a market index:*

$$\sigma_i^2 = \beta_i^2 \sigma_M^2 + \sigma_{\epsilon i}^2 \tag{9.12}$$

---

[14]There are a variety of other indices of common stock prices that are commonly reported in the daily press. Many of these are components of the major indices. For example, *The Wall Street Journal* reports on a daily basis not only the level of the S&P 500 but also the levels of the Standard & Poor's Industrials, Transportations, Utilities, and Financials. These last four indices reflect the performance of particular sectors of the stock market. Their components, 500 stocks in total, make up the S&P 500. See Chapters 24 and 25 for a more thorough discussion of stock market indices.

[15]Charles Dow started this index in 1884 by simply adding the prices of 11 companies and then dividing the sum by 11. In 1928, securities were added to bring the total number up to 30, and since then the composition of these 30 has been changed periodically. Due to factors such as stock dividends and splits, the divisor is no longer simply equal to the number of stocks in the index.

As with the market model, the total risk of security i, measured by its variance and denoted σ_i^2, is shown to consist of two parts. The first component is the portion related to moves of the market portfolio. It is equal to the product of the square of the beta of the stock and the variance of the market portfolio, and is also often referred to as the **market risk** of the security. The second component is the portion not related to moves of the market portfolio. It is denoted $\sigma_{\epsilon i}^2$ and can be considered **non-market risk**. Under the assumptions of the market model, it is also unique to the security in question and hence is termed *unique risk*. Note that if β_{iI} is treated as an estimate of β_i, then the decomposition of σ_i^2 is the same in equations (7.8) and (9.12).

An Example

From the earlier example, the betas of Able, Baker, and Charlie were calculated to be .66, 1.11, and 1.02, respectively. As the standard deviation of the market portfolio was equal to 15.2%, this means that the market risk of the three firms is equal to $(.66^2 \times 15.2^2) = 100$, $(1.11^2 \times 15.2^2) = 285$, and $(1.02^2 \times 15.2^2) = 240$, respectively.

The non-market risk of any security can be calculated by solving equation (9.12) for $\sigma_{\epsilon i}^2$:

$$\sigma_{\epsilon i}^2 = \sigma_i^2 - \beta_i^2 \sigma_M^2 \tag{9.13}$$

Thus, equation (9.13) can be used to calculate the non-market risk of Able, Baker, and Charlie, respectively:

$$\sigma_{\epsilon 1}^2 = 146 - 100$$
$$= 46$$
$$\sigma_{\epsilon 2}^2 = 854 - 285$$
$$= 569$$
$$\sigma_{\epsilon 3}^2 = 289 - 240$$
$$= 49$$

Non-market risk is sometimes expressed as a standard deviation. This is calculated by taking the square root of $\sigma_{\epsilon i}^2$ and would be equal to $\sqrt{46} = 6.8\%$ for Able, $\sqrt{569} = 23.9\%$ for Baker, and $\sqrt{49} = 7\%$ for Charlie.

Motivation for the Partitioning of Risk

At this point one may wonder: why partition total risk into two parts? For the investor, it would seem that risk is risk—whatever its source. The answer lies in the domain of expected returns.

Market risk is related to the risk of the market portfolio and to the beta of the security in question. Securities with larger betas will have larger amounts of market risk. In the world of the CAPM, securities with larger betas will have larger expected returns. These two relationships together imply that securities with larger market risks should have larger expected returns.

Non-market risk is not related to beta. This means that there is no reason why securities with larger amounts of non-market risk should have larger expected returns. Thus, according to the CAPM, investors are rewarded for bearing market risk but not for bearing non-market risk.

Summary

1. The Capital Asset Pricing Model (CAPM) is based on a specific set of assumptions about investor behaviour and the existence of perfect security markets.
2. Based on these assumptions, all investors will hold the same efficient portfolio of risky assets.
3. Investors will differ only in the amounts of risk-free borrowing or lending they undertake.
4. The risky portfolio held by all investors is known as the market portfolio.
5. The market portfolio consists of all securities, each weighted in proportion to its market value relative to the market value of all securities.
6. The linear efficient set of the CAPM is known as the Capital Market Line (CML). The CML represents the equilibrium relationship between the expected return and standard deviation of efficient portfolios.
7. Under the CAPM the relevant measure of risk for a security is its covariance with the market portfolio.
8. The linear relationship between market covariance and expected return is known as the Security Market Line (SML).
9. The beta of a security is an alternative way of measuring the risk that a security adds to the market portfolio. Beta is a measure of covariance relative to the market portfolio's variance.
10. The beta from the CAPM is similar in concept to the beta from the market model. However, the market model is not an equilibrium model of security prices as is the CAPM. Furthermore, the market model uses a market index, which is a subset of the CAPM's market portfolio.
11. Under the CAPM, the total risk of a security can be separated into market risk and non-market risk. Under the market model, each security's non-market risk is unique to that security and hence is termed its unique risk.

APPENDIX A

SOME EXTENDED VERSIONS OF THE CAPM

The original capital asset pricing model makes strong assumptions and gives strong implications. In the years since it was developed, more complex models have been proposed. These models generally involve relaxing some of the assumptions associated with the original CAPM, and are often referred to as *extended versions of the CAPM* (or extended capital asset pricing models). Some of them are described in this appendix.

Efficient Investment Policies When Borrowing Is Restricted or Expensive

The Capital Market Line

The original CAPM assumes that investors can lend or borrow at the same risk-free rate of interest. In reality, such borrowing is likely to be either unavailable or restricted in amount. What impact might the relaxation of this risk-free borrowing assumption have on the CAPM?

A useful way to answer the question makes the following alternative assumptions: (1) investors can lend money risklessly—that is, they can purchase assets that provide a risk-free return of r_{fL}; or (2) investors can borrow money without limit at a higher rate of interest, r_{fB}. These risk-free rates are shown on the vertical axis of Figure 9.3; the "umbrella area" represents risk-return combinations available from investment solely in risky assets.[16]

If there are no opportunities to borrow or lend at the risk-free rate, the efficient set would be the curve WT_LT_BY, and many combinations of risky securities would be efficient. However, the availability of risk-free lending at the rate r_{fL} makes the risky portfolios between W and T_L inefficient, since combinations of risk-free lending and the portfolio plotting at T_L provide more return for the same risk.

Similarly, the ability to borrow money at rate r_{fB} makes another portfolio, denoted by T_B, of special interest. Risky portfolios between T_B and Y are now inefficient, since levered holdings of T_B dominate them by providing more return for the same risk.

Investors with attitudes towards risk that suggest neither borrowing nor lending should hold efficient combinations of risky securities plotting along curve T_LT_B. Accordingly, their holdings should be tailored to be consistent with differences in their degrees of aversion to risk.

In this situation the CML is now two lines and a curve, corresponding to the line going from r_{fL} to T_L, then the curve from T_L to T_B, and then the line from T_B on out to the northeast in Figure 9.3.

● The Security Market Line

What becomes of the Security Market Line when the risk-free borrowing rate exceeds the risk-free lending rate? The answer depends on whether or not the market portfolio is in fact one of the efficient combinations of risky securities along the boundary between T_L and T_B in Figure 9.3.[17] If it is not, little more can be said. If it is, a great deal can be said.

Figure 9.4 shows a case in which the market portfolio (shown by point M) is efficient. In part (a) a line has been drawn that is tangent to the efficient set at point M. When this line is extended to the vertical axis, the resulting intercept is denoted $\bar{r}_z$. In panel (b) only this tangency line is shown.

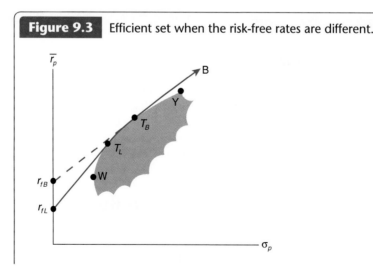

Figure 9.3 Efficient set when the risk-free rates are different.

---

[16]A more rigorous development of this figure is presented in Appendix A to Chapter 8.

[17]If investors could obtain the proceeds from short sales and there were no restrictions on such sales, then the market portfolio would definitely plot on the efficient set between T_L and T_B.

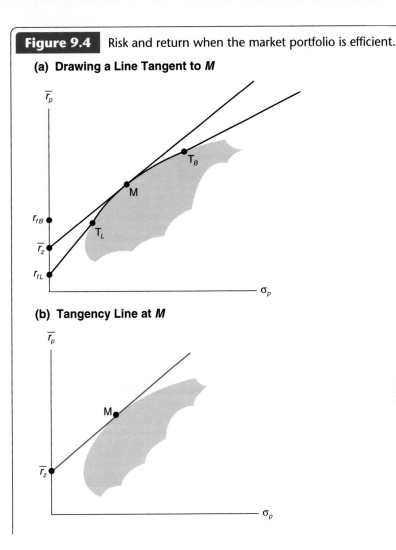

Figure 9.4 Risk and return when the market portfolio is efficient.

(a) Drawing a Line Tangent to M

(b) Tangency Line at M

A striking characteristic of Figure 9.4(b) is that it is precisely the same picture that would be produced in a market in which investors could borrow and lend without limit at a hypothetical risk-free rate equal in value to $\bar{r}_z$. Whereas only point M along the line emanating from $\bar{r}_z$ would be attainable, the expected returns of risky securities would be the same as they would be in a hypothetical market with borrowing and lending at $\bar{r}_z$. That is, all risky securities (and portfolios consisting of these securities) would plot along an SML going through point $\bar{r}_z$, as shown in Figure 9.5.

The vertical intercept of the SML indicates the expected return on a security or portfolio with a beta of zero. Accordingly, this extension of the CAPM is termed the *zero-beta capital asset pricing model*. This version of the CAPM implies that the SML will be flatter than implied by the original version, since $\bar{r}_z$ will be above r_{fL}. As a practical matter, it means that $\bar{r}_z$ must be inferred from the prices of risky securities, since it cannot simply be found in the quotations of current prices on, for example, Treasury bills. Many organizations both in Canada and the United States that estimate the SML generally find that it conforms more to the zero-beta CAPM than to the original CAPM.

Cases in which borrowing is either impossible or costs more as one borrows larger amounts lead to only minor modifications in the conclusions. As long as the market portfolio is efficient, all securities will plot along an SML, but the "zero-beta return" will exceed the risk-free rate at which funds can be invested.

The Capital Asset Pricing Model   **231**

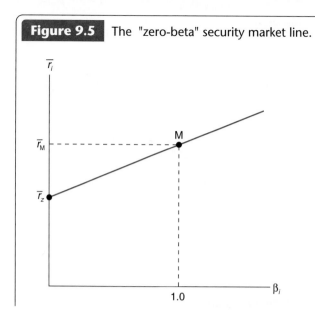

Figure 9.5 The "zero-beta" security market line.

Introducing Heterogeneous Expectations

A number of researchers have examined the implications of assuming that different investors have different perceptions about expected returns, standard deviations, and covariances. More specifically, the assumption of homogeneous expectations has been replaced by these researchers with an assumption of *heterogeneous expectations*.

In one such study, it was noted that each investor would face an efficient set that was unique to him.[18] This means that the tangency portfolio (denoted by T in Chapter 8) is unique to each investor, since the optimal combination of risky assets for an investor depends on that investor's perceptions about expected returns, standard deviations, and covariances. Furthermore, an investor will likely determine that his tangency portfolio does not involve an investment in some securities (that is, certain securities may have zero proportions in the tangency portfolio). Nevertheless, the SML will still exist. This was shown by aggregating the holdings of all investors, and remembering that in equilibrium each security's price has to be at a level where the amount of the security demanded equals the supply of the security. Now, however, the equilibrium expected return for each security will be a complex weighted average of all investors' perceptions of its expected return. That is, from the viewpoint of a representative, or average, investor, each security will be priced fairly, so its expected return (as perceived by this investor) will be linearly and positively related to its beta.

Liquidity

The original CAPM assumes that investors are concerned only with risk and return. However, other characteristics may also be important to investors. For example, *liquidity*

---

[18]John Lintner, "The Aggregation of Investors' Diverse Judgements and Preferences in Purely Competitive Security Markets," *Journal of Financial and Quantitative Analysis* 4, no. 4 (December 1969): 347–400.

may be important. Here, liquidity refers to the cost of selling or buying a security "in a hurry." For example, a house is regarded as a relatively illiquid investment, since usually a "fair" price for it cannot be obtained quickly. In terms of securities, liquidity may be measured by the size of the spread between the bid and ask prices, with smaller spreads suggesting greater liquidity. Furthermore, it is reasonable to assume that many investors would find more liquid portfolios to be more attractive, keeping everything else the same. However, investors undoubtedly differ in their attitudes towards liquidity. For some it is very important; for others, somewhat important; and for yet others, of little importance.

Under these conditions, security prices would adjust until, overall, investors would be content to hold the outstanding securities. The expected return of a security would be based on two characteristics of the security:

1. The marginal contribution of the security to the risk of an efficient portfolio. This would be measured by the familiar beta (β_i) of the security.
2. The marginal contribution of the security to the liquidity of an efficient portfolio. This would be measured by the liquidity (L_i) of the security.

Now, other things equal, investors dislike large values of β_i but like large values of L_i. This means that two securities with the same beta but different liquidities would not have the same level of expected return. To understand why they would have different levels of expected return, consider what would happen if they had the same level of expected return. In such a situation investors would buy the security with the greater liquidity and sell the one with the lesser liquidity. This would push the price of the first security up and the second one down. Ultimately, in equilibrium the quantity demanded would equal the quantity supplied and the security with the greater liquidity would have a relatively lower expected return. Similarly, two securities with the same liquidity but different betas would not have the same level of expected return. Instead, the security with the higher beta would have a higher expected return.[19]

Figure 9.6 shows the equilibrium relationship one might expect among $\bar{r}_i$, β_i, and L_i. For a given level of β_i, more liquid securities have lower expected returns. And for a given level of L_i, more risky securities have higher expected returns as in the original CAPM. Lastly, there are securities with various levels of β_i and L_i that provide the same level of $\bar{r}_i$. The figure is three-dimensional, since now expected returns are related to two characteristics of securities. Accordingly, it is sometimes referred to as a *Security Market Plane*.[20]

If expected returns are based on beta, liquidity, and a third characteristic, then a four-dimensional CAPM would be necessary to describe the corresponding equilibrium. Whether or not liquidity is an important characteristic of securities has not been demonstrated in a Canadian context. Taxes, however, have been shown to affect before-tax returns

[19]Investors possess completely illiquid assets in the form of human capital. This means that the ability that an investor has to produce a stream of income by working shows that the investor possesses an asset known as human capital and that different investors have different amounts of human capital. As slavery is outlawed, this asset cannot be sold and hence is non-marketable. Nevertheless, because human capital is an asset, certain researchers have argued that it is relevant to each investor in identifying her optimal portfolio. Accordingly, the market portfolio should consist of all marketable and non-marketable assets (like human capital), and each security's beta should be measured relative to it. See David Mayers, "Nonmarketable Assets and Capital Market Equilibrium Under Certainty," in *Studies in the Theory of Capital Markets*, ed. Michael C. Jensen (New York: Praeger Publishers, 1972), and "Nonmarketable Assets and the Determination of Capital Asset Prices in the Absence of a Riskless Asset," *Journal of Business* 46, no. 2 (April 1973): 258–267.

[20]The term Security Market Plane is a trademark of Wells Fargo Bank. For more on the relationship between liquidity and stock returns, see Yakov Amihud and Haim Mendelson, "Liquidity and Stock Returns," *Financial Analysts Journal* 42, no. 3 (May–June 1986): 43–48, and "Asset Pricing and the Bid-Ask Spread," *Journal of Financial Economics* 17, no. 2 (December 1986): 223–249; and "Liquidity, Asset Prices and Financial Policy," *Financial Analysts Journal* 47, no. 6 (November–December 1991): 56–66.

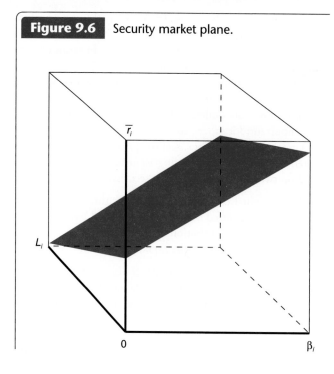

Figure 9.6 Security market plane.

on Canadian stocks in a similar way to that found in the United States.[21] Although a diagram cannot be drawn for this type of extended CAPM, an equation can be written for it. Such an equation, by analogy to the three-dimensional plane, is termed a *hyperplane.*

> In equilibrium, all securities will plot on a *Security Market Hyperplane,* where each axis measures the contribution of a security to a characteristic of efficient portfolios that matter (on average) to investors.

The relationship between the expected return of a security and its contribution to a particular characteristic of efficient portfolios depends on the attitudes of investors to the characteristic:

> If, on the average, a characteristic (such as liquidity) is liked by investors, then those securities that contribute more to that characteristic will, other things equal, offer lower expected returns. Conversely, if a characteristic (such as beta) is disliked by investors, then those securities that contribute more to that characteristic will offer higher expected returns.

In a capital market with many relevant characteristics, the task of tailoring a portfolio for a specific investor is more complicated, since only an investor with average attitudes and circumstances should hold the market portfolio. In general:

---

[21]In the United States taxes were thought to be such a characteristic before the Tax Reform Act of 1986, when the tax rate on income from capital gains was less than the tax rate on dividend income. In considering such taxes, one study found that the before-tax expected return of a security was a positive linear function of its beta and its dividend yield. That is, the higher a security's beta or dividend yield, the higher its before-tax expected return. The reason securities with higher dividend yields would have had higher before-tax expected returns was because they would be taxed more heavily. See M. J. Brennan, "Taxes, Market Valuation and Corporate Financial Policy," *National Tax Journal* 23, no. 4 (December 1970): 417–427. The issue of whether or not dividends influence before-tax expected returns has been contentious; it is discussed in Chapters 15 and 16 of Thomas E. Copeland and J. Fred Weston, *Financial Theory and Corporate Policy* (Reading, MA: Addison-Wesley, 1988). See I. G. Morgan, "Dividends and Stock Price Behavior in Canada," *Journal of Business Administration* 12 (Fall 1980): 91–106.

If an investor likes a characteristic more (or dislikes it less) than the average investor, he should generally hold a portfolio with relatively more of that characteristic than is provided by holding the market portfolio. Conversely, if an investor likes a characteristic less (or dislikes it more) than the average investor, he should generally hold a portfolio with relatively less of that characteristic than is provided by holding the market portfolio.

For example, consider an investor who likes having a relatively liquid portfolio. Such an investor should hold a portfolio consisting of relatively liquid securities. Conversely, an investor who has relatively little need for liquidity should hold a portfolio of relatively illiquid securities.

The right combination of "tilt" away from market proportions will depend on the extent of the differences between the investor's attitudes and those of the average investor and on the added risk involved in such a strategy. A complex capital market requires all the tools of modern portfolio theory for managing the money of any investor who is significantly different from the "average investor." On the other hand, in such a world, investment management should be relatively passive: after the selection of an initial portfolio, there should be minor and infrequent changes.

APPENDIX B

A DERIVATION OF THE SECURITY MARKET LINE

Figure 9.7 shows the location of the feasible set of the Markowitz model, along with the risk-free rate and the associated efficient set that represents the Capital Market Line. Within the feasible set of the Markowitz model lies every individual risky security. An arbitrarily chosen risky security, denoted by I, has been selected for analysis and is shown on the figure.

Consider any portfolio, p, that consists of the proportion X_i invested in security i and the proportion $1 - X_i$ invested in the market portfolio M. Such a portfolio will have an

Figure 9.7 Deriving the Security Market Line.

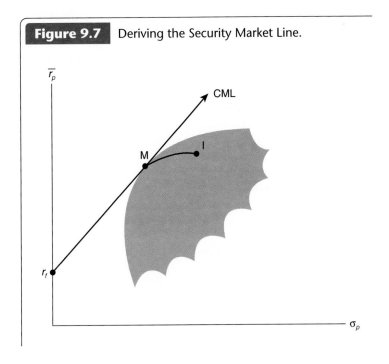

expected return equal to

$$\bar{r}_p = X_i \bar{r}_i + (1 - X_i)\bar{r}_M \tag{9.14}$$

and a standard deviation equal to

$$\sigma_p = [X_i^2 \sigma_i^2 + (1 - X_i)^2 \sigma_M^2 + 2X_i(1 - X_i)\sigma_{iM}]^{1/2} \tag{9.15}$$

All such portfolios will lie on a curved line, such as the one shown in Figure 9.7 connecting I and M.

Of concern is the slope of this curved line. Since it is a curved line, its slope is not a constant. However, its slope can be determined with the use of calculus. First, using equation (9.14), the derivative of $\bar{r}_p$ with respect to X_i is taken:

$$\frac{d\bar{r}_p}{dX_i} = \bar{r}_i - \bar{r}_M \tag{9.16}$$

Second, using equation (9.15), the derivative of σ_p with respect to X_i is taken:

$$\frac{d\sigma_p}{dX_i} = \frac{X_i\sigma_i^2 - \sigma_M^2 + X_i\sigma_M^2 + \sigma_{iM} - 2X_i\sigma_{iM}}{[X_i^2 \sigma_i^2 + (1 - X_i)^2 \sigma_M^2 + 2X_i(1 - X_i)\sigma_{iM}]^{1/2}} \tag{9.17}$$

Third, the slope of the curved line IM, $d\bar{r}_p/d\sigma_p$, can be written as

$$\frac{d\bar{r}_p}{d\sigma_p} = \frac{d\bar{r}_p/dX_i}{d\sigma_p/dX_i} \tag{9.18}$$

Finally, the slope of IM can be calculated by substituting equations (9.16) and (9.17) into the numerator and denominator of equation (9.18), respectively:

$$\frac{d\bar{r}_p}{d\sigma_p} = \frac{[\bar{r}_i - \bar{r}_M][X_i^2 \sigma_i^2 + (1 - X_i)^2 \sigma_M^2 + 2X_i(1 - X_i)\sigma_{iM}]^{1/2}}{X_i\sigma_i^2 - \sigma_M^2 + X_i\sigma_M^2 + \sigma_{iM} - 2X_i\sigma_{iM}} \tag{9.19}$$

Of interest is the slope of the curved line IM at the endpoint M. Since the proportion X_i is zero at this point, the slope of IM can be calculated by substituting zero for X_i in equation (9.19). After doing so, many terms drop out, leaving

$$\frac{d\bar{r}_p}{d\sigma_p} = \frac{[\bar{r}_i - \bar{r}_M][\sigma_M]}{\sigma_{iM} - \sigma_M^2} \tag{9.20}$$

At M, the slope of the CML, $(\bar{r}_M - r_f)/\sigma_M$, must equal the slope of the curved line IM. This is because the slope of the curved line IM increases when moving from the endpoint I, converging to the slope of the CML at the endpoint M. Accordingly, the slope of the curve IM at M, as shown on the right-hand side of equation (9.20), is set equal to the slope of the CML:

$$\frac{[\bar{r}_i - \bar{r}_M][\sigma_M]}{\sigma_{iM} - \sigma_M^2} = \frac{\bar{r}_M - r_f}{\sigma_M} \tag{9.21}$$

Solving equation (9.21) for r_i results in the covariance version of the SML:

$$\bar{r}_i = r_f + \left[\frac{\bar{r}_M - r_f}{\sigma_M^2}\right]\sigma_{iM} \tag{9.6}$$

The beta version of the SML is derived by substituting β_i for σ_{iM}/σ_M^2 in equation (9.6).

1. Describe the key assumptions underlying the CAPM.
2. Many of the underlying assumptions of the CAPM are violated to some degree in the "real world." Does that fact invalidate the model's conclusions? Explain.
3. What is the separation theorem? What implications does it have for the optimal portfolio of risky assets held by investors?
4. What constitutes the market portfolio? What problems does one confront in specifying the composition of the true market portfolio? How have researchers and practitioners circumvented these problems?
5. In the equilibrium world of the CAPM, is it possible for a security not to be part of the market portfolio? Explain.
6. Describe the price adjustment process that equilibrates the market's supply and demand for securities. What conditions will prevail under such an equilibrium?
7. Will an investor who owns the market portfolio have to buy and sell units of the component securities every time the relative prices of those securities change? Why?
8. Given an expected return of 12% for the market portfolio, a risk-free rate of 6%, and a market portfolio standard deviation of 20%, draw the Capital Market Line.
9. Explain the significance of the Capital Market Line.
10. Assume that two securities constitute the market portfolio. Those securities have the following expected returns, standard deviations, and proportions:

Security	Expected Return	Standard Deviation	Proportion
A	10%	20%	.40
B	15	28	.60

Based on this information, and given a correlation of .30 between the two securities and a risk-free rate of 5%, specify the equation for the Capital Market Line.
11. Distinguish between the Capital Market Line and the Security Market Line.
12. The market portfolio is assumed to be composed of four securities. Their covariances with the market and their proportions are shown below:

Security	Covariance with Market	Proportion
A	242	.20
B	360	.30
C	155	.20
D	210	.30

Given these data, calculate the market portfolio's standard deviation.
13. Explain the significance of the slope of the SML. How might the slope of the SML change over time?
14. Why should the expected return for a security be directly related to the security's covariance with the market portfolio?
15. The risk of a well-diversified portfolio to an investor is measured by the standard deviation of the portfolio's returns. Why shouldn't the risk of an individual security be calculated in the same manner?
16. The risk-free rate is 5% while the market portfolio's expected return is 12%. If the standard deviation of the market portfolio is 13%, what is the equilibrium expected return on a security that has a covariance with the market portfolio of 186?

17. A security with a high standard deviation of returns is not necessarily highly risky to an investor. Why might you suspect that securities with above-average standard deviations tend to have above-average betas?

18. Oliver Smith, an investments student, argued, "A security with a positive standard deviation must have an expected return greater than the risk-free rate. Otherwise, why would anyone be willing to hold the security?" Based on the CAPM, is Oliver's statement correct? Why?

19. The standard deviation of the market portfolio is 15%. Given the covariances with the market portfolio of the following securities, calculate their betas.

Security	Covariance
A	292
B	180
C	225

20. Kitty Bransfield owns a portfolio composed of three securities. The betas of those securities and their proportions in Kitty's portfolio follow. What is the beta of Kitty's portfolio?

Security	Beta	Proportion
A	.90	.30
B	1.30	.10
C	1.05	.60

21. Assume that the expected return on the market portfolio is 15% and its standard deviation is 21%. The risk-free rate is 7%. What is the standard deviation of a well-diversified (no non-market risk) portfolio with an expected return of 16.6%?

22. Given that the expected return on the market portfolio is 10%, the risk-free rate of return is 6%, the beta of stock A is .85, and the beta of stock B is 1.20:
   a. Draw the SML.
   b. What is the equation for the SML?
   c. What are the equilibrium expected returns for stocks A and B?
   d. Plot the two risky securities on the SML.

23. You are given the following information on two securities, the market portfolio, and the risk-free rate:

	Expected Return	Correlation with Market Portfolio	Standard Deviation
Security 1	15.5%	0.90	20.0%
Security 2	9.2	0.80	9.0
Market Portfolio	12.0	1.00	12.0
Risk-free Rate	5.0	0.00	0.0

   a. Draw the SML.
   b. Identify the betas of the two securities.
   c. Plot the two securities on the SML.

24. The SML describes an equilibrium relationship between risk and expected return. Would you consider a security that plotted above the SML to be an attractive investment? Why?

25. Assume that two securities, A and B, constitute the market portfolio. Their proportions and variances are .39, 160, and .61, 340, respectively. The covariance of the two securities is 190. Calculate the betas of the two securities.

26. The CAPM permits the standard deviation of a security to be segmented into market and non-market risk. Distinguish between the two types of risk.

27. Is an investor who owns any portfolio of risky assets other than the market portfolio exposed to some non-market risk? Explain.

28. Based on the risk and return relationships of the CAPM, supply the missing values in the following table.

Security	Expected Return	Beta	Standard Deviation	Non-market Risk ($\sigma_{\varepsilon i}^2$)
A	_____%	0.8	_____%	81
B	19.0	1.5	_____	36
C	15.0	_____	12	0
D	7.0	0	8	_____
E	16.6	_____	15	_____

29. (Appendix Question) Describe how the SML is altered when the risk-free borrowing rate exceeds the risk-free lending rate.

CFA Exam Question

30. The following information describes the expected return and risk relationship for the stocks of two of WAH's competitors.

	Expected Return	Standard Deviation	Beta
Stock Y	12.0%	20%	1.3
Stock Y	9.0	15	0.7
Market Index	10.0	12	1.0
Risk-free rate	5.0		

Using only the data shown above:

a. Draw and label a graph showing the Security Market Line and position stocks X and Y relative to it.

b. Compute the alphas both for stock X and for stock Y. Show your work.

c. Assume that the risk-free rate increases to 7% with the other data in the matrix remaining unchanged. Select the stock providing the higher expected risk-adjusted return and justify your selection. Show your calculations.

KEY TERMS

normative economics (p. 214)
positive economics (p. 214)
Capital Asset Pricing Model (CAPM) (p. 214)
homogeneous expectations (p. 215)
perfect market (p. 215)
separation theorem (p. 216)

market portfolio (p. 218)
Capital Market Line (CML) (p. 218)
Security Market Line (SML) (p. 222)
beta coefficient (p. 223)
market risk (p. 228)
non-market risk (p. 228)

1. Credit for the initial development of the CAPM is usually given to:

   William F. Sharpe, "Capital Asset Prices: A Theory of Market Equilibrium Under Conditions of Risk," *Journal of Finance* 19, no. 3 (September 1964): 425–442.

   John Lintner, "The Valuation of Risk Assets and the Selection of Risky Investments in Stock Portfolios and Capital Budgets," *Review of Economics and Statistics* 47, no. 1 (February 1965): 13–37; and "Security Prices, Risk, and Maximal Gains from Diversification," *Journal of Finance* 20, no. 4 (December 1965): 587–615.

   Jan Mossin, "Equilibrium in a Capital Asset Market," *Econometrica* 34, no. 4 (October 1966): 768–783.

2. The Sharpe and Lintner papers were compared in:

   Eugene F. Fama, "Risk, Return, and Equilibrium: Some Clarifying Comments," *Journal of Finance* 28, no. 1 (March 1968): 29–40.

3. Some extended versions of the CAPM are described in:

   Gordon J. Alexander and Jack Clark Francis, *Portfolio Analysis* (Englewood Cliff, NJ: Prentice Hall, 1986), Chapter 8.

   Edwin J. Elton and Martin J. Gruber, *Modern Portfolio Theory and Investment Analysis* (New York: John Wiley, 1995), Chapter 14.

4. For a comparison of the market model and CAPM betas, see:

   Harry M. Markowitz, "The 'Two Beta' Trap," *Journal of Portfolio Management* 11, no. 1 (Fall 1984): 12–20.

5. It has been argued that the CAPM is virtually impossible to test because (a) the only testable hypothesis of the CAPM is that the "true" market portfolio lies on the efficient set (when this happens securities' expected returns and betas have a positive linear relationship) and (b) the "true" market portfolio cannot be meaningfully measured. See:

   Richard Roll, "A Critique of the Asset Pricing Theory's Tests: Part I. On Past and Potential Testability of the Theory," *Journal of Financial Economics* 4, no. 2 (March 1977): 129–176.

6. In spite of Roll's critique, several tests of the CAPM have been conducted. Some of them are summarized in:

   Gordon J. Alexander and Jack Clark Francis, *Portfolio Analysis* (Englewood Cliffs, NJ: Prentice Hall, 1986), Chapter 10.

   Edwin J. Elton and Martin J. Gruber, *Modern Portfolio Theory and Investment Analysis* (New York: John Wiley, 1995), Chapter 15.

7. Recently some people have concluded that the CAPM is no longer relevant based on the following test results that show that the relationship between beta and average stock returns is flat:

   Eugene F. Fama and Kenneth R. French, "The Cross-Section of Expected Stock Returns," *Journal of Finance* 47, no. 2 (June 1992): 427–465.

   Eugene F. Fama and Kenneth R. French, "Common Risk Factors in the Returns on Stocks and Bonds," *Journal of Financial Economics* 33, no. 1 (February 1993): 3–56.

   James L. Davis, "The Cross-Section of Realized Stock Returns: The Pre-COMPUSTAT Evidence," *Journal of Finance* 49, no. 5 (December 1994): 1579–1593.

Eugene F. Fama and Kenneth R. French, "The CAPM is Wanted, Dead or Alive," *Journal of Finance* 51, no. 5 (December 1996): 1947–1958.

8. However, these test results have been challenged by others, such as those listed below. For example, the fourth study shows that average returns and betas have a positive linear relationship when the market portfolio includes human capital and betas are allowed to vary over the business cycle:

Louis K. C. Chan and Josef Lakonishok, "Are the Reports of Beta's Death Premature?" *Journal of Portfolio Management* 19, no. 4 (Summer 1993): 51–62.

Fischer Black, "Beta and Return," *Journal of Portfolio Management* 20, no. 1 (February 1993): 8–18.

S. P. Kothari, Jay Shanken, and Richard D. Sloan, "Another Look at the Cross-Section of Expected Stock Returns," *Journal of Finance* 50, no. 1 (March 1995): 185–224.

Ravi Jagannathan and Zhenyu Wang, "The Conditional CAPM and the Cross-Section of Expected Returns," *Journal of Finance* 51, no. 1 (March 1996): 3–53.

9. For an assertion that the use of modern portfolio theory does not depend upon successful testing of the CAPM, see:

Harry M. Markowitz, "Nonnegative or Not Nonnegative: A Question about CAPMs," *Journal of Finance* 38, no. 2 (May 1983): 283–295.

10. For a Canadian perspective on the topics covered in this chapter, see:

Roger Morin, "Market Line Theory and the Canadian Equity Market," *Journal of Business Administration: Capital Markets in Canada* 12, no. 1 (Fall 1980).

M. J. Brennan and E. S. Schwartz, *Canadian Estimates of the Capital Asset Pricing Model*, Corporate Finance Division, Department of Finance (July 1982).

A. L. Calvet and J. Lefoll, "Risk and Return in Canadian Capital Markets," *Canadian Journal of Administrative Sciences* 5, no. 1 (March 1988): 1–12.

M. J. Robinson, "Univariate Canadian CAPM Tests," in M. J. Robinson and B. F. Smith, eds., *Canadian Capital Markets* (London, ON: Western Business School, 1993).

CHAPTER 10

Factor Models

The objective of modern portfolio theory is to provide a means by which the investor can identify her optimal portfolio when there are an infinite number of possibilities. The investor needs to estimate the expected return and standard deviation for each security under consideration for inclusion in the portfolio, along with all the covariances between securities. With these estimates the investor can derive the curved efficient set of Markowitz. Then for a given risk-free rate the investor can identify the tangency portfolio and determine the location of the linear efficient set. Finally, the investor can proceed to invest in this tangency portfolio and borrow or lend at the risk-free rate, with the amount of borrowing or lending depending on the investor's risk-return preferences.

Factor Models and Return-Generating Processes

Return-generating Process A statistical model that describes how the returns on a security are produced.

The task of identifying the curved Markowitz efficient set can be greatly simplified by introducing a **return-generating process**. A return-generating process is a statistical model that describes how the return on a security is produced. Chapter 7 presented a type of return-generating process known as the market model. The market model states that a security's return is a function of the return on a market index. However, there are many other types of return-generating processes for securities.

▶ Factor Models

Factor Model A return generating process that attributes the return on a security to the security's sensitivity to the movements of various common factors.

Factor models or index models assume that the return on a security is sensitive to the movements of various factors or indices. The market model assumes that there is one factor—the return on a market index. However, in attempting to accurately estimate expected returns, variances, and covariances for securities, multiple-factor models are potentially more useful than the market model. They have this potential because it appears that actual security returns are sensitive to more than movements in a market index. This means that there is probably more than one pervasive factor in the economy that affects security returns.

As a return-generating process, a factor model attempts to capture the major economic forces that systematically move the prices of all securities. Implicit in the construction of a factor model is the assumption that the returns on two securities will be correlated—that is, will move together—only through common reactions to one or more of the factors specified in the model. Any aspect of a security's return unexplained by the factor model is assumed to be unique or specific to the security and therefore uncorrelated with the unique

Sensitivity A measure of
the responsiveness of a
security's returns to a
particular common factor.

elements of returns on other securities. As a result, a factor model is a powerful tool for portfolio management. It can supply the information needed to calculate expected returns, variances, and covariances for every security—a necessary condition for determining the curved Markowitz efficient set. It can also be used to characterize a portfolio's **sensitivity** to movements in the factors.

Application

As a practical matter, all investors employ factor models, whether they do so explicitly or implicitly. It is impossible to consider separately the interrelationship of every security with every other. The problem of calculating covariances among securities rises exponentially as the number of securities analyzed increases.[1]

Conceptually, thinking about the tangled web of security variances and covariances becomes mind-boggling even when dealing with just a few securities, let alone hundreds or thousands. Even the vast data-processing capabilities of high-speed computers are strained when they are called upon to construct efficient sets from a large number of securities.

Abstraction is therefore essential in identifying the curved Markowitz efficient set. Factor models supply the necessary level of abstraction. They provide investment managers with a framework to identify important factors in the economy and the marketplace and to assess the extent to which different securities and portfolios will respond to changes in these factors.

Given the belief that one or more factors influence security returns, a primary goal of security analysis is to determine these factors and the sensitivities of security returns to movements in these factors. A formal statement of such a relationship is termed a *factor model of security returns*. The discussion begins with the simplest form of such a model, a one-factor model.

One-factor Models

Some investors argue that the return-generating process for securities involves a single factor. For example, they may contend that the returns on securities respond to the predicted growth rate in the gross domestic product (GDP). Table 10.1 and Figure 10.1 illustrate one way of providing substance for such statements.

Table 10.1	Factor Model Data.		
Year	Growth Rate In GDP	Rate of Inflation	Return on Widget Stock
1	5.7%	1.1%	14.3%
2	6.4	4.4	19.2
3	7.9	4.4	23.4
4	7.0	4.6	15.6
5	5.1	6.1	9.2
6	2.9	3.1	13.0

---

[1]See Appendix B to Chapter 7.

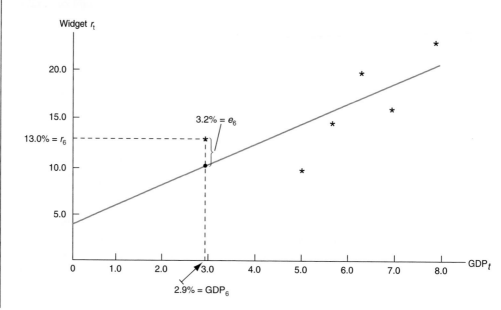

Figure 10.1 A one-factor model.

An Example

The horizontal axis of Figure 10.1 shows the predicted growth rate in GDP, while the vertical axis measures the return on Widget's stock. Each point in the graph represents the combination of Widget's return and GDP growth rate for a particular year as reported in Table 10.1. A line has been statistically fitted to the data by using a technique known as *simple-regression analysis*. (*Simple* refers to the fact that there is one variable—GDP in this example—on the right-hand side of the equation).[2] This line has a positive slope of 2, indicating that there exists a positive relationship between GDP growth rates and Widget's returns. Higher rates of GDP growth are associated with higher returns.

In equation form, the relationship between predicted GDP growth and Widget's return can be expressed as follows:

$$r_t = a + bGDP_t + e_t \tag{10.1}$$

where:

$$r_t = \text{the return on Widget in period } t$$
$$GDP_t = \text{the predicted rate of growth in GDP in period } t$$
$$e_t = \text{the unique or specific return on Widget in period } t$$
$$b = \text{the sensitivity of Widget to predicted GDP growth}^{3}$$
$$a = \text{the zero factor for GDP}$$

Factor Loading or **Attribute** A measure of the responsiveness of a security's returns to a particular common factor.

[2]Only six data points are shown in the figure for ease of exposition. The standard statistical procedure of simple linear regression is discussed in Chapter 16 and in Mark Kritzman, ". . . About Regression," *Financial Analysts Journal* 47, no. 3 (May–June 1991): 12–15. It can be found in most statistics books, such as David Levine, Mark Berenson, and David Stephan, *Statistics for Managers Using Microsoft Excel*, Second Edition (Upper Saddle River, NJ: Prentice Hall, 1999).

[3]Sometimes b is referred to as the **factor loading**, or **attribute**, of the security.

In Figure 10.1 the zero factor is 4% per period. This is the return that would be expected for Widget if predicted GDP growth equalled zero. The sensitivity of Widget to predicted GDP growth b is 2, and is the same as the slope of the line in Figure 10.1. This value indicates that, in general, higher predicted growth in GDP is associated with higher returns for Widget. If predicted GDP growth equalled 5%, Widget should generate a return of $4\% + (2 \times 5\%) = 14\%$. If predicted GDP growth were 1% higher—that is, 6%—Widget's return should be 2% higher, or 16%.[4]

In this example, predicted GDP growth in year 6 was 2.9%, and Widget actually returned 13%. Therefore Widget's unique return (given by e_t) in this particular year was +3.2%. This was determined by subtracting an amount that represents Widget's expected return, given that GDP was predicted to grow by 2.9%, from Widget's actual return of 13%. In this case, Widget would have an expected return of $4\% + (2 \times 2.9\%) = 9.8\%$, thereby resulting in a unique return of $13\% - 9.8\% = +3.2\%$.

In effect, the one-factor model presented in Figure 10.1 and equation (10.1) attributes Widget's return in any particular period to three elements:

1. An effect common in any period (the term a)
2. An effect that differs across periods depending on the predicted growth rate of GDP (the term $b\text{GDP}_t$)
3. An effect specific to the particular period observed (the term e_t)

Generalizing the Example

This example of a one-factor model can be generalized in equation form for any security i in period t:

$$r_{it} = a_i + b_i F_t + e_{it} \tag{10.2}$$

where F is the predicted value of the factor in period t and b_i is the sensitivity of security i to this factor. If the predicted value of the factor were zero, the return on the security would equal $a_i + e_{it}$. Note that e_{it} is a random error term just like the random error term discussed in Chapter 7. This means that it is a random variable with an expected value of zero and a standard deviation σ_{ei}. It can be thought of as the outcome occurring from a spin of a roulette wheel.

Expected Return

According to the one-factor model, the expected return on security i can be written as

$$\bar{r}_i = a_i + b_i \overline{F} \tag{10.3}$$

where $\overline{F}$ denotes the expected value of the factor.

This equation can be used to estimate the expected return on the security. For example, if the expected growth rate in GDP is 3%, then the expected return for Widget equals $4\% + (2 \times 3\%) = 10\%$.

Variance

With the one-factor model, it can also be shown that the variance of any security i is equal to

$$\sigma_i^2 = b_i^2 \sigma_F^2 + \sigma_{ei}^2 \tag{10.4}$$

---

[4]It is more appropriate to state that security returns respond to expectations (and deviations from those expectations) about the future values of factors such as GDP growth as opposed to merely the realized values of those factors. This subtle (but important) distinction will be addressed later in the chapter.

where σ_F^2 is the variance of the factor F and σ_{ei}^2 is the variance of the random error term e_i. Thus if the variance of the factor σ_F^2 equals 3 and the residual variance σ_{ei}^2 equals 15.2, then according to this equation Widget's variance equals

$$\sigma_i^2 = (2^2 \times 3) + 15.2$$
$$= 27.2$$

Covariance

With a one-factor model the covariance between any two securities i and j can be shown to equal

$$\sigma_{ij} = b_i b_j \sigma_F^2 \tag{10.5}$$

In the example of Widget, equation (10.5) can be used to estimate the covariance between Widget and another hypothetical security, such as the stock of Whatever Company. Assuming that the factor sensitivity of Whatever is 4.0, the covariance between Widget and Whatever equals

$$\sigma_{ij} = 2 \times 4 \times 3$$
$$= 24$$

Assumptions

Equations (10.4) and (10.5) are based on two critical assumptions. The first assumption is that the random error term and the factor are uncorrelated. This means that the outcome of the factor has no bearing on the outcome of the random error term.

The second assumption is that the random error terms of any two securities are uncorrelated. This means that the outcome of the random error term of one security has no bearing on the outcome of the random error term of any other security. In other words, the returns of two securities will be correlated—that is, will move together only through common responses to the factor. If either of these two assumptions is invalid, then the model is an approximation, and a different factor model (perhaps one with more factors) will theoretically be a more accurate model of the return-generating process.

The Market Model

The market model can now be shown to be a specific example of a one-factor model where the factor is the return on a market index. In Chapter 7, the market model appeared as

$$r_i = \alpha_{iI} + \beta_{iI} r_I + \epsilon_{iI} \tag{7.3}$$

The similarity between equation (7.3) and the general form of the one-factor model in equation (10.2) is readily apparent. The intercept term α_{iI} from the market model equation corresponds to the zero factor term a_i from equation (10.2). Furthermore, the slope term β_{iI} from the market model equates to the sensitivity term b_i from the generalized one-factor model. Each equation has a random error term: e_{it} in the factor model and ϵ_{iI} in the market model.[5] Finally, the market index return plays the role of the single factor.

However, as mentioned earlier, the concept of a one-factor model does not restrict the investor to using a market index as the factor. Many other factors are plausible, such as predicted GDP or industrial production.

---

[5] The time subscript t was deleted from the market model simply for ease of exposition. Technically speaking, the random error term should be written as ϵ_{iIt}.

Two Important Features of One-factor Models

Two features of one-factor models are of particular interest.

The Tangency Portfolio

First, the assumption that the returns on all securities respond to a single common factor greatly simplifies the task of identifying the tangency portfolio. To determine the composition of the tangency portfolio, the investor needs to estimate all the expected returns, variances, and covariances. This can be done with a one-factor model by estimating a_i, b_i, and σ_{ei} for each of the N risky securities.[6]

Also needed are the expected value of the factor $\overline{F}$ and its standard deviation, σ_F. With these estimates, equations (10.3), (10.4), and (10.5) can be used to calculate expected returns, variances, and covariances for the securities. Using these values, the curved efficient set of Markowitz can be derived. Finally, the tangency portfolio can be determined for a given risk-free rate.

The common responsiveness of securities to the factor eliminates the need to estimate directly the covariances between the securities. Those covariances are captured by the securities' sensitivities to the factor and the factor's variance.

Diversification

The second interesting feature of one-factor models has to do with diversification. Earlier it was shown that diversification leads to an averaging of market risk and a reduction in unique risk. This feature is true of any one-factor model, except that instead of market and unique (or non-market) risk, the words factor and nonfactor risk are used. In equation (10.4) the first term on the right-hand side ($b_i^2 \sigma_F^2$) is known as the **factor risk** of the security, and the second term (σ_{ei}^2) is known as the **nonfactor** (or idiosyncratic) **risk** of the security.

Factor Risk That part of a security's total risk that is related to moves in various common factors and, hence, cannot be diversified away.

Nonfactor Risk That part of a security's total risk that is not related to moves in various common factors and, hence, can be diversified away.

With a one-factor model, the variance of a portfolio is given by

$$\sigma_P^2 = b_P^2 \sigma_F^2 + \sigma_{ep}^2 \tag{10.6a}$$

where:

$$b_p = \sum_{i=1}^{N} X_i b_i \tag{10.6b}$$

$$\sigma_{ep}^2 = \sum_{i=1}^{N} X_i^2 \sigma_{ei}^2 \tag{10.6c}$$

Equation (10.6a) shows that the total risk of any portfolio can be viewed as having two components similar to the two components of the total risk of an individual security shown in equation (10.4). In particular, the first and second terms on the right-hand side of equation (10.6a) are the factor risk and nonfactor risk of the portfolio, respectively.

As a portfolio becomes more diversified (meaning that it contains more securities), each proportion X_i will become smaller. However, this will not cause b_p to either decrease or increase significantly unless a deliberate attempt is made to do so by adding securities with values of b_i that are either relatively low or high. As equation (10.6b) shows, this is because b_p is simply a weighted average of the sensitivities of the securities b_i with the values of X_i serving as the weights. Thus, *diversification leads to an averaging of factor risk.*

However, as a portfolio becomes more diversified, there is reason to expect σ_{ep}^2, the nonfactor risk, to decrease. This can be shown by examining equation (10.6c). Assuming

---

[6]This is shown in more detail in Appendix B to Chapter 7.

that the amount invested in each security is equal, then this equation can be rewritten by substituting $1/N$ for X_i:

$$\sigma_{ep}^2 = \sum_{i=1}^{N} \left(\frac{1}{N}\right)^2 \sigma_{ei}^2$$

$$= \left(\frac{1}{N}\right)\left[\frac{\sigma_{e1}^2 + \sigma_{e2}^2 + \cdots + \sigma_{eN}^2}{N}\right]$$

The value inside the square brackets is the average nonfactor risk for the individual securities. But the portfolio's nonfactor risk is only one-Nth as large as this because the term $1/N$ appears outside the brackets. As the portfolio becomes more diversified, the number of securities in it, N, becomes larger. This means that $1/N$ becomes smaller, which in turn reduces the nonfactor risk of the portfolio. Simply stated, *diversification reduces nonfactor risk.*[7]

Multiple-Factor Models

The health of the economy affects most firms. Thus, changes in expectations concerning the future of the economy can be expected to have profound effects on the returns of most securities. However, the economy is not a simple, monolithic entity. Several common influences with pervasive effects can be identified.

1. The growth rate of GDP
2. The level of interest rates on Treasury bills
3. The yield spread between long-term Government of Canada bonds and Treasury bills
4. The yield spread between long-term corporate and Government of Canada bonds
5. The inflation rate
6. The level of oil prices

Two-factor Models

Instead of a one-factor model, a multiple-factor model for security returns that considers these various influences may be more accurate. As an example of a multiple-factor model, consider a two-factor model. This assumes that the return-generating process contains two factors.

In equation form, the two-factor model for period t is

$$r_{it} = a_i + b_{i1}F_{1t} + b_{i2}F_{2t} + e_{it} \tag{10.7}$$

where F_{1t} and F_{2t} are the two factors that are pervasive influences on security returns and b_{i1} and b_{i2} are the sensitivities of security i to these two factors. As with the one-factor model, e_{it} is a random error term and a_i is the expected return on security i if each factor has a value of zero.

Figure 10.2 provides an illustration of Widget Company's stock, whose returns are affected by expectations concerning both the growth rate in GDP and the rate of inflation. As was the case in the one-factor example, each point in the figure corresponds to a particular year. This time, however, each point is a combination of Widget's return, the rate of inflation, and the growth of GDP in that year, as given in Table 10.1. To this scatter of

---

[7]Actually, all that is necessary for this reduction in nonfactor risk to occur is for the maximum amount invested in any one security to continually decrease as N increases. An example based on the market model is given in Chapter 7.

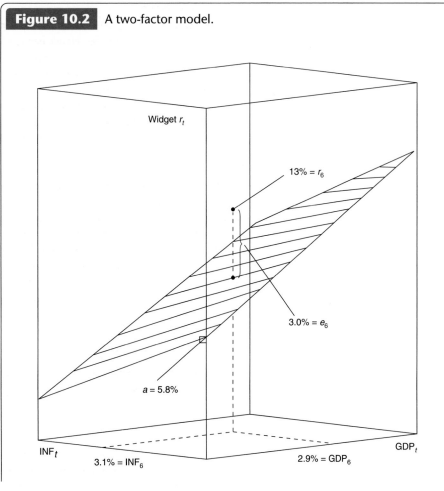

Figure 10.2 A two-factor model.

Widget r_t

13% = r_6

3.0% = e_6

$a = 5.8\%$

INF$_t$

3.1% = INF$_6$

2.9% = GDP$_6$

GDP$_t$

points is fitted a two-dimensional plane using the statistical technique of *multiple-regression analysis*. (*Multiple* refers to the fact that there are two predicted variables—GDP and inflation in this example—on the right-hand side of the equation.) The plane for a given security is described by the following adaptation of equation (10.7):

$$r_t = a + b_1\text{GDP}_t + b_2\text{INF}_t + e_t$$

The slope of the plane in the GDP growth-rate direction (the term b_1) represents Widget's sensitivity to changes in GDP growth. The slope of the plane in the inflation rate direction (the term b_2) is Widget's sensitivity to changes in the inflation rate. Note that the sensitivities b_1 and b_2 in this example are positive and negative, respectively, having corresponding values of 2.2 and −.7.[8] This indicates that as predicted GDP growth or inflation rises, Widget's return should increase or decrease, respectively.

The intercept term (the zero factor) of 5.8% in Figure 10.2 indicates Widget's expected return if both GDP growth and inflation are zero. Finally, in a given year the distance from Widget's actual point to the plane indicates its unique return (e_{it}), the portion of Widget's

---

[8]These values were arrived at by applying multiple regression (see David Levine, Mark Berenson, and David Stephan, *Statistics for Managers Using Microsoft Excel*, second edition (Upper Saddle River, NJ: Prentice Hall, 1999) to the data given in Table 10.1.

return not attributed to either GDP growth or inflation. For example, given that GDP grew by 2.9% and inflation was 3.1%, Widget's expected return in year 6 equals 5.8% + (2.2 × 2.9%) − (.7 × 3.1%) = 10%. Hence its unique return for that year is equal to 13% − 10% = 3%.

Four parameters need to be estimated for each security with the two-factor model: a_i, b_{i1}, b_{i2}, and the standard deviation of the random error term denoted σ_{ei}. For each of the factors, two parameters need to be estimated. These parameters are the expected value of each factor ($\overline{F}_1$ and $\overline{F}_2$) and the variance of each factor (σ_{F1}^2 and σ_{F2}^2). Finally, the covariance between the factors [$COV(F_1, F_2)$] needs to be estimated.

Expected Return

With these estimates, the expected return for any security i can be determined by using the following formula:

$$\overline{r}_i = a_i + b_{i1}\overline{F}_1 + b_{i2}\overline{F}_2 \tag{10.8}$$

For example, the expected return for Widget equals 5.8% + (2.2 × 3%) − (.7 × 5%) = 8.9% provided that the expected increases in GDP and inflation are 3% and 5%, respectively.

Variance

According to the two-factor model, the variance for any security i is

$$\sigma_i^2 = b_{i1}^2\sigma_{F1}^2 + b_{i2}^2\sigma_{F2}^2 + 2b_{i1}b_{i2}COV(F_1, F_2) + \sigma_{ei}^2 \tag{10.9}$$

If, in the example, the variances of the first (σ_{F1}^2) and second (σ_{F2}^2) factors are equal to 3 and 2.9, respectively, and their covariance $COV(F_1, F_2)$ equals .65, then the variance of Widget equals $(2.2^2 × 3) + (−.7^2 × 2.9) + (2 × 2.2 × −.7 × .65) + 18.2 = 32.1$, since its two sensitivities and random error term variance are 2.2, −.7, and 18.2, respectively.

Covariance

Similarly, according to the two-factor model the covariance between any two securities i and j can be determined by

$$\sigma_{ij} = b_{i1}b_{j1}\sigma_{F1}^2 + b_{i2}b_{j2}\sigma_{F2}^2 + (b_{i1}b_{j2} + b_{i2}b_{j1})COV(F_1, F_2) \tag{10.10}$$

Thus, continuing with the example, the covariance between Widget and Whatever is estimated to equal (2.2 × 6 × 3) + (−.7 × −5 × 2.9) + [(2.2 × −5) + (−.7 × 6)] × .65 = 39.9 if the sensitivities of Whatever to the two factors are 6 and −5, respectively.

The Tangency Portfolio

As with the one-factor model, once the expected returns, variances, and covariances have been determined using these equations, the investor can proceed to use an *optimizer* (a special kind of mathematical routine) to derive the curved efficient set of Markowitz. Then the tangency portfolio can be identified for a given risk-free rate, after which the investor can determine her optimal portfolio.

Diversification

Everything said earlier regarding one-factor models and the effects of diversification applies here as well.

1. Diversification leads to an averaging of factor risk.
2. Diversification can substantially reduce nonfactor risk.
3. For a *well-diversified portfolio*, nonfactor risk will be insignificant.

As with a one-factor model, the sensitivity of a portfolio to a particular factor in a multiple-factor model is a weighted average of the sensitivities of the securities where the weights are equal to the proportions invested in the securities. This can be seen by remembering that the return on a portfolio is a weighted average of the returns of its component securities:

$$r_{pt} = \sum_{i=1}^{N} X_i r_{it} \tag{10.11}$$

Substituting the right-hand side of equation (10.7) for r_{it} on the right-hand side of equation (10.11) results in

$$r_{pt} = \sum_{i=1}^{N} X_i(a_i + b_{i1}F_{1t} + b_{i2}F_{2t} + e_{it})$$

$$= \left[\sum_{i=1}^{N} X_i a_i\right] + \left[\sum_{i=1}^{N} X_i b_{i1} F_{1t}\right] + \left[\sum_{i=1}^{N} X_i b_{i2} F_{2t}\right] + \left[\sum_{i=1}^{N} X_i e_{it}\right] \tag{10.12}$$

$$= a_p + b_{p1}F_{1t} + b_{p2}F_{2t} + e_{pt}$$

where:

$$a_p = \sum_{i=1}^{N} X_i a_i$$

$$b_{p1} = \sum_{i=1}^{N} X_i b_{i1}$$

$$b_{p2} = \sum_{i=1}^{N} X_i b_{i2}$$

$$e_{pt} = \sum_{i=1}^{N} X_i e_{it}$$

Note that the portfolio sensitivities b_{p1} and b_{p2} are weighted averages of the respective individual sensitivities b_{i1} and b_{i2}.

The Importance of Expectations

Security prices reflect investors' estimates of the present values of firms' future prospects. At any given time the price of Widget stock is likely to depend on the projected growth rate of GDP, the projected rate of inflation, and other factors. If investors' projections of such fundamental economic conditions change, so too will the price of Widget. Because the return on a stock is influenced heavily by changes in its price, stock returns are expected to be more highly correlated with changes in expected future values of fundamental economic variables than with the actual changes that occur contemporaneously.

For example, a large increase in inflation that was fully anticipated might have no effect on the stock price of a company whose earnings are highly sensitive to inflation. However, if the consensus expectation was for a low inflation rate, then the subsequent large increase would have a large effect on the company's stock price.

For this reason, whenever possible it is desirable to select factors that measure changes in expectations rather than realizations, as the latter typically include both changes that were anticipated and those that were not. One way to accomplish this goal is to rely on variables that involve changes in market prices. Thus, the difference in the returns on two portfolios—one consisting of stocks thought to be unaffected by inflation and the other consisting of stocks thought to be affected by inflation—can be used as a factor that measures revisions in inflation expectations. Those who construct factor models using the time-series approach often rely on market-based surrogates for changes in forecasts of fundamental economic variables in this manner.

Sector-factor Models

Sector-factor Model A special kind of multiple-factor model in which the factors are particular industries or economic sectors.

The prices of securities in the same industry or economic sector often move together in response to changes in prospects for that sector. Some investors acknowledge this by using a special kind of multiple-factor model referred to as a **sector-factor model**. To create a sector-factor model, each security under consideration must be assigned to a sector. For a two-sector-factor model, there are two sectors and each security must be assigned to one of them.

For example, let sector-factor 1 consist of all industrial companies and sector-factor 2 consist of all non-industrial companies (such as utility, transportation, and financial companies). Thus, F_1 and F_2 can be thought of as representing the returns on an industrial stock index and a non-industrial stock index, respectively. (They could, for example, be components of the TSE 300.) Keep in mind, however, that both the number of sectors and what each sector consists of is an open matter that is left to the investor to decide.[9]

With this two-sector-factor model, the return-generating process for securities is of the same general form as the two-factor model given in equation (10.7). However, with the two-sector-factor model, F_1 and F_2 now denote sector-factors 1 and 2, respectively. Furthermore, any particular security belongs to either sector-factor 1 or sector-factor 2 but not both. By definition, a value of zero is given to the sensitivity term corresponding to the sector-factor to which the security is not assigned. This means that either b_{i1} or b_{i2} is set equal to zero, depending on the sector-factor to which security i is not assigned. The value of the other sensitivity term must be estimated. (To make matters simple, some people simply give it a value of one.)

As an illustration, consider Alcan (AL) and Air Canada (AC). The two-sector-factor model for AL (the time subscript t has been deleted for ease of exposition here) would be

$$r_{AL} = a_{AL} + b_{AL1}F_1 + b_{AL2}F_2 + e_{AL} \tag{10.13}$$

However, because AL belongs to sector-factor 1 as an industrial security, the coefficient b_{AL2} is assigned a value of zero. Once this assignment is made, equation (10.13) reduces to

$$r_{AL} = a_{AL} + b_{AL1}F_1 + e_{AL} \tag{10.14}$$

Thus only the values of a_{AL}, b_{AL1}, and σ_{eAL} need to be estimated for AL with the two-sector-factor model. In comparison with the two-factor model, values of a_{AL}, b_{AL1}, b_{AL2}, and σ_{eAL} need to be estimated.

Similarly, as AC belongs to the non-industrial sector, it would have the following two-sector-factor model:

$$r_{AC} = a_{AC} + b_{AC1}F_1 + b_{AC2}F_2 + e_{AC} \tag{10.15}$$

which would reduce to

$$r_{AC} = a_{AC} + b_{AC2}F_2 + e_{AC} \tag{10.16}$$

as b_{AC1} would be assigned a value of zero. Thus only the values of a_{AC}, b_{AC2}, and σ_{eAC} need to be estimated with the two-sector-factor model.

---

[9]Attempts have been made to identify stock groups, or clusters, where stocks within any group have returns that are more highly correlated with one another than the returns of stocks from different groups. See, for example, Benjamin F. King, "Market and Industry Factors in Stock Price Behavior," *Journal of Business* 39, no.1 (January 1966): 139–170; James L. Farrell, Jr., "Analyzing Covariation of Returns to Determine Stock Groupings," *Journal of Business* 47, no. 2 (April 1974): 186–207; "Homogeneous Stock Groupings: Implications for Portfolio Management," *Financial Analysts Journal* 31, no. 3 (May–June 1975): 50–62; and Robert D. Arnott, "Cluster Analysis and Stock Price Co-movement," *Financial Analysts Journal* 36, no. 6 (November–December 1980): 56–62.

In general, whereas four parameters need to be estimated for each security with a two-factor model (a_i, b_{i1}, b_{i2}, and σ_{ei}), only three parameters need to be estimated with a two-sector-factor model (a_i, σ_{ei}, and either b_{i1} or b_{i2}). With these estimates in hand, along with estimates of $\overline{F}_1$, $\overline{F}_2$, σ_{F1}, and σ_{F2}, the investor can use equations (10.8) and (10.9) to estimate expected returns and variances for each security. Pairwise covariances can be estimated using equation (10.10). This will then enable the investor to derive the curved efficient set of Markowitz from which the tangency portfolio can be determined for a given risk-free rate.

Extending the Model

Once the discussion is extended to more than two factors, diagrams are no longer useful, as the analysis moves beyond three dimensions. Nevertheless, the concepts are the same. If there are k factors, the multiple-factor model can be written as

$$r_{it} = a_i + b_{i1}F_{1t} + b_{i2}F_{2t} + \cdots + b_{ik}F_{kt} + e_{it} \tag{10.17}$$

where each security has k sensitivities, one for each of the k factors.

It is possible to have both factors and sector factors represented in equation (10.17). For example, F_1 and F_2 could represent GDP and inflation as in Table 10.1, whereas F_3 and F_4 could represent the returns on industrial stocks and non-industrial stocks, respectively. Hence, each stock would have three sensitivities: b_{i1}, b_{i2}, and b_{i3} for industrials and b_{i1}, b_{i2}, and b_{i4} for non-industrials.[10]

An Alternative

As an alternative to equation (10.17), factor models are sometimes written as follows:

$$r_{it} = \bar{r}_{it} + c_{i1}FD_{1t} + c_{i2}FD_{2t} + \cdots + c_{ik}FD_{kt} + e_{it} \tag{10.18}$$

Here $\bar{r}_{it}$ denotes the expected return of stock i in period t and the terms $FD_{1t}\ldots FD_{kt}$ denote the deviations of factors 1 through k from their expected values in period t. For example, in the case of the first factor, $FD_{1t} = F_{1t} - \bar{F}_{1t}$, which represents the difference between the actual value of the first factor and its expected value (and perhaps the change in projections of the first factor's future value). Hence, if this factor is the rate of inflation, then FD_{1t} would denote the unexpected rate of inflation since it is equivalent to the difference between the actual rate of inflation and the expected inflation rate. Lastly, the terms $c_{i1}\ldots c_{ik}$ denote the response coefficients in the rate of return of stock i to these factor deviations. Note that the random error term e_{it} and the factor deviation terms $FD_{1t}\ldots FD_{kt}$ all have expected values of zero.[11]

As an example, assume that there are two factors: the growth rate in gross domestic product and the rate of inflation. Thus, the factor model would describe Digit's rate of return in period t as follows:

$$r_t = \bar{r}_t + c_{GDP}FD_{GDP_t} + c_{INF}FD_{INF_t} + e_t \tag{10.19}$$

indicating that there are four components to Digit's actual return:

---

[10]Another example of such a model expands the market model to include sector factors where the sectors are selected to represent "industries." Hence each stock has two sensitivities that indicate how the stock responds to returns on the stock index and an industry index to which the stock belongs. See Gordon J. Alexander and Jack Clark Francis, *Portfolio Analysis* (Englewood Cliffs, NJ: Prentice Hall): 83–92.

[11]Equations (10.17) and (10.18) can be reconciled as follows: for ease of exposition, the analysis deletes the time subscript t and assumes that there is one factor. Note that equation (10.17) implies $\bar{r}_i = a_i + b_i\bar{F}_1$, where $\bar{r}_i$ and $\bar{F}_1$ are the expected return for security i and the expected value of the factor, respectively. Substituting $\bar{r}_i - b_i\bar{F}_1$ for a_i results in $r_i = \bar{r}_i + b_i(F_1 - \bar{F}_1) + e_i$. Letting $FD_1 = F_1 - \bar{F}_1$ produces an alternative formulation of a one-factor model that corresponds to equation (10.18): $r_i = \bar{r}_i + b_iFD_1 + e_i$.

1. Digit's expected return $\bar{r}_t$, which is determined by Equation (10.8)
2. Digit's response to the growth rate in gross domestic product turning out to be different from what was expected, $c_{GDP}FD_{GDP_t}$
3. Digit's response to the rate of inflation turning out to be different from what was expected, $c_{INF}FD_{INF_t}$
4. Digit's random error return, e_t

Imagine that the expected growth rate in GDP was 2% and the expected inflation rate was 4%, but that the actual growth rate in GDP turned out to be 1% and the actual inflation rate was 5%. Hence, $FD_{GDP_t} = 1\% - 2\% = -1\%$, and $FD_{INF_t} = 5\% - 4\% = 1\%$. Assume c_{GDP} and c_{INF} are equal to 3 and -2, respectively, and that Digit had an expected return at the beginning of the period of 10%. If its actual return for the period ended up being 8%, then this return would have the following four components:

1. An expected return of 10%
2. A return attributable to GDP turning out to be different than initially expected, amounting to $3 \times -1\% = -3\%$
3. A return attributable to inflation turning out to be different that initially expected, amounting to $-2 \times 1\% = -2\%$
4. A random error return of $+3\%$

Note that the 8% actual return equals the sum of its components, $10\% - 3\% - 2\% + 3\%$ (actually, the random error return of 3% is determined in order for the sum to equal 8%).

Estimating Factor Models

Methods of estimating factor models can be grouped into three primary approaches:

1. Time-series approaches
2. Cross-sectional approaches
3. Factor-analytic approaches

▶ Time-series Approaches

Time-series approaches are perhaps the most intuitive.[12] The model builder begins with the assumption that he knows in advance the factors that influence security returns. Identification of the relevant factors typically proceeds from an economic analysis of the firms involved. Aspects of macroeconomics, microeconomics, industrial organization, and fundamental security analysis will play a major role in the process.

For example, as discussed earlier, certain macroeconomic variables might be expected to have a pervasive impact on security returns, including such things as predicted growth in GDP, inflation, interest rates, and oil prices. With these factors specified, the model builder collects information concerning the values of the factors and security returns from period to period. Using these data, the model builder can calculate the sensitivities of the securities' returns to the factors, the securities' zero factors and unique returns, and the standard deviations of the factors and their correlations. In this approach, accurate measurement of factor values is crucial. In practice, this can be quite difficult.

As discussed earlier, security prices are highly dependent on investors' projections of the future prospects for the issuing firms. Desirable factors therefore will incorporate these expectations. Yet it is generally difficult to directly obtain accurate information regarding investors' expectations. Thus those who construct factor models using the time-series approach often rely on market-based surrogates for changes in forecasts of fundamental

---

[12]The examples given earlier in the chapter are examples of this approach.

The Barra US and Canadian Equity Multiple-factor Model

For the quantitatively inclined investment professional, multiple-factor models are intuitively appealing tools. They capture the essence of the fundamental economic and financial forces that affect security returns in a concise and readily testable form. However, moving from abstract discussions to the development of factor models that are sufficiently comprehensive and robust to serve the varied needs of institutional investors is a difficult task. An overview of the BARRA US equity multiple-factor model offers insights into the complex elements of factor model implementation.

The BARRA model is based on the pioneering work of Barr Rosenberg, an econometrician and former finance professor. In the early 1970s while at the University of California, Berkeley, he and Vinay Marathe formulated a sophisticated factor model. The model related common stock returns to a variety of factors derived primarily from the underlying companies' business operations.

Rosenberg is more than your typical ivory tower academic. Instead of being content to publish his results and receive the accolades of his colleagues, he recognized the commercial applications of his model. He formed a firm, now called BARRA, to enhance and sell the model to institutional investors.

Both the model and the firm proved successful beyond anyone's imagination. BARRA has grown into a worldwide consulting organization with annual revenues exceeding $100 million. Its stock is publicly traded and today has a market capitalization of over $300 million. Although Rosenberg left the firm in 1985 to pursue his own investment management ambitions, BARRA has continued to leverage off of its factor-model expertise by designing additional factor models for the global equity market and various foreign stock markets. The firm has also built factor models for the US and several foreign bond markets.

Rosenberg's original US equity multiple-factor model underwent major revisions in 1982 and 1997 and is referred to by factor-model aficionados as the E3 model. Currently hundreds of institutional investors (more than half of them outside of the United States) subscribe to the E3 model service

(and its predecessor, the E2 model). These investors range from large investment managers to pension funds, and in total they manage over one trillion dollars of US common stocks.

All factor models are based on the assumption that securities with similar exposures to specific factors will exhibit similar investment behaviour. The factor model-builder must translate this basic concept into practice. The process of constructing factor models is far from an exact science. While certain statistical tests can be applied to gauge the explanatory power of a particular factor model, the model-builder retains wide latitude to include or exclude potential factors.

It is instructive, therefore, to review how BARRA developed the E3 model. The process by which the model was specified is summarized by five steps.

1. Data collection and checking
2. Factor selection
3. Creation of composite factors
4. Estimation of factor returns and the factor variance-covariance matrix
5. Model testing

The E3 model's construction began with the collection of relevant security data. BARRA gathered monthly components of security returns, such as prices, dividends, and shares outstanding over an extended period of time for stocks to comprise the "estimation universe." This group included the largest 1500 US common stocks, with another roughly 400 stocks added to ensure adequate industry representation. BARRA also acquired a wide array of income and balance sheet information on the underlying companies. This financial data came largely from the annual and quarterly financial statements issued by the companies.

As part of this collection process, BARRA checked the data for quality. Although this task may seem mundane, it was a critical step, as a small amount of bad data can produce a disproportionately large impact on a factor model's accuracy.

The second step involved factor selection. Literally hundreds of potential factors were available for inclusion in the model. BARRA sought to identify those factors that had a pervasive influence on the returns and risks of individual securities. Using historical security return data, BARRA isolated 39 market-related, income statement, and balance sheet factors that demonstrated statistically significant relationships with security prices.

The particular factors selected by BARRA ranged from the obvious to the novel. Examples included a company's historical equity beta, its consensus forecast earnings growth, its historical variability in earnings, the relative performance of its stock, its stock's book-to-price and earnings-to-price ratios, its debt to total assets, its earnings payout ratio, and the sensitivity of its stock to movements in foreign currency values.

The third step in the E3 model's construction entailed creating a set of composite fundamental factors from the individual factors. BARRA employed 13 composite factors: Volatility, Momentum, Size, Size Non-linearity, Trading Activity, Growth, Earnings/Yield, Value, Earnings Variability, Leverage, Currency Sensitivity, Dividend Yield, and Non-estimation Universe Estimator. The individual factors were assigned to and weighted within the composite factors based on both judgment and statistical analyses. The weights of the factors may change over time as BARRA refits the model periodically.

The purpose of creating these composite fundamental factors was largely statistical convenience. As the text describes, a factor model-builder must estimate the variance of each factor and the covariances among all the factors. The number of variances and covariances grows exponentially as the number of factors increases. Therefore, instead of having to calculate variances and covariances for dozens of factors, BARRA's task was considerably reduced by combining the individual factors into a handful of composite factors.

To these 13 composite factors, BARRA added 13 sector-factors. Like the composite fundamental factors, the sector-factors are composed of smaller items, in this case 52 individual industries. (In the E3 model, a security can be assigned to as many as six industries, with total weights summing to 1, based on analysis of the company's sales, earnings, and assets. While the defined sectors remain constant

over time, the number and definitions of the industries evolve as economic forces dictate. For example, the computer software industry was unimportant in the 1970s, but is a large industry today.) Thus in its final form, the BARRA E3 factor model contains 26 fundamental and industry factors.

The fourth step involved estimating factor returns for each of the 26 factors and developing forecasts of nonfactor risk. Given return data on the model's estimation universe, for every month in its test period BARRA effectively estimated the returns on 26 portfolios that each had unit exposure to one particular factor and zero exposure to all other 25 factors. The returns to these unit-exposure portfolios represented the monthly returns to the respective factors. Using these factor returns, the factor variance-covariance matrix was computed. Further, nonfactor returns were separated from the factor returns and a nonfactor risk forecasting model was estimated.

The last step involved testing the performance of the E3 model. BARRA was concerned with how effective its forecasts of security risk were outside of the test period. Cutting through the statistical jargon, BARRA found that the model performed well.

The BARRA E3 model and its predecessors are applied by institutional investors in a variety of situations. Investment managers use the model to forecast the variability of their portfolios' returns, both in an absolute sense and relative to a benchmark. The model allows the managers to dissect this forecast risk into factor and nonfactor components.

Managers can make informed judgments about the expected rewards offered by their particular portfolio strategies relative to the forecast risks. Managers and their clients also use the E3 model for performance attribution (see Chapter 24). Here an analyst uses the model to calculate a portfolio's historical exposure to the various factors. Then using BARRA's calculated factor returns, the contribution of each of those exposures to the portfolio's total return is computed. Finally, comparing the portfolio's exposures and the contributions of those exposures to the portfolio's performance against a relevant benchmark provides clues to the success or failure of the manager's strategies.

Institutional investors also use the E3 model to characterize the investment styles of their managers.

Similar investment styles tend to exhibit similar E3 factor exposures. For example, large capitalization growth managers typically have large Size and Growth exposures and low Value exposures. By analyzing a series of past returns for various portfolios with the E3 model, a client can more accurately identify the investment styles of its current and potential managers. This process aids in both performance evaluation (see Chapter 24) and manager structuring (see Chapters 23).

The BARRA US equity multiple-factor model has contributed to the rigour and sophistication with which institutional investors approach the task of managing large pools of US common stocks. Perhaps the most impressive testament to the model's utility and robustness is that in the highly competitive and fickle world of investments, no alternative factor model has gained the widespread acceptance that the BARRA models have achieved.

BARRA has also developed the *Canadian Equity Risk Model*, an analogue of the US E3 Multiple-factor Risk Model. The Canadian model uses 10

composite risk indices: Variability in Markets, Momentum, Size, Liquidity, Profitability, Growth, Value, Yield, US Sensitivity, and a non-TSE indicator. The last of these captures the behaviour of smaller firms that are not in the model's estimation universe. The composite indices, in turn, consist of linear combinations of anywhere from two to five fundamental factors. All told, 29 fundamental factors are required to develop the model.

It is interesting to note that not all the risk indices correspond to those used in the E3 model, although the index named "US Sensitivity" presumably includes many of the US factors not included in the Canadian model. In addition, BARRA adds 19 industry factors that are composites constructed from the 40 TSE industry classes, for a total of 30 variables. The model is then applied in the same way as the US model. Tests of an earlier version of this model showed that it explained equity returns better than either a single-factor CAPM or an industry sectoral model.

BARRA, Inc.
www.barra.com

economic variables in this manner. For example, the single factor in the market model is the return on a market index. That return represents investors' consensus expectations regarding the financial outlook for the companies whose stocks constitute the index. Changes in those expectations will be reflected in price changes for the index's securities.

An Example

Table 10.1 and Figure 10.2 presented an example of how to use the time-series approach to estimate a factor model. In this example, returns on individual stocks such as Widget were related to two factors—gross domestic product and inflation—by comparing over time each stock's returns to the predicted values of the factors.

Recently, Fama and French conducted a study that used a time-series approach to identify the factors that explain stock and bond returns.[13] In their study, monthly stock returns were found to be related to three factors: a market factor, a size factor, and a book-to-market equity factor. In equation form, their factor model for stocks appears as

$$r_{it} - r_{ft} = a_i + b_{i1}(r_{Mt} - r_{ft}) + b_{i2}\text{SMB}_t + b_{i3}\text{HML}_t + e_{it} \qquad (10.20)$$

The first factor $(r_{Mt} - r_{ft})$ is simply the monthly return on a broad stock market index over and above the return on one-month Treasury bills. The size factor (SMB_t) can be

---

[13]Eugene F. Fama and Kenneth R. French, "Common Risk Factors in the Returns on Stocks and Bonds," *Journal of Financial Economics* 33, no. 1 (February 1993): 3–56. Other time series examples are presented in Chapter 11. It should be noted that attempts to relate the Fama-French factor model to an asset pricing model of market equilibrium have been controversial. See, for example, A. Craig MacKinlay, "Multifactor Models Do Not Explain Deviations from the CAPM," *Journal of Financial Economics* 38 no. 1 (May 1995): 3–28.

thought of as the difference in the monthly return on two stock indices—a small-stock index and a big-stock index. (Here a stock's size is measured by its share price at the end of June each year times the number of shares it has outstanding at that time. The small-stock index consists of stocks that are below the median NYSE size and the big-stock index consists of stocks that are above the median.) The book-to-market equity factor (HML_t) is also the difference in the monthly return on two stock indices—an index of stocks with high book-to-market equity ratios and an index of stocks with low book-to-market equity ratios. (Here book equity is shareholders' equity taken from the firm's balance sheet and market equity is the same as the stock's size used in determining the previous factor. The high ratio index consists of stocks that are in the top third, and the low ratio index consists of stocks that are in the bottom third.)

Fama and French also identified two factors that seem to explain monthly bond returns. In equation form, their factor model for bonds appears as

$$r_{it} - r_{ft} = a_i + b_{i1}\text{TERM}_t + b_{i2}\text{DEF}_t + e_{it} \qquad (10.21)$$

These two factors are a term-structure factor and a default factor.[14] The term-structure factor (TERM_t) is simply the difference in the monthly returns on long-term Treasury bonds and one-month Treasury bills. The default factor (DEF_t) is the difference in the monthly returns on a portfolio of long-term corporate bonds and long-term Treasury bonds.[15]

▶ Cross-sectional Approaches

Cross-sectional approaches are less intuitive than time-series approaches but can often be just as powerful a tool. The model builder begins with estimates of securities' sensitivities to certain factors. Then, in a particular time period, the values of the factors are estimated based on securities' returns and their sensitivities to the factors. This process is repeated over multiple time periods, thereby providing an estimate of the factors' standard deviations and their correlations.

Note that the cross-sectional approach is entirely different from the time-series approach. With the latter approach, the values of the factors are known and the sensitivities are estimated. Furthermore, the analysis is conducted for one security over multiple time periods, then another security, then another, and so on. With the former approach the sensitivities are known and the values of the factors are estimated. Accordingly, the sensitivities in the cross-sectional approach are sometimes referred to as attributes. Furthermore, the analysis is conducted over one time period for a group of securities, then another time period for the same group, then another, and so on. Examples of one-factor and two-factor models will be shown next to illustrate the cross-sectional approach.[16]

One-factor Models

Figure 10.3 provides a hypothetical example of the relationship between the returns for a number of different stocks in a given time period and one security attribute—dividend

---

[14]Speculative-grade bonds were also found to be related to the three stock factors.

[15]Interestingly, Fama and French also found that the market factor ($r_{Mt} - r_{ft}$) was related to these two bond factors. In light of this, they constructed a revised market factor that basically consisted of the market factor less the influence of the two bond factors and the two other stock factors, and they found that stock returns were related to five factors: the revised market factor, SML_t, HML_t, $TERM_t$, and DEF_t. Bond returns continued to be related to just the two bond factors.

[16]Note that in the time-series approach, a security's sensitivity to a factor is its "attribute," and the factor is a given macroeconomic variable. Hence the attribute's value is unknown and must be estimated, whereas the value of the factor is known. In the cross-sectional approach, a security's attribute is usually some microeconomic variable measuring the security's exposure to the factor (a stock's dividend yield and market capitalization can be thought of as examples of attributes). Hence the attribute's value is known whereas the factor is unknown and must be estimated.

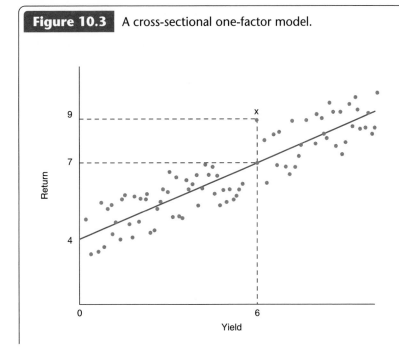

Figure 10.3 A cross-sectional one-factor model.

yield—for each stock. Each point represents one particular stock, showing its return and dividend yield for the time period under evaluation. In this case, stocks with higher-dividend yields tended to do better—that is, have higher returns—than those with lower-dividend yields. Figure 10.3 (an example of the cross-sectional approach) is based on many stocks for one time period, whereas Figure 10.1 (an example of the time-series approach) is based on one stock for many time periods.

To quantify the relationship shown in Figure 10.3, a straight line has been fitted to the diagram by using the statistical technique of simple-regression analysis. The equation of the line in Figure 10.3 is

$$\bar{r}_{it} = 4 + .5 b_{it} \qquad (10.22)$$

or, more generally,

$$\bar{r}_{it} = a_t + b_{it} F_t \qquad (10.23)$$

where:

$$\bar{r}_{it} = \text{the expected return on stock } i \text{ in period } t$$
$$\text{given that the factor had an actual value of } F_t$$
$$a_t = \text{the zero factor in period } t$$
$$b_{it} = \text{the dividend yield of stock } i \text{ in period } t$$
$$F_t = \text{the actual value of the factor in period } t$$

The vertical intercept a_t indicates the expected return on a typical stock with a dividend yield of zero. Hence, it is called the zero factor, as in equation (10.1). In Figure 10.3 it is equal to 4%. The slope of .5 indicates the increase in expected return for each percent of dividend yield. Hence, it represents the actual value of the dividend yield factor (F_t) in this time period.

From this example it can be seen that the cross-sectional approach uses sensitivities to estimate the values of the factors. Hence, these factors are known as *empirical factors*. In comparison, it was shown earlier that the time-series approach uses known values of factors to provide estimates of a security's sensitivities. These factors are known as *fundamental factors.*

The actual return on any given security may lie above or below the line due to its non-factor return. A complete description of the relationship for this one-factor model is

$$r_{it} = 4 + .5b_{it} + e_{it} \tag{10.24}$$

where e_{it} denotes the nonfactor return during period t on security i. In Figure 10.3, security x had a dividend yield of 6%. Hence, from equation (10.20), it had an expected return during this time period of $4 + (.5 \times 6) = 7\%$. Because it actually had a return of 9%, its nonfactor return was $9\% - 7\% = +2\%$.

In periods such as the one shown in Figure 10.3, high-yield stocks tended to outperform low-yield stocks. This indicates that the yield factor F_t was positive at this time. However, in another time period it is possible that low-yield stocks will tend to outperform high-yield stocks. The regression line in the corresponding diagram will be downward-sloping, and the yield factor will be negative. In still other time periods, there will be no relationship between yield and return, resulting in a flat regression line and a yield factor of zero.

A Two-factor Example

In some time periods small stocks tend to outperform large stocks. In other months the converse is true. Hence, many cross-sectional models use a *size attribute* that is often computed by taking the logarithm of the total market value of the firm's outstanding equity measured in millions, which is, in turn, calculated by taking the firm's share price, multiplying it by the number of shares outstanding, and then dividing the resulting figure by one million.[17] Thus, a $1-million stock would be assigned a size attribute value of zero; a $10-million stock a size attribute value of one; a $100-million stock a size attribute value of two, and so on. This convention is based on the empirical observation that the impact of the size factor on a security with a large total market value is likely to be twice as great as that on a security with one-tenth the value. More succinctly, the size effect appears to be *linear in the logarithms.*

To estimate the size factor in a given month, the procedure used in Figure 10.3 to estimate the yield factor can be employed. The size attributes of securities can be plotted on the horizontal axis and their returns for the given time period plotted (as in Figure 10.3) on the vertical axis. The slope of the resultant regression line provides an estimate of the size factor for the time period.

This procedure has drawbacks, however. Large stocks tend to have high yields. Thus, differences in returns between large and small stocks may be due to some extent to differences in yield, not size. The estimated size factor may be in part a reflection of a true yield factor. The problem is symmetrical in that the estimated yield factor may also be in part a reflection of the true size factor.

To mitigate this problem, returns can be compared with both size and yield attributes simultaneously by using the statistical technique of multiple regression. Figure 10.4 provides an illustration. Each security is represented by a point in a three-dimensional graph with return during the time period shown on the vertical axis, dividend yield for the time period shown on one of the bottom axes, and size for the period shown on the other.

Multiple-regression analysis is typically used to fit a plane to the data. In the example shown in Figure 10.4, this results in the following regression equation:

$$r_{it} = 7 + .4b_{i1t} - .3b_{i2t} + e_{it} \tag{10.25}$$

---

[17]Size has also been used as a factor in the time-series approach but in a different manner. See the previous discussion of the Fama and French study that is mentioned in footnote 12.

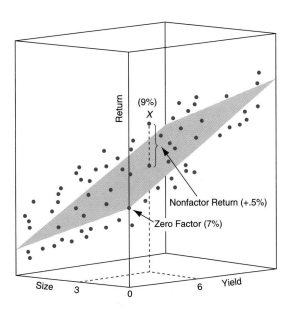

Figure 10.4 A cross-sectional two-factor model.

where b_{i1t} and b_{i2t} denote, respectively, the dividend yield and size of stock i in time period t. In general, the regression equation for a two-factor model is

$$r_{it} = a_t + b_{i1t}F_{1t} + b_{i2t}F_{2t} + e_{it} \qquad (10.26)$$

where a_t denotes the zero factor in time period t and the two factors are denoted F_{1t} and F_{2t}.

The equation of the plane shown in Figure 10.4 is

$$\bar{r}_{it} = 7 + .4b_{i1t} - .3b_{i2t} \qquad (10.27)$$

or, more generally,

$$\bar{r}_{it} = a_t + b_{i1t}F_{1t} + b_{i2t}F_{2t} \qquad (10.28)$$

This means that the zero factor a_t was 7%, indicating that a stock with zero-dividend yield and zero size (meaning a market value of \$1 million) would have been expected to have a return of 7%. Note that the estimated values of the dividend yield-factor (F_{1t}) and size factor (F_{2t}) are .4 and $-.3$, respectively. Thus, during this time period, higher-dividend yields and smaller sizes were both associated with larger returns.

Using equations (10.25) and (10.27), a given security X with a dividend yield of 6% and a size of 3 would have been expected to have a return of $7 + (.4 \times 6) - (.3 \times 3)$ = 8.5%. With an actual return of 9%, its nonfactor return e_{it} is thus 9% − 8.5% = +.5% during this time period, as shown in Figure 10.4.

The inclusion of size and dividend yield along with the use of multiple-regression analysis can help sort out the effects of differences in yield and size on differences in security returns. It cannot deal adequately with influences that are not represented at all, nor can it guarantee that the included attributes are not simply serving as *proxies* for other, more fundamental attributes. Statistical tests can indicate the ability of the variables included in the analysis to explain or predict past security returns. But judgment and luck are required to identify variables that can help predict future security returns, risks, and covariances. The extension to more than two variables follows in a straightforward manner from what has been indicated in equations (10.25) through (10.28).[18]

⬤ Factor-analytic Approaches

Finally, with factor-analytic approaches the model builder knows neither the factor values nor the securities' sensitivities to those factors. A statistical technique called *factor analysis* is used to extract the number of factors and securities' sensitivities based simply on a set of securities' past returns. Factor analysis takes the returns over many time periods on a sample of securities and attempts to identify one or more statistically significant factors that could have generated the covariances of returns observed within the sample. In essence, the return data tell the model builder about the structure of the factor model. Unfortunately, factor analysis does not specify what economic variables the factors represent.

⬤ Limitations

There is no reason to assume that a good factor model for one period will be a good one for the next period. Key factors change, as in the effect of energy prices on security markets in the 1970s and, more recently, during the US war in the Persian Gulf. The risks and returns associated with various factors and the sensitivities of securities to factors can change over time.[19]

It would be convenient if neither the relevant factors nor their magnitudes were to change from period to period. If this were so, mechanical procedures could be applied to security returns over an extended past period and the factor model inferred along with all the needed magnitudes. As it is, statistical estimation methods should be tempered by the judgment of the model builder to account for the dynamic nature of the investment environment.

Factor Models and Equilibrium

It should be kept in mind that a factor model is not an equilibrium model of asset pricing. Compare, for example, the expected return on a stock using a one-factor model from equation (10.3) with that of the Capital Asset Pricing Model (CAPM) from equation (9.7):[20]

$$\bar{r}_i = a_i + b_i\overline{F} \tag{10.3}$$

$$\bar{r}_i = r_f + (\bar{r}_M - r_f)\beta_i \tag{9.7}$$

Both equations show that the expected return on the stock is related to a characteristic of the stock, b_i or β_i. Assuming that the expected return on the factor $\overline{F}$ and $\bar{r}_M - r_f$ is positive, the larger the size of the characteristic, the larger the security's expected return. Hence, at this point there appears to be little to differentiate these two equations of expected return.

The key is in the other term on the right-hand side of each equation: a_i and r_f. The only characteristic of the stock that determines its expected return according to the CAPM

---

[18]One of the first studies to use the cross-sectional approach with more than two factors is William F. Sharpe, "Factors in New York Stock Exchange Security Returns, 1931–1979." *Journal of Portfolio Management* 8, no. 4 (Summer 1982): 5–19. A subsequent application is presented in Blake R. Grossman and William F. Sharpe, "Financial Implications of South African Divestment." *Financial Analysis Journal* 42, No. 4 (July–August 1986): 15–29.

[19]One study found that the factors that appear to explain security returns on even dates generally do not explain security returns on odd dates. See Dolores A. Conway and Marc R. Reinganum, "Stable Factors in Security Returns: Identification Using Cross Validation," *Journal of Business and Economics* 6, no. 1 (January 1988): 1–15.

[20]Time subscripts have been removed for ease of exposition. In Chapter 11, the relationship between a factor model's sensitivities and the CAPM's beta is examined.

is β_i, as r_f denotes the risk-free rate and is the same for all securities. However, with the factor model there is a second characteristic of the stock that needs to be estimated to determine the stock's expected return—namely, a_i. As the size of a_i differs from one stock to another, it prevents the factor model from being an equilibrium model.

Stated differently, two stocks with the same value of b_i can have dramatically different expected returns according to a factor model. For example, if GDP is expected to rise by 5%, then the expected return on Widget is 14% because a_i and b_i for Widget are 4 and 2 $[14\% = 4\% + (2 \times 5\%)]$. In comparison, even though ABC has the same sensitivity to GDP as Widget ($b_i = 2$), if ABC has an a_i of -2% then its expected return is only $-2\% + (2 \times 5\%) = 8\%$.

In contrast, two stocks with the same value of β_i will have the same expected return according to the equilibrium-based CAPM. If Widget and XYZ both have a beta of 1.2, then they both will have an expected return of 14%, given that the risk-free rate is 8% and the expected return on the market is 13% [since $8\% + (13\% - 8\%) \times 1.2 = 14\%$].

Having established that a factor model is not an equilibrium model, it seems appropriate to investigate the relationship between the parameters a_i and b_i of the one-factor model and the single parameter β_i of the CAPM.

For example, if actual returns can be viewed as being generated by a one-factor model where the factor F is the return on the market portfolio r_M, then according to equation (10.3), expected returns will be equal to

$$\bar{r}_i = a_i + b_i \bar{r}_M \qquad (10.29)$$

because $\overline{F} = \bar{r}_M$. But if equilibrium exists according to the CAPM, then equation (9.7) can be rewritten to state that expected returns will also be equal to

$$\bar{r}_i = (1 - \beta_i)r_f + \bar{r}_M\beta_i \qquad (10.30)$$

This means that the parameters of the one-factor model and the CAPM must have the following relationships:

$$a_i = (1 - \beta_i)r_f \qquad (10.31)$$

$$b_i = \beta_i \qquad (10.32)$$

This means that if expected returns are determined according to the CAPM and actual returns are generated by the one-factor market model, then a_i and b_i must be equal to $(1 - \beta_i)r_f$ and β_i, respectively.[21]

Summary

1. A factor model is a return-generating process that relates returns on securities to the movement in one or more common factors.
2. Any aspect of a security's return unexplained by the factor model is assumed to be unique to the security and therefore uncorrelated with the unique element of returns on other securities.
3. The market model is a specific example of a factor model where the factor is the return on a market index.
4. The assumption that the returns on securities respond to common factors greatly simplifies the task of calculating the curved Markowitz efficient set.

---

[21]If the factor in a one-factor world is the return on the market portfolio (as shown here), then technically the random error term for any security cannot be completely uncorrelated with the factor. This is because the market portfolio consists of all securities and hence is influenced by the nonfactor return of each security. See Eugene F. Fama, *Foundations of Finance* (New York: Basic Books, 1976), Chapter 3.

5. The sensitivity of a portfolio to a factor is the weighted average of the sensitivities of the component securities, with the securities' proportions in the portfolio serving as weights.
6. The total risk of a security is composed of factor risk and nonfactor risk.
7. Diversification leads to an averaging of factor risk.
8. Diversification reduces nonfactor risk.
9. Three basic methods are used to estimate factor models: the time-series approach, the cross-sectional approach, and the factor-analytic approach.
10. A factor model is not an equilibrium model of asset prices as is the CAPM. However, if equilibrium exists, certain relationships will hold between the factor model and the equilibrium asset-pricing model.

QUESTIONS AND PROBLEMS

1. Included among the factors that might be expected to be pervasive are expectations regarding growth in real GDP, real interest rates, inflation, and oil prices. For each factor, provide an example of an industry that is expected to have a high (either positive or negative) sensitivity to the factor.
2. Why do factor models greatly simplify the process of deriving the curved Markowitz efficient set?
3. Many investment management firms assign each of their security analysts to research a particular group of stocks. (Usually these assignments are organized by industry.) How are these assignments an implicit recognition of the validity of factor-model relationships?
4. What are two critical assumptions underlying any factor model? Cite hypothetical examples of violations of those assumptions.
5. Mary Childs, a wise investment statistician, once said with respect to factor models, "Similar stocks should display similar returns." What did Mary mean by this statement?
6. Based on a one-factor model, consider a security with a zero-factor value of 4% and a sensitivity to the factor of .50. The factor takes on a value of 10%. The security generates a return of 11%. What portion is related to nonfactor elements?
7. Based on a one-factor model, consider a portfolio of two securities with the following characteristics:

Security	Factor Sensitivity	Nonfactor Risk (σ_{ei}^2)	Proportion
A	.20	49	.40
B	3.50	100	.60

a. If the standard deviation of the factor is 15%, what is the factor risk of the portfolio?
b. What is the nonfactor risk of the portfolio?
c. What is the portfolio's standard deviation?
8. Recalculate the answers to Problem 7 assuming that the portfolio is also invested in the risk-free asset so that its investment proportions are:

Security	Proportion
Risk-free	.10
A	.36
B	.54

9. Based on a one-factor model, security A has a sensitivity of −.50, whereas security B has a sensitivity of 1.25. If the covariance between the two securities is −312.50, what is the standard deviation of the factor?

10. Based on a one-factor model, for two securities A and B:

$$r_A = 5\% + .8F + e_A$$

$$r_B = 7\% + 1.2F + e_B$$

$$\sigma_F = 18\%$$

$$\sigma_{eA} = 25\%$$

$$\sigma_{eB} = 15\%$$

Calculate the standard deviation of each security.

11. Based on a one-factor model, if the average nonfactor risk (σ_{ei}^2) of all securities is 225, what is the nonfactor risk of a portfolio with equal weights assigned to its 10 securities? 100 securities? 1000 securities?

12. Based on the discussion of factor and nonfactor risk and given a set of securities that can be combined into various portfolios, what might be a useful measure of the relative diversification of each of the alternative portfolios?

13. With a five-factor model (assuming uncorrelated factors) and a 30-stock portfolio, how many parameters must be estimated to calculate the expected return and standard deviation of the portfolio? How many additional parameter estimates are required if the factors are correlated?

14. Beyond the factors discussed in the text, speculate as to other factors that could reasonably be expected to pervasively affect security returns.

15. Based on a three-factor model, consider a portfolio composed of three securities with the following characteristics:

Security	Factor 1 Sensitivity	Factor 2 Sensitivity	Factor 3 Sensitivity	Proportion
A	−.20	3.60	.05	.60
B	.50	10.00	.75	.20
C	1.50	2.20	.30	.20

What are the sensitivities of the portfolio to factors 1, 2, and 3?

16. Len Murray, a quantitative security analyst, remarked, "The structure of any factor model concerns surprise, in particular the nature of correlations between surprises in different securities' returns." What does Len mean by this statement?

17. Filippo Cesario owns a portfolio of two securities. Based on a two-factor model, the two securities have the following characteristics:

Security	Zero Factor	Factor 1 Sensitivity	Factor 2 Sensitivity	Nonfactor Risk (σ_{ei}^2)	Proportion
A	2%	.30	2.0	196	.70
B	3	.50	1.8	100	.30

The factors are uncorrelated. Factor 1 has an expected value of 15% and a standard deviation of 20%. Factor 2 has an expected value of 4% and a standard deviation of 5%. Calculate the expected return and standard deviation of Filippo's portfolio. [Hint: Think about how equation (10.6a) could be extended to a two-factor model by considering equation (10.9).]

18. Compare the three approaches to estimating factor models.

19. Consider a factor model with earnings yield (or earnings/price ratio) and book-price (or book value/market price ratio) as the two factors. Stock A has an earnings yield of 10% and a book-price of 2. Stock B's earnings yield is 15% and its book-price is .90. The zero factors of stocks A and B are 7% and 9%, respectively. If the expected returns of stocks A and B are 18% and 16.5%, respectively, what are the expected earnings-yield and book-price factor values?

20. Why are investor expectations about future factor values more relevant to security returns than the historical value of the factors?

21. The return on security A can be expressed as a one-factor model of the form:

$$r_{At} = -4\% + 2.6F_1 + e_{At}$$

The response coefficient of security A (c_A) to unanticipated change in the factor is +1.5. During the period security A returned 13%. If the expected value of the factor was 8% and security A's random error term (e_{At}) during the period was +1%, what must have been the unexpected change in the factor (FD_t)?

22. Based on a two-factor model, consider two securities with the following characteristics:

Characteristic	Security A	Security B
Factor 1 sensitivity	1.5	.7
Factor 2 sensitivity	2.6	1.2
Nonfactor risk (σ_{ei}^2)	25.0	16.0

The standard deviations of factor 1 and factor 2 are 20% and 15%, respectively, and the factors have a covariance of 225. What are the standard deviations of securities A and B? What is their covariance?

23. Are the factor models consistent with the CAPM? If returns are determined by a one-factor model (where that factor is the return on the market portfolio) and the CAPM holds, what relationships must exist between the two models?

KEY TERMS

return-generating process (p. 242)
factor models (p. 242)
sensitivity (p. 243)
factor loading (p. 244)

attributes (p. 244)
factor risk (p. 247)
nonfactor risk (p. 247)
sector-factor model (p. 252)

REFERENCES

1. General discussions of factor models can be found in:

William F. Sharpe, "Factors in New York Stock Exchange Security Returns, 1931–1979," *Journal of Portfolio Management* 8, no. 4 (Summer 1982): 5–19; and "Factor Models, CAPMs, and the ABT [*sic*]," *Journal of Portfolio Management* 11, no. 1 (Fall 1984): 21–25.

Mark Kritzman, "…About Factor Models," *Financial Analysts Journal* 49, no. 1 (January–February 1993): 12–15.

Gregory Connor, "The Three Types of Factor Models: A Comparision of Their Explanatory Power," *Financial Analysis Journal* 51, no. 3 (May–June 1995): 42–46.

Richard C. Grinold and Ronald N. Kahn, *Active Portfolio Management* (Chicago: Probus Publishing, 1995), Chapter 3.

2. Empirical papers that attempt to identify relevant factors and estimate the magnitudes of the associated values include:

Benjamin F. King, "Market and Industry Factors in Stock Price Behavior," *Journal of Business* 39, no. 1 (January 1966): 139–170.

George J. Feeney and Donald D. Hester, "Stock Market Indices: A Principal Components Analysis," in Donald D. Hester and James Tobin, eds., *Risk Aversion and Portfolio Choice* (New York: John Wiley, 1967).

Edwin J. Elton and Martin J. Gruber, "Estimating the Dependence Structure of Share Prices—Implications for Portfolio Selection," *Journal of Finance* 28, no. 5 (December 1973): 1203–1232.

James J. Farrell, Jr., "Analyzing Covariation of Returns to Determine Homogeneous Stock Groupings," *Journal of Business* 47, no. 2 (April 1974): 186–207.

Barr Rosenberg and Vinay Marathe, "The Prediction of Investment Risk: Systematic and Residual Risk," in *Proceedings of the Seminar on the Analysis of Security Prices* (Center for Research in Security Prices, Graduate School of Business, University of Chicago, November 1975).

Robert D. Arnott, "Cluster Analysis and Stock Price Movement," *Financial Analysts Journal* 36, no. 6 (November–December 1980): 56–62.

Tony Estep, Nick Hanson, and Carl Johnson, "Sources of Value and Risk in Common Stocks," *Journal of Portfolio Management* 9, no. 4 (Summer 1983): 5–13.

Nai-Fu Chen, Richard Roll, and Stephen A. Ross, "Economic Forces and the Stock Market," *Journal of Business* 59, no. 3 (July 1986): 383–403.

Robert D. Arnott, Charles M. Kelso, Jr., Stephen Kiscadden, and Rosemary Macedo, "Forecasting Factor Returns: An Intriguing Possibility," *Journal of Portfolio Management* 16, no. 1 (Fall 1989): 28–35.

Eugene F. Fama and Kenneth F. French, "The Cross-section of Expected Stock Returns," *Journal of Finance* 47, no. 2 (June 1992): 427–465.

Eugene F. Fama and Kenneth R. French, "Common Risk Factors in the Returns on Stocks and Bonds," *Journal of Financial Economics* 33, no. 1 (February 1993): 3–56.

James L. Davis, "The Cross-Section of Realized Stock Returns: The Pre-COMPUSTAT Evidence," *Journal of Finance* 49, no. 5 (December 1994): 1579–1593.

Eugene F. Fama and Kenneth R. French, "Size and Book-to-Market Factors in Earnings and Returns," *Journal of Finance* 50, no. 1 (March 1995): 131–155.

S. P. Kothari, Jay Shanken, and Richard G. Sloan, "Another Look at the Cross-section of Expected Stock Returns," *Journal of Finance* 50, no. 1 (March 1995): 185–224.

Eugene F. Fama and Kenneth R. French, "Multifactor Explanations of Asset Pricing Anomalies," *Journal of Finance* 51, no 1 (March 1996): 55–84.

William C. Barbee Jr., Sandip Mukherji, and Gary A. Raines, "Do Sales-price and Debt-equity Explain Stock Returns Better than Book-market and Firm Size?" *Financial Analysts Journal* 52, no. 2 (March–April 1996): 56–60.

Kent Daniel and Sheridan Titman, "Evidence on the Characteristics of Cross Sectional Variation in Stock Returns," *Journal of Finance* 52, no. 1 (March 1997): 1–33.

3. There have been several recent papers that have argued that a factor model that distinguished value stocks from growth (or "glamour") stocks is more appropriate than the Fama-French model:

Josef Lakonishok, Andrei Shleifer, and Robert W. Vishny, "Contrarian Investment, Extrapolation, and Risk," *Journal of Finance* 49, no. 5 (December 1994): 1541–1578.

Louis K. C. Chan, Narasimhan Jegadeesh, and Josef Lakonishok, "Evaluating the Performance of Value Versus Glamour Stocks: The Impact of Selection Bias," *Journal of Financial Economics* 38 no. 3 (July 1995): 269–296.

Rafael La Porta, Josef Lakonishok, Andrei Shleifer, and Robert Vishny, "Good News for Value Stocks: Further Evidence on Market Efficiency," *Journal of Finance* 52, no. 2 (June 1997): 859–874.

4. Fixed-income factor models are discussed in:

Ronald N. Kahn and Deepak Gulrajani, "Risk and Return in the Canadian Bond Market," *Journal of Portfolio Management* 19, no. 3 (Spring 1993): 86–92.

5. For a Canadian perspective on the topics discussed in this chapter, see:

L. Kryzanowski and M. C. To, "General Factor Models and the Structure of Security Returns," *Journal of Financial and Quantitative Analysis* 18, no. 1 (March 1983): 31–52.

Peter Muller, "Building a Canadian Equities Risk Model," *Canadian Investment Review* II, no. 1 (Spring 1989): 39–43.

M. J. Robinson, "An Empirical Examination of the Market Model," in M. J. Robinson and B. F. Smith, eds., *Canadian Capital Markets* (London, ON: Western Business School, 1993).

B. F. Smith, "An Analysis of the Usefulness of Multi-Index Models in Explaining Canadian Equity Returns," in M. J. Robinson and B. F. Smith, eds., *Canadian Capital Markets* (London, ON: Western Business School, 1993).

CHAPTER 11

Arbitrage Pricing Theory

The Capital Asset Pricing Model (CAPM) is an equilibrium model that describes why different securities have different expected returns. In particular, this positive economic model of asset pricing asserts that securities have different expected returns because they have different betas. However, there exists an alternative model of asset pricing that was developed by Stephen Ross. It is known as **Arbitrage Pricing Theory** (APT), and in some ways it is less complicated than the CAPM.

The CAPM requires a large number of assumptions, including those initially made by Harry Markowitz when he developed the basic mean-variance model. For example, each investor is assumed to choose his optimal portfolio by the use of indifference curves based on portfolio expected returns and standard deviations. In contrast, APT makes fewer assumptions. One primary APT assumption is that each investor, when given the opportunity to increase the return of her portfolio without increasing its risk, will do so. The mechanism for doing so involves the use of arbitrage portfolios.

Arbitrage Pricing Theory (APT) An equilibrium model of asset pricing that states that the expected return on a security is a linear function of the security's sensitivity to various common factors.

Factor Models

APT starts out by making the assumption that security returns are related to an unknown number of unknown factors.[1] For ease of exposition, imagine that there is only one factor and that factor is the predicted rate of increase in industrial production. In this situation, security returns are related to the following one-factor model:

$$r_i = a_i + b_i F_1 + e_i \qquad (11.1)$$

where:

$$r_i = \text{rate of return on security } i$$

$$F_1 = \text{the value of the factor, which in this case is the predicted}$$
$$\text{rate of growth in industrial production}$$

$$e_i = \text{random error term}$$

Sensitivity A measure of the responsiveness of a security's returns to a particular common factor.

In this equation, b_i is known as the **sensitivity** of security i to the factor. (It is also known as the factor loading for security i or the attribute of security i.)[2]

---

[1]Factor models are discussed in detail in Chapter 10.

[2]As noted in Equation (10.18) of Chapter 10, there are other ways to write the equation for a factor model.

Imagine that an investor owns three stocks and the current market value of his holdings in each one is $4 000 000. In this case, the investor's current investable wealth (W_0) is equal to $12 000 000. Everyone believes that these three stocks have the following expected returns and sensitivities:

i	$\bar{r}_i$	b_i
Stock 1	15%	.9
Stock 2	21	3.0
Stock 3	12	1.8

Do these expected returns and factor sensitivities represent an equilibrium situation? If not, what will happen to stock prices and expected returns to restore equilibrium? The answers to these questions will be addressed in the next sections.

Principle of Arbitrage

In recent years, baseball card conventions have become commonplace events. Collectors gather to exchange baseball cards with one another at negotiated prices. Suppose that Ms. A attends such a gathering where in one corner she finds S offering to sell a 1951 Mickey Mantle rookie card for $400. Exploring the convention further, she finds B bidding $500 for the same card. Recognizing a financial opportunity, Ms. A agrees to sell the card to B, who gives her $500 in cash. She races back to give $400 to S, receives the card, and returns with it to B, who takes possession of the card. Ms. A pockets the $100 in profit from the two transactions and moves on in search of other opportunities. Ms. A has engaged in a form of arbitrage.

Arbitrage The simultaneous purchase and sale of the same, or essentially similar, security in two different markets for advantageously different prices.

Arbitrage is the earning of riskless profit by taking advantage of differential pricing for the same physical asset or security. As a widely applied investment tactic, arbitrage typically entails the sale of a security at a relatively high price and the simultaneous purchase of the same security (or its functional equivalent) at a relatively low price.

Arbitrage activity is a critical element of modern, efficient security markets. Because arbitrage profits are by definition riskless, all investors have an incentive to take advantage of them whenever they are discovered. Granted, some investors have greater resources and inclination to engage in arbitrage than others. However, it takes relatively few of these active investors to exploit arbitrage situations and, by their buying and selling actions, eliminate these profit opportunities.

The nature of arbitrage is clear when discussing different prices for an individual security. However, "almost arbitrage" opportunities can involve "similar" securities or portfolios. That similarity can be defined in many ways. One interesting way is the exposure to pervasive factors that affect security prices.

A factor model implies that securities or portfolios with equal-factor sensitivities will behave in the same way except for nonfactor risk. Therefore, securities or portfolios with the same factor sensitivities should offer the same expected returns. If not, then "almost arbitrage" opportunities exist. Investors will take advantage of these opportunities, causing their elimination. That is the essential logic underlying APT.

Arbitrage Portfolios

Arbitrage Portfolio A portfolio that requires no investment, has no sensitivity to any factor, and has a positive expected return. More strictly, a portfolio that provides inflows in some circumstances and requires no outflows under any circumstances.

According to APT, an investor will explore the possibility of forming an **arbitrage portfolio** to increase the expected return of his current portfolio without increasing its risk. Just what is an arbitrage portfolio? First of all, it is a portfolio that does not require any additional funds from the investor. If X_i denotes the *change* in the investor's holdings of security i (and hence the weight of security i in the arbitrage portfolio), this requirement of an arbitrage portfolio can be written as

$$X_1 + X_2 + X_3 = 0 \tag{11.2}$$

Second, an arbitrage portfolio has no sensitivity to any factor. In its terminology, an arbitrage portfolio has "zero factor exposures." Because the sensitivity of a portfolio to a factor is just a weighted average of the sensitivities of the securities in the portfolio to that factor, this requirement of an arbitrage portfolio can be written as

$$b_1 X_1 + b_2 X_2 + b_3 X_3 = 0 \tag{11.3a}$$

or, in the current example,

$$.9 X_1 + 3.0 X_2 + 1.8 X_3 = 0 \tag{11.3b}$$

Thus, in this example, an arbitrage portfolio will have no sensitivity to industrial production.

Strictly speaking, an arbitrage portfolio should also have zero nonfactor risk. However, the APT assumes that such risk is small enough to be ignored.

At this point, many potential arbitrage portfolios can be identified. These candidates are simply portfolios that meet the conditions given in equations (11.2) and (11.3b). Note that there are three unknowns (X_1, X_2, and X_3) and two equations in this situation, which means that there is an infinite number of combinations of values for X_1, X_2, and X_3 that satisfy these two equations.[3] As a way of finding one combination, consider arbitrarily assigning a value of .1 to X_1. Doing so results in two equations and two unknowns:

$$.1 + X_2 + X_3 = 0 \tag{11.4a}$$
$$.09 + 3.0 X_2 + 1.8 X_3 = 0 \tag{11.4b}$$

The solution to equations (11.4a) and (11.4b) is $X_2 = .075$ and $X_3 = -.175$. Hence, a potential arbitrage portfolio is one with these weights.

In order to see if this candidate is indeed an arbitrage portfolio, its expected return must be determined. If it is positive, then an arbitrage portfolio will have been identified.[4] Mathematically, this third and last requirement for an arbitrage portfolio is

$$X_1 \bar{r}_1 + X_2 \bar{r}_2 + X_3 \bar{r}_3 > 0 \tag{11.5a}$$

or, for this example,

$$15 X_1 + 21 X_2 + 11 X_3 > 0 \tag{11.5b}$$

Using the solution for this candidate, it can be seen that its expected return is $(15\% \times .1) + (21\% \times .075) + (12 \times -.175) = .975\%$. Because this is a positive number, an arbitrage portfolio has indeed been identified.

The arbitrage portfolio just identified involves buying $1 200 000 of stock 1 and $900 000 of stock 2. How were these dollar figures arrived at? The solution comes from taking the current market value of the portfolio ($W_0 = \$12\ 000\ 000$) and multiplying it by the weights for the arbitrage portfolio of $X_1 = .1$ and $X_2 = .075$. Where does the money come from to make these purchases? It comes from selling $2 100 000 of stock 3. (Note that $X_3 W_0 = -.175 \times \$12\ 000\ 000 = -\$2\ 100\ 000$.)

In summary, this arbitrage portfolio is attractive to any investor who desires a higher return and is not concerned with nonfactor risk. It requires no additional dollar investment, it has no factor risk, and it has a positive expected return.

---

[3] There will always be an infinite number of solutions whenever there are more unknowns than equations. For example, consider a situation where there is one equation with two unknowns: $Y = 3X$. Note that there is an infinite number of paired values of X and Y that solve this equation, such as (1, 3), (2, 6), and (3, 9).

[4] If its expected return is negative, then simply changing the signs of the weights will cause the expected return to become positive. Note that the new weights will also sum to zero and will still represent a portfolio that has zero sensitivity to the factor. Thus, the new weights will represent an arbitrage portfolio.

The Investor's Position

At this juncture the investor can evaluate his position from either one of two equivalent viewpoints: (1) holding both the old portfolio and the arbitrage portfolio or (2) holding a new portfolio. Consider, for example, the weight in stock 1. The old portfolio weight was .333 and the arbitrage portfolio weight was .100, with the sum of these two weights being equal to .433. Note that the dollar value of the holdings of stock 1 in the new portfolio rises to $5 200 000 ($4 000 000 + $1 200 000), so its weight is $5 200 000/$12 000 000 = .433, equivalent to the sum of the old and arbitrage portfolio weights.

Similarly, the portfolio's expected return is equal to the sum of the expected returns of the old and arbitrage portfolios, or 16% + .975% = 16.975%. Equivalently, the new portfolio's expected return can be calculated using the new portfolio's weights and the expected returns of the stocks, or (.433 × 15%) + (.408 × 21%) + (.158 × 12%) = 16.975%.

The sensitivity of the new portfolio is (.433 × .9) + (.408 × 3.0) + (.158 × 1.8) = 1.9. This is the same as the sum of the sensitivities of the old and arbitrage portfolios (= 1.9 + 0.0).

What about the risk of the new portfolio? Assume that the standard deviation of the old portfolio was 11%. The variance of the arbitrage portfolio will be small because its only source of risk is nonfactor risk. Similarly, the variance of the new portfolio will differ from that of the old only as a result of changes in its nonfactor risk. Thus, it can be concluded that the risk of the new portfolio will be approximately 11%.[5] Table 11.1 summarizes these observations.

Table 11.1	How an Arbitrage Portfolio Affects an Investor's Position.				
	Old Portfolio	+	Arbitrage Portfolio	=	New Portfolio
Weights					
X_1	.333		.100		.433
X_2	.333		.075		.408
X_3	.333		−.175		.158
Properties					
$\bar{r}_p$	16.000%		.975%		16.975%
b_p	1.900		.000		1.900
σ_p	11.000%		small		approx. 11.000%

Pricing Effects

What are the consequences of buying stocks 1 or 2 and selling stock 3? As everyone will be doing this, their market prices will be affected and, accordingly, their expected returns will adjust. Specifically, the prices of stocks 1 and 2 will rise because of increased buying pressure. In turn, this will cause their expected returns to fall. Conversely, the selling pressure put on stock 3 will cause its stock price to fall and its expected return to rise.

---

[5]The APT ignores nonfactor risk. Because the total risk of a portfolio σ_p^2 is equal to $b_p^2\sigma_F^2 + \sigma_{ep}^2$ according to the one-factor model [see equation (10.6a) in Chapter 10], and given that the arbitrage portfolio has no factor risk by design, meaning that $b_p^2\sigma_F^2 = 0$ because $b_p = 0$, this means that the arbitrage portfolio must be sufficiently diversified so as to have insignificant nonfactor risk and, consequently, insignificant total risk.

This can be seen by examining the equation for estimating a stock's expected return:

$$\bar{r} = \frac{\bar{P}_1}{P_0} - 1 \qquad (11.6)$$

where P_0 is the stock's current price and $\bar{P}_1$ is the stock's expected end-of-period price. Buying a stock such as stock 1 or 2 will push up its current price P_0 and thus result in a decline in its expected return $\bar{r}$. Conversely, selling a stock such as stock 3 will push down its current price and result in a rise in its expected return.

This buying-and-selling activity will continue until *all* arbitrage possibilities are significantly reduced or eliminated. At this point there will exist an approximately linear relationship between expected returns and sensitivities of the following sort:

$$\bar{r}_i = \lambda_0 + \lambda_1 b_i \qquad (11.7)$$

where λ_0 and λ_1 are constants. This equation is the asset pricing equation of the APT when returns are generated by one factor.[6] Note that it is the equation of a straight line, meaning that in equilibrium there will be a linear relationship between expected returns and sensitivities.

In the example, one possible equilibrium setting could have $\lambda_0 = 8$ and $\lambda_1 = 4$.[7] Consequently, the pricing equation is

$$\bar{r}_1 = 8 + 4b_i \qquad (11.8)$$

This would result in the following equilibrium levels of expected returns for stocks 1, 2, and 3:

$$\bar{r}_1 = 8 + (4 \times .9) = 11.6\%$$
$$\bar{r}_2 = 8 + (4 \times 3.0) = 20.0\%$$
$$\bar{r}_3 = 8 + (4 \times 1.8) = 15.2\%$$

As a result, the expected returns for stock 1 and 2 will have fallen from 15% and 21%, respectively, to 11.6% and 20% because of increased buying pressure. Conversely, increased selling pressure will have caused the expected return on stock 3 to rise from 12% to 15.2%. The bottom line is that the expected return on any security is, in equilibrium, a linear function of the security's sensitivity to the factor b_i.[8]

A Graphical Illustration

Figure 11.1 illustrates the asset pricing equation of equation (11.7). Any security that has a factor sensitivity and expected return such that it lies off the line will be mispriced according to the APT and will present investors with the opportunity of forming arbitrage portfolios. Security B is an example. If an investor buys security B and sells security S in equal dollar amounts, then the investor will have formed an arbitrage portfolio.[9] How can this be?

First of all, by selling an amount of security S to pay for the long position in security B the investor will not have committed any new funds. Second, because securities B and S

---

[6]Technically, this pricing equation is only approximately true and may be significantly wrong for a small number of assets.

[7]Why choose 8 and 4 for λ_0 and λ_1, respectively? The magnitudes that these two parameters assume in equilibrium will depend on many things, such as investors' relative degrees of risk aversion, wealth, and time preferences.

[8]To demonstrate that equation (11.8) is indeed an equilibrium situation, the reader is encouraged to try setting various values for X_1, X_2, and X_3 and show that the resulting potential arbitrage portfolios will all have expected returns of zero.

[9]If B were to plot below the APT asset pricing line, then investors would do just the opposite of what is described here. This means that they would buy S and sell B.

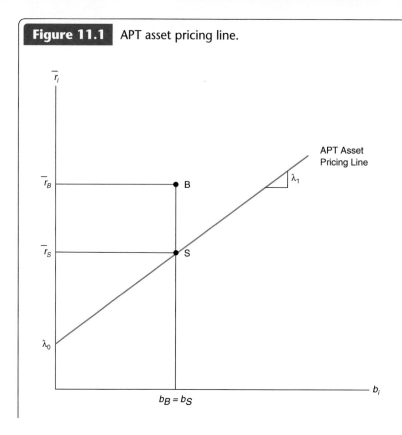

Figure 11.1 APT asset pricing line.

have the same sensitivity to the factor, the selling of security S and buying of security B will constitute a portfolio with no sensitivity to the factor. Finally, the arbitrage portfolio will have a positive expected return because the expected return of security B is greater than the expected return of security S.[10] As a result of investors buying security B, its price will rise and, in turn, its expected return will fall until it is located on the APT asset pricing line.[11]

Interpreting the APT Pricing Equation

How can the constants λ_0 and λ_1 that appear in the APT pricing equation (11.7) be interpreted? Assuming that there is a risk-free asset in existence, such an asset will have a rate of return that is a constant. Therefore, this asset will have no sensitivity to the factor. From equation (11.7) it can be seen that $\bar{r}_i = \lambda_0$ for any asset with $b_i = 0$. In the case of the risk-free asset, it is also known that $\bar{r}_i = r_f$, implying that $\lambda_0 = r_f$. Hence the value of λ_0 in equation (11.7) must be r_f, allowing this equation to be rewritten as

$$\bar{r}_i = r_f + \lambda_1 b_i \qquad (11.9)$$

Pure Factor Portfolio A portfolio that possesses a unit sensitivity to one factor, no sensitivity to any other factor, and has zero nonfactor risk.

In terms of λ_1, its value can be seen by considering a **pure factor portfolio** (or pure factor play), denoted p^*, that has unit sensitivity to the factor, meaning $b_{p^*} = 1.0$. (If there were

---

[10]A simpler way of viewing this transaction is as a stock swap where S is being swapped for B. Because it is a swap, no new funds are needed. Furthermore, because both B and S have the same factor sensitivity, the swap will not alter the sensitivity of the currently held portfolio. Finally, the replacement of S and B will increase the currently held portfolio's expected return because B has a higher level of expected return than S.

[11]Technically, the APT asset pricing line would shift upward a bit due to the selling of S.

other factors, such a portfolio would be constructed so as to have no sensitivity to them.) According to equation (11.9), such a portfolio will have the following expected return:

$$\bar{r}_{p^*} = r_f + \lambda_1 \qquad (11.10a)$$

Note that this equation can be rewritten as

$$\bar{r}_{p^*} - r_f = \lambda_1 \qquad (11.10b)$$

Thus, λ_1 is the expected excess return (meaning the expected return over and above the risk-free rate) on a portfolio that has unit sensitivity to the factor. Accordingly, it is known as a **factor risk premium** (or factor-expected return premium). Letting $\delta_1 = \bar{r}_{p^*}$ denote the expected return on a portfolio that has unit sensitivity to the factor, equation (11.10b) can be rewritten as

Factor Risk Premium
The expected return over and above the risk-free rate on a portfolio that has unit sensitivity to a particular factor and zero sensitivity to all other factors.

$$\delta_1 - r_f = \lambda_1 \qquad (11.10c)$$

Inserting the left-hand side of equation (11.10c) for λ_1 in equation (11.9) results in a second version of the APT pricing equation:

$$\bar{r}_1 = r_f + (\delta_1 - r_f)b_i \qquad (11.11)$$

In the example, because $r_f = 8\%$ and $\lambda_1 = \delta_1 - r_f = 4\%$, it follows that $\delta_1 = 12\%$. This means that the expected return on a portfolio that has unit sensitivity to the first factor is 12%.

In order to generalize the pricing equation of APT, the case where security returns are generated by more than one factor needs to be examined. This is done by considering a two-factor model next and then expanding the analysis to k factors where $k > 2$.

Two-Factor Models

In the case of two factors, denoted F_1 and F_2 and representing, for example, predicted industrial production and inflation, each security will have two sensitivities, b_{i1} and b_{i2}. Thus, security returns are generated by the following factor model:

$$r_i = a_i + b_{i1}F_1 + b_{i2}F_2 + e_i \qquad (11.12)$$

Consider a situation where there are four securities that have the following expected returns and sensitivities:

i	$\bar{r}_i$	b_{i1}	b_{i2}
Stock 1	15%	.9	2.0
Stock 2	21	3.0	1.5
Stock 3	12	1.8	.7
Stock 4	8	2.0	3.2

In addition, consider an investor who has $5 000 000 invested in each of the securities. (Thus, the investor has initial wealth W_0 of $20 000 000.) Are these securities priced in equilibrium?

▶ Arbitrage Portfolios

To answer this question, the possibility of forming an arbitrage portfolio must be explored. First of all, an arbitrage portfolio must have weights that satisfy the following equations:

$$X_1 + X_2 + X_3 + X_4 = 0 \tag{11.13}$$

$$.9X_1 + 3X_2 + 1.8X_3 + 2X_4 = 0 \tag{11.14}$$

$$2X_1 + 1.5X_2 + .7X_3 + 3.2X_4 = 0 \tag{11.15}$$

This means that the arbitrage portfolio must not involve an additional commitment of funds by the investor and must have zero sensitivity to each factor.

Note that there are three equations that need to be satisfied and that each equation involves four unknowns. Because there are more unknowns than equations, there are an infinite number of solutions. One solution can be found by setting X_1 equal to .1 (an arbitrarily chosen amount) and then solving for the remaining weights. Doing so results in the following weights: $X_2 = .088$, $X_3 = -.108$, and $X_4 = -.08$.

These weights represent a potential arbitrage portfolio. What remains to be seen is if this portfolio has a positive expected return. Calculating the expected return of the portfolio reveals that it is equal to $(.1 \times 15\%) + (.088 \times 21\%) + (-.108 \times 12\%) + (-.08 \times 8\%) = 1.41\%$. Hence, an arbitrage portfolio has been identified.

This arbitrage portfolio involves the purchase of stocks 1 and 2, funded by selling stocks 3 and 4. Consequently, the buying-and-selling pressures will drive the prices of stocks 1 and 2 up and stocks 3 and 4 down. In turn, this means that the expected returns of stocks 1 and 2 will fall and stocks 3 and 4 will rise. Investors will continue to create such arbitrage portfolios until equilibrium is reached. This means that equilibrium will be attained when any portfolio that satisfies the conditions given by equations (11.13), (11.14), and (11.15) has an expected return of zero. This will occur when the following linear relationship between expected returns and sensitivities exists:

$$\bar{r}_i = \lambda_0 + \lambda_1 b_{i1} + \lambda_2 b_{i2} \tag{11.16}$$

As in equation (11.7), this is a linear equation except that it now has three dimensions, $\bar{r}_i$, b_{i1}, and b_{i2}. Hence, it corresponds to the equation of a plane instead of a line.

In the example, one possible equilibrium setting is where $\lambda_0 = 8$, $\lambda_1 = 4$, and $\lambda_2 = -2$. Thus the pricing equation is

$$\bar{r}_i = 8 + 4b_{i1} - 2b_{i2} \tag{11.17}$$

As a result, the four stocks have the following equilibrium levels of expected returns:

$$\bar{r}_1 = 8 + (4 \times .9) - (2 \times 2) = 7.6\%$$

$$\bar{r}_2 = 8 + (4 \times 3) - (2 \times 1.5) = 17.0\%$$

$$\bar{r}_3 = 8 + (4 \times 1.8) - (2 \times .7) = 13.8\%$$

$$\bar{r}_4 = 8 + (4 \times 2) - (2 \times 3.2) = 9.6\%$$

The expected returns of stocks 1 and 2 have fallen from 15% and 21% while the expected returns of stocks 3 and 4 have risen from 12% and 8%, respectively. Given the buying-and-selling pressures generated by investing in arbitrage portfolios, these changes are in the predicted direction.

One consequence of equation (11.17) is that a stock with higher sensitivity to the first factor than another stock will have a higher expected return if the two stocks also have the same sensitivity to the second factor, because $\lambda_1 > 0$. Conversely, since $\lambda_2 < 0$, a stock with higher sensitivity to the second factor will have a lower expected return than another stock with a lower sensitivity to the second factor, provided that both stocks have the same sensitivity to the first factor. However, the effect of two stocks having different sensitivities to both factors can be confounding. For example, stock 4 has a lower expected return than stock 3, even though both of its sensitivities are larger. This is because the advantage of having a higher sensitivity to the first factor ($b_{41} = 2.0 > b_{31} = 1.8$) is not of sufficient magnitude to offset the disadvantage of having a higher sensitivity to the second factor ($b_{42} = 3.2 > b_{32} = .7$).

Pricing Effects

Extending the one-factor APT pricing equation (11.7) to this two-factor situation is relatively uncomplicated. As before, λ_0 is equal to the risk-free rate. This is because the risk-free asset has no sensitivity to either factor, meaning that its values of b_{i1} and b_{i2} are both zero. Hence it follows that $\lambda_0 = r_f$. Thus equation (11.16) can be rewritten more generally as

$$\bar{r}_i = r_f + \lambda_1 b_{i1} + \lambda_2 b_{i2} \tag{11.18}$$

In the example given in equation (11.16), it can be seen that $r_f = 8\%$.

Next, consider a well-diversified portfolio that has unit sensitivity to the first factor and zero sensitivity to the second factor. As mentioned earlier, such a portfolio is known as a pure factor portfolio or pure factor play because it has: (1) unit sensitivity to one factor, (2) no sensitivity to any other factor, and (3) zero nonfactor risk. Specifically, $b_1 = 1$ and $b_2 = 0$. It can be seen from equation (11.18) that the expected return on this portfolio, denoted δ_1, will be equal to $r_f + \lambda_1$. As it follows that $\delta_1 - r_f = \lambda_1$, equation (11.18) can be rewritten as

$$\bar{r}_i = r_f + (\delta_1 - r_f) b_{i1} + \lambda_2 b_{i2} \tag{11.19}$$

In the example given in equation (11.17), it can be seen that $\delta_1 - r_f = 4$.

This means that $\delta_1 = 12$, because $r_f = 8$. In other words, a portfolio that has unit sensitivity to predicted industrial production (the first factor) would have an expected return of 12%, or 4% more than the risk-free rate of 8%.

Finally, consider a portfolio that has zero sensitivity to the first factor and unit sensitivity to the second factor, meaning that $b_1 = 0$ and $b_2 = 1$. It can be seen from equation (11.18) that the expected return on this portfolio, denoted δ_2, will be equal to $r_f + \lambda_2$. Accordingly, $\delta_2 - r_f = \lambda_2$, thereby allowing equation (11.19) to be rewritten as

$$\bar{r}_i = r_f + (\delta_1 - r_f) b_{i1} + (\delta_2 - r_f) b_{i2} \tag{11.20}$$

In the example given in equation (11.17), it can be seen that $\delta_2 - r_f = -2$. This means that $\delta_2 = 6$ since $r_f = 8$. In other words, a portfolio that has zero sensitivity to predicted industrial production (the first factor) and unit sensitivity to predicted inflation (the second factor) would have an expected return of 6%, or 2% less than the risk-free rate of 8%.

Multiple-Factor Models

When returns were generated by a two-factor model instead of a one-factor model, APT pricing equations (11.7) and (11.11) were simply expanded to accommodate the additional factor in equations (11.16) and (11.20). What happens to these APT pricing equations when returns are generated by a multiple-factor model where the number of factors k is greater than two? It turns out that the basic pricing equations are expanded once again in a relatively straightforward manner.

In the case of k factors (F_1, F_2, ..., F_k) each security will have k sensitivities (b_{i1}, b_{i2}, ..., b_{ik}) in the following k-factor model:

$$r_i = a_i + b_{i1} F_1 + b_{i2} F_2 + \ldots + b_{ik} F_k + e_i \tag{11.21}$$

In turn, this suggests that securities will be priced by the following equation, which is similar to equations (11.7) and (11.16):

$$\bar{r}_i = \lambda_0 + \lambda_1 b_{i1} + \lambda_2 b_{i2} + \ldots + \lambda_k b_{ik} \tag{11.22}$$

As before, this is a linear equation, except now it is in $k + 1$ dimensions with the dimensions being $\bar{r}_i$, b_{i1}, b_{i2}, ..., and b_{ik}.

Extending the APT pricing equations (11.11) and (11.20) to this situation is relatively uncomplicated. As before, λ_0 is equal to the risk-free rate as the risk-free asset has no sensitivity to any factor. Each value of δ_j represents the expected return on a portfolio of stocks that has unit sensitivity to factor j and zero sensitivity to all the other factors. As a result, equations (11.11) and (11.20) can be expanded as follows:

$$\bar{r}_i = r_f + (\delta_1 - r_f)b_{i1} + (\delta_2 - r_f)b_{i2} + \ldots + (\delta_k - r_f)b_{ik} \tag{11.23}$$

Hence, a stock's expected return is equal to the risk-free rate plus k risk premiums based on the stock's sensitivities to the k factors.

A Synthesis of the APT and the CAPM

Unlike the APT, the CAPM does not assume that returns are generated by a factor model. However, this does not mean that the CAPM is inconsistent with a world in which returns are generated by a factor model. Indeed, it is possible to have a world where returns are generated by a factor model, where the remaining assumptions of the APT hold, and where all the assumptions of the CAPM hold. This situation will now be examined.

One-factor Models

Consider what happens if returns are generated by a one-factor model and that factor is the market portfolio. In such a situation, δ_1 will correspond to the expected return on the market portfolio and b_i will represent the beta of stock i measured relative to the market portfolio. Hence the CAPM will hold.

What if returns are generated by a one-factor model and that factor is *not* the market portfolio? Now δ_1 will correspond to the expected return on a portfolio with unit sensitivity to the factor, and b_i will represent the sensitivity of stock i measured relative to the factor.[12] However, if the CAPM also holds, then security i's expected return will be related to both its beta *and* its sensitivity:

$$\bar{r}_i = r_f + (\bar{r}_M - r_f)\beta_i \tag{11.24}$$

$$\bar{r}_i = r_f + (\delta_1 - r_f)b_i \tag{11.25}$$

This suggests that betas and sensitivities must somehow be related to each other; just how they are related is shown next.

Beta Coefficients and Factor Sensitivities

How can expected returns be linearly related to both betas and factor sensitivities? This will happen because betas and factor sensitivities will be related to each other in the following manner;

$$\beta_i = \frac{COV(F_1, r_M) + COV(e_i, r_M)}{\sigma_M^2} b_i \tag{11.26a}$$

$$= (\beta_{F_1} + \beta_{e_i})b_i \tag{11.26b}$$

where $COV(F_1, r_M)$ denotes the covariance between the factor and the market portfolio. $COV(e_i, r_M)$ denotes the covariance between the residual return of the factor model for security i and the return on the market portfolio, σ_M^2 denotes the variance of the return on the market portfolio, and β_{F_1} and β_{e_i} are defined as being equal to $COV(F_1, r_M)/\sigma_M^2$ and

---

[12]If the factor is a market index (instead of the market portfolio) such as the TSE 300, then δ_1 will correspond to the expected return on the index and b_i will represent the beta of stock i measured relative to the index, denoted previously in Chapter 7 as β_{iI}.

$COV(e_i, r_M)/\sigma_M^2$, respectively.[13] Hence, β_{F_1} denotes the beta of the factor and β_{e_i} denotes the beta of security i's residual returns; both of these betas are measured relative to the market portfolio. What if each security's residual return is uncorrelated with the market's return? In this situation, $COV(e_i, r_M) = 0$, which in turn means that $\beta_{e_i} = 0$. Thus, equation (11.26b) reduces to:

$$\beta_i = \beta_{F_1} b_i \tag{11.27}$$

Because the quantity β_{F_1} is a constant that does not change from one security to another, equation (11.27) is equivalent to saying that β_i will be equal to a constant times b_i when equations (11.24) and (11.25) both hold. Hence if the factor is industrial production, then equation (11.27) states that each security's beta is equal to a constant times the security's sensitivity to industrial production when the security's residual return is uncorrelated with the market's return. The constant will be a positive number if industrial production and the returns on the market portfolio are positively correlated, as then β_{F_1} will be positive.[14] Conversely, the constant will be negative if the correlation is negative because then β_{F_1} will be negative.

Factor Risk Premiums

Continuing with this discussion, note what happens if the right-hand side of equation (11.27) is substituted for β_i on the right-hand side of equation (11.24):

$$\bar{r}_i = r_f + [(\bar{r}_M - r_f)\beta_{F_1}]b_i \tag{11.28}$$

Comparing this equation with equation (11.9) reveals that if the assumptions of both APT (with one factor) and the CAPM hold and each security's residual return is uncorrelated with the market's return, then the following relationship must hold:

$$\lambda_1 = (\bar{r}_M - r_f)\beta_{F_1} \tag{11.29}$$

By itself, APT says nothing about the size of the factor risk premium λ_1. However, if the CAPM also holds, it can provide some guidance. This guidance is given in equation (11.29), which has been shown to hold if the assumptions of both APT and the CAPM are taken as given and each security's residual return is uncorrelated with the market's return.

Imagine that the factor moves with the market portfolio, meaning that it is positively correlated with the market portfolio so that β_{F_1} is positive.[15] As $(\bar{r}_M - r_f)$ is positive, it follows that the right-hand side of equation (11.29) is positive and hence λ_1 is positive. Furthermore, because λ_1 is positive, it can be seen in equation (11.9) that the higher the value of b_i the higher will be the expected return of the security.[16] To generalize, if a factor is positively correlated with the market portfolio but the residual return of each security is uncorrelated with the market return, then each security's expected return will be a positive function of the security's sensitivity to that factor.

Using the same kind of argument, if the factor moves against the market portfolio, meaning that F_1 is negatively correlated with $\bar{r}_M$ then λ_1 will be negative. This means that the higher the value of b_i the lower will be the expected return on the security. Generalizing, if a factor is negatively correlated with the market portfolio, then a security's expected return will be a negative function of the security's sensitivity to that factor.

---

[13]This can be seen by noting that $COV(r_i, r_M) = COV(a_i + b_iF_1 + e_i, r_M)$, which simplifies to $COV(r_i, r_M) = b_iCOV(F_1, r_M) + COV(e_i, r_M)$. Dividing both sides by σ_M^2 and recognizing from Chapter 9 that $COV(r_i, r_M)/\sigma_M^2 = \beta_i$ produces equation (11.26a).

[14]$COV(F_1, r_M)$ will be positive if the correlation is positive because it is equal to the product of the correlation and the standard deviations of F_1 and r_M.

[15]See footnote 14.

[16]The greater the extent to which the factor moves with the market portfolio (meaning the higher the correlation between F_1 and r_M), the greater will be the associated expected return premium λ_1.

A Market Index as the Factor

What if returns are generated by a one-factor model and instead of industrial production, the factor is the return on a market index such as the TSE 300? Consider a situation where the following two conditions are met: (1) the returns on the index and market portfolio are perfectly correlated and (2) the variance of the returns on the market portfolio and the market index are identical.

First of all, a stock's beta will be equal to its sensitivity. This can be seen by examining equation (11.26b). Given the two conditions just described, $COV(F_1, r_M) = \rho_{F_1,M}\sigma_{F_1}\sigma_M = \sigma_M^2$ so that $COV(F_1, r_M)/\sigma_M^2 = \beta_{F_1} = 1$ and $\beta_{ei} = 0$. Hence equation (11.26b) would reduce to $\beta_i = b_i$.

Second, λ_1 will equal $\bar{r}_M - r_f$ under these two conditions. This can be seen by again noting that $\beta_{F_1} = COV(F_1, r_M)/\sigma_M^2 = 1$, which in turn means that equation (11.29) reduces to $\lambda_1 = \bar{r}_M - r_f$. Because equation (11.10c) states that $\delta_1 - r_f = \lambda_1$, this means that $\delta_1 = \bar{r}_M$. Hence the expected return on a portfolio that has unit sensitivity to the returns on the TSE 300 equals the expected return on the market portfolio.

In summary, if a proxy for the market portfolio could be found such that the two conditions given previously were met, then the CAPM would hold where the role of the market portfolio could be replaced by the proxy. Unfortunately, because the true market portfolio is unknown, it cannot be verified whether or not any proxy meets the two conditions.

Multiple-factor Models

It is possible for the CAPM to hold even though returns are generated by a multiple-factor model such as a two-factor model. Again equations (11.24) and (11.25) can be extended to show that security i's expected return will be related to its beta and two sensitivities:

$$\bar{r}_i = r_f + (\bar{r}_M - r_f)\beta_i \tag{11.30}$$

$$\bar{r}_i = r_f + (\delta_1 - r_f)b_{i1} + (\delta_2 - r_f)b_{i2} \tag{11.31}$$

In this situation, equation (11.26a) can be extended to show that betas will be linearly related to sensitivities in the following manner (when each security's residual return is uncorrelated with the market return):

$$\beta_i = \frac{COV(F_1, r_M)}{\sigma_M^2}b_{i1} + \frac{COV(F_2, r_M)}{\sigma_M^2}b_{i2} \tag{11.32b}$$

$$= \beta_{F_1}b_{i1} + \beta_{F_2}b_{i2} \tag{11.32b}$$

Here $COV(F_1, r_M)$ and $COV(F_2, r_M)$ denote the covariance between the first factor and the returns on the market portfolio and covariance between the second factor and the returns on the market portfolio, respectively. As the quantities $COV(F_1, r_M)/\sigma_M^2 = \beta_{F_1}$ and $COV(F_2, r_M)/\sigma_M^2 = \beta_{F_2}$ are constants, it can be seen from equation (11.32b) that β_i *will* be a function of b_{i1} and b_{i2} when equation (11.30) and (11.31) hold and each security's residual return is uncorrelated with the market return. This means that a stock's beta will be a linear combination of its sensitivities to the two factors, which means that in this example, the size of a stock's beta will be dependent on the size of its sensitivities to industrial production and inflation.

Note what happens if the right-hand side of equation (11.32b) is substituted for β_i on the right-hand side of equation (11.30):

$$\bar{r}_i = r_f + (\bar{r}_M - r_f)[\beta_{F_1}b_{i1} + \beta_{F_2}b_{i2}] \tag{11.33a}$$

which can be rewritten as:

$$\bar{r}_i = r_f + [(\bar{r}_M - r_f)\beta_{F_1}]b_{i1} + [(\bar{r}_M - r_f)\beta_{F_2}]b_{i2} \tag{11.33b}$$

Applying APT

Since its inception in the mid-1970s, Arbitrage Pricing Theory (APT) has provided researchers and practitioners with an intuitive and flexible framework through which to address important investment management issues. As opposed to the Capital Asset Pricing Model (CAPM), with its specific assumptions concerning investor preferences as well as the critical role played by the market portfolio, APT operates under relatively weaker assumptions. Because of its emphasis on multiple sources of systematic risk, APT has attracted considerable interest as a tool for better explaining investment results and more effectively controlling portfolio risk.

Despite its attractive features, APT has not been widely applied by the investment community. The reason lies largely with APT's most significant drawback: the lack of specificity regarding the multiple factors that systematically affect security returns as well as the long-term return associated with each of these factors. Rightly or wrongly, the CAPM unambiguously states that a security's covariance with the market portfolio is the only systematic source of its investment risk within a well-diversified portfolio. APT, conversely, is conspicuously silent regarding the particular systematic factors affecting a security's risk and return. Investors must fend for themselves in determining those factors.

The number of institutional investors actually using APT to manage assets is small. The most prominent organization is Roll & Ross Asset Management Corporation (R&R). As Stephen Ross invented the APT, it is interesting to briefly review how R&R translates this theory into practice.

R&R begins with a statement of the systematic sources of risk (or factors) that it believes are *currently* relevant in the capital markets. Specifically, R&R has identified five factors that pervasively affect common stock returns:

- the business cycle
- interest rates
- investor confidence
- short-term inflation
- long-term inflationary expectations

R&R quantifies these factors by designating certain measurable macroeconomic variables as proxies.

For example, the business-cycle factor is represented by real (inflation-adjusted) percentage changes in the index of industrial production, whereas short-term inflation is measured by monthly percentage changes in the Consumer Price Index.

At the heart of the R&R approach are several assumptions. First, each source of systematic risk has a certain current volatility and reward. Factor volatilities and rewards, and even the factors themselves, may change over time. Second, individual securities and portfolios possess different sensitivities to each factor. These sensitivities may also vary through time. Third, a well-diversified portfolio's exposure to the factors will determine its expected return and total risk. Fourth, a portfolio should be constructed that offers the most attractive total reward-to-risk ratio, given the current rewards and volatilities exhibited by the factors.

R&R has developed a security database (updated monthly) that covers roughly 15 000 individual common stocks across 17 countries. For each country's stock market, R&R applies the database to create a pure factor portfolio (discussed in this chapter) for each of the five factors. R&R uses the historical returns on these pure factor portfolios not only to estimate the sensitivity of every security in its database to each of the factors, but also to estimate factor standard deviations, correlations, and risk premiums as well as calculate nonfactor returns and risk for every security.

Attention at this point turns to a client's benchmark. Typically, a US institutional investor will select a market index such as the S&P 500 as its common stock benchmark. R&R's standard assignment is to devise a more efficient portfolio that exceeds the benchmark's expected return by a prespecified (reasonable) amount, yet maintains a similar standard deviation. R&R does this by employing portfolio optimization techniques (see Chapter 7) that combine securities in a way that attempts to set portfolio standard deviation near that of the benchmark; reduce nonfactor risk to minimal levels; emphasize stocks with high market-to-book and market-to-earnings ratios as well as positive recent returns relative to other stocks; increase exposure to risk factors with attractive reward-to-risk; and minimize buying and selling of securities (to control transaction costs). The process is repeated monthly to keep the portfolio aligned with the benchmark.

The R&R approach is highly quantitative and, intriguingly, involves no judgmental forecasts of factor returns or risks. Rather, historical data on the factors and securities' factor sensitivities is mechanically manipulated to determine the desired portfolio composition. This approach may prove effective if the future mimics the past, but it can produce disap-

pointing results if past factor data display no stable relationship with future values.

R&R has captured considerable institutional investor interest since the firm was organized in 1986. Furthermore, the firm has expanded to take on foreign partners who now apply its techniques abroad. Thus R&R provides an interesting example of converting theoretical investment concepts into practical investment products.

Comparing this equation with equation (11.18) reveals that if the assumptions of both APT (with two factors) and the CAPM hold and each security's residual return is uncorrelated with the market return, then the following relationships must hold:

$$\lambda_1 = (\bar{r}_M - r_f)\beta_{F_1} \tag{11.34a}$$

$$\lambda_2 = (\bar{r}_M - r_f)\beta_{F_2} \tag{11.34b}$$

Hence the size of λ_1 and λ_2 will be dependent upon both the market premium $(\bar{r}_M - r_f)$, a positive number, and the beta of the factor with the market portfolio, which may be positive or negative. This means that λ_1 and λ_2 will have positive values if the factors are positively correlated with the returns on the market portfolio.[17] However, if either factor is negatively correlated with the returns on the market portfolio, then the corresponding value of λ will be negative (as was the case with λ_2 in the example).

Identifying the Factors

Left unanswered by APT are the number and identity of the factors that are "priced"—that is, have values of lambda (λ) that are sufficiently positive or negative in magnitude that they need to be included when estimating expected returns. Several researchers have investigated stock returns and estimated that there are anywhere from three to five factors. Subsequently, various people attempted to identify these factors.[18] In one paper by Chen, Roll, and Ross, the following factors were identified:

1. Growth rate in industrial production,
2. Rate of inflation (both expected and unexpected),
3. Spread between long-term and short-term interest rates,
4. Spread between low-grade and high-grade bonds.[19]

---

[17]For the reasoning behind this assertion, see footnote 14.

[18]In Chapter 10 a three-factor model that was developed by Fama and French was described. In their model, the factors represented returns on (1) a general market index, (2) the difference between small and large stock indices, and (3) the difference between high and low book-to-market equity ratio stock indices.

[19]Note that the third factor can be interpreted as a measure of the term structure of interest rates, and the fourth factor can be interpreted as a measure of the default risk premium that investors demand for holding risky corporate bonds instead of government bonds.

Another paper by Berry, Burmeister, and McElroy identifies five factors. Of these five factors, three correspond closely to the last three identified by Chen, Roll, and Ross. The other two are the growth rate in aggregate sales in the economy and the rate of return on the S&P 500.[20]

In a series of tests using Canadian data, Otuteye found that two distinct models using different macroeconomic factors performed equally well. The first model included the same factors used by Chen, Roll, and Ross plus a value-weighted market index. The second included the value-weighted market index, the yield spread between high- and low-grade corporate bonds, the growth rate of unemployment, and the Canada/US exchange rate.

Finally, consider the five factors used by Salomon Brothers in what they refer to as their Fundamental Factor Model. Only one factor, inflation, is in common with the factors identified by the others. The remaining factors are as follows:

1. Growth rate in gross domestic product,
2. Rate of interest,
3. Rate of change in oil prices,
4. Rate of growth in defence spending.[21]

In summary, it is interesting to note that the sets of factors have some common characteristics. First, they contain some indication of aggregate economic activity (industrial production, aggregate sales, and GDP). Second, they contain inflation. Third, they contain some type of interest rate factor (either spreads or a rate itself). Considering the fact that stock prices can be thought of as being equal to the discounted value of future dividends, the factors make intuitive sense.[22] Future dividends will be related to aggregate economic activity, and the discount rate used to determine present value will be related to inflation and interest rates.

Salomon Brothers
www.salomon.com

Summary

1. Arbitrage Pricing Theory (APT) is an equilibrium model of security prices, as is the Capital Asset Pricing Model (CAPM).
2. APT makes different assumptions than does the CAPM.
3. APT assumes that security returns are generated by a factor model, but does not identify the factors.
4. An arbitrage portfolio includes long and short positions in securities. It must have a net market value of zero, no sensitivity to any factor, and a positive expected return.
5. Investors will invest in arbitrage portfolios if they exist, driving up the prices of the securities held in long positions and driving down the prices of securities held in short positions, until all arbitrage possibilities are eliminated.
6. When all arbitrage possibilities are eliminated, the equilibrium-expected return on a security will be a linear function of its sensitivities to the factors.
7. A factor risk premium is the equilibrium return over the risk-free rate expected to be generated by a portfolio with a unit sensitivity to the factor and no sensitivity to any other factor.
8. APT and the CAPM are not necessarily inconsistent with each other. If security returns are generated by a factor model and the CAPM holds, then a security's beta will depend

---

[20]Technically, they used the part of the rate of return of the S&P 500 that could not be attributed to the other four factors.

[21]They used inflation-adjusted figures for all the variables except the rate of interest.

[22]Dividend discount models are discussed in depth in Chapter 17.

on the security's sensitivity to the factors and the beta values of the factors with the market portfolio.

9. APT does not specify the number or identity of the factors that affect expected returns nor the magnitudes or signs of the risk premiums. Most research into factors focuses on indicators of aggregate economic activity, inflation, and interest rates.

QUESTIONS AND PROBLEMS

1. In what significant ways does APT differ from the CAPM?
2. Why would an investor wish to form an arbitrage portfolio?
3. What three conditions define an arbitrage portfolio?
4. Assuming a one-factor model, consider a portfolio composed of three securities with the following factor sensitivities:

Security	Factor Sensitivity
1	0.09
2	3.00
3	1.80

If the proportion of security 1 in the portfolio is increased by .2, how must the proportion of the other two securities change if the portfolio is to maintain the same factor sensitivity?

5. Assuming a one-factor model of the form:

$$r_i = 4\% + b_i F + e_i$$

consider three well-diversified portfolios (zero nonfactor risk). The expected valued of the factor is 8%.

Portfolio	Factor Sensitivity	Expected Return
A	0.80	10.4%
B	1.00	10.0
C	1.20	13.6

Is one of the portfolio's expected returns not in line with the factor model relationship? Which one? Can you construct a combination of the other two portfolios that has the same factor sensitivity as the "out-of-line" portfolio? What is the expected return of that combination? What action would you expect investors to take with respect to these three portfolios?

6. Gunnar Seybold owns a portfolio with the following characteristics (assume that returns are generated by a one-factor model):

Security	Factor Sensitivity	Proportion	Expected Return
A	2.0	.20	20%
B	3.5	.40	10
C	0.5	.40	5

Gunnar decides to create an arbitrage portfolio by increasing his holdings of security A by .20 (Hint: Remember, X_B must equal $-X_C - X_A$.)

a. What must be the weights of the other two securities in Gunnar's arbitrage portfolio?
b. What is the expected return on the arbitrage portfolio?

c. If everyone follows Gunnar's buy-and-sell decisions, what will be the effects on the prices of the three securities?

7. Assume that security returns are generated by a one-factor model. Hap Morse holds a portfolio whose component securities have the following characteristics:

Security	Factor Sensitivity	Proportion	Expected Return
A	.60	.40	12%
B	.30	.30	15
C	1.20	.30	8

Specify an arbitrage portfolio in which Hap might invest. (Remember that there are an infinite number of possibilities—choose one.) Demonstrate that this portfolio satisfies the conditions of an arbitrage portfolio.

8. Why must the variance of a well-diversified arbitrage portfolio be small?

9. Why is the concept of arbitrage central to the asset-pricing mechanism of the APT?

10. Based on a one-factor model, Wyeville Labs' stock has a factor sensitivity of 3. Given a risk-free rate of 5% and a factor risk premium of 7%, what is the equilibrium expected return on Wyeville stock?

11. According to the APT, why must the relationship between a security's equilibrium return and its factor sensitivities be linear?

12. Based on a one-factor model, two portfolios, A and B, have equilibrium expected returns of 9.8% and 11.0%, respectively. If the factor sensitivity of portfolios A and B is 0.80 and 1.00, respectively, what must be the risk-free rate?

13. What is a pure factor portfolio? How may such a portfolio be constructed?

14. Based on a one-factor model, assume that the risk-free rate is 6% and the expected return on a portfolio with unit sensitivity to the factor is 8.5%. Consider a portfolio of two securities with the following characteristics:

Security	Factor Sensitivity	Proportion
A	4.0	.30
B	2.6	.70

According to the APT, what is the portfolio's equilibrium expected return?

15. Assume that security returns are generated by a factor model in which two factors are pervasive. The sensitivities of two securities and of the risk-free asset to each of the two factors is shown below, along with the expected return on each security.

Security	b_{i1}	b_{i2}	Expected Return
A	0.50	0.80	16.2%
B	1.50	1.40	21.6
r_f	0.00	0.00	10.0

a. If Dorothy Miller has $100 to invest and sells short $50 of security B and purchases $150 of security A, what is the sensitivity of Dorothy's portfolio to the two factors? (Ignore margin requirements.)

b. If Dorothy now borrows $100 at the risk-free rate and invests the proceeds of the loan along with the original $100 in securities A and B in the same proportions as described in part (a), what is the sensitivity of this portfolio to the two factors?

c. What is the expected return on the portfolio created in part (b)?

d. What is the expected return premium of factor 2?

16. Claus Pfeffer owns a portfolio with the following characteristics:

Security	Factor 1 Sensitivity	Factor 2 Sensitivity	Proportion	Expected Return
A	2.50	1.40	.30	13%
B	1.60	0.90	.30	18
C	0.80	1.00	.20	10
D	2.00	1.30	.20	12

Assume that the returns are generated by a two-factor model. Claus decides to create an arbitrage portfolio by increasing the holding of security B by .05.

a. What must be the weights of the other three securities in Claus's portfolio?

b. What is the expected return on the arbitrage portfolio?

17. Is it true if one believes that the APT is a correct theory of asset pricing, then the risk-return relationship derived from the CAPM is necessarily incorrect? Why?

18. If the CAPM and APT both hold, why must it be the case that the factor risk premium is negative for a factor that is negatively correlated with the market portfolio? Explain both mathematically and intuitively.

19. Some people have argued that the market portfolio can never be measured and that the CAPM is therefore untestable. Others have argued that the APT specifies neither the number of factors nor their identity and, hence, is also untestable. If these views are correct, does this mean that the theories are of no value? Explain.

20. Although the APT does not specify the identity of the relevant factors, most empirical APT research has focused on certain types of factors. What are some of the common characteristics of those factors?

21. Assume that the CAPM holds and that returns on securities are generated by a single-factor model. You are given the following information:

$$\sigma_M^2 = 400 \qquad b_A = 0.70 \qquad b_B = 1.10 \qquad COV(F, r_M) = 370$$

a. Calculate the beta coefficients of securities A and B.

b. If the risk-free rate is 6% and the expected return on the market portfolio is 12%, what is the equilibrium expected return on securities A and B?

22. Assume that the CAPM holds and that returns are generated by a two-factor model. You are given the following information:

$$\sigma_M^2 = 324 \qquad b_{A1} = .80 \qquad b_{B1} = 1.00 \qquad COV(F_1, r_M) = 156$$
$$b_{A2} = 1.10 \qquad b_{B2} = .70 \qquad COV(F_2, r_M) = 500$$

Calculate the beta coefficients of securities A and B.

CFA Exam Question

23. As the manager of a large, broadly diversified portfolio of stocks and bonds, you realize that changes in certain macroeconomic variables may directly affect the performance of your portfolio. You are considering using an arbitrage pricing theory (APT) approach to strategic portfolio planning and want to analyze the possible impacts of the following four factors:

- industrial production
- inflation
- risk premiums or quality spreads
- yield curve shifts

a. Indicate how each of these four factors influences the cash flows and the discount rates in the traditional discounted cash flow valuation model. Explain how unanticipated changes in each of these four factors could affect portfolio returns.

b. You now use a constant-proportion allocation strategy of 60% stocks and 40% bonds, which you rebalance monthly. Compare and contrast an active portfolio approach that incorporates macroeconomic factors, such as the four factors listed above, to the constant-proportion strategy currently in use.

KEY TERMS

Arbitrage Pricing Theory (APT) (p. 269)   arbitrage portfolio (p. 270)
sensitivity (p. 269)   pure factor portfolio (p. 274)
arbitrage (p. 270)   factor risk premium (p. 275)

REFERENCES

1. Credit for the initial development of the APT belongs to:

Stephen A. Ross, "The Arbitrage Theory of Capital Asset Pricing," *Journal of Economic Theory* 13, no. 3 (December 1976): 341–360; and "Risk, Return, and Arbitrage," in *Risk and Return in Finance*, Vol. I, eds. Irwin Friend and James L. Bicksler (Cambridge, MA: Ballinger Publishing, 1977), Section 9.

2. Ross's initial presentation of the APT was clarified in:

Gur Huberman, "A Simple Approach to Arbitrage Pricing Theory," *Journal of Economic Theory* 28, no. 1 (October 1982): 183–191.

3. The fundamental asset pricing equation of Ross's APT is approximately correct for all but a small number of assets. By making additional assumptions all assets will be priced with, at most, negligible error. Some of the papers (also see the papers cited in references 7 and 8) that address this issue are:

Nai-fu Chen and Jonathan E. Ingersoll, Jr., "Exact Pricing in Linear Factor Models with Finitely Many Assets: A Note," *Journal of Finance* 38, no. 3 (June 1983): 985–988.

Gary Chamberlain and Michael Rothschild, "Arbitrage, Factor Structure, and Mean-Variance Analysis on Large Asset Markets," *Econometrica* 51, no. 5 (September 1983): 1281–1304.

Gary Chamberlain, "Funds, Factors, and Diversification in Arbitrage Pricing Models," *Econometrica* 51, no. 5 (September 1983): 1305–1323.

Philip H. Dybvig, "An Explicit Bound on Individual Assets' Deviations from APT Pricing in a Finite Economy," *Journal of Financial Economics* 12, no. 4 (December 1983): 483–496.

Mark Grinblatt and Sheridan Titman, "Factor Pricing in a Finite Economy," *Journal of Financial Economics* 12, no. 4 (December 1983): 497–507.

Gregory Connor, "A Unified Beta Pricing Theory," *Journal of Economic Theory* 34, no. 1 (October 1984): 13–31.

Robert A. Jarrow, "Preferences, Continuity, and the Arbitrage Pricing Theory," *Review of Financial Studies* 2, no. 1 (Summer 1988): 159–172.

4. Nontechnical descriptions of the APT can be found in:

Richard W. Roll and Stephen A. Ross, "Regulation, the Capital Asset Pricing Model, and the Arbitrage Pricing Theory," *Public Utilities Fortnightly* 111, no. 11 (May 26, 1983): 22–28.

Richard Roll and Stephen A. Ross, "The Arbitrage Pricing Theory Approach to Strategic Portfolio Planning," *Financial Analysts Journal* 40, no. 3 (May–June 1984): 14–26.

Dorothy H. Bower, Richard S. Bower, and Dennis E. Logue, "A Primer on Arbitrage Pricing Theory," *Midland Corporate Finance Journal* 2, no. 3 (Fall 1984): 31–40.

Richard C. Grinold and Ronald N. Kahn, *Active Portfolio Management* (Chicago: Probus Publishing, 1995), Chapter 7.

5. Some of the attempts to identify the number of factors that are priced are:

Richard Roll and Stephen A. Ross, "An Empirical Investigation of the Arbitrage Pricing Theory," *Journal of Finance* 35, no.5 (December 1980): 1073–1103.

Stephen J. Brown and Mark I. Weinstein, "A New Approach to Testing Asset Pricing Models: The Bilinear Paradigm," *Journal of Finance* 38, no. 3 (June 1983): 711–743.

Phoebus J. Dhyrmes, Irwin Friend, and N. Bulent Gultekin, "A Critical Reexamination of the Empirical Evidence on the Arbitrage Pricing Theory," *Journal of Finance* 39, no. 2 (June 1984): 323–346.

Richard Roll and Stephen A. Ross, "A Critical Reexamination of the Empirical Evidence on the Arbitrage Pricing Theory: A Reply," *Journal of Finance* 39, no. 2 (June 1984): 347–350.

Phoebus J. Dhrymes, Irwin Friend, Mustafa N. Gultekin, and N. Bulent Gultekin, "New Tests of the APT and Their Implications," *Journal of Finance* 40, no. 3 (July 1985): 659–674.

Charles Trzcinka, "On the Number of Factors in the Arbitrage Pricing Model," *Journal of Finance* 41, no. 2 (June 1986): 347–368.

Dolores A. Conway and Marc R. Reinganum, "Stable Factors in Security Returns: Identification Using Cross Validation," *Journal of Business and Economic Statistics* 6, no. 1 (January 1988): 1–15.

Bruce N. Lehmann and David M. Modest, "The Empirical Foundations of the Arbitrage Pricing Theory," *Journal of Financial Economics* 21, no. 2 (September 1988): 213–254.

Gregory Connor and Robert A. Korajczyk, "Risk and Return in an Equilibrium APT: Application of a New Test Methodology," *Journal of Financial Economics* 21, no. 2 (September 1988): 255–289.

Stephen J. Brown, "The Number of Factors in Security Returns," *Journal of Finance* 44, no. 5 (December 1989): 1247–1262.

Ravi Shukla and Charles Trzcinka, "Sequential Tests of the Arbitrage Pricing Theory: A Comparison of Principal Components and Maximum Likelihood Factors," *Journal of Finance* 45, no. 5 (December 1990): 1541–1564.

Eugene F. Fama and Kenneth R. French, "Common Risk Factors in the Returns on Stocks and Bonds," *Journal of Financial Economics* 33, no. 1 (February 1993): 3–56.

Jianping Mei, "A Semiautoregression Approach to the Arbitrage Pricing Theory," *Journal of Finance* 48, no. 2 (June 1993): 599–620.

Gregory Connor and Robert A. Korajczyk, "A Test for the Number of Factors in an Approximate Factor Model," *Journal of Finance* 48, no. 4 (September 1993): 1263–1291.

Jianping Mei, "Explaining the Cross-Section of Returns via a Multi-Factor APT Model," *Journal of Financial and Quantitative Analysis* 28, no. 3 (September 1993): 331–345.

John Geweke and Guofu Zhou, "Measuring the Pricing Error of the Arbitrage Pricing Theory," *Review of Financial Studies* 9, no. 2 (Summer 1996): 557–587.

6. A few of the previous papers also identified factors. Some other papers that identified factors are:

Tony Estep, Nick Hansen, and Cal Johnson, "Sources of Value and Risk in Common Stocks," *Journal of Portfolio Management* 9, no. 4 (Summer 1983): 5–13.

Nai-fu Chen, Richard Roll, and Stephen A. Ross, "Economic Forces and the Stock Market," *Journal of Business* 59, no. 3 (July 1986): 383–403.

Marjorie B. McElroy and Edwin Burmeister, "Arbitrage Pricing Theory as a Restricted Nonlinear Multivariate Regression Model," *Journal of Business and Economic Statistics* 6, no. 1 (January 1988): 29–42.

Michael A. Berry, Edwin Burmeister, and Marjorie B. McElroy, "Sorting Out Risks Using Known APT Factors," *Financial Analysts Journal* 44, no. 2 (March–April 1988): 29–42.

7. It has been argued that the APT cannot be meaningfully tested and hence is of questionable practical use. These arguments and their rebuttals have been provided by:

Jay Shanken, "The Arbitrage Pricing Theory: Is It Testable?" *Journal of Finance* 37, no. 5 (December 1982): 1129–1140.

Phoebus J. Dhrymes, "The Empirical Relevance of Arbitrage Pricing Models," *Journal of Portfolio Management* 10, no. 4 (Summer 1984): 35–44.

Stephen A. Ross, "Reply to Dhrymes: APT is Empirically Relevant," *Journal of Portfolio Management* 11, no. 1 (Fall 1984): 54–56.

Phoebus J. Dhrymes, "On the Empirical Relevance of APT: Comment," *Journal of Portfolio Management* 11, no. 4 (Summer 1985): 70–71.

Stephen A. Ross, "On the Empirical Relevance of APT: Reply," *Journal of Portfolio Management* 11, no. 4 (Summer 1985): 72–73.

Philip H. Dybvig and Stephen A. Ross, "Yes, the APT Is Testable," *Journal of Finance* 40, no. 4 (September 1985): 1129–1140.

Christian Gilles and Stephen F. LeRoy, "On the Arbitrage Pricing Theory," *Economic Theory* 1, no. 3 (1991): 213–229.

Jay Shanken, "The Current State of Arbitrage Pricing Theory," *Journal of Finance* 47, no. 4 (September 1992): 1569–1574.

8. For a discussion of the relationships between the APT and the CAPM, see:

Robert Jarrow and Andrew Rudd, "A Comparison of the APT and CAPM: A Note," *Journal of Banking and Finance* 7, no. 2 (June 1983): 295–303.

William F. Sharpe, "Factor Models, CAPMs and the ABT," *Journal of Portfolio Management* 11, no. 1 (Fall 1984): 21–25.

Jay Shanken, "Multi-Beta CAPM or Equilibrium-APT? A Reply," *Journal of Finance* 40, no. 4 (September 1985): 1189–1196.

K. C. John Wei, "An Asset-Pricing Theory Unifying the CAPM and APT," *Journal of Finance* 43, no. 4 (September 1988): 881–892.

9. For a discussion of the APT in an international context, see:

Bruno Solnik, "International Arbitrage Pricing Theory," *Journal of Finance* 38, no. 2 (May 1982): 449–457.

10. For a Canadian perspective on the topics covered in this chapter, see:

Patricia J. Hughes, "A Test of the Arbitrage Pricing Theory," *Canadian Journal of Administrative Sciences* 1, no. 2 (December 1984): 195–214.

Eben Otuteye, "How Economic Forces Explain Canadian Stock Returns," *Canadian Investment Review* IV, no. 1 (Spring 1991): 93–99.

B. F. Smith, "A Study of the Arbitrage Pricing Theory Using Daily Returns of Canadian Stocks," in M. J. Robinson and B. F. Smith, eds., *Canadian Capital Markets* (London, ON: Western Business School, 1993).

CHAPTER 12

Taxes and Inflation

Neither taxation nor inflation should be regarded as an unmitigated evil. Each provides benefits to some individuals that may outweigh the associated costs that others have to bear. Regardless of whether or not the benefits outweigh the costs, both taxes and inflation have an impact on investment decisions and investment results and they are sufficiently important in present-day societies to warrant considerable discussion.

Federal and provincial tax laws play a major role in the way securities are priced in the marketplace, since, understandably, investors are concerned with after-tax returns, rather than before-tax returns. Accordingly, the investor should determine the tax rate applicable to her before making any investment decision. This tax rate is not the same for all securities for a given individual investor; when both federal and provincial taxes are considered in 1998, it can be as low as 6.6% in the case of dividends paid on eligible Canadian shares in excess of 52% for corporate bonds. After determining the applicable tax rate, the investor can estimate a security's expected after-tax return and risk.

Taxes in Canada

Revenue Canada
www.rc.gc.ca

In Canada, personal and corporate taxes are levied by the federal, the 10 provincial, and 2 territorial governments. In all provinces except Quebec, the federal government acts as a collection agency for personal income taxes; individuals file a single tax return with the federal government, which then distributes the appropriate amount to the provinces. Residents of Quebec must file two separate tax returns, one with Revenue Canada and one with the Quebec Ministry of Finance.

Many of the specific tax rates and provisions cited in this chapter are contained in the amendments to the Income Tax Act that were passed in September 1988. Changes occur from year to year, and current regulations should, of course, be consulted when preparing tax returns or considering major investment decisions. However, the material given here can be considered broadly representative of current taxation in Canada.

Generally speaking, the most important taxes for investment decision making are personal and corporate income taxes. The essential elements of each will be described, and the manner in which they influence the pricing of securities will be considered.

● Corporate Income Taxes

There are three forms of business organizations in Canada and in many other countries—corporations, partnerships, and single proprietorships. The corporate form of organization is the largest in terms of the dollar value of assets owned, even though there are more firms organized as partnerships or single proprietorships. Legally, a corporation is regarded as a separate entity, whereas a proprietorship or partnership is considered an extension of its owner or owners. Income earned by proprietorships and partnerships is taxed primarily through the personal income tax levied on their owners. Income earned by a corporation may be taxed twice—once when it is earned, via the corporate income tax, and again when it is received as dividends by holders of the firm's securities, via the personal income tax.[1]

This double taxation of corporate income may at first seem inefficient, if not unfair. It also raises questions about the efficiency of the corporate form of organization. Suffice it to say that limited liability and the ability to subdivide ownership and to transfer shares of that ownership appear to be of sufficient value to more than offset the tax law disadvantages. Moreover, without the corporate income tax, personal tax rates would have to be increased if the level of government expenditures were to remain constant without increasing the national debt.

Corporate Tax Rates (Federal and Provincial)

The corporate income tax is relatively simple in one respect. There are only a few basic rates applicable to all taxable income. The rates vary depending on the size of the corporation and the nature of its operations. Table 12.1 shows the federal and provincial tax rates that were in effect on January 1, 1998.

The federal and provincial rates are additive. Thus, a large Manitoba non-manufacturing corporation pays 46.12% of all its reported income in combined taxes. As demonstrated in Table 12.1 the tax system favours firms in the manufacturing sector. This is

Table 12.1 Federal and Provincial Corporate Tax Rates, 1998.				
	Small Cdn.-Controlled Corporations[a]		Other Cdn. Corporations	
Jurisdiction	Mfg.	Non-mfg.	Mfg.	Non-mfg.
Federal[b]	13.12%	13.12%	22.12%	29.12%
Provincial:				
Alberta	6.0	6.0	14.5	15.5
British Columbia	9.0	9.0	16.5	16.5
Manitoba	9.0	9.0	17.0	17.0
New Brunswick	7.0	7.0	17.0	17.0
Newfoundland	5.0	5.0	5.0	14.0
Northwest Terr.	5.0	5.0	14.0	14.0
Nova Scotia	5.0	5.0	16.0	16.0
Ontario	9.0	9.0	13.5	15.5
Quebec	5.91	5.91	9.15	9.15
Prince Edward I.	7.5	7.5	7.5	16.0
Saskatchewan	8.0	8.0	17.0	17.0
Yukon Terr.	2.5	6.0	2.5	15.0

[a] Certain Canadian-controlled private corporations are eligible for these rates.
[b] Includes the 4% surtax.

SOURCE: KPMG, *Tax Facts, 1998–99* (Toronto, July 1998), p. 52.

---

[1] The Income Tax Act attempts to minimize the effects of double taxation on dividends through the Dividend Tax Credit—an issue that will be discussed in more detail later.

Table 12.2	Capital Tax Rates for General Corporations.	

General Corporations

Jurisdiction[a]	Current Rate	Capital Deduction[b]
Federal Government	0.225%	$10 million
British Columbia	0.300	1.5 million
Manitoba	0.300	3 million
New Brunswick	0.300	5 million
Nova Scotia	0.250	None
Ontario	0.300	2 million
Quebec	0.640	None

[a]Not all jurisdictions in Canada levy this tax.
[b]This represents the amount that may be deducted from capital before calculating the tax.

SOURCE: KPMG, *Tax Facts, 1998–99* (Toronto, July 1998), p. 60.

Marginal Tax Rate The amount of taxes, expressed as a percentage, paid on each additional dollar of taxable income received.

Average Tax Rate The amount of taxes paid expressed as a percentage of the total income subject to tax.

intended to stimulate employment. The system of tax rates is also simple in the sense that the **marginal tax rates** and **average tax rates** are equal because there is a single rate applicable to a given corporation. The marginal tax rate is the tax rate it would pay on an additional dollar of income. The average tax rate is equal to the total amount of taxes paid divided by the total income subject to tax. The average rate measures the overall impact of taxes, but the marginal rate is more relevant for most decisions.

Corporations are also subject to a capital tax paid as a percentage on the capital of the firm. Table 12.2 shows the applicable rates and the deductions from capital permitted by the different jurisdictions for general corporations. Financial institutions pay this tax at a different rate from general corporations. The applicable rates and regulations are considerably more complicated in the case of financial institutions.

Defining Income

Corporate income is partly a philosophic concept, partly an artifact of legal requirements, partly a result of accounting conventions, partly an indication of the hopes of the firm's management, and sometimes only incidentally related to underlying economic factors.

For tax purposes, corporate income is defined as revenues minus expenses. However, a problem arises in measuring these two elements. Simply put, this problem involves determining when to recognize revenues and expenses as having occurred. If a company sells an airplane this year but payment is to be made in instalments over the next 5 years, when is the sales price to be considered taxable revenue? If a new plant is to be built and paid for this year but is to be used to produce goods for the next 20 years, when is the outlay to be considered as an expense? Accountants have a set of procedures, known as generally accepted accounting principles (GAAP), that can be used to handle these and many more subtle cases. However, there is extremely wide latitude within these principles.

The government has prescribed certain limits on the procedures that can be used to calculate income when determining a corporation's income tax liability. In some cases, the firm is required to use the same procedures when reporting its income to its shareholders; in other cases it can (and often does) use different procedures, sometimes resulting in a noticeably different income figure.[2]

---

[2]Differences of this sort are usually described in the firm's annual report.

Deductibility of Interest Payments

In Canada, interest is regarded as a business expense and can be deducted from revenue when calculating taxable income. For example, consider two firms, each with revenues of $25 000 and noninterest expenses of $15 000. Firm A is financed by both debt and equity and pays $5000 in interest to its creditors. As shown in Table 12.3, its net income after taxes is $4250, which is available to be paid as dividends, if desired. Thus, a total amount of $9250 ($5000 + $4250) can be paid to those who provided the firm's capital.

The other part of the table shows the results for firm B, which differs only with respect to financing. All its capital was provided by common stock financing. Thus, the entire $10 000 of income is subject to tax, leaving only $8500 for distribution to those who provided the firm's capital.

The deductibility of interest payments provides an apparent tax advantage for the use of debt over equity funds. For this reason, it may seem surprising that firms do not choose to obtain more of their capital by issuing bonds. Indeed, the dramatic difference in tax treatment raises substantial questions about the definition of debt and interest, on the one hand, and stocks and dividend payments, on the other. Revenue Canada pays considerable attention to any arrangement designed to provide the tax characteristics of debt with the financial characteristics of equity. To qualify as debt, there must be a definite lender, a definite borrower, a definite ascertainable obligation (a specific amount), and a time of maturity (date when the debt must be repaid). That is, debt should be represented by an instrument (a legal document such as a contract) that contains an unconditional legal obligation to pay a certain sum either on demand or on a specific date, with interest. Payments made under any other arrangement are not likely to be deductible for purposes of income taxation.

Failure to make interest payments may have serious consequences for the firm and its management. In many cases bankruptcy results, with mandatory and costly corporate reorganization. The greater the magnitude of interest payments in relation to dividend payments, the greater the probability of this type of unfortunate event. This risk of bankruptcy, along with the associated costs of bankruptcy, provides a constraint on the use of debt financing, despite its obvious tax advantage.

Corporate Income from Dividends, Interest, and Capital Gains

The full amount of the dividends *received* by a corporation can be excluded from income when calculating the corporation's income tax liability. The recipient corporation is regarded as a *conduit* between the issuing corporation and individual investors. This special treatment of dividends avoids the partial triple taxation of income. Consider how dividends would be taxed if this exclusion did not exist. Corporation A is taxed on its income and then pays dividends to one of its shareholders, corporation B. Corporation B then pays taxes on its income, which includes the dividends received from A. Finally, the sharehold-

---

Table 12.3 The Effects of Deducting Interest Payments.

	Firm A	Firm B
Revenue	$25 000	$25 000
Cost of goods sold	15 000	15 000
Revenue minus expense	10 000	10 000
Interest paid	5 000	0
Taxable income	5 000	10 000
Tax (at 15%)	750	1 500
Available for dividends	$ 4 250	$ 8 500

ers of B pay income taxes on the dividends received from B. Thus, a dollar of income earned by A would be taxed three times (a tax on A, then a tax on B, then a tax on the shareholders of B) if the dividend exclusion did not exist. With the dividend exclusion, a dollar of income earned by A is taxed, for all practical purposes, only twice. Despite the existence of the Dividend Tax Credit that applies to dividends received by individual investors in Canada, some degree of double taxation still exists.

Interest received by a corporation is simply added to income and taxed at the regular rate. This means that the effective tax rate on interest received from bonds is substantially greater than the rate received on dividends from common and preferred shares. This differential tax treatment has an effect on the relative prices that corporate investors are willing to pay for these securities, since their concern is with relative after-tax yields. As preferred shares are generally viewed as being riskier than bonds, the after-tax yield on preferred shares needs to be higher in order for investors to be interested in purchasing them. Given the favourable tax treatment on preferred shares for corporate investors, it is possible for preferred shares to have a lower before-tax yield than bonds while still enabling the corporate investor who buys the more risky preferred shares to be rewarded by earning a higher after-tax yield relative to bonds.

Tax-exempt Organizations

Many organizations are wholly or partly exempt from federal income taxes. Non-profit religious, charitable, or educational foundations generally qualify. Such foundations are required to pay out to their beneficiaries a minimum percentage of the value of their assets (4.5% in 1998). Failure to do so can result in a punitive and confiscatory tax.

Investment companies, often called *mutual funds*, may elect to be treated as regulated investment companies for tax purposes. This privilege is granted if certain conditions are met. For example, the funds of the investment company must be invested primarily in securities, without undue concentration in any one. Thus, its income takes the form of dividends and interest received on its investments, as well as capital gains from price appreciation realized when investments are sold at a price that is higher than their purchase price. A regulated investment company pays income tax only on income and capital gains not distributed to its shareholders. As a result of this tax treatment, such companies distribute substantially all income and gains and, in doing so, end up not having to pay any taxes.

Employee pension, profit-sharing, and share-ownership plans may also qualify for tax-exempt status. Such a plan may entrust its assets, which are usually securities, to a *fiduciary* (for example, a trust company). The fiduciary receives new contributions, makes required payments, and manages the investments owned by the plan. A fiduciary under a qualified plan (that is, a plan that meets all the requirements of applicable legislation) pays no taxes on either income or capital gains.

Another example of a tax-exempt entity is the *personal trust*. Here, funds are provided for the benefit of one or more individuals by another individual or individuals with a fiduciary serving as a trustee. Some trusts are created by wills, others by a contract among living persons. Whatever the origin, trusts generally pay taxes only on income that is not distributed to the designated beneficiaries. It is important, however, to have adequate legal and tax advice when establishing these trusts to avoid Revenue Canada's *income attribution rules*, which will be discussed later in this chapter.

Income and capital gains earned by investment companies, pension funds, and personal trusts do not go untaxed forever. Payments made to investment company shareholders, pension fund beneficiaries, and the beneficiaries of personal trusts are subject to applicable personal income tax rules. The exemptions apply only to taxes that might otherwise be levied at the previous stage.

Personal Income Taxes

Although the corporate income tax is an important feature of the investment scene, its effect on most individuals is indirect. This is not so for the personal income tax. Few investors can avoid dealing with it in detail, at both an economic and an emotional level. Its provisions have major and direct effects on investment behaviour.

Personal Tax Rates (Federal)

Taxes must be paid on an individual's worldwide income as defined in the Income Tax Act.[3] Capital gains were not included in income for tax purposes until the Income Tax Act of 1972 came into force. Certain items may be deducted from income before computing the tax due and capital gains and losses are subject to special procedures that are described in a later section. Deductions of special importance for investment purposes are described in this section as well as in later sections.

Three definitions are relevant for tax purposes. *Total income* is the sum of income received from all sources including self-employment (reported as gross income less expenses). *Net income* is total income less certain allowable expenses (for example, contributions to certain retirement funds, union and/or professional dues, alimony payments). *Taxable income* is net income less other specified deductions.

Despite the 1988 changes to the Income Tax Act, many people are still of the opinion that little is simple about personal income taxes in Canada. Table 12.4 shows the federal tax rates in effect in 1998.

These figures are used to calculate the *gross federal tax*. Each taxpayer is entitled to a non-refundable tax credit that is subtracted directly from the gross federal tax to obtain the *basic federal tax*. Finally, the following surtaxes must be added to arrive at the *total federal tax payable:*

3% of the basic federal tax plus an additional 5% on any amount over $12 500.

The 1998 federal budget introduced a reduction in the 3% surtax up to a maximum of $250. This maximum is reached when the basic federal tax is $8333 (equivalent to a taxable income of about $50 000). The $250 maximum then declines at a rate of 3% of the basic federal tax in excess of $8333 up to a maximum of $12 500. When the federal tax is over $12 500 the surtax reverts to 3%.

Provincial and Territorial Income Taxes

All provinces levy personal income taxes that, except for those in Quebec, are calculated as a percentage of the basic federal tax. These rates vary from 42.75% in Ontario to 69% in Newfoundland. Ontario's rate will be used in subsequent examples. In addition, some provinces also levy provincial surtaxes on high-income taxpayers.

In any investment decision, the important figure to know is the total federal plus provincial tax payable. Table 12.5 shows the detailed tax calculation for an unmarried res-

Table 12.4	Personal Federal Income Tax Rates, 1998.
Taxable Income	*Tax Rate*
$29 590 or less	$0 + 17% on next $29 590
29 590 to 59 180	5003 + 26% on next $29 590
59 180 or more	12 724 + 29% on remainder

[3]For more details see S. B. Fisher and P. B. Hickey, eds., *KPMG Personal Tax Planning Guide 1999* (Scarborough, ON: Thomson Canada Ltd., 1998).

Table 12.5   Detailed Tax Calculation for an Ontario Resident in 1998.

Taxable Income	$90 000	
On the first	$59 180 tax is	$12 724.00
On the remaining	$30 820 tax at 29% is	8 937.80
Gross federal tax		21 661.80
Less non-refundable tax credit		1 098.00
Basic federal tax		20 563.80
Federal surcharge:		
3% of basic federal tax*		616.91
5% on basic federal tax in excess of $12 500		403.19
Total federal tax payable		21 583.90
Provincial tax calculation:		
Basic tax – 42.75% of basic federal tax		8 791.02
Surcharge – (1) 20% of basic tax over $4 058		946.60
– (2) 33% of basic tax over $5 218		1 179.10
Total provincial tax payable		10 916.72
Total tax collected		$32 500.62
Marginal tax rate		50.29%
Average tax rate		36.11%

*This calculation includes the adjustment introduced in the 1998 federal budget as described on p. 296.

ident of Ontario (or a married resident with a spouse earning more than $5918 per year and with no children) with a taxable income of $90 000 derived from employment and interest bearing securities and with a non-refundable tax credit of $1098.[4]

Some taxpayers may be able, in addition, to claim a marriage allowance of $ 5380 and other amounts for dependent children, disability allowance, tuition fees, etc. The non-refundable tax credit is 17% of the sum of all these allowances. It is referred to as non-refundable because it can be used to reduce the tax bill to zero but not to generate a refund.

The combined federal and Ontario provincial tax rates are plotted in Figure 12.1. The top line shows the marginal tax (i.e., the tax rate payable on any additional dollar earned). The lower line shows the average tax rate, which is the ratio of total tax paid to total taxable income.

As can be seen in Figure 12.1, the average rate, a measurement of the overall impact of taxes, is below the marginal rate. The latter, however, is more relevant for most investment decisions. The larger an investor's taxable income, the closer the average tax rate comes to the marginal tax rate. Consider an investor with a taxable income of $90 000 who is evaluating an investment opportunity that is expected to increase his taxable income by $3000. Using the figures for the combined federal and provincial tax rates, this opportunity will have the following effect on the taxes payable:

---

[4]Dividends are subject to a different tax treatment from interest payments, as described in a later section. In 1998, *all* taxpayers were allowed to claim a basic personal allowance of $6456 in order to calculate their non-refundable tax credit.

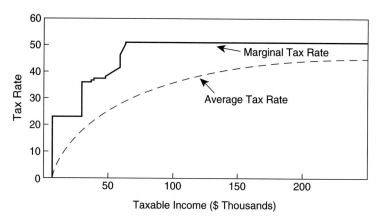

Figure 12.1 Marginal and average personal tax rates on employment income,* 1998.

*Rates shown apply to an Ontario resident.

	Before Increase	After Increase	Difference
Taxable income	$90 000	$93 000	$3 000
Tax payable	32 009	33 578	1 509
Spendable income	$57 991	$59 492	$1 491

Marginal tax rate = ($33 578 − $32 009)/$3000 = $1509/$3000 = 50.3%

As shown in this table, the increase of $3000 in taxable income will result in an increase of $1509 in taxes, leaving a net increase in spendable income of $1491. The calculations for this particular example are simple because the change in taxable income left the taxpayer in the same bracket. Thus, 50.29% of the additional income will be taxed away, leaving 49.71% to be spent. The fact that the average tax rate is 32 009/90 000 = 35.57% before the increase and 33 578/93 000 = 36.00% after the increase is irrelevant to this individual in deciding whether or not to make the investment.

When a decision moves income into a higher bracket (a situation that generally applies to taxpayers in lower tax brackets) the computations are more complex. The effective marginal tax rate on such an investment is a weighted average of the two (or more) applicable rates.

Dividend Tax Credit

Dividend Tax Credit A credit applicable to the tax payable on dividend income that lowers the effective tax rate.

The **dividend tax credit** (DTC) has a long and honourable history in Canadian tax law. It is designed to mitigate the effects of double taxation (corporate plus personal) on dividend income from taxable Canadian corporations.[5] Prior to the 1972 tax reforms, application of the DTC was simple. The full amount of the dividend was included in taxable income and the gross tax payable computed accordingly. The net tax was then the gross tax less 20% of the dividend.

[5]Investors who receive dividends from foreign corporations are generally permitted to deduct any foreign tax paid from their Canadian tax payable but may not claim the DTC. These provisions do not mitigate any double taxation that may occur in the source country.

Since 1972 the system has been more complicated. The following steps must be followed: first, the dividend is *grossed up* by a factor, g; second, the grossed up dividend is included in taxable income and the gross federal tax payable is calculated; third, a factor, q, of the grossed up dividend is allowed as a tax credit and subtracted from gross tax to arrive at the basic federal tax; fourth and fifth, the federal surtax and provincial tax (including surtax, where applicable) are then computed as a fraction of the basic federal tax. The fractions, g and q, are prescribed in the Income Tax Act and its amendments and, therefore, may change from year to year. Table 12.6 shows a sample calculation of the DTC for an Ontario investor in the highest tax bracket of 50.29% who receives a dividend of $1000. For 1998, g is 0.25 and q is 0.1333.

The DTC system can be expressed algebraically as follows:

$$T = (1 + g)(t_f - q)(1 + t_p + t_s) \qquad (12.1)$$

where:

T is the total tax payable per dollar of dividend

g is the gross-up factor

t_f is the marginal federal tax rate net of surtax

q is the DTC factor

t_p is the provincial tax rate (including any surtax) as a fraction of the basic federal tax

t_s is the federal surtax rate

Substituting the figures used in the table into equation (12.1) results in a tax payable of $0.3396 per dollar of dividend that agrees very closely with the marginal tax rate on dividend income of 33.97% obtained above in Table 12.6. This marginal tax rate is substantially smaller than the rate that the same investor would pay on interest income (50.29%). It is clear that, in the absence of any risk considerations, a dividend yield of 7.26% provides the above investor with the same after-tax return as an interest payment of 10%. The relationship between dividend yield and interest payment, however, varies according to the investor's tax bracket.

When both corporate and individual taxes are considered it becomes evident that the DTC offers only a partial mitigation of the double taxation problem. A large corporation in Ontario need earn only $100 in order to provide our investor with a before-tax interest payment of $100, but must earn $112.75 if it is in manufacturing and $131.09 if it is a non-manufacturing concern in order to provide the same investor with a dividend payment of $72.60. In the absence of the DTC even more would have to be earned: $155.30 and $180.57 respectively. The situation is different for a small Canadian-controlled corporation, which needs to earn only $93.22 in order to provide the investor with the same after-tax return as an interest payment of $100. In this case there is some over-compensation for double taxation.

Table 12.6	Sample Calculation of the Dividend Tax Credit.
Dividend received	$1 000.00
Grossed-up dividend	1 250.00
Gross federal tax payable @ 29%	362.50
Less: DTC—0.133333 of $1250	166.63
Basic federal tax	195.87
Federal surtax—8% of basic tax	15.67
Provincial tax and surtax—65.41% of basic tax	128.11
Extra tax payable on the dividend	339.65
Marginal tax rate on dividend income	33.97%

Stock dividends are treated in the same way as cash dividends. The cash equivalent of the shares received is grossed up and added to taxable income, and the tax calculation is completed as before, even though the investor has received no cash. This procedure is followed in order to prevent stock dividends from being treated as capital gains for tax purposes, thereby deferring the tax.

Capital Gains and Losses

Prior to the 1972 tax reform, the situation was simple—capital gains were not taxed and capital losses were not deductible. The provisions of the personal income tax laws, introduced in 1972, dealing with the treatment of capital gains and losses have had a great impact on investor behaviour. The taxation of capital gains is now an extremely complex topic. For this reason only the basic elements of these tax provisions will be described here.

A change in the market value of a capital asset is not relevant for tax purposes until it is **realized** as a **capital gain** (or loss) by sale or exchange. If a security purchased for $50 appreciates to a value of $100 in a year, no tax is due on the **unrealized capital gain**. But if it is sold for $120 two years after purchase, the difference of $70 must be declared as a capital gain realized at the time of sale and tax must be paid at the applicable rate.

This rule makes the end of the year an interesting time for stockbrokers. Depending on their situations, their taxpayer-clients may be either anxious or reluctant to realize capital gains or losses before a new tax year begins.

Consider, for example, a taxpayer who earlier in the year sold 1000 shares of stock A for $50 per share, having purchased them three years previously for $20 per share. This investor is liable for taxes on a capital gain of $30 000 ($1000 \times [\$50 - \$20]$). In December, the investor considers the 1000 shares of stock B, purchased four years ago for $95 per share, now selling for $65 per share. The investor has an unrealized loss of $30 000 ($1000 \times [\$65 - \$95]$) on the investment in B. The investor believes that stock B will rebound in the near future and, therefore, wants to continue owning it. It might seem that the investor should sell B on December 31 and then buy it back January 1, thereby establishing a capital loss of $30 000 on B to offset the capital gain on A. This would remove the tax liability while essentially maintaining her position in B. The tax laws, however, preclude a deduction associated with a superficial loss on a **wash sale** where a security is sold and a "substantially identical" one is bought within 30 days.

Brokerage firms publish lists pairing similar stocks for those investors who wish to sell a particular stock for tax purposes; by selling a stock and simultaneously purchasing the matching stock, the investor will continually be able to maintain a portfolio with similar investment characteristics. In the previous example, a brokerage firm may have stocks B and C matched together. These two stocks have different issuers but may be in the same industry and, in the opinion of the brokerage firm, be poised for a similar rebound next year. Accordingly, the investor might sell B and purchase C.

End-of-year sales and purchases motivated by tax considerations are fairly common. At this time, securities that experienced substantial price changes during the year tend to have large numbers of trades as holders sell to realize gains or losses. If buyers recognize that the sellers are motivated by knowledge of the tax laws and not some previously unrecognized bad news affecting the company in question, such "selling pressure" should not seriously depress the company's stock price.

Capital gains and losses are those realized on **capital property**, but the Income Tax Act has a specific definition of capital property. For tax purposes, four different kinds of assets are included in capital property: the taxpayer's *principal residence, personal use property, listed personal property*, and *investment and fixed assets in a business*. Gains or losses on current assets that are an integral part of a taxpayer's business (for example, inventories) are considered regular income. The tax treatment of the four kinds of assets is described below. The capital gain or loss realized when an asset is sold or exchanged is the difference between

Realized Capital Gain (Loss) A capital gain (or loss) on an asset that is recognized, for tax purposes, through the sale or exchange of the asset.

Unrealized Capital Gain (or Loss) A capital gain (or loss) on an asset that has not yet been recognized for tax purposes through the sale or exchange of the asset.

Wash Sale The sale and subsequent purchase of a "substantially identical" security solely for the purpose of generating a tax deductible capital loss.

Capital Property Capital property includes the taxpayer's principal residence, personal use property, listed personal property, and investment and fixed assets in a business.

Capital Gain (or Loss) The difference between the current market value of an asset and the original cost of the asset, with the cost adjusted for any improvement or depreciation in the asset.

Adjusted Cost Base (ACB)
For an asset purchased outright, the (initial) ACB is equal to the actual cost of the asset plus any costs or commissions incurred in making the acquisition.

the value received and the asset's **adjusted cost base** (**ACB**). For an asset purchased outright, the (initial) ACB is equal to the actual cost of the asset plus any costs or commissions incurred in making the acquisition. Any costs associated with the disposal of the asset simply reduce the size of the capital gain. The treatment of assets received as a gift or inheritance is described below.

While an asset is held, improvements may be made and their costs added to the ACB. On the other hand, any return of capital must be deducted from the ACB, as must depreciation. The accounting required can become complicated. When identical properties such as common shares are purchased at different times and at different prices, these must be pooled in order to determine the ACB. For example, if an investor buys 100 shares at $40 each, then buys another 100 at $50, and later sells 100 shares at $60, what is the realized capital gain? As an adequate identification of the lots is not possible, the ACB used is the average acquisition cost of the shares—$45—and the gain is $15 per share.

The ability to control the realization of capital gains and losses has obvious advantages. Most important, tax can be paid at the most opportune time. The clearest case involves the realization of capital gains around the time of retirement. Shortly before retirement is usually a time when the taxpayer's income is relatively high, which in turn means that the taxpayer's marginal tax rate is relatively high. After retirement the taxpayer's income and, in turn, marginal tax rate are usually substantially lower. Accordingly, it is generally advantageous for the taxpayer who is near retirement to wait until after retirement to realize any capital gains.

Tax Treatment of Capital Gains and Losses

The tax treatment on disposal of each of the four types of assets included in capital property will be discussed next.

The taxpayer's family home or *principal residence* is not subject to capital gains tax during the owner's lifetime. Unmarried individuals may own a family home that is tax exempt, but married couples are entitled to only one principal residence per family unit. A vacation home (unless it is the only property the family owns) is, therefore, not exempted from capital gains tax and is treated as *personal use property*.

This is any asset that is primarily for the personal use or enjoyment of the taxpayer and would not normally be considered an investment asset. If the ACB of personal use property is less than $1000 then, for tax purposes, it is deemed to be $1000. If the selling price of the asset is less than $1000 then no tax is payable. If, on the other hand, the selling price exceeds $1000 then three-quarters of the difference between that price and the ACB must be included in taxable income. Losses may not be claimed on the disposal of personal use property.

The third category, *listed personal property* consists predominantly of collectibles (works of art, rare books, jewelry, etc.). Capital gains realized on the disposal of listed personal property are treated in the same manner as gains on investment assets. Capital losses may only be used to offset gains realized from the sale of other listed personal property.

The final category is *investment and fixed assets in a non-incorporated business*.

All capital gains and losses are brought together to obtain a net capital gain or net capital loss figure. If there are net gains, three-quarters of these are included in taxable income whereas three-quarters of net losses (referred to as allowable capital losses) may be used to reduce capital gains in the three immediately preceeding years.[6] As a net result, capital gains are taxed at a preferential rate. In the case of an investor in the maximum marginal tax bracket of 50.29%, the capital gains are taxed at an effective rate of 37.72%. Capital losses may be used to offset capital gains.

---

[6]If any allowable losses are left after extinguishing all prior capital gains then the residue may be carried forward indefinitely.

Reporting on Capital or Income Account

The gain or loss on the disposition of an investment asset can be taxed either as a gain or loss of income, or as a capital gain or loss at the taxpayer's option. In other words, the taxpayer must choose whether any gains or losses incurred will receive "income or capital treatment." Once the decision has been made, all current and subsequent gains and losses must receive the treatment selected. Certain taxpayers (security dealers, professional traders, and financial institutions) can only report on their income account. The regulations further specify that certain security transactions *must* receive income treatment regardless of the taxpayer's election. Most of these are specialized transactions; however, two of them are noteworthy:

1. The appreciation of a fixed-income security issued at a significant discount (for example, a 91-day Treasury bill) is considered to be income, since it is more akin to interest than to a capital gain.
2. The gain or loss on the short sale of a security is considered to be income.

If Revenue Canada rules that a taxpayer's actions are such that she could be considered to be "in the business" of trading securities then all transactions must be reported on the income account. Table 12.7 shows a list of some of the factors that Revenue Canada considers in determining whether or not a taxpayer should be deemed to be carrying on such a business.

Investors who undertake frequent transactions or who regularly trade in "exotic" securities should recognize that the proceeds of their trading activities may receive income treatment.

Deductible Expenses

Certain interest payments may be deducted from an individual's income to determine taxable income. As a general rule, interest paid on funds borrowed in order to earn business or investment income is tax deductible. This deduction significantly lowers the effective cost of financing an investment by borrowing. To qualify for this deduction, the investment does not have to be profitable, but it must have a reasonable expectation of generating a profit. Borrowing money at 6% in order to buy Canada Savings Bonds paying 4% has no

---

Table 12.7 Factors Used by Revenue Canada to Determine a Taxpayer's Status.

(a) Frequency of transactions—a history of extensive buying and selling of securities or of a quick turnover of properties.

(b) Period of ownership—securities are usually owned only for a short period of time.

(c) Knowledge of securities markets—the taxpayer has some knowledge or experience in the securities market.

(d) Security transactions form a part of a taxpayer's ordinary business.

(e) Time spent—a substantial part of a taxpayer's time is spent studying the securities markets and investigating potential purchases.

(f) Financing—security purchases are financed primarily on margin or by some other form of debt.

(g) Advertising—the taxpayer has advertised or otherwise made it known that he is willing to purchase securities.

(h) Shares owned are normally speculative in nature or of a non-dividend type.

SOURCE: Revenue Canada, *Interpretation Bulletin IT-479R, Transactions in Securities* (Ottawa, February 24, 1984, revised February 21, 1985).

reasonable expectation of producing a profit and, therefore, a portion of the interest payment will be disallowed as a deduction. Other expenses associated with investing may be deducted from income if they are ordinary and necessary, and in line with reasonable expectations of a profitable return. Thus, fees paid for investment advice or safekeeping of securities (e.g., a safety deposit box) may be deducted.

Investments that habitually produce financial losses but non-financial pleasure may be considered hobbies by Revenue Canada and may, therefore, not qualify for some or all of the associated deductions. This possibility should concern the racehorse owner, for example, but not the serious investor.

Alternative Minimum Tax

There has long been a suspicion that certain wealthy individuals are able to use tax shelters and other legitimate deductions to pay out only a small fraction of their income in taxes. An *Alternative Minimum Tax* (AMT) has, therefore, been introduced. The calculation of AMT is complicated. As a rule of thumb, a taxpayer may be liable for the AMT if the following condition holds:

$$\text{Tax Payable} < 0.17 \times (\text{Total Income} - \$40\ 000)$$

One tax advisor has put forward the following advice for those in the top tax bracket: One, if you are pleased with the small amount of tax that you calculate this year, you may have an AMT problem. Two, if you think you may be subject to the AMT, then get professional advice.[7]

Tax Reduction Techniques

Tax avoidance is a legitimate activity, whereas tax evasion is illegal. Legal procedures for reducing immediate taxes fall into the following classifications: tax deferrals and tax shelters. As the name implies, the former are methods for delaying the payment of taxes to a time when the taxpayer expects to face a lower marginal tax rate. The latter, on the other hand, purportedly provide methods totally shielding income from taxation.

Tax Deferrals

The two principally used forms of tax deferral will be described here.

The best known and most popular tax deferral technique in Canada is the **Registered Retirement Savings Plan** (RRSP). In any year, taxpayers are permitted to contribute a specified fraction (18% in 1998) of *earned income* (to a specified maximum, $13 500 in 1998) to an RRSP established at a financial institution and to deduct the amount from that year's taxable income.[8] Furthermore, the investment returns can accumulate within the plan tax-free. Withdrawals from the plan are permitted at any time, but the amount withdrawn must be added to that year's taxable income.

Full withdrawal or conversion of an RRSP, usually on retirement, must occur by the end of the year in which the owner turns 69 years of age. Full withdrawal means that the RRSP account is deregistered and the full value is added to the owner's taxable income in that year. For all practical purposes this means that tax must be paid at the owner's maximum marginal rate on all the funds in the account. Alternatively the owner has two conversions options. First, the retiree may remove the full amount from the RRSP and

Registered Retirement Savings Plan (RRSP) A tax deferral arrangement that allows investors to deduct from income any contributions to a registered plan account. In addition, investment returns accumulate within the account free of tax. Taxable withdrawals must start no later than the year following that in which the investor reaches age 69.

---

[7]Richard Birch, *The Canadian Price Waterhouse Personal Tax Advisor, 1990* (Toronto: McClelland-Bantam, Inc.), 1989.

[8]Earned income is defined to include employment income, business income, rental income, and some others. The upper contribution limit is expected to remain unchanged until the year 2003. The upper limit is less for taxpayers whose employer provides a pension plan. This reduction is consistent with the stated objectives of an RRSP, which is to provide retirement income.

purchase an *annuity* that pays the proceeds out over a number of years. Only the annual annuity payment need be included in taxable income. This procedure significantly reduces the overall tax burden on retirement.

Second, the retiree can convert the account into a Registered Retirement Income Fund (RRIF). The funds in an RRIF can be invested in a wide range of securities of the owner's choice, thereby giving her a large measure of control over the management of these funds. The only stipulation is that a specified percentage of the value of the fund must be withdrawn each year and added to the individual's taxable income. The investment returns continue to accumulate within the plan free of tax, the withdrawals represent the only tax liability incurred. This option also effectively reduces the overall tax burden after retirement. Not surprisingly, the conversion options are much more popular than full withdrawal.

On the death of the owner of either an RRSP or a RRIF the account passes to the individual's beneficiary. If the beneficiary is the surviving spouse the transfer is made free of tax. If anyone else is the beneficiary then the account is deregistered and the full tax liability is paid as part of the deceased's final income tax return.

An RRSP is a vehicle for accumulating investment returns at a before-tax rate. Suppose that an individual, in the highest tax bracket of 50.29%, wishes to put aside $1200 per year for the next 30 years in an investment that will earn 6% per year. In the absence of an RRSP the investment returns will be taxed each year so that the effective rate of interest will be 2.9826%. At the end of 30 years the individual will have $61 744 on which no further tax is payable. By utilizing an RRSP, the individual can contribute $2372.48 each year to the plan and maintain the same annual disposable income. After 30 years the amount in the plan is $187 564. In the worst case scenario, if this is withdrawn as a lump sum and full tax paid, the net receipt is $94 870, a gain of almost 54%. It is not surprising, therefore, that many Canadians have established RRSPs.

A similar device is a *Deferred Profit Sharing Plan*. This is essentially the same as an RRSP except that the employer makes the contributions directly into the employee's plan. The upper contribution limit in 1998 was $6750. The employer's contribution reduces the amount that the employee can contribute to an RRSP.

Tax Shelters

Income splitting between spouses is an effective way to shelter a portion of investment income and thereby reduce the family's aggregate tax payments. The idea is simple and consists of transferring ownership of income-producing assets from the higher tax bracket family member to the lower tax bracket member or members. Revenue Canada has, however, established a number of rules which must be observed if the income is not to be attributed back to the original owner, thereby negating the purpose of the exercise. It pays to read the regulations carefully if income splitting is contemplated. One relatively straightforward way to split income is to establish a **spousal RRSP**. The higher tax bracket family member makes the contributions to the plan in the normal way, but ownership of the plan is vested in the lower tax bracket family member. If, however, a withdrawal is made in the following two calendar years, then the amount withdrawn is attributed back to the higher income spouse. The benefits of such a plan will be evident at retirement, providing that the plan owner is then in a lower tax bracket than the contributor.

Other tax shelters are also available. Many advertisements exhort high tax bracket investors to put their money in frontier oil and gas exploration, multiple unit real estate, films and videos produced in Canada, and other investments with purportedly attractive tax characteristics. Such "tax shelters" are devised to take advantage of tax provisions allowing large deductions to create a "tax loss" in the present, to be followed by a subsequent profit, generally in the form of a capital gain. The higher the taxpayer's marginal tax rate, the more attractive these investments become.

Spousal RRSP A spousal registered retirement savings plan allows the higher tax bracket family member to contribute to the plan, but ownership of the plan is vested in the lower tax bracket family member.

Therefore, only those in the highest brackets should find such investments interesting. These enterprises are generally formed as limited partnerships. A promoter, or general partner, puts together the operation, with individual investors as limited partners. The hoped-for results are tidy profits for the promoter and the investors, at the expense of the tax collector.

◗ Estate and Gift Taxes

As of September 1998, there are neither explicit federal nor provincial estate or gift taxes in Canada. Some gifts and estate bequests are taxed as capital gains and losses.

A gift of cash or securities to a spouse incurs no tax liability at the time of transfer; the recipient assumes the asset at the donor's ACB. If the spouse disposes of the asset while the donor is still alive then any capital gain or loss must be reported by the donor in the year of its disposal. For example, in 1987 an investor purchases 500 shares at a price of $6.25 per share plus commissions of $0.25 per share making a total ACB of $6.50 per share. In 1991, she makes a gift of these shares, currently priced at $12.00 per share, to her husband. In 1996, he sells the shares at $15.00 per share, realizing a capital gain of $500 \times (15 - 6.5) = \$4250$ that his wife must report in her 1996 tax return. If instead he waits until 1998 (after his wife's demise) to sell the shares for $15.00 per share then he must report the capital gain of $4250.

Gifts to other people, including children, are deemed to have taken place at the fair market value at the time of transfer. The donor, therefore, must report, in the year in which the gift is made, the difference between the fair market value and the ACB, and the recipient must use the fair market value as his ACB. If, in the example above, the investor had given the shares to her daughter instead of to her husband she would report an immediate capital gain of $500 \times (12 - 6.5) = \$2750$ in 1991 and the daughter would report a capital gain of $500 \times (15 - 12) = \$1500$ in the year in which she sells them for $15.00.

When a taxpayer dies, he is deemed to have sold all assets immediately prior to death. A capital gains tax liability will exist against the estate except in the case of assets willed to the spouse, which carry the original ACB and, therefore, attract no immediate tax.

The estate must file an income tax return for a deceased taxpayer. This will be a terminal settlement of all unpaid taxes.

Inflation in Canada

The story is told of the modern-day Rip Van Winkle, who awoke in the year 2050 and immediately called his broker. (Fortunately, pay phones at the time permitted a call of up to three minutes without charge.) He first asked what had happened to the $10 000 he had instructed the broker to put in short-term Treasury bills, continually reinvesting the proceeds. The broker promptly informed him that due to high interest rates and the power of compounding, his initial $10 000 investment had grown to be worth over $1 million. Stunned, Mr. Van Winkle inquired about his stocks, which were also worth about $10 000 when he dozed off. The broker told him that he was in for an even more pleasant surprise: they were now worth $2.5 million. "In short, Mr. Van Winkle," said the broker, "you are a millionaire 3.5 times over."

Inflation The rate of change in a price index over a certain period of time. Equivalently, the percentage change in the purchasing power of a unit of currency over a certain period of time.

At this point an operator cut in: "Your three minutes are over, please deposit $100 for an additional three minutes." While this clearly overstates the case, there is no doubt that **inflation** is a major concern for investors. By and large, people have come to fear significant inflation, particularly when it is unpredictable.

This section begins by describing how inflation is typically measured. Then the benefits and costs of inflation are discussed, along with who gains and who loses when it is present.

Taxing Pension Funds and RRSPs

The battle over reducing the federal budget deficit continues unabated. Two of the last unexploited sources of significant tax revenue are private pension plans and RRSPs. Virtually all such pension plans conform to specific government regulations and as a result offer their sponsors and participants several important tax advantages:

1. Employers may treat pension fund contributions as tax-deductible expenses.
2. Employees defer paying taxes on contributions that their employers make to the pension funds on their behalf.
3. Pension fund investment earnings are not taxed until they are withdrawn.

Under present laws, employers (and in some cases employees) make tax-deductible contributions to a pension plan to prefund pension benefits that are to be paid upon employees' subsequent retirements. These employer contributions clearly represent a form of income to employees. After all, employers could just as easily increase the employees' paycheques by the amount of the contributions and let the employees invest those dollars for themselves. Moreover, this income is invested and grows untaxed over the employees' working lives. Eventually, the employees pay taxes on their invested pension contributions, but not until they receive their pension benefits during their retirement years. Private individuals derive similar benefits from their RRSP contributions.

Proponents of taxing pension plans contend that the costs of exempting pension plans from taxation far exceed the benefits. Their primary argument is that pension funds do not increase national savings significantly. This contention may seem counterintuitive at first. Pension fund taxation proponents believe that employees save less outside of their pension funds because of the savings that accumulate inside the pension funds. That is, pension savings offset other personal savings. Proponents estimate that this offset, while not dollar-for-dollar, effectively reduces net savings from pension plans to about the same amount that Revenue Canada forgoes in lost tax revenues each year.

Taxation proponents also contend that exempting pension funds from taxation violates fundamental tax fairness principles. Not all of the Canadian working population is covered by pension plans. Moreover, those persons covered tend to be in the higher income categories. Further, as these higher income persons are subject to higher marginal tax rates, the benefit of tax-exempt pension funds is greatest for them. (The existence of RRSPs, however, weakens this argument as an employee not covered by a pension plan can design a "homemade" pension plan within an RRSP.)

Most proposals to tax pension funds involve levying a tax on each pension plan expressed as a percentage of the plan's annual contributions and investment earnings. Benefits would then not be subject to tax. As a transition to the tax scheme, a one-time tax on the plans' assets would be charged, thus taxing employees who have already accrued benefits tax-free.

Opponents of taxing pension funds take issue with the crowding-out theory of taxation proponents. That theory is difficult to substantiate empirically, and the crowding-out effect may be much less than proponents contend.

They go on to argue that, as savings ultimately have a multiplier effect on national income, accepting a $1 revenue loss for $1 of additional savings may be a sound long-term trade-off.

As for the equity issue, taxation opponents point out that higher income persons in all economies always provide the bulk of the economies' savings. It may be unrealistic and counterproductive to add to the existing disincentives to save in the name of wealth equity.

Opponents also point to the technical difficulties of taxing pension plans. A large fraction of pension assets are held by provincial and local pension plans. The employers get no tax benefit from contributions, while taxing the employees would be politically tricky.

Taxation of pension funds, if and when it ever occurs, may not take the form of radical legislation. Rather, it may begin with seemingly innocuous dips into pension fund coffers, such as taxes on pension fund holdings of foreign securities above a certain threshold, or taxes on pension funds' security transactions as well as on their capital gains.

Measuring Inflation

There is no completely satisfactory way to summarize the price changes that have occurred over a given time period for the large number of goods and services available in Canada. Nevertheless, Statistics Canada has attempted to do so by measuring the cost of a specific mix of major items (a "basket of goods") at various points in time. The "overall" price level computed for this representative combination of items is termed a **cost-of-living index**. The percentage change in this index over a given time period can then be viewed as a measure of the inflation (or deflation) that took place from the beginning of the period to the end of the period.

Whether or not this measure of inflation is relevant for a given individual depends to a major extent on the similarity of his or her purchases to the mix of items used to construct the index. Even if an individual finds the mix to be appropriate at the beginning of a period, the rate of increase in the mix over the time period is likely to overstate the increase in the cost of living for the individual. There are two reasons for this. First, improvements in the quality of the items in the mix are seldom taken adequately into account. This means the end-of-period price for a good is not comparable to the beginning-of-period price, since the good is different. For example, a new Toyota may have a 5% higher sticker price than a similar model had the previous year, but the newer model may have better tires on it than the older model. Hence, it would be inaccurate to conclude that the price of this particular model rose by 5% over the year.

Second, and perhaps more important, little or no adjustment is made in the mix as relative prices change. The rational customer can reduce the cost of attaining a given standard of living as prices change by substituting relatively less expensive goods for those that have become relatively more expensive. For example, if the price of beef rises 20% over a given year while the price of chicken rises only 10% over the same year, then the customer may start to eat more chicken and less beef. Failure to take into account this change in the mix will result in an overstatement in the rate of inflation. Despite these two drawbacks, cost-of-living indices provide at least rough estimates of changes in prices.[9]

Price Indices

Most governments compute a number of alternative indices to provide a wider choice for analysis. Nevertheless, many people tend to focus on one index as an indicator of the price level. In Canada, the **Consumer Price Index** (CPI) often fills this role, despite attempts to discourage its widespread use.[10] Recognizing its importance, Statistics Canada has changed the composition of the market basket of goods used to make up the CPI from time to time in order to provide a more representative index. Furthermore, the process by which the relevant data are gathered and verified has periodically been improved

In Chapter 1, Table 1.1 provided some historical perspective on the rate of inflation in Canada. It showed the annual rate of increase in the CPI from 1950 through 1997. As an aid to interpretation, these rates are plotted on a graph, shown in Figure 12.2(a). As can be seen in the figure, the CPI did not grow at a constant rate over the period of 1950 to 1997. However, prices increased in almost every year. Generally speaking, there were

[9]In 1997, a commission in the US headed by former White House chief economist Barry Boskin examined the accuracy of the Consumer Price Index (CPI) in measuring inflation. The Boskin commission estimated that the CPI overstates inflation by roughly 1%–1.5% per year. This conclusion generated considerable controversy. How it will affect public policy remains to be seen. For a summary of the report, see Michael J. Boskin, "Prisoner of Faulty Statistics," *The Wall Street Journal*, December 5, 1996, p. A20. See also the entire issue of the May–June 1997 *Federal Reserve Bank of St. Louis Review*, which is devoted to discussing the Boskin report and its implications.

[10]A number of authorities prefer "deflators" derived from gross domestic product figures, but such indices have not received the publicity accorded the CPI.

Cost-of-Living Index A collection of goods and services, and their associated prices, designed to reflect changes over time in the cost of making normal consumption expenditures.

Consumer Price Index A cost-of-living index which is representative of the goods and services purchased by Canadian consumers.

Statistics Canada
www.statcan.ca

Figure 12.2 Inflation, nominal, and real returns on short–term default-free investments, 12-month periods ending December 1950–December 1997.

(a) Changes in the Consumer Price Index, 1950–1997

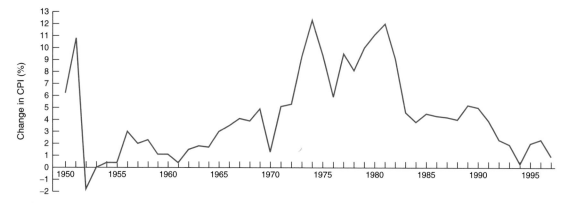

(b) Nominal Returns on Canadian T-bills, 1950–1997

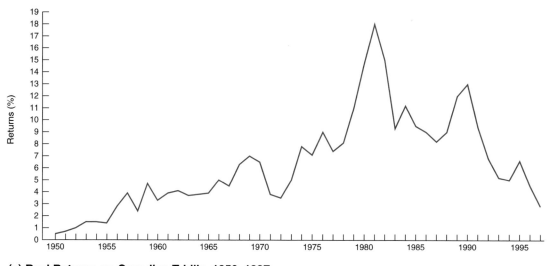

(c) Real Returns on Canadian T-bills, 1950–1997

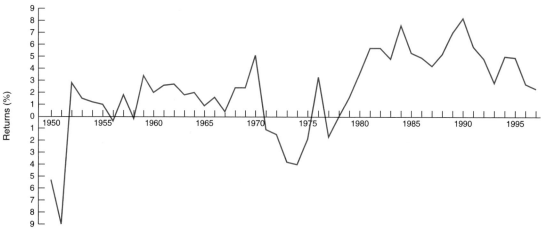

SOURCE: See Table 1.1

| Table 12.8 | Growth Rates of the Canadian Consumer Price Index. | |
From	To	Rate of Growth (% Per Year)
1950	1951	8.4
1952	1965	1.3
1966	1982	7.3
1983	1991	4.3
1992	1997	1.5

four subperiods with different rates of inflation: high inflation in 1950 and 1951, mild inflation from 1952 to 1965, high (but uneven) inflation from 1966 to 1982, followed by moderate inflation from 1983 to 1991 and low inflation from 1992 to 1997. Interestingly, the recent moderation in Canadian inflation has occurred almost simultaneously in many other countries as well, leading some observers to contend (perhaps erroneously) that inflation is no longer a serious macroeconomic problem.

Geometric Mean Return The compounded per-period average rate of return on a financial asset over a specified time interval.

Table 12.8 shows the average annual rate of growth of the CPI for each of these subperiods, measured by what is known as the **geometric mean** growth rate of the CPI. This growth rate, when compounded over the subperiod and applied to the beginning index value, results in the ending index value. For example, at the end of 1977, the CPI was 53.3, and at the end of 1991, it was at 126.4 (the CPI was adjusted so that its average monthly value in 1986 was 100). Thus, the geometric mean growth rate was 6.36%, since 53.3, when compounded at this rate over 14 years, equals 126.4:

$$126.4 = 53.3 \times (1 + .0636)^{14}$$

More generally, the geometric mean (g) can be calculated by solving the following equation for g:

$$C_e = C_b(1 + g)^y \tag{12.2}$$

which results in

$$g = \left(\frac{C_e}{C_b} \right)^{1/y} - 1 \tag{12.3}$$

where y denotes the number of years and C_e and C_b denote the ending and beginning CPI values, respectively.

Nominal and Real Returns

Nominal Returns

Modern economies gain much of their efficiency through the use of money—a generally agreed-upon medium of exchange. Instead of trading corn for a stereo to be delivered in one year, as in a barter economy, the citizen of a modern economy can trade her corn for money and then trade this "current" money for "future" money by investing it. Later, the "future" money can be used to buy a stereo. The rate at which the citizen can trade current money for future money depends on the investment she makes and is known as the **nominal return** (also known as the nominal rate).

Nominal Return The percentage change in the value of an investment in a financial asset, where the beginning and ending values of the asset are not adjusted for inflation over the time of the investment.

Fisher Model of Real Returns

Real Return The percentage change in the value of an investment in a financial asset, where the beginning and ending values of the asset are adjusted for inflation over the time of the investment.

In times of changing prices, the nominal return on an investment may be a poor indicator of the **real return** (also known as the real rate) obtained by the investor.[11] This is because part of the additional dollars received from the investment may be needed to recoup the citizen's lost purchasing power due to inflation that has occurred over the investment period. As a result, the nominal return needs to be adjusted to remove the effect of inflation in order to determine the real return. Frequently, the CPI is used for this purpose.

For example, assume that at the start of a given year the CPI is at a level of 121 and that at the end of the year it is at a level of 124. This means that it costs $124 at the end of the year to buy the same amount of the CPI market basket of goods that at the start of the year could have been purchased for $121. Assuming the nominal return is 8% for this year, the individual who started the year with $121 and invested it would have $121 × 1.08 = $130.68 at year-end. At this point, the individual could purchase ($130.68/$124) − 1 = .0539 = 5.39% more of the CPI market basket of goods than at the beginning of the year. Thus, the real return for this investment was 5.39%, after allowing for inflation.

These calculations can be summarized in the following formula:

$$\left(C_0 \times \frac{1 + NR}{C_1} \right) - 1 = RR \tag{12.4}$$

where:

C_0 = CPI at the beginning of the year
C_1 = CPI at the end of the year
NR = the nominal return
RR = the real return

Alternatively, the individual could note that an increase in the CPI from 121 to 124 can be translated into an inflation rate of (124/121) − 1 = .0248, or 2.48%. Denoting this inflation rate as CCL (Change in the Cost of Living) the real return can be calculated using the following formula, known as the Fisher model.

$$\left(\frac{1 + NR}{1 + CCL} \right) - 1 = RR \tag{12.5}$$

Note that for the example, RR = (1.08/1.0248) − 1 = .0539, or 5.39%.

For a quick calculation involving the Fisher model,[12] the real return can be estimated by simply subtracting the inflation rate from the nominal return:

$$NR - i \cong RR \tag{12.6}$$

where $\cong$ means "is approximately equal to." In this example, the quick method results in an estimate of the real return of .08 − .0248 = .0552, or 5.52%. Thus, the error resulting from use of this method is .0552 − .0539 = .0013, or .13%.[13]

---

[11]Here, real return refers to the increase in purchasing power that the citizen has received as a result of making a particular investment.

[12]The Fisher model is named after its creator, Irving Fisher, who derived the model in *The Theory of Interest* (New York: Macmillan, 1930).

[13]This error will be larger for higher rates of inflation. Thus, in those countries with "hyperinflation," the quick method will have a substantial amount of error associated with it. For example, if the nominal return is 110% and the inflation rate is 100%, then the true real return is 5%, but the quick method will indicate it is twice as large, 10%.

The Effect of Investor Expectations

The simplest view of investors' attitudes towards inflation is that they are concerned with real returns, not nominal returns, and that a single price index is adequate to characterize the difference. Looking to the future, investors do not know what the rate of inflation will be, nor do they know what the nominal return on an investment will be. However, in both cases they have expectations, which are denoted as $E(CCL)$ (expected inflation rate) and $E(NR)$ (expected nominal return), respectively. Thus, the expected real return on an investment can be approximated by

$$E(RR) \cong E(NR) - E(CCL) \tag{12.7}$$

If a security is to provide a given expected real return, the expected nominal return must be larger by the expected rate of inflation for the relevant holding period. This can be seen by rearranging equation (12.7):

$$E(NR) \cong E(RR) + E(CCL) \tag{12.8}$$

For example, if the expected rate of inflation is 4% and a given security is to provide investors with an expected real return of 6%, then the security must be priced in the marketplace so that its expected nominal return is 10%. Furthermore, if the expected real rate remains constant, then a 1% increase in the expected rate of inflation from 4% to 5% will result in a 1% increase in the nominal rate of return from 10% to 11%. In summary, if investors are concerned with real returns, all securities will be priced by the actions of the marketplace so that expected nominal returns incorporate the expected rate of inflation.[14]

Interest Rates and Inflation

At the start of a given investment holding period, nominal interest rates for securities having no risk of default should cover both a requisite expected real return and the expected rate of inflation for the period in question. At the end of the period, the real return actually received will be the difference between the nominal return and the rate of inflation actually experienced. Only when actual inflation equals expected inflation will the actual real return equal the expected real return on such securities.

As mentioned earlier, Figure 12.2(a) indicates the annual rate of inflation, as measured by changes in the CPI, over the 48-year period 1950–1997. Part (b) shows how short-term nominal interest rates varied over this time period; Treasury bill rates, taken from Table 1.1, are used for this purpose. Part (c), obtained by using equation (12.5), represents real returns.

One cannot help being struck by the fact that those who invested in short-term securities over this period frequently ended up with less purchasing power than they started with, since the real return was negative in 11 of the 48 years. Perhaps even more surprising, the average real return over the period 1950 to 1979 was close to zero.

Although expected real returns may vary from year to year, the variation is relatively small. Otherwise investors would not be willing to invest in short-term, highly liquid securities even though they expected to earn close to nothing in real terms. If they are currently willing to do so, such securities will be priced to give a very low expected real return.[15]

---

[14]The model given in equation (12.8) can be written more precisely as $E(NR) = E(RR) + E(CCL) + IRP$ where IRP denotes inflation risk premium. This is because investors will demand to be compensated for not only the expected inflation rate but also for the risk they bear in that the inflation rate is uncertain, that is, inflation risk. Thus, if the expected rate of inflation is 4% and a given security is to provide investors with an expected real return of 6% then the security must be priced in the marketplace so that its expectged nominal return is more than 10% such as 10.5% if the inflation risk premium is 5%. Similar adjustments can also be made to equations (12.4) through (12.6) by replacing RR with $RR + IRP$.

[15]However, there apparently are periods of time when such securities have an expected real return that is positive. For example, in the 1980–1987 period, Treasury bill returns actually exceeded the rate of change in the CPI by over 5%. This suggests that investors probably expected a positive real return over the latter part of the period.

If this assumption is made, the "market's" predicted rate of inflation over the near future can be estimated by simply subtracting the estimated expected real rate, say 1%, from the nominal interest rate (also known as the yield) on short-term government securities, namely, Treasury bills. In a sense, this Treasury bill rate represents a consensus prediction of inflation—a prediction that an average investor in this market would make and one that is likely to be more accurate than the predictions of any single forecaster.

The Effect of Inflation on Borrowers and Lenders

Although deviations of actual inflation from expected inflation may have relatively little effect on the real return on investments in general, they may have a significant effect on specific investments. In fact, one would expect a direct effect on the real returns associated with investments whose payments are fixed in terms of dollars to be received.

A simple example will illustrate the relationship. Assume that everyone currently expects the rate of inflation to be 5% over the next year and that a lender has agreed to make loans at a nominal rate of 5% (that is, the lender is content with having an expected real return of zero). Thus, one can borrow $100 now and, one year later, pay back $100 \times 1.05 = $105 for a one-year loan. That is, if actual inflation equals expected inflation, a one-year loan would require a payment equivalent to $100 in constant (current) dollars a year hence. In this case, the real rate of interest would turn out to be zero.

Now, imagine that an individual takes advantage of the lender's offer, borrowing $100 for one year. How will the borrower and lender be affected if the actual rate of inflation differs from the expected rate of inflation?

Assume that in the first year, prices rise by 9% instead of the expected 5%, meaning that unexpected inflation is 9% − 5% = 4%. In this situation, the short-term borrower gains at the expense of the lender because the borrower still must repay $105, but this is only $105/1.09 = $96.33 in constant-dollar terms, less than the amount of the loan. As a result, the lender receives a real rate of interest of ($96.33 − $100)/$100 = −3.67%, instead of the anticipated rate of 0%.

What if first-year prices had risen by only 3%, meaning that unexpected inflation is −2% = 3% − 5%? In this situation, the short-term lender gains at the expense of the borrower. Although the borrower must repay $105, in constant-dollar terms this amounts to $105/1.03 = $101.94, greater than the amount of the loan. As a result, the lender receives a real rate of interest of ($101.94 − $100)/$100 = 1.94% instead of the anticipated rate of 0%.

These results can be generalized: when the actual rate of inflation exceeds the expected rate of inflation, those with commitments to make payments that are fixed in nominal terms (debtors) gain in real terms at the expense of those to whom payments are to be made (creditors). Conversely, when actual inflation is less than expected inflation, creditors gain and debtors lose.[16] This uncertainty in the real return on fixed-income securities that is due to uncertain inflation is frequently referred to as **purchasing-power risk**.

Purchasing-power Risk
The risk experienced by investors in financial assets due to uncertainty concerning the impact of inflation on the real returns produced by those financial assets.

Indexation

The previous section suggests that in a world of uncertain inflation, even default-free bonds are subject to purchasing-power risk. Contractual nominal interest rates can cover expected inflation, but the subsequent real return from any investment with fixed nominal payments

---

[16]More specifically, it can be shown that long-term borrowers are likely to gain somewhat more than short-term borrowers when actual inflation exceeds expected inflation and lose somewhat more when actual inflation falls below expectations. Similarly, long-term lenders are likely to lose somewhat more than short-term lenders when actual inflation exceeds expectations and gain somewhat more when actual inflation falls below expectations.

will depend on the actual amount of inflation. As long as the two differ, the expected real return will be uncertain. However, there is a way to design a bond so that its expected real return is certain. This involves the use of **indexation**.

Government Bonds

If a specified price index can adequately measure purchasing power, there is no reason why a contract cannot be written with specified real payments instead of specified nominal payments. Thus, if the CPI currently stands at C_0 and will be C_1 one year later, C_2 two years later, and so on, in return for a 10-year loan of $100 a borrower might promise to pay $\$4 \times C_1 C_0$ one year later, $\$4 \times C_2 C_0$ two years later, ..., and $\$104 \times C_{10} C_0$ ten years later. The values C_1/C_0, C_2/C_0, ..., C_{10}/C_0, are known as *index ratios*, and represent the quantity of 1 + the rate of inflation from the time that the bond was issued (time 0) to the time a given payment is to be made. To convert these payments to constant (or real) dollars, each one must be divided by the corresponding quantity of 1 + the rate of inflation since the bond was issued, which is equivalent to C_t/C_0 for a payment at time t.

Time	Amount in Nominal Dollars	Price Level (CPI)	Amount in Real Dollars
1	$4 \times C_1/C_0$	C_1	4
2	$4 \times C_2/C_0$	C_2	4
*	*	*	*
*	*	*	*
*	*	*	*
10	$104 \times C_{10}/C_0$	C_{10}	104

The real value of each payment is the amount shown in the final column, regardless of what happens to prices (that is, regardless of the actual values of C_1, C_2, and so on). Thus, the loan is said to be fully indexed, since all amounts are tied to a stated price index on a one-for-one basis. This means that when the price index goes up by 10%, for example, all the subsequent payments go up by 10%. Thus, any investor who buys this bond at issuance at $100 and holds it to maturity will receive an annual *real* return of 4%. In December 1991, the Canadian government introduced its first indexed bonds, known as Real Return Bonds. They are described in some detail in the next chapter.

Indexing Other Contracts

In some countries, a great many contracts are tied to standard price indices (two notable examples are Israel and Brazil). Government bonds, returns on savings accounts, wage contracts, pension plans, insurance contracts—all have been indexed at various times and places. In Canada, Canada Pension Plan benefits are indexed, as are the pension plans of civil servants, MPs, and some employees. Some of these are fully indexed, while others are only partially indexed, meaning that payments might be increased by, for example, 75% of the price index increases. Table 12.9 indicates the experience of six countries with similar securities. Note that Israel has made the greatest use of such securities, which is not surprising given its history of relatively high inflation.

The key advantage of indexation is its role in reducing or eliminating purchasing power risk. Typically, higher expected inflation is accompanied by increased uncertainty about the actual rate of inflation. This increased uncertainty means that the potential gains and losses to both non-indexed borrowers and non-indexed lenders are larger. Since both borrowers and lenders dislike the prospect of losses more than they like the prospect of gains, there will be increased pressure for indexation by both borrowers and lenders when a country moves into periods of high inflationary expectations.

The Taxation of Investment Returns

Economists agree that taxing any commodity or activity reduces the output of that commodity or activity. Taxing gains on capital assets, therefore, reduces the amount of capital assets "produced." Other things remaining the same (always a tenuous assumption), lower tax rates will encourage saving, increase investment, and thus enhance economic productivity. However, as the vast proportion of taxable capital assets is directly or indirectly held by a minority of relatively affluent people, proponents of wealth redistribution view capital gains taxes as symbolic of their effort to create a more egalitarian society.

Certain general features of the Canadian tax system lead to movements of wealth from the private sector to the federal government that increase with the rate of inflation. Thus, one of the potential beneficiaries of inflation is the federal government.

Consider a one-year security with an expected real pre-tax return of 7% that is held by someone in a 30% marginal tax bracket. In the absence of inflation, the investor would expect to receive a real return of $(1 - .3) \times 7\% = 4.9\%$. Now, assume that the expected rate of inflation is 2%, so that the expected pre-tax nominal return on the security is $(1.07 \times 1.02) - 1 = 9.14\%$. In this case, the investor's expected after-tax nominal return is $(1 - .3) \times 9.14\% = 6.40\%$, but in real terms this is $(1.0640/1.02) - 1 = 4.31\%$. Similarly, if expected inflation is 4%, then the expected pre-tax nominal return will be 11.28%, the investor's expected after-tax nominal return will be 7.90%, and his or her expected after-tax real return will be 3.75%.

Since it is reasonable to assume that, over time, actual inflation rates will approximately equal expected inflation rates, it can be seen that the higher the actual inflation rate, the lower the actual real after-tax return. In this example, the after-tax real return decreased from 4.9% with no inflation to 4.31% with 2% inflation and to 3.75% with 4% inflation. Thus, taxation of interest income can be viewed as being equivalent to an effective tax rate on real returns that increases with inflation; that is, the higher the inflation rate, the larger the portion of the real pre-tax return that is being allocated to the government. This phenomenon could be avoided by levying taxes on real returns instead of nominal returns.

The tax assessed on your capital, as distinguished from the tax imposed on the profits from your capital, is more akin to a property tax than an income tax. Moreover, the level of that tax changes with the inflation rate, producing an arbitrary and capricious tax structure. Over some holding periods, a capital asset's value may actually suffer a decline in real terms, yet inflation boosts its nominal value sufficiently to generate a gain for tax reporting purposes. An investor selling this asset could find himself paying capital gains taxes on an inflation-adjusted capital loss.

The solution to this inequity involves indexing the base value (that is, the original cost) of the capital asset to the inflation rate. The base value is adjusted upward by the inflation rate experienced over the period the capital asset is held. Only gains above this adjusted base are subject to tax.

Pension funds and RRSPs are big businesses that pay no taxes until the funds are withdrawn by the beneficiaries. In 1996 pension funds held assets worth $528.1 billion and individuals held $223.8 billion in their RRSPs. Allowing a quite conservative investment return of 8% and an average tax rate across beneficiaries of 45% this represents an immediate tax loss to Revenue Canada of $27 billion—more if the tax deductibility of contributions is also ended. This sum is enough to make an accumulated dent in the federal deficit. It must be conceded that taxes will ultimately be paid on these funds but that only occurs later and probably at a reduced tax rate.

The fairness and simplicity of adjusting capital gains taxes for inflation seems indisputable. Why has such a proposal not received popular support? Several explanations are plausible. First, in periods of relatively low inflation, such as we have seen since the early 1980s, the inflation-compensation component of capital gains is relatively small, making the issue less pressing. Second, in periods of large budget deficits, any cut in taxes, even in the name of equity and increased long-term investment, causes short-term problems. Current government spending would have to be reduced or other taxes increased if the budget deficit were not to grow in the short term due to the effective capital gains tax cut. Finally, if one accepts the argument for adjusting capital gains for inflation, should not the same logic apply to interest income as well? After all, this investment income has its own inflation-compensation component. However, the tax revenue lost from such a change in the taxation of interest income would far exceed the revenue losses caused by altering the capital gains tax structure.

Table 12.9 Inflation-Indexed Securities in Six Countries.

Year First Issued	Israel 1955	UK 1981	Sweden 1994	Australia 1985	Canada 1991	New Zealand 1995
Amount outstanding (in billions of US dollars)	$27.9	$71.1	$5.7	$2.7	$4.3	$ .1
Indexed debt as percent of country's total marketable debt	79.0%	17.8%	4.5%	3.8%	1.4%	.7%

SOURCE: Jeffrey M. Wrase, "Inflation-Indexed Bonds: How Do They Work?" *Federal Reserve Bank of Philadelphia Business Review* (July–August 1997), p. 7.

Thus, when uncertainty about inflation is substantial, one would expect indexation to become widespread. However, laws regulating interest rates frequently prevent the issuance of fully indexed debt, since these laws usually place a ceiling on the nominal rate but not the real rate. This leads to predictable inefficiencies when expected inflation increases, since rationing of credit that is subject to such ceilings would be required. Rationing would be necessary because a ceiling on the nominal rate means that the real rate declines as inflationary expectations increase, which in turn makes this type of credit attractive to borrowers.[17]

A notable example occurred in Canada in the 1960s. At that time, ceilings placed on nominal rates paid by banks, coupled with increased inflationary expectations, caused a substantial outflow of funds from such companies and a corresponding reduction in the amount of money made available by them for home mortgages. On the other side were those issuers of securities that were not subject to rate ceilings and who offered an appropriate nominal rate and, thus, had little difficulty in attracting funds. The term **disintermediation** was invented to describe this pattern of funds' flow.

Since inflation is generally harder to predict for longer time periods relative to shorter time periods, uncertainty about inflation often leads to a reduction in the average term-to-maturity of newly issued fixed-income securities. Here term-to-maturity refers to the length of time from the date of issue of the security until the date that last payment is to be made. For example, the average term-to-maturity of fixed-coupon debt issued in periods of great inflationary uncertainty is usually shorter than in more stable times.

Alternatively, debt with long maturities can be written with **variable rates** (also known as floating rates) of interest. Such instruments provide long-term debt at short-term rates.

Disintermediation A pattern of funds' flow whereby investors withdraw funds from financial intermediaries, such as banks and savings and loans, because market interest rates exceed the maximum interest rates that these organizations are permitted to pay. The investors reinvest their funds in financial assets that pay interest rates not subject to ceilings.

Variable Rate A rate of interest on a financial asset that may vary over the life of the asset, depending on changes in a specified indicator of current market interest rates.

---

[17]Actually, rationing might not occur, since lenders may simply refuse to make those kinds of loans that are subject to ceilings when inflationary expectations are high.

Interest payments are allowed to vary, with each one determined by adding a fixed number of percentage points (say, 2%) to a specified base rate that changes periodically. Two base rates frequently used are the prime rate and the yield on 91-day Treasury bills. If short-term interest rates anticipate inflation reasonably well, such a variable rate security is a reasonable substitute for a fully indexed bond.

Stock Returns and Inflation

Long-term Historical Relationships

It is reasonable to assume that investors are more concerned with real returns than with nominal returns because real returns reflect how much better off they are after adjusting for inflation. Accordingly, real returns of securities need to be analyzed. This is done in Table 12.10 for US common stocks and Treasury bills for the long-term period of 1802 to 1996 and five relatively long subperiods, and for the period 1950 to 1997 in Canada.

Column (2) of the table shows that, on average, the rate of return on common stocks in the US has substantially exceeded the rate of inflation, providing a real return of nearly 8% for the entire period examined and in excess of 7% in all of the subperiods. In comparison, the rate of return on Treasury bills exceeded the rate of inflation by over 3% in the entire period. However, the subperiods show substantial variation, as the real return ranged from .67% over the period from 1926 to 1996 to 5.62% in the period from 1802 to 1888.

Also of interest is the **equity premium** shown in column (4), which is simply the difference between the real rates of return on stocks and bills. Although less than 2% from 1802 to 1888, it has since then been nearly 7%, an amount that some researchers believe is inexplicably large. In summary, Table 12.10 shows that common stocks have historically returned substantially more than the rate of inflation and Treasury bills. That is, in the long run, common stocks have had a large positive real return.

A comparison of the Canadian data with that of the US over the 1950–1996 period shows that Canadian T-bills have provided substantially higher real returns than US T-bills whereas the real returns on Canadian equities have been as attractive as those in the US. Not surprisingly the equity premium in Canada has also been lower, but is close to the US historical average. Despite these differences, Canadian equities have offered investors more attractive real returns than T-bills over the post-war period.

Equity Premium The difference between the expected rate of return on common stocks and the risk-free return.

| **Table 12.10** | Rates of Return on Stocks, Bills, and the Equity Premium in the US and Canada. |

Period (1)	Real Return on Stocks (2)	Real Return on Bills (3)	Equity Premium (2) − (3) = (4)
US Data			
1802–1996[1,2]	8.03%	3.14%	4.89%
1802–1888[1]	7.52	5.62	1.90
1889–1996[1,2]	8.59	1.18	7.41
1926–1996[2]	9.35	0.67	8.68
1950–1996[2]	9.65	.99	8.66
Canadian Data			
1950–1996[3]	7.59	2.12	5.47

[1] SOURCE: Andrew B. Abel, "The Equity Premium Puzzle," *Federal Reserve Bank of Philadelphia Business Review* (September–October 1991), p. 8.
[2] SOURCE: Sharpe, Alexander, and Bowley, *Investments*, 6th Ed., 1998, Table 1.1.
[3] Table 1.1, Chapter 1.

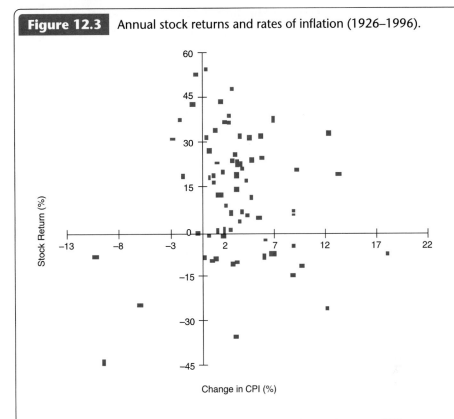

Figure 12.3 Annual stock returns and rates of inflation (1926–1996).

Stock Return (%)

Change in CPI (%)

Short-term Historical Relationships

Another interesting question to investigate is the relationship between the short-term rate of return on stocks and the rate of inflation. Conventional wisdom suggests that stock returns should be relatively high when inflation is relatively high and relatively low when inflation is relatively low. Why? Because stocks represent claims on real assets that should increase in value with inflation.

Figure 12.3 displays the relationship between annual stock returns and rates of inflation in the US from 1926 to 1996. The figure shows that there is no discernible relationship between the rate of inflation and stock returns. Indeed, the correlation coefficient between these two variables is −.01, which for all practical purposes is equal to zero and indicates that there is no significant statistical relationship between the rate of inflation and stock returns.[18] That is, when inflation is relatively high, there is no tendency for stock returns to be either relatively high or relatively low. Similarly, when inflation is relatively low, there is no tendency for stock returns to be either relatively high or relatively low.[19] Accordingly, stocks are not good hedges against inflation in the short term.

---

[18]The correlation coefficient for the period from 1950 to 1996 is equal to −0.26. Similar results occur when monthly data are used. Hence, some people argue that there is an inverse relationship between historical rates of inflation and stock returns.

[19]Interestingly, there appears to be a significantly negative relationship between the real return on stocks and the rate of inflation. That is, higher rates of inflation seem to be accompanied by lower real stock returns. A number of explanations (some of them conflicting) have been offered to account for this observation. For a survey, see David P. Ely and Kenneth J. Robinson, "The Stock Market and Inflation: A Synthesis of the Theory and Evidence," *Federal Reserve Bank of Dallas Economic Review* (March 1989): 17–29.

Relationships Involving Expected Inflation

The previous results used historical (or *ex post*) rates of inflation and stock returns. Also of interest are tests of the relationship between expected (or *ex ante*) rates of inflation and stock returns. For example, if expected inflation for the forthcoming year is relatively high, what effect does that have on stock returns over the forthcoming year?

One study explored this relationship by using time horizons of one and five years.[20] The major difficulty in performing such a test is that expected inflation rates are not observable—only subsequent actual inflation rates are observed. This was overcome by constructing and testing four models for arriving at estimates of expected inflation. These models used past inflation rates and interest rates as "instrumental variables" to estimate expected inflation.

To simplify, the tests involved the following model:

$$r_t = \alpha + \beta \pi_t + e_t \tag{12.9}$$

where r_t and π_t denote, respectively, the rate of return on stocks and the expected inflation rate over time period t. In this equation the variable of interest is the coefficient β. If there is a one-for-one relationship between expected inflation and stock returns, then the estimated value of β will be approximately equal to 1.0. In such a situation, an increase of 1% in the expected inflation rate would result in a 1% increase in stock returns.

Equation (12.9) was first tested using one-year stock returns and inflation rates from 1802 to 1990 and then tested again using overlapping five-year returns and rates.[21] Table 12.11 presents the results. In two of the four cases involving one-year expectations, the value of β appears to be significantly less than 1.0. This suggests that, in the short term, stock returns do not respond to changes in expected rates of inflation. However, in all four cases involving five-year expectations, the value of β is not significantly different from 1.0, suggesting that stock returns do respond to changes in expected rates of inflation over long horizons.

Table 12.11	Testing the Relationships Between Expected Inflation Rates and US Stock Returns, 1802–1990.		
Instrumental Variables Used		Estimated Value of β	
One-Year	Five-Year	One-Year	Five-Year
ST int rates	LT int rates	−2.781	1.394
ST inf rates	LT inf rates	−.048[a]	1.820
ST int rates	ST, LT int rates	−2.531	2.072
ST inf rates	ST, LT inf rates	.061[a]	.380

Notes: ST = past year; LT = past five years; int = interest; inf = inflation.
[a] Denotes number is significantly different from 1.0 at .10 level of significance.

SOURCE: Jacob Boudoukh and Matthew Richardson, "Stock Returns and Inflation: A Long-Horizon Perspective," *American Economic Review* 83, no. 5 (December 1993): 1352.

---

[20] Jacob Boudoukh and Matthew Richardson, "Stock Returns and Inflation: A Long-Horizon Perspective," *American Economic Review* 83, no. 5 (December 1993): 1346–1355.

[21] Equation (12.9) was also tested using actual inflation rates and stock returns from 1802 through 1990. The estimated value of β when one-year rates were used was .07, which was significantly less than 1.0 and not significantly different from zero. When five-year rates were used, its estimated value was .52, which was not significantly different from 1.0. These results are consistent with the earlier results about the observed short-term and long-term relationship between inflation rates and stock returns.

Hence, the Fisher model appears to be validated when applied over long horizons but not when applied over short horizons.[22] That is, there appears to be a positive relation between expected rates of inflation and stock returns over long periods of time but not over short periods. These findings are consistent with those observed when actual rates of inflation were compared with stock returns.

Summary

1. Because investors concern themselves with after-tax returns, federal and provincial tax laws play a major role in the way securities are priced.

2. Income earned by a corporation may be taxed twice—once when it is earned, via the corporate income tax, and again when it is received as dividends by the shareholders, via the personal income tax. The dividend tax credit in Canada, however, mitigates the effect of this double taxation.

3. In the case of both individuals and corporations, the marginal tax rate is more relevant than the average tax rate for making investment decisions.

4. Capital gains need only be included in taxable income when they are realized.

5. The Income Tax Act identifies four kinds of assets to be included in capital property— the taxpayer's personal residence, personal use property, listed personal property, and investment and fixed assets in a business. Capital gains on a taxpayer's personal residence are not taxable and losses are not deductible.

6. The calculation of capital gains taxes involves netting all gains and losses for each kind of asset included in the definition of capital property. Each asset type must be treated separately.

7. Some tax shelters, such as RRSPs, permit the deferment of taxes on the investor's wage income and investment earnings.

8. Inflation measures the percentage change in a specific cost-of-living index at various points in time.

9. Whether a measure of inflation is relevant for a given individual depends to a large extent on the similarity of her purchases to the composition of the Consumer Price Index.

10. An investor's real return is a function of the difference between the investor's nominal return and the inflation rate.

11. Real returns are important to an investor because they represent how much the investor's purchasing power has increased (or decreased) and thus how much better (or worse) off the investor is.

12. If investors are concerned with real returns, securities will be priced so that expected nominal returns incorporate the expected inflation rate.

13. When the actual inflation rate exceeds the expected inflation rate, debtors gain in real terms at the expense of creditors. The opposite is the case when actual inflation is less than expected inflation.

14. Investment returns can be indexed by tying security payments to changes in the price level. Indexation reduces or removes an investment's purchasing-power risk.

15. Over long periods of time, common stocks have generated large, positive real returns. Treasury bills have produced much lower, but still positive, real returns.

16. Over short periods of time, stock returns are not positively related to either actual or expected rates of inflation. However, over long periods of time, stock returns are positively related to both actual and expected rates of inflation.

---

[22]Similar results were obtained when both subperiods and UK data were analyzed.

1. Why is the marginal tax rate more relevant to investment decision making than the average tax rate?

2. Given the following income tax schedule, draw a graph illustrating the marginal and average tax rates as a function of income level.

Income	Tax Rate
$ 0 – $10 000	10%
$10 001 – $20 000	13
$20 001 – $30 000	15
$30 001 – $50 000	20
$50 001 and above	25

3. Why would a corporation report one annual income figure to their shareholders and another to the tax authorities?

4. Given that interest payments are tax deductible for a corporation while dividend payments are not, why don't corporations finance all of their operations with debt?

5. Preferred shares have several fixed-income characteristics, yet generally provide lower after-tax yields to individual investors than do straight-debt securities. However, corporations seem to find preferred-share investments particularly attractive. Why?

6. Heinz Groh expects consumer prices to rise at a 7% rate next year, and has negotiated a 9.5% pay increase. Given a 35% marginal income tax bracket, will this pay increase cause Heinz's real income (that is, purchasing power) to grow? Explain.

7. Is the following statement true or false? Dividends from taxable Canadian corporations are subject to the dividend tax credit. Therefore, shares of these corporations are more attractive investments for inclusion in an RRSP than the bonds of the same corporations. Explain your answer.

8. A corporate bond is selling for $950. It matures in a year, at which time the holder will receive $1000. In addition, the bond will pay $50 in interest during the year. What would be the after-tax return on the bond to an investor in the 50% marginal income tax bracket if capital gains do not receive preferential tax treatment? Recalculate the return assuming that only 75% of any capital gain is taxable.

9. Consider a stock in a taxable Canadian corporation that provides a dividend yield of 6%. To an investor in the following marginal tax brackets, what is the equivalent before-tax yield on a taxable bond? Use the values for g and q given in the text.
   a. 17%
   b. 26%
   c. 34%

10. What is a wash sale? Why does Revenue Canada prohibit such transactions for tax calculation purposes?

11. Jean Lalonde lives in a province where the tax payable is 60% of the basic federal rate. Jean's marginal basic federal tax rate is 26%. There is a federal surtax of 5% but none provincially.
   a. What is Jean's effective provincial marginal tax rate?
   b. What is Jean's effective federal marginal tax rate?
   c. What is Jean's effective combined marginal tax rate?

12. Given the following beginning and ending values for a particular price index, and the respective number of years between the measurement of the two values, calculate the annual compounded (geometric mean) inflation rate.

	Price Index Beginning Value	Price Index Ending Value	Years Covered
a.	100	115	1
b.	115	170	3
c.	170	150	2

13. Why do cost-of-living indices frequently overstate the true economic impact of inflation on typical consumers?

14. Distinguish between the nominal and the real rate of return on an investment.

15. Ken Higgins started 1997 with investments valued at $11 500. At the end of 1998 those same investments were worth $16 000. During the same time period the price index rose from 210 to 250. What was Ken's real rate of return over the two-year period?

16. Why is it reasonable to assume that rational investors will build an expected inflation premium into the returns they require from their investments?

17. In the late 1970s and early 1980s, a period of unexpectedly high inflation, Harry Fell referred to long-term bonds issued by corporations and the government as "certificates of confiscation." Why would Harry make such a comment?

18. Why is it often argued that the federal government is the greatest beneficiary of inflation?

19. Many economists contend that during periods of inflation, taxes on investment income reflect, in part, a tax on the return of capital and, hence, are inequitable. Explain the reasoning behind this argument.

20. Explain why the returns on bonds are found to be negatively correlated with unexpected inflation. Why does this relationship become progressively more negative as one considers longer lived bonds?

21. How are economywide inflation rates calculated? Are all consumers affected equally by the increase in overall prices measured by the price index? Explain.

22. Assume that your portfolio grows 9% in value per year and annual inflation is 5%. How many years will it take for the nominal value of your portfolio to triple? How many years will it take for the real value of your portfolio to triple?

23. Common stocks, somewhat surprisingly, do not appear to be effective hedges against either expected or unexpected inflation. Explain why the stocks of some companies might be better hedges against inflation than others.

KEY TERMS

marginal tax rate (p. 293)
average tax rate (p. 293)
dividend tax credit (DTC) (p. 298)
realized capital gain (p. 300)
unrealized capital gain (p. 300)
wash sale (p. 300)
capital gains and losses (p. 300)
capital property (p. 300)
adjusted cost base (ACB) (p. 301)
Registered Retirement Savings Plan (RRSP) (p. 303)
spousal RRSP (p. 304)

inflation (p. 305)
cost-of-living index (p. 307)
Consumer Price Index (CPI) (p. 307)
geometric mean (p. 309)
nominal return (p. 309)
real return (p. 310)
purchasing-power risk (p. 312)
indexation (p. 313)
disintermediation (p. 315)
variable rates (p. 315)
equity premium (p. 316)

REFERENCES

1. For a valuable book that provides a framework for analyzing how tax rules affect decision-making, see:

   Myron S. Scholes and Mark A. Wolfson, *Taxes and Business Strategy* (Englewood Cliffs, NJ: Prentice Hall, 1992).

2. Portfolio management and taxation are discussed in:

   Robert H. Jeffrey and Robert D. Arnott, "Is Your Alpha Big Enough to Cover Its Taxes?" *Journal of Portfolio Management* 19, no. 3 (Spring 1993): 15–25.

   Laurence B. Siegel and David Montgomery. "Stocks, Bonds, and Bills after Taxes and Inflation." *Journal of Portfolio Management* 21, no. 2 (Winter 1995): 17–25.

   Roberto Apelfeld, Gordon B. Fowler, Jr., and James P. Gordon Jr., "Tax-Aware Equity Investing," *Journal of Portfolio Management* 22, no. 2 (Winter 1996): 18–28.

   William Ghee and William Reichenstein, "The After-Tax Returns from Different Savings Vehicles," *Financial Analysts Journal* 52, no. 4 (July–August 1996): 62–72.

3. The seminal work linking interest rates and inflationary expectations is:

   Irving Fisher, *The Theory of Interest* (New York: Macmillan, 1930).

4. For a review article and test of this linkage, see, respectively:

   Herbert Taylor, "Interest Rates: How Much Does Expected Inflation Matter?" *Federal Reserve Bank of Philadelphia Business Review* (July–August 1982): 3–12.

   Jacob Boudoukh and Matthew Richardson, "Stock Returns and Inflation: A Long-Horizon Perspective," *American Economic Review* 83, no. 5 (December 1993): 1346–1355.

5. The relationship between real interest rates and inflation is discussed in:

   George G. Pennachi, "Identifying the Dynamics of Real Interest Rates and Inflation: Evidence Using Survey Data," *Review of Financial Studies* 4, no. 1 (1991): 53–86.

6. The following papers present an analysis of the effect of inflation on the accounting treatment of corporate earnings:

   Franco Modigliani and Richard A. Cohn, "Inflation and the Stock Market," *Financial Analysts Journal* 35, no. 2 (March–April 1979): 24–44.

   Kenneth R. French, Richard S. Ruback, and G. William Schwert, "Effects of Nominal Contracting on Stock Returns," *Journal of Political Economy* 91, no. 1 (February 1983): 70–96.

   William H. Beaver, Paul A. Griffin, and Wayne R. Landsman, "How Well Does Replacement Cost Income Explain Stock Return [*sic*]?" *Financial Analysts Journal* 39, no. 2 (March–April 1983): 26–30, 39.

   William C. Nordby, "Applications of Inflation-Adjusted Accounting Data," *Financial Analysts Journal* 39, no. 2 (March–April 1983): 33–39.

   Charles G. Callard and David C. Kleinman, "Inflation-Adjusted Accounting: Does It Matter?" *Financial Analysts Journal* 41, no. 3 (May–June 1985): 51–59.

7. For a discussion of the U.S. Treasury's inflation-indexed securities, see:

   Richard Roll, "U.S. Treasury Inflation-Indexed Bonds: The Design of a New Security," *Journal of Fixed Income* 6, no. 3 (December (1996): 28.

Jeffrey M. Wrase, "Inflation-Indexed Bonds: How Do They Work?" *Federal Reserve Bank of Philadelphia Business Review* (July–August 1997): 3–16.

8. For a discussion of the relationship of the inflation rate to the returns on stocks, bonds, and real estate, see:

Eugene F. Fama and G. William Schwert, "Asset Returns and Inflation," *Journal of Financial Economics* 5, no. 2 (November 1977): 115–146.

9. Other papers dealing with the relationship between inflation and stock returns can be found at the end of the following survey articles:

David P. Ely and Kenneth J. Robinson, "The Stock Market and Inflation: A Synthesis of the Theory and Evidence," *Federal Reserve Bank of Dallas Economic Review* (March 1989): 17–29.

Andrew B. Abel, "The Equity Premium Puzzle," *Federal Reserve Bank of Philadelphia Business Review* (September–October 1991): 3–14.

10. The equity premium has also been reviewed and analyzed in:

Jeremy J. Siegel, "The Equity Premium: Stock and Bond Returns Since 1802," *Financial Analysts Journal* 48, no. 1 (January–February 1992): 28–38, 46.

Narayana Kocherlakota, "The Equity Premium: It's Still a Puzzle," *Journal of Economic Literature* 34, no. 1 (March 1996): 42–71.

11. The tendency of certain types of common stocks to offer better inflation hedges is discussed in:

Douglas K. Pearce and V. Vance Roley, "Firm Characteristics, Unanticipated Inflation, and Stock Returns," *Journal of Finance* 43, no. 4 (September 1988): 965–981.

Christopher K. Ma and M. E. Ellis, "Selecting Industries as Inflation Hedges," *Journal of Portfolio Management* 15, no. 4 (Summer 1989): 45–48.

Yaman Asikoglu and Metin R. Ercan, "Inflation Flow-Through and Stock Prices," *Journal of Portfolio Management* 18, no. 3 (Spring 1992): 63–68.

12. International evidence on the relationship between stock returns and inflation is provided by:

Bruno Solnik, "The Relation Between Stock Prices and Inflationary Expectations: The International Evidence," *Journal of Finance* 38, no. 1 (March 1983): 35–48.

N. Bulent Gultekin, "Stock Market Returns and Inflation: Evidence From Other Countries," *Journal of Finance* 38, no. 1 (March 1983): 49–65.

13. For a Canadian perspective on the topics covered in this chapter, see:

I. G. Morgan, "Dividends and Stock Price Behaviour in Canada," *Journal of Business Administration: Capital Markets in Canada* 12, no. 1 (Fall 1980).

J. Pesando, "Inflation-Indexed Pensions: Investment Policy Implications," *Canadian Investment Review* I, no. 1 (Fall 1988).

D. Peters, "Government of Canada Real Return Bonds," *Proceedings*, Administrative Sciences Association of Canada Conference, Montreal, June 1996.

B. Amoako-Adu, M. Rashid, and M. Stebbins, "Capital Gains Taxes and Equity Values: An Empirical Test of Stock Price Reactions to the Introduction and Reduction of a Capital Gains Tax Exemption," *Journal of Banking and Finance* 16, no. 2 (April 1992).

F. Adjaoud and D. Zéghal, "Fiscalité et Politique de Dividend Au Canada: Nouveaux Résultats," *Finéco 3*, no. 2 (2e semestre 1993).

S. Brian Fisher and Paul B. Hickey, eds., *KPMG Personal Tax Planning Guide, 1998* (Scarborough, ON: Carswell, Thomson Professional Publishing Company, 1998).

Fixed-income Securities

Pure-discount Security A fixed-income security that promises to make only one payment to its owner.

Coupon Payments The periodic payment of interest on a bond.

Maturity Date The date upon which a bond issuer repays investors the principal of the bond.

Principal The nominal value of a bond that is repaid to bondholders at the maturity date.

T his chapter provides a broad survey of the major types of fixed-income securities, with an emphasis on those currently popular in Canada. A security is a contract giving the investor certain rights to the future prospects of the issuer. These rights can differ from one security to another and the future prospects of issuers can also differ substantially; therefore, the number of different types of fixed-income securities is too high to allow a complete survey to be included.

The term *fixed-income* is commonly used to cover the types of securities discussed in this chapter, but it can be misleading. Typically, these securities promise the investors that they will receive certain specified cash flows at certain specified times in the future. If a security provides only a single cash flow, it is known as a **pure-discount security**. Alternatively, it may involve multiple cash flows. If all these cash flows (except for the last one) are of the same size, they are generally referred to as **coupon payments**. The specified date beyond which the investor will no longer receive cash flows is known as the **maturity date**. On this date the investor receives the **principal** (also known as the *par value* or *face value*) associated with the security, along with the last coupon payment. All the cash flows *promised*, however, may not be received. That is, there is some risk, however small, that a promised payment will not be made in full and on time.

Savings Deposits

Perhaps the most familiar type of fixed-income investment is the personal savings account at a chartered bank, trust company, credit union, or caisse populaire. Such an account provides substantial (if not complete) safety of principal, low probability of failure to receive interest, high liquidity, and a relatively low return.

Chartered Banks

Demand Deposit A chequing account at a financial institution.

Many people maintain a chequing account in a chartered bank. Formally, these accounts are termed **demand deposits**, since money can be withdrawn on demand by the depositors. While the bookkeeping required to keep track of withdrawals and deposits is costly to the bank, the balance in such an account is available to support interest-earning loans made by the bank. Banks offer an array of chequing accounts with different terms and conditions. Figure 13.1 shows the different types of demand deposits offered by a chartered bank. In general, customers with small balances who write many cheques pay the bank, whereas those with large balances who write few cheques are paid by the bank. This is because the

Figure 13.1 Typical chartered bank deposit accounts.

FINANCIAL RATE LETTER

TD GUARANTEED INVESTMENT CERTIFICATES

Effective: AUG 27, 1998

LONG TERM	Minimum $5,000 %	Minimum $1,000 %	Minimum $1,000 %	Minimum $1,000 %	SHORT TERM	Minimum $5,000 %
1 year	3.800	3.925	4.050	4.050	30 - 59 days	3.250
2 years	4.050	4.175	4.300	4.050	60 - 89 days	3.300
3 years	4.200	4.325	4.450	4.200	90 - 119 days	3.300
4 years	4.300	4.425	4.550	4.300	120 - 179 days	3.300
5 years	4.550	4.675	4.800	4.550	180 - 269 days	3.750
	(Interest paid monthly)	(Interest paid semi-annually)	(Interest paid annually)	(Interest compounded annually and paid at maturity)	270 - 365 days	3.850
						(Interest paid at maturity)

GIC RSPS

LONG TERM	Minimum $500 %	Minimum $500 %	SHORT TERM	Minimum $2,000 %
1 year	4.050	4.050	90 - 179 days	3.300
2 years	4.300	4.300	180 - 269 days	3.750
3 years	4.450	4.450	270 - 365 days	3.850
4 years	4.550	4.550		(Interest paid at maturity)
5 years	4.800	4.800		
	(Interest paid annually and at maturity)	(Interest compounded annually and paid at maturity)		

TD TERM DEPOSITS

LONG TERM	Minimum $1,000 %	SHORT TERM	Minimum $5,000 %
1 year	3.800	30 - 59 days	3.000
2 years	4.050	60 - 89 days	3.050
3 years	4.200	90 - 119 days	3.050
4 years	4.300	120 - 179 days	3.050
5 years	4.550	180 - 269 days	3.500
	(Interest paid semi-annually)	270 - 365 days	3.600
		(Interest paid at maturity)	

GIC RIFS

LONG TERM	Minimum $500 %	Minimum $500 %	SHORT TERM	Minimum $2,000 %
1 year	4.050	4.050	90 - 179 days	3.300
2 years	4.300	4.300	180 - 269 days	3.750
3 years	4.450	4.450	270 - 365 days	3.850
4 years	4.550	4.550		(Interest paid at maturity)
5 years	4.800	4.800		
	(Interest paid annually and at maturity)	(Interest compounded annually and paid at maturity)		

U.S. DOLLAR GICS

	Minimum $1,000 US %	
1 year	4.500	
2 years	4.500	US$ Term Deposits also available
3 years	4.625	
4 years	4.625	
5 years	4.625	
	(Interest paid annually)	

ANNUITIES

FIXED TERM Registered and Non-Registered %	PRESCRIBED Non-Registered Only %
6 - 12 years 4.750	6 - 12 years 4.750
13 - 17 years 5.000	13 - 17 years 5.000
18 - 25 years 5.250	18 - 25 years 5.250

INVESTMENT BUILDER™ ACCOUNT

Interest paid monthly

	Daily Closing Balance $	%
- on totals:	0 - < 5,000	0.350
	5,000 - < 10,000	1.250
	10,000 - < 25,000	1.400
	25,000 - < 60,000	2.750
- plus on portion:	60,000 - < 100,000	3.850
	100,000 - < 150,000	3.900
	150,000 +	3.900

SOURCE: The Toronto-Dominion Bank (August 27, 1998). For illustrative purposes only. Rates do not reflect current information. ™Trademark of TD Mortgage Corporation.

---

bank pays interest on the customer's deposit (either on the daily closing balance or on the minimum balance maintained in the account over a specified period) and at the same time charges for handling the customer's cheques and for other services. In some cases accounts with larger minimum balances are paid higher interest rates.

An alternative to a chequing account is a savings account. This type of account typically earns a higher rate of interest than a chequing account but offers no chequing privileges. Cash withdrawals may be made at any time. Service charges and interest are determined in the same manner as for a chequing account. Almost any amount may be invested in a savings account. No security is issued; instead, the current balance plus interest earned is either posted to the depositor's passbook or recorded in a monthly statement.

Credit unions offer accounts similar to those described above, and many investment companies (described in Chapter 21) provide at least limited cheque-writing services.

Time deposits, also known as **guaranteed investment certificates** (GICs) or *term deposits*, have a stated maturity date (for example, one year after the initial deposit), with interest paid at maturity on short-term (less than one year) deposits and either annually or

Time Deposit A savings account at a financial institution.

Guaranteed Investment Certificates (GICs) These deposits have a stated maturity date.

semiannually on long-term deposits. In practice, such deposits can be withdrawn at any time. A penalty must be paid, however, when this is done prior to maturity. Often, the penalty takes the form of recomputing the interest earned using a lower rate. Most types of time deposits require a minimum investment, for example, $1000 each.[1]

Trust and Mortgage Loan Companies

In general, trust and mortgage loan companies accept demand and shorter-term deposits (up to five years), then use the money primarily to make longer-term loans, often for home mortgages. Trust companies offer accounts and services that are very similar to those provided by chartered banks and are therefore referred to as *near banks*.

The interest rates and maturities on deposits offered by these institutions are generally similar to those offered by the chartered banks. Figure 13.2 shows the short- and medium-term retail rates offered by various financial institutions, as reported weekly in *The Toronto Star*.

Credit Unions

A credit union accepts deposits from members of the credit union (membership is limited to individuals sharing some kind of common bond, often a common employer) and uses them to make loans to other members. Typically, loans are relatively small and relatively short-term (for example, to finance the purchase of an automobile). Excess funds are invested in highly liquid short-term assets.

Each credit union is owned by its members, who elect a board of directors. The interest rates and maturities on deposits are generally similar to those on savings accounts in banks or trust companies, but earn dividends instead of interest. Many credit unions also offer GICs and chequing accounts to their members.

Other Types of Personal Savings Accounts

A number of institutions similar to those described above also exist. In some countries, the government-run post office accepts savings deposits. In Canada, some provincial governments operate savings banks, such as *The Province of Ontario Savings Office*. Certain kinds of life insurance policies include a savings component—payments often exceed the amount strictly required to pay for the insurance involved. The cash value of such a policy may be obtained by cancellation; alternatively, some or all of it may be borrowed without cancelling the policy. The implicit rate of return on the cash value of an insurance policy is typically low, reflecting the extremely low risk to the policyholder and the length of the insurance company's commitment.

Deposit Insurance

In 1967, the *Canadian Deposit Insurance Corporation* (CDIC) was created by the federal government to guarantee deposits in all federally incorporated chartered banks, and trust and loan companies and all provincially incorporated trust and loan companies, with the exception of those in Quebec. The Quebec Deposit Insurance Board (QDIB) was established to insure deposits of all deposit-accepting institutions in Quebec as well as deposits accepted outside Quebec by institutions incorporated in that province. In 1990,

---

[1]One recent innovation is the issuance of "equity linked term deposits" that provide the investor with a return based on the performance of a given market index, coupled with a guarantee that the investor will not experience a loss (some even guarantee the investor some minimal interest rate if the market index performs poorly).

What your savings earn

The rates shown are for October 9, 1998, and change without notice. The sample changes weekly. The chart is prepared by **Fiscal Agents,** which supplies free consumer information on these investments. Phone (905) 844-7700.

CHARTERED BANKS

	SAVINGS A/CS* MONTHLY	DAILY	SHORT TERM DEPOSITS MINIMUM DEPOSIT	30-59 DAYS	60-89 DAYS	90-119 DAYS	FIXED TERM DEPOSITS INTEREST PAID ANNUALLY MINIMUM DEPOSIT	1 YR.	2 YRS.	3 YRS.	4 YRS.	5 YRS.
Amex Bank of Canada	-	0.25	-	-	-	-	1,000	4.05	4.55	4.65	4.70	5.00
BCI Bank	0.75	0.50	5,000	4.00	4.00	4.00	1,000	3.95	4.10	4.25	4.40	4.55
Bank of Montreal	-	0.35	5,000	3.75	3.75	3.75	1,000	3.75	3.85	3.95	4.00	4.25
Bank of Nova Scotia	-	0.35	5,000	3.75	3.75	3.75	500	3.75	3.85	3.95	4.00	4.25
CIBC	-	0.25	5,000	3.75	3.75	3.75	1,000	3.75	3.85	3.95	4.00	4.25
Citizens Bank	-	0.50	5,000	4.00	4.00	4.25	500	4.50	4.50	4.50	4.50	4.75
Hongkong Bank	-	0.25	5,000	3.75	3.75	3.75	1,000	4.15	4.35	4.50	4.25	4.50
ING Direct	-	4.75	-	-	-	-	0	4.60	4.65	4.80	4.85	5.00
Laurentian Bank	-	0.05	5,000	3.55	3.55	3.55	1,000	3.85	4.10	4.20	4.25	4.50
Manulife Bank	-	-	25,000	4.95	4.95	4.80	500	4.40	4.40	4.50	4.55	4.60
National Bank	-	0.02	5,000	3.50	3.50	3.50	1,000	4.10	4.35	4.57	4.62	4.87
National Bank of Greece	0.75	1.00	5,000	3.75	3.75	3.75	1,000	3.80	3.85	3.95	4.00	4.50
Royal Bank	-	0.15	5,000	3.75	3.75	3.75	500	3.75	3.85	3.95	4.00	4.25
Toronto Dominion Bank	-	0.35	5,000	3.75	3.75	3.75	1,000	3.75	3.85	3.95	4.00	4.25

TRUST & LOAN COMPANIES

	MONTHLY	DAILY	MINIMUM DEPOSIT	30-59 DAYS	60-89 DAYS	90-119 DAYS	MINIMUM DEPOSIT	1 YR.	2 YRS.	3 YRS.	4 YRS.	5 YRS.
Canada Trust	-	0.75	5,000	3.75	3.75	3.75	1,000	3.75	3.85	3.95	4.00	4.25
Canadian Western Trust	-	-	25,000	3.75	4.00	4.00	5,000	4.00	4.25	4.35	4.40	4.65
Community Trust	-	-	5,000	2.00	2.00	2.12	5,000	4.75	5.00	5.00	5.00	5.20
Co-operative Trust	-	-	5,000	3.50	3.50	3.50	500	4.00	4.10	4.20	4.25	4.50
Equitable Trust	-	-	5,000	4.50	4.75	4.75	5,000	4.75	5.00	5.05	5.10	5.20
Home Savings & Loan	-	-	5,000	4.00	4.50	4.50	1,000	4.65	4.75	4.75	4.75	5.20
Household Trust	-	0.50	5,000	1.25	1.25	1.25	500	1.50	2.00	2.50	2.75	3.00
London Trust & Savings	-	-	5,000	4.00	4.00	4.25	5,000	4.60	4.75	4.75	4.85	5.00
Montreal Trust	-	0.35	5,000	3.75	3.75	3.75	500	3.75	3.85	3.95	4.00	4.25
Mutual Trust	-	2.25	10,000	3.25	3.25	3.25	1,000	3.85	3.95	4.05	4.10	4.35
National Trust	-	-	1,000	3.75	3.75	3.75	500	3.75	3.85	3.95	4.00	4.25
Royal Trust	-	0.15	5,000	3.75	3.75	3.75	500	3.75	3.85	3.95	4.00	4.25
Standard Life Trust	-	-	5,000	3.62	3.75	3.75	1,000	4.37	4.50	4.62	4.62	4.75
Sun Life Trust	-	-	25,000	4.25	4.25	4.25	1,000	4.37	4.37	4.50	4.50	4.50
Trimark Trust	-	1.00	5,000	4.10	4.10	4.10	1,000	4.50	4.60	4.65	4.70	4.90

OTHER FINANCIAL INSTITUTIONS

	MONTHLY	DAILY	MINIMUM DEPOSIT	30-59 DAYS	60-89 DAYS	90-119 DAYS	MINIMUM DEPOSIT	1 YR.	2 YRS.	3 YRS.	4 YRS.	5 YRS.
Duca Credit Union	1.25	1.00	1,000	3.65	3.65	3.75	1,000	4.45	4.65	4.75	4.85	5.00
GTA Savings & C.U.	-	0.25	5,000	3.50	3.50	3.50	1,000	3.75	3.85	3.95	4.00	4.25
Hepcoe Credit Union	-	-	5,000	3.75	3.75	3.75	1,000	3.75	3.85	3.95	4.00	4.25
Manulife Financial	-	1.00	-	-	-	-	1,000	4.25	4.37	4.37	4.62	4.75
Maritime Life	-	2.50	-	-	-	-	1,000	4.00	4.00	4.00	4.00	4.12
mbanx	-	3.69	-	-	-	-	-	-	-	-	-	-
Prov. of Ont. Savings	-	0.75	1,000	4.00	4.00	4.00	500	4.35	4.35	4.45	4.50	4.55
Royal & SunAlliance	-	3.12	-	-	-	-	500	3.87	3.87	3.87	3.87	4.25
Standard Life	-	2.50	5,000	3.25	-	3.37	1,000	4.25	4.37	4.37	4.50	4.50
Transamerica Life	-	-	-	-	-	-	1,000	3.85	3.85	3.95	4.10	4.35

NOTE: R.O.R. —— Rates on request. * Savings Account rates are based on minimum dollar balance levels in account. Some institutions may pay premium rates on higher dollar balance levels.

SOURCE: *The Toronto Star* (Sunday, October 11, 1998).

the CDIC had 151 insured member institutions—116 federally and 35 provincially incorporated.

The CDIC was created to achieve several objectives:

1. protection of small depositors
2. provision of last resort facilities
3. improvement in the minimum financial standards of deposit-taking institutions across the country
4. maintenance of confidence and stability in the financial system

The deposit insurance system was designed to operate much like a casualty insurance company. The premiums collected from the insured member institutions, together with income from investments, are used to cover operating expenses and losses, with any excess contributing to an increase in reserves. In a properly functioning deposit insurance system the premium plus investment income should be sufficient to cover expenses and anticipated losses together with an amount budgeted for unforeseen losses.

The insured limit under the Canada Deposit Insurance Act on Canadian dollar deposits with an original term to maturity of five years or less was set at $60 000 in 1983 and has remained at that level since. Judicious use of multiple accounts in different financial institutions makes it possible to increase the total amount covered by deposit insurance. Member institutions were originally required to pay an annual insurance premium of 1/30th of 1% of insured deposits, but this was raised to 0.1% in 1988. All member institutions pay the same premium with no risk differential.

Money Market Instruments

Money Market Instrument A short-term fixed-income security.

Certain types of short-term (meaning, arbitrarily, one year or less), highly marketable loans play a major role in the investment and borrowing activities of industrial corporations and financial intermediaries. Individual investors with substantial funds may invest in such **money market instruments** directly or indirectly via money market accounts at various financial institutions.[2]

Some money market instruments are negotiable and are traded in active secondary dealer markets; others are not. Some may be purchased by anyone with adequate funds, others only by particular types of institutions. Many are sold on a discount basis; for example, a 91-day Treasury bill with a face value of $100 000 might be sold for $98 800—where the face value of $100 000 is to be paid to the investor at maturity and the difference of $1200 represents interest income.

Annualized Rate Basis A method for calculating the annualized return on a Treasury bill with a maturity of less than one year.

Interest rates on such money market instruments are often reported on an **annualized rate basis**. This means that in the example above, the T-bill will be described in the media as providing a rate of 4.87% per year calculated as follows:

$$(\$1200/\$98\ 800) \times (365/91) \times 100 = 4.87\%$$

Over the 91-day period the investor receives a return of $1200/$98 800, or 1.215%. If, however, the proceeds were reinvested at the same rate four times over, the actual return or **annual percentage rate** (APR) would be $1.01215^4 - 1 = 4.95\%$. Both *The Globe and*

Annual Percentage Rate (APR) With respect to a loan, the APR is the yield-to-maturity of the loan computed using the most frequent time between payments as the compounding interval.

---

[2]Short-term obligations and bonds of the Government of Canada and its agencies that mature in less than three years are also considered to be money market instruments. Useful descriptions of the various types of money market instruments are contained in W. T. Hunter, *Canadian Financial Markets* (Peterborough, ON: Broadview Press Ltd., 1988); and James E. Hatch and Robert W. White, *Canadian Stocks, Bonds, Bills, and Inflation: 1950–1987* (Charlottesville, VA: The Research Foundation of The Institute of Chartered Financial Analysts, 1988).

Financial Post

www.canoe.com/FP/home.
html

Mail: Report on Business and *The Financial Post* publish a daily list of the current interest rates on a number of Canadian, US, and international money market instruments. Figure 13.3 presents samples of these lists. Table 13.1 shows the size of the Canadian money market broken down by type of instrument. Most of these are described in the next section.

Table 13.1	Money Market Instruments Held Outside the Bank of Canada, December 1996.	
Type of Instrument	Amount (in millions)	
Treasury bills:		
Government of Canada	$117 464	
Provincial governments	15 908	
Municipal governments	306	
Subtotal Treasury bills		$133 678
Short-term paper:		
Bankers' acceptances	$ 33 965	
Finance paper	10 639	
Commercial paper	24 226	
Subtotal short-term paper		68 830
Total Money Market		$202 508

SOURCE: *Bank of Canada Review*, Autumn 1997.

Figure 13.3   Canadian and US money market rates quoted in the financial press.

MONEY RATES

ADMINISTERED RATES

Bank of Canada 5.00%
Central bank call range
           4.50-5.00%
Canadian prime 6.50%

MONEY MARKET RATES
(for transactions
of $1-million or more)

3-mo. T-bill(when-issued) 4.94%
1-month treasury bills 4.62%
2-month treasury bills 4.78%
3-month treasury bills 4.85%
6-month treasury bills 5.14%
1-year treasury bills 5.34%
10-year Canada bonds 5.60%
30-year Canada bonds 5.73%
1-month banker's accept. 5.02%
2-month banker's accept. 5.10%
3-month banker's accept. 5.16%
   Commercial Paper (R-1 Low)
1-month 5.03%
2-month 5.12%
3-month 5.19%
Call money 4.76%

FEDERAL BILL YIELDS
The average yield at this week's auction of $3.5-billion of 98-day Government of Canada treasury bills was 4.876 per cent, down from 5.068 per cent at the previous auction held on Aug. 4.
   Accepted yields for the 98-day bills ranged from a high of 4.882 per cent for a price equivalent of 98.70618 to a low of 4.868 per

cent for a price equivalent of 98.70984. The average yield of 4.876 per cent provided a price equivalent of 98.70778.
   For an offering of $1.7-billion of 182-day treasury bills, accepted yields ranged from a high of 5.173 per cent for a price equivalent of 97.48545 to a low of 5.165 per cent for a price equivalent of 97.48924. The average yield of 5.169 per cent provided a price equivalent of 97.48716.
   For an offering of $1.6-billion of 364-day treasury bills, accepted yields ranged from a high of 5.363 per cent for a price equivalent of 94.92322 to a low of 5.345 per cent for a price equivalent of 94.93939 per cent. The average yield of 5.356 per cent provided a price equivalent of 95.92954.

Dow Jones Markets
UNITED STATES
NEW YORK (AP) — Money rates for Tuesday as reported by Bridge Telerate as of 4 p.m.:
   Bridge Telerate interest rate index: 5.453
   Prime Rate: 8.50
   Discount Rate: 5.00
   Broker call loan rate: 7.25
   Federal funds market rate:
   High 5.5625; low 5.5625; last 5.5625
   Dealers commercial paper:

30-180 days: 5.52-5.48
   Commercial paper by finance company: 30-270 days: 5.52-5.39
   Bankers acceptances dealer indications: 30 days, 5.51; 60 days, 5.50; 90 days, 5.49; 120 days, 5.47; 150 days, 5.46; 180 days, 5.46
   Certificates of Deposit Primary: 30 days, 4.68; 90 days, 4.99; 180 days, 5.17
   Certificates of Deposit by dealer: 30 days, 5.56; 60 days, 5.57; 90 days, 5.58; 120 days, 5.59; 150 days, 5.62; 180 days, 5.63
   Eurodollar rates: Overnight, 5.46875-5.3125; 1 month, 5.53125-5.5625; 3 months, 5.5625-5.59375; 6 months, 5.59375-5.65625; 1 year, 5.59375-5.65625
   London Interbank Offered Rate: 3 months, 5.69; 6 months, 5.72; 1 year, 5.72
   Treasury Bill auction results: average discount rate: 3-month as of Aug. 17: 4.910; 6-month as of Aug. 17: 4.945; 52-week as of Aug. 18: 5.000
   Treasury Bill annualized rate on weekly average basis, yield adjusted for constant maturity, 1-year, as of Aug. 17: 5.23
   Treasury Bill market rate, 1-year: 5.00-4.98
   Treasury Bond market rate, 30-year: 5.55

SOURCE: Reprinted by permission of *The Globe and Mail: Report on Business* (August 19, 1998).

Finance Company and Commercial Paper

Finance Company Paper Short-term unsecured, negotiable debt issued by finance or acceptance companies.

Commercial Paper A type of money instrument. It represents unsecured promissory notes of large, financially sound corporations.

Finance paper is an unsecured short-term promissory note issued in either Canadian dollars or other currencies (usually US dollars) by sales finance and consumer loan companies. Commercial and industrial corporations issue **commercial paper** with characteristics similar to that of finance paper but offering slightly higher rates.[3] Finance paper is secured by the pledge of the installment obligations that the company will receive. Commercial paper is often backed by either a standby line of credit at a bank or a guarantee from a parent company or affiliate to insure that the loan will be paid off when it comes due. The interest rates on finance and commercial paper reflect this low risk, being relatively low compared to other corporate fixed-income securities and slightly higher than Treasury bills.

Finance and commercial paper is issued in minimum denominations of $50 000, with maturities of 30 to 365 days for the former and one to 365 days for the latter (but typically less than 90 days). The secondary market for both types of paper is limited. Therefore, they are usually held to maturity. Commercial paper often has a 24-hour prepayment provision, whereby the company can repay the note on one day's notice.

Bankers' Acceptances

Bankers' Acceptance A type of money market instrument. It is a promissory note issued by a corporation, with a stated maturity date, that is endorsed by a bank. The bank, by endorsing the note, assumes the obligation that may subsequently be traded.

In Canada, a **bankers' acceptance** is a pure-discount security that is a substitute for commercial paper as a source of financing. It can be regarded as a negotiable, certified cheque made out to the bearer. The firm seeking financing must write a bill for $100 000 or a multiple thereof payable to itself within 180 days or less for acceptance by its bank. *Acceptance* means that the bank will guarantee payment. Once accepted, the company can endorse the bill to the bearer and sell it (at a discount) in the money market. At maturity the bank is obliged to redeem the bill and it collects the necessary funds from the issuing company. The effective rate of interest is only slightly higher than that on T-bills, reflecting the high credit-worthiness of the company and the bank's guarantee. In addition to the interest, the issuing corporation must also pay the bank a fee for accepting the bill.

In the United States, banker's acceptances were created to finance goods in transit, but currently they are generally used to finance foreign trade. A company buying goods imported from abroad makes out a bill payable to itself as described above, then has it accepted by its bank and turns it over to the seller. The seller of the goods, having received the accepted bill, need not wait until it is due in order to receive payment. It can be sold in the money market at a discount.

Term Deposits Issued by Financial Institutions

Negotiable Deposits

Bearer Deposit Notes (BDNs) are the only short-term instruments issued by the Canadian chartered banks that are traded in the money market. These negotiable deposits are issued in multiples of $100 000 with maturities ranging from 30 to 365 days. They are transferable but not redeemable before maturity and, therefore, marketable. US banks issue similar securities, known as **Certificates of Deposit** (CDs) (or Jumbo CDs when they are in large denominations).

Certificate of Deposit A form of time deposit issued by banks and other financial institutions

Non-negotiable Deposits

The chartered banks also issue Certificates of Deposit that are similar to BDNs but are neither transferable nor negotiable. These are also called *Term Deposit Receipts* or *Term Notes*

---

[3]About 25% of all finance and commercial paper outstanding at the end of 1996 was denominated in a foreign currency.

and are issued in denominations ranging from $5000 to $100 000 with maturities ranging from one day to five years.

Trust and mortgage loan companies issue similar instruments under a variety of names (Deposit Receipts, Guaranteed Trust Certificates, Guaranteed Investment Certificates, and Guaranteed Investment Receipts). In general, term deposits have a minimum denomination of $5000 with one-day to one-year maturities, and receipts or certificates have a minimum denomination of $500 with one- to five-year maturities.

Eurodollars

Eurodollar Certificate of Deposit A certificate of deposit denominated in US dollars and issued by banks domiciled outside North America.

Eurodollar Deposit A US dollar-denominated time deposit held in a bank domiciled outside North America.

In the world of international finance, large short-term CDs denominated in dollars and issued by banks outside North America (most often in London) are known as **Eurodollar CDs** (or simply Euro CDs). Dollar-denominated time deposits in banks outside North America are known as **Eurodollar deposits**. A key distinction between Euro CDs and Eurodollar deposits is that Euro CDs are negotiable, meaning they can be traded, whereas Eurodollar deposits are non-negotiable, meaning they cannot be traded.

The demand and supply conditions for such instruments may differ from the conditions for other Canadian and US money market instruments, owing to restrictions imposed (or likely to be imposed) by the Canadian and US governments. Enough commonality exists, however, to keep interest rates from markedly diverging from those available in North America. Euro CDs are not covered by deposit insurance as are deposits issued by Canadian financial institutions.

Repurchase Agreements

Repurchase Agreement A type of money market instrument. It involves the sale of a financial asset from one investor to another. The investor selling the asset simultaneously agrees to repurchase it from the purchaser on a stated future date at a predetermined price, which is higher than the original transaction price.

Repo Rate The rate of interest involved in a repurchase agreement.

Sometimes one investor (often a financial institution) will sell another investor (often another financial institution) a money market instrument and agree to repurchase it for an agreed-upon price at a later date. For example, investor A might sell investor B, for a price of $20 million, a number of Treasury bills that mature in 180 days. Investor A signs a **repurchase agreement** with investor B specifying that after 30 days, investor A will repurchase these Treasury bills for $20.1 million. Thus, investor A will be paying investor B $100 000 in interest for a 30-day loan of $20 million. Investor B is, in essence, purchasing a money market instrument that matures in 30 days. The annualized interest rate is known as the **repo rate**, which in this case is equal to ($100 000/$20 000 000) × (365/30) = 6.09%.

Note that this repurchase agreement is like a collateralized loan from B to A, with the Treasury bills serving as the collateral. Such loans involve very little risk to the lender (B), because the money market instruments typically used in repurchase agreements are of high quality.

Canadian Government Securities

Debt Refunding The issuance of new debt for the purpose of paying off currently maturing debt.

Export Development Corporation
www.edc.ca

Until 1997 the Canadian government relied heavily on debt to finance its budget deficits. The recent budget surpluses have reduced this need, but new debt must be issued in order to raise the necessary funds to pay off old debts that mature, an operation known as **debt refunding**. In addition to issuing its own debt, the Canadian government implicitly guarantees the debts of certain federal agencies such as the Export Development Corporation, the Farm Credit Corporation, and the Federal Business Development Bank. The bonds of these agencies are generally regarded as being of high quality but low liquidity. In the past, the government has also unconditionally guaranteed the principal and interest of debt securities of certain Crown Corporations.

Some idea of the magnitude and ownership of Canadian government marketable term debt (one year or more) can be gained by examining Table 13.2. The federal government,

Table 13.2	Ownership of Outstanding Government of Canada Marketable Term Debt, December 1996.[a]		
Held By	Amount (in millions)	Percentage of Total
Chartered banks	$ 51 319	17.5%
Thrift institutions	5 155	1.8
Life insurance companies	25 170	8.6
Property and casualty insurance companies	13 282	4.5
Trusteed pension funds	51 450	17.5
Mutual funds	16 794	5.7
Investment dealers	443	0.2
Non-financial private corporations	2 108	0.7
Misc. private financial institutions	1 338	0.5
Foreign investors	93 909	32.0
Individuals and non-incorporated business	108	neg.
Subtotal — privately held federal bonds	$261 076	88.8%
Non-financial government enterprise	$ 142	neg.
Public financial institutions	6 798	2.3
Social security funds	3 464	1.2
Provincial and local governments	14 332	4.9
Bank of Canada	7 963	2.7
Federal government	103	neg.
Subtotal publicly held federal bonds	$ 32 802	11.2%
Total federal marketable bonds	$293 878	100.0%

[a]Excludes Treasury bills but includes federal government guaranteed issues.

SOURCE: Statistics Canada, *National Balance Sheet Accounts: System of National Accounts, Annual Estimates,* 1984–1996, Ottawa, March 1997.

Bank of Canada
www.bank-banque-
canada.ca

**Federal Business
Development Bank**
www.bdc.ca

through the Bank of Canada, is a moderately large debt holder, as are provincial and local governments. The vast majority of these bonds, however, are held by the private sector; notably by foreign investors and trusteed pension funds. The remainder are fairly uniformly distributed amongst the various Canadian institutions and individuals. Over 97% of these bonds are denominated in Canadian dollars with the remainder issued predominantly in Eurodollars or Japanese yen. Nearly 90% of the total public debt is marketable, meaning it is represented by securities that can be sold at any time by the original purchaser through investment dealers. The major non-marketable issues are held by individuals in the form of Canada Savings Bonds. Marketable issues include Treasury bills and bonds of different maturities. Table 13.3 shows the amounts in each category and the maturity structure of the marketable securities in December 1996.

The Bank of Canada has considerable latitude in selecting maturities for new issues and makes a practice of providing bonds of different maturities with each issue—presumably to appeal to investors with different horizons. At the end of 1996 more than 56% of the total debt was short-term, maturing in three years or less, and about 64% had a maturity date within five years.[4]

---

[4]The effective maturity of the non-marketable debt is not easy to determine because Canada Savings Bonds are redeemable by the buyer on demand at any time.

Table 13.3	Maturity Structure of Marketable Interest-Bearing Government of Canada Debt, December 1996.		
Type and Maturity		Amount (in millions)	Percentage of Total
Non-marketable issues:			
Canada Savings Bonds		$ 53 409	7.5%
Foreign series		6 928	1.6
Other*		3 785	0.9
Total Non-marketable Debt		$ 44 122	9.9%
Marketable issues:			
Treasury bills		$117 464	26.5%
Under 3 years		91 199	20.6
3–5 years		58 895	13.3
5–10 years		71 838	16.2
10 years and over		60 222	13.6
Total Marketable Debt		$399 618	90.1%
Total Debt		$443 740	100.0%

*All of these bonds are held by the Canadian Pension Plan Investment Fund.
SOURCE: *Bank of Canada Review*, Autumn 1997.

The three principal types of debt issued by the Canadian government as well as two derivative securities are discussed next.

Government of Canada Treasury Bills

Treasury bills are issued on a discount basis, with maturities of up to 52 weeks, in denominations of $5000, $25 000, $100 000, and $1 million (although at times denominations as small as $1000 have been offered). All are issued as **bearer bonds** only. This means that the buyer's name is neither recorded in the Bank of Canada's books nor on the security itself. The face value is payable at maturity to the current holder of the security. Although Treasury bills are sold at a discount, their dollar yield (that is, the difference between the purchase price and face value if the bill is held to maturity) is treated as interest income for tax purposes.

Offerings of 91-day and 182-day bills are made once each week, 364-day bills are offered most weeks, and occasionally shorter maturities are also offered. All are sold at auction every Tuesday at noon (Monday if Tuesday is a holiday) by the Bank of Canada acting as an agent of the Minister of Finance. The Bank of Canada itself and **primary distributors** (specified chartered banks and investment dealers) are eligible to bid on bills intended for resale, but others may bid on their own account. Bids may be entered on either a competitive or non-competitive basis. With a competitive bid, the investor states a price she is willing to pay. For example, an investor might enter a bid for a stated number of 91-day bills at a price of 99.098. If the bid is accepted, the investor will pay $99 098.00 for each $100 000 of face value, meaning that an investment of $99 098.00 will generate a receipt of $100 000 if held to maturity 91 days later. With a non-competitive bid, the investor agrees to pay the average price of all bids that will be accepted by the Bank of Canada.

The results of the auction are announced by the Bank of Canada at about 2:00 p.m. on Tuesday. Generally, bids are received for more bills than are being offered, so some bidders are not successful. All non-competitive bids are accepted, with the balance of the issue allocated between the highest competitive bidders. Every Wednesday *The Globe and Mail* publishes the results of the auction that took place on the previous day. Figure 13.3 presents the results of the auction that took place on August 18, 1998, of 98-day T-bills in this case.

Bearer Bond A bond with attached coupons that represent the right to receive interest payments. The owner submits each coupon on its specified date to receive payment. Ownership is transferred by the seller endorsing the bond over to the buyer.

Primary Distributor An institution that issued a security to be sold in the primary market.

Individuals may purchase Treasury bills indirectly from a bank or investment dealer, or through a mutual fund, all of whom offer them at a slightly higher price than that paid at the auction (i.e., at a lower yield). Figure 13.4 shows the yields quoted by a financial institution for common maturities of Treasury bills as well as Bankers' Acceptances.

There is an active secondary market where institutions may trade Treasury bills with investment dealers. The bid-ask spread on these transactions varies between 1 and 5 basis points (for example, a dealer may quote bid 3.96% and ask 3.92%, meaning that the dealer is willing to pay a price that will earn him an annualized rate of 3.96%) depending on the size of the transaction and the volatility of the market.

Government of Canada Short-Term Bonds

These consist of bonds and government guaranteed bonds with a residual maturity of three years or less and may consist of either medium-term (maturity between three and ten years) or long-term bonds that are approaching maturity, or newly issued short-term bonds. Short-term bonds are traded in the money market, although the characteristics and marketing of newly issued bonds with a maturity of three years are more like those of medium-term and long-term bonds, discussed on the next page.

Prices and yields on short-term bonds are quoted in the newspapers along with other Government of Canada bonds. The following is a typical bond quotation, reported in *The Globe and Mail* on August 20, 1998:

Aug. 19 1998	Coupon Rate %	Maturity Date	Bid Price $	Yield
Canada	9.25	Dec. 1 99	104.62	5.45

This indicates that this short-term bond maturing on December 1, 1999, carries a coupon rate of 9.25% and a quoted price of $104.62. This quoted price is the bid price. The effective yield to maturity based on the quoted price is approximately 5.45%. A purchaser of this bond could expect to pay the ask price while a seller would receive the bid price. As the bid-ask spread is generally $0.10 to $0.15 for government bonds, the seller could expect to receive $104.62 and the buyer could expect to pay $104.77.

Accrued Interest Interest earned, but not yet paid.

In practice, the situation facing a potential buyer (or seller) is somewhat more complicated. The buyer is required to pay the seller not only the ask price (say, $104.77) but also any **accrued interest**. For example, on August 19, 80 days have elapsed since the last coupon payment and 103 days remain until the next. Therefore, an amount equal to $80/183 = 0.4372$ of the semiannual coupon ($0.4372 \times 46.25 = 20.22$) is added to the ask price to arrive at the settlement price (in this case, $104.77 + 20.22 = 124.99$). Similarly if an investor were to sell this bond the dealer would pay the bid price plus accrued interest ($104.62 + 20.22 = 124.84$). This procedure is commonly followed with all bonds.

Figure 13.4	Money market and fixed income investments.

Rates as of Aug. 27/98	30 D	60 D	90 D	180 D	365 D
G of C T-Bills (>$25 000)	4.10%	4.15%	4.20%	4.45%	4.90%
Bankers' Acceptances (>$100 000)	5.00	5.05	5.10	5.25	5.35
	2 Y	3 Y	5 Y	7 Y	10 Y
Mortgage-backed Securities	5.04%	5.24%	5.47%	5.60%	5.64%
G of C Strips	5.00	5.17	5.37	5.48	5.54%
Provincial Bonds	4.99	5.16	5.49	5.55	5.61%

SOURCE: The Toronto Dominion Bank (August 28, 1998). For illustrative purposes only. Rates do not reflect current information.

Government of Canada Medium- and Long-term Bonds

Medium-term bonds have maturities from three to 10 years at the time of issue. Long-term bonds are those with initial maturities greater than 10 years. Interest or coupon payments are generally made semi-annually at a set rate. Bonds may be issued as either bearer or **registered bonds**, commonly in denominations of $1000, $5000, $25 000, $100 000, or $1 million. Bonds issued in bearer form have numbered and dated coupons attached to the bond certificate that may be detached and cashed on the due date (but not before). The name of the owner of a registered bond is recorded at the Bank of Canada in Ottawa and also appears on the bond certificate. Interest is paid by cheque directly to the owner. Transfer of ownership of a registered bond is somewhat more complicated than for a bearer bond, although the former provides security in the event of a theft.[5]

Some issues may have a *call* or *redemption feature* that allows them to be "called" on specified notice (30 to 60 days typically). The Bank of Canada has the right to force the investor to sell the bonds back to the government at a predetermined price (par or slightly above). These issues usually provide call protection, in that the call provision does not come into effect for several years after the date of issue.

For callable issues, the yield-to-maturity is calculated using the stated price. If this price is greater than par, then the calculation of yield-to-maturity is based on an assumption that the bond will be called at the earliest allowable date.

Several issues also include a purchase fund, under whose provisions the Government of Canada undertakes to retire a specified fraction of the issue prior to maturity by purchasing the bonds in the open market at prices not exceeding a specified value (usually par or slightly below).

Many Government of Canada bonds trade in an active secondary market. Prices and yields of more heavily traded Government of Canada, provincial, and corporate bonds are quoted daily in *The Globe and Mail* and *The Financial Post.* Figure 13.5 illustrates typical information provided in the former publication.

Canada Savings Bonds

Once a year, generally for about two weeks ending on November 1, non-marketable *Canada Savings Bonds* (CSBs) are offered—only to individuals, estates, and specified trusts. No more than a specified amount may be purchased by any one person in a single year, but the amount may vary from year to year (for example, $20 000 in 1987, $75 000 in 1991). Term to maturity varies from issue to issue. In the early 1980s seven-year terms prevailed, but the 1991 series had a twelve-year term. Term to maturity is not an important feature, because the valuable option CSBs provide is the possibility of redemption, at face value plus accrued interest, at any time prior to maturity by presenting the bonds at any financial institution.

Two types of CSBs are available. Simple interest bonds pay interest annually on November 1 each year. Compound interest bonds are essentially pure-discount bonds, meaning that no interest is paid on them prior to maturity, at which time a lump sum representing principal plus interest is paid.

In October 1998 the Government of Canada introduced Canada Premium Bonds. The first series of these (Series 3) went on sale with a November 1 issue date and further series went on sale each month until April 1, 1999 (Series 8). Canada Premium Bonds are similar to Canada Savings Bonds except that they offer a slightly higher coupon (about 0.25%) and are only redeemable once a year on the anniversary of the issue date and during the 30 days thereafter.

---

[5]Some bonds currently in existence are registered as to principal only. These carry coupons like a bearer bond but the owner's name is recorded on the bond certificate. Such bonds are no longer issued.

Figure 13.5 Price quotations for actively traded Canadian bonds.

CANADIAN BONDS

Provided by RBC Dominion Securities

Selected quotations, with changes since the previous day, on actively traded bond issues yester-day. Yields are calculated to full maturity. Price is the final bid-side price as of 5 pm yesterday.

Issuer	Coupon	Maturity	Price	Yield	Price $ Chg
GOVERNMENT OF CANADA					
Canada	7.750	Sep 01/99	102.28	5.44	-0.04
Canada	4.750	Sep 15/99	99.30	5.43	-0.04
Canada	9.250	Dec 01/99	104.62	5.45	-0.06
Canada	5.500	Feb 01/00	100.09	5.43	-0.05
Canada	8.500	Mar 01/00	104.39	5.46	-0.06
Canada	5.000	Mar 15/00	99.47	5.35	-0.05
Canada	10.500	Jul 01/00	108.73	5.49	-0.08
Canada	7.500	Sep 01/00	103.73	5.53	-0.07
Canada	5.000	Dec 01/00	99.11	5.42	-0.08
Canada	10.500	Mar 01/01	111.46	5.58	-0.07
Canada	7.500	Mar 01/01	104.50	5.57	-0.06
Canada	9.750	Jun 01/01	110.57	5.59	-0.09
Canada	7.000	Sep 01/01	103.88	5.59	-0.09
Canada	9.750	Dec 01/01	112.24	5.60	-0.12
Canada	8.500	Apr 01/02	109.33	5.60	-0.12
Canada	5.500	Sep 01/02	99.75	5.57	-0.10
Canada	11.750	Feb 01/03	123.73	5.63	-0.17
Canada	7.250	Jun 01/03	106.70	5.63	-0.14
Canada	5.250	Sep 01/03	98.66	5.56	-0.13
Canada	7.500	Dec 01/03	108.42	5.63	-0.16
Canada	10.250	Feb 01/04	121.33	5.64	-0.19
Canada	6.500	Jun 01/04	104.21	5.63	-0.16
Canada	9.000	Dec 01/04	117.53	5.64	-0.19
Canada	8.750	Dec 01/05	118.29	5.65	-0.20
Canada	14.000	Oct 01/06	153.58	5.66	-0.32
Canada	7.000	Dec 01/06	108.82	5.65	-0.20
Canada	7.250	Jun 01/07	110.92	5.65	-0.21
Canada	6.000	Jun 01/08	102.72	5.63	-0.22
Canada	10.000	Jun 01/08	132.20	5.66	-0.27
Canada	9.500	Jun 01/10	132.38	5.69	-0.30
Canada	9.000	Mar 01/11	129.24	5.70	-0.30
Canada	10.250	Mar 15/14	146.37	5.71	-0.27
Canada	9.750	Jun 01/21	150.18	5.76	-0.39
Canada	8.000	Jun 01/23	129.50	5.75	-0.30
Canada	9.000	Jun 01/25	143.76	5.77	-0.39
Canada	8.000	Jun 01/27	131.38	5.75	-0.39
Canada	5.750	Jun 01/29	100.70	5.70	-0.71
CMHC	5.500	Mar 03/02	99.43	5.66	-0.10
PROVINCIAL					
Alberta	6.250	Mar 01/01	101.52	5.60	-0.06
Alberta	6.375	Jun 01/04	103.15	5.72	-0.15
B C	9.000	Jan 09/02	109.75	5.78	-0.11
B C	7.750	Jun 16/03	108.03	5.81	-0.14
B C	9.000	Jun 21/04	115.35	5.85	-0.18
B C	6.000	Jun 09/08	100.60	5.92	-0.21
B C	8.500	Aug 23/13	123.91	6.05	-0.32
B C	6.150	Nov 19/27	100.18	6.14	-0.25
B C Mun Fin	7.750	Dec 01/05	110.73	5.91	-0.18
B C Mun Fin	5.500	Mar 24/08	97.01	5.91	-0.20
Hydro Quebec	10.875	Jul 25/01	113.46	5.79	-0.15
Hydro Quebec	5.500	May 15/03	98.30	5.92	-0.15
Hydro Quebec	7.000	Jun 01/04	104.98	5.96	-0.21
Hydro Quebec	10.250	Jul 16/12	136.90	6.24	-0.50
Hydro Quebec	9.625	Jul 15/22	140.45	6.32	-0.45
Manitoba	7.875	Apr 07/03	108.46	5.76	-0.14
Manitoba	5.750	Jun 02/08	98.98	5.89	-0.21
Manitoba	7.750	Dec 22/25	123.51	5.99	-0.29
New Brunswic	8.000	Mar 17/03	108.75	5.79	-0.14
New Brunswic	5.700	Jun 02/08	98.61	5.89	-0.21
New Brunswic	6.000	Dec 27/17	99.63	6.03	-0.22
Newfoundland	6.150	Apr 17/28	98.11	6.29	-0.24
Nova Scotia	5.250	Jun 02/03	97.70	5.81	-0.12
Nova Scotia	6.600	Jun 01/27	105.53	6.19	-0.26
Ontario	10.875	Jan 10/01	111.30	5.72	-0.10
Ontario	8.000	Mar 11/03	108.68	5.80	-0.14
Ontario	8.750	Apr 22/03	111.84	5.81	-0.15
Ontario	7.750	Dec 08/03	108.74	5.80	-0.16
Ontario	9.000	Sep 15/04	115.90	5.84	-0.18
Ontario	8.250	Dec 01/05	113.81	5.89	-0.19
Ontario	7.500	Jan 19/06	109.56	5.89	-0.18
Ontario	7.750	Jul 24/06	111.55	5.90	-0.20
Ontario	6.125	Sep 12/07	101.58	5.90	-0.19
Ontario	9.500	Jul 13/22	142.29	6.11	-0.31
Ontario	7.600	Jun 02/27	119.82	6.13	-0.29
Ontario	6.500	Mar 08/29	105.07	6.13	-0.26
Ontario Hyd	10.000	Mar 19/01	110.09	5.72	-0.09

Issuer	Coupon	Maturity	Price	Yield	Price $ Chg
Ontario Hyd	8.625	Feb 06/02	108.83	5.77	-0.11
Ontario Hyd	9.000	Jun 24/02	110.95	5.77	-0.12
Ontario Hyd	5.375	Jun 02/03	98.24	5.80	-0.12
Ontario Hyd	7.750	Nov 03/05	110.79	5.89	-0.18
Ontario Hyd	5.600	Jun 02/08	97.73	5.91	-0.21
Ontario Hyd	8.250	Jun 22/26	128.20	6.13	-0.30
Quebec	10.000	Apr 26/00	106.88	5.62	-0.09
Quebec	10.250	Oct 15/01	112.60	5.80	-0.15
Quebec	5.250	Apr 01/02	98.10	5.84	-0.10
Quebec	7.500	Dec 01/03	106.94	5.94	-0.20
Quebec	7.750	Mar 30/06	110.20	6.05	-0.25
Quebec	6.500	Oct 01/07	102.75	6.10	-0.29
Quebec	11.000	Apr 01/09	137.40	6.15	-0.44
Quebec	8.500	Apr 01/26	128.00	6.34	-0.45
Quebec	6.000	Oct 01/29	95.40	6.34	-0.39
Saskatchewan	6.125	Oct 10/01	101.17	5.71	-0.09
Saskatchewan	5.500	Jun 02/08	97.18	5.88	-0.21
Saskatchewan	8.750	May 30/25	134.40	6.12	-0.30
Toronto -Met	6.100	Aug 15/07	101.00	5.95	-0.21
Toronto -Met	6.100	Dec 12/17	100.09	6.09	-0.22
CORPORATE					
AGT Limited	8.800	Sep 22/25	131.16	6.37	-0.35
Associates	5.400	Sep 04/01	98.39	5.99	-0.07
Avco Fin	5.750	Jun 02/03	98.63	6.08	-0.13
Bank Of Mont	5.550	Aug 27/02	98.52	5.97	-0.10
Bank Of Mont	5.650	Dec 01/03	98.52	5.98	-0.13
Bank Of N S	6.000	Dec 04/01	100.23	5.92	-0.09
Bank Of N S	5.400	Apr 01/03	97.67	5.99	-0.12
Bank Of N S	6.250	Jul 16/07	100.86	6.12	-0.19
Bank Of N S	5.650	Jul 22/08	96.60	6.11	-0.21
Can Cred Tst	5.625	Mar 24/05	97.71	6.05	-0.05
Can Trust M	5.450	Dec 03/01	98.53	5.95	-0.08
Cards Trust	5.510	Jun 21/03	98.27	5.93	-0.04
Cards Trust	5.630	Dec 21/05	97.76	6.01	-0.07
Cdn Occ Pet	6.300	Jun 02/08	93.87	7.18	-0.25
Crestar En	6.450	Oct 01/07	94.71	7.25	-0.17
Domtar Inc	10.000	Apr 15/11	115.39	8.04	-0.25
Grtr TTO Air	5.400	Dec 03/02	98.19	5.88	-0.10
Grtr TTO Air	5.950	Dec 03/07	99.13	6.07	-0.19
Grtr TTO Air	6.450	Dec 03/27	101.65	6.32	-0.30
Gtc Trans	6.200	Jun 01/07	98.65	6.40	-0.18
Interprv Pip	8.200	Feb 15/24	123.51	6.33	-0.32
Legacy	5.930	Nov 15/02	98.38	6.37	-0.10
Loblaws Co	6.650	Nov 08/27	101.22	6.55	-0.30
Loewen	6.100	Oct 01/02	92.73	8.22	-0.08
London Ins	9.375	Jan 08/02	110.16	6.00	-0.12
Morguard Ret	6.600	Oct 09/07	95.69	7.25	-0.17
Mstr Cr Trus	5.760	Aug 21/02	99.51	5.90	-0.03
Mstr Cr Trus	5.700	Nov 21/03	98.84	5.96	-0.05
Mstr Cr Trus	6.150	Dec 21/04	100.82	5.99	-0.05
Nav Canada	7.560	Mar 01/27	115.26	6.39	-0.27
Oxford	6.860	Jul 21/04	95.68	7.78	-0.13
Renaissance	6.850	Feb 06/07	101.93	6.55	-0.18
Rogers Cable	8.750	Jul 15/07	98.17	9.05	-0.16
Rogers Cant	10.500	Jun 01/06	109.42	8.80	-0.17
Royal Bank	5.400	Sep 03/02	98.01	5.96	-0.10
Royal Bank	5.400	Apr 07/03	97.78	5.96	-0.12
Royal Bank	6.500	Sep 12/06	102.52	6.10	-0.18
Royal Bank	6.750	Jun 04/07	104.20	6.12	-0.19
Royal Bank	5.600	Apr 22/08	96.51	6.08	-0.20
Sask Wheat	6.100	Jul 18/07	98.99	6.75	-0.18
Strait Cross	6.170	Sep 15/31	96.39	6.43	-0.30
T D Bank	5.600	Sep 05/01	99.15	5.91	-0.08
T D Bank	6.450	Oct 17/01	101.53	5.91	-0.09
Trizec Hahn	7.950	Jun 01/07	100.28	7.90	-0.80
Union Gas	8.650	Nov 10/25	128.04	6.45	-0.34
West Fraser	6.800	Nov 19/07	97.64	7.15	-0.18
Weston Geo	7.450	Feb 09/04	106.64	6.00	-0.15
Wstcoast Ene	6.750	Dec 15/27	104.12	6.43	-0.31
York Receiv	5.670	Apr 21/02	99.22	5.91	-0.03
Real Return	4.250	Dec 01/21	102.90	4.06	-0.40
Real Return	4.250	Dec 01/26	103.41	4.05	-0.43

DS Barra indexes

Index	Level	Daily Total Return % Chg	Daily Price Return % Chg	MTD Total Return % Chg
Market	307.70	-0.14	-0.15	-0.71
Short	262.21	-0.06	-0.08	0.00
Intermed	311.21	-0.15	-0.17	-0.71
Long	379.50	-0.24	-0.25	-1.85
Govts	305.88	-0.14	-0.15	-0.66
Canadas	298.21	-0.13	-0.14	-0.51
Provs	325.87	-0.16	-0.18	-1.10
Munis	112.52	-0.14	-0.16	-0.90
Corps	327.11	-0.13	-0.15	-0.93

Scotia Capital Markets indexes

Index	Close	% chg	Yield	Chg	52 wk High	52 wk Low
Short	312.74	-0.02	5.580	0.01	313.43	299.95
Mid	370.88	-0.03	5.772	0.01	377.06	347.86
Long	453.36	-0.07	5.957	0.01	468.38	398.57
Universe	371.01	-0.03	5.740	0.01	376.43	345.34

Benchmarks

Issuer	Coupon	Maturity	Price	Yield	$ chg
U.S. Treasury	5.5	Aug/28	99 4/32	5.56	-2/32
British gilt	7.25	Dec/07	111 23/32	5.60	-6/32
German	4.75	Jan/08	102.48	4.43	-0.08
Japan #182	3.0	Sept/05	111.77	1.195	-0.30

SOURCE: Reprinted by the permission of *The Globe and Mail: Report on Business* (August 20, 1998).

All CSBs are floating-rate bonds with an annual adjustment period. The interest rate payable is announced for the first year at the time of issue. In subsequent years the interest rate is equal to the rate paid on the newly issued CSBs. In any given year, therefore, all CSB series pay the same interest rate. Both types are fully registered and may be neither transferred nor assigned, although some banks will accept CSBs as collateral for loans. These bonds are available in denominations from $100 to $10 000, and may be purchased from chartered banks and other financial institutions. Some employers allow their employees to obtain them through payroll savings plans.[6]

Income from CSBs is taxed in the same manner as any other fixed income security—payments from simple interest bonds must be reported in the year in which they are received and accrued interest on compound interest bonds must be reported, despite the fact that no interest has actually been received. Each year the Bank of Canada publishes tables showing the amount of accrued interest that must be reported for compound interest bonds.

Zero-coupon or Strip Bonds

Zero-coupon Bond A fixed-income security that promises to make only one payment to its owner.

A non-callable Government of Canada bond is, in effect, a portfolio of pure-discount or **zero-coupon bonds**. That is, each coupon payment, as well as the principal, can be viewed as a bond in itself; the investor who owns the bond can therefore be viewed as holding a number of individual pure-discount bonds. In 1982, a number of brokerage firms began separating these components, using a process known as **coupon stripping**, described in Chapter 5.

Coupon Stripping The process of separating and selling the individual cash flows of Treasury notes or bonds.

Figure 13.6 shows typical market prices for a set of stripped default-free securities, where price is expressed as a percent of maturity value. As the figure shows, the longer the investor has to wait until maturity, the lower the price of the security. In Canada, strip bonds are derived from federal and provincial securities and trade in the OTC market, but prices are not quoted in the business press. Investors wishing to trade these securities may approach the chartered banks or dealers who specialize in them to obtain quotes. Figure 13.4 also shows a bank's quotation for Government of Canada stripped coupons.

Real Return Bonds

Real Return Bond A Government of Canada bond whose coupon payments and face value are indexed to the Consumer Price Index, thereby providing investors with a known real return if held to maturity.

Real Return Bonds are designed to provide a specified real return over their lifetime; that is, they are indexed so as to offer an inflation protected return. On December 10, 1991, the Government of Canada issued $700 million of non-callable 4.25% Real Return Bonds that mature on December 1, 2021. These are the first example of their kind in North America, although index-linked bonds have been issued by other governments, notably in the UK and Israel. In 1996 the Government of Canada issued a second series of 4.25% Real Return Bonds maturing on December 1, 2026. Prices for and yields for both these series are quoted in the financial press as shown in Figure 13.5.

While the nominal yield to maturity and nominal cash flows are known in advance for conventional bonds (for example, an 8% Government of Canada bond purchased at par has a nominal yield of 8% per annum), the real yield depends on the rate of inflation throughout the term of the bonds. Even though the nominal amount due on maturity is known in advance, the purchasing power of that amount is uncertain and may be more or less than the purchasing power of the original principal.

---

[6]In times of rapidly rising interest rates the Bank of Canada has been forced to change rates during the year in an effort to stem the flood of redemptions, but has not always been successful. In 1990, redemptions exceeded the new issue by over $8 billion.

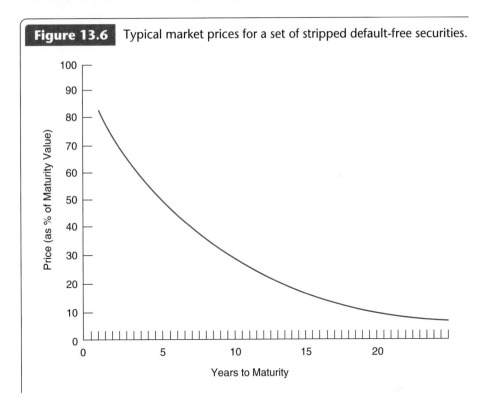

Figure 13.6 Typical market prices for a set of stripped default-free securities.

In the case of Real Return Bonds the real yield to maturity and real cash flows are known in advance. The nominal yield, however, depends on the rate of inflation throughout the term of these bonds and, while the purchasing power of the amount due at maturity is known in advance, the actual nominal amount due at maturity is uncertain and may be more or less than the nominal amount of the original principal.

A Real Return Bond offers investors the following advantages:

- guaranteed real yield to maturity
- preservation of purchasing power of principal and coupons
- automatic reinvestment of inflation compensation, thereby reducing reinvestment risk
- better matching of inflation-indexed liabilities
- improved portfolio risk/return characteristics

For a more detailed description of the Government of Canada's Real Return Bond offerings see the Institutional Issues section on page 340.

Mortgage-backed Securities

Technically, *mortgage-backed securities* are not Government of Canada securities but they are guaranteed by the government and so are described here. A mortgage-backed security (MBS) is a flow-through security that represents an ownership interest in a pool of residential first mortgages with similar terms to maturity (usually five years) and similar interest rates. The mortgages must be individually guaranteed under the National Housing Act (NHA). They are assembled by a financial institution (such as a bank, trust company, credit union, etc.), into an MBS that is underwritten by the Canada Mortgage and Housing Corporation (CMHC)—a federal government agency—then subdivided into individual units and sold to the general public in minimum denominations of $5000.

Canada Mortgage and Housing Corporation
www.cmhc-schl.gc.ca

Real Return Bonds

Summary of the Offering

Issue:	4.25% Real Return Bonds due 2021 (the "Bonds"), with a rate of return linked to the Consumer Price Index for Canada.
Issue Amount:	$700 000 000
Issue Price:	100%
Real Yield:	4.25%
Rank:	The Bonds constitute direct, unsecured, unconditional obligations of Her Majesty in right of Canada. Principal and interest on the Bonds (interest consisting of coupon interest and inflation compensation) are direct charges on, and payable out of, the Consolidated Revenue Fund of Canada.
Date of Maturity:	December 1, 2021 ("Maturity")
Date of Closing:	December 10, 1991 ("Date of Closing")
Consumer Price Index:	The Consumer Price Index for purposes of the Bonds is the All-items Consumer Price Index for Canada (1986 = 100), not seasonally adjusted, as published by Statistics Canada.
Indexing Process:	An index ratio (the "Index Ratio") is applied to calculate both Coupon Interest and Inflation Compensation. The Index Ratio for any date ("Date") is defined as the ratio of the reference CPI ("Ref CPI$_{\text{Date}}$") applicable to such date divided by the reference CPI applicable to the Date of Closing ("Ref CPI$_{\text{Base}}$").

$$\text{Index Ratio}_{\text{Date}} = \left[\frac{\text{Ref CPI}_{\text{Date}}}{\text{Ref CPI}_{\text{Base}}} \right]$$

The reference CPI for the first day of any calendar month is the CPI for the third preceding calendar month. For example, the reference CPI for January 1, 1992 will be the CPI for October 1991. The reference CPI for any other day in a month is calculated by linear interpolation between the reference CPI applicable to the first day of the month in which such day falls and the reference CPI applicable to the first day of the month immediately following.

Interest and Final Payment:	The Bonds bear interest adjusted in relation to the Consumer Price Index for Canada ("CPI") which interest consists of both an inflation compensation component ("Inflation Compensation") calculated based on Principal and payable at Maturity and a cash entitlement ("Coupon Interest") calculated based on Principal and accrued Inflation Compensation, which Coupon Interest is payable in semi-annual instalments on June 1 and December 1 (the "Coupon Payment Dates"), commencing June 1, 1992. Coupon Interest is calculated by multiplying one-half of the coupon of 4.25% per annum by the sum of the Principal and the Inflation Compensation which has accrued from the date of issue of the Bonds to the relevant Coupon Payment Date. At Maturity, in addition to Coupon Interest payable on such date, a final payment (the "Final Payment") equal to the sum of Inflation Compensation accrued from the date of issue of the Bonds to Maturity (whether positive or negative) and Principal will be made.

Final Payment = Principal + Inflation Compensation

Calculation of Interest: Inflation Compensation accrued to any Date is calculated by first multiplying the Principal by the Index Ratio applicable to that Date ("Index Ratio$_{Date}$") and then subtracting the Principal.

$$\text{Inflation Compensation}_{Date} = \{[\text{Principal} \times \text{Index Ratio}_{Date}] - \text{Principal}\}$$

or

$$\text{Inflation Compensation}_{Date} = \left\{\left[\text{Principal} \times \frac{\text{Ref CPI}_{Date}}{\text{Ref CPI}_{Base}}\right] - \text{Principal}\right\}$$

Coupon Interest is calculated by multiplying one-half of the coupon of 4.25% per annum by the sum of the Principal and the Inflation Compensation accrued from the date of issue of the Bonds to the relevant Coupon Payment Date.

$$\text{Coupon Interest}_{Date} = \frac{4.25\%}{2} \times [\text{Principal} + \text{Inflation Compensation}_{Date}]$$

Sample Calculation

Assumptions for purposes of illustration:

Issue Date:	December 1, 1991	Ref CPI$_{Base}$:	126.7000 (Ref CPI$_{December\ 1991}$)
Maturity Date:	March 1, 2021	Ref CPI$_{December\ 1,\ 1991}$:	CPI$_{September\ 1991}$
Annual Coupon:	4.25%	Principal:	100

Coupon Interest—June 1, 1992

Ref CPI$_{June\ 1,\ 1992}$ = 127.5000 (or CPI$_{March\ 1992}$)

$$\text{Index Ratio}_{September\ 1,\ 1991} = \left[\frac{127.5000}{126.7000}\right] = 1.00631$$

$$\text{Inflation Compensation}_{June\ 1,\ 1992} = \left\{\left[\text{Principal} \times \frac{\text{Ref CPI}_{June\ 1,\ 1992}}{\text{Ref CPI}_{December\ 1991}}\right] - \text{Principal}\right\}$$

$$\text{Inflation Compensation}_{June\ 1,\ 1992} = [100 \times 1.00631] - 100 = 0.631$$

$$\text{Coupon Interest}_{Date} = \frac{4.25\%}{2} \times [\text{Principal} + \text{Inflation Compensation}_{Date}]$$

$$\text{Coupon Interest}_{June\ 1,\ 1992} = \frac{4.25\%}{2} \times [100 + 0.631] = \$2.1384$$

Final Payment—March 1, 2021:

Ref CPI$_{March\ 1,\ 2021}$ = 395.8500 = CPI$_{December\ 2020}$

$$\text{Index Ratio}_{March\ 1,\ 2021} = \left[\frac{395.8500}{126.7}\right] = 3.1243$$

$$\text{Inflation Compensation}_{March\ 1,\ 2021} = [100 \times 3.1243] - 100 = 212.4309$$

$$\text{Final Payment} = \text{Principal} + \text{Inflation Compensation}$$

$$\text{Final Payment}_{March\ 1,\ 2021} = 100 + 212.4309 = 312.4309$$

Source: Excerpts from the original *Offering Circular*, October 1991 and material provided by Daniel Kelly, CIBC Wood Gundy.

Unlike most bonds, MBSs pay investors, on a monthly basis, an amount that represents a *pro rata* return of principal as well as interest on the underlying mortgages. For example, a holder of a $25 000 certificate from a $1 million pool would indirectly "own" 2.5% of each mortgage in the pool. Each month the homeowners make mortgage payments that are part principal and part interest. In turn, each month the investor receives 2.5% of the aggregate amount paid by the homeowners, less a small service charge. The mortgages are free from default risk because timely payment to the investor is guaranteed by CMHC, whether or not the issuer receives payment from the homeowner.

Two types of MBS are available—those consisting of non-prepayable mortgages and those consisting of prepayable mortgages.

There is a risk associated with the latter. When interest rates fall, homeowners prepaying or paying off their mortgages reduce the investor's return because both the term to maturity and the interest payments are reduced. MBSs based on prepayable mortgages would, therefore, be expected to sell at lower prices (higher yields) than those based on non-prepayable mortgages. The quoted prices and yields presented in Figure 13.7 show that this is the case. However, the yield differences are quite small, suggesting that prepayment risk is not perceived to be high.

Provincial, Territorial, and Local Government Securities

Provincial Bond A bond issued by one of the provinces of Canada

Municipal Bond A bond issued by a local unit of government.

Provincial, territorial, and municipal governments all borrow money to finance their investments and operations. In aggregate, the provincial and territorial governments have more term debt outstanding than the federal government. The securities issued by the first two are collectively referred to as **provincial bonds** or "provincials," while those of the third group are called **municipal bonds**, or simply "municipals" (the securities of the Canadian

---

Figure 13.7   Quoted prices and yields of mortgage-backed securities.

NHA Mortgage Backed Securities

Supplied by RBC Dominion Securities Inc. Bid side levels on minimum $1 million. Indicated yields assume no prepayments. All MBS are priced to their weighted average maturity date.

Pool #	Issuer	Coupon	Maturity	Price	Yield
Non-prepayable					
99005779	Bank Of NS	6.375	Nov 01/98	99.99	5.47
99007213	National Bnk	5.500	Mar 01/99	99.81	5.47
99007122	CIBC Mort	6.000	Mar 01/99	100.08	5.47
96600465	Equitble Tst	6.625	Jan 01/01	101.89	5.61
99007205	Peoples Tst	6.375	Mar 01/01	101.62	5.57
99007411	TD Bank	5.125	Jan 01/02	98.47	5.58
99007585	ManufCan Tst	5.000	Dec 01/02	97.64	5.58
99006355	Sun Life Ass	9.250	Sep 01/04	117.50	5.62
96600895	Pafco Ins	5.875	Nov 01/07	100.88	5.71
96600945	Maritime Lfe	5.000	Dec 01/07	95.42	5.71
Prepayable					
96409412	Wstmster Svg	6.375	Oct 01/98	99.90	5.62
96407911	Frstline Tst	7.750	Mar 01/00	102.09	5.72
97000038	Canada Trust	6.500	Jan 01/01	101.00	5.74
97000004	Canada Trust	5.750	Sep 01/01	99.84	5.73
97000012	Canada Trust	5.700	Jan 01/02	99.67	5.75
96412408	Sun Life Tst	5.500	Mar 01/02	99.35	5.68
97000327	National Bnk	5.250	Jul 01/02	98.44	5.75
97000608	Royal Bank	5.375	Oct 01/02	98.81	5.72
97000657	Royal Bank	5.125	Jan 01/03	97.95	5.72
96702204	Frstline Tst	5.500	Jan 01/08	98.40	5.83

SOURCE: Reprinted by permission of *The Financial Post* (August 6, 1998).

government are referred to as "Canadas"). Table 13.4 shows the distribution of ownership of provincial, territorial, and municipal term debt as of the end of 1996.

Provincial and Territorial Bonds

Provincials are issued to finance public works and, recently, social welfare programs. The payments on these securities are supported by provincial tax revenues. Many provinces also guarantee the bonds issued by provincial authorities and commissions, notably their hydro-electric commissions. As Figure 13.5 indicates, Hydro-Quebec and Ontario Hydro bonds

Hydro-Quebec
www.hydroquebec.com

Ontario Hydro
www.hydro.on.ca

Table 13.4 Ownership of Outstanding Provincial, Territorial, and Municipal Term Debt, December 1996.[a]

Held by	Provincials		Municipals	
	Amount[b]	Percentage of Total	Amount[b]	Percentage of Total
Chartered banks	$ 7 709	2.2%	$ 693	1.8%
Thrift institutions	3 414	1.0	143	0.4
Life insurance companies	18 716	5.4	3 766	9.6
Property and casualty insurance companies	4 883	1.4	1 221	3.1
Trusteed pension funds	59 084	17.1	3 158	8.0
Mutual funds	5 395	1.6	598	1.5
Investment dealers	1 221	0.4	654	1.7
Non-financial private corporations	152	neg.	—	—
Misc. private financial institutions	376	0.1	—	—
Foreign investors	151 756	44.0	5 082	13.0
Individuals and non-incorporated business	20 048	5.8	9 368	23.9
Subtotal — privately held term debt	$ 272 754	79.1%	$ 24 683	62.9%
Non-financial government enterprise	2 996	0.9	97	0.2
Public financial institutions	7 258	2.1	994	2.5
Social security funds	30 748	8.9	—	—
Provincial and local governments	31 045	9.0	13 458	34.3
Federal government	5	neg.	1	neg.
Subtotal publicly held term debt	$ 72 052	20.9%	$14 550	37.1%
Total term debt	$344 806	100.0%	$ 39 233	100.0%

[a]Excludes Treasury bills but includes provincial government guaranteed issues.
[b]in millions of dollars.

SOURCE: Statistics Canada, *National Balance Sheet Accounts: System of National Accounts, Annual Estimates*, 1984–1993, Ottawa, March 1997.

are listed among the more actively traded issues. The three principal holders of provincials are the trusteed pension plans, social security funds (notably the Canada Pension Plan) and foreign investors. The provinces have, in general, been more aggressive than the federal government in tapping foreign markets for funds, which provide better borrowing rates and conditions. A significant fraction of the outstanding issues are denominated in foreign currencies, predominantly US dollars, Swiss francs, and Japanese yen. At the time of issue their coupon rates were significantly below those prevailing in the domestic market. As a result, the provinces have assumed a degree of foreign exchange risk.

To assist municipalities, the provinces raise funds through government agencies such as the Alberta Municipal Financing Corporation and the Ontario Municipal Improvements Corporation. These agencies float large bond issues (guaranteed by the province) at advantageous rates and then distribute the proceeds to small municipalities that would otherwise have difficulty raising funds. An investor purchasing these bonds is effectively investing in a portfolio of municipal bonds that are guaranteed by the provincial government.

❍ Municipal Bonds

Installment Debentures A bond issued with different portions of the issue maturity at different dates.

Term Debentures A bond issued where all of the bonds mature on the same date.

Municipals are usually issued by larger cities as **installment debentures**, where specified groups of debentures mature in each succeeding year. The largest cities, such as Montreal, Toronto, and Vancouver may issue **term debentures** (that is, debentures that all mature on the same date) or a mixture of serial and term bonds. These issues are generally underwritten by an investment dealer who specializes in municipals or they are sold through a private placement. Table 13.4 indicates that the holders of municipal bonds are more widely varied than those of federal and provincial bonds. It should be noted, however, that no municipals appear in Figure 13.5 where actively traded issues are listed.

In recent years municipalities have, more frequently, been using non-market sources of capital such as the provincial agencies mentioned above, senior levels of government, and the Canada Pension Plan and provincial pension plan funds. Foreign sources, predominantly in the US, have also been used, but these represented only about 10% of the total at the end of 1997.

Corporate Bonds

Corporate bonds are similar to other kinds of fixed-income securities in that they carry the promise of specified payments at specified times and provide legal remedies in the event of default. Restrictions are often placed on the activities of the issuing corporation in order to provide additional protection for bondholders (for example, there may be restrictions on the amount of additional bonds that can be issued in the future).

From the viewpoint of the issuing corporation, debt differs from equity in two crucial respects. First, principal and interest payments are obligatory. Failure to make any payment in full and on time can expose the issuer to expensive, time-consuming, and potentially disruptive legal actions. Second, unlike dividend payments, interest payments are considered expenses to the corporation, and hence can be deducted from earnings before calculating the corporation's income tax liability. As a result, each dollar paid in interest reduces earnings before taxes by a dollar, thereby reducing corporate taxes by $0.40 for a firm in the 40% marginal tax bracket. This leads to less than a dollar decline in earnings after taxes (in the 40% tax bracket example, the decline in earnings is $0.60).

The Indenture

An issue of bonds is generally covered by a **trust indenture** or **trust deed**, in which the issuing corporation promises a specified **trustee** that it will comply with a number of stated provisions. Chief among these is the timely payment of required coupons and principal on the issue. Other terms are often included to control the sale of pledged property, the issuance of other bonds, and the like.

The trustee for a bond issue, usually a trust company, acts on behalf of the bondholders. Some actions may be required by the indenture, whereas others, such as acting in response to a request from specific bondholders, may be done at the trustee's discretion.

If the corporation defaults on an interest payment, after a relatively short period of time (perhaps one to six months) the entire principal typically becomes due and payable—a procedure designed to enhance the bondholders' status in any forthcoming bankruptcy or related legal proceedings.

Types of Bonds

An exhaustive list of the names used to describe bonds would be intolerably long. Different names are often used for the same type of bond, and occasionally the same name will be used for two quite different bonds. A few major types do predominate, however, with relatively standard nomenclature.

Mortgage Bonds

Bonds of this type represent debt that is secured by the pledge of specific property. In the event of default, the bondholders are entitled to obtain the property in question and sell it to satisfy their claims on the firm. In addition to the property itself, the holders of mortgage bonds have an unsecured claim or floating charge on all the other assets of the corporation.

Mortgage bondholders are usually protected by terms included in the bond indenture. The corporation may be constrained from pledging property for other bonds (or such bonds, if issued, must be "junior," or "second," mortgages, with only a secondary claim on the property). Certain property acquired by the corporation after the bonds were issued may also be pledged to support the bonds.

Collateral Trust Bonds

These bonds are backed by other securities that are usually held by the trustee. A common situation of this sort arises when the securities of a subsidiary firm are pledged as collateral by the parent firm.

Equipment Obligations

These securities (also known also as equipment trust certificates) are backed by specific pieces of equipment; for example, railway cars or commercial aircraft. If necessary, the equipment can be readily sold and delivered to a new owner. The legal arrangements used to facilitate the issuance of such bonds can be very complex. The most popular procedure uses the *Philadelphia plan*, in which the trustee initially holds the equipment, issues obligations, and leases the equipment to a corporation. Money received from the lessee is subsequently used to make interest and principal payments to the holders of the obligations; ultimately, if all payments are made on schedule, the leasing corporation takes title to the equipment.

Debentures

These are general obligations of the issuing corporation and thus represent unsecured credit. To protect the holders of such bonds, the indenture will usually limit the future issuance of secured debt as well as any additional unsecured debt.

Subordinated Debentures

When more than one issue of debentures is outstanding, a hierarchy may be specified. For example, subordinated debentures are junior to unsubordinated debentures, meaning that in the event of bankruptcy, junior claims are to be considered only after senior claims have been fully satisfied.

Other Types of Bonds

Income Bond A bond for which the size of the interest payments varies, based on the income of the issuer.

Income bonds are more like preferred shares (described in a later section) than bonds. Payment of interest in full and on schedule is not absolutely required, and failure to do so need not send the corporation into bankruptcy. Since 1978, interest on such bonds has qualified as a tax deductible expense in Canada for the issuing corporation. Except in reorganizations, this type of bond is rarely used.

Guaranteed Bond A bond issued by one corporation but backed by another corporation.

Guaranteed bonds are issued by one corporation but backed in some way by another (for example, by a parent firm). **Participation bonds** require stated interest payments and provide additional amounts if earnings exceed some stated level. In **serial bonds**, different portions of the issue mature at different dates.

Participation Bond A bond that promises to pay a stated rate of interest to its owner, but may also pay additional interest if the issuer's earnings exceed a specified level.

Convertible bonds may, at the holder's option, be exchanged for other securities, often common shares. Such bonds, which have become very popular in recent years, are discussed in more detail in Chapter 19.

Extendible bonds give the bondholder the option of extending the term to maturity of the bond on a specific date. For example, a five-year extendible bond may allow the investor, within six months of maturity, to extend the maturity by five years at the same or a slightly higher interest rate.

Serial Bond A bond issue with different portions of the issue maturing at different dates.

Retractable bonds give the bondholder the option of reducing the term to maturity of the bond on a specified date.

Convertible Bond A bond which may, at the holder's option, be exchanged for other securities, often common stock.

Call Provisions

Management would like to have the right to pay off the corporation's bonds at par at any time prior to maturity. Reducing debt or altering maturity by refunding provides desirable flexibility. Most important, expensive high-coupon debt issued during a time of high interest rates can be replaced with cheaper low-coupon debt if rates decline.

Extendible Bond A bond that includes a provision giving the owner the option to extend the maturity day by a specified number of years.

Not surprisingly, investors hold a different opinion on the matter. The issuer's ability to redeem an issue at par at any time virtually precludes a rise in price over par and robs the holder of potential gains from the price appreciation associated with declining interest rates; moreover, it introduces a new form of uncertainty. A bond with such a feature will almost certainly sell for less than one without it.

Retractable Bond A bond that includes a provision giving the owner the option to retract the maturity day by a specified number of years.

Despite the cost of obtaining this sort of flexibility, many corporations include call provisions in their bond indentures that give the corporation the option to call some or all of the bonds from their holders at stated prices during specified periods prior to maturity. In a sense, the firm sells a bond and simultaneously buys an option from the holders. The net price of the bond, therefore, is the difference between the value of the bond and the option. (Note that retractable bonds give the investor the option of forcing the issuer to call the security.)

Call Premium The difference between the call price of a bond and the par value of the bond.

Investors are often given some call protection: during the first few years after being issued, a bond may not be callable. When a bond is callable, a **call premium** may be specified in the call provision. If the issue is called when a call premium is specified then the issuer must pay the bondholders a **call price** that is a stated amount above par. Generally, the call premium declines as the maturity date approaches.

An entire issue may be called, or only specific bonds that are chosen randomly by the trustee may be called. In either case, a notice of redemption will appear in advance in the financial press.

Call features are not popular with Canadian institutional investors, probably because the relative illiquidity of the corporate bond market makes it difficult to replace a called bond with one having similar characteristics. For many years an alternative form of call protection was used that included a provision stating that the issue was non-refundable for financial advantage. This meant that the corporation could not call the bonds in order to replace them with bonds carrying a lower coupon rate but could call them to retire the issue without replacing them. This provision proved to be unenforceable so it was replaced with the **Canada Call**. The Canada Call required the issuer to pay a call premium such that the investor could enter the long Canada market to replace the bond with one that provided an equivalent cash flow. It soon became evident, however, that the investors benefitted from this provision because they were able to obtain higher quality bonds as replacements. Currently the **Canada plus x call** feature is standard on practically all corporate bonds issued. Under this provision the call premium is calculated using the corresponding Canada bond yield plus x basis points to reflect the quality differential.

Sinking Funds

A bond indenture will often require the issuing corporation to make annual payments into a **sinking fund**. Each payment covers part of the principal as well as the interest, thereby reducing the amount outstanding at maturity.

Sinking funds operate by having the corporation transfer cash to the trustee, who then purchases bonds in the open market. Alternatively, the corporation may obtain the bonds, by either purchase or call, and deposit them with the trustee. Call prices for sinking fund purchases may differ from those specified when the entire issue is to be repaid prior to maturity.

Required contributions to a sinking fund may or may not be the same each year. In some cases, the required amount may depend on earnings or output; in others, the goal is to make the annual payments equal.

Private Placements

Bonds intended for eventual public sale are usually issued in denominations of $1000 each. Both bearer and registered forms may be utilized. Often, however, a single investor (or a small group of investors) will buy an entire issue. Such **private placements** are typically purchased by large financial institutions.

Bankruptcy

When a corporation fails to make a scheduled coupon or principal payment on a bond, the corporation is said to be in default on that obligation. If the payment is not made within a relatively short period, litigation will usually follow.

A corporation unable to meet its obligatory debt payments is said to be technically insolvent (or insolvent in the equity sense). If the value of the firm's assets falls below its liabilities, it is said to be insolvent (or insolvent in the bankruptcy sense).

If voluntary agreements with creditors cannot be obtained, bankruptcy—usually "voluntary"—is filed by the corporation itself. Subsequent developments involve, among others, courts, court-appointed officials, representatives of the firm's creditors, and the management of the firm.

Distressed Securities

Investments in fixed-income securities have traditionally encompassed investment-grade bonds—securities rated Baa (or BBB) or higher by the major credit rating agencies. In the 1980s, the universe of popular fixed-income investments expanded to include below-investment grade bonds, called high-yield bonds. As interest rates fell in the early and mid-1990s, high-yield bonds became increasingly inviting to portfolio managers seeking to maintain attractive interest payouts to their clients.

Even in prosperous times, a surprisingly large percentage of high-yield bond issuers default on their debt. Although the high-yield bond category technically includes securities whose issuers have defaulted on their debt, high-yield bond portfolio managers in practice do not usually purchase bonds already in default. Rather, they focus their efforts on issuers who they anticipate can avoid default and therefore make the high yields paid on the issuers' bonds attractive relative to alternative fixed-income investments.

The securities of firms that have defaulted on their debt and who either (1) have filed for legal bankruptcy protection or (2) are negotiating out-of-court with creditors in the hope of avoiding bankruptcy are called *distressed securities*. These securities include publicly traded bonds as well as privately traded debt owed to commercial banks (known as bank debt) or suppliers of goods and services to the distressed companies (called trade debt). In addition, distressed securities can also include common stock, as one likely resolution to a bankruptcy is for holders of the company's debt to be compensated, in part, with newly issued equity.

Most companies that restructure their debt do so out of court. Those that do enter legal bankruptcy either reorganize their debt or investors in distressed securities will often prefer a reorganization as opposed to an out-of-court restructuring because the reorganized company must file considerable financial information with the court. This makes a valuation of the company's debt less difficult.

For those companies that do enter bankruptcy, each situation is unique. Nevertheless, there tend to be common aspects to most bankruptcies. Figure 13.8 provides an overview of the bankruptcy process from a company's initial financial problems to its ultimate reorganization.

It is often argued that distressed securities represent a more inefficient sector of the fixed-income market than either investment-grade or high-yield bonds. The reasoning is several-fold. First, there may be a market segmentation effect. Many institutional investors are prohibited from owning bankrupt securities. Thus, when a company enters bankruptcy, these investors are forced to sell their holdings, potentially driving down the price of the company's debt. Second, the process of bankruptcy is time consuming and unpredictable. Debt holders of a company near, or in, bankruptcy may wish to avoid these complications and sell their holdings cheaply to investors who are willing see the process through to reorganization. Third, there is a lack of research coverage on bankrupt companies. Analysts at major brokerage firms typically suspend their coverage when a company becomes bankrupt, leaving investors to secure their own information about the company's financial condition. Finally, there is the issue of limited liquidity. Only a few organizations are willing to make a market in distressed securities, resulting in wider bid-ask spreads.

Investors use different strategies to invest in distressed securities. Some follow a non-participatory approach in which they do not attempt to influence the bankruptcy proceedings. They simply purchase the debt of bankrupt companies that they view to be attractively priced and hold that debt until it can be sold at an anticipated higher price later in the bankruptcy process. Other investors follow a proactive approach, serving on creditors committees that are charged with negotiating the terms of the company's reorganization. Through these committees, they hope to secure outcomes favourable to the value of their holdings. At the most aggressive end of the spectrum, some investors attempt to impose their solutions on other creditors by acquiring "blocking" positions in certain classes of a bankrupt company's debt. As two-thirds of each class of debt must concur with the bankruptcy settlement, holding at least a one-third position in a strategically located debt class

Figure 13.8 Time line of the bankruptcy process.

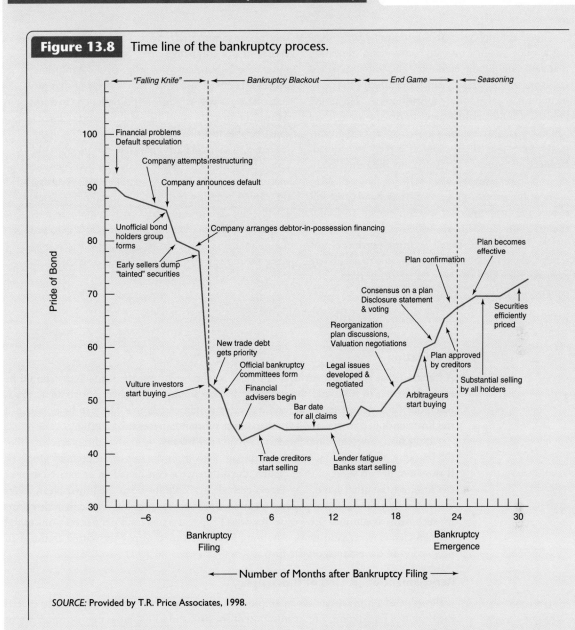

SOURCE: Provided by T.R. Price Associates, 1998.

gives an investor effective veto power over a settlement. Applied strategically, this power can be translated into an outcome that favours the holders of the position.

Some distressed securities investors prefer to own the most senior debt in a bankrupt company's financial structure. Their reasoning is that bankruptcy rules require that creditors be paid in order of seniority (although in practice this rule is not always followed to the letter). Thus, owning senior debt provides more of a valuation cushion in the event that the company's value in reorganization turns out to be worth less than originally expected. Other investors prefer to own more junior claims. Their logic is that junior debt is the most likely to appreciate significantly in value if a successful reorganization plan can be developed and implemented. In the reorganization, more senior claims tend to receive cash and newly issued debt, while more junior claims tend to receive more common stock.

The bankruptcy court is responsible for assigning a value to the company's assets and allocating that value among the creditors. The court's assigned value may not necessarily equal the value of the company's assets after the reorganization. Therefore, holders of junior claims stand to benefit more if the bankruptcy court assigns a greater value to the company's assets, as their claim is largely a residual. Holders of more senior claims, on the other hand, prefer a lower assigned asset value as that will leave more of the company's assets in their hands and will reduce the proportion of assets allocated to junior claims.

A successful distressed securities investor possesses a blend of skills. He must be able to accurately estimate the value of the company's assets that the bankruptcy court will assign. This is critical to determining an appropriate price to pay for different classes of the company's debt. Second, the investor must have a thorough knowledge of the bankruptcy process. There are many intricate aspects of that process that can easily trip up an inexperienced investor. Third, the investor must be a skillful negotiator. He must be able to strike deals with a disparate group of creditors, who may have financial agendas quite different from his own. Negotiations that become stalemated can quickly drag down an investor's returns as his capital remains tied up in unproductive assets. Finally, the investor must be a savvy trader. He must understand the market for the company's debt and maintain access to sources of liquidity, both in initiating positions in the company's debt and in exiting those positions as well.

Liquidation

A question that arises in many bankruptcies is whether or not the firm's assets should be liquidated (that is, sold) and the proceeds divided among the creditors. Such an action is taken only if the court feels the resulting value would exceed that likely to be obtained if the firm continued in operation (perhaps after substantial reorganization).

If the firm's assets are liquidated in a *straight bankruptcy*, secured creditors receive either the property pledged for their loans or the proceeds from the sale of the secured property. If this amount falls short of their claims, the difference is considered an unsecured debt of the firm; on the other hand, any excess is made available for other creditors. Next, assets are used to pay the claims of priority creditors to the extent possible. These include claims for such items as administrative expenses, wages (up to a stated limit per person), uninsured pension claims, taxes, and rents. Anything left over is used to pay unsecured creditors in proportion to their claims on the firm.

Reorganization in Lieu of Bankruptcy

If the value of a firm's assets, when employed as part of a going concern, appears to exceed their value in liquidation, a reorganization of the firm and its liabilities may be undertaken. Such proceedings, conducted under the provisions of The Bankruptcy and Insolvency Act, may be voluntary (initiated by the firm) or involuntary (initiated by three or more creditors). A number of parties must concur in the proposed reorganization, including the holders of two-thirds of the value in each general class of creditor that is affected by the reorganization.

Among the goals of reorganization are "fair and equitable" treatment of various classes of securities and the elimination of "burdensome" debt obligations. Typically, creditors are given new claims on the reorganized firm, with the amounts of the new claims intended to be at least equal in value to the amounts that the creditors would have received in liquidation. For example, holders of debentures might receive bonds of longer maturity, holders of subordinated debentures might become shareholders, and shareholders might be left without any claims on the firm.

Some Financial Aspects of Bankruptcy

Although the subject is far too complex for detailed treatment here, two aspects of bankruptcy deserve some discussion. First, the choice between continuation of a firm and liquidation of its assets should be unrelated to the reasons for its bankruptcy. If an asset can be sold for more than the present value of its future earnings, it should be. Management may have to be taken to court to be forced to do this, but the issue is not one of solvency or lack thereof.

Second, the definition of insolvency is rather vague. Assume, for example, that assets can be adequately valued at liquidating or going-concern value, whichever is greater. A firm is said to be insolvent if this value is less than that of the firm's liabilities. How should these liabilities be valued? Their current market value will frequently be less than the value of the assets, whereas their book value may be greater than the value of the assets.

Ownership of Corporate Bonds

At the end of 1996, investors held more than $153 billion of corporate and foreign bonds. As can be seen in Table 13.5, the largest investors were life insurance companies, pension funds, and foreign investors. Over 50% of these bonds were issued in foreign currencies, the principal ones being US dollars, Eurodollars, Swiss francs and Japanese yen.

Some firms use foreign denominated bond issues in order to hedge their foreign exchange exposure in the product market. For example, a Canadian pulp and paper company with substantial US sales, whose product prices are quoted in US dollars, loses revenue when the Canadian dollar rises vis-à-vis the US dollar. If its debt is US-dollar denominated then the Canadian-dollar value of its interest payments will also fall providing at least a partial off-set.

Table 13.5	Ownership of Outstanding Corporate and Foreign Bonds, December 1996.	
Held by	Amount (in millions)	Percentage of Total
Chartered banks	$ 10 654	4.8%
Thrift institutions	1 416	0.6
Life insurance companies	38 212	17.1
Property and casualty insurance companies	4 322	1.9
Trusteed pension funds	18 110	8.1
Mutual funds	9 348	4.2
Investment dealers	560	0.3
Non-financial private corporations	3 918	1.8
Misc. private financial institutions	3 113	1.4
Foreign investors	97 387	43.6
Individuals and non-incorporated business	30 414	13.6
Subtotal — privately held corporate bonds	$217 454	97.3%
Non-financial government enterprise	145	0.1
Public financial institutions	1 866	0.8
Provincial and local governments	3 917	1.8
Federal government	5	neg.
Subtotal — publicly held bonds	$ 5 933	2.7%
Total corporate bonds	$223 387	100.0%

SOURCE: Statistics Canada, *National Balance Sheet Accounts: System of National Accounts, Annual Estimates, 1984–1993*, Ottawa, March 1997.

The Secondary Bond Market

Most trading in corporate bonds takes place through dealers in the over-the-counter market. A small number of debentures are listed on the Alberta, Vancouver, and Toronto Stock Exchanges. About 100 dealers and a few banks and trust companies are active in the OTC market. The major dealers and large institutional clients are electronically linked—bid and offer prices for a wide range of bonds are displayed on video screens located in their offices. Some dealers issue periodic quotation sheets that are reported in the daily business press, such as that shown in Figure 13.5.

Foreign Bonds

The foreign bond market refers to bonds issued and denominated in the currency of a country other than the one in which the issuer is primarily located. Foreign bonds that are issued in the United States and are denominated in US dollars are referred to as Yankee bonds, and foreign (that is, non-Japanese) bonds that are issued in Japan are referred to as Samurai bonds.

In issuing foreign bonds, the issuer must abide by the rules and regulations imposed by the government of the country in which the bonds are issued. This may be relatively easy or difficult, depending on the countries involved.

One of the main advantages of purchasing foreign bonds is the opportunity to obtain international diversification of the default risk of a bond portfolio while not having to be concerned about foreign exchange fluctuations. For example, a Canadian investor might be able to buy a Toyota bond in Japan that is denominated in yen, but in doing so would have to worry about the yen-dollar exchange rate. This is because the coupon payments and ultimately the principal would be paid to the investor in yen, which would then have to be converted into dollars at a currently unknown exchange rate. However, the investor could avoid such worries by purchasing a Toyota bond that is denominated in Canadian dollars.

Eurobonds

Eurobond A bond that is offered outside the country of the borrower and usually outside the country in whose currency the security is denominated.

Owing in part to government restrictions on investment in foreign securities, a number of borrowers have found it advantageous to sell securities in other countries. The term **Eurobond** is loosely applied to bonds that are offered outside the country of the borrower and usually outside the country in whose currency the securities are denominated. Thus, a bond issued by a Canadian corporation that is denominated in Japanese yen and sold in Germany and Switzerland would be referred to as a Eurobond.[7]

Since the Eurobond market is neither regulated nor taxed, it offers substantial advantages for many issuers and buyers of bonds. For example, a foreign subsidiary of a Canadian corporation may issue a Eurobond in "bearer" form. No tax is withheld by the corporation, and the tax (if any) paid by the purchaser depends on her country of residence. Because of these regulatory and tax advantages, interest rates on Eurobonds tend to be somewhat lower than those on domestic bonds denominated in the same currency.

Global Issue A debt issue that is sold in several countries simultaneously.

A recent development has been the appearance of **global issues**. These are large issues that appear simultaneously in several countries and are underwritten by investment dealers in those countries. For example, a recent Ontario Hydro issue of $1.5 billion was issued in

---

[7]There are also fixed-income securities of this nature that have shorter lives; they are sometimes referred to as Euronotes or Euro-commercial paper. The market where they (and Eurobonds) are issued and traded is known as the Eurocredit market.

Canadian dollars and underwritten in the US, the UK, Japan, several European countries, and Australia, among other markets. With worldwide distribution of this kind it is possible to maintain a 24-hour market in these securities, thereby enhancing their liquidity.

Tax Treatment of Fixed-Income Securities

The tax treatment of coupon-bearing securities is not complicated—the coupon payment must be reported as income in the year that it is received and tax is payable at the regular rate.

Coupon-bearing securities bought at either a discount or a premium in the marketplace, if held to maturity, affect the investor's income tax because the difference between the purchase price and the par value must be treated as a capital gain or loss at maturity.

Revenue Canada also requires that taxes be paid annually on the accrued interest on zero-coupon or pure-discount securities.

Economic Accrual Method This method results in a lower reported interest income in the first year and a larger one in the second and, therefore, reduces the present value of the investor's two tax bills.

For example, a stripped bond that matures in two years for $1000 can be purchased currently for $850. Thus, the investor will earn $150 in interest over two years, realizing it only when the bond matures. Revenue Canada, however, requires that the investor pay taxes on a portion of the $150 each year, but has no specific rules as to how the accrual should be calculated as long as the method used is "reasonable." One simple alternative is to allocate an equal fraction of the implied interest to each year to maturity. The investor would then report $75 ($150/2) per year as interest income. An alternative is to use the **economic accrual method**. In this method the yield is calculated, which in this case is $(\$1000/\$850)^{1/2} - 1 = 8.46\%$. This means that the implied value of the bond at the end of the first year is $850 \times 1.0846 = \$921.91$; thus, the amount of interest income to be recognized that year is $\$921.91 - \$850 = \$71.91$ or $\$850 \times 0.0846$. The amount of interest income to be recognized in the second year, assuming the bond is held to maturity, will be $\$1000 - \$921.91 = \$78.09$ or $\$921.21 \times 0.0846$ (note that $\$1000 = \$921.91 \times 1.0846$). This method results in a lower reported interest income in the first year and a larger one in the second and, therefore, reduces the present value of the investor's two tax bills. Compound interest Canada Savings Bonds are taxed in a similar way, except that the government publishes annually the amount of accrued interest that must be reported.

With zero-coupon bonds the investor has a cash outflow when purchasing the bond and also has to pay tax on the accrued interest every year until it matures. The investor only receives a cash inflow at maturity. As a result, such securities are attractive primarily for tax-exempt or low tax-bracket investors (for example, as RRSP investments).

The taxation of Real Return Bonds presents some special features. Adjusted coupon payments must be reported in the normal manner in the year they are received. In addition, the inflationary adjustment to the principal that accrues during the year must be included in taxable income. Thus, for taxation year T, the amount Principal $\times [IR_T - IR_{T-1}]$ must be reported as income. The taxation of these bonds resembles that of strip bonds in that tax must be paid on an amount that has not yet been received, a factor that makes them less attractive to taxed investors.

Preferred Shares

Preferred Shares A hybrid form of security that has characteristics of both common shares and bonds.

In some respects, **preferred shares** are like perpetual bonds. A given annual dollar amount is promised by the issuer to the investor. This amount may be stated as a percent of the stock's par value (for example, 8% of $100, meaning $8 per year), or directly as a dollar figure (for example, $2.75 per year). Since the security is a stock, such payments are called dividends rather than interest. They do not qualify as a tax-deductible expense for the issuing corporation, but do qualify for the personal dividend tax credit. Furthermore, failure to make such payments does not constitute grounds for bankruptcy proceedings.

Floating Rate Preferred Shares A preferred share whose dividend is not fixed but tied to an administered interest rate such as the Bank of Canada's prime rate.

A recent innovation is variable or **floating rate preferred shares** (known as adjustable rate preferred stock, or ARPS, in the US), where the dividend is reset periodically in terms of an established market rate with an underlying floor (or minimum payment). For example, the annualized "percent of par" for the minimum payment may be set at 8% and the quarterly dividends reset every three months to equal half the prevailing Bank of Canada rate plus 1.5%. Any difference between 8% and the actual dividends paid must be made up in the final quarter.

Related to variable rate preferred are money market or auction preferred shares (known as Dutch auction rate preferred stock, DARPS, in the US).[8] The price of these shares is fixed but the dividend is reset periodically (usually every calendar month) at a level that is determined at an auction between current and potential owners. If the auction is not successful, then a minimum dividend rate is triggered. This rate is predetermined in relation to an established market-based rate such as the prime rate or the current bankers' acceptance yield.

Preferred shares are generally "preferred as to dividends." Specified payments must be made on the preferred shares before any dividends may be paid to holders of the firm's common stock. Failure to pay a preferred dividend in full does not constitute default, but unpaid dividends are usually cumulative. This means that all previously unpaid preferred share dividends must be paid (but seldom with interest) before any dividends may be paid on the common stock.

No indenture is provided with a preferred share issue. Various provisions protecting the preferred shareholders against potentially harmful actions, however, may be written into the corporation's charter. For example, one provision may limit the dollar amount of senior securities that can be issued in the future. Although preferred shareholders typically do not have voting rights, there may be another provision that gives them voting rights when the corporation is in arrears on its preferred dividends.

Many issues of preferred shares are callable, often at a premium; such stock is sometimes said to be redeemable at a stated redemption price. *Retractable preferred* provide the investor with an option to force the redemption of the issue by the company at a specified date and price. *Participating preferred* shares entitle the holder to receive extra dividends when earnings permit. *Convertible preferred* shares may, at the option of the holder, be converted into another security (usually the firm's common stock) on stated terms. Some firms issue more than one class of preferred shares, with preference accorded the various classes in a specified order.

In the event of a dissolution of the firm, preferred shares take precedence over common stock in the liquidation of assets. Generally this means that preferred shareholders are entitled to receive the share's par value before any payment is made to common shareholders.

Since preferred shares have many features of a bond without the substantial tax advantage that bonds give to the issuer, they are used less often than debt. In 1990, $0.942 billion of such shares were issued, compared with $8.6 billion of publicly offered corporate debt.[9]

As indicated in Chapter 12, interest income from bonds held by a corporate investor is subject to corporate income tax at an effective rate in excess of 40%, while dividend income is generally tax exempt. For this reason, preferred shares tend to sell at prices that give lower before-tax returns than long-term bonds, even though the latter may be considerably lower in risk. As a result, preferred shares are generally unattractive holdings for tax-exempt non-corporate investors.

---

[8]Presumably these are referred to as dutch auction preferred because the lowest bidder is the winner. For a discussion of ARPS and DARPS, see Michael J. Alderson, Keith C. Brown, and Scott L. Lummer, "Dutch Auction Rate Preferred Stock," *Financial Management* 16, no. 2 (Summer 1987): 68–73.

[9]*Bank of Canada Review*, November 1991.

Many preferred shares are traded on major exchanges in a manner similar to common stocks. Typically, they are assigned to the market-maker responsible for the firm's common stock. Trading prices are reported in the financial press in the same format as that used for common stocks.

Summary

1. The most familiar types of fixed-income securities are personal savings deposits. These include demand deposits, time deposits, and guaranteed investment certificates issued by chartered banks, trust companies, caisses populaires, and credit unions.

2. Highly marketable, short-term securities are referred to as money market instruments. These securities include commercial paper, large-denomination certificates of deposit, bankers' acceptances, repurchase agreements, and Eurodollars CDs.

3. The Bank of Canada issues debt securities to finance the government's borrowing needs. These securities are issued in various maturities—from short-term Treasury bills to intermediate-term and long-term bonds. The Bank of Canada also issues Canada Savings Bonds to individual investors.

4. Canada bonds can be converted into a set of pure-discount bonds by issuing marketable receipts entitling the holder to a specific coupon payment or the bond's principal payment. Separating a bond into its component payments is known as coupon stripping.

5. Government agencies also issue securities to finance their operations. In some cases this debt is explicitly backed by the federal or provincial governments. In other cases the government guarantee is implicit.

6. The Government of Canada has issued a series of index-linked Real Return Bonds that are inflation protected.

7. Provincial governments issue a wide variety of fixed-income securities, generally backed solely by the full faith and credit of the issuer.

8. Municipal bonds, especially for smaller municipalities, are issued by provincial municipal finance corporations.

9. Corporate bonds, such as mortgage bonds or equipment obligations, may be backed by specific assets. Alternatively, corporate bonds, such as debentures, may represent general obligations of the issuing corporation.

10. Corporate bonds (and some federal government and municipal bonds) may contain call provisions, giving the issuer the right to redeem the security prior to maturity under specified terms.

11. Corporations entering bankruptcy may undergo liquidation or reorganization, or enter into arrangements.

12. Foreign bonds are those that are issued and denominated in the currency of a country other than that of the issuer.

13. Eurobonds are those that are issued in a country other than that of the issuer and in a currency different from that of the country where they are offered.

14. Preferred share dividends are generally fixed but do not represent legal obligations of the issuers. Most preferred share dividends are cumulative, requiring payment of all unpaid preferred dividends before common stock dividends can be paid.

1. What is the annual equivalent yield on a 13-week Treasury bill selling at a price of 96?

2. Consider a 13-week Treasury bill, issued today, which is selling for $9675. (Its face value is $10 000.)

   a. What is the annual discount based on the selling price of the security?

   b. What is the annual equivalent yield of the security?

3. If a three-month Treasury bill sells for a price of 98, whereas a six-month Treasury bill sells for 96, is the equivalent yield (unannualized) for the six-month bill twice that of the three-month bill? Why?

4. Rank the various money market instruments discussed in the text in terms of default risk. Explain the reasoning behind your rankings. Find the latest interest rates for these securities. Do they correspond with your default-risk rankings?

5. Bonds may be issued in either bearer or registered form. Given the characteristics of bearer and registered bonds, discuss the relative merits of each.

6. Using *The Globe and Mail* as a data source, identify a particular Canada bond. What is its coupon rate? What is its maturity date? What is the security's yield-to-maturity?

7. Describe the standard practice by which sellers of government and corporate bonds are compensated for accrued interest.

8. What is the rationale for including a call provision in the indenture of a bond issue? How do bond investors typically respond to the inclusion of a call provision?

9. How do zero-coupon fixed-income securities provide returns to investors?

10. Consider a 10-year zero-coupon Treasury security selling for a price of $300, with a face value of $1000. What is the before-tax annual rate of return to an investor who buys and holds this security to maturity?

11. Why does Revenue Canada treat the difference between the price of a strip bond purchased at a discount and its face value as ordinary income to the investor, as opposed to treating it as a capital gain?

12. Bonds issued by federal agencies carry an explicit or implicit promise that the federal government will ensure payment of interest and principal. Why then are these securities usually priced by the market to offer yields above Canada securities?

13. What is a mortgage-backed security? What is the primary risk that such securities present to investors?

14. Cary Dolan, an amateur investor, said "I prefer investing in mortgage-backed securities. Their government guarantee gives me a risk-free return." Comment on Cary's remark.

15. Labrador Airlines was in difficult financial shape owing to ongoing recession and labour problems. To this point the firm had issued no debt, but management believed that borrowing in the bond market was the only way to get through the tough times. Because of its poor financial condition, Labrador's investment bankers advised management that a debenture issue would not be well received. What other bond issuance options might Labrador pursue?

16. Is any mortgage bond necessarily a more secure investment than any debenture? Explain.

17. A callable bond is sometimes described as a combination of a non-callable bond and an option. Explain why this description is appropriate. Further, explain the impact of these two features on the price of a callable bond.

18. Chris Dolan is considering purchasing one of two bonds: a corporate bond with a 9% coupon interest rate, selling at par, or a preferred share, with a 6% dividend rate. Given that Chris lives in Ontario, is in the 26% federal tax bracket, and assuming that all other relevant factors are the same between the two securities, which should Chris select? (Ignore any surtaxes and use the dividend tax credit factors given in Chapter 12.)

19. Is it true that most corporations that default on their debt eventually enter bankruptcy and see their assets liquidated to repay creditors? Explain.

20. Eurobonds have become very popular forms of financing in recent years. What features of the Eurobond market make Eurobonds attractive to issuers and bondholders?

21. In trying to explain the concept of preferred shares to a novice investor, Lisa Mototsune referred to it as a "hybrid" security. What did Lisa mean by this term?

22. What is the purpose of the cumulative restriction of most preferred shares?

CFA Exam Question

23. A portfolio manager at Superior Trust Company is structuring a fixed-income portfolio to meet the objectives of a client. The client plans to retire in 15 years and wants a substantial lump sum at that time. The client has specified the use of AAA-rated securities.

The portfolio manager compares coupon Canadas with zero-coupon stripped Canadas and observes a significant yield advantage for the stripped bonds.

Maturity	Coupon Canadas	Zero-Coupon Stripped Canadas
3 year	5.50%	5.80%
5 year	6.00	6.60
7 year	6.75	7.25
10 year	7.25	7.60
15 year	7.40	8.80
30 year	7.75	7.75

Briefly discuss two reasons why zero-coupon stripped Canadas could yield more than coupon Canadas with the same final maturity.

KEY TERMS

pure-discount security (p. 325)
coupon payment (p. 325)
maturity date (p. 325)
principal (p. 325)
demand deposit (p. 325)
time deposit (p. 326)
guaranteed investment certificate (GIC) (p. 326)
money market instrument (p. 329)
annualized rate basis (p. 329)
annual percentage rate (APR) (p. 329)
finance company paper (p. 331)
commercial paper (p. 331
bankers' acceptance (p. 331)
Certificate of Deposit (CD) (p. 331)
Eurodollar CDs (p. 332)
Eurodollar deposit (p. 332)
repurchase agreement (p. 332)
repo rate (p. 332)
debt refunding (p. 332)
bearer bond (p. 334)

primary distributor (p. 334)
accrued interest (p. 335)
registered bond (p. 336)
zero-coupon bond (p. 338)
coupon stripping (p. 338)
Real Return Bond (p. 338)
provincial bond (p. 342)
municipal bond (p. 342)
installment debenture (p. 344)
term debenture (p. 344)
trust indenture (p. 345)
trust deed (p. 345)
trustee (p. 345)
income bond (p. 346)
guaranteed bond (p. 346)
participation bond (p. 346)
serial bond (p. 346)
convertible bond (p. 346)
extendible bond (p. 346)
retractable bond (p. 346)
call premium (p. 346)

call price (p. 347)
Canada Call (p. 347)
Canada plus x Call (p. 347)
sinking fund (p. 347)
private placement (p. 347)

Eurobond (p. 352)
global issue (p. 352)
economic accrual method (p. 353)
preferred share (p. 353)
floating rate preferred share (p. 354)

REFERENCES

1. A concise summary description of the various types of US money market instruments is contained in:

   Timothy Q. Cook and Timothy D. Rowe, *Instruments of the Money Market* (Federal Reserve Bank of Richmond, 1986).

2. The following contain thorough descriptions of the various types of US fixed-income securities discussed in this chapter:

   Frank J. Fabozzi and Franco Modigliani, *Capital Markets: Institutions and Instruments* (Englewood Cliffs, NJ: Prentice Hall, 1992), Chapters 13–18.

   Suresh Sundaresan, *Fixed Income Markets and Their Derivatives* (Cincinnati, OH: South-Western College Publishing, 1997), Chapters 1–2, 8–10.

   Frank J. Fabozzi, Franco Modigliani, and Michael G. Ferri, *Foundations of Financial Markets and Institutions* (Englewood Cliffs, NJ: Prentice Hall, 1998), Chapters 16, 17, 20–25.

3. For a discussion of coupon stripping in the US, see:

   Miles Livingston and Deborah Wright Gregory, *The Stripping of US Treasury Securities*, Monograph Series in Finance and Economics #1989–1, New York University Salomon Center, Leonard N. Stern School of Business.

   Deborah W. Gregory and Miles Livingston, "Development of the Market for US Treasury STRIPS," *Financial Analysts Journal* 48, no. 2 (March–April 1992): 68–74.

   Phillip R. Daves, Michael C. Ehrhardt, and John M. Wachowicz, Jr., "A Guide to Investing in US Treasury STRIPS," *AAII Journal* 15, no. 1 (January 1993): 6–10.

   Phillip R. Daves and Michael C. Ehrhardt, "Liquidity, Reconstitution, and the Value of US Treasury STRIPS," *Journal of Finance* 47, no. 1 (March 1993): 315–329.

4. For a discussion of the market for securities issued by the US Treasury, see:

   Peter Wann, *Inside the US Treasury Market* (New York: Quorum Books, 1989).

   Saikat Nandi, "Treasury Auctions: What Do the Recent Models Tell Us?" Federal Reserve Bank of Atlanta *Economic Review* 82, no. 4 (Fourth Quarter 1997): 4–15.

5. For discussion of mortgage-backed securities, see:

   Earl Baldwin and Saundra Stotts, *Mortgage-Backed Securities: A Reference Guide for Lenders & Issuers* (Chicago: Probus Publishing, 1990).

   Sean Becketti and Charles S. Morris, *The Prepayment Experience of FNMA Mortgage-backed Securities*, Monograph Series in Finance and Economics #1990–3, New York University Salomon Center, Leonard N. Stern School of Business.

   Eduardo S. Schwartz and Walter N. Torous, "Prepayment, Default, and the Valuation of Mortgage Pass-through Securities," *Journal of Business* 65, no. 2 (April 1992): 221–239.

Andrew Carron, "Understanding CMOs. REMICs, and Other Mortgage Derivatives," *Journal of Fixed Income* 2, no. 1 (June 1992): 25–43.

Albert J. Golly, Jr., "An Individual Investor's Guide to the Complex World of CMOs," *AAII Journal* 14, no. 6 (July 1992): 7–10.

Frank J. Fabozzi and Franco Modigliani, *Mortgage and Mortgage-backed Securities Markets* (Boston: Harvard Business School Press, 1992).

Michael D. Joehnk and Matthew J. Hasset, "Getting a Grip on the Risks of CMO Prepayments," *AAII Journal* 15, no. 5 (June 1993): 8–12.

Frank J. Fabozzi, Charles Ramsey, and Frank R. Ramirez, *Collateralized Mortgage Obligations: Structure and Analysis* (Summit, NJ: Frank J. Fabozzi Associates, 1993).

6. For a discussion of the foreign bond and Eurobond markets, see:

J. Orlin Grabbe, *International Financial Markets* (New York: Elsevier Science Publishing, 1991), Chapters 16–18.

Bruno Solnik, *International Investments* (Reading, MA: Addison-Wesley, 1991), Chapters 6–7.

7. For a discussion of the Eurocredit market, see:

Arie L. Melnik and Steven E. Plaut, *The Short-Term Eurocredit Market*, Monograph Series in Finance and Economics #1991–1, New York University Salomon Center, Leonard N. Stern School of Business.

8. For a discussion of how government bond markets function in the United Kingdom, Japan, and Germany, see:

Thomas J. Urich, *UK, German and Japanese Government Bond Markets*, Monograph Series in Finance and Economics #1991–2, New York University Salomon Center, Leonard N. Stern School of Business.

9. The accuracy of reported prices for corporate bonds is analyzed in:

Kenneth P. Nunn, Jr., Joanne Hill, and Thomas Schneeweis, "Corporate Bond Price Data Sources and Risk/Return Measurement," *Journal of Financial and Quantitative Analysis* 21, no. 2 (June 1986): 197–208.

Oded Sarig and Arthur Warga, "Bond Price Data and Bond Market Liquidity," *Journal of Financial and Quantitative Analysis* 24, no. 3 (September 1989): 367–378.

Arthur D. Warga, "Corporate Bond Price Discrepancies in the Dealer and Exchange Markets," *Journal of Fixed Income* 1, no. 3 (December 1991): 7–16.

10. The market for preferred shares is discussed in:

Arthur L. Houston, Jr., and Carol Olson Houston, "Financing with Preferred Stock," *Financial Management* 19, no. 3 (Autumn 1990): 42–54.

11. An extensive discussion of the US private placement market for corporate debt is contained in:

Mark Carey, Stephen Prowse, John Rea, and Gregory Udell, "The Economics of Private Placements: A New Look," *Financial Markets, Institutions & Instruments* 2, no. 3 (1993).

12. For a Canadian perspective on the topics covered in this chapter, see:

C. R. Dipchand and R. J. Hanrahan, "Exit and Exchange Option Values on Government of Canada Retractable Bonds," *Financial Management* 8, no. 3 (Autumn 1979).

A. L. Ananthanarayanan and E. Schwartz, "Retractable and Extendible Bonds: The Canadian Experience," *Journal of Finance* 35, no. 1 (March 1980).

J. Cooperman, M. Gagnon, H. Hinkle, P. Kearns and V. Rao, "Canadian Mortgage Securities: A Primer," *Journal of Fixed Income* 4, no. 3 (December 1994).

Bond Analysis

C onsider an investor who believes that there are situations where public information can be used to identify mispriced bonds. To translate that belief into action about which bonds to buy and sell, an analytical procedure is needed. One procedure involves comparing a bond's yield-to-maturity with a yield-to-maturity that the investor feels is appropriate, based on the characteristics of the bond as well as current market conditions. If the yield-to-maturity is higher than the appropriate yield-to-maturity, then the bond is said to be underpriced (or undervalued) and is a candidate for buying. Conversely, if the yield-to-maturity is lower than the appropriate one, then the bond is said to be overpriced (or overvalued) and is a candidate for selling (or even short selling).

Alternatively, the investor could estimate the bond's "true," or "intrinsic," value, and compare it with the bond's current market price. Specifically, if the current market price is less than the bond's intrinsic value, then the bond is underpriced, and if it is greater, then the bond is overpriced. Both procedures for analyzing bonds are based on the capitalization of income method of valuation.[1] The first procedure, involving yields, is analogous to the internal rate of return method that is discussed in most introductory finance textbooks, whereas the second procedure, involving intrinsic value, is analogous to the net present value method that also appears in such books. Although the focus in those books is on making an investment decision involving some type of real asset (such as whether or not a new piece of machinery should be purchased), the focus here is on making an investment decision involving a particular type of financial asset—bonds.[2]

Applying the Capitalization of Income Method to Bonds

Capitalization of Income Method Valuation An approach to valuing financial assets. It is based on the concept that the "true" or intrinsic value of a financial asset is equal to the discounted value of future cash flows generated by that asset.

The **capitalization of income method of valuation** states that the intrinsic value of any asset is based on the discounted value of the cash flows that the investor expects to receive in the future from owning the asset. As mentioned earlier, one way that this method has

---

[1]The capitalization of income approach to valuation is also known as the discounted cash flow approach; its usefulness is discussed in Steven N. Kaplan and Richard S. Ruback. "The Valuation of Cash Flow Forecasts: An Empirical Analysis," *Journal of Finance* 50, no. 4 (September 1995): 1059–1093.

[2]With complex cash flows (such as a mix of positive and negative cash flows), the IRR method can be misleading. However, this is not a problem when it is applied to bonds (or stocks—see Chapter 17). For a discussion of potential problems in other contexts, see Richard A. Brealey and Stewart C. Myers, *Principles of Corporate Finance* (New York: McGraw-Hill, 1996), Chapter 5.

been applied to bond valuation is to compare the bond's yield-to-maturity (y) with the yield-to-maturity the investor deems appropriate (y^*). Specifically, if $y > y^*$, then the bond is underpriced, and if $y < y^*$, then the bond is overpriced. However, if $y = y^*$, then the bond is said to be fairly priced.

Promised Yield-to-maturity

Letting P denote the current market price of a bond with a remaining life of n years and promising cash flows to the investor of C_1 in year 1, C_2 in year 2, and so on, the yield-to-maturity (more specifically, the **promised yield-to-maturity**) of the bond is the value of y that solves the following equation:

$$P = \frac{C_1}{(1 + y)^1} + \frac{C_2}{(1 + y)^2} + \frac{C_3}{(1 + y)^3} + \cdots + \frac{C_n}{(1 + y)^n}$$

Using summation notation, this equation can be rewritten as

$$P = \sum_{t=1}^{n} \frac{C_t}{(1 + y)^t} \tag{14.1}$$

For example, consider a bond that is currently selling for $900 and has a remaining life of three years. For ease of exposition, assume it makes annual coupon payments amounting to $60 per year and has a par value of $1000. That is, $C_1 = \$60$, $C_2 = \$60$, and $C_3 = \$1060 = \$1000 + \$60$. Using equation (14.1), the yield-to-maturity on this bond is the value of y that solves the following equation:

$$\$900 = \frac{\$60}{(1 + y)^1} + \frac{\$60}{(1 + y)^2} + \frac{\$1060}{(1 + y)^3}$$

which is $y = 10.02\%$. If subsequent analysis indicates that the yield-to-maturity should be 9.00%, then this bond is underpriced, since $y = 10.02\% > y^* = 9.00\%$.

Intrinsic Value

Alternatively, the intrinsic value of a bond can be calculated using the following formula:

$$V = \frac{C_1}{(1 + y^*)^1} + \frac{C_2}{(1 + y^*)^2} + \frac{C_3}{(1 + y^*)^3} + \cdots + \frac{C_n}{(1 + y^*)^n}$$

or, using summation notation,

$$V = \sum_{t=1}^{n} \frac{C_t}{(1 + y^*)^t} \tag{14.2}$$

After estimating V, it should be compared to the bond's market price P in order to determine whether $V > P$, in which case the bond is underpriced, or if $V < P$ then the bond is overpriced. Alternatively, the **net present value** (NPV) can be calculated as the difference between the value of the bond and the purchase price:

$$NPV = V - P$$

$$= \left[\sum_{t=1}^{n} \frac{C_t}{(1 + y^*)^t} \right] - P \tag{14.3}$$

The NPV of the bond in the previous example is the solution to the following equation:

$$NPV = \left[\frac{\$60}{(1 + .09)^1} + \frac{\$60}{(1 + .09)^2} + \frac{\$1060}{(1 + .09)^3} \right] - \$900$$

$$= \$24.06$$

Since this bond has a positive NPV, it is underpriced. This will always be the case when a bond has a yield-to-maturity that is more than appropriate (earlier, it was shown that this bond's yield-to-maturity was 10.02%, which is more than 9.00%, the appropriate yield-to-maturity). That is, in general, any bond with $y > y^*$ will always have a positive NPV and vice versa, so that under either method it would be underpriced.[3]

Alternatively, if the investor had determined that y^* was equal to 11.00%, then the bond's NPV would have been −$22.19. This would suggest the bond was overpriced, just as would have been noted when the yield-to-maturity of 10.02% was compared with 11.00%. This will always be the case—a bond with $y < y^*$ will always have a negative NPV and vice versa, so that under either method it would be found to be overpriced.

It should also be pointed out that if the investor had determined that y^* had a value of approximately the same magnitude as the bond's yield-to-maturity of 10%, then the NPV of the bond would be approximately zero. In such a situation, the bond would be viewed as being fairly priced.

Note that in order to use the capitalization of income method of valuation, the values of C_t, P, and y^* must be determined. It is generally quite easy to determine the values for C_t and P, since they are the bond's promised cash flows and current market price, respectively. However, determining the value of y^* is difficult, since the investor must estimate an appropriate value for the bond. Such a decision will depend on the characteristics of the bond, as well as on current market conditions. Given that the key ingredient in bond analysis is determining the appropriate value of y^*, the next section discusses the attributes that should be considered in making such a determination.

Bond Attributes

Six primary attributes of a bond are important in bond valuation:

- length of time until maturity
- coupon rate
- call provisions
- taxation
- marketability
- likelihood of default

Yield Structure The set of yields-to-maturity across bonds differing in terms of a number of attributes. These attributes include term-to-maturity, coupon rate, call provisions, tax status, marketability, and likelihood of default.

Term Structure The set of yields-to-maturity across bonds that possess different terms-to-maturity, but are similar with respect to other attributes.

Risk Structure The set of yields-to-maturity across bonds that possess different degrees of default risk, but are similar with respect to other attributes.

Yield Spread The difference in the promised yields-to-maturity of two bonds.

At any time, the structure of market prices for bonds differing in these dimensions can be examined and described in terms of yields-to-maturity. This underlying structure is sometimes referred to as the **yield structure**. Often, attention is confined to differences along a single dimension, holding the other attributes constant. For example, the set of yields of bonds of different maturities constitutes the **term structure** (discussed in Chapter 5), and the set of yields of bonds of different default risk is referred to as the **risk structure**.

Most bond analysts consider the yields-to-maturity for default-free bonds to form the term structure. "Risk differentials" are then added to obtain the relevant yields-to-maturity for bonds of lower quality. While subject to some criticism, this procedure makes it possible to think about a complicated set of relationships sequentially.

The differential between the yields of two bonds is usually called a **yield spread**. Most often, it involves a bond that is under analysis and a comparable default-free bond (that is,

---

[3]A more accurate method of determining a bond's intrinsic value involves the use of spot rates. That is, in determining the NPV of this bond, the investor might have determined that the relevant spot rates for the one-year, two-year, and three-year cash flows are 8.24%, 8.69%, and 9.03%, respectively. Using these values, the bond's intrinsic value would be equal to $60/1.0824 + $60/1.0869^2 + $1060/1.0903^3 = $924.06. Although V is the same in this example when either spot rates or y^* are used in the calculations, this need not always be the case.

Basis Point 1/100th of 1%.

a government security of similar maturity and coupon rate). Yield spreads are sometimes measured in **basis points**, where one basis point equals .01%. If the yield-to-maturity for one bond is 8.50% and that of another is 8.90%, the yield spread is 40 basis points.

Coupon Rate and Length of Time Until Maturity

These attributes of a bond are important because they determine the size and timing of the cash flows that are promised to the bondholder by the issuer. Given a bond's current market price, these attributes can be used to determine the bond's yield-to-maturity, which will subsequently be compared with what the investor thinks it should be. More specifically, if the market for Canada bonds is viewed as being efficient, then the yield-to-maturity on a Canada bond that is similar to the bond under evaluation can form a starting point for the analysis.

Consider the previously mentioned bond selling for $900 that has promised cash flows over the next three years of $60, $60, and $1060, respectively. Suppose there is a Canada bond that provides a cash flow over the next three years of $50, $50, and $1050 and is selling for $912.89. The yield-to-maturity on this second security is 8.5%, information that can be used to determine what the yield-to-maturity should be on the $900 bond. In this situation, the yield spread between the bond and the government security is 10.02% − 8.50% = 1.52% and the analyst must then consider whether or not this spread is appropriate. Figure 14.1 shows the yield spreads between indexes of bonds of four different qualities (AAA, AA, A, and BBB) from January 1985 to December 1994. Note that these spreads can vary significantly through time.[4]

Call Provisions

Call Provision A provision in some bond indentures that permits an issuer to retire some or all of the bonds in a particular bond issue prior to the bonds' stated maturity date.

Call Price The price that an issuer must pay bondholders when an issue is retired prior to its stated maturity date.

Call Premium The difference between the call price of a bond and the par value of the bond.

At first glance, bonds issued when yields-to-maturity are relatively high may appear to be unusually attractive investments. However, this is not necessarily the case because many corporate bonds have a **call provision** that enables the issuer to redeem the bonds prior to maturity, usually for a price somewhat above par.[5] This price is known as the **call price**, and the difference between it and the par value of the bond is known as the **call premium**. An issuer will often find it financially advantageous to call the existing bonds if yields drop substantially after the bonds were initially sold, since the issuer will be able to replace them with lower yielding securities that are less costly.

For example, consider a 10-year bond issued at par ($1000) that has a coupon rate of 12% and is callable at $1050 any time after it has been outstanding for five years.[6] If, after five years, yields on similar five-year bonds were 8%, the bond would probably be called. This means that an investor who had planned on receiving annual coupon payments of $120 for ten years would instead actually receive the call price of $1050 after five years. At this time, the investor could take the $1050 and reinvest it in the 8% bonds, thereby receiving $84 per year in coupon payments over the last five years (it is assumed here that the investor can purchase a fraction of a bond, so that the full $1050 can be invested in the 8% bonds), and $1050 at the end of the tenth year as a return of principal. Given this pat-

---

[4]The yield spread series for AAA bonds is truncated in October 1993. This was the month that the last AAA corporate bond in Canada was downgraded to AA.

[5]Many corporate bonds have, in addition to a call provision, a provision for a sinking fund where each year the issuer retires a pre-specified portion of the original bond issue.

[6]In this example, the **yield-to-call** (or, to be more specific, the **yield-to-first-call**) is 12.78%. That is, 12.78% is the discount rate that makes the present value of $120 received after each of the first four years and $1170 ($1050 + $120) at the end of five years equal to the issue price of the bond, $1000. Note that the yield-to-first-call is greater than the bond's promised yield-to-maturity at the time of issue (12%).

Yield-to-call The yield-to-maturity of a callable bond calculated assuming that the bond is called at the earliest possible time.

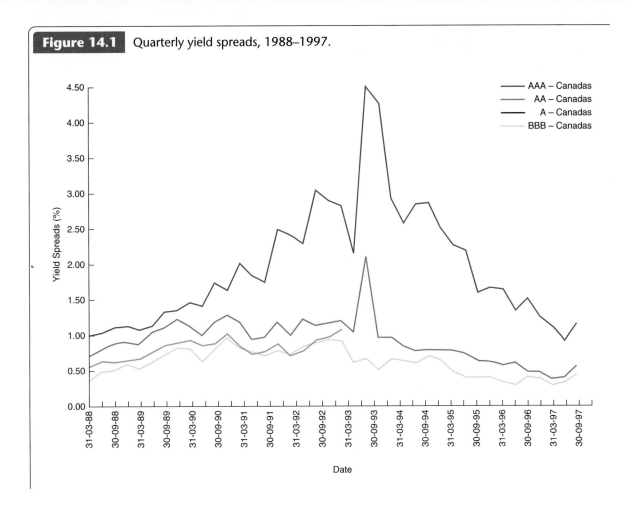

Figure 14.1 Quarterly yield spreads, 1988–1997.

tern of cash flows, the actual yield-to-maturity (otherwise known as the *realized return*) over the ten years would be 10.96% rather than 12%.[7]

This example suggests that the higher the coupon rate of a callable bond, the greater is the likely divergence between actual and apparent yields. This is borne out by experience. Figure 14.2 plots the coupon rate, set at time of issue, on the horizontal axis. Since most bonds are initially sold at (or very close to) par, the coupon rate is also a measure of the yield-to-maturity that an investor may have thought was obtainable by purchasing one of the newly issued bonds.

The vertical axis in this figure plots the actual yield-to-maturity obtained up to the original maturity date by an investor, assuming that the payments received in the event of a call were reinvested in non-callable bonds with appropriate maturities. The curve is based on experience for a group of callable bonds issued by utility companies during a period of fluctuating interest rates. As can be seen, the coupon rate and actual yield are quite similar in magnitude until the coupon rate approaches 5%. At this point, higher coupon rates are no longer associated with higher actual yields, since these coupon rates were relatively high

---

[7]This situation is less likely to occur in Canada where The Canada Call + x (see Chapter 13) is frequently used. With this call provision redemption is not an attractive proposition when interest rates fall. It should be noted, however, that a number of recent corporate bond issues have included conventional call provisions.

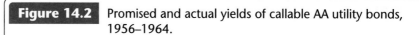

Figure 14.2 Promised and actual yields of callable AA utility bonds, 1956–1964.

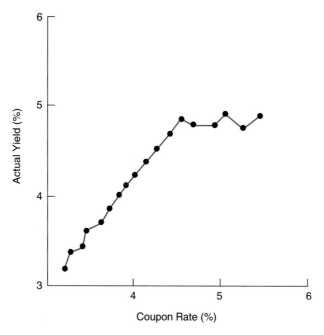

SOURCE: Frank C. Jen and James E. Wert, "The Effect of Call Risk on Corporate Bond Yields," *Journal of Finance* 22, no. 4 (December 1967): 646.

during the time period examined; as a consequence, most of the bonds with coupon rates above 5% were ultimately called.

The upshot is that bonds with a greater likelihood of being called should have a higher yield-to-maturity. That is, the higher the coupon rate or the lower the call premium, the higher the yield-to-maturity should be. Equivalently, bonds with higher coupon rates or lower call premiums will have lower intrinsic values, all else being equal.

Taxation

Taxation affects bond prices and yields in other ways. For example, low-coupon bonds selling at a discount provide returns in two forms: coupon payments and capital gains. In Canada, coupon payments are taxed as ordinary income, and capital gains are taxed at a reduced rate. Furthermore, taxes on the latter may be deferred until the bond is either sold or matures. This means that such **deep discount bonds** have a double tax advantage. Other things being equal they should, therefore, have lower before-tax yields than high-coupon bonds. That is, low-coupon bonds have a higher intrinsic value than high-coupon bonds.

Marketability

Marketability (sometimes also referred to as liquidity) refers to the ease with which an investor can sell an asset quickly without having to make a substantial price concession. An example of an illiquid asset is a *collectible*, such as a piece of artwork. An investor who owns a Van Gogh painting may have to settle for a relatively low price if she has to sell it within an hour. If the sale can be postponed for a length of time in order to set up a public auction, a much higher price could probably be obtained. Alternatively, an investor with

Deep Discount Bond A bond whose coupon interest rate is considerably below those of other bonds that otherwise possess similar attributes. Hence, these bonds sell at prices significantly below the other bonds.

Marketability The ability of investors to convert securities to cash at a price similar to the price of the previous trade in the security, assuming no significant new information has arrived since the previous trade. Equivalently, the ability to sell an asset quickly without having to make a substantial price concession.

$1 000 000 worth of BCE common shares who has to sell these shares within an hour will probably be able to receive a price close to the price that other sellers of BCE shares received recently. Furthermore, it is unlikely that waiting would increase the expected selling price of such securities.

Since most bonds are bought and sold in dealer markets, one measure of a bond's marketability is the bid-ask spread that the dealers are quoting on the bonds. Bonds that are actively traded tend to have lower bid-ask spreads than bonds that are inactive. This is because the dealer is more exposed to risk when making a market in an inactive security than when making a market in an active security. The source of this risk is the inventory that the dealer holds and the fact that interest rates in general may move in a way that causes the dealer to lose money on his inventory. Accordingly, bonds that are actively traded should have a lower yield-to-maturity and a higher intrinsic value than bonds that are inactive, everything else being equal.

● Likelihood of Default

In Canada, two corporations—the Canadian Bond Rating Service (CBRS) and Dominion Bond Rating Service (DBRS)—provide ratings of the creditworthiness of many corporate, municipal, and provincial bonds. In the US, Standard & Poor's Corporation and Moody's Investors Service, Inc. provide similar information.[8] These **bond ratings** are often used by investors as an indication of the likelihood of default by the issuer. Figures 14.3 and 14.4 provide details of the CBRS and DBRS ratings.[9]

A broader categorization is often employed, with bonds classified as being of either **investment grade** or **speculative grade**. Typically, investment-grade bonds are bonds that have been assigned to one of the top four ratings (AAA through BBB by DBRS; A++ through B++ by CBRS). In contrast, speculative-grade bonds are bonds that have been assigned to one of the lower ratings (BB and below by DRBS; B+ and below by CBRS). Sometimes these low-rated securities are called **junk bonds**.[10] Investment-grade bonds whose quality has fallen to junk levels are referred to as **fallen angels**.

Certain regulated financial institutions (such as trust companies, insurance companies, and pension plans) are prohibited from purchasing bonds that are not of investment grade. Because an important group of investors is encouraged or forced to purchase them, investment grade bonds are believed to command "superpremium" prices, and hence disproportionately low yields. If this were true, a major disparity in yields would attract many new issuers, thereby increasing the supply of such bonds and causing the prices to fall and yields to rise. For a significant superpremium to persist, substantial market segmentation on both the buying and the selling side would be required. As there is no clear evidence that segmentation exists, it seems likely that the differences in yields between investment-grade bonds and speculative-grade bonds are roughly proportional to differences in default risk.

Ratings are designed "to provide investors with a readily identifiable measure of the financial strength of a debt issue. In this way its relative level of risk and hence the required return may be compared to other types of securities throughout a diversified portfolio."[11] Moreover:

Canadian Bond Rating Service
www.cbrs.com

Dominion Bond Rating Service
www.dbrs.com

Moody's Investors Service
www.moodys.com

Bond Ratings An indicator of the creditworthiness of specific bond issues. These ratings provide an indication of a bond issuer's likelihood of default.

Investment-grade Bonds Bonds that possess bond ratings that permit them to be purchased by the vast majority of institutional investors, particularly regulated financial institutions. Usually, investment grade bonds have a BBB (Dominion Bond Rating Service), B++ (Canadian Bond Rating Service) or higher bond rating.

Speculative-grade Bonds (Also known in the US as **Junk Bonds**.) Bonds that are not investment grade bonds. Usually, speculative bonds have a BB (Dominion Bond Rating Service) or B+ (Canadian Bond Rating Service) or lower rating.

Fallen Angel A junk bond that was of investment grade when originally issued.

---

[8]Both Moody's and Standard & Poor's have made a practice of rating Canadian government bonds as well as selected Canadian corporate bonds.

[9]Both rating agencies use finer gradations than those shown in the figures. The ratings may be augmented by the addition of the qualifiers "high" or "low" to indicate both the relative ranking and the trend within a classification.

[10]For a primer on junk bonds and their analysis, see Stanley Block, "High-Yielding Securities: How Appropriate Are They?" *AAII Journal* 11, no. 10 (November 1989): 7–11; and Glen E. Atkins and Ben Branch, "A Qualitative Look at High-Yield Bond Analysis," *AAII Journal* 13, no. 12 (October 1991): 12–15. Also see the articles cited in notes 14 and 15.

[11]*The CBRS Method of Rating* (Montreal: Canadian Bond Rating Service, Inc., 1989): 6.

Highest Quality A++

This category encompasses bonds of outstanding quality. They possess the highest degree of protection of principal and interest. Companies with debt rated A++ are generally large national and/or multinational corporations whose products or services are essential to the Canadian economy.

These companies are the acknowledged leaders in their respective industries and have clearly demonstrated their ability to best withstand adverse economic or trade conditions either national or international in scope. Characteristically, these companies have had a long and creditable history of superior debt protection, in which the quality of their assets and earnings has been constantly maintained or improved, with strong evidence that this will continue.

Very Good Quality A+

Bonds rated A+ are similar in characteristics to those rated A++ and can also be considered superior in quality. These companies have demonstrated a long and satisfactory history of growth with above-average protection of principal and interest on their debt securities.

These bonds are generally rated lower in quality because the margin of assets or earnings protection may not be as large or as stable as those rated A++. In both these categories the nature and quality of the assets and earnings coverages are more important than the numerical values of the ratios.

Good Quality A

Bonds rated A are considered to be good quality securities and to have favourable long-term investment characteristics. The main feature that distinguishes them from the higher rated securities is that these companies are more susceptible to adverse trade or economic conditions. Consequently, the protection is lower than for the categories of A++ and A+.

In all cases the A-rated companies have maintained a history of adequate asset and earnings protection. There may be certain elements that may impair this protection sometime in the future. Confidence that the current overall financial position will be maintained or improved is slightly lower than for the securities rated above.

Medium Quality B++

Issues rated B++ are classified as medium or average grade credits and are considered to be investment grade. These companies are generally more susceptible than any of the higher rated companies to swings in economic or trade conditions that would cause a deterioration in protection should the company enter a period of poor operating conditions.

There may be factors present either from within or without the company that may adversely affect the long-term level of protection of the debt. These companies bear closer scrutiny but in all cases both interest and principal are adequately protected at the present time.

Figure 14.3 (Continued)

Lower Medium Quality B+

Bonds that are rated B+ are considered to be lower medium grade securities and have limited long-term protective investment characteristics. Assets and earnings coverage may be modest or unstable.

A significant deterioration in interest and principal protection may occur during periods of adverse economic or trade conditions. During periods of normal or improving economic conditions, assets and earnings protection are adequate. However, the company's ability to continually improve its financial position and level of debt protection is at present limited.

Poor Quality B

Securities rated B lack most qualities necessary for the long-term fixed income investment. Companies in this category have a general history of volatile operating conditions, and the assurance has been in doubt that principal and interest protection will be maintained at an adequate level. Current coverages may be below industry standards and there is little assurance that debt protection will significantly improve.

Speculative Quality C

Securities in this category are clearly speculative. The companies are generally junior in many respects and there is little assurance that the adequate coverage of principal and interest can be maintained uninterruptedly over a period of time.

Default D

Bonds in this category are in default of some provisions in their trust deed and the companies may or may not be in the process of liquidation.

Rating Suspended

A company which has its rating currently suspended is experiencing severe financial or operating problems of which the outcome is uncertain. The company may or may not be in default but at present there is uncertainty as to the company's ability to pay off its debt.

Note: (High) and (Low) designations after a rating indicate an issuer's relative strength within a rating category.

SOURCE: *The CBRS Method of Rating: Corporate and Government Securities* (Canadian Bond Rating Service Inc., 1989): 16, 17.

Ratings involve judgments about the future on the one hand, and they are used by investors as a means of protection on the other, therefore, an effort is made when assigning ratings to look at the "worst" potential outcomes in the "visible" future, as well as the past record and the present status. Investors using the ratings should not expect to find in them a reflection of statistical factors alone. They are an appraisal of long-term risks, including the recognition of many non-statistical factors.[12]

Despite this disclaimer, the influence of "statistical factors" on the ratings is apparently significant. Several studies have investigated the relationship between historical measures of

---

[12] *Moody's Bond Record* (New York: Moody's Investors Service, Inc., January 1997), p. 3.

a firm's performance and the ratings assigned its bonds. Many of the differences in the ratings accorded various bonds can, in fact, be attributed to differences in the issuers' situations, measured in traditional ways. For corporate bonds, better ratings are generally associated with:

1. **Lower financial leverage**, for example, having a smaller debt to total assets (or debt to equity) ratio and a larger current (or quick) ratio (measured by dividing current assets by current liabilities or, in the case of the quick ratio, dividing current assets except inventory by current liabilities).
2. **Larger firm size**, for example, having a larger amount of total assets.
3. **Larger and steadier profits**, for example, having a consistently high rate of return on equity or rate of return on total assets (often earnings before interest and taxes is used as the numerator in such ratios when evaluating a firm's debt) and coverage ratio, such as times interest earned (measured by dividing earnings before interest and taxes by interest).
4. **Larger cash flow**, for example, having a large cash flow to debt ratio.
5. **Lack of subordination to other debt issues.**

The results obtained by Canadian studies are similar to those of US studies. One use of these findings is in the development of models for predicting the initial ratings that will be given to forthcoming bond issues as well as for predicting changes in the ratings of outstanding bonds.

Taking Advantage of the Bond Rating Process

"Your bond rating: don't try to issue debt without it," might read the motto of both US and Canadian bond rating agencies. Receiving a bond rating has long been a prerequisite for any debt issuer desiring easy access to the domestic bond market. Without such a rating, debt issuers are forced to seek financing from more expensive sources; banks or the market for privately placed debt.

Once they have acquired a bond rating, debt issuers strive to maintain that rating or even to improve it. The benefits of an improved rating (and the costs of a lower rating) can be substantial. The difference in yields between the highest and the lowest rated investment-grade bonds fluctuates over time, but it is often well over a full percentage point (as is illustrated in Figure 14.5). Yield differences between investment-grade and below-investment-grade bonds typically are even greater. As corporations have increased the amount of debt on their balance sheets in recent decades, the financial ramifications of bond rating changes have increased commensurately.

Most institutional bond investors focus their efforts on forecasting changes in interest rates and structuring their portfolios to benefit from those expected movements. However, the emphasis placed by the bond market on both a debt issue's initial rating and subsequent changes in that rating present insightful investors with another approach to bond management: searching for bonds whose "true" credit quality is different from their assigned ratings. In discussing those opportunities, we first consider some additional information on the bond rating process.

In the US two companies dominate the bond rating business. Standard & Poor's and Moody's. Virtually every corporate debt security that comes to the public market is rated by at least one of these organizations. Over 2000 debt issuers submit financial data to these organizations. For all practical purposes, no bond can be considered an investment-grade security without the acquiescence of S&P's or Moody's.

In Canada, Canadian Bond Rating Service, Inc. and Dominion Bond Rating Service, Ltd. rate the

Figure 14.5 Quarterly Canadian corporate bond yields by ratings, 1977–1997.

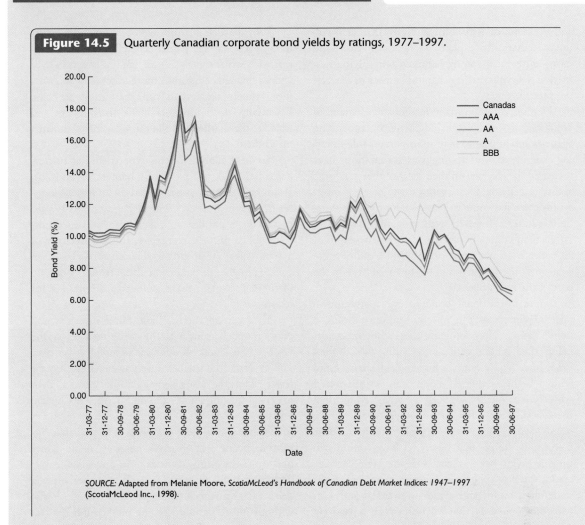

SOURCE: Adapted from Melanie Moore, *ScotiaMcLeod's Handbook of Canadian Debt Market Indices: 1947–1997* (ScotiaMcLeod Inc., 1998).

majority of corporate issues. In recent years, however, an increasing number of Canadian corporate issues have been rated by S&P's and/or Moody's and the trend seems to be increasing. The former company maintains a small office in Toronto. The ratings assigned by the Canadian rating agencies are frequently higher than those assigned by the US raters to the same issues. A study of 55 Canadian issues that were rated by a least one US and one Canadian rating agency showed that the latter assigned a higher rating in 45 cases, lower in 4 and the same in 6. On average the ratings by the Canadian raters were one quality level higher.[13] This has led some analysts to conclude that the Canadian bond raters are systematically biased. Other analysts, however, point out that the Canadian firms are more familiar with the domestic market and may uncover aspects of the debt issuer's financial condition overlooked by S&P's and Moody's.

The text describes many of the financial factors that rating agencies use in assigning bond ratings, including the issuers' leverage, earnings variability,

---

[13]See Greg Ip, "Are Canadian Bond Raters Biased?" *The Globe and Mail: Report on Business,* December 13, 1995.

and profitability. Research has shown that such factors systematically "explain" a large portion of bond rating differences among debt issues, implying that there is a significant "mechanical" aspect to the rating process.

Despite this dominant formulistic element of bond ratings, qualitative judgments by the rating agencies still appear to play an important role in rating assignments. Interestingly, as corporations have increased the leverage on their balance sheets, a firm's ability to generate future cash flow to meet its interest expenses has come to play a major role in setting bond ratings. However, evaluating the prospective rather than contemporaneous, cash flow strength of an issuer is an uncertain process and requires more subjective interpretations of the financial data on the part of the rating agencies.

Some institutional bond investors attempt to take advantage of the uncertainty surrounding a bond's rating. They recognize that, all other factors being equal, a bond with a lower rating will sell for a lower price (equivalently, a higher yield) than a bond with a higher rating. If bonds can be discovered whose credit quality supports a higher rating, then these bonds will offer premium yields relative to bonds with the same "actual" credit quality. Conversely, bonds that deserve a lower rating will provide yields below those with the same "actual" credit quality. Thus an investor who purchases underrated bonds and avoids overrated bonds can construct a portfolio that will outperform a passively managed portfolio of similar risk.

Owners of underrated bonds may benefit even further if their bonds are subsequently upgraded by the rating agencies. Such upgrades are usually associated with substantial price increases, although those increases usually occur before rating changes rather than after them.

Why do such institutional bond investors expect to beat the ratings game? They believe that with intensive security analysis they can understand a debt issuer's financial condition more accurately and on a more timely basis than can the rating agencies. Essentially, these investors make their moves and wait for the market and the rating agencies to catch up to them.

Security analysis of this type is similar to fundamental stock analysis (see Chapters 17 and 22), although less emphasis is placed on an issuer's long-term growth prospects and more attention is paid to the issuer's ability to cover near- and medium-term obligations. Nevertheless, an interpretation of a debt issuer's "true" financial condition is based on a wide range of disparate variables, from the quality of the debt issuer's management to the market for its products.

To a certain extent, these bond investors also play a numbers game with the rating agencies. In the US both S&P and Moody's each employ fewer than 100 analysts (the smaller rating agencies employ far fewer). Thus the rating agencies cannot cover all debt issuers at all times and the same is true in Canada. Further, they devote the majority of their resources to evaluating new debt offerings. It is true that significant positive or negative news about an issuer may cause the rating agencies to immediately reevaluate their bond ratings. However, at other times a debt issuer's financial condition may change slowly, without full recognition by the market and the rating agencies.

Of course, as with successful common stock analysis, identifying misrated bonds consistently and accurately requires skills possessed by few investors in an efficient market. But also as with common stock analysis, the potential profits to bond investors who correctly diverge from the current consensus can be large.

Default Premiums

Since common stocks do not "promise" any cash flows to the investor, they are not subject to default. To assess the investment prospects for a common stock, all possible holding-period returns might be considered. By multiplying each return by its perceived probability of occurrence and then adding up the products, an estimate of the expected holding-period return can be determined.

Expected Yield-to-maturity The yield-to-maturity on a bond calculated as a weighted average of all possible yields that the bond might produce under different scenarios of default or late payments, where the weights are the probabilities of each scenario occurring.

Default Premium The difference between the promised and expected yield-to-maturity on a bond arising from the possibility that the bond issuer might default on the bond.

A similar procedure can be employed with bonds, with the analysis usually focusing on yield-to-maturity. Formally, all possible yields are considered, along with their respective probabilities, and a weighted average is computed to determine the **expected yield-to-maturity**. As long as there is any possibility of default or late payment, the expected yield will fall below the promised yield. In general, the greater the risk of default and the greater the amount of loss in the event of default, the greater will be this disparity.

This is illustrated in Figure 14.6 for a hypothetical risky bond. Its promised yield-to-maturity is 12% but, owing to a high default risk, the expected yield is only 9%. The 3% difference between the promised and expected yields is the **default premium**. Any bond that has some probability of default should offer such a premium, and the greater the probability of default, the larger the premium should be.

Just how large should a bond's default premium be? According to one model, the answer depends on both the probability of default and the likely financial loss to the bondholder in the event of default.[14] Consider a bond that is perceived to be equally likely to default in each year (given it did not default in the previous year), with the probability that it will default in any given year denoted by p_d. Assume that if the bond does default, a payment equal to $(1 - \lambda)$ times its market price a year earlier will be made to the owner of each bond. According to this model, a bond will be fairly priced if its promised yield-to-maturity (y) is

$$y = \frac{\bar{y} + \lambda p_d}{1 - p_d} \tag{14.4}$$

where $\bar{y}$ denotes the bond's expected yield-to-maturity. The difference (d) between a bond's promised yield-to-maturity (y) and its expected yield-to-maturity $(\bar{y})$ was referred to earlier as the bond's default premium. Using equation (14.4), this difference for a fairly priced bond will be equal to

$$d = y - \bar{y}$$
$$= \left[\frac{\bar{y} + \lambda p_d}{1 - p_d} \right] - \bar{y} \tag{14.5}$$

As an example, consider the bond illustrated in Figure 14.6. Assume that this bond has a 6% annual default probability and that it is estimated that if the bond does default, each bondholder will receive an amount equal to 60% of the bond's market price a year earlier (meaning that $1 - \lambda = .60$, which in turn means that $\lambda = .40$). Using equation (14.5), this bond would be fairly priced if its default premium were equal to

$$d = \left[\frac{.09 + (.40 \times .06)}{1 - .06} \right] - .09$$
$$= .0313$$

or 3.13%. Because the actual default premium earlier was estimated to be 3%, it can be seen that the two figures are similar. This suggests the actual default premium is appropriate, according to this model.

What sort of default experience might the long-run bond investor anticipate? And how is this experience likely to be related to the ratings of the bonds held? In a massive US study of all large bond issues and a sample of small bond issues, Hickman attempted to answer these questions.[15] He analyzed investor experience for each bond from 1900 through 1943 to determine the actual yield-to-maturity, measured from the date of issuance to the date

---

[14]The model was developed by Gordon Pye in "Gauging the Default Premium," *Financial Analysts Journal* 30 no. 1 (January–February 1974): 49–52.

[15]W. Braddock Hickman, *Corporate Bond Quality and Investor Experience* (Princeton, NJ: Princeton University Press, 1958).

Figure 14.4 Dominion Bond Rating Service's bond rating scale.

AAA "Near Perfection"

Bonds that are rated AAA are of the highest investment quality. The degree of protection afforded principal and interest is of the highest order. Earnings are relatively stable, the structure of the industry in which the Company operates is very strong, and the outlook for future profitability is extremely favourable. There are few qualifying factors present that would detract from the performance of the Company, and the strength of liquidity ratios is unquestioned for the industry in which the Company operates.

AA Well Above Average

Bonds rated AA are of superior investment quality, and protection of interest and principal is considered high. In many cases, they differ from bonds rated AAA to a small degree.

A Up to High Average, Upper Medium Grade

Bonds rated A are upper medium grade securities. Protection of interest and principal is still substantial, but the degree of strength is less than with AA rated companies. Companies in this category may be more susceptible to adverse economic conditions.

BBB Up to Low Average, Medium Grade

Bonds rated BBB are medium grade securities. Protection of interest and principal is considered adequate, but the Company may be more susceptible to economic cycles, or there may be other adversities present which reduce the strength of these bonds.

BB Mildly Speculative

Bonds rated BB are lower medium grade obligations, and are considered mildly speculative and below average. The degree of protection afforded interest and principal is uncertain, particularly during periods of economic recession, and the size of the Company may be relatively small.

B Middle Speculative

Bonds rated B are "middle" speculative. Uncertainty exists as to the ability of the Company to pay interest and principal on a continuing basis in the future, especially in periods of economic recession.

CCC Highly Speculative

Bonds rated CCC are considered highly speculative and are in danger of default of interest and principal. The degree of adverse elements present is more severe than bonds rated B.

CC In Default

Bonds rated CC are in default of either interest or principal, and other severe adverse elements are present.

Figure 14.4
 (Continued)

C Second Tier of Debt of a Company in Default

C is the lowest rating provided. Bonds rated C differ from bonds rated CC with respect to the relative liquidation values.

"NR"

For certain companies, we may complete the editorial, yet not rate the Company formally, in which case we would rate it NR, or "not rated".

High or Low

In addition to the above, our ratings may be modified by the quotation "high" or "low" to indicate the relative standing within a rating classification.

Highest Rating

Please note: the rating quoted at the top left of the front page of a report indicates the rating of the highest order or securities issued by the Company.

SOURCE: DBRS, Dominion Bond Rating Service Limited, 1992: 7.

on which the bond matured, defaulted, or was called—whichever came first. He then compared this actual yield with the promised yield-to-maturity based on the price at time of issue. Every bond was also classified according to the ratings assigned at time of issue. Part (a) of Table 14.1 shows the major results.

As might be expected, Hickman found that, in general, the riskier the bond, the higher the promised yield at time of issue and the higher the percentage of bonds that subsequently defaulted. However, a surprise was uncovered when the actual yields-to-maturity were compared with promised yields-to-maturity. As the last column on the right of the table shows, in four out of five rating classifications, the actual yield was found to *exceed* the promised yield. Fortunately, a convenient explanation exists for this finding—the period studied by Hickman was one where a substantial drop in interest rates occurred. This is important because the drop made it attractive for issuers to call their outstanding bonds, paying the bondholders a call premium in the process and resulting in an actual yield above the promised yield.

Figure 14.6 Yield-to-maturity for a risky bond.

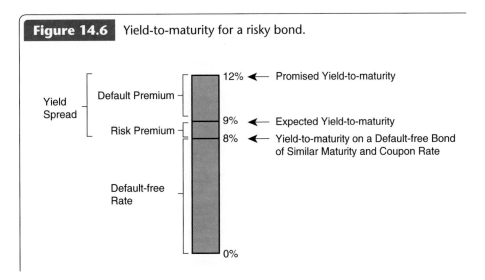

Table 14.1   Actual and Realized Bond Yields-to-Maturity, 1900–1943.

(a) All Large and a Sample of Small Issues

Composite Rating	Comparable Moody's Rating	Promised Yield-to-Maturity at Issue	Percent Defaulting Prior to Maturity	Actual-Yield-to-Maturity
I	AAA	4.5%	5.9%	5.1%
II	AA	4.6	6.0	5.0
III	A	4.9	13.4	5.0
IV	BAA	5.4	19.1	5.7
V–IX	below BAA	9.5	42.4	8.6

(b) All Large Issues

Composite Rating	Comparable Moody's Rating	Promised Yield-to-Maturity	Actual Yield-to-Maturity	Modified Actual Yield-to-Maturity
I	AAA	4.5%	5.1%	4.3%
II	AA	4.5	5.1	4.3
III	A	4.9	5.0	4.3
IV	BAA	5.4	5.8	4.5

SOURCE: (a) W. Braddock Hickman, *Corporate Bond Quality and Investor Experience* (Princeton, NJ: Princeton University Press, 1953):10. (b) Harold G. Fraine and Robert H. Mills, "The Effect of Defaults and Credit Deterioration on Yields of Corporate Bonds," *Journal of Finance* 16, no. 3 (September 1961): 433.

To see what might have happened had this not been the case, Fraine and Mills reanalyzed the data for large investment-grade issues.[16] Their results are shown in part (b) of Table 14.1. The initial columns differ from those in part (a) because smaller issues were excluded. The major difference between the parts appears in the right-hand column, where Fraine and Mills substituted a bond's promised yield for its actual yield whenever the latter was larger, thereby removing the effects of most calls. Unlike Hickman, their results suggest that there was little difference in actual yields within the highest rating classifications.[17]

More recently, Edward Altman examined the default experience of corporate bonds over the period from 1971 through 1990.[18] His methodology was somewhat different from Hickman's in that for each bond he noted its rating when it was originally issued and then how many years later it went into default (if at all). From this he compiled "mortality tables," such as Table 14.2, which shows the percentage of bond issues that went into default within various numbers of years after issuance.

There are several interesting observations that can be made upon inspection of this table. First, in looking down any particular column, it can be seen that the cumulative rate of default increases as one moves further from the date of issuance. Second, with the exception of those bonds originally rated AA, lower rated bonds had higher default rates. Third,

---

[16]Harold G. Fraine and Robert H. Mills, "The Effect of Defaults and Credit Deterioration on Yields of Corporate Bonds," *Journal of Finance* 16, no. 3 (September 1961): 423–434.

[17]While Fraine and Mills work may appear dated, it has been reported that the "work holds up extremely well a generation or so after its publication," according to Martin S. Fridson, "Fraine's Neglected Findings: Was Hickman Wrong?" *Financial Analysts Journal* 50, no. 5 (September–October 1994): 52.

[18]Edward I. Altman, "Defaults and Returns on High-yield Bonds Through the First Half of 1991," *Financial Analysts Journal* 47, no. 6 (November–December 1991): 67–77.

Table 14.2 Default Rates of US Bonds, 1971–1990.

Years After Issuance	Original Rating						
	AAA	AA	A	BBB	BB	B	CCC
1	.00%	.00%	.00%	.03%	.00%	.87%	1.31%
2	.00	.00	.30	.57	.93	3.22	4.00
3	.00	1.11	.60	.85	1.36	9.41	19.72
4	.00	1.42	.65	1.34	3.98	16.37	36.67
5	.00	1.70	.65	1.54	5.93	20.87	38.08
6	.14	1.70	.73	1.81	7.38	26.48	40.58
7	.19	1.91	.87	2.70	10.91	29.62	NA
8	.19	1.93	.94	2.83	10.91	31.74	NA
9	.19	2.01	1.28	2.99	10.91	39.38	NA
10	.19	2.11	1.28	3.85	13.86	40.86	NA

SOURCE: Edward I. Altman, "Defaults and Returns on High-yield Bonds Through the First Half of 1991," *Financial Analysts Journal* 47, no. 6 (November–December 1991): Table X, pp. 74–75.

the default rates for the speculative grades of bonds are strikingly high. Indeed, it raises the question of whether or not such bonds make good investments, as their higher yields might not make up for their higher default rates.[19] This question will be addressed shortly.

Risk Premiums

It is useful to compare the expected return of a risky security with the certain return of a default-free security. In an efficient market, the difference in these returns will be related to the relevant risk of the security. Consider common stocks, where the investor has a holding period of one year or less. In this situation, the expected return on a share is typically compared with the yield of a Treasury bill having a maturity date corresponding with the end of the holding period (note that the yield on such a Treasury bill is equal to its holding-period return).

Traditionally, a risky bond's expected yield-to-maturity is compared with that of a default-free bond of similar maturity and coupon rate. The difference between these yields is known as the bond's **risk premium**. In the example shown in Figure 14.5, default-free bonds of similar maturity and coupon rate offer a certain 8% yield-to-maturity. Since the risky bond's expected yield-to-maturity is 9%, its risk premium is 1% (that is, 100 basis points).

Every bond that might default should offer a default premium. But the risk premium is another matter. Any security's expected return should be related only to its contribution to the risk of a well-diversified portfolio (i.e., its systematic risk); its total risk is not directly relevant.

For example, if a group of companies all faced the possibility of bankruptcy, but from totally unrelated causes, a portfolio that included all their bonds would subsequently provide an actual return very close to its expected return. This is because the default premiums earned on the bonds that did not default would offset the losses incurred from those bonds

Risk Premium The difference between the expected yield-to-maturity of a risky bond and the expected yield-to-maturity of a similar default-free bond.

---

[19]Interestingly, one study found that investors who purchased the equity of B-rated firms at the time that they issued debt subsequently received relatively poor returns over the next three years, while those who bought the equity of Ba or higher-rated firms received a normal return. See Jeff Jewell and Miles Livingston, "The Long-run Performance of Firms Issuing Debt," *Journal of Fixed Income* 7, no. 2 (September 1997): 61–66.

that did default. Consequently, there would be little reason for this expected return to differ significantly from that of a default-free bond, since there is little doubt concerning what its actual return will be. Accordingly, each bond should be priced to offer little or no risk premium (but each bond should have a substantial default premium).

However, the risks associated with bonds are not unrelated. Figure 14.7 shows for each year from 1900 to 1965 the ratio of the par value of corporate bonds defaulting during the year to the par value outstanding at the beginning of the year. Not surprisingly, the peaks coincide with periods of economic distress.[20] When business is bad, most firms are affected. The market value of a firm's common stock will decline when an economic downturn is anticipated. If the likelihood of default on its debt also increases, the market value of its outstanding bonds will follow suit. Thus, the holding-period return on a bond may be correlated with the returns of other bonds and with those of stocks. Most important, a risky bond's holding-period return is likely to be correlated to at least some extent with the return on a widely diversified market portfolio that includes both corporate bonds and stocks. This part of the risk of a bond should command a risk premium in the form of a higher expected return, because it is not diversifiable.

Bonds with greater likelihood of default will have greater potential sensitivity to market declines that represent lowered assessments of prospects for the economy as a whole. This is illustrated in Table 14.3, which summarizes the investment performance of three portfolios of US bonds, known as bond funds, in the Keystone group.[21] All values shown in the table are based on annual returns earned over a 24-year period by each portfolio. As might be anticipated, the most risky bond portfolio (fund B4) had the highest average

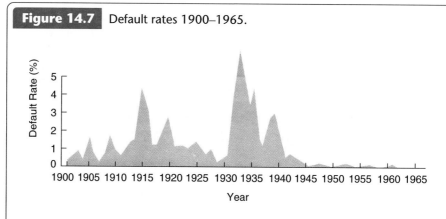

Figure 14.7 Default rates 1900–1965.

SOURCE: Adapted from Thomas R. Atkinson and Elizabeth T. Simpson, *Trends in Corporate Bond Quality* (Columbia University Press, 1967), p. 5.

[20]See Marshall E. Blume and Donald B. Keim, "Realized Returns and Defaults on Low-grade Bonds: The Cohort of 1977 and 1978," *Financial Analysts Journal* 47, no. 2 (March–April 1991): 63–72; Marshall E. Blume, Donald B. Keim, and Sandeep A. Patel, "Returns and Volatility of Low-grade Bonds, 1977–1989," *Journal of Finance* 46, no. 1 (March 1991): 49–74; and Marshall E. Blume and Donald B. Keim, "The Risk and Return of Low-grade Bonds: An Update," *Financial Analysts Journal* 47, no. 5 (September–October 1991).

[21]For an in-depth analysis of such bond portfolios, see Bradford Cornell and Kevin Greene, "The Investment Performance of Low-grade Bond Funds," *Journal of Finance* 46, no. 1 (March 1991): 29–48; and Bradford Cornell, "Liquidity and the Pricing of Low-grade Bonds," *Financial Analysts Journal* 48, no. 1 (January–February 1992): 63–67, 74.

Table 14.3 Risk and Return, Keystone Bond Funds, 1968–1991.

	Fund B1	Fund B2	Fund B4
	Conservative Bonds	Investment Grade Bonds	Discount Bonds
Average return (% per year)	7.84	8.53	8.64
Standard deviation of return (% per year)	8.27	9.35	13.68
Beta value, relative to S&P 500	.26	.38	.54
Proportion of variance explained by S&P 500	.28	.45	.42

return and highest standard deviation of return, whereas the least risky bond portfolio (fund B1) had the lowest average return and lowest standard deviation.

To estimate each portfolio's sensitivity to changes in stock prices, each portfolio's returns were compared with those of Standard & Poor's 500. Specifically, a beta was calculated for each portfolio in order to measure the sensitivity of each portfolio to swings in the stock market. As can be seen, the riskier the portfolio, the higher the estimated beta, indicating that riskier bonds moved more with stocks and thus should have had higher average returns.

The final row in the table shows the proportion of the year-to-year variation in bond portfolio returns that were associated with stock market swings. As indicated, relatively more of the B2 and B4 portfolios' variation was associated with the stock market than was the case with the B1 portfolio. Thus, for less-risky bonds, interest-rate risk appears to be more important than stock market risk.[22]

The Risk Structure of Interest Rates

The greater a bond's risk of default, the greater its default premium. This alone will cause a bond with a higher default risk to offer a higher promised yield-to-maturity. If it is also true that the greater a bond's risk of default, the greater its risk premium, then the promised yield-to-maturity will have to be even higher. Bonds with lower agency ratings should have higher promised yields-to-maturity if these ratings in fact reflect the risk of default.

Figure 14.5 shows that this is indeed the case. Each of the curves plots the promised yield-to-maturity for a group of corporate bonds assigned the same ratings. It is clear that bonds are priced so that higher promised yields are associated with lower ratings. The yield differences between rating categories vary considerably over time, however, suggesting that agency ratings indicate *relative* levels of risk instead of *absolute* levels of risk.

If an absolute level of risk were indicated by a rating classification, then each classification would be associated with a particular probability of default (or, more accurately, a range of probabilities of default). Consequently, as the economy became more uncertain (for example, an increased probability of a recession), bonds would be reclassified as necessary, with most moving to lower ratings. In this situation, yield spreads between classifications would change only slightly, since each classification would still reflect bonds having

---

[22]In a study of preferred shares, it was found that the price movements of low-rated preferred shares were related more to the price movements of common stocks than to the price movements of bonds; for high-rated preferred shares, the findings were just the opposite. See John S. Bildersee, "Some Aspects of the Performance of Non-convertible Preferred Stocks," *Journal of Finance* 28, no. 5 (December 1973): 1187–1201.

the same probability of default. However, Figure 14.1 shows that these spreads change considerably over time, an observation that can be interpreted as evidence that the bond market does not believe that the ratings reflect absolute levels of risk.

Further evidence is provided in Table 14.4, which shows the historical difference in the returns on junk bonds and US Treasuries for various holding periods. As shown in the table, at times these differences are positive and at other times they are negative. (For example, the average annual differences for 1978–1983 and 1984–1991 are +5.82% and −2.31%, respectively.)

Rating agencies appear to prefer to avoid making a large number of rating changes as the economy becomes more uncertain. Instead, they prefer to use the classifications to indicate relative levels of risk. This means that an overall increase in economic uncertainty does not result in a significant number of reclassifications. Thus, the probability of default associated with bonds in a given rating classification is greater at such a time. In turn, the yield spreads between classifications of corporate bonds and the yield spreads between corporate and government bonds both increase. Indeed, there is evidence that the spread between the promised yields of bonds of different rating classifications increases when uncertainty about the economy increases.

Some models have attempted to take advantage of this observation in order to predict the amount of economic uncertainty. In particular, these models use the size of the yield spread between, say, bonds rated AAA and those rated BBB as an indication of the degree of economic uncertainty. For example, if this spread is widening, then that might be taken as an indication that the near-term future of the economy was becoming more uncertain. There are also models that look not at yield spreads but at differences in the holding-period returns of AAA and BBB bonds.

Table 14.4 Historical Return Differences Between Junk Bonds and US Treasuries.

Terminal Period (December 31)

Base Period (Jan. 1)	1978	1979	1980	1981	1982	1983	1984	1985	1986	1987	1988	1989	1990	1991
1978	8.68%	6.60%	5.01%	5.51%	3.17%	5.82%	4.13%	2.70%	1.59%	2.22%	2.41%	0.98%	(0.04%)	1.37%
1979		4.55	3.23	4.48	1.71	5.22	3.32	1.77	0.62	1.44	1.73	0.23	(0.82)	0.74
1980			1.96	4.45	0.67	5.39	3.05	1.24	(0.02)	1.01	1.38	(0.25)	(1.35)	0.37
1981				7.08	(0.13)	6.74	3.36	1.07	(0.42)	0.85	1.29	(0.54)	(1.73)	0.19
1982					(9.63)	6.49	1.93	(0.69)	(2.16)	(0.33)	0.36	(1.60)	(2.80)	(0.60)
1983						19.57	6.62	1.84	(0.56)	1.22	1.74	(0.65)	(2.11)	0.26
1984							(6.32)	(7.60)	(7.73)	(3.48)	(1.89)	(4.06)	(5.19)	(2.31)
1985								(9.03)	(8.50)	(2.50)	(0.76)	(3.60)	(5.00)	(1.70)
1986									(7.99)	0.34	1.64	(2.41)	(4.30)	(0.54)
1987										7.34	5.89	(0.76)	(3.49)	0.93
1988											4.27	(5.16)	(7.31)	(1.04)
1989												(14.37)	(12.76)	(3.11)
1990													(11.24)	4.34
1991*														19.01

*First six months of 1991.

SOURCE: Edward I. Altman, "Defaults and Returns on High-Yield Bonds Through the First Half of 1991." *Financial Analysts Journal 47, no. 6* (November–December 1991): Table XIV, p. 77.

Matrix Bond Pricing

Many institutional investors must periodically determine the market values of their bond portfolios. For example, a pension fund may wish to keep beneficiaries abreast of the value of their fixed-income investments. Further, the pension fund needs accurate market valuations to evaluate fixed-income managers' investment results and to compute their compensation. (Managers' fees are typically based on the market values of their portfolios.)

In some cases, valuing a bond portfolio is a straightforward matter. Prices of most government bonds, many government agency bonds, and certain actively traded corporate bonds are available through real-time electronic quotation systems and the print media. Unlike common stocks, however, where an active market usually exists for all but the smallest issues, many bond issues (even some with large face values outstanding) do not trade frequently. It is not uncommon to find entire bond issues held to maturity by investors. The limited trading of these securities inhibits efforts to accurately determine their current market prices.

How can an institutional investor establish market prices for thinly traded fixed-income securities in its possession? It could ask its fixed-income managers to supply their best estimates of the bonds' market prices. After all, these managers constantly compare their perceptions of the bonds' intrinsic values to the bonds' estimated market prices as part of their portfolio management processes. However, a manager has an inherent conflict of interest in providing such valuations because his financial well-being is directly related to those values.

Alternatively, the pension fund might canvass bond dealers who trade the bonds under question (or similar securities) and solicit representative bid prices. Unfortunately, this procedure is too time-consuming to conduct on a regular basis for hundreds of bonds. Furthermore, the dealers have no incentive to participate.

In response to this dearth of pricing data, institutional investors have turned to various commercial bond valuation services. For a fee, these organizations provide third-party security valuations for tens of thousands of fixed-income securities on a daily, weekly, or monthly basis.

Some bond pricing services "lever off" of their own trading operations. They use their bond traders to submit bid-side valuations daily for any securities that the traders regularly see traded in the market. This "hand pricing" by traders offers perhaps the best estimate that institutional investors can readily obtain of the "true" market price, or liquidation value, of their bonds. Note, however, that the pricing services do not offer to transact at their price quotations. An actual bid for an institutional investor's fixed-income portfolio would involve an assessment by the trader of many factors, including the trader's current inventory, the price risk of the portfolio, and available hedges on the portfolio.

Oftentimes, however, a bond pricing service does not have immediate access to current prices for certain securities, either because it does not maintain a trading desk or because its traders do not deal in the securities. In those cases, various mechanical procedures, generally known as *matrix pricing*, are used to estimate market prices. The particular matrix pricing formulas vary among the pricing services and among the types of bonds valued by the services. Nevertheless, the pricing of corporate bonds provides a good example of the essential aspects of matrix bond pricing.

The price matrix for investment-grade corporate bonds is typically three-dimensional, with sector, quality, and term-to-maturity as the three primary variables. Each cell in the matrix represents a unique three-way combination of these variables. For example, one cell might contain industrial bonds with A ratings and three years to maturity. Each cell in the matrix is assigned an incremental yield (or "spread") over comparable maturity government securities, based on an analysis of current market conditions. (For example, three-year, A-rated industrial bonds might be assigned a 100-basis-point spread over Canadas.) These spreads may change over time at the discretion of the pricing service.

Once the matrix spreads are established, a corporate bond is priced by finding the cell in which it resides and using the associated yield to discount the bond's promised cash flows and thereby compute an estimated price. Adjustments may be made for special factors, such as coupon rates, call features, and sinking fund provisions.

Mortgage pass-through securities create particular problems for matrix pricing systems, especially complex mortgage-backed bonds, such as various forms of collaterial obligations (CMOs). There exist literally hundreds of variations of mortgage pass-through securities that differ in terms of coupon rate, payment terms, years since issuance (called "seasoning"), underlying collateral, and expected prepayment speed. The existing matrix pricing procedures are relatively primitive compared to the state-of-the-art option-adjusted pricing models used by many fixed-income managers.

For standard mortgage pass-through securities, the bond pricing services may supply valuations for various generic securities based on issuer type, coupon rate, and seasoning. Any mortgage pass-through security that matches the characteristics of

one of the generic securities is assigned the same price.

Current matrix-pricing procedures for pass-through securities have been criticized for not explicitly accounting for the embedded option contained in those securities (that is, the ability of homeowners to prepay their mortgages at their discretion). This option has an implicit value, and failing to adequately incorporate it into a pass-through securities price will produce systematic errors.

As one might expect, the accuracy of matrix bond pricing depends on the comparability of the security under analysis. Those securities that do not deviate significantly in terms of investment characteristics from their actively traded counterparts are relatively easy to price accurately. Securities with unique or relatively complicated features are more difficult to price accurately, and their matrix prices are often considered suspect by fixed-income managers.

Determinants of Yield Spreads

As mentioned previously, when bond analysts refer to a corporate bond's yield spread, they are typically referring to the difference between the corporate bond's promised yield-to-maturity and that of another bond (often a default-free government security) having similar maturity and coupon rate. The greater the risk of default, the greater this spread should be. Moreover, bonds that have more marketability might command an additional "premium" in price and hence offer a lower yield-to-maturity with a corresponding lower spread. Given a large enough sample of bonds, it should be possible to see if these relationships really do exist.

A US study of corporate bond prices did this.[23] Four measures were used to assess the probability of default:

1. The extent to which the firm's net income had varied over the preceding nine years (measured by the coefficient of variation of earnings—that is, the ratio of standard deviation of earnings to average earnings)
2. The length of time that the firm had operated without forcing any of its creditors to take a loss
3. The ratio of the market value of the firm's equity to the par value of its debt
4. The market value of the firm's outstanding debt

---

[23]Lawrence Fisher, "Determinants of Risk Premiums on Corporate Bonds," *Journal of Political Economy* 67, no. 3 (June 1959): 217–237.

First, these measures were calculated, along with the yield spread, for each one of 366 bonds. Second, the logarithm of every yield spread and measure was calculated. Third, statistical methods were used to analyze the relationship between a bond's yield spread and these measures. The one that was found to describe this relationship most accurately was:

$$\text{Yield spread} = .987 + .307 \text{ (earnings variability)} \\ - .253 \text{ (time without default)} \\ - .537 \text{ (equity/debt ratio)} \\ - .275 \text{ (market value of debt)} \tag{14.6}$$

This form of the relationship accounted for roughly 75% of the variation in the bonds' yield spreads.

The advantage of an equation such as this is that the coefficients can be easily interpreted. Since all yield spreads and values had been converted to logarithms, the effect is similar to that of using ratio scales on all axes of a diagram. This means that a 1% increase in a bond's earnings variability can be expected to bring about an increase of .307% in the bond's yield spread, other things being equal. Similarly, a 1% increase in a bond's time without default can be expected to cause a decrease of approximately .253% in the bond's yield spread, and so on. Each coefficient is an elasticity, indicating the percentage change in a bond's yield spread likely to accompany a 1% change in the associated measure. Since every measure was found to be related in the expected direction to the yield spread, the study provides substantial support for the notion that bonds with higher default risk and less marketability have higher yield spreads.

Financial Ratios as Predictors of Default

For years, security analysts have used accounting ratios to indicate the probability that a firm will fail to meet its financial obligations. Specific procedures have been developed to predict default with such ratios. Univariate analysis attempts to find the best single predictor for this purpose, whereas multivariate analysis searches for the best combination of two or more predictors.

Univariate Methods

Cash inflows can be viewed as contributions to the firm's cash balance, and cash outflows can be viewed as drains on this balance. When the balance falls below zero, default is likely to occur. This means that the probability of default will be greater for the firm when (1) the existing cash balance is smaller; (2) the expected net cash flow (measured before payments to creditors and shareholders) is smaller; and (3) the net cash flow is more variable.

In an examination of various measures used to assess these factors, it was found that the ratio of net cash flow (income before depreciation, depletion, and amortization charges) to total debt was particularly useful.[24] Figure 14.8(a) shows the mean value of this ratio for a group of firms that defaulted on a promised payment and for a companion group that did not. As early as five years before default the two groups' ratios diverged, and the spread widened as the year of default approached.

---

[24]William H. Beaver, "Market Prices, Financial Ratios and the Prediction of Failure," *Journal of Accounting Research* 6, no. 2 (Autumn 1968): 1979–1992. For a more recent study, see James M. Gahlon and Robert L. Vigeland, "Early Warning Signs of Bankruptcy Using Cash Flow Analysis," *Journal of Commercial Bank Lending* 71, no. 4 (December 1988): 4–15.

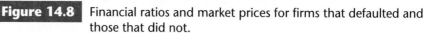

Figure 14.8 Financial ratios and market prices for firms that defaulted and those that did not.

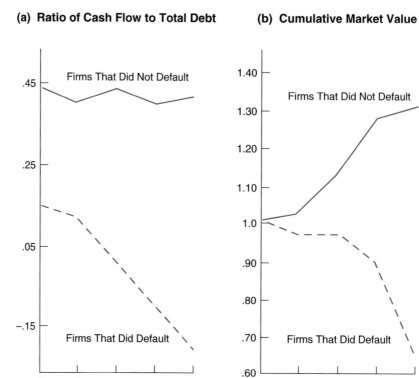

(a) Ratio of Cash Flow to Total Debt

Firms That Did Not Default

Firms That Did Default

Years Before Default

(b) Cumulative Market Value

Firms That Did Not Default

Firms That Did Default

Years Before Default

SOURCE: William H. Beaver, "Market Prices, Financial Ratios and the Prediction of Failure," *Journal of Accounting Research* 6, no. 2 (Autumn 1968): 182, 185.

This changing spread suggests that the probability of default may not be constant through time. Instead, warning signals may indicate an increase in the probability, which should, in turn, cause a fall in the market price of the firm's bonds along with a fall in the market price of its common stock. Figure 14.8(b) shows that such signals are indeed recognized in the marketplace. The median market value of common stock in the firms that did not default went up, while that of the firms that subsequently defaulted went down as the date of default approached.

Canadian stock market data were used to compare the characteristics of a sample of 25 firms that failed with those of a matched sample of firms that did not fail. This showed that impending failure was characterized by: decreasing common stock returns starting about 12 months prior to failure; increasing total risk (increasing variance of returns) also starting about 12 months prior to failure; and a shift from systematic to unsystematic risk as evidenced by a decrease in beta starting about 24 months prior to failure. They concluded that market participants could use their techniques to anticipate failure, on average, 14 months before its occurrence.[25]

---

[25]Vijay M. Jog and Allan L. Riding, "Canadian Stock Market Reactions to Impending Corporate Failure," *Proceedings*, Administrative Sciences Association of Canada Conference, Whistler, BC (June 1988): 226–240.

Multivariate Methods

Combinations of certain financial ratios have been considered as possible predictors of default.[26] Statistical analysis has indicated that the most accurate method of predicting default has been to calculate a firm's *Z-score* from some of its financial ratios as follows:

$$Z = 1.2X_1 + 1.4X_2 + 3.3X_3 + .6X_4 + .99X_5 \qquad (14.7)$$

where the following ratios are calculated from information contained in the firm's most recent income statement and balance sheet:

X_1 = (current assets − current liabilities)/total assets
X_2 = retained earnings/total assets
X_3 = earnings before interest and taxes/total assets
X_4 = market value of equity/book value of total debt
X_5 = sales/total assets

Any firm with a *Z*-score below 1.8 is considered a likely candidate for default, and the lower the score, the greater the likelihood.

A corresponding Canadian study found that the following financial ratios were significant:[27]

X_1 = sales/total assets
X_2 = total debt/total assets
X_3 = current assets/current liabilities
X_4 = net profits after tax/total debt
X_5 = rate of growth of equity − rate of asset growth.

In this case a critical score of −0.33 indicates a significant probability of default.

Investment Implications

The preceding discussion does not mean that securities of firms whose cash-flow-to-total-debt ratio or *Z*-score had declined should be avoided. It should be remembered that the firms represented by the dashed lines in Figure 14.8 were chosen because they eventually defaulted. Had all firms with declining ratios been selected, corresponding decreases in their market price would undoubtedly have been observed, reflecting the increased probability of future default. However, only some of these firms would have ultimately defaulted, whereas the others would have recovered. Consequently, the gains on the firms that recovered might well have offset the losses on the firms that defaulted. In summary, the net result from purchasing a portfolio of stocks with declining ratios or *Z*-scores is that the investor would have received an average return.

What about purchasing bonds of companies that have just had their ratings increased and selling (or avoiding) bonds of companies that have just had their ratings decreased? After all, such changes in ratings should be related to a change in the default risk of the issuer. In a US study that looked at the behaviour of bond prices around the time of ratings changes, some evidence was found that the bond price adjustment to a rating change

---

[26]Edward I. Altman, "Financial Ratios, Discriminant Analysis and the Prediction of Corporate Bankruptcy," *Journal of Finance* 23, no. 4 (September 1968): 589–609.

[27]Edward I. Altman and Mario Y. Lavallee, "Business Failure Classification in Canada, *Journal of Business Administration: Capital Markets in Canada* 12, no. 1 (Fall 1980): 147–164. Subsequent refinements to this model have been made, leading to a revised procedure known as *zeta analysis*. See Edward I. Altman, Robert G. Haldeman, and P. Narayanan, "Zeta Analysis: A New Model to Identify Bankruptcy Risk of Corporations," *Journal of Banking and Finance* 1, no. 1 (June 1977): 29–54.

occurred in the period from 18 to 7 months *before* the rating change.[28] Little or no evidence of a substantive price change was found either during the month of the rating change or in the period from six months before to six months after the rating change. These findings are consistent with the notion that the bond market is semistrong-form efficient, since bond ratings are predictable from publicly available information.

While the previous study looked primarily at ratings changes within investment-grade categories, a recent paper also looked at what happened around the time of ratings changes for bonds that (1) were not investment grade and were downgraded, or (2) were investment grade and were downgraded to no longer be investment grade.[29] Care was taken to ensure that there were no other firm announcements, and that the downgrades were issued at the same time by both Moody's and Standard & Poor's. In both of these cases, there was a strong negative price reaction during the month of the downgrade and during the previous six months. The reaction before the downgrade is again consistent with semistrong-form market efficiency, but the reaction during the month of the downgrade might not be, since it is unclear whether the reaction occurred, at least in part, on or after the day of the downgrade. If there was a significant negative price reaction after the day of the downgrade, this would be evidence of an inefficiency since investors could short sell such bonds on the announcement date and make abnormal profits. However, if most of the reaction was before the announcement, then there would not be any way to profit from trading after the announcement was made.

Summary

1. The capitalization of income method of valuation is a commonly used approach to identifying mispriced bonds. It is based on the discounted value of the cash flows that the investor expects to receive from owning a bond.
2. Given the bond's current market price and promised cash flows, the investor can calculate the bond's promised yield-to-maturity and compare it to an appropriate discount rate.
3. Alternatively, the investor can use an appropriate discount rate to discount the bond's promised cash flows. The sum of the present value of these cash flows is compared to the bond's market price.
4. Six primary attributes are of significance in bond valuation: length of time to maturity, coupon rate, call provisions, tax status, marketability, and likelihood of default.
5. Time to maturity, call provisions, tax status, and likelihood of default tend to be directly related to promised yield-to-maturity. Coupon rate and marketability tend to be inversely related to promised yield-to-maturity.
6. Several organizations provide ratings of the creditworthiness of corporate and municipal bonds. These ratings are often interpreted as an indication of the issuer's likelihood of default.
7. Bond ratings indicate relative levels of risk instead of absolute levels of risk.

---

[28]Mark I. Weinstein, "The Effect of a Rating Change Announcement on Bond Price," *Journal of Financial Economics* 5, no. 3 (December 1977): 329–350. Another study that examined rating change announcements that were "noncontaminated by other news releases found a small but statistically significant upward movement in daily bond prices around upgrades; downgrades produced no significant movements." See John R. M. Hand, Robert W. Holthausen, and Richard W. Leftwich, "The Effect of Bond Rating Agency Announcements on Bond and Stock Prices," *Journal of Finance* 47, no. 2 (June 1992): 733–752.

[29]Gailen Hite and Arthur Warga, "The Effect of Bond-rating Changes on Bond Price Performance." *Financial Analysts Journal* 53, no. 3 (May–June 1997): 35–51. It should be noted that the authors looked at other rating change scenarios in addition to the two mentioned here.

8. A bond's promised yield-to-maturity can be subdivided into a default-free yield-to-maturity and a yield spread. Furthermore, the yield spread can be subdivided into a risk premium and a default premium.

9. Various statistical models have been developed to predict the probability that a bond issuer will default. These models typically use financial ratios derived from the issuer's balance sheet and income statement.

QUESTIONS AND PROBLEMS

1. Philip Wong owns a $1000 face-value bond with three years to maturity. The bond makes annual interest payments of $75, the first to be made one year from today. The bond is currently priced at $975.48. Given an appropriate discount rate of 10%, should Philip hold or sell the bond?

2. A broker has advised Jane Ens to purchase a 10-year $10 000 face-value bond that makes 8% annual coupon payments. The appropriate discount rate is 9%. The first interest payment is due one year from today. If the bond currently sells for $8560, should Jane follow the broker's advice?

3. Pierre Thibeau is considering investing in a bond currently selling for $8785.07. The bond has four years to maturity, a $10 000 face value, and an 8% coupon rate. The next annual interest payment is due one year from today. The appropriate discount rate for investments of similar risk is 10%.
   a. Calculate the intrinsic value of the bond. Based on this calculation, should Pierre purchase the bond?
   b. Calculate the yield-to-maturity of the bond. Based on this calculation, should Pierre purchase the bond?

4. Consider two bonds with $1000 face values that carry coupon rates of 8%, make annual coupon payments, and exhibit similar risk characteristics. However, the first bond has five years to maturity whereas the second has ten years to maturity. The appropriate discount rate for investments of similar risk is 8%. If this discount rate rises by two percentage points, what will be the respective percentage price changes of the two bonds?

5. Why is it convenient to use Government of Canada securities as a starting point for analyzing bond yields?

6. Bond A's yield-to-maturity is 9.80%; bond B's yield-to-maturity is 8.73%. What is the difference in yields stated in basis points?

7. Eli Falk recently purchased a bond with a $1000 face value, a 10% coupon rate, and four years to maturity. The bond makes annual interest payments, the first to be received one year from today. Eli paid $1032.40 for the bond.
   a. What is the bond's yield-to-maturity?
   b. If the bond can be called two years from now at a price of $1100, what is its yield-to-call?

8. Beverly Grimaldi purchased at par a bond with a face value of $1000. The bond had five years to maturity and a 10% coupon rate. The bond was called two years later for a price of $1200, after making its second annual interest payment. Beverly then reinvested the proceeds in a bond selling at its face value of $1000, with three years to maturity and a 7% coupon rate. What was Beverly's actual yield-to-maturity over the five-year period?

9. Nellie Fox acquired at par a bond for $1000 that offered a 9% coupon rate. At the time of purchase, the bond had four years to maturity. Assuming annual interest payments, calculate Nellie's actual yield-to-maturity if she reinvested all the interest payments in an investment earning 14% per year. What would Nellie's actual yield-to-maturity be if she spent all the interest payments upon receipt?

10. Distinguish between yield-to-first-call and yield-to-maturity.
11. What is the effect of a call provision on a bond's potential for price appreciation?
12. What is the purpose of bond ratings? Given the importance attached to bond ratings by bond investors, why don't common stock investors focus on quality ratings of entire companies in making their investment decisions?
13. According to Dave Cross, "Agency ratings indicate *relative* levels of risk instead of *absolute* levels of risk." Explain the meaning of Dave's statement.
14. Based on the default premium model presented in the text, what is the fair value default premium for a bond with an expected yield-to-maturity of 8.5%, a 10% annual default probability, and an expected loss as percent of market value of 60%?
15. Corporate default appears to be an event specific to an individual company. Yet despite the apparently diversifiable nature of corporate default (meaning that relatively few bonds would default in a well-diversified portfolio), the bond market systematically adds default premiums when valuing corporate bonds. Explain why.
16. Junk bonds are often viewed by investors as having financial characteristics much more akin to common stocks than to high-grade corporate bonds. Why?
17. Examine equation (14.6) and explain the rationale underlying the observed relationship (positive or negative) between each of the variables and the yield spread.
18. How would you expect yield spreads to respond to the following macroeconomics events: recession, high inflation, tax cuts, stock market decline, improved trade balance? Explain the reasoning behind each of your answers.
19. Ursula Schmidt has noted that the spread between yield-to-maturity on BBB-rated bonds and that on AAA-rated bonds has recently widened considerably. Explain to Ursula what this change might indicate.

CFA Exam Questions

20. [In 1990,] Barney Gray, CFA, is Director of Fixed-income Securities at Piedmont Security Advisors. In a recent meeting, one of his major endowment clients suggested investing in corporate bonds yielding 9%, rather than US government bonds yielding 8%. Two bond issues—one US Treasury and one corporate—were compared to illustrate the point.

US Treasury bond	8% due 6/15/2010	Priced at 100
AJAX Manufacturing	9.5% due 6/15/2015	Priced at 105
Rated AAA		
Callable @ 107.5 on 6/15/1995		

Gray wants to prepare a response based upon his expectation that long-term US Treasury interest rates will fall sharply (at least 100 basis points) over the next three months. Evaluate the return expectations for each bond, and support your evaluation of which bond would be the superior performer. Discuss the price-yield measures that affected your conclusion.

21. One common goal among fixed-income managers is to earn high incremental returns on corporate bonds versus government bonds of comparable durations. The approach of some corporate bond portfolio managers is to find and purchase those corporate bonds having the largest initial spreads over comparable-duration government bonds. John Ames, HFS's fixed-income manager, believes that a more rigorous approach is required if incremental returns are to be maximized.

Table 14.9 below presents data relating to one set of corporate/government spread relationships presents in the market at a given date:

| | Table 14.9 | Current and Expected Spreads and Durations of High-Grade Corporate Bonds (One-Year Horizon). | | | |

Bond Rating	Initial Spread Over Governments	Expected Horizon Spread	Initial Duration	Expected Duration One Year from Now
AAA	31 b.p.	31 b.p.	4 years	3.1 years
AAA	40 b.p.	50 b.p.	4 years	3.1 years

Recommend purchase of either Aaa or Aa bonds for a one-year investment horizon given a goal of maximizing incremental returns. Show your calculations. (Base your decision only on the information presented in Table 14.9 above.)

Ames chooses not to rely solely on initial spread relationships. His analytical framework considers a full range of other key variables likely to impact realized incremental returns including:

- call provisions
- potential changes in interest rates

Describe two variables in addition to those identified above, that Ames should include in his analysis and explain how each of these two variables could cause realized incremental returns to differ from those indicated by initial spread relationships.

KEY TERMS

capitalization of income method of
  valuation (p. 361)
promised yield-to-maturity (p. 362)
net present value (p. 362)
yield structure (p. 363)
term structure (p. 363)
risk structure (p. 363)
yield spread (p. 363)
basis points (p. 364)
call provisions (p. 364)
call price (p. 364)
call premium (p. 364)

yield-to-call (p. 364)
deep discount bond (p. 366)
marketability (p. 366)
bond ratings (p. 367)
investment-grade bond (p. 367)
speculative-grade bond (p. 367)
junk bond (p. 367)
fallen angel (p. 367)
expected yield-to-maturity (p. 373)
default premium (p. 373)
risk premium (p. 377)

REFERENCES

1. For a detailed discussion of bond valuation and the attributes of bonds that are important in their pricing, see:

   Karlyn Mitchell, "The Call, Sinking Fund, and Term-to-Maturity Features of Corporate Bonds: An Empirical Investigation," *Journal of Financial and Quantitative Analysis* 26, no. 2 (June 1991): 201–222.

   James C. Van Horne, *Financial Market Rates and Flows* (Englewood Cliffs, NJ: Prentice Hall, 1994).

   Frank J. Fabozzi, *Valuation of Fixed-Income Securities* (Summit, NJ: Frank J. Fabozzi Associates, 1994).

   Frank J. Fabozzi, ed., *Advances in Fixed Income Valuation Modeling and Risk Management* (New Hope, PA: Frank J. Fabozzi Associates, 1997).

2. Some of the many studies that have investigated the relationship between historical measures of a firm's performance and its bond ratings are:

Thomas F. Pogue and Robert M. Soldofsky, "What's in a Bond Rating?" *Journal of Financial and Quantitative Analysis* 4, no. 2 (June 1969): 201–228.

R. R. West, "An Alternative Approach to Predicting Corporate Bond Ratings," *Journal of Accounting Research* 8, no. 1 (Spring 1970): 118–125.

George E. Pinches and Kent A. Mingo, "A Multivariate Analysis of Industrial Bond Ratings," *Journal of Finance* 30, no. 1 (March 1975): 201–206.

Robert S. Kaplan and Gabriel Urwitz, "Statistical Models of Bond Ratings: A Methodological Inquiry," *Journal of Business* 52, no. 2 (April 1979): 231–261.

Ahmed Belkaoui, *Industrial Bonds and the Rating Process* (Westport, CT: Quorum Books, 1983).

3. Changes in bond ratings have been studied in:

Steven Katz, "The Price Adjustment Process of Bonds to Rating Reclassification: A Test of Bond Market Efficiency," *Journal of Finance* 29, no. 2 (May 1974): 551–559.

Paul Grier and Steven Katz, "The Differential Effects of Bond Rating Changes Among Industrial and Public Utility Bonds by Maturity," *Journal of Business* 49, no. 2 (April 1976): 226–239.

Mark I. Weinstein, "The Effect of a Rating Change Announcement on Bond Price," *Journal of Financial Economics* 5, no. 3 (December 1977): 329–350.

Douglas J. Lucas and John G. Lonski, "Changes in Corporate Credit Quality 1970–1990," *Journal of Fixed Income* 1, no. 4 (March 1992): 7–14.

Edward I. Altman and Duen Li Kao, "Rating Drift in High-yield Bonds," *Journal of Fixed Income* 1, no. 4 (March 1992): 15–20.

Edward I. Altman, "The Implications of Bond Ratings Drift," *Financial Analysts Journal* 48, no. 3 (May–June 1992): 64–75.

John R. M. Hand, Robert W. Holthausen, and Richard W. Leftwich, "The Effect of Bond Rating Agency Announcements on Bond and Stock Prices," *Journal of Finance* 47, no. 2 (June 1992): 733–752.

Lea V. Carty and Jerome S. Fons, "Measuring Changes in Corporate Credit Quality," *Journal of Fixed Income* 4, no. 1 (June 1994): 27–41.

Richard Cantor and Frank Packer, "The Credit Rating Industry," *Journal of Fixed Income* 5, no. 3 (December 1995): 10–34.

Gailen Hite and Arthur Warga, "The Effect of Bond-rating Changes on Bond Price Performance," *Financial Analysts Journal* 53, no. 3 (May–June 1997): 35–51.

4. Default premiums and risks are discussed in:

W. Braddock Hickman, *Corporate Bond Quality and Investor Experience* (Princeton, NJ: Princeton University Press, 1958).

Harold G. Fraine and Robert H. Mills, "The Effects of Defaults and Credit Deterioration on Yields of Corporate Bonds," *Journal of Finance* 16, no. 3 (September 1961): 423–434.

Thomas R. Atkinson and Elizabeth T. Simpson, *Trends in Corporate Bond Quality* (New York: Columbia University Press, 1967).

Gordon Pye, "Gauging the Default Premium," *Financial Analysis Journal* 30, no. 1 (January–February 1974): 49–52.

Ricardo J. Rodriguez, "Default Risk, Yield Spreads, and Time to Maturity," *Journal of Financial and Quantitative Analysis* 23, no. 1 (March 1988): 111–117.

Edward I. Altman, "Measuring Corporate Bond Mortality and Performance," *Journal of Finance* 44, no. 4 (September 1989): 909–922.

Jerome S. Fons and Andrew E. Kimball, "Corporate Bond Defaults and Default Rates 1970–1990," *Journal of Fixed Income* 1, no. 1 (June 1991): 36–47.

Edward I. Altman, "Defaults and Returns on High-yield Bonds Through the First Half of 1991," *Financial Analysts Journal* 47, no. 6 (November–December 1991): 67–77.

Edward I. Altman, "Revisiting the High-yield Bond Market," *Financial Management* 21, no. 2 (Summer 1992): 79–92.

Paul Asquith, David W. Mullins, Jr., and Eric D. Wolff, "Original Issue High Yield Bonds: Aging Analysis of Defaults, Exchanges, and Calls," *Journal of Finance* 44, no. 4 (September 1989): 923–952.

Marshall E. Blume and Donald B. Keim, "Realized Returns and Defaults on Low-Grade Bonds: The Cohort of 1977 and 1978," *Financial Analysts Journal* 47, no. 2 (March–April 1991): 63–72.

Marshall E. Blume, Donald B.Keim, and Sandeep A. patel, "Returns and Volatility of Low-Grade Bonds, 1977–1989," *Journal of Finance* 46, no. 1 (March 1991): 49–74.

Bradford, Cornell, "Liquidity and the Pricing of Low-Grade Bonds," *Financial Analysts Journal* 48, no. 1 (January–February 1992): 63–67, 74.

Martin S. Fridson, "Frame's Neglected Findings: Was Hickman Wrong?" *Financial Analysts Journal* 50, no. 5 (September–October 1994): 43–53.

5. The classic study on yield spreads is:

Lawrence Fisher, "Determinants of Risk Premiums on Corporate Bonds," *Journal of Political Economy* 67, no. 3 (June 1959): 217–237.

6. Yield spreads are also discussed in:

George Foster, *Financial Statement Analysis* (Englewood Cliffs, NJ: Prentice Hall, 1986), pp. 510–511.

Martin S. Fridson and Jeffrey A. Bersh, "Spread Versus Treasuries as a Market-timing Tool for High-yield Investors," *Journal of Fixed Income* 4, no. 1 (June 1994): 63–69.

Martin S. Fridson and Jon G. Jonsson, Spread Versus Treasuries and the Riskiness of High-yield Bonds," *Journal of Fixed Income* 5, no. 3 (December 1995): 79–88.

7. Predicting bankruptcy has been a subject of much research; see the following papers and their citations:

William H. Beaver, "Financial Ratios as Predictors of Failure," *Empirical Research in Accounting: Selected Studies, 1966*, supplement to *Journal of Accounting Research*: 71–111.

William H. Beaver, "Market Prices, Financial Ratios and the Prediction of Failure," *Journal of Accounting Research* 6, no. 2 (Autumn 1968): 179–192.

Edward I. Altman, "Financial Ratios, Discriminant Analysis and the Prediction of Corporate Bankruptcy," *Journal of Finance* 23, no. 4 (September 1968): 589–609.

Edward B. Deakin, "A Discriminant Analysis of Predictors of Business Failure," *Journal of Accounting Research* 10, no. 1 (Spring 1972): 167–179.

R. Charles Moyer, "Forecasting Financial Failure: A Re-examination," *Financial Management* 6, no. 1 (Spring 1977): 11–17.

Edward I. Altman, Robert G. Haldeman, and P. Narayanan, "Zeta Analysis: A New Model to Identify Bankruptcy Risk of Corporations," *Journal of Banking and Finance* 1, no. 1 (June 1977): 29–54.

James A. Ohlson, "Financial Ratios and the Probabilistic Prediction of Bankruptcy," *Journal of Accounting Research* 18, no. 1 (Spring 1980): 109–131.

Joseph Aharony, Charles P. Jones, and Itzhak Swary, "An Analysis of Risk and Return Characteristics of Corporate Bankruptcy Using Capital Market Data," *Journal of Finance* 35, no. 4 (September 1980): 1001–1016.

Edward I. Altman, "The Success of Business Failure Prediction Models: An International Survey," *Journal of Banking and Finance* 8, no. 2 (June 1984): 171–198.

Cornelius Casey and Norman Bartczak, "Using Operating Cash Flow Data to Predict Financial Distress: Some Extensions," *Journal of Accounting Research* 23, no. 1 (Spring 1985): 384–401.

James A. Gentry, Paul Newbold, and David T. Whitford, "Classifying Bankrupt Firms with Funds Flow Components," *Journal of Accounting Research* 23, no. 1 (Spring 1985): 146–160.

James A. Gentry, Paul Newbold, and David T. Whitford, "Predicting Bankruptcy: If Cash Flow's Not the Bottom Line, What Is?" *Financial Analysts Journal* 41, no. 5 (September–October 1985): 47–56.

Maggie Queen and Richard Roll, "Firm Morality: Using Market Indicators to Predict Survival," *Financial Analysts Journal* 43, no. 3 (May–June 1987): 9–26.

Ismael G. Dambolena and Joel M. Shulman, "A Primary Rule for Detecting Bankruptcy: Watch the Cash," *Financial Analysts Journal* 44, no. 5 (September–October 1988): 74–78.

James M. Gahlon and Robert L. Vigeland, "Early Warning Signs of Bankruptcy Using Cash Flow Analysis," *Journal of Commercial Bank Lending* 71, no. 4 (December 1988): 4–15.

Abdul Aziz and Gerald H. Lawson, "Cash Flow Reporting and Financial Distress Models: Testing of Hypothesis," *Financial Management* 18, no. 1 (Spring 1989): 55–63.

Douglas J. Lucas, "Default Correlation and Credit Analysis," *Journal of Fixed Income* 4, no. 4 (March 1995): 76–87.

Jean Helwege and Paul Kleinman, "Understanding Aggregate Default Rates of High-yield Bonds," *Journal of Fixed Income* 7, no. 1 (June 1997): 55–61.

Martin S. Fridson, M. Christopher Garman, and Sheng Wu, "Real Interest Rates and the Default Rate on High-yield Bonds," *Journal of Fixed Income* 7, no. 2 (September 1997): 29–34.

8. For a Canadian perspective on the topics covered in this chapter, see:

A. Thibeault and L. Wynant, "Investor Reaction to the Political Environment in Quebec," *Canadian Public Policy* (Spring 1979).

Edward I. Altman and Mario Y. Lavallee, "Business Failure Classification in Canada," *Journal of Business Administration* 12, no. 1 (Fall 1980): 147–164.

Halim Bishara, "Determinants of Canadian Corporate Bond Ratings: A Multivariate Analysis," *Proceedings*, Administrative Sciences Association of Canada Conference, Halifax, June 1988.

T. Barnes and T. Byng, "The Prediction of Corporate Bond Ratings: The Canadian Case," *Canadian Journal of Administrative Sciences* 5, no. 3 (September 1988).

M. Brennan, J. Detemple et A. Kalay, "Une Nouvelle Optique D'Evaluation de la Dette Contractuelle," *Finéco* 2, no. 2 (2e *Semestre 1992*).

R. N. Kahn and D. Gulrajani, "Risk and Return in the Canadian Bond Market," *Journal of Portfolio Management* 19, no. 3 (Spring 1993).

D. Gulrajani and B. Chui, "Measuring Risk in the Canadian Bond Market," *Canadian Investment Review* VI, no. 3 (Fall 1993).

R. Deaves, "Forecasting Canadian Short-Term Interest Rates," *Canadian Journal of Economics* 29, no. 3 (August 1996).

V. Miller, "Inflation Uncertainty and Optimal Debt Maturity: An Empirical Look at Canadian and U.S. Government Bonds," *Canadian Journal of Administrative Sciences* 14, no. 3 (September 1997).

CHAPTER 15

Bond Portfolio Management

The methods currently in use for managing bond portfolios can be divided into two general categories—passive and active. Methods in the passive category rest on the basic assumption that bond markets are semistrong-form efficient. That is, current bond prices are viewed as accurately reflecting all publicly available information. Thus, bonds are felt to be priced fairly in the marketplace, providing a return that is commensurate with the risk involved. In addition to believing that individual bonds are not mispriced, passive investors also believe that attempting to predict interest rates is, in general, futile. In summary, passive management rests on the belief that attempts at both security selection (that is, identifying mispriced bonds) and market timing (for example, buying long-term bonds when interest rates are predicted to fall and replacing them with short-term bonds when interest rates are predicted to rise) will be unsuccessful in providing the investor with above-average returns.

Active methods of bond portfolio management are based on the assumption that the bond market is not so efficient, thereby giving some investors the opportunity to earn above-average returns. Active management is based on the ability of the portfolio manager either to identify mispriced bonds or to "time" the bond market by accurately predicting interest rates.

This chapter discusses these two general approaches to bond portfolio management. It begins by reviewing some of the findings regarding the efficiency of the bond market.

Bond Market Efficiency

In assessing the efficiency of the bond market, a sample of the major US studies and the few Canadian studies available are mentioned. The impression obtained from reading them is that US bond markets appear to be highly, but not perfectly, semistrong-form efficient. That is, bond prices tend to reflect almost all publicly available information. Not surprisingly, this impression is similar to the one obtained from studies of the efficiency of stock markets.

Canadian markets are less active. Therefore, some inefficiencies that may not be economically significant appear to exist. These are discussed below.

● Price Behaviour of Treasury Bills

An early study of bond market efficiency focused on the price behaviour of Treasury bills. In particular, the prices of Treasury bills were analyzed on a weekly basis from October

1946 through December 1964, a total of 796 weeks. The study found that knowledge of how Treasury bill prices changed in the past was of little use in trying to predict how they would change in the future. Consequently, the results from this study are consistent with the notion that the market for Treasury bills is weak-form efficient.[1]

Experts' Predictions of Interest Rates

Bond market efficiency has also been studied by examining the accuracy of interest rate predictions made by experts. These people use a wide range of techniques and a number of different sources of information. Since it is reasonable to assume their information is publicly available, such studies can be viewed as tests of semistrong-form efficiency.

One way these tests have been conducted involves the building of statistical models that are based on what the experts have said about how interest rates should be predicted. Once these models have been constructed, their predictive accuracy can be evaluated. In one study, six different models were constructed and then their one-month-ahead predictions were tested over the two-year period of 1973 through 1974. Consistent with the notion of efficient markets, it was found that a simple model of "no change" was more accurate in predicting interest rates than any of the six statistical models.[2]

Another way these tests have been conducted involves comparing a set of explicit predictions with what subsequently actually occurred. One source of such predictions is the quarterly survey of interest rate expectations that appears in the *Goldsmith-Nagan Bond and Money Market Newsletter*, published by Goldsmith-Nagan, Inc. Specifically, this survey reports the predictions made by a number (roughly 50) of "money market professionals" regarding three-month ahead and six-month ahead levels of 10 different interest rates. In one study, the predictions made from September 1969 through December 1972 (that is, 14 sets of quarterly predictions) were compared with those of a "no-change" model—that is, a model that forecasts no change from the current level of interest rates.[3] Interestingly, the professionals seemed to forecast better than the no-change model for short-term interest rates (such as forecasting what the three-month Treasury bill rate will be three months in the future) but did worse than the no-change model for longer-term interest rates (such as forecasting what the intermediate-term Treasury note rate will be three months in the future).

A subsequent study examined the Goldsmith-Nagan predictions of three-month Treasury bill rates six months in the future during the time period from March 1970 through September 1979 (39 predictions).[4] These predictions were compared with those of

---

[1]For details, see Richard Roll, *The Behavior of Interest Rates* (New York: Basic Books, 1970). Interestingly, this study also produced evidence rejecting the unbiased expectations theory of the term structure of interest rates (see Chapter 5). Also of interest is that U.S. Treasury bonds appear to have been mispriced in May and June of 1986. See Bradford Cornell and Alan C. Shapiro. "The Mispricing of U.S. Treasury Bonds: A Case Study," *Review of Financial Studies* 2 no. 3 (1989): 297–310.

[2]J. Walter Elliott and Jerome R. Baier, "Econometric Models and Current Interest Rates: How Well Do They Predict Future Rates?" *Journal of Finance* 34, no. 4 (September 1979): 975–986. It should be noted that the models used by major economic forecasting firms tend to have similar amounts of accuracy. See Stephen K. McNees, "Forecasting Accuracy of Alternative Techniques: A Comparison of US Macroeconomic Forecasts," *Journal of Business & Economic Statistics* 4, no. 1 (January 1986): 5–15, particularly Table 6 where 90-day Treasury bill rate forecasts are evaluated; and Dean Croushore, "Introducing The Survey of Professional Forecasters," Federal Reserve Bank of Philadelphia *Business Review* (November–December 1993): 3–15.

[3]Michael J. Prell, "How Well Do the Experts Forecast Interest Rates?" Federal Reserve Bank of Kansas City *Monthly Review* (September–October 1973): 3–13.

[4]Adrian W. Throop, "Interest Rate Forecasts and Market Efficiency," Federal Reserve Bank of San Francisco *Economic Review* (Spring 1981): 29–43. This article contains a useful reference list of other studies concerning the prediction of interest rates.

three "simple" models, the first one being the no-change model. The second simple model was based on the liquidity preference theory of the term structure of interest rates (discussed in Chapter 5). According to this theory, the forward rate implicit in current market rates should be equal to the expected future interest rate plus a liquidity premium. Thus, the expected future interest rate can be forecast by subtracting an estimate of the liquidity premium from the forward rate. The third simple model was what statisticians refer to as an autoregressive model. Basically, a forecast of the future Treasury bill rate was formed from the current Treasury bill rate as well as what the Treasury bill rate was one, two, three, and six quarters ago. The study found that the professionals were more accurate than both the no-change model and the liquidity premium model but were less accurate than the autoregressive model.

Another study evaluated the six-month-ahead predictions of three-month Treasury bill rates that were made by nine economists and reported semiannually in *The Wall Street Journal*. Evaluating the forecasts published from December 1981 through June 1986, it was found that the no-change model was more accurate.[5] An update of this study looked at six-month-ahead predictions of three-month Treasury bill and 30-year Treasury bond yields made by economists from 1982 through 1996 in surveys conducted by *The Wall Street Journal*. Yields moved in the opposite direction of the economists' consensus prediction 53% of the time for the Treasury bill forecasts and 67% of the time for the Treasury bond forecasts. Furthermore, a no-change model produced smaller forecast errors. Lastly, no evidence was uncovered that the best forecasters in one period were able to demonstrate superior forecasting ability in the next period.[6]

An extensive Canadian study was triggered by the observation that October 1979 ushered in a regime of high and volatile interest rates that lasted several years. The hypothesis that forecasters might perform better in such an environment was tested. The study went on to compare the performance of the simple no-change model with consensus forecasts of short- and long-term interest rates provided by three institutions (McLeod, Young, Weir and Company [now ScotiaMcLeod Inc.]; The Conference Board of Canada; and Data Resources Incorporated of Canada) over the second quarter of 1975 to the third quarter of 1979 and the fourth quarter of 1979 to the fourth quarter of 1984.[7] These institutions report interest rate forecasts for each of the following two quarters as part of their regular quarterly macroeconomic forecasts. The McLeod, Young, Weir forecasts perform as well or slightly better than the simple model in both time periods, but both the Conference Board and Data Resources forecasts deteriorate noticeably in the second period. A significant observation is the deterioration of the accuracy of all short-term interest rate forecasts (including the simple model) in the second period.

It appears from this evidence that the no-change model sometimes provides the most accurate forecasts of future interest rates, while occasionally the experts are more accurate. On balance, a reasonable interpretation of these results is that the bond market is nearly semistrong-form efficient. While the bond market may not be perfectly efficient, the evi-

Wall Street Journal
www.wsj.com

Conference Board of Canada
www.conferenceboard.ca

---

[5]Forecasts implicit in the futures market (discussed in Chapter 20) for Treasury bills were also found to be more accurate than those of the economists but less accurate than those of the no-change model over this time period. For a longer time period, the futures market and no-change model forecasts were of comparable accuracy. See Michael T. Belognia, "Predicting Interest Rates: A Comparison of Professional and Market-Based Forecasts," *Federal Reserve Bank of St. Louis Review* 69, no. 3 (March 1987): 9–15.

[6]See Kevin Stephenson,"Just How Bad are Economists at Predicting Interest Rates? (And What Are the Implications for Investors?" *Journal of Investing* 6, no. 2 (Summer 1997): 8–10.

[7]James E. Pesando and Andre Plourde, "The October 1979 Change in the US Monetary Regime: Its Impact on the Forecastability of Canadian Interest Rates," *Journal of Finance* 43, no.1 (March 1988): 217–239.

dence clearly suggests that it is hard to consistently forecast interest rates with greater accuracy than a no-change model.[8]

Price Reaction to Bond Rating Changes

A different type of test of market efficiency concerned the reaction of bond prices to rating changes. If ratings are based on public information, then any rating change would follow the release of such information. This suggests that in a semistrong-form efficient market, a bond's price would react to the release of the public information rather than the subsequent announcement of the rating change. Thus, an announcement of a rating change should not trigger a subsequent adjustment in the associated bond's price.

In a study that examined 100 rating changes that took place during the period of 1962 through 1974, no significant changes in bond prices were detected in the period from six months before through six months after the announcement of the change. However, a significant change was observed in the period from 18 months through 7 months before the announcement. Specifically, rating increases were preceded by price increases, and rating decreases were preceded by price decreases.[9]

In a second study that looked at downgrades to a non-investment grade rating during 1985–1995, it was found that there was a large abnormal downward price movement in the bond over the six-month period before the downgrade. Furthermore, there was a smaller but still significant abnormal downward price movement during the month of the downgrade.[10] However, it is unknown if this downward price movement occurred during the days before or after the day of the downgrade.

No comparable Canadian study is available, but the similarity between the bond rating processes in the two countries suggests that Canadian investors are also likely to anticipate bond rating changes.

---

[8]The reported accuracy of macroeconomic forecasters in regard to Treasury bill rates (see the Early Quarter results for a two-quarter horizon in Table 6 of McNees, "Forecast Accuracy") can be compared to the reported accuracy of the no-change model (see Table 1 of Belognia, "Predicting Interest Rates"). While such a comparison should be done with caution, it does suggest that the no-change model is of similar, and in some cases, superior, accuracy. There is also indirect evidence of the superiority of the no-change model in that bond portfolio managers apparently have not been able to generate returns exceeding those of bond market indices. See Christopher R. Blake, Edwin J. Elton, and Martin J. Gruber, "The Performance of Bond Mutual Funds," *Journal of Business* 66, no. 3 (July 1993): 371–403. It also appears that the record of the experts in predicting the level of the stock market is of little value. See Werner F. De Bondt, "What Do Economists Know About the Stock Market?" *Journal of Portfolio Management* 17, no. 2 (Winter 1991): 84–91.

[9]See Mark I. Weinstein, "The Effect of a Rating Change Announcement on Bond Price," *Journal of Financial Economics* 5, no. 3 (December 1977): 329–350. A study of the prices of the common stocks associated with bonds that had rating changes reported similar results—share prices tended to change several months prior to the announcement dates of the rating changes. See George E. Pinches and J. Clay Singleton, "The Adjustment of Stock Prices to Bond Rating Changes," *Journal of Finance* 33, no. 1 (March 1978): 29–44. Another study that examined rating change announcements that were "noncontaminated" by other news releases found a small but statistically significant upward movement in daily bond prices around upgrades; downgrades produced no significant movements. Oddly, these findings were reversed when stock prices were examined in that no significant movements were found around upgrades but marginally significant downward movements were observed around downgrades. See John R. M. Hand, Robert W. Holthausen, and Richard W. Leftwich, "The Effect of Bond Rating Agency Announcements on Bond and Stock Prices," *Journal of Finance* 47, no. 2 (June 1992): 733–752. Further analysis revealed that one type of downgrade—namely, "downgrades associated with deteriorating financial prospects"—resulted in a significant downward movement in the price of the associated firm's stock. See Jeremy C. Goh and Louis H. Ederington, "Is a Bond Downgrade Bad News, Good News, or No News for Stockholders?" *Journal of Finance* 48, no. 5 (December 1993): 2001–2008.

[10]Gailen Hite and Arthur Warga, "The Effect of Bond-Rating Changes on Bond Price Performance," *Financial Analysts Journal* 53, no. 3 (May–June 1997): 35–51. It should be noted that the authors looked at other rating change scenarios in addition to the downgrades mentioned here.

Money Supply Announcements

Every week, generally on Thursday, the Federal Reserve Board announces the current size of the money supply in the US economy. Now, it is known that interest rates are related to, among other things, the availability of credit and that the money supply affects this availability. This means that if the money supply figures are surprisingly high or low, then the announcement should trigger adjustments in the levels of various interest rates.[11] Furthermore, such adjustments should take place rapidly in a semistrong-form efficient market. Past studies indicate that such adjustments are indeed rapid, generally taking place within a day after the announcement.[12]

In October 1979, the US Federal Reserve set monetary growth as one of its principal macroeconomic targets and started controlling the money supply. Given the inter-relationship of the US and Canadian economies, changes in the US money supply should also affect Canadian interest rates. A study by Bailey reports that, since that date, Canadian short-term interest rates and bond prices (as well as share prices) respond to unanticipated changes in the level of the US money supply.[13] This result is consistent with semistrong-form efficiency.

Performance of Bond Portfolio Managers

Perhaps the best test of bond market efficiency is to examine the performance record of those professionals who manage bond portfolios. After all, if the people who make their living by investing other people's money in fixed-income securities cannot, on average, generate abnormal returns for their clients, then it would be difficult to argue that these markets are not highly efficient. One study that carefully examined the performance of 41 bond funds from 1979–1988 found that depending on the model of performance used, between 27 (66%) and 33 (80%) of the funds had negative abnormal returns. Furthermore, the underperformance ranged from –.023% to –.069% per month (or –.3% to –.8% per year).

In spite of the evidence that the average fund was not able to generate positive abnormal returns, it is still possible that some of the managers were consistently able to do so. One way of testing whether this is true is to examine whether the top performing funds in one time period continued being top performers in the next period. More specifically, the managers were ranked based on their funds performance during the five-year period of 1979–1983 and then ranked again based on their performance during the next five-year period of 1984–1988. If the top managers have a special talent for "betting the market," then these two sets of rankings should be highly correlated. However, depending on the model used to generate the rankings, the correlations ranged from .234 to –.111; none were statistically significantly different from zero.

To slightly cloud the issue of bond market efficiency, 223 bond funds were analyzed over the period of 1987–2991. The average fund had negative abnormal returns of between

---

[11]For an explanation of this adjustment process, see Richard G. Sheehan, "Weekly Money Announcements: New Information and Its Effects," Federal Reserve Bank of St. Louis *Review* 67, no. 7 (August–September 1985): 25–34; and Anthony M. Santomero, "Money Supply Announcements: A Retrospective," *Journal of Economics and Business* 43, no. 1 (February 1991): 1–23.

[12]See, for example, Thomas Urich and Paul Wachtel, "Market Response to Weekly Money Supply Announcements in the 1970s," *Journal of Finance* 36, no. 5 (December 1981): 1063–1072; "The Effects of Inflation and Money Supply Announcements on Interest Rates," *Journal of Finance* 39, no. 4 (September 1984): 1177–1188; Bradford Cornell, "Money Supply Announcements and Interest Rates: Another View," *Journal of Business* 56, no. 1 (January 1983): 1–23.

[13]W. Bailey, "The Effect of US Money Supply Announcements on Canadian Stock, Bond, and Currency Prices," *Canadian Journal of Economics* 22, no. 3 (August 1989): 607–618.

−.077% to −.107% per month (or −.9% to −1.3% per year). However, relative performance was observed to persist as the performance rankings from the first three-year period had a significantly positive correlation ranging from .212 to .451 with the rankings for the following two years.[14]

A Direct Test of Bond Market Efficiency

A direct test of the efficiency of both the US and Canadian bond markets was carried out by Appelt and Schulman.[15] They calculated zero-coupon yield curves for both markets on the same days using the prices of available coupon bonds. Figure 15.1(a) shows the US term structure for March 31, 1988, and Figure 15.1(b) shows the Canadian term structure on the same day. Using these data they calculated "revealed spot rates" by following a simple arbitrage procedure that can be applied when there is more than one bond issue with the same maturity but different coupon rates. For example, consider the following two bonds:

	Coupon	Maturity	Price	Principal
Bond 1:	10.5 %	95.02.15	$110.78	$100.00
Bond 2:	11.25	95.02.15	114.63	100.00

Shorting bond 1 and buying bond 2 in the correct proportions results in an arbitrage portfolio with a zero net coupon income. This can be achieved by selling $1125 of face value of bond 1 and buying $1050 of face value of bond 2 with the following result:

	Coupon Stream	Current Investment	Receipt at Maturity
Bond 1:	$−118.125	$−1246.48	$−1125.00
Bond 2:	118.125	1203.62	1050.00
Net	0.000	42.66	−75.00

The net result is the same as borrowing $42.66 on March 31, 1988, and repaying $75.00 on February 15, 1995. The implied interest rate is 8.37% (neglecting transaction costs)—about 21 basis points lower than the risk-free spot rate for a 6.88 year bond. By examining all possible combinations in both markets, the revealed spot rates across the maturity spectrum could be calculated. Figures 15.2(a) and (b) show these revealed rates for US Treasury securities and Canadas respectively. Figure 15.2(a) shows that there are some arbitrage opportunities to be exploited in the US market, especially at the longer end of the maturity spectrum, but these are relatively small. Figure 15.2(b) shows that there are substantially larger arbitrage opportunities in the Canadian market. Two factors may explain the differences: first, transactions costs in Canada are higher than those in the US and second, the returns on low-coupon bonds receive more favourable tax treatment in Canada than in the US. The authors argue that the transaction costs in Canada would have to be two to three times the levels observed in the US to explain the differences and that taxation alone cannot explain the degree of mispricing of low-coupon bonds. They conclude that there are arbitrage opportunities in both markets but more so in Canada. For

[14]See Christopher R. Blake, Edwin J. Elton, and Martin J. Gruber, "The Performance of Bond Mutual Funds," *Journal of Business* 66, no. 3 (July 1993): 371–403.

[15]T. Appelt and E. Schulman, "The Government of Canada Bond Market: Is it Efficiently Priced?" *Canadian Investment Review* I, no.1 (Fall 1988): 63–70.

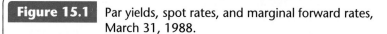

Figure 15.1 Par yields, spot rates, and marginal forward rates, March 31, 1988.

(a) US Treasuries

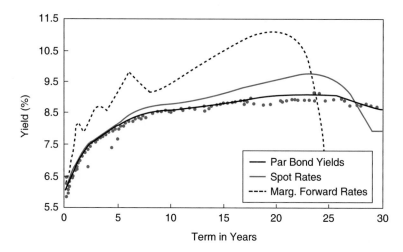

(b) Canadas

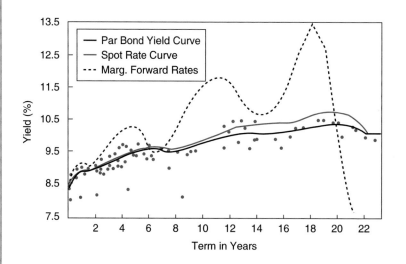

SOURCE: T. Appelt and E. Schulman, "The Government of Canada Bond Market: Is It Efficiently Priced?" *Canadian Investment Review* I, no. I (Fall 1988): 63–72.

these to be exploitable, however, it must be possible to borrow the securities (with margin requirements that are not onerous) that should be sold short.

◗ Summary

In summary, the evidence on the efficiency of the bond market is consistent with the notion that it is highly, but not perfectly, semistrong-form efficient.[16] Statistical tests of past

---

[16]Like the stock market, the bond market has some anomalies. However, they are fewer in number and less pronounced. These anomalies are briefly discussed in the Appendix.

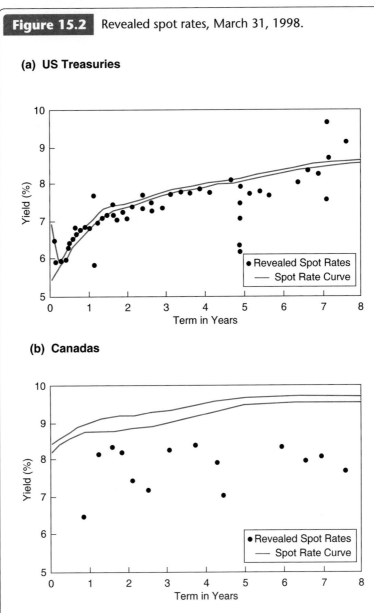

Figure 15.2 Revealed spot rates, March 31, 1998.

(a) US Treasuries

Yield (%) / Term in Years

- Revealed Spot Rates
- Spot Rate Curve

(b) Canadas

Yield (%) / Term in Years

- Revealed Spot Rates
- Spot Rate Curve

SOURCE: T. Appelt and E. Schulman, "The Government of Canada Bond Market: Is It Efficiently Priced?" *Canadian Investment Review* I, no. I (Fall 1988): 63–72.

prices of Treasury bills suggest it is efficient. It appears that corporate bonds reflect the information leading to a rating change in a timely fashion and that interest rates change rapidly when there is a surprise in the announced size of the money supply, observations that are also consistent with the notion of efficiency.

There is some evidence, however, suggesting that certain professionals are occasionally able to make accurate interest rate forecasts. It also appears that there are some limited arbitrage opportunities available. With this in mind, it is not surprising that some bond managers have opted to follow a passive approach to investing, while others have decided to be more active. These two approaches are presented next, beginning with a discussion of some bond pricing theorems. In turn, these theorems will be related to a concept known as duration, which is the basis for one method of passively managing a bond portfolio.

Bond-Pricing Theorems

Bond-pricing theorems deal with how bond prices move in response to changes in their yields-to-maturity. Before presenting the theorems, a brief review of some terms associated with bonds will be useful.

The typical bond is characterized by a promise to pay the investor two types of cash flows. The first involves the payment of a fixed dollar amount periodically (usually every six months), with the last payment being on a stated date. The second type of cash flow involves the payment of a lump sum on this stated date. The periodic payments are known as **coupon payments**, and the lump sum payment is known as the bond's principal (or par value or face value). A bond's **coupon rate** is calculated by dividing the dollar amount of the coupon payments a bondholder would receive over the course of a year by the principal of the bond. Lastly, the amount of time left until the last promised payment is made is known as the bond's **term-to-maturity**, whereas the discount rate that makes the present value of all the cash flows equal to the market price of the bond is known as the bond's **yield-to-maturity** (or, simply, yield).

Note that if a bond has a market price that is equal to its par value, then its yield-to-maturity will be equal to its coupon rate. However, if the market price is less than par value (a situation where the bond is said to be selling at a discount), then the bond will have a yield-to-maturity that is greater than the coupon rate. Conversely, if the market price is greater than par value (a situation where the bond is said to be selling at a premium), then the bond will have a yield-to-maturity that is less than the coupon rate. Summarizing:

Discount:	Market price < Par value	Yield-to-maturity > Coupon rate
Par:	Market price = Par value	Yield-to-maturity = Coupon rate
Premium:	Market price > Par value	Yield-to-maturity < Coupon rate

With this in mind, five theorems that deal with bond pricing have been derived.[17] For ease of exposition, it is assumed that there is one coupon payment per year (that is, coupon payments are made every 12 months). The theorems are as follows:

1. *If a bond's market price increases, then its yield must decrease; conversely, if a bond's market price decreases, then its yield must increase.*

As an example, consider bond A that has a life of five years and a par value of $1000 and pays coupons annually of $80. Its yield is 8%, since it is currently selling for $1000. However, if its price increases to $1100, then its yield will fall to 5.76%. Conversely, if its price falls to $900, then its yield will rise to 10.68%.

2. *If a bond's yield does not change over its life, then the size of its discount or premium will decrease as its life gets shorter.*

This can be seen by examining Figure 15.3. Note how the price of a bond that is selling at either a premium or a discount today will converge over time to its par value. Ultimately the premium or discount will completely disappear at the maturity date.

As an example, consider bond B that has a life of five years and a par value of $1000 and pays coupons annually of $60. Its current market price is $883.31, indicating it has a yield of 9%. After one year, if it still has a yield of 9%, it will be selling for $902.81. Thus,

[17]Burton G. Malkiel, "Expectations, Bond Prices, and the Term Structure of Interest Rates," *Quarterly Journal of Economics* 76, no. 2 (May 1962): 197–218.

Sidebar definitions:

Coupon Payments The periodic payment of interest on a bond.

Coupon Rate The annual dollar amount of coupon payments made by a bond expressed as a percentage of the bond's par value.

Term-to-maturity The time remaining until a bond's maturity date.

Yield-to-maturity For a particular fixed-income security, the single interest rate (with interest compounded at some specified interval) that, if paid by a bank on the amount invested in the security, would enable the investor to obtain all the payments made by that security. Equivalently, the discount rate that equates the present value of future cash flows from the security to the current market price of the security.

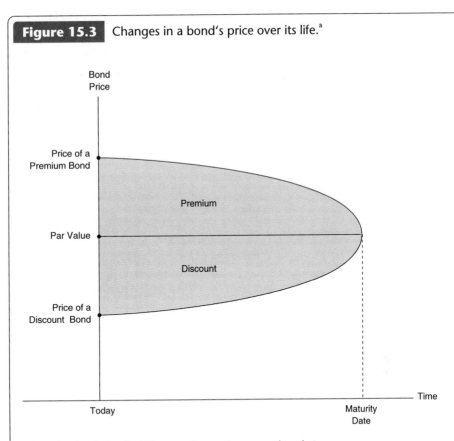

Figure 15.3 Changes in a bond's price over its life.[a]

Bond Price

Price of a Premium Bond

Premium

Par Value

Discount

Price of a Discount Bond

Today

Maturity Date

Time

[a]Assuming that the bond's yield-to-maturity remains constant through time.

its discount has decreased from $1000 − $883.31 = $116.69 to $1000 − $902.81 = $97.19, for a change of $116.69 − $97.19 = $19.50.

An equivalent interpretation of this theorem is that if two bonds have the same coupon rate, par value, and yield, then the one with the shorter life will sell for a smaller discount or premium. Consider two bonds, one with a life of five years and the other with a life of four years. Both bonds have a par value of $1000, pay annual coupons of $60, and yield 9%. In this situation, the one with a five-year life has a discount of $116.69, whereas the one with a four-year life has a smaller discount of $97.19.

3. *If a bond's yield does not change over its life, then the size of its discount or premium will decrease at an increasing rate as it approaches maturity.*

Figure 15.3 can also be used to illustrate this theorem. Note that, at first, the premium or discount does not change much with time. In contrast, however, the size changes much more rapidly with time as the maturity date approaches.

As an example, consider bond B again. After two years, if it still has a yield of 9%, it will be selling for $924.06. Thus, its discount has decreased to $1000 − $924.06 = $75.94. Now, the amount of the change in the discount from five years to four years was $116.69 − $97.19 = $19.50, for a percentage change from par of 1.95%. However, the amount of the change from four years to three years is larger, going from $97.19 to $75.94, for a dollar change of $21.25 and a percentage change from par of 2.125%.

4. *A decrease in a bond's yield will raise the bond's price by an amount that is greater in size than the corresponding fall in the bond's price that would occur if there were an equal-sized increase in the bond's yield.*

As an example, consider bond C that has a life of five years and a coupon rate of 7%. Since it is currently selling at its par value of $1000, its yield is 7%. If its yield rises by 1% to 8%, then it will be selling for $960.07, a change of $39.93. Alternatively, if its yield falls by 1% to 6%, then it will be selling for $1042.12, a change of $42.12, which is of greater magnitude than the $39.93 associated with the 1% rise in the bond's yield.

5. *The percentage change in a bond's price due to a change in its yield will be smaller if its coupon rate is higher.* (*Note:* This theorem does not apply to bonds with a life of one year or to bonds that have no maturity date, known as consols, or perpetuities.)

As an example, compare bond D with bond C. Bond D has a coupon rate of 9%, which is 2% larger than C's. However, bond D has the same life (five years) and yield (7%) as C. Thus, D's current market price is $1082.00. If the yield on both C and D increases to 8%, then their prices will be $960.07 and $1039.93, respectively.

This represents a decrease in the price of C equal to $1000 − $960.07 = $39.93, or 3.993% (*note:* $39.93/$1000 = 3.993%). For D, the decrease in price is equal to $1082 − $1039.93 = $42.07, or 3.889% (*note:* $42.07/$1082 = 3.889%). Since D has the higher coupon rate, it has the smaller percentage change in price.

It is important for a bond analyst to understand these properties of bond prices thoroughly because they are valuable in forecasting how bond prices will respond to changes in interest rates.

Convexity

Convexity The tendency for bond prices to change asymmetrically relative to yield changes. Typically, for a given yield change, a bond will rise in price more if the yield change is negative than it will fall in price if the yield change is positive.

The first and fourth bond pricing theorems have led to the concept in bond valuation known as **convexity**. Consider what happens to the price of a bond if its yield increases or decreases. According to Theorem 1, bond prices and yields are inversely related. However, this relationship is not linear, according to Theorem 4: the size of the rise in a bond's price associated with a given decrease in its yield is greater than the drop in the bond's price for a similar-sized increase in the bond's yield.

This can be seen by examining Figure 15.4. The current yield-to-maturity and the price for the bond are denoted by y and P, respectively. Consider what would happen to the bond's price if the yield increased or decreased by a fixed amount (for example, 1%), denoted y^+ and y^-. The associated bond prices are denoted by P^- and P^+, respectively.

Two observations can be made about this figure. First, an increase in the yield to y^+ is associated with a drop in the bond's price to P^-, and a decrease in the yield to y^- is associated with a rise in the bond's price to P^+. This is in accord with the first bond theorem. (Hence, the symbols + and − are paired inversely so that, for example, y^+ is associated with P^-.) Second, note that the size of the rise in the bond's price ($P^+ - P$) is greater than the size of the drop in the bond's price ($P - P^-$). This is in accord with the fourth bond theorem.

The curved line in the figure that shows the relationship between bond prices and yields is convex because it opens upward. Accordingly, the relationship is frequently referred to as convexity. Although this relationship is true for standard types of bonds, it should be mentioned that the degree of curvature (or convexity) is not the same for all bonds. Instead, it depends on (among other things) the size of the coupon payments, the life of the bond, and its current market price. Furthermore, if the bond has a call provision, then the convexity will disappear at sufficiently low yields. This is because a drop in the yield may trigger a call, thereby limiting the rise in the bond's price to the call price and no further.

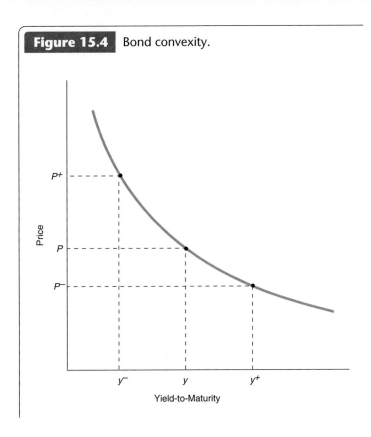

Figure 15.4 Bond convexity.

·····

Duration

Duration A measure of the average maturity of the stream of payments generated by a financial asset. Mathematically, duration is the weighted average of the lengths of time until the asset's remaining payments are made. The weights in this calculation are the proportion of the asset's total present value of the respective cash flows.

Duration is a measure of the "average maturity" of the stream of payments associated with a bond. More specifically, it is a weighted average of the lengths of time until the remaining payments are made. Consider, for example, a bond with annual coupon payments of $80, a remaining life of three years, and a par value of $1000. Since it has a current market price of $950.25, it has a yield-to-maturity of 10.00%. As shown in Table 15.1, its duration is 2.78 years. This is calculated by taking the present value of each cash flow, multiplying each one by the respective amount of time until it is received, summing the resulting figures up, and then dividing this sum ($2639.17) by the market price of the bond ($950.25).

Table 15.1 Calculation of Duration.

Time Until Receipt of Cash Flow	Amount of Cash Flow	Present Value Factor	Present Value of Cash Flow	Present Value of Cash Flow × Time
1	$ 80	.9091	$ 72.73	$ 72.73
2	80	.8264	66.12	132.23
3	1080	.7513	811.40	2434.21
			$950.25	$2639.17

$$\text{Duration} = \frac{\$2639.17}{\$950.25} = 2.78 \text{ years}$$

The Formula

Specifically, the formula for a bond's duration (D) is

$$D = \frac{\sum_{t=1}^{T} PV(C_t) \times t}{P_0} \tag{15.1}$$

where $PV(C_t)$ denotes the present value of the cash flow to be received at time t, calculated using a discount rate equal to the bond's yield-to-maturity; P_0 denotes the current market price of the bond; and T denotes the bond's remaining life.[18]

Why is duration thought of as the "average maturity of the stream of payments associated with a bond?" The current market price of the bond, P_0, is equal to the sum of the present values of the cash flows, $PV(C_t)$, where the discount rate is the bond's yield-to-maturity:

$$P_0 = \sum_{t=1}^{T} PV(C_t) \tag{15.2}$$

Thus, there is an equivalent method for calculating a bond's duration that can be seen by rewriting equation (15.1) in a slightly different manner:

$$D = \sum_{t=1}^{T} \left[\frac{PV(C_t)}{P_0} \times t \right] \tag{15.3}$$

First, the present value of each cash flow $[PV(C_t)]$ is expressed as a proportion of the market price (P_0). Second, these proportions are multiplied by the respective amount of time until the cash flows are received. Third, these figures are added, with the sum being equal to the bond's duration.

In the example shown in Table 15.1, note that $\$72.73/\$950.25 = .07653$ of the bond's market price is to be received in one year. Similarly $\$66.12/\$950.25 = .06958$ is to be received in two years, and $\$811.40/\$950.25 = .85388$ is to be received in three years. Note how these proportions sum to one, which means that they can be interpreted as weights in calculating a weighted average. Thus, to calculate the average maturity of the payments associated with a bond, each weight needs to be multiplied by the respective amount of time until the corresponding cash flow is to be received, and then the products need to be summed up: $(1 \times .07653) + (2 \times .06958) + (3 \times .85388) = 2.78$ years.

A zero-coupon bond will have a duration equal to its remaining life, T, since there is only one cash flow associated with such a bond. That is, since $P_0 = PV(C_T)$ for such bonds, equation (15.3) reduces to

$$D = \frac{PV(C_T)}{P_0} \times T$$
$$= 1 \times T$$
$$= T$$

For any coupon-bearing bond, its duration will always be less than the amount of time to its maturity date, T. Again, examination of equation (15.3) indicates why this is so. Since

---

[18]There are other methods of calculating a bond's duration. For example, instead of using the bond's yield to calculate $PV(C_t)$, the appropriate current spot rate could be used. The concept of duration was initially developed in 1938 by Frederick R. Macaulay, a Canadian actuary, in *Some Theoretical Problems Suggested by the Movements of Interest Rates, Bond Yields, and Stock Prices in the United States Since 1856* (New York: National Bureau of Economic Research). For an interesting article describing the development of the concept of duration (as well as immunization), see Roman L. Weil, "Macaulay's Duration: An Appreciation," *Journal of Business* 46, no. 4 (October 1973): 589–592.

the largest value that t can have is T, and each value of t is multiplied by a weight equal to $PV(C_t)/P_0$, it follows that D must be less than T.

Relationship to Bond Price Changes

One implication of Theorem 5 is that bonds having the same maturity date but different coupon sizes may react differently to a given change in interest rates. That is, the prices of these bonds may adjust by notably different amounts when there is a given change in interest rates. However, bonds with the same duration will react quite similarly.

Specifically, the percentage change in a bond's price is related to its duration in the following fashion:

Percentage change in price $\cong -D \times$ percentage change in $(1 +$ the bond's yield$)$ (15.4a)

where the symbol $\cong$ means "is approximately equal to." This formula implies that when the yields of two bonds having the same duration change by the same percentage, then the prices of the two bonds will change by approximately equal percentages. Equivalently, equation (15.4a) is written as

$$\frac{\Delta P}{P} \cong -D\left(\frac{\Delta y}{1+y}\right) \tag{15.4b}$$

where ΔP denotes the change in the bond's price, P is the bond's initial price, Δy is the change in the bond's yield-to-maturity, and y is the bond's initial yield-to-maturity.

As an example, consider a bond that is currently selling for \$1000 with a yield-to-maturity of 8%. Given that the bond has a duration of 10 years, by how much will the bond's price change if its yield increases to 9%? Using equation (15.4b), it can be seen that $\Delta y = 9\% - 8\% = 1\% = .01$, so that $\Delta y/(1 + y) = .01/1.08 = .00926 = .926\%$ and $= -D[\Delta y/(1 + y)] = -10[.926\%] = -9.26\%$. Hence the one-percentage-point rise in the yield will cause approximately a 9.26% drop in the bond's price to \$1000 $-$ (.0926 $\times$ \$1000) $=$ \$907.40.

Equation (15.4b) can be rewritten by rearranging terms, resulting in:

$$\frac{\Delta P}{P} = -\left[\frac{D}{(1+y)}\right] \times \Delta y \tag{15.4c}$$

The quantity $D/(1 + y)$ is sometimes referred to as a bond's **modified duration**—it reflects the bond's percentage change in price for a 1% change in its yield, and hence is a better measure of the price risk of a bond than Macaulay's D. Thus, the link between these two measures of duration is:

$$D_m = \frac{D}{(1+y)} \tag{15.4d}$$

As an illustration of why some people prefer D_m over D as the measure of a bond's price risk, consider the previous example. Since the bond's duration was 10 years, its modified duration is $10/(1 + .08) = 9.26$ years. Thus, a 1% change in yields will cause the bond's price to change in an opposite direction [note the minimum sign in equation (15.4c)] by 9.26%, as stated earlier. That is:

$$+.01 \times (-9.26) = -0.926$$

or equivalently:

$$+1\% \times (-9.26) = -9.26\%$$

An important assumption has been made in presenting equations (15.4a) through (15.4d). These equations reflect the price risk of a bond only when the yield curve is horizontal and any shifts in it up or down are parallel in nature. Hence, in the example the current yield curve is assumed to initially be flat at 8%, and then to shift either up to 9%

Modified Duration and Key Rate Durations

Issues concerning the term structure of interest rates stand at the top of most bond managers' decision-making hierarchies. Shifts in, and changes in the shape of, the yield curve affect the value of investment-grade bond portfolios to a far greater extent than do other factors. Whether bond managers follow strategies that attempt to actively benefit from interest rate changes or simply desire to neutralize the impact of those changes on their portfolios, controlling interest rate risk is of paramount importance.

If we were to poll bond managers and ask them what single measure best indicates their interest rate risk exposure, they would be nearly unanimous in answering (modified) duration. As the text discusses, modified duration gauges the sensitivity of the market value of a bond (or a portfolio of bonds) to changes in the level of interest rates. Modified duration represents the approximate percentage change in a bond's price caused by a 100-basis-point change in the bond's yield. Thus, for example, if you own a four-year duration bond and its yield rises by 100 basis points, your bond's price should fall by roughly 4%.

An active bond manager attempting to outperform an assigned benchmark may adjust her portfolio's modified duration in anticipation of changes in interest rates. Expectations of falling interest rates call for maintaining a modified duration greater than that of the benchmark. Conversely, a bond manager anticipating rising interest rates will want to hold his portfolio's modified duration less than that of the benchmark. A bond index fund manager similarly pays close attention to modified duration. If the manager lets the portfolio's modified duration differ significantly from that of the index, the portfolio's returns likely will fail to track the index's returns adequately. Other passive bond management strategies, such as immunization, also rely on matching a portfolio's modified duration with that of a target.

Despite its importance to bond portfolio management, modified duration does have certain practical limitations that restrict its ability to accurately measure how a bond's price will respond to a change in yields. Those limitations relate to the underlying assumptions made in calculating a bond's duration. Of particular consequence is the assumption that interest rate changes take the form of parallel shifts along a flat yield curve. In actuality, such shifts are unusual. Various segments of the yield curve usually move by different amounts. In some instances one or more segments may move in the opposite direction of other segments. When these non-parallel shifts occur, two bonds with the same durations may respond quite differently depending on the pattern of their cash flows. As a simple example, if long-term interest rates rise and short-term interest rates fall (referred to as a yield curve *steepening*) then a portfolio holding a single zero-coupon bond with a five-year modified duration may respond quite differently than a portfolio with an equal weighting in two zero-coupon bonds, one with a two-year and the other with an eight-year modified duration, even though the modified durations of both portfolios are the same. What is needed are alternative measures of interest-rate risk that can account for the valuation effect of more complex changes in the yield curve. One such tool is known as key rate durations.

Essentially, key rate durations are a means of breaking apart a bond's modified duration. Instead of one number summarizing the bond's interest rate sensitivity, key rate durations are a set of numbers identifying the sensitivity of the bond to interest rate changes at various points along the yield curve. As the name implies, key rate durations entail specifying certain key rates and associated terms on the yield curve. Thus, a bond manager might select four key rates at ninety days, one year, five years, and thirty years. (In practice, more are usually chosen. Regardless of the number chosen, the key rates must extend across the entire yield curve—effectively from zero to thirty years. Further, the larger the number of key rates, the greater is the ability of the key rate analysis to capture the diverse nature of yield curve shifts, but the more complex becomes that analysis.) The shape of a yield curve shift is indicated by measuring the yield change at each key rate and linearly interpolating the change in between key rates.

At each key rate, the sensitivity of a bond's value to a small shift in the yield curve is estimated. That is, the modified duration of the bond at that point is calculated. For example, if the yield curve at one year were to move by .01 percentage point (one basis point) and the bond's value changes in the opposite direction by .02%, then the bond's one-year key rate duration is 2. Carrying out this calculation at all key rates provides a *profile* of the bond's sensitivity to changes in the yield curve.

By construction, the sum of all key rate durations equals the modified duration of the entire bond. Further, key rate durations combine in a portfolio of bonds in the same way that modified duration does; that is, the key rate duration of a bond at a particular term is the weighted average of the individual bonds' key rate durations at that term, where the weights are the proportion of the portfolio invested in each bond.

Key rate durations enhance the ability of bond managers to fine tune interest rate risk in their portfolios. For example, XYZ Financial Management is an active bond manager who attempts to outperform a market bond index benchmark while keeping tight control over interest-rate risk. XYZ maintains a modified duration close to that of the index, 4.69 years versus 4.49 years. However, the manager is willing to place small interest rate "bets" at various points along the yield curve. The table below shows how a portfolio managed by XYZ compares to the index in terms of key rate durations.

The portfolio's key rate durations are greater than those of the benchmark at the long end of the yield curve. For example, at the 30-year term, the portfolio's key rate duration is .40 years against the benchmark's .14 years. A 100-basis-point decline in the 30-year term, the portfolio's key rate would cause the portfolio to outperform the benchmark by $(.40 - .14) \times 100 = .26\%$. The portfolio is also tilted in favour of rates declining at the 10-year term. Because XYZ maintains a modified duration near that of the benchmark, the key rate duration bets at the long end of the yield curve and at the 10-year term must be largely offset by opposite bets at other key rates along the yield curve. This is the case particularly at the 3-, 7-, and 20-year terms.

Use of key rate durations is not limited to active bond managers. By constructing an indexed portfolio whose key rate durations match those of the assigned index, a bond index fund manager can have greater confidence that yield curve shifts will not result in unacceptable levels of tracking error.

Key rate durations as an analytical tool are not without deficiencies. Because they involve a set of numbers, their application is more complex than is modified duration with its single summary statistic. Key rate durations also ignore potentially valuable information about the covariance of different segments of the yield curve by assuming that all the segments move independently. Nevertheless, key rate durations are a valuable additional arrow in the quiver of bond managers seeking to effectively control interest rate risk.

Key Rate Durations

	.25	1	2	3	5	7	10	15	20	25	30	Modified Duration
Portfolio	.02	.11	.33	.43	.69	.56	.99	.43	.31	.43	.40	4.69
Benchmark	.02	.15	.31	.52	.66	.71	.71	.46	.46	.34	.14	4.49
Gap	.00	(.04)	.02	(.09)	.03	(.15)	.27	(.04)	(.15)	.09	.26	0.20

or down to 7% so it remains horizontal afterwards. Since yield curves are seldom horizontal and infrequently shift in a parallel manner, these equations are best viewed as approximations. There are other reasons why they are approximations, as will be seen next.

● Relationship Between Convexity and Duration

At this point it is useful to consider just what kind of relationship the concepts of convexity and duration have to each other. After all, both have something to do with measuring the association of the change in a bond's price with a change in the bond's yield-to-maturity. Figure 15.5 shows the nature of the relationship. Like Figure 15.4, this figure represents a bond that is currently selling for P and has a yield-to-maturity of y. Note the straight line that is tangent to the curve at the point associated with the current price and yield.

If the bond's yield increases to y^+ then the associated price of the bond will fall to P^-. Conversely, if the bond's yield decreases to y^-, then the associated price of the bond will rise to P^+. However, by using equation (15.4b), the estimated prices will be P_D^- and P_D^+, respectively. This is because the equation, as mentioned earlier, is not exact. Instead, it is an approximation that states that the percentage change in the bond's price is a linear function of its duration. Hence the equation approximates the new price in a linear fashion represented by the straight line and leading to an error that is a consequence of convexity. [In the example, the sizes of the respective errors are $(P^- - P_D^-)$ and $(P^+ - P_D^+)$.] That is, because the relationship between yield changes and bond price changes is convex, not linear, the use of equation (15.4b) will underestimate the new price associated with either an

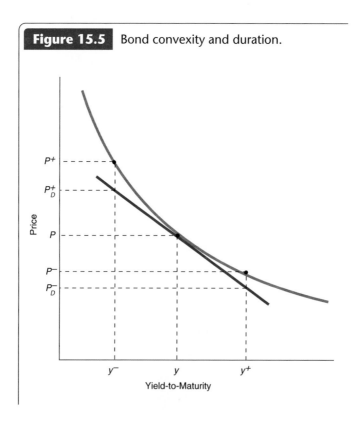

Figure 15.5 Bond convexity and duration.

increase or a decrease in the bond's yield.[19] However, for small changes in yields the error is relatively small, and thus, as an approximation, equation (15.4b) works reasonably well. Figure 15.5 shows that the size of the pricing error becomes smaller as the size of the yield change gets smaller. (Note that the distance between the linear approximating line and the convex curve will be smaller for smaller changes in yields from y.)

Changes in the Term Structure

As mentioned earlier, when yields change, most bond prices also change, but some react more than others. Even bonds with the same maturity date can react quite differently to a given change in yields. However, it was shown in equations (15.4a) and (15.4b) that the percentage change in a bond's price is related to its duration. Hence, the prices of two bonds that have the same duration will react similarly to a given change in yields.

For example, the bond shown in Table 15.1 has a duration of 2.78 and a yield of 10%. If its yield changes to 11%, then the percentage change in (1 + the bond's yield) is $(1.11 - 1.10)/1.10 = .91\%$. Thus its price should change by approximately $-2.78 \times .91\% = -2.53\%$. Using a discount rate of 11%, its price can be calculated to equal $926.69, for an actual price change of $926.69 - $950.25 = -$23.56$ and a percentage change of $-$23.56/$950.25 = -2.48\%$. Any other bond having a duration of 2.78 years will experience a similar price change if it has a similar percentage change in its yield. Any other bond with a modified duration of $2.78/1.10 = 2.53$ will experience a similar price change in response to a similar change in its yield.

Consider a bond with a maturity of four years that also has a duration of 2.78 years. When there is a shift in interest rates, and the yields on the three-year and four-year bonds change by the same amount, then their prices will change similarly. For example, if the yield on the four-year bond goes from 10.8% to 11.81% and at the same time the yield on the three-year bond goes from 10% to 11%, then the percentage change in the present value of the four-year bond will be approximately $-2.78 \times (1.1181 - 1.108)/1.108 = 2.78 \times .91\% = -2.53\%$, which is the same percentage as the three-year bond. Here the difference in the two bonds' modified durations ($2.78/1.10 = 2.53$ for the three-year bond; $2.78/1.108 = 2.51$ for the four-year bond) is exactly offset by the different changes in yield (1% of the three-year bond; 1.01% for the four-year bond.)

What if the percentage change in (1 + the bond's yield) is different? That is, what happens if the term structure shifts in a manner so that the percentage change in (1 + the bond's yield) is not the same for all bonds? Perhaps when the three-year bond goes from a yield of 10% to a yield of 11% [a percentage change of $(1.11 - 1.10)/1.10 = .91\%$] the four-year bond will go from a yield of 10.8% to a yield of 11.5% [a percentage change of $(1.115 - 1.108)/1.108 = .63\%$]. In this case the percentage change in price for the four-year bond will be approximately $-2.78 \times [(1.115 - 1.108)/1.108] = 1.75\%$, which is a smaller change than the -2.53% associated with the three-year bond. Accordingly, even though the two bonds have the same duration, or modified duration, it does not automatically follow that their prices will react identically to any change in yields, as these yield changes can be different for two bonds having the same duration.

---

[19]It follows that if there are two bonds that are identical in all aspects except that one has "more convexity," then the one with more convexity would be more desirable. This is because if yields rise, its price will drop by a smaller amount than the other bonds. Conversely, if yields drop, its price will rise by a larger amount than the other bonds. In either case, the investor is better off with the bond having more convexity.

Immunization

Immunization A bond portfolio management technique that permits an investor to meet a promised stream of cash outflows with a high degree of certainty.

The introduction of the concept of duration has led to the development of the technique of bond portfolio management known as **immunization**.[20] Specifically, this technique allegedly allows a bond portfolio manager to be relatively certain of being able to meet a given promised stream of cash outflows. Thus, once the portfolio has been formed, it is "immunized" from any adverse effects associated with future changes in interest rates.

How Immunization Is Accomplished

Immunization is accomplished by calculating the duration of the promised outflows and then investing in a portfolio of bonds that have an identical duration. In doing so, this technique takes advantage of the observation that *the duration of a portfolio of bonds is equal to the weighted average of the durations of the individual bonds in the portfolio.* For example, if one-third of a portfolio's funds are invested in bonds having a duration of six years and two-thirds of its funds are in bonds having a duration of three years, then the portfolio itself has a duration of $[(1/3) \times 6] + [(2/3) \times 3] = 4$ years.

Consider a simple situation where a portfolio manager has one and only one cash outflow to make from his portfolio—an amount equal to $1 000 000 that is to be paid in two years. Since there is only one cash outflow, its duration is simply two years. Now, the bond portfolio manager is considering investing in two different bond issues. The first bond issue is the one shown in Table 15.1, where the bonds have a maturity of three years. The second bond issue involves a set of bonds that mature in one year, providing the holder of each bond with a single payment of $1070 (consisting of a single coupon payment of $70 and a par value of $1000). Since these bonds are currently selling for $972.73, their yield-to-maturity is 10%.

Consider the choices open to the portfolio manager. All the portfolio's funds could be invested in the one-year bonds, with the notion of reinvesting the proceeds from the maturing bonds one year from now in another one-year issue. However, doing so would entail risks. In particular, if interest rates were to decline over the next year, then the funds from the maturing one-year bonds will have to be reinvested at a lower rate than the currently available 10%. Thus, the portfolio manager faces reinvestment-rate risk due to the possibility that the funds one year from now can only be reinvested at a lower rate.[21]

A second alternative would be for the portfolio manager to invest all the funds in the three-year issue. However, this also entails risks. In particular, the three-year bonds will have to be sold after two years in order to come up with the $1 000 000. The risk is that interest rates will have risen before then, meaning that bond prices, in general, will have fallen and the bonds will not have a selling price that is equal to or greater than $1 000 000. Thus, the portfolio manager faces interest-rate risk with this strategy.

One proposed solution is to invest part of the portfolio's funds in the one-year bonds and the rest in the three-year bonds. How much should be placed in each issue? If immunization is to be used, the solution can be found by simultaneously solving a set of two equations involving two unknowns:

---

[20]For the initial development, see F. M. Redington, "Review of the Principles of Life-Office Valuations," *Journal of the Institute of Actuaries* 78, no. 3 (1952): 286–315. A useful book that discusses duration-based investment strategies is Gerald O. Bierwag, *Duration Analysis* (Cambridge, MA: Ballinger Publishing Company, 1987).

[21]If there were two-year coupon-bearing bonds available for investment, then there would be no reinvestment-rate risk associated with the principal. However, the investor would still face reinvestment-rate risk in terms of the coupon payments received after one year. Although such risk appears to be relatively minor in this example, it becomes much more substantial in situations involving promised cash outflows that are more than two years into the future.

$$W_1 + W_3 = 1 \qquad\qquad (15.5)$$
$$(W_1 \times 1) + (W_3 \times 2.78) = 2 \qquad\qquad (15.6)$$

Here, W_1 and W_3 denote the weights (or proportions) of the portfolio's funds that are to be invested in the bonds with maturities of one and three years, respectively. Note how equation (15.5) states that the sum of the weights must equal 1, whereas equation (15.6) states that the weighted average of the durations of the bonds in the portfolio must equal the duration of the cash outflow, which is two years.

The solution to these two equations is easily found. First, equation (15.5) is rewritten as

$$W_1 = 1 - W_3 \qquad\qquad (15.7)$$

Then, $1 - W_3$ is substituted for W_1 in equation (15.6), resulting in

$$[(1 - W_3) \times 1] + (W_3 \times 2.78) = 2 \qquad\qquad (15.8)$$

Since this is one equation with one unknown, W_3, it can be easily solved. Doing so results in $W_3 = .5618$. Inserting this value into equation (15.7) indicates that $W_1 = .4382$. Thus, the portfolio manager should put 43.82% of the portfolio's funds in the one-year bonds and 56.18% in the three-year bonds.

In this case, the portfolio manager would need $\$1\ 000\ 000/(1.10^2) = \$826\ 446$ in order to purchase bonds that would create a fully immunized portfolio. With this money, $.4382 \times \$826\ 446 = \$362\ 149$ would be used to buy one-year bonds and $.5618 \times \$826\ 446 = \$464\ 297$ would be used to buy three-year bonds. Since the current market prices of the one-year and three-year bonds are $972.73 and $950.25, respectively, this means that $\$362\ 149/\$972.73 = 372$ one-year bonds and $\$464\ 297/\$950.25 = 489$ three-year bonds would be purchased.

What does immunization accomplish? According to theory, if yields rise, then the portfolio's losses due to the selling of the three-year bonds at a discount after two years will be exactly offset by the gains from reinvesting the maturing one-year bonds (and first-year coupons on the three-year bonds) at the higher rate. Alternatively, if yields fall, then the loss from being able to reinvest the maturing one-year bonds (and first-year coupons on the three-year bonds) at a lower rate will be exactly offset by being able to sell the three-year bonds after two years at a premium. Thus, the portfolio is immunized from the effect of any movements in interest rates in the future.

Table 15.2 shows more explicitly what would happen to the portfolio. The second column shows what the portfolio would be worth at the end of two years if yields remained at 10% over the next two years. As can be seen, the value of the portfolio of one-year and three-year bonds would be approximately equal to the promised cash outflow of $1 000 000.

Alternatively, if yields fell to 9% or rose to 11% before one year had passed and remained at the new level, then the value of the portfolio would be slightly more than the needed $1 000 000.[22]

● Problems with Immunization

The previous paragraph described what immunization accomplishes in theory. This leaves open the possibility that it might not work quite as well in practice. What can cause it to work less than perfectly? In terms of the example, what can cause the value of the portfolio to be less than $1 000 000 at the end of two years?

---

[22]The value is more than $1 000 000 due to the convexity property of bonds, discussed earlier.

Table 15.2 An Example of an Immunized Portfolio.

	Yield-to-Maturity at the End of One Year		
	9%	10%	11%
Value at $t = 2$ from reinvesting one-year bond proceeds:			
[$1070 × 372.3 × (1 + y)] =	$ 434 213	$438 197	$ 442 181
Value at $t = 2$ of three-year bonds:			
Value from reinvesting coupons received at $t = 1$:			
[$80 × 488.6 × (1 + y)] =	42 606	42 997	43 388
Coupons received at $t = 2$:			
[$80 × 488.6] =	39 088	39 088	39 088
Selling price at $t = 2$:			
[$1080 × 488.6/(1 + y)] =	484 117	479 716	475 395
Aggregate portfolio value at $t = 2$	$1 000 024	$999 998	$1 000 052

Default and Call Risk

To begin with, immunization is based on the belief that all the bonds' promised cash flows will be paid in full and on time. This means that immunization is based on the assumption that the bond will not default and will not be called before maturity—that is, the bonds are assumed to be free from both call risk and default risk. Consequently, if a bond in the portfolio either enters into default or is called, the portfolio will not be immunized.

Because of problems with the use of the traditional measure of duration in forming immunized portfolios, an alternative measure known as **effective duration** has been introduced.[23] Specifically, this measure is of use in evaluating any bond that contains *embedded options*, meaning that either the bond issuer or bondholder has the ability to cause the actual stream of cash payments to differ from that which would be received if the bond were paid off as promised over its entire life. Examples of embedded options include the option of the issuer to go into default or to prepay the bond before maturity by exercising the bond's call provision, and the option of bondholders of *putable bonds* to force the issuer to pay them off before maturity.

Effective Duration A measure of a bond's duration that accounts for the ability of either the bond's issuer or the bondholder to cause stream of cash payments to differ from that which would be received if the bond were paid off as promised over its entire life.

The formula for calculating a bond's effective duration D_e is:

$$D_e = \frac{P^+ - P^-}{2P\Delta y} \tag{15.9}$$

where P^+ and P^- denote the bond's price if its yield decrease and increases by a given amount (say, 1%), such as shown in Figure 15.2. For example, consider a default-free bond with a 7% coupon paid annually that has 15 years left until maturity, but can be called at any time for $1050. The bond is currently selling for par, so if its yield increases by 1% to 8%, the bond's price will be $914.41 as no embedded options will be exercised. However, if its yield drops by 1% to 6%, then it is believed that the call option will be exercised so the value of the bond will be $1050 instead of $1097.12. Thus, the effective duration for this bond can be approximated by using equation (15.9), and will be ($1050 − $914.41)/(2 × $1000 × .01) = 6.8 years, in contrast to the traditional duration and modified duration measures of 9.75 and 9.11, respectively.

---

[23]The concept of *effective convexity* has also been introduced to take into consideration such issues as default and call risk when measuring a bond's convexity. See, for example, Frank J. Fabozzi, *Bond Market Analysis and Strategies* (Upper Saddle River, NJ: Prentice Hall, 1996), pp. 344–345, 358.

Multiple Nonparallel Shifts in a Nonhorizontal Yield Curve

Immunization is also based on the assumption that the yield curve is horizontal and that any shifts in it will be parallel and will occur before any payments are received from the bonds that were purchased. In the example, both the one-year and three-year bonds had the same 10% yield-to-maturity at the start, and the shift of 1% in yields was assumed to be the same for both bond issues. Furthermore, this shift was assumed to occur sometime before one year had passed.

In reality, the yield curve will not be horizontal at the start, and shifts in it are not likely to be either parallel or restricted as to when they occur. Perhaps the one-year and three-year bonds will have initial yields of 10% and 10.5%, respectively, with the yields on the one-year and three-year bonds falling by 1% and .8%, respectively, after one year. Indeed, there is evidence that there is greater volatility in yields of shorter-term securities.[24] If these kinds of shifts occur, then it is possible that the portfolio will not be immunized.

Cash Matching A form of immunization that involves the purchase of bonds that generate a stream of cash inflows identical in amount and timing to a set of expected cash outflows over a given period of time.

Dedicated Portfolio A portfolio of bonds that provides its owner with cash inflows that are matched against a specific stream of cash outflows.

If the bond portfolio manager followed a special kind of immunization known as **cash matching**, then frequent nonparallel shifts in a nonhorizontal yield curve would have no adverse effect on the portfolio. This is because cash matching involves the purchase of bonds so that the cash received each period from the bonds is identical in size to the promised cash outflow for that period.

Such a cash-matching portfolio of bonds is often referred to as a **dedicated portfolio**. Note that there is no need to reinvest any cash inflows in the future with a dedicated portfolio, so there is no reinvestment-rate risk. Furthermore, since bonds do not have to be sold prior to maturity, there is no interest-rate risk either.

In the simplest situation where there is one promised cash outflow, the dedicated portfolio would consist of zero-coupon bonds, where each bond has a life corresponding to the date of the promised cash outflow. In the previous example where there was a promised cash outflow of $1 000 000 after two years, this would be accomplished by purchasing the requisite number of zero-coupon bonds having a maturity of two years.

However, cash matching is often not so easily accomplished because the promised cash outflows may involve an uneven stream of payments for which no zero-coupon bonds exist. It can be difficult (if not impossible) and expensive to match cash inflows exactly with promised outflows.

Another potential way around the problem of having nonhorizontal yield curves that have nonparallel shifts is to use one of a variety of more complicated immunization models. These models involve various other assumptions about the current shape of the yield curve and how it will shift in the future. Consequently, the bond portfolio manager must choose the one that he deems most accurate. Interestingly, various studies have found that the best performer was the version of immunization that has been described in this chapter, and not the more complicated models. For this reason, some researchers argue that the portfolio manager interested in immunization would be well advised to use this version.[25]

---

[24]See the articles by Jeffrey Nelson and Stephen Schaefer, "The Dynamics of the Term Structure and Alternative Portfolio Immunization Strategies," pp. 61–101; and Jonathan E. Ingersoll, Jr., "Is Immunization Feasible? Evidence from the CRSP Data," pp. 163–182 in George G. Kaufman, G.O. Bierwag, and Alden Toevs, eds., *Innovations in Bond Portfolio Management: Duration Analysis and Immunization* (Greenwich, CT: JAI Press 1983); and Robert R. Reitano, "Non-parallel Yield Curve Shifts and Spread Leverage," *Journal of Portfolio Management* 17, no. 3 (Spring 1991): 82–87.

[25]For a summary and set of references, see G. O. Bierwag, George G. Kaufman, Robert Schweitzer, and Alden Toevs, "The Art of Risk Management in Bond Portfolios," *Journal of Portfolio Management* 7, no. 3 (Spring 1981): 27–36; G. O. Bierwag, George G. Kaufman, and Alden Toevs, "Duration: Its Development and Use in Bond Portfolio Management," *Financial Analysts Journal* 39, no. 4 (July–August 1983): 15–35; and Stephen M. Schaefer, "Immunization and Duration: A Review of Theory, Performance, and Applications," *Midland Corporate Finance Journal* 2, no. 3 (Fall 1984): 41–58.

Regardless of the model being used, the bond portfolio manager must recognize that there is a risk being incurred—the risk that the yield curve will shift in a way that does not correspond with the way assumed by the model. For example, if the model presented here is used, then the bond portfolio is facing the risk that the yield curve may not shift in a parallel manner. Consequently, some people have argued that none of the immunization models are useful.[26] Others have argued that there are ways to use immunization in the presence of such risk, which has been called **stochastic process risk**.[27]

Stochastic Process Risk

In the context of immunization, the risk that the yield curve will shift in a way that prevents an immunized bond portfolio from producing its expected cash inflows.

Rebalancing

Another problem with the use of immunization is the effect of the passage of time on the duration of the bonds held and on the duration of the promised cash outflows. As time passes and yields change, these durations can change at different rates so that the portfolio is no longer immunized. This means that the portfolio may need to be rebalanced fairly often.

Here, rebalancing refers to selling some bonds currently held and replacing them with others so that, afterward, the duration of the portfolio matches the duration of the promised cash outflows. However, since rebalancing causes the portfolio manager to incur transaction costs, the manager might not want to rebalance whenever the durations do not match, since the costs might outweigh the perceived gains from rebalancing. Ultimately, the bond portfolio manager will have to decide how frequently to rebalance the portfolio, taking into consideration the risk of being unbalanced along with the transaction costs associated with rebalancing.

Choosing Among Many Candidates

Usually, many portfolios have a duration of the requisite length. Which one is the bond portfolio manager to choose? In the example, imagine that in addition to the one-year and three-year bonds, there is a zero-coupon bond having a life of four years (thus, its duration is also four years) that the manager is considering. Now the manager faces a choice of which portfolio to hold, since there are many with the requisite duration of two years. In addition to the one previously described that consisted of just one-year and three-year bonds, there is also one where two-thirds and one-third of the portfolio's funds are invested in one-year bonds and four-year bonds, respectively. [Note how the duration of this portfolio is also two years: $(2/3 \times 1) + (1/3 \times 4) = 2$.] Furthermore, there are many other candidate portfolios.

One solution is to choose the portfolio with the highest average yield-to-maturity. Here, the yield of each issue is multiplied by the percentage of the portfolio's funds that are invested in that issue. Another solution is to choose the portfolio that most closely resembles a "bullet," or "focused," portfolio, since it has been argued that such a portfolio has less stochastic process risk than any other. Such a portfolio is one where the bonds in it have

---

[26]See N. Bulent Gultekin and Richard J. Rogalski, "Alternative Duration Specifications and the Measurement of Basis Risk," *Journal of Business* 57, no. 2 (April 1984): 241–264. For rebuttals and responses, see G. O. Bierwag, George G. Kaufman, Cynthia M. Latta, and Gordon S. Roberts, "Duration: Response to Critics," *Journal of Portfolio Management* 13, no. 2 (Winter 1987): 48–52; N. Bulent Gultekin and Richard J. Rogalski, "Duration: Response to Critics: Comment," *Journal of Portfolio Management* 15, no. 3 (Spring 1989): 83–87; G. O. Bierwag, George G. Kaufman, Cynthia M. Latta, and Gordon S. Roberts, "Duration as a Measure of Basis Risk: The Wrong Answer at Low Cost—Rejoinder," *Journal of Portfolio Management* 15, no.4 (Summer 1989): 82–85; and N. Bulent Gultekin and Richard J. Rogalski, "Duration as a Measure of Basis Risk: The Wrong Answer at Low Cost—Answer to Rejoinder," *Journal of Portfolio Management* 15, no. 4 (Summer 1989): 86–87.

[27]G. O. Bierwag, George G. Kaufman, and Alden Toevs, "Bond Portfolio Immunization and Stochastic Process Risk," *Journal of Bank Research* 13 (Winter 1983): 282–291; and G. O. Bierwag, George G. Kaufman, and Cynthia M. Latta, "Duration Models: A Taxonomy," *Journal of Portfolio Management* 15, no. 1 (Fall 1988): 50–54.

Surplus Management

Corporate pension funds are established to secure the funding of retirement benefits promised to corporate employees. Therefore, the primary investment objective of these funds is to accumulate sufficient assets, through contributions and investment income, to satisfy all pension obligations on a timely basis.

The management of corporate pension funds has traditionally focused solely on the asset side of the asset-liability equation. Those organizations charged with the oversight of pension funds (often referred to as "plan sponsors") have typically defined their investment policies in terms of seeking maximum returns subject to their tolerance for volatility of returns (see Chapter 23). This philosophy has led many plan sponsors to invest heavily in equity assets, particularly common stocks, based on their perceived superior long-run risk-return characteristics (see Chapter 1).

The foundation of this investment philosophy received a jolt in 1986 when the US Financial Accounting Standards Board issued FAS 87, a directive requiring US corporations to more fully disclose pension obligations on their financial statements beginning in 1989. Prior to FAS 87, corporate reporting on pension obligations was consigned to annual report footnotes. This level of disclosure seemed inadequate, given that pension assets and liabilities would represent the largest items on many corporations' balance sheets if they were reported there, and that annual pension expenses often represent a large portion of a corporation's earnings. FAS 87 was designed to address this deficiency.

FAS 87 requires that US companies report any negative difference between their pension assets and their pension liabilities on their balance sheets as liabilities. (There is no corresponding balance sheet asset if pension assets exceed pension liabilities.) Moreover, the way in which companies state pension expenses on their income statements was redefined. The expense includes costs associated with pension benefits earned in the current year, plus interest on past obligations, plus the amortization of any unfunded liabilities (that is, liabilities not offset by pension assets), less the expected earnings on the pension fund's assets.

As a result of FAS 87, the earnings of US corporations have become sensitive to changes in their pension fund's surplus, which is the difference in value between the fund's assets and liabilities. A significant decrease in pension surplus will result in an earnings reduction, whereas a significant increase can boost earnings. Thus, FAS 87 created for the first time a source of reported earnings variability directly attributable to changes in a pension fund's assets and liabilities.

This new source of earnings variability has caused some companies to emphasize control of pension surplus volatility through a process known as *surplus management*. How does a plan sponsor manage pension surplus? By developing an investment strategy that causes the value of the pension fund's assets to move more closely with the pension fund's liabilities. That is, the plan sponsor tries to "immunize" the pension fund's liabilities by creating an appropriately structured portfolio of assets. In this way, the variability of changes in pension surplus will be reduced, thereby lowering the pension fund's impact on the variability of the corporation's earnings.

To specify the appropriate composition of the pension fund's portfolio that will immunize the fund's pension liabilities, the plan sponsor must determine what factors can cause the value of these liabilities to change. In the short run, when promised pension benefits can be viewed as fixed, only movements in interest rates will alter the value of pension liabilities. FAS 87 mandates that the value of pension liabilities be calculated as the discounted value of pension benefits earned to date by the company's employees (plus, in some cases, projected salary increases for current employees). The discount rate applied to these earned pension benefits is related to current market interest rates. Therefore, as those interest rates fluctuate, so too does the value of a company's pension liabilities. Interest-rate increases reduce the value of pension liabilities, whereas interest-rate declines increase pension liabilities.

As described in the text, a simple means of at least partially immunizing a set of interest-sensitive liabilities is to create a portfolio of bonds whose duration equals that of the liabilities. As interest rates change, the value of the assets will rise and fall more or less in line with the value of the liabilities, maintaining a relatively constant pension surplus.

FAS 87 has given rise to numerous sophisticated strategies designed to reduce pension surplus volatility. To implement these strategies, some plan sponsors have significantly reduced their pension funds' allocations to equity assets and purchased fixed-income securities.

Such shifts in asset allocation have led critics of surplus management to argue that by maintaining large fixed-income investments, pension plans are sacrificing the superior returns available from equity assets. These critics contend that surplus management is shortsighted. If one views pension liabilities on a longer-term basis, they are not fixed. Rather, they grow with inflation and worker productivity (which translate into pay raises and higher benefits). Thus, in the long run, equity assets may be more effective in hedging against these changes in pension liabilities than fixed-income investments.

To date, no legislation similar to FAS 87 has been proposed in Canada. However, many observers feel it is only a matter of time before the issue arises here as well.

durations (or, alternatively, terms-to-maturity) most closely matching the duration of the promised outflows. In the example, the portfolio consisting of just one-year and three-year bonds is more focused than the one consisting of the one-year and four-year bonds.

Two Canadian studies have found that the simple Macaulay measure of duration, despite stochastic process risk, explains about 80% of the variability in Government of Canada bond returns. Furthermore, a simple portfolio construction procedure worked as effectively as the bullet portfolio. The simple procedure consisted of first choosing a bond with a maturity equal to the horizon date and then adding a second bond with a longer duration in the appropriate proportions to make the portfolio duration equal to the horizon.[28]

Active Management

As mentioned earlier, active management of a bond portfolio is based on the belief that the bond market is not perfectly efficient. Such management can involve security selection, where attempts are made at identifying mispriced bonds. Alternatively, it can involve market timing, i.e., attempts to forecast general movements in interest rates. It is also possible for an active portfolio manager to be involved in both security selection and market timing. While there are a large number of methods of actively managing a bond portfolio, some general types of active management can be described.

---

[28]For a discussion of how to select the best immunizing portfolio, see Alexander and Resnick, "Using Linear and Goal Programming to Immunize Bond Portfolios," *Journal of Banking and Finance* 9, no.1 (March 1985): 35–54; I. Fooladi and G. Roberts, "How Effective are Duration-based Bond Strategies in Canada?" *Canadian Investment Review*, II, no. 1 (Spring 1989): 57–62; G. O. Bierwag, I. Fooladi and G. Roberts, "Designing an Immunized Portfolio: Is M-squared the Key?" *Journal of Banking and Finance* 17, no. 6 (December 1993): 1147–1170.

Horizon Analysis

The return on a bond over any given holding period depends on its price at the beginning of the period and its price at the end of the period, as well as its coupon rate. Thus, the return on a bond over a one-year period will depend on the yield structure at the beginning of the year and the yield structure at the end of the year, since the price of the bond at these two points in time will depend on these structures. It follows that possible changes to the beginning-of-period yield structure must be analyzed in order to analyze possible bond returns over a given holding period. Bond portfolio managers who believe they (or their staffs) are able to identify such changes will want to translate their beliefs into action.

Horizon Analysis A form of active bond management in which a single holding period is selected for analysis and possible yield structures at the end of the period are considered. Bonds with the most attractive expected returns under the alternative yield structures are selected for the portfolio.

One way of doing this is known as **horizon analysis**, where a single holding period is selected for analysis and possible yield structures at the end of the period (that is, at the "horizon") are considered.[29] The possible returns for two bonds—one currently held and one candidate to replace it—are then analyzed. In doing so, neither bond is assumed to default up to the horizon date. In the process of the analysis, the sensitivities of the returns to changes in key assumptions regarding yields are estimated, allowing at least a rough assessment of some of the relevant risks.

Horizon analysis can be viewed as another way of implementing the capitalization-of-income method of valuation that was discussed in Chapter 14. By focusing on the estimated end-of-period price of a bond, it seeks to determine if the current market price is relatively high or low. That is, for a given estimated end-of-period price, a bond will have a relatively high expected return if its current price is relatively low. Conversely, a bond will have a relatively low expected return if its current price is relatively high.

Figure 15.6 represents a page from a standard yield book for bonds with a 4% coupon. As indicated, a 4% bond with 10 years remaining to maturity that is currently priced at $67.48 (for ease of exposition, a par of $100 is used here) will have a 9% promised annual yield-to-maturity (or 4.5% semiannually). Five years into the future, such a bond's term-to-maturity will have decreased and the relevant promised yield-to-maturity will probably have changed. Thus, as time passes, the bond might follow a path through the table such as that shown by the dashed line. If so, it would end up at a price of $83.78 at the *horizon* (five years hence), with an 8% promised annual yield-to-maturity (or 4% semiannually).

Over any holding period, a bond's return typically will be affected by both the passage of time and a change in yields. Horizon analysis breaks this into two parts: one due solely to the passage of time, with no change in yields, and the other due solely to a change in yield, with no passage of time. This is illustrated in Figure 15.6. The total price change from $67.48 to $83.78 (or $16.30) is broken into a change from $67.48 to $80.22 (or $12.74), followed by an instantaneous change from $80.22 to $83.78 (or $3.56). The intermediate value is the price the bond would command at the horizon if its promised yield-to-maturity had remained unchanged at its initial level of 9%. The actual price is that which it commands at its actual yield-to-maturity of 8%. In summary, the total price change can be broken into two parts, representing the two effects:

$$\text{Price change} = \text{time effect} + \text{yield change effect} \qquad (15.10)$$

So far, no account has been taken of the coupon payments to be received before the horizon date. In principle, one should consider all possible uses of such cash flows or at least analyze possible alternative yield structures during the period to determine likely reinvestment opportunities. In practice, this is rarely done. Instead, a single reinvestment rate is

---

[29]See Martin L. Leibowitz, "Horizon Analysis for Managed Bond Portfolios," *Journal of Portfolio Management* 1, no. 3 (Spring (1975): 23–34; and "An Analytic Approach to the Bond Market," in *Financial Analyst's Handbook*, ed. Sumner N. Levine (Homewood, IL: Dow Jones-Irwin, Inc., 1975), pp. 226–277.

Figure 15.6 The effect of time and yield change on a 4% coupon bond.
Note: Y_0 and P_0 denote the bond's yield-to-maturity and price at the beginning of the period; Y_H and P_H denote the bond's yield-to-maturity and price at the horizon (that is, at the end of the period); P_A denotes the bond's price at the horizon if its yield had remained at $Y_0 = 9\%$; yields are compounded semiannually.

| Yield to Maturity (%) | **YEARS TO MATURITY** | | | | |
	10 Yrs	9 Yrs	5 Yrs	1 Yr	0 Yrs
7.00	78.68	80.22	87.53	97.15	100.00
7.50	75.68	77.39	85.63	96.69	100.00
Y_H (8.00)	72.82	74.68	(83.78) ← P_H	96.23	100.00
8.50	70.09	72.09	81.98	95.77	100.00
		Actual Price Pattern Over Time		Yield Change Effect	
Y_0 (9.00) P_0 (67.48)	69.60		(80.22) → P_A	95.32	100.00
		Time Effect			
9.50	64.99	67.22	78.51	94.87	100.00
10.00	62.61	64.92 ...	76.83 ...	94.42	100.00
10.50	60.34	62.74	75.21	93.98	100.00
11.00	58.17	60.64	73.62	93.54	100.00

SOURCE: Martin L. Leibowitz, "Horizon Analysis for Managed Bond Portfolios," *Journal of Portfolio Management* 1, no. 3 (Spring 1975): 26.

assumed and the future value of all coupon payments at the horizon date is determined by compounding each one using this rate.[30]

For example, if $2 is received every six months (as in Figure 15.6) with the first payment occurring six months from now and the last one occurring five years from now, and each payment is reinvested at 4.25% per six months, then the value at the end of five years will be approximately $24.29. Of this amount, $20 can be considered interest (coupon payments of $2 for 10 six-month periods) with the remaining $4.29 being "interest on interest."

In summary, a bond's overall dollar return has four components—the time effect, the yield change effect, the coupons, and the interest from reinvesting the coupons. In the example, the overall dollar return is

$$
\begin{aligned}
\frac{\text{Overall}}{\text{dollar return}} &= \frac{\text{time}}{\text{effect}} + \frac{\text{yield}}{\text{change effect}} + \text{coupons} + \frac{\text{interest}}{\text{on coupons}} \\
&= (\$80.22 - \$67.48) + (\$83.78 - \$80.22) + \$20.00 + \$4.29 \\
&= \$12.74 + \$3.56 + \$20.00 + \$4.29 \\
&= \$40.59
\end{aligned}
$$

---

[30]The longer the horizon, the greater the importance of the size of the reinvestment rate in determining a bond's return. This means that if the investor's horizon is greater than 10 years, for example, then alternative reinvestment rates should be considered. See Richard W. McEually, "Rethinking Our Thinking About Interest Rates," *Financial Analysts Journal* 41, no. 2 (March–April 1985): 62–67.

This overall dollar return can be converted into an overall rate of return by dividing it by the market price of the bond at the beginning of the period, $67.48. In doing so, it can be seen that a bond's overall rate of return consists of four components:

$$\begin{aligned} \text{Overall} \atop \text{dollar return} &= \frac{\$12.74}{\$67.48} + \frac{\$3.56}{\$67.48} + \frac{\$20.00}{\$67.48} + \frac{\$4.29}{\$67.48} \\ &= .1888 + .0528 + .2964 + .0635 \\ &= .6015 \end{aligned}$$

or 60.15%. The first term is the return due to the passage of time, the second term is the return due to yield change, the third term is coupon return, and the fourth term is the return due to the reinvestment of the coupon payments.

Because the second term is uncertain, it is important to analyze it further. In the example, a change in yield from 9.0% to 8.0% will result in a change in the market price from $80.22 to $83.78. Given 8.0% was the expected yield at the horizon, an expected overall rate of return of 60.15% was computed. By using different end-of-period yields, different overall rates of return can be calculated. Then, with estimates of the probabilities of these yields occurring, a feel for the bond's risk can be obtained. Indeed, it can now be seen why bond portfolio managers devote a great deal of attention to making predictions of future yields.

Bond Swaps

Bond Swapping A form of active bond management that entails the replacement of bonds in a portfolio with other bonds so as to enhance the yield of the portfolio.

Substitution Swap A type of bond swap in which an investor exchanges one bond with a lower yield for another with a higher yield, yet both bonds have essentially the same financial characteristics.

Intermarket Spread Swap A type of bond swap in which an investor moves out of one market segment and into another because the investor believes that one segment is significantly underpriced relative to the other.

Given a set of predictions about future bond yields, holding-period returns over one or more horizons for one or more bonds can be estimated. The goal of **bond swapping** is to manage a portfolio actively by exchanging bonds to take advantage of any superior ability to predict such yields.[31] In making a swap, the portfolio manager believes that an over-priced bond is being exchanged for an underpriced bond. Some swaps are based on the belief that the market will correct for its mispricing in a short period of time, whereas other types of swaps are based on a belief that corrections will either never take place or will take place over a long period of time.

There are many categories for classifying swaps, and the distinctions between the categories are often blurred. Nevertheless, many bond swaps can be placed in one of four general categories:

1. **Substitution swap:** Ideally, this swap is an exchange of a bond for a perfect substitute or "twin" bond. The motivation here is temporary price advantage, presumably resulting from an imbalance in the relative supply and demand conditions in the marketplace.
2. **Intermarket spread swap:** This type of swap involves a more general movement out of one market component and into another with the intention of exploiting a currently advantageous yield relationship. The idea here is to benefit from a forecasted changing relationship between the two market components. Although such swaps will almost always have some sensitivity to the direction of the overall market, the idealized focus of this type of swap is the spread relationship itself.

---

[31]Bond swaps should not be confused with interest rate swaps, where two issuers of debt keep the respective amounts raised but make each other's coupon payments. That is, issuer A makes the coupon payments on issuer B's debt, and issuer B makes the coupon payments on issuer A's debt, perhaps because A has fixed-rate debt and B has floating-rate debt. See, for example, Stuart M. Turnbull, "Swaps: A Zero Sum Game?" *Financial Management* 16, no. 1 (Spring 1987): 15–21; Clifford W. Smith, Jr., Charles W. Smithson, and D. Sykes Wilford, *Managing Financial Risk* (New York: Harper & Row, 1990), Chapters 9–12; John F. Marshall and Kenneth R. Kapner, *The Swaps Market* (Miami: Kolb Publishing, 1993); and Bernadette A. Minton, "An Empirical Examination of Basic Valuation Models for Plain Vanilla U.S. Interest Rate Swaps," *Journal of Financial Economics* 44, no. 2 (May 1997): 251–277. Interest rate swaps are discussed in Chapter 23.

3. **Rate anticipation swap:** Such swaps, on the other hand, are geared towards profiting from an anticipated movement in overall market rates.
4. **Pure yield pickup swap:** These swaps are oriented towards yield improvements over the long term, with little heed being paid to interim price movements in either the respective market components or the market as a whole.[32]

Consider a hypothetical portfolio manager who holds some of a 30-year, AA utility bond issue that has a 7% coupon rate. Since these bonds are currently selling at par, their yield-to-maturity is 7%. Now, imagine that there is another 30-year, AA utility bond issue with a 7% coupon rate that is being made available to the manager at a price so that its yield-to-maturity is 7.10%. The manager could exchange a given dollar amount of the currently held bonds for an equivalent dollar amount of the second bond issue in a substitution swap, thereby picking up 10 basis points in yield.

Alternatively, the manager might note that there is a 10-year, AA utility bond issue outstanding that carries a 6% coupon and is priced at par; thus, its yield is 6%. In this case, there is a 100-basis-point yield spread between the currently held 30-year bonds and the 10-year bonds. If the manager feels this spread is too low, then she might initiate an intermarket spread swap by exchanging some of the 30-year bonds for an equivalent dollar amount of the 10-year bonds. Since the manager expects the spread to increase in the future, she believes the yield on the 10-year bonds will fall. This means the price on these bonds should rise by an abnormal amount, resulting in an abnormally high holding-period return.

Another possibility is that the manager feels that yields in general are going to rise. In such a situation, the manager will recognize that the currently held portfolio is very risky because longer-term bonds generally move downward further in price for a given rise in yields than do shorter-term bonds. Accordingly, the manager might use a rate anticipation swap to exchange a given dollar amount of the 30-year bonds for an equivalent amount of some short-term bonds.

Lastly, the manager might not want to make any predictions about future yields or yield spreads. Instead, she might simply note that some 30-year, AA industrial bonds are currently priced to yield 8%. In this case, the manager might want to enter a pure-yield pickup swap, where some of the 7% utility bonds are exchanged for an equivalent dollar amount of the 8% industrial bonds, the motivation being to earn the extra 100 basis points in yield from the industrials.

Contingent Immunization

One method of bond portfolio management that has both passive and active elements is **contingent immunization.** In the simplest form of contingent immunization, the portfolio is actively managed as long as favourable results are obtained. However, if unfavourable results occur, then the portfolio is immediately immunized.

As an illustration, consider the earlier example where the portfolio manager had to come up with $1 000 000 at the end of two years, and the current yield curve was horizontal at 10%. It was explained that the portfolio manager could immunize the portfolio by investing $826 446 in one-year and three-year bonds. However, the portfolio manager may convince the client that the portfolio should be *contingently* immunized with $841 680. This means that the portfolio manager must be certain that the portfolio will be worth at least $1 000 000 at the end of the two years, with any excess going to the client and the manager being compensated accordingly. Equivalently, the portfolio manager must earn a minimum average return of 9% (note that $841 680 \times 1.09^2 = \$1\ 000\ 000$) over the two years. Here, the client is willing to settle for a return as low as 9% but hopes that

---

[32]See Sidney Homer and Martin L. Leibowitz, *Inside the Yield Book* (Englewood Cliffs, NJ: Prentice Hall, 1972) and Chapter 16 in Marcia Stigum and Frank J. Fabozzi, *The Dow Jones-Irwin Guide to Bond and Money Market Investments* (Homewood, IL: Dow Jones-Irwin, Inc., 1987).

the portfolio manager will be able to exceed the 10% return that could have been locked in with an immunized portfolio.

The manager would proceed to manage the portfolio actively by attempting to engage either in selectivity or timing (or both). Perhaps the arrangement with the client is that the status of the portfolio will be reviewed weekly, and yields that are currently available will be determined.

Consider how the review would be conducted after one year has elapsed and the yield curve is still horizontal, but at 11%. First of all, $1 000 000/(1.11) = $900 901 would be needed to immunize the portfolio at that point. Second, the market value of the current portfolio is determined to be $930 000. Now, in this example, the arrangement between the client and portfolio manager is that the manager can continue to manage the portfolio actively as long as it is worth at least $10 000 more than the amount needed for immunization. Since it is worth $930 000, an amount greater than $900 901 + $10 000 = $910 901, the portfolio manager can continue being active. However, if the portfolio were worth less than $910 901, then, according to the agreement, the manager would have immediately immunized the portfolio.

Riding the Yield Curve

Riding the yield curve is a method of bond portfolio management sometimes used by people who, having liquidity as a primary objective, invest in short-term fixed-income securities. One way of investing is simply to purchase these securities, hold them until they mature, and then reinvest them. An alternative way is to ride the yield curve, provided certain conditions exist.

One condition is that the yield curve be upward sloping, indicating that longer-term securities have higher yields. Another condition is that the investor believes that the yield curve will remain upward sloping. Given these two conditions, the investor who is riding the yield curve will purchase securities that have a somewhat longer term-to-maturity than desired and then sell them before they mature, thereby capturing some capital gains.

For example, consider an investor who prefers investing in 91-day Treasury bills. Currently, such bills are selling for $98.25 per $100 of face value, yielding 7.14% $[($100 − 98.25)/98.25) \times (100 \times 365/91)] = 7.14\%$. However, 182-day Treasury bills are currently selling for $96.20, providing a higher yield of 7.92% $[($100 − 96.2)/96.2) \times (100 \times 365/182) = 7.92\%]$. If this investor believes that the yield curve will remain upward sloping over the next three months, he may choose to ride the yield curve for a higher return than would be possible from simply buying and holding 91-day Treasury bills.

If the investor buys and holds the 91-day Treasury bills, then the resulting annualized rate of return will be 7.14% (as calculated above). Alternatively, if the investor buys 182-day Treasury bills and subsequently sells them after 91 days, then the expected selling price will be $98.25 (note that this is the same as the current price of 91-day bills, since it is assumed that the yield curve will not have changed after 90 days have elapsed). This means that the expected return is

$$[(\$98.25 − \$96.20)/\$96.00] \times (100 \times 365/91) = 8.55\%$$

The expected return from riding the yield curve, therefore, is higher. This is because the investor expects to benefit from a decline in yield that is due to the shortening of the maturity of the Treasury bills that were initially purchased and not to a shift in the yield curve.

It should be kept in mind that if the yield curve changes adversely, then this strategy can reduce the investor's return.[33] That is, riding the yield curve is riskier than simply

---

[33]According to the unbiased expectations theory (discussed in Chapter 5), the yield curve would be expected to shift in such a manner that the expected return on both strategies (in the example, buy and hold the 91-day Treasury bills versus buy and sell the 182-day Treasury bills 91 days later) would be the same.

buying securities that mature at the appropriate time. Similarly, there are two transactions necessary (buying and then selling the security) when riding the yield curve, whereas a maturity strategy has only one transaction (buying the security). Thus, there will be larger transaction costs associated with riding the yield curve.

Passive Management

The previous discussion of active management assumes that there are inefficiencies in the market that can be exploited. Examples include the ability to find mispriced bonds and the ability to discern when certain market sectors are likely to outperform others (for example, when short-term Treasuries are likely to outperform long-term Treasuries and vice versa). However, if one believes that bond markets are highly efficient, then a passive approach to investing in bonds is in order.

Indexation A method of linking the payments associated with a bond to the price level in order to provide a certain real return on the bond.

The most common passive approach involves **indexation**. With this approach, an investor selects a bond index that is consistent with her risk-return preferences. the objective indexation is to invest in a portfolio of bonds whose performance *tracks* (that is, closely follows) that of the index. Three broad-based US indices commonly used by investors creating indexed bond portfolios are:

1. Lehman Brothers Aggregate Index
2. Merrill Lynch Domestic Market Index
3. Salomon Brothers Broad Investment-Grade Bond Index

Each one of these indexes contains over 5000 bonds that have maturities of greater than one year and are rated BBB or above. In addition, Lehman Brothers, Merrill Lynch, and Salomon Brothers as well as other organizations, such as Morgan Stanley and First Boston, publish more narrow market indices.[34]

Investing in a portfolio of bonds whose performance tracks that of a given index is not simple. Indeed, it is quite challenging. Why? First of all, buying all the bonds in the index is impractical since, as mentioned earlier, there are thousands of bonds in each of the broad-based indices. Indeed, even the narrower bond indices are typically composed of many bonds. Second, transaction costs are not reflected in the performance of a bond index, but will be incurred in buying and selling bonds in an attempt to manage a portfolio whose performance tracks the index. Third, each of the bonds held will provide the investor with coupon payments periodically that need to be reinvested. However, it is impractical to take, say $3000 of coupon payments received during a given week, and invest these coupons in all the bonds that are currently held in the portfolio.

As a consequence, most approaches to constructing indexed bond portfolios involve sampling techniques. That is, a subset of all the bonds in the index (plus, possibly, some bonds that are outside the index) is selected for investment such that the *tracking error* of the portfolio is minimal. That is, the portfolio is designed so that its rate of return has minimal deviations from the return on the bond index. Assuming an investment-grade corporate index is to be tracked, one method known as *stratified sampling* initially involves dissecting the index by determining, for example:

1. What bonds in the index have a duration of zero to three years, three to six years, and over six years.
2. What bonds in the index are issued by companies in one of three economic sectors: industrials, utilities, and financial.

---

[34] For more information on bond market indices, see Frank K. Reilly, G. Wenchi Kao, and David J. Wright, "Alternative Bond Market Indices," *Financial Analysts Journal* 48, no. 3 (May–June 1992): 44–58.

3. What bonds in the index are in each of the four investment-grade rating categories (AAA, AA, A, and BAA.)

Note that in total there are $3 \times 3 \times 4 = 36$ categories, referred to as cells. Next, the percent of the bond index's value associated with each cell is calculated. Finally, some but not all of the bonds in each cell are selected for purchase such that the weight in the category for the portfolio is the same as the weight for the index. Thus, if 3% of the index consists of AAA-rated financial bonds with three- to six-year durations and the portfolio is worth $200 000 000, then $6 000 000 of the portfolio will be invested in a subset of those bonds in the index that are rated AAA, are issued by financial companies, and have a duration between three and six years.

Tracking error will be related to the number of different cells that are defined. At first, more cells lead to closer tracking, but after a point more categories lead to poorer tracking as transaction costs begin to overwhelm the benefits of more precise cell definitions. This can be seen by considering two extreme cases. At one extreme, the number of cells is one (in the above example, the category would be "corporates"), which would result in large tracking errors since all that would be done would be to select a subset of the bonds in the index. At the other extreme, the categories are drawn up so narrowly that the number of categories equals the number of bonds in the index, which would result in large tracking errors due to the large amount of transaction costs incurred. Somewhere in between these two extremes lies the optimal number of cells, determined by both art and science.[35]

Bond Versus Stocks

Bonds and stocks are different kinds of securities, with quite different characteristics. Making an investment decision between them should not be based on some simple one-dimensional comparison. In many cases this decision, known as **asset allocation**, will involve investing in both bonds and stocks.[36]

Asset Allocation The process of determining the optimal division of an investor's portfolio among available asset classes.

While historical relationships may not be useful for accurately predicting future relationships, it is instructive to examine the average values, standard deviations, and correlations of past stock and bond returns. The US statistics presented in Table 15.3 are based on quarterly excess returns during one time period, 1926–1985, and two subperiods, 1926–1945 and 1946–1985. The Canadian results cover a single time period, 1950–1989. The similarity in the results obtained in both countries is notable with the exception of the correlation coefficient. Based on average returns, stocks appear to have a substantial advantage for the investor with a reasonably long horizon.[37] However, there is good reason to believe that the average returns on long-term bonds are not representative of investors'

---

[35]A hybrid approach to indexation is known as enhanced indexation. It involves managing a portfolio with the objective of earning a return that is at least equal to and sometimes slightly better than the return on a chosen index. For more on enhanced indexation, passive management, and stratified sampling, see Frank J. Fabozzi, *Bond Markets, Analysis and Strategies* (Upper Saddle River, NJ: Prentice Hall, 1996), Chapter 18 and pp. 423–424.

[36]Chapter 23 presents some methods for making the asset allocation decision. For a model of how to measure the interest rate sensitivity of a portfolio consisting of both stocks and bonds, see Martin L. Leibowitz, "Total Portfolio Duration: A New Perspective on Asset Allocation," *Financial Analysts Journal* 42, no. 5 (September–October 1986): 18–29.

[37]Another US study involving simulation found that, based on historical returns, an investor with a 20-year horizon had about a 5% probability of earning less when investing in a common stock index as opposed to investing in a long-term Treasury bond index. For a 10-year horizon the probability was 11%. See Kirt C. Butler and Dale L. Domian, "Risk, Diversification, and the Investment Horizon," *Journal of Portfolio Management* 17, no. 3 (Spring 1991): 41–47.

Table 15.3 Historical Relationships Between Bonds and Shares.

	Shares	Bonds	Correlation
1. US Data			
A. 1926–1996:			
Average annual excess return	8.90%	1.67%	
Standard deviation	20.67	9.01	
Correlation			0.21
B. 1926–1945:			
Average annual excess return	9.86%	3.75%	
Standard deviation	28.43	5.07	
Correlation			0.19
C. 1946–1996:			
Average annual excess return	8.52%	0.85%	
Standard deviation	17.05	10.07	
Correlation			0.25
2. Canadian Data[a]			
D. 1950–1997:			
Average annual excess return	5.63%	1.63%	
Standard deviation	17.41	9.75	
Correlation			0.20

[a] Based on annual data.

SOURCES: US data adapted from Meir Statman and Neal L. Ushman, "Bonds Versus Stocks: Another Look," *Journal of Portfolio Management* 13, no. 2 (Winter 1987): 33–38. Canadian data adapted from Melanie Moore, *ScotiaMcLeod's Handbook of Canadian Debt Market Indices: 1947–1997*, ScotiaMcLeod Inc., February 1998.

expectations for future returns. The returns show the results obtained by purchasing a long-term bond, holding it for a period of time, and then replacing it with another long-term bond. The total returns include both income and capital gains or losses. In the US, during the postwar subperiod, bond price changes were frequently negative, averaging roughly –.7% per year.[38] A better estimate of investors' expectations might be obtained by assuming that the price would be as likely to increase as to decrease (that is, the expected price change is zero). Expected future returns on bonds might then have been roughly .5% per year greater than shown in the table.

Bond returns have been less variable than stock returns in both the full period and the two subperiods. However, the standard deviation of bonds in the postwar subperiod is double that of the earlier subperiod. It is likely that the increased uncertainty concerning the rate of inflation during the postwar subperiod has increased the variability of bond returns.

The correlation between stock and bond returns has been low, and during various multiyear subperiods it has even had negative values. This indicates that portfolios combining both stocks and bonds benefited considerably from the resulting diversification. More recently, however, correlations have been considerably more positive than in the past, owing in part to common reactions to changes in inflationary expectations. Consequently,

---

[38]Another study involving simulation found that, based on historical returns, an investor with a 20-year horizon had about a 5% probability of earning less when investing in a common stock index as opposed to investing in a long-term Treasury bond index. For a 10-year horizon the probability was 11%. See Kirt C. Butler and Dale L. Domian. "Risk, Diversification, and the Investment Horizon," *Journal of Portfolio Management* 17 no. 3 (Spring 1991): 41–47.

the gains from diversification have recently been reduced substantially. Nevertheless, from the historical record it would be reasonable to expect that, in the future, bonds will still offer diversification benefits.

The average return on equity investment in Canada from 1950 to 1997 was lower than that in the US with an equal standard deviation over an approximately comparable period. Corporate bonds, on the other hand, have shown a slightly higher return with a comparable standard deviation.

The correlation coefficient between bonds and shares is quite low at 0.2 suggesting that bonds can provide attractive diversification opportunities. It should be noted, however, that the correlation coefficient between the two sets of returns has been substantially higher since 1989 at 0.62, probably due to a common reaction to changing inflationary expectations on the part of investors. If the correlation coefficient between the two series reverts to its historical value close to zero as it was in the period from 1950 to 1989 then bonds will again become useful diversification vehicles.

Summary

1. Like the common stock markets, Canadian and US bond markets appear to be highly, but not perfectly, semistrong-form efficient.
2. For a typical bond, making periodic interest payments and a final principal repayment on a stated date, five bond pricing theorems apply:
   a. If a bond's market price increases, then its yield must decrease; conversely, if a bond's market price decreases, then its yield must increase.
   b. If a bond's yield does not change over its life, then the size of its discount or premium will decrease as its life gets shorter.
   c. If a bond's yield does not change over its life, then the size of its discount or premium will decrease at an increasing rate as its life gets shorter.
   d. A decrease in a bond's yield will raise the bond's price by an amount that is greater in size than the corresponding fall in the bond's price that would occur if there were an equal-sized increase in the bond's yield. (That is, the price-yield relationship is convex.)
   e. The percentage change in a bond's price owing to a change in its yield will be smaller if its coupon rate is higher.
3. Duration is a measure of the "average maturity" of the stream of payments associated with a bond. It is a weighted average of the length of time until the bond's remaining payments are made, with the weights equal to the present value of each cash flow relative to the price of the bond.
4. The duration of a portfolio of bonds is equal to the weighted average of the durations of the individual bonds in the portfolio.
5. A bond portfolio manager can be fairly confident of being able to meet a given promised stream of cash outflows by creating a bond portfolio with a duration equal to the liabilities. This procedure is known as immunization.
6. Problems with immunization include default and call risk, multiple nonparallel shifts in a nonhorizontal yield curve, costly rebalancings, and a wide range of candidate bond portfolios.
7. Active bond management may involve security selection, market timing (where attempts are made to forecast general movements in interest rates), or combinations of the two.
8. Active management strategies include horizon analysis, bond swaps, contingent immunization, and riding the yield curve.
9. The most common passive management strategy involves indexation, where a portfolio is formed whose performance tracks that of a chosen index.

10. Portfolios consisting of both stocks and bonds benefit from the resulting diversification due to the relatively low correlation of returns between the two asset classes.

APPENDIX A

EMPIRICAL REGULARITIES IN THE BOND MARKET

Certain empirical regularities in the stock market are well known among investment professionals.[39] The principal regularities observed are the January effect and the day-of-the-week effect. It has been noted in the stock market that returns are higher in January than in any other month and that returns on Mondays are generally negative, while returns on Fridays are generally positive. Because these regularities cannot be explained by any of the currently known asset pricing models, they are referred to as "anomalies." An interesting question to ponder is this: do such regularities also exist in the bond market? One study looked at this question by examining the daily performance from January 1963 through December 1986 of the Dow Jones Composite Bond Average. (This bond index consists of 20 investment-grade US corporate bonds, divided evenly between industrials and utilities.)[40]

The January Effect

Table 15.4 presents evidence that, as with common stocks, there is a January effect in bonds—that is, on average, corporate bonds have a notably higher return during the month of January than during the other 11 months of the year. Furthermore, this table also shows that this observation was true across all investment-grade (Aaa to Baa) and two speculative-grade (Ba and B) risk classes. Interestingly, the effect is extremely pronounced for the speculative classes.

Table 15.4 Seasonality in Bond Returns.	Average Return in January	Average Monthly Return in Other Months
(a) 1963–1986	4.34%	–.56%
(b) 1963–1979		
Aaa	1.15	.22
Aa	1.21	.29
A	1.18	.30
Baa	1.55	.30
Ba	3.32	.27
B	5.09	.36

SOURCE: Susan D. Jordan and Bradford D. Jordan, "Seasonality in Daily Bond Returns," *Journal of Financial and Quantitative Analysis* 26, no. 2 (June 1991): Table 5, p. 281; Eric C. Chang and Roger D. Huang, "Time-Varying Return and Risk in the Corporate Bond Market," *Journal of Financial and Quantitative Analysis* 25, no. 3 (September 1990): Table 1, p. 331.

---

[39]Some of these regularities are discussed in the Appendix to Chapter 16.

[40]Susan D. Jordan and Bradford D. Jordan, "Seasonality in Daily Bond Returns," *Journal of Financial and Quantitative Analysis* 26, no. 2 (June 1991): 269–285. Note that this study did not examine the bond market in order to see whether the "size effect" (observed for common stocks) was present. Hence, only two of the anomalies discussed in the Appendix to Chapter 16 are discussed here.

The Day-of-the-Week Effect

Table 15.5 presents US average daily returns for each business day of the week over the period from 1963 to 1986. As with common stocks, the average return on Monday is negative. However, it is also negative for every day except Thursday, and the average returns for all five days are not statistically significantly different from one another.[41] Hence, in contrast to common stocks, the day-of-the-week effect does not appear to exist for corporate bonds.

Table 15.5	Analysis of Daily Return.
Day of Week	*Average Daily Return*
Monday	−0.0020%
Tuesday	−0.0093
Wednesday	0.0000
Thursday	+0.0044
Friday	0.0000

SOURCE: Susan D. Jordan and Bradford D. Jordan, "Seasonality in Daily Bond Returns," *Journal of Financial and Quantitative Analysis* 26, no. 2 (June 1991): Table 5, p. 281.

QUESTIONS AND PROBLEMS

1. A $10 000 face-value pure-discount bond with a 10-year term-to-maturity currently sells so as to produce an 8% yield-to-maturity. What is the bond's price? Calculate the bond's price if its yield rises to 10% and if its yield falls to 5%.

2. Both bonds A and B have $10 000 face values, have 10% coupon rates, and sell with yields-to-maturity of 9%. However, bond A has a 20-year term-to-maturity while bond B has a 5-year term-to-maturity. Calculate the prices of the two bonds. Despite having the same yields, why is one bond's price different from the other's?

3. Consider three pure-discount bonds, each with a $1000 face value; 7% yield-to-maturity; and terms-to-maturity of 5, 10, and 20 years, respectively. Calculate each bond's price. Graph the bond's discounts versus their terms-to-maturity. Is the relationship linear? Why?

4. Consider two bonds with 10% coupon rates and $1000 face values. One of the bonds has a term-to-maturity of 4 years, whereas the other has a term-to-maturity of 15 years. Both make annual interest payments. Assuming that yields on the two bonds rise from 10% to 14%, calculate the intrinsic values of the two bonds before and after the change in interest rates. Explain the difference in percentage price changes.

5. Consider a five-year term-to-maturity bond with a $1000 face value and $100 annual coupon interest payments. The bond sells at par. What is the bond's percentage price change if the yield-to-maturity rises to 12%; if it falls to 8%?

6. Consider two bonds, one with 5 years to maturity and the other with 20 years to maturity. Both have $1000 face values and 8% coupon rates (with annual interest payments), and both sell at par. Assume that the yields of both bonds fall to 6%. Calculate the dollar increases in the bonds' prices. What percentage of this increase in each case

---

[41]The returns on Wednesday and Friday are shown to be zero, but this is only because of rounding, as they are slightly negative.

comes from a change in the present value of the bonds' principals, and what percentage comes from a change in the present value of the bonds' interest payments?

7. Both bonds A and B have $10 000 face values, 8% yields-to-maturity, and 10-year terms-to-maturity. However, bond A has a 10% coupon rate whereas bond B sells at par. (Both make annual interest payments.) If the yields on both bonds decline to 6%, calculate the percentage price changes of the two bonds.

8. Consider a bond selling at its par value of $1000, with six years to maturity and a 7% coupon rate (with annual interest payments). Calculate the bond's duration and its modified duration.

9. If the yield-to-maturity on the bond in Problem 8 increases to 8%, what happens to the bond's duration? Why does this change occur?

10. Why must the duration of a coupon-bearing bond always be less than the time to its maturity date?

11. Liz Fiorello owns a portfolio of four bonds with the following durations and proportions:

Bond	Duration	Proportion
A	4.5 years	.20
B	3.0	.25
C	3.5	.25
D	2.8	.30

What is the duration of Liz's bond portfolio?

12. Rank order the following bonds in terms of duration. Explain the rationale behind your rankings. (You do not have to actually calculate the bonds' durations. Logical reasoning will suffice.)

Bond	Term-to-maturity	Coupon Rate	Yield-to-maturity
1	30 years	10.0%	10.0%
2	30	0.0	10.0
3	30	10.0	7.0
4	5	10.0	10.0

13. What impact would you expect the option features of callable bonds and mortgage-backed securities to have on the expected durations of such bonds as opposed to the durations calculated based on the bonds' stated maturity dates?

14. Consider a bond with a 3.5-year duration. If its yield-to-maturity increases from 8.0% to 8.3%, what is the expected percentage change in the price of the bond?

15. Distinguish between modified duration and effective duration.

16. Referring to equation 15.9, show why a bond with no embedded options will have an effective duration equal to its modified duration. [Hint: Think about what the relationship is between $(P^+ - P^-)$ and ΔP.]

17. The price-yield relationship for a typical bond is convex, opening upward as shown in Figure 15.4. Investment professionals often describe the price-yield relationship of mortgage pass-through securities as being "negatively convex"—that is, a graph of the relationship opens downward. What features of these securities could produce such a relationship?

18. Explain why immunization permits a bond investor to be confident of meeting a given liability on a predetermined future date.

19. What are the advantages and disadvantages of meeting promised cash outflows through cash matching as opposed to duration matching?

20. Why can nonparallel shifts in the yield curve cause problems for an investor seeking to construct an immunized bond portfolio?

21. Beatrice Richardson is planning to offset a single-payment liability with an immunized bond portfolio. Beatrice is considering buying either bonds with durations close to that of the liability (a "bullet" strategy) or bonds with durations considerably above and below that of the liability (a "barbell" strategy). Why is the "bullet" strategy a lower risk strategy for Beatrice? What are its disadvantages relative to the "barbell" strategy?

22. Describe the four components of return on a bond investment over a given holding period.

23. Consider a bond with a $1000 face value, 10 years to maturity, and $80 annual coupon interest payments. The bond sells so as to produce a 10% yield-to-maturity. That yield is expected to decline to 9% at the end of four years. Interest income is assumed to be invested at 9.5%. Calculate the bond's four-year holding period return and the four components of that return.

24. Distinguish between a substitution swap and an intermarket swap.

25. Compare contingent immunization to the strategy of using stop orders (discussed in Chapter 2) to protect a portfolio's value.

CFA Exam Questions

26. Bill Peters is the investment officer of a $60 million pension fund. He has become concerned about the big price swings that have occurred lately in the fund's fixed-income securities. Peters has been told that such price behaviour is only natural given the recent behaviour of market yields. To deal with the problem, the pension fund's fixed-income money manager keeps track of exposure to price volatility by closely monitoring bond duration. The money manager believes that price volatility can be kept to a reasonable level as long as portfolio duration is maintained at approximately seven to eight years.

    Discuss the concepts of duration and convexity and explain how each fits into the price/yield relationship. In the situation described above, explain why the money manager should have used both duration and convexity to monitor the bond portfolio's exposure to price volatility.

27. You have been asked to evaluate two specific bond issues held in your company's pension fund. The characteristics of these are shown in the following table. Note that these bonds are both issued by the same firm.

    a. Using the duration and yield information in the table, compare the price and yield behaviour of the two bonds under each of the following two scenarios:
       • Scenario 1—strong economic recovery with rising inflation expectations
       • Scenario 2—economic recession with reduced inflation expectations

    b. Using the information in the table, calculate the projected price change for Bond B if the yield-to-maturity for this bond falls by 75 basis points.

    c. Describe the shortcoming of analyzing bond A strictly to call or to maturity. Explain an approach to remedy this shortcoming.

	Bond A (Callable)	Bond B (Noncallable)
Maturity	2002	2002
Coupon	11.50%	7.25%
Current price	125.75	100.00
Yield-to-maturity	7.70%	7.25%
Modified duration to maturity	6.20	6.80
Convexity to maturity	0.50	0.60
Call date	1996	—
Call price	105	—
Yield-to-call	5.10%	—
Modified duration to call	3.10	—
Convexity to call	0.10	—

28. Identify and briefly explain the three conditions that must be satisfied to immunize a portfolio.

KEY TERMS

coupon payments (p. 402)
coupon rate (p. 402)
term-to-maturity (p. 402)
yield-to-maturity(p. 402)
convexity (p. 404)
duration (p. 405)
modified duration (p. 407)
immunization (p. 412)
effective duration (p. 414)
cash matching (p. 415)
dedicated portfolio (p. 415)

stochastic process risk (p. 416)
horizon analysis (p. 419)
bond swapping (p. 421)
substitution swap (p. 421)
intermarket spread swap (p. 421)
rate anticipation swap (p. 422)
pure yield pickup swap (p. 422)
contingent immunization (p. 422)
riding the yield curve (p. 423)
indexation (p. 424)
asset allocation (p. 425)

REFERENCES

1. There have been many tests of efficiency in the bond market. Footnotes1 through 11 contain citations of several of them. Some of the others are cited in:

Frank J. Fabozzi and T. Dessa Fabozzi, *Bond Markets, Analysis, and Strategies* (Englewood Cliffs, NJ: Prentice Hall, 1989), p. 300–303. Chapter 4 also contains an extensive discussion of the concepts of convexity and duration.

2. Books that discuss convexity, duration, and many related investment strategies are:

Gerald O. Bierwag, *Duration Analysis* (Cambridge, MA: Ballinger Publishing, 1987).

Frank J. Fabozzi, *Bond Markets, Analysis, and Strategies* (Upper Saddle River, NJ: Prentice Hall, 1996).

Kenneth D. Garbade, *Fixed-income Analytics* (Cambridge, MA: MIT Press, 1996).

Suresh Sundaresan, *Fixed-income Markets and Their Derivatives* (Cincinnati, OH: South-Western Publishing, 1997).

3. A method for measuring convexity is given by:

Robert Brooks and Miles Livingston, "A Closed-form Equation for Bond Convexity," *Financial Analysts Journal* 45, no. 6 (November–December 1989): 78–79.

4. The concept of duration and its use to measure interest rate risk was initially developed by:

Frederick R. Macaulay, *Some Theoretical Problems Suggested by the Movement of Interest Rates, Bond Yields, and Stock Prices in the United States Since 1856* (New York: National Bureau of Economic Research, 1938).

J. R. Hicks, *Value and Capital* 2nd ed. (Oxford, England: Clarendon Press, 1946; the first edition was published in 1939).

Michael H. Hopewell and George G. Kaufman, "Bond Price Volatility and Term to Maturity: A Generalized Respecification," *American Economic Review* 63, no. 4 (September 1973): 4749–4753.

5. For interesting articles describing the development of the concept of duration (as well as immunization), see:

Roman L. Weil, "Macaulay's Duration: An Appreciation," *Journal of Business* 46, no. 4 (October 1973): 589–592.

Frank K. Reilly and Rupinder S. Sidhu, "The Many Uses of Bond Duration," *Financial Analysts Journal* 36, no. 4 (July–August 1980): 58–72.

G. O. Bierwag, George G. Kaufman, and Alden Toevs, "Duration: Its Development and Use in Bond Portfolio Management," *Financial Analysts Journal* 39, no. 4 (July–August 1983): 15–35.

6. For alternative methods of calculating duration, see:

Jess H. Chua, "A Generalized Formula for Calculating Bond Duration," *Financial Analysts Journal* 44, no. 5 (September–October 1988): 65–67.

Sanjay K. Nawalkha and Nelson J. Lacey, "Closed-form Solutions of Higher-order Duration Measures," *Financial Analysts Journal* 44, no. 6 (November–December 1988): 82–84.

7. For the initial development and subsequent supportive tests of immunization, see:

F. M. Redington, "Review of the Principles of Life-office Valuations," *Journal of the Institute of Actuaries* 78, no. 3 (1952): 286–315.

Lawrence Fisher and Roman L. Weil, "Coping with the Risk of Interest-rate Fluctuations: Returns to Bondholders from Naive and Optimal Strategies," *Journal of Business* 44, no. 4 (October 1971): 408–431.

G. O. Bierwag and George G. Kaufman, "Coping with the Risk of Interest-rate Fluctuations: A Note," *Journal of Business* 50, no. 3 (July 1977): 364–370.

Charles H. Gushee, "How to Immunize a Bond Investment," *Financial Analysts Journal* 37, no. 2 (March–April 1981): 44–51.

G. O. Bierwag, George G. Kaufman, Robert Schweitzer, and Alden Toevs, "The Art of Risk Management in Bond Portfolios," *Journal of Portfolio Management* 7, no. 2 (Spring 1981): 27–36.

Gerald O. Bierwag, *Duration Analysis* (Cambridge, MA: Ballinger Publishing, 1987), Chapter 12.

Donald R. Chambers, Willard T. Carleton, and Richard W. McEnally, "Immunizing Default-free Bond Portfolios with a Duration Vector," *Journal of Financial and Quantitative Analysis* 23, no. 1 (March 1988): 89–104.

Iraj Fooladi and Gordon S. Roberts, "Bond Portfolio Immunization," *Journal of Economics and Business* 44, no. 1 (February 1992): 3–17.

8. For some interesting articles on the relationship of duration and convexity, see:

Mark L. Dunetz and James M. Mahoney, "Using Duration and Convexity in the Analysis of Callable Bonds," *Financial Analysts Journal* 44, no. 3 (May–June 1988): 53–72.

Bruce J. Grantier, "Convexity and Bond Portfolio Performance: The Benter the Better," *Financial Analysts Journal* 44, no. 6 (November–December 1988): 79–81.

Jacques A. Schnabel, "Is Benter Better: A Cautionary Note on Maximizing Convexity," *Financial Analysts Journal* 46, no. 1 (January–February 1990): 78–79.

Robert Brooks and Miles Livingston, "Relative Impact of Duration and Convexity on Bond Price Changes," *Financial Practice and Education* 2, no. 1 (Spring–Summer 1992): 93–99.

Mark Kritzman, "… About Duration and Convexity," *Financial Analysts Journal* 48, no. 6 (November–December 1992): 17–20.

Gerald O. Bierwag, Iraj Fooladi, and Gordon S. Roberts, "Designing an Immunized Portfolio: Is M-squared the Key?" *Journal of Banking and Finance* 17, no. 6 (December 1993): 1147–1170.

Edward J. Kane and Stephen A. Kane, "Teaching Duration of Annuities and Portfolio Net Worth from a Financial Engineerin Perspective," *Financial Practice and Education* 5, no. 2 (Fall–Winter 1995): 144–148.

Don M. Chance and James V. Jordan, "Duration, Convexity, and Time as Components of Bond Returns," *Journal of Fixed Income* 6, no. 2 (September 1996): 88–96.

Nicola Carcano and Silverio Foresi, "Hedging Against Interest-rate Risk: Reconsidering Volatility-adjusted Immunization," *Journal of Banking and Finance* 21, no. 2 (February 1997): 127–141.

Joel R. Barber and Mark L. Copper, "Is Bond Convexity a Free Lunch?" *Journal of Portfolio Management* 24, no. 1 (Fall 1997): 113–119.

Antony C. Cherin and Robert C. Hanson, "Consistent Treatment of Interest Payments in Immunization Examples," *Financial Practice and Education* 7, no. 1 (Spring–Summer 1997): 122–126.

9. Some of the research that is critical of the use of duration, convexity, and immunization is mentioned in footnote 26. Other critical research includes:

Jonathan E. Ingersoll, Jr., Jeffrey Skelton, and Roman L. Weil, "Duration Forty Years Later," *Journal of Financial and Quantitative Analysis* 13, no. 4 (November 1977): 627–650.

Ronald N. Kahn and Roland Lochoff, "Convexity and Exceptional Return," *Journal of Portfolio Management* 16, no. 2 (Winter 1990): 43–47.

Antti Ilmanen, "How Well Does Duration Measure Interest-rate Risk?" *Journal of Fixed Income* 1, no. 4 (March 1992): 43–51.

10. For a discussion of how to use non-default-free bonds in an immunized portfolio, see:

Gordon J. Alexander and Bruce G. Resnick, "Using Linear and Goal Programming to Immunize Bond Portfolios," *Journal of Banking and Finance* 9, no. 1 (March 1985): 35–54.

G. O. Bierwag and George G. Kaufman, "Durations of Nondefault-free Securities," *Financial Analysts Journal* 44, no. 4 (July–August 1988): 39–46, 62.

Gerald O. Bierwag, Charles J. Corrado, and George G. Kaufman, "Computing Durations for Bond Portfolios," *Journal of Portfolio Management* 17, no. 1 (Fall 1990): 51–55.

Gerald O. Bierwag, Charles J. Corrado, and George G. Kaufman, "Duration for Portfolios of Bonds Priced on Different Term Structures," *Journal of Banking and Finance* 16, no. 4 (August 1992): 705–714.

Antti Ilmanen, Donald McGuire, and Arthur Warga. "The Value of Duration as a Risk Measure for Corporate Debt," *Journal of Fixed Income* 4, no. 1 (June 1994): 70–76.

Martin Leibowitz, Stanley Kogelman, and Lawrence N. Bader, "Spread Immunization: Portfolio Improvements Through Dollar-duration Matching," *Journal of Investing* 4, no. 3 (Fall 1995): 49–56.

Iraj J. Fooladi, Gordon S. Roberts, and Frank Skinner, "Duration for Bonds with Default Risk," *Journal of Banking and Finance* 21, no. 1 (January 1997): 1–16.

11. For a discussion of the effect of call risk on duration (and immunization), see:

Kurt Winkelmann, "Uses and Abuses of Duration and Convexity," *Financial Analysts Journal* 45, no. 5 (September–October 1989): 72–75.

12. For a discussion of how to use duration to measure the risk of foreign bonds, see:

Steven I. Dym, "Measuring the Risk of Foreign Bonds," *Journal of Portfolio Management* 17, no. 2 (Winter 1991): 56–61.

Steven I. Dym, "Global and Local Components of Foreign Bond Risk," *Financial Analysts Journal* 48, no. 2 (March–April 1992): 83–91.

13. Dedicated bond portfolios and contingent immunization are discussed in:

Martin L. Leibowitz and Alfred Weinberger, "Contingent Immunization—Part I: Risk Control Procedures," *Financial Analysts Journal* 38, no. 6 (November–December 1982): 17–31.

Martin L. Leibowitz and Alfred Weinberger, "Contingent Immunization—Part II: Problem Areas," *Financial Analysts Journal* 39, no. 1 (January–February 1983): 39–50.

Martin L. Leibowitz, "The Dedicated Bond Portfolio in Pension Funds—Part I: Motivations and Basics," *Financial Analysts Journal* 42, no. 1 (January–February 1986): 69–75.

Martin L. Leibowitz, "The Dedicated Bond Portfolio in Pension Funds—Part II: Immunization, Horizon Matching, and Contingent Procedures," *Financial Analysts Journal* 42, no. 2 (March–April 1986): 47–57.

14. For a discussion of horizon analysis and bond swaps, see:

Sidney Homer and Martin L. Leibowitz, *Inside the Yield Book* (Englewood Cliffs, NJ: Prentice Hall, 1972), Chapters 6–7.

Martin L. Leibowitz, "Horizon Analysis for Managed Bond Portfolios," *Journal of Portfolio Management* 1, no. 3 (Spring 1975): 23–34.

Martin L. Leibowitz, "An Analytic Approach to the Bond Market," in *Financial Analyst's Handbook*, ed. Sumner N. Levine (Homewood, IL: Dow Jones-Irwin, 1975), pp. 226–277.

Marcia Stigum and Frank J. Fabozzi, *The Dow Jones-Irwin Guide to Bond and Money Market Investments* (Homewood, IL: Dow Jones-Irwin, 1987), Chapter 15.

15. For discussion of various yield curve strategies, see:

Jerome S. Osteryoung, Gordon S. Roberts, and Daniel E. McCarty, "Ride the Yield Curve When Investing Idle Funds in Treasury Bills?" *Financial Executive* 47, no. 4 (April 1979): 10–15.

Edward A. Dyl and Michael D. Joehnk, "Riding the Yield Curve: Does It Work?" *Journal of Portfolio Management* 7, no. 3 (Spring 1981): 13–17.

Marcia Stigum and Frank J. Fabozzi, *The Dow Jones-Irwin Guide to Bond and Money Market Investments* (Homewood, IL: Dow Jones-Irwin, 1987), pp. 270–272.

Frank J. Jones, "Yield Curve Strategies," *Journal of Fixed Income* 1, no. 2 (September 1991): 43–51.

Robin Grieves and Alan J. Marcus, "Riding the Yield Curve: Reprise," *Journal of Portfolio Management* 18, no. 4 (Summer 1992): 67–76.

16. More on bond investment strategies is contained in:

Ehud I. Ronn, "A New Linear Programming Approach to Bond Portfolio Management," *Journal of Financial and Quantitative Analysis* 22, no. 4 (December 1987): 439–466.

Michael C. Ehrhardt, "A New Linear Programming Approach to Bond Portfolio Management: A Comment," *Journal of Financial and Quantitative Analysis* 24, no. 4 (December 1989): 533–537.

Randall S. Hiller and Christian Schaack, "A Classification of Structured Bond Portfolio Modeling Techniques," *Journal of Portfolio Management* 17, no. 1 (Fall 1990): 37–48.

Frank J. Fabozzi, *Bond Markets, Analysis and Strategies* (Englewood Cliffs, NJ: Prentice Hall, 1993), in particular Chapters 20–22.

Antti Ilmanen, "Market Rate Expectations and Forward Rates," *Journal of Fixed Income* 6, no. 2 (September 1996): 8–22.

Antti Ilmanen, "Does Duration Extension Enhance Long-term Expected Returns?" *Journal of Fixed Income* 6, no. 2 (September 1996): 23–36.

17. For an interesting discussion of what mix of bonds and stocks is appropriate for investors, see:

Martin L. Leibowitz and William S. Krasker, "The Persistence of Risk: Stocks Versus Bonds Over the Long Term," *Financial Analysts Journal* 44, no. 6 (November–December 1988): 40–47.

Paul A. Samuelson, "The Judgment of Economic Science on Rational Portfolio Management: Indexing, Timing, and Long-horizon Effects," *Journal of Portfolio Management* 16, no. 1 (Fall 1989): 4–12.

Martin L. Leibowitz and Terence C. Langetieg, "Shortfall Risk and the Asset Allocation Decision: A Simulation Analysis of Stock and Bond Profiles," *Journal of Portfolio Management* 16, no. 1 (Fall 1989): 61–68.

Keith P. Ambachtscheer, "The Persistence of Investment Risk," *Journal of Portfolio Management* 16, no. 1 (Fall 1989): 69–71.

Kirt C. Butler and Dale L. Domian, "Risk, Diversification, and the Investment Horizon," *Journal of Portfolio Management* 17, no. 3 (Spring 1991): 41–47.

Peter L. Bernstein, "Are Stocks the Best Place to Be in the Long Run?" *Journal of Investing* 5, no. 2 (Summer 1996): 6–9.

Ravi Jagannathan and Narayana R. Kotcherlakota, "Why Should Older People Invest Less in Stocks Than Younger People?" Federal Reserve Bank of Minneapolis *Quarterly Review* 20, no. 3 (Summer 1996): 11–23.

18. Pension fund management is discussed in:

Martin L. Leibowitz, "Total Portfolio Duration: A New Perspective on Asset Allocation," *Financial Analysts Journal* 42, no. 5 (September–October 1986): 18–29, 77.

Martin L. Leibowitz and Roy D. Henriksson, "Portfolio Optimization Within a Surplus Framework," *Financial Analysts Journal* 44, no. 2 (March–April 1988): 43–51.

William F. Sharpe, "Liabilities—A New Approach," *Journal of Portfolio Management* 16, no. 2 (Winter 1990): 4–10.

19. Empirical regularities in the bond market have been investigated by:

Eric C. Chang and J. Michael Pinegar, "Return Seasonality and Tax-loss Selling in the Market for Long-term Government and Corporate Bonds," *Journal of Financial Economics* 17, no. 2 (December 1986): 391–415.

Eric C. Chang and Roger D. Huang, "Time-varying Return and Risk in the Corporate Bond Market," *Journal of Financial and Quantitative Analysis* 25, no. 3 (September 1990): 323–340.

Susan D. Jordan and Bradford D. Jordan, "Seasonality in Daily Bond Returns," *Journal of Financial and Quantitative Analysis* 26, no. 2 (June 1991): 269–285.

Kam C. Chan and H. K. Wu, "Another Look at Bond Market Seasonality: A Note," *Journal of Banking and Finance* 19, no. 6 (September 1995): 1047–1054.

20. Key rate durations are discussed in:

Robert R. Reitano, "Non-parallel Yield Curve Shifts and Durational Leverage," *Journal of Portfolio Management* 26, no. 4 (Summer 1990): 62–67.

Thomas S. Y. Ho, "Key Rate Durations: Measures of Interest-rate Risks," *Journal of Fixed Income* 2, no. 2 (September 1992): 29–44.

Bennett W. Golub and Leo M. Tilman, "Measuring Yield Curve Risk Using Principal Components Analysis, Value at Risk, and Key Rate Durations," *Journal of Portfolio Management* 23, no. 4 (Summer 1997): 72–84.

21. For a Canadian perspective on the topics covered in this chapter, see:

I. J Fooladi, G. S. Roberts, and F. Skinner, "Duration for Corporate and Provincial Bonds with Default Risk," *Proceedings*, Administrative Sciences Association of Canada Conference, Lake Louise, June 1993.

E. Z. Prisman and Y. Tian, "Immunization in Markets with Tax-clientele Effects: Evidence from the Canadian Market," *Journal of Financial and Quantitative Analysis* 29, no. 2 (June 1994).

G. Athanassakos and Y. Tian, "Seasonality in Canadian Government Bond Returns: An Institutional Explanation," *Proceedings*, Administrative Sciences Association of Canada Conference, Halifax, June 1994.

G. Edwards, "A Simple Model for Bond Portfolio Attribution," *Canadian Investment Review* X, no. 1 (Spring 1997).

C. Guo, "Mapping the Term Structure of Interest Rates into a Three-dimensional Simplex," *Canadian Journal of Administrative Sciences* 14, no. 1 (March 1997).

Y. Tian and B. Warrack, "Testing for Monthly Seasonality in Canadian Government Bond Markets," *Proceedings,* Adminstrative Sciences Association of Canada Conference, St. John's, June 1997.

H. Marmer, M. Den Heyer and B. McInerney, "The Uses of Real Return Bonds," *Canadian Investment Review* X, no. 4 (Winter 1997–1998).

Lawrence Booth, "The Case Against Foreign Bonds," *Canadian Investment Review* XI, no. 2 (Summer 1998).

CHAPTER 16

Common Shares

C ommon shares are easier to describe than fixed-income securities such as bonds, but are harder to analyze. Fixed-income securities almost always have a limited life and an upper dollar limit on cash payments to investors. Common shares have neither. Although the basic principles of valuation apply to both, the role of uncertainty is larger for common shares, so much so that it often dominates all other elements in their valuation.

Common Shares Legal representation of an equity (or ownership) position in a corporation.

Common shares represent equity, or an ownership position, in a corporation. It is a residual claim, in the sense that creditors and preferred shareholders must be paid as scheduled before common shareholders can receive any payments. In bankruptcy, common shareholders are in principle entitled to any value remaining after all other claimants have been satisfied. (However, in practice courts sometimes violate this principle.)

Limited Liability An aspect of the corporate form of organization that prevents common shareholders from losing more than their investment if the corporation should default on its obligation.

The great advantage of the corporate form of organization is the **limited liability** of its owners. Common shares are generally "fully paid and nonassessable," meaning that common shareholders may lose their initial investment, but no more. That is, if the corporation fails to meet its obligations, the shareholders cannot be forced to give the corporation the funds that are needed to pay off the obligations. However, as a result of such a failure, it is possible that the value of a corporation's shares will be negligible. This will result in the shareholders having lost an amount equal to the price previously paid to buy the shares.

The Corporate Form

Charter (Alternatively, **Certificate of Incorporation**.) A document issued by a government to a corporation that specifies the rights and obligations of the corporation's shareholders.

A corporation exists only when it has been granted a **charter**, or certificate of incorporation, by the federal government or a provincial government. This document specifies the rights and obligations of shareholders. It may be amended with the approval of the shareholders, perhaps by a majority or two-thirds vote, where each share of stock generally entitles its owner to one vote. Both the initial terms of the charter and the terms of any amendment must also be approved by the jurisdiction in which the corporation is chartered.

◗ Share Certificates

The ownership of a firm's shares has typically been represented by a single certificate, with the number of shares held by the particular investor noted on it. Such a share certificate is usually registered, with the name, address, and holdings of the investor included on the corporation's books. Dividend payments, voting material, annual and quarterly reports, and other mailings are then sent directly to the investor, taking into account the size of her holdings.

Transfer Agent A designated agent of a corporation, usually a trust company, that administers the transfer of shares of a corporation's stock between old and new owners.

Registrar A designated agent of a corporation responsible for cancelling and issuing shares of stock in the corporation as these shares are issued or traded.

Proxy A power of attorney that authorizes a designated party to cast all of a shareholder's votes on any matter brought up at the corporation's annual meeting.

Proxy Fight An attempt by dissident shareholders to solicit proxies to vote against corporate incumbents.

Cumulative Voting System In the context of a corporation, a method of voting in which a shareholder is permitted to give any one candidate for the board of directors a maximum number of votes equal to the number of shares owned by that shareholder times the number of directors being elected.

Majority Voting System (Alternatively, **Straight Voting System**.) In the context of a corporation, a method of voting in which a shareholder is permitted to give any one candidate for the board of directors a maximum number of votes equal to the number of shares owned by that shareholder.

Shares of stock held by an investor may be transferred to a new owner with the assistance of either the issuing corporation or, more commonly, its designated **transfer agent**. This agent cancels the old share certificate and issues a new one in its place, made out to the new owner. Frequently a **registrar** will make sure that the cancellation and issuance of certificates has been done properly.

Usually banks and trust companies act as transfer agents and registrars. Many shareholders have chosen to avoid these rather cumbersome procedures. Instead, clearing arrangements (discussed in Chapter 3) are used to substitute computerized records for embossed certificates.

Voting

Since an owner of a share of common stock is one of the owners of a corporation, he is entitled to vote on matters brought up at the corporation's annual meeting and to vote for the corporation's directors. Any owner may attend and vote in person, but most choose instead to vote by **proxy**. That is, the incumbent directors and senior management typically solicit all the shareholders, asking each one to sign a proxy statement. Such a statement is a power of attorney authorizing the designated party listed on the statement to cast all of the investor's votes on any matter brought up at the meeting. Occasionally, desired positions on specific issues may be solicited on the proxy statement. However, most of the time the positions held by the incumbents are made known with the proxy solicitation. Since the majority of votes are generally controlled by the incumbents via proxy statements, the actual voting turns out to be perfunctory, leaving little if any controversy or excitement.[1]

Proxy Fight

Once in a while, however, a **proxy fight** develops. Insurgents from outside the corporation solicit proxies to vote against the incumbents, often in order to effect a takeover of some sort. Shareholders are deluged with literature and appeals for their proxies. The incumbents often win, but the possibility of a loss in such a skirmish tends to curb activities clearly not in the shareholders' best interests.[2]

When proposals are to be voted on, the number of votes given an investor equals the number of shares held. Thus, when a yes or no vote is called for, anyone controlling a majority of the shares can ensure that the outcome he favours will receive a majority of the votes. When directors are to be elected, however, there are two types of voting systems that can be used, one of which does not give a majority owner complete control of the outcome. This type of voting system is known as a **cumulative voting system**, whereas the type of voting system that does allow a majority owner to control the outcome completely is known as a **majority voting system**.

Under both systems, the winners of the election are those candidates who have received the highest vote totals. Thus, if six candidates were running for the three directorships, the three receiving the largest number of votes would be elected.

---

[1]For more information on proxies, see Paul Jessup and Mary Bochnak, "Exercising Your Rights: How to Use Proxy Material," *AAII Journal* 14, no. 9 (October 1992): 8–11.

[2]For an interesting discussion of proxy fights, see David Ikenberry and Josef Lakonishok, "Corporate Governance Through the Proxy Contest: Evidence and Implications," *Journal of Business* 66, no. 3 (July 1993): 405–435. In examining proxy contests that dealt with the election of directors, the authors found that such contests followed a period of below-average performance for both the firm's earnings and share price. If management had its nominees elected, then afterward the firm's performance reverted to average. However, if the dissidents' nominees were elected, then the firm's performance continued its deterioration for another two years, with the deterioration being most acute if the dissidents took control of the board.

Majority Voting System

With both voting systems, a shareholder receives a total number of votes that is equal to the number of directors to be elected times the number of shares owned. However, with the majority voting system, the shareholder may only give any one candidate, as a maximum, a number of votes equal to the number of shares owned. This means that in a situation where three directors are to be elected, a shareholder with 400 shares would have 1200 votes but could give no more than 400 of these votes to any one candidate. Note that if there are a total of 1000 shares outstanding and one shareholder owns (or has proxies for) 501 shares, then she can give 501 votes to each of the three candidates she favours. In doing so, this shareholder will be certain they are elected, regardless of how the remaining 499 shares are voted. The majority shareholder's candidates would each have 501 votes, whereas the *most* any other candidate could receive is 499 votes. Thus, with a majority voting system, a shareholder owning (or controlling with proxies) one share more than 50% can be certain of electing all the candidates she favours.

Cumulative Voting System

The cumulative voting system differs from the majority voting system in that a shareholder can cast his votes in any manner. As a result, a minority shareholder can be certain of having some representation on the board of directors, provided the number of shares owned is sufficiently large. In the previous example, the minority owner of the 400 shares could cast all his 1200 votes for one candidate. Suppose that this owner wanted director A to be elected, but the majority owner of 501 shares wanted candidates B, C, and D to be elected. In this situation, the minority shareholder could give all 1200 votes to A and be certain that A would be one of the three directors elected, regardless of what the majority shareholder does. Now suppose that the majority owner holds the remaining 600 shares; he has 1800 votes. Candidate A, favoured by the minority shareholder, can never come in lower than second place in the vote totals. This is because A will receive 1200 votes, and there is no way that the 1800 votes of the majority shareholder can be cast to give more than one of his favoured candidates a vote total in excess of 1200. Thus, the minority shareholder can be certain that A will be elected, whereas the majority shareholder can be certain that only two of his favourites will be elected.

In general, the formula for determining the minimum number of shares a shareholder must own in order to be able to elect a certain number of candidates under a cumulative voting system is

$$n = \left(\frac{ds}{D+1} \right) + 1 \qquad (16.1)$$

where:

n = the minimum number of shares that must be owned

d = the number of directors the shareholder wants to be certain of electing

s = the number of shares outstanding

D = the number of directors to be elected

Thus, the minimum number of shares a shareholder needs in order to be certain of electing one director when three are to be elected and there are 1000 shares outstanding is $[(1 \times 1000)/(3 + 1)] + 1 = 251$. Since the minority shareholder in the example owned 400 shares, he is certain of being able to elect one director. Note that the minimum number of shares that must be owned in order to be certain of electing two directors is $[(2 \times 1000)/(3 + 1)] + 1 = 501$. The minimum number owned to be certain of electing all three directors is $[(3 \times 1000)/(3 + 1)] + 1 = 751$.

In summary, the cumulative voting system gives minority shareholders the right to have some representation on the board of directors, provided the number of shares owned

Takeover An action by an individual or firm to acquire controlling interest in a corporation.

Tender Offer A form of corporate takeover in which a firm or individual offers to buy some or all of the shares of a target firm at a stated price. This offer is publicly advertised and material describing the bid is mailed to the target's stockholders.

Bidder In the context of a corporate takeover, the firm making a tender offer to the target firm.

Target Firm A firm that is the subject of a takeover attempt.

White Knight Another firm, favourably inclined towards a target firm's current management, that during the process of a hostile takeover of that corporation, agrees to make a better offer to the corporation's shareholders.

Greenmail An offer by the management of a corporation that is the target of a hostile takeover to repurchase its shares from the hostile bidder at an above-market price.

Repurchase Offer An offer by the management of a corporation to buy back some of its own stock.

Pac-Man Defence A strategy used by corporations to ward off hostile takeovers. The targeted company reverses the takeover effort and seeks to acquire the firm making the initial takeover attempt.

is sufficiently large. In contrast, the majority voting system does not give the minority shareholder the right to such representation, even if she owns 49.9% of the shares.

The voting system that a corporation decides to use depends not only on the desires of the corporate founders but also on the jurisdiction in which the firm is incorporated. Under Alberta, British Columbia, Ontario, or federal incorporation, cumulative voting is permitted providing there are specific provisions in the company's articles or bylaws.

Takeovers

Periodically, a firm or a wealthy individual who is convinced that the management of a corporation is not fully exploiting its opportunities will attempt a **takeover**. This is frequently done with a **tender offer** being made by a **bidder** to a **target firm**.[3] Before this offer is announced, a small number of the target firm's shares are usually acquired by the bidder in the open market through the use of brokers (if the firm's shares are traded in Ontario then once 10% of the stock has been acquired, the bidder becomes an "insider" under the Ontario Securities Act and must report all further trades to the Ontario Securities Commission).

Then, in the bidder's quest to acquire a substantial number of the target's shares, the bid is announced to the public. Advertisements to purchase shares are placed in the financial press, and material describing the bid is mailed to the target's shareholders. The bidder generally offers to buy, at a stated price, some or all shares offered ("tendered") by the current shareholders of the target. This buying offer is usually contingent on the tender of a minimum number of shares by the target's shareholders by a fixed date. When the buying offer is first made, the offered price ("tender price") is generally set considerably above the current market price, although the offer itself usually leads to a subsequent price increase.

Management of the target firm frequently responds to tender offers with advertisements, mailings, and the like, urging its shareholders to reject the bidder's offer. Sometimes a **white knight** will be sought: another firm that is favourably inclined towards current management will be invited to make a better offer to the target's shareholders. Another type of response by management is to pay **greenmail** to the bidder, meaning that any shares held by the bidder will be bought by the target firm at an above-market price. Still another type of response is for management of the target firm to issue a tender offer of its own, known as a **repurchase offer**, where the firm offers to buy back some of its own stock. (Occasionally repurchase offers are made by firms that have not received tender offers from outside bidders.) Other types of corporate defences include the **Pac-Man defence**, where the initial target turns around and makes a tender offer for the initial acquirer, the **crown jewel defence**, where the target sells its most attractive assets to make the firm less attractive, and the use of **poison pills**, where the target gives its shareholders certain rights that can be exercised only in the event of a subsequent takeover and that, once exercised, will be extremely onerous to the acquirer.

---

[3]Another form of a takeover is a **merger**. A merger occurs when two firms combine their operations, the result being that only one firm exists. Mergers usually are negotiated by the management of the two firms. Tender offers differ in that the management of the bidder makes a direct appeal to the shareholders of the target firm for their shares. Tender offers also differ in that afterward both firms will still exist, because most tender offers are not for all the shares of the target. **Management buyouts** are a special kind of tender offer, where the current management of the firm uses borrowed funds to buy the company. (Hence they are a type of **leveraged buyout**. LBOs can be executed by anyone, including incumbent management.)

Ownership Versus Control

Much has been written about the effects of the separation of ownership and control of the modern corporation.[4] This separation gives rise to what is known as a principal-agent problem. In particular, shareholders can be viewed as principals who hire management to act as their agents. The agent is to make decisions that maximize shareholder wealth as reflected in the firm's share price. No problem would exist if shareholders could monitor the managers without cost, since the shareholders would then be capable of determining for certain whether or not management had acted in their best interests. However, monitoring is not costless, and complete monitoring of every decision is, practically speaking, impossible.[5] As a result some, but not complete, monitoring is done. This gives management a certain degree of latitude in making decisions and leaves open the possibility that some decisions will be made that are not in the shareholders' best interests.[6] However, the possibility of a proxy fight or tender offer provides at least some check on such decisions.

To align the interests of management with their own, shareholders frequently offer certain incentives to management. An example is the use of stock options. These options are given to certain high-level managers and allow them to purchase a specified number of shares at a stated price (often above the market price when the options are initially issued) by a stated date. This motivates managers to make decisions that will increase the share price of the firm as much as possible. Furthermore, given their relatively long initial lifespan (in comparison with listed options, discussed in Chapter 19), stock options implicitly exert pressure on management to take a long-term view in making decisions.

Shareholders' Equity

Par Value

When a corporation is first chartered, it is authorized to issue up to a stated number of shares of common stock, each of which will often carry a specified **par value**. Legally, a corporation may be precluded from making payments to common shareholders if doing so would reduce the balance sheet value of shareholders' equity below the amount represented by the par value of outstanding stock. For this reason the par value is typically low relative to the price for which the stock is initially sold. Some corporations issue no-par shares (if so, a stated value must be recorded in place of the par value).

When shares are initially sold for more than their par value, the difference may be carried separately on the corporation's books under shareholders' equity. Frequently, the entry is for "capital contributed in excess of par value" or "paid-in capital." The par value of the stock is carried in a separate account, generally entitled "common stock," with the amount equal to the number of shares outstanding times the par value per share (for no-par shares, the stated value).

---

[4]See, for example, Michael C. Jensen and William H. Meckling, "Theory of the Firm: Managerial Behavior, Agency Costs, and Ownership Structure," *Journal of Financial Economics* 3, no. 4 (October 1976): 305–360; Eugene F. Fama, "Agency Problems and the Theory of the Firm," *Journal of Political Economy* 88, no. 2 (April 1980): 288–307; Eugene F. Fama and Michael C. Jensen, "Separation of Ownership and Control," *Journal of Law and Economics* 26 (June 1983): 301–325; Eugene F. Fama and Michael C. Jensen, "Agency Problems and Residual Claims," *Journal of Law and Economics* 26 (June 1983): 327–349; the entire issues of vol. 11 (April 1983) and vol. 20 (January–March 1988) of the *Journal of Financial Economics*; and Michael C. Jensen, "Eclipse of the Public Corporation," *Harvard Business Review* 89, no. 5 (September–October 1989): 61–74.

[5]An example of monitoring is having the firm's financial statements independently audited.

[6]For example, management may decide to procure lavishly furnished offices and an executive jet when the conduct of business suggests that these actions are not merited. Furthermore, management may invest in negative net present value investment projects when the firm has "free cash flow" instead of paying it to the shareholders. See Michael C. Jensen, "Agency Costs of Free Cash Flow, Corporate Finance, and Takeovers," *American Economic Review* 76, no. 2 (May 1986): 323–329.

Book Value

With the passage of time, a corporation will generate income, much of which is paid out to creditors (as interest) and shareholders (as dividends). Any remainder is added to the amount shown as cumulative retained earnings on the corporation's books. The sum of the cumulative retained earnings and other entries (such as "common stock" and "capital contributed in excess of par value") under shareholders' equity equals the **book value of the equity**. The **book value per share** is obtained by dividing the book value of the equity by the number of shares outstanding.

Treasury Shares

Typically, a corporation issues only a part of its authorized stock. Some of the remainder may be specifically reserved for outstanding options, convertible securities, and so on. If a corporation wishes to issue new stock in excess of the amount originally authorized, the charter must be amended. This requires approval by both the chartering jurisdiction and the shareholders.

When a corporation repurchases some of its own shares, either in the open market through the services of a broker or with a tender offer, the shares may be "held in the treasury." Such **treasury shares** do not carry votes or receive dividends and are equivalent economically (though not legally) to unissued shares.

A major US study of over 1300 stock repurchases found that nearly 90% of the repurchases analyzed were executed in the open market, with the remainder being "self-tender offers."[7] Two types of self-tender offers occurred with approximately equal frequency. The first type was a "fixed-price" self-tender offer, where the corporation makes an offer to repurchase a stated number of shares at a set, predetermined price. The second type was a "Dutch-auction" self-tendered offer, where the corporation again makes an offer to repurchase a stated number of shares, but at a price that is determined by inviting existing shareholders to submit offers to sell. The ultimate repurchase price is the lowest offered price at which the previously stated number of shares can be repurchased from those shareholders that have submitted offers.[8]

Figure 16.1 shows the average stock price behaviour surrounding the announcement date for the three types of stock repurchases just mentioned. For each repurchase, the stock's "abnormal" return was determined by relating daily returns on the stock to the corresponding returns on the stock market index. This was done for the 50-day period immediately prior to the repurchase announcement and the 50-day period immediately following it. These abnormal returns were averaged across firms for each day relative to the announcement and then cumulated across time. The figure shows that open-market repurchases are typically made after the stock price has had an abnormal decline. However, fixed-price and Dutch-auction repurchases are made after a period of fairly normal returns. Also of interest is the observation that the stock price jumped upward on the announcement of the repurchase offer for all three types. (The average size of the abnormal return on the announcement date was 11% for fixed-price, 8% for Dutch-auction, and 2% for open-market repurchases.) Finally, after the repurchase offer expired, the stock price did not tend to fall back to its preannouncement level.

Interestingly, two other studies found that investors could form profitable investment strategies to take advantage of the observed abnormal return associated with the announce-

Book Value of the Equity The sum of the cumulative retained earnings and other balance sheet entries classified under shareholders' equity such as common stock and capital contributed in excess of par value.

Book Value per Share A corporation's book value of the equity divided by the number of its common shares outstanding.

Treasury Shares Common shares that have been issued by a corporation and then later purchased by the corporation in the open market or through a tender offer. These shares do not include voting rights or rights to receive dividends and are equivalent economically to unissued stock.

---

[7] Robert Comment and Gregg A. Jarrell, "The Relative Signalling Power of Dutch-auction and Fixed-price Self-tender Offers and Open-market Share Repurchases," *Journal of Finance* 46, no. 4 (September 1991): 1243–1271.

[8] It should be noted that formerly there were similar numbers of fixed-price and Dutch-auction tender offers, however, the Dutch-auction method is becoming increasingly popular, particularly among larger corporations.

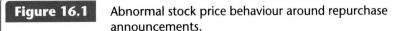

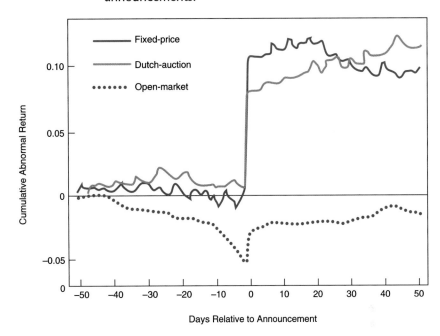

Figure 16.1 Abnormal stock price behaviour around repurchase announcements.

SOURCE: Robert Comment and Gregg A. Jarrell, "The Relative Signalling Power of Dutch-auction and Fixed-price Self-tender Offers and Open-market Share Repurchases," *Journal of Finance* 46, no. 4 (September 1991): 1254.

Council of Institutional Investors
www.ciicentral.com

ment of a share repurchase.[9] Specifically, the strategy involves fixed-price self-tender offers where the shares are purchased by the investor in the open market shortly before the offer's expiration date if it is selling at least 3% below the repurchase price. Then the investor tenders the shares to the firm on the expiration date. If the repurchase is oversubscribed (meaning that more shares are submitted for repurchase than the corporation has indicated it will buy), then the number of shares that the corporation does not buy are sold in the marketplace shortly after the expiration date. The result is that for an investment of less than a week, this strategy will generate an abnormal return of more than 9%.

In the second study, investors who bought shares of a firm's stock upon hearing of the firm's announcement of an open-market repurchase program would have made an abnormal return of about 12% over the next three years (or 4% per year). Furthermore, if these investors limited their purchases to those firms that had low book-value-to-market-value ratios, the abnormal returns were even higher, being about 45% over three years (or about 15% per year)[10] Clearly, both of these studies have uncovered investment strategies that appear to be inconsistent with the notion of efficient markets.

Why do firms repurchase their shares? Previously it was mentioned that one motive was to repel a takeover attempt. Two other explanations have been offered. First, management may be attempting to send a signal to the shareholders (and the public) that the corporation's stock is undervalued in the marketplace. Second, it may provide the current

---

[9]See Josef Lakonishok and Theo Vermaelen, "Anomalous Price Behavior Around Repurchase Tender Offers," *Journal of Finance* 45, no. 2 (June 1990): 455–477.

[10]See David Ikenbery, Josef Lakonishok, and Theo Vermaelen, "Market Underreaction to Open Market Share Repurchases," *Journal of Financial Economics* 29, nos. 2 and 3 (October–November): 181–208.

Corporate Governance

Conflicts between corporate managements and institutional shareholders first surfaced as a major public policy issue in the 1980s. The potentially adversarial principal-agent relationship between corporate owners and managers has long been recognized. In the last decade, however, two major developments brought this issue to greater prominence.

First, corporate managements, responding to a wave of hostile corporate takeovers, instituted various defensive strategies such as poison pill provisions, the sale of key corporate assets, and staggered board of directors' terms. These defences were designed to prevent the target companies from being acquired easily, thereby protecting the jobs of existing management. Indeed, they appear to have had the intended result of making hostile takeovers more difficult. However, to the extent that they entrench inefficient corporate managements, the defences also may have reduced the value of the companies to their existing shareholders.

In Canada the situation described above is exacerbated by the existence of many companies with a dominant shareholder or shareholders and the introduction of dual classes of shares with differential voting rights. In both of these cases the minority shareholders or those with restricted voting rights are at the mercy of the control group. On at least one occasion the Ontario Securities Commission has chosen to intervene to disallow the egregious abuse of the non-voting shareholders by the voting shareholders.[11]

Second, institutional shareholders now wield considerable corporate voting power. The growth of institutional investors has concentrated corporate ownership in the hands of a relatively few organizations. (See *Institutional Issues: Institutional Investors* in Chapter 1.) The resources of these large organizations enabled them to actively oppose management decisions that diminished the value of their investments. *Corporate governance,* a particularly bureau-cratic-sounding term, has become the catchall description for institutional investor efforts to influence the fundamental relationships between corporate managements and their shareholders.

Until recently, the attitude of most company managements towards shareholders was simply, "If you don't like the way we run the company, then sell our stock and quit complaining." Institutional investors, however, came to realize that they had nowhere else to go. For example, they place hundreds of billions of dollars in *indexed* portfolios designed to track the US stock market (see Chapter 23). As a result, they effectively hold permanent positions in all large US corporations. Corporate governance (or "shareholder rights") activities expressed institutional investors' desires to stand and fight for their financial interest.

In both Canada and the US pension funds are the leading shareholder rights proponents. Their activism can be traced to the early and mid-1980s, when many of them sponsored shareholder resolutions that urged corporations to end their involvement in South Africa. Although none of those resolutions passed, their mere introduction embarrassed the confronted corporate managements. Many prominent US companies voluntarily sold their South African business investments or considerably lowered their profile in the country.

The organizational lessons acquired in this South African "divestment" debate proved valuable when the battle against corporate takeover defences began soon after. In 1984 several public pension funds, along with various union pension funds, formed the Council of Institutional investors (CII). The goal of the CII is to provide a forum for Institutional investors to discuss and organize efforts to encourage enlightened shareholder rights policies by corporate managements. Although the CII is still dominated by public and union pension funds, several large corporate pension funds have joined. Today the CII has

---

[11]For an extensive discussion of the issues associated with corporate governance in Canada see Ronald J. Daniels and Randall Mørck (eds.), *Corporate Decision Making in Canada* (Calgary: University of Calgary Press, 1995) and Jeffrey MacIntosh, "If It Ain't Broke ... ," *Canadian Investment Review* VII, no. 4 (Winter 1994–1995).

over 100 members who, in total, control more than $1 trillion in assets.

The CII and other shareholder rights organizations have become forces to be reckoned with on corporate governance issues. Shareholder victories have begun to mount. In the early 1990s, under pressure from institutional investors, chief executives from such large organizations as General Motors, American Express, and Westinghouse were ousted. IBM restructured its board of directors to give more power to outsiders. Sears revamped its business strategy, eliminating unprofitable operations. To date no organization similar to the CII has been formed in Canada.

Many large corporations have come to see the handwriting on the wall and have moved to negotiate directly with their large institutional shareholders. Although direct victories by institutional investors in proxy battles remain rare, shareholder rights proponents are increasingly accomplishing their objectives away from the publicity of annual meetings. The mere threat of introducing corporate governance proposals at a company's annual meeting now often is sufficient to force concessions from corporate management. In several cases, institutional investors have produced target lists of poorly performing companies and focused their reform efforts on those companies.

Interestingly, the motives of institutional shareholders in the corporate governance debate are not always clear-cut. For example, public pension funds may be sensitive to political pressures to support companies domiciled in their states or localities, regardless of the companies' shareholder rights records. Managers of corporate pension funds may wish to avoid opposing other corporations' shareholder rights practices for fear that their own companies may face similar pressures some day. Insurance companies and mutual funds, newcomers

to the corporate governance debate, may be directly employed by the companies whose shareholder policies they might oppose.

Given these potentially conflicting motivations, it is perhaps surprising that the shareholder rights movement has achieved its current prominence. Actions on the part of the federal government seem likely to ensure that the debate continues. In 1992 the Securities and Exchange Commission issued regulations making it easier for institutional investors to communicate with one another to enlist support for various shareholder proposals. Also in 1992 the US Department of Labor strongly reaffirmed an early ruling that a pension fund's proxy votes are a plan asset and must be managed accordingly. Congress, on occasion, has considered legislation formalizing certain shareholder rights, although no such action is currently pending.

Institutional investors have been encouraged enough by their successes to take their corporate governance proposals abroad. They have begun to challenge corporate practices that disenfranchise shareholders and protect managements in Canada, Europe, and Japan. Further, in the United States, while shareholder rights activists still oppose blatantly antishareholder takeover defences, they have begun to focus their attention on subtler issues, such as executive compensation, independent boards of directors, and secret balloting in proxy fights. The future may see debates moving to such nonshareholder issues as product liability, health care, and the environment. To what extent institutional investors should involve themselves with corporate business decision making remains a hotly contested subject, as is the issue of whether such activities actually enhance shareholder value. One thing is certain, however: Corporate managements will never again be able to run their businesses oblivious to the wishes of their largest shareholders.

shareholders with a tax benefit for the firm to use excess cash to repurchase shares instead of using it to pay a cash dividend.

For example, consider a shareholder who bought 10 shares of stock at $40 per share that are now worth $50 per share, resulting in an unrealized capital gain of $10 per share, or $100 in total. Furthermore, the shareholder could receive a $10 per share cash dividend from the firm as part of a general disbursement of excess cash. As a result, the stock price will drop $10 per share, removing the capital gain, but all of this dividend will be treated as taxable income (subject to the dividend tax credit) to the shareholder. Alternatively, the corporation could spend the same amount to repurchase its shares. If the shareholder tenders her *pro rata* share, then the investor will receive $100 for two shares of stock (= $100 cash dividend/$50 share price, assuming perfect markets) and have to pay capital gains on only the amount of $100 that exceeds the 2 shares × $40 = $80 cost of the two shares that were repurchased. Hence the shareholder would have to pay capital gains taxes on only $20 or the $100 at that time but would have unrealized capital gains of $10 per share on the eight shares still owned (as the stock price would remain at $50 per share), upon which capital gains taxes will have to be paid at some later date when they are sold. Thus, the shareholder benefits from a repurchase in that a *smaller* amount is taxed at the capital gains tax rate.

Restricted Shares

Restricted Shares Equity shares whose voting rights are in some way diminished or curtailed. Restricted voting shares each carry the requisite number of votes per share but the shareholder is not permitted to vote the full number of shares he or she owns. Subordinate voting shares are those with fewer votes per share than regular common shares and non-voting shares are those with no voting rights.

Some corporations issue two or more classes of common shares, one or more of which may be restricted. **Restricted shares** are defined under the Ontario Securities Act as equity shares that are not common shares. Equity shares, in turn, are defined as shares of a company that carry a residual right to participate to an unlimited degree in the earnings of the issuing corporation and in its assets upon liquidation. The important feature of this definition is the fact that they participate in the earnings and assets. Common shares are those with unrestricted voting rights per share that are not less than the voting rights of any other outstanding issue.

The Act goes on to recognize three types of restricted shares:

i. Restricted voting shares are those that carry a right to vote that is subject to some restriction on the number or percentage of shares that may be voted by the owner.
ii. Subordinate voting shares are those that carry a right to vote, where there is another class of shares outstanding that carry a greater right to vote.
iii. Non-voting shares are those that carry no right to vote (or a right to vote in certain limited circumstances).

Subordinate and non-voting shares frequently have a preferred position over the voting shares in regard to dividends (and sometimes in liquidation). These shares are unlike preferred shares in that they participate in the earnings of the corporation and do not have a prescribed dividend.

At the end of August 1998, there were 144 issues listed on the Toronto Stock Exchange that involved restricted shares. Of these, 79 were subordinate voting, 52 were non-voting, 12 were restricted or limited voting, and one was not classified. Ownership of Canadian corporations is closely held, so the issuance of restricted or non-voting shares is seen as a means of raising additional equity capital without diluting control. Their existence has raised concerns that concentrated voting power with a low investment in the corporation could lead to abuse of other shareholders by the owners of the control block(s). One area of particular concern has been the distribution of the control premium in the event of a takeover. In the absence of any specific provisions, a potential acquirer need only negotiate with the holders of voting or superior voting shares, ignoring the other shareholders. Following considerable controversy, most issuers of restricted voting shares have incorporated *coattail* provisions in their bylaws to allow the holders of restricted voting shares to participate in the takeover premium.

A typical example of subordinate voting shares is Ivaco Inc., which has 22.0 million Class A shares that are entitled to one vote each and 6.7 million Class B shares entitled to 10 votes each. The Class A shares will receive 120% of the dividend declared on Class B shares and are protected against any subdivision or consolidation (but not stock dividends). The coattail provision described in the 1990 *Annual Report* reads as follows:

> In the event an offer is made to holders of Class B shares and a similar offer is not made to Class A shareholders then each Class A share will, for the purposes of such an offer only, be deemed to have been converted to Class B shares in order that the Class A shares will be treated equally with the Class B shares.

In Ivaco's case the Ivanier family plus the company's officers and directors hold over 60% of the votes primarily through holdings of Class B shares. Furthermore, the Class B shares may be freely converted into Class A shares on a one-for-one basis. Absolute control of Ivaco can be secured by owning 4.5 million Class B shares or about 15.5% of the total equity.[12]

The valuation of restricted voting shares presents some interesting challenges given the existence of dividend preferences and coattail provisions. Considerable research has been undertaken that indicates that the value of a vote is worth between 1% and 16% of the equity value. The value of a vote is manifested in a premium paid for the voting over the non-voting or restricted voting shares. This voting premium, however, is sometimes obscured by the effect of the dividend preference. In the case of Ivaco, for example, the Class A shares closed at $3.75 and the Class B at $5.00 on August 31, 1998. On the face of it there appears to be a large voting premium. It should be noted that the Class B voting shares trade very infrequently, as a result the recorded price was probably established several days before the month-end. It is likely, therefore, that the apparent premium overstates the "true" premium. Robinson and White estimated that the expected net present value of the dividend difference is larger than the price difference; therefore, the existence of a premium cannot be ruled out.[13]

Split Common Shares

The principle behind the structure of these securities is quite simple but the details can be complicated.

An underwriter floats a new investment corporation and issues two types of securities: *capital shares* and *preferred shares*. The proceeds from the sale of these securities are used to purchase the shares of a large and creditworthy company (such as BCE, Inc.) or group of companies, such as telecommunications firms. The investment corporation is designed to be unwound or liquidated at the end of a specified period, either 5 years or 10 years.

Generally, the owner of the preferred shares is entitled to the cash dividends (less a management fee) that the underlying company pays to the underwriter and the owner of the capital shares is entitled to the price appreciation on the underlying shares at liquidation. The two securities are priced such that the dividend yield on the preferred shares is higher than that of the underlying shares and the capital shares can expect to receive an enhanced capital gain (if any). Both of these securities are listed on the Toronto Stock Exchange and can be freely bought or sold through a broker. The company that issues the

---

[12]Ivaco is not an extreme example; absolute control of Canadian Tire Corporation can be secured with ownership of about 2.1% of the equity.

[13]C. Robinson and A. White, "Empirical Evidence on the Relative Valuation of Voting and Restricted Voting Shares," *Canadian Journal of Administrative Sciences* 7, no. 4 (December 1990): 9–18. For a summary of the issues and a comprehensive literature review, see E. Maynes, C. Robinson, and A. White, "How Much Is a Share Vote Worth?" *Canadian Investment Review* III, no. 1 (Spring 1990): 49–55. It is worth noting that on August 31, 1998, the Canadian Tire voting shares closed at $31.00 while the non-voting shares closed at $30.70. Both classes of shares trade regularly on the TSE.

underlying shares has nothing to do with either the creation or subsequent trading of the derivative securities.

The complications arise because dividend increases subsequent to issuance of the derivative can be either attributed to the preference shares or to the capital shares or retained by the underwriter. In addition, there may be retraction privileges assigned to the capital shares and the preferred shares may be subject to redemption by the underwriter. Any prospective investor in split common shares should read the prospectus with care to determine the precise terms and conditions attached to each type of share offered.

A specific example involves BCE, Inc. The corporation is known as B Split with the preferred shares listed as BST.PR.A and the capital shares as BST. On September 29, 1998, when the underlying BCE, Inc. shares closed at $43.90 per share the preferred closed at $25.00 and the capital shares at $19.30. As the redemption price of the preferred is $25.00 it is unlikely that their price will fall much below this value; therefore, the full effect of any changes in the price of the underlying BCE shares will be experienced by the capital shares.

Cash Dividends

Dividends Cash payments made to shareholders by the corporation.

Date of Record The date, established quarterly by a corporation's board of directors, on which the shareholders of record are determined for the purpose of paying a cash or stock dividend.

Ex-dividend Date The date on which ownership of stock is determined for purposes of paying dividends. Owners purchasing shares before the ex-dividend date receive the dividend in question. Owners purchasing shares on or after the ex-dividend date are not entitled to the dividend.

Payments made in cash to shareholders are termed **dividends**. These are typically declared quarterly by the board of directors and paid to the shareholders of record at a date, known as the **date of record**, specified by the board. The dividends may be of almost any size, subject to certain restrictions contained in the charter or in documents given to creditors. Dividends may even be larger than the current earnings of the corporation, although this is unusual. (If so, they are usually paid out of past earnings.)

Compiling a list of shareholders to receive the dividend is not as simple as it may initially seem, since for many firms the list changes almost constantly as shares are bought and sold. The way of identifying those shareholders who are to receive the dividend is by use of an **ex-dividend date**. Because settlement must be made three business days after the transaction, major stock exchanges specify an ex-dividend date that is two business days before the date of record. Shares purchased before an ex-dividend date are entitled to receive the dividend in question; those purchased on or after the ex-dividend date are not entitled to the dividend.

For example, a dividend may be declared on April 15 with a date of record of Friday, May 15. In this situation Wednesday, May 13, is the ex-dividend date. If an investor bought shares on Friday, May 8, he would subsequently receive the cash dividend (unless the shares were sold later in the day on the 8th). However, if the shares were bought on Wednesday, May 13, the investor would not receive the cash dividend. Besides a declaration date (April 15), an ex-dividend date (May 13), and a date-of-record (May 15), there is also a fourth date, the payment date. On this date (perhaps May 25) the cheques for the cash dividends are put in the mail or the funds are deposited electronically in the custodian's account.

Summarizing the example:

April 15 →	May 13 →	May 15 →	May 25
Declaration Date	Ex-dividend Date	Date of Record	Payment Date

Stock Dividends and Stock Splits

Occasionally, the board of directors decides to forgo a cash dividend and declares a **stock dividend** instead. For example, if a 5% stock dividend is declared, the owner of 100 shares receives five additional shares issued for this occasion. The accounting treatment of a stock dividend is to increase the "common stock" and "capital contributed in excess of par" accounts by an amount equal to the market value of the stock at the time of the dividend times the number of new shares issued (the "common stock" account would increase by an amount equal to the par value times the number of new shares; the remainder of the increase would go into the "capital contributed in excess of par" account). In order to keep the total book value of shareholders' equity the same, the "retained earnings" account is reduced by a equivalent amount.

A **stock split** is similar to a stock dividend in that the shareholder owns more shares afterward. However, it differs in both magnitude and accounting treatment. With a stock split, all the old shares are destroyed and new ones are issued with a new par value; afterward, the number of new shares outstanding is usually larger than the previous number of old shares by 25% or more, with the exact amount depending on the size of the split. In contrast, a stock dividend usually results in an increase of less than 25%. While a stock dividend results in adjustments to the dollar figures in certain shareholders' equity accounts, no adjustments are made for a split. For example, if a stock with par value $1 is split 2-for-1, the holder of 200 old shares will receive 400 new shares with par value $0.50, and none of the dollar figures in shareholders' equity would change.

A **reverse stock split** or consolidation reduces the number of shares and increases the par value per share. For example, in a reverse 2-for-1 split, the holder of 200 shares with par value $1 would exchange them for 100 shares with par value $2. Again, there would not be any change in the dollar figures in shareholders' equity.

Stock dividends and splits must be taken into account when following the price of a company's shares. For example, a fall in price per share may be due solely to a large stock dividend. To reduce confusion, most financial services provide data adjusted for at least some of these changes. Thus, if a stock split 2-for-1 on a particular date, prices prior to that date might be divided by two to facilitate comparison.

Ex-distribution Dates

Similar to the payment of cash dividends, the corporation specifies three dates associated with either stock dividends or stock splits: a declaration date, a date of record, and a payment date. However, there is now an **ex-distribution date** instead of an ex-dividend date. For stock dividends, the procedure is identical to the one described previously for cash dividends—the ex-distribution date is two business days before the date of record, meaning that if you buy the stock after that date, you do not get the additional shares.

For stock splits, the procedure is a bit different in that the ex-distribution date is usually the business day after the payment date (which, in turn, is after the date of record). Hence, if a stock split is declared on April 15 with a date of record of May 15 and a payment date of May 25, then anyone buying before May 26 will receive the additional shares. However, those who wait until May 26 to buy will not receive the additional shares.[14]

Reasons for Stock Dividends and Splits

Why do corporations issue stock dividends and split their stocks? Nothing of importance would appear to be changed, since such actions do not increase revenues or reduce expenses. All that changes is the size of the units in which ownership may be bought and sold. Moreover, since the process involves administrative effort and costs something to execute, one wonders why it is done.

---

[14]For more on "ex-dates," see "Dividends and Interest: Who Gets Payments After a Trade?" *AAII Journal* 12, no. 4 (April 1990): 8–11.

It is sometimes argued that shareholders respond positively to "tangible" evidence of the growth of their corporation. Another view holds that splits and stock dividends, by decreasing the price per share, may bring the stock's price into a more desirable trading range and hence, by increasing the liquidity of the stock and subsequently its price, increase the total value of the amount outstanding. A related view is that there is a desirable trading range for the stock that is based on the minimum tick size that is allowed (currently 1/16 for all stocks priced over $1 in the US). This is because lower prices result in larger spreads relative to the stock's price, thereby benefiting brokers and dealers but costing investors.[15] Figure 16.2 presents the average behaviour of stock returns for 1275 2-for-1 stock splits that occurred between 1975 and 1990.[16] For each split, the stock's "abnormal" return was determined by relating monthly returns on the stock to the corresponding returns in the stock market. This was done for (1) the 12-month period before the split announcement month; (2) the five-day period running from two days before to two days after the split announcement; and (3) the three years after the split announcement. These abnormal returns were first averaged across firms for each day relative to the announcement of the firm's split and then cumulated across time.

As the figure shows, the stocks tended to have a positive abnormal return of about 54% during the year prior to announcement of the split. Thus, it appears that unexpected positive developments (such as unexpected large increases in earnings) caused abnormal increases in the stock prices of these firms, after which the firms decided to split their stock. The announcement of the stock split appears to have triggered a boost in the firm's stock, as it had an abnormal increase of a bit over 3% in the period from two days before to two days after the announcement. The behaviour of the post-split prices indicates that over the following year investors continued to receive significantly positive abnormal returns amounting to about 8%, and that thereafter no notable returns occurred.[17] Apparently the prices of firms whose stocks split did rise, but they did not rise to an equilibrium level on the announcement date. Such an underreaction to the announcement of a stock split can be interpreted as evidence of a market inefficiency. However, it should be noted that other studies, using different stocks and time periods, found either slightly negative abnormal returns, no abnormal returns, or slightly positive abnormal returns after the split.[18]

A comparable Canadian study of 177 stock splits that occurred between 1963 and 1975 shows a similar but not identical pattern of abnormal returns. A disturbing feature of this study, however, is the finding that the maximum abnormal return is recorded about six months *after* the announcement, as shown in Figure 16.3. A further study of 241 stock splits recorded between 1977 and 1985 using weekly data produced results closer to Figure

[15]Some evidence in support of the optimal trading explanation is provided by Josef Lakonishok and Baruch Lev, "Stock Splits and Stock Dividends: Why, Who, and When," *Journal of Finance* 42, no. 4 (September 1987): 913–932. The tick size explanation has been put forth by James J. Angel in "Tick Size, Share Prices, and Stock Splits," *Journal of Finance* 52, no. 2 (June 1997): 655–681 and "Picking Your Tick: Toward a New Theory of Stock Splits," *Journal of Applied Corporate Finance* 10, no. 3 (Fall 1997): 59–68.

[16]David Ikenberry, Graeme Rankine, and Earl K. Stice, "What Do Stock Splits Really Signal?" *Journal of Financial and Quantitative Analysis* 10, no. 3 (September 1996): 357–375.

[17]Interestingly, a study of reverse stock splits found that for the typical firm (1) the stock had average performance before the announcement, (2) the announcement was associated with an abnormal return of about –6%, and (3) the stock continued to perform somewhat poorly after the announcement. See J. Randall Woolridge and Donald R. Chambers, "Reverse Splits and Shareholder Wealth," *Financial Management* 12, no. 4 (Autumn 1983): 5–15.

[18]See Eugene F. Fama, Lawrence Fisher, Michael C. Jensen, and Richard Roll, "The Adjustment of Stock Prices to New Information," *International Economic Review* 10, no. 1 (February 1969): 1–21: Sasson Bar-Josef and Lawrence D. Brown, "A Re-examination of Stock Splits Using Moving Betas," *Journal of Finance* 32, no. 4 (September 1977): 1069–1080; and Guy Charest, "Split Information, Stock Returns, and Market Efficiency—I," *Journal of Financial Economics* 6, no. 2–3 (June–September 1978): 265–296.

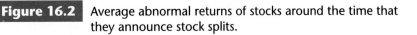

Figure 16.2 Average abnormal returns of stocks around the time that they announce stock splits.

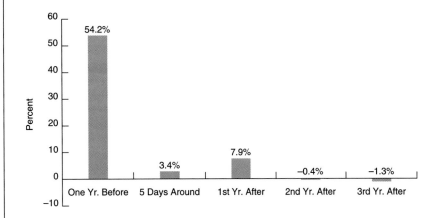

SOURCE: Adapted from David Ikenberry, Graeme Rankine, and Earl K. Stice, "What Do Stock Splits Really Signal?" *Journal of Financial and Quantitative Analysis* 31, no. 3 (September 1996): 360, 362, 367.

16.2, with the maximum abnormal return occurring at week minus one.[19] The overall effect of stock splits in Canadian markets is an unresolved issue.

US evidence also suggests that rather than *decreasing* transaction costs, stock splits actually *increased* them. A study of pre-split and post-split behaviour showed that after splits, trading volume rose less than proportionately, and both commission costs and bid-ask spreads, expressed as a percentage of value, increased—hardly reactions that are favourable to shareholders.[20] For example, after a 2-for-1 stock split, there will be twice as many shares outstanding, so it is reasonable to expect the daily number of shares that are traded to double and also to expect the commission for buying 200 shares after the split to be the same as the commission for buying 100 shares before the split. Instead, it was found that after the split the number of shares traded daily was less than twice as large and the commission was larger.

Another study of stock splits and stock dividends uncovered an apparent market inefficiency.[21] This study examined the performance of stocks around the "ex" dates associated with their stock splits and dividends. If an investor bought shares of a firm the day before its ex date and sold them the day after the ex date, then on average the investor would make an abnormal return of roughly 2% for stock dividends and 1% for stock splits. Such an observance appears to violate the notion of efficient markets because it suggests that an investor can make abnormal returns by trading stocks using a simple strategy based on publicly available information.

---

[19]See Guy Charest, "Returns to Splitting Stocks on the Toronto Stock Exchange," *Journal of Business Administration* 12, no. 1 (Fall 1980): 19–37; Halim Bishara, "Stock Splits, Stock Returns, and Trading Benefits on Canadian Stock Markets," *Akron Business and Economic Review* 19, no. 3 (Fall 1988): 57–65.

[20]See Thomas E. Copeland, "Liquidity Changes Following Stock Splits," *Journal of Finance* 34, no. 1 (March 1979): 115–141; and Robert M. Conroy, Robert S. Harris, and Bruce A. Benet, "The Effects of Stock Splits on Bid-ask Spreads," *Journal of Finance* 45, no. 4 (September 1990): 1285–1295.

[21]Mark S. Grinblatt, Ronald W. Masulis, and Sheridan Titman, "The Valuation Effects of Stock Splits and Stock Dividends," *Journal of Financial Economics* 13, no. 4 (December 1984): 461–490.

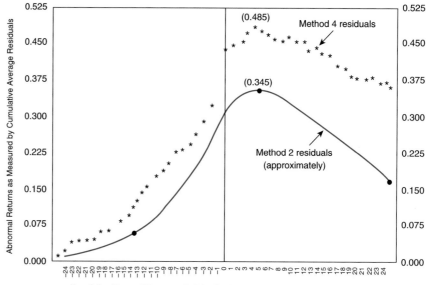

Figure 16.3 Cumulative abnormal returns to splitting stocks on the Toronto Stock Exchange, 1963–1975.

Cumulative Abnormal Returns to Splitting Stocks on the TSE (1963–1975, Methods 2 and 4)

Note: This study uses four different methods for computing abnormal returns that give different absolute values, but the shapes of the curves are similar. The results for Methods 2 and 4 only are reported.

SOURCE: G. Charest, "Returns to Splitting Stocks on the Toronto Stock Exchange," *Journal of Business Administration* 12, no. 1 (Fall 1980): 28.

Preemptive Rights

Preemptive Rights When a corporation plans an issuance of new common shares, the right of existing shareholders to purchase the new shares in proportion to the numbers of shares that they currently own.

Under common law (and most provincial laws), a shareholder has an inherent right to maintain his or her proportionate ownership of the corporation. The existence of these **preemptive rights** means that when new shares are to be sold, the current shareholders must be given the right of first refusal in regard to the purchase of the shares.[22] This is accomplished by issuing a certificate to each shareholder that indicates the number of new shares he is authorized to purchase. This number will be proportional to the number of existing shares currently owned by the shareholder. Usually, the new shares will be priced below the current market price of the stock, making such *rights* valuable. The shareholder can exercise the rights by purchasing his allotted amount of new shares, thereby maintaining his proportional ownership in the firm, but at the cost of providing additional capital. Alternatively, the rights can be sold to someone else.[23]

Oversubscription Privilege The opportunity given shareholders who have exercised their rights in a rights offering to buy shares that were not purchased in the offering.

---

[22]Current shareholders may not be given this right if there is a provision in the charter denying it or if it is denied by the shareholders at the annual meeting.

[23]The investor could simply let the rights expire, causing that investor's proportion in the corporation to decline as others are given ownership in the expanded firm in return for the provision of new capital. Sometimes there is an **oversubscription privilege** given to the subscribing shareholders. This means that those shareholders who have exercised their rights will be given an opportunity to buy the shares that were not purchased.

For example, if a firm needs $10 000 000 for new equipment, it may decide to sell new shares in order to raise the capital. Given that the current market price of the stock is $60 per share, a *rights offering* may be used to raise the capital, in which the **subscription price** is set at $50 per share.[24] Accordingly, $10 000 000/$50 = 200 000 new shares are to be sold. Assuming the firm has 4 000 000 shares outstanding, this means that the owner of one share will receive the right to buy 200 000/4 000 000 = 1/20 of a new share. Since the number of rights received is equal to the number of shares owned, 20 shares must be owned in order to be able to buy one new share. Thus, if a shareholder owns 100 shares, he will receive 100 rights, allowing him to buy $(1/20) \times 100 = 5$ new shares. These rights are valuable because the owner of them can buy stock at $50 a share when the market price is significantly higher. The current owner of 100 shares can either use the 100 rights by coming up with cash equal to $5 \times \$50 = \$250$ or sell the 100 rights to someone else. But this raises a question: what is a fair price for the rights?

Subscription Price The price at which holders of rights are permitted to purchase shares of stock in a rights offering.

Rights are distributed in a manner similar to cash dividends. That is, there is a date of record and, two business days earlier, an **ex-rights date**. Before the ex-rights date, the value of a right can be calculated by using the following equation:

$$C_o - (RN + S) = R \qquad (16.2)$$

where:

Ex-rights Date The date on which ownership of stock is determined for purposes of granting rights to purchase new stock in a rights offering. Owners purchasing shares before the ex-rights date receive the rights in question. Owners purchasing shares on or after the ex-rights date are not entitled to the rights.

C_o is the "rights-on" market price of the stock
R is the value of a right
N is the number of rights needed to buy one share
S is the subscription price

This equation can be interpreted in the following manner. If an investor purchases one share before the ex-rights date, by definition she pays the market price of C_o, shown on the left-hand side of the equation. Alternatively, the investor could purchase the number of rights necessary to buy one share of the new stock at a cost of RN and set aside an amount of money equal to the subscription price S. The total cost of doing this is $RN + S$. The only difference between the two alternatives is that the first one gives the investor not only one share of stock but also one right. Thus, the difference in the cost of the two alternatives, $C_o - (RN + S)$, must equal the value of a right, R, as shown in equation (16.2).

Equation (16.2) can be rewritten as

$$R = \frac{C_o - S}{N + 1} \qquad (16.3)$$

Thus, in the previous example, the value of a right when a share is selling for $60 would be equal to approximately ($60 − $50)/(20 + 1) = $.48.

On or after the ex-rights date, the value of a right can be calculated by using the following equation:

$$C_e - (RN + S) = 0 \qquad (16.4)$$

where C_e is the ex-rights market price of a share. The reasoning behind this equation is similar to the reasoning behind equation (16.2). That is, an investor can purchase one share by either buying it in the open market at a cost of C_e or by purchasing the requisite number of rights and setting aside the subscription price, for a total cost of $RN + S$. Since the purchase of one share ex-rights means the investor does not receive a right, the two alternatives provide the investor with the same item. Thus, the cost of these two alternatives should be equivalent, so the difference in their cost should be zero.

---

[24]The subscription price is usually set at roughly 80% of the current market price of the stock.

Equation (16.4) can be rewritten as

$$R = \frac{C_e - S}{N} \qquad (16.5)$$

In the previous example, if a share is selling for $56 after the ex-rights date, then the value of a right at that time would be approximately ($56 − $50)/20 = $.30.

Share Price Quotations

Figures 16.4, 16.5, and 16.6 provide examples of quotations summarizing a day's transactions in stocks traded over the counter, on the TSE, and on foreign exchanges respectively.

Active stocks that traded on the previous day, reported by the Canadian Dealing Network, Inc., are shown in the top section of Figure 16.4. After the security's name, the trading volume, highest, lowest, and closing prices recorded the previous day are shown together with the change in price from the prior trading day. Bid and asked offers for issues that traded in the past five days are shown in the bottom section of Figure 16.4 following the security's name.

Regular activity in shares traded on the Toronto Stock Exchange, reported daily (except Mondays), is shown in Figure 16.5. The accompanying instructions in the table, entitled *How to Read the Stock Tables*, describe the information that is provided. The Saturday report presents the same information but includes a weekly summary.

The Financial Post also provides share price quotations for companies listed on the Montreal and Vancouver exchanges in Canada, the New York and other US stock exchanges, as well as on NASDAQ.

International Stock Exchanges

Figure 16.6 displays the trading activities in various foreign stock markets. The complete table shows the trading activities in the major European markets, the major Mexican market (Mexico City), Chile, Australia, and South Africa, as well as closing values for a wide range of international indices. The prices shown in the figure are stated in the local currency of the country in which the exchange is located.

Ex Ante and *Ex Post* Values

Ex Ante Before the fact; future.

Ex Post After the fact; historical.

Equilibrium theories such as the Capital Asset Pricing Model and Arbitrage Pricing Theory imply that in the opinion of well-informed investors, securities with certain attributes will, other things being equal, have large expected returns, whereas those with other attributes will have small expected returns. Thus, the focus of these theories is on future, or *ex ante* (Latin for "before the fact"), expected returns. However, only historical, or *ex post* (Latin for "after the fact"), returns are observed. These historical returns are undoubtedly different from the expected returns, making it extremely difficult to tell whether security attributes and expected returns do, in fact, go together in the manner implied by either the CAPM or APT. Moreover, such theories are relatively silent concerning simple ways in which a security's future, or *ex ante*, attributes and expected returns might be estimated by examining historical, or *ex post*, returns.

To bridge this gap, a number of investigators have used the average historical return of a security as an estimate of its expected return. This requires an assumption that the expected return did not change over some arbitrary time period and that this time period contains a sufficient number of historical returns to make a reasonably accurate estimate of the expected return. However, expectations almost certainly would have changed over the

Figure 16.4 Summary of shares quoted on the CDN.

CDN Unlisted Wed., Aug. 5, 1998

Figures supplied by Star Data Systems Inc.

Stock	Ticker	Vol 00s	High	Low	Cls	Net chg
A&E Cap B♦	AECF	4	1.00	1.00	1.00	
AMT Fine	AMTE	286	2.10	2.10	2.10	
ActiveCtl	ATIV	110	0.80	0.80	0.80	
AftonFood	AFTN	100	0.15	0.15	0.15	
AllegncEq	ALGN	75	1.00	1.00	1.00	
Altaur	AAGE	1938	0.01	0.01	0.01	−0.01
Alterra	ALRI	160	0.04	0.04	0.04	−0.02
Ambrex	AMBX	550	0.095	0.09	0.09	
Arlington	ARLL	25	0.35	0.35	0.35	+0.05
Asian TV	ATNL	60	0.80	0.70	0.80	−0.05
Asquith	ASQH	30	0.10	0.10	0.10	
AtlanSys	ASGT	50	0.35	0.35	0.35	
BevrlyGln	**BGCC**	**183**	**1.20**	**0.80**	**1.10**	**−0.15**
Blk Pearl	BLKP	175	0.08	0.08	0.08	−0.01
BorealsEx	**BSXC**	**10**	**4.00**	**4.00**	**4.00**	**−0.25**
Brazilian	BZIN	240	0.20	0.17	0.20	
CLN Vent	CLNV	100	0.35	0.35	0.35	
CdnBlood	**CBBC**	**10**	**1.00**	**1.00**	**1.00**	**+0.10**
CantexEn	CTXE	1535	1.20	1.00	1.20	+0.05
Canuc Res	CANC	6170	0.05	0.04	0.045	+0.01
CastleCapp	CCAP	450	0.11	0.10	0.10	−0.03
Channel i	CNLI	1000	0.02	0.02	0.02	
Complex	COPX	30	0.15	0.15	0.15	
Concopper	CCPP	20	0.50	0.50	0.50	−0.10
CntrlAdv	CADV	175	1.00	0.95	1.00	−0.05
Copperqst	COPQ	100	0.13	0.13	0.13	−0.02
Cryptlogic	CRYP	276	7	6 1/4	6 1/2	−1/4
DitekSftwr	DITK	z300	0.85	0.85	0.85	
Divrsfile	DVFL	50	0.15	0.15	0.15	
DuraProds	DURP	1560	2.70	2.55	2.61	−0.07
ENPAR	ENPR	100	0.25	0.20	0.25	+0.03
EP2000Con	EPCI	658	1.35	1.20	1.25	

Stock	Ticker	Vol 00s	High	Low	Cls	Net chg
EWMC Intl	EWMI	848	0.51	0.50	0.50	
EastAsia	EAGC	50	0.10	0.10	0.10	−0.05
Eloro Res	ELOR	150	0.28	0.25	0.25	−0.05
EmrgAfrica	EAGI	z700	0.06	0.06	0.06	
EnginPwr	**EPSX**	**81**	**3.25**	**3.25**	**3.25**	**−0.25**
EuroDisney	EDIS	8	2.40	2.40	2.40	−0.10
EuroNevBwt	ERNM	90	14 5/8	14 5/8	14 5/8	+5/8
FalcnWell	FWSL	50	0.20	0.20	0.20	
Fareport	FARE	120	0.80	0.80	0.80	
FariniCos	FRNI	74	0.20	0.20	0.20	
Footmaxx	FTMX	140	0.60	0.60	0.60	−0.05
FrstHill	FHCC	40	0.40	0.40	0.40	+0.05
FrcmstrIR(-)	FMAN	20	1.50	1.50	1.50	
GalaVu	GENI	130	0.22	0.20	0.22	−0.02
Gemstar	GSTR	44	0.90	0.80	0.90	+0.05
GibSpring	GSPR	70	0.50	0.50	0.50	
Glassmstr	GMTR	200	0.10	0.10	0.10	
Goldmint	GMEX	229	0.40	0.20	0.40	
GolfNorth	GFNP	959	3.15	3.00	3.15	
Granite A	GRNT	2	3.50	3.50	3.50	+0.50
GuyanaG	GGFI	91	0.60	0.60	0.60	−0.01
Harte Res	HTRC	90	0.13	0.13	0.13	
Heartland	HRTL	25	0.25	0.25	0.25	
Hyberlab	HLAB	500	0.22	0.17	0.21	+0.04
IMI Intl	**IMIN**	**50**	**1.50**	**1.50**	**1.50**	**−0.10**
Innomat	INAT	200	0.04	0.04	0.04	+0.01
IntHsptlty*	IWIN	905	0.20	0.15	0.15	
Interoil	INOL	60	3.00	2.95	3.00	
IntrpVent	IVCC	117	0.70	0.70	0.70	
Interquest	IQIT	6	0.50	0.50	0.50	
JannaSys	JANA	109	2.05	2.00	2.00	−0.04
JavaJoes	JVAJ	85	1.00	1.00	1.00	

Stock	Ticker	Vol 00s	High	Low	Cls	Net chg
Jetcom	JTCM	70	0.155	0.15	0.15	−0.01
KazkstnGld	KGFC	1350	0.045	0.04	0.04	
King Prod	KINK	50	1.15	1.15	1.15	
KinglyEnt	KIEN	150	0.25	0.25	0.25	−0.05
Lasrmedia	LMCD	209	0.50	0.40	0.50	+0.10
Leisure	LCAN	165	2.60	2.45	2.45	
LifeTECH	LFTK	30	0.40	0.40	0.40	+0.05
LyndexExp	LYDX	1250	0.12	0.11	0.11	−0.01
LynxGolf*	LYGI	3900	0.08	0.05	0.08	+0.03
MagAlloy*	MGAC	11	0.35	0.30	0.30	−0.05
Magra	MGRA	2233	0.81	0.70	0.81	+0.01
Manitex	MNTX	10	0.45	0.45	0.45	−0.15
Masswippi	MSVR	e1	700	700	700	−100
MedResort	MDRE	8994	0.16	0.13	0.15	−0.01
MicrslvCm	MSLV	163	1.20	1.20	1.20	
Millstream	MLSM	575	0.33	0.25	0.28	−0.05
Minpro	MINO	50	0.43	0.43	0.43	
Monyswrth	WRTH	295	3.20	2.90	2.95	−0.10
MultMed A♦	MWTM	120	0.75	0.60	0.75	
MustangGd	MUST	200	0.27	0.25	0.25	+0.01
NSI Comms	NSII	80	0.45	0.40	0.40	−0.15
Navitrak	NVTK	40	0.92	0.90	0.90	−0.10
Neotel	NTLI	100	0.05	0.05	0.05	−0.05
NeuroBio	NBIO	10	0.40	0.40	0.40	
NA Detect	NADI	540	0.70	0.65	0.65	
NuCanolan	NCRL	13825	0.78	0.29	0.78	
OlympROM	ORWI	80	0.20	0.20	0.20	−0.10
OptRobot	OPMR	z40	12	12	12	
OroPeru	OROP	107	0.38	0.38	0.38	+0.01
PalletPal	PPAL	1310	0.10	0.08	0.08	−0.03
PrtnrJet	PJET	99	1.00	0.90	1.00	
Pelangio	PLLM	300	0.08	0.08	0.08	

Stock	Ticker	Vol 00s	High	Low	Cls	Net chg
Pharmex	PRXI	722	0.38	0.35	0.35	−0.03
Pinetree	PICA	75	1.15	1.15	1.15	
Plasma	PLAS	560	0.18	0.16	0.16	−0.01
PointsNth	PNTS	20	3.60	3.60	3.60	−0.10
Polyphalt	PLYF	5	0.65	0.65	0.65	
Primenet	PMNT	250	0.10	0.10	0.10	
Prospctor	PALL	z400	0.16	0.16	0.16	
Radiant	MELT	4	1.40	1.40	1.40	
RallyEnrg	RALY	490	1.30	1.30	1.30	+0.05
RenGolf	RGCI	5500	0.25	0.20	0.25	+0.05
Renco	RNRS	130	0.02	0.02	0.02	−0.01
St Lucie	LUCE	40	0.45	0.42	0.42	−0.06
SandRiver	SRIV	775	0.33	0.29	0.31	−0.01
SkyPhrm	SKYE	62	2.65	2.50	2.50	−0.05
SftwrGamng	SGMS	1065	0.16	0.14	0.15	

Stock	Ticker	Vol 00s	High	Low	Cls	Net chg
SthnReef	REEF	681	1.26	1.18	1.26	+0.05
Spartec	SPTC	100	0.04	0.04	0.04	
Sparton	SPTN	z414	0.15	0.15	0.15	
SprceRidg	SPRG	20	0.20	0.20	0.20	
Stamford	**STFD**	**1155**	**1.00**	**0.95**	**1.00**	**+0.10**
SwiDent	**SWIN**	**5**	**4.50**	**4.50**	**4.50**	**+0.50**
Syscan	SYSN	200	0.55	0.50	0.50	+0.10
TKN Inter	TKNI	3280	0.18	0.15	0.17	+0.01
TNK Res	TNKR	20	0.32	0.32	0.32	+0.02
TecnoPetrl*	TPTE	800	0.35	0.35	0.35	+0.01
TomaNetA♦	TOMA	80	0.75	0.70	0.70	−0.05
Trnsarctic	**TARC**	**80**	**2.55**	**2.40**	**2.40**	**−0.20**
Transpacific	TRNP	185	0.01	0.01	0.01	
TriLaterl	TRII	161	0.07	0.07	0.07	
TriarxGld	TXTX	100	0.03	0.03	0.03	

Stock	Ticker	Vol 00s	High	Low	Cls	Net chg
Tropika	TPIL	3440	0.10	0.09	0.09	
UngavaMnl	UNGV	120	0.03	0.03	0.03	−0.10
UniRom	UROM	100	0.06	0.06	0.06	
VedronGld	VDGI	250	0.08	0.08	0.08	−0.01
VengaAero	VAAV	3200	0.015	0.015	0.015	+0.01
VerenaMnl	VMCO	z100	0.25	0.25	0.25	
VikingGld	VGCN	1000	0.22	0.22	0.22	−0.01
Virtek	VRTK	260	1.30	1.25	1.25	−0.02
Westhope	WHCC	456	0.90	0.90	0.90	
WrldSp	WSMI	175	0.18	0.18	0.18	+0.02
WrldWdIntr	WWID	300	0.55	0.55	0.55	+0.15
WrldWise	WWTI	295	0.23	0.20	0.23	
York Bay	YBCG	100	0.16	0.16	0.16	−0.04
Zamora	ZMRA	10	0.04	0.04	0.04	
Ztest	ZTST	120	1.25	1.20	1.25	

CDN Unlisted Bid/Ask

Quotes for stocks traded in past five days

Stock	Ticker	Bid	Ask	Last
A&E Cap A♦	AECF	0.75	1.25	1.00
AVL Info	AVLL	0.17	0.22	0.22
AkroAshnti	AAGM	0.13	0.18	0.15
AlphaGrp	ALFG	0.10	0.12	0.10
Anatolia*	AMCD	0.23	0.28	0.27
Augusta	AUGC	0.30	0.65	0.40
Bactech	BACO	0.60	0.75	0.65
Bid.Com wt	BIII	0.25	0.75	0.60
BlackMtn	BKMT	1.55	1.75	1.75
Brecknrdg	BREK	0.05	0.15	0.10
Brigadier	BRIG	0.70	0.95	0.95
Brownstn	BWNI	0.15	0.23	0.20
CD ROM	CDRN	0.25	0.30	0.25
CME Telmet	CMET	2.50	3.25	3.00
Canargo	CNAR	1.55	2.50	1.55
Canfibre	CFGL	1.85	1.95	1.85
ChampGld♦	CHPG	1.00	1.40	1.00
CitadelGld	CIGD	0.08	0.13	0.10
ColumMtls	COML	0.13	0.18	0.15
ComLgist	CLOG	1.00	1.25	1.15
CondorGld	CGFI	0.51	0.60	0.51
CopprHill	CUHL	0.15	0.25	0.25

Stock	Ticker	Bid	Ask	Last
Cross Cda	CRSS	0.005	0.02	0.01
DavdsnTis	DDTS	0.01	0.05	0.01
Divrsnet	DVNT	2.25	2.75	2.90
Envrtreat	ETSI	0.005	0.02	0.005
EuropnGld	EGRI	0.35	0.45	0.45
FT Cap pf	FTCL	0.10	0.20	0.10
Foodquest	FDQI	0.15	0.20	0.19
FgnCrrncy	FCEC	2.45	2.60	2.50
Forsys	FORS	0.03	0.07	0.07
FrNevBwt	FRNV	18 1/2	19 1/2	18 1/2
Futureline	FTLN	0.01	0.30	0.05
GDL Evrgn	GDLM	1.10	1.15	1.15
Gammon Lk	GAML	1.20	1.50	1.30
GeneVest	GEVE	1.15	1.35	1.20
Goderich	GDRE	27	...	27
GoldcrpAwt	GCRP	0.25	0.50	0.25
Goldeye	GEYE	0.26	0.35	0.26
Greenlight	GLCT	0.23	0.28	0.25
Grntree	GGOL	0.23	0.28	0.28
GriffinMn	GRFM	0.30	0.40	0.41
HallTrain	HTRN	0.05	0.07	0.05
HighAmGld	HIAM	0.02	0.05	0.05

Stock	Ticker	Bid	Ask	Last
HighNorth	HNRI	0.10	0.11	0.10
HornbyBay	HBBY	0.25	0.30	0.30
HurricHwt	HUHY	0.50	2.00	3.00
HydrometA	HMEA	0.03	0.035	0.03
ImpPlasTch	IPLC	0.80	1.00	0.85
IntLarder	LRDR	0.02	0.03	0.02
IntTelepr	ITLP	0.06	0.08	0.07
Java Gld	JVAG	0.09	0.11	0.09
Kelnick	KLNK	0.30	0.50	0.30
Kinbauri	KNBR	0.05	0.15	0.10
KrystalBd	KBON	1.50	1.70	1.60
Lakefield	LKFD	0.25	0.75	0.25
Lassie RL	LRLG	1.00	1.50	1.50
LenoxPoly	LENP	0.80	0.85	0.85
Lignex	LGNX	0.02	0.04	0.02
LinkMnrl	LMVL	0.04	0.07	0.05
London Lf	LLIN	3100	3300	3300
Louvicourt	LVCT	0.10	0.15	0.10
MCK Mng♦	MCKM	0.35	0.45	0.42
MacdOil	MACO	0.04	0.07	0.04
Mantaur	MTUR	0.06	0.07	0.07

Stock	Ticker	Bid	Ask	Last
MapleMnrl	MAPM	0.13	0.18	0.17
Merch	MRCH	0.40	0.60	0.55
MeridianR	MRDS	0.09	0.13	0.13
NFX Gold	NFXG	0.75	0.85	0.85
NatlSeaCpf	NLSP	3.25	...	3.25
New Inca	NIGL	0.08	0.10	0.08
NoblHouse	NBLH	0.43	0.50	0.45
Nthampton	NHGI	0.62	0.70	0.62
NorthfldA♦	NFDC	1.60	1.80	1.70
Nthpoint	NOPT	0.05	0.10	0.05
NovaGrwth	NGCO	0.12	0.30	0.20
Ont&QueRR	OQRL	2100	2200	2100
PearlRiv	PRHL	0.20	0.25	0.20
PetroFlwA♦	PFNG	0.20	0.25	0.20
Phenex	PHEN	0.80	1.10	0.80
PrismEqty	PREQ	1.25	1.50	1.35
QuadraRs*	QDRA	0.12	0.18	0.18
RES Intl	RESZ	0.045	0.055	0.05
RampartM	RAMP	0.50	0.53	0.53
ReclmtnM	RMLL	0.01	0.02	0.02
Regal Gld	REGL	0.10	0.12	0.11

Stock	Ticker	Bid	Ask	Last
RichcoB♦	RCHO	0.50	0.80	0.55
RomiosGld	RGRI	0.30	0.40	0.40
San-Mar	SMEC	0.10	0.12	0.105
ShrdnResv	SHRI	0.85	1.25	1.00
SiritTech	SIRT	0.60	0.70	0.65
SkyPhrm wt	SKYE	0.50	0.75	0.50
SlovGm	GRAM	0.32	0.38	0.38
Stratic	SECO	0.50	1.00	1.00
Tagalder	TAGI	0.02	0.04	0.02
TalsmnEnt	TALS	0.32	0.38	0.38
Telehop	THOP	0.45	0.50	0.50
Templtn96	TMPR	59	...	60
Tragoes	TRGO	0.05	0.15	0.10
Transgold	TEII	0.12	0.16	0.16
UruGldfld	UGIL	0.15	0.25	0.17
WheatHills	WHRI	0.01	0.10	0.10
Winchster	WING	0.04	0.07	0.05
Wollasco	WOLL	0.07	0.20	0.07
Woodview	WODV	0.20	0.28	0.25
Zenda	ZNDA	0.05	0.10	0.05
01Commun	OONE	0.47	0.50	0.50
Zlin Aero	ZLIN	0.25	0.50	0.25

SOURCE: Reprinted with permission of *The Financial Post* (August 6, 1998).

Figure 16.5 Summary of activity of shares traded on the TSE.

How to read the stock tables

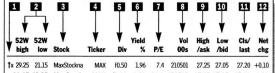

1	2	2	3	4	5	6	7	8	9	10	11	12
	52W high	**52W low**	**Stock**	**Ticker**	**Div**	**Yield %**	**P/E**	**Vol 00s**	**High /ask**	**Low /bid**	**Cls/ last**	**Net chg**
↑x	29.25	21.15	MaxStockna	MAX	f0.50	1.96	7.4	210501	27.25	27.05	27.20	+0.10
n	**39.25**	**31.15**	**MaxStockna**	**MAX**	**f1.00**	**2.83**	**10.3**	**210501**	**37.25**	**37.05**	**37.20**	**+0.10**
↓s	49.25	41.15	MaxStockna	MAX	f1.50	3.30	13.2	210501	47.25	47.05	47.20	+0.10

Equities on Canadian exchanges are shown in decimals. NYSE, Amex, Nasdaq, and Unlisted stocks closing at less than $5 are shown in decimals, those closing at more than $5 are shown in fractions.

Stocks in bold type closed at least 5% higher or lower than the previous board lot closing price. Stocks must close at a minimum $1 and trade at least 500 shares to qualify.

Underlined stocks have traded 500% or more above their 60-day average daily volume.

1. Up/down arrows indicate a new 52-week high or low in the day's trading

2. 52-week high/low: Highest and lowest inter-day price reached in the previous 52 weeks

3. Stock names have been abbreviated

4. Ticker: Basic trading symbol for primary issues (usually common)

5. Dividend: Indicated annual rate. See footnotes

6. Yield %: Annual dividend rate or amount paid in past 12 months as a percentage of closing price in past 12 months

7. P/E: Price earnings ratio, closing price divided by earnings per share in past 12 months. Figures reported in US$ converted to C$

8. Volume: Number of shares traded in 00s; **nt** – no trade; **z** – odd lot; **e** – exact no. of shares

9. High/ask: Highest inter-day trading price or last asking price if no trades. If no asking price ... shown

10. Low/bid: Lowest inter-day trading price or last bid price if no trades. If no bid price ... shown

11. Close/last: Closing price or last board lot closing price in past 12 months. If no last closing price ... shown

12. Net change: Change between board lot closing price and previous board lot closing price

Footnotes:
* – traded in $US
x – stock is trading ex-dividend
n – stock is newly listed on exchange in past year
s – stock has split in past year
c – stock has consolidated in past year
a – spinoff company distributed as shares
♦ – shares carry unusual voting rights

Dividend footnotes:
r – dividend in arrears
u – US$
p – paid in the past 12 months including extras
y – dividend paid in stock, cash equivalent
f – floating rate, annualized
v – variable rate, annualized based on last payment

Data supplied by Star Data Systems (905) 479-STAR and Financial Post Data-Group (416) 350-6500. Historical Nasdaq supplied by DataStream

Toronto continued

52W high	52W low	Stock	Ticker	Div	Yield %	P/E	Vol 00s	High /ask	Low /bid	Cls/ last	Net chg
1.50	0.15	EdenRoc	EDN				216	0.25	0.25	0.25	
30.10	21.50	EdprBrasA♦	EBC	0.98	4.2	5.4	1087	23.50	23.10	23.40	−0.10
26.00	23.00	Edper1pf		f1.05	4.6		nt	24.85	22.00	23.00	
23.40	21.00	Edper2pf		f1.13	4.9		10	23.00	23.00	23.00	
24.00	21.00	Edper4pf		f1.13	4.9		nt	23.40	23.05	23.20	
27.00	25.50	Edper8pf		1.56	6.0		531	26.20	26.05	26.15	+0.05
200.00	155.00	Edper7%db					nt	170.00	150.00	166.00	
5.90	2.30	EiconTech	EIC				172	3.71	3.69	3.71	+0.01
↓ 4.43	0.47	Eldorado	ELD				3845	0.55	0.47	0.49	−0.01
0.17	0.005	Eldrdo wt					nt	0.005	...	0.005	
n 18.50	12.50	ElcthmBrdX	EBI				100	14.25	14.25	14.25	
n 19.25	12.50	ElcthmBrdY♦					51	14.35	14.35	14.35	−0.15
n 4.00	**1.30**	**ElcthmLtdX**	**ELL**				**123**	**1.50**	**1.30**	**1.30**	**−0.20**
↓n 3.50	**1.25**	**ElcthmLtdY♦**					**2265**	**1.35**	**1.25**	**1.25**	**−0.10**
↓ 10.60	**3.40**	**ElkPoint**	**ELK**				**34**	**3.50**	**3.40**	**3.40**	**−0.20**
↓ 17.90	9.70	Emco	EML			10.7	17	9.75	9.70	9.70	−0.25
114.50	96.20	Emco6.5db					nt	99.50	97.50	99.00	
30.75	18.10	EmpireA♦	EMP	0.25	0.9	12.4	1257	28.85	28.70	28.80	−0.05
25.25	23.75	Empire2pf		f1.20	4.8		nt	25.25	24.80	25.00	
27.00	24.55	Empire3pf		2.00	7.4		nt	...	25.40	27.00	
6.15	4.00	EncalEn	ENL				74	5.50	5.30	5.30	−0.20
3.65	**1.56**	**Enerchem**	**ECH**			**8.5**	**10**	**2.30**	**2.30**	**2.30**	**−0.25**
45.60	27.00	Enerflex	EFX	0.40	1.3	17.4	1674	31.00	30.00	30.70	−0.30
7.45	5.00	EnerMark	EIF	p0.85	17.1	26.6	885	5.10	5.00	5.00	−0.05
↓ 4.80	3.10	EnerplusFd	ERF	p0.50	16.3	11.9	23	3.20	3.10	3.10	−0.10
21.50	7.50	EnertecRs	ERS			8.6	144	7.50	7.50	7.50	
n 9.90	5.65	EnerVstun	EIT	p0.86	14.8	6.7	139	6.20	5.75	5.80	
n 17.70	12.50	Enghouse	ESL			15.9	8	13.00	13.00	13.00	
57.00	18.00	EnsignRs	ESI	0.45	2.5	4.8	3384	18.50	18.00	18.20	−0.45
n 4.77	**3.20**	**EnvoyComm**	**ECG**			**22.2**	**468**	**4.00**	**3.60**	**4.00**	**+0.25**
n 2.50	1.80	EnvReclam	EVM				5	1.89	1.89	1.89	
15.50	5.35	EpicData	EKD			17.8	5	10.15	10.15	10.15	−0.50
9.95	6.85	Equisure	EFN			56.7	138	8.75	8.50	8.50	−0.40
39.00	28.00	EquisrApf		0.60	1.7		nt	35.00	33.50	35.00	
↓n 0.90	0.35	EssexRes	ESX				260	0.36	0.35	0.35	−0.04
6.50	2.50	Etruscan	EET				1362	2.80	2.79	2.79	−0.01
s 28.25	13.60	EuroNev	EN	0.05	0.3	83.2	364	18.50	18.10	18.30	−0.05
3.50	0.26	Eurogas	EUG				201	0.28	0.27	0.27	−0.02
0.54	0.22	ExallRs	EXL				131	0.28	0.28	0.28	−0.02
s 12.00	8.75	ExcoTech	XTC			18.0	6	9.25	9.00	9.25	+0.35
23.75	10.25	Extdcare♦	EXE			13.6	nt	11.25	10.75	11.00	
23.40	10.05	ExtdcareA♦				13.4	318	10.85	10.25	10.85	+0.45
23.00	22.00	Extdcare2pf		f1.15	5.2		nt	23.00	22.00	22.00	
23.15	20.55	Extdcare3pf		f1.23	5.9		5	21.00	21.00	21.00	+0.45
22.50	20.00	Extdcare4pf		f1.17	5.9		nt	22.00	20.00	20.00	
22.75	18.00	ExtdcareII		f1.29	6.4		nt	20.90	20.00	20.10	

F G

52W high	52W low	Stock	Ticker	Div	Yield %	P/E	Vol 00s	High /ask	Low /bid	Cls/ last	Net chg
n 10.65	9.75	FACS Rec un	FXS	p0.97	10.0		1	9.75	9.75	9.75	
7.70	5.35	FPI	FPL			11.5	119	6.15	6.10	6.10	
x 31.75	23.00	FahnstckA♦	FHV	u0.28	1.7	7.4	11	25.25	25.25	25.25	−0.45
603.00	253.00	FairfaxFin♦	FFH			25.4	90	560.00	542.00	560.00	−25.00
1.85	0.65	FairfieldM	FFD				nt	0.65	0.60	0.65	
n 26.00	25.60	GrWLifecoDpf		1.25	4.9		nt	...	25.25	25.70	
0.80	0.21	GrLenora	GEN				305	0.26	0.25	0.25	−0.01
↓ 14.25	**3.50**	**Greenstne**	**GRE**				**865**	**3.70**	**3.50**	**3.50**	**−0.20**
6.00	1.15	Greenstnwt					15	1.30	1.30	1.30	
n 1.50	0.65	Greystar	GSL				477	0.70	0.67	0.67	−0.03
2.19	0.70	Greyvest	GFI	0.04	5.0		nt	0.80	0.73	0.80	
s 23.00	11.67	GuardnCap	GCG	0.08	0.4	48.2	nt	21.10	21.00	21.05	
↓s 16.08	**10.10**	**GuardnCapA♦**		**0.08**	**0.7**	**25.0**	**18**	**10.90**	**10.10**	**10.90**	**+0.65**
↓ 13.75	4.30	GulfCda	GOU			14.2	8034	4.75	4.30	4.40	−0.20
↓ 4.85	3.50	GulfCda pf		f0.26	7.4		198	3.60	3.50	3.58	−0.02
14.20	3.65	Gulfstrm	GUR	p0.02	0.5	34.1	316	3.85	3.70	3.75	+0.10
3.95	**1.14**	**GuyanorB**	**GRL**				**37**	**1.75**	**1.65**	**1.65**	**−0.10**
5.00	2.50	Gwil	GWS			83.0	nt	4.45	4.00	4.15	

H I

52W high	52W low	Stock	Ticker	Div	Yield %	P/E	Vol 00s	High /ask	Low /bid	Cls/ last	Net chg
n 12.30	10.50	H&R RE un	HR	p0.81	7.5	12.8	77	10.95	10.85	10.95	
0.08	0.03	HMH China	HMH				nt	0.045	0.02	0.04	
7.50	2.00	Haemacure	HAE				12	5.75	5.70	5.70	−0.30
7.50	3.45	Haley	HLY			13.4	15	5.75	5.50	5.50	
18.00	7.50	Hallmark	HTI			12.3	3	7.60	7.60	7.60	−0.15
n 10.20	9.05	HltrmIF un	HAL	p0.97	10.4		149	9.70	9.35	9.35	−0.30
6.95	6.95	Hammersn♦	HPD	p0.29	4.3	18.7	nt	...	6.50	6.95	
2.49	1.50	HammndA♦	HMM			6.6	nt	1.98	1.80	1.90	
↓ 1.08	0.11	HarbourP	HRP				100	0.15	0.11	0.11	−0.04
14.40	7.30	HarmacPac	HRC				35	8.00	7.90	7.90	
112.00	94.00	Harmacdeb					nt	95.00	92.50	94.00	
13.25	9.00	HarrisStA♦	HSG	0.24	2.1	7.7	10	11.50	11.50	11.50	
12.50	9.45	HarrisStB		0.24	1.9	8.4	nt	13.00	12.50	12.50	
6.50	**4.60**	**HarowstnA**	**HRW**			**19.6**	**18**	**4.80**	**4.70**	**4.70**	**−0.30**
17.70	9.30	Hartco	HTC	0.18	1.2	15.4	nt	14.50	14.00	15.40	
n 12.00	7.00	HrtlndPpln	HAR				40	7.15	7.05	7.15	−0.25
5.50	2.10	HawkrSid	HSC	p1.50	42.9		nt	3.80	3.40	3.50	
8.75	5.75	Hlth&Bio un	HCB	p0.23	3.9		55	6.20	6.00	6.00	
0.80	0.21	HelixBio	HBP				nt	0.295	0.25	0.25	
3.90	**1.50**	**Hemosol**	**HML**				**30**	**2.80**	**2.80**	**2.80**	**−0.19**
0.25	0.075	HeritgCpt	HCI				103	0.085	0.085	0.085	+0.01
n 3.50	2.55	Hi-Alta	HIA			35.4	nt	2.75	2.55	2.55	
3.30	0.65	HighRiver	HRG				21	0.70	0.70	0.70	
5.20	**3.40**	**HighridgEx**	**HRE**			**25.4**	**20**	**3.55**	**3.55**	**3.55**	**−0.45**
1.04	0.51	HighwdRs	HWD			14.0	z284	0.52	0.52	0.52	
1.85	0.40	Hillsbrgh	HLB			2.4	723	0.42	0.40	0.40	−0.02
11.50	**7.30**	**HllngrCdnS***	**HCP**				**745**	**9.00**	**8.50**	**9.00**	**−0.75**
19.35	11.40	Hollngr	HLG	0.60	3.4	7.2	1229	17.40	17.00	17.40	−0.10
n 9.85	8.80	HollngrIIpf		0.70	7.4		16	9.45	9.40	9.40	
1.90	0.10	Hollinger wt					16	0.75	0.75	0.75	
138.50	134.00	Hollngr db					e10	137.50	137.50	137.50	
1.03	0.17	Holmer	HGM				nt	0.195	0.17	0.18	
4.45	1.71	HomCapB♦	HCG			10.3	69	3.35	3.00	3.30	−0.10
38.00	25.60	HudsnBay	HBC	0.72	2.4		7395	29.70	28.90	29.60	−0.40
n 19.90	**7.75**	**HudsnBayIR**		**p0.72**	**7.0**		**2086**	**11.00**	**10.35**	**10.35**	**−1.00**
↓ 69.90	32.25	Hmngbrd	HUM			11.8	876	33.30	32.25	32.95	−0.45
14.40	**3.55**	**HurricnA**	**HHL**			**3.9**	**1165**	**5.20**	**4.00**	**4.45**	**+0.35**
7.30	4.30	Hy&Zel	HZI	p0.30	5.0	8.7	25	6.00	5.75	6.00	+0.25
5.60	0.17	HyalPhar	HPC				1021	2.08	2.02	2.05	−0.05
6.10	2.75	IAMGOLD	IMG			15.5	55	3.40	3.25	3.30	+0.15
n 10.50	9.45	IAT AirUN	ACF	p1.09	11.1		15	9.90	9.85	9.90	−0.10
7.15	0.76	IBEX Tech	IBT				304	0.99	0.93	0.95	−0.03
7.25	3.00	ID Bio	IDB				133	4.75	4.40	4.75	+0.10

SOURCE: Reprinted with permission of *The Financial Post (August 6, 1998).*

Figure 16.6 Summary closing prices on selected international exchanges.

International Wed., Aug. 5, 1998

Figures supplied by Reuter

Stock	Close	Chg
London (in British pence)		
AA Corp.	33.15	-0.03
Abbey Nat.	1126.00	-13.00
Airtours	403.00	-24.50
Allied Domecq	557.50	2.00
Ass Br Foods	530.00	-12.00
Avocet Mining	32.50	-2.00
BAA	688.00	-5.00
BPB Inds	326.00	-15.00
BAT Ind	675.00	-19.00
BG	381.00	9.50
BICC	121.50	-3.00
BOC Group	738.50	-15.00
BTR	158.00	1.25
Barclays Bank	1708.00	-18.00
Bass	993.00	10.00
Beazer Homes	169.00	-7.00
Blue Circle	354.00	-4.00
Body Shop	131.50	-4.50
Boots	1019.00	-1.00
Br Aerospace	453.50	-1.00
Br Airways	594.50	-10.00
Br Petroleum	783.00	-31.00
Br Sky Brdcst	416.00	-2.00
Br Steel	132.75	-2.75
Br Telecom	820.00	-21.00
Bunzl	270.00	-6.50
Burmah Castrol	1053.00	-18.00
Cable & Wire	730.00	-30.00
Cad Schweppes	843.50	27.00
Caradon	163.50	-3.50
Centrica	94.00	-2.00
CGU	1196.00	-8.00
Charter Cons.	572.00	-12.00
Coats Viyella	69.50	
Cookson Grp	167.50	-4.00
Cordiant	129.50	-3.00
Courtaulds	448.00	-1.00
Daily Mail Trst	2708.00	-105.00
Devro Int'l	309.00	-8.50
Diageo	697.00	4.00
Dixons Group	538.50	-15.50
EMAP	1119.00	-65.00
Electrocomp	409.00	
English China	177.00	-7.50
Enterprise Oil	481.50	-18.00
Eurotunnel	66.50	-4.00
Flextech	464.00	-16.50
GKN	754.00	-23.00
General Electric	463.50	-13.50
Glaxo	1834.00	-47.00
Granada	958.00	-7.00
Gr Universal	700.50	-12.50
Guardian Royal	336.00	-4.50
HSBC Hldg	1450.00	27.00
Hammerson Ppty	387.00	-6.50
Hanson	343.00	13.00
Hillsdown	167.50	-3.00
House of Fraser	138.50	-4.00
ICI	754.00	-14.00
Jardine Strategic	1.63	-0.01
Johnson Matthey	423.50	-5.50
Kingfisher	446.50	8.00
Ladbroke	286.25	2.00
Land Sec	817.00	-13.00
Laporte	640.00	-16.00
Lasmo	214.25	-2.00
Legal & Gen	706.00	-30.00
Lloyds Bank	796.50	-27.00
Lonrho	271.00	-10.00
MEPC	470.00	-4.00
Marks & Spenc	503.00	
Mirror Grp News	211.00	-5.00
NFC	139.50	-1.50
Nat'l Power	502.50	-11.50
Nat Westminster	1147.00	-6.00
Next	480.50	-24.00
Norwich Union	434.25	-11.00
Oriflame Int'l	380.00	-5.00
P & O	930.00	-10.00
Pearson	1131.00	-13.00
Pilkington	93.50	-4.00
Powergen	770.00	-8.00
Proudfoot	38.50	-1.00
Prudential	815.50	-33.50
RMC	845.00	-14.00
Racal Electronic	381.50	-18.50
Rank	320.00	7.50
Reckitt & Colman	1159.00	12.00
Reed Intl	535.00	-13.00
Rentokil	358.50	-14.50
Reuters Hldgs	595.50	-10.00
Rexam	228.50	-1.50
Rio Tinto	740.00	-1.00
Rolls Royce	223.50	3.00
Royal & Sun All	637.00	-15.00
Royal Bk of Scot	936.00	-8.00
Royal Doulton	167.50	-8.00
Safeway	363.00	2.50
Sainsbury J	504.00	-14.00
Salvesen Christian	117.50	-3.00
Scottish & New	815.50	-14.00
Scottish Pwr	586.50	-10.00
Sears	224.50	-7.50
Sedgwick Grp	161.50	
Severn Trent	1053.50	12.00
Shell Transport	384.00	-9.50
Smith & Nephew	162.00	-2.00
Smithkline Beech	671.50	-9.00
Stagecoach Hldgs	1146.00	-30.00
Stand Chart Bk	620.00	-20.00
Storehouse	244.50	-2.00
TI Group	408.00	-4.00
Tarmac	99.50	3.00
Tate & Lyle	540.00	-2.00
Tesco	178.50	-7.00
Thomson Travel	171.50	-6.00
Thorne EMI	245.50	0.50
Unigate	593.50	-7.00
Unilever	593.50	-3.50
United Biscuits	216.75	-9.00
Vodafone Gr	778.50	-35.00
WPP	363.00	-19.00
Whitbread	867.00	-12.00
Williams	365.25	-4.25
Zeneca	2406.00	-45.00
Amsterdam (in Dutch guilders)		
ABN-AMRO	49.80	-1.20
AMEV	141.30	-3.30
Aegon	180.50	-6.00
Ahold	59.80	-1.40
Akzo	100.80	-2.30
Baan Co	77.90	0.20
Beers Zonen	129.90	-4.10
Bolswessanen	28.00	-0.40
Boskalis	30.70	-1.10
CSM	107.90	-0.70
DSM	201.50	0.40
Dordse Petr	94.40	-2.60
Draka Hldg	67.70	-2.10
Drie Electric	24.10	-0.30
EVC Int'l	27.00	-1.00
Elsevier-NDU	31.40	-0.60
Fortis Amev	141.30	-3.30
GTI Hldg	70.20	-1.80
Geveke	112.40	-0.60
Gist Brocades	62.50	-4.00
Grolsch	49.50	-0.50
Heineken	86.10	-2.20
Hoogovens	92.30	6.00
Hunter Douglas	100.60	0.50
ING	142.80	-5.70
KLM	81.90	0.10
KNP	46.50	-0.80
Kon PTT NL	82.40	1.20
Koninklijke PTT	82.40	1.20
NKF Holding	52.00	-1.80
Nedlloyd Groep	39.30	0.10
Neways Elect	38.40	-0.50
OCE Grinten	85.40	-1.90
Ommeren	77.50	
Otra	26.30	-0.70
Pakhoed	58.90	-1.30
Philips	163.20	-1.00
Polygram	109.10	
Polynorm	207.00	-0.90
Randstad Hldg	150.00	-5.50
Robeco	217.40	-7.40
Rodamco	49.90	-1.00
Rolinco	187.50	-8.80
Rorento	124.80	-0.10
Royal Dutch	99.90	-2.90
Samas	111.50	-2.60
Sphinx Kon	23.90	-0.30
Stork	63.00	-1.30
Unilever	138.50	-4.40
VNU	79.00	-1.50
Vendex Int'l	78.90	1.30
Vredestein	22.00	-0.40
Wolters Kluwer	302.30	-4.80
Brussels (in Belgian francs)		
Ackermans	14350	-475
Barco	9780	30
Bekaert	26750	225
Belcofi	4790	-110
CBR	3580	-70
CFE	10900	-250
CMB Act	2415	-5
Cobepa	2635	-30
Cofinimmo	3950	-10
Colruyt	26100	-275
Deceuninck	10550	-350
Delhaize	2865	-40
Electrabel	11900	375
Electrafina	4530	-70
Electrorail	57	
Finoutremer	8310	260
Fortis	10800	-475
GBL	7350	-80
Glaverbel	4875	-325
Generale Bk	19250	300
Gen Belgique	6180	-300
Immobel	2600	
Kredietbank	3255	-85
Nat'l Portefeu	3200	-30
Petrofina	13950	-525
Powerfin	9900	-100
Recticel	470	-25
Royale Belge	13900	-150
Sidro	3000	
Sofina Opt	1805	-5
Solvay	2820	
Spector	1650	-40
Tessenderlo	2150	-50
Tractebel	5990	-50
UCB	214900	-2100
Union Miniere	2120	35
Frankfurt (in German marks)		
AA & Mu Bet	224.00	-2.00
AGIV	45.25	-0.45
Adidas	242.00	-10.00
Allianz	618.50	-18.50
BASF	78.20	-1.80
BMW	1644.00	13.00
Bayer	79.10	-0.40
Bayer Vereinsbk	160.20	-6.30
Bayerische	120.50	-5.00
Beiersdorf	112.50	1.00
Bremer Vulkan	0.90	-0.08
Ceag Inds	380.00	-19.00
Commerzbank	64.20	-1.80
Continental	57.40	-0.80
DLW Ag Aktier	57.40	-0.80
Daimler Benz	173.00	-2.50
Degussa	107.50	-2.00
Depfa Bank	154.50	-2.50

International Indexes

— 52 week — high	low		Close	Net chg	% chg
Japan					
19702.07	14664.44	Nikkei	15992.16	-31.42	-0.20
1507.63	1120.61	Tokyo Topix	1235.78	1.17	0.09
Britain					
3984.00	3072.60	FT Ordinaries	3619.00	-43.80	-1.20
6179.00	4711.00	FT SE 100	5632.50	-103.60	-1.81
5458.80	1647.57	FT 500	2691.20	-52.16	-1.90
2885.17	2238.43	FT Act. All Share	2643.40	-50.65	-1.88
Germany					
1940.80	1207.81	FAZ Aktien	1762.74	-43.82	-2.43
5712.60	3532.10	Commerzbank	5197.80	-128.70	-2.42
6171.43	3567.22	DAX Aktien	5632.51	-123.69	-2.15
Australia					
2881.40	2299.20	All Ordinaries	2640.20	-42.10	-1.57
4964.50	3835.80	All Industrials	4644.60	-81.90	-1.73
855.20	541.10	Metals & Minerals	559.20	-10.10	-1.77
Hong Kong					
16673.27	7462.56	Hang Seng Bank	7466.43	-114.37	-1.51
Taiwan					
10116.84	7089.56	Taiwan Weighted	7499.73	-93.41	-1.23
China					
441.04	312.73	Shenzhen Composite	392.45	4.45	1.15
1420.00	1041.97	Shanghai Composite	1307.44	13.98	1.08
Indonesia					
699.86	339.54	JKSE Index	441.78	-19.57	-4.24
Philippines					
2694.79	1511.44	PHS Composite	1524.75	13.31	0.88
Singapore					
1958.62	1042.44	Straits Times	1052.13	-12.86	-1.21
Thailand					
638.04	254.07	SET Index	254.07	-3.97	-1.54
France					
4388.48	2651.33	CAC 40	3976.40	-71.48	-1.77
Italy					
1654.36	877.20	Banca Commercial	1477.09	-41.88	-2.76
38860	21142	MIB 30 Index	35250	-731.00	-2.03
Switzerland					
8412.00	5216.70	Swiss Market Index	7943.20	-227.00	-2.78
Netherlands					
845.10	572.00	CBS Gen. All Share	769.70	-17.30	-2.20
Belgium					
22348.33	12720.34	Brussels General	20734.43	-370.93	-1.76
Sweden					
3955.60	2775.00	Affarsvarlden	3622.20	-86.00	-2.32
Spain					
947.62	531.19	Madrid Exchange	896.96	-16.76	-1.83
South Africa					
7232.40	4708.10	Johannesburg All Share	5653.90	-197.40	-3.37
Mexico					
5369.48	4048.99	General IPC	4055.32	-16.63	-0.41
Argentina					
866.47	538.36	BUSE Merval	552.57	0.31	0.05
Brazil					
13016	7822	BRSP Bovespa	9828	-31	-0.32
Venezuela					
10817.13	4539.78	CCS Bursatil	4539.78	-116.27	-2.50
Chile					
135.01	82.30	Santiago IPSA	87.15	-0.36	-0.42
India					
4523.01	3037.34	Bombay BSE Sensex	3133.42	13.88	0.44
Turkey					
4530.99	1925.00	IMKB National-100	3977.38	-150.98	-3.66
Malaysia					
951.74	380.29	KLSE Composite	380.29	-6.15	-1.59
Israel					
337.43	263.12	TA-100 Index	306.26	-6.38	-2.04
Greece					
2825.52	1331.04	Athens General	2692.77	-91.05	-3.27

SOURCE: Reprinted with permission of *The Financial Post* (August 6, 1998).

time period needed to obtain a reasonably useful estimate of the expected return for any given security.[25] Despite this objection, it is worthwhile examining historical returns to see how they can be used to come up with meaningful predictions about the future.[26] The next section explores the prediction of a firm's beta. It begins by discussing the estimation of the firm's historical beta by use of the market model.

Common Stock Betas

For purposes of portfolio management, the relevant risk of a security concerns its impact on the risk of a well-diversified portfolio. In the world of the CAPM, such portfolios would be subject primarily to market risk. This suggests the importance of a security's beta, which measures its sensitivity to future market movements. To estimate beta, in principle the possible sources of such movements should be considered. Then, the reaction of the security's price to each of these sources should be estimated, along with the probability of each reaction. In the process, the economics of the relevant industry and firm, the impact of both operating and financial leverage on the firm, and other fundamental factors should be taken into account.

But what about investigating the extent to which the security's price moved with the market in the past? Such an approach ignores the myriad possible differences between the past and the future. However, it is easily done and provides a useful starting point.

As shown in Chapter 9, a security's beta can be regarded as the slope of the security's market model. If this line were constant over time, meaning it did not change from period to period, then the **historical beta** for a security could be estimated by examining the historical relationship between the excess returns on the security and on the market portfolio. The statistical procedure used for making such estimates of *ex post* betas is **simple linear regression**, also known as ordinary least squares (OLS).[27]

As an example, consider estimating the *ex post* beta for Widget Manufacturing (WM) using a hypothetical market index. Table 16.1 presents the most recent 16 quarterly returns on both WM and the index, and the calculations necessary to determine WM's *ex post* beta and alpha, as well as certain other statistical parameters. As can be seen, WM's beta and alpha were equal to .63 and .79%, respectively, over this period.[28]

Given these values for alpha and beta, the market model for WM is

$$r_{WM} = .79\% + .63r_I + \epsilon_{WM} \tag{16.6}$$

Historical Beta An estimate of a security's beta, derived solely from historical returns. Equivalently, the slope of the *ex post* characteristic line.

Simple Linear Regression (Alternatively, **Ordinary Least Squares**.) A statistical model of the relationship between two random variables in which one variable is hypothesized to be linearly related to the other. This relationship is depicted by a regression line that is a straight line, "fitted" to pairs of values of the two variables, so that the sum of the squared random error terms is minimized.

---

[25]It has been argued that roughly 300 months (25 years) of historical returns are needed in order for a simple averaging technique to produce reasonably useful estimates of expected returns, provided that the "true" but unobserved expected return is constant during this entire period. See J. D. Jobson and Bob Korkie, "Estimation for Markowitz Efficient Portfolios," *Journal of the American Statistical Association* 75, no. 371 (September 1980): 544–554 and "Putting Markowitz Theory to Work," *Journal of Portfolio Management* 7, no. 4 (Summer 1981): 70–74.

[26]In doing so, a number of researchers have uncovered certain "empirical regularities" in common stock returns; Appendix A discusses a number of these. For a more detailed summary, see Donald B. Keim, "The CAPM and Equity Return Regularities," *Financial Analysts Journal* 42, no. 3 (May–June 1986): 19–34; Douglas K. Pearce, "Challenges to the Concept of Market Efficiency," Federal Reserve Bank of Kansas City *Economic Review* 72, no. 8 (September–October 1987): 16-33; and Robert A. Haugen and Josef Lakonishok, *The Incredible January Effect* (Homewood, IL: Dow Jones-Irwin, 1988).

[27]For a discussion of regression, see Peter Tryfos, *Business Statistics* (Toronto, ON: McGraw-Hill Ryerson, 1989).

[28]WM's beta and alpha would have been equal to .63 and .17%, respectively, if excess returns (that is, returns less the risk-free rate) had been used in the calculations instead of returns. Using returns or excess returns (as well as including or ignoring dividends in calculating returns) appears to make little difference in the estimated size of beta. However, there is a substantive difference in the estimated size of alpha. See William F. Sharpe and Guy M. Cooper, "Risk-return Classes of New York Stock Exchange Common Stocks, 1931–1967," *Financial Analysts Journal* 28, no. 2 (March–April 1972): 46–54.

Table 16.1 Market Model for Widget Manufacturing.

(A) Data

Quarter		WM Returns = Y (1)	Index Returns = X (2)	Y^2 (3)	X^2 (4)	$Y \times X$ (5)
1	1	−13.38%	2.52%	178.92	6.35	−33.71
	2	16.79	5.45	282.00	29.71	91.54
	3	−1.67	0.76	2.77	0.57	−1.26
	4	−3.46	2.36	11.99	5.58	−8.18
2	5	10.22	8.56	104.53	73.36	87.57
	6	7.13	8.67	50.79	75.19	61.80
	7	6.71	10.80	45.07	116.59	72.49
	8	7.84	3.33	61.47	11.08	26.10
3	9	2.15	−5.07	4.62	25.66	−10.89
	10	7.95	7.10	63.22	50.42	56.46
	11	−8.05	−11.57	64.74	133.87	93.09
	12	7.68	4.65	58.97	21.58	35.67
4	13	4.75	14.59	22.55	212.97	69.29
	14	7.55	2.66	57.03	7.05	20.05
	15	−2.36	3.81	5.58	14.54	−9.01
	16	4.98	7.99	24.78	63.85	39.78
Sum(Σ) =		54.84 = ΣY	66.62 = ΣX	1039.03 = ΣY²	848.38 = ΣX²	590.80 = ΣXY

(B) Calculations

1. Beta:

$$\frac{(T \times \sum XY) - (\sum Y \times \sum X)}{(T \times \sum X^2) - (\sum X)^2} = \frac{(16 \times 590.80) - (54.84 \times 66.62)}{(16 \times 848.38) - (66.62)^2} = .63$$

2. Alpha:

$$[\sum Y]/T] - [\text{Beta} \times (\sum X/T)] = [54.84/16] - [.63 \times (66.62/16)] = .79\%$$

3. Standard Deviation of Random Error Term:

$$\{[\sum Y^2 - (\text{Alpha} \times \sum Y) - (\text{Beta} \times \sum XY)]/[T - 2]\}^{1/2}$$
$$= \{[1039.03 - (.79 \times 54.84) - (.63 \times 590.80)]/[16 - 2]\}^{1/2} = 6.67\%$$

4. Standard Error of Beta:

$$\text{Standard Deviation of Random Error Term}/\{\sum X^2 - [(\sum X)^2/T]\}^{1/2}$$
$$= 6.67/\{848.38 - [(66.62)^2/16]\}^{1/2} = .28$$

5. Standard Error of Alpha:

$$\text{Standard Deviation of Random Error Term}/\{T - [(\sum X)^2/\sum X^2]\}^{1/2}$$
$$= 6.67/\{16 - [(66.62)^2/848.38]\}^{1/2} = 2.03$$

6. Correlation Coefficient:

$$\frac{(T \times \sum XY) - (\sum Y \times \sum X)}{\{[(T \times \sum Y^2) - (\sum Y)^2] \times [(T \times \sum X^2) - (\sum X)^2]\}^{1/2}}$$
$$= \frac{(16 \times 590.80) - (54.84 \times 66.62)}{\{[(16 \times 1039.03) - (54.84)^2] \times [(16 \times 848.38) - (66.62)^2]\}^{1/2}} = .52$$

7. Coefficient of Determination:

$$(\text{Coefficient of Determination})^2 = (.52)^2 = .27$$

8. Coefficient of Nondetermination:

$$1 - \text{Coefficient of Determination} = 1 - .27 = .73$$

NOTE: All summations are to be carried out over t where t goes from 1 to T (in this example, $t = 1, 2, ..., 16$).

Figure 16.7 presents a scatter diagram of the returns on WM (r_{WM}) and the index r_I. Also shown in the figure is a graph of the market model with the random error term deleted—that is, the figure has a graph of the following line:

$$r_{WM} = .79\% + .63r_I \tag{16.7}$$

The vertical distance of each point in the scatter diagram from this line represents an estimate of the size of the random error term for the corresponding quarter. The exact distance can be found by rewriting equation (16.6) as

$$r_{WM} - (.79\% + .63r_I) = \epsilon_{WM} \tag{16.8}$$

For example, looking at part (A) of Table 16.1, three quarters ago (quarter 14) the return on WM and the index were 7.55% and 2.66%, respectively. The value of ϵ_{WM} for that quarter can be calculated by using equation (16.8) as follows:

$$7.55\% - [.79\% + (.63 \times 2.66\%)] = 5.08\%$$

The values of ϵ_{WM} can be similarly calculated for the other 15 quarters of the estimation period. The standard deviation of the resulting set of 16 numbers is an estimate of the **standard deviation of the random error term** (or residual standard deviation), and is shown in Table 16.1 to be equal to 6.67%. This number can be viewed as an estimate of the historical unique risk of WM.

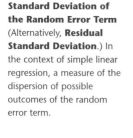

Standard Deviation of the Random Error Term (Alternatively, **Residual Standard Deviation**.) In the context of simple linear regression, a measure of the dispersion of possible outcomes of the random error term.

The market model for WM that is shown in Figure 16.7 corresponds to the regression line for the scatter diagram. Recalling that a straight line is defined by its intercept and slope, it can be shown that there are no other values for alpha and beta that will define a straight line that fits the scatter diagram any better than the regression line. This means that there is no line that could be drawn that would result in a smaller standard deviation of the random error term. Thus, the regression line is often referred to as the line of "best fit."

Equivalently, the line of best fit is the line that has the smallest sum of squared values of the random error terms. That is, the 16 random error terms associated with the regression line can each be squared and then summed. This sum (the sum of squared errors) is smaller for the line of best fit than the sum associated with any other line.

For example, in equation (16.8) if alpha equalled 1.5% and beta equalled .8, then the random error term ϵ_{WM} could be calculated for each of the 16 quarters. With these 16 values, the standard deviation of the random error term could be calculated by squaring each value, summing up the squared values, and dividing the sum by 14 (16 − 2). The standard

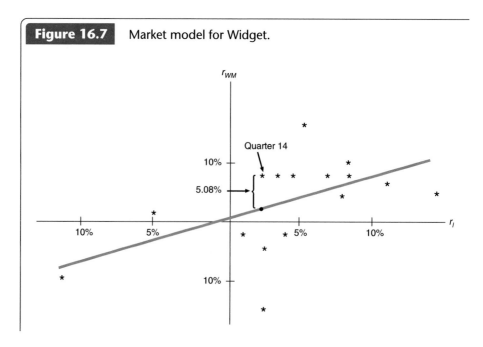

Figure 16.7   Market model for Widget.

deviation of the random error term would then be the squared root of this number. However, it would be larger than 6.67%, which is the standard deviation of the random error term associated with the line of best fit— that is, the line with an alpha of .79% and a beta of .63.

It should be remembered that a security's "true" historical beta cannot be observed. All that can be done is to estimate its value. Thus even if a security's "true" beta remained the same forever, its estimated value, obtained in the manner shown in Table 16.1, would still change from time to time because of mistakes (known as sampling errors) in estimating it. For example, if a different set of 16 quarters were examined, the resulting estimated beta for WM would almost certainly be different from .63, the estimated value for the set of 16 quarters given in Table 16.1. The **standard error of beta** shown in Table 16.1 attempts to indicate the extent of such estimation errors. Given a number of necessary assumptions (for example, the "true" beta did not change during the 16-quarter estimation period), the chances are roughly two out of three that the "true" beta is within a standard error, plus or minus, of the estimated beta. Thus, Widget's "true" beta is likely to be larger than .63 − .28 = .35 and smaller than .63 + .28 = .91. Similarly, the **standard error of alpha** provides an indication of the magnitude of the possible sampling error that has been made in estimating alpha.

The **correlation coefficient** that is shown in Table 16.1 provides an indication of how closely the returns on Widget were associated with the returns on the index. Because its range is between −1 and +1, the value for WM of .52 indicates a mildly strong positive relationship between WM and the index. This means that larger returns for Widget seem to be associated with larger returns on the index.

The **coefficient of determination** represents the proportion of variation in the return on WM that is related to the variation in the return on the index. That is, it shows how much of the movements in Widget's returns can be explained by movements in the returns on the index. The table shows that 27% of the movements in the return on Widget during the 16-quarter estimation period can be attributed to movements in the return on the index.

Because the **coefficient of nondetermination** is 1 minus the coefficient of determination, it represents the proportion (73%) of movements in the return on Widget that is not due to movements in the return on the index.

Figure 16.8 shows a page from the Security Risk Evaluation report prepared by Merrill Lynch, Pierce, Fenner & Smith Inc. Percentage price changes for many stocks, calculated for each of 60 months (when available), were compared by means of the corresponding percentage changes in the Standard & Poor's 500 using the market model in Table 16.1. Seven of the resulting values from this analysis are of interest for each stock.

The values shown under *Beta* and *Alpha* indicate the slope and intercept, respectively, of the straight line that is the best fit for the scatter diagram of the percentage price changes for the stock and index. For example, during the 60-month period covered, the stock of Ask Computer had a beta and alpha of 1.65 and −.06%, respectively.

The value of *R-Sqr*, short for **R-squared**, is equivalent to the coefficient of determination shown in Table 16.1.[29] Having a value of .37 means that 37% of the variation in Ask Computer's price changes could be attributed to changes in the market index over the 60-month period.

The value of *Resid Std Dev-n* (**residual standard deviation**) corresponds to the standard deviation of the random error term in Table 16.1. Ask Computer can be seen to have a residual standard deviation of 10.82%.

---

[29] *R* is used here to denote the correlation coefficient; sometimes (as in Chapter 7) the Greek letter rho (ρ) is used instead. Thus *R*-squared is equivalent to ρ-squared, or the square of the correlation coefficient.

Figure 16.8 Sample page from security risk evaluation by Merrill Lynch, Pierce, Fenner & Smith Inc.

Ticker Symbol	Security Name	92/04 Close Price	Beta	Alpha	R-Sqr	Resid Std Dev-n	Std. Err. of Beta	Std. Err. of Alpha	Adjusted Beta	Number of Observ
AOI	AOI COAL CO	0.500	1.11	−1.79	0.07	19.23	0.49	2.51	1.07	60
APAT	APA OPTICS INC	4.875	0.60	0.80	0.08	9.66	0.25	1.26	0.73	60
APIE	API ENTERPRISES INC	0.688	1.00	2.51	0.02	26.90	0.69	3.51	1.00	60
ASKI	ASK COMPUTER SYS INC	14.875	1.65	−0.06	0.37	10.82	0.28	1.41	1.43	60
ATV	ARC INTL CORP	0.813	1.22	−1.38	0.07	20.71	0.53	2.70	1.15	60
ASTA	AST RESEARCH INC	16.750	1.47	1.66	0.16	16.75	0.43	2.19	1.31	60
ARX	ARX INC	1.875	1.02	−1.90	0.07	17.02	0.43	2.22	1.01	60
ASAA	ASA INTL LTD	1.875	0.79	−1.03	0.01	23.55	0.60	3.07	0.86	60
RCH	ARCO CHEM CO	45.375	1.33	0.03	0.47	7.35	0.19	1.00	1.22	55
ANBC	ANB CORP	36.375	−0.02	1.80	0.10	1.90	0.13	0.56	0.32	12
ATCE	ATC ENVIRONMENTAL INC	2.813	−0.02	0.68	0.02	21.22	0.75	3.22	0.32	46
ATI	ATI MED INC	3.750	0.26	0.07	0.01	19.11	0.49	2.49	0.51	60
ATCIC	ATC INC	1.750	0.61	0.38	0.00	26.63	0.68	3.47	0.74	60
ATNN	ATNN INC	0.219	1.38	1.51	0.00	50.89	1.30	6.64	1.25	60
ATTNF	ATTN AVECA ENTERTAINMENT COR	1.750	2.81	0.39	0.05	42.49	1.59	6.97	2.20	39
AVSY	AVTR SYS INC	0.203	−0.54	6.23	0.06	55.49	3.33	14.41	−0.02	18
AWCSA	AW COMPUTER SYS INC CLASS A	5.875	1.23	7.08	0.01	71.41	1.85	9.29	1.15	60
ARON	AARON RENTS INC	13.125	0.92	−0.23	0.16	10.30	0.26	1.34	0.95	60
ABIX	ABATIX ENVIRONMENTAL CORP	1.750	0.00	0.36	0.03	17.54	0.67	2.96	0.34	37
ABT	ABBOTT LABS	66.000	0.87	0.87	0.51	4.31	0.11	0.56	0.92	60
ABERF	ABER RES LTD	0.969	1.53	3.52	0.02	29.18	1.11	4.93	1.35	37
AANB	ABIGAIL ADAMS NATL BANCORP I	11.000	−1.50	1.81	0.14	12.61	0.70	2.80	−0.66	24
ABBK	ABINGTON BANCORP INC	5.875	1.37	−0.15	0.09	20.09	0.51	2.62	1.24	60
ABD	ABIOMED INC	13.000	1.08	1.04	0.07	18.21	0.47	2.43	1.05	57
ABY	ABITIBI PRICE INC	12.625	0.65	−1.42	0.23	6.00	0.15	0.80	0.77	57
ABRI	ABRAMS INDS INC	4.313	1.28	1.90	0.07	20.91	0.53	2.73	1.18	60
ACAP	ACAP CORP	0.500	0.05	0.88	0.02	13.80	0.35	1.80	0.37	60
ACLE	ACCEL INTL CORP	6.750	1.12	−0.66	0.20	11.10	0.28	1.45	1.08	60
AKLM	ACCLAIM ENTHT INC	6.375	1.29	0.02	0.03	23.62	0.84	3.58	1.19	46
ACCU	ACCUHEALTH INC	5.438	0.53	0.60	0.00	13.47	0.49	2.17	0.69	41

Based on S&P 500 Index. Using Straight Regression   Page 3

Adjusted Beta An estimate of a security's future beta, derived initially from historical data, but modified by the assumption that the security's "true" beta has a tendency over time to move towards the market average of 1.0.

Std. Err. of Beta (standard error of beta) indicates that there is roughly a two-out-of-three chance that the "true" beta for Ask Computer is between 1.65 − .28 = 1.37 and 1.65 + .28 = 1.93. Similarly, the value under *Std. Err. of Alpha* indicates that there is roughly a two out of three chance that the "true" alpha for Ask Computer lies between −.06 − 1.41 = −.147 and −.06 + 1.41 = 1.35.

The seventh value in Figure 16.8 that is of particular interest is the **adjusted beta** value, representing an estimate of the *ex ante* (or future) beta of the firm's stock. Typically, these values are obtained by simply adjusting the estimated *ex post* (or historical) beta by: (1) multiplying the *ex post* value by .66 and (2) adding .34 to the product. Thus, a firm with an *ex post* beta of 1.5 would have an adjusted beta of (1.5 × .66) + .34 = 1.33. Appendix B discusses procedures for adjusting *ex post* betas in more detail.

Growth Versus Value

Growth Stock A stock that has experienced or is expected to experience rapidly increasing earnings per share. It is often characterized as having low earnings-to-price and book-value-to-market-value ratios.

Value Stock Typically, a stock that has experienced relatively poor past price performance, or whose issuing company has experienced relatively poor past earnings results. It is often characterized as having high earnings-to-price and book-value-to-market-value ratios.

Common stocks are often divided into two categories—**growth stocks** and **value stocks**. Although there are no hard-and-fast rules on how they are divided and disagreement exists among investment professionals as to what category certain stocks belong to, there are two financial measures that are often used to distinguish growth stocks from value stocks. These are the book-value-to-market-value ratio (BV/MV) and the earnings-to-price ratio (E/P).[30]

Book-value-to-Market-value Ratio

This ratio is typically calculated as follows. First, the book value of the firm's common stock is determined by using the most recent balance sheet data and calculating the total value of shareholders' equity. Second, the market capitalization of the firm's common stock is determined by taking the most recent market price for the firm's common stock and multiplying it by the number of shares outstanding. Lastly, the book value of shareholders' equity is divided by the market capitalization to arrive at their BV/MV ratio. Relatively low values of this ratio characterize growth stocks, and relatively high values characterize value stocks.[31]

An interesting question is whether there is a relationship between stock returns and their BV/MV ratios. Fama and French examined this issue and found that there was such a relationship.[32] Specifically, they found that on average the larger the size of the BV/MV ratio, the larger the rate of return. Table 16.2 presents their findings.

Panel (a) of Table 16.2 was constructed as follows. First, at the end of June 1963, the book value was determined for each stock on the NYSE, AMEX, and NASDAQ using the annual financial statements for the fiscal year ending in 1962. This value was then divided by the market capitalization for each firm, based on the market price for each firm at the end of December 1962. Second, using these BV/MV ratios, the firms were ranked from smallest to largest and formed into 12 portfolios. Third, the return on each portfolio was tracked monthly from July 1963 through June 1964. Fourth, the entire process was updated by a year so that returns were calculated from July 1964 to June 1965 on 12 BV/MV-ranked portfolios that were formed based on data as of the end of 1963. The process was repeated until a set of monthly returns was available from July 1963 through December 1990 for each of the 12 portfolios.

Table 16.2(a) shows a clear relationship between average monthly return and the BV/MV ratio—higher values of the ratio are associated with higher average returns. Remembering that growth stocks tend to have low BV/MV ratios and value stocks tend to have high BV/MV ratios, this suggests that over the period analyzed, value stocks tended to outperform growth stocks.

---

[30]In general, growth stocks are stocks having rapid increases in earnings whereas value stocks are stocks whose market price seems to be low relative to measures of their worth. Hence, other ratios (such as dividend yield) are sometimes used in sorting out these two types of stocks.

[31]The S&P/BARRA Value Stock Index and the S&P/BARRA Growth Stock Index involve dividing the S&P 500 stocks into two groups based on the size of their BV/MV ratios every six months. The stocks in each group are then used to form these two market-capitalization-weighted indices. The construction of market indices is discussed in more detail in Chapter 24.

[32]Eugene F. Fama and Kenneth R. French, "The Cross-section of Expected Stock Returns," *Journal of Finance* 47, no. 2 (June 1992): 427–465. Also see Barr Rosenberg, Kenneth Reid, and Ronald Lanstein, "Persuasive Evidence of Market Inefficiency," *Journal of Portfolio Management* 11, no. 3 (Spring 1985): 9–16.

Table 16.2 Growth Versus Value Stocks.

	Portfolio Number[a]											
	1	2	3	4	5	6	7	8	9	10	11	12
(a) Portfolios Based on BV/MV Ratio												
Return	.30	.67	.87	.97	1.04	1.17	1.30	1.44	1.50	1.59	1.92	1.83
BV/MV	.11	.22	.34	.47	.60	.73	.87	1.03	1.23	1.52	1.93	2.77
(b) Portfolios Based on E/P Ratio[b]												
Return	1.04	.93	.94	1.03	1.18	1.22	1.33	1.42	1.46	1.57	1.74	1.72
E/P	.01	.03	.05	.06	.08	.09	.11	.12	.14	.16	.20	.28
(c) Portfolios Based on Size												
Return	1.64	1.16	1.29	1.24	1.25	1.29	1.17	1.07	1.10	.95	.88	.90
ln (MV)	1.98	3.18	3.63	4.10	4.50	4.89	5.30	5.73	6.24	6.82	7.39	8.44

[a] Portfolios formed based on rankings of indicated financial measure for stocks from smallest (1) to largest (12); return indicates the average monthly return, in percent, from July 1963 through December 1990.

[b] The portfolio of stocks that had negative earnings had an average monthly return of 1.46.

SOURCE: Eugene F. Fama and Kenneth R. French, "The Cross-section of Expected Stock Returns," *Journal of Finance* 47, no. 2 (June 1992): Table II, pp. 436–437; Table IV, pp. 442–443.

◗ Earning-to-price Ratio

This ratio is typically calculated as follows. First, the accounting value of the firm's earnings per share is determined by using the most recent income statement and dividing the firm's earnings after taxes by the number of shares outstanding. Second, the market price of the firm's common stock is determined by taking the most recent price at which the firm's common stock was traded. Lastly, the earnings-per-share figure is divided by the market price of the stock to arrive at the E/P ratio. Relatively low values of this ratio characterize growth stocks, and relatively high values characterize value stocks.

Is there a relationship between stock returns and their E/P ratios? Fama and French examined this issue and discovered such a relationship does exist.[33] Specifically, they found that, on average, the larger the size of the E/P ratio, the larger the rate of return. Their results are shown in Table 16.2(b), which was constructed in the same manner as part (a) except that at the end of each June, firms were ranked and assigned to portfolios on the basis of their E/P ratios.

Except for portfolio 1, part (b) shows a clear relationship between average monthly returns and the E/P ratio—higher values of the ratio are associated with higher average returns. Since growth stocks tend to have low E/P ratios and value stocks tend to have high E/P ratios, this data reinforces the conclusions drawn from the BV/MV data—namely, that value stocks tended to outperform growth stocks over the period analyzed.

There is one other interesting feature of this panel. When Fama and French assigned stocks to portfolios based on their E/P ratios, they assigned those stocks that had negative earnings and hence a negative E/P ratio to a separate portfolio. This portfolio had an average monthly return of 1.46%. Thus, if one considers a portfolio with a negative E/P ratio

---

[33]Also see S. Basu, "Investment Performance of Common Stocks in Relation to Their Price-earnings Ratios: A Test of the Efficient Market Hypothesis," *Journal of Finance* 32, no. 3 (June 1977): 663–682; and "The Relationship Between Earnings' Yield, Market Value, and Return for NYSE Common Stocks: Further Evidence," *Journal of Financial Economics* 12, no. 1 (June 1983): 129–156.

to be the lowest E/P portfolio, then it can be seen from the table that as E/P gets larger, average returns at first decline and then rise. This has led Fama and French to refer to the relationship between average returns and the E/P ratio as being "U-shaped."

Size

Although firm size is not generally used as a criterion for distinguishing growth from value stocks, it is often used to sort stocks. For example, many investment professionals think of stocks in terms of two dimensions, as follows:

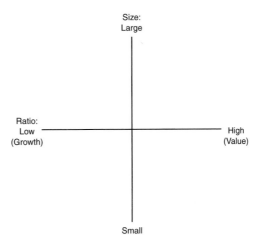

Hence, stocks could be classified as growth or value using the BV/MV ratio and as larger or small using their size. The result is that each stock could be located in a diagram like the one shown.

Typically a stock's market capitalization is used as the measure of its size. This is what Fama and French did when they assigned stocks to one of 12 portfolios after ranking them at the end of each June based on size. Proceeding in a manner analogous to that discussed previously, they tracked the monthly returns for these 12 size-based portfolios from July 1963 to December 1990. Table 16.2(c) displays the average returns and sizes of these portfolios.

In contrast to parts (a) and (b), it can be seen that there is a clear inverse relationship between size and average return. That is, stocks of smaller firms tend to have higher returns than stocks of larger firms. Even more notable is the average return for the smallest portfolio (1). This return is significantly higher than for the next smaller portfolio (2) or for any other. Hence, when some people refer to a **size effect** in stock returns, they are really referring to a "small firm effect."[34]

Interrelationships

The existence of a relationship between any one of three financial variables (BV/MV ratio, E/P ratio, and firm size) and stock returns suggests that at least one missing factor is needed

Size Effect (Alternatively, **Small Firm Effect**.) An empirical regularity whereby stock returns appear to differ consistently across the spectrum of market capitalization. Over extended periods of time, smaller capitalization stocks have outperformed larger capitalization stocks on a risk-adjusted basis.

---

[34]Other studies of the size effect include Rolf Banz, "The Relationship Between Return and Market Value of Common Stocks," *Journal of Financial Economics* 9, no. 1 (March 1981): 3–18; and Marc R. Reinganum, "Misspecification of Capital Asset Pricing: Empirical Anomalies Based on Earnings Yields and Market Values," *Journal of Financial Economics* 9, no. 1 (March 1981): 19–46. One explanation of the size effect is that small firms have high discount rates because they are riskier than large firms, thereby causing them to have higher average returns over long time periods; see Jonathan Berk, "Does Size Really Matter?" *Financial Analysts Journal* 53, no. 5 (September–October 1997): 12–18 and "A Critique of Size-related Anomalies," *Review of Financial Studies* 8, no. 2 (Summer 1995): 275–286.

to explain the differences in returns.[35] Hence, it is of interest to examine the interrelationships between the BV/MV ratio, the E/P ratio, firm size, and average returns. The joint effect of E/P ratio and firm size on stock returns is examined next.

E/P, Size, and Average Returns

In order to examine the joint effect of these two financial variables on stock returns, one study noted at each year-end the breakpoints formed by sorting NYSE and AMEX stocks in quintiles based on just size and then on just the E/P ratio.[36] Then, using both of these sets of breakpoints, stocks were assigned to one of 25 size-E/P portfolios for the next year. That is, each stock in the smallest size quintile was assigned to one of five E/P portfolios, then each stock in the next-to-smallest quintile was assigned to one of five E/P portfolios, and so on until there were 5 sizes × 5 E/P ratios = 25 size-E/P portfolios. The process was repeated year after year until a set of daily returns was available for each one of the 25 portfolios from 1963 through 1977.

When average returns for the 25 portfolios were compared, it was found that there was a clear inverse relationship between size and average returns for any E/P quintile. For example, consider the five size-ranked portfolios that were formed from the lowest E/P quintile. It was found that when comparing these five portfolios, the larger the size, the smaller the average return.

However, there was no clear relationship between E/P ratios and average returns for any size quintile. For example, consider the five E/P-ranked portfolios that were formed from the smallest size quintile. In this case the largest and third-largest average returns were associated with the lowest and next-to-lowest E/P portfolios. This was contrary to previous observations of the relationship between E/P ratios and average returns. As a consequence, it appears that there is a missing factor that is needed to explain differences in stock returns, and that this factor is more closely related to size than to the E/P ratio.[37]

BV/MV, Size, and Average Returns

Fama and French were interested in the joint effect of the BV/MV ratio and firm size on stock returns.[38] Accordingly, they formed 100 portfolios annually based on the rankings of stocks using size and the BV/MV ratio. Monthly returns on these portfolios were then recorded for the period from July 1963 through the end of 1990.

When average returns for the 100 portfolios were compared, it was found that there was an inverse relationship between size and average return for almost every BV/MV decile. For example, comparing the 10 size-ranked portfolios that were formed from the largest BV/MV decile, it was found that, in general, the larger the size, the smaller the average return. The only exceptions were the two smallest BV/MV deciles, in which there was no apparent relationship between size and return.

---

[35]The missing variable apparently is not beta, as the relationship between these variables and stock returns has been found to exist independent of differences in beta. See Fama and French, "The Cross-section of Expected Stock Returns." Also see the following three papers by Fama and French: "Common Risk Factors in the Returns on Stocks and Bond," *Journal of Financial Economics* 33, no. 1 (February 1993): 3–56: "Size and Book-to-market Factors in Earnings and Returns," *Journal of Finance* 50, no. 1 (March 1995): 131–155; and "Multifactor Explanations of Asset Pricing Anomalies," *Journal of Finance* 51, no. 1 (March 1996): 55–84.

[36]Marc R. Reinganum, "Misspecification of Capital Asset Pricing." Also see Rolf W. Banz and William J. Breen, "Sample-dependent Results Using Accounting and Market Data: Some Evidence," *Journal of Finance* 41, no. 4 (September 1986): 779–793.

[37]It should be noted that this view is not universally held. See Jeffrey Jaffe, Donald B. Keim, and Randolph Westerfield, "Earnings Yields, Market Values, and Stock Returns," *Journal of Finance* 44, no. 1 (March 1989): 135–138.

[38]Fama and French, "The Cross-section of Expected Stock Returns." Also see Peter J. Knez and Mark J. Ready, "On the Robustness of Size and Book-to-market in Cross-sectional Regressions," *Journal of Finance* 52, no. 4 (September 1997): 1355–1382.

Furthermore, there was a clear direct relationship between BV/MV ratios and average returns for any size quintile. For example, a comparison of the ten BV/MV-ranked portfolios that were formed from the smallest size decile showed that the larger the BV/MV ratio, the larger the average return. Fama and French concluded that at least two missing factors are needed to explain differences in stock returns, and that those factors are closely related to size and the BV/MV ratio.

Primary Distributions

Underwriter (Alternatively, **Investment Dealer**) An organization that acts as an intermediary between issuers and the ultimate purchasers of securities in the primary security market.

The discussion so far has focused on secondary markets for securities, where securities that were initially issued at some previous point in time are subsequently traded. The focus now shifts to the primary market for securities, which is the name given to the markets where the initial issuance itself takes place. Some issuers deal directly with purchasers in this market, but many rely on **investment dealers** who act as **underwriters** by serving as intermediaries between issuers and the ultimate purchasers of their securities.[39]

Private Placements

Private Placement The direct sale of a newly issued security to one or a small number of large institutional investors.

In some instances, issuers decide that only a few large institutional investors should be solicited, and the entire issue is sold to one or more of them. Such **private placements** are frequently used for bond issues, with the dealer acting as an agent for the issuing corporation. As long as the minimum cash value of the issue is greater than $150 000 and relatively few potential buyers are contacted (say, less than 25), requirements for detailed disclosure, public notice, and so on may be waived, thereby considerably reducing the cost of floating an issue. These placements are often announced after the fact, via advertisements in the financial press.

Such investments, however, are illiquid because the investor is typically prohibited from selling the security within two years of the purchase date. This has resulted in few equities being sold in this manner. Instead, most private placements involve fixed-income securities that are purchased by investors who are attracted by their coupon payments, not the prospect of capital gains.

Public Sale

Banking Group A group of investment dealers, each of which assumes financial responsibility for part of a new issue of securities.

Selling Group A group of investment banking organizations who, as part of a security underwriting are responsible for selling the security.

Competitive Bidding With respect to selecting an underwriter, the process of an issuer soliciting bids on the underwriting and choosing the underwriter offering the best overall terms.

When a public sale is contemplated, much more must be done. Many dealers and brokers may serve as intermediaries in the process. One, acting as the "lead" underwriter, will put together a **banking group** and a **selling group**. The banking group includes firms that purchase the securities from the issuing corporation and thus underwrite part of the offering. The selling group includes firms that contact potential buyers and do the actual selling, usually on a commission basis.

The process begins with discussions between the issuing corporation and one or more investment dealers. Some issuers utilize **competitive bidding** and then select the investment dealer offering the best overall terms. This procedure is used for many government bond issues. Many corporations, however, maintain a continuing relationship with a single

---

[39]Outside Canada underwriters are generally referred to as *investment bankers*. For more on investment banking, see Richard A. Brealey, Stewart C. Myers, Gordon Sick, and Robert Gianmarino, *Principles of Corporate Finance*, 2nd Canadian ed. (Toronto: McGraw-Hill Ryerson, 1992); and Stephen Ross, Randolph Westerfield, Jeffrey Jaffe and Gordon Roberts, *Corporate Finance*, 1st Canadian ed. (Toronto: Irwin, 1995). For the US situation see the January–February 1986 issue of the *Journal of Financial Economics*, which contains papers presented at a symposium on investment banking.

Prospectus The official selling circular that must be given to purchasers of new securities registered with the provincial regulator. The prospectus provides information about the issuer's business, its financial condition, and the nature of the security being offered.

Red Herring A preliminary prospectus that provides much of the information in the final prospectus, but is not an offer to sell the security, nor does it display an actual offering price.

Firm Commitment An arrangement between underwriters and a security issuer whereby the underwriters agree to purchase, at the offering price, all of the issue not bought by the public.

Rights Offering The sale of new stock conducted by first offering the stock to existing shareholders in proportion to the number of shares owned by each shareholder.

Standby Agreement An arrangement between a security issuer and an underwriter as part of a rights offering. The underwriter agrees to purchase at a fixed price all securities not purchased by current stockholders.

Best-efforts Basis An agreement under which the investment dealer or underwriter agrees to use its best effort to sell a new issue of securities without guaranteeing that any or all of these securities will be sold.

Pegging The process by which investment bankers attempt to stabilize the price of an underwritten security in the secondary market for a period of time after the initial offering date.

underwriter and negotiate the terms of each new offering with that firm. The underwriter is usually heavily involved in the planning of an offering, the terms involved, the amount to be offered, and so on, serving, in effect, as a financial consultant to the corporation.

Once the basic characteristics of an offering have been established, a preliminary **prospectus** disclosing material relevant to the prospective buyer is filed with the provincial securities commission in provinces where these are required. (This prospectus is often referred to as a **red herring** since it has a disclaimer printed in red ink across the first page that informs the reader that it is not an offer to sell.) The actual price of the security is not usually included in the preliminary prospectus, and no final sales may be made until the registration has been approved and a final prospectus issued, indicating the offer price at which the shares will be sold. The final prospectus may be issued about three weeks after all *deficiencies* regarding adequate disclosure have been resolved to the satisfaction of the securities commission. The securities commission, however, does not take a position regarding the investment merits of an offering or the reasonableness of the price.

A security issue may be completely underwritten by an investment dealer and the other members of the syndicate. If it is, the issuing corporation receives the public offering price less a stated percentage spread (although underwriters will occasionally be compensated with some combination of shares and warrants, perhaps in addition to a smaller spread). The underwriters, in turn, sell the securities at the public offering price (or less) and may take some of the securities themselves. Underwriters who provide this sort of **firm commitment** bear the major part of the risk, since the public may not be willing to buy the entire issue. The underwriter may be able to escape the effects of an unexpected market downturn if the contract includes a *market-out* clause. A variant on a firm commitment underwriting in Canada is a *bought deal* where the underwriter buys all the shares from the firm before releasing them to the public, thereby financing the full amount of the issue for a period of time.

Not all agreements are of this type. In the case of a **rights offering** where the current shareholders are given the opportunity to buy the new shares first), an underwriter may agree to purchase, at a fixed price, all securities not take by current shareholders. This is termed a **standby agreement**. In the case of a non-rights offering (where the shares are offered to the general public first), members of a selling group may serve as agents instead of dealers, agreeing only to handle an offering on a **best-efforts basis**.

During the period when new securities remain unsold, the underwriter is allowed to attempt to "stabilize" the price of the security in the secondary market by standing ready to make purchases at a particular price. Such **pegging** may continue up to 10 days after the official offering date. There is a limit to the amount that can be purchased in this manner, usually stated in the agreement under which the underwriting syndicate is formed, since the members typically share the cost of such transactions. If there is to be any pegging, a statement to that effect must be included in the prospectus.

In any security transaction, there may be explicit and implicit costs. In a primary distribution, the explicit cost is the underwriting spread and the implicit cost is any difference between the public offering price and the price that might have been obtained otherwise. The spread provides the underwriter with compensation for selling the issue and bearing the risk that the issue may not be completely sold to the public, thereby leaving them with ownership of the unsold shares. The lower the public offering price, the smaller the risk that the issue will not be sold quickly at that price. If an issue is substantially underpriced, the selling group can be assured that the securities will sell rapidly, requiring little or no support in the secondary market. Since many corporations deal with only one underwriter and since the larger investment dealers rely on one another for inclusion in syndicates, it has been alleged that issuers pay too much in spreads, given the prices at which their securities are offered. In other words, the returns to underwriting are alleged to be overly large relative to the risks involved, owing to ignorance on the part of issuers or the existence of an informal cartel among investment dealers.

Underpricing of Ipo's

Initial Public Offering (IPO) (Alternatively, **Unseasoned Offering**.) The first offering of the shares of a company to the public.

Whether or not returns to underwriting are overly large, a number of **initial public offerings** (ipo's) appear to be underpriced. Ipo's are the first offerings of shares of a company to the public and are sometimes referred to as **unseasoned offerings**. The abnormal returns for a sample of ipo's in the US are show in Figure 16.9. Each one of the first 60 months after the initial offering is shown on the horizontal axis, and the corresponding average abnormal return, meaning the average return over and above that of stocks of equal risk, is show on the vertical axis. The leftmost point indicates the average abnormal return obtained by an investor who purchased such a stock at its offering price and sold it for the bid price at the end of the month during which it was offered. The average abnormal return was substantial: 11.4%. The remaining points show the average abnormal returns that could have been obtained by an investor who purchased the security in the secondary market at the beginning of the month indicated and then sold it in the secondary market at the end of that particular month. Some of these post-offering abnormal returns were positive, but most were negative.

A subsequent study found that the initial abnormal return, measured over the time period beginning with the offering and ending when the first closing price was reported, was 14.1%.[40] Although there is evidence that the average abnormal returns remained positive over the next two months, the average abnormal return over the three-year period after

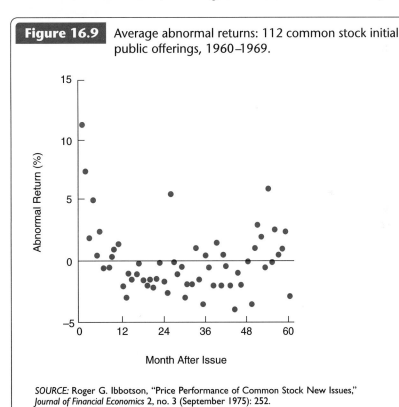

Figure 16.9 Average abnormal returns: 112 common stock initial public offerings, 1960–1969.

SOURCE: Roger G. Ibbotson, "Price Performance of Common Stock New Issues," *Journal of Financial Economics* 2, no. 3 (September 1975): 252.

---

[40]Investors who quickly sell their shares in order to capture this price spurt are known as "flippers." See Jay R. Ritter, "The Long-run Performance of Initial Public Offerings," *Journal of Finance,* 46, no. 1 (March 1991): 3–27. Also, set Roger G. Ibbotson, Jody L. Sindelat, and Jay R. Ritter, "Initial Public Offerings," *Journal of Applied Corporate Finance* 1, no. 2 (Summer 1998): 37–45. An interesting explanation for the initial underpricing is provided by Kevin Rock, "Why New Issues Are Underpriced," *Journal of Financial Economics* 15, no. 1–2 (January–February 1986): 187–212.

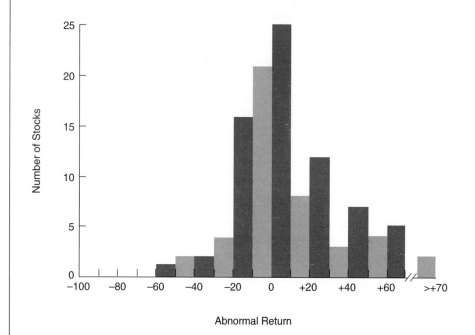

Figure 16.10 Average abnormal returns from offering price to bid price at the end of the offering month: 112 common stock initial offerings, 1960–1969.

SOURCE: Roger G. Ibbotson, "Price Performance of Common Stock New Issues," *Journal of Financial Economics* 2, no. 3 (September 1975): 248.

the first close was −37.4%. Three other interesting observations were that (1) offerings of smaller firms had lower three-year abnormal returns than those of larger firms, (2) firms that had the highest positive initial abnormal return had the worst performance over the subsequent three-year period, and (3) younger firms going public had both higher initial abnormal returns and lower subsequent three-year abnormal returns than older firms going public.

On the average, offerings of these unseasoned securities appear to have been underpriced. Investors able to purchase a cross-section of such shares at their offering prices might thus expect better performance than those holding other securities of equal risk. It is not surprising that such offerings are often rationed by the members of the selling group to "favoured" customers. It is "not uncommon for underwriters to receive, prior to the effective date, 'public indication of interest' for five times the number of shares available."[41] Unfavoured customers are presumably allowed to buy only the new issues that are not substantially underpriced. Since costs may be incurred in becoming a favoured customer, it is not clear that even such an investor obtains abnormally large returns overall.

Whereas the return obtained by the purchaser of a new issue may be substantial on average, the amount may be very good or very bad in any particular instance, as Figure 16.10 shows. Although the odds may be in the purchaser's favour, a single investment of this type is far from a sure bet.

A Canadian study examined 115 ipo's in the period 1971 to 1983. The average *first trading day* return was 11.6% with a standard deviation of 40.2%. The minimum first day

---

[41]Securities and Exchange Commission, *Report on Special Study on Security Markets* 1973. Also see Roger G. Ibboston, "Price Performance of Common Stock New Issues," *Journal of Financial Economics* 2, no. 3 (September 1975): 235–272.

return was −81.7% and the maximum 196.7%. This duplicates the US finding that ipo's are, on average, significantly underpriced but no single investment of this type is a certain winner. The range of first-day returns recorded, however, is surprisingly large.[42]

Seasoned Offerings

Interestingly, the announcement of a seasoned US stock offering seems to result in a decline of roughly 2% to 4% in the firm's stock price. This could be because managers tend to issue stock when they think it is overpriced in the marketplace. Thus, the announcement of the offering causes investors to revise downward their assessment of the value of the stock, leading to a price decline. A Canadian study that examined seasoned offerings found that the issuing firm's share price declined, on average, by about 1%, but reported finding little support for the theoretical asymmetric information models of Myers and Majiluf, and Lucan and McDonald.[43] In the US this decline is larger for stocks of industrial firms than for stocks of public utilities, probably due to the fact that the typical utility has seasoned offerings far more often then the typical industrial firm.[44]

Figure 16.11 displays the average post-issue abnormal price performance of a sample of seasoned equity offerings.[45] In particular, it shows the average abnormal return over the six-month and one-year periods beginning with the first post-issue price recorded on the exchange on which the security is listed. Also shown are the average abnormal returns for the second, third, fourth, and fifth year after issuance. As the figure shows, for the first six months after a seasoned equity offering, nothing unusual happens to the typical firm's stock price. However, over the first year there is a −6.3% abnormal return, suggesting that the stocks performed poorly during the second six-month period after the offering. The second, third, fourth, and fifth years show continued poor performance. Overall, the seasoned equity offerings had an abnormal return of roughly −8% per year for the five years after the offering. This leaves a puzzle: why do many firms issue equity when they ultimately provide investors with such low returns over the next five years? Equivalently, who do investors buy such offerings? Indeed, these two questions can be asked not only about seasoned offerings, but also about ipo's.

---

[42]I. Krinsky and W. Rotenberg, "The Valuation of Initial Public Offerings," *Contemporary Accounting Research* 5, no. 2 (Spring, 1989); 500–514. See also V. Jog and A. Riding, "Underpricing in Canadian IPOs," *Financial Analysts Journal* (November–December 1987), who reported similar results for a sample of 100 firms. Also see V. Jog and A. Srivastava, "La Sous-evaluation des emissions premières au Canada: Une mise à jour," *Finéco* 4, no. 1 1ère semestre, 1994).

[43]See Stewart C. Myers and Nicholas S. Majluf, "Corporate Financing and Investment Decisions Where Firms Have Information That Investors Do Not Have," *Journal of Financial Economics* 13, no. 2 (June 1984): 187–221; Wayne H. Mikkelson and M. Megan Partch, "Valuation Effects of Security Offerings and the Issuance Process," *Journal of Financial Economics* 15, no. 1–2 (January–February 1986): 31–60; D. Lucas and R. McDonald, "Equity Issues and Stock Price Dynamics," *Journal of Finance*, 1990; and V. Jog and H. Schaller, "Share Price Behavior Around the Announce of New Equity Issues: A New Test of the Asymmetric Information Models," Carleton University, Working Paper, 1994.

[44]See Ronald W. Masulis and Ashok N. Korwar, "Seasoned Equity Offerings: An Empirical Investigation," *Journal of Financial Economics* 15, nos. 1 and 2 (January–February 1986): 91–118.

[45]See Tim Loughran and Jay R. Ritter, "The New Issues Puzzle," *Journal of Finance* 50, no. 1 (March 1995): 23–51. This study also looked at 4753 ipo's that were issued during 1970–1990, and found that they too had significant negative abnormal returns over the five-year period after issuance. Also see D. Katherine Spiess and John Affeck-Graves, "Underperformance in Long-run Stock Returns Following Seasoned Equity Offerings," *Journal of Financial Economics* 38, no. 3 (July 1995): 243–267.

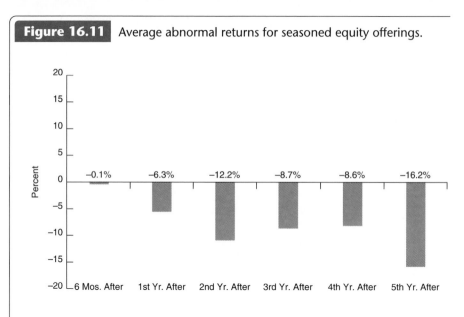

Figure 16.11 Average abnormal returns for seasoned equity offerings.

SOURCE: Adapted from Tom Loughran and Jay R. Ritter, *Journal of Finance* 50, no. 1 (March 1995): 33.

⬧ Shelf Registration

A recent change in Canadian regulations has made it possible for corporations to foster greater competition among underwriters. In May 1991, National Policy 44 came into force to allows firms to register securities in advance of issuance. With such a **shelf registration** securities may be sold up to two years later. With securities "on the shelf," the corporation can request competitive bids from investment bankers and refuse to sell shares if acceptable bids are not forthcoming. There is not yet any evidence to indicate what effect this change has had on underwriting costs in Canada. Shelf registration has, however, been allowed in the US since 1982, where the evidence suggests that issuing costs have been reduced.[46]

Shelf Registration Under National Policy 44, issuers may register securities in advance of their issuance and sell these securities up to two years later.

....

Secondary Distributions

As mentioned earlier, an individual or institution wishing to sell a large block of stock can do so through a secondary distribution. An investment banking group buys the block from the seller and then offers the shares to the public through an organized exchange.

All the Securities Commissions in Canada (except Quebec) require that the sale of securities from a *control position* be accompanied by a prospectus and an underwriter. A control position is one in which the person offering the shares owns a sufficient number to materially affect control of the company. In most provinces a 20% holding is deemed to represent control, although there are circumstances under which a smaller holding may be ruled to be a control position. The distribution then proceeds in the same way as a primary distribution.

The impact of the sale of a large block on the market price of the shares provides information on the resiliency of the capital market. The results of a US study are described

---

[46]See Sanjai Bhagat, M. Wayne Matt, and G. Rodney Thompson, "The Rule 415 Experiment: Equity Markets," *Journal of Finance* 40 no. 5 (December 1985): 1385–1401.

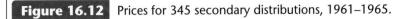

Figure 16.12 Prices for 345 secondary distributions, 1961–1965.

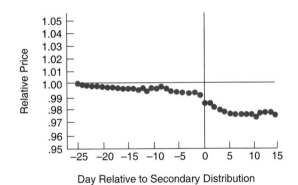

SOURCE: Myron S. Scholes, "The Market for Securities: Substitution Versus Price Pressure and the Effects of Information on the Share Prices," *Journal of Business* 45, no. 2 (April 1972): 193.

below.[47] Figure 16.12 shows the average price (adjusted for market changes) for 345 secondary distributions, with the price 25 days prior to the distribution taken as 1.0. On the average, a secondary distribution leads to a 2% to 3% decline in price. since there is no evidence of a subsequent price rebound, this decline is most likely due to the information contained in the fact that someone has decided to sell. Additional analysis of these results, as shown in Table 16.3 supports the assertion. The size of the decline was related to the identity of the seller—being the greatest for sellers likely to be information-motivated and smallest for sellers likely to be liquidity-motivated.[48]

Table 16.3 Average Price Decline Versus Type of Seller: 345 Secondary Distributions, 1961–1965.

Type of Seller	Percentage Change in Adjusted Price from 10 Days Before the Distribution to 10 Days After the Distribution
Corporations and officers	2.9%
Investment companies and mutual funds	2.5
Individuals	1.1
Estates	.7
Banks and insurance companies	.3

SOURCE: Myron S. Scholes, "The Market for Securities: Substitution Versus Price Pressure and the Effects of Information on Share Prices," *Journal of Business* 45, no. 2 (April 1972): 202.

[47]Myron S. Scholes, "The Market for Securities: Substitution Versus Price Pressures and the Effects of Information on Share Prices," *Journal of Business* 45, no. 2 (April 1972): 193.

[48]A more recent study has confirmed these findings; see Wayne H. Mikkelson and M. Megan Partch, "Stock Price Effects and Costs of Secondary Distributions," *Journal of Financial Economics* 14, no. 2 (June 1985): 165–194.

Summary

1. Common stock represents an ownership position in a corporation. Common shareholders possess a residual claim on the corporation's earnings and assets. Furthermore, their liability for the corporation's obligations is limited.

2. Common shareholders elect the corporation's directors through either a majority or a cumulative voting system.

3. Corporations may at times repurchase some of their outstanding shares either in the open market or through a tender offer. Such actions may involve an attempt to repel a takeover, a signal to shareholders that the shares are undervalued, or a taxwise distribution of cash to shareholders.

4. Stock dividends and splits involve the issuance of additional shares of common stock to current shareholders, proportional to their ownership positions. No change in the total value of the corporation is caused by a stock dividend or split.

5. Preemptive rights give existing shareholders the right of first refusal to purchase new shares. Such shares are purchased in a rights offering.

6. Daily information regarding transactions in publicly traded shares can be found in business newspapers and the business sections of most local newspapers.

7. A security's *ex-post* beta can be estimated using historical return data for the security and a market index. The beta is the slope of the security's market model, calculated by using simple linear regression.

8. Beta estimates based on historical return data are sometimes adjusted to account for a tendency of betas to drift towards an average value of 1.0 over time.

9. Firms that have either low book-value-to-market-value or earnings-to-price ratios or both, are generally referred to as growth stocks, whereas firms that have either high book-value-to-market-value or earnings-to-price ratios, or both, are generally referred to as value stocks.

10. Firms that have either high book-value-to-market-value ratios, high earnings-to-price ratios, or are of smaller firm size historically have had higher stock returns.

11. When viewed jointly, there seems to be a relationship between stock returns and both firm size and the book-to-value-to-market-value ratio.

12. The primary market involves the initial issuance of securities.

13. Although some issuers deal directly with investors, most hire investment bankers to assist them in the sale of securities.

APPENDIX A

EMPIRICAL REGULARITIES IN THE STOCK MARKET

Empirical Regularities Differences in returns on securities that occur with regularity from period to period.

Anomaly An empirical regularity that is not predicted by any known asset pricing model.

Researchers have uncovered certain **empirical regularities** in common stocks. That is, certain cross-sectional differences among stock returns have been found to occur with regularity. Some regularities should occur according to certain asset pricing models. For example, the CAPM asserts that different stocks should have different returns because different stocks have different betas. What makes the regularities that are about to be discussed of special interest is that they are not predicted by any of the traditional asset pricing models. Accordingly, they are sometimes also referred to as **anomalies**.

Earlier it was mentioned that returns were related to a firm's size as well as its book-value-to-market-value and earnings-to-price ratios. Hence these relationships are often used as examples of anomalies.[49] This appendix will examine some calendar anomalies and present some international evidence that indicates that such anomalies also exist in other countries.

Seasonality in Stock Returns

January Effect An empirical regularity whereby stock returns appear to be higher in January as opposed to other months of the year.

Day-of-the-week Effect (Alternatively, **Weekend Effect**.) An empirical regularity whereby stock returns appear to be lower on Mondays as opposed to other days of the week.

The desire of individuals for liquidity may be thought to change from day to day and from month to month. If so, there may be seasonal patterns in stock returns. One might presume that such patterns would be relatively unimportant. Indeed, according to the notion of efficient markets, such patterns should be quite minor (if they exist at all), because they are not suggested by traditional asset pricing models. However, the evidence indicates that at least two are significant: the **January effect** and the **day-of-the-week effect**.[50]

January Effect

There is no obvious reason to expect stock returns to be higher in certain months than in others. However, in a study that looked at average monthly returns on NYSE-listed common stocks, significant seasonalities were found.[51] In particular, the average return in January was higher than the average return in any other month. Table 16.4 indicates the average stock return in January and the other 11 months for various time periods. Although the difference in returns was minor in the early part of the century, more recently it appears that the average return in January has been approximately 3% higher than the average monthly returns in February through December.[52]

Table 16.4	Seasonality in Stock Returns.		
Time Period	Average Stock Return in January	Average Stock Return in Other Months	Difference in Returns
1904–1928	1.30%	.44%	.86%
1929–1940	6.63	−.60	7.23
1941–1974	3.91	.70	3.21
1904–1974	3.48	.42	3.06

SOURCE: Michael S. Rozeff and William R. Kinney, Jr., "Capital Market Seasonality: The Case of Stock Returns," *Journal of Financial Economics* 3, no. 4 (October 1976): 388.

---

[49]Another anomaly involves financial leverage. More specifically, the stocks of firms with larger debt-to-equity ratios have, on average, larger stock returns. See Laxmi Chand Bhandari, "Debt/Equity Ratio and Expected Common Stock Returns: Empirical Evidence," *Journal of Finance* 43, no. 2 (June 1988): 507–528.

[50]There is also evidence of a "weather effect" in that NYSE stock returns appear to be related to the amount of cloud cover in New York City. More specifically, the average daily return was .13% when the cloud cover was 0–20% and .02% when the cloud cover was 100%. This has been interpreted to mean that investor psychology influences asset prices. See Edward M. Saunders, Jr., "Stock Prices and Wall Street Weather," *American Economic Review* 83, no. 5 (December 1993): 1337–1345.

[51]Michael S. Rozeff and William R. Kinney, Jr., "Capital Market Seasonality: The Case of Stock Returns," *Journal of Financial Economics* 3, no. 4 (October 1976): 379–402. For an argument that the market does not have a January effect, see Jay R. Ritter and Navin Chopra, "Portfolio Rebalancing and the Turn-of-the-year Effect," *Journal of Finance* 44, no. 1 (March 1989): 149–166.

Turn-of-the-month Effect The observation that average stock returns have been abnormally high during a four-day period beginning on the last trading day of the month.

[52]Interestingly, it appears that the returns over the first half of any month (defined to include the last day of the previous month) are significantly higher than the returns over the second half of the month. See Robert A. Ariel, "A Monthly Effect in Stock Returns," *Journal of Financial Economics* 18, no. 1 (March 1987): 161–164. Another study found this effect to be concentrated in the first three trading days (plus the last trading day of the previous month) and labelled it the **turn-of-the-month effect**. See Josef Lakonishok and Seymour Smidt, "Are Seasonal Anomalies Real? A Ninety-year Perspective," *Review of Financial Studies* 1, no. 4 (Winter 1988): 403–425.1

Day-of-the-week Effect

It is often assumed that the expected daily returns on stocks are the same for all days of the week. That is, the expected return on a given stock is the same for Monday as it is for Tuesday as it is for Wednesday as it is for Thursday as it is for Friday. However, a number of studies have uncovered evidence that refutes this belief. Two early studies looked at the average daily return on NYSE-listed securities and found that the return on Monday was quite different.[53] In particular, the average return on Monday was found to be much lower than the average return on any other day of the week. Furthermore, the average return on Monday was negative, whereas the other days of the week had positive average returns. Table 16.5 displays these findings.

Table 16.5	Analysis of Daily Returns.				
	Monday	Tuesday	Wednesday	Thursday	Friday
A. French Study					
January 1953–December 1977	−.17%	.02%	.10%	.04%	.09%
B. Gibbons & Hess Study					
July 1962–December 1978	−.13%	.00%	.10%	.03%	.08%

SOURCE: Kenneth R. French, "Stock Returns and the Weekend Effect," *Journal of Financial Economics* 8, no. 1 (March 1980): 58; and Michael R. Gibbons and Patrick Hess, "Day-of-the-week Effects and Asset Returns," *Journal of Business* 54, no. 4 (October 1981): 582–583.

The rate of return on a stock for a given day of the week is typically calculated by subtracting the closing price on the previous trading day from the closing price on that day, adding any dividends for that day to the difference, and then dividing the resulting number by the closing price as of the previous trading day:

$$r_t = \frac{(P_t - P_{t-1}) + D_t}{P_{t-1}} \tag{16.9}$$

where P_t and P_{t-1} are the closing prices on days t and $t-1$, and D_t is the value of any dividends assumed to be paid on the ex-dividend day t. This means that the return for Monday uses the closing price on Monday as P_t and the closing price on Friday as P_{t-1}. Thus, the change in price of a stock for Monday $(P_t - P_{t-1})$ actually represents the change in price *over the weekend*, as well as during Monday. This observation has caused some people to refer to the day-of-the-week effect as the *weekend effect*. Other people use the *weekend effect* to refer to price behaviour from Friday close to Monday open, and the *Monday effect* to refer to price behaviour from Monday open to Monday close.

A refinement of the day-of-the-week effect involved an examination of NYSE stock returns over 15-minute intervals during trading hours over the period of December 1, 1981,

---

[53]Kenneth R. French, "Stock Returns and the Weekend Effect," *Journal of Financial Economics* 8, no. 1 (March 1980): 55–69; and Michael R. Gibbons and Patrick Hess, "Day-of-the-week Effects and Asset Returns," *Journal of Business* 54, no. 4 (October 1981): 579–596. It has been contended that the Weekend Effect was actually first discovered in the late 1920s. See Edwin D. Maberly, "Eureka! Eureka! Discovery of the Monday Effect Belongs to the Ancient Scribes," *Financial Analysts Journal* 51, no. 5 (September–October 1995): 10–11. For an argument that this effect disappeared in the mid 1970s, see Robert A. Connolly, "An Examination of the Robustness of the Weekend Effect," *Journal of Financial and Quantitative Analysis* 24, no. 2 (June 1989): 133–169. It has been observed that NYSE trading volume is lower on Monday than any other day of the week, but that trading by individuals is highest on Mondays (and thus institutional trading is much lower), and that individuals tend to be net sellers on Monday. This is offered as a possible explanation for the day-of-the-week effect; see Josef Lakonishok and Edwin Maberly, "The Weekend Effect: Trading Patterns of Individual and Institutional Investors," *Journal of Finance* 45, no. 1 (March 1990): 231–243.

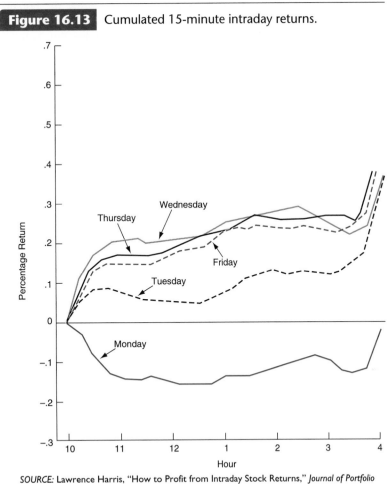

Figure 16.13 Cumulated 15-minute intraday returns.

SOURCE: Lawrence Harris, "How to Profit from Intraday Stock Returns," *Journal of Portfolio Management* 12, no. 2 (Winter 1986): 63.

through January 31, 1983.[54] Figure 16.13 displays the results when these returns were cumulated and examined on a day-of-the-week basis. Several observations can be made. First, the negative returns during trading hours on Monday occurred within an hour of the opening. Afterward, the behaviour of stock prices on Monday was similar to the other days of the week. Second, on Tuesdays through Fridays there was a notable upward movement in prices in the first hour of trading. Third, on all days of the week there was a notable upward movement in prices during the last hour of trading.[55] Hence, most of the daily price movement in a stock typically comes near the open and close.

Somewhat related to the day-of-the-week effect is the **holiday effect**. A study of this effect found that average stock returns on trading days immediately before US federal holidays (the market is closed on these holidays; there are eight per year) are 9 to 14 times

Holiday Effect The observation that average stock returns have been abnormally high on the trading day immediately before a federal holiday in the US.

---

[54]Lawrence Harris, "How to Profit from Intradaily Stock Returns," *Journal of Portfolio Management* 12, no. 2 (Winter 1986): 61–64; and "A Transaction Data Study of Weekly and Intradaily Patterns in Stock Returns," *Journal of Financial Economics* 16, no. 1 (May 1986): 99–117.

[55]This rise in prices at the end of the day appears to be primarily due to a large price rise between the next-to-last and last trades; this observation appears to be widespread over firms and days of the week. See Lawrence Harris, "A Day-End Transaction Price Anomaly," *Journal of Financial and Quantitative Analysis* 24, no. 1 (March 1989): 29–45.

higher than the average daily returns during the rest of the year.[56] Furthermore, this abnormally high return is spread out from the closing price two days before the holiday to the opening price on the day after the holiday. Tests indicate that it is unrelated to the size, January, or day-of-the-week effects.

Interrelationships

Researchers have attempted to see whether there are any interrelationships among these regularities. For example, is the January effect more pronounced for small firms? A brief discussion of this interrelationship follows.[57]

Size and January Effects

Having observed that small firms have higher returns than large firms, and that returns are higher in January than in any other month of the year, it is interesting to ponder whether or not these two effects are somehow interrelated. One study that examined this issue found that the two effects were strongly interrelated.[58] All NYSE-listed and AMEX-listed stocks over the 16-year period of 1963 to 1979 were examined in this study. At the end of each year, each firm was ranked by the size of the aggregate market value of its equity (that is, the year-end market price per share times the number of shares outstanding). Ten portfolios were then formed based on size, with portfolio 1 containing the smallest 10% of the firms, portfolio 2 the next smallest 10%, and so on.

Abnormal returns were calculated subsequently for each portfolio on a monthly basis over the 17-year period and averaged for each month. Figure 16.14 displays the results.

It can be seen from this figure that the size effect was most pronounced in January because the line for this month slopes down sharply from left to right. The other 11 months of the year appear to be quite similar to each other. Generally, each one of these months displays a slight downward slope, indicating that the size effect also existed for these months, but only to a minor degree. Also of interest is the observation that large firms had a negative abnormal return in January. Thus, the January effect has been due primarily to the behaviour of small firms, and the size effect has been concentrated mainly in the month of January.

Further examination of this interrelationship between the size effect and the January effect has revealed that it is concentrated in the first five trading days of January.[59] In particular, the difference in returns between the smallest firm portfolio and the largest firm portfolio over these five days was 8.0%, whereas over the entire year it was 30.4%. Thus, 8.0%/30.4% = 26.3% of the annual size effect occurred during these five days. (If the size

---

[56]Robert A. Ariel, "High Stock Returns Before Holidays: Existence and Evidence on Possible Causes," *Journal of Finance* 45, no. 5 (December 1990): 1611–1626. Also see Paul Brockman, "A Review and Analysis of the Holiday Effect." *Financial Markets, Institutions & Instruments* 4 No. 5 (1995): 37–58. The holiday effect also exists in Japan and the UK. See Chan-Wang Kim and Jinwoo Park, "Holiday Effects and Stock Returns: Further Evidence," *Journal of Financial and Quantitative Analysis* 29, no. 1 (March 1994): 145–157.

[57]Other interrelationships are discussed in an earlier edition of this book; see pp. 437–440.

[58]Donald B. Keim, "Size-related Anomalies and Stock Returns Seasonality: Further Empirical Evidence," *Journal of Financial Economics* 12, no. 1 (June 1983): 13–32.

[59]Rogalski also finds that the anomalous price behaviour of stocks in January mostly occurs in the first five trading days. Roll has observed that the largest daily differences in the returns between small firms and large firms occur over the last trading day of the year and the first four days of the year. Furthermore, eight of the subsequent ten trading days also have notably large differences in returns. See Richard Rogalski, "New Findings Regarding Day-of-the-week Returns Over Trading and Non-trading Periods: A Note," *Journal of Finance* 39, no. 5 (December 1984): 1603–1614; and Richard Roll, "Vas ist das?" *Journal of Portfolio Management* 9, no. 2 (Winter 1983): 18–28.

Figure 16.14 Interrelationship between the size effect and the January effect.

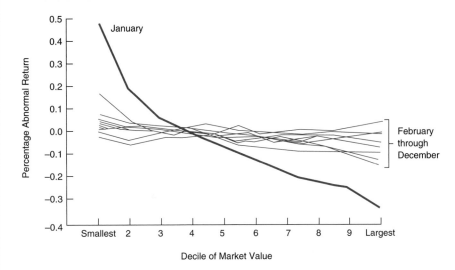

SOURCE: Donald B. Keim, "Size-Related Anomalies and Stock Return Seasonality: Further Empirical Evidence," *Journal of Financial Economics* 12, no. 1 (June 1983): 21.

effect had been spread evenly over the year, then .4% of it would have been attributed to these five days.)

Attempts have been made to explain this interrelationship between the January effect and the size effect. One explanation that appears to have some merit has to do with "tax selling." This explanation begins by arguing that stocks that have declined during the year have downward pressure on their prices near year-end as investors sell them to realize capital losses in order to minimize tax payments. After the end of the year, this pressure is removed and the prices jump back to their "fair" values. A related argument asserts that some professional money managers wish to sell those stocks that have performed poorly during the past year in order to avoid their appearance on year-end reports. Such activity is often referred to as "window dressing." Note that these arguments fly in the face of the notion of efficient markets. (The notion of efficient markets would suggest that this cannot be true, because if investors sensed that stocks were becoming undervalued at year-end, they would flood the market with buy orders, thereby preventing any substantive undervaluation from occurring.) Nevertheless, it does appear to have some merit, in that those stocks that declined during the previous year had the largest appreciation in January.[60] However, this association between January returns and the previous year's stock-price

---

[60]See Roll, "Vas ist das?" Edward A. Dyl, "Capital Gains Taxation and Year-end Stock Market Behavior," *Journal of Finance* 32, no. 1 (March 1977): 165–175; Ben Branch, "A Tax-loss Trading Rule," *Journal of Business* 50, no. 2 (April 1977): 198–207; Dan Givoly and Arie Ovadia, "Year-end Tax-induced Sales and Stock Market Seasonality," *Journal of Finance* 38, no. 1 (March 1983): 171–185; Marc R. Reinganum, "The Anomalous Stock Market Behavior of Small Firms in January: Empirical Tests for Tax-loss Selling Effects," *Journal of Financial Economics* 12, no. 1 (June 1983): 89–104; Josef Lakonishok and Seymour Smidt, "Capital Gain Taxation and Volume of Trading," *Journal of Finance* 41, no. 4 (September 1986): 951–974; Jay R. Ritter, "The Buying and Selling Behavior of Individual Investors at the Turn of the Year," *Journal of Finance* 43, no. 3 (July 1988): 701–717; Joseph P. Ogden, "Turn-of-month Evaluations of Liquid Profits and Stock Returns: A Common Explanation for the Monthly and January Effects," *Journal of Finance* 45, no. 4 (September 1990): 1259–1272; and Greggory A. Brauer and Eric C. Chang, "Return Seasonality in Stocks and Their Underlying Assets: Tax-loss Selling Versus Information Explanations," *Review of Financial Studies* 3, no. 2 (1990): 255–280.

declines does not appear to be attributable solely to such downward tax-selling price pressure, because the biggest "losers" during a year appear to have abnormally high returns for as long as five Januaries thereafter.[61] In addition, the January effect exists in Japan, yet Japan has no capital gains tax and disallows any deduction for capital losses.[62] Rebutting this evidence is the observation that the January effect apparently did not exist prior to the imposition of income taxes in the United States.[63]

A second possible explanation is that small stocks may be relatively riskier in January than during the rest of the year. If this is true, then they should have a relatively higher average return in January. A study finding that the betas of small stocks tend to increase at the beginning of the year lends support to this explanation.[64]

Empirical Regularities in Canadian Equity Markets

The Canadian situation with respect to the study of empirical regularities is similar to that in the US—many observations but little explanation. This section will briefly discuss those anomalies that have been identified in Canada and list references so that interested readers may pursue the subject further.[65]

The Size Effect in Canada

Data presented by Hatch and White, reproduced in Table 16.6, strongly suggests the existence of a small-firm effect in Canada. A rigorous study examined this phenomenon in considerable detail. The study, which included adjustments for the effects of non-synchronous trading, discovered the existence of a significant size effect. Other studies (described on the next page) that examine interrelationships between the size effect and other regularities also confirm its existence. Mittoo, however, argues that the small-firm effect disappeared from both US and Canadian markets after published research documented its existence and institutions started offering small capitalization investment funds. Table 16.7 shows that the differential returns to small firms effectively disappeared from both US and Canadian markets after May 1982.[66]

---

[61]See K. C. Chan, "Can Tax-loss Selling Explain the January Seasonal in Stock Returns?" *Journal of Finance* 41, no. 5 (December 1986): 1115–1128; Werner F. M. DeBondt and Richard Thaler, "Does the Stock Market Overreact?" *Journal of Finance* 40, no. 3 (July 1985): 793–805; and "Further Evidence on Investor Over-reaction and Stock Market Seasonality," *Journal of Finance* 42, no. 3 (July 1987): 557–581.

[62]A similar observation has been made regarding Canada. See Angle Berges, John J. McConnell, and Gary G. Schlarbaum, "The Turn-of-the-year in Canada," *Journal of Finance* 39, no. 1 (March 1984): 185–192.

[63]See Steven L. Jones, Winson Lee, and Rudolf Apenbrink, "New Evidence on the January Effect Before Personal Income Taxes," *Journal of Finance* 46, no. 5 (December 1991): 1909–1924.

[64]Richard J. Rogalski and Seha M. Tinic, "The January Size Effect: Anomaly or Risk Mismeasurement?" *Financial Analysts Journal* 42, no. 6 (November–December 1986): 63–70. See also Avner Arbel, "Generic Stocks: An Old Product in a New Package," *Journal of Portfolio Management* 11, no. 4 (Summer 1985): 4–13; and K. C. Chan and Nai-fu Chen, "Structural and Return Characteristics of Small and Large Firms," *Journal of Finance* 46, no. 4 (September 1991): 1467–1484.

[65]For an excellent summary, marred only by the lack of an adequate bibliography, see V. M. Jog, "Stock Pricing Anomalies: Canadian Experience," *Canadian Investment Review* I, no.1 (Fall 1988): 55–62.

[66]I. G. Morgan, A. L. MacBeth, and D. J. Novak, "The Relationship Between Equity Value and Abnormal Returns in the Canadian Stock Market," Kingston: Queen's University School of Business Working Paper; U. R. Mittoo, "Do Financial Markets Learn from Academic Research?" *Canadian Investment Review* IV, no. 1 (Spring 1991): 83–86.

Table 16.6	Small- and Large-stock Performance, 1950–1987.		
		Small Stocks	Large Stocks
Value Weighted			
Average monthly return		1.30%	0.98%
Monthly standard deviation		5.05%	4.45%
Equally Weighted			
Average monthly return		1.69%	1.07%
Monthly standard deviation		5.40%	4.47%

SOURCE: Reprinted, with permission, from J. E. Hatch and R. W. White, *Canadian Stocks, Bonds, Bills and Inflation: 1957–1987.* Copyright 1988, The Research Foundation of The Institute of Chartered Financial Analysts, Charlottesville, VA.

Table 16.7	Change in the Size Effect.

(a) US Market

Period	Pre-Information July 62–April 82	Post-Information May 82–Sept 87
Annual Size Effect	9.4%	–3.0%
T-statistics	5.5	–0.8

(b) Canadian Market

Period	Pre-Information Jan 53–April 82	Post-Information May 82–May 90
Size Effect	4.5%	–0.8%
T-statistics	3.7	–0.3

SOURCE: U. R. Mittoo, "Do Financial Markets Learn from Academic Research?" *Canadian Investment Review* IV, no. 1 (Spring 1991).

Seasonality in Canadian Stock Returns

Several time-related effects have been identified in Canadian stock markets, the best known of which is the January or turn-of-the-year effect. This empirical regularity has been investigated and documented by several researchers. The results of a typical study are summarized in Table 16.8 and show that there is a pronounced January effect in all stocks, large and small, but smaller stocks earn higher returns in January than other firms. Morgan et al. report that the January return accounts for practically all the annual abnormal returns earned by small firms. They conclude that there are no abnormal returns to small firms except in January.

Evidence on the tax loss selling hypothesis, however, is mixed. Canada should provide an excellent testing ground for this hypothesis because the capital gains tax was only introduced in 1972. It would be reasonable to expect, therefore, that there should be no January effect prior to 1972. The results presented in Table 16.8, however, clearly show that this effect predates the introduction of the capital gains tax.[67]

[67]A. J. Berges, J. J. McConell and G. Schlarbaum, "The Turn-of-the-year in Canada," *Journal of Finance* 39, no. 1 (March 1984): 185–92; S. M. Tinic, G. Barone-Adessi, and R. R. West, "Seasonality in Canadian Stock Prices: A Test of the 'Tax-loss-selling' Hypothesis," *Journal of Financial and Quantitative Research* 22, no.1 (March 1987): 51–63.

Table 16.8 Average Monthly Returns on the TSE 300, on the Market-value-weighted Laval Index (MVWI), and on the Equally Weighted Laval Index (EWI).

| Period | TSE 300 | | MVWI | | EWI | |
	January	Other Months	January	Other Months	January	Other Months
1963–1971	9.98%	0.58%	2.64%	0.92%	3.66%	0.91%
1972–1986	3.13	0.82	3.51	1.54	5.90	0.97

SOURCE: V. M. Jog, "Stock Pricing Anomalies: Canadian Experience," *Canadian Investment Review* I, no.1 (Fall 1988): 56.

Unlike the US, however, the turn-of-the-year effect in Canada should manifest itself during the last week of December rather than in January. In Canada, share ownership must be transferred from seller to buyer before a capital gain or loss may be reported for tax purposes. This means that a trade must be executed three trading days before year-end in order to qualify. In most years, the cut-off date is December 27 or 28 (in contrast, in the US simple execution is sufficient to qualify). Stock prices should, therefore, "rebound" during the last week in December if tax loss selling is a significant factor. Two studies have found that this is, in fact, the case.[68]

Table 16.9 Average Percentage Returns by Day of the Week.

Researchers	Index	Period	Mon.	Tues.	Wed.	Thurs.	Fri.
(a) Canada							
Jaffe & Westerfield	TSE 300[b]	1976–1983	−.14	.02	.12	.11	.14
Chamberlain et al.	TSE 300[b]	1978–1985	−.15	.07	.13	.11	.14
	TSE 300[c]	1978–1985	−.10	.05	.08	.07	.11
Bishara	TSE 300[b]	1968–1987[d]	−.49	.01	.06	.24	.21
(b) International							
Jaffe & Westerfield	US	1962–1983[a]	−.13	.02	.11	.03	.08
	Japan	1970–1983[a]	−.02	−.09	.15	.03	.06
	UK	1950–1983[a]	−.14	.09	.08	.05	.06
	Australia	1973–1983[a]	−.05	−.13	.04	.17	.13

[a] Close-to-close [c] Open-to-close
[b] Close-to-open [d] Only till March 1987

SOURCE: V. M. Jog, "Stock Pricing Anomalies: Canadian Experience," *Canadian Investment Review* I, no. 1 (Fall 1988): 56.

The day-of-the-week effect has also been reported by several Canadian researchers, as shown in Table 16.9. Returns are significantly negative on Mondays and positive on Fridays with positive but insignificant returns on other days. Despite the existence of these regularities it is probable that transaction costs would eliminate any profit from a trading

---

[68]C. B. Cadsby, "Canadian Calendar Anomalies and the Capital Asset Pricing Model," in *A Reappraisal of the Efficiency of Financial Markets*, eds. R. M. C. Guimarães, B. G. Kingsman, and S. J. Taylor (Berlin: Springer-Verlag; 1989) reports that the turn-of-the-year effect in Canada lasts from December 21 to January 5. See also M. D. Griffiths, "Systematic Changes in Investor Trading Behavior at the Turn-of-the-year: An Intraday Study," Milwaukee: University of Wisconsin-Milwaukee School of Business Administration, Working Paper, 1991. Griffiths also reports that informed investors not subject to capital gains also engage in year-end trading; see M. D. Griffiths, "The Role of Informed Traders in the Canadian Turn-of-the-year Effect," *Proceedings, Administrative Sciences Association of Canada,* Whistler, BC, 1990.

rule based on these results. Discretionary traders, however, may find it useful to purchase on Monday and to advance sales from Monday to the previous Friday.[69]

Table 16.10	Average Wealth Relatives and Tests of Deviations from the Mean.	
Day in Trading Month	Average Daily Wealth Relative	T-test Statistic[a]
−9	0.075%	0.68
−8	0.019	−0.65
−7	0.026	−0.41
−6	0.084	0.33
−5	0.022	−0.51
−4	0.006	−1.88
−3	0.033	−0.36
−2	0.040	−0.23
−1	0.041	−0.19
1	0.160	1.70[b]
2	0.159	1.27
3	0.230	2.16[b]
4	0.012	−0.70
5	0.015	−0.56
6	0.000	−1.02
7	0.014	−0.58
8	0.061	0.01
9	0.110	1.77

[a]Test: H_0: Average return for trading day = overall average daily return, against
H_1: Average return for trading day < overall average daily return.
[b]Statistically significant at the 5% level.

SOURCE: V. Jog and A. L. Riding, "The Month-end Effect in Canadian Stock Prices: Some Anomalous Findings," *Canadian Journal of Administrative Sciences* 6, no. 4 (December 1989): 7-17.

Jog and Riding have reported a month-end effect similar to that reported in US markets, shown in Table 16.10. They find that abnormally high returns are recorded on the last trading day of the calendar month and the first two trading days of the subsequent month. The returns from these three days of each month account for about 60% of the total returns on the TSE 300 for the period 1976–1984. A subsequent study indicates that a strategy based on this regularity would probably not be profitable because of transaction costs. An international study finds that the turn of the month effects are significant in Canada, the UK, Australia, Switzerland, and West Germany, whereas pre-holiday effects (similar to the Friday anomaly) are only found in Canada, Japan, Hong Kong and Australia.[70]

[69]T. Chamberlain, C. S. Cheung, and C. Kwan, "Day-of-the-week Patterns in Stock Returns: The Canadian Evidence," *Canadian Journal of Administrative Sciences* 5, no. 4 (December 1988); H. Bishara, "Stock Returns and the Weekend Effect in Canada," *Akron Business and Economic Review* 20, no. 2 (Summer 1989): 62–71; J. F. Jaffe and R. Westerfield, "A Twist on the Monday Effect in Stock Prices: Evidence from the US and Foreign Stock Markets," *Journal of Banking and Finance* 13, no. 4–5 (September 1989): 641–50.

[70]V. Jog and A. L. Riding, "The Month-end Effect in Canadian Stock Prices: Some Anomalous Findings," *Canadian Journal of Administrative Sciences* 6, no. 4 (December 1989): 7–17; V. Jog and A. L. Riding, "Lunar Cycles in Stock Prices," *Financial Analysts Journal* 45, no. 2 (March–April 1989): 63–68; C. B. Cadsby and M. Ratner, "Turn-of-the-month and Pre-holiday Effects on Stock Returns: Some International Evidence," *Journal of Banking and Finance* 16, June 1992.

Summary of Empirical Regularities

On balance, what do these regularities suggest that the investor should do? First, investors who want to buy shares should avoid doing so late on Friday or early on Monday. Conversely, investors who want to sell stocks should try to sell late on Friday or early on Monday. Second, if the stocks of small firms are to be purchased they should be purchased in late December or somewhat earlier. If the stocks of small firms are to be sold, they should be sold in mid-January or somewhat later. Third, if the stocks of large firms are to be purchased, they should be purchased in early February or somewhat later. If the stocks of large firms are to be sold, they should be sold in late December or somewhat earlier.[71]

Two words of caution are in order here. First, none of these empirical regularities is of a sufficient magnitude to suggest that riches are to be made by exploiting them. Indeed, transaction costs would devour most if not all of any profits that might be made.[72] All that they suggest is that if, for whatever reason, a buy or sell order is to be placed, there are some times when it may be more advantageous to do so. Second, although these regularities have been found to exist in the past, and in some instances for long periods of time and in several foreign markets, there is no guarantee that they will continue to exist in the future.[73] It may be the case that as more investors become aware of them and time their trades accordingly, such regularities will cease to exist.

APPENDIX B

ADJUSTING BETA

Without any information at all, it would be reasonable to estimate the beta of a stock to be equal to 1.0, the average size of beta. Given a chance to see how the stock moved relative to the market over some time period, a modification of this prior estimate would seem appropriate. Such a modification would sensibly produce a final estimate of beta that would lie between the value of 1.0 and its estimated value based purely on historical price changes.

Formal procedures for making such modifications have been adopted by most investment firms that estimate betas. The specific adjustments made may differ from time to time and, in some cases, from stock to stock. For example Merrill Lynch calculates *adjusted beta* values by giving approximately 66% weight to the historical estimate of beta and approximately 34% weight to the prior value of beta of 1.0 for each stock. More generally,

$$\beta_a = (.66 \times \beta_h) + (.34 \times 1.0) \tag{16.10}$$

where β_a and β_h are the adjusted and historical betas, respectively.[74] Examination of equa-

---

[71]These recommendations are based on studies that typically involved exchange-listed stocks. For over-the-counter stocks, Richard D. Fortin and O. Maurice Joy ["Buying and Selling OTC Stock: Fine-tuning Your Trade Date," *AAII Journal* 15, no. 3 (March 1993): 8–10] recommend (1) buying just before and selling just after the end of the month, (2) buying on Tuesday and selling on Friday, and (3) buying within two days on either side of a holiday and avoiding selling during this period.

[72]See Donald B. Keim, "Trading Patterns, Bid-ask Spreads, and Estimated Security Returns: The Case of Common Stocks at Calendar Turning Points," *Journal of Financial Economics* 25, no. 1 (November 1989): 75–97.

[73]The Appendix to Chapter 15 discusses regularities in the bond market.

[74]Adjusted betas are also published in the *Value Line Investment Survey*; their adjusted beta is equal to $(.35 \times 1.0) + (.65 \times \beta_h)$. Thus, the adjustment procedures of Value Line and Merrill Lynch are quite similar. See Meir Statman, "Betas Compared: Merrill Lynch Versus Value Line," *Journal of Portfolio Management* 7, no. 2 (Winter 1981): 41–44; and Frank K. Reilly and David J. Wright, "A Comparison of Published Betas," *Journal of Portfolio Management* 14, no. 3 (Spring 1988): 64–69.

tion (16.10) indicates that this procedure takes the historical beta for a security and adjusts it by giving it a value closer to 1.0. Thus, historical betas less than 1.0 are made larger but are still less than 1.0, and historical betas greater than 1.0 are made smaller but are still greater than 1.0. The adjustments are in this direction because the weights (.66 and .34) are positive and add up to 1.0, indicating the adjustment procedure is an averaging technique. A share's adjusted beta, therefore, is a weighted average of 1.0 and the share's historical beta.

Table 16.14 shows the extent to which this procedure anticipates differences between historical and future betas. The second column lists the unadjusted historical betas for eight portfolios of 100 securities each, based on monthly price changes from July 1947 through June 1954 (the portfolios were designed to have significantly different betas during this period). The third column of the table shows the values obtained when an adjustment of the type used by Merrill Lynch was applied. The betas in the fourth column are based on price changes over the subsequent seven years. For a majority of the portfolios, the adjusted betas are closer in magnitude to the subsequent historical betas than are the unadjusted betas. This suggests that the adjusted historical beta is a more accurate estimate of the future beta than the unadjusted historical beta.

The fifth column of Table 16.11 shows the historical betas estimated using data from a third seven-year period. Comparing the unadjusted betas in columns 2, 4, and 5, it can be seen that there is a continuing tendency for betas to revert toward the mean value of 1.0 over time. Thus, adjustment procedures seem to have some usefulness when it comes to estimating betas for a future time period.

It seems plausible that true betas not only vary over time but have a tendency to move back towards average levels, since extreme values are likely to be moderated over time. A firm whose operations or financing make the risk of its equity considerably different from that of other firms is more likely to move back towards the average than away from it. Such changes in betas are due to real economic phenomena, not simply an artifact of overly simple statistical procedures. There is, however, no reason to expect every stock's true beta to move to the same average in the same manner at the same speed. In this regard, some fundamental analysis of the firm may prove more useful than the adoption of more sophisticated statistical methods for processing past price changes in estimating beta.

Although historical betas for portfolios can provide useful information about future betas, historical betas for individual securities are subject to great error and should be

| **Table 16.11** | *Ex Ante* and *Ex Post* Beta Values for Portfolios of 100 Securities Each. |

| | July 1947–June 1954 | | | |
Portfolio (1)	Unadjusted (2)	Adjusted (3)	July 1954–June 1961 (4)	July 1961–June 1968 (5)
1	.36	.48	.57	.72
2	.61	.68	.71	.79
3	.78	.82	.88	.88
4	.91	.93	.96	.92
5	1.01	1.01	1.03	1.04
6	1.13	1.10	1.13	1.02
7	1.26	1.21	1.24	1.08
8	1.47	1.39	1.32	1.15

SOURCE: Marshall E. Blume, "Betas and Their Regression Tendencies," *Journal of Finance* 30, no. 3 (June 1975): 792.

treated accordingly. Note the magnitude of the standard errors of the betas shown in Figure 16.14.

Table 16.11 provides another view. Every stock listed on the New York Stock Exchange was assigned to one of ten classes in each year from 1931 through 1967, based on the magnitude of its historical beta calculated using data from the preceding five years. The stocks in the top 10% of each January's ranking were assigned to class 10, the next 10% to class 9, and so on. The table shows the percent of the stocks that were in the same class and within one risk class five years later. Also shown are the entries that would be expected if there were no relationship between such past and future beta classes. Examination of the table reveals that individual security betas have some but not a great deal of predictive value.

Figure 16.15 shows that the predictive ability of historical portfolio betas improves with the amount of diversification in a portfolio. The vertical axis plots the percentage of the differences in (measured) portfolio betas (based on weekly price changes) in one year that can be attributed to differences in their (measured) betas in the prior year. The horizontal axis indicates the number of securities in each portfolio. It can be seen in the figure that the historical betas for portfolios containing roughly 10 to 20 securities or more have a high degree of predictive ability. Thus, individual security betas are worth estimating even though they are rather inaccurate when viewed by themselves. This is because their individual inaccuracies seem to cancel out one another when the beta of a diversified portfolio is calculated, resulting in quite an accurate estimate of the portfolio's beta.

Table 16.12 Movement of Stocks Among Beta Classes.

Risk Class	Percentage of Stocks in the Same Beta Class Five Years Later		Percentage of Stocks in the Same Beta Class or Within One Risk Class Five Years Later	
	Actual	Expected If There Were No Relationship	Actual	Expected If There Were No Relationship
10 (highest beta values)	35.2%	10%	69.3%	20%
9	18.4	10	53.7	30
8	16.4	10	45.3	30
7	13.3	10	40.9	30
6	13.9	10	39.3	30
5	13.6	10	41.7	30
4	13.2	10	40.2	30
3	15.9	10	44.6	30
2	21.5	10	60.9	30
1 (lowest beta values)	40.5	10	62.3	20

SOURCE: William F. Sharpe and Guy M. Cooper, "Risk-return Classes of New York Stock Exchange Common Stocks, 1931–1967," *Financial Analysts Journal* 28, no. 2 (March–April 1972): 53.

Leverage and Beta

The beta of a *firm* represents the sensitivity of the aggregate value of the firm to changes in the value of the market portfolio. It depends on both the demand for the firm's products and the firm's operating costs. However, most firms have both debt and equity outstanding. This means that the beta of a firm's *equity* (that is, stock) depends on the beta of the firm and the firm's financial leverage. For example, imagine that there are two firms that are

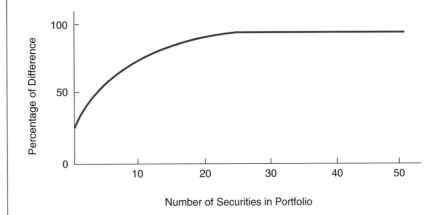

Figure 16.15 Percentage of differences in beta values attributable to differences in prior year's betas.

SOURCE: Robert A. Levy, "On the Short-term Stationarity of Beta Coefficients," *Financial Analysts Journal* 27, no. 6 (November–December 1971): 57.

identical in every way except that firm A has debt while firm B is free of debt. This means that even though they have the same earnings before interest and taxes (EBIT), they will have different earnings after taxes (EAT) because A, unlike B, has to make interest payments. In this situation, the firm betas for A and B are the same, but the stock beta for A will be greater than the stock beta for B. The difference in their debt levels is the reason for the difference in their stock betas. This is because the debt makes the earnings available to common shareholders more variable for A than for B. Thus, the stock beta for A could be viewed as being equal to the stock beta it would have if it had no debt (that is, the beta of B) plus an adjustment for the amount of debt it actually has outstanding.

One method that has been suggested for determining the influence of debt on the beta of the stock of a firm involves a four-step procedure.[75] First, the current market values of the firm's outstanding debt D and equity E must be determined. Once this is done, the current market value of the levered firm V_L can be determined:

$$V_L = D + E \qquad (16.11)$$

Second, the market value of the firm *if it were unlevered* must be determined, using the following formula:

$$V_u = V_L - \tau D \qquad (16.12)$$

where:

V_u is the market value of the firm if it was unlevered

τ is the average corporate tax rate for the firm

D is the market value of the firm's debt

Third, the beta of the firm can be calculated after estimating the betas of the firm's debt β_{debt} and equity β_{equity} by using the following formula:

---

[75]The method is developed more fully in Stephen A. Ross, Randolph W. Westerfield, Jeffrey F. Jaffe, and Gordon S. Roberts, *Corporate Finance: First Canadian Edition* (Toronto: Richard D. Irwin, Inc., 1995) pp. 351–352, 500–502, and Thomas E. Copeland and J. Fred Weston, *Financial Theory and Corporate Policy* (Reading, MA: Addison-Wesley, 1988), Chapter 13.

$$\beta_{firm} = \beta_{debt}\frac{(1-\tau)D}{V_u} + \beta_{equity}\frac{E}{V_u} \qquad (16.13)$$

Fourth, the effect of any degree of leverage on the equity beta of the firm can be determined by restating equation (16.13). Specifically, solving the equation for β_{equity} results in[76]

$$\beta_{equity} = \beta_{firm} + (\beta_{firm} - \beta_{debt})\left(\frac{D}{E}\right)(1-\tau) \qquad (16.14)$$

In evaluating equation (16.14), it should be noted that the value of β_{firm} does not change as the firm's debt-equity ratio (D/E) is changed. Assuming that the value of β_{debt} also does not change, then increasing the firm's debt-equity ratio will increase the beta of the firm's equity. This makes intuitive sense, because a higher debt-equity ratio will make a firm's EAT more volatile. Conversely, lowering a firm's debt-equity ratio should lower the firm's equity beta because it makes EAT less volatile.

This property of beta can be useful in estimating the beta of a firm's equity if the firm has recently altered its debt-equity ratio (or is contemplating increasing the ratio). For example, imagine that until last month ABC Inc. had $60 000 000 of equity and $40 000 000 of debt outstanding for a total firm value of $100 000 000; its tax rate is 30%. Using the market model shown in Table 16.1, but applied to data before the recent equity issuance, it is determined that the equity beta and debt beta of ABC are 1.40 and .20, respectively. However, ABC has just issued $20 000 000 of equity and used the proceeds to retire some of the debt so that the current values of ABC's debt and equity are $74 000 000 and $20 000 000, respectively. (The $74 000 000 value of equity represents the sum of $20 000 000 in new equity and $54 000 000 in old equity, which has decreased in value by $6 000 000 due to the loss of tax shields resulting from the $20 000 000 reduction in ABC's debt.) What is the equity beta of ABC likely to be in the immediate future?

The previously described four-step procedure can be used to answer this question. First, it is noted from equation (16.11) that the value of ABC before the new equity issuance was $100 000 000. Second, it is noted from equation (16.12) that the value of ABC if the firm were unlevered would be equal to $100 000 000 - (.3 \times $40 000 000) = $88 000 000. Third, the beta of the firm can be estimated using equation (16.13):

$$\beta_{firm} = .20\left[\frac{(1-.3)\$40\ 000\ 000}{\$88\ 000\ 000}\right] + 1.40\left(\frac{\$60\ 000\ 000}{\$88\ 000\ 000}\right)$$
$$= 1.02$$

Lastly, the current equity beta (that is, the equity beta after the recent issuance of $20 000 000 of equity) can be estimated by using equation (16.14).

$$\beta_{equity} = 1.02 + 91.02 - .20)\left(\frac{\$20\ 000\ 000}{\$74\ 000\ 000}\right)(1-.3)$$
$$= 1.17$$

Hence, the reduction in the amount of debt that ABC has outstanding has reduced the beta of the equity from 1.40 to 1.17.[77]

---

[76]To derive equation (16.14), note that equation (16.12) can be written as $V_u = D + E - \tau D$ since $V_L = D + E$. Hence the quantity $D + E - \tau D$ can be substituted for V_u in equation (16.13), and then the altered equation can be solved for β_{equity} and simplified, resulting in equation (16.14).

[77]It is assumed here that ABC's bond beta and average tax were unaffected by the new issuance of equity. More complex analyses are sometimes utilized to take into account the possible impact of capital structure changes upon them.

Industry Beta Values

Firms in industries having highly cyclical demand or large fixed costs might be expected to have higher firm betas than those in industries with more stable demand or greater variable costs, since the former will have greater variability in EBIT. Differences in financial leverage could wholly offset such factors, leaving few, if any, differences among the stock betas of firms in different industries. However, this does not seem to be the case. Firms in certain industries do tend to have higher stock betas than those in other industries, and, by and large, the classifications agree with prior expectations.

Table 16.13 shows the predicted average values of beta for stocks in various industry classifications. Stock prices of firms whose products are termed necessities tend to respond less than the stock prices of most other firms when expectations about the future health of the economy are revised. That is, firms producing necessities (such as utilities or food) tend to have lower betas because they tend to have more stable earnings. On the other hand, stock prices of firms that manufacture luxuries tend to respond more than most others when expectations about the future health of the economy are revised. That is, firms in luxuries (such as travel or electronics) tend to have high betas, because they tend to have cyclical earnings. The mining industries also have high betas reflecting the cyclical nature of their earnings.

Table 16.13 Predicted Betas by Industry in Canada, November 1998.

Industry	Beta	Industry	Beta
Integrated Mines	1.06	Mining	1.06
Gold & Precious Minerals	1.16	Integrated Oils	0.89
Oil & Gas Producers	0.89	Oil & Gas Services	0.89
Paper & Forest Products	1.03	Food Processing	0.82
Tobacco	0.82	Distilleries	0.82
Breweries & Beverages	0.82	Household Goods	0.82
Autos & Parts	0.82	Biotech & Pharmaceutical	0.78
Steel	1.29	Fabrication & Engineer.	0.93
Transportation Equipment	0.93	Technology — Hardware	0.92
Building Materials	0.93	Chemicals & Fertilizers	0.93
Business Services	0.93	Technology — Software	0.92
Real Estate	0.86	Transport & Environment	0.99
Pipelines	0.66	Telephone Utilities	0.82
Gas & Electric Utilities	0.82	Broadcasting	0.77
Cable & Entertainment	0.77	Publishing & Printing	0.85
Wholesale Distributors	0.88	Food Stores	0.88
Department Stores	0.88	Specialty Stores	0.88
Hospitality	0.88	Banks & Trusts	1.19
Investment Co. & Funds	1.16	Insurance	1.16
Financial Management	1.16	Conglomerates	1.09

SOURCE: Data provided by *BARRA International* (Canada), St. Laurent, Quebec, November 1998.

Forecasting Beta

Information of the type shown in Table 16.16 can be used to adjust historical equity betas. For example, the knowledge that a corporation is in the steel industry suggests that a reasonable prior estimate of its equity beta is 1.25. Thus, it makes more sense to adjust its historical equity beta towards a value of 1.25 than 1.0, the average for all stocks, as was suggested in equation (16.10).

The procedure used to adjust historical betas involves an implicit prediction equation for future betas. Equation (16.10) can be written more generally as:

$$\beta_a = a + b\beta_h \qquad (16.15)$$

where a and b are constants. One way to consider the differences in industry betas is to alter equation (16.15) as follows:

$$\beta_a = a\beta_{ind} + b\beta_h \qquad (16.16)$$

where β_{ind} denotes the average equity beta of the industry to which the stock belongs.

For example, consider the values of .33 and .67 for a and b, respectively. Biopharm is a pharmaceutical firm whose historical beta is 0.93. What is its adjusted beta? Noting that the average equity beta for stocks in the pharmaceutical industry is 0.69, its adjusted beta can be calculated by using equation (16.16) as follows:

$$\beta_a = (.33 \times 0.69) + (.67 \times 0.93)$$
$$= 0.85$$

Thus, Biopharm has an adjusted beta of 0.85, which lies between its historical beta of 0.93 and the average beta in its industry of 0.69. Indeed, this is what equation (16.16) accomplishes: it alters a historical beta to give an adjusted beta lying between β_h and β_{ind}.

Multiple-industry Firms

What happens if the firm has divisions that are in different industries? When there are two industries involved, equation (16.16) is modified as follows:

$$\beta_a = a(E_{ind1}\beta_{ind1} + E_{ind2}\beta_{ind2}) + b\beta_h \qquad (16.17)$$

where E_{ind1} and E_{ind2} denote the percentages of the firm's earnings that are from industries 1 and 2, respectively, and β_{ind1} and β_{ind2} are the betas for industries 1 and 2, respectively.[78]

As an example, consider United Industries, a firm that has half of its earnings coming from a division that is in the gold mining industry and half coming from a division that is in the oil and gas industry. Assuming that a and b are equal to .33 and .67, respectively, and that the historical beta for United Industries is 1.3, its adjusted beta can be calculated in two steps.

First, the value of $E_{ind1}\beta_{ind1} + E_{ind2}\beta_{ind2}$ needs to be calculated. Doing so produces a value of $(.5 \times 1.4) + (.5 \times 0.91) = 1.16$. This can be interpreted as the average equity beta for any stock whose firm has equal business interests in the gold and oil and gas industries.

Second, the adjusted beta of United Industries can be calculated using equation (16.16) as $(.33 \times 1.16) + (.67 \times 1.3) = 1.25$. Note that this value lies between the firm's historical beta of 1.3 and its "industry" beta of 1.16.

Adjustments Based on Financial Characteristics

Various financial characteristics can also be used to estimate an adjusted beta. For example, stocks with high dividend yields might have lower betas because more of their value is associated with near-term than far-term dividends. Equation (16.17) could thus be augmented to

$$\beta_a = a(E_{ind1}\beta_{ind1} + E_{ind2}\beta_{ind2}) + b\beta_h + cY \qquad (16.18)$$

where c is a constant and Y is the dividend yield of the firm's stock.

---

[78]The term $(E_{ind1}\beta_{ind1} + E_{ind2}\beta_{ind2})$ would simply be expanded if more than two industries were involved.

Table 16.14 shows a beta prediction equation of this form, using US historic data from 1928 through 1982.[79] To estimate the beta of a security using this prediction equation, start with a constant based on the industry (referred to as the "sector") in which the security is classified. Add to this constant an amount equal to the security's historical beta times 0.576. Note that this is similar to the historical beta shown in equation (16.10). Finally, add (1) the security's dividend yield times −.019, and (2) the security's "size attribute" times −.105.[80] Algebraically, the model is:

$$\beta_a = a_s + (.576 \times \beta_h) + (-.019 \times Y) + (-.105 \times S) \tag{16.19}$$

where a_s denotes the constant associated with the sector to which the stock belongs, β_h is the historical beta, Y is the dividend yield, and S is the size of the firm. With this formula, securities having higher yields are predicted to have lower betas, as are those with larger market values of equity outstanding.

Table 16.14	A Beta Prediction Equation Derived from a Factor Model.

Constant Term	
Sector	*Value*
Basic industry	.455
Capital goods	.425
Consumer staple	.307
Consumer cyclical	.443
Credit cyclical	.429
Energy	.394
Finance	.398
Transportation	.255
Utilities	.340

Variable Term	
Attribute	*Coefficient*
Beta	.576
Yield	−.019
Size	−.105

SOURCE: Blake Grossman and William F. Sharpe, "Factors in Security Returns," paper presented at the Center for the Study of Banking and Financial Markets, University of Washington, March 1984.

An Example

As an example, consider a stock that is classified as belonging to "basic industry." It has a historical beta of 1.2, a dividend yield over the previous 12 months of 4%, and an aggregate market value of $7 billion (that is, the firm has 100 million shares outstanding and the stock is selling for $70 per share). Using equation (17.18), its adjusted beta is

[79] In this method, both historical and adjusted betas are calculated relative to a value-weighted index of the returns on all stocks listed on the New York Stock Exchange. All attributes were calculated using data available a full month prior to the beginning of the month in which stock returns are measured. This avoids statistical problems and provides results that can be used for actual portfolio management.

[80] The dividend yield is measured in percent per year. The "size attribute" is calculated by taking the logarithm (to the base 10) of the total market value of equity outstanding (that is, price per share times shares outstanding), expressed in billions of dollars.

$$\beta_a = .455 + (.576 \times 1.2) + (-.019 \times 4) + [-.105 \times (\log 7)]$$
$$= .455 + .69 - .08 - .09$$
$$= .98$$

Such prediction equations, based on multifactor models, fit historical data considerably better than those that use only historical betas. One study reported an improvement of 86% over the more simple adjusted beta approach.[81] However, such figures describe only the extent to which the equations fit a given set of data. Since the true test of a prediction equation is its ability to *predict*, only extensive experience with such approaches can, in the final analysis, determine how well various factor models can predict beta values.

Beta Services

Services providing betas on a regular basis in published form are available in several countries. Many use only past price changes to form estimates. Some derive their estimates from more general factor models. One service uses weekly data for two years; another, monthly data for five years. One estimates betas for US securities relative to Standard & Poor's 500; another, relative to the New York Stock Exchange Composite Index; and so on. In each case, estimates for individual securities are subject to error. Thus, it is hardly surprising that estimated values for a given security obtained by different services using different procedures are not the same. This does not indicate that some are useless, only that they should be used appropriately and with caution.

In Canada, betas are provided by *The Polymetric Report, The Value Line Investment Survey: Canadian Edition,* and the *Beta Book* published by BARRA International, Ltd.

QUESTIONS AND PROBLEMS

1. What is the significant advantage of the corporate form of business organization? Why would you expect that this advantage would be important to the success of a capitalist economy?

2. Fall Creek is conducting the annual election for its five-member board of directors. The firm has 1 500 000 shares of voting common stock outstanding.
   a. Under a majority voting system, how many shares must a shareholder own to ensure being able to elect his choices to each of the five director seats?
   b. Under a cumulative voting system, how many shares must a shareholder own to ensure being able to elect her choices to two of the director seats?
   c. Andy Latham holds 20% of Fall Creek's outstanding shares. How many directors can Andy elect under a cumulative voting system?

3. The issue of corporate ownership versus control has become quite controversial. Discuss the principal-agent problem as it relates to shareholder-management relations. Specifically, why is there a potential conflict between the two groups? What steps can be taken to mitigate this problem?

[81]Barr Rosenberg and Vinay Marathe, "The Prediction of Investment Risk: Systematic and Residual Risk," *Proceedings of the Seminar on the Analysis of Security Prices,* University of Chicago, November 1975. Also see Barr Rosenberg, "Prediction of Common Stock Investment Risk," *Journal of Portfolio Management* 11, no. 1 (Fall 1984): 44–53, and "Prediction of Common Stock Betas," *Journal of Portfolio Management* 11, no. 2 (Winter 1985): 5–14.

4. When a bidder makes a tender offer for a target firm, what types of defences are often applied to fend off the bidder? Do these defences generally seem to be in the best interests of the target firm's shareholders? Why?

5. Why might a corporation wish to issue more than one class of common shares?

6. With respect to the payment of corporate dividends, distinguish between declaration date, ex-dividend date, and date of record.

7. Theoretical arguments and empirical research support the case that stock dividends and splits do not enhance shareholder wealth. However, corporations continue to declare stock dividends and splits. Summarize the arguments for and against stock dividends and splits from the perspective of the shareholder.

8. Menomonie Publishing stock currently sells for $40 per share. The company has 1 200 000 shares outstanding. What would be the effect on the number of shares outstanding and on the share price of the following:
   a. 15% stock dividend
   b. 4-for-3 stock split
   c. Reverse 3-for-1 stock split

9. St. Paul Corporation is planning to raise $35 000 000 through the sale of new common stock under a rights offering. The subscription price is $70 per share while the stock currently sells for $80 per share, rights on. Total outstanding shares equal 10 000 000. Of this amount, Annie Joss owns 100 000 shares.
   a. How many shares will each right permit its owner to purchase?
   b. What will be the total value of Annie's rights a day before the ex-rights date, assuming that the market price of St. Paul stock remains $80?
   c. After the ex-rights date, if the market value of each St. Paul right equals $20, what must be the ex-rights market price of St. Paul's shares?

10. Pete Van Vleet owns stock in DeKalb Dairy. DeKalb is planning a rights offering in which seven shares must be owned to buy one additional share at a price of $15. DeKalb shares currently sell for $63.
   a. What is the value of a DeKalb right?
   b. At the time of the offering announcement, Pete's assets consisted of $1500 in cash and 490 shares of DeKalb. List and show the value of Pete's assets prior to the ex-rights date.
   c. List and show the value of Pete's assets on the ex-rights date if DeKalb stock sells for $60 on that date.
   d. List and show the value of Pete's assets if Pete sells the DeKalb rights on the ex-right date.

11. Using a recent *Globe and Mail: Report on Business* as a data source, select a TSE-listed stock whose name begins with the same letter as the first letter of your last name. For this stock, calculate its rate of return for that day of the week. What was the stock's trading volume that day?

12. Tomah Electronics' stock price at the end of several quarters, along with the market index value for the same periods, is shown below. Tomah pays no dividends. Calculate the beta of Tomah's stock over the eight quarters.

Quarter	Quarter-end Tomah Share Price	Quarter-end Market Index Value
0	60.000	210.00
1	62.500	220.50
2	64.375	229.87
3	59.875	206.88
4	56.875	190.33
5	61.500	209.36
6	66.500	238.67
7	69.750	257.76
8	68.375	262.92

13. Using the data from Problem 8 in Chapter 1, calculate the beta of the small stock portfolio over the 20-year period. Use the common stock returns from Table 1.1 as the returns on the market index.

14. Shown here are ten quarters of return data for Baraboo Associates stock, as well as return data over the same period for a broad stock market index. Using this information, calculate the following statistics for Baraboo Associates stock.
    a. beta
    b. alpha
    c. standard deviation of random error term
    d. coefficient of determination

Quarter	Baraboo Return	Market Return
1	3.8%	2.7%
2	5.3	3.1
3	−7.2	−4.9
4	10.1	9.9
5	1.0	2.7
6	2.5	1.2
7	6.4	3.8
8	4.8	4.0
9	6.0	5.5
10	2.2	2.0

15. Why are liquid and continuous secondary security markets important to the effective functioning of primary security markets?

16. Describe the role of an underwriting syndicate in a public security offering.

17. Distinguish between a competitive bid underwriting and a negotiated underwriting.

18. Investment bankers frequently attempt to stabilize the price of a newly issued security in the secondary market.
    a. How is this stabilization accomplished?
    b. What is the purpose of the stabilization?
    c. What can go wrong with the stabilization attempts?

19. Why must companies that publicly issue securities file a prospectus with the SEC? What does the SEC's acceptance of the prospectus imply?

20. Discuss why ipo's appear to generate abnormal returns for investors. Are these returns a "sure thing"? What are the economic implications of these high returns for ipo issuers?

21. (Appendix Question) The empirical regularities cited in this chapter have potentially troubling implications for the Capital Asset Pricing Model and the concept of highly efficient markets. Discuss some of these implications.

22. (Appendix Question) Benita Del Vecchio, an astute investment observer, wrote, "Testing for empirical regularities is conceptually difficult because it is really a two-hypothesis test. One test relates to the validity of the underlying asset pricing model, and the other test relates to the existence of the empirical regularity." What does Benita mean by this statement?

23. (Appendix Question) Sugar Grove Technologies has debt and equity with total market values of $120 million and $230 million, respectively. With a 35% corporate tax, what is the firm's unlevered value?

24. (Appendix Question) The market value of Oswego Computers' total debt outstanding is $10 million. Further, the unlevered market value of Oswego is $40 million. The firm's average corporate tax rate is 35%.
   a. If the beta of the firm's debt is .40 and the beta of its equity is 1.20 what is the firm's beta?
   b. If the firm borrows another $10 million and uses the proceeds to purchase an equivalent amount of its own equity, what will be the effect on the beta of is equity?

25. (Appendix Question) Necedah Power is an electric utility company. Its historical beta is .70. Its stock offers a dividend yield of 7.6%. The market value of its outstanding equity is currently $140 million. Based on the data from Table 16.17, calculate Necedah's beta.

CFA Exam Questions

26. You ask John Statdud, your research assistant, to analyze the relationship between the return on Coca-Cola Enterprises (CCE) common stock and the return on the market using the Standard & Poor's 500 Stock Index as a proxy for the market. The data include monthly returns for both CCE and S&P 500 over a recent five-year period. The results of the regression are indicated below:

$$R_{CCE,t} = .59 + .94(R_{S\&P,t}) + e_{CCE,t}$$

$$(.81) \quad (3.10)$$

where:

$R_{CCE,t}$ is the return on CCE common shares in month t

$R_{S\&P,t}$ is the return on S&P 500 stock index in month t

$e_{CCE,t}$ is the residual error in month t

The numbers in parentheses are the t-statistics (the .01 critical value is 2.66). The coefficient of determination R^2 for the regression is .215.

Statdud wrote the following summary of the regression results:
   a. The regression statistics indicate that during the five-year period under study, when the annual return on the S&P 500 was zero, CCE had an average annual return of 0.59%.
   b. The alpha value of .59 is a measure of the variability of the return on the market.
   c. The coefficient of .94 indicates CCE's sensitivity to the return on the S&P 500 and suggests that the return on CCE's common stock is less sensitive to market movements than the average stock.
   d. The t-statistic of 3.10 for the slope coefficient indicates that the coefficient is not statistically significant at the .01 level.
   e. The R^2 for the regression of .215 indicates that the average estimate deviates from the actual observation by an average of 21.5%.
   f. There is no concern that the slope coefficient lacks statistical significance since beta values tend to be less stable (and therefore less useful) than alpha values.

g. The regression should be rerun using 10 years of data. This would improve the reliability of the estimated coefficients while not sacrificing anything.

Identify which of the seven statements made by Statdud are incorrect and justify your answer(s).

27. You are a portfolio manager meeting a client. During the conversation that followed your formal review of her account, your client asked the following question: "My granddaughter, who is studying investments, tells me that one of the best ways to make money in the stock market is to buy the stocks of small-capitalization firms on a Monday morning late in December and to sell the stocks one month later." What is she talking about?

a. Identify the apparent market anomalies (empirical regularities) that would justify the proposed strategy.

b. Explain why you believe such a strategy might or might not work in the future.

KEY TERMS

common shares (p. 439)
limited liability (p. 439)
charter (p. 439)
transfer agent (p. 440)
registrar (p. 440)
proxy (p. 440)
proxy fight (p. 440)
cumulative voting system (p. 440)
majority voting system (p. 440)
takeover (p. 442)
tender offer (p. 442)
bidder (p. 442)
target firm (p. 442)
white knight (p. 442)
greenmail (p. 442)
repurchase offer (p. 442)
Pac-Mac defence (p. 442)
crown jewel defence (p. 443)
poison pill defence (p. 443)
merger (p. 443)
management buyout (p. 443)
leveraged buyout (p. 443)
par value (p. 443)
book value of the equity (p. 444)
book value per share (p. 444)
treasury shares (p. 444)
restricted shares (p. 448)
dividends (p. 450)
date of record (p. 450)
ex-dividend date (p. 450)
stock dividend (p. 450)
stock split (p. 451)
reverse stock split (p. 451)
ex-distribution date (p. 451)
preemptive rights (p. 454)

oversubscription privilege (p. 454)
subscription price (p. 455)
ex-rights date (p. 455)
ex ante (p. 456)
ex post (p. 456)
historical beta (p. 460)
simple linear regression (p. 460)
standard deviation of the random error term (p. 462)
standard error of beta (p. 463)
standard error of alpha (p. 463)
correlation coefficient (p. 463)
coefficient of determination (p. 463)
coefficient of nondetermination (p. 463)
R-squared (p. 463)
residual standard deviation (p. 463)
adjusted beta (p. 464)
growth stocks (p. 465)
value stocks (p. 465)
size effect (p. 467)
investment dealer (p. 469)
underwriters (p. 469)
private placements (p. 469)
banking group (p. 469)
selling group (p. 469)
competitive bidding (p. 469)
prospectus (p. 470)
red herring (p. 470)
firm commitment (p. 470)
rights offering (p. 470)
standby agreement (p. 470)
best-efforts basis (p. 470)
pegging (p. 470)
initial public offerings (p. 471)
unseasoned offerings (p. 471)

REFERENCES

1. Corporate governance issues are discussed in:

   Bevis Longstreth, "Corporate Governance: There's Danger in New Orthodoxies," *Journal of Portfolio Management* 21, no. 3 (Spring 1995): 47–52.

   Andrei Shliefer, and Robert W. Vishny, "A Survey of Corporate Governance," *Journal of Finance* 52, no. 2 (June 1997): 737–783.

2. For a discussion of the motivations for takeovers and the associated consequences, see:

   Michael C. Jensen and Richard S. Ruback, "The Market for Corporate Control: The Scientific Evidence," *Journal of Financial Economics* 11, nos. 1–4 (April 1983): 5–50.

   Richard Roll, "The Hubris Hypothesis of Corporate Takeovers," *Journal of Business* 59, no. 1, pt. 2 (April 1986): 197–216

   J. Fred Weston, Kwang S. Chung, and Susan E. Hoag, *Mergers, Restructuring, and Corporate Control* (Englewood Cliffs, NJ: Prentice Hall, 1990).

   Michael C. Jensen, "Corporate Control and the Politics of Finance," *Journal of Applied Corporate Finance* 4, no. 2 (Summer 1991): 13–33.

   Andrei Shliefer and Robert W. Vishny, "The Takeover Wave of the 1980s," *Journal of Applied Corporate Finance* 4, no. 3 (Fall 1991): 49–56.

   Jack Treynor, "The Value of Control," *Financial Analysts Journal* 49, no. 5 (July–August 1993): 6–9.

   J. Fred Weston, Kwang S. Chung, and Susan E. Hoag, *Mergers, Restructuring, and Corporate Control* (Englewood Cliffs, NJ: Prentice Hall, 1998).

3. For a study of how risk arbitrageurs (investors who buy and sell shares of firms involved in takeovers and divestitures) are able to earn substantial returns, see:

   David F. Larcker and Thomas Lys, "An Empirical Analysis of the Incentives to Engage in Costly Information Acquisition: The Case of Risk Arbitrage," *Journal of Financial Economics* 18, no. 1 (March 1987): 111–126.

4. Several interesting studies of stock repurchases are:

   Larry Y. Dann, "Common Stock Repurchases: An Analysis of Returns to Bondholders and Stockholders," *Journal of Financial Economics* 9, no. 2 (June 1981): 113–138.

   Theo Vermaelen, "Common Stock Repurchases and Market Signaling: An Empirical Study," *Journal of Financial Economics* 9, no. 2 (June 1981): 139–183.

   Aharon R. Ofer and Anjan V. Thakor, "A Theory of Stock Price Responses to Alternative Corporate Cash Disbursement Methods: Stock Repurchases and Dividends," *Journal of Finance* 42, no. 2 (June 1987): 365–394.

   George M. Constantinides and Bruce D. Grundy, "Optimal Investment with Stock Repurchase and Financing as Signals," *Review of Financial Studies* 2, no. 4 (1989): 445–465.

   Josef Lakonishok and Theo Vermaelen, "Anomalous Price Behavior Around Repurchase Tender Offers," *Journal of Finance* 45, no. 2 (June 1990): 455–477.

Robert Comment and Gregg A. Jarrell, "The Relative Signalling Power of Dutch-auction and Fixed-price Self-tender Offers and Open-market Share Repurchases," *Journal of Finance* 46, no. 4 (September 1991): 1243–1271.

Laurie Simon Bagwell, "Dutch Auction Repurchases: An Analysis of Shareholder Heterogeneity," *Journal of Finance* 47, no. 1 (March 1992): 71–105.

David Ikenberry, Josef Lakonishok, and Theo Vermaelen, "Market Underreaction to Open Market Share Repurchases," *Journal of Financial Economics* 39, nos. 2–3 (October–November 1995): 181–208.

5. Stock splits and stock dividends are examined in:

Eugene F. Fama, Lawrence Fisher, Michael C. Jensen, and Richard Roll, "The Adjustment of Stock Prices to New Information," *International Economic Review* 10, no. 1 (February 1969): 1–21.

Sasson Bar-Yosef and Lawrence D. Brown, "A Re-examination of Stock Splits Using Moving Betas," *Journal of Finance* 32, no. 4 (September 1977): 1069–1080.

Guy Charest, "Split Information, Stock Returns, and Market Efficiency—I," *Journal of Financial Economics* 6, nos. 2–3 (June–September 1978): 265–296.

Thomas E. Copeland, "Liquidity Changes Following Stock Splits," *Journal of Finance* 34, no. 1 (March 1979): 115–141.

J. Randall Woolridge, "Ex-date Stock Price Adjustment to Stock Dividends: A Note," *Journal of Finance* 38, no. 1 (March 1983): 247–255.

J. Randall Woolridge and Donald R. Chambers, "Reverse Splits and Shareholder Wealth," *Financial Management* 12, no. 3 (Autumn 1983): 5–15.

Mark S. Grinblatt, Ronald W. Masulis, and Sheridan Titman, "The Valuation Effects of Stock Splits and Stock Dividends," *Journal of Financial Economics* 13, no. 4 (December 1984): 461–490.

Josef Lakonishok and Baruch Lev, "Stock Splits and Stock Dividends: Why, Who, and When," *Journal of Finance* 42, no. 4 (September 1987): 913–932.

Christopher G. Lamoreux and Percy Poon, "The Market Reaction to Stock Splits," *Journal of Finance* 42, no. 5 (December 1987): 1347–1370.

Michael J. Brennan and Thomas E. Copeland, "Stock Splits, Stock Prices, and Transactions Costs," *Journal of Financial Economics* 22, no. 1 (October 1988): 83–101.

Maureeen McNichols and Ajay Dravid, "Stock Dividends, Stock Splits, and Signaling," *Journal of Finance* 45, no. 3 (July 1990): 857–879.

Robert S. Conroy, Robert S. Harris, and Bruce A. Benet, "The Effects of Stock Splits on Bid-ask Spreads," *Journal of Finance* 45, no. 4 (September 1990): 1285–1295.

David A. Dubofsky, "Volatility Increases Subsequent to NYSE and AMEX Stock Splits," *Journal of Finance* 46, no. 1 (March 1991): 421–431.

Michael J. Brennan and Patricia J. Hughes, "Stock Prices and the Supply of Information," *Journal of Finance,* 46, no. 5 (December 1991): 1665–1691.

Michael T. Maloney and J. Harold Mulherin, "The Effects of Splitting on the Ex: A Microstructure Reconcilliation," *Financial Management* 21, no. 4 (Winter 1992): 44–59.

H. Kent Baker, Aaron L. Phillips, and Gary E. Powell, "The Stock Distribution Puzzle: A Synthesis of the Literature on Stock Splits and Stock Dividends," *Financial Practice and Education* 5, no. 1 (Spring–Summer 1995): 24–37.

Eugene Pilotte and Timothy Manuel, "The Market's Response to Recurring Events: The Case of Stock Splits," *Journal of Financial Economics* 42, no. 1 (September 1996): 3–26.

Chris J. Muscarella and Michael R. Vetsuypens, "Stock Splits: Signaling or Liquidity? The Case of ADR 'Solo Splits'," *Journal of Financial Economics* 41, no. 1 (May 1996): 111–127.

David L. Ikenberry, Graeme Rankine, and Earl K. Stice, "What Do Stock Splits Really Signal?" *Journal of Financial and Quantitative Analysts* 31, no. 3 (September 1996): 357–375.

James J. Angel, "Tick Size, Share Prices, and Stock Splits," *Journal of Finance* 52, no. 2 (June 1997): 655–681.

James J. Angel, "Picking Your Tick: Toward a New Theory of Stock Splits," *Journal of Applied Corporate Finance* 10, no. 3 (Fall 1997): 59–68.

6. References for the relationship between size and return are contained in the endnotes. The characteristics of value and growth stocks are described in:

Ken Gregory, "Fund Investment Strategies: Growth versus Value Investing," *AAII Journal* 11, no. 9 (October 1989): 22–25.

David E. Tierney and Kenneth J. Winston, "Using Generic Benchmarks to Present Manager Styles," *Journal of Portfolio Management* 17, no. 4 (Summer 1991): 33–36.

John Bajkowski, "A Question of Style: Growth and Value Investing," *AAII Journal* 14, no. 5 (June 1992): 33–37.

John Bajkowski, "Creating Stock Screens That Make Practical Sense," *AAII Journal* 15, no. 6 (July 1993): 34–37.

Rafael La Porta, Josef Lakonishok, Andrei Shliefer, and Robert Vishny, "Good News for Value Stocks: Further Evidence on Market Efficiency," *Journal of Finance* 52, no. 2 (June 1997): 859–874.

Louis K. C. Chan, Narasimhan Jegadeesh, and Josef Lakonishok, "Evaluating the Performance of Value Versus Glamour Stocks: The Impact of Selection Bias," *Journal of Financial Economics* 38, no. 3 (July 1995): 269–296.

7. For more on investment banking, see the citations given in the footnotes and:

Richard A. Brealey, Ron Giammarino, Elizabeth Maynes, Stewart C. Myers, and Ian J. Marcus, *Fundamentals of Corporate Finance, First Canadian Edition* (Toronto: McGraw-Hill Ryerson, 1996), Chapter 15.

Stephen A. Ross, Randolph W. Westerfield, and Jeffrey F. Jaffee, *Corporate Finance* (Boston: Irwin McGraw-Hill, 1996), Chapters 19–20.

8. Many of the studies conducted concerning various empirical regularities are cited in the footnotes. Also see:

Donald B. Keim, "The CAPM and Equity Return Regularities," *Financial Analysts Journal* 42, no. 3 (May–June 1986): 19–34.

Michael Smirlock and Laura Starks, "Day-of-the-week and Intraday Effects in Stock Returns," *Journal of Financial Economics* 17, no. 1 (September 1986): 197–210.

Richard H. Thaler, "Anomalies: The January Effect," *Journal of Economic Perspectives* 1, no. 1 (Summer 1987): 197–201; and "Anomalies: Seasonal Movements in Security Prices—Weekend, Holiday, Turn-of-the-month, and Intraday Effects," *Journal of Economic Perspectives* 1, no. 2 (Fall 1987): 169–177.

Douglas K. Pearce, "Challenges to the Concept of Market Efficiency," Federal Reserve Bank of Kansas City *Economic Review* 72, no. 8 (September–October 1987): 16–33.

Elroy Dimson, ed., *Stock Market Anomalies* (Cambridge, England: Cambridge University Press, 1988).

Robert A. Haugen and Josef Lakonishok, *The Incredible January Effect* (Homewood, IL: Dow Jones-Irwin, 1988).

Burton G. Malkiel, *A Random Walk Down Wall Street* (New York: W. W. Norton, 1990), Chapter 8.

Eugene F. Fama, "Efficient Capital Markets: II," *Journal of Finance* 46, no. 5 (December 1991): 1575–1617.

Narasimhan Jegadeesh, "Does Market Risk Really Explain the Size Effect?" *Journal of Financial and Quantitative Analysis* 27, no. 3 (September 1992): 337–351.

Mark D. Griffiths and Robert W. White, "Tax-induced Trading and the Turn-of-the-year Anomaly: An Intraday Study," *Journal of Finance* 48, no. 2 (June 1993): 575–598.

Rick A. Cooper and Joel M. Shulman, "The Year-end Effect in Junk Bond Prices," *Financial Analysts Journal* 50, no. 5 (September–October 1994): 61–65.

Josef Lakonishok, Andrei Shliefer, and Robert W. Vishny, "Contrarian Investment, Extrapolation, and Risk," *Journal of Finance* 49, no. 5 (December 1994): 1541–1578.

Richard W. Sias and Laura T. Starks, "Institutions and Individuals at the Turn-of-the-year," *Journal of Finance* 52, no. 4 (September 1997): 1543–1562.

David K. Musto, "Portfolio Disclosures and Year-end Price Shifts," *Journal of Finance* 52, no. 4 (September 1997): 1563–1588.

9. For a tongue-in-cheek article on anomalies that shows that market returns are influenced by superstition because returns on Friday the 13th are, on average, abnormally low, see:

Robert W. Kolb and Ricardo J. Rodriguez, "Friday the Thirteenth: 'Part VII'—A Note," *Journal of Finance* 42, no. 5 (December 1987): 1385–1387.

10. The behaviour of beta coefficients has been extensively studied. See, for example:

Marshall Blume, "On the Assessment of Risk," *Journal of Finance* 26, no. 1 (March 1971): 1–10.

Robert A. Levy, "On the Short-term Stationarity of Beta Coefficients," *Financial Analysts Journal* 27, no. 6 (November–December 1971): 55–62.

William F. Sharpe and Guy M. Cooper, "Risk-return Classes of New York Stock Exchange Common Stocks, 1931–1967," *Financial Analysts Journal* 28, no. 2 (March–April 1972): 46–54.

Robert S. Hamada, "The Effect of the Firm's Capital Structure on the Systematic Risk of Common Stocks," *Journal of Finance* 27, no. 2 (May 1972): 435–452.

Marshall Blume, "Betas and Their Regression Tendencies," *Journal of Finance* 30, no. 3 (June 1975): 785–795.

Barr Rosenberg and Vinay Marathe, "The Prediction of Investment Risk: Systematic and Residual Risk," *Proceedings of the Seminar on the Analysis of Security Prices*, Center for Research in Security Prices, Graduate School of Business, University of Chicago, November 1975.

Barr Rosenberg and James Guy, "Prediction of Beta from Investment Fundamentals,"

Financial Analysts Journal 32, no. 3 (May–June 1976): 60–72, and no. 4 (July–August 1976): 62–70.

Meir Statman, "Betas Compared: Merrill Lynch Versus Value Line," *Journal of Portfolio Management* 7, no. 2 (Winter 1981): 41–44.

Diana R. Harrington, "Whose Beta is Best?" *Financial Analysts Journal* 39, no. 5 (July–August 1983): 67–73.

Barr Rosenberg, "Prediction of Common Stock Investment Risk," *Journal of Portfolio Management* 11, no. 1 (Fall 1984): 44–53.

Barr Rosenberg, "Prediction of Common Stock Betas," *Journal of Portfolio Management* 11, no. 2 (Winter 1985): 5–14.

Gordon J. Alexander and Jack Clark Francis, *Portfolio Analysis* (Englewood Cliffs, NJ: Prentice Hall, 1986): 185–192.

George Foster, *Financial Statement Analysis* (Englewood Cliffs, NJ: Prentice Hall, 1986), Chapter 10.

Frank K. Reilly and David J. Wright, "A Comparison of Published Betas," *Journal of Portfolio Management* 14, no. 3 (Spring 1988): 64–69.

Thomas E. Copeland and J. Fred Weston, *Financial Theory and Corporate Policy* (Reading, MA: Addison-Wesley, 1988), Chapter 13.

Richard A. Brealey and Stewart C. Myers, *Principles of Corporate Finance* (New York: McGraw-Hill, 1991), pp. 191–192, 468–469.

Louis K. C. Chan and Josef Lakonishok, "Robust Measurement of Beta Risk," *Journal of Financial and Quantitative Analysts* 27, no. 2 (June 1992): 265–282.

Stephen A. Ross, Randolph W. Westerfield, and Jeffrey Jaffe, *Corporate Finance* (Chicago: Irwin, 1996), pp. 322, 469.

11. For a Canadian perspective on the topics covered in this chapter, see:

B. Smith and A. Amoako-Adu, "Financing Canadian Corporations with Restricted Voting Shares," *NCMRD Working Paper*, London, ON, 1991.

G. Athanassakos, "Portfolio Rebalancing and the January Effect," *Financial Analysts Journal* 48, no. 6 (November–December 1992).

J. B. Berk, "A Critique of Size-related Anomalies," *Review of Financial Studies* 8, no. 1 (Summer 1993).

S. R. Foerster and D. C. Porter, "Calendar and Size-based Anomalies in Canadian Stock Returns," in M. J. Robinson and B. F. Smith, eds., *Canadian Capital Markets* (London, ON: Western Business School, 1993).

D. C. Porter, "Stock Splits and Changing Betas," in M. J. Robinson and B. F. Smith, eds., *Canadian Capital Markets* (London, ON: Western Business School, 1993).

W. J. McNally, "Le Rachat D'Actions Signale-t-il Une Variation Du Risque," *Fineco* 4, no. 1 (1[er] semestre 1994).

P. M. Clarkson and J. Merkley, "Ex-ante Uncertainty and the Underpricing of Initial Public Offerings: Further Canadian Evidence," *Canadian Journal of Administrative Sciences* 11, no. 1 (March 1994).

G. Athanassakos and M. J. Robinson, "The Day-of-the-week Anomaly: The Toronto Stock Exchange Experience," *Journal of Business Finance and Accounting* 21, no. 6 (September 1994).

G. Athanassakos, "How to Predict the Likelihood of the January Effect," *Canadian Investment Review* VIII, no. 1 (Spring 1995).

V. Jog and B. Li, "Price Related Anomalies on the Toronto Stock Exchange," *Proceedings, Administrative Sciences Association of Canada Conference,* Windsor, June 1995.

G. F. Tannous, "Management Compensation and Shareholder Value," *Proceedings, Administrative Sciences Association of Canada Conference,* Windsor, June 1995.

N. Ursel, "Deregulation in Investment Banking and Underwriting Fees for Seasoned Common Equity Offerings on the Toronto Stock Exchange," *Proceedings, Administration Sciences Association of Canada Conference,* Windsor (June 1995).

R. Atindéhou, G. Bernier, and G. Charest, "Annonces de Dividende et Évolution du Risque Systématique: Une Estimation pas les Modéles ARCH," *Administrative Sciences Association of Canada Conference,* Montreal, June 1996.

D. Domian, D. Louton, and E. Yobaccio, "Psychological Barriers in Canada and US Stock Indices," *Proceedings, Administrative Sciences Association of Canada Conference,* Montreal, June 1996.

L. Kryzanowski and I. Rakita, "The Short-run Intraday Behviour of Canadian IPOs," *Proceedings, Administrative Sciences Association of Canada Conference,* Montreal, June 1996.

C. Mossman, "Can Investors Realize Abnormal Returns at Year-end? A Toronto Stock Exchange Study," *Proceedings, Administrative Sciences Association of Canada Conference,* Montreal, June 1996.

C. Robinson, J. Rumsey, and A. White, "Market Efficiency in the Valuation of Corporate Control: Evidence from Dual Class Equity," *Canadian Journal of Administrative Sciences* 13, no. 3 (September 1996).

L. Kryzanowski and H. Zhang, "Is the Day-of-the-week Effect Still Valid?" *Canadian Investment Review* XI, no. 2 (Summer 1997).

G. Athanassakos, "Seasons for Stocks," *Canadian Investment Review* X, no. 3 (Fall 1997).

V. Jog and A. Srivastava, "The Mixed Results of Canadian IPOs," *Canadian Investment Review* X, no. 4 (Winter 1997–98).

D. Domian and D. Louton, "Canadian Stock Market Responses to Interest Rate Changes," *Proceedings, Administrative Sciences Association of Canada Conference,* Saskatoon, June 1998.

G. Tannous and A. Chehab, "Short Position Announcements and Stock Price Reactions," *Proceedings, Administrative Sciences Association of Canada Conference,* Saskatoon, June 1998.

N. Ursel and D. Trepanier, "A Time-series Analysis of Rights Usages in Canada," *Proceedings, Administrative Sciences Association of Canada Conference,* Saskatoon, June 1998.

Steve Foerster, "Canadian Market Anomalies," *Canadian Investment Review* XI, no. 2 (Summer 1998).

S. Clearly and M. Inglis, "Momentum in Canadian Stock Returns," *Canadian Journal of Administrative Sciences* 15, no. 3 (September 1998).

Lucy Ackert and George Athanassakos, "The Seasonal Impact of Institutional Investors," *Canadian Investment Review* XI, no. 3 (Fall 1998).

CHAPTER 17

The Valuation of Common Shares

I n Chapter 16, it was noted that one purpose of financial analysis is to identify mispriced securities. Fundamental analysis was mentioned as one approach for conducting a search for such securities. With this approach, the security analyst makes estimates of such things as the firm's future earnings and dividends. If these estimates are substantially different from the average estimates of other analysts but are viewed as being more accurate, then the security is considered to be mispriced. If it is also felt that the market price of the security will adjust to reflect these more accurate estimates, then the analyst will issue either a buy or sell recommendation, depending upon the direction of the anticipated price adjustment. Based upon the capitalization of income method of valuation (also known as the discounted cash flow approach), dividend discount models have been frequently used by fundamental analysts as a means of identifying mispriced common stocks.[1] This chapter will examine dividend discount models and show how they can be related to models based on price-earnings ratios.

Capitalization of Income Method of Valuation

Capitalization of Income Method of Valuation An approach to valuing financial assets. It is based on the concept that the ``true'' or intrinsic value of a financial asset is equal to the discounted value of future cash flows generated by that asset.

There are many ways to implement the fundamental analysis approach to identifying mispriced securities. A number of them are either directly or indirectly related to what is sometimes referred to as the **capitalization of income method of valuation.**[2] This method states

---

[1] The usefulness of this method of valuation is shown in Steven N. Kaplan and Richard S. Ruback, "The Valuation of Cash Flow Forecasts: An Empirical Analysis," *Journal of Finance* 50, no. 4 (September 1995): 1059–1093.

[2] Some fundamental analysts use a model for identifying winners (that is, underpriced common stocks) that is not directly related to the capitalization of income method of valuation. Instead, stocks are identified as candidates for purchase if certain of their financial ratios exceed predetermined values. For example, the first screen might identify every stock whose price was less than 2/3 of its net current asset value (that is, the per share value of current assets less total debt) and the second screen might identify stocks that also had a debt-to-equity ratio greater than one. Articles that discuss such screening methods include J. Ronald Hoffmeister and Edward A. Dyl, "Dividends and Share Value: Graham and Dodd Revisited," *Financial Analysts Journal* 41, no. 3 (May–June 1985): 77–78; and Lewis D. Johnson, "Dividends and Share Value: Graham and Dodd Revisited, Again," *Financial Analysts Journal* 41, no. 5 (September–October 1985): 79–80. For the most recent edition of the book, see Sidney Cottle, Roger F. Murray, and Frank E. Block, *Graham and Dodd's Security Analysis* 5th ed. (New York: McGraw-Hill, 1988). For a brief discussion of their approach to investing, see Roger F. Murray, "Graham and Dodd: A Durable Discipline," *Financial Analysts Journal* 40, no. 5 (September–October 1984): 18–23; Paul Blustein, "Ben Graham's Last Will and Testament," *Forbes*, August 1, 1977, pp. 43–45; and James B. Rea, "Remembering

(continued on next page)

that the true, or intrinsic, value of any asset is based on the cash flows that the investor expects to receive in the future from owning the asset. Since these cash flows are expected in the future, they are discounted to reflect the time value of money, with the **discount rate** reflecting not only the time value of money but also the riskiness of the cash flows. Chapter 14 introduced the capitalization of income method of valuation and applied it to fixed-income securities. In this chapter the method is considered in more detail and then applied to common shares.

Algebraically, the intrinsic value of the asset (V) is equal to the sum of the present values of the expected cash flows:

$$V = \frac{C_1}{(1+k)^1} + \frac{C_2}{(1+k)^2} + \frac{C_3}{(1+k)^3} + \cdots = \sum_{t=1}^{\infty} \frac{C_t}{(1+k)^t} \qquad (17.1)$$

where C_t denotes the expected cash flow associated with the asset at time t and k is the appropriate discount rate for cash flows of this degree risk. In this equation, the discount rate is assumed to be the same for all periods. Since the symbol ∞ above the summation sign in the equation denotes infinity, all expected cash flows, from immediately after making the investment until infinity, are discounted at the same rate in determining V.[3]

Net Present Value

For the sake of convenience, let the current moment in time be denoted by zero, or $t = 0$. If the cost of purchasing an asset at $t = 0$ is P, then its **net present value** (**NPV**) is equal to the difference between its intrinsic value and cost, or

$$NPV = V - P = \left[\sum_{t=1}^{\infty} \frac{C_t}{(1+k)^t} \right] - P \qquad (17.2)$$

The NPV calculation shown here is conceptually the same as the NPV calculation made for capital budgeting decisions that has long been advocated in introductory finance textbooks. Capital budgeting decisions involve deciding whether or not a given investment project should be undertaken (for example, whether to buy a new machine). In such decisions, the focal point is the NPV of the project. Specifically, an investment project will likely be viewed favourably if its NPV is positive and unfavourably if its NPV is negative. For a simple project involving a cash outflow now (at $t = 0$) and expected cash inflows in the future, a positive NPV means that the present value of all the expected cash inflows is greater than the cost of making the investment. Conversely, a negative NPV means that the present value of all the expected cash inflows is less than the cost of making the investment.

The same views about NPV apply when financial assets (such as a common share) instead of real assets (such as a new machine) are being considered for purchase. That is, a financial asset is viewed favourably and said to be underpriced, or undervalued, if NPV > 0. Conversely, a financial asset is viewed unfavourably and said to be overpriced, or overvalued, if NPV < 0. From equation (17.2), this is equivalent to stating that a finan-

[2] *(continued)* Benjamin Graham—Teacher and Friend," *Journal of Portfolio Management* 3, no. 4 (Summer 1977): 66–72; Henry R. Oppenheimer, "A Test of Ben Graham's Stock Selection Criteria," *Financial Analysts Journal* 40, no. 5 (September–October 1984): 68–74; Henry R. Oppenheimer, "Ben Graham's Net Current Asset Values: A Performance Update," *Financial Analysts Journal* 42, no. 6 (November–December 1986): 40–47; Marc R. Reinganum, "The Anatomy of Stock Market Winners," *Financial Analysts Journal* 44, no. 2 (March–April 1988): 16–28.

[3] Sometimes the expected cash flows after some time period will be equal to zero, meaning that the summation only needs to be carried out to that point. Even if they are never equal to zero, in many cases the denominator in equation (17.1) will become so large as t gets large (for example, if t is 40 or more for a discount rate of 15%) that the present value of all expected cash flows past an arbitrary time in the future will be roughly zero and can be safely ignored. In addition, the discount rate may vary from period to period. It is assumed constant here for ease of exposition.

cial asset is underpriced if $V > P$:

$$\sum_{t=1}^{\infty} \frac{C_t}{(1+k)^t} > P \tag{17.3}$$

Conversely, the asset is overvalued if $V < P$:

$$\sum_{t=1}^{\infty} \frac{C_t}{(1+k)^t} < P \tag{17.4}$$

Internal Rate of Return

Internal Rate of Return (IRR) (Alternatively, **Implied Return**.) The discount rate that equates the present value of future cash flows expected to be received from a particular investment to the cost of that investment.

Another way of making capital budgeting decisions that is similar to NPV involves calculating the **internal rate of return** (IRR) associated with the investment project. With IRR, the NPV in equation (17.2) is set equal to zero and the discount rate becomes the unknown that must be calculated. That is, the IRR for a given investment is the discount rate that makes the net present value of the investment equal to zero. Algebraically, the procedure involves solving the following equation for the internal rate of return, denoted by k^*:

$$0 = \sum_{t=1}^{\infty} \frac{C_t}{(1+k^*)^t} - P \tag{17.5}$$

Equivalently, equation (17.5) can be rewritten as

$$P = \sum_{t=1}^{\infty} \frac{C_t}{(1+k^*)^t} \tag{17.6}$$

The decision rule for IRR involves comparing the project's IRR, denoted by k^*, with the required rate of return for an investment of similar risk (denoted by k). Specifically, the investment would be viewed favourably if $k^* > k$ and unfavourably if $k^* < k$. As with NPV, the same decision rule applies if either a real asset or a financial asset is being considered for possible investment.[4]

An Application to Common Shares

Dividend Discount Model (DDM) The term used for the capitalization of income method of valuation as applied to common shares. All variants of dividend discount models assume that the intrinsic value of a share of common stock is equal to the discounted value of the dividends forecast to be paid on the shares.

This chapter is concerned with using the capitalization of income method to determine the intrinsic value of common shares. Since the cash flows associated with an investment in any particular common share are the dividends that are expected to be paid in the future, the models suggested by this method of valuation are often known as **dividend discount models** (DDMs).[5] Accordingly, D_t will be used instead of C_t to denote the expected cash flow

---

[4]With complex cash flows (such as a mix of positive and negative cash flows), the IRR method can be misleading. However, this is not a problem when it is applied to securities such as stocks and bonds. For a discussion of potential problems in other contexts, see Richard A. Brealey and Stewart C. Myers, *Principles of Corporate Finance* (New York: McGraw-Hill, 1996), Chapter 5.

[5]Since the focus of DDMs is on predicting dividends, there is a particular situation where using DDMs to value common shares is exceptionally difficult. This is the situation when the firm has not paid dividends on its shares in the recent past, which results in a complete lack of a historical record on which to base a prediction of dividends. Examples include valuing the shares of a firm being sold to the public for the first time (known as an initial public offering, or ipo) and valuing the shares of a firm that has not paid dividends recently (perhaps the firm has never paid dividends, or perhaps it has suspended paying them). A more extensive discussion of DDMs is contained in the entire November–December 1985 issue of the *Financial Analysts Journal*. For articles that describe some of the current applications of DDMs, see Barbara Donnelly, "The Dividend Discount Model Comes into Its Own," *Institutional Investor* 19, no. 3 (March 1985): 77–82, and Kent Hickman and Glen H. Petry, "A Comparison of Stock Price Predictions Using Court Accepted Formulas, Dividend Discount, and P/E Models," *Financial Management* 19, no. 2 (Summer 1990): 76–87.

in period t associated with a particular share of common stock, resulting in the following restatement of equation (17.1):

$$V = \frac{D_1}{(1 + k)^1} + \frac{D_2}{(1 + k)^2} + \frac{D_3}{(1 + k)^3} + \cdots$$
$$= \sum_{t=1}^{\infty} \frac{D_t}{(1 + k)^t} \tag{17.7}$$

Usually the focus of DDMs is on determining the true, or intrinsic, value of one share of a particular company's common stock, even if larger-size purchases are being contemplated. This is because it is usually believed that larger-size purchases can be made at a cost that is a simple multiple of the cost of one share (for example, the cost of 1000 shares is usually assumed to be 1000 times the cost of one share). Thus, the numerator in DDMs is the cash dividends per share that are expected in the future.

However, there is a complication in using equation (17.7) to determine the intrinsic value of a share of common stock. In particular, in order to use this equation the investor must forecast *all* future dividends. Since common shares do not have a fixed lifetime, this suggests that an infinitely long stream of dividends must be forecast. While this may seem to be an impossible task, with the addition of certain assumptions, the equation can be made tractable (that is, usable).

These assumptions centre around dividend growth rates. That is, the dividend per share at any time t can be viewed as being equal to the dividend per share at time $t - 1$ times a dividend growth rate of g_t:

$$D_t = D_{t-1}(1 + g_t) \tag{17.8}$$

or, equivalently,

$$\frac{D_t - D_{t-1}}{D_{t-1}} = g_t \tag{17.9}$$

For example, if the dividend per share expected at $t = 2$ is $4 and the dividend per share expected at $t = 3$ is $4.20, then $g_3 = (\$4.20 - \$4)/\$4 = 5\%$.

The different types of tractable DDMs are presented next. Each reflects a different set of assumptions about dividend growth rates. The discussion begins with the simplest case, the zero-growth model.

The Zero-growth Model

One assumption that could be made about future dividends is that they will remain at a fixed dollar amount. That is, the dollar amount of dividends per share that were paid over the past year (D_0) will also be paid over the next year (D_1), the year after that (D_2), the year after that (D_3), and so on. That is,

$$D_0 = D_1 = D_2 = D_3 = \cdots$$

Zero-growth Model
(Alternatively, **No-growth Model**.) A type of dividend discount model in which dividends are assumed to maintain a constant value in perpetuity.

This is equivalent to assuming that all the dividend growth rates are zero, since if $g_t = 0$, then $D_t = D_{t-1}$ in equation (17.8). Accordingly, this model is often referred to as the **zero-growth** (or no-growth) **model**.

▶ **Net Present Value**

The impact of this assumption on equation (17.7) can be analyzed by noting what happens when D_t is replaced by D_0 in the numerator:

$$V = \sum_{t=1}^{\infty} \frac{D_0}{(1 + k)^t} \tag{17.10}$$

Fortunately, equation (17.10) can be simplified by noting that D_0 is a fixed dollar amount, which means it can be written outside the summation sign:

$$V = D_0 \left[\sum_{t=1}^{\infty} \frac{1}{(1+k)^t} \right]$$

(17.11)

The next step involves using a property of infinite series from mathematics. If $k > 0$, then it can be shown that

$$\sum_{t=1}^{\infty} \frac{1}{(1+k)^t} = \frac{1}{k}$$

(17.12)

Applying this property to equation (17.11) results in the following formula for the zero-growth model:

$$V = \frac{D_0}{k}$$

(17.13)

Since $D_0 = D_1$, equation (17.13) is sometimes written as

$$V = \frac{D_1}{k}$$

(17.14)

An Example

As an example of how this DDM can be used, assume that the Zinc Company is expected to pay cash dividends amounting to $8 per share into the indefinite future and has a required rate of return of 10%. Using either equation (17.13) or equation (17.14), it can be seen that the value of a share of Zinc stock is equal to $8/.10 = $80. With a current stock price of $65 per share, equation (17.2) would suggest that the NPV per share is $80 − $65 = $15. Equivalently, since $V = \$80 > P = \$65$, the stock is underpriced by $15 per share and would be a candidate for purchase.

Internal Rate of Return

Equation (17.13) can be reformulated to solve for the IRR on an investment in a zero-growth security. First, the current price of the security is substituted for V; second, k^* is substituted for k. Doing so results in

$$P = \frac{D_0}{k^*}$$

which can be rewritten as

$$k^* = \frac{D_0}{P}$$

(17.15a)

$$= \frac{D_1}{P}$$

(17.15b)

An Example

Applying this formula to the shares of Zinc indicates that $k^* = \$8/\$65 = 12.3\%$. Since the IRR from an investment in Zinc exceeds the required rate of return on Zinc (12.3% > 10%), this method also indicates that Zinc is underpriced.[6]

---

[6] A share of common stock has a positive NPV if and only if it has an IRR greater than its required rate of return. Thus, there can never be inconsistent signals given by the two approaches. That is, there will never be a situation where one approach indicates a share is underpriced and the other approach indicates it is overpriced. This is true not only for the zero-growth model but for all DDMs.

An Application

The zero-growth model may seem quite restrictive. After all, it does not seem reasonable to assume a given stock will pay a fixed dollar-size dividend forever. While such a criticism has validity for common stock valuation, there is one particular situation where this model is quite useful. Specifically, whenever the intrinsic value of a preferred share is to be determined, this DDM is often appropriate. It is appropriate because most preferred shares are nonparticipating, meaning they pay a fixed dollar-size dividend that will not be changed as earnings-per-share changes. Furthermore, for high-grade preferred shares these dividends are expected to be paid regularly into the foreseeable future. Why? Because preferred stock does not have a fixed lifetime and, by restricting the application of the zero-growth model to high-grade preferred shares, the chance of a suspension of dividends is remote.[7]

The Constant-growth Model

Constant-growth Model
A type of dividend discount model in which dividends are assumed to exhibit a constant growth rate.

The next type of DDM to be considered is one that assumes dividends grow from period to period at the same rate forever, and that is therefore known as the **constant-growth model**.[8] Specifically, the dividends per share that were paid over the previous year (D_0) are expected to grow at a given rate g, so that the dividends expected over the next year (D_1) are expected to be equal to $D_0(1 + g)$. Dividends the year after that are again expected to grow by the rate g, meaning that $D_2 = D_1(1 + g)$. Since $D_1 = D_0(1 + g)$, this is equivalent to assuming that $D_2 = D_0(1 + g)^2$ and, in general,

$$D_t = D_{t-1}(1 + g) \qquad (17.16a)$$
$$= D_0(1 + g)^t \qquad (17.16b)$$

Net Present Value

The impact of this assumption on equation (17.7) can be analyzed by noting what happens when D_t is replaced by $D_0(1 + g)^t$ in the numerator:

$$V = \sum_{t=1}^{\infty} \frac{D_0(1 + g)^t}{(1 + k)^t} \qquad (17.17)$$

Fortunately, equation (17.17) can be simplified by noting that D_0 is a given dollar amount, which means it can be written outside the summation sign:

$$V = D_0 \left[\sum_{t=1}^{\infty} \frac{(1 + g)^t}{(1 + k)^t} \right] \qquad (17.18)$$

The next step involves using a property of infinite series from mathematics. If $k > g$, then it can be shown that

---

[7]The formula for valuing *consols* (these are bonds that make regular coupon payments but have no maturity date) is identical to equation (17.13), where the numerator now represents the annual coupon payment. Because it has been found that the price behaviour of high-grade preferred shares is very similar to that of bonds, it is not surprising that the zero-growth model can be used to value high-grade preferred stocks. See John S. Bildersee, "Some Aspects of the Performance of Non-convertible Preferred Stocks," *Journal of Finance* 28, no. 5 (December 1973): 1177–1201; and Enrico J. Ferreira, Michael F. Spivey, and Charles E. Edwards, "Pricing New-issue and Seasoned Preferred Stock: A Comparison of Valuation Models," *Financial Management* 21, no. 2 (Summer 1992): 52–62. For another method of valuing preferred stock, see Pradipkumar Ramanlal, "A Simple Algorithm for the Valuation of Preferred Stock," *Financial Practice and Education* 7, no. 1 (Spring–Summer 1997): 11–19.

[8]For an extension of this model that introduces capital gains taxes, see Raymond Chiang and Ricardo J. Rodriguez, "Personal Taxes, Holding Period, and the Variation of Growth Stocks," *Journal of Economics and Business* 42, no. 4 (November 1990): 303–309.

$$\sum_{t=1}^{\infty} \frac{(1+g)^t}{(1+k)^t} = \frac{1+g}{k-g} \tag{17.19}$$

Substituting equation (17.19) into equation (17.18) results in the valuation formula for the constant-growth model:

$$V = D_0 \left[\frac{1+g}{k-g} \right] \tag{17.20}$$

Sometimes equation (17.20) is rewritten as

$$V = \frac{D_1}{k-g} \tag{17.21}$$

since $D_1 = D_0(1+g)$.

An Example

As an example of how this DDM can be used, assume that during the past year the Copper Company paid dividends amounting to $1.80 per share. The forecast is that dividends on Copper shares will increase by 5% per year into the indefinite future. Thus, dividends over the next year are expected to equal $1.80(1 + .05) = $1.89. Using equation (17.20) and assuming the required rate of return of 11%, it can be seen that the value of a share of Copper stock is equal to $1.80[(1 + .05)/(.11 − .05)] = $1.89/(.11 − .05) = $31.50. With a current stock price of $40 per share, equation (17.2) would suggest that the NPV per share is $31.50 − $40 = −$8.50. Equivalently, since $V = $31.50 < P = 40, the stock is overpriced by $8.50 per share and would be a candidate for sale if currently owned.

Internal Rate of Return

Equation (17.20) can be reformulated to solve for the internal rate of return on an investment in a constant growth security. First, the current price of the security is substituted for V and then k^* is substituted for k. Doing so results in

$$P = D_0 \left[\frac{1+g}{k^*-g} \right] \tag{17.22}$$

which can be rewritten as

$$k^* = \frac{D_0(1+g)}{P} + g \tag{17.23a}$$

$$= \frac{D_1}{P} + g \tag{17.23b}$$

An Example

Applying this formula to the shares of Copper indicates that $k^* = [$1.80(1 + .05)/$40] + .05 = [$1.89/$40] + .05 = 9.725\%$. Since the required rate of return on Copper exceeds the IRR from an investment in Copper (11% > 9.725%), this method also indicates that Copper is overpriced.

Relationship to the Zero-growth Model

The zero-growth model of the previous section can be shown to be a special case of the constant-growth model. In particular, if the growth rate g is assumed to be 0, then dividends will be a fixed dollar amount forever, which is the same as saying that there will be zero growth. Letting $g = 0$ in equations (17.20) and (17.23a) results in two equations that are identical to (17.13) and (17.15a), respectively.

While assuming constant growth may seem less restrictive than assuming no growth, it may still be unrealistic in many cases. However, as will be shown next, the constant-growth model is important because it is embedded in the multiple-growth model.

The Multiple-growth Model

Multiple-growth Model
A type of dividend discount model in which dividends are assumed to grow at different rates over specifically defined time periods.

The most general DDM for valuing common stocks is the **multiple-growth model**. With this model, the focus is on a time in the future after which dividends are expected to grow at a constant rate g. Although the investor is still concerned with forecasting dividends, these dividends do not need to have any specific pattern until this time, after which they will be assumed to have the specific pattern of constant growth. If this time is denoted by T, then dividends $D_1, D_2, D_3, \ldots, D_T$ will be forecast separately by the investor (the investor also forecasts when this time T will occur). Thereafter, dividends are assumed to grow by a constant rate g that the investor must also forecast, meaning that

$$D_{T+1} = D_T(1 + g)$$
$$D_{T+2} = D_{T+1}(1 + g) = D_T(1 + g)^2$$
$$D_{T+3} = D_{T+2}(1 + g) = D_T(1 + g)^3$$

and so on. Figure 17.1 presents a time line of dividends and growth rates associated with the multiple-growth model.

Net Present Value

In determining the value of a share of common stock with the multiple-growth model, the present value of the forecasted stream of dividends must be determined. This can be done by dividing the stream into two parts, finding the present value of each part, and then adding these two present values together.

The first part consists of finding the present value of all the forecasted dividends up to and including T. Denoting this present value by V_{T-}, it is equal to

$$V_{T-} = \sum_{t=1}^{T} \frac{D_t}{(1 + k)^t} \tag{17.24}$$

The second part consists of finding the present value of all the forecasted dividends after T and involves the application of the constant-growth model. The application begins by imagining that the investor is not at time zero ($t = 0$) but is at time T ($t = T$) and has not changed his forecast of dividends for the shares. This means that next period's dividend, D_{T+1}, and all those thereafter are expected to grow at the rate g. Thus, the investor would

---

Figure 17.1 Time line for multiple growth model.

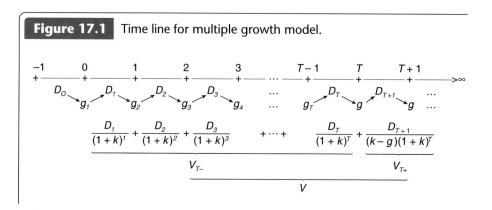

be viewing the stock as having a constant growth rate, and its value *at time T* (V_T) could be determined with the constant-growth model of equation (17.21):

$$V_T = D_{T+1} \left[\frac{1}{k - g} \right] \qquad (17.25)$$

One way to view V_T is that it represents a lump sum that is just as desirable as the stream of dividends after T. That is, an investor would find a lump sum of cash equal to V_T, to be received at T, to be equally desirable to the stream of dividends D_{T+1}, D_{T+2}, D_{T+3}, and so on. Now, given that the investor is at time zero ($t = 0$), not at T, the present value at $t = 0$ of the lump sum V_T must be determined. This is done by discounting it for T periods at the rate k, resulting in the following formula for finding the present value at time zero for all dividends after T, denoted by V_{T+}:

$$V_{T+} = V_T \left[\frac{1}{(1 + k)^T} \right]$$

$$= \frac{D_{T+1}}{(k - g)(1 + k)^T} \qquad (17.26)$$

Having found the present value of all dividends up to and including T with equation (17.24) and the present value of all dividends after T with equation (17.26), the value of a share can be determined by summing these two amounts:

$$V = V_{T-} + V_{T+}$$

$$= \sum_{t=1}^{T} \frac{D_t}{(1 + k)^t} + \frac{D_{T+1}}{(k - g)(1 + k)^T} \qquad (17.27)$$

Figure 17.1 illustrates the valuation procedure for the multiple-growth DDM that is given in equation (17.27).

An Example

As an example of how this DDM can be used, assume that during the past year the Magnesium Company paid dividends amounting to $.75 per share. Over the next year Magnesium is expected to pay dividends of $2 per share. Thus, $g_1 = (D_1 - D_0)/D_0 = (\$2 - \$.75)/\$.75 = 167\%$. The year after that dividends are expected to amount to $3 per share, indicating that $g_2 = (D_2 - D_1)/D_1 = (\$3 - \$2)/\$2 = 50\%$. At this time, the forecast is that dividends will grow by 10% per year into the indefinite future, indicating that $T = 2$ and $g = 10\%$. Consequently, $D_{T+1} = D_3 = \$3(1 + .10) = \$3.30$.

Given a required rate of return on Magnesium shares of 15%, the value of V_{T-} and V_{T+} can be calculated, respectively, as follows:

$$V_{T-} = \frac{\$2}{(1 + .15)^1} + \frac{\$3}{(1 + .15)^2}$$

$$= \$4.01$$

$$V_{T+} = \frac{\$3.30}{(.15 - .10)(1 + .15)^2}$$

$$= \$49.91$$

Summing V_{T-} and V_{T+} results in a value for V of $4.01 + $49.91 = $53.92. With a current stock price of $55 per share, Magnesium appears to be fairly priced. That is, since V and P are nearly of equal size, Magnesium is not mispriced.

Internal Rate of Return

The zero-growth and constant-growth models had equations for V that could be reformulated in order to solve for the internal rate of return on an investment in a share.

Unfortunately, a convenient expression similar to equations (17.15a), (17.15b), (17.23a), and (17.23b) is not available for the multiple-growth model. This can be seen by noting that the expression for IRR is derived by substituting P for V and k^* for k in equation (17.27):

$$P = \sum_{t=1}^{T} \frac{D_t}{(1 + k^*)^t} + \frac{D_{T+1}}{(k^* - g)(1 + k^*)^T} \tag{17.28}$$

This equation cannot be rewritten with k^* isolated on the left-hand side, meaning that a closed-form expression for IRR does not exist for the multiple-growth model.

However, all is not lost. It is still possible to calculate the IRR for an investment in a share conforming to the multiple-growth model by using an "educated" trial-and-error method. The basis for this method is the observation that the right-hand side of equation (17.28) is simply equal to the present value of the dividend stream, where k^* is used as the discount rate. Hence, the larger the value of k^*, the smaller the value of the right-hand side of equation (17.28). The trial-and-error method proceeds by initially using an estimate for k^*. If the resulting value on the right-hand side of equation (17.28) is larger than P, then a larger estimate of k^* is tried. Conversely, if the resulting value is smaller than P, then a smaller estimate of k^* is tried. Continuing this search process, the investor can hone in on the value of k^* that makes the right-hand side equal P on the left-hand side. Fortunately, it is a relatively simple matter to program a computer to conduct the search for k^* in equation (17.28). Most spreadsheets include a function that does so automatically.

An Example

Applying equation (17.28) to the Magnesium Company results in

$$\$55 = \frac{\$2}{(1 + k^*)^1} + \frac{\$3}{(1 + k^*)^2} + \frac{\$3.30}{(k^* - .10)(1 + k^*)^2} \tag{17.29}$$

Initially a rate of 14% may be used in attempting to solve this equation for k^*. Inserting 14% for k^* in the right-hand side of equation (17.29) results in a value of $67.54. Earlier 15% was used in determining V and resulted in a value of $53.92. This means that k^* must have a value between 14% and 15%, since $55 is between $67.54 and $53.92. If 14.5% is tried next, the resulting value is $59.97, suggesting a higher rate should be tried. If 14.8% and 14.9% are subsequently tried, the respective results are $56.18 and $55.03. Since $55.03 is the closest to P, the IRR associated with an investment in Magnesium is 14.9%. Given a required return of 15% and an IRR of approximately that amount, the stock of Magnesium appears to be fairly priced.

Relationship to the Constant-growth Model

The constant-growth model can be shown to be a special case of the multiple-growth model. In particular, if the time when constant growth is assumed to begin is set equal to zero, then

$$V_{T-} = \sum_{t=1}^{T} \frac{D_t}{(1 + k)^t} = 0$$

and

$$V_{T+} = \frac{D_{T+1}}{(k - g)(1 + k)^T} = \frac{D_1}{k - g}$$

since $T = 0$ and $(1 + k)^0 = 1$. Given that the multiple-growth model states that $V = V_{T-} + V_{T+}$, setting $T = 0$ results in $V = D_1/(k - g)$, a formula that is equivalent to the formula for the constant-growth model.

◗ Two-stage and Three-stage Models

Two dividend discount models that are sometimes used are the two-stage and the three-stage models.[9] The two-stage model assumes a constant growth rate (g_1) exists only until some time T, when a different growth rate (g_2) is assumed to begin and continue thereafter. The three-stage model assumes a constant growth rate (g_1) exists only until some time T_1, when a second growth rate is assumed to begin and last until a later time T_2, when a third growth rate is assumed to begin and last thereafter. By letting V_{T+} denote the present value of all dividends after the last growth rate has begun and V_{T-} denote the present value of all the preceding dividends, it can be seen that these models are just special cases of the multiple-growth model.

In applying the capitalization of income method of valuation to common shares, it might seem appropriate to assume that they will be sold at some point in the future. In this case, the expected cash flows would consist of the dividends up to that point as well as the expected selling price. Since dividends after the selling date would be ignored, the use of a dividend discount model may seem to be improper. However, as is shown next, this is not so.

Valuation Based on a Finite Holding Period

The capitalization of income method of valuation involves discounting all dividends that are expected in the future. Since the simplified models of zero growth, constant growth, and multiple growth are based on this method, they too involve a future stream of dividends. Upon reflection, it may seem that such models are relevant only for an investor who plans to hold a stock forever, since such an investor would expect to receive this stream of future dividends.

But what about an investor who plans to sell the shares in a year?[10] In such a situation, the cash flows that the investor expects to receive from purchasing a share of the stock are equal to the dividend expected one year from now (for ease of exposition, it is assumed that common shares pay dividends annually) and the expected selling price of the shares. Thus, it would seem appropriate to determine the intrinsic value of the shares to the investor by discounting these two cash flows at the required rate of return as follows:

$$
\begin{aligned}
V &= \frac{D_1 + P_1}{(1 + k)} \\
&= \frac{D_1}{1 + k} + \frac{P_1}{1 + k}
\end{aligned}
\tag{17.30}
$$

where D_1 and P_1 are the expected dividend and selling price at $t = 1$, respectively.

In order to use equation (17.30), the expected price of a share at $t = 1$ must be estimated. The simplest approach assumes that the selling price will be based on the dividends that are expected to be paid after the selling date, $t = 1$. Thus, the expected selling price at $t = 1$ is

---

[9]For a discussion of these models, see Russell J. Fuller and Chi-Cheng Hsia, "A Simplified Common Stock Valuation Model," *Financial Analysts Journal* 40, no. 5 (September–October 1984): 49–56; Eric H. Sorensen and David A. Williamson, "Some Evidence on the Value of Dividend Discount Models," *Financial Analysts Journal* 41, no. 6 (November–December 1985): 60–69; Richard W. Taylor, "A Three-phase Quarterly Dividend Discount Model," *Financial Analysts Journal* 44, no. 5 (September–October 1988): 79–80, and "A Three-phase Quarterly Earnings Model," *Financial Analysts Journal* 45, no. 5 (September–October 1989): 79; and Michael S. Rozeff, "The Three-phase Dividend Discount Model and the ROPE Model," *Journal of Portfolio Management* 16, no. 2 (Winter 1990): 36–42.

[10]The analysis is similar if it is assumed that the investor plans to sell the stock after some other length of time, such as six months or two years.

$$P_1 = \frac{D_2}{(1+k)^1} + \frac{D_3}{(1+k)^2} + \frac{D_4}{(1+k)^3} + \cdots$$

$$= \sum_{t=2}^{\infty} \frac{D_t}{(1+k)^{t-1}} \qquad (17.31)$$

Substituting equation (17.31) for P_1 in the right-hand side of equation (17.30) results in

$$V = \frac{D_1}{1+k} + \left[\frac{D_2}{(1+k)^1} + \frac{D_3}{(1+k)^2} + \frac{D_4}{(1+k)^3} + \cdots \right] \left[\frac{1}{1+k} \right]$$

$$= \frac{D_1}{(1+k)^1} + \frac{D_2}{(1+k)^2} + \frac{D_3}{(1+k)^3} + \frac{D_4}{(1+k)^4} + \cdots$$

$$= \sum_{t=1}^{\infty} \frac{D_t}{(1+k)^t}$$

which is exactly the same as equation (17.7). Thus, valuing a share of common stock by discounting its dividends up to some point in the future and its expected selling price at that time is equivalent to valuing a share by discounting all future dividends. Simply stated, the two are equivalent because the expected selling price is itself based on dividends to be paid after the selling date. Thus, equation (17.7)—as well as the zero-growth, constant-growth, and multiple-growth models that are based on it—is appropriate for determining the intrinsic value of a share of common stock regardless of the length of the investor's planned holding period.

An Example

As an example, reconsider the common shares of the Copper Company. Over the past year it was noted that Copper paid dividends of $1.80 per share, with the forecast that the dividends would grow by 5% per year forever. This means that dividends over the next two years (D_1 and D_2) are forecast to be $1.80(1 + .05) = 1.89 and $1.89(1 + .05) = 1.985, respectively. If the investor plans to sell the shares after one year, the selling price can be estimated by noting that at $t = 1$, the forecast of dividends for the forthcoming year would be D_2, or $1.985. Thus, the anticipated selling price at $t = 1$, denoted by P_1, would be equal to $1.985/(.11 − .05) = $33.08. Accordingly, the intrinsic value of Copper to such an investor would be equal to the present value of the expected cash flows, which are $D_1 = 1.89 and $P_1 = 33.08. Using equation (17.30) and assuming a required rate of 11%, this value is equal to ($1.89 + $33.08)/(1 + .11) = $31.50. Note that this is the same amount that was calculated earlier when all the dividends from now to infinity were discounted using the constant-growth model: $V = D_1/(k − g) = $1.89/(.11 − .05) = $31.50.

Models Based on Price-earnings Ratios

Price-earnings Ratio A corporation's current stock price divided by its earnings per share.

Despite the inherent sensibility of DDMs, many security analysts use a much simpler procedure to value common shares. First, a stock's earnings per share over the forthcoming year (E_1) are estimated, and then the analyst (or someone else) will estimate a "normal" **price-earnings ratio** for the stock. The product of these two numbers gives the estimated future price (P_1). Using this value, together with estimated dividends to be paid during the period (D_1) and current price (P), the estimated return on the stock over the period can be determined:

$$\text{Expected return} = \frac{(P_1 − P) + D_1}{P} \qquad (17.32)$$

where

$$P_1 = (P_1/E_1) \times E_1$$

Some security analysts expand this procedure, estimating earnings per share and price-earnings ratios for optimistic, most likely, and pessimistic scenarios to produce a rudimentary probability distribution of a security's return. Other analysts determine whether a share is underpriced or overpriced by comparing its actual price-earnings ratio with its normal price-earnings ratio, as is shown next.[11]

In order to make this comparison, equation (17.7) must be rearranged and some new variables must be introduced. To begin, it should be noted that earnings per share (E_t) are related to dividends per share (D_t) by the firm's **payout ratio** (p_t):

$$D_t = p_t E_t \tag{17.33}$$

Payout Ratio The percentage of a firm's earnings paid to shareholders in the form of cash dividends.

Note that if an analyst has forecast earnings per share and payout ratios, then she has implicitly forecast dividends.

Equation (17.33) can be used to restate the various DDMs so as to focus on what the share's price-earnings ratio should be instead of on its intrinsic value. In order to do so, $p_t E_t$ is substituted for D_t on the right-hand side of equation (17.7), resulting in a general formula for determining a stock's intrinsic value that involves discounting earnings:

$$
\begin{aligned}
V &= \frac{D_1}{(1+k)^1} + \frac{D_2}{(1+k)^2} + \frac{D_3}{(1+k)^3} + \cdots \\
&= \frac{p_1 E_1}{(1+k)^1} + \frac{p_2 E_2}{(1+k)^2} + \frac{p_3 E_3}{(1+k)^3} + \cdots \\
&= \sum_{t=1}^{\infty} \frac{p_t E_t}{(1+k)^t}
\end{aligned}
\tag{17.34}
$$

Earlier, it was noted that dividends in adjacent time periods could be viewed as being "linked" to each other by a dividend growth rate, g_t. Similarly, earnings per share in any year t can be linked to earnings per share in the previous year $t-1$ by a growth rate in earnings per share, g_{et}:

$$E_t = E_{t-1}(1 + g_{et}) \tag{17.35}$$

This implies that

$$
\begin{aligned}
E_1 &= E_0(1 + g_{e1}) \\
E_2 &= E_1(1 + g_{e2}) = E_0(1 + g_{e1})(1 + g_{e2}) \\
E_3 &= E_2(1 + g_{e3}) = E_0(1 + g_{e1})(1 + g_{e2})(1 + g_{e3})
\end{aligned}
$$

and so on, where E_0 is the actual level of earnings per share over the past year, E_1 is the expected level of earnings per share over the forthcoming year, E_2 is the expected level of earnings per share for the year after E_1, and E_3 is the expected level of earnings per share for the year after E_2.

These equations relating expected future earnings per share to E_0 can be substituted into equation (17.34), resulting in

$$
V = \frac{p_1[E_0(1 + g_{e1})]}{(1+k)^1} + \frac{p_2[E_0(1 + g_{e1})(1 + g_{e2})]}{(1+k)^2} + \frac{p_3[E_0(1 + g_{e1})(1 + g_{e2})(1 + g_{e3})]}{(1+k)^3} + \cdots \tag{17.36}
$$

Earnings-price Ratio The reciprocal of the price-earnings ratio.

[11]Alternatively, some analysts focus on the **earnings-price ratio**, which is the reciprocal of the price-earnings ratio. Accordingly, the formulas for a share's normal earnings-price ratio can be found by simply taking the reciprocal of the forthcoming formulas for determining its normal price-earnings ratio. In cases where earnings are close to zero, the earnings-price ratio is computationally preferred by analysts to the price-earnings ratio. This is because it approaches zero in such a situation, whereas the price-earnings ratio approaches infinity.

Since V is the intrinsic value of a share of stock, it represents what the share should be selling for if it were fairly priced. It follows that V/E_0 represents what the price-earnings ratio should be for the share if it were fairly priced; it is sometimes referred to as the share's normal price-earnings ratio. Dividing both sides of equation (17.36) by E_0 and simplifying results in the formula for determining the normal price-earnings ratio:

$$\frac{V}{E_o} = \frac{p_1[(1 + g_{e1})]}{(1 + k)^1} + \frac{p_2[(1 + g_{e1})(1 + g_{e2})]}{(1 + k)^2} + \frac{p_3[(1 + g_{e1})(1 + g_{e2})(1 + g_{e3})]}{(1 + k)^3} + \cdots \tag{17.37}$$

This shows that, other things being equal, a share's normal price-earnings ratio will be *higher*:

1. The *greater* the expected payout ratios (p_1, p_2, p_3, ...),
2. The *greater* the expected growth rates in earnings per share (g_{e1}, g_{e2}, g_{e3}, ...), and
3. The *smaller* the required rate of return (k).

The qualifying phrase "other things being equal" should not be overlooked. For example, a firm cannot increase the value of its shares by simply planning on having greater payouts. This will increase p_1, p_2, p_3, ... but will decrease the expected growth rates in earnings per share g_{e1}, g_{e2}, g_{e3}, ... Assuming the firm's investment policy is not altered, the effects of the reduced growth in earnings per share will just offset the effects of the increased payouts, leaving value per share unchanged.

Earlier, it was noted that a share was viewed as being underpriced if $V > P$ and overpriced if $V < P$. Since dividing both sides of an inequality by a positive constant will not change the direction of the inequality, a share can be viewed as being underpriced if $V/E_0 > P/E_0$ and overpriced if $V/E_0 < P/E_0$. Thus, a share will be underpriced if its normal price-earnings ratio is greater than its actual price-earnings ratio and overpriced if its normal price-earnings ratio is less than its actual price-earnings ratio.

Unfortunately, equation (17.37) is intractable, meaning it cannot be used to estimate the normal price-earnings ratio for any share. However, simplifying assumptions can be made that result in tractable formulas for estimating normal price-earnings ratios. These assumptions, along with the formulas, parallel those made previously regarding dividends and are discussed next.

The Zero-growth Model

The zero-growth model assumed that dividends per share remained at a fixed dollar amount forever. This is equivalent to assuming that earnings per share remain at a fixed dollar amount forever, with the firm maintaining a 100% payout ratio. It is assumed to be 100% because if a lesser amount were paid out, it would mean that the firm was retaining part of its earnings. These retained earnings would be put to some use and would thus be expected to increase future earnings per share, and consequently dividends per share.

Accordingly, the zero-growth model assumes $p_t = 1$ for all time periods and $E_0 = E_1 = E_2 = E_3$ and so on. This means that $D_0 = E_0 = D_1 = E_1 = D_2 = E_2$ and so on, allowing valuation equation (17.13) to be restated as

$$V = \frac{E_0}{k} \tag{17.38}$$

Dividing equation (17.38) by E_0 results in the formula for the normal price-earnings ratio for a stock having zero growth:

$$\frac{V}{E_0} = \frac{1}{k} \tag{17.39}$$

An Example

Earlier, it was assumed that the Zinc Company was a zero-growth firm paying dividends of $8 per share, selling for $65 a share, and having a required rate of return of 10%. Since Zinc is a zero-growth company, this means that it has a 100% payout ratio, which, in turn, means that $E_0 = \$8$. At this point, equation (17.38) can be used to note that a normal price-earnings ratio for Zinc is $1/.10 = 10$. Since Zinc has an actual price-earnings ratio of $\$65/\$8 = 8.1$ and since $V/E_0 = 10 > P/E_0 = 8.1$, Zinc shares are underpriced.

The Constant-growth Model

Earlier, it was noted that dividends in adjacent time periods could be viewed as being connected to each other by a dividend growth rate, g_t. Similarly, it was noted that earnings per share can be connected by an earnings growth rate, g_{et}. The constant-growth model assumes that the growth rate in dividends per share will be the same throughout the future. An equivalent assumption is that earnings per share will grow at a constant rate (g_e) throughout the future, with the payout ratio remaining at a constant level (p). This means that

$$E_1 = E_0(1 + g_e)$$
$$E_2 = E_1(1 + g_e) = E_0(1 + g_e)(1 + g_e)$$
$$E_3 = E_2(1 + g_e) = E_0(1 + g_e)(1 + g_e)(1 + g_e)$$

and so on. In general, earnings in year t can be connected to E_0 as follows:

$$E_t = E_0(1 + g_e)^t \tag{17.40}$$

Substituting equation (17.40) into the numerator of equation (17.34) and recognizing that $p_t = p$ results in the following:

$$V = \sum_{t=1}^{\infty} \frac{pE_0(1 + g_e)^t}{(1 + k)^t}$$

$$= pE_0 \left[\sum_{t=1}^{\infty} \frac{(1 + g_e)^t}{(1 + k)^t} \right] \tag{17.41}$$

The same mathematical property of infinite series given in equation (17.19) can be applied to equation (17.41), resulting in

$$V = pE_0 \left[\frac{1 + g_e}{k - g_e} \right] \tag{17.42}$$

It can be noted that the earnings-based constant-growth model has a numerator identical to the numerator of the dividend-based constant-growth model, since $pE_0 = D_0$. Furthermore, the denominators of the two models are identical if the growth rates in earnings and dividends are the same (that is, if $g_e = g$). Examining the assumptions of the models reveals that these growth rates must be equal. This can be seen by recalling that constant earnings growth means

$$E_t = E_{t-1}(1 + g_e)$$

When both sides of this equation are multiplied by the constant payout ratio, the result is

$$pE_t = pE_{t-1}(1 + g_e)$$

Since $pE_t = D_t$ and $pE_{t-1} = D_{t-1}$, this equation reduces to:

$$D_t = D_{t-1}(1 + g_e)$$

which indicates that dividends in any period $t - 1$ will grow by the earnings growth rate, g_e. Since the dividend-based constant-growth model assumed dividends in any period $t - 1$ would grow by the dividend growth rate g, it can be seen that the two growth rates must be equal for the two models to be equivalent.

Equation (17.42) can be restated by dividing each side by E_0, resulting in the following formula for determining the normal price-earnings ratio for a stock with constant growth:

$$\frac{V}{E_0} = p\left[\frac{1 + g_e}{k - g_e}\right] \tag{17.43}$$

An Example

Earlier, it was assumed that the Copper Company had paid dividends of \$1.80 per share over the past year, with a forecast that dividends would grow by 5% per year forever. Furthermore, it was assumed that the required rate of return on Copper was 11%, and the current stock price was \$40 per share. Now, assuming E_0 was \$2.70, it can be seen that the payout ratio was equal to \$1.80/\$2.70 = $66\frac{2}{3}\%$. This means that the normal price-earnings ratio for Copper, according to equation (17.43), is equal to $.6667[(1 + .05)/(.11 - .05)] = 11.67$. Since this is less than Copper's actual price-earnings ratio of \$40/\$2.70 = 14.81, it follows that the shares of Copper Company are overpriced.

The Multiple-growth Model

Earlier it was noted that the most general DDM is the multiple-growth model, where dividends are allowed to grow at varying rates until some point in time T, after which they are assumed to grow at a constant rate. In this situation the present value of all the dividends is found by adding the present value of all dividends up to and including T, denoted by V_{T-}, and the present value of all dividends after T, denoted by V_{T+}:

$$V = V_{T-} + V_{T+}$$

$$= \sum_{t=1}^{T} \frac{D_t}{(1 + k)^t} + \frac{D_{T+1}}{(k - g)(1 + k)^T} \tag{17.27}$$

In general, earnings per share in any period t can be expressed as being equal to E_0 times the product of all the earnings growth rates from time zero to time t:

$$E_t = E_0(1 + g_{e1})(1 + g_{e2}) \cdots (1 + g_{et}) \tag{17.44}$$

Because dividends per share in any period t are equal to the payout ratio for that period times the earnings per share, it follows from equation (17.44) that

$$D_t = p_t E_t$$

$$= p_t E_0(1 + g_{e1})(1 + g_{e2}) \cdots (1 + g_{et}) \tag{17.45}$$

Replacing the numerator in equation (17.37) with the right-hand side of equation (17.45) and then dividing both sides by E_0 gives the following formula for determining a share's "normal" price-earnings ratio with the multiple-growth model:

$$\frac{V}{E_0} = \frac{p_1(1 + g_{e1})}{(1 + k)^1} + \frac{p_2(1 + g_{e1})(1 + g_{e2})}{(1 + k)^2} + \cdots$$

$$+ \frac{p_T(1 + g_{e1})(1 + g_{e2}) \cdots (1 + g_{eT})}{(1 + k)^T}$$

$$+ \frac{p(1 + g_{e1})(1 + g_{e2}) \cdots (1 + g_{eT})(1 + g)}{(k - g)(1 + k)^T} \tag{17.46}$$

An Example

Consider the Magnesium Company again. Its share price is currently $55, and per share earnings and dividends over the past year were $3 and $.75, respectively. For the next two years, forecast earnings and dividends, along with the earnings growth rates and payout ratios, are:

$$D_1 = \$2.00 \qquad E_1 = \$5.00 \qquad g_{e1} = 67\% \qquad p_1 = 40\%$$
$$D_2 = \$3.00 \qquad E_2 = \$6.00 \qquad g_{e2} = 20\% \qquad p_2 = 50\%$$

Constant growth in dividends and earnings of 10% per year is forecast to begin at $T = 2$, which means that $D_3 = \$3.30$, $E_3 = \$6.60$, $g = 10\%$, and $p = 50\%$.

Given a required return of 15%, equation (17.46) can be used as follows to estimate a "normal" price-earnings ratio for Magnesium:

$$\frac{V}{E_0} = \frac{.40(1 + .67)}{(1 + .15)^1} + \frac{.50(1 + .67)(1 + .20)}{(1 + .15)^2} + \frac{.50(1 + .67)(1 + .20)(1 + .10)}{(.15 - .10)(1 + .15)^2}$$
$$= .58 + .76 + 16.67$$
$$= 18.01$$

Because the actual price-earnings ratio of $55/$3 = 18.33 is close to the "normal" ratio of 17.01, the shares of the Magnesium Company can be viewed as fairly priced.

Sources of Earnings Growth

So far, no explanation has been given as to why earnings or dividends can be expected to grow in the future. One explanation uses the constant-growth model. Assuming that no new capital is obtained externally and no shares are repurchased (meaning the number of shares outstanding does not increase or decrease), the portion of earnings not paid to shareholders as dividends will be used to pay for the firm's new investments. Given that p_t denotes the payout ratio in year t, then $(1 - p_t)$ is equal to the portion of earnings not paid out, known as the **retention ratio**. Furthermore, the firm's new investments, stated on a per-share basis and denoted by I_t, will be

$$I_t = (1 - p_t)E_t \tag{17.47}$$

Retention Ratio The percentage of a firm's earnings that are not paid to shareholders, but instead are retained by the firm. Equivalently, one minus the payout ratio.

If these new investments have an average return on equity of r_t in period t and every year thereafter, they will add $r_t I_t$ to earnings per share in year $t + 1$ and every year thereafter. If all previous investments also produce perpetual earnings at a constant rate of return, next year's earnings will equal this year's earnings plus the new earnings resulting from this year's new investments:

$$E_{t+1} = E_t + r_t I_t$$
$$= E_t + r_t(1 - p_t)E_t$$
$$= E_t[1 + r_t(1 - p_t)] \tag{17.48}$$

Because it was shown earlier that the growth rate in earnings per share is

$$E_t = E_{t-1}(1 + g_{et}) \tag{17.35}$$

it follows that

$$E_{t+1} = E_t(1 + g_{et+1}) \tag{17.49}$$

A comparison of equations (17.48) and (17.49) indicates that

$$g_{et+1} = r_t(1 - p_t) \tag{17.50}$$

If the growth rate in earnings per share (g_{et+1}) is to be constant over time, then the average return on equity for new investments (r_t) and payout ratio (p_t) must also be constant over time. In this situation, equation (17.50) can be simplified by removing the time subscripts:

$$g_e = r(1 - p) \tag{17.51a}$$

Since the growth rate in dividends per share (g) is equal to the growth rate in earnings per share (g_e), this equation can be rewritten as

$$g = r(1 - p) \tag{17.51b}$$

From this equation it can be seen that the growth rate g depends on (1) the proportion of earnings that is retained $(1 - p)$, and (2) the average return on equity for the earnings that are retained (r).

The constant-growth valuation formula given in equation (17.20) can be modified by replacing g with the expression on the right-hand side of equation (17.51b), resulting in

$$\begin{aligned} V &= D_0 \left(\frac{1 + g}{k - g} \right) \\ &= D_0 \left[\frac{1 + r(1 - p)}{k - r(1 - p)} \right] \\ &= D_1 \left[\frac{1}{k - r(1 - p)} \right] \end{aligned} \tag{17.52}$$

In terms of price-earnings ratios, the formula in equation (17.43) becomes

$$\begin{aligned} \frac{V}{E_0} &= p \left(\frac{1 + g_e}{k - g_e} \right) \\ &= p \left[\frac{1 + r(1 - p)}{k - r(1 - p)} \right] \end{aligned} \tag{17.53}$$

Under these assumptions, a share's value, and hence its price, should be greater, the greater its average return on equity for new investments, other things being equal.

An Example

Continuing with the Copper Company, recall that $E_0 = \$2.70$ and $p = 66\ 2/3\%$. This means that 33 1/3% of earnings per share over the past year were retained and reinvested, an amount equal to $.3333 \times \$2.70 = \$.90$. The earnings per share in the forthcoming year (E_1) are expected to be $\$2.70(1 + .05) = \$2.835$, since the growth rate (g) for Copper is 5%. The source of the increase in earnings per share of $\$2.835 - \$2.70 = \$.135$ is the $\$.90$ per share that was reinvested at $t = 0$. The average return on equity for new investments (r) is 15%, since $\$.135/\$.90 = 15\%$. That is, the reinvested earnings of $\$.90$ per share can be viewed as having generated an annual increase in earnings per share of $\$.135$. This increase will occur not only at $t = 1$ but also at $t = 2$, $t = 3$, and so on. Equivalently, a $\$.90$ investment at $t = 0$ will generate a perpetual annual cash inflow of $\$.135$ beginning at $t = 1$.

Expected dividends at $t = 1$ can be calculated by multiplying the expected payout ratio (p) of 66 2/3% times the expected earnings per share (E_1) of $\$2.835$, or $.6667 \times \$2.835 = \$1.89$. It can also be calculated by multiplying 1 plus the growth rate (g) of 5% times the past amount of dividends per share (D_0) of $\$1.80$, or $1.05 \times \$1.80 = \$1.89$. It can be seen that the growth rate in dividends per share of 5% is equal to the product of the retention rate (33 1/3%) and the average return on equity for new investments (15%), an amount equal to $.3333 \times .15 = 5\%$.

Two years from now $(t = 2)$, earnings per share are anticipated to be $\$2.835 \times (1 + .05) = \$2.977$, a further increase of $\$2.977 - \$2.835 = \$.142$ that is due to the retention and reinvestment of $.3333 \times \$2.835 = \$.945$ per share at $t = 1$. This

Figure 17.2 Growth in earnings for Copper Company.

$$
\begin{array}{llll}
-1 & 0 & 1 & 2 \\
\end{array}
$$

		$2.700	$2.700 ...
	$.90 × .15 = .135	.135 ...
	E_1 = $2.835	$.945 × .15 = .142 ...
		E_2 = $2.977 ...

I_0 = $ .90	I_1 = $ .945	I_2 = $ .992 ...
D_0 = 1.80	D_1 = 1.890	D_2 = 1.985 ...
E_0 = $2.70	E_1 = $2.835	E_2 = $2.977 ...

expected increase in earnings per share of $.142 is the result of earning 15% on the reinvested $.945, since $.15 \times \$.945 = \$.142$.

The expected earnings per share at $t = 2$ have three components. The first is the earnings attributable to the assets held at $t = 0$, an amount equal to $2.70. The second is the earnings attributable to the reinvestment of $.90 at $t = 0$, earning $.135. The third is the earnings attributable to the reinvestment of $.945 at $t = 1$, earning $.142. These three components, when summed, equal $E_2 = \$2.70 + \$.135 + \$.142 = \$2.977$. Dividends at $t = 2$ are expected to be 5% larger than at $t = 1$, or $1.05 \times \$1.89 = \$1.985$ per share. This amount corresponds to the amount calculated by multiplying the payout ratio times the expected earnings per share at $t = 2$, or $.6667 \times \$2.977 = \$1.985$. Figure 17.2 summarizes the example.

A Three-stage DDM

As this chapter's Institutional Issues section discusses, the three-stage DDM is the most widely applied form of the general multiple-growth DDM. Consider analyzing the ABC Company.

Making Forecasts

Over the past year, ABC has had earnings per share of $1.67 and dividends per share of $40. After carefully studying ABC, a security analyst has made the following forecasts of earnings per share and dividends per share for the next five years.

$E_1 = \$2.67$	$E_2 = \$4.00$	$E_3 = \$6.00$	$E_4 = \$8.00$	$E_5 = \$10.00$
$D_1 = \$.60$	$D_2 = \$1.60$	$D_3 = \$2.40$	$D_4 = \$3.20$	$D_5 = \$5.00$

These forecasts imply the following payout ratios and earnings-per-share growth rates:

$p_1 = 22\%$	$p_2 = 40\%$	$p_3 = 40\%$	$p_4 = 40\%$	$p_5 = 50\%$
$g_{e1} = 60\%$	$g_{e2} = 50\%$	$g_{e3} = 50\%$	$g_{e4} = 33\%$	$g_{e5} = 25\%$

Furthermore, the analyst believes that ABC will enter a transition stage at the end of the fifth year (that is, the sixth year will be the first year of the transition stage), and that the transition stage will last three years. Earnings per share and the payout ratio for year 6 are forecast to be $E_6 = \$11.90$ and $p_6 = 55\%$.

Thus $g_{e6} = (\$11.90 - \$10.00)/\$10.00 = 19\%$ and $D_6 = .55 \times \$11.90 = \$6.55$. The last stage, known as the maturity stage, is forecast to have an earnings-per-share growth rate of 4% and a payout ratio of 70%. Now, it was shown in equation (17.51b) that with the

Applying Dividend Discount Models

Over the last 30 years, dividend discount models (DDMs) have achieved broad acceptance among professional common stock investors. Although few investment managers rely solely on DDMs to select stocks, many have integrated DDMs into their security valuation procedures.

The reasons for the popularity of DDMs are twofold. First, DDMs are based on a simple, widely understood concept: the fair value of any security should equal the discounted value of the cash flows expected to be produced by that security. Second, the basic inputs for DDMs are standard outputs for many large investment management firms—that is, these firms employ security analysts who are responsible for projecting corporate earnings.

Valuing common stocks with a DDM technically requires an estimate of future dividends over an infinite time horizon. Given that accurately forecasting dividends 3 years from today, let alone 20 years in the future, is a difficult proposition, how do investment firms actually go about implementing DDMs?

One approach is to use constant or two-stage dividend growth models, as described in the text. However, although such models are relatively easy to apply, institutional investors typically view the assumed dividend growth assumptions as overly simplistic. Instead, these investors generally prefer three-stage models, believing that they provide the best combination of realism and ease of application.

Whereas many variations of the three-stage DDM exist, in general, the model is based on the assumption that companies evolve through three stages during their lifetimes. (Figure 17.3 portrays these stages.)

1. **Growth stage:** Characterized by rapidly expanding sales, high profit margins, and abnormally high growth in earnings per share. Because of highly profitable expected investment opportunities, the payout ratio is low. Competitors are attracted by the unusually high earnings, leading to a decline in the growth rate.

2. **Transition stage:** In later years, increased competition reduces profit margins and earnings growth slows. With fewer new investment opportunities, the company begins to pay out a larger percentage of earnings.

3. **Maturity (steady-state) stage:** Eventually the company reaches a position where its new investment opportunities offer, on average, only

---

Figure 17.3 The three stages of the multiple-growth model.

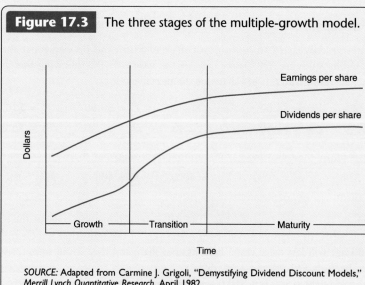

SOURCE: Adapted from Carmine J. Grigoli, "Demystifying Dividend Discount Models," *Merrill Lynch Quantitative Research*, April 1982.

slightly attractive returns on equity. At that time its earnings growth rate, payout ratio, and return on equity stabilize for the remainder of its life.

The forecasting process of the three-stage DDM involves specifying earnings and dividend growth rates in each of the three stages. Although one cannot expect a security analyst to be omniscient in his growth forecast for a particular company, one can hope that the forecast pattern of growth—in terms of magnitude and duration—resembles that actually realized by the company, particularly in the short run.

Investment firms attempt to structure their DDMs to make maximum use of their analysts' forecasting capabilities. Thus, the models emphasize specific forecasts in the near term, when it is realistic to expect security analysts to project earnings and dividends more accurately. Conversely, the models emphasize more general forecasts over the longer term, when distinctions between companies' growth rates become less discernible. Typically, analysts are required to supply the following for their assigned companies:

1. expected annual earnings and dividends for the next several years;
2. after these specific annual forecasts end, earnings growth and the payout ratio forecasts until the end of the growth stage;
3. the number of years until the transition stage is reached;
4. the duration (in years) of the transition stage—that is, once abnormally high growth ends, the number of years until the maturity stage is reached.

Most three-stage DDMs assume that during the transition stage, earnings growth declines and payout ratios rise linearly to the maturity-stage steady-state levels. (For example, if the transition stage is 10 years long, earnings growth at the maturity stage is 5% per year, and earnings growth at the end of the growth stage is 25%, then earnings growth will decline 2% in each year of the transition stage.) Finally, most three-stage DDMs make standard assumptions that all companies in the maturity stage have the same growth rates, payout ratios, and returns on equity.

With analysts' inputs, plus an appropriate required rate of return for each security, all the necessary information for the three-stage DDM is available. The last step involves merely calculating the discounted value of the estimated dividends to determine the stock's "fair" value.

The seeming simplicity of the three-stage DDM should not lead one to believe that it is without its implementation problems. Investment firms must strive to achieve consistency across their analysts' forecasts. The long-term nature of the estimates involved, the substantial training required to make even short-term earnings forecasts accurately, and the coordination of a number of analysts covering many companies severely complicate the problem. Considerable discipline is required if the DDM valuations generated by a firm's analysts are to be sufficiently comparable and reliable to guide investment decisions. Despite these complexities, if successfully implemented, DDMs can combine the creative insights of security analysts with the rigour and discipline of quantitative investment techniques.

constant-growth model, $g = r(1 - p)$, where r is the average return on equity for new investment and p is the payout ratio. Given that the maturity stage has constant growth, this equation can be reformulated and used to determine r:

$$r = g/(1 - p)$$

Thus, r for ABC has an implied value of $4\%/(100\% - 70\%) = 13.33\%$, which is assumed to be consistent with the long-run growth forecasts for similar companies.

At this point there are only two missing pieces of information that are needed to determine the value of ABC—the earnings-per-share growth rates and the payout ratios for the transition stage. Taking earnings per share first, it has been forecast that $g_{e6} = 19\%$ and $g_{e9} = 4\%$. One method of determining how 19% will "decay" to 4% is to note that there are three years between the sixth and ninth years, and 15% between 19% and 4%. A "linear decay" rate is determined by noting that 15%/3 years = 5% per year. This rate of 5% is deducted from 19% to get g_{e7}, resulting in 19% − 5% = 14%. Then it would be deducted from 14% to get g_{e8}, resulting in 14% − 5% = 9%. As a check it can be noted that 9% − 5% = 4% is the value that was forecast for g_{e9}.

A similar procedure can be used to determine how the payout ratio of 55% in year 6 will grow to 70% in year 9. The "linear growth" rate will be (70% − 55%)/3 years = 15%/3 years = 5% per year, indicating that p_7 = 55% + 5% = 60% and p_8 = 60% + 5% = 65%. Again, a check indicates that 65% + 5% = 70% is the value that was forecast for p_9.

With these forecasts of earnings-per-share growth rates and payout ratios in hand, forecasts of dividends per share can now be made:

$$
\begin{aligned}
D_7 &= p_7 E_7 \\
&= p_7 E_6 (1 + g_{e7}) \\
&= .60 \times \$11.90 \times (1 + .14) \\
&= .60 \times \$13.57 \\
&= \$8.14 \\
D_8 &= p_8 E_8 \\
&= p_8 E_6 (1 + g_{e7})(1 + g_{e8}) \\
&= .65 \times \$11.90 \times (1 + .14) \times (1 + .09) \\
&= .65 \times \$14.79 \\
&= \$9.61 \\
D_9 &= p_9 E_9 \\
&= p_9 E_6 (1 + g_{e7})(1 + g_{e8})(1 + g_{e9}) \\
&= .70 \times \$11.90 \times (1 + .14) \times (1 + .09) \times (1 + .04) \\
&= .70 \times \$15.38 \\
&= \$10.76
\end{aligned}
$$

Estimating the Intrinsic Value

Given a required rate of return on ABC of 12.4%, all the necessary inputs for the multiple-growth model have been determined. It is now possible to estimate ABC's intrinsic (or fair) value. To begin, it can be seen that $T = 8$, indicating that V_{T-} involves determining the present value of D_1 through D_8:

$$
\begin{aligned}
V_{T-} =\ & \left[\frac{\$.60}{(1 + .124)^1}\right] + \left[\frac{\$1.60}{(1 + .124)^2}\right] + \left[\frac{\$2.40}{(1 + .124)^3}\right] \\
& + \left[\frac{\$3.20}{(1 + .124)^4}\right] + \left[\frac{\$5.00}{(1 + .124)^5}\right] + \left[\frac{\$6.55}{(1 + .124)^6}\right] \\
& + \left[\frac{\$8.14}{(1 + .124)^7}\right] + \left[\frac{\$9.61}{(1 + .124)^8}\right] \\
=\ & \$18.89
\end{aligned}
$$

Then V_{T+} can be determined using D_9:

$$
V_{T+} = \frac{\$10.76}{(.124 - .04)(1 + .124)^8}
$$
$$
= \$50.28
$$

Combining V_{T-} and V_{T+} results in the intrinsic value of ABC:

$$V = V_{T-} + V_{T+}$$
$$= \$18.89 + \$50.28$$
$$= \$69.17$$

Given a current market price for ABC of $50, it can be seen that its stock is underpriced by $69.17 − $50 = $19.17 per share. Equivalently, it can be noted that the actual price-earnings ratio for ABC is $50/$1.67 = 29.9 but that a "normal" price-earnings ratio would be higher, equal to $69.17/$1.67 = 41.4, again indicating that ABC is underpriced.

Implied Returns

As shown in the previous example, once the analyst has made certain forecasts, it is relatively easy to determine a company's expected dividends for each year up through the first year of the maturity stage. Then the present value of these predicted dividends can be calculated for a given required rate of return. However, many investment firms use a computerized trial-and-error procedure to determine the discount rate, which equates the present value of the stock's expected dividends with its current price. Sometimes this long-run internal rate of return is referred to as the security's **implied return**. In the case of ABC its implied return is 14.8%.

Implied Return The discount rate that equates the present value of future cash flows expected to be received from a particular investment to the cost of that investment.

The Security Market Line

After implied returns have been estimated for a number of stocks, the associated beta for each stock can be estimated. Then, for all the stocks analyzed, this information can be plotted on a graph that has implied returns on the vertical axis and estimated betas on the horizontal axis.

There are several methods for estimating the security market line (SML).[12] One method involves determining a line of best fit for this graph by using a statistical procedure known as simple regression (described in Chapter 16). That is, the values of an intercept term and a slope term are determined from the data, thereby indicating the location of the straight line that best describes the relationship between implied returns and betas.[13]

Figure 17.4 provides an example of an estimated SML. In this case, the SML has been determined to have an intercept of 8% and a slope of 4%, indicating that, in general, securities with higher betas are expected to have higher implied returns in the forthcoming period. Depending on the sizes of the implied returns, such lines can have steeper or flatter slopes or even negative slopes.

The second method of estimating the SML involves calculating the implied return for a portfolio of common stocks. This is done by taking a value-weighted average of the implied returns of the stocks in the portfolio, with the resulting return being an estimate of the implied return on the market portfolio. Given this return and a beta of 1, the market portfolio can be plotted on a graph having implied returns on the vertical axis and betas on the horizontal axis. Next, the risk-free rate, having a beta of 0, can be plotted on the same graph. Finally, the SML is determined by simply connecting these two points with a straight line.

Either of these SMLs can be used to determine the required return on a stock. However, they will probably result in different numbers, since the two lines will probably have different intercepts and slopes. For example, note that in the first method the SML

---

[12]There are numerous methods besides those described here. Some of them are based on more complicated versions of the CAPM, whereas others are based on the APT (discussed in Chapter 11).

[13]There are ways of forcing the intercept of the line to go through the risk-free rate in order to agree with the implications of the traditional CAPM.

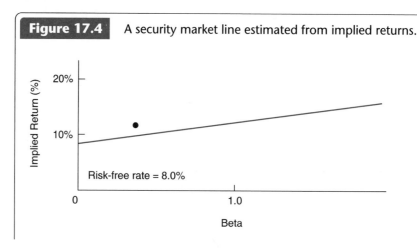

Figure 17.4 A security market line estimated from implied returns.

Risk-free rate = 8.0%

may not go through the risk-free rate, whereas the second method forces the SML to go through this rate.

Required Returns and Alphas

Once a security's beta has been estimated, its required return can be determined from the estimated SML. For example, the equation for the SML shown in Figure 17.4 is:

$$k_i = 8 + 4\beta_i$$

Thus, if ABC has an estimated beta of 1.1, then it would have a required return equal to $8 + (4 \times 1.1) = 12.4\%$.

Once the required return on a stock has been determined, the difference between its implied return (from the dividend discount model) and this required return can be calculated. This difference can then be viewed as an estimate of the stock's *alpha* and represents "… the degree to which a stock is mispriced. Positive alphas indicate undervalued securities and negative alphas indicate overvalued securities."[14] In the case of ABC, its implied and required returns were 14.8% and 12.4%, respectively. Thus, its estimated alpha is $14.8\% - 12.4\% = 2.4\%$. Since this is a positive number, ABC can be viewed as being underpriced.

The Implied Return on the Stock Market

Another product of this analysis is that the implied return for the portfolio of shares can be compared with expected returns on bonds. Specifically, the difference between the stock and bond returns can be used as an input for recommendations concerning asset allocation between stocks and bonds. That is, it can be used to form recommendations regarding what percentage of an investor's money should go into stocks and what percentage should go into bonds. Typically, the greater the implied return on stocks relative to bonds, the larger the percentage of the investor's money that should be placed in common shares.

---

[14]Carmine J. Grigoli, "Common Stock Valuation," *Merrill Lynch Quantitative Analysis* (May–June 1984). A subsequent procedure divides the estimated alpha by an estimate of the security's unique risk (that is, non-market or unsystematic risk) to obtain a standardized alpha. Then, based on the magnitude of the standardized alpha, the security is classified into one of 10 standardized alpha deciles. See also Marshall E. Blume, "The Use of Alphas' to Improve Performance," *Journal of Portfolio Management* 11, no. 1 (Fall 1984): 86–92.

Multiple Valuation Models

Despite the simple elegance and compelling logic of the dividend discount model (DDM), few investment management firms use it as a means of identifying mispriced common stocks. In general, managers have always been leery of the DDM approach. Most view with skepticism the notion that the market makes a long-term forecast of a company's dividends and then discounts that expected dividend stream at some appropriate discount rate to arrive at a "fair" value for the stock.

Some managers firmly believe that the market is highly inefficient and that any valuation method, including a DDM, that is based on the rationality of market participants will prove ineffective. They often rely on various technical stock selection tools (discussed in Chapter 22).

Most managers do concede that the market is very efficient, but they contend that enough inefficiencies exist to warrant the search for mispriced stocks. Yet rather than use a DDM to funnel their fundamental research into an objective estimate of a stock's intrinsic value, most of these managers prefer to use alternative methods of identifying mispricings that do not involve long-term forecasts. For example, some divide a stock's current price-earnings ratio by that of the market's price-earnings ratio. This *relative* price-earnings ratio is then compared to the stock's historic range of relative price-earnings. A stock whose relative price-earnings ratio is near or below the low end of its historic range is seen as undervalued.

Why do many managers prefer these alternative valuation methods to the DDM? Some believe that it is futile to forecast dividends for more than a few years in the future. In particular, they question the assumptions required to make a dividend growth forecast tractable (for example, the growth assumptions underlying the constant growth DDM or the three-state DDM). Others are concerned that DDMs exhibit certain biases. Probably the most disconcerting problem is a tendency for DDMs to calculate high expected returns for stocks that currently pay high dividends and to calculate low expected returns for stocks that currently pay low or zero dividends. Because the earnings growth rates of companies with high current payout ratios tend to be lower than those with low current payout ratios, managers are naturally concerned that DDMs show a favourable bias towards low-growth, high-dividend stocks.

A small group of managers have responded to the problems of the DDM not by rejecting the concept but rather by incorporating DDMs into a broader framework of multiple valuation models. The basic idea behind this approach is that many different valuation models contain information about security mispricings. Some of these valuation models are based on perceived market anomalies, such as an overreaction to unexpected news about a company. Other models may be cousins of the DDM, such a relative price-earnings comparisons mentioned earlier. If DDMs and these models do contain mispricing information, and if their mispricing estimates are not perfectly correlated, then a combination of the models' forecasts can produce estimates of mispricings superior to any single model. A brief look at one investment manager gives a sense of how a multiple valuation model approach is applied.

Franklin Portfolio Associates (FPA) is a Boston-based investment management firm. It manages common stock portfolios for roughly two dozen clients, including some of the largest pension funds in the US, such as General Motors, AT&T, and Amoco. The firm also manages the Growth and Income Fund for the Vanguard Group. Total assets under management exceed $13 billion. FPA has used a multiple valuation model approach for stock selection since the firm's formation in 1982.

FPA divides its valuation models into four primary groups:
- fundamental momentum
- relative value
- future cash flow
- supplementary

The fundamental momentum models are based on data regarding earnings revisions and surprises. FPA purchases earnings estimates made by various brokerage house securities analysts. (Services that supply analysts' earnings estimates to firms such as FPA are the subject of Chapter 18's Institutional Issues.) On a stock-by-stock basis, FPA computes the change (if any) in the average earnings estimate (called an *earnings revision*). The firm also compares a company's reported earnings against analysts' estimates. (The difference is called an *earnings surprise* and is discussed in Chapter 18.) Stocks with large earnings revisions or surprises are potentially misvalued. Relative value models compare a stock's current price to some base measure such as book value, dividends, or earnings. Future cash flow models are various versions of DDMs. The models differ in terms of the assumptions made about the path of dividend growth over time as well as the sources of dividend growth estimates. Finally, the supplementary models use measures of insider trading and relative strength to identify under and overvalued stocks. (See Chapter 22 for more on these two valuation indicators.)

In total, FPA uses over 30 different valuation models. Twice a month, each model is used to rank roughly 3500 (primarily) US common stocks by relative attractiveness. In order to create a composite rank, weights or importance must be assigned to the individual models. One solution is to give all of the models an equal weight. (Thus with 30 models, each model would contribute 1/30 to a stock's composite rank). FPA combines this approach with statistical techniques based on the past performances of the models to develop the most effective combination of model weights.

After calculating the composite rank of each stock, FPA divides the 3500 stocks into deciles based on those ranks. Only the first decile stocks are considered for purchase in the firm's portfolios, while any holdings that have slipped down below the fifth

decile are considered to be sale candidates. Stocks in the second through fifth deciles can continue to be held if previously purchased. The composite rankings of the eligible stocks are then used as inputs into a portfolio "Optimizer"—a statistical procedure for combining stocks to produce mean-variance efficient portfolios (see the Institutional Issues discussion in Chapter 7). FPA uses the optimizer to control the amount of expected variability in its portfolios' returns relative to the portfolios' assigned benchmarks.

Over the years, FPA's multiple valuation model methodology has successfully differentiated between high and low return stocks. For the 15-year period from 1982 through 1997, stocks ranked in the first decile by the FPA valuation process earned 29.5% per year, while stocks ranked in the tenth decile earned a 7.0% annual return. In between the first and tenth deciles, returns were inversely related to the ranking deciles. The costs of transacting in securities makes it difficult to translate these differences in decile performance directly into portfolio returns. Nevertheless, in its flagship "core" accounts that are assigned a broad market index as the benchmark, FPA has been able to outperform the benchmark in 32 out of 39 rolling three-year periods from April 1985 through September 1997, while taking on no more systematic risk than the benchmark. Cumulatively, during the period the firm's portfolios earned 18.6% per year versus 17.5% for the benchmark, a record that attests to the usefulness of the multiple model valuation approach to investing.

Dividend Discount Models and Expected Returns

The procedures described here are similar to those employed by a number of brokerage firms and portfolio managers.[15] A security's implied return, obtained from a dividend discount model, is often treated as an expected return, which in turn can be divided into two components—the security's required return and alpha. However, the expected return on a stock over a given holding period may differ from its DDM-based implied rate, k^*. A simple set of examples will indicate why this difference can exist.

---

[15]An example of a similar procedure that has been used by Wells Fargo Investment Advisors is described by George Foster in *Financial Statement Analysis* (Englewood Cliffs, NJ: Prentice Hall, 1986): 428–30.

Assume that a security analyst predicts that a stock will pay a dividend of $1.10 per share per year forever. On the other hand, the consensus opinion of "the market" (most other investors) is that the dividend will equal $1.00 per year forever. This suggests that the analyst's prediction is a deviant, or nonconsensus, prediction.

Assume that both the analyst and other investors agree that the required rate of return for a stock of this type is 10%. Using the formula for the zero-growth model, the value of a share is $D_1/.10 = 10D_1$, meaning that a share should sell for 10 times its expected dividend. Since other investors expect to receive $1.00 per year, the stock has a current price (P) of $10 per share. The analyst feels the stock has a value of $1.10/.10 = $11 and thus feels it is underpriced by $11 - $10 = $1 per share.

Rate of Convergence of Investors' Predictions

In this situation the implied return according to the analyst is $1.10/$10 = 11%. If the analyst buys a share now with a plan to sell it a year later, what rate of return might the analyst expect to earn? The answer depends on what assumption is made regarding the *rate of convergence of investors' predictions*—that is, the expected market reaction to the mispricing that the analyst believes currently exists.

The cases shown in Table 17.1 are based on an assumption that the analyst is confident that her forecast of future dividends is correct. That is, in all of the cases, the analyst expects that at the end of the year, the stock will pay the predicted dividend of $1.10.

Table 17.1	Alpha and the Convergence of Predications.		
	Expected Amount of Convergence		
	0% (A)	100% (B)	50% (C)
Dividend predictions D_2			
Consensus of other investors	1.00	1.10	1.05
Analyst	1.10	1.10	1.10
Expected stock price P_1	10.00	11.00	10.50
Expected return:			
Dividend yield D_1/P	11%	11%	11%
Capital gain $(P_1 - P)/P$	0	10	5
Total expected return	11%	21%	16%
Less required return	10	10	10
Alpha	1%	11%	6%

NOTE: P_1 is equal to the consensus dividend prediction at $t = 1$ divided by the required return of 10%. The example assumes that the current stock price P is $10, and dividends are forecast by the consensus at $t = 0$ to remain constant at $1.00 per share, where as the analyst forecasts the dividends at $t = 0$ to remain constant at $1.10 per share.

No Convergence

In column (A), it is assumed that other investors will regard the higher dividend as a fluke and steadfastly refuse to alter their projections of subsequent dividends from their initial estimate of $1.00. As a result, the security's price at $t = 1$ can be expected to remain at $1.00/.10 = $10. In this case the analyst's total return is expected to be $1.10/$10 = 11%, which will be attributed entirely to dividends as no capital gains are expected.

The 11% expected return can also be viewed as consisting of the required return of 10% plus an alpha of 1% that is equal to the portion of the dividend unanticipated by other investors, \$.10/\$10. Accordingly, if it is assumed that there will be no convergence of predictions, the expected return would be set at the implied rate of 11% and the alpha would be set at 1%.

Complete Convergence

Column (B) shows a very different situation. Here it is assumed that the other investors will recognize their error and completely revise their predictions. At the end of the year, it is expected that they too will predict future dividends of \$1.10 per year thereafter; thus, the stock is expected to be selling for \$1.10/.10 = \$11 at $t = 1$. Under these conditions, the analyst can expect to achieve a total return of 21% by selling the stock at the end of the year for \$11, obtaining \$1.10/\$10 = 11% in dividend yield and \$1/\$10 = 10% in capital gains.

The 10% expected capital gains result directly from the expected repricing of the security because of the complete convergence of predictions. In this case the fruits of the analyst's superior prediction are expected to be obtained all in one year. Instead of 1% "extra" per year forever, as in column (A), the analyst expects to obtain \$.10/\$10 = 1% in extra dividend yield plus \$1/\$10 = 10% in capital gains this year. By continuing to hold the stock in subsequent years, the analyst would expect to earn only the required return of 10% over those years. Accordingly, the expected return is 21% and the alpha is 11% when it is assumed that there is complete convergence of predictions.

Partial Convergence

Column (C) shows an intermediate case. Here, the predictions of the other investors are expected to converge only halfway towards those of the analyst (that is, from \$1.00 to \$1.05 instead of to \$1.10). Total return in the first year is expected to be 16%, consisting of \$1.10/\$10 = 11% in dividend yield plus \$.50/\$10 = 5% in capital gains.

Since the stock is expected to be selling for \$1.05/.10 = \$10.50 at $t = 1$, the analyst will still feel that it is underpriced at $t = 1$ because it will have an intrinsic value of \$1.10/.10 = \$11 at that time. To obtain the remainder of the "extra return" owing to this underpricing, the stock would have to be held past $t = 1$. Accordingly, the expected return would be set at 16% and the alpha would be set at 6% when it is assumed that there is halfway convergence of predictions.

In general, a security's expected return and alpha will be larger the faster the assumed rate of convergence of predictions.[16] Many investors use the implied rate (that is, the internal rate of return k^*) as a surrogate for a relatively short-term (for example, one year) expected return, as in column (A). In doing so, they are assuming that the dividend forecast is completely accurate, but that there is no convergence. Alternatively, investors could assume that there is some degree of convergence, thereby raising their estimate of the security's expected return. Indeed, investors could further alter their estimate of the security's expected return by assuming that the security analyst's deviant prediction is less than perfectly accurate, as will be seen next.[17]

---

[16]In a perfectly efficient market (in the semistrong-form sense), these analysts would sometimes be right and sometimes be wrong, so that on balance their predictions would be of no value. In such a situation, the expected return for any security would be its required return and the alpha would be zero.

[17]As an example of how to estimate alpha if it is assumed that the analyst has less than perfect forecasting ability and there is less than 100% convergence, reconsider the example given in Table 17.1. First, assume that the forecast accuracy of the security analyst is 60%. Remembering that the analyst's forecast of D_1 is \$1.10, but the consensus forecast is \$1.00, then 60% accuracy means that the forecast that should be used is $\$1.00 + .60 \times (\$1.10 - \$1.00) = \$1.06$. Second, assume that there will be 50% convergence. This means that the security's price at $t = 1$ is expected to be $[\$1.00 + .50 \times (\$1.06 - \$1.00)]/.10 = \$10.30$. Hence the expected return under 60% forecast accuracy and 50% convergence is $[(\$10.30 - \$10) + \$1.06]/\$10 = 13.6\%$, which translates into an alpha of $13.6\% - 10\% = 3.6\%$.

Predicted Versus Actual Returns

An alternative approach does not simply use outputs from a model "as is," but *adjusts* them, based on relationships between previous predictions and actual outcomes. Figure 17.5 provides examples.

Each point in Figure 17.5(a) plots *predicted return* on the stock market as a whole (on the horizontal axis) and the subsequent *actual return* for that period (on the vertical axis). The line of best fit (determined by simple regression) through the points indicates the general relationship between prediction and outcome. If the current prediction is 14%, history suggests that an estimate of 15% would be superior.

Each point in Figure 17.5(b) plots a predicted alpha value for a security (on the horizontal axis) and the subsequent abnormal return for that period (on the vertical axis). Such a diagram can be made for a given security, or for all the securities that a particular analyst makes predictions about, or for all the securities that the investment firm makes predictions about. Again a line of best fit can be drawn through the points. In this case, if the current prediction of a security's alpha is +1%, this relationship suggests that an "adjusted" estimate of +2.5% would be superior.

An important by-product of this type of analysis is the measure of correlation between predicted and actual outcomes, indicating the nearness of the points to the line. This **information coefficient (IC)** can serve as a measure of predictive accuracy. If it is too small to

Information Coefficient (IC) The correlation coefficient between a security analyst's predicted returns and subsequent actual returns that is used to measure the accuracy of the analyst's predictions.

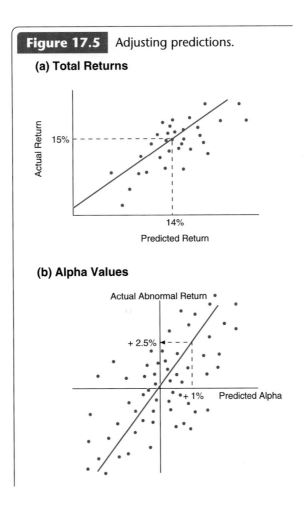

Figure 17.5 Adjusting predictions.

(a) Total Returns

(b) Alpha Values

be significantly different from zero in a statistical sense, the value of the predictions is subject to considerable question.[18]

Summary

1. The capitalization of income method of valuation states that the intrinsic value of any asset is equal to the sum of the discounted cash flows investors expect to receive from that asset.
2. Dividend discount models (DDMs) are a specific application of the capitalization of income method of valuation to common shares.
3. To use a DDM, the investor must implicitly or explicitly supply a forecast of all future dividends expected to be generated by a security.
4. Investors typically make certain simplifying assumptions about the growth of common stock dividends. For example, a common share's dividends may be assumed to exhibit zero growth or growth at a constant rate. More complex assumptions may allow for multiple growth rates over time.
5. Instead of applying DDMs, many security analysts use a simpler method of security valuation that involves estimating a share's "normal" price-earnings ratio and comparing it with the share's actual price-earnings ratio.
6. The growth rate in a firm's earnings and dividends depends on its earnings retention rate and its average return on equity for new investments.
7. Determining whether a security is mispriced using a DDM can be done in one of two ways. First, the discounted value of expected dividends can be compared with the share's current price. Second, the discount rate that equates the share's current price to the present value of forecast dividends can be compared with the required return for stocks of similar risk.
8. The rate of return that an analyst with accurate non-consensus dividend forecasts can expect to earn depends on the rate of convergence of other investors' predictions to the predictions of the analyst.

QUESTIONS AND PROBLEMS

1. Consider five annual cash flows (the first occurring one year from today):

Year	Cash Flow
1	$5
2	$6
3	$7
4	$8
5	$9

Given a discount rate of 10%, what is the present value of this stream of cash flows?

---

[18]It has been argued that a value of .15 for an IC is indicative of good performance with regard to stock forecasting, and that several different forecasters have recorded ICs of this magnitude (a value of zero would be expected in a perfectly efficient market). See Keith P. Ambachtsheer, "Profit Potential in an 'Almost Efficient' Market," *Journal of Portfolio Management* 1, no. 1 (Fall 1974): 84–87, and "Where Are the Customers' Alphas?" *Journal of Portfolio Management* 4, no. 1 (Fall 1977): 52–56; Keith P. Ambachtsheer and James L. Farrell, Jr., "Can Active Management Add Value?" *Financial Analysts Journal* 35, no. 6 (November–December 1979): 39–47; and S. D. Hodges and R. A. Brealey, "Portfolio Selection in a Dynamic and Uncertain World," *Financial Analysts Journal* 29, no. 2 (March–April 1973): 50–65.

2. Amy Cohen is considering buying a machine to produce baseballs. The machine costs $10 000. With the machine, Amy expects to produce and sell 1000 baseballs per year for $3 per baseball, net of all costs. The machine's life is five years (with no salvage value). Based on these assumptions and an 8% discount rate, what is the net present value of Amy's investment?

3. Hugh Collins has invested in a project that promised to pay $100, $200, and $300, respectively, at the end of the next three years. If Hugh paid $513.04 for this investment, what is the project's internal rate of return?

4. Afton Products currently pays a dividend of $4 per share on its common stock.
   a. If Afton Products plans to increase its dividend at a rate of 5% per year indefinitely, what will be the dividend per share in 10 years?
   b. If Afton Products' dividend per share is expected to be $5.87 per share at the end of five years, at what annual rate is the dividend expected to grow?

5. Hammond Pipes has issued preferred stock that pays $12 per share. The dividend is fixed and the stock has no expiration date. What is the intrinsic value of Hammond preferred shares, assuming a discount rate of 15%?

6. Milton Information Services currently pays a dividend of $4 per share on its common stock. The dividend is expected to grow at 4% per year forever. Stocks with similar risk currently are priced to provide a 12% expected return. What is the intrinsic value of Milton stock?

7. Spring Valley Bedding stock currently sells for $53 per share. The stock's dividend is expected to grow at 6% per year indefinitely. Spring Valley just paid a dividend of $3 per share. Given this information, calculate the stock's internal rate of return.

8. Select a stock whose name begins with the first letter of your last name. From the *Value Line Investment Survey, Canadian Edition*, find the average annual compounded growth rate in the stock's dividend over the last five years. Assume that this growth rate will continue indefinitely. Also from the same *Value Line Investment Survey* find the beta of the stock. Using the current risk-free rate (90-day Treasury bills as found in *The Globe and Mail*) and a 6% expected market risk premium, calculate the SML and the required return on the stock. Finally, using the dividend growth rate and the required return, calculate the intrinsic value of the stock. (*Note:* If the data for your stock is incompatible with the constant-growth DDM, select another stock.) Compare this intrinsic value to the latest closing price for the stock. Is the stock underpriced or overpriced? What potential problems are involved with this approach to making investment decisions?

9. The constant-growth model is an overly simplistic means of valuing most corporations' stocks. However, a number of market analysts believe that it is a useful means of estimating a fair value for the stock market as a whole. Why might the constant-growth DDM be a more reasonable valuation tool for the market in aggregate than for individual stocks?

10. This year Monona Air Cleaners Inc. will pay a dividend on its stock of $6 per share. The following year the dividend is expected to be the same, increasing to $7 the year after. From that point on, the dividend is expected to grow at 4% per year indefinitely. Stocks with similar risk are currently priced to provide a 10% expected return. What is the intrinsic value of Monona stock?

11. Knapp Carpet recently paid an annual dividend on its stock of $2 per share. The dividend is expected to grow at $1 per share for the next four years. Thereafter the dividend is expected to grow at 5% per year indefinitely. The required return on stocks with similar risk is 12%. What is the intrinsic value of Knapp stock?

12. Chief Medical Inc. is a little-known producer of heart pacemakers. The earnings and dividend growth prospects of the company are disputed by analysts. Albert Bender is forecasting 5% growth in dividends indefinitely.

However, his brother John is predicting a 20% growth in dividends, but only for the next three years, after which the growth rate is expected to decline to 4% for the indefinite future. Chief dividends per share are currently $3. Stocks with similar risk are currently priced to provide a 14% expected return.

a. What is the intrinsic value of Chief stock according to Albert?

b. What is the intrinsic value of Chief stock according to John?

c. Assume that Chief stock now sells for $39-3/4 per share. If the stock is fairly priced at the present time, what is the implied perpetual dividend growth rate? What is the implied P/E (price-earnings ratio) on next year's earnings, based on this perpetual dividend growth assumption and assuming a 25% payout ratio?

13. Elk Mound Candy Company currently pays a dividend of $3 per share. That dividend is expected to grow at a 6% rate indefinitely. Stocks with similar risk provide a 10% expected return. Calculate the intrinsic value of Elk Mound stock today using an interim computation based on the sale of the stock at its expected intrinsic value three years from now.

14. How would an increase in the perceived riskiness of a common stock's future cash flows affect its price-earnings ratio? Explain intuitively and mathematically.

15. Roberts Roofing currently earns $4 per share. Its return on equity is 20% and it retains 50% of its earnings (both figures are expected to be maintained indefinitely). Stocks of similar risk are priced to return 15%. What is the intrinsic value of Roberts' stock?

16. Osseo Operations recently paid an annual dividend of $4 per share. Earnings for the same year were $8 per share. The required return on stocks with similar risk is 11%. Dividends are expected to grow 6% per year indefinitely. Calculate Osseo's "normal" price-earnings ratio.

17. Reedsburg Associates is currently paying a dividend of $2 per share on earnings of $4 per share. Its stock is selling for $200 per share. Stocks of similar risk are priced to return 15%. What kind of return on equity could explain investors' willingness to pay a price equal to 50 times earnings on this stock?

18. Rochelle Corp. is expected to pay out 40% of its earnings and to earn an average of 15% per year on its incremental reinvestment earnings forever. Stocks with similar risk are currently priced to provide a 12% expected return. By what percentage can Rochelle's earnings be expected to grow each year? What is an appropriate price-earnings multiple for the stock? What portion of the return on Rochelle stock is expected to come from capital gains?

19. A three-stage DDM has become a very popular common stock valuation model. It is used by a number of institutional investors and brokerage firms. What advantages does it offer relative to a simple constant-growth DDM? Despite its increased sophistication compared to the constant-growth DDM, what disadvantages does it still retain?

20. What explanations can you offer for the fact that the SML shown in Figure 17.4 is so flat?

21. Fay Thomas, a financial analyst, once remarked: "Even if your dividend estimates and discount rate assumption are correct, dividend discount models identify stocks that will produce positive risk-adjusted returns only if other investors eventually come to agree with the DDM's valuation conclusions." Is this statement correct? Why?

22. Some people assert that a "true" growth company is one whose dividends grow at a rate greater than its required rate of return. Why is the constant-growth DDM incapable of valuing such a "true" growth stock?

CFA Exam Questions

23. The constant-growth dividend discount model can be used for both the valuation of companies and the estimation of the long-term total return of a stock.

Assume : $20 = the price of a stock today,

8% = the expected growth rate of dividends,

$0.60 = the annual dividend one year forward.

   a. Using only the above data, compute the expected long-term total return on the stock using the constant-growth dividend discount model. Show calculations.
   b. Briefly discuss three disadvantages of the constant-growth dividend discount model in its application to investment analysis.
24. As a firm operating in a mature industry, Arbot Industries is expected to maintain a constant dividend payout ratio and constant growth rate of earnings for the foreseeable future. Earnings were $4.50 per share in the recently completed fiscal year. The dividend payout ratio has been a constant 55% in recent years and is expected to remain so. Arbot's return on equity (ROE) is expected to remain at 10% in the future, and you require an 11% return on stock.
   a. Using the constant-growth dividend discount model, calculate the current value of Arbot common stock. Show your calculations.
   After an aggressive acquisition and marketing program, it now appears that Arbot's earnings per share and ROE will grow rapidly over the next two years. You are aware that the dividend discount model can be useful in estimating the value of common stock even when the assumption of constant growth does not apply.
   b. Calculate the current value of Arbot's common stock, using the dividend discount model, assuming that Arbot's dividend will grow at a 15% rate for the next two years, returning in the third year to the historical growth rate and continuing to grow at the historical rate for the foreseeable future. Show your calculations.

KEY TERMS

capitalization of income method of
   valuation (p. 505)
discount rate (p. 506)
net present value (NPV) (p. 506)
internal rate of return (IRR) (p. 507)
dividend discount model (DDM) (p. 507)
zero-growth model (p. 508)
constant-growth model (p. 510)

multiple-growth model (p. 512)
price-earnings ratio (p. 516)
earnings-price ratio (p. 517)
payout ratio (p. 517)
retention ratio (p. 521)
implied return (p. 527)
information coefficient (IC) (p. 533)

REFERENCES

1. The foundation for dividend discount models was laid out in:

   John Burr Williams, *The Theory of Investment Value* (Amsterdam: North-Holland Publishing, 1964). The original edition was published in 1938.

2. The constant-growth and multiple-growth models were subsequently developed by, respectively:

   M. J. Gordon, "Dividends, Earnings, and Stock Prices," *Review of Economics and Statistics* 41, no. 2 (May 1959): 99–105.

   Nicholas Molodovsky, Catherine May, and Sherman Chottiner, "Common Stock Valuation: Principles, Tables, and Application," *Financial Analysts Journal* 21, no. 2 (March–April 1965): 104–123.

3. For interesting extensions of the multiple-growth DDM, see:

   Patricia M. Fairfield, "P/E, P/B, and the Present Value of Future Dividends," *Financial Analysts Journal* 50, no. 4 (July–August 1994): 23–31.

   Joseph R. Gordon and Myron J. Gordon, "The Finite Horizon Expected Return Model," *Financial Analysts Journal* 53, no. 3 (May–June 1997): 52–61.

   William J. Hurley and Lewis D. Johnson, "Stochastic Two-phase Dividend Discount Models," *Journal of Portfolio Management* 23, no. 4 (Summer 1997): 91–98.

   Yulin Yao, "A Trinomial Dividend Valuation Model," *Journal of Portfolio Management,* 23, no. 4 (Summer 1997): 99–103.

4. For more on DDMs, see the entire November–December 1985 issue of the *Financial Analysts Journal* and *Damodaran on Valuation: Security Analysis for Investment and Corporate Finance* by Aswath Damodaran (New York: John Wiley, 1994), particularly Chapter 6. Some of the problems involved in using dividend discount models are discussed in:

   Richard O. Michaud and Paul L. Davis, "Valuation Model Bias and the Scale Structure of Dividend Discount Returns," *Journal of Finance* 38, no. 2 (May 1982): 563–573.

   Adam K. Gehr, Jr., "A Bias in Dividend Discount Models," *Financial Analysts Journal* 48, no. 1 (January–February 1992): 75–80.

5. For a discussion of how to estimate the discount rate k used with DDMs, see the entire issue of *Financial Markets, Institutions & Instruments* 3, no. 3 (1994) and:

   Eugene F. Fama and Kenneth R. French, "Industry Costs of Equity," *Journal of Financial Economics* 43, no. 2 (February 1997): 153–193.

   Bradford Cornell, John I. Hirshleifer, and Elizabeth P. James, "Estimating the Cost of Equity Capital," *Contemporary Finance Digest* 1, no. 1 (Autumn 1997): 5–26.

6. For more on how to measure and use P/E ratios, see:

   John Markese, "Will the Real P/E Please Stand Up?" *AAII Journal* 11, no. 9 (October 1989): 32–34.

   Robert J. Angell and Alonzo Redman, "How to Judge a P/E? Examine the Expected Growth Rate," *AAII Journal* 12, no. 3 (March 1990): 16–17.

   John Baijkowski, "Price-Earnings Ratios and Fundamental Stock Valuation," *AAII Journal* 13, no. 6 (July 1991): 33–36.

7. For an interesting note on why Japanese P/E ratios appear to be overstated, see:

   Harold Bierman, Jr., "Price/Earnings Ratios Restructured for Japan," *Financial Analysts Journal* 47, no. 2 (March–April 1991): 91–92.

8. The issue of market volatility has been studied by utilizing dividend discount models. In essence, these studies compare the actual levels of various stock market indices with their intrinsic values, calculated by determining the present value of rational forecasts of subsequent dividends paid on the stocks in the indices. The main observation is that the actual levels fluctuate far more over time than the intrinsic values. A conclusion that some people draw from these studies is that there is excess volatility in stock prices and hence markets are not efficient. This hotly debated topic was introduced in:

   Stephen F. LeRoy and Richard D. Porter, "The Present-value Relation: Tests Based on Implied Variance Bounds," *Econometrica* 49, no. 3 (May 1981): 555–574.

Robert J. Shiller, "Do Stock Prices Move Too Much to Be Justified by Subsequent Changes in Dividends?" *American Economic Review* 71, no. 3 (June 1981): 421–436.

9. For more on market volatility, see:

Robert J. Shiller, "Theories of Aggregate Stock Price Movements," *Journal of Portfolio Management* 10, no. 2 (Winter 1984): 23–37.

Robert J. Shiller, *Market Volatility* (Cambridge, MA: MIT Press, 1989).

Stephen F. LeRoy, "Efficient Capital Markets and Martingales," *Journal of Economic Literature* 27, no. 4 (December 1989): 1583–1621.

Stephen F. LeRoy, "Capital Market Efficiency: An Update," Federal Reserve Bank of San Francisco *Economic Review* (Spring 1990): 29–40.

Lucy F. Ackert and Brian F. Smith, "Stock Price Volatility, Ordinary Dividends, and Other Cash Flows to Shareholders," *Journal of Finance* 48, no. 4 (September 1993): 1147–1160.

Bong-Soo Lee, "The Response of Stock Prices to Permanent and Temporary Shocks to Dividends," *Journal of Financial and Quantitative Analysis* 30, no. 1 (March 1995): 1–22.

10. For a Canadian perspective on the dividend discount model, see:

L. Ackert and J. Schnabel, "The Dividend Discount Model: A Victim of the Tumultuous Eighties?" *Canadian Investment Review* VI, no. 3 (Fall 1993): 7–10.

Paul J. N. Halpern (ed.), *Financing Growth in Canada* (Calgary, University of Calgary Press, 1997) contains several articles that discuss the cost of capital and the cost of equity in Canada and internationally.

CHAPTER 18

Earnings

Chapter 17 discussed how the intrinsic value of a share of common stock can be determined by discounting expected dividends per share at a rate of return that is appropriate for a security of similar risk. Alternatively, the implied return on a share of common stock can be determined by finding the discount rate that makes the present value of all the expected dividends equal to the current market price of the stock. In either case, a forecast of dividends per share is necessary. Because dividends per share are equal to earnings per share times a payout ratio, dividends can be forecast by forecasting earnings per share and payout ratios. Currently there are numerous methods that are used by security analysts for forecasting either earnings or dividends. This chapter presents a discussion of some of the important features of dividends and earnings that the analyst must be aware of in making such forecasts. It begins with a discussion of the relationship among earnings, dividends, and investment.

Stock Valuation Based on Earnings

A continual controversy in the investment community concerns the relevance of dividends versus earnings as the underlying source of value of common shares. Clearly, earnings are important to shareholders because earnings provide the cash flow necessary for paying dividends.[1] However, dividends are also important because dividends are what shareholders actually receive from the firm, and they are the focus of the dividend discount models discussed in Chapter 17. Indeed, it would seem that an increase in the proportion of earnings per share paid out as dividends would make shareholders wealthier, suggesting that the **dividend decision** (deciding on the amount of dividends to pay) is a very important one.

Dividend Decision The process of determining the amount of dividends that a corporation will pay its shareholders.

Considerable light was shed on this controversy in 1961 when Merton Miller and Franco Modigliani published a seminal paper arguing that the underlying source of value of common shares was earnings, not dividends. An implication of this conclusion is that the dividend decision is relatively unimportant to the shareholders, as it will not affect the value of their investment in the firm.

In the course of a year, a firm generates revenues and incurs costs. With cash accounting, the difference between revenues and costs would be termed *cash flow*. With accrual

---

[1]It should be remembered that while earnings and cash flow are typically highly correlated, they are not perfectly correlated. Thus, there can be instances where earnings rise and cash flow falls. Hence, earnings do not always provide the cash flow necessary for paying dividends. For more on cash flow analysis, see Chapter 22.

accounting, used by almost all firms, both revenues and costs are likely to include estimates made by accountants of the values of non-cash items. Items such as depreciation charges are deducted from cash flow to obtain earnings. Moreover, each year some amount is invested in the business. Of the total (gross) investment, a portion will be equal in value to the estimated depreciation of various real assets (such as machines and buildings); the rest is new (net) investment.

The dollar amount of new investment each year should be based on the investment opportunities that are available to the firm, and they should be unaffected by the dollar amount of dividends that are to be paid out. In particular, any investment opportunity whose net present value (NPV) is positive should be undertaken. This means that the future prospects of the firm can be described by a stream of expected earnings (E_1, E_2, E_3, ...) and the expected net investment required to produce such earnings (I_1, I_2, I_3, ...). Taking these two streams as given, it can be shown that management can set the total dollar amount of current dividends (D_0) at any level without making the current shareholders either better or worse off.[2] This will be done next, with the focus on earnings and how they can be used to pay for new investments and dividends.

Earnings, Dividends, and Investment

Figure 18.1(a) shows one way that the firm can use total earnings for the current year (E_0). In this situation, new investment (I_0) is financed out of earnings, and the firm uses the remainder of the earnings to pay dividends (D_0) to its shareholders. For example, if the Plum Company has just earned \$5000 and has new investments it would like to make that cost \$3000, then Plum could pay for these investments out of earnings and declare a dividend of \$2000.

Issuing Shares

Whereas earnings are exactly equal to dividends and investment ($E_0 = D_0 + I_0$) in Figure 18.1(a), this need not be the case. In the situation shown in Figure 18.1(b), earnings are less than dividends and investment ($E_0 < D_0 + I_0$). Because the amount of investment has

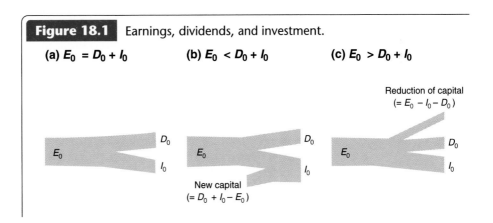

Figure 18.1 Earnings, dividends, and investment.

(a) $E_0 = D_0 + I_0$ (b) $E_0 < D_0 + I_0$ (c) $E_0 > D_0 + I_0$

---

[2]In Chapter 17, D_0 denoted the per-share dividends that had been paid over the past year. Now D_0 is used to denote the aggregate amount of dividends that is about to be paid. Similarly, the quantities of earnings (E_t) and new investment (I_t) are measured for the firm on an aggregate basis, not a per-share basis. Note that dividends cannot be set at an arbitrarily high value relative to earnings (for example, earnings of \$10 million and dividends of \$100 million), because the firm would then find it practically impossible to obtain the necessary funds to pay the dividends.

been determined by the number of positive NPV projects available to the firm, the reason for this inequality is that the firm has decided to pay its current shareholders a higher dividend than was paid in Figure 18.1(a). However, in order for higher dividends to be paid, additional funds must be obtained from outside the firm. This is accomplished by a new sale of common shares (it is assumed that the flotation costs associated with a new sale of common shares are negligible).

The reason the funds are obtained through a new sale of common shares instead of through a new sale of debt is a desire to avoid the confounding effects of a change in the firm's debt-equity ratio. That is, if debt financing is to be allowed, then two things would be changing at the same time—the amount of the dividend and the debt-equity ratio for the firm. As a result, if shareholders appear to be made better off by a change in the amount of the dividend, their betterment may actually be due to a change in the debt-equity ratio. By prohibiting debt financing, the debt-equity ratio will remain constant, and only the amount of the dividend will be allowed to change. That is, each additional dollar in equity funds raised by issuing new shares is offset by a dollar in dividend payments. Thus if shareholders appear to be better off, it has to be due to the change in the amount of the dividend, because everything else (specifically, the amount of investment and the debt-equity ratio) has remained fixed.

Note that if investment is financed out of earnings, as in Figure 18.1(a), then it has been financed with equity obtained internally. In Figure 18.1(b), investment has also been financed with equity, but here some of the equity has been obtained externally. As a result, the debt-equity ratio for the firm is the same in both situations.

In the case of Plum, instead of paying dividends amounting to $2000, the firm could decide to pay dividends amounting to $3000. Because investment is equal to $3000, Plum will have a cash outflow of $3000 + $3000 = $6000, with earnings amounting to only $5000. This means that Plum will have to sell $6000 − $5000 = $1000 of new common shares.

Repurchasing Shares

In Figure 18.1(c), the situation is reversed from 18.1(b) as earnings are now greater than dividends and investment ($E_0 > D_0 + I_0$). Given that the amount of investment has been determined by the number of positive NPV projects available to the firm, the reason for this inequality is that the firm has decided to pay its shareholders a lower dividend than was paid in Figure 18.1(a). In paying this smaller dividend, the firm will be left with excess cash. It is assumed that the firm will use this cash to repurchase some of its outstanding shares in the marketplace (and that the transaction costs associated with such repurchases are negligible).

The reason for this assumption is the desire to keep the situation comparable to the two earlier ones. Allowing the firm to keep the excess cash would be tantamount to letting the firm invest the cash, an investment decision that was not made in the two earlier cases and therefore does not have a positive NPV (remember that I_0 consists of all positive NPV projects). Allowing the firm to keep the excess cash would also mean that the firm has made a decision to lower its debt-equity ratio. This is because retention of the excess cash would increase the amount of equity for the firm, thereby decreasing the amount of debt outstanding relative to the amount of equity.

Continuing with the Plum Company, dividends could be set at $1000 instead of $2000 or $3000. In this case, the firm would have a cash outflow for dividends and investment amounting to $1000 + $3000 = $4000. With earnings of $5000, this means that there would be $5000 − $4000 = $1000 of cash left for the firm to use to repurchase its own shares.

The Dividend Decision

The firm has a decision to make regarding the size of its current dividends. The amount of current earnings E_0 and the amount of new investment I_0 have been determined. What is left to be decided is the amount of dividends, D_0. They can be set equal to earnings less investment as in Figure 18.1(a), or greater than this amount as in Figure 18.1(b), or less than this amount as in Figure 18.1(c). The question that remains to be answered is, will one of these three levels of dividends make the current shareholders better off than the other two? That is, which level of dividends—$1000, $2000, or $3000—will make the current shareholders better off?

The simplest way to answer this question is to consider a shareholder who presently holds 1% of the common shares of the firm and is determined to maintain this percentage ownership in the future.[3] If the firm follows a dividend policy as shown in Figure 18.1(a), the shareholder's current dividends will equal $.01 D_0$ or, equivalently, $.01(E_0 - I_0)$. Similarly, the shareholder's future dividends will be equal to $.01 D_t$ or, equivalently, $.01(E_t - I_t)$.

If the firm follows a dividend policy as shown in Figure 18.1(b), however, the shareholder must invest additional funds in the firm's common shares in order to avoid a diminished proportional ownership position in the firm. Why? Because in this situation the firm must raise funds by selling additional shares in order to pay for the larger cash dividends. As $E_0 < D_0 + I_0$, the total amount of funds that the firm needs to raise is the amount F_0 such that

$$E_0 + F_0 = D_0 + I_0 \tag{18.1}$$

or

$$F_0 = D_0 + I_0 - E_0 \tag{18.2}$$

The amount of the additional investment that the shareholder needs to make in order to maintain a 1% position in the firm is $.01 F_0$, which from equation (18.2) is equal to $.01(D_0 + I_0 - E_0)$. Because the shareholder receives 1% of the dividends, the net amount the shareholder receives at time zero is equal to $.01 D_0 - .01 F_0$, or

$$.01 D_0 - .01(D_0 + I_0 - E_0) = .01 E_0 - .01 I_0. \tag{18.3}$$

Interestingly, the net amount the shareholder receives, $.01 E_0 - .01 I_0$, is the same as in the first situation. This is because the amount of the extra cash dividend received is exactly offset by the amount the shareholder needs to spend to maintain his ownership position in the firm.

If the firm follows a dividend policy as shown in Figure 18.1(c), then the firm will repurchase shares. Accordingly, the shareholder must sell some shares back to the firm in order to avoid having an increased ownership position in the firm. As $E_0 > D_0 + I_0$, the total amount of funds that the firm will spend on repurchasing its own shares is the amount R_0 such that

$$E_0 = D_0 + I_0 + R_0 \tag{18.4}$$

or

$$R_0 = E_0 - D_0 - I_0 \tag{18.5}$$

The number of shares that the shareholder needs to sell back to the firm to maintain a 1% position in the firm is $.01 R_0$, which from equation (18.5) is equal to $.01(E_0 - D_0 - I_0)$.

---

[3]The use of such a shareholder is for ease of exposition. The same answer would be obtained if other types of shareholders (such as those who are not interested in maintaining a constant proportional ownership position in the firm in the future) are considered.

Because the shareholder receives 1% of the dividends, the net amount the shareholder receives at time zero is equal to $.01D_0 + .01R_0$, or

$$.01D_0 + .01(E_0 - D_0 - I_0) = .01E_0 - .01I_0 \qquad (18.6)$$

Again this net amount, $.01E_0 - .01I_0$, is the same as in the first situation. That is, in the third situation, the smaller amount of the cash dividend received by the shareholder is exactly made up for by the amount of cash received from the repurchase of shares by the firm.

Thus, no matter what the firm's dividend policy, a shareholder choosing to maintain a constant proportional ownership will be able to spend the same amount of money on consumption at time zero. This amount will be equal to the proportion times the quantity $E_0 - I_0$. Furthermore, this will also be true in the future. That is, in any year t the shareholder will be able to spend on consumption an amount that is equal to the proportion times the quantity $E_t - I_t$.

Earnings Determine Market Value

In determining the value of 1% of the current shares outstanding, remember that the firm is about to declare and pay current dividends. Regardless of the magnitude of these dividends, the shareholder will only be able to spend on consumption an amount equal to $.01(E_0 - I_0)$.

Furthermore, the shareholder will be able to spend on consumption an amount equal to $.01(E_t - I_t)$ in any future year t. Discounting these expected amounts by a (constant) rate k reveals that the value (V) of 1% of the current shares outstanding will be

$$.01V = \frac{.01(E_0 - I_0)}{(1 + k)^0} + \frac{.01(E_1 - I_1)}{(1 + k)^1} + \frac{.01(E_2 - I_2)}{(1 + k)^2} + \cdots$$

Multiplying both sides of this equation by 100 results in the following expression for the total market value of all shares outstanding:

$$V = \frac{(E_0 - I_0)}{(1 + k)^0} + \frac{(E_1 - I_1)}{(1 + k)^1} + \frac{(E_2 - I_2)}{(1 + k)^2} + \cdots \qquad (18.7)$$

Equation (18.7) shows that the aggregate market value of equity is equal to the present value of expected earnings net of investment. Note how the size of the dividends does not enter into the formula. This indicates that the market value of the stock is *independent* of the dividend decision made by the firm, meaning that the dividend decision is irrelevant to stock valuation. Instead, the market value of the firm is related to the earnings prospects of the firm, along with the required amounts of new investment needed to produce those earnings.[4]

Dividend Discount Models

In Chapter 17 it was shown that the value of a share of common stock was equal to the present value of all dividends expected in the future. Hence it is tempting to believe that, contrary to the assertion above, the market value of a firm's shares is *dependent* on the div-

---

[4] It has been argued that if the tax rate on dividends is greater than the tax rate on capital gains, then shareholders will earn more on an after-tax basis if the firm has a relatively low payout ratio. An additional benefit to shareholders if the firm has a low payout ratio is that capital gains taxes are paid only when the shares are sold, and can therefore be deferred. Thus, it appears that shareholders will be better off if the firm has a relatively low payout ratio. For a more detailed discussion of the issue, along with the relevant citations, see pp. 128–135 of Gordon J. Alexander and Jack Clark Francis, *Portfolio Analysis* (Englewood Cliffs, NJ: Prentice Hall, 1986). Also see James S. Ang, David W. Blackwell, and William L. Megginson, "The Effect of Taxes on the Relative Valuation of Dividends and Capital Gains: Evidence from Dual-class British Investment Trusts," *Journal of Finance* 46, no. 1 (March 1991): 383–399.

idend decision. However, it turns out that there is nothing inconsistent between valuation being based on dividend discount models and the irrelevancy of the dividend decision.

The dividend irrelevancy argument suggests that if the firm decides to increase its current dividend, then new shares will need to be sold. This, in turn, suggests that future dividends will be smaller because the aggregate amount of dividends will have to be divided among an increased number of shares outstanding. Ultimately, the current shareholders will be neither better off nor worse off, as the increased current dividend will be exactly offset by the decreased future dividends. Conversely, if the firm decides to decrease its current dividend, then shares will be repurchased and future dividends will be increased due to the fewer shares outstanding. Ultimately, the decreased current dividend will be exactly offset by the increased future dividends, again leaving current shareholders neither better off nor worse off.

An Example

All this can be illustrated with the earlier example of the Plum Company. Because Plum currently has reported earnings of $5000 and investments totalling $3000, if dividends amounting to $2000 were paid, then the shareholder owning 1% of the firm would receive cash amounting to $.01 \times \$2000 = \$20$.

Alternatively, if dividends amounting to $3000 were paid, then Plum would have to raise $1000 from the sale of new common shares. The shareholder would receive $.01 \times \$3000 = \$30$ in dividends, but would have to pay $.01 \times \$1000 = \$10$ to purchase 1% of the new shares, thereby maintaining her 1% ownership position. Consequently, the net cash flow to the shareholder would be $\$30 - \$10 = \$20$, the same amount as in the previous situation.

Lastly, if dividends amounting to $1000 were paid, then Plum would have cash amounting to $1000 to use to repurchase common shares. The shareholder, desirous of maintaining a 1% position, would thus sell shares amounting to $.01 \times \$1000 = \$10$. As a result, the shareholder would have a cash inflow totalling $\$10 + \$10 = \$20$, again the same amount as in the two previous situations.

Under all three situations, the 1% shareholder would receive the same cash flow at the present time ($20) and have the same claim on the future earnings of Plum. That is, in all three cases, the shareholder would still own 1% of Plum and would therefore receive the same amount of dividends in the future. Accordingly, the 1% shareholder (and all the others) would be neither better off nor worse off if Plum pays a dividend amounting to $1000, $2000, or $3000. In summary, the dividend decision is a non-event—whatever the level of dividends, current shareholders will be neither better off nor worse off. This result is sometimes referred to as the "dividend irrelevancy theorem."

Determinants of Dividends

Few firms attempt to maintain a constant ratio of dividends to current earnings because doing so would result in a fluctuating dollar amount of dividends. The reason the dividends would fluctuate is that earnings on a year-to-year basis are likely to be quite variable. Instead, firms attempt to maintain a desired ratio of dividends to earnings over some relatively long period, meaning that there is a target payout ratio of dividends to long-run or sustainable earnings. As a result, dividends are usually kept at a constant dollar amount and are increased only when management is confident that it will be relatively easy to keep paying this increased amount in the future.[5] Nonetheless, larger earnings are likely to be accompanied by some sort of increase in dividends, as Table 18.1 shows.

---

[5]In addition to a regular dividend, sometimes a firm will declare a "special" or "extra" dividend, usually at year-end. By calling it a special dividend, the firm is conveying a message to its shareholders that such a dividend is a one-time event.

Table 18.1 Earnings and Dividend Changes.[a]

Earnings Changes			Percentage of Cases in Which Firms:		
Current Year	Previous Year	Percentage of Cases	Increased Dividends	Did Not Change Dividends	Decreased Dividends
+		59.3%	65.8%	13.9%	20.3%
−		40.7	42.8	17.9	39.5
+	+	33.4	74.8	11.4	13.8
+	−	25.9	54.1	17.2	28.7
−	+	24.7	49.7	16.9	33.4
−	−	16.0	31.8	19.4	48.8

[a] Based on 392 firms during the period 1946–1964.

SOURCE: Eugene F. Fama and Harvey Babiak, "Dividend Policy: An Empirical Analysis," *Journal of the American Statistical Association* 63, no. 324 (December 1968): 1134.

Changes in Earnings and Dividends

The first two lines of Table 18.1 indicate that 59.3% of the time the earnings of the firms examined rose, and the remaining 40.7% of the time earnings fell. The majority of the times when current earnings rose, firms increased their current dividends. However, whenever current earnings fell, firms would increase their current dividends as frequently as they would decrease their current dividends (note that, roughly speaking, 42.8% ≅ 39.5%).

The next two lines of the table suggest that firms are more likely to increase current dividends if they have had two consecutive years of rising earnings than if they have had falling and then rising earnings (74.8% > 54.1%). The last two lines of the table suggest that firms are more likely to decrease current dividends if they have had two consecutive years of falling earnings than if they have had rising and then falling earnings (48.8% > 33.4%). Overall, the table shows that firms in general are more likely to increase dividends than to decrease them.

The Lintner Model

A formal representation of the kind of behaviour implied by a constant long-run target payout ratio begins by assuming that the goal of the firm is to pay out p^* (for example, $p^* = 60\%$) of long-run earnings. If this target ratio were maintained every year, total dividends paid in year t would be

$$D_t^* = p^* E_t \tag{18.8}$$

where D_t^* denotes the target amount for dividends to be paid in year t and E_t is the amount of earnings in year t. The difference between target dividends in year t and the previous year's actual dividends is determined by subtracting D_{t-1} from both sides of equation (18.8), resulting in

$$D_t^* - D_{t-1} = p^* E_t - D_{t-1} \tag{18.9}$$

Although firms would like to change their dividends from D_{t-1} to D_t^*, few (if any) firms would actually change their dividends by this amount. Instead, the actual change in dividends will be a proportion of the desired change:

$$D_t - D_{t-1} = a(D_t^* - D_{t-1}) \tag{18.10}$$

where a is a "speed of adjustment" coefficient, a number between zero and one.

For example, if a firm has just earned $5 million ($E_t$ = $5 million) and has a target payout ratio of 60%, then it would like to pay dividends amounting to .6 × $5 million = $3 million. Assuming that it paid dividends of $2 million last year, this represents an increase of $3 million − $2 million = $1 million. However, if a = 50%, then the firm will actually increase the dividends by .5 × $1 million = $500 000. Thus actual dividends will be equal to $2 million + $500 000 = $2.5 million, an amount equal to last year's dividends plus the change in dividends from last year to this year.

This model can be summarized by substituting p^*E_t for D_t^* in equation (18.10) and then solving the resulting expression for D_t:

$$D_t = ap^*E_t + (1 - a)D_{t-1} \qquad (18.11)$$

Equation (18.11) indicates that the amount of current dividends is based on the amount of current earnings and the amount of the last year's dividends.[6] In the previous example, a = 50%, p^* = 60%, E_t = $5 million, and D_{t-1} = $2 million. Thus actual dividends D_t would be equal to (.5 × .6 × $5 million) + (1 − .5) × $2 million = $2.5 million.

By subtracting D_{t-1} from both sides of equation (18.11), it can be seen that the change in dividends is equal to

$$D_t - D_{t-1} = ap^*E_t - aD_{t-1} \qquad (18.12)$$

When written in this form, the model suggests that the size of the *change* in dividends will be positively related to the current amount of earnings (because ap^* is a positive number) and negatively related to the amount of the previous period's dividends (since $-aD_{t-1}$ is a negative number). Thus, the larger current earnings are, the larger the change in dividends, but the larger the previous period's dividends, the smaller the change in dividends.

▸ Test Results

Statistical analysis has been used to test how well this model describes the way a sample of firms set the amount of their dividends. Table 18.2 summarizes some of the values obtained in one such study. The average firm had a target payout ratio of 59.1% and adjusted dividends 26.9% of the way towards its target each year. However, most firms' dividends varied substantially from the pattern implied by their targets and adjustment factors. Somewhat less than half (42%) of the annual variance in the typical firm's dividends could be explained in this manner. This means that the model, although explaining a portion of the changes in dividends that occurred, leaves a substantial portion unexplained.

A refinement of the model presented in equation (18.12) uses an alternative definition of earnings. Specifically, the term E_t in equation (18.8) can be defined as the *permanent* earnings of the firm in year t instead of total earnings. Here total earnings can be thought of as having two components—permanent earnings, which are likely to be repeated, and transitory earnings, which are not likely to be repeated. Accordingly, the refinement is based on the idea that management ignores the transitory component of earnings in arriving at its target amount of dividends. Hence, the target amount is based on the permanent earnings of the firm, not the total earnings, and the change in dividends shown in equation (18.12) is related to the past level of dividends and permanent earnings. A test of this

---

[6]Looking backward in time, it can be shown that current dividends, D_t, are a linear function of past earnings E_{t-1}, E_{t-2}, E_{t-3}, and so on. More specifically, it can be shown that:

$$D_t = ap^*[(1 - a)^0E_{t-0} + (1 - a)^1E_{t-1} + (1 - a)^2E_{t-2} + (1 - a)^3E_{t-3} + \ldots]$$

Because the quantity $(1 - a)$ is a positive fraction (for example, 1/3), when it is raised to a power it becomes smaller in value, with larger powers resulting in values closer to zero. Thus, current dividends depend more on recent past earnings than on distant past earnings, and the equation can be approximated by using an arbitrary number of past earnings (the accuracy of the approximation depends on the number used).

Table 18.2 Target Payout Ratios and Speed of Dividend Adjustment Factors.[a]

Speed of Adjustment Coefficient		Target Payout Ratio		Percentage of Variance Explained	
Value	Percentage of Firms with Smaller Value	Value	Percentage of Firms with Smaller Value	Value	Percentage of Firms with Smaller Value
.104	10%	.401	10%	11%	10%
.182	30	.525	30	32	30
.251	50	.584	50	42	50
.339	70	.660	70	54	70
.470	90	.779	90	72	90
average .269		average .591		average 42	

[a] Based on 298 firms during the period 1946–1968.

SOURCE: Eugene F. Fama, "The Empirical Relationship Between the Dividend and Investment Decisions of Firms," *American Economic Review* 64, no. 3 (June 1974): 310.

model found that it described changes in dividends better than the previously described model that was based on total earnings.[7]

The results from a comparable Canadian study of 40 companies in the manufacturing sector from 1947 to 1970 are shown in Table 18.3. In this case, however, current dividends were regressed against cash flow (rather than earnings) and the dividend paid in the prior period. The average target payout ratio and speed of adjustment coefficient were 0.316 and 0.379 respectively. The cash flow model used here appears to describe the firms' dividend behaviour better than the earnings model used in the US in that it explains about 77% of the variance of the typical firm's dividend compared with 42%. The behaviour of a few Canadian firms, however, does not conform well to this model in that these firms have low

Table 18.3 Target Payout Ratios and Speed of Dividend Adjustment Factors for 40 Canadian Firms, 1947–1970.

Speed of Adjustment Coefficient		Target Payout Ratio		Percentage of Variance Explained	
Value	Percentage of Firms with Smaller Value	Value	Percentage of Firms with Smaller Value	Value	Percentage of Firms with Smaller Value
.204	25%	.244	25%	72%	25%
.324	50	.313	50	85	50
.506	75	.374	75	93	75
average .379		average .316		average 77	

SOURCE: J-P. D. Chateau, "La Politique de distribution de dividends des sociétés: Une étude microéconométrique," *Canadian Journal of Economics* 9, no. 2 (1976): 255–277.

[7] See Bong-Soo Lee, "Time Series Implications of Aggregate Dividend Behavior," *Review of Financial Studies* 9, no. 2 (Summer 1996): 589–618.

speed of adjustment coefficients, implying that they make little or no adjustment to their dividends in response to changes in cash flow.

The Information Content of Dividends

It is reasonable to believe that management has more information about the future earnings of the firm than does the public (including its own shareholders). This situation of **asymmetric information** suggests that managers will seek to convey the information to the public if they have an incentive to do so. Assuming that they have such an incentive, one way of doing so is by announcing a change in the amount of the firm's dividends. When used in this manner, dividend announcements are said to be a signaling device.[8]

Signaling

A relatively simple view of dividend changes is that an announced increase in dividends is a signal that management has increased its assessment of the firm's future earnings. The announced increase in dividends is therefore good news and will, in turn, cause investors to raise their expectations regarding the firm's future earnings. Conversely, an announced decrease in dividends is a signal that management has decreased its assessment of the firm's future earnings. The announced decrease in dividends is therefore bad news and will, in turn, cause investors to lower their expectations regarding the firm's future earnings. An implication is that an announced increase in dividends will cause the firm's share price to rise, and an announced decrease will cause it to fall.

This simple model of dividend changes can be thought of as a special case of the model given in equation (18.12), where the speed of adjustment, a, is zero. With this model, the expected change in dividends, $D_t - D_{t-1}$, is zero, suggesting that a simple increase in dividends will be viewed as good news. Conversely, a simple decrease in dividends will be viewed as bad news.

One way of testing to see if dividend changes do indeed convey information to the public is to see how share prices react to announcements of changes in dividends. However, care must be exercised in conducting such a study because the firm's announcement of dividends is often made at the same time as the firm announces its earnings. Thus, when such announcements are made at the same time, any price change in the firm's common shares may be attributable to either (or both) announcements.

One study attempted to avoid this problem of contamination by looking only at cases where the announcement of earnings was at least 11 trading days apart from the announcement of dividends. Figure 18.2 provides an illustration of the average abnormal return associated with a firm's dividend announcement for those firms that announced their dividends 11 or more days after they announced their earnings (similar results were obtained when the authors examined those cases where dividend announcements preceded earnings announcements).

In those cases where firms announced an increase in their dividends, there is a significant positive reaction in their share prices. Conversely, in those cases where firms announced a decrease in their dividends, there is a significant negative reaction in their

---

[8]Other signaling devices include changes in the firm's capital structure (for example, announcing an issuance of debt with the proceeds being used to repurchase stock). It has been argued that in order for the signal to be useful to the public (1) management must have an incentive to send a truthful signal; (2) the signal cannot be imitated by competitors in different financial positions; and (3) there cannot be a cheaper means of conveying the same information. See Stephen A. Ross, "The Determination of Financial Structure: The Incentive Signalling Approach," *Bell Journal of Economics* 8, no. 1 (Spring 1977): 23–40.

(a) Dividend Decrease

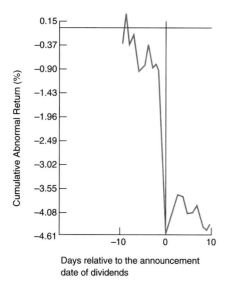

(b) Dividend Increase

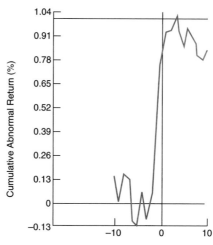

Days relative to the announcement date of dividends

SOURCE: Joseph Aharony and Itzhak Swary, "Quarterly Dividend and Earnings Announcements and Stockholders' Returns: An Empirical Analysis," *Journal of Finance* 35, no. 1 (March 1980): 8.

Information Content of Dividends Hypothesis
The proposition that dividend announcements contain inside information about a corporation's future prospects.

share prices. These findings strongly support the **information content of dividends hypothesis**, where dividend announcements are asserted to contain inside information about the firm's future prospects.

A study by Charest, that was not free of possible contamination by earnings announcements, found that dividend changes in Canada are anticipated by the market several months in advance of the announcement, as shown in Figure 18.3.[9] Here also dividend increases (decreases) are accompanied by positive (negative) reactions in the stock prices. These findings are also consistent with the information content of dividends hypothesis.

It should be noted that dividends being used as a signal is not inconsistent with the dividend irrelevancy argument of Miller and Modigliani that was made earlier. In particular, shareholders will be neither better nor worse off if the *level* of dividends, relative to earnings, is high or low. *Changes* in dividends may, however, be important because they convey information to the public about the future earnings prospects for the firm.

Dividend Initiations and Omissions

One study looked at the relationship between dividend changes and past, current, and future changes in earnings.[10] Specifically, it focused on the most dramatic dividend announcements possible—dividend initiations and omissions—because the information being conveyed in these announcements is clearly unambiguous.

---

[9]G. Charest, "Returns to Dividend Changing Stocks on the Toronto Stock Exchange," *Journal of Business Administration* 12, no. 1 (Fall 1980): 1–18.

[10]Paul M. Healy and Krishna G. Palepu, "Earnings Information Conveyed by Dividend Initiations and Omissions," *Journal of Financial Economics* 21, no. 2 (September 1988): 149–175.

Figure 18.3

Cumulative abnormal returns starting 24 months before a dividend announcement.

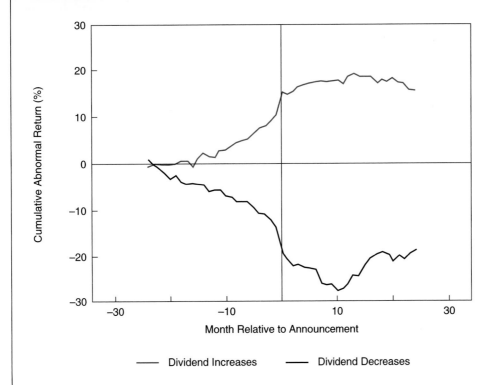

Month Relative to Announcement

——— Dividend Increases   ——— Dividend Decreases

SOURCE: Adapted from G. Charest, "Returns to Dividend Changing Stocks on the Toronto Stock Exchange," *Journal of Business Administration* 12, no. 1 (Fall 1980): 7–8.

That is, if the information content of dividends hypothesis is correct, then firms that start to pay dividends for the first time in at least 10 years must be signaling that they believe that earnings have recently increased to a permanently higher level, and that earnings may increase even more in the near future. The question to be addressed is this: have firms actually experienced notably higher earnings around the time of such initiations and afterward?

Conversely, firms that have paid dividends for at least 10 years and that suddenly stop paying any dividends must believe that their earnings have recently decreased to a permanently lower level, and that earnings may decrease even more in the future. For them the question is this: have firms actually experienced notably lower earnings around the time of such omissions and afterward?

The answer supported the information content of dividends hypothesis. Specifically, the study found that earnings tended to increase for at least one year leading up to dividend initiations and to decrease for up to two years leading up to dividend omissions. Furthermore, earnings continued to increase for at least one year after initiations and to decrease for one year after omissions, and such changes appear to be permanent. Interestingly, the larger the change in the firm's share price when the dividend initiation or omission is announced, the larger the change in the firm's earnings in both the year of the announcement and the year thereafter. Thus, it seems that dividends do indeed convey information about earnings.

A second study also focused on the share price movements of firms around the time that they either initiated or omitted dividends.[11] Examining a sample of New York Stock Exchange and American Stock Exchange-listed firms, 887 occurrences of dividend omissions and 561 initiations were uncovered during 1964–1988. The following observations were made:

1. Firms that initiated dividends had on average an abnormal rise of 15.1% in their share price over the year up to the time of the dividend announcement. The corresponding figure for firms that omitted dividends was −31.8%. Hence, firms that initiated dividends seem to have been prior "winners" while firms that omitted dividends seem to have been prior "losers."

2. Over the three-day period centred on the initial announcement of a dividend, the average firm had its shares rise by an abnormal 3.4%. The corresponding figure for omissions was −7.0%.

3. The average share of firms that initiated a dividend rose by an abnormal 24.8% in the three years afterwards, while the average share price of firms that omitted a dividend fell by an abnormal 15.0% over the subsequent two years, and thereafter had normal returns. Because of the lagged response to the dividend initiations and omissions, it appears that the market is underreacting to these dividend announcements, implying a market inefficiency.

4. The average dividend yield at the time a dividend was initiated was .9%, while the average dividend yield just before an omission was 6.7%.

Dividends and Losses

In a similar vein to dividend initiations and omissions, it is interesting to examine situations where firms that have had a string of at least 10 years of positive earnings and dividend payments suddenly experience negative earnings. In particular, do dividends in such a situation convey information about future earnings?

One study examined this situation by looking at firms that had at least one year of negative earnings during the 1980–1985 period but previously had at least 10 consecutive years of positive earnings and dividend payments; 167 firms ("loss" firms) were uncovered meeting these criteria.[12] A comparison sample of 440 firms ("non-loss" firms) that had positive earnings during the 1980–1985 period as well as during a previous 10-year period was also formed.

Approximately half the "loss" firms reduced or omitted their dividends in the four subsequent quarters after the fiscal year-end of the loss. In comparison, fewer than 1% of the "non-loss" firms either reduced or omitted their dividends during the six-year period of 1980–1985. Further examination revealed that:

1. The "loss" firms that did not reduce their dividends were more likely to have unusual income items, indicating that their earnings problems were more likely to be temporary.

2. The "loss" firms that reduced their dividends had deeper losses than the "loss" firms that did not reduce their dividends.

3. The "loss" firms that reduced their dividends were much more likely to have negative earnings in the next two years than the nonreducing "loss" firms.

---

[11] See Roni Michaely, Richard H. Thaler, and Kent L. Womack, "Price Reactions to Dividend Initiations and Omissions: Overreaction or Drift?" *Journal of Finance* 50, no. 2 (June 1995): 573–608.

[12] Harry DeAngelo, Linda DeAngelo, and Douglas J. Skinner, "Dividends and Losses," *Journal of Finance* 47, no. 5 (December 1992): 1837–1863. Also see Harry DeAngelo and Linda DeAngelo, "Dividend Policy and Financial Distress: An Empirical Investigation of Troubled NYSE Firms," *Journal of Finance* 45, no. 5 (December 1990): 1415–1431.

Hence, knowing what happened to dividends for a "loss" firm tends to make it easier to predict its future earnings, thereby indicating that dividends have information content when a firm suddenly has negative earnings.

Accounting Earnings Versus Economic Earnings

Because the prediction of earnings is of critical importance in security analysis and investment research, a review of what is known about earnings and the relationship between earnings and security prices is essential. At a fundamental level, consideration of the concept of "earnings" itself is needed. Specifically, just what is meant by "earnings" to those who produce the figures, and how does this affect the valuation process?

● Accounting Earnings

Accounting Earnings (Alternatively, **Reported Earnings**.) A firm's revenues less its expenses. Equivalently, the change in the firm's book value of the equity plus dividends paid to shareholders.

Earnings per Share (EPS) A corporation's accounting earnings divided by the number of its common shares outstanding.

Return on Equity (ROE) The earnings per share of a firm divided by the firm's book value per share.

A firm's accountants operate under constraints and guidelines imposed by regulatory authorities and professional organizations such as the Ontario Securities Commission (OSC) and the Canadian Institute of Chartered Accountants (CICA). In cooperation with management, the accountants produce, on a quarterly basis, a set of financial statements for the firm that ends with a figure for the firm's **accounting earnings** (also known as the firm's **reported earnings**). In a broad sense, such earnings represent the difference between revenues and expenses, including the expenses associated with non-equity sources of funds (such as debt). This difference, the "total earnings available for common stock," is divided by the number of shares outstanding to calculate **earnings per share** (EPS). It may also be divided by the book value per share to calculate the **return on equity** (ROE).

A basic principle of accounting makes the book value of a firm's equity at the end of a period (such as a quarter or a year) equal to (1) its value at the end of the previous period, plus (2) the portion of accounting earnings for the period that is retained by the firm (here it is assumed that there has been no change in the number of shares outstanding during the period).[13] Letting B_t denote the book value of the equity of the firm at the end of period t, E_t^a denote the accounting earnings for period t, and D_t denote the dividends paid during period t, this relationship can be expressed algebraically as

$$B_t = B_{t-1} + E_t^a - D_t \qquad (18.13)$$

From equation (18.13), it can be seen that accounting earnings equal the change in book value of equity plus dividends paid:

$$E_t^a = B_t - B_{t-1} + D_t \qquad (18.14)$$

● Economic Earnings

Economic Earnings The change in the economic value of the firm plus dividends paid to shareholders.

Economic Value of the Firm The aggregate market value of all securities issued by the firm.

Economic earnings (E_t^e) may be defined as the amount that would be obtained in equation (18.14) if the change in the book value of the firm equalled the change in the **economic value of the firm**:

$$E_t^e = V_t - V_{t-1} + D_t \qquad (18.15)$$

Here the change in the economic value of the firm during period t, $V_t - V_{t-1}$, is defined

---

[13]Book value of the firm's equity is also called shareholders' equity, particularly when the discussion refers to a company's balance sheet. Shareholders' equity is discussed further in Chapter 22.

as the change in the market value of the firm's common shares (assuming that there is no change in the market value of the firm's other securities).[14]

It is easy to show that reported book values and market values (that is, economic values) of stocks are often considerably different. Figure 18.4 shows the ratio of (1) the year-end market price per share for Standard & Poor's Industrial Stock Index to (2) the corresponding year-end book value per share. It can be seen that the ratio is typically greater than 1.0 and has fluctuated considerably from year to year.

Figure 18.4 indicates that there can be sizeable differences between market and book values. Because equations (18.14) and (18.15) show that accounting and economic earnings will be equal only if market and book values are equal, the evidence thus suggests that accounting and economic earnings differ by varying amounts for different firms.

It is sometimes contended that investors estimate the value of a firm's common stock by directly applying a formula to the firm's current and past accounting earnings.[15] Such a belief may tempt a firm's managers to try to "manage" such earnings in order to make a firm appear more valuable than it is, thereby fooling investors, at least temporarily. This is permissible since the **generally accepted accounting principles (GAAP)** set by the regulatory authorities (such as CICA) allow a large amount of discretion in how certain items are accounted for (examples include methods for depreciation and inventory valuation). As a result, management may pressure accountants to use those principles that maximize the level of reported earnings, or that result in a high growth rate of reported earnings, or that "smooth" earnings by reducing the year-to-year variability of earnings around a growth rate.[16] Some of these activities can be continued only for a limited number of years; others can go on indefinitely.

To obtain a truly independent estimate of value, analysts must dissect reported earnings. In doing so, they should not be fooled by any accounting illusions, meaning that they should ignore any manipulations that may have been made by the accountants at management's request.[17] Anyone who estimates value by applying a formula (no matter how complex) to reported earnings is not producing an estimate that is completely free from all possible manipulations by management. This is not to say that reported earnings are irrelevant for security valuation. Instead, they should be viewed as one source of information about the future prospects of a firm.

Generally Accepted Accounting Principles (GAAP) Accounting rules established by recognized authorities, such as the Canadian Institute of Chartered Accountants (CICA).

Price-earnings Ratios

Chapter 17 discussed how dividend discount models could be used to determine if stocks were either underpriced or overpriced. One means of making this determination was to

---

[14]Sir John R. Hicks, winner in 1972 of the Nobel Prize in Economics, defined the weekly economic income of an individual as "the maximum value which he can consume during a week and still be as well off at the end of the week as he was at the beginning" (*Value and Capital*, London: Oxford University Press, 1946, p. 172). The definition of the economic earnings of a firm that is given in equation (18.15) can be viewed as an extension of Hicks's definition for an individual.

[15]Two assertions that have been made in regard to what investors look at when valuing shares are known as the *mechanistic hypothesis* and the *myopic hypothesis*. The former asserts that investors look only at reported earnings, and the latter asserts that investors look only at the short-term future. Both these assertions seem to be invalid when data are analyzed. For an in-depth discussion, see George Foster, *Financial Statement Analysis* (Englewood Cliffs, NJ: Prentice Hall, 1986), pp. 443–445.

[16]For a discussion of a number of related issues, see Ross Watts, "Does It Pay to Manipulate EPS?" in *Issues in Corporate Finance* (New York: Stern Stewart Putnam & Macklis, 1983).

[17]There is evidence that investors in publicly held firms are not fooled by such manipulations. See, for example, John R. M. Hand and Patricia Hughes, "The Motives and Consequences of Debt-Equity Swaps and Defeasances: More Evidence That It Does Not Pay to Manipulate Earnings," *Journal of Applied Corporate Finance* 3, no. 3 (Fall 1990): 77–81.

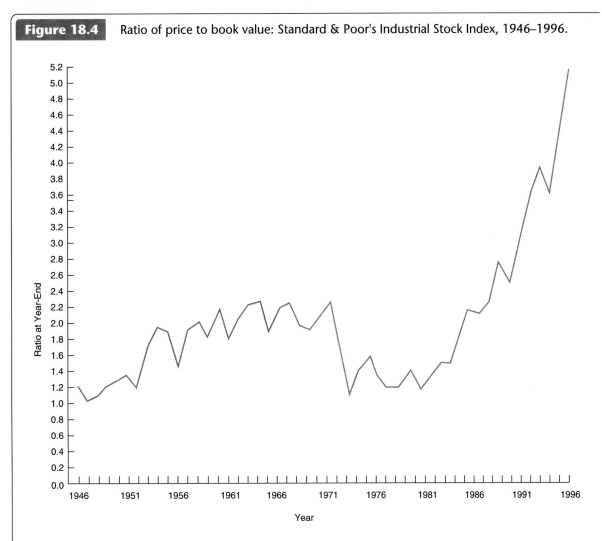

Figure 18.4 Ratio of price to book value: Standard & Poor's Industrial Stock Index, 1946–1996.

SOURCE: Standard & Poor's *Statistical Service*, various issues.

compare the actual price-earnings ratio for a firm with what the security analyst had determined it should be. In view of this use of price-earnings ratios, some evidence on the behaviour of overall earnings, prices, and price-earnings ratios will now be presented.

The Historical Record

Figure 18.5(a) presents a plot of the year-end price-earnings ratios for the Standard & Poor's 500. It can be seen from this plot that the variation in the ratio on a year-to-year basis is considerable, suggesting that investors do not simply apply a standard multiple to earnings in order to determine an appropriate value.

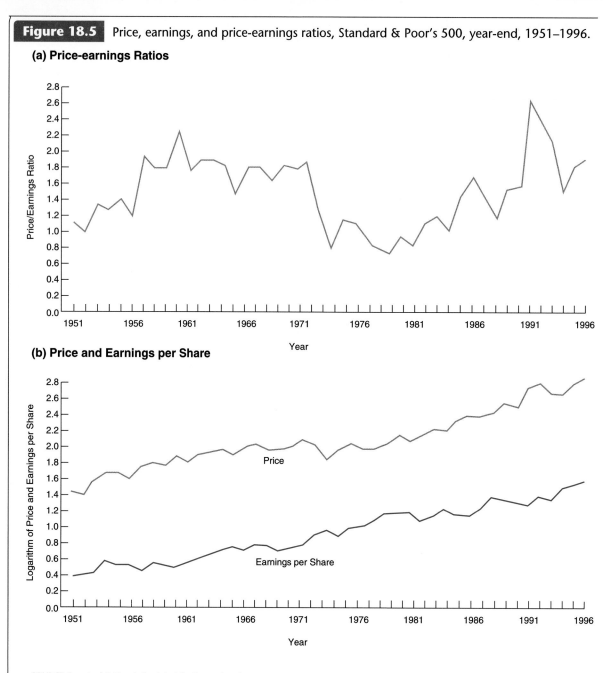

Figure 18.5 Price, earnings, and price-earnings ratios, Standard & Poor's 500, year-end, 1951–1996.

(a) Price-earnings Ratios

Price/Earnings Ratio

Year

(b) Price and Earnings per Share

Logarithm of Price and Earnings per Share

Price

Earnings per Share

Year

SOURCE: Standard & Poor's *Statistical Service*, various issues.

Figure 18.5(b) presents a plot of earnings per share (the lower jagged line) and price (the upper jagged line) for the Standard & Poor's 500.[18] Both lines generally move upward to the

---

[18]The vertical axis of this figure actually measures the logarithm of earnings per share and of the price index. In this type of diagram, a given vertical distance represents the same percentage change, no matter where it appears. If prices, for example, changed by the same percentage every year (like $10 to $20 to $40 to $80), then the plot of log prices would be a straight line sloping upward to the right whereas the plot of prices would curve upward.

right, showing a general trend for both earnings per share and prices to increase over time. However, the two lines are not parallel. This means that earnings per share and prices do not move together in a lockstep manner, an observation that is also apparent in Figure 18.5(a).

Figure 18.6 presents a similar plot of price-earnings ratios for the TSE 300. This also shows a wide variation from year to year, particularly in 1992 and 1993 when the ratio rose sharply. Several large Canadian companies reported huge losses in those years, mainly writedowns related to closing inefficient operations or revising asset values. The firms had not exercised due diligence in control of operations, or had paid too much for assets in the 1980s. When total earnings returned to normal levels in 1994, the price-earnings ratio plummeted.

● Permanent and Transitory Components of Earnings

When individual common stocks are analyzed, they too show considerable variation in their price-earnings ratios over time. Furthermore, their ratios are quite different from each other at any point in time. One possible explanation notes that reported earnings can be viewed as having two components. The *permanent component* is the component that is likely to be repeated in the future, whereas the *transitory component* is not likely to be repeated.

Earlier, it was argued that the intrinsic value of a share depends on the firm's future earnings prospects. This suggests that changes in a share's intrinsic value, and in turn its price, will be correlated with changes in the permanent component of its earnings but not with changes in the transitory component. If the transitory component is positive, then the price-earnings ratio would be relatively low due to a relatively large number in the denominator. Conversely, if the transitory component is negative, then the price-earnings ratio would be relatively high due to a relatively small number in the denominator.

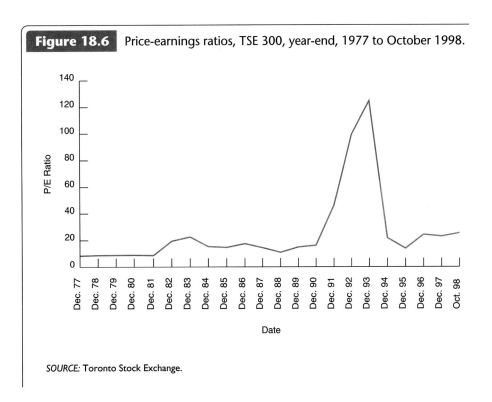

| **Figure 18.6** | Price-earnings ratios, TSE 300, year-end, 1977 to October 1998.

SOURCE: Toronto Stock Exchange.

As an example, consider a firm whose current share price is $30. Its permanent component of earnings per share over the past year is $4, and its transitory component is $1, resulting in reported earnings of $4 + $1 = $5 and a price-earnings ratio of $30/$5 = 6. Remember that the stock's current price is based on its future prospects, which are in turn based on the permanent component of earnings per share over the past year. Thus, if the firm had the same permanent component of $4 but had a transitory component of −$1 instead of +$1, the stock would still have a current price of $30 per share. However, its reported earnings would have been $4 − $1 = $3 and its price-earnings ratio would have been $30/$3 = 10.

The permanent component of earnings will change over time, causing investors to revise their forecasts. This will lead to a change in a firm's share price and, in turn, its price-earnings ratio. However, changes in the transitory component will have an even greater effect on the price-earnings ratio because this component will sometimes be positive and sometimes be negative. As a result, a firm's price-earnings ratio will be variable over time, as was shown in Figure 18.5(a) for the S&P 500. This also means that at any point in time, the transitory component of earnings for a group of firms will have varying sizes, some being positive and some being negative. As a result, at any point in time, firms will have a range of different price-earnings ratios.

If this were a complete explanation for the considerable variation in price-earnings ratios over time and across firms, then most of the variation in a firm's price-earnings ratio would itself be transitory. That is, the ratio would vary over time around some average value. However, the evidence suggests that this is not the case. Figure 18.7 shows the

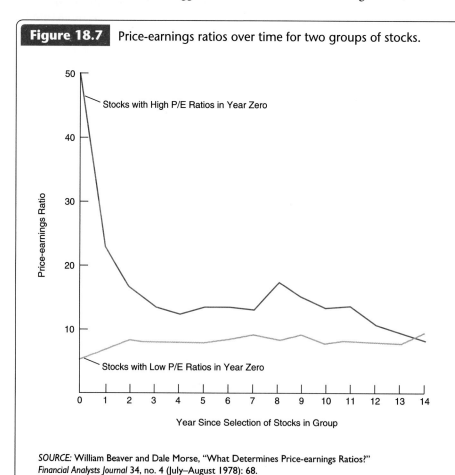

Figure 18.7 Price-earnings ratios over time for two groups of stocks.

SOURCE: William Beaver and Dale Morse, "What Determines Price-earnings Ratios?" *Financial Analysts Journal* 34, no. 4 (July–August 1978): 68.

behaviour over time of price-earnings ratios for two groups of stocks. The first group includes stocks with high price-earnings ratios at the beginning of the period (that is, during a portfolio formation period). The other group includes stocks with low price-earnings ratios at the beginning of the period.

Over time, the price-earnings ratios tend to revert to an average ratio for the market as a whole. The changes are substantial in the first two years, owing undoubtedly to the influence of transitory components of earnings. That is, those stocks in the high price-earnings ratio group apparently had, on average, a negative transitory component in their earnings in the portfolio formation period. (Remember that such a component would tend to give a stock a high ratio.) Conversely, those stocks in the low price-earnings ratio group apparently had, on average, a positive transitory component. (Remember that such a component would tend to give a stock a low ratio.) Over future periods, each group of stocks would tend to have an equal number of stocks with positive and negative transitory components, resulting in an average transitory component for each group of roughly zero.

However, Figure 18.7 shows that the two groups of stocks have different price-earnings ratios for many years after the portfolio formation period. Three explanations can be offered for this persistent difference.

1. Appropriate discount rates (that is, required returns) differ because of differences in security attributes. For two firms with the same current and expected future earnings, the firm with the lower discount rate will have a higher share price and hence a higher price-earnings ratio.
2. There may be permanent differences between economic and reported earnings due to the use of different accounting methods. As mentioned earlier, there is evidence that the market sees through such differences in reported earnings.
3. There may be persistent differences in the forecasts of long-term permanent earnings growth rates by security analysts. That is, firms with high price-earnings ratios may have high forecast long-term permanent earnings growth rates and hence relatively high prices. Conversely, firms with low price-earnings ratios may have low forecast long-term permanent earnings growth rates and hence relatively low prices.[19] If such forecasts persist over time, then firms with high price-earnings ratios would tend to continue having high ratios over time, while firms with low ratios would tend to continue having low ratios over time. Evidence suggests that indeed this is the case.

Relative Growth Rates of Firms' Earnings

Because security analysis typically involves forecasting earnings per share, it is useful to examine the historical record to see how earnings per share have changed over time. An interesting question about growth rates in firm earnings over time focuses on growth stocks. The very idea of a growth stock suggests that growth in some firms' earnings will exceed the average growth of all firms' earnings in most years, while other firms' earnings will grow less than the average.

Earnings Growth Rates

The results of a study of the earnings growth rates for 610 industrial companies from 1950 to 1964 are shown in Table 18.4. In every year, each firm's earnings were compared with

---

[19]This suggests that firms will have high price-earnings ratios if they have either negative transitory current earnings or high forecasted long-term permanent earnings, or both. The converse holds for firms with low price-earnings ratios.

Table 18.4	Earnings Growth Rates.[a]		
Length of Run	Actual Number of Good Runs	Actual Number of Bad Runs	Number of Good or Bad Runs Expected if the Odds Each Year Were 50–50 Regardless of Past Performance
1	1152	1102	1068
2	562	590	534
3	266	300	267
4	114	120	133
5	55	63	67
6	24	20	33
7	23	12	17
8	5	6	8
9	3	3	4
10	6	0	2
11	2	0	1
12	1	0	1
13	0	0	0
14	0	1	0

[a]Based on 610 firms during the period 1950–1964.

SOURCE: Richard A. Brealey, *An Introduction to Risk and Return from Common Stocks* (Cambridge, MA: MIT Press, 1983), p. 89.

its earnings in the previous year and the percentage change calculated. The year was counted as "good" for the firm if its percentage change was in the top half of the changes for all firms that year, and "bad" if it was in the bottom half. If some firms tend to experience above-average earnings growth rates, then fairly long runs of good years should occur for these firms. Conversely, if some firms tend to experience below-average earnings growth rates, then they should have fairly long runs of bad years.

The middle two columns of Table 18.4 indicate the actual number of runs of various lengths. The right-hand column shows the number that would be expected if there were a 50–50 chance of either a good year or a bad year. The three columns are remarkably similar. Above-average earnings growth in the past does not appear to indicate above-average growth in the future; and below-average growth in the past does not appear to indicate below-average growth in the future. Flipping a coin seems to be as reliable a predictor of future growth as looking at past growth rates.

A study using longer time periods for measuring growth reached generally similar conclusions.[20] For each of 323 companies with positive earnings in each year from 1946

---

[20]John Lintner and Robert Glauber, "Higgledy Piggledy Growth in America," in James Lorie and Richard Brealey, eds., *Modern Developments in Investment Management* (Hinsdale, IL: Dryden Press, 1978). However, a more recent study came to a different conclusion concerning the predictability of earnings changes. This study divided a large number of companies into five groups based on their earnings-to-price (E/P) ratios, and found that lower E/P stock groups exhibited consistently higher long-term earnings growth rates. See two articles by Russell J. Fuller, Lex C. Huberts, and Michael Levinson, "It's Not Higgledy-Piggledy Growth!" *Journal of Portfolio Management* 18, no. 2 (Winter 1992): 38–45, and "Predictability Bias in the US Equity Market," *Financial Analysts Journal* 51, no. 2 (March–April 1995): 12–28. Also see H. Bradlee Perry, "Analyzing Growth Stocks: What's a Good Growth Rate?" *AAII Journal* 13, no. 9 (October 1991): 7–10.

through 1965, average growth rates were computed for (1) the period from 1946 through 1955 and (2) the period from 1956 through 1965. Differences among firms' earnings growth rates in the first period accounted for less than 1% of the variation in the differences among their earnings growth rates in the second period.

Annual Earnings

The results of these and other studies suggest that *annual reported earnings* follow what is known in statistics as a **random walk model**. That is, annual earnings for the forthcoming year (E_t) can be thought of as being equal to annual earnings over the past year (E_{t-1}) plus a random error term. (Remember that a random error term can be thought of as a roulette wheel where the numbers on the wheel are distributed around zero.) Accordingly, next year's earnings can be described by the following statistical model:

$$E_t = E_{t-1} + \epsilon_t \qquad (18.16)$$

where ϵ_t is the random error term. With this model, the estimate of next year's earnings is simply the past year's earnings, E_{t-1}. Another way of viewing a random walk model for earnings is that the change in earnings is independent and identically distributed:

$$E_t - E_{t-1} = \epsilon_t \qquad (18.17)$$

This means that the change in earnings, $E_t - E_{t-1}$, is unrelated to past changes in earnings and can be thought of as a spin from a roulette wheel that is perhaps unique to the firm but, more importantly, is used year after year. Because the expected outcome from a spin of the roulette wheel is zero, the expected change in earnings is zero. This implies that the expected level of earnings is equal to the past year's earnings, as was suggested earlier.[21]

Quarterly Earnings

In terms of *quarterly reported earnings*, consideration must be given to the fact that there is typically a seasonal component to a firm's earnings (for example, many firms have high earnings during the quarter that includes Christmas). As a result, a slightly different model appears to be best for forecasting purposes. This model forecasts the growth in earnings for the forthcoming quarter relative to the same quarter one year ago, a quantity denoted $QE_t - QE_{t-4}$. It does so by relating this growth to the growth during the most recent quarter relative to the comparable quarter one year before it, $QE_{t-1} - QE_{t-5}$. Formally, the model for the "seasonally differenced series" of quarterly earnings is known as an *autoregressive model of order one*, and is as follows:

$$QE_t - QE_{t-4} = a(QE_{t-1} - QE_{t-5}) + b + e_t \qquad (18.18)$$

where a and b are constants and e_t is a random error term.

Alternatively, the model can be rewritten by moving the term QE_{t-4} to the right-hand side:

$$QE_t = QE_{t-4} + a(QE_{t-1} - QE_{t-5}) + b + e_t \qquad (18.19)$$

---

[21]Some people [for example, Jane Ou and Stephen H. Penman, "Financial Statement Analysis and the Prediction of Stock Returns," *Journal of Accounting and Economics* 11, no. 4 (November 1989): 295–329] think that a "random walk with drift" model as follows is more accurate:

$$E_t - E_{t-1} = \delta + \epsilon_t$$

where δ is a positive constant that represents the "drift" term. With this model, the expected change in earnings is equal to δ. Note how the random walk model given in equation (18.17) is a special case where $\delta = 0$.

By estimating the constants a and b, this model can be used to forecast quarterly earnings.[22]

For example, assuming estimates for a and b of .4 and .05, respectively, the forecast of a firm's earnings for the next quarter would be equal to $QE_{t-4} + .4(QE_{t-1} - QE_{t-5}) + \$.05$. Thus, if a firm had earnings per share for the last quarter ($t - 1$) of \$3, for four quarters before now ($t - 4$) of \$2, and for five quarters before now ($t - 5$) of \$2.60, then its forecasted earnings for the forthcoming quarter would be equal to $\$2 + .4(\$3 - \$2.60) + \$.05 = \$2.21$. Note how the forecast consists of three components—a component equal to quarterly earnings a year ago (\$2); a component that considers the year-to-year quarterly growth in earnings ($.4[\$3 - \$2.60] = \$.16$); and a component that is a constant (\$.05).[23]

Earnings Announcements and Price Changes

A number of studies have shown large price changes for stocks of companies that report earnings that differ substantially from consensus expectations. One study looked at three groups of 50 stocks.[24] The first group consisted of the 50 stocks listed on the New York Stock Exchange (NYSE) that experienced the greatest price rise during 1970. The second group consisted of 50 stocks chosen randomly from all those listed on the NYSE during 1970. The third group consisted of the 50 stocks listed on the NYSE that experienced the greatest price decline during 1970. As shown in Figure 18.8, the median changes in the prices of the shares in the top, random, and bottom groups were 48.4%, −3.2%, and −56.7%, respectively.

Next, the study looked at the actual change in earnings per share from 1969 to 1970 for each stock in each group. As shown in Figure 18.8, the median changes in earnings per share for the top, random, and bottom groups were 21.4%, −10.5%, and −83.0%, respectively.

Lastly, the study determined the forecasted change in earnings per share at the beginning of 1970 for each stock in each group. This was done by using the predictions contained in Standard & Poor's *Earnings Forecaster*, where estimates made by a number of investment research organizations are reported. The median forecasted changes in earnings per share for the top, random, and bottom groups are shown in Figure 18.8 to be 7.7%, 5.8%, and 15.3%, respectively.

Interestingly, the forecasts of earnings per share hardly correspond to the price movements of the shares. In fact, the earnings of the stocks in the bottom group were expected to increase more than the earnings of the stocks in the top group (15.3%, compared with 7.7%). However, the prediction for the bottom group was disastrously wrong, with a

---

[22]This model can also be used to forecast annual earnings by working forward one quarter at a time and then adding up the forecasts for the forthcoming four quarters. Doing so would result in a forecast of annual earnings (E_t) equal to $E_{t-1} + c(QE_{t-1} - QE_{t-5}) + d$, where $c = a^1 + a^2 + a^3 + a^4$ and $d = 4b + 3ab + 2a^2b + a^3b$. Note that the random walk model is a special case where a and b are equal to zero, thereby making c and d equal to zero.

[23]It has been argued that an improvement can be made in this model by either (1) adding to the right-hand side the term $c(QE_{t-4} - QE_{t-8})$ where c is a constant or (2) by multiplying the constant b term by the random error term that occurred four quarters ago now (e_{t-4}). See P. A. Griffin, "The Time-series Behavior of Quarterly Earnings: Preliminary Evidence," *Journal of Accounting Research* 15, no. 1 (Spring 1977): 71–83; Lawrence D. Brown and Michael S. Rozeff, "Univariate Time-series Models of Quarterly Accounting Earnings per Share: A Proposed Model," *Journal of Accounting Research* 17, no. 1 (Spring 1979): 179–189; and Allen W. Bathke, Jr. and Kenneth S. Lorek, "The Relationship Between Time-series Models and the Security Market's Expectations of Quarterly Earnings," *Accounting Review* 59, no. 2 (April 1984): 163–176.

[24]Victor Niederhoffer and Patrick J. Regan, "Earnings Changes, Analysts' Forecasts, and Stock Prices," *Financial Analysts Journal* 28, no. 3 (May–June 1972): 65–71. It should be noted that the entire June–September 1992 issue of the *Journal of Accounting and Economics* is devoted to an examination of how share prices are related to earnings and other financial statement information.

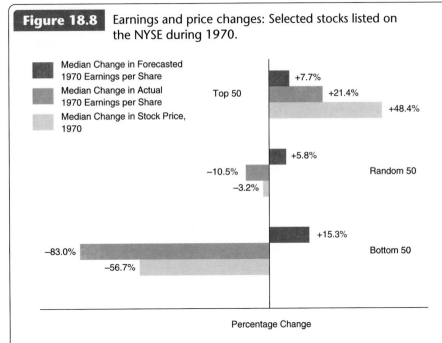

Figure 18.8 Earnings and price changes: Selected stocks listed on the NYSE during 1970.

Median Change in Forecasted 1970 Earnings per Share

Median Change in Actual 1970 Earnings per Share

Median Change in Stock Price, 1970

Top 50

+7.7%
+21.4%
+48.4%

Random 50

+5.8%
−10.5%
−3.2%

Bottom 50

+15.3%
−83.0%
−56.7%

Percentage Change

SOURCE: Victor Niederhoffer and Patrick J. Regan, "Earnings Changes, Analysts' Forecasts, and Stock Prices," *Financial Analysts Journal* 28, no. 3 (May–June 1972): 67.

median earnings-per-share decline of 83.0%. And, as Figure 18.8 shows, prices definitely followed suit. Overall, it appears that unexpected changes in earnings do indeed affect security prices.[25]

But do earnings surprises affect prices before or after their announcement? In a completely efficient market, such information would be reflected in prices as soon as it had been disseminated to a few major market participants. The reaction of security prices around the time of earnings announcements has been examined by a number of authors and will be discussed next.

Deviations from Time-series Models of Earnings

A comprehensive study involving 2053 firms from 1974 through 1981 provided evidence concerning the speed of response of security prices to earnings announcements.[26] For each company, an expected earnings figure was computed for each quarter by using the model of the time-series behaviour of earnings shown in equation (18.19). With this model, the expected earnings for a firm during period t was equal to $QE_{t-4} + a(QE_{t-1} - QE_{t-5}) + b$. For example, the earnings expected for the firm in the second quarter of 1999 would equal

---

[25]Another study using data from 1980 and 1981 reached similar conclusions. That is, the top 50 stocks had forecasted and actual earnings growth rates of 14.3% and 31.3%, respectively. For the bottom 50 stocks the respective rates were 17.4% and −10.3%. See Gary A. Benesh and Pamela P. Peterson, "On the Relation Between Earnings Changes, Analysts' Forecasts, and Stock Price Fluctuations," *Financial Analysts Journal* 42, no. 6 (November–December 1986): 29–39, 55.

[26]George Foster, Chris Olsen, and Terry Shevlin, "Earnings Releases, Anomalies, and the Behavior of Security Returns," *Accounting Review*, 59, no. 4 (October 1984): 574–603. For a related paper, see Roger Kormendi and Robert Lipe, "Earnings Innovations, Earnings Persistence, and Stock Returns," *Journal of Business* 60, no. 3 (July 1987): 323–345.

(1) the firm's earnings in the second quarter of 1998, plus (2) the change in earnings from the first quarter of 1998 to the first quarter of 1999 times the parameter a, plus (3) the parameter b. The values of a and b would be determined by analysis of the behaviour of earnings prior to the second quarter of 1999.

Given actual earnings and an estimate of expected earnings, a forecast error (FE_t) can be computed for the firm:

$$FE_t = QE_t - \overline{QE}_t \tag{18.20}$$

where QE_t are the actual earnings for quarter t and $\overline{QE}_t$ are the expected earnings for quarter t, forecast at time $t - 1$. Simply stated, equation (18.20) indicates that the forecast error for a quarter is the difference between actual earnings for that quarter and expected earnings.

The forecast error provides a measure of the "surprise" in the quarterly earnings announcement, but it fails to differentiate between stocks for which large forecast errors are routine and those for which they are rare. The important surprises are those associated with forecast errors that are large by historical standards. To account for this, a forecast error can be related to previous errors to obtain a measure of **standardized unexpected earnings** (**SUE**):

$$SUE_t = \frac{FE_t}{\sigma_{FE_t}} \tag{18.21}$$

where σ_{FE_t} is the standard deviation of forecast errors over the 20 quarterly earnings of the firm prior to t. (That is, forecast errors were determined for each one of the 20 quarters before t, then the standard deviation for this set of 20 errors was estimated.)

For example, a firm with a forecast of earnings per share of $3 that subsequently reports actual earnings of $5 will have a forecast error of $5 − $3 = $2. That is, the earnings announcement will "surprise" people by $2. Now, if the standard deviation of past errors is $.80, this surprise will be notable, as the standardized unexpected earnings (SUE) equal $2/$.80 = 2.50.[27] However, if the standard deviation is $4, then this surprise will be minor, because SUE will equal $2/$4 = .50. Thus, a large positive value for SUE would indicate that the earnings announcement contained significant good news, whereas a large negative SUE would indicate that the earnings announcement contained significant bad news.

In the study, the SUEs associated with all the earnings announcements for all the sampled firms were ranked from smallest to largest. Then they were divided into 10 equal-sized groups based on the ranking. Group 1 consisted of those announcements resulting in the most negative SUEs, and group 10 consisted of those with the most positive SUEs.

After forming these 10 groups, the stock returns for each firm in each group were measured for the period from 60 days before its earnings announcement through 60 days after its announcement. Figure 18.9 shows the **abnormal return** for the average firm in each of the 10 groups for three different time periods.

Figure 18.9(a) shows the average abnormal return for the period from 60 days before the earnings announcement through the day the announcement appeared in the *Wall Street Journal*. This period is denoted (−60, 0).

Standardized Unexpected Earnings (SUE) The difference between a firm's actual earnings over a given period less an estimate of the firm's expected earnings, with this quantity divided by the standard deviation of the firm's previous earnings forecast errors.

Abnormal Return The return earned on a financial asset in excess of that required to compensate for the risk of the asset.

---

[27] Assume that a firm's earnings are normally distributed and that this distribution remains unchanged over time. Accordingly, 67% of the actual earnings should fall within one standard deviation of the firm's expected earnings. Equivalently, 67% of the SUEs should be less than 1.0. Similarly, 95% of the SUEs should be less than 2.0. One study has argued that most forecast errors are too large for the forecast to be useful; see David N. Dreman and Michael A. Berry, "Analyst Forecasting Errors and Their Implications for Security Analysis," *Financial Analysts Journal* 51, no. 3 (May–June 1995): 30–41. For a refutation, see Lawrence D. Brown, "Analyst Forecasting Errors and Their Implications for Security Analysis: An Alternative Perspective," *Financial Analysts Journal* 52, no. 16 (January–February 1996): 40–47.

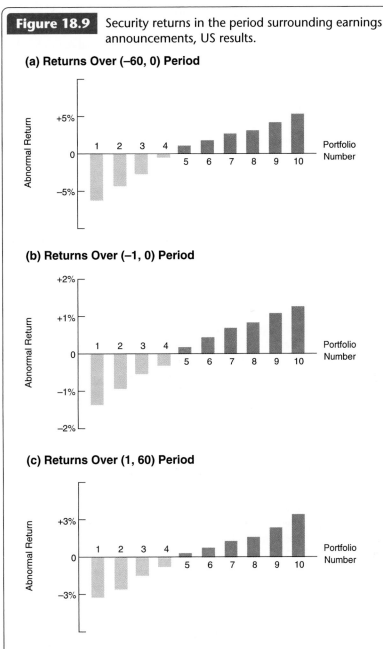

Figure 18.9 Security returns in the period surrounding earnings announcements, US results.

(a) Returns Over (–60, 0) Period

(b) Returns Over (–1, 0) Period

(c) Returns Over (1, 60) Period

SOURCE: George Foster, Chris Olsen, and Terry Shevlin, "Earnings Releases, Anomalies, and the Behavior of Security Returns," *Accounting Review* 59, no. 4 (October 1984): 587.

Figure 18.9(b) shows the average abnormal return for the two-day period consisting of the day before the announcement appeared in the *Wall Street Journal* and the day the announcement appeared, a period that is denoted (–1, 0). Because day 0 is the day the announcement appeared in the *Wall Street Journal*, day –1 is the day the announcement was made to the public. If this announcement was made after trading hours on day –1, investors would not have been able to buy or sell the stock until the next day, day 0. If the announcement was made during trading hours on day –1, then investors could have acted on that day. Due to the inability to pinpoint the hour of the announcement, the return over the two-day period was examined to see the immediate impact of the announcement on the price of the security.

Figure 18.9(c) shows the average abnormal return for the period from the day after the announcement through 60 days after the announcement, a period that is denoted (1, 60).

Figure 18.9(a) shows that prices of firms that announced unexpectedly high earnings (such as SUE group 10) tended to increase *prior* to the announcement (day 0), suggesting that information relevant to the earnings announcement was becoming available to the market prior to the actual announcement. Conversely, prices of firms that announced unexpectedly low earnings (such as SUE group 1) tended to decrease *prior* to the announcement, undoubtedly for the same reason. In general, there seems to be a strong direct correspondence between the size of the unexpected earnings and the size of the abnormal return. Note that if an investor knew what the earnings were going to be 60 days before the announcement, then he could exploit this information by either buying the stock (if the firm was going to announce unexpected large earnings), or short selling the stock (if the firm was going to announce unexpected low earnings). However, because investors typically do not have prior access to earnings, such exploitation is generally impossible. Thus, the existence of abnormal returns prior to the announcement date does not necessarily indicate some sort of market inefficiency.

Figure 18.9(b) shows that the larger the size of the unexpected earnings, the larger the price movement during the two-day period surrounding the announcement. For example, firms in SUE group 1 had an abnormal return of −1.34%, while those in SUE group 10 had an abnormal return of 1.26%. As in (a), there is a direct relationship between the size of the unexpected earnings and the abnormal stock return.[28]

Thus, it appears that the market reacted in a predictable fashion, pushing up the share prices of those firms announcing good news and pushing down the share prices of those firms announcing bad news.

As shown in (c), the changes in share prices after the announcement dates are quite remarkable in that they appear to suggest a market inefficiency. Prices of shares of firms announcing unexpectedly high earnings tended to increase for many days *after* the announcement (the average abnormal return over the 60-day period after the announcement was 3.23% for SUE group 10). Conversely, the prices of firms announcing unexpectedly low earnings tended to decrease for many days *after* the announcement (the average abnormal return over the 60-day period subsequent to the announcement was −3.08% for SUE group 1).

As was noted in (a) and (b), there seems to be a strong direct correspondence between the size of the unexpected earnings and the size of the abnormal return. This observation suggests that an investor could make abnormal returns by simply looking at quarterly earnings announcements and, based on the magnitude and sign of the unexpected component, acting appropriately. That is, if the firm announced earnings that were notably above expectations, the investor should subsequently purchase some of the firm's shares. In contrast, if the announced earnings were notably below expectations, the investor should subsequently sell any holdings and perhaps even short-sell the firm's shares. Announcements of earnings that were reasonably close to expectations would not motivate either a buy or a sell order.

---

[28]Studies have shown that earnings announcements containing good news are often made earlier than expected, while those containing bad news are often made later than expected. These studies also show that the "timeliness" (defined as the difference between the actual announcement date and the expected announcement date) affects the size of the abnormal return. Interestingly, around the time of earnings announcements there appears to be both increased trading volume and increased variability in security returns. See George Foster, *Financial Statement Analysis* (Englewood Cliffs, NJ: Prentice Hall, 1986), pp. 377–386; and V. V. Chari, Ravi Jagannathan, and Aharon Ofer, "Seasonalities in Security Returns: The Case of Earnings Announcements," *Journal of Financial Economics* 21, no. 1 (May 1988): 101–121.

Accordingly, the "post-earnings-announcement drift" can be viewed as an empirical anomaly that is inconsistent with the notion of semistrong efficient markets.[29]

Figure 18.10 shows the TSE's reaction to earnings announcements for 400 earnings increases and 300 earnings decreases over the 1980–1984 period.[30] A simple no-change forecasting model was used to determine the magnitude of the earnings' "surprises." Positive (negative) and significant forecast errors were observed following earnings increases (decreases). The upward drift following the announcement of the increases suggests that some inefficiencies may exist in the Canadian market. Whether or not these can be profitably exploited remains a moot question.

Unexpected Earnings and Abnormal Returns

One plausible explanation for the abnormal returns associated with large SUEs concerns the cost of information transfer. "New news" must reach a large number of investors before the appropriate new equilibrium price can be completely established. Although large insti-

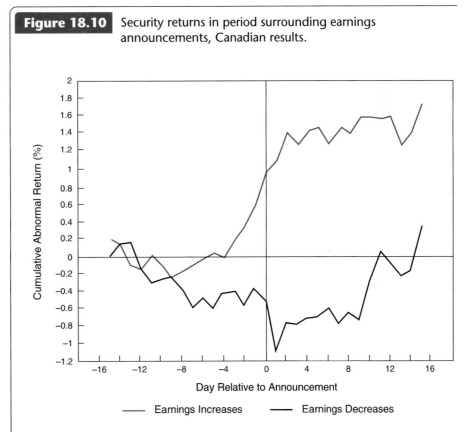

Figure 18.10 Security returns in period surrounding earnings announcements, Canadian results.

SOURCE: Adapted from J. Desrochers, "Bénefice annuel et réaction boursière au Canada," *Finéco* 1, no. 1 (automne 1991): 72.

---

[29]One article argues that the post-earnings-announcement drift should be listed with the set of empirical regularities described in the appendix to Chapter 16. See Charles P. Jones and Bruce Bublitz, "The CAPM and Equity Return Regularities: An Extension," *Financial Analysts Journal* 43, no. 3 (May–June 1987): 77–79.

[30]J. Desrochers, "Bénéfice annuel et réaction boursière au Canada," *Finéco,* 1, no. 1 (automne 1991): 61–80.

tutional investors can obtain news quickly, it may take some time before it reaches smaller institutional investors and individuals. Thus, after an earnings announcement there can be a period of abnormal price movement that is related in sign and magnitude to the nature of the announcement.

Alternatively, perhaps the measurement of "abnormal" returns has been in error. In making such a measurement, a determination of what is a "normal" return must be made. Such a determination is not straightforward but instead is fraught with difficulty. This means that the estimated abnormal returns could actually be due to measurement errors, leaving open the possibility that a more accurate measure of "normal return" would have resulted in no significant abnormal returns.

Nevertheless, there appear to be striking differences in subsequent stock returns for firms with different SUEs. Although the magnitudes of the return differences may be too small to warrant extensive trading, they do suggest the consideration of such things as SUE values and forecast revisions when money must be invested or a portion of an existing portfolio must be liquidated.

Security Analysts' Forecasts of Future Earnings

In using only the historical record of past earnings to forecast future earnings, it was mentioned earlier that an autoregressive model of order one, as shown in equation (18.19), seemed to work about as well as any other model. However, security analysts do not restrict themselves to just past earnings when developing their forecasts. Instead, they look at many different pieces of information. This raises several interesting questions. How well can analysts forecast earnings? And do their forecasts incorporate information other than that contained in past earnings? The results of two studies that provide some answers to these questions are shown in Tables 18.5 and 18.6.

Forecasts of Analysts

In one study, illustrated in Table 18.5, two sets of forecasts were examined for the quarterly earnings of 50 firms over the period from 1971 through 1975.[31] The first set was obtained by applying sophisticated mechanical models, such as the autoregressive model of equation (18.19), to each firm's previous earnings history. The second set was obtained from the

Table 18.5 Accuracy of Mechanical and Judgmental Earnings Forecasts.

Earnings Forecast Error as a Percentage of Actual Earnings	Percentage of Forecasts with a Smaller Error	
	Mechanical Model	Analysts' Forecasts
5%	15.0%	18.0%
10	26.5	32.0
25	54.5	63.5
50	81.0	86.5
75	87.5	90.5
100	89.5	92.0

SOURCE: Lawrence D. Brown and Michael S. Rozeff, "The Superiority of Analyst Forecasts as Measures of Expectations: Evidence from Earnings," *Journal of Finance* 33, no. 1 (March 1978): 7–8.

---

[31]Lawrence D. Brown and Michael S. Rozeff, "The Superiority of Analyst Forecasts as Measures of Expectations: Evidence from Earnings," *Journal of Finance* 33, no. 1 (March 1978): 1–16.

Table 18.6 Forecast Accuracy of Time-series Models and Security Models.

	Days Before Annual Announcement Date			
Model	240	180	120	60
Random walk	$.963	$.781	$.620	$.363
Autoregressive	.975	.780	.592	.350
Average analyst	.747	.645	.516	.395
Current analyst	.742	.610	.468	.342

SOURCE: Adapted from Patricia C. O'Brien, "Analysts' Forecasts as Earnings Expectations," *Journal of Accounting and Economics* 10, no. 1 (January 1988): Table 4.

earnings forecasts of security analysts as reported in the *Value Line Investment Survey*.[32] The results suggest that the analysts outperformed the mechanical model. For example, 63.5% of the analysts' forecasts were within 25% of the actual earnings values, while only 54.4% of the forecasts made via mechanical models came as close. Analysts appear to base their forecasts on both past earnings and other information, and the latter appears to help.

In another study, forecasts of annual earnings made by security analysts approximately 240, 180, 120, and 60 days before the announcement date of actual earnings were examined.[33] Typically these days correspond to dates in each of the year's fiscal quarters before the announcement date. Hence, 240 days falls roughly between last year's earnings announcement and this year's first quarter earnings announcement, 180 days falls roughly between the first quarter and second quarter earnings announcement, and so on. These forecasts, made over the period from 1975 to 1982 by analysts at between 50 and 130 brokerage firms, were obtained from the Institutional Brokers Estimate System (I/B/E/S) database developed by the brokerage firm of Lynch, Jones, & Ryan.

Table 18.6 presents a comparison of the accuracy of four forecasts. The first forecast, denoted *RW*, is the annual forecast generated by using a model like the random walk model of equation (18.16). The second, denoted *AR*, is the annual forecast produced by using an autoregressive model like the one shown in equation (18.19). The third is the average forecast published by I/B/E/S, and the fourth is the single most current individual forecast published by I/B/E/S.

Forecast accuracy for a particular model and firm is measured by absolute forecast error, or

$$FE = |A - F| \qquad (18.22)$$

where F denotes the forecast and A denotes the subsequent actual earnings of the firm.

There are several interesting observations to be made from Table 18.6. First, as the announcement date gets closer, all of the forecasting models become more accurate. This is hardly surprising, because more information is available as the announcement date gets closer. Second, for long horizons both the average and most current forecasts are more accurate than either of the time-series models. Third, the current forecast is more accurate than any of the other models. However, subsequent examination of the forecasts indicates that the average forecast was more accurate than the most current forecast, provided that

[32]Value Line also ranks stocks in terms of their relative attractiveness as investments. For a discussion of the usefulness of the Value Line rankings, see Table 22.8 and the end-of-chapter references in Chapter 22.

[33]Patricia C. O'Brien, "Analysts' Forecasts as Earnings Expectations," *Journal of Accounting and Economics* 10, no. 1 (January 1988): 53–83.

Consensus Earnings Expectations

Reference is frequently made in the financial press to "market" or "consensus" expectations. We may read that the "market" expects inflation to remain stable or that the "market" expects the Bank of Canada to raise interest rates. Given that the market is the amalgam of a large, diverse group of investors, how does anyone determine what the market really expects?

Of course, the most important market expectations are established and published daily—that is, the expected values of corporate assets as reflected in security prices. But what about market expectations regarding economic and financial variables that underlie security prices? In general, these expectations are reported anecdotally, perhaps through interviews with prominent investors or through a variety of surveys.

Investing based on such ambiguous information is problematic. Abnormal returns can be earned only by staking out positions based on expectations contrary to those of the market. Superior investors will consistently identify securities for which market expectations are somehow in error. But unless these investors can correctly interpret the market's expectations, they will not know whether their expectations are significantly different from those of the market.

As the text discusses, earnings expectations are the most important determinant of common share prices. If an investor can identify companies for which the market is under- or overestimating future earnings, the investor can appropriately buy and sell these stocks to produce portfolio returns superior to those of the market on a risk-adjusted basis.

Many organizations publish earnings estimates, including Standard & Poor's, Value Line, and brokerage houses. However, individually these estimates do not represent market expectations; they are merely the opinions of specific analysts. What is needed is a way to collect the earnings estimates of many analysts following a particular company. That need has been satisfied for 30 years by a firm called Institutional Brokers Estimate System, or I/B/E/S.

While I/B/E/S is not the only company collecting earnings expectations data (Zacks Investment Research is a prominent competitor), it was the first and it remains the leader in the field. I/B/E/S was formed in 1971.

Its initial objectives were modest—to collect timely earnings estimates from brokerage firms on several hundred large, well-followed companies. These estimates were then compiled and the distributions of earnings estimates (high, low, median, measure of dispersion) were periodically reported to subscribers.

For example, suppose that an institutional investment firm was estimating earnings next year of $2.50 per share for XYZ company and $3.30 per share for ABC company. Through I/B/E/S, the institutional investor might find that the consensus earnings estimates for XYZ and ABC were currently $1.50 and $3.50, respectively. Further, the coefficient of variation (standard deviation divided by mean—a measure of the estimates' relative dispersion) was 0.20 for XYZ and 0.80 for ABC. If the institutional investor has confidence in its own estimates, then it should expect XYZ stock to perform relatively well. The market's earnings expectations are tight around the $1.50 level, which is $1.00 less than the investor's estimate. If the market comes to realize that $2.50 is the actual level of XYZ earnings, it will likely bid the company's share price up.

ABC shares are much less attractive. The institutional investor's estimate is less than the consensus by $0.20, so it might wish to sell ABC out of its portfolio if it owned the stock or perhaps even short sell the stock. However, the relatively high dispersion of estimates around the median indicates that the market's expectations are not firm. If ABC's earnings actually come in at $3.30, the result may not be a particularly unpleasant surprise to the market, and therefore may have little impact on ABC's stock price.

The advantages of using consensus earnings expectations in common stock analysis quickly caught on among institutional investors. Today, I/B/E/S receives, compiles, and distributes earnings estimates from over 6000 equity analysts in nearly 600 research departments in over 33 countries. Although by far the most intense analyst earnings coverage is for US companies, the contributing I/B/E/S analysts now cover over 13 000 companies in 39 equity markets around the world. Even companies in emerging equity markets such as the People's Republic of China, Sri Lanka, and Chile have attracted institutional analysts' coverage and have been included in the I/B/E/S service.

I/B/E/S collects earnings estimates in a number of ways, including faxes, diskettes, telephone calls, and printed reports. Many research firms now provide I/B/E/S with data directly by computer. Upon receipt of analysts' earnings estimates, I/B/E/S staffers perform several quality checks to ensure the integrity of the data. At that point, the estimates are entered into the firm's database. Summary consensus numbers are updated daily and made available to I/B/E/S subscribers.

The original I/B/E/S reports were simply printed books containing summary data on individual company earnings estimates. Although the original printed format is still available, I/B/E/S now provides data through a variety of electronic vendors.

For example, I/B/E/S data can be accessed through an optical disk data delivery system that can easily bring earnings expectation data into an electronic spreadsheet for detailed analysis.

Customers can now receive I/B/E/S data diced and sliced in a number of ways. The firm makes available to subscribers analyst-by-analyst data, daily alerts of analyst changes, and custom-designed reports. The firm also provides commentaries and analyses of market trends that it discerns from the earnings estimate data.

The systematic collection of earnings estimates is an excellent example of the forces that have been increasing the efficiency of security markets. Before I/B/E/S collected such data, consensus earnings estimates were difficult to obtain and highly ambiguous. Now those estimates are rigorously quantified and widely distributed, decreasing the likelihood of investors acting on incomplete or erroneous information.

none of the individual forecasts used to determine the average was "stale" (that is, more than roughly a week old). This is because such averaging reduces the forecast error by having individual forecast errors offset each other (that is, positive errors will offset negative errors, resulting in a smaller error for the average forecast). In summary, it appears that analysts on average are better forecasters of earnings than sophisticated mechanical models.[34]

Another interesting observation that has been uncovered about security analysts' forecasts is that they tend to be too optimistic, meaning that they tend to have an upward bias (more on this shortly). Hence most of the typical analysts' revisions are downward. One interpretation of this observation is that many of the analysts work for brokerage firms and thus find it in their employers' best interest (and thus their own) to avoid antagonizing any corporation that is or might become an investment banking client.[35]

---

[34]In one study it was found that sophisticated investors (such as big institutional investors) placed more weight on analysts forecasts relative to mechanical models in forming their expectations about earnings. See Beverly R. Walther, "Investor Sophistication and Market Earnings Expectations," *Journal of Accounting Research* 35, no. 2 (Autumn 1997): 157–179.

[35]The observation that analysts (1) tend to be too optimistic in their EPS forecasts, (2) tend to revise these forecasts downward, and (3) issue far more buy than sell recommendations has been documented in several places. See, for example, John C. Groth, Wilbur G. Lewellen, Gary Schlarbaum, and Ronald C. Lease, "An Analysis of Brokerage House Recommendations," *Financial Analysts Journal* 35, no. 1 (January–February 1979): 32–40; and Werner F. De Bondt and Richard H. Thaler, "Do Security Analysts Overreact?" *American Economic Review* 80, no. 2 (May 1990): 52–57. For a counterview, see Michael P. Keane and David E. Runkle, "Are Analysts' Forecasts Rational?" *Journal of Political Economy* (June 1997).

All-American Analysts

The monthly publication *Institutional Investor* announces each October its "All-American" Research Team by querying 2000 money managers.[36] These managers are asked to evaluate security analysts on the basis of (1) stock recommendations, (2) earnings forecasts, (3) written reports, and (4) overall performance. From these evaluations, analysts are selected for the Team (there is a First Team, a Second Team, a Third Team, and Runners-up) in over 60 industries as well as in such areas as portfolio strategy, quantitative analysis, economics, and market timing.

One study looked at the relative forecasting ability of All-American and non-All-American industry analysts for the fiscal years 1981–1985. Each EPS forecast of an All-American was matched with a forecast by a non-All-American for the same firm, where each forecast was made an identical number of days before the fiscal year-end. Forecast accuracy was measured by using equation (18.22). Table 18.7(a) indicates that the average

Table 18.7 EPS Forecast Accuracy of All-American and Non-All-American Analysts.

	Average Absolute Forecast Error[a]		
(a) While on Team	*Non-All-Americans*	*All-Americans*	*Difference*
	$.98	$.95	$.03
	(3.7%)	(3.6%)	(.1%)
		Future	
(b) Before Gaining Membership:	*Non-All-Americans*	*All-Americans*	*Difference*
One Year Before	$.97	$.97	$.00
	(3.1%)	(3.1%)	(.0%)
Two Years Before	.95	.94	.01
	(3.2%)	(3.2%)	(.0%)
Three Years Before	.96	.94	.02
	(3.5%)	(3.5%)	(.0%)
	Former *All-Americans*	*Remaining* *All-Americans*	*Difference*
(c) Before Losing Membership:			
One Year Before	$1.03	$1.01	$.02
	(3.8%)	(3.7%)	(.1%)
Two Years Before	.91	.88	.03
	(3.3%)	(3.3%)	(.0%)
Three Years Before	.91	.87	.04
	(2.8%)	(2.7%)	(.1%)

[a] The numbers shown in parentheses below the average absolute forecast error represent the average of the percentage absolute forecast errors where the percentage is calculated as $|A - F|/A$ where A = actual and F = forecast.

SOURCE: Scott E. Stickel, "Reputation and Performance Among Security Analysts," *Journal of Finance* 47, no. 5 (December 1992): 1818, 1819, 1821.

---

[36]The discussion that follows draws from Scott E. Stickel, "Reputation and Performance Among Security Analysts," *Journal of Finance* 47, no. 5 (December 1992): 1811–1836.

forecast error for All-Americans was $.95, while non-All-Americans had an error of $.98. Hence, All-American EPS forecasts were more accurate by approximately $.03 per share.

Also examined in the study were the records of analysts in the three-year period before they became All-Americans ("future" All-Americans) and the records of All-Americans in the three-year period before they lost their exalted status and became non-All-Americans ("former" All-Americans).[37] This was done as follows.

1. The track records of future All-Americans were matched with analysts who were and remained non-All-Americans. Table 18.7(b) indicates that future All-Americans were only slightly more accurate [by ($.00 + $.01 + $.02)/3 = $.01 per share, on average] than non-All-Americans in the three-year period before they became All-Americans.

2. The track records of former All-Americans were matched with All-Americans who maintained their Team membership ("remaining" All-Americans). Table 18.7(c) indicates that former All-Americans were less accurate than the remaining All-Americans by between $.04 and $.02 per share in the three-year period before removal.

Given the nearly indistinguishable differences in earnings forecasting performance between All-Americans and non-All-Americans, the reasons for Team membership appear to be explained by other factors, such as high-quality company research or good personal relationships with money managers.

The study also documented the existence of forecast bias. This bias was measured by the average forecast error, where the forecast error for a given analyst is

$$FE = A - F \tag{18.23}$$

As before, F denotes the forecast and A denotes the subsequent actual earnings of the firm. Note how equation (18.23) is identical to equation (18.22), except that absolute values are no longer used. The average forecast error for All-Americans was $-.73 per share (or 2.9% of the actual EPS). For non-All-Americans the comparable figure was $-.74 (or 3.0%). Given that the average FE was negative, this means that both types of analysts tended to overestimate the level of EPS. As mentioned earlier, this is clear evidence of both All-Americans' and non-All-Americans' being too optimistic in forecasting EPS.

Management Forecasts of Future Earnings

Often management itself will make a forecast of next year's earnings for the firm. Generally, the forecasts of security analysts are not as accurate as the forecasts of management when both sets of forecasts are made about the same time, as shown in Table 18.8.[38] Here, average security analysts' forecasts, as reported weekly by Zacks Investment Research's Icarus Service, were compared with corresponding management forecasts.[39] The objective was to see who was the more accurate forecaster. To do this, forecast errors (FE) were calculated for both sets of forecasts as

$$FE = |(F - A)/A| \tag{18.24}$$

where F is the earnings forecast and A is the actual earnings subsequently reported by the

---

[37]The study also found that the median number of firms analyzed by All-Americans and non-All-Americans was 14 and 8, respectively, and that All-Americans revised their forecasts within a given fiscal year on average every 86 days whereas non-All-Americans revised them every 93 days.

[38]John M. Hassell and Robert H. Jennings, "Relative Forecast Accuracy and the Timing of Earnings Forecast Announcements," *Accounting Review* 61, no. 1 (January 1986): 58–75.

[39]Similar to I/B/E/S, Zacks Investment Research provides weekly summaries of earnings forecasts for over 2000 firms that are provided by analysts at roughly 50 brokerage firms. While Zacks dates forecasts by the date of issuance by the analysts' employers, I/B/E/S dates forecasts by when they receive them.

	Table 18.8	Security Analyst and Management Forecast Errors.	

Week	Average Analyst Forecast Error	Average Analyst Forecast Error– Average Management Forecast Error[a]
−12	.224	.074
−11	.222	.072
−10	.221	.071
−9	.221	.071
−8	.214	.064
−7	.221	.071
−6	.222	.072
−5	.216	.066
−4	.210	.060
−3	.208	.058
−2	.211	.061
−1	.209	.059
0	.195	.045
+1	.186	.036
+2	.177	.027
+3	.174	.024
+4	.171	.021
+5	.166	.016
+6	.160	.010
+7	.153	.003
+8	.150	.000
+9	.141	−.009
+10	.133	−.017
+11	.129	−.021
+12	.124	−.026

[a] The size of the average management forecast error was .150.

SOURCE: Adapted from John M. Hassell and Robert H. Jennings, "Relative Forecast Accuracy and the Timing of Earnings Forecast Announcements," *Accounting Review* 61, no. 1 (January 1986): Tables 2 and 3.

firm. Hence, an earnings forecast of $3 per share that subsequently turned out to be $4 would have $FE = |(\$3 - \$4)/\$4| = .25$ or 25%.

Letting $t = 0$ denote the date that the management forecast is released, analysts' forecasts were collected weekly from 12 weeks before to 12 weeks after $t = 0$. As Table 18.8 shows in the note, the average forecast error for management was .150. Analyst forecast errors ranged from .224 at week −12 (meaning 12 weeks prior to the date of the management forecast) to .124 at week +12. Hence, as was shown in Table 18.6, analysts' forecasts became more accurate the closer they were to the date the actual earnings were announced, because the size of the average forecast error decreases fairly steadily from $t = -12$ to $t = +12$.

Most important, however, is the observation that management forecasts were more accurate than analyst forecasts from $t = -12$ to $t = +8$ (the difference was found to be statistically significant through $t = +4$). That is, forecasts issued by analysts before, coincident to, or up to four months after management's forecast were less accurate. This observation is not surprising up to $t = 0$, as management has private information about the firm that is not available to the analysts. However, it is surprising that management forecasts were superior from $t = +1$ through $t = +4$ because it suggests that analysts could improve their accuracy simply by using management's previously released forecast. After $t = +4$, the analysts' forecasts were more accurate (the difference was statistically significant beginning nine weeks after the release date of the management forecast)—a finding that is not surprising, because the analysts probably had access to more timely information upon which to base their forecast.

These results leave a question: why does management occasionally produce an earnings forecast for the firm? Is it to reduce *information asymmetry* in the marketplace? That is, management might want to tell investors about the firm's prospects when it feels the prevailing view of the investing public is in serious error. One way to examine this issue is to look at the firm's bid-ask spread. In Chapter 3 it was noted that specialists tend to widen the bid-ask spread if they sense an increase in information asymmetry, since they tend to sustain losses from trading with informed investors. One study examined the bid-ask spreads of firms whose management issued forecasts and a matching sample of firms whose management did not issue forecasts.[40]

Interestingly, the study found that the firms issuing forecasts had significantly wider spreads than those that did not issue forecasts before the forecasts were made, and that afterwards the spreads of the two were equivalent. Thus, it appears that the management tends to issue forecasts when it senses an increased level of information asymmetry is present, and that the forecast reduces the amount of the asymmetry.

Sources of Errors in Forecasting

As security analysts' forecasts are not perfect, it is interesting to consider the major source of their errors. One study examined the I/B/E/S database and attempted to break down the forecast errors into three components: (1) errors that could be traced to misjudgments about the economy; (2) errors that could be traced to misjudgments about the firm's particular industry; and (3) errors that were purely due to misjudgments about the firm.[41]

The results indicated the following: less than 3% of the typical error was due to a misjudgment about the economy; roughly 30% of the typical error was due to a misjudgment about the industry; and over 65% of the typical error was due to a misjudgment about the firm.

Summary

1. Assuming that a firm undertakes positive NPV projects and maintains a constant debt-equity ratio, shareholders will be indifferent to the level of dividends.
2. If dividends and new investment are greater than earnings, the firm may issue new equity. If dividends and new investment are less than earnings, the firm may repurchase equity. In either case, a shareholder maintaining constant proportional ownership will be able to spend the same amount on consumption, regardless of the level of dividends.
3. Earnings, not dividends, are the source of a firm's value.
4. Few firms attempt to maintain a constant ratio of dividends to current earnings. It is often assumed that firms establish a long-run payout ratio and adjust current actual dividends based on the difference between current target dividends and the last period's actual dividends.

[40]Maribeth Collier and Teri Lombardi Yohn, "Management Forecasts and Information Asymmetry: An Examination of Bid-ask Spreads," *Journal of Accounting Research* 35, no. 2 (Autumn 1997): 181–191.

[41]Edwin J. Elton, Martin J. Gruber, and Mustafa N. Gultekin, "Professional Expectations: Accuracy and Diagnosis of Errors," *Journal of Financial and Quantitative Analysis* 19, no. 4 (December 1984): 351–363.

5. Corporate management often uses dividend changes as a signaling device, raising or lowering dividends based on its assessment of the firm's future earnings.

6. A firm has considerable discretion in calculating its accounting earnings. These accounting earnings may differ substantially from the firm's economic earnings. Similarly, a firm's book value may differ considerably from its market value.

7. Firms initiate paying dividends after a period during which their share price has risen by an abnormally large amount and earnings have increased. The announcement of the initiation is associated with an abnormal increase in the share's price, with earnings and the price continuing to move upward afterward.

8. Firms omit paying dividends after a period during which their share price has fallen by an abnormally large amount and earnings have decreased. The announcement of the omission is associated with an abnormal decrease in the share's price, with earnings and the price continuing to move downward afterward.

9. Earnings can be divided into permanent and transitory components. A firm's intrinsic value will be based on the permanent component of earnings. The transitory component is a significant factor in short-run changes in a firm's price-earnings ratio.

10. Stocks with the highest returns typically have earnings that are substantially greater than expected, whereas those with the lowest returns have earnings substantially below expectations.

11. Share prices tend to correctly anticipate earnings announcements by moving in the appropriate direction beforehand.

12. Share prices tend to react correctly, but not fully, to earnings announcements immediately afterward.

13. Share prices continue to move in a direction similar to their initial reaction for several months afterward. This phenomenon is known as post-earnings-announcement drift.

14. Analysts appear to forecast earnings better than sophisticated mechanical models.

15. Analysts tend to overestimate when forecasting earnings per share.

16. Management earnings forecasts are generally more accurate than analysts' forecasts.

QUESTIONS AND PROBLEMS

1. For a given level of earnings (E), net new investment (I), and dividends (D), explain why a firm must issue new stock if $E < D + I$ and it desires to maintain a constant debt-equity ratio. Similarly, why must it repurchase shares if $E > D + I$ and it desires to maintain a constant debt-equity ratio?

2. Merrillan Motors had earnings of $8 million last year. It made $5 million of investments in projects with positive net present values. Asra Singh owns 20% of the firm's common shares. Assume that Asra desires no change in proportional ownership of Merrillan and the firm wishes to maintain a constant debt-equity ratio. What will be Asra's action in response to:
   a. Merrillan's paying out dividends of $5 million?
   b. Merrillan's paying out dividends of $1 million?
   c. Merrillan's paying out dividends of $3 million?

3. Why is an individual shareholder indifferent between the firm retaining $1 of earnings or paying out the $1 of earnings as a dividend, assuming that the firm and the shareholder maintain a constant debt-equity ratio and a constant proportional ownership position, respectively?

4. If the dividend decision is irrelevant to the valuation of a firm, then aren't dividend discount models irrelevant to valuing common shares? Why?

5. Patrick Cooney, a confused investment student, commented, "I understand the irrelevance of the dividend decision to the value of the firm. As a result, I calculate the value

of a firm's shares based on the present value of the firm's expected earnings per share."
Is Patrick correct? Why?

6. Why do most corporations not maintain a constant payout ratio? What payout strategy do most firms pursue?

7. Hixton Farms has a target payout ratio of 50%. Dividends paid last year amounted to $10 million. Its earnings were $20 million. Hixton's "speed of adjustment" factor for dividends is 60%. Calculate its dividend payments over the next five years if its earnings display the path shown in the following table.

Year	Earnings
I	$30 million
2	35 million
3	30 million
4	25 million
5	30 million

Draw a graph of Hixton's actual dividends paid versus the desired dividend payments over this five-year period.

8. Rockton Plastics has made changes to its dividends over the last 14 years. Based on a target payout ratio of 30%, according to the Lintner Model the firm would have preferred to make a different set of dividend changes. Both the actual and preferred dividend changes are shown in the following table. What "speed of adjustment" factor is implied by these two dividend change series? (Use of a computer regression program, such as one provided with an electronic spreadsheet, is recommended.)

Year	Actual Change in Dividends	Preferred Change in Dividends
I	$-0.28	$-0.47
2	-0.09	-0.16
3	-0.05	-0.08
4	-0.01	-0.02
5	0.01	0.02
6	0.04	0.07
7	0.01	0.01
8	0.03	0.05
9	0.03	0.05
10	0.01	0.02
11	0.04	0.07
12	0.03	0.06
13	0.03	0.05

9. How are dividends used as a signaling device by corporate management? To the extent that dividends are a signaling device, how are dividend changes related to share prices?

10. Discuss why there generally does not exist a one-to-one relationship between corporations' book values and their market values.

11. The price per share of the Dells Deli Corporation is less than its book value. Does this indicate that those who now hold the firm's shares have lost money in the past? Does it indicate that they are likely to lose money in the future? Does it indicate that the Dells Deli should not undertake any further capital investment? Explain your answers.

12. Why might a steady trend in a firm's reported earnings from year to year suggest that the figures do not represent the firm's economic earnings?

13. Reported earnings typically differ, sometimes considerably, from economic earnings. Nevertheless, it is often argued that reported earnings are intended simply to provide a "source of information" to investors about the value of the firm. If so, might there not be many alternative accounting procedures of equal use to investors? How might one go about evaluating the usefulness of such procedures?

14. Distinguish between permanent and transitory earnings. Would you expect companies across industries to differ in terms of the relative importance of transitory earnings to total earnings? Explain.

15. Price-earnings ratios for individual companies vary over time and across firms. Discuss some of the possible reasons for this variability.

16. Harry Clift once wrote in a market newsletter that, "I focus my research on consensus earnings forecasts. Those companies that the consensus believes will produce the largest earnings increases next year are most likely to produce the best returns." Is Harry's opinion consistent with empirical evidence? Explain why or why not.

17. Calculate the relationship among the following series of quarterly earnings using an autoregressive model of order one (use of a computer regression program is recommended). What is your forecast for earnings in Quarter 21?

Quarter	Earnings	Quarter	Earnings
1	$4.00	11	$4.25
2	4.10	12	4.49
3	3.95	13	4.59
4	4.20	14	4.58
5	4.30	15	4.39
6	4.29	16	4.63
7	4.11	17	4.73
8	4.35	18	4.72
9	4.44	19	4.54
10	4.43	20	4.78

18. Oakdale Orchards has produced the following earnings over the last nine quarters:

Quarter	Earnings per Share
1	$2.00
2	1.95
3	2.05
4	2.10
5	2.40
6	2.24
7	2.67
8	2.84
9	2.64

The expected earnings for the current quarter are based on the equation $QE_t = QE_{t-4} + .75(QE_{t-1} - QE_{t-5})$. Calculate the standardized unexpected earnings in each of the last four quarters, given a standard deviation of $0.35.

19. Why might the price of a stock react only partially to an "earnings surprise" on the first day or two after the earnings announcement?

KEY TERMS

dividend decision (p. 540)
asymmetric information (p. 549)
information content of
   dividends hypothesis (p. 550)
accounting earnings (p. 553)
earnings per share (EPS) (p. 553)
return on equity (ROE) (p. 553)
economic earnings (p. 553)

economic value of the firm (p. 553)
generally accepted accounting
   principles (GAAP) (p. 554)
random walk model (p. 561)
standardized unexpected earnings
   (SUE) (p. 564)
abnormal return (p. 564)

REFERENCES

1. The seminal paper on dividend policy that established both the "dividend irrelevancy theorem" and the notion that earnings are the basis for the market value of the firm was written by two Nobel laureates in economics:

Merton H. Miller and Franco Modigliani, "Dividend Policy, Growth, and the Valuation of Shares," *Journal of Business* 34, no. 4 (October 1961): 411–433.

2. The Lintner Model of dividend behaviour and some studies that empirically tested it are found in:

John Lintner, "Distribution of Incomes of Corporations Among Dividends, Retained Earnings, and Taxes," *American Economic Review* 46, no. 2 (May 1956): 97–113.

John A. Brittain, *Corporate Dividend Policy* (Washington, DC: The Brookings Institution, 1966).

Eugene F. Fama and Harvey Babiak, "Dividend Policy: An Empirical Analysis," *Journal of the American Statistical Association* 63, no. 324 (December 1968): 1132–1161.

Eugene F. Fama, "The Empirical Relationship Between the Dividend and Investment Decisions of Firms," *American Economic Review* 64, no. 3 (June 1974): 304–318.

Terry A. Marsh and Robert C. Merton, "Dividend Behavior for the Aggregate Stock Market," *Journal of Business* 60, no. 1 (January 1987): 1–40.

Bong-Soo Lee, "Time-series Implications of Aggregate Dividend Behavior," *Review of Financial Studies* 9, no. 2 (Summer 1996): 589–618.

3. The determinants of recent dividend behaviour appear to be similar to those in the Lintner Model from the 1950s, according to:

H. Kent Baker, Gail E. Farrelly, and Richard B. Edelman, "A Survey of Management Views on Dividend Policy," *Financial Management* 14, no. 3 (Autumn 1985): 78–84.

4. A summary of the literature on signaling can be found in:

Thomas E. Copeland and J. Fred Weston, *Financial Theory and Corporate Policy* (Reading, MA: Addison-Wesley, 1988), pp. 501–507, 584–588.

5. The information content of dividends hypothesis, closely linked to the signaling literature, has been the subject of much research. Some of the more important papers are:

R. Richardson Pettit, "Dividend Announcements, Security Performance, and Capital Market Efficiency," *Journal of Finance* 27, no. 5 (December 1972): 993–1007.

Ross Watts, "The Information Content of Dividends," *Journal of Business* 46, no. 2 (April 1973): 191–211.

Joseph Aharony and Itzak Swary, "Quarterly Dividend and Earnings Announcements and Stockholders' Returns: An Empirical Analysis," *Journal of Finance* 35, no. 1 (March 1980): 1–12.

Clarence C. Y. Kwan, "Efficient Market Tests of the Informational Content of Dividend Announcements: Critique and Extension," *Journal of Financial and Quantitative Analysis* 16, no. 2 (June 1981): 193–206.

Paul Asquith and David W. Mullins, Jr., "The Impact of Initiating Dividend Payments on Shareholders' Wealth," *Journal of Business* 56, no. 1 (January 1983): 77–96.

James A. Brickley, "Shareholder Wealth, Information Signaling, and the Specially Designated Dividend: An Empirical Study," *Journal of Financial Economics* 12, no. 2 (August 1983): 187–209.

J. Randall Woolridge, "Dividend Changes and Stock Prices," *Journal of Finance* 38, no. 5 (December 1983): 1607–1615.

Terry E. Dielman and Henry R. Oppenheimer, "An Examination of Investor Behavior During Periods of Large Dividend Changes," *Journal of Financial and Quantitative Analysis* 19, no. 2 (June 1984): 197–216.

Paul M. Healy and Krishna G. Palepu, "Earnings Information Conveyed by Dividend Initiations and Omissions," *Journal of Financial Economics* 21, no. 2 (September 1988): 149–175.

P. C. Venkatesh, "The Impact of Dividend Initiation on the Information Content of Earnings Announcements and Returns Volatility," *Journal of Business* 62, no. 2 (April 1989): 175–197.

Larry H. P. Lang and Robert H. Litzenberger, "Dividend Announcements: Cash Flow Signaling Versus Free Cash Flow Hypothesis," *Journal of Financial Economics* 24, no. 1 (September 1989): 181–191.

Harry DeAngelo, Linda DeAngelo, and Douglas J. Skinner, "Dividends and Losses," *Journal of Finance* 47, no. 5 (December 1992): 1837–1863.

Keith M. Howe, Jia He, and G. Wenchi Kao, "One-time Cash Flow Announcements and Free Cash-flow Theory: Share Repurchases and Special Dividends," *Journal of Finance* 47, no. 5 (December 1992): 1963–1975.

Roni Michaely, Richard H. Thaler, and Kent L. Womack, "Price Reactions to Dividend Initiations and Omissions: Overreaction or Drift?" *Journal of Finance* 50, no. 2 (June 1995): 573–608.

6. The relationship between economic and accounting earnings is discussed in:

Fischer Black, "The Magic in Earnings: Economic Earnings Versus Accounting Earnings," *Financial Analysts Journal* 36, no. 6 (November–December 1980): 19–24.

7. For a study on the timing of dividend announcements as well as a listing of other studies concerning dividend announcements, see:

Avner Kalay and Uri Loewenstein, "The Informational Content of the Timing of Dividend Announcements," *Journal of Financial Economics* 16, no. 3 (July 1986): 373–388.

Aharon R. Ofer and Daniel R. Siegel, "Corporate Financial Policy, Information, and Market Expectations: An Empirical Investigation of Dividends," *Journal of Finance* 42, no. 4 (September 1987): 889–911.

8. For a review of the literature dealing with dividends, see:

James S. Ang, *Do Dividends Matter? A Review of Corporate Dividend Theories and Evidence*, Monograph Series in Finance and Economics #1987–2, New York University Salomon Center, Leonard N. Stern School of Business.

9. For a discussion of price-earnings ratios, see:

William Beaver and Dale Morse, "What Determines Price-earnings Ratios?" *Financial Analysts Journal* 34, no. 4 (July–August 1978): 65–76.

William H. Beaver, *Financial Reporting: An Accounting Revolution* (Englewood Cliffs, NJ: Prentice Hall, 1981), Chapters 4 and 5.

George Foster, *Financial Statement Analysis* (Englewood Cliffs, NJ: Prentice Hall, 1986), pp. 437–442.

Paul Zarowin, "What Determines Earnings-price Ratios: Revisited," *Journal of Accounting, Auditing, and Finance* 5, no. 3 (Summer 1990): 439–454.

Peter D. Easton and Trevor S. Harris, "Earnings as an Explanatory Variable for Returns," *Journal of Accounting Research* 29, no. 1 (Spring 1991): 19–36.

William H. Beaver, Mary Lea McAnally, and Christopher H. Stinson, "The Information Content of Earnings and Prices: A Simultaneous Equations Approach," *Journal of Accounting and Economics* 23, (1997): 53–81.

10. Time-series models of annual and quarterly earnings per share are discussed in:

George Foster, "Quarterly Accounting Data: Time-Series Properties and Predictive-Ability Results," *Accounting Review* 52, no. 1 (January 1977): 1–21.

George Foster, *Financial Statement Analysis* (Englewood Cliffs, NJ: Prentice Hall, 1986), Chapter 7.

Ross L. Watts and Jerold L. Zimmerman, *Positive Accounting Theory* (Englewood Cliffs, NJ: Prentice Hall, 1986), Chapter 6.

11. The relationship between earnings announcements and share prices has been documented in many studies. See the following as well as their citations:

Ray Ball and Philip Brown, "An Empirical Evaluation of Accounting Income Numbers," *Journal of Accounting Research* 6, no. 2 (Autumn 1968): 159–178.

William H. Beaver, "The Information Content of Annual Earnings Announcements," *Empirical Research in Accounting: Selected Studies*, Supplement to *Journal of Accounting Research* 6 (1968): 67–92.

Leonard Zacks, "EPS Forecasts—Accuracy Is Not Enough," *Financial Analysts Journal* 35, no. 2 (March–April 1979): 53–55.

Dale Morse, "Price and Trading Volume Reaction Surrounding Earnings Announcements: A Closer Examination," *Journal of Accounting Research* 19, no. 2 (Autumn 1981): 374–383.

James M. Patell and Mark A. Wolfson, "The *Ex Ante* and *Ex Post* Effects of Quarterly Earnings Announcements Reflected in Stock and Option Prices," *Journal of Accounting Research* 19, no. 2 (Autumn 1981): 434–458.

Richard J. Rendleman, Jr., Charles P. Jones, and Henry A. Latane, "Empirical Anomalies Based on Unexpected Earnings and the Importance of Risk Adjustments," *Journal of Financial Economics* 10, no. 3 (November 1982): 269–287.

James M. Patell and Mark A. Wolfson, "The Intraday Speed of Adjustment of Stock Prices to Earnings and Dividend Announcements," *Journal of Financial Economics* 13, no. 2 (June 1984): 223–252.

George Foster, Chris Olsen, and Terry Shevlin, "Earnings Releases, Anomalies, and the Behavior of Security Returns," *Accounting Review* 59, no. 4 (October 1984): 574–603.

Catherine S. Woodruff and A. J. Senchack, Jr., "Intradaily Price-volume Adjustments of NYSE Stocks to Unexpected Earnings," *Journal of Finance* 43, no. 2 (June 1988): 467–491.

The entire issue of the *Journal of Accounting and Economics* 15, no. 2/3 (June–September 1992).

Anthony Bercel, "Consensus Expectations and International Equity Returns," *Financial Analysts Journal* 50, no. 4 (July–August 1994): 76–80.

Beverly R. Walther, "Investor Sophistication and Market Earnings Expectations," *Journal of Accounting Research* 35, no. 2 (Autumn 1997): 157–179.

12. Some of the studies that have examined possible explanations for the "post-earnings-announcement drift" in share prices are:

Richard J. Rendleman, Jr., Charles P. Jones, and Henry A. Latane, "Further Insight into the Standardized Unexpected Earnings Anomaly: Size and Serial Correlation Effects," *Financial Review* 22, no. 1 (February 1987): 131–144.

Victor L. Bernard and Jacob K. Thomas, "Post-earnings-announcement Drift: Delayed Price Response or Risk Premium?" *Journal of Accounting Research* 27 (Supplement 1989): 1–36.

Robert N. Freeman and Senyo Tse, "The Multiperiod Information Content of Accounting Earnings: Confirmations and Contradictions of Previous Earnings Reports," *Journal of Accounting Research* 27 (Supplement 1989): 49–79.

Victor L. Bernard and Jacob K. Thomas, "Evidence That Stock Prices Do Not Fully Reflect the Implications of Current Earnings for Future Earnings," *Journal of Accounting and Economics* 13, no. 4 (December 1990): 305–340.

Richard R. Mendenhall, "Evidence on the Possible Underweighting of Earnings-Related Information," *Journal of Accounting Research* 29, no. 1 (Spring 1991): 170–179.

Ray Ball, "The Earnings-price Anomaly," *Journal of Accounting and Economics* 15, no. 2/3 (June–September 1992): 319–345.

Jeffrey S. Abarbanell and Victor L. Bernard, "Tests of Analysts' Overreaction/Underreaction to Earnings Information as an Explanation for Anomalous Stock Price Behavior," *Journal of Finance* 47, no. 3 (July 1992): 1181–1207.

Ray Ball and Eli Bartov, "How Naive is the Stock Market's Use of Earnings Information?" *Journal of Accounting and Economics* 21, no. 3 (June 1996): 319–337.

13. There have been numerous studies concerning the earnings forecasts made by security analysts and management. Some of the studies are:

Lawrence D. Brown and Michael S. Rozeff, "The Superiority of Analyst Forecasts as Measures of Expectations: Evidence from Earnings," *Journal of Finance* 33, no. 1 (March 1978): 1–16.

Lawrence D. Brown and Michael S. Rozeff, "Analysts Can Forecast Accurately!" *Journal of Portfolio Management* 6, no. 3 (Spring 1980): 31–34.

John G. Cragg and Burton G. Malkiel, *Expectations and the Structure of Share Prices* (Chicago: University of Chicago Press, 1982), particularly pp. 85–86 and 165.

Dan Givoly and Josef Lakonishok, "Properties of Analysts' Forecasts of Earnings: A Review and Analysis of the Research," *Journal of Accounting Literature* 3 (Spring 1984): 117–152.

Dan Givoly and Josef Lakonishok, "The Quality of Analysts' Forecasts of Earnings," *Financial Analysts Journal* 40, no. 5 (September–October 1984): 40–47.

Philip Brown, George Foster, and Eric Noreen, *Security Analyst Multi-year Earnings Forecasts and the Capital Markets* (Sarasota, FL: American Accounting Association, 1985).

John M. Hassell and Robert H. Jennings, "Relative Forecast Accuracy and the Timing of Earnings Forecast Announcements," *Accounting Review* 61, no. 1 (January 1986): 58–75.

Gary A. Benesh and Pamela P. Peterson, "On the Relation Between Earnings Changes, Analysts' Forecasts and Stock Price Fluctuations," *Financial Analysts Journal* 42, no. 6 (November–December 1986): 29–39, 55.

Lawrence D. Brown, Robert L. Hagerman, Paul A. Griffin, and Mark Zmijewski, "Security Analyst Superiority Relative to Univariate Time-series Models in Forecasting Quarterly Earnings," *Journal of Accounting and Economics* 9, no. 1 (April 1987): 61–87.

Robert Conroy and Robert Harris, "Consensus Forecasts of Corporate Earnings: Analysts' Forecasts and Time-series Methods," *Management Science* 33, no. 6 (June 1987): 725–738.

Lawrence D. Brown, Robert L. Hagerman, Paul A. Griffin, and Mark Zmijewski, "An Evaluation of Alternative Proxies for the Market's Assessment of Unexpected Earnings," *Journal of Accounting and Economics* 9, no. 2 (July 1987): 159–193.

Patricia C. O'Brien, "Analysts' Forecasts as Earnings Expectations," *Journal of Accounting and Economics* 10, no. 1 (January 1988): 53–83.

Werner F. De Bondt and Richard H. Thaler, "Do Security Analysts Overreact?" *American Economic Review* 80, no. 2 (May 1990): 52–57.

Lawrence D. Brown and Kwon-Jung Kim, "Timely Aggregate Analyst Forecasts as Better Proxies for Market Earnings Expectations," *Journal of Accounting Research* 29, no. 2 (Autumn 1991): 382–385.

Ashiq Ali, April Klein, and James Rosenfeld, "Analysts' Use of Information About Permanent and Transitory Earnings Components in Forecasting Annual EPS," *Accounting Review* 67, no. 1 (January 1992): 183–198.

Scott E. Stickel, "Reputation and Performance Among Security Analysts," *Journal of Finance* 47, no. 5 (December 1992): 1811–1836.

David N. Dreman and Michael A. Berry, "Analyst Forecasting Errors and Their Implications for Security Analysis," *Financial Analysts Journal* 51, no. 3 (May–June 1995): 30–41.

Lawrence D. Brown, "Analyst Forecasting Errors and Their Implications for Security Analysis: An Alternative Perspective," *Financial Analysts Journal* 52, no. 1 (January–February 1996): 40–47.

David N. Dreman, "Analyst Forecasting Errors," *Financial Analysts Journal* 52, no. 3 (May–June 1996): 77–80.

Robert A. Olsen, "Implications of Herding Behavior for Earnings Estimation, Risk Assessment, and Stock Returns," *Financial Analysts Journal* 52, no. 4 (July–August 1996): 37–41.

Maribeth Collier and Teri Lombardi Yohn, "Management Forecasts and Information Asymmetry: An Examination of Bid-ask Spreads," *Journal of Accounting Research* 35, no. 2 (Autumn 1997): 181–191.

Lawrence D. Brown, "Analyst Forecasting Errors: Additional Evidence," *Financial Analysts Journal* 53, no. 6 (November–December 1997): 81–88.

14. For a Canadian perspective on the topics covered in this chapter, see:

N. Betts and L. Johnson, "The Determinants of the P/E Ratio: Theory and Evidence," *Proceedings, Administrative Sciences Association of Canada Conference,* Lake Louise, June 1993.

S. Hennessey, "Using Tests of the Rationality of Canadian Analysts' Earnings Forecasts," *Proceedings, Administrative Sciences Association of Canada Conference,* Lake Louise, June 1993.

J. Bourgeois and J. Lussier, "P/Es and Performance in the Canadian Market," *Canadian Investment Review* VII, no. 1 (Spring 1994).

S. Hennessey, "Using Analysts' Revised Forecasts as a Stock Selection Tool," *Canadian Investment Review* VIII, no. 4 (Winter 1995–1996): 23–28.

L. Ackert and G. Athanassakos, "Expectations of the Herd," *Canadian Investment Review* IX, no. 4 (Winter 1996–1997): 7–11.

Options

In the world of investments, an **option** is a type of contract between two people in which one person grants the other person the right to buy a specific asset at a specific price within a specific time period. Alternatively, the contract may grant the other person the right to sell a specific asset at a specific price within a specific time period. The person who has received the right, and thus has a decision to make, is known as the option buyer because he must pay for this right. The person who has sold the right, and thus must respond to the buyer's decision, is known as the option writer.

Option A contract between two investors in which one investor grants the other the right to buy (or sell) a specific asset at a specific price within a specific time period.

The variety of contracts containing an option feature is enormous. Even within the domain of publicly traded securities, many types can be found. Traditionally only certain instruments are referred to as options; the others, though similar in nature, are designated differently. This chapter presents an introduction to the institutional features of option contracts, along with some basics regarding how they are valued in the marketplace.

Types of Option Contracts

Call Option A contract that gives the buyer the right to buy a specific number of shares of a company from the option writer at a specific purchase price during a specific time period.

The two most basic types of option contracts are known as calls and puts. Currently such contracts are traded on many exchanges around the world. Furthermore, many of these contracts are created privately (that is, "off exchange" or "over the counter"), typically involving financial institutions or investment banking firms and their clients. A brief introduction to calls and puts follows.

Exercise Price (Alternatively, **Striking Price**.) In the case of a call option, the price at which an option buyer may purchase the underlying asset from the option writer. In the case of a put option, the price at which an option buyer may sell the underlying asset to the option writer.

Call Options

The most common type of option contract is the **call option** for stocks. It gives the buyer the right to buy ("call away") a specific number of shares of a specific company from the option writer at a specific purchase price at any time up to and including a specific date. Note how the contract specifies four items:

1. the company whose shares can be bought;
2. the number of shares that can be bought;
3. the purchase price for those shares, known as the **exercise price** (or striking price);
4. the date when the right to buy expires, known as the **expiration date**.

Expiration Date The date on which the right to buy or sell a security under an option contract ceases.

An Example

Consider a simple hypothetical example where investors B and W are thinking about signing a call option contract. This contract will allow B to buy 100 shares of Widget from W for $50 per share at any time during the next six months. Currently Widget is selling for $45 per share on an organized exchange. Investor B, the potential option buyer, believes that the price of Widget's common shares will rise substantially over the next six months. Investor W, the potential option writer, has a different opinion about Widget, believing that its stock price will not rise above $50 over this time period.

Will investor W be willing to sign this contract without receiving something in return from investor B? No. W is running a risk by signing the contract and would demand compensation for doing so. The risk is that Widget's share price will subsequently rise above $50 per share, in which case W will have to buy the shares at that price and then turn them over to B for only $50 per share. Perhaps the shares will rise to $60, costing W $60 × 100 shares = $6000 to buy the stock. Then W will give the 100 shares to B and receive in return $50 × 100 shares = $5000. Consequently W will have lost $6000 − $5000 = $1000.

The point is that the buyer of a call option will have to pay the writer something in order to get the writer to sign the contract. The amount paid is known as the **premium**, although *option price* is a more appropriate term. In the example, perhaps the premium is $3 per share, meaning that investor B will pay $3 × 100 shares = $300 to investor W in order to induce W to sign the contract. Because investor B expects Widget's share price to rise in the future, she would expect to make money by purchasing shares of Widget at $45 per share. The attraction of purchasing call options instead of shares is that investor B can apply a high degree of leverage, since only $3 per share needs to be spent in order to purchase the option.

At some point in time after investors B and W have signed the call option contract, investor W might like to get out of the contract. But breaching the contract is illegal, so how can this be done? Investor W could buy the contract back from investor B for a negotiated amount of money and then destroy the document. If Widget rises in one month to $55 per share, perhaps the amount will be $7 per share or, in total, $7 × 100 shares = $700. In this case, W will have lost $300 − $700 = $400 and B will have made $400. Alternatively, if Widget falls to $40 per share, perhaps the amount will be $.50 per share or, in total, $.50 × 100 shares = $50, in which case W will have made $300 − $50 = $250 and B will have lost $250.

Another way that W can get out of the contract is to find someone else to take his position in the contract (assuming that the contract has a provision that allows this to be done). For example, if Widget has risen to $55 per share after one month, perhaps investor W will find an investor, denoted WW, who is willing to become the option writer if W will pay him $7 per share (or $700 in total). Assuming that they both agree, the contract will be amended so that WW is now the option writer, with W no longer being a party in the contract.

What if investor B subsequently wants to get out of the contract? In this case, B could look and see if someone is willing to pay an agreeable sum of money in order to possess the right to buy Widget stock under the terms of the contract—that is, B could attempt to sell the contract to someone else. In this situation, perhaps investor B will find another investor, denoted BB, who is willing to pay B $7 per share (or $700 in total) in return for the right to buy Widget under the terms of the call option contract. Provided that B is agreeable, the call option contract will be sold to BB and amended, making BB the option buyer.

In this example, both of the original parties, W and B, have "closed out" (or "offset" or "unwound") their positions and are no longer involved in the call option contract. However, the example suggests that the original writer and buyer must meet face to face in order to draw up the terms of the contract. It also suggests that if either the original writer or buyer wants to get out of the contract, then he must reach an agreeable price with the other original party or, alternatively, find a third investor to whom he can transfer the position in the contract. Thus, it would appear that dealing in options involves a great deal of effort.

Closing Sale The sale of an option contract by an investor that is designed to offset, and thereby cancel, the previous purchase of the same option contract by the investor.

Closing Purchase The purchase of an option contract by an investor that is designed to offset, and thereby cancel, the previous sale of the same option contract by the investor.

Role of Exchanges

Fortunately this is not the case in Canada and the United States because of the introduction of *standardized contracts* and the maintenance of a relatively liquid marketplace by organized exchanges for listed options.[1] The Canadian Derivatives Clearing Corp. (CDCC), formerly known as Trans-Canada Options, Inc., a company that is jointly owned by the Montreal Exchange and the Toronto and Vancouver Stock Exchanges, greatly facilitates trading in these options. (The Options Clearing Corporation (OCC) performs the same function in the United States.) It maintains a computer system that keeps track of all of these options by recording the position of each investor in each one. Although the mechanics are rather complex, the principles are simple enough. As soon as a buyer and a writer decide to trade a particular option contract and the buyer pays the agreed-upon premium, the CDCC steps in, becoming the effective writer as far as the buyer is concerned and the effective buyer as far as the writer is concerned. Thus, at this time all direct links between original buyer and writer are severed. If a buyer chooses to exercise an option, the CDCC will randomly choose a writer who has not closed her position and assign the exercise notice accordingly. The CDCC also guarantees delivery of stock if the writer is unable to come up with the shares.

The CDCC makes it possible for buyers and writers to "close out" their positions at any time. If a buyer subsequently becomes a writer of the same contract, meaning that the buyer later "sells" the contract to someone else, the CDCC computer will note the offsetting positions in this investor's account and will simply cancel both entries. Consider an investor who buys a contract on Monday and then sells it on Tuesday. The computer will note that the investor's net position is zero and will remove both entries. The second trade is a **closing sale** because it serves to close out the investor's position from the earlier trade. Closing sales thus allow buyers to sell options rather than exercise them.

A similar procedure allows a writer to pay to be relieved of the potential obligation to deliver stock. Consider an investor who writes a contract on Wednesday and buys an identical one on Thursday. The latter is a **closing purchase** and, analogous to a closing sale, serves to close out the investor's position from the earlier trade.

Stock-split and Dividend Protection

Call options are protected against stock splits and stock dividends on the underlying stock. In the example where the option was on 100 shares of Widget stock with an exercise price of $50, a two-for-one stock split would cause the contract to be altered so that it was for 200 shares at $25 per share. The reason for this protection has to do with the effect that stock splits and stock dividends have on the share price of the firm. Since either of these events will cause the share price to fall below what it otherwise would have been, without adjustment they would work to the disadvantage of the call option buyer and to the advantage of the call option writer.

In terms of cash dividends, there is no protection for listed call options.[2] That is, the exercise price and the number of shares are unaffected by the payment of cash dividends. For example, the terms of the Widget call option would remain the same if Widget declared and paid a $4 per share cash dividend.

---

[1]Prior to 1973 in the US and 1975 in Canada, options were traded over the counter through the efforts of dealers and brokers in a relatively illiquid market. These dealers and brokers brought buyers and writers together, arranged terms, helped with the paperwork, and charged fees for their efforts.

[2]However, there is protection for any cash dividend that is formally designated a "return of capital." Furthermore, options that are traded over the counter typically are protected from any type of cash dividend. In both cases the protection is in the form of a reduction in the exercise price.

⟩ Put Options

A second type of option contract for stocks is the **put option**. It gives the buyer the right to sell ("put away") a specific number of shares of a specific company to the option writer at a specific selling price at any time up to and including a specific date. Note how the contract specifies four items that are analogous to those for call options:

1. the company whose shares can be sold;
2. the number of shares that can be sold;
3. the selling price for those shares, known as the exercise price (or striking price);
4. the date when the right to sell expires, known as the expiration date.

An Example

Consider an example where investors B and W are thinking about signing a put option contract. This contract will allow B to sell 100 shares of XYZ Company to W for $30 per share at any time during the next six months. Currently XYZ is selling for $35 per share on an organized exchange. Investor B, the potential option buyer, believes that the price of XYZ's common shares will fall substantially over the next six months. Investor W, the potential option writer, has a different opinion about XYZ, believing that its share price will not fall below $30 over this time period.

As with the call option on Widget, investor W would be running a risk by signing the contract and would demand compensation for doing so. The risk is that XYZ's share price will subsequently fall below $30 per share, in which case W will have to buy the shares at $30 per share from B when they are not worth that much in the marketplace. Perhaps XYZ will fall to $20, costing W $30 × 100 shares = $3000 to buy shares that are worth only $20 × 100 shares = $2000. Consequently W would have lost $3000 − $2000 = $1000. In this case B would make $1000, purchasing XYZ in the marketplace for $2000 and then selling the shares to W for $3000.

As with a call option, the buyer of a put option will have to pay the writer an amount of money known as a premium in order to get the writer to sign the contract and assume this risk. Also as with call options, the buyer and writer may "close out" (or "offset" or "unwind") their positions at any time by simply entering an offsetting transaction. As with calls, this is easily done for listed put options in Canada because these contracts are standardized.

Again, the CDCC facilitates trading in listed puts, as these options exist only in the memory of its computer system. As with calls, as soon as a buyer and a writer decide to trade a particular put option contract and the buyer pays the agreed-upon premium, the CDCC steps in, becoming the effective writer as far as the buyer is concerned and the effective buyer as far as the writer is concerned. If a buyer chooses to exercise an option, the CDCC will randomly choose a writer who has not closed her position and assign the exercise notice accordingly. The CDCC also guarantees delivery of the exercise price if the writer is unable to come up with the necessary cash.

Like calls, puts are protected against stock splits and stock dividends on the underlying stock. In the example where the option was on 100 shares of XYZ with an exercise price of $30, a two-for-one stock split would cause the contract to be altered so that it was for 200 shares at $15 per share. In terms of cash dividends, there is no protection for listed puts.

Option Trading in Canada

Before January 1992, TSE traded options were introduced on a nine-month cycle (as is done in US markets). Beginning in January 1992, a new set of options on a given stock began trading on the TSE every month. Figure 19.1 shows the available expiry dates listed by cycle and by month. Each underlying stock is assigned to a given cycle and options are

Figure 19.1 Options expiry cycles.

OPTION EXPIRIES AVAILABLE – LISTED BY CYCLE AND BY MONTH

CYCLE 5(1)	JAN	FEB	MAR	APR	MAY	JUN	JUL	AUG	SEP	OCT	NOV	DEC
	JAN	FEB	MAR	APR	MAY	JUN	JUL	AUG	SEP	OCT	NOV	DEC
	FEB	MAR	APR	MAY	JUN	JUL	AUG	SEP	OCT	NOV	DEC	JAN
	APR	APR	JUL	JUL	JUL	OCT	OCT	OCT	JAN	JAN	JAN	APR
	JUL	JUL	OCT	OCT	OCT	JAN	JAN	JAN	APR	APR	APR	JUL

CYCLE 5(2)	JAN	FEB	MAR	APR	MAY	JUN	JUL	AUG	SEP	OCT	NOV	DEC
	JAN	FEB	MAR	APR	MAY	JUN	JUL	AUG	SEP	OCT	NOV	DEC
	FEB	MAR	APR	MAY	JUN	JUL	AUG	SEP	OCT	NOV	DEC	JAN
	MAY	MAY	MAY	AUG	AUG	AUG	NOV	NOV	NOV	FEB	FEB	FEB
	AUG	AUG	AUG	NOV	NOV	NOV	FEB	FEB	FEB	MAY	MAY	MAY

CYCLE 5(3)	JAN	FEB	MAR	APR	MAY	JUN	JUL	AUG	SEP	OCT	NOV	DEC
	JAN	FEB	MAR	APR	MAY	JUN	JUL	AUG	SEP	OCT	NOV	DEC
	FEB	MAR	APR	MAY	JUN	JUL	AUG	SEP	OCT	NOV	DEC	JAN
	MAR	JUN	JUN	JUN	SEP	SEP	SEP	DEC	DEC	DEC	MAR	MAR
	JUN	SEP	SEP	SEP	DEC	DEC	DEC	MAR	MAR	MAR	JUN	JUN

HOW TO USE THIS CHART: Look up the cycle and the month, e.g. Canadian Pacific is a Cycle 5(2). In March the options available are March, April, May and August. After the March expiry, move to the April column, March has been deleted, and November added on.

The Toronto Futures Exchange

The Exchange

SOURCE: Reprinted by permission of the Toronto Stock Exchange, Derivative Markets Division.

introduced according to the schedule shown. For example, in January, options on Canadian Pacific [a cycle 5(2) stock] will be introduced with an August expiry such that contracts with January, February, May, and August expiries will be available. In February, contracts expiring in March will be introduced to replace the January options that expired and so on. The object is to maintain contracts with expiry in the two near months and two more distant months in existence at all times. The maximum term to expiry is eight months. The exercise prices of the new options are determined using the schedule shown in Table 19.1 and the proviso that their prices should bracket the current market price.

Table 19.1 Exercise Price Intervals for New Options for Different Prices of the Underlying Stock.

Stock Price	Exercise Price Interval
Less than $20	$1.00
$20 to $30	$1.00 or $2.50 (optional)
$30 to $75	$2.50
Over $75	$5.00

SOURCE: Information provided by Derivatives Markets, Marketing, Toronto Stock Exchange, January 1996.

For example, if in January Canadian Pacific is selling for $31.40, then the two August call options introduced have exercise prices of $30 and $32.50; similarly, the two August put options have exercise prices of $30 and $32.50. Exchange officials acting in conjunction with the market makers have some latitude in setting the price and introduction date of additional options on a volatile stock.

The exchange also offers long-lived options that are known as *Long-term Equity Participation Securities* or LEAPS. These may be either calls or puts with a maximum of two years to expiration when issued. All LEAPS expire in January and become part of the regular option class at nine months or less to expiry.

An option remains listed until its expiry date. Listed options on common stocks generally expire on the Saturday after the third Friday of the specified month. Index options (to be discussed later) expire on the third Friday of the month. Trading ends on the last business day prior to the expiry date.

Trading Activity

The bulk of options trading in Canada takes place on the Toronto Stock Exchange.[3] Figure 19.2 shows a portion of the daily listing of the trading activity of Trans-Canada Options. The first row for each company shows the name of the company, the closing price of its shares, the total volume, and the total open interest. The total volume is the total number of contracts of all series of options on that stock that traded during the previous trading day. Below the name are the expiry month and exercise price (P for put, otherwise call) for each series followed by the bid and ask prices for each series, the last recorded premium, the number of contracts traded, and the open interest. The open interest is the number of contracts outstanding in that series. For example, on October 28, 1998, Alcan Aluminum common stock closed at $39.45. The prices for the last trades of Alcan November 1998 and January 1999 call options (with an exercise price of $40 per share) were $0.75 and $1.55, respectively. Similarly, the price for the last trades of Alcan November put options (with an exercise price of $40) that stop trading on the third Friday of November was $1.65. The bid and ask prices were $1.55 and $1.70 respectively. If on a particular day some options are not traded there will be no record.

The last entries show the total volume (the number of contracts traded) and total open interest (the number of contracts outstanding) for calls and puts. The first entries of Figure 19.2 indicate the five "most active" options.

Trading on Exchanges

Investors may place the same kinds of orders for options as for stocks—market, limit, and stop orders (these were discussed in Chapter 2). However, the way the orders for options are executed on the exchanges is, in some ways, different from the way that orders for stocks are executed.

As mentioned in Chapter 2, trading on stock exchanges centres around market-makers. On the options trading floor of the TSE there are are also market-makers known as **specialists**. They serve two functions, acting as both dealers and brokers. As dealers, they set the bid and ask prices and keep an inventory of the options (and the underlying stocks) that are assigned to them. They buy into and sell from that inventory as required to maintain a market. As brokers, they keep the limit order book and execute the orders in it as

Specialist A dealer who acts as a market maker on the New York Stock Exchange. The term is also used to describe the market makers on the Canadian options exchanges.

---

[3]In the US option trading activity is rather more extensive than in Canada, with common stock options traded on the Chicago Board Options Exchange (CBOE) and on the American, Pacific, and Philadelphia Stock Exchanges. For a detailed description of how options are created and traded in the US, see Chapter 3 of John C. Cox and Mark Rubinstein, *Options Markets* (Englewood Cliffs, NJ: Prentice Hall, 1985).

Figure 19.2 Listed options quotations (excerpts).

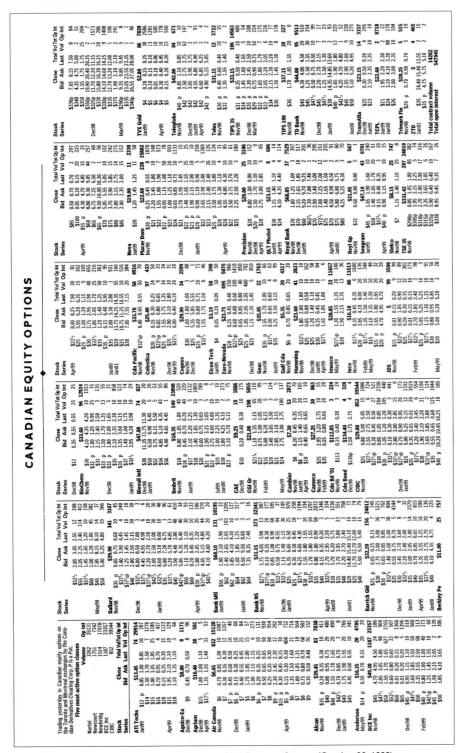

CANADIAN EQUITY OPTIONS

SOURCE: Reprinted with permission of *The Globe and Mail: Report on Business* (October 29, 1998).

Open Outcry

Is it a scene from a Fellini movie? Or perhaps the crowd at a 90% off sale at Bloomingdale's? No, it is simply the members of the Chicago Board Options Exchange (CBOE) participating in the time-honoured tradition of open outcry.

As the text describes, at the CBOE and other option exchanges (as well as futures exchanges—see Chapter 20), members come together in various trading pits to conduct transactions in specific option contracts. Like the trading posts of the New York Stock Exchange (see Chapter 3), the CBOE trading pits serve as central locations where market-clearing prices for option contracts are continually determined through an auction process. Unlike the NYSE trading posts, however, the CBOE and most other option exchanges do not use a specialist system. No one individual acts as a monopolistic dealer and auctioneer, ensuring the setting of market-clearing prices. Instead, those prices are established through *open outcry*, a public auction method involving verbal bids and offers initiated by the exchange members in the pit.

Open outcry is a raucous and colourful trading mechanism that combines the mental gymnastics of rapid-fire decision making with a set of physical skills ranging from strategic positioning in the trading pit to shouting instructions to frenetic hand signaling.

To describe the open outcry system as "the pits" is no exaggeration. The process begins in the trading pits, large depressions in the exchange floor surrounded by several levels of stairs on which the members stand. Although no formal rules are involved, traders generally behave very territorially in the pit. Floor traders usually have certain market-makers with whom they prefer to trade, and these individuals position themselves to make convenient contact with one another. Further, the most senior and important traders take positions in the pit where they have most efficient access to their counterparts. Junior members must stand in less desirable positions, where they are less likely to catch the attention of other traders.

The trading pits are often crowded, noisy, and uncomfortable. Members may jostle each other for position. Hence such attributes as voice strength and physical endurance are important. The pits are dominated by men, and the disadvantages endured by women in this physical environment are not lost on critics of the open outcry system.

Members deliver their trading intentions through a system of verbal orders and hand signals. For example, a floor broker may enter the IBM trading pit and verbally announce her intention to purchase June IBM call option contracts at a specified price. At the same time, she will typically repeat the buy order and desired price through hand signals. A market-maker who wishes to sell at that price will signal the desired quantity by hand.

To the uninitiated, the hand gestures used by members appear wild and unintelligible. In actuality, the signals are simple and highly efficient. Buy and sell orders are indicated by the position of the trader's palms. If the trader's palms are facing her, a buy is signaled. The trader signals a sell by keeping her palms facing outward.

The trader indicates the bid or ask price by holding her hand in a vertical position and using fingers to indicate the fraction of a dollar involved. For example, one finger indicates an eighth of a dollar, whereas a closed fist indicates a full dollar.

Traders likewise display their quantity intentions with their hands. In this case, however, fingers pointed vertically indicate one through five contracts, while fingers pointed horizontally indicate six through nine contracts. One finger to the forehead indicates 10 contracts.

At any given time, members in the pit may be trading in different option contracts, shouting in an attempt to make their voices heard above the din, and flailing their arms about to signal their trading intentions. Add to this scene runners milling about the edge of the pit, time and sale clerks, price reporters, order book officials keeping track of transactions, and persons situated away from the pit signaling in orders to the floor brokers, and pandemonium hardly seems an adequate description of the trading process.

Open outcry is a controversial trading mechanism. It has been criticized as an archaic method designed primarily to perpetuate control over lucrative option trading by the exchanges' members. In an age of advanced electronics, there are readily available computer systems that could facilitate electronic auctions and permit wider access to the auction process. (For example, in mid-1992 the Chicago Board of Trade and the Chicago Mercantile Exchange initiated a trading system known as Globex. This system involves electronic trading in certain futures contracts that are listed on various exchanges during times when those exchanges are closed. When the exchanges are open, they use an open outcry system that is essentially the same as that used on the

CBOE.) The benefits of such electronic auction systems would appear to be lower trading costs and greater liquidity.

Defenders of the open outcry system claim that it is the most efficient method of price discovery. They believe that the system's face-to-face contact permits traders to better ascertain the "true" intentions of buyers and sellers. Moreover, the defenders contend that price manipulation is less likely in an open environment. Whether or not this is true remains an open question.

Chicago Board Options Exchange
www.cboe.com

Chicago Board of Trade
www.cbot.com

Chicago Mercantile Exchange
www.cme.com

market prices move up and down. There are also competitive option traders (COTs), who trade solely for their own account, hoping to buy low and sell high, and *floor traders*, who handle orders from the public.

Orders may be executed either by means of an auction at the trading post with "open outcry," (meaning that the auction is conducted orally) or entered electronically through the *Market Order System of Trading* (MOST). Option trading is, therefore, a hybrid system in the process of evolving towards full automation. The MOST system guarantees a complete fill at the current bid or offer price for every market and tradeable limit order for 10 contracts or less, and provides immediate price confirmation electronically. In addition, MOST orders are transmitted to the floor. If a price that is better than the current bid or ask is available from a trader on the floor then a delayed but improved fill will be confirmed.

More than one specialist may be assigned to the options on a given stock (a few have as many as four). The specialists have the choice of maintaining either an open or a closed limit order book that, unlike the stock exchange limit order book, has manual entries. The information in an open book is available to all market participants, whereas that in a closed book is known only to the specialists. Specialists must provide a minimum guaranteed fill (MGF) that is generally 10 contracts, but some offer an MGF as large as 25 contracts. In addition, they must ensure that the maximum spread between the bid and ask prices of options on a particular stock is not exceeded. A typical schedule is shown in Table 19.2.

Table 19.2	Maximum Spread Between Bid and Ask Prices for Option Contracts.

Option Price	Maximum Spread[a]
under $2.00	$0.25
over $2.00	$0.50

[a]For LEAPS and index options, maximum spreads are double those shown.

In North America all options are traded in continuous markets, meaning that orders can be executed any time the exchanges are open. Trading in options, however, is frequently far from continuous. In the financial press, it is not unusual to find prices for various options that appear to be out of line with one another or with the price of the underlying stock. It should be remembered that each listed price is that of the last trade recorded in the day and that these trades may have taken place at different times. Observed price disparities may simply reflect trading that occurred before and after major news, rather than concurrent values at which arbitrage trades could have been made.

Commissions

Whereas a commission must be paid to a stockbroker whenever an option is either written, bought, or sold, the size of the commission has been reduced substantially since options began to be traded on organized exchanges in 1973. Furthermore, this commission is typically smaller than the commission that would be paid if the underlying stock had been purchased instead of the option. This is probably because clearing and settling are easier with options than with stocks (with options there are no share certificates that have to change hands with every trade) and the order size is smaller (the total dollar amount paid for the option is much less than the total dollar amount of the underlying stock).

However, the investor should be aware that exercising an option will typically result in the buyer's having to pay a commission equivalent to the commission that would be incurred if the stock itself were being bought or sold.

Margin

In contrast to a stock buyer, a call or put buyer is not allowed to use margin. The option buyer is required to pay 100% of the option's purchase price. The buyer of an option, however, would like some assurance that the writer can deliver as required if the option is exercised. Specifically, the buyer of a call option would like some guarantee that the writer is capable of delivering the requisite shares, and the buyer of a put option would like some guarantee that the writer is capable of delivering the necessary cash. Since all option contracts are with Canadian Derivatives Clearing Corp., Inc., the CDCC is also concerned about the ability of the writer to fulfill the terms of the contract.

To relieve the CDCC of this concern, margin requirements have been set by the exchanges where the options are traded. However, brokerage firms, since they are ultimately liable to the CDCC for the actions of their clients, are allowed to impose stricter requirements if they wish.

If a call is exercised, shares are delivered by the writer in exchange for the exercise price. If a put is exercised, cash is delivered in exchange for shares. In either case, the cost to the option writer is the difference between the exercise price and the stock's market value at the time of exercise. Since the CDCC is at risk if the writer is unable to bear this cost, it is not surprising that the CDCC has a system in place to protect itself. This system is known as margin, and it is similar in some ways to the notion of margin associated with short sales of stocks (discussed in Chapter 2).

Valuation of Options

Valuation at Expiration

The value of an option is related to the value of the underlying security in a manner that is most easily seen just prior to expiration (which for simplicity will be referred to as "at expiration"). Figure 19.3(a) relates the value of a call option with an exercise price of $100 to the price of the underlying stock at expiration. If the stock price is below $100, the option will be worthless when it expires. If the price is above $100, the option can be exercised for $100 to obtain a security with a greater value, resulting in a net gain to the option

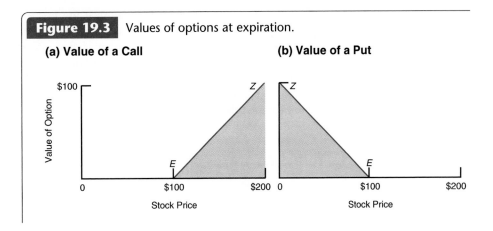

Figure 19.3 Values of options at expiration.

(a) Value of a Call

(b) Value of a Put

buyer that will equal the difference between the security's market price and the $100 exercise price. However, there is no need for the option buyer to actually exercise the option. Instead, the option writer can simply pay the buyer the difference between the security price and the $100 exercise price, thereby allowing both parties to avoid the inconvenience of exercise. This is commonly done for listed options (by using the services of the CDCC), although a minority of investors choose to exercise their options, possibly for tax purposes.

Figure 19.3(b) shows the value at expiration of a put option with an exercise price of $100. If the stock price is above $100, the option will be worthless when it expires. If the price is below $100, the option can be exercised to obtain $100 for stock having a lower value, resulting in a net gain to the option buyer that will equal the difference between the $100 exercise price and the stock's market price. As with a call option, neither the put option buyer nor the writer need actually deal in the stock. Instead, the writer of any put option that is worth exercising at expiration can simply pay the buyer of the option the difference between the stock price and the $100 exercise price.

In both panels of Figure 19.3, the lines indicating the value of a call and a put at expiration can also be interpreted to be the value of a call or a put *at the moment the option is exercised*, no matter when that occurs during the life of the option. In particular, for calls the kinked line connecting points 0, E, and Z is known as the **intrinsic value** of the call. Similarly, for puts the kinked line connecting points Z, E, and $200 is known as the intrinsic value of the put.

Intrinsic Value of an Option The value of an option if it were exercised immediately. Equivalently, the market price of the asset upon which a call option is written less the exercise price of the option (or the exercise price less the market price of the asset in the case of a put option).

The kinked lines representing the intrinsic values of calls and puts such as those shown in Figure 19.3 can be expressed as IV_c and IV_p, respectively, as follows:

$$IV_c = \max\{0, P_s - E\} \tag{19.1a}$$

$$IV_p = \max\{0, E - P_s\} \tag{19.1b}$$

where P_s denotes the market price of the underlying stock and E denotes the exercise price of the option. (Here max means to use the larger of the two values in braces.)

Consider the call option in Figure 19.3(a). Its intrinsic value, according to equation (19.1a), is $\max\{0, P_s - \$100\}$ because its exercise price is $100. Note that for any market price of the stock that is below $100, such as $50, its intrinsic value is $\max\{0, \$50 - \$100\} = 0$. Hence $IV_c = 0$ in such situations. Next imagine that the market price of the stock is above $100, for example, $150. In this situation its intrinsic value is $\max\{0, \$150 - \$100\} = \$50$. Hence $IV_c = P_s - E$. Thus, the kinked intrinsic value line has its kink at E, as it has two components that meet there: a horizontal line going through the origin out to the value E, and then a 45-degree line (and therefore having a slope of 1) going northeast from E. Similar analysis reveals that the kinked intrinsic value line for the put also has its kink at E, as shown in Figure 19.3(b).

Calls and puts will not sell for less than their intrinsic values, owing to the actions of shrewd investors. If an option sold for less than its intrinsic value, then such investors could instantaneously make riskless profits. For example, if the stock price was $150 and the call was selling for $40, which is $10 less than its intrinsic value of $50, then these investors would simultaneously buy these calls, exercise them, and sell the shares received from the writers. In doing so they would spend $140 on each call and exercise price and get $150 in return for each share sold, resulting in a net riskless profit of $10 per call. As a consequence, the call will not sell for less than $50 if the stock price is $150.

❯ Profits and Losses on Calls and Puts

Figure 19.3 shows the values of call and put options at expiration. However, in order to determine profits and losses from buying or writing these options, the premiums involved must be taken into consideration.[4] Figure 19.4 does this for investors who engage in some of the more complicated option strategies. Each strategy assumes that the underlying stock is selling for $100 at the time an option is initially bought or written. It is also assumed that closing transactions are made just prior to the expiration date for the option being considered. Outcomes are shown for each of 10 strategies. Because the profit obtained by a buyer is the writer's loss and vice versa, each diagram in the figure has a corresponding mirror image.

Panels (a) and (b) in Figure 19.4 show the profits and losses associated with buying and writing a call, respectively. Similarly, panels (c) and (d) show the profits and losses associated with buying and writing a put, respectively.

Consider panels (a) and (c) first. The kinked lines representing profits and losses in these two panels are simply graphs of the intrinsic value equations, equations (19.1a) and (19.1b), shown in Figure 19.3, less the premiums on the options. Thus, they are graphs of the following equations:

$$\pi_c = IV_c - P_c$$
$$= \max\{0, P_s - E\} - P_c$$
$$= \max\{-P_c, P_s - E - P_c\} \tag{19.2a}$$

$$\pi_p = IV_p - P_p$$
$$= \max\{0, E - P_s\} - P_p$$
$$= \max\{-P_p, E - P_s - P_p\} \tag{19.2b}$$

where π_c and π_p denote the profits associated with buying a call and a put, and P_c and P_p denote the premiums on the call and the put, respectively. This means that the kinked profit line for the call is simply the same kinked line for the intrinsic value but lowered by an amount equal to the call premium P_c. Similarly, the kinked profit line for the put is simply the kinked intrinsic value line for the put, lowered by an amount equal to the put premium P_p.

If the premium on the call and put options shown in Figure 19.3 were $5, then their profit lines would be graphs of the following two equations:

$$\pi_c = \max\{-\$5, P_s - \$100 - \$5\}$$
$$= \max\{-\$5, P_s - \$105\}$$
$$\pi_p = \max\{-\$5, \$100 - P_s - \$5\}$$
$$= \max\{-\$5, \$95 - P_s\}$$

---

[4]Because the premium is paid by the buyer to the writer at the time the option is created, its value should be compounded to the expiration date using an appropriate rate of interest when calculating profits and losses.

Figure 19.4   Profits and losses from various strategies.

(a) Buy a Call

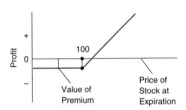

(b) Write a Call

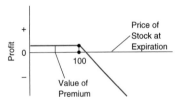

(c) Buy a Put

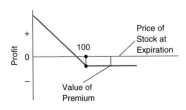

(d) Write a Put

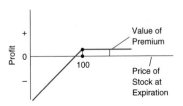

(e) Buy a Put and a Call (i.e., a Straddle)

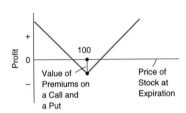

(f) Write a Put and a Call (i.e., a Straddle)

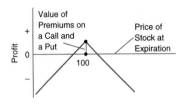

(g) Buy Stock

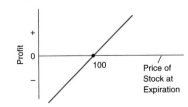

(h) Short Sell Stock

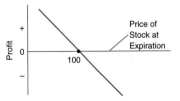

(i) Buy Stock and Write a Call

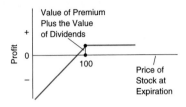

(j) Short Sell Stock and Buy a Call

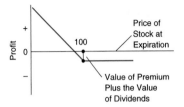

Therefore the kinked line for the call would be a horizontal line intersecting the vertical axis at −$5, and it would have a kink at a stock price of $100, where it would turn upward to intersect the horizontal axis at $105. This indicates that the call buyer would not make a profit unless the stock price was above the breakeven point of $105 at expiration. Each dollar that the stock price is above $105 represents an additional dollar of profit. (Hence a price of $108 would represent a profit of $3, since the call buyer pays a premium of $5 and an exercise price of $100 to procure a share of stock that is worth $108.)

Similarly, the kinked line for the put would be a downward-sloping line that would have a kink at a stock price of $100 after intersecting the horizontal axis at $95. At the kink the line would become horizontal so that if this part of the line were extended left to the vertical axis, it would intersect it at −$5. This indicates that the put buyer would not make a profit unless the stock price was below the breakeven point of $95 at expiration. Each dollar that the stock price is below $95 represents an additional dollar of profit. (Hence, a price of $92 would represent a profit of $3, since the put buyer pays a premium of $5 and gives up a share of stock worth $92 in order to receive $100 in return.)

Panels (b) and (d) of Figure 19.4 are mirror images of panels (a) and (c), respectively. This is because options are zero-sum games, where the profits to one party occur at the expense of the other party. Hence, if the stock price is at $108 so that the call buyer has a $3 profit, then the call writer has a $3 loss (because the writer receives the $5 premium and $100 exercise price but must give up a share of stock worth $108). Similarly, if the put buyer has a $3 profit, then the put writer has a loss of $3.

Profits and Losses from Some Option Strategies

Straddle An options strategy that involves buying (or writing) both a call and a put on the same asset, with the options having the same exercise price and expiration date.

Panels (e) and (f) of Figure 19.4 illustrate a more complicated options strategy known as a **straddle**. This strategy involves buying (or writing) both a call and a put on the same stock, with the options having the same exercise price and expiration date.[5] Note how panel (e) can be derived by adding the profits and losses shown in panels (a) and (c), whereas panel (f) can be derived by adding the profits and losses shown in panels (b) and (d). It can also be seen that panels (e) and (f) are mirror images of each other, again reflecting the fact that the profits to buyers equal the losses to writers and vice versa.

Panel (g) of Figure 19.4 shows the profit or loss made by an investor who avoids options entirely but buys a share of the underlying stock (at $100) at the same time that others buy or write options and sells the stock when the options expire. Assuming that no dividends are paid in the interim, the relationship is that shown by the solid line.[6] Similarly, panel (h) shows the profit or loss obtained by an investor who short sells the stock at the initial date and then buys it back at the expiration date.

Covered Call Writing The process of writing a call option on an asset owned by the option writer.

Panel (i) of Figure 19.4 shows the results obtained by an investor who buys one share of stock and simultaneously writes a call on it, a strategy known as **covered call writing**. These results can be derived by adding the profits and losses shown in panels (b) and (g). In contrast, the writer who does not hold the underlying stock, depicted in panel (b), is said to have written a naked option.

---

[5]Strips and straps are option strategies similar to a straddle. The former involves combining two puts with one call, and the latter involves combining two calls with one put. Another kind of strategy is known as a spread, where one call is bought while another is written on the same underlying security. Specifically, a price spread involves two calls having the same expiration date but different exercise prices. A time spread involves two calls having the same exercise price but different expiration dates.

[6]If there are dividends, they should be expressed as a compounded value at the expiration date associated with the options (as they would have been previously received) and added to the line, thereby shifting it upward.

Panel (j) of Figure 19.4 shows the results obtained by an investor who short sells one share of stock and simultaneously buys a call option, and it can be derived by adding the profits and losses in panels (a) and (h). Note that this panel is the mirror image of panel (i).

Comparison of the diagrams in Figure 19.4 suggests that similar results can be obtained via alternative strategies. Panels (c) and (j) are similar, as are (d) and (i). Neither the premiums involved nor the initial investments required need be equal in every case. Nonetheless, the similarity of the results obtained with different "packages" of securities suggests that the total market values of the packages will be similar.

Having discussed the value of options (and option-based strategies) when they expire, it is appropriate to discuss next the value of options before they expire. Specifically, what is the fair (or true) value of an option today if it expires at some future date? The binomial option pricing model can be used to answer such a question. It is presented next.

The Binomial Option Pricing Model

European Option An option that can only be exercised on its expiration date.

American Option An option that can be exercised any time through its expiration date.

The binomial option pricing model (BOPM) can be used to estimate the fair value of a call or put option. It is best presented through an example in which it is assumed that the options are **European options**, meaning that they can be exercised only on their expiration dates. In addition, it is assumed that the underlying stock does not pay any dividends during the life of the option. It should be noted that the model can be modified to value **American options**, which are options that can be exercised any time during their life and can also be used to value options on stocks that pay dividends during the life of the option.

Call Options

Assume that the price of Widget stock today ($t = 0$) is $100, and that after one year ($t = T$) its stock will be selling for either $125 or $80, meaning that the stock will either rise by 25% or fall by 20% over the year. In addition, the annual risk-free rate is 8% compounded continuously. Investors are assumed to be able to either lend (by purchasing these 8% bonds) or borrow (by short-selling the bonds) at this rate.

Now consider a call option on Widget that has an exercise price of $100 and an expiration date of one year from now. This means that on the expiration date the call will have a value of either $25 (if Widget is at $125) or $0 (if Widget is at $80). Panel (a) of Figure 19.5 illustrates the situation by use of a "price tree." It can be seen from this tree why this is called a binomial model, as there are only two branches that represent prices at the expiration date.

Valuation

What is a fair value for the call at time 0? The binomial option pricing model is designed to answer this question.

There are three investments that are of interest here: the share, the option, and a risk-free bond. The prices and payoffs for the share are known. It is also known that $100 invested in a risk-free bond will grow to approximately $108.33 given interest that is continuously compounded at an annual rate of 8%.[7] Finally, the end-of-period payoffs associated with the option are known. What is to be determined is a fair selling price for the option for now.

---

[7] In general, $1 will grow to 1e^{RT}$ at the end of T periods if it is continuously compounded at a rate of R. Here e represents the base of the natural logarithm, which is equal to approximately 2.71828. For a more detailed discussion, see the Appendix to Chapter 5.

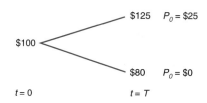

Figure 19.5 Binomial model of prices for Widget.

(a) Annual Analysis

$100

$125 $P_0 = \$25$

$80 $P_0 = \$0$

$t = 0$

$t = T$

(b) Semi-annual Analysis

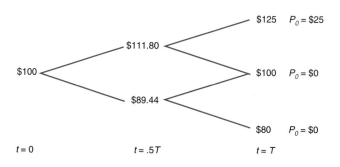

$100

$111.80

$89.44

$125 $P_0 = \$25$

$100 $P_0 = \$0$

$80 $P_0 = \$0$

$t = 0$

$t = .5T$

$t = T$

The key to understanding the situation is the observation that there are two possible future *states of nature*. The share's price may go up or down. For simplicity, these two states are called the "up state" and the "down state," respectively. This essential information is summarized as follows:

Security	Payoff in Up State	Payoff in Down State	Current Price
Share	$125.00	$80.00	$100.00
Bond	108.33	108.33	100.00
Call	25.00	0.00	???

Note that at this juncture the current price of the call is unknown.

Replicating Portfolios

Although the Widget call option may seem exotic, its characteristics can in fact be replicated with an appropriate combination of the Widget stock and the risk-free bond. Moreover, the cost of this *replicating portfolio* constitutes the fair value of the option. Why? Because otherwise there would be an *arbitrage opportunity*—an investor could buy the cheaper of the two alternatives and sell the more expensive one, thereby achieving a guaranteed profit. (Just how this is done will be shown shortly.)

The composition of a portfolio that will precisely replicate the payoffs of the Widget call option needs to be determined. Consider a portfolio with N_s shares of Widget stock and N_b risk-free bonds. In the up state such a portfolio will have a payoff of $125N_s + \$108.33N_b$, whereas in the down state it will have a payoff of $80N_s + \$108.33N_b$. The call option is worth $25 in the up state. Thus N_s and N_b need to have values so that

$$\$125N_s + \$108.33N_b = \$25 \qquad (19.3a)$$

The call option is worthless in the down state. Thus, N_s and N_b need to have values so that

$$\$80N_s + \$108.33N_b = \$0 \qquad (19.3b)$$

These two linear equations, (19.3a) and (19.3b), have two unknowns and can easily be solved. Subtracting the second equation from the first gives

$$(\$125 - \$80)N_s = \$25 \qquad (19.3c)$$

so that N_s equals .5556. Substituting this value in either equation (19.3a) or equation (19.3b) gives the remainder of the solution, $N_b = -.4103$.

What does this mean in financial terms? It means that an investor can replicate the payoffs from the call by *short selling* $41.03 of the risk-free bonds (note that investing $-.4103$ in $100 bonds is equivalent to short selling $41.03 of the bonds or borrowing $41.03 at the risk-free rate) and *purchasing* .5556 shares of Widget stock. This is indeed the case, as can be seen here:

Portfolio Component	Payoff in Up State	Payoff in Down State
Share investment	.5556 × $125 = $69.45	.5556 × $80 = $44.45
Loan repayment	−$41.03 × 1.0833 = −$44.45	−$41.03 × 1.0833 = −$44.45
Net payoff	$25.00	$0.00

Because the replicating portfolio provides the same payoffs as the call, only its cost needs to be calculated in order to find the fair value of the option. To obtain the portfolio, $55.56 must be spent to purchase .5556 shares of Widget stock (at $100 per share). However, $41.03 of this amount is provided by the proceeds from the short sale of the bond. Thus, only $55.56 − $41.03 = $14.53 of the investor's own funds must be spent. Accordingly, this is the fair value of the call option.

More generally, the value of the call option will be

$$V_o = N_s P_s + N_b P_b \qquad (19.4)$$

where V_o represents the value of the option, P_s is the price of the stock, P_b is the price of a risk-free bond, and N_s and N_b are the number of shares and risk-free bonds required to replicate the option's payoffs.

Overpricing

To show that equilibrium will be attained if the call is selling for $14.53, consider what a shrewd investor would do if the call were selling for either more or less than this amount. Imagine that the call is selling for $20, so it is overpriced. In this case the investor would consider writing one call, buying .5556 shares, and borrowing $41.03. The net cash flow when this is done (that is, at $t = 0$) would be $20 − (.5556 × $100) + $41.03 = 5.47, indicating that the investor has a net cash inflow. At the end of the year (that is, at $t = T$) the investor's net cash flow will be as shown in the following table:

Portfolio Component	Payoff in Up State	Payoff in Down State
Written call	−$25.00	$0.00
Share investment	.5556 × $125 = $69.45	.5556 × $80 = $44.45
Loan repayment	−$41.03 × 1.0833 = −$44.45	−$41.03 × 1.0833 = −$44.45
Net payoff	$0.00	$0.00

Because the net aggregate value is zero regardless of the ending stock price, the investor has no risk of loss from this strategy. Thus, the investor currently has a means for generating free cash as long as the call is priced at $20, since the investment strategy does not require any cash from the investor later on. This cannot represent equilibrium, as anyone can get free cash by investing similarly.

Underpricing

Next, imagine that the call is selling for $10 instead of $20, so it is underpriced. In this case the investor would consider buying one call, short selling .5556 shares, and investing $41.03 at the risk-free rate. The net cash flow when this is done (that is, at $t = 0$) would be $−\$10 + (.5556 \times \$100) − \$41.03 = \$4.53$, indicating that the investor has a net cash inflow. At the end of the year (that is, at $t = T$) the investor's net cash flow will be as follows:

Portfolio Component	Payoff in Up State	Payoff in Down State
Call investment	$25.00	$0.00
Repay shorted shares	−.5556 × $125 = −$69.45	−.5556 × $80 = −$44.45
Risk-free investment	$41.03 × 1.0833 = $44.45	$41.03 × 1.0833 = $44.45
Net payoff	$0.00	$0.00

Once again, the net aggregate value is zero regardless of the ending stock price, indicating that the investor has no risk of loss from this strategy. Hence, the investor currently has a means for generating free cash as long as the call is priced at $10. This cannot represent equilibrium, however, as anyone can get free cash by investing similarly.

The Hedge Ratio

Hedge Ratio
(Alternatively, **Delta**.) The expected change in the value of an option per dollar change in the market price of the underlying asset.

To replicate the Widget call option, imagine borrowing $41.03 and purchasing .5556 shares of Widget stock. Now, consider the effect of a change in the price of the stock tomorrow (not a year from now) on the value of the replicating portfolio. Because .5556 shares of stock are included in the portfolio, the value of the portfolio will change by $.5556 for every $1 change in the price of Widget stock. But because the call option and the portfolio should sell for the same price, it follows that the price of the call should also change by $.5556 for every $1 change in the price of the stock. This relationship is defined as the option's **hedge ratio**. It is equal to the value of N_s that was determined in equation (19.3c).

In the case of the Widget call option, the hedge ratio was equal to .5556, which equals the value of ($25 − $0)/($125 − $80). Note that the numerator equals the difference between the option's payoffs in the up and down states, and the denominator equals the difference between the stock's payoffs in the two states. More generally, in the binomial model:

$$h = \frac{P_{ou} - P_{od}}{P_{su} - P_{sd}} \qquad (19.5)$$

where P represents the end-of-period price and the subscripts indicate the instrument (o for option, s for stock) and the state of nature (u for up, d for down).

To replicate a call option in a binomial world, h shares of stock [where h represents the hedge ratio determined by using equation (19.5)] must be purchased. Simultaneously, an amount must be risklessly borrowed by short selling bonds; this amount is equal to

$$B = PV(hP_{sd} - P_{od}) \qquad (19.6)$$

where PV refers to taking the present value of the figure calculated in the parentheses that follow. (Note that the figure in parentheses is the value of the bond at the end of the period.)[8]

To summarize, the value of a call option is given to be

$$V_o = hP_s - B \qquad (19.7)$$

where h and B are the hedge ratio and the current value of a short bond position in a portfolio that replicates the payoffs of the call, and they are calculated by using equations (19.5) and (19.6).

More Than Two Prices

At this juncture it is reasonable to wonder about the accuracy of the BOPM if it is based on an assumption that the price of Widget shares can assume only one of two values at the end of a year. Realistically, Widget shares can assume any one of a great number of prices at year-end. It turns out that this is not a problem, as the model can be extended in a straightforward manner.

In the case of Widget, divide the year into two six-month periods. In the first period, assume that Widget can go up to $111.80 (an 11.80% increase) or down to $89.44 (a 10.56% decrease). For the second six-month period, the price of Widget can again go either up by 11.80% or down by 10.56%. Hence, the price of Widget will follow one of the paths of the price tree shown in panel (b) of Figure 19.5 over the coming year. Widget can now assume one of three prices at year-end: $125, $100, or $80. The associated value of the call option is also given in the figure for each of these stock prices.

How can the value of the Widget call option at time 0 be calculated from the information given in the figure? The answer is remarkably simple. The problem is broken down into three parts, each of which is solved in a manner similar to that shown earlier when panel (a) was discussed. The three parts must be approached sequentially by working backward in time.

First, imagine that six months have passed and the price of Widget stock is $111.80. What is the value of the call option at this node in the price tree? The hedge ratio h is calculated to be ($25 − $0)/($125 − $100) = 1.0, and the amount of the borrowing B is calculated to be (1 × $100 − $0)/1.0408 = $96.08. (The 8% risk-free rate compounded continuously corresponds to a discrete discount rate of 4.08% for the six-month period.) Using equation (19.7), the value of the call is determined to be 1 × $111.80 − $96.08 = $15.72.

Second, again imagine that six months have passed but the price of Widget is $89.44. While equations (19.5), (19.6), and (19.7) could be used to determine the value of the call at this node in the price tree, intuition gives the answer more quickly: the call has to be selling for $0. This is because in six months the price of Widget will be either $100 or $80,

---

[8]Equations (19.5) and (19.6) can be derived by solving the set of equations (19.3a) and (19.3b) using symbols instead of numbers.

and regardless of which it is, the call will still be worthless. That is, investors will realize that the call will be worthless at the end of the year if the stock price is at $89.44 after six months, and hence they will be unwilling to pay anything for the call option.

Third, imagine that no time has elapsed, so that it is time 0. In this case the price tree can be simplified to

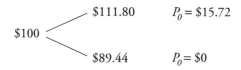

$$\$100 \quad \nearrow \quad \$111.80 \quad\quad P_0 = \$15.72$$
$$\searrow \quad \$89.44 \quad\quad P_0 = \$0$$

Applying equations (19.5) and (19.6) indicates that the hedge ratio h is equal to ($\$15.72 - \$0$)/($\$111.80 - \$89.44$) = .7030 and the amount of borrowing B is equal to (.7030 × $\$89.44 - \$0$)/1.0408 = $\$60.41$. Applying equation (19.7) results in a value for the call at $t = 0$ of .7030 × $\$100 - \$60.41 = \$9.89$.

There is no need to stop here. Instead of analyzing two six-month periods, four quarterly periods can be analyzed, or 12 monthly periods. Note that the number of year-end stock prices for Widget is equal to one more than the number of periods in a year. Hence, when annual periods were used in panel (a) of Figure 19.5, there were two year-end prices, and when semi-annual prices were used, there were three year-end prices. It follows that if quarterly or monthly periods had been used, there would have been 5 or 13 year-end prices, respectively.

▶ Put Options

Can the BOPM be used to value puts? Because the formulas cover any set of payoffs, they can be applied directly. Consider Widget once again from an annual perspective, where the put option has an exercise price of $100 and an expiration date of one year. Its price tree will be

$$\$100 \quad \nearrow \quad \$125 \quad\quad P_0 = \$0$$
$$\searrow \quad \$80 \quad\quad P_0 = \$20$$

Applying equation (19.5) gives the hedge ratio for the put option as ($\$0 - \$20$)/($\$125 - \$80$) = −.4444. Note that this is a negative number, indicating that a rise in the price of the stock will lower the price of the put.

Applying equation (19.6) shows that B equals −$51.28, which is the present value of the year-end value of −$55.55. Because these are negative numbers, they denote the amount of bonds to be purchased (that is, the negative value of a short position should be interpreted as the value of a long position).

To replicate the put option, then, one *sells short* .4444 shares of Widget and *lends* (that is, invests in the risk-free bond) $51.28. As the short sale will generate $44.44 while the bond purchase will cost $51.28, the net cost of the replicating portfolio will be $51.28 − $44.44 = $6.84. Accordingly, this is the fair value of the put.

This is the same value that is obtained when equation (19.7) is used: −.4444 × $100 − (−$51.28) = $6.84, where h = .4444, B = −$51.28, and P_s = $100. Hence equations (19.5), (19.6), and (19.7) can be used to value not only calls but also puts. Furthermore, the procedure for extending the valuation of puts to the situation where there is more than one period between now and the expiration date is analogous to the one that was given for calls.

Put-call Parity

Earlier it was shown that the call on Widget had a hedge ratio of .5556. Note that .5556 − 1 = −.4444, the hedge ratio for the put. This is not a coincidence. The hedge ratios of a European put and call having the same exercise price and expiration date are related in the following manner:

$$h_c - 1 = h_p \tag{19.8}$$

where h_c and h_p denote the hedge ratios for the call and the put, respectively.

Of even greater interest is the relationship between the market prices of a call and a put on a given stock that have the same exercise price and expiration date. Again consider the example involving Widget options that have an exercise price of $100 and an expiration date of one year. Two investment strategies need to be compared. Strategy A involves buying a put and a share of stock. (This strategy is sometimes known as a "protective put" or a "married put.") Strategy B involves buying a call and investing an amount of money in the risk-free asset that is equal to the present value of the exercise price.

At the expiration date the values of these two investment strategies can be calculated under two scenarios: the price of Widget being below its exercise price of $100, and the price of Widget being above its exercise price. (The case where it is exactly equal to its exercise price can be added to either scenario without affecting the results.) Table 19.3 does this. Note that if the stock of Widget is selling for less than the $100 exercise price on the expiration date, both strategies have a payoff of $100 in cash. Alternatively, if the price of Widget stock is above $100, both strategies result in the investor having possession of a share of stock that is worth more than $100. Hence, because both strategies have the same payoffs, they must cost the same amount in equilibrium:

$$P_p + P_s = P_c + E/e^{RT} \tag{19.9}$$

Put-call Parity The relationship between the market price on a put and a call that have the same exercise price, expiration date, and underlying stock.

where P_p and P_c denote the current market prices of the put and the call, respectively.

This equation represents what is known as **put-call parity**. In Table 19.3 it can be seen that the cost of each strategy is $106.84, just as was suggested previously by the calculations using equations (19.5), (19.6), and (19.7).

Table 19.3 Put-call Parity Involving Widget.

Strategy	Initial Cost	Value at Expiration Date	
		$P_s < E = \$100$	$E = \$100 > P_s$

A: Buy put
   Buy share of stock
	$P_p + P_s$
	  $= \$6.84 + \$100$
	  $= \$106.84$
		Exercise put, get $100	Throw away put, have stock worth P_s

B: Buy call
   Invest present value
   of E in risk-free asset
	$P_c + E/e^{RT}$
	  $= \$14.53 + \$92.31$
	  $= \$106.84$
		Throw away call, get $100 from risk-free asset	Exercise call, get stock worth P_s

---

The Black-Scholes Model for Call Options

Consider what would happen with the binomial option pricing model if the number of periods before the expiration date were allowed to increase. For example, with Widget's option for which the expiration date was a year in the future, there could be a price tree with periods for each one of the approximately 250 trading days in a year. Hence there would be 251 possible year-end prices for Widget stock. Needless to say, the fair value of any call associated with such a tree is found by using a computer to quickly perform calculations such as those shown earlier for Widget. If the number of periods was even larger, with each one representing a specific hour of each trading day, then there would be about $7 \times 250 = 1750$ hourly periods (and 1751 possible year-end prices). Note that the number of periods in a year gets larger as the length of each period gets shorter. In the limit there will be an infinite number of infinitely small periods (and, consequently, an infinite number of possible year-end prices). In this situation the BOPM given in equation (19.7) reduces to the Black-Scholes model, so named in honour of its originators.[9]

The Formula

In the absence of taxes and transaction costs, the fair value of a call option can be estimated by using the valuation formula developed by Black and Scholes. It has been widely used by those who deal with options to search for situations where the market price of an option differs substantially from its fair value. A call option that is found to be selling for substantially less than its Black-Scholes value is a candidate for purchase, whereas one that is found to be selling for substantially more is a candidate for writing. The Black-Scholes formula for estimating the fair value of a call option V_c is

$$V_c = N(d_1)P_s - \frac{E}{e^{RT}}N(d_2) \tag{19.10}$$

where:

$$d_1 = \frac{\ln(P_s/E) + (R + .5\sigma^2)T}{\sigma\sqrt{T}} \tag{19.11}$$

$$d_2 = \frac{\ln(P_s/E) + (R - .5\sigma^2)T}{\sigma\sqrt{T}} \tag{19.12a}$$

$$= d_1 - \sigma\sqrt{T} \tag{19.12b}$$

and where:

P_s = current market price of the underlying stock
E = exercise price of the option
R = continuously compounded risk-free rate of return expressed on an annual basis
T = time remaining before expiration, expressed as a fraction of a year
σ = risk of the underlying common stock, measured by the standard deviation of the continuously compounded annual rate of return on the stock

Note that E/e^{RT} is the present value of the exercise price where a continuous discount rate is used. The quantity $\ln(P_s/E)$ is the natural logarithm of P_s/E. Finally, $N(d_1)$ and $N(d_2)$ denote the probabilities that outcomes of less than d_1 and d_2, respectively, will occur in a normal distribution that has a mean of 0 and a standard deviation of 1.

Table 19.4 provides values of $N(d_1)$ for various levels of d_1.[10] Only this table and a

---

[9]Fischer Black and Myron Scholes, "The Pricing of Options and Corporate Liabilities," *Journal of Political Economy* 81, no. 3 (May–June 1973): 637–654. Also see Fischer Black, "How We Came Up with the Option Formula," *Journal of Portfolio Management* 15, no. 2 (Winter 1989): 4–8, and "How to Use the Holes in Black-Scholes," *Journal of Applied Corporate Finance* 1, no. 4 (Winter 1989): 67–73. For an intuitive explanation of the Black-Scholes formula, see Dwight Grant, Gautam Vora, and David Weeks, "Teaching Option Valuation: From Simple Discrete Distributions to Black-Scholes Via Monte Carlo Simulation," *Financial Practice and Education* 5, no. 2 (Fall–Winter 1995): 149–155. It should be noted that Scholes and Robert Merton were the co-recipients of the 1997 Nobel Prize in Economic Science, largely for their contributions in this area. Undoubtedly, Black would have shared the Prize with them had he not suffered an untimely death.

[10]Table 19.4 is an abbreviated version of a standard cumulative normal distribution table. More detailed versions can be found in most statistics textbooks.

Table 19.4 Values of N(d) for Selected Values of d.

d	N(d)	d	N(d)	d	N(d)
		−1.00	.1587	1.00	.8413
−2.95	.0016	−.95	.1711	1.05	.8531
−2.90	.0019	−.90	.1841	1.10	.8643
−2.85	.0022	−.85	.1977	1.15	.8749
−2.80	.0026	−.80	.2119	1.20	.8849
−2.75	.0030	−.75	.2266	1.25	.8944
−2.70	.0035	−.70	.2420	1.30	.9032
−2.65	.0040	−.65	.2578	1.35	.9115
−2.60	.0047	−.60	.2743	1.40	.9192
−2.55	.0054	−.55	.2912	1.45	.9265
−2.50	.0062	−.50	.3085	1.50	.9332
−2.45	.0071	−.45	.3264	1.55	.9394
−2.40	.0082	−.40	.3446	1.60	.9452
−2.35	.0094	−.35	.3632	1.65	.9505
−2.30	.0107	−.30	.3821	1.70	.9554
−2.25	.0122	−.25	.4013	1.75	.9599
−2.20	.0139	−.20	.4207	1.80	.9641
−2.15	.0158	−.15	.4404	1.85	.9678
−2.10	.0179	−.10	.4602	1.90	.9713
−2.05	.0202	−.05	.4801	1.95	.9744
−2.00	.0228	.00	.5000	2.00	.9773
−1.95	.0256	.05	.5199	2.05	.9798
−1.90	.0287	.10	.5398	2.10	.9821
−1.85	.0322	.15	.5596	2.15	.9842
−1.80	.0359	.20	.5793	2.20	.9861
−1.75	.0401	.25	.5987	2.25	.9878
−1.70	.0446	.30	.6179	2.30	.9893
−1.65	.0495	.35	.6368	2.35	.9906
−1.60	.0548	.40	.6554	2.40	.9918
−1.55	.0606	.45	.6736	2.45	.9929
−1.50	.0668	.50	.6915	2.50	.9938
−1.45	.0735	.55	.7088	2.55	.9946
−1.40	.0808	.60	.7257	2.60	.9953
−1.35	.0885	.65	.7422	2.65	.9960
−1.30	.0968	.70	.7580	2.70	.9965
−1.25	.1057	.75	.7734	2.75	.9970
−1.20	.1151	.80	.7881	2.80	.9974
−1.15	.1251	.85	.8023	2.85	.9978
−1.10	.1357	.90	.8159	2.90	.9981
−1.05	.1469	.95	.8289	2.95	.9984

pocket calculator are needed in order to use the Black-Scholes formula for valuing a call option. It should be noted that with this formula the interest rate R and the stock volatility σ are assumed to be constant over the life of the option. (More recently people have developed formulas where these assumptions have been relaxed.) For example, consider a call option that expires in three months and has an exercise price of $40 (thus $T = .25$ and $E = 40$). Furthermore, the current price and the risk of the underlying common stock are $36 and 50%, respectively, whereas the risk-free rate is 5% (thus $P_s = 36$, $R = .05$, and $\sigma = .50$). Solving equations (19.11) and (19.12b) provides the following values for d_1 and d_2:

$$d_1 = \frac{\ln(36/40) + [.05 + .5(.50)^2].25}{.50\sqrt{.25}} = -.25$$

$$d_2 = -.25 - .50\sqrt{.25} = -.50$$

Now Table 19.4 can be used to find the corresponding values of $N(d_1)$ and $N(d_2)$:

$$N(d_1) = N(-.25) = .4013$$

$$N(d_2) = N(-.50) = .3085$$

Finally, equation (19.10) can be used to estimate the fair value of this call option:

$$V_c = (.4013 \times \$36) - \left(\frac{\$40}{e^{.05 \times .25}} \times .3085 \right)$$

$$= \$14.45 - \$12.19 = \$2.26$$

If this call option is currently selling for $5, the investor should consider writing some of them. This is because they are overpriced (according to the Black-Scholes model), suggesting that their price will fall in the near future. Thus, the writer would receive a premium of $5 and would expect to be able to enter a closing buy order later for a lower price, making a profit on the difference. Conversely, if the call option were selling for $1, the investor should consider buying some of them. This is because they are underpriced and can be expected to rise in value in the future.

Comparison to BOPM

At this juncture the BOPM formula given in equation (19.7) where V_0 is now denoted V_c can be compared with the Black-Scholes option pricing formula given in equation (19.10):

$$V_c = hP_s - B \tag{19.7}$$

$$V_c = N(d_1)P_s - \frac{E}{e^{RT}}N(d_2) \tag{19.10}$$

In comparing the two equations, the quantity $N(d_1)$ in equation (19.10) can be seen to correspond to h in equation (19.7). Remembering that h is the hedge ratio, the quantity $N(d_1)$ in the Black-Scholes formula can be interpreted in a similar manner. That is, it corresponds to the number of shares that an investor would need to purchase in executing an investment strategy that was designed to have the same payoffs as a call option. Similarly, the quantity $EN(d_2)/e^{RT}$ corresponds to B, the amount of money that the investor borrows as the other part of the strategy. This means that the quantity $EN(d_2)$ corresponds to the face amount of the loan, because it is the amount that must be paid back to the lender at time T, the expiration date. Hence e^{RT} is the present value (or discount) factor, indicating that the interest rate on the loan is R per period and that the loan is for T periods. Thus, the seemingly complex Black-Scholes formula can be seen to have an intuitive interpretation. It simply involves calculating the cost of a buy-stock-and-borrow-money investment strategy that has the same payoffs at T as a call option.

In the example, $N(d_1)$ was equal to .4013 and $EN(d_2)/e^{RT}$ was equal to $12.19. Hence, an investment strategy that involves buying .4013 shares and borrowing $12.19 at time 0 will have payoffs exactly equal to those associated with buying the call.[11] Because this strategy costs $2.26, it follows that in equilibrium the market price of the call must also be $2.26.

---

[11]It should be pointed out that the investment strategy is more complicated than it might appear because the number of shares that are to be held will change over time as the share price changes and the expiration date gets closer. Similarly, the amount of the loan will change over time. Hence, it is a *dynamic strategy*..

Static Analysis

Close scrutiny of the Black-Scholes formula reveals some interesting features of European call option pricing. In particular, the fair value of a call option is dependent on five inputs—the market price of the common stock P_s, the exercise price of the option E, the length of time until the expiration date T, the risk-free rate R, and the risk of the common stock σ. What happens to the fair value of a call option when one of these inputs is changed while the other four remain the same?

1. The higher the price of the underlying stock P_s, the higher the value of the call option.
2. The higher the exercise price E, the lower the value of the call option.
3. The longer the time to the expiration date T, the higher the value of the call option.
4. The higher the risk-free rate R, the higher the value of the call option.
5. The greater the risk σ of the common stock, the higher the value of the call option.

Of these five factors, the first three (P_s, E, and T) are readily determined. The fourth factor, the risk-free rate R, is often estimated by using the yield-to-maturity on a Treasury bill having a maturity date close to the expiration date of the option. The fifth factor, the risk of the underlying stock σ, is not readily observed; consequently various methods for estimating it have been proposed. Two of these methods will be presented next.

Estimating a Stock's Risk from Historical Prices

One method for estimating the risk of the underlying common stock associated with a call option involves analyzing historical prices of the stock. Initially a set of $n + 1$ market prices on the underlying stock must be obtained from either financial publications such as *The Globe and Mail* or a computer database. These prices are then used to calculate a set of n continuously compounded returns as follows:

$$r_t = \ln\left(\frac{P_{st}}{P_{st-1}}\right) \tag{19.13}$$

where P_{st} and P_{st-1} denote the market price of the underlying stock at times t and $t - 1$, respectively. Here, ln denotes taking the natural logarithm of the quantity P_{st}/P_{st-1}, which thus results in a continuously compounded return.

For example, the set of market prices for the stock might consist of the closing price at the end of each of 53 weeks. If the price at the end of one week was $105 and the price at the end of the next week was $107, then the return for that week r_t will be equal to $\ln(107/105) = 1.886\%$. Similar calculations will result in a set of 52 weekly returns.

Having calculated a set of n returns on the stock, the next step involves using them to estimate the stock's average return:

$$r_{av} = \frac{1}{n}\sum_{t=1}^{n} r_t \tag{19.14}$$

The average return is then used in estimating the per-period variance—that is, the square of the per-period standard deviation:

$$s^2 = \frac{1}{n-1}\sum_{t=1}^{n}(r_t - r_{av})^2 \tag{19.15}$$

This is called the per-period variance because its size is dependent on the length of time over which each return is measured. In the example, weekly returns were calculated and would lead to the estimation of a weekly variance. Alternatively, daily returns could have been used, leading to a daily variance that would be of smaller magnitude than the weekly variance. However, what is needed is not a weekly or daily variance, but an annual variance. This is obtained by multiplying the per-period variance by the number of periods in a year.

Thus an estimated weekly variance would be multiplied by 52 in order to estimate the annual variance σ^2 (that is, $\sigma^2 = 52s^2$).[12]

Alternative methods of estimating a stock's total risk exist. One such method involves subjectively estimating the probabilities of possible future stock prices. Another method involves combining the historical and subjective risk estimates.

For any estimate of future uncertainty, historical data are likely to prove more helpful than definitive. And because recent data may prove more helpful than older data, some analysts study daily price changes over the most recent 6 to 12 months, sometimes giving more weight to more recent data than to earlier ones. Others take into account the price histories of related stocks and the possibility that a stock whose price has recently decreased may be more risky in the future than it was in the past. Still others make explicit subjective estimates of the future, taking into account changes in uncertainty concerning the economy in general as well as uncertainty in specific industries and in stocks.

In some cases an analyst's estimate of a stock's risk over the next three months may differ from that for the following three months, leading to the use of different values of σ for call options on the same stock that have different expiration dates.

The Market Consensus of a Stock's Risk

Implicit (or Implied) Votality The risk of an asset derived from an options valuation model, assuming that an option on the asset is fairly priced by the market.

Another way to estimate a stock's risk is based on the assumption that a currently outstanding call option is fairly priced in the marketplace. Because this means that $P_c = V_c$, the current market price of the call P_c can be entered on the left-hand side of equation (19.10) in place of the fair value of the call V_c. Next all the other factors except for σ are entered on the right-hand side, and a value for σ, the only unknown variable, is found that satisfies the equation. The solution for σ can be interpreted as representing a consensus opinion in the marketplace on the size of the stock's risk, and it is sometimes known as the stock's **implicit** (or implied) **volatility**.[13]

For example, assume that the risk-free rate is 6%, and that a six-month call option with an exercise price of $40 sells for $4 when the price of the underlying stock is $36. Different estimates of σ can be "plugged into" the right-hand side of equation (19.10) until a value of $4 for this side of the equation is obtained. In this example an estimated value of .40 (that is, 40%) for σ will result in a number for the right-hand side of equation (19.10) that is equal to $4, the current market price of the call option that is on the left-hand side.

The procedure can be modified by applying it to several call options on the same stock. For example, σ can be estimated for each of several call options on the same stock that have different exercise prices but the same expiration date. Then the resulting estimates for σ can be averaged and, in turn, used to determine the fair value of another call option on the same stock having yet another exercise price but a similar expiration date.

In the example, σ can be estimated not only for a six-month option having an exercise price of $40, but also for six-month options having exercise prices of $35 and $45. Then the three estimates of σ can be averaged to produce a "best estimate" of σ that is used to value a six-month $50 option on the same stock.

---

[12]If daily data are used, it is best to multiply the daily variance by 250 instead of 365 because there are about 250 trading days in a year. See Mark Kritzman, "About Estimating Volatility: Part I," *Financial Analysts Journal* 47, no. 4 (July–August 1991): 22–25; and "About Estimating Volatility: Part II," *Financial Analysts Journal* 47, no. 5 (September–October 1991): 10–11. For a method of estimating σ that uses high, low, opening, and closing prices as well as trading volume, see Mark B. Garman and Michael J. Klass, "On the Estimation of Security Price Volatilities from Historical Data," *Journal of Business* 53, no. 1 (January 1980): 67–78.

[13]Alternatively, equation (19.10) could be solved for the interest rate R; doing so gives an estimate of the *implied interest rate*. See Menachem Brenner and Dan Galai, "Implied Interest Rates," *Journal of Business* 59, no. 3 (July 1986): 493–507.

Alternatively, the procedure can be modified by averaging the estimates for σ associated with each of several expiration dates. In the example, σ can be estimated not only for a six-month option having an exercise price of $40 but also for a three-month and a nine-month option that each have an exercise price of $40. The three estimates of σ can be averaged to produce a best estimate of σ that will subsequently be used to determine the fair value of a one-month $40 option on the same stock.

There are other ways of using a set of estimates of σ that correspond to different call options on the same stock. Perhaps σ will be estimated for a set of calls having different expiration prices and different exercise prices, and then averaged. Perhaps σ will be estimated from historical returns using equation (19.15), with the resulting figure averaged with one or more estimates of the stock's implicit volatility. Although the evidence is still unclear, it appears that methods based on calculating implicit volatility are better than methods based on historical returns.[14] It should be remembered, however, that all of these methods assume that volatility remains constant over the life of the option—an assumption that can be challenged.

More on Hedge Ratios

The slope of the Black-Scholes value curve at any point represents the expected change in the value of the option per dollar change in the price of the underlying common stock. This amount corresponds to the hedge ratio of the call option and is equal to $N(d_1)$ in equation (19.10). As can be seen in Figure 19.6 (assuming that the market price of the call is equal to its Black-Scholes value), the slope (that is, the hedge ratio) of the curve is always positive. Note that if the stock has a relatively low market price, the slope will be near zero. For higher stock prices the slope increases and ultimately approaches a value of 1 for relatively high prices.

Because the hedge ratio is typically less than 1, a $1 increase in the stock price will typically result in an increase in a call option's value of less than $1. However, the percentage change in the value of the call option will generally be much greater than the percentage change in the price of the stock. It is this relationship that leads people to say that options offer high leverage.

The reason for referring to the slope of the Black-Scholes value curve as the hedge ratio is that a "hedge" portfolio, meaning a nearly risk-free portfolio, can be formed by simultaneously writing one call option and purchasing a number of shares equal to the hedge ratio, $N(d_1)$. For example, assume that the hedge ratio is .5, indicating that the hedge portfolio consists of writing one call and buying .5 shares of stock. Now if the stock price rises by $1, the value of the call option will rise by approximately $.50. This means that the hedge portfolio would lose approximately $.50 on the written call option but gain $.50 from the rise in the stock's price. Conversely, a $1 decrease in the stock's price would result in a $.50 gain on the written call option but a loss of $.50 on the half-share of stock. Overall, it can be seen that the hedge portfolio will neither gain nor lose value when the price of the underlying common stock changes by a relatively small amount.[15]

Even if the Black-Scholes model is valid and all the inputs have been correctly specified, it should be noted that risk is not permanently eliminated in the hedge portfolio when

---

[14]For a further discussion of these methods, see any of the options textbooks cited at the end of the chapter, or see Menachem Brenner and Marti Subrahmanyam, "A Simple Formula to Compute the Implied Standard Deviation," *Financial Analysts Journal* 44, no. 5 (September–October 1988): 80–83, and Charles J. Corrado and Thomas W. Miller, Jr., "A Note on a Simple Accurate Formula to Compute Implied Standard Deviations," *Journal of Banking and Finance* 20, no. 3 (April 1996): 595–603.

[15]This explanation of a hedge ratio follows from the BOPM-based interpretation of the Black-Scholes formula that was given earlier. That is, if a call's payoffs can be duplicated by buying shares and borrowing at the risk-free rate, it follows that buying shares and writing a call will duplicate investing in the risk-free asset.

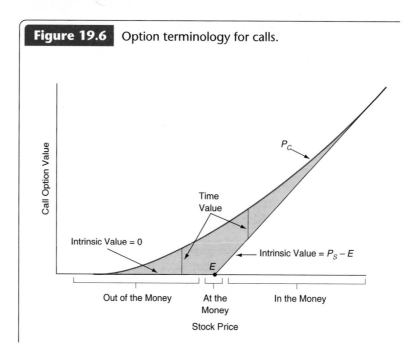

Figure 19.6 Option terminology for calls.

the portfolio is first formed (or, for that matter, at any time). This is because the hedge ratio will change as the stock price changes and as the life of the option decreases with the passage of time. In order to eliminate risk from the hedge portfolio, the investor will have to alter its composition continually. Altering it less often will reduce but not completely eliminate risk.

Limitations on Its Use

At first this model might seem to have limited use, because almost all options in North America are American options that can be exercised at any time up to their expiration date whereas the Black-Scholes model applies only to European options. Furthermore, strictly speaking, the model is applicable only to options on stocks that will not pay any dividends over the life of the option. However, most of the common stocks on which options are written do in fact pay dividends.

The first drawback of the Black-Scholes model—that it is only applicable to European options—can be dispensed with rather easily when the option is a call and the underlying stock does not pay dividends. This is because it can be shown that it is unwise for an investor holding an American call option on a non-dividend-paying stock to exercise it prior to maturity.[16] As there is no reason for exercising such an option prior to maturity, the opportunity to do so is worthless. Consequently there will be no difference in the values of an American and a European call option. In turn, this means that the Black-Scholes model can be used to estimate the fair value of American call options on non-dividend-paying stocks.

---

[16]See Robert C. Merton, "Theory of Rational Option Pricing," *Bell Journal of Economics and Management Science* 4, no. 1 (Spring 1973): 141–183.

The reason for this can be seen in Figure 19.6, but first some terminology must be introduced. A call option is said to be **at the money** if the underlying stock has a market price roughly equal to the call's exercise price. If the stock's market price is below the exercise price, the call is said to be **out of the money**, and if the market price is above the exercise price, the call is said to be **in the money**. Occasionally, finer gradations are invoked, and one hears of "near the money," "deep in the money," or "far out of the money."

As mentioned earlier, the value of an option if it were exercised immediately is known as its intrinsic value. This value is equal to zero if the option is out of the money. However, it is equal to the difference between the stock price and the exercise price if the option is in the money. The excess of the option's price over its intrinsic value is the option's **time value** (or time premium). The time value of a call option at expiration is zero, but is positive before then. Note that a call option's premium is simply the sum of its intrinsic and time values.

An investor considering exercising a call option on a non-dividend-paying stock prior to its expiration date will always find it cheaper to sell the call option and purchase the stock in the marketplace. This is because exercising the call will result in the investor's losing the time value of the option (hence the expression that call options are "worth more alive than dead").

For example, consider a stock that has a current price of $110. If this stock has a call option with an exercise price of $100 that is selling for $14, then the intrinsic and time values of this option are $110 − $100 = $10 and $14 − $10 = $4, respectively. An investor who owns one of these calls could exercise it by spending an additional $100. However, it would be cheaper for the investor to get the share of stock by selling the call option and buying the share of stock in the marketplace, because the additional cost would be only $110 − $14 = $96.

The second drawback of the Black-Scholes model—that it is only applicable to non-dividend-paying stocks—cannot be easily dismissed, as many call options are written on stocks that will pay dividends over the life of the option. Some procedures have been suggested for amending this formula to value call options on such stocks.[17] As will be seen shortly, European options on dividend-paying stocks can generally be valued using the Black-Scholes formula by making one simple alteration, but American options are more problematic.

Adjustments for Dividends

Thus far, the issue of dividend payments on the underlying stock during the life of an option has been avoided. Other things being equal, the greater the amount of the dividends to be paid during the life of a call option, the lower the value of the call option. This is because the greater the dividend that a firm declares, the lower its stock price will be. Since options are not "dividend protected," this lower stock price will result in a lower value for the call option (and a higher value for put options).

The simplest case is valuing European call options on dividend-paying stocks when the future dividends can be accurately forecast, both in size and date. This is often possible, since most options have an expiration date of within nine months. In such cases, all that is done in valuing European call options is to take the current stock price, subtract from it the discounted value of the dividends (using the ex-dividend date and the risk-free rate for discounting), and insert the resulting adjusted price in the Black-Scholes call option formula along with the other inputs. The reason for this is quite straightforward. The current stock price can be viewed as consisting of two components—the present value of the

---

[17]These procedures are reviewed in the options textbooks cited at the end of the chapter.

known dividends that will be paid over the life of the option, and the present value of all the dividends thereafter (see the discussion of dividend discount models in Chapter 17). Since the option is only exercisable at expiration, it is only applicable to the second component, whose current value is just the adjusted price. Thus, if the stock previously discussed that is currently priced at $36 will pay a dividend in six months of $1, its adjusted price is $35.025 since the risk-free rate is $36 − ($1/e^{.05 × .5}) = 5%. Consequently any calls that expire in more than six months but before the next ex-dividend date can be valued by using the Black-Scholes call option formula and a current price of $35.025. When it comes to American call options, things are much more complicated because it may pay to exercise such an option just prior to an ex-dividend date. Earlier it was mentioned that in the absence of dividends, an American call option would be worth at least as much "alive" (not exercised) as "dead" (exercised). When dividends are involved, however, the situation may be different. This is shown in Figure 19.7.

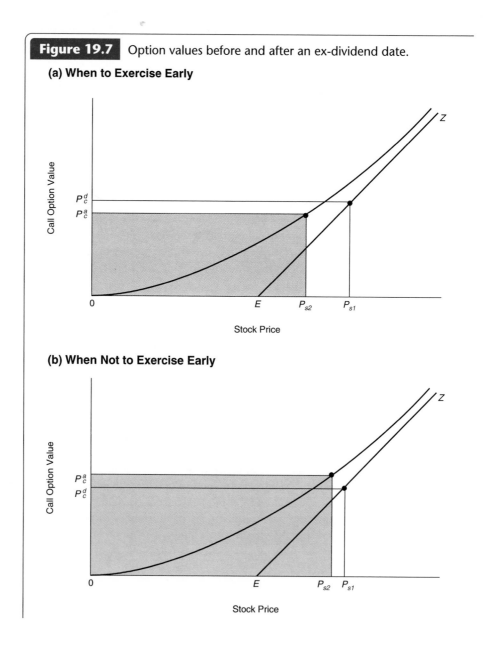

Figure 19.7 Option values before and after an ex-dividend date.

(a) When to Exercise Early

(b) When Not to Exercise Early

The call option's value if exercised immediately, referred to as the option's "intrinsic value," lies along the lower boundary $0EZ$. If allowed to live, the option's value will lie along the higher Black-Scholes curve, as shown in the figure. Imagine that the stock is currently priced at P_{s1} and is about to go ex-dividend for the last time prior to the option's expiration. Afterward it can be expected to sell for a lower price P_{s2}. The Black-Scholes formula can be used to estimate the option's value if it remains "alive" just after the ex-dividend date. In Figure 19.7, this alive value is P_c^a. If instead the option is exercised just before the ex-dividend date while the stock price is still P_{s1}, the investor will obtain the "dead" value (that is, the intrinsic value) of P_c^d. If P_c^d is greater than P_c^a [as is the case in panel (a)], the option should be exercised now, just before the ex-dividend date; if P_c^d is less than P_c^a [as is the case in panel (b)], the option should not be exercised. Hence for an American call option on a dividend-paying stock, the possibility of early exercise must be taken into consideration.[18] Fortunately, the BOPM is capable of handling such a situation.

The Valuation of Put Options

Similar to a call option, a put option is said to be at the money if the underlying stock has a market price roughly equal to the put's exercise price. However, the terms "out of the money" and "in the money" have, in one sense, *opposite meanings* for puts and calls. In particular, a put option is out of the money if the underlying stock has a market price above the exercise price and is in the money if the market price is below the exercise price. Figure 19.8 provides an illustration of how these terms apply to a put option.

An option's intrinsic value is equal to zero if the option is out of the money, and is equal to the difference between the stock price and the exercise price if the stock is in the money. Thus in another sense, the terms "out of the money" and "in the money" have *similar meanings* for puts and calls.

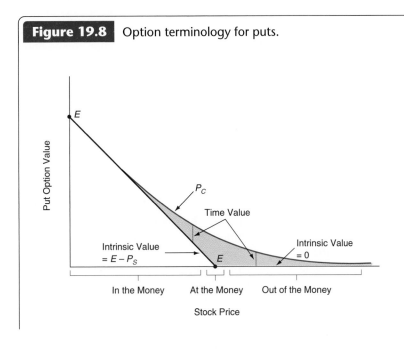

Figure 19.8 Option terminology for puts.

---

[18]See footnote 17. Also see Thomas J. Finucane, "An Empirical Analysis of Common Stock Call Exercise: A Note," *Journal of Banking and Finance* 21, no. 4 (April 1997): 563–571.

Option Overwriting

Option overwriting is one of the oldest options-related portfolio management strategies. In its basic form it is a relatively simple technique that conveniently illustrates certain fundamental aspects of options and demonstrates how options can be used to control the shape of a portfolio distribution of returns.

Option overwriting is a type of covered call writing. The owner of an asset (for purposes of discussion, assume that asset is a portfolio of common stocks) writes out-of-the-money or at-the-money calls on the asset and receives premium income in exchange. The option overwriter stands to gain relative to a strategy of merely holding the portfolio if the portfolio should either decline in value or not rise in value significantly. In that case, the premium helps to either cushion the decline in the portfolio's value or enhance any small price appreciation. On the other hand, the option overwriter loses if the portfolio's value rises above the option's exercise price by more than the amount of the premium received. In that case, the option will be exercised at a loss to the overwriter.

Option overwriting can be done on an individual security basis. However, writing one index option on an entire common stock portfolio is more cost effective than writing many options on individual stocks. Further, index options provide for cash settlement, a feature that eliminates the risk that the overwritten asset will be called away. Consequently, it was the introduction of equity index options in 1983 that encouraged institutional investors to first engage in option overwriting programs on their common stock portfolios.

Option overwriting serves two principle objectives: risk reduction and return enhancement. The first objective is unambiguous: an overwritten portfolio has less risk than the portfolio without option writing. The premium reduces potential downside returns while the existence of the call limits upside price appreciation for the overwriter. The second objective is more controversial. In an efficient market, an option overwriter should not stand to gain on a risk-adjusted basis. The lower risk of option overwriting should be offset by a lower expected return.

However, if option markets are not perfectly efficient, then the opportunity may exist for enhanced returns if the option overwriter can identify situations when index calls are overvalued. In that case, the option overwriter would selectively sell calls when they appear overpriced and buy them back when they appear underpriced.

There are many different variations on the option overwriting theme. A passively managed index fund (see Chapter 23), designed to match the performance of an index on which options are actively traded, is the ideal underlying asset for option overwriting. Out-of-the-money index call options (with exercise prices usually at least 1% to 5% above the current level of the index) are often used to reduce the likelihood of call losses if market prices should rise, although at-the-money options may be sold as they offer higher premiums. Short-term options (usually three months to expiration) are used to maximize the capture of time value decay. That is, the time value of an option (the difference between the option's market value and its intrinsic value) declines most rapidly near expiration. Thus a seller captures the greatest amount of time value decay by selling near expiration. Some option overwriters may sell calls against the entire value of the portfolio, while others may overwrite only a fraction. Some overwriters continually sell calls against the portfolio, while others are more selective in their timing. As American options are more expensive than European options (because they can be exercised any time up to expiration), and as the option writer does not expect to have the call exercised, American options are the preferred instrument, where appropriate.

Option overwriters typically estimate the relative attractiveness of selling covered calls by examining the implied volatility of the available options. (As the text discusses, implied volatility is the standard deviation of a stock's return that equates the "fair" value of an option to its current market price.) Option values vary directly with the volatility of the underlying asset. Overwriters contend that the market is prone to periods of overreaction, usually around times of market instability, such as October 1987 and the 1990 Persian Gulf War. The overwriters hope to benefit from a mean reversion effect, selling calls when implied volatilities (and prices) are abnormally high and buying when implied volatilities (and prices) have fallen back to "normal" levels. Overwriters will often compare an option's implied volatility to a historical range of volatility for the index. If the implied volatility lies outside of that range it indicates that the option may be significantly mispriced.

Consider a hypothetical institutional investor XYZ who has hired manager ABC to conduct an option overwriting program on XYZ's $300 million portfolio of US common stocks. Examining XYZ's portfolio indicates that it most closely resembles the S&P 500, so ABC decides to concentrate on S&P 500 index options. The S&P 500 is currently at 950 and March options (the contract with three months to expiration) with an exercise price of $1000 (5% out-of-the-money) are selling for $2450 per contract. Assuming a risk-free rate of 5%, ABC calculates an implied volatility for the S&P 500 of 21%. As the historical average volatility is 17%, with a standard deviation of 3% around that mean, it appears that the market is overvaluing the March option. ABC decides to overwrite 25% of XYZ's common stock portfolio, or $75 million. ABC sells 790 contracts and receives $1 935 500 in premiums, equal to .65% of XYZ's total common stock portfolio's value. Three months later, implied volatilities have declined to 18% and the S&P 500 has risen in value to 980, still below the exercise price of the option, which expires worthless. ABC chooses not to roll over the option and to let the portfolio remain unwritten for the time being. Consequently, the option overwriting program has boosted the return on XYZ's portfolio by .65%.

The biggest risk to an options overwriting program is that the stock market rises sharply for an extended period of time. The relatively small amount of premium income can quickly be overwhelmed by the losses incurred when the market moves against the overwriting strategy. In fact, that situation occurred in the mid-1990s. Option overwriting strategies generally worked well from 1990 through 1994, when the market had several down or modestly positive return years. The success of those strategies led a number of institutional investors to enter into option overwriting programs. Overwritten assets in the US were estimated to be over $17 billion at their peak in 1995. However, these programs generally produced disappointing results as stock prices rose sharply from 1995 through 1997. As a result, most of the institutional investors who had entered into option overwriting in the early 1990s had abandoned the strategy by 1997. In hindsight, one is left to conclude that many of these investors either did not understand the risk-reward tradeoffs involved in option overwriting or overestimated the active management skills of overwriting managers.

The excess of the price of a call or a put over this intrinsic value is the option's time value (or time premium). As shown for calls and puts in panels (a) and (b) of Figure 19.3, respectively, the time value is 0 at expiration. However, Figures 19.6 and 19.8 show that the time value is generally positive before expiration. Note that an option's premium is simply the sum of its intrinsic value and its time value.

▶ Put-call Parity

Consider a put and a call on the same underlying stock that have the same exercise price and expiration date. It was shown in equation (19.9) that their market prices should be related, with the nature of the relationship known as put-call parity. This relationship, however, is valid only for European options on non-dividend-paying stocks.

Equation (19.9) can be rearranged to estimate the value of European put options:

$$P_p = P_c + \frac{E}{e^{RT}} - P_s \qquad (19.16)$$

Thus, the value of a put can be estimated by using either the BOPM or the Black-Scholes formula to estimate the value of a matching call option, then adding an amount equal to the present value of the exercise price to this estimate, and finally subtracting from this sum an amount that is equal to the current market price of the underlying common stock.

For example, consider a put option that expires in three months and has an exercise price of $40, while the current market price and the risk of the underlying common stock are $36 and 50%, respectively. Assuming that the risk-free rate is 5%, it was shown earlier that the Black-Scholes estimate of the value for a matching call option was $2.26. Because the 5% risk-free rate is a continuously compounded rate, the present value of the exercise price is equal to $40/($e^{.05 \times .25}$) = $39.50. At this point, since it has been determined that P_c = $2.26, E/e^{RT} = $39.50, and P_s = $36, equation (19.16) can be used to estimate the value of the put option as $2.26 + $39.50 − $36 = $5.76.

Alternatively, the Black-Scholes formula for estimating the value of a call given in equation (19.10) can be substituted for P_c in equation (19.16). After simplifying, the equation can be used directly for estimating the value of a put:

$$P_p = \frac{E}{e^{RT}} N(-d_2) - P_s N(-d_1) \tag{19.17}$$

where d_1 and d_2 are given in equations (19.11) and (19.12a), respectively.

In the previous example, d_1 = −.25 and d_2 = −.50; thus $N(-d_1)$ = $N(.25)$ = .5987 and $N(-d_2)$ = $N(.50)$ = .6915. Applying equation (19.17), the value of this put can be estimated directly:

$$P_p = \left(\frac{\$40}{e^{.05 \times .25}} \times .6915 \right) - (\$36 \times .5987)$$
$$= \$27.31 - \$21.55 = \$5.76$$

which is the same estimated value as indicated earlier when equation (19.16) was used.

▸ Static Analysis

Close scrutiny of the put-call parity equation reveals some interesting features of European put option pricing. In particular, the value of a put option is dependent on the values of the same five inputs used for call valuation—the market price of the common stock P_s, the exercise price of the option E, the length of time until the expiration date T, the risk-free rate R, and the risk of the common stock σ. What happens to the value of a put option when one of these inputs is changed while the other four remain the same?

1. The higher the price of the underlying stock P_s, the lower the value of the put option.
2. The higher the exercise price E, the higher the value of the put option.
3. Generally, the longer the time to the expiration date T, the higher the value of the put option.
4. The higher the risk-free rate R, the lower the value of the put option.
5. The greater the risk σ of the common stock, the higher the value of the put option.

The relationships for the underlying stock price P_s, exercise price E, and risk-free rate R are in the opposite direction from those shown earlier for call options, while the relationships for the time to the expiration date T and risk σ are in the same direction. It should be noted that exceptions can occur with T when the put is deep in the money. In such a situation a longer time to expiration could actually decrease the value of the put.

▸ Early Exercise and Dividends

Equations (19.16) and (19.17) apply to a European put on a stock that will not pay dividends prior to the option's expiration. As with call options, it is straightforward to handle European puts if there are dividends that will be paid on the underlying common stock during the option's life, provided they can be accurately forecast. All that needs to be done is to follow the same procedure as described earlier for calls: reduce the current stock price by the present value of the dividends that are to be paid during the option's life, and then use this adjusted price in the Black-Scholes put option formula along with the other inputs. However, complications arise when it is recognized that most put options are American, meaning that they can be exercised before expiration, and that often dividends on the underlying common stock will be paid before the expiration date.

Consider first the ability to exercise a put option at any time up to its expiration date. Earlier it was shown that if there were no dividends on the underlying stock, then a call option was worth more "alive" than "dead," meaning that call options should not be exercised prior to expiration. Such an argument does *not* hold for put options.

Specifically, if a put option is in the money, meaning that the market price of the stock is less than the exercise price, then the investor may want to exercise the put option. In doing so, the investor will receive an additional amount of cash equal to $E - P_s$. In turn, this cash can be invested at the risk-free rate to earn money over the remaining life of the option. Because these earnings may be greater than any additional profits received by the investor if the put option were held, it may be advantageous to exercise the put early and thereby receive the earnings.

An example can be used to illustrate the point. Consider a put option on Widget that has a year left until its expiration date. The exercise price on the put is $100, and the annual risk-free rate is 10%. Imagine that the stock price of Widget is now at $5 per share, having recently plunged in value. If an investor owned such a deep-in-the-money option, it would be in his best interest to exercise it immediately. The logic is as follows.

The intrinsic value of the put is currently $100 − $5 = $95, indicating that if the put is exercised immediately, the buyer will receive $95. That is, the buyer will spend $5 to buy a share of Widget and then turn the share and the put over to the writer in return for the exercise price of $100. The net cash inflow to the put buyer of $95 could be invested in the risk-free asset so that in one year it would be worth $95 × 1.10 = $104.50. Alternatively, if the put is held, what is the best that the buyer can hope to earn at year-end? If the stock price of Widget drops to $0, the buyer will receive $100 at expiration from the put writer. Clearly the buyer would be better off exercising the put now instead of holding onto it. Hence, early exercise is merited in such a situation.

What will happen to the market price of the put in such a situation? In equilibrium it will be equal to the put's intrinsic value $E - P_s$ (in this instance, $95). Hence, the put's time premium would be zero, because nobody would pay more than the intrinsic value for the put, knowing that they could get a better return by investing in the risk-free asset. In addition, nobody would be willing to sell a put for less than its intrinsic value because this would open up the opportunity for immediately earning risk-free profits by purchasing the put and exercising it right away. Therefore, the only price that the put could sell for would be its intrinsic value.

Consider next the impact of dividends on put valuation. Previously it was shown that the owner of a call may find it optimal to exercise just *before* an ex-dividend date, as doing so allowed the investor to receive the forthcoming dividends on the stock. With respect to a put, the owner may find it optimal to exercise just *after* the ex-dividend date, as the corresponding drop in the stock price will cause the value of the put to rise.[19]

[19]See Robert Geske and Kuldeep Shastri, "The Early Exercise of American Puts," *Journal of Banking and Finance* 9, no. 2 (June 1985): 207–219.

Index Options

Not all options are written on individual issues of common stock. In recent years many new options have been created that have as an underlying asset something other than the stock of a particular company. One of them—index options—is discussed here. The appendix discusses others, while the next chapter discusses what are known as futures options.

Cash Settlement

Inco
www.incoltd.com

A call option on Inco stock is a relatively simple instrument. Upon exercise, the call buyer literally calls away 100 shares of Inco stock. The call writer is expected to physically deliver the shares. In practice, both the buyer and the writer may find it advantageous to close their positions in order to avoid the costs associated with the physical transfer of shares. In this event the buyer may expect a gain (and the seller a loss) approximately equal to the difference between the current market price of the security and the option's exercise price, with a net gain equal to this amount less the premium that was paid to purchase the call.

It would be entirely feasible to use only a "cash settlement" procedure upon expiration for any option contract. Here, the writer would be required to pay the buyer an amount equal to the difference between the current price of the security and the call option's exercise price (provided that the current price is larger than the exercise price). Similarly for puts, the writer could be expected to pay the buyer an amount equal to the difference between the option's exercise price and the current market price (provided that the exercise price is larger than the current price).

Although listed options on individual securities retain the obligation to "deliver," the realization that cash settlement can serve as a substitute has allowed the creation of index options.

The Contract

An index option is based on the level of an index of stock prices and thus allows investors to take positions in the market that the index represents. Some indices are designed to reflect movements in the stock market, broadly construed. Other "specialized" indices are intended to capture changes in the fortunes of particular industries or sectors. Some of the indices are highly specialized, consisting of only a few stocks. Others are broadly representative of major portions of the stock market.

In Canada the only index options traded are those based on the Toronto 35 Index that was designed by the TSE in 1987 specifically for trading derivative securities (i.e., predominantly options and futures). These are European options that can only be exercised on the expiry date—the third Friday of the expiry month. The companies included in this index are among the largest listed firms with the most heavily traded issues on the TSE. Trading details for these options, identified as TSE 35 Index, are included with other CDCC options in Figure 19.2.

Contracts for index options are not stated in terms of numbers of shares. Instead, the size of a contract is determined as the product of the level of the index and a multiplier specified by the exchange on which the option is traded. The premium (price) of an index option times the applicable multiplier indicates the total amount paid.

For example, on October 28, 1998, the call option on the TSE 35 Index with an exercise price of $330 (when the index was at $331.42) that expires in December had an indicated premium of $16.15. Since the multiplier for TSE 35 option contracts is 100, an investor has to pay $16.15 \times 100 = \$1615$ (plus a commission) for this contract.

Subsequently, the investor could either exercise or sell the contract for its cash settlement value. Suppose that, at the end of November the TSE 35 is at 360, then the investor could exercise the call and receive its intrinsic value of $(360 - 330) \times 100 = \$3000$.

Alternatively, the investor could simply sell the contract on the exchange and could expect to receive an amount greater than $3000 because it would sell for a price that is equal to the sum of its intrinsic value and its time value (see Figure 19.6).

A related contract is the *Toronto 35 Index Participation Option* (TIPS 35 Options). TIPS 35s (described in Chapter 14) are in effect units of a fund, managed by the TSE, that mimics the TSE 35 Index. These units and their related options are traded on the exchange. The price of a TIPS 35 unit is approximately 1/10 of the value of the index. These options are treated in the same way as ordinary stock options and their trading details are shown in Figure 19.2. TIPS 100 options are also traded, but typically have low volume and open interest.

Flex Options

In an effort to counteract the growing off-exchange market for customized call and put options in the US, the Chicago Board Options Exchange (CBOE) has recently started to list "flexible option contracts," called "flex options" for short. These contracts are on indices, and they allow an investor (typically an institution) to specify the exercise price and expiration date. In addition, the investor can specify whether the option is American (exercisable at any time) or European (exercisable only at expiration). Once the investor places the order, it is executed on the CBOE, where someone else takes the other side of the contract. Because the OCC is in the middle between the buyer and the writer, there is little risk of default on the contract. This is an advantage to these customized options, since options created off-exchange (say between investors A and B) are only as good as the creditworthiness of the parties themselves. (The possibility that the writer of one of these off-exchange options may default on his obligations is referred to as **counterparty risk**.[20])

Counterparty Risk The risk posed by the possibility that the person or organization with which an investor has entered into a financial arrangement may fail to make required payments.

Portfolio Insurance

Portfolio Insurance An investment strategy designed to guarantee a minimum rate of return while allowing the investor to benefit substantially from the positive returns generated by an investment in a risky portfolio.

In the mid-1980s one of the more popular uses of options, procuring **portfolio insurance**, was developed. This is a way of synthetically creating a put on a given portfolio. Consider an investor who holds a highly diversified portfolio. This investor would like to be able to benefit from any upward movements that may subsequently occur in the stock market but would also like to be protected from any downward movements.[21] There are, in principle, at least two ways this might be accomplished.[22]

Purchase a Protective Put

Assume that the investor's portfolio is currently worth $100 000 and that a put option is available on a stock market index that closely resembles the investor's portfolio. The kinked line *ADE* in Figure 19.9(a) shows the value to a buyer of such a put at the expiration date, where the put has an exercise price of $100 000 [note how it corresponds to part (b) in

---

[20]For a discussion of how the possibility of default by the writer affects the prices of such options, see Herb Johnson and Rene Stulz, "The Pricing of Options with Default Risk," *Journal of Finance 42*, no. 2 (June 1987): 267–280.

[21]In an efficient market, investors with "average" attitudes towards risk should not purchase portfolio insurance. Those who are especially averse to "downside risk" (relative to "upside potential") may find it useful to buy insurance. The key is the nature of the investor's attitudes towards risk and return. See Hayne E. Leland, "Who Should Buy Portfolio Insurance?" *Journal of Finance* 35, no. 2 (May 1980): 581–594.

[22]Some people would argue that the use of stop orders or getting an insurance company to sell the investor a policy represent two other ways.

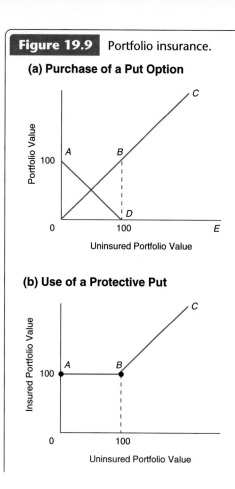

Figure 19.9 Portfolio insurance.

(a) Purchase of a Put Option

Portfolio Value

Uninsured Portfolio Value

(b) Use of a Protective Put

Insured Portfolio Value

Uninsured Portfolio Value

Figure 19.3]. Line $0BC$ is the value of the portfolio on the expiration date, assuming that the put was not purchased.

What would happen to an investor who (1) held the portfolio and (2) purchased this put? Figure 19.9(b) shows the answer. The value of the portfolio (ABC) is simply the sum of the values $0BC$ and ADE shown in Figure 19.9(a).

In this case the purchase of a put provides protection against declines in portfolio value. In this role it is termed a protective put (or "married put"). In practice, stock indices may not closely correspond with an investor's portfolio.

Thus, the purchase of a put on a stock index may provide only imperfect insurance. In a graph such as that shown in Figure 19.9(b), the resulting curve would be somewhat fuzzy owing to the possible divergence of values of the portfolio and the index. For example, the portfolio may decline in value by $25 000 whereas the index declines only by $10 000. In this case the portfolio would be insured for only $10 000/$25 000 = 40% of its decline in value.

What if neither explicit insurance nor an appropriate put were available? Can something still be done to insure the portfolio's value against market declines? Yes, if the allocation of funds between the portfolio and a riskless security can be altered frequently enough (and at reasonable cost). This type of portfolio insurance involves the creation of a **synthetic put**, and its application involves the use of a dynamic strategy for asset allocation, which will be discussed next.

Synthetic Put A form of portfolio insurance that emulates the investment outcomes of a put option through the use of a dynamic asset allocation strategy.

Create a Synthetic Put

Insuring a portfolio by creating a synthetic put can most easily be described with an example.[23] Assume that the investor has $100 000 and is considering the purchase of a portfolio of common stocks. It is believed that the market value of this portfolio will either increase to $125 000 or decrease to $80 000 in six months. If it does increase to $125 000, then it will end up being worth either $156 250 or $100 000 after another six months. Alternatively, if it decreases to $80 000, then it will subsequently end up being worth either $100 000 or $64 000. Each one of these possible "states of nature" is indicated by a letter in Figure 19.10(a), with the current state being denoted as state A.

Figure 19.10(a) also shows two sets of terminal portfolio values (that is, portfolio values after 12 months) on the assumption that the common stock portfolio is purchased. The first set gives the values of the portfolio if it is uninsured. The second shows the desired portfolio values—that is, the values of an insured portfolio. In this example the investor wants to be certain that the ending portfolio is worth at least $100 000, while also being able to earn the returns associated with state D, should that state occur.[24]

What should the investor do initially in order to be certain of this? Clearly, the investor cannot simply purchase the portfolio of stocks because the portfolio could be worth only $64 000 if state G occurs. However, the investor could consider purchasing portfolio insurance—that is, creating a synthetic put—by investing in both the stock portfolio and risk-free bonds.

The way this is done is to imagine that six months have passed and that state B has occurred. In this situation, how might one be certain to have $156 250 if the final state is D and $100 000 if the state is E? The answer is simple—if state B occurs, make sure that the portfolio at that point is worth $125 000. Thus, an initial investment strategy is required that will provide $125 000 if the six-month state turns out to be state B.

It is also possible that after the first six months state C will occur. In this situation, how might one be certain to have $100 000 regardless of the final state? Assuming that risk-free bonds return 5% (compounded discretely) per six months, the investor should purchase $100 000/1.05 = $95 238 of these bonds if state C occurs. This means that an initial investment strategy is required that will provide $95 238 if the six-month state turns out to be state C.

Figure 19.10(b) shows the investments and the amounts required in situations B and C. It remains only to determine an appropriate initial set of investments (at point A).

An amount of $1 invested in the common stock portfolio at A will grow to $1.25 after six months if the state at that time is B. More generally, s invested in the common stock portfolio at A will grow to 1.25s if the six-month state is B. Similarly, b invested in bonds at A will grow to 1.05b after six months. Thus, a set of initial investments that will provide $125 000 if state B occurs can be found by solving the following equation for s and b:

$$1.25s + 1.05b = \$125\ 000 \tag{19.18}$$

---

[23]For an exposition, see Mark Rubinstein and Hayne E. Leland, "Replicating Options with Positions in Stock and Cash," *Financial Analysts Journal* 37, no. 4 (July–August 1981): 63–72; Mark Rubinstein, "Alternative Paths to Portfolio Insurance," *Financial Analysts Journal* 41, no. 4 (July–August 1985): 42–52; Robert Ferguson, "How to Beat the S&P 500 (Without Losing Sleep)," *Financial Analysts Journal* 42, no. 2 (March–April 1986): 37–46; and Thomas J. O'Brien, "The Mechanics of Portfolio Insurance," *Journal of Portfolio Management* 14, no. 3 (Spring 1988): 40–47.

[24]In this example, portfolio insurance is sought for a one-year horizon with a floor of 0% (meaning that the investor does not want to lose any of the initial investment over the next 12 months). Other horizons and floors, such as a two-year horizon with a floor of –5% (meaning that the investor does not want to lose more than 5% of the initial investment over the next 24 months), are possible. Note the parallel to the discussion of the BOPM, which provides a theoretical basis for the development of portfolio insurance.

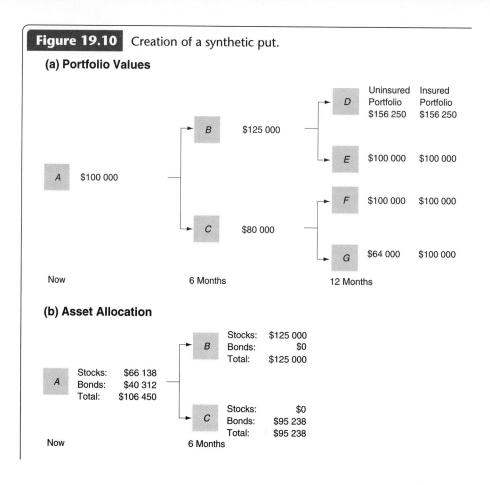

Figure 19.10 Creation of a synthetic put.

(a) Portfolio Values

		Uninsured Portfolio	Insured Portfolio
D		$156 250	$156 250
E		$100 000	$100 000
F		$100 000	$100 000
G		$64 000	$100 000

B $125 000

C $80 000

A $100 000

Now   6 Months   12 Months

(b) Asset Allocation

B — Stocks: $125 000 / Bonds: $0 / Total: $125 000

A — Stocks: $66 138 / Bonds: $40 312 / Total: $106 450

C — Stocks: $0 / Bonds: $95 238 / Total: $95 238

Now   6 Months

If the six-month state is C, then s invested in the common stock portfolio will be worth $.8s$, while b invested in bonds will be worth $1.05b$. Thus a set of initial investments that will provide $95 238 if state C occurs can be found by solving the following equation for s and b:

$$.8s + 1.05b = \$95\ 238 \qquad (19.19)$$

Solutions for s and b can now be found because there are two equations and two unknowns. The solution, shown in Figure 19.10(b), is that the investor should initially put $66 138 in common stocks and $40 312 in bonds (that is, $s = \$66\ 138$ and $b = \$40\ 312$), for a total initial investment of $66 138 + $40 312 = $106 450.

Making this initial investment is equivalent to investing $100 000 in the common stock portfolio and buying a protective put option (or an insurance policy) for $6450. Indeed, this analysis could be used to determine the appropriate price for such an option or insurance policy. Equivalently, the actions of the investor have resulted in the creation of a synthetic put where the stocks being held are the underlying asset.

By design, this initial investment will provide precisely the desired ending values, but only if the "mix" is altered as values change. The goal is achieved by using a *dynamic strategy* in which investments are bought and sold at intermediate points, depending on the returns of the underlying assets.

In the example, if state B occurs, the stocks will be worth $66 138 × 1.25 = $82 672, and the bonds will be worth $40 312 × 1.05 = $42 328, for an aggregate value of $125 000. In this situation the $42 328 of bonds would be sold and the proceeds used to make an additional investment in the common stock portfolio so that the investor is entirely invested in common stocks for the last six months.

However, if state C occurs, the stocks will be worth $66\ 138 \times .8 = \$52\ 910$, and the bonds will be worth $40\ 312 \times 1.05 = \$42\ 328$, for an aggregate value of $95 238. In this situation the $52 910 of stocks would be sold and the proceeds used to make an additional investment in the risk-free bonds for the last six months.

Thus, more money is invested in common stocks if the initial portfolio rises in value, with the money obtained by selling bonds. However, if the initial portfolio falls in value, more money is invested in bonds, with the money obtained by selling stocks. In this example, the percentage invested in stocks is initially $66 138/$106 450 = 62.13% and subsequently goes to either 100% (if stocks go up) or 0% (if stocks go down) with the reverse happening to the initial 37.87% investment in bonds.

More realistic applications involve many time intervals within the one-year period, with smaller stock price movements in each interval. Consequently there would be more changes in the mix of stocks and bonds after each interval, but the changes would be of smaller magnitude. Nevertheless, the essential nature of the strategy would be the same:

> *When stock prices rise, sell some bonds and buy more stocks.*
> *When stock prices fall, sell some stocks and buy more bonds.*

Computers are often used to monitor stock price movements of investors who have obtained portfolio insurance in this manner. When these movements are of sufficient magnitude, the computer is used to place the requisite buy and sell orders electronically. Because much of this monitoring and ordering is programmed into a computer, portfolio insurance is often referred to as a form of **program trading**.[25]

Program Trading The purchase or sale of a collection of securities as if the collection were one security. Program trades are predominantly employed in portfolio insurance and index arbitrage strategies.

If there are only two states of nature in each interval, and reallocation is possible after every interval, and there are no transaction costs, then the values associated with any desired "insured portfolio" can be replicated exactly with a dynamic strategy. In practice, however, the results are likely to be only approximately equal. First, there are transaction costs associated with buying and selling securities for the dynamic strategy.[26] Second, if an interval is defined as a length of time over which only two alternative states may occur, then the amount of time to an interval may be so short that reallocation is impossible after each interval.

In practice, arbitrary rules are applied to avoid frequent revisions and the associated transaction costs while being reasonably certain of providing the portfolio with the desired level of insurance.[27] Unfortunately, these arbitrary rules did not work very well on Black Monday and Terrible Tuesday (October 19 and 20, 1987). During these two days stock prices moved downward so fast that reallocation could not be performed in a timely fashion, resulting in a situation where portfolio insurance did not provide the anticipated protection. As a result, dynamic strategies have been used much less frequently, and to some extent have been replaced by index puts.[28]

---

[25]The next chapter discusses another form of program trading that is known as index arbitrage.

[26]There is another dynamic strategy for insuring the portfolio that is often preferred because it has smaller transaction costs. It involves index futures, which are a type of financial contract that is discussed in the next chapter. For a survey of dynamic trading strategies, see Robert R. Trippi and Richard B. Harriff, "Dynamic Asset Allocation Rules: Survey and Synthesis," *Journal of Portfolio Management* 17, no. 4 (Summer 1991): 19–26.

[27]For a discussion of transaction costs, see John E. Gilster, Jr., and William Lee, "The Effects of Transactions Costs and Different Borrowing and Lending Rates on the Option Pricing Model: A Note," *Journal of Finance* 39, no. 4 (September 1984): 1215–1222; Hayne E. Leland, "Option Pricing and Replication with Transactions Costs," *Journal of Finance* 40, no. 5 (December 1985): 1283–1301; Fischer Black and Robert Jones, "Simplifying Portfolio Insurance," *Journal of Portfolio Management* 14, no. 1 (Fall 1987): 48–51; and Phelim P. Boyle and Ton Vorst, "Option Replication in Discrete Time with Transactions Costs," *Journal of Finance* 47, no. 1 (March 1992): 271–293.

[28]See Mark Rubinstein, "Portfolio Insurance and the Market Crash," *Financial Analysts Journal* 44, no. 1 (January–February 1988): 38–47. For a discussion of various types of dynamic strategies, see André F. Perold and William F. Sharpe, "Dynamic Strategies for Asset Allocation," *Financial Analysts Journal* 44, no. 1 (January–February 1988): 16–27; and Philip H. Dybvig, "Inefficient Dynamic Portfolio Strategies or How to Throw Away a Million Dollars in the Stock Market," *Review of Financial Studies* 1, no. 1 (Spring 1988): 67–88.

Summary

1. An option is a contract between two investors that grants one investor the right (but not the obligation) to sell to or buy from the other investor a specific asset at a specific price within a specific time period.

2. A call option for a stock gives the buyer the right to buy a specific number of shares of a specific company from the option writer at a specific purchase price at any time up to and including a specific date.

3. A put option for a stock gives the buyer the right to sell a specific number of shares of a specific company to the option writer at a specific selling price at any time up to and including a specific date.

4. Option trading is facilitated by standardized contracts traded on organized exchanges. These exchanges employ the services of a clearing corporation, which maintains records of all trades and acts as a buyer from all option writers and a writer to all option buyers.

5. Option writers are required to deposit margin to ensure performance of their obligations. The amount and form of the margin will depend on the particular option strategy involved.

6. The intrinsic value of a call option equals the difference between the stock's price and the option's exercise price, if this difference is positive. Otherwise the option's intrinsic value is zero.

7. The intrinsic value of a put option equals the difference between its exercise price and the stock's price, if this difference is positive. Otherwise, the option's intrinsic value is zero.

8. Calls and puts will not sell for less than their intrinsic values. However, they may sell for more than their intrinsic values owing to their time values.

9. The binomial option pricing model can be used to determine the fair value of an option based on the assumption that the underlying asset will attain one of two possible known prices at the end of each of a finite number of periods, given its price at the start of each period.

10. An option's hedge ratio indicates the change in the option's value resulting from a one-dollar change in the value of the underlying asset.

11. The Black-Scholes option valuation model shows that the fair value of an option is determined by five factors: the market price of the stock, the exercise price, the life of the option, the risk-free rate, and the risk of the common stock. It assumes that the risk-free rate and common stock risk are constant over the option's life.

12. Put-call parity states that buying both a put option on a stock and a share of the stock will produce the same payoff as buying both a call option on the stock and a risk-free bond (assuming that both options have the same exercise price and expiration date).

13. In addition to put and call options on individual common stocks, options on other assets are traded, such as options on stock indices, debt instruments, and foreign currency.

14. Synthetic options can be created by holding the underlying asset and a risk-free asset in relative amounts that vary with the market price of the underlying asset.

SECURITIES WITH OPTIONLIKE FEATURES

Many securities have features that are similar to stock options, particularly call options. In some cases the optionlike features are explicit. Examples include options on stock market indices (discussed earlier in the chapter), debt instruments, and foreign currencies.[29] These options let investors take positions based on their forecasts of movements of the stock market, interest rates, and foreign exchange rates. In other cases more subtle optionlike features are involved. This appendix discusses some of these securities.

Warrants

A stock purchase warrant (or, more simply, a warrant) is a call option issued by the firm whose stock serves as the underlying security. At the time of issue, a warrant usually has a longer time to expiration (for example, five or more years) than a typical call option. Some perpetual warrants, with no expiration date, have also been issued. Generally, warrants may be exercised before expiration—that is, they are like American call options—but some require an initial waiting period.

The exercise price may be fixed, or it may change during the life of the warrant, usually increasing in steps. The initial exercise price is typically set to exceed the market price of the underlying security at the time the warrant is issued, often by a substantial amount.

At the time of issue, one warrant typically entitles the holder to purchase one share of stock for the appropriate exercise price. However, most warrants are protected against stock splits and stock dividends. This means that any warrant with such protection will enable the investor to buy more or less than one share at an altered exercise price if a stock dividend or stock split is declared. For example, a two-for-one stock split would allow the warrant holder to purchase two shares at one-half the original exercise price, whereas a one-for-two reverse stock split would allow the warrant holder to purchase one-half share at twice the original exercise price.

Warrants may be distributed to shareholders in lieu of a stock or cash dividend or sold directly as a new security issue. Alternatively, warrants may be issued in order to "sweeten" an offering of some other kind of security. For example, a bond may be sold by the firm with warrants attached to it. In some cases, the warrants are nondetachable, except upon exercise. This means that if an investor wants to sell one of the bonds, the warrants must be either exercised or sold with the bond. In other cases the warrants are detachable, meaning that after the initial sale of the bonds an investor may sell either the bonds or the warrants (or both).

Terms associated with a warrant are contained in a warrant agreement, which serves the same function as an indenture for a bond issue. In this agreement the scope of the warrant holder's protection is defined (for example, the treatment of warrants in the event of a merger). It may also specify certain restrictions on corporate behaviour.

Some warrants that are issued with bonds have an additional attribute. Although they may be detached and exercised by paying cash to the corporation, an alternative method of

---

[29]See the textbooks cited at the end of the chapter for more on these types of options. For more on foreign exchange options, see Ian Giddy, "The Foreign Exchange Option as a Hedging Tool," *Midland Corporate Finance Journal* 1, no. 3 (Fall 1983): 32–42; Niso Abauf, "Foreign Exchange Options: The Leading Hedge," *Midland Corporate Finance Journal* 5, no. 2 (Summer 1987): 51–58; and Mark Kritzman, "About Option Replication," *Financial Analysts Journal* 48, no. 1 (January–February 1992): 21–23.

payment is provided. This alternative allows bonds from the initial issue to be used in lieu of cash to pay the exercise price, with the bonds being valued at par for this purpose.

One difference between warrants and call options is the limitation on the amount of warrants that are outstanding. A specific number of warrants of a particular type will be issued. The total generally cannot be increased, and typically will be reduced as the warrants are exercised. In contrast, a call option can be created whenever two people wish to create one. Thus, the number outstanding is not fixed. Exercise of a call option on its stock has no more effect on a corporation than a transaction in its stock on the secondary market. However, the exercise of a warrant does have an effect. In particular, it leaves the corporation with more cash, fewer warrants outstanding, and more stock outstanding.

Warrants are traded on major stock exchanges and on the over-the-counter market. Quotations for those with active markets are provided in the financial press in the sections devoted primarily to stocks.

Rights

A right is similar to a warrant in that it also is like a call option issued by the firm whose stock serves as the underlying security. Rights, also known as subscription warrants, are issued to give existing shareholders their preemptive right to subscribe to a new issue of common stock before the general public is given an opportunity. Each share receives one right. A stated number of rights plus cash equal to a specified subscription price are required in order to obtain one new share. To ensure the sale of the new stock, the subscription price is usually set below the stock's market price at the time the rights are issued. This does not mean that new subscribers get a bargain, as they must pay old shareholders for the required number of rights, which become valuable as a result.

Rights generally have short lives (from 2 to 10 weeks when issued) and may be freely traded prior to exercise. Up to a specified date, old shares of the stock trade *cum rights*, meaning that the buyer of the stock is entitled to receive the rights when issued. Afterward the stock trades *ex rights* at a correspondingly lower price. Rights for popular issues of stock are sometimes traded on exchanges; others are available in the over-the-counter market. Often trading begins prior to actual availability, with the rights sold for delivery on a *when-issued* basis.

A right is, in effect, a warrant, although one with a rather short time before expiration. It also differs with regard to exercise price, which is typically set above the stock's market price at issuance for a warrant and below it for a right. Because of their short lives, rights need not be protected against stock splits and stock dividends. Otherwise they have all the attributes of a warrant and can be valued in a similar manner.[30]

Bond Call Provisions

Many firms issue bonds with call provisions that allow the firm to repurchase the bonds before maturity, usually at a price above par value. This amounts to the simultaneous sale of a straight bond and purchase of a call option that is paid by the corporation in the form of a relatively lower selling price for the bond. The writer of the option is the bond purchaser.

---

[30]Rights are also discussed in Chapter 16. Valuation of rights is relatively simple if it is assumed that there is no chance that they will end up being out of the money on the expiration date and the time value of money is ignored (meaning that the risk-free rate is assumed to be zero).

Bond call provisions usually can be exercised only after some specified date (for example, five years after issue). Moreover, the exercise price, known as the call premium, may be different for different exercise dates (typically shrinking in size the longer the bond is outstanding). The implicit call option associated with such a bond is thus both longer lived and more complex than those traded on the listed option markets.[31]

Convertible Securities

A particularly popular financial instrument is a security that can be converted into a different security of the same firm under certain conditions. The typical case involves a bond or a preferred share convertible into shares of the firm's common stock, with a stated number of shares received for each bond or preferred share. Usually no cash is involved: the old security is simply traded in, and the appropriate number of new securities is issued in return. Convertible preferred shares are issued from time to time, but like other preferred shares, tax effects make them attractive primarily to corporate investors. For other investors many issues of convertible bonds are more attractive.

If a $1000 par-value bond can be converted into 20 common shares, the *conversion ratio* is 20. Alternatively, the *conversion price* may be said to be $1000/20 = $50, because $50 of the bond's par value must be given up to obtain one common share. Neither the conversion ratio nor the conversion price is affected by changes in a bond's market value.

Conversion ratios are typically set so that conversion will not prove attractive unless the stock price increases substantially from its value at the time the convertible security was first issued. This is similar to the general practice used in setting exercise prices for warrants.

A convertible bond's *conversion value*, obtained by multiplying the conversion ratio by the stock's current market price, is the value that would be obtained by conversion; it is the bond's current "value as stock." The *conversion premium* is the amount by which the bond's current market price exceeds its conversion value, expressed as a percent of the latter. A related amount is the convertible's *investment value*. This value is an estimate—based on the convertible's maturity date, coupon rate, and credit rating—of the amount for which the bond might sell if it were not convertible. Equivalently, it is the convertible's "value as a straight bond."

Consider a $1000 par-value bond convertible into 20 shares of stock. If the market price of the shares is $60 per share, then the conversion value of the bond is $60 × 20 = $1200. If the current market price of the convertible bond is $1300, then its conversion premium is $1300 − $1200 = $100. Its investment value might be estimated to be, say, $950, meaning that the bond would sell for this much if it did not provide the investor with the option of convertibility.

Convertible securities of great complexity can be found in the marketplace. Some may be converted only after an initial waiting period. Some may be converted up to the bond's maturity date; others, only for a stated, shorter period. Some have different conversion ratios for different years. A few can be converted into packages of two or more different securities; others require the additional payment of cash upon conversion.

Convertible bonds are usually protected against stock splits and stock dividends via adjustments in the conversion ratio. For example, a bond with an initial conversion ratio of 20 could be adjusted to have a ratio of 22 following a 10% stock dividend. Protection against cash dividends is not generally provided, but some indentures require that the holders of convertible bonds be notified prior to payment of cash dividends so that they may convert before the resultant fall in the stock's market price.

---

[31]Bond call provisions are also discussed in Chapters 13 and 14.

Convertible securities often contain a call provision, which may be used by the corporation to force conversion when the stock's market price is sufficiently high to make the value of the shares obtained on conversion exceed the call price of the bond. For example, if the conversion value of the bond is $1200 (the bond is convertible into 20 shares of stock that are currently selling for $60 per share) and the call price is $1100, the firm can force conversion by calling the bond. This is because a bondholder faces two choices when the call is received—either convert and receive 20 shares collectively worth $1200 or receive cash of $1100—and should choose the shares because they have a higher value.

A convertible bond is, for practical purposes, a bond with nondetachable warrants plus the restriction that *only* the bond is usable (at par) to pay the exercise price. If the bond were not callable, the value of this package would equal the value of a straight non-callable bond (that is, the estimated investment value) plus that of the warrants. However, most convertible bonds are callable and thus involve a double option: the holder has an option to convert the bond to shares, and the issuing corporation has an option to buy the bond back from the investors.

QUESTIONS AND PROBLEMS

1. Why have organized options exchanges been so important to the growth in options trading?
2. How do organized options exchanges permit option buyers and writers to open and close positions without having to contact one another directly?
3. Consider the following stocks selling for the prices listed in the following table:

Stock	Current Price
A	$ 26
B	$ 73
C	$215

   Specify the likely exercise prices that will be set for newly created options on these stocks.
4. From the latest two consecutive issues of *The Globe and Mail: Report on Business*, find the price of the NorTel call option with the nearest expiration date and the exercise price closest to the current price of NorTel stock. What is the premium on the call option? What has been the percentage change in the option's price from the previous day? From another part of the *Report*, calculate the percentage change in the price of NorTel stock from the previous day. Compare this number to the option's percentage price change.
5. Draw a profit-loss graph for the following option strategies:
   a. Buy a put, $2 premium, $70 exercise price.
   b. Write a call, $3 premium, $40 exercise price.
   c. Buy a stock for $80 and buy a put on the same stock, $1 premium, $70 exercise price.
6. Elizabeth Stroud has only a few hours left to decide whether to exercise a call option on Carson Company stock. The call option has an exercise price of $54. Elizabeth originally purchased the call six months ago for $400 (or $4 per share).
   a. For what range of stock prices should Elizabeth exercise the call on the last day of the call's life?
   b. For what range of stock prices would Elizabeth realize a net loss (including the premium paid for the call)?
   c. If Elizabeth had purchased a put instead of a call, how would your answers to parts (a) and (b) change?

7. On November 18, three call options on Eden Prairie Associates stock, all expiring in December, sold for the following prices:

Exercise Price	Option Price
$50	7\frac{1}{2}$
$60	$3
$70	1\frac{1}{2}$

Fred Marberry is considering a "butterfly spread" that involves the following positions:
Buy one call at $50 exercise price.
Sell (write) two calls at $60 exercise price.
Buy one call at $70 exercise price.

a. What would be the values at expiration of Fred's spread if Eden Prairie Associates' stock price is below $50? Between $50 and $60? Between $60 and $70? Above $70?

b. What dollar investment would be required of Fred to establish the spread?

8. What is the time value of an option? Why does an option's time value decline as the option approaches expiration?

9. Shorewood Systems stock currently sells for $50 per share. One year from today the stock will be worth either $58.09 or $43.04. The continuously compounded risk-free rate is 5.13% for one year. Based on the binomial option pricing model, what is the fair value for a call option on Shorewood stock with one year to expiration and a $50 exercise price?

10. Hopkins Pharmaceuticals stock is currently priced at $40 per share. Six months from now its price will be either $44.21 or $36.19. If the price rises to $44.21, then six months later the price will be either $48.86 or $40. If, however, the price initially falls to $36.19, then six months later the price will be either $40 or $32.75. The risk-free rate (continuously compounded) is 3.05% over each six-month period. Using the binomial option pricing model, what is the fair value of a one-year call option on Hopkins stock?

11. Given the information below, calculate the three-month call option price that is consistent with the Black-Scholes model:

$$P_s = \$47, \qquad E = \$45, \qquad R = .05, \qquad \sigma = .40$$

12. If the premium on a call option has recently declined, does this indicate that the option is a better buy than it was previously? Why?

13. List the variables needed to estimate the value of a call option. Describe how changes in the values of these variables affect the value of a call option.

14. Calculate the hedge ratio of a call option for a stock with a current price of $40, an exercise price of $45, a standard deviation of 34%, and a time to expiration of six months, given a risk-free return of 7% per annum.

15. Using the Black-Scholes model, calculate the implicit volatility of a stock with a three-month call option currently selling for $8.54 and:

$$P_s = \$83, \qquad E = \$80, \qquad R = .05$$

16. Amir Gutman owns 20 000 shares of Merrimac Monitoring Equipment stock. This stock makes up the bulk of Amir's wealth. Concerned about the stock's near-term prospects, Amir wishes to fully hedge the risk of the stock. Given a hedge ratio of .37 and a premium of $2.50 for the near Merrimac put option, how many put options should Amir buy?

17. A six-month call option with an exercise price of $40 is selling for $5. The current price of the stock is $41.25. The hedge ratio of the option is .65.

a. What percentage change in the option's price is likely to accompany a 1% change in the stock's price?

b. If the beta of the stock is 1.10, what is the beta of the option? (*Hint*: Recall what the beta of a stock implies about the relationship between the stock's price and that of the market.)

18. The fair value of a three-month call option on Portage Industries stock is $1.50. The exercise price of the call option is $30. The risk-free rate is 5%, and the stock price of Portage is currently $28 per share. What is the fair value of a three-month put option on Portage stock with the same exercise price as the call option?

19. Given the following information, calculate the three-month put option price that is consistent with the Black-Scholes model:

$$P_s = \$32, \qquad E = \$45, \qquad R = .06, \qquad \sigma = .35$$

20. Explain why call options on non-dividend-paying stocks are "worth more alive than dead."

21. In February George Gardner sold a September 55 call on Dane Corporation stock for $4.375 per share and simultaneously bought a September 55 put on the same stock for $6 per share. At the time, Treasury bills coming due in September were priced to yield 12.6%, and Dane stock sold for $53 per share.
    a. What value would put-call parity suggest was appropriate for the Dane put?
    b. Dane was expected to make three dividend payments between February and September. Could that account for the discrepancy between your answer to part (a) and the actual price of the put? Why or why not?
    c. If Dane stock were to fall to a very low value before September, might it pay for George to exercise the put? Why?

22. Why does a stock index option sell at a lower price than the cost of a portfolio of options on the constituent stocks (assuming that the index call option and the portfolio of call options control the same dollar value of stocks)?

23. Distinguish between portfolio insurance implemented through a protective put and through dynamic asset allocation.

24. (Appendix Question) What is the primary advantage to an investor of a warrant compared to a call option?

25. (Appendix Question) Wheeling Corp. has a 10% subordinated convertible debenture outstanding, maturing in eight years. The bond's face value is $1000. It currently sells for 99% of par. The bond is convertible into 15 shares of common stock. The company's common stock currently sells for $50 per share. Nonconvertible bonds of similar risk have a yield of 12%.
    a. What is the bond's conversion value?
    b. What is the bond's conversion premium?
    c. What is the bond's investment value?

option (p. 585)
call option (p. 585)
exercise price (p. 585)
expiration date (p. 585)
premium (p. 586)
closing sale (p. 587)
closing purchase (p. 587)
put option (p. 588)
specialists (p. 590)
intrinsic value (p. 595)
straddle (p. 598)
covered call writing (p. 598)
European option (p. 599)

American option (p. 599)
hedge ratio (p. 602)
put-call parity (p. 605)
implicit volatility (p. 610)
at the money (p. 613)
out of the money (p. 613)
in the money (p. 613)
time value (p. 613)
counterparty risk (p. 621)
portfolio insurance (p. 621)
synthetic put (p. 622)
program trading (p. 625)

REFERENCES

1. Investment strategies involving options are discussed in many papers. Here are three of the most notable ones:

   Robert C. Merton, Myron S. Scholes, and Mathew L. Gladstein, "The Returns and Risk of Alternative Call Option Portfolio Investment Strategies," *Journal of Business* 51, no. 1 (April 1978): 183–242.

   Robert C. Merton, Myron S. Scholes, and Mathew L. Gladstein, "The Returns and Risk of Alternative Put-option Portfolio Investment Strategies," *Journal of Business* 55, no. 1 (January 1982): 1–55.

   Aimee Gerberg Ronn and Ehud I. Ronn, "The Box Spread Arbitrage Conditions: Theory, Tests, and Investment Strategies," *Review of Financial Studies* 2, no. 1 (1989): 91–107.

2. The binomial option pricing model was initially developed in:

   William F. Sharpe, *Investments* (Englewood Cliffs, NJ: Prentice Hall, 1978), Chapter 14.

3. A short while later the following two papers expanded upon Sharpe's model:

   John C. Cox, Stephen A. Ross, and Mark Rubinstein, "Option Pricing: A Simplified Approach," *Journal of Financial Economics* 7, no. 3 (September 1979): 229–263.

   Richard J. Rendleman, Jr., and Brit J. Bartter, "Two-state Option Pricing," *Journal of Finance* 34, no. 5 (December 1979): 1093–1110.

4. For more on the theory of binomial models, see:

   Daniel B. Nelson and Krishna Ramaswamy, "Simple Binomial Processes as Diffusion Approximations in Financial Models," *Review of Financial Studies* 3, no. 3 (1990): 393–430.

5. Two seminal papers on option pricing are:

   Robert C. Merton, "Theory of Rational Option Pricing," *Bell Journal of Economics and Management Science* 4, no. 1 (Spring 1973): 141–183.

   Fischer Black and Myron Scholes, "The Pricing of Options and Corporate Liabilities," *Journal of Political Economy* 81, no. 3 (May–June 1973): 637–654.

6. The Black-Scholes option pricing model assumes that the risk-free rate is constant over the life of the option. Four interesting papers that relax this assumption are:

Ramon Rabinovitch, "Pricing Stock and Bond Options When the Default-free Rate Is Stochastic," *Journal of Financial and Quantitative Analysis* 24, no. 4 (December 1989): 447–457.

Stuart M. Turnbull and Frank Milne, "A Simple Approach to Interest-rate Option Pricing," *Review of Financial Studies* 4, no. 1 (1991): 87–121.

Jason Z. Wei, "Valuing American Equity Options with a Stochastic Interest Rate: A Note," *Journal of Financial Engineering* 2, no. 2 (June 1993): 195–206.

T. S. Ho, Richard C. Stapleton, and Marti G. Subrahmanyam, "The Valuation of American Options with Stochastic Interest Rates: A Generalization of the Geske-Johnson Technique," *Journal of Finance* 52, no. 2 (June 1997): 827–840.

7. The Black-Scholes model also assumes that the volatility of the underlying asset is constant over the life of the option. For papers that relax this assumption, see:

John Hull and Alan White, "The Pricing of Options on Assets with Stochastic Volatilities," *Journal of Finance* 42, no. 2 (June 1987): 281–300.

Herb Johnson and David Shanno, "Option Pricing When the Variance Is Changing," *Journal of Financial and Quantitative Analysis* 22, no. 2 (June 1987): 143–151.

Louis O. Scott, "Option Pricing When the Variance Changes Randomly: Theory, Estimation, and an Application," *Journal of Financial and Quantitative Analysis* 22, no. 4 (December 1987): 419–438.

James B. Wiggins, "Option Values Under Stochastic Volatility: Theory and Empirical Estimates," *Journal of Financial Economics* 19, no. 2 (December 1987): 351–372.

Marc Chesney and Louis Scott, "Pricing European Currency Options: A Comparison of the Modified Black-Scholes Model and a Random Variance Model," *Journal of Financial and Quantitative Analysis* 24, no. 3 (September 1989): 267–284.

Thomas J. Finucane, "Black-Scholes Approximations of Call Option Prices with Stochastic Volatilities: A Note," *Journal of Financial and Quantitative Analysis* 24, no. 4 (December 1989): 527–532.

Steven L. Heston, "A Closed-form Solution for Options in Stochastic Volatility with Applications to Bond and Currency Options," *Review of Financial Studies* 6, no. 2 (1993): 327–343.

Stephen Figlewski, "Forecasting Volatility," *Financial Markets, Institutions, & Instruments* 6, no. 1 (1997): 1–88.

8. For an interesting paper on static analysis of calls, see:

Don M. Chance, "Translating the Greek: The Real Meaning of Call Option Derivatives," *Financial Analysts Journal* 50, no. 4 (July–August 1994): 43–49.

9. Portfolio insurance has received much attention. In addition to the citations given in the chapter, see:

M. J. Brennan and R. Solanki, "Optimal Portfolio Insurance," *Journal of Financial and Quantitative Analysis* 16, no. 3 (September 1981): 279–300.

Ethan S. Etzioni, "Rebalance Disciplines for Portfolio Insurance," *Journal of Portfolio Management* 13, no. 1 (Fall 1986): 59–62.

Richard J. Rendelman, Jr., and Richard McEnally, "Assessing the Costs of Portfolio Insurance," *Financial Analysts Journal* 43, no. 3 (May–June 1987): 27–37.

C. B. Garcia and F. J. Gould, "An Empirical Study of Portfolio Insurance," *Financial Analysts Journal* 43, no. 4 (July–August 1987): 44–54.

Robert Ferguson, "A Comparison of the Mean-variance and Long-term Return Characteristics of Three Investment Strategies," *Financial Analysts Journal* 43, no. 4 (July–August 1987): 55–66.

Fischer Black and Robert Jones, "Simplifying Portfolio Insurance," *Journal of Portfolio Management* 14, no. 1 (Fall 1987): 48–51.

Yu Zhu and Robert C. Kavee, "Performance of Portfolio Insurance Strategies," *Journal of Portfolio Management* 14, no. 3 (Spring 1988): 48–54.

Fischer Black and Robert Jones, "Simplifying Portfolio Insurance for Corporate Pension Plans," *Journal of Portfolio Management* 14, no. 4 (Summer 1988): 33–37.

Thomas J. O'Brien, *How Option Replicating Portfolio Insurance Works: Expanded Details*, Monograph Series in Finance and Economics no. 1988–4, New York University Salomon Center, Leonard N. Stern School of Business.

Erol Hakanoglu, Robert Koppraseh, and Emmanuel Roman, "Constant Proportion Portfolio Insurance for Fixed-income Investment," *Journal of Portfolio Management* 15, no. 4 (Summer 1989): 58–66.

Michael J. Brennan and Eduardo Schwartz, "Portfolio Insurance and Financial Market Equilibrium," *Journal of Business* 62, no. 4 (October 1989): 455–472.

Sanford J. Grossman and Jean-Luc Vila, "Portfolio Insurance in Complete Markets: A Note," *Journal of Business* 62, no. 4 (October 1989): 473–476.

Robert R. Trippi and Richard B. Harriff, "Dynamic Asset Allocation Rules: Survey and Synthesis," *Journal of Portfolio Management* 17, no. 4 (Summer 1991): 19–26.

Charles J. Jacklin, Allan W. Kleidon, and Paul Pfleiderer, "Underestimation of Portfolio Insurance and the Crash of October 1987," *Review of Financial Studies* 5, no. 1 (1992): 35–63.

10. A great deal has been written on warrants and convertibles. For an introduction to this literature, see:

Richard A. Brealey and Stewart C. Myers, *Principles of Corporate Finance* (New York: McGraw-Hill, 1996), Chapter 22.

Stephen A. Ross, Randolph W. Westerfield, and Jeffrey Jaffe, *Corporate Finance* (Boston: Irwin McGraw Hill, 1996), Chapter 22.

11. Many textbooks are devoted exclusively to options or have options as one of their primary subjects. Most cover everything discussed in this chapter, but in more detail and with a more complete list of citations. Here are a few:

Robert A. Jarrow and Andrew Rudd, *Option Pricing* (Homewood, IL: Richard D. Irwin, 1983).

John C. Cox and Mark Rubinstein, *Options Markets* (Englewood Cliffs, NJ: Prentice Hall, 1985).

Richard M. Bookstaber, *Option Pricing and Investment Strategies* (Chicago: Probus Publishing, 1987).

Peter Ritchken, *Options: Theory, Strategy, and Applications* (Glenview, IL: Scott, Foresman, 1987).

Robert W. Kolb, *Options: An Introduction* (Miami, FL: Kolb Publishing, 1991).

Alan L. Tucker, *Financial Futures, Options, and Swaps* (St. Paul, MN: West Publishing, 1991).

David A. Dubofsky, *Options and Financial Futures* (New York: McGraw-Hill, 1992).

Hans R. Stoll and Robert E. Whaley, *Futures and Options* (Cincinnati, OH: South-Western Publishing, 1993).

Don M. Chance, *An Introduction to Derivatives* (Fort Worth, TX: The Dryden Press, 1995).

Fred D. Arditti, *Derivatives* (Boston: Harvard Business School Press, 1996).

Robert Jarrow and Stuart Turnbull, *Derivative Securities* (Cincinnati, OH: South-Western Publishing, 1996).

John C. Hull, *Options, Futures, and Other Derivative Securities* (Upper Saddle River, NJ: Prentice Hall, 1997).

12. A useful software package and manual for valuing options is:

Stuart M. Turnbull, *Option Valuation* (Toronto: Holt, Rinehart and Winston of Canada, 1987).

13. For a Canadian perspective on the topics covered in this chapter, see:

P. Halpern and S. Turnbull, "Empirical Tests on Boundary Conditions for Toronto Stock Exchange Options," *Journal of Finance* 40, no. 2 (June 1985): 481–500.

A. Mandron, "Some Empirical Evidence about Canadian Stock Options, Part I: Valuation; Part II: Market Structure," *Canadian Journal of Administrative Sciences* 5, no. 2 (June 1988): 1–21.

L. Gagnon, "Empirical Investigation of the Canadian Government Bond Option Market," *Canadian Journal of Administrative Sciences* 11, no. 1 (March 1994): 2–11.

D. Cyr, "Expiration Day Effects on Individual Index Stocks: Evidence from the Toronto 35 Index," *Proceedings, Administrative Sciences Association of Canada Conference,* St. John's (June 1997): pp. 41–50.

C. Doidge and J. Wei, "Volatility Forecasting and the Efficiency of the Toronto 35 Index Options Market," *Canadian Journal of Administrative Sciences* 15, no. 1 (March 1998): 28–38.

Futures

Consider a contract that involves the delivery of some specific asset by a seller to a buyer at an agreed-upon future date. While such a contract also specifies the purchase price, the asset is not to be paid for until the delivery date. However, the buyer and the seller will both be requested to make a security deposit at the time the contract is signed. The reason for this deposit is to protect each person from experiencing any losses, should the other person renege on the contract. Hence, the size of the deposit is checked daily to see that it provides sufficient protection. If it is insufficient, it will have to be increased. If it is more than sufficient, the excess can be withdrawn.

These contracts are often referred to as **futures** (short for futures contract), and in the United States they involve assets such as agricultural goods (for example, wheat), natural resources (for example, copper), foreign currencies (for example, Swiss francs), fixed-income securities (for example, Treasury bonds), and market indices (for example, the Standard & Poor's 500).[1] As with options, standardization of the terms in these contracts makes it relatively easy for anyone to create and subsequently trade the contracts.

Futures contracts are available on exchanges in Canada on agricultural products (cereals), bankers' acceptances, long Canada Bonds, and the Toronto 35 index. Canadian investors can readily trade futures contracts on other commodities on US exchanges. The Canadian business press provides price quotations for contracts traded in both countries.

Futures (Futures Contract) An agreement between two people under which the seller promises to deliver a specific asset on a specific future date to the buyer for a predetermined price to be paid on the delivery date.

Hedges and Speculators

There are two types of people who deal in futures (and options)—speculators and hedgers. **Speculators** buy and sell futures for the sole purpose of making a profit by closing out their positions at a price that is better than the the initial price (or so they hope). Such people neither produce nor use the asset in the ordinary course of business. In contrast, **hedgers** buy and sell futures to offset an otherwise risky position in the spot market. In the ordinary course of business, they either produce or use the asset.

Speculator An investor in future contracts whose primary objective is to make a profit from buying and selling these contracts.

Hedger An investor in futures contracts whose primary objective is to offset an otherwise risky position.

---

[1]The term *commodity futures* is often used to refer to futures on agricultural goods and natural resources. The term *financial futures* is typically used in reference to futures on financial instruments such as Treasury bonds, foreign currencies, and stock market indices.

Example of Hedging

For example, consider wheat futures. A farmer might note today that the market price for a wheat futures contract with delivery around harvest time is $105 per tonne, a price that is high enough to ensure a profitable year. Although the farmer could sell wheat futures today, alternatively the farmer could wait until harvest and sell the wheat on the spot market at that time.[2] However, waiting until harvest entails risk because the spot price of wheat could fall by then, perhaps to $85 per tonne, which would bring financial ruin to the farmer. In contrast, selling wheat futures today will allow the farmer to "lock in" a $105-per-tonne selling price. Doing so would remove an element of risk from the farmer's primary business of growing wheat. Thus, a farmer who sells futures is known as a hedger or, more specifically, a **short hedger**.

Perhaps the buyer of the farmer's futures contract is a baker who uses wheat in making bread. Currently the baker has enough wheat in inventory to last until harvest season. In anticipation of the need to replenish the inventory at that time, the baker could buy a wheat futures contract today at $105 per tonne. Alternatively, the baker could simply wait until the inventory runs low and then buy wheat in the spot market. However, there is a chance that the spot price will be $125 per tonne at that time. Should this happen, the baker would have to raise the selling price of bread and perhaps lose sales in doing so. Alternatively, by purchasing wheat futures, the baker can "lock in" a $105 per tonne purchase price, thereby removing an element of risk from the bread business. Thus, a baker who buys futures is also known as a hedger or, more specifically, a **long hedger**.

Example of Speculating

The farmer and the baker can be compared with a speculator—a person who buys and sells wheat futures, based on the forecast price of wheat, in the pursuit of relatively short-term profits. As mentioned earlier, such a person neither produces nor uses the asset in the ordinary course of business.

A speculator who thinks that the price of wheat is going to rise substantially will buy wheat futures. Later this person will enter a **reversing trade** by selling wheat futures. If the forecast was accurate, a profit will have been made an increase in the wheat futures price.

For example, consider a speculator expecting at least a $20 per tonne rise in the spot price of wheat. Whereas this person could buy wheat, store it, and hope to sell it later at the anticipated higher price, it would be easier and more profitable to buy a wheat futures contract today at $105 per tonne. Later, assuming that the spot price of wheat rises by $20, the speculator would enter a reversing trade by selling the wheat futures contract for perhaps $125 per tonne. (A $20 rise in the spot price of wheat will cause the futures price to rise by about $20.) Thus the speculator will make a profit of $20 per tonne, or $400 in total, because these contracts are for 20 tonnes.[3] As will be shown later, the speculator might need to make a security deposit of $100 at the time the wheat futures contract is bought. As this is returned when the reversing trade is made, the speculator's rate of return is quite high (400%) relative to the percentage rise in the price of wheat (19%).

Alternatively, if a speculator forecasts a substantial price decline, then initially wheat futures would be sold. Later, the person would enter a reversing trade by purchasing wheat futures. Assuming that the forecast was accurate, a profit will be made on the decrease in the wheat futures price.

Short Hedger A hedger who offsets risk by selling futures contracts.

Long Hedger A hedger who offsets risk by buying futures contracts.

Reversing Trade The purchase or sale of a futures (or options) contract designed to offset, and thereby cancel, the previous sale or purchase of the same contract.

Spot Market The market for an asset that involves the immediate exchange of the asset for cash.

Spot Price The purchase price of an asset in the spot market.

---

[2]The **spot market** involves the immediate exchange of an asset for cash. The purchase price of the asset is known as its **spot price**.

[3]Prices quoted in the business press refer to 20 tonne contracts (a *job lot*) although a board lot is generally 100 tonnes.

The Futures Contract

Winnipeg Commodity Exchange
www.wce.mb.ca

Futures contracts are standardized in terms of delivery as well as the type of asset that can be delivered. For example, *The Winnipeg Commodity Exchange* (WCE) specifies the following requirements for its wheat contracts:

1. The seller agrees to deliver 20 tonnes of No. 3 CWRS wheat at the agreed-upon price. Alternatively, three other grades can be delivered at $5.00 per tonne discounts from the agreed-upon price. In any case, the seller is allowed to decide which grade shall be delivered.
2. The grain will be delivered by registered warehouse receipts issued by approved warehouses in Thunder Bay, Ontario.
3. Delivery will take place during the contract month, with the seller allowed to decide the actual date. Delivery must be completed by the last business day of the contract month. Alternative delivery points are permitted for some cereals, but delivery at these must be completed by the eighth business day before the end of the contract month.
4. Upon delivery of the warehouse receipt from the seller to the buyer, the latter will pay the former the agreed-upon price in cash.

After an organized exchange has set all the terms of a futures contract except for its price, the exchange will authorize trading in the contract.[4] Buyers and sellers (or their representatives) meet at a specific place on the floor of the exchange and try to agree on a price at which to trade. If they succeed, one or more contracts will be created, with all the standard terms plus an additional one—the price involved. Prices are normally stated on a per-unit basis. Thus, if a buyer and seller agree to a price of $105 per tonne for a contract of 20 tonnes of wheat, the amount of money involved is $2100.

Figure 20.1 shows a set of daily quotations of the prices at which commodity futures contracts were traded on the Winnipeg Exchange and the total volume of sales for each type of contract. Such listings of active futures markets are published regularly in the financial press, with each item for delivery having a heading that indicates the number of units per contract (e.g., 20 metric tonnes for oats) and the terms on which prices are stated (dollars per tonne).

Below the heading for the asset are certain details for each type of contract. In Figure 20.1, for example, there are six different futures contracts for canola, having different delivery dates that are shown in the third column. The first two columns show the *seasonal high (SeaHi)* and the *seasonal low (SeaLow)* that are the highest and lowest prices recorded during the lifetime of the contract. In the fourth, fifth, sixth, and seventh columns are the *open*, denoting the price at which the first transaction was made; the *high* and *low*, representing the highest and lowest prices recorded during the preceeding trading day; and the **settle**, a price (for example, the average of the high and low prices) that is representative of trades executed during the "closing period" designated by the exchange (for example, the last two minutes of trading). The eighth and ninth columns show the *change* from the previous day's settlement price and the **open interest** (the number of outstanding contracts) on the previous day.

For each futures contract, information is summarized below the figures for the last delivery date and indicates the estimated and previous sales (that is, the number of contracts traded on that day and on the previous trading day) as well as the total open inter-

---

Settle Price The representative price for a futures contract determined during the closing period of the futures exchange.

Open Interest The number of a particular futures contract outstanding at a particular point in time.

---

[4]For a relatively complete description of the terms for many exchange-traded futures contracts, see the *Commodity Trading Manual* (Chicago Board of Trade, 1989); Malcolm J. Robertson, *Directory of World Futures and Options* (Englewood Cliffs, NJ: Prentice Hall, 1990); and the extensive literature published by The Winnipeg Commodity Exchange. The first two of these books also contain descriptions of various futures exchanges.

Figure 20.1 Quotations for commodity futures contracts.

Winnipeg Commodity Exchange
Futures

SeaHi	SeaLow	Mth.	Open	High	Low	Settle	Chg.	Opint
CANOLA 20 tonnes, can $/tonne								
397.5	349.6	Nov98	372.2	374.9	372.0	374.7	+2.8	12182
401.0	354.1	Jan99	377.2	380.5	377.2	380.2	+3.0	23954
403.5	359.0	Mar99	380.3	384.0	380.3	383.5	+3.2	7255
405.0	364.0	May99	388.5	388.9	388.5	388.7	+3.6	1959
392.0	367.0	Jul99	390.9	391.6	390.9	391.2	+3.1	371
380.0	349.0	Nov99	361.8	362.5	361.0	362.5	+1.5	3060

Est sales		Prv Sales		Prv Open Int				Chg.
		6521		48851				−1430

SeaHi	SeaLow	Mth.	Open	High	Low	Settle	Chg.	Opint
FLAXSEED 20 tonnes, can $/tonne								
332.0	294.0	Nov98	324.5	325.5	321.5	322.0	−2.0	4143
332.0	303.0	Jan99	327.5	329.4	326.5	326.7	−0.8	1906
335.5	308.1	Mar99	331.5	332.5	330.0	330.0	−1.5	1434
338.5	316.0	May99	336.0	336.0	336.0	336.0	+0.5	410

Est sales		Prv Sales		Prv Open Int				Chg.
		663		8258				−20

OATS 20 tonnes, can $/tonne

SeaHi	SeaLow	Mth.	Open	High	Low	Settle	Chg.	Opint
114.5	83.0	Oct98				95.0	−89	100
119.5	83.0	Dec98				95.0		625
95.0	89.5	Mar99				97.2	−0.1	400
95.0	94.0	May99				100.0		50
		Jul99				103.0		

Est sales		Prv Sales		Prv Open Int				Chg.
		0		1175				

WESTERN BARLEY 20 tonnes, can $/tonne

SeaHi	SeaLow	Mth.	Open	High	Low	Settle	Chg.	Opint
150.5	114.9	Dec98	126.0	126.7	126.0	126.6	+0.2	6909
142.5	118.1	Mar99	129.0	129.3	129.0	129.1	+0.1	3520
141.2	120.5	May99	131.0	131.1	131.0	131.1	+0.1	458

Est sales		Prv Sales		Prv Open Int				Chg.
		798		11149				+20

WHEAT 20 tonnes, can $/tonne

SeaHi	SeaLow	Mth.	Open	High	Low	Settle	Chg.	Opint
170.0	136.6	Dec98	145.5	145.9	145.5	145.7	+0.5	5454
164.0	141.3	Mar99	147.1	147.8	147.1	147.6	+0.6	1712
167.0	143.1	May99	149.0	149.4	148.7	148.7	+0.1	2622

Est sales		Prv Sales		Prv Open Int				Chg.
		512		10297				+138

SOURCE: Reprinted with permission of *The Globe and Mail: Report on Business* (October 29, 1998).

est in those contracts on the previous day and the change in total open interest from the previous day (in the case of canola, these summary figures are below the November 1999 delivery date figures).

Futures Markets

The futures contracts shown in Figure 20.1 were traded on The Winnipeg Commodity Exchange, the only agricultural exchange in Canada. In the United States, futures contracts are traded on various organized exchanges, notably the Chicago Board of Trade (CBT), currently the largest futures exchange in the world. The method of trading futures on organized exchanges is similar in some ways and different in other ways from the way that stocks and options are traded. Like stocks and options, customers can place market, limit, and stop orders. Furthermore, once an order is transmitted to an exchange floor, it must be taken to a designated spot for execution by a member of the exchange, just as is done for stocks and options. This spot is known as a "pit" because of its shape, which is circular with a set of interior descending steps on which members stand. What transpires in the pit is what distinguishes trading in futures from trading in stocks and options.

First of all, there are no specialists or market-makers on futures exchanges. Trading is carried out by floor brokers, who may trade for their own personal account in an attempt to make profits by buying low and selling high, or for the firm they work for, or they may execute customers' orders. In doing so, they (or their phone clerks) each keep a file of any stop or limit orders that cannot be immediately executed. All orders are treated equally on the floor regardless of where they originate. Floor brokers are in some ways similar to market-makers, since a floor broker may have an inventory of futures contracts and may act as a dealer. However, unlike a market-maker, a floor broker is not required to do so.

Second, all futures orders must be announced by "open outcry," meaning that any member wishing to buy or sell any futures contract must verbally announce the order and a price at which the member is willing to trade. By doing so, the order is exposed to everyone in the pit, thereby enabling an auction to take place that will lead to the order being filled at the best possible price.

The Clearinghouse

Each futures exchange has an associated clearinghouse that becomes the "seller's buyer" and the "buyer's seller" as soon as a trade is concluded. The procedure is similar to that used for options, which is not surprising, since the first market in listed options was set up by people associated with a futures exchange (specifically, the Chicago Board Options Exchange was set up by the Chicago Board of Trade). In Winnipeg the clearing house is Winnipeg Commodity Clearing Ltd.

In order to understand how a clearinghouse operates, consider the futures market for wheat. Assume that on the first day of trading in July wheat, buyer B agrees to purchase 20 tonnes (one contract) from seller S for $105 per tonne (actually, what happens is that a floor broker working for B's brokerage firm and a floor broker working for S's brokerage firm meet in the wheat pit and agree on a price). In this situation, B believes that the price of wheat is going to rise, whereas S believes it is going to fall.

After B and S reach their agreement, the clearinghouse will immediately step in and break the transaction apart. That is, B and S no longer deal directly with each other. Now it is the obligation of the clearinghouse to deliver the wheat to B and to accept delivery from S. At this point, there is an open interest of one contract (20 tonnes) in July wheat, since only one contract exists at this time (technically, there are two, since the clearinghouse has separate contracts with B and S). Figure 20.2 summarizes the creation of this contract.

It is important to realize that if nothing else is done at this point, the clearinghouse is in a potentially risky position. For example, if the price of wheat rises to $125 per tonne by July, what happens if S does not deliver the wheat? The clearinghouse would have to buy the wheat on the spot market for $20 \times \$125 = \$2500$ and then deliver it to B. Because the clearinghouse will receive the selling price of $20 \times \$105 = \$2100$ from B in return, it will have lost $400. Although the clearinghouse has a claim on S for the $400, it faces protracted legal battles in trying to recover this amount and may end up with little or nothing from S.

Alternatively, if the price of wheat falls to $85 per tonne by July, then B will be paying $2100 for delivery of wheat that is only worth $20 \times \$85 = \$1700$ on the spot market. What happens if B refuses to make payment? In this case, the clearinghouse will not deliver the wheat that it received from S. Instead, it will have to sell the wheat for $1700 on the spot market. Since the clearinghouse paid $2100 for the wheat, it has lost $400. Again, although the clearinghouse has a claim on B for the $400, it may end up with little or nothing from B.

The procedures that protect the clearinghouse from such potential losses involve having brokers (1) impose initial margin requirements on both buyers and sellers; (2) mark to market the accounts of buyers and sellers every day; and (3) impose daily maintenance margin requirements on both buyers and sellers.

Figure 20.2 Creating a futures contract.

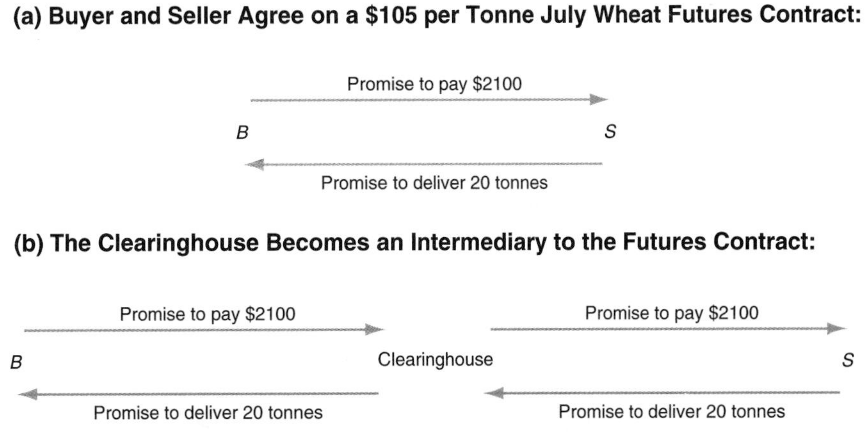

(a) Buyer and Seller Agree on a $105 per Tonne July Wheat Futures Contract:

Promise to pay $2100

B → S

Promise to deliver 20 tonnes

(b) The Clearinghouse Becomes an Intermediary to the Futures Contract:

Promise to pay $2100   Promise to pay $2100

B   Clearinghouse   S

Promise to deliver 20 tonnes   Promise to deliver 20 tonnes

Initial Margin

Performance Margin The initial margin that must be posted by a futures buyer or seller.

In order to buy and sell futures, an investor must open a commodity account with a brokerage firm. This type of account must be kept separate from other accounts (such as a cash account or a margin account) that the investor might have. Whenever a futures contract is signed, both the buyer and seller are required to post initial margin. That is, both the buyer and seller are required to make security deposits that are intended to guarantee that they will in fact be able to fulfill their obligations; accordingly, initial margin is often referred to as **performance margin**. The amount of this margin is roughly 5% to 15% of the total purchase price of the futures contract. In Winnipeg, however, it is stated as a given dollar amount regardless of the purchase price, $100 for speculators and $70 for hedgers per 20 tonne contract.[5]

For example, a July wheat futures contract for 20 tonnes at $105 per tonne would have a total purchase price of $20 \times \$105 = \$2100$. To meet the initial margin requirement, buyer B and seller S (both speculators) would each have to make a deposit of $100 (approximately 5% of the total purchase price). This deposit can be made in the form of cash, cash equivalents (such as Treasury bills), or a bank line of credit, and forms the equity in the account on the first day.

Although initial margin provides some protection to the clearinghouse, it does not provide complete protection. As indicated earlier, if the price of wheat rises to $125 per tonne by July, the clearinghouse faces a potential loss of $400, only $100 of which can be quickly recovered using the margin deposit. This is where the use of marking to market, coupled with a maintenance margin requirement, provides the requisite amount of additional protection.

Marking to Market

Marked (Marking) to Market The process of calculating, on a daily basis, the actual margin in an investor's account. Equivalently, the daily process of adjusting the equity in an investor's account to reflect the daily changes in the market value of the account's assets and liabilities.

In order to understand marking to market, the previous example, where B and S were, respectively, a buyer and a seller of a 20-tonne wheat futures contract at $105 per tonne, is continued. Assume now that on the second day of trading the settle price of July wheat is $107 per tonne. In this situation, S has lost $40 due to the rise in the price of wheat from $105 to $107 per tonne, whereas B has made $40. Thus, the equity in the account of S is reduced by $40 and the equity in the account of B is increased by $40. Since the initial equity was equal to the initial margin requirement of $100, this means that S has equity of $60, and B has equity of $140. This process of adjusting the equity in an investor's commodity account in order to reflect the change in the settle price of the futures contract is known as **marking to market**. It should also be noted that each day, as part of the marking-to-market process, the clearinghouse replaces each existing futures contract with a new one that has the settle price as reported in the financial press as the purchase price in the new contract.

In general, the equity in either a buyer's or seller's commodity account is the sum of (1) the initial margin deposit and (2) the sum of all daily gains, less losses, on open positions in futures. Since the amount of the gains (less losses) changes every day, the amount of equity changes every day.

In the example, if the settle price of the July wheat futures contract had fallen to $103.50 per tonne the day after rising to $107, then B would have lost $20 \times (\$107 - \$103.50) = \$70$,

---

[5]Since Black Monday and Terrible Tuesday (October 19 and 20, 1987), a number of people have advocated an increase in the size of the initial margin deposit for certain futures contracts (particularly stock index futures, which will be discussed later). The levels of initial and maintenance margins are set by each exchange, with brokers being allowed to set them higher. Typically, higher amounts of margin are required on futures contracts that have greater price volatility, since the clearinghouse faces larger potential losses on such contracts.

whereas S would have made $70 on that day. When their accounts are marked to market at the end of the day, the equity in B's account would have dropped from $140 to $70, and S's equity would have risen from $60 to $130.

Maintenance Margin

Variation Margin The amount of cash that an investor must provide to meet a margin call on a futures contract.

Another key concept is the requirement of maintenance margin. According to this requirement, the investor must keep the commodity account's equity equal to or greater than a certain percentage of the amount deposited as initial margin. In Winnipeg this percentage is 70% for speculators and 100% for hedgers; therefore, the speculator must have equity equal to or greater than 70% of the initial margin. If this requirement is not met, the investor will receive a margin call from her broker. This call is a request for an additional deposit of cash (nothing else can be deposited for this purpose), known as **variation margin**, to bring the equity up to the initial margin level. If the investor does not (or cannot) respond, then the broker will close out the investor's position by entering a reversing trade in the investor's account.

For example, reconsider investors B and S who had, respectively, bought and sold a July wheat futures contract at $105 per tonne; each investor had made a deposit of $100 in order to meet the initial margin requirement. The next day, the price of the wheat futures contract rose to $107 per tonne, or $2140. Thus, B's equity had increased to $140, whereas S's equity had decreased to $60. With the maintenance margin requirement set at 70% of initial margin, both B and S are required to have equity of at least $.70 \times $100 = 70 in their accounts every day. Since the actual level of equity for B clearly exceeds this amount, B does not need to do anything. Indeed, B may withdraw an amount of cash equal to the amount by which the equity exceeds the initial margin; in this example, B can withdraw $40.

However, S is undermargined and will be asked to make a cash deposit of at least $40, since this would increase the equity from $60 to $100, the level of the initial margin. In the event that S refuses to make this deposit, the broker will enter a reversing trade for S by purchasing a July wheat futures contract. The result is that S will simply receive an amount of money approximately equal to the account's equity, $60, and the account will be closed. Since S initially deposited $100, this represents a personal loss of $40.

Reversing Trades

Suppose that on the next day, B finds that people are paying $108 per tonne for July wheat. This represents an additional profit to B of $1.00 per tonne, since the price was $107 the previous day. If B believes that the price of July wheat will not go any higher, then B might sell a July wheat futures contract for $108 to someone else. In this situation, B has made a reversing trade, since B now has offsetting positions with respect to July wheat (equivalently, B is said to have unwound, or closed out, his position in July wheat).

At this point, the benefit to B of having a clearinghouse involved can be seen. Nominally, B is obligated to deliver 20 tonnes of wheat to the clearinghouse in July, which is in turn obligated to deliver it back to B. This situation occurs because B is involved in two July wheat contracts, one as a seller and one as a buyer. However, the clearinghouse will note that B has offsetting positions in July wheat and will immediately cancel both of them. Furthermore, once the reversing trade had been made, B will be able to withdraw the initial margin of $100 as well as the $20 \times ($108 - $105) = 60 profit that has been made.

In effect, a futures contract is replaced every day by (1) adjusting the equity in the investor's commodity account and (2) drawing up a new contract that has a purchase price equal to the current settle price. This daily marking-to-market procedure, coupled with margin requirements, results in the clearinghouse always having a security deposit of sufficient size to protect it from losses due to the actions of the individual investors.[6]

These rather complex arrangements make it possible for futures traders to think in very simple terms. In the example, B bought a contract of July wheat at $105 and sold it two days later for $108, making a profit of $3 per tonne. If S, having initially sold a contract of July wheat at $105, later made a reversing trade for $107, then S's position can also be thought of in simple terms—specifically, S sold July wheat for $105 and later bought it back for $107, suffering a loss of $2 per tonne in the process.

Futures Positions

In the previous example, B was the person who initially bought a July wheat futures contract. Accordingly, B now has a long position and is said to be long one contract of July wheat. In contrast, S, having initially sold a July wheat futures contract, has a short position and is said to be short one contract of July wheat.

The process of marking to market every day means that changes in the settle price are realized as soon as they occur. When the settle price rises, those with long positions realize profits equal to the change and those who are short realize losses. When the settle price falls, those with long positions realize losses, whereas those with short positions realize profits. In either event, total profits always equal total losses. Thus, either the buyer gains and the seller loses, or the seller gains and the buyer loses because both parties are involved in a "zero-sum game" (as was also the case with buyers and writers of options, discussed in Chapter 19).

Open Interest

When trading is first allowed in a contract, there is no open interest, since no contracts are outstanding. Subsequently, as people begin to make transactions, the open interest grows. At any time, open interest equals the amount that those with short positions (the sellers) are currently obligated to deliver. It also equals the amount that those with long positions (the buyers) are obligated to receive.

Open interest figures are typically shown with futures prices in the financial press. For example, Figure 20.1 indicates that on October 28, 1998, a total of 23 954 contracts in January 1999 canola were outstanding on The Winnipeg Commodity Exchange (WCE). Note the substantial differences in the open interest figures for the other canola contracts on the WCE that day. This is quite typical of agricultural commodities around the world. Figure 20.3 shows why. Open interest in a corn contract on the Chicago Board of Trade is shown for every month from the preceding January until the contract expired at the end of the delivery month, December. From January until the end of October, more trades were generally made to open new positions than to reverse old ones, and open interest continued to increase. As the delivery month came closer, reversing trades began to outnumber those intended to open new positions, and the open interest began to decline.[7] The amount remaining at the beginning of December was the maximum number of bushels of corn that could have been delivered against futures contracts at that time, but most of these contracts were also settled by reversing trades instead of delivery.

---

[6]Actually, only brokerage firms belong to a clearinghouse, and it is *their* accounts that are settled by the clearinghouse at the end of every day. Each brokerage firm acts in turn as a clearinghouse for its own clients. For more information on clearing procedures, see Chapter 6 of the *Commodity Trading Manual*.

[7]Interestingly, it has been observed that typically the volatility of the futures price changes increases as the contract approaches its delivery date. This phenomenon is known as the "Samuelson hypothesis"; see Paul A. Samuelson, "Proof That Properly Anticipated Prices Fluctuate Randomly," *Industrial Management Review* 6, no. 2 (Spring 1965): 41–49. Also see Hendrik Bessembinder, Jay F. Coughenour, Paul J. Seguin, and Margaret Monroe Smoller, "Is There a Term Structure of Futures Volatilities? Re-evaluating the Samuelson Hypothesis," *Journal of Derivatives* 4, no. 2 (Winter 1996): 45–58.

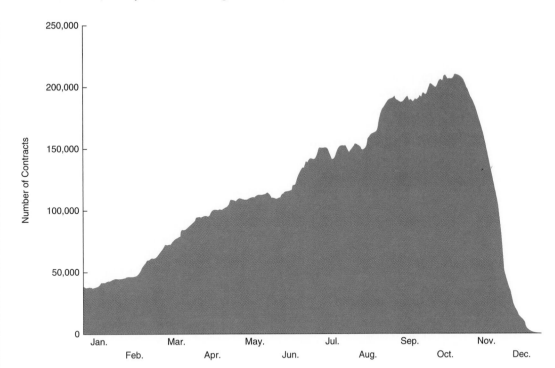

Relatively few futures positions—less than 3% of the total—end in actual delivery of the asset involved.[8] However, the fact that delivery is a possibility makes a contract's value in the delivery month differ only slightly, if at all, from the spot price (that is, the current market price) of the asset.

If not reversed, most futures contracts require delivery of the corresponding asset. Notable exceptions are market index futures, since they do not require delivery of the set of securities comprising the corresponding index. Instead, *cash settlement* is required where an amount equal to the difference between the level of the index and the purchase price must be paid in cash on the delivery date. Nevertheless, as with other types of futures, most positions in market index futures are closed out with reversing trades prior to the date at which delivery (in cash) is required.

Price Limits

The by-laws of the WCE place dollar limits on the extent to which futures prices are allowed to vary from day to day. These price limits on futures are imposed so that traders who might overreact to major news are protected from voluntarily entering into agreements under such conditions. For example, if July wheat contracts had closed at $105 on the previous day and the daily price limit was $5, then only contracts for July wheat at prices in the range from $100 to $110 would be allowed. If news during the day led traders

---

[8]Merrill Lynch, Pierce, Fenner & Smith, Inc., *Speculating on Inflation: Futures Trading in Interest Rates, Foreign Currencies, and Precious Metals*, July 1979.

to consider $115 a reasonable price for the contract, they would have to (1) trade privately, foregoing the advantages offered by the exchange; or (2) trade on the exchange at the limit price of $110; or (3) wait until the next day, when the range of acceptable prices would be from $105 to $115.

One negative result of this "limit move" up to $110 or down to $100 is that all traders may choose option 3 and, therefore, no July wheat contracts will be traded on that day. This is because nobody will want to sell these wheat contracts for a below-market price of $110, preferring to wait until the next day when the range of acceptable prices is raised. Indeed, if the news is important enough (such as hail storms in Saskatchewan, which destroy the wheat crop and dramatically increase the price of wheat futures), the daily limit moves could prevent trading from taking place for several days. In an attempt to avoid this situation the WCE has ruled that when two of the three nearest contracts close at the normal limit (up or down) then the daily price limit is immediately expanded by 50% and remains there for the next three days. If after three days trading at the expanded limit continues then the expanded limit remains in force until two of the three nearest contracts close within the expanded limit.

Interestingly, initial margins are usually set at an amount that is roughly equal to the price limit times the size of the contract. In the case of wheat having a $5 price limit and a contract for 20 tonnes, the initial margin is $5 \times 20 = 100. Thus, if the price of wheat moves the limit against the investor, no more than the initial margin of $100 will be lost on the day of the adverse limit move. In a sense, the price limit protects the investor from losing more than $100 on that day. However, it is possible that the investor cannot enter a reversing trade after prices have reached the limit, meaning that much larger losses could be incurred later.

Basis

Basis The difference between the spot price of an asset and the futures price of the same asset.

The difference between the current spot price on an asset (that is, the price of the asset for immediate delivery) and the corresponding futures price (that is, the purchase price stated in the futures contract) is known as the **basis** for the futures:

$$\text{Basis} = \text{current spot price} - \text{futures price} \qquad (20.1)$$

Speculating on the Basis

Since the futures price will equal the spot price on the delivery date, the basis will ultimately narrow and disappear on the delivery date. However, before then it can widen or narrow, opening up the opportunity for profitable investing if such changes in the basis can be accurately forecasted. Typically, depending on whether the basis is positive or negative and if the basis is forecasted to widen or narrow, an investor will want to either be (1) short in the futures contract and long in the underlying deliverable asset or (2) long in the futures contract and short in the underlying deliverable asset. The risk that the basis will narrow or widen, causing gains or losses to these investors, is known as **basis risk.** The only type of uncertainty investors face concerns the difference between the spot price of the deliverable asset and the price of the futures contract. Such a person is said to be speculating on the basis.[9]

Basis Risk The risk to a futures investor of the basis widening or narrowing.

---

[9]For more on the relationship between spot and futures prices as reflected in the basis, see the *Commodity Trading Manual*, Chapter 8. It should be noted that sometimes basis is defined as the futures price less the current spot price—the reverse of what is shown in equation (20.1).

● Spreads

It is quite possible to take a long position in a futures contract and a short position in another futures contract in the same asset, but with a different delivery date. The person who does this is speculating on changes in the difference between the prices of the two contracts, a difference that constitutes the "basis" for these particular positions.

Others attempt to profit from temporary imbalances among the prices of futures contracts on different but related assets. For example, one might take a long position in soybeans along with a short position in an item produced from soybeans, such as soybean meal. Another possibility involves a position in wheat with an offsetting position in corn, which serves as a substitute for wheat in many applications.

Such people are known as *spreaders*, and, like those who speculate on the basis, they reduce or eliminate the risk associated with general price moves. Instead, they take on the risk associated with changes in price *differences* in the hope that superior knowledge will enable them to consistently make profits from such changes.

Returns on Futures

During the period from 1950 through 1976, a portfolio made up of positions in 23 different commodity futures contracts was compared with a diversified portfolio of common stocks.[10] The average rates of return and risk level of the two portfolios were found to be of similar magnitude:

Portfolio	Average Annual Return	Standard Deviation
Futures	13.83%	22.43%
Common stocks	13.05	18.95

Given these results, an investor might view the two alternatives as equally desirable. Better yet, during the period from 1950 to 1976, a combination of the two portfolios was found to be more desirable than either portfolio by itself. This resulted from the fact that the returns of the commodity futures and stock portfolios were negatively correlated, suggesting that the return on a combined portfolio would have had considerably less variation than on either portfolio separately. Specifically, the correlation coefficient was −.24, resulting in the following standard deviations for portfolios with different combinations:

Percentage in Stocks	Percentage in Futures	Standard Deviation	Average Annual Return
0%	100%	22.43%	13.83%
20	80	17.43	13.67
40	60	13.77	13.52
60	40	12.68	13.36
80	20	14.74	13.21
100	0	18.95	13.05

---

[10]The futures contracts consisted of agricultural goods and natural resources. See Zvi Bodie and Victor Rosansky, "Risk and Return in Commodity Futures," *Financial Analysts Journal* 36, no. 3 (May–June 1980): 27–39. Similar conclusions were reached when the period from 1978 to 1981 was examined. See Cheng F. Lee, Raymond M. Leuthold, and Jean E. Cordier, "The Stock Market and the Commodity Futures Market: Diversification and Arbitrage Potential," *Financial Analysts Journal* 41, no. 4 (July–August 1985): 53–60.

Whereas there was little difference in the average returns of the various portfolios, there was a noticeable difference in their risks. In particular, the portfolio with 60% in stocks and 40% in futures seems to have had much less risk than the others.

Also of interest was the observation that commodity futures have been at least a partial hedge against inflation. During the period from 1950 to 1976, the returns on the portfolio of 23 futures were positively correlated with changes in the Consumer Price Index, having a correlation coefficient of .58. In contrast, the returns on the portfolio of common stocks were negatively correlated with changes in the Consumer Price Index, having a correlation coefficient of −.43. (See the accompanying *Institutional Issues* section for a further discussion of commodity futures returns.)

At this point it is appropriate to discuss the pricing of futures contracts. Specifically, what is the relationship between the futures price and investors' expectations of what the spot price will be on the delivery date? And what is the relationship between the futures price and the current spot price of the deliverable asset? The next two sections explore these relationships and provide some answers to the questions.

Futures Prices and Expected Spot Prices

Certainty

If future spot prices could be predicted with certainty, there would be no reason for anyone to be either a buyer or a seller of a futures contract. To understand why, imagine what a futures contract would look like in a world of certainty. First, the purchase price of the futures contract would simply equal the (perfectly predictable) expected spot price on the delivery date. This means that neither buyers nor sellers would be able to make profits from the existence of futures. Second, the purchase price would not change as the delivery date got closer.[11] Finally, no margin would be necessary because there would not be any unexpected "adverse" price movements.

Uncertainty

While it is useful to know something about the way in which futures prices and expected spot prices are related to each other in a world of certainty where forecasting is done with complete accuracy, the real world is uncertain. Given this, how are futures prices related to expected spot prices? While there are several possible explanations, no definitive answer has been provided.

Expectations Hypothesis

Expectations Hypothesis
A hypothesis that the futures price of an asset is equal to the expected spot price of the asset on the delivery date of the futures contract.

One possible explanation is given by the **expectations hypothesis**: the current purchase price of a futures contract equals the consensus expectation of the spot price on the delivery date. In symbols:

$$P_f = \overline{P}_s$$

where P_f is the current purchase price of the futures contract and $\overline{P}_s$ is the expected spot price of the asset on the delivery date. Thus, if a July wheat futures contract is currently selling for $105 per tonne, then it can be inferred that the consensus opinion is that in July the spot price of wheat will be $105.

---

[11]These first two points do not mean that the current spot price will not change as time passes. For futures involving a seasonal commodity (such as wheat), the spot price will sometimes be greater than and sometimes be less than the futures price during the life of the contract. Furthermore, sometimes a futures contract involving a more distant delivery date will sell for more than one with a nearer delivery date, whereas at other times it will sell for less.

If the expectations hypothesis is correct, a speculator should not expect to either win or lose from a position in the futures market, be it long or short. Neglecting margin requirements, a speculator who takes a long position in futures agrees to pay P_f at the delivery date for an asset that is expected to be worth $\overline{P}_s$ at that time. Thus the long speculator's expected profit is $\overline{P}_s - P_f$, which equals zero. Conversely, a speculator with a short position will have sold an asset at a price of P_f and will expect to enter a reversing trade at $\overline{P}_s$ on the delivery date. Thus, the short speculator's expected profit is $P_f - \overline{P}_s$, which also equals zero.

The expectations hypothesis is often defended on the grounds that speculators are indifferent to risk and are thus happy to accommodate hedgers without any compensation in the form of the risk premium. The reason for their indifference has to do with the belief that the impact of a specific futures position on the risk of a diversified portfolio that includes many types of assets will be very small. As a result, speculators holding diversified portfolios may be willing to take over some risk from hedgers with little (if any) compensation in the form of a risk premium.

Figure 20.4 shows the pattern of futures prices implied by the expectations hypothesis, given that the expected spot price $\overline{P}_s$ does not change during the life of the contract.

Normal Backwardation

John Maynard Keynes
www.drexel.edu/top/prin/
txt/Intro/keynes.html

Normal Backwardation

An expected relationship between the futures price of an asset and the expected spot price of the asset on the delivery date of the contract. Normal backwardation states that the futures price will be less than the expected spot price.

The famous economist John Maynard Keynes felt that the expectations hypothesis did not correctly explain futures prices.[12] He argued that, on balance, hedgers will want to be short in futures, and therefore they will have to entice the speculators to be long in futures. Because there are risks associated with being long, Keynes hypothesized that the hedgers would have to entice the speculators by making the expected return from a long position greater than the risk-free rate. This requires the futures price to be less than the expected spot price:

$$P_f < \overline{P}_s$$

Thus, a speculator who bought a futures contract at a price P_f would expect to be able to sell it on (or near) the delivery date at a higher price $\overline{P}_s$. This relationship between the futures price and the expected spot price has been referred to as **normal backwardation** and implies that the price of a futures contract can be expected to rise during its life, as shown in Figure 20.4.

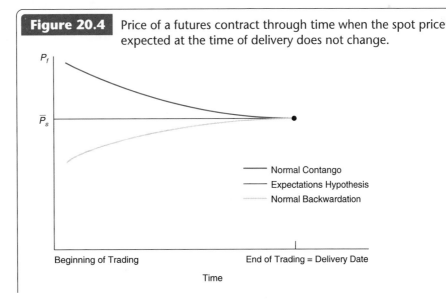

Figure 20.4 Price of a futures contract through time when the spot price expected at the time of delivery does not change.

Normal Contango
Expectations Hypothesis
Normal Backwardation

Beginning of Trading   End of Trading = Delivery Date

Time

---

[12]J. M. Keynes, *Treatise on Money*, vol. 2 (London: Macmillan, 1930), pp. 142–144.

A contrary hypothesis holds that, on balance, hedgers will want to be long in futures and therefore they will have to entice speculators to be short in futures. Because there are risks associated with being short, it can be hypothesized that the hedgers will have to entice the speculators by making the expected return from a short position greater than the risk-free rate. This requires the futures price to be greater than the expected spot price:

$$P_f > \overline{P}_s$$

Thus, a speculator who short sold a futures contract at a price P_f would expect to be able to buy it back on (or near) the delivery date at a lower price, $\overline{P}_s$. This relationship between the futures price and the expected spot price has been referred to as **normal contango** and implies that the price of a futures contract can be expected to fall during its life, as shown in Figure 20.4.[13]

Normal Contango An expected relationship between the futures price of an asset and the expected spot price of the asset on the delivery date of the contract. Normal contango states that the futures price will be greater than the expected spot price.

Futures Prices and Current Spot Prices

The previous section discussed the relationship between the futures price associated with an asset and the expected spot price of the asset on the delivery date given in the futures contract. What about the relationship between the futures price and the current spot price of the asset? In general, they will be different, but is there some explanation for why these prices are different? Is there some model that can be used to forecast how the size of the difference will change over time? This section attempts to answer these questions.[14]

Introducing the Problem

Consider the owner of a circa 1910 Honus Wagner baseball card who is getting ready to sell the card. The owner knows that the current market price of the card is $100 000 because there are very few (reputedly fewer than five) of these cards available. (One actually sold for $451 000 in 1990.) Furthermore, an investor has offered to buy it but wants to pay for it a year from now. The buyer is willing to take delivery of the card then and wants to sign the contract for sale today. More specifically, she would like to sign a futures contract with the owner in which the delivery date is one year from now.

No Costs or Benefits of Ownership

What price should the owner ask for in the futures contract? Assume that there is no risk that either party will default on the contract, and that there are no benefits (such as from showing the card) or costs (such as insurance) associated with owning the card. Given that the current one-year interest rate is 4%, the owner could sell the card today on the spot market for $100 000, put the proceeds in the bank to earn 4%, and have $104 000 in one year. Hence the owner would not be willing to sign the futures contract for any futures price that is less than $104 000. The buyer, on the other hand, is unwilling to pay more than $104 000 because she could pay $100 000 now and get the card immediately but

---

[13]There are other hypotheses regarding the relationship between futures prices and expected spot prices. See, for example, Paul H. Cootner, "Speculation and Hedging," Stanford University, *Food Research Institute Studies*, Supplement, 1967.

[14]This section and the next one borrow from Kenneth R. French, "Pricing Financial Futures Contracts: An Introduction," *Journal of Applied Corporate Finance* 1, no. 4 (Winter 1989): 59–66. It ignores the apparently minor effect that daily marking to market has on the futures price that is stated in futures contracts (see p. 65 and footnotes 5 and 6 in French's paper).

Commodity Futures: The Selling of an Asset Class

When institutional investors discuss investments in futures, we can safely assume that they are referring to *financial futures*—that is, futures contracts on, for example, stock market indices or Treasury bonds. Commodity futures, on the other hand, play only an insignificant role in institutional investors' portfolios.

Given the history of the futures markets, this situation might seem somewhat surprising. After all, financial futures are mere fledglings compared to commodity futures. The oldest futures exchange, the Chicago Board of Trade, was organized in 1848 for the sole purpose of trading futures contracts on agricultural commodities. The first financial futures contracts (a futures contract on foreign currencies) were established in 1972. The most popular financial futures contracts today, S&P 500 futures, were not created until 1981.

The dollar volume of trading in financial futures contracts now far exceeds the trading volume in commodity futures. Traditional users of commodity futures contracts have not become less enamoured of those products. Rather, directly and indirectly institutional investors have helped create a gigantic market for financial futures.

The question then is not why institutional investors have become extensively involved in financial futures. The application of financial futures to the activities of institutional investors, in terms of both hedging and speculating, are obvious. More intriguing is why institutional investors have not entered the commodity futures market in any substantial way.

Institutional investors, particularly pension funds, in recent years have expanded the range of asset types (or classes) in which they invest. Whereas once they restricted themselves to domestic common stocks, high-grade bonds, and cash equivalents, institutional investors now own foreign securities, junk bonds, real estate, and oil and gas wells, to mention just a few. With some notable exceptions, however, institutional investors have been unwilling to add commodity futures to their asset class toolboxes.

Financial services providers have recognized the tremendous profit potential if institutional investors could be enticed to invest in commodities. If those investors chose to place just 2% to 3% of their immense wealth in commodities, the accompanying fees to brokers and money managers would easily run into the hundreds of millions of dollars.

How to convince institutional investors to trade in commodities? One potential means is to help publicize the risk-reward opportunities historically offered by investments in commodities. Institutional investors have generally shown a reluctance to become involved in investments lacking a quantifiable track record. By developing an index of a diversified investment in commodity futures, institutional investors would have performance data that could be compared against the results of investments in other asset classes. Furthermore, institutional investors would be able to construct simulated past portfolios that included commodity futures, thus emphasizing the diversification benefits of this asset class.

Beyond the industrywide benefit of stimulating institutional investor interest in commodity futures, a unique benefit accrues to the creator of an investable commodity futures index. If that index were to become widely accepted, the creator would have a considerable advantage in designing and trading products based on that index. That advantage could translate into significant revenue.

In 1991 Goldman Sachs, the large New York brokerage firm, with considerable fanfare introduced its own commodity futures index. Other organizations had previously developed such indices. Goldman Sachs, however, directly targeted institutional investors by designing its index to be more truly reflective of the commodity futures investment opportunities available to large investors. Furthermore, Goldman Sachs developed detailed simulated performance data for the index extending back to 1970.

The Goldman Sachs Commodities Index (GSCI) is composed of "near" futures commodity contract prices for which active liquid markets exist. ("Near" refers to the contract in a given commodity with the shortest time remaining until delivery.) This liquidity requirement allows large investors to replicate the index by buying its individual components.

Weights in the index are based on world production of the respective commodities. Thus, the most economically important commodities receive the most weight in the index.

Currently, 18 commodities constitute the index, which is dominated by various energy, livestock, and grain futures (with weights of roughly 50%, 25%, and 15%, respectively). Historically the composition of the index has changed over time as new commodity futures contracts were created or met the GSCI liquidity requirements. In the 1970s the livestock and grain futures made up most of the index. Energy-related futures did not begin trading until 1983 and were not added to the index until 1987.

The reported historical performance of the GSCI has been impressive in terms of both return and risk. Ibbotson Associates reports the following returns, standard deviations, and correlations for the GSCI and comparative asset classes over the period of 1970 through the first quarter of 1992:

	Annual Return	Annual Standard Deviation	Correlation with GSCI
GSCI	14.8%	18.3	1.00
US stocks	11.5	16.2	−.42
Foreign stocks	13.1	17.6	−.27
US long-term bonds	9.0	11.5	−.32
US Treasury bills	7.5	0.8	−.20
US inflation	6.0	1.4	.26

The GSCI has produced returns exceeding those of US and foreign stocks while offering only slightly more variability. Also impressive has been the GSCI's negative correlation with other asset classes and its positive correlation with inflation. The conclusions one draws from this data are that commodities offer equitylike returns, are excellent portfolio diversifiers, and are a good inflation hedge.

How Goldman Sachs has calculated the GSCI returns has generated some controversy. Those returns have three components: the spot return, the Treasury-bill return, and the roll yield. The first two components are straightforward. The spot yield is how much the price of the underlying commodity changes. The Treasury-bill yield is the interest earned if the investor were to post as collateral the full dollar value (that is, the notional principal) of the investment in the commodities at the time of the futures contract purchase.

The roll yield is more complicated. It represents the change in the futures price over the life of the contract. If futures are priced according to normal backwardation (discussed in this chapter), then futures prices are expected to rise towards the spot price of the commodity over time. Therefore, the process of "rolling" over expiring futures will be profitable on average.

Which is the correct explanation of the relationship between futures and expected spot prices: the expectations hypothesis, normal backwardation, or normal contango? As historically about one-third of the GSCI's return has come from roll yield, this question is more than academic. Goldman Sachs argues that the markets for commodities that are normally consumed as they are produced (such as energy or livestock) are typically subject to backwardation. Only if this will be the case in the future can a positive roll yield for the GSCI (and the resulting high GSCI total returns) be expected to persist.

Equally problematic is whether institutional investors can be expected to increase their investments in commodities. Current indications are that institutions are beginning to dip their toes in commodity futures through accounts called *managed futures*. In these accounts money managers actively take long and short positions in commodity and financial futures. The accounts gain only if their managers are adept at anticipating the direction of various futures price changes. Over $2 billion is now invested in managed futures accounts. Are these investments the harbingers of increased institutional activity, or a mere passing fancy? The jury is still out.

forgo $4000 of interest that would have been earned had the $100 000 been left in the bank where it earned 4%. Since the seller wants to receive at least $104 000 and the buyer will pay no more than $104 000, they will settle at a futures price of $104 000.

To generalize, let P_s denote the current spot price of the asset (in this case, $100 000) and I the dollar amount of interest corresponding to the period of time from the present to the delivery date (in this case, $4000). If P_f denotes the futures price, then

$$P_f = P_s + I \qquad (20.2)$$

This equation shows that the futures price will be greater than the spot price by the amount of the interest that the owner forgoes by holding onto the asset, provided that there are no costs or benefits associated with ownership.

Benefits from Ownership

To add a complication to the model, imagine that a baseball card exhibition will be held in 12 months, just before the delivery date. The exhibitor is willing to pay the card owner $1000 in order to have the card displayed at the exhibition. How will this benefit of ownership affect the futures price?

As mentioned earlier, if the owner sells the card now, then she will receive $100 000 immediately, which could be invested right away and be worth $104 000 in 12 months. Alternatively, the owner could hold on to the card and receive the $1000 exhibitor fee as well as the futures price. Hence, the futures price must be at least $103 000 in order for the owner to be as well off financially by selling the card by means of a futures contract as by selling it immediately in the spot market. On the other side, the buyer will accept a futures price of no more than $103 000. This is because she could buy the card on the spot market for $100 000, thereby forgoing $4000 of interest but receiving the $1000 exhibitor fee. Consequently, the futures price will be $103 000, as this is the only price that is agreeable to both buyer and seller.

What if the exhibition were to be held in six months instead of one year? In that case the owner of the card would receive the $1000 exhibitor fee in six months and would be able to invest it risklessly at 2% for the remaining six months until the delivery date. Thus, the $1000 in six months is equivalent to $1020 in 12 months, and the futures price would be $100 000 + $4000 − $1020 = $102 980.

Let B denote the value of the benefits of ownership (sometimes known as the convenience yield of the asset) as of the delivery date (in this case, $1020). When such benefits are present, the futures price can be calculated as

$$P_f = P_s + I - B \qquad (20.3)$$

This equation shows that the futures price can be greater or less than the spot price, depending on whether the net amount of interest forgone less benefits received is positive or negative and provided that there are no costs associated with ownership of the asset.

Costs of Ownership

What if the owner of the baseball card decides that it must be insured at an annual cost of $100? How will this affect the futures price? The easiest way to think of such costs of ownership as insurance and storage is to view them as the opposite of benefits of ownership. Because the benefits of ownership result in cash inflows to the owner, the costs of ownership result in cash outflows. Hence the previously calculated futures price of $102 980 would have to be increased by the $100 cost of insurance to $103 080. If C denotes the costs of ownership (in this example, $100), then the futures price will be

$$P_f = P_s + I - B + C \qquad (20.4)$$

Cost of Carry The differential between the futures and spot prices of a particular asset. It equals the interest forgone less the benefits plus the costs of ownership.

The total value of interest less benefits received plus cost of ownership, $I - B + C$, is known as the **cost of carry** associated with the futures contract. Note that the futures price can be greater or lower than the spot price, depending upon whether the cost of carry is positive or negative.

Financial Futures

Until the 1970s, futures contracts were limited to those on agricultural goods and natural resources. Since then, financial futures based on foreign currencies, fixed-income securities, and market indices have been introduced on major exchanges. Indeed, in terms of trading volume, they are now far more important than both the underlying assets and traditional futures contracts. Unlike other types of futures that permit delivery any time during a given month, most financial futures have a specific delivery date. (The exceptions involve some fixed-income futures.)

Foreign Currency Futures

Anyone who has crossed a national border knows that there is an active spot market for foreign currency, and that the rate at which one currency can be exchanged for another varies over time. At any particular point in time, however, all such rates must be in conformance or else a riskless profit-making situation may arise. For example, it is usually possible to exchange US dollars for British pounds, then exchange the British pounds for French francs, and, finally, exchange the French francs for US dollars. If all three exchange rates were not in line, an investor might end up with more dollars at the end of this chain of transactions than at the beginning. Such an opportunity would attract large amounts of money, placing pressure on exchange rates and rapidly restoring balance. Although transaction costs and certain exchange restrictions might limit the ability of people to exploit such imbalances among exchange rates, they would nevertheless force the rates into being closely aligned.

The familiar market in foreign currency, operated by banks, travel agents, and others, is in effect a spot market, because both the agreement on terms and the actual exchange of currencies occur at the same time. There are also markets for agreements involving the future delivery of foreign currency.

The largest such market is operated by banks and specialized brokers that maintain close communications with each other throughout the world. Corporations, institutions, and some individuals deal in this market via large banks. Substantial amounts of money are involved, and every agreement is negotiated separately. Typical rates are quoted daily in the financial press, as shown in Figure 20.5. This network of large institutions is generally termed the *market for forward exchange* because there is no marking to market. Furthermore, because the contracts are not standardized, no organized secondary market for them exists. However, there is a market that deals in standardized futures contracts for foreign currency.[15] Procedures are similar to those used for commodity futures.

---

[15]The prices of foreign currency forward and futures contracts appear to be quite similar. See Bradford Cornell and Marc Reinganum, "Forward and Futures Prices: Evidence from the Foreign Exchange Market," *Journal of Finance* 36, no. 5 (December 1981): 1035–1045. Their findings are challenged by Michael A. Polakoff and Paul C. Grier, "A Comparison of Foreign Exchange Forward and Futures Prices," *Journal of Banking and Finance* 15, no. 6 (December 1991): 1057–1079, but supported by Carolyn W. Chang and Jack S. K. Chang, "Forward and Futures Prices: Evidence From the Foreign Exchange Markets," *Journal of Finance* 45, no. 4 (September 1990): 1333–1336. See Kenneth R. French, "A Comparison of Futures and Forward Prices," *Journal of Financial Economics* 12, no. 3 (November 1983): 311–342 for a discussion of the difficulties encountered when testing to see whether the prices of forward and futures contracts are similar.

Figure 20.5 Quotations for foreign exchange rates.

Major Currencies

Supplied by Royal Bank of Canada – indicative wholesale late afternoon rates

Per US$	Latest	Prev day	Week ago	4 wks ago	% chg on day	% chg in wk	% chg in 4 wk
Canadian $	1.5448	1.5240	1.5495	1.5150	1.36	-0.30	1.97
Deutschemark	1.6353	1.6147	1.6471	1.6820	1.27	-0.71	-2.78
Japanese yen	119.23	120.68	135.68	134.28	-1.20	n.a.	n.a.
British pound *	1.7112	1.7040	1.7055	1.6905	0.43	0.34	1.22
French franc	5.4841	5.4174	5.5230	5.6395	1.23	-0.70	-2.76
Swiss franc	1.3174	1.3085	1.3587	1.3840	0.68	-3.04	-4.81
Australian $ *	0.6162	0.6215	0.5982	0.5981	-0.84	3.02	3.03
Mexican peso	10.2600	10.2850	10.3750	10.5450	-0.24	-1.11	-2.70
Hong Kong $	7.7470	7.7470	7.7483	7.7495	0.00	-0.02	-0.03
Singapore $	1.6460	1.6375	1.6910	1.7290	0.52	-2.66	-4.80
Chinese renminbi	8.28	8.28	8.28	8.28	-0.00	-0.00	-0.03

Per C$							
U.S. $	0.6473	0.6562	0.6454	0.6601	-1.35	0.30	-1.93
Deutschemark	1.0586	1.0595	1.0630	1.1103	-0.09	-0.41	-4.66
Japanese yen	77.18	79.18	87.56	88.63	-2.53	n.a.	n.a.
British pound *	2.6435	2.5968	2.6426	2.5610	1.80	0.03	3.22
French franc	3.5500	3.5547	3.5644	3.7226	-0.13	-0.40	-4.63
Swiss franc	0.8528	0.8586	0.8769	0.9136	-0.68	-2.74	-6.65
Australian $ *	0.9519	0.9471	0.9268	0.9060	0.51	2.71	5.07
Mexican peso	6.6416	6.7487	6.6957	6.9606	-1.59	-0.81	-4.58
Hong Kong $	5.0149	5.0833	5.0005	5.1154	-1.35	0.29	-1.96
Singapore $	1.0655	1.0745	1.0913	1.1413	-0.83	-2.36	-6.64
Chinese renminbi	5.36	5.43	5.34	5.47	-1.35	0.30	-1.96

* inverted

Currency Cross Rates

Supplied by Royal Bank of Canada – indicative wholesale late afternoon rates

	C$	US$	DM	Yen	£	Fr. fr.	Sw. fr.	A$
Canadian $	...	1.54480	0.94466	0.01296	2.64346	0.28169	1.17261	0.95191
U.S.$	0.64733	...	0.61151	0.00839	1.71120	0.18235	0.75907	0.61620
Deutschmark	1.05858	1.63530	...	0.01372	2.79833	0.29819	1.24131	1.00767
Japanese yen	77.18	119.23	72.91	...	204.02	21.74	90.50	73.47
British pnd.	0.37829	0.58439	0.35736	0.00490	...	0.10656	0.44359	0.36010
French franc	3.55004	5.48410	3.35357	0.04600	9.38439	...	4.16282	3.37930
Swiss franc	0.85280	1.31740	0.80560	0.01105	2.25433	0.24022	...	0.81178
Australian $	1.05052	1.62285	0.99239	0.01361	2.77702	0.29592	1.23186	...
Gold	463.52	300.05	490.67	35773.46	175.34	1645.50	395.29	486.94

SOURCE: Reprinted with permission of *The Financial Post* (October 9, 1998).

For example, one of the currency futures contracts traded on the International Monetary Market (IMM) of the Chicago Mercantile Exchange requires the seller to deliver 12 500 000 Japanese yen to the buyer on a specific date for a number of US dollars agreed upon in advance. Only the price of the transaction (expressed in both dollars per yen and yen per dollar) is negotiated by the parties involved; all other terms are standard. Clearing procedures allow positions to be covered by reversing trades, and few contracts result in the actual delivery of foreign currency. As shown in Figure 20.6, prices and volumes for such contracts are quoted daily in the financial press along with those for other futures.

Markets for foreign currency futures attract both hedgers and speculators. Hedgers wish to reduce or possibly eliminate the risk associated with planned future transfers of funds from one country to another.

An Example

For example, a US importer might know on October 8, 1998, that he will have to make a payment of 50 million yen to a Japanese exporter in March 1999. The current exchange rate is $.008387 per yen (or, equivalently, 119.23 yen per dollar), so the anticipated dollar size of the payment is $.008387 \times 50\,000\,000 = \$419\,350$. The risk the importer faces

Figure 20.6 Quotations for foreign currency futures contracts.

— Lifetime —				— Daily —				Previous
High	Low	Month	Open	High	Low	Settle	Chg	open int.

Currency

Australian Dollar (IMM)
A$100,000, US$ per A$; 0.0001 = $10 per contract

High	Low	Month	Open	High	Low	Settle	Chg	open int.
0.6690	0.5470	Dec98	0.6215	0.6251	0.6100	0.6179	−0.0053	20,686
Est. vol.	2,098			Prev. vol.	15,797		Prev. open int.	20,716

British Pound (IMM)
62,500 pounds, US$ per pound; 0.0002 = $12.50 per contract

1.7300	1.5630	Dec98	1.6984	1.7300	1.6908	1.7052	+0.0056	54,831
Est. vol.	14,520			Prev. vol.	14,774		Prev. open int.	55,341

Canadian Dollar (IMM)
C$100,000, US$ per C$; 0.0001 = $10 per contract

0.7400	0.6300	Dec98	0.6552	0.6610	0.6455	0.6468	−0.0092	46,037
0.7247	0.6290	Mar99	0.6540	0.6565	0.6455	0.6470	−0.0092	2,651
0.7170	0.6300	June99	0.6545	0.6545	0.6470	0.6472	−0.0092	1,152
Est. vol.	13,055			Prev. vol.	15,642		Prev. open int.	50,207

European Currency (CME)
125,000 ECUs, US$ per unit; 0.0001 = $12.50 per contract

Est. vol.	0			Prev. vol.	0		Prev. open int.	1

French Franc (IMM)
500,000 francs, US$ per franc; 0.00002 = $10 per contract

0.1868	0.1656	Dec98	0.1859	0.1867	0.1822	0.1828	−0.0037	2,061
Est. vol.	5			Prev. vol.	7		Prev. open int.	2,061

German Mark (IMM)
125,000 marks, US$ per mark; 0.0001 = $12.50 per contract

0.6320	0.5496	Dec98	0.6217	0.6320	0.6112	0.6130	−0.0089	146,067
Est. vol.	47,051			Prev. vol.	33,600		Prev. open int.	146,631

Japanese Yen (IMM)
12.5 million yen, US$ per yen (scaled .00); 0.0001 = $12.50 per contract

0.8787	0.6890	Dec98	0.8364	0.8787	0.8165	0.8462	+0.0075	91,301
0.8891	0.6997	Mar99	0.8380	0.8891	0.8360	0.8567	+0.0076	2,769
0.8700	0.7086	June99	...	0.8700	...	0.8665	+0.0078	1,305
Est. vol.	68,636			Prev. vol.	88,889		Prev. open int.	95,463

Mexican Peso (IMM)
500,000 new pesos, US$ per peso; 0.000025 = $12.50 per contract

0.1144	0.0800	Dec98	0.0910	0.0925	0.0896	0.0924	+0.0011	18,997
0.1056	0.0755	Mar99	0.0840	0.0858	0.0835	0.0860	+0.0012	6,268
0.1022	0.0690	June99	0.0786	0.0810	0.0786	0.0810	+0.0012	2,541
0.0951	0.0635	Sept99	...	0.0772	0.0748	0.0772	+0.0012	778
Est. vol.	4,601			Prev. vol.	2,504		Prev. open int.	28,584

Swiss Franc (IMM)
125,000 francs, US$ per franc; 0.0001 = $12.50 per contract

0.7920	0.6569	Dec98	0.7695	0.7920	0.7600	0.7644	−0.0084	65,071
Est. vol.	24,130			Prev. vol.	18,399		Prev. open int.	65,433

U.S. Dollar Index (FINEX)
1000 x index points and US cents; 0.01 = $10 per contract

102.60	90.74	Dec98	92.45	93.65	90.74	93.35	+1.01	6,024
102.03	91.60	Mar99	92.30	92.30	91.60	93.17	+1.02	2,029
				Prev. vol.	2,082		Prev. open int.	8,062

SOURCE: Reprinted with permission of *The Financial Post* (October 9, 1998).

by simply waiting until March to make this payment is that the exchange rate will change in an unfavourable manner—perhaps rising to $.0105 per yen, in which case the dollar cost to the importer will have risen to $.0105 × 50 000 000 = $525 000. The importer can hedge this risk by purchasing four March futures contracts for yen. The settlement price on October 8, 1998, for these contracts was $.008567, meaning that the dollar cost of one contract is $.008567 × 50 000 000 = $428 350. Thus, the importer can remove the risk of the yen's appreciating by more than $.00018 against the dollar before the payment date by purchasing the four yen futures contracts.

A Canadian firm needing to hedge future Japanese yen liability would have to proceed differently because yen/CAD futures contracts do not exist. One way to set up such a hedge would be to buy an over-the-counter six-month forward contract. These contracts can be negotiated through the firm's bank at a price close to that quoted in the financial press. Alternatively, the firm could arrange a cross-hedge by simultaneously buying yen/USD contracts and selling CAD/USD contracts. The optimal way to proceed would, of course, depend on the relative costs of the two approaches.

Speculators are attracted to the foreign currency futures market when they believe that the current price of the futures contract is substantially different from what they expect the spot rate to be on the delivery date.

For example, a speculator might believe that the price of the March futures contract for Japanese yen is too high. Perhaps a speculator might believe that when March comes around, the exchange rate will be $.0080 per yen (or, equivalently, 125 yen per dollar). By selling (that is, short selling) a March futures contract for yen, the speculator will be selling yen for $.008567, the settlement price on October 8, 1998. At the time delivery has to be made, the speculator believes that yen can be bought on the spot market for $.0080, thereby allowing a profit to be made on the difference between the selling and buying prices.[16] Specifically, the speculator expects to be able to make a profit of ($.008567 − $.0080) × 12 500 000 = $7087.50 per futures contract.

Pricing

Futures contracts involving foreign currencies are priced according to the notion of **interest rate parity**, which is merely a special application of the model of futures pricing given in equation (20.4).

Imagine that it is October 1998 and you are planning to invest some money for one year. You could simply invest in a one-year US risk-free security and then receive the principal and interest a year later in the form of US dollars. Alternatively, you could exchange the dollars for German marks and use the marks to buy a one-year German risk-free security. In addition, you would short sell the requisite number of one-year German mark futures contracts so that a year later, when you receive the principal and interest in the form of German marks, you know exactly how many US dollars you would receive for them.

Both of these strategies—investing in US risk-free securities or investing in German risk-free securities—have no risk associated with them in that you know exactly how many US dollars they will yield after one year. If the German strategy had a higher return per dollar invested, Americans would not buy the US risk-free securities because they could earn the same amount for a smaller investment by buying the German risk-free securities. Similarly, if the US strategy had a higher return per dollar invested, Germans would not buy the German risk-free securities because they could earn the same amount for a smaller investment by buying US dollars in the spot market, purchasing US risk-free securities, and buying a one-year German mark futures contract. As a consequence, in equilibrium the two strategies must have the same cost if they have the same dollar payoffs.

Consider what would happen per dollar invested. The strategy of investing $1 in a US risk-free security that has a return of R_{US} will provide a cash inflow of $1(1 + R_s) after one year. The strategy of investing $1 in a German risk-free security that has a return of R_G, where the current spot rate of exchange is P_s and the futures price is P_f, will provide a dollar cash inflow of ($1/P_s$)(1 + R_G)P_f after one year. (Here both P_s and P_f are stated in dollars per mark.) Given that these two strategies cost the same ($1), their payoffs must be equal:

$$\$1(1 + R_{US}) = \left(\frac{\$1}{P_s}\right)(1 + R_G)P_f \tag{20.5}$$

Hence, the futures price of the mark can be determined by rewriting equation (20.5) as the interest-rate parity equation:

$$P_f = P_s\left(\frac{1 + R_{US}}{1 + R_G}\right) \tag{20.6}$$

Interest Rate Parity An explanation for why spot and futures exchange rates differ. It asserts that such differences result from different interest rates in the two countries.

---

[16]Actually, the typical speculator will plan to realize this profit by entering a reversing trade instead of buying yen on the spot market and then making delivery. Similarly, the previously mentioned hedging importer will typically plan to enter a reversing trade.

Thus if the current spot rate of exchange for the German mark is $.6115, and the US and German one-year risk-free rates are 4% and 5%, respectively, then the one-year futures price of the mark will be $.6115 × 1.04/1.05 = $.6057.

In relation to equation (20.4), the cost of carry is $.6057 − .6115 = −$.0058. In the case of foreign currency, the costs of ownership C are zero. However, the net benefits of ownership $I − B$ amount to the −$.0058 cost of carry. More generally, the cost of carry will equal

$$\text{carry} = P_s \left(\frac{R_{US} − R_G}{1 + R_G} \right) \tag{20.7}$$

for foreign currency futures, where R_G now denotes the risk-free rate in the foreign currency under consideration. From equation (20.7) it can be seen that because carry = $I − B$, it follows that

$$I = \frac{P_s R_{US}}{1 + R_G} \tag{20.8a}$$

$$B = \frac{P_s R_G}{1 + R_G} \tag{20.8b}$$

Hence, in the example I, the amount of interest forgone by the owner by selling marks in the futures market instead of the spot market, equals $.6115 × .04/1.05 = $.0233, whereas B, the benefit of owning marks instead of selling them, equals $.6115 × .05/1.05 = $.0291. Consequently, the cost of carry equals $.0233 − .0291 = −$.0058, as shown earlier.

Equation (20.4) indicates that the futures price will be less than the current spot price when the cost of carry is negative. This will occur when the US risk-free rate is less than the foreign risk-free rate, because the numerator on the right-hand side of equation (20.7) is negative whereas the denominator is positive in such a situation. Conversely, the futures price will be greater than the current spot price when the cost of carry is positive, which will occur when the US risk-free rate is greater than the foreign risk-free rate. Hence, the reason why futures prices are different from spot prices is that risk-free interest rates between countries are different.

▶ Interest-rate Futures

Futures involving fixed-income securities are often referred to as interest-rate futures because their prices are greatly influenced by the current and forecast interest rates. More specifically, their pricing can be related to the term structure of interest rates, which in turn is related to the concept of forward rates.[17]

An Example

Just how the pricing of interest-rate futures is related to the concept of forward rates can be illustrated with an example. Consider the futures market for US Treasury bonds, which is the most popular long-term interest rate futures contract in the US. As Figure 20.7 indicates, on October 8, 1998, any purchaser of a futures contract calling for delivery in December 1998 of a $100 000 face value Treasury bond would have paid a settlement price of 130-04, meaning 130-4/32 of par, or $130 125.[18] However, the actual amount that the purchaser would pay equals the settlement price times a *conversion factor*, plus accrued interest. The conversion factor varies depending on which Treasury bond is delivered to satisfy the contract, since the contract calls for delivery of a Treasury bond that

---

[17]See Chapter 5 for a discussion of term structure and forward rates.

[18]Delivery on Treasury bond futures can take place on any business day in the delivery month even though the trading ceases when there are seven business days left in the month.

Figure 20.7 Quotations for interest-rate futures contracts.

— Lifetime —				— Daily —				Previous		— Lifetime —				— Daily —				Previous
High	Low	Month	Open	High	Low	Settle	Chg	open int.		High	Low	Month	Open	High	Low	Settle	Chg	open int.

Interest Rate

										94.41	91.58	June06	...	...	93.91	93.88	−0.33	5,319

Canadian Govt. Bonds 5 Year (ME)
$100,000, points of 100%; 0.01 = $10 per contract

105.15	100.62	Dec98	...	...	...	104.70	−0.30	2,991
Vol.	0		Prev. vol.	865		Prev. open int.		2,991

Canadian Govt. Bonds 10 Year (ME)
$100,000, points of 100%; 0.01 = $10 per contract

130.35	120.55	Dec98	129.28	129.70	128.00	128.06	−1.22	58,485
Vol.	8,081		Prev. vol.	8,710		Prev. open int.		58,485

Canadian 3 Month Bankers' Acceptance (ME)
$1,000,000, points of 100%; 0.01 = $25 per contract

94.80	94.06	Oct98	94.75	94.76	94.72	94.72	+0.02	2,980
95.69	93.70	June99	95.60	95.69	95.47	95.48	−0.08	42,721
95.69	93.80	Sept99	95.65	95.69	95.46	95.47	−0.11	23,573
95.49	93.77	Dec99	95.49	95.49	95.49	95.30	−0.11	11,950
95.48	93.85	Mar00	95.48	95.48	95.27	95.28	−0.12	11,770
95.30	93.87	June00	95.20	95.20	95.20	95.18	−0.12	3,981
95.22	94.36	Sept00	...	...	...	95.12	−0.12	1,558
Vol.	27,666		Prev. vol.	29,643		Prev. open int.		275,309

Eurodollars (CME)
US$1,000,000, points of 100%; 0.01 = $25 per contract

94.85	94.06	Oct98	94.72	94.80	94.72	94.74	+0.04	39,362
95.00	94.16	Nov98	94.94	95.00	94.72	94.94	+0.06	12,733
95.17	91.33	Dec98	95.02	95.17	95.00	95.10	+0.08	492,320
95.35	94.32	Jan99	95.29	95.35	95.28	95.29	+0.08	3,067
95.48	94.43	Feb99	95.48	95.48	95.41	95.41	+0.06	941
95.60	91.36	Mar99	95.44	95.60	95.41	95.48	+0.03	505,008
95.72	91.31	June99	95.58	95.72	95.52	95.53	−0.04	412,854
95.76	91.26	Sept99	95.62	95.76	95.52	95.53	−0.09	323,787
95.62	91.15	Dec99	95.48	95.62	95.35	95.36	−0.14	283,183
95.67	91.19	Mar00	95.54	95.64	95.38	95.39	−0.16	226,549
95.58	91.14	June00	95.51	95.52	95.25	95.25	−0.19	140,820
95.48	91.10	Sept00	95.37	95.38	95.09	95.10	−0.23	115,428
95.30	91.00	Dec00	95.14	95.18	94.92	94.89	−0.26	108,703
95.28	91.05	Mar01	95.13	95.17	94.83	94.87	−0.26	87,777
95.20	91.01	June01	95.05	95.09	94.82	94.78	−0.27	70,427
95.12	90.98	Sept01	94.95	95.01	94.74	94.70	−0.27	65,677
94.98	90.90	Dec01	94.82	94.82	94.52	94.56	−0.28	50,230
94.98	90.95	Mar02	94.83	94.83	94.53	94.56	−0.28	48,453
94.92	90.93	June02	94.76	94.76	94.46	94.49	−0.29	51,288
94.87	90.91	Sept02	94.71	94.72	94.41	94.43	−0.29	30,341
94.79	90.83	Dec02	94.59	94.59	94.29	94.32	−0.30	31,265
94.79	90.87	Mar03	94.60	94.60	94.30	94.33	−0.30	29,220
94.75	90.84	June03	94.56	94.56	94.26	94.29	−0.30	19,879
94.72	90.82	Sept03	94.51	94.51	94.22	94.25	−0.31	16,906
94.63	90.73	Dec03	94.35	94.38	94.12	94.14	−0.31	12,218
94.65	90.77	Mar04	94.40	94.40	94.14	94.16	−0.31	10,939
94.62	90.74	June04	94.34	94.37	94.11	94.13	−0.31	11,681
94.59	90.71	Sept04	94.32	94.35	94.09	94.11	−0.31	10,175
94.51	91.12	Dec04	94.23	94.23	94.00	94.01	−0.32	10,703
94.53	91.14	Mar05	94.25	94.25	94.02	94.03	−0.32	8,673
94.53	91.50	June05	94.22	94.22	93.99	94.00	−0.32	7,666
94.50	91.67	Sept05	94.20	94.20	93.97	93.98	−0.32	7,988
94.42	91.60	Dec05	...	...	...	93.91	93.88	−0.33	4,236
94.44	91.61	Mar06	...	...	...	93.93	93.90	−0.33	5,724

94.38	91.86	Sept06	...	...	93.89	93.86	−0.33	5,380
94.30	91.78	Dec06	...	...	93.75	93.76	−0.34	6,019
94.32	91.79	Mar07	...	...	93.77	93.78	−0.34	5,254
94.29	92.28	June07	...	...	93.75	93.76	−0.34	4,943
94.27	92.58	Sept07	...	...	93.73	93.74	−0.34	4,439
94.27	92.98	Dec07	...	...	93.64	93.64	−0.35	4,675
94.75	93.19	Mar08	...	...	93.67	93.67	−0.35	4,199
95.22	93.16	June08	...	...	93.64	93.64	−0.35	3,441
94.14	93.62	Sept08	...	...	93.62	93.62	−0.35	1,967
Est. vol. 1,142,164			Prev. vol. 785,848			Prev. open int. 3,301,857		

Libor - 1 Month (CME)
US$3,000,000, points of 100%; 0.01 = $25 per contract

94.800	93.890	Oct98	94.630	94.685	94.630	94.655	+0.0400	19,570
94.930	94.005	Nov98	94.825	94.920	94.825	94.880	+0.0550	12,193
94.895	93.970	Dec98	94.820	94.865	94.790	94.790	+0.0200	7,406
95.280	94.155	Jan99	95.225	95.280	95.205	95.205	+0.0600	1,936
95.420	94.125	Feb99	95.410	95.420	95.360	95.360	+0.0400	1,418
95.510	94.110	Mar99	95.440	95.510	95.430	95.415	+0.0350	657
Est. vol.	6,415		Prev. vol.	9,558		Prev. open int.		43,288

U.S. Treasury Bills 3 Month (CME)
US$1,000,000, points of 100%; 0.01 = $25 per contract

96.220	94.880	Dec98	96.000	96.220	96.000	96.110	+0.1600	1,525
Est. vol.	429		Prev. vol.	69		Prev. open int.		1,716

U.S. Treasury Bonds 30 Year 8% (CBOT)
US$100,000, points and 32nds of 100%; 1/32nd = $31.25 per contract

135-08	103-13	Dec98	132-11	132-19	130-02	130-04	−2-29	749,445
134-26	103-04	Mar99	132-00	132-05	129-22	129-24	−2-30	80,244
134-02	111-24	June99	129-27	129-27	129-04	129-04	−3-00	736
131-06	111-15	Sept99	...	...	...	128-19	−3-00	4,295
				Prev. vol. 754,181		Prev. open int.		834,764

U.S. Treasury Notes 2 Year (CBOT)
US$200,000, points and 32nds of 100%; 1/32nd = $31.25 per contract

107-01	104-04	Dec98	106-22	107-01	106-15	106-16	−0-02	36,002
			Prev. vol.	5,308		Prev. open int.		36,002

U.S. Treasury Notes 5 Year (CBOT)
US$100,000, points and 32nds of 100%; 1/32nd = $62.50 per contract

116-07	108-30	Dec98	115-14	115-18	114-11	114-12	−0-28	374,577
116-15	109-23	Mar99	...	...	114-20	−0-29		1,200
			Prev. vol.	100,245		Prev. open int.		375,777

U.S. Treasury Notes 10 Year (CBOT)
US$100,000, points and 32nds of 100%; 1/32nd = $31.25 per contract

123-19	111-15	Dec98	121-23	121-29	119-31	120-03	−1-23	460,054
123-22	112-04	Mar99	122-03	122-03	120-10	120-14	−1-24	16,347
			Prev. vol.	178,565		Prev. open int.		476,605

30 Day Interest Rate (CBOT)
US$5,000,000, points of 100%; 0.01 = $41.67 per contract

94.890	94.320	Oct98	94.770	94.835	94.770	94.815	+0.050	11,722
95.010	94.270	Nov98	94.920	95.010	94.920	94.980	+0.050	8,214
95.200	94.350	Dec98	95.160	95.200	95.140	95.150	+0.050	7,227
95.300	94.250	Jan99	95.250	95.300	95.240	95.250	+0.050	2,235
95.510	94.370	Feb99	95.490	95.510	95.450	95.460	+0.060	1,727
95.540	94.440	Mar99	95.540	95.540	95.510	95.510	+0.050	636
				Prev. vol.	7,334		Prev. open int.	31,829

SOURCE: Reprinted with permission of *The Financial Post* (October 9, 1998).

either (1) if not callable, has a maturity of at least 15 years from December 1 or (2) if callable, has a first call date of at least 15 years after December 1.[19] Specifically, the conversion factor is the proportion of par the delivered Treasury bond would be selling for on the first day of the delivery month if it had a yield-to-maturity of 8%. Thus, deliverable bonds with coupons of less than 8% will have conversion factors of less than one, and those with coupons of greater than 8% will have conversion factors of greater than one.

As an example, a noncallable 7% coupon Treasury bond that matures 20 years after the delivery month would be selling for $90.10 per $100 of par value [computed as $20.83 (the present value of the $100 par value of the bond) plus $69.27 (the present value of a

---

[19]For this and certain other interest-rate futures contracts there is flexibility in just what the seller has to deliver, known as the *quality option*. The short position in the contract will usually decide on the *cheapest-to-deliver* Treasury bond, and deliver it to the long position. Sometimes there is also some flexibility regarding when during a business day an intention to deliver must be announced, known as the *wild card option*.

stream of 40 coupon interest payments of $3.50 each)]. Thus, the conversion value for this bond is 90.10/$100 = .9010. Given there is no accrued interest on this bond on the delivery date, the purchaser of the futures would pay $130 125 × .9010 = $117 243 for this Treasury bond on the December delivery date. This price corresponds with a 5.6% yield-to-maturity. If the market yield on this bond on the delivery date is less than 5.6%, then the purchaser of the futures will have made a profit as his purchase price is less than the spot price of the bond.

As with commodity futures, neither the buyers nor the sellers of such contracts must maintain their positions until the delivery date. Reversing trades can be made at any time, and relatively few contracts result in actual delivery.

Actively traded interest rate futures involve underlying securities ranging from short term (such as 90-day Treasury bills) to intermediate term (such as 10-year Treasury notes) to long term (such as the 20-year Treasury bonds just described). In Canada, the two actively traded contracts are on 3-month bankers' acceptances and 10-year Government of Canada bonds. Prices are generally stated in terms of percentages of par values for the corresponding securities.

Pricing

In general, pricing of interest rate futures contracts involves applying the cost-of-carry model given in equation (20.4). As an example, consider a 90-day Treasury bill futures contract that calls for delivery in six months. Note that nine-month Treasury bills will be equivalent to 90-day Treasury bills after six months have passed. Hence, they could be delivered as the underlying assets in 90-day Treasury bill futures contracts where the delivery date is six months from now. What futures price is fair for these contracts?

Assume that the current market price of a nine-month Treasury bill is $95.24, providing a yield of $4.76/$95.24 = 5% over the nine months. (This yield and those that follow are not annualized.) If an owner sold this security now, he would be able to risklessly earn 3% on the proceeds over the next six months. This means that the owner should not short sell a futures contract calling for delivery in six months of a 90-day Treasury bill, where the price to be received is less than $95.24 × 1.03 = $98.10. For example, if the price of the futures contract was $97, then the owner would be making only 1.85% on his initial investment of $95.24 over the subsequent six months. This is less than the 3% that could be earned by selling the nine-month Treasury bill now and investing in a six-month Treasury bill.

Conversely, the buyer should not agree to a price that is more than $98.10. This is because the buyer could buy the nine-month Treasury bill in the spot market today for $95.24 and receive $100 in nine months, or the buyer could risklessly invest the $95.24 for six months at 3% and then use the $98.10 proceeds to pay the futures price for a 90-day Treasury bill that pays $100 at maturity. If the futures price were greater than $98.10 then the buyer would have to invest more than $95.24 today. For example, if the futures price was $99, then $99/1.03 = $96.12 would have to be invested today, so that the principal plus 3% interest for six months would be sufficient to pay the futures price ($99) after six months. In such a situation, nobody would choose to be long in the futures contract, because he would be better off buying a nine-month Treasury bill in the spot market for $95.24 instead of investing more at 3% for six months in order to be able to pay the futures price upon delivery of the Treasury bill. Consequently, the futures price must be $98.10, because this is the only price that is acceptable to both parties to the futures contract.

Generalizing, the futures price, P_f, must equal the spot price, P_s, plus the forgone interest I, just as shown in equation (20.2), because the benefits B and costs of ownership C are zero with such assets. Equivalently, letting R denote the risk-free interest rate that exists on Treasuries that mature on the delivery date, the futures price is

$$P_f = P_s(1 + R) \qquad (20.9)$$

The futures price will be greater than the spot price as long as the risk-free rate R is positive. Similarly, note that the cost of carry equals

$$\text{carry} = P_s R \qquad (20.10)$$

because both B and C are equal to zero. In this example, carry = $95.24 × .03 = $2.86. Note that the difference between the futures price of $98.10 and the spot price of $95.24 also equals $2.86.

Market Index Futures

Figure 20.8 shows a set of quotations for futures contracts on a variety of market indices. Each of these contracts involves the payment of *cash* on the delivery date of an amount equal to a *multiplier* times the difference between (1) the value of the index at the close of the last trading day of the contract and (2) the purchase price of the futures contract. If the index is above the futures price, those with short positions pay those with long positions. If the index is below the futures price, those with long positions pay those with short positions.

In practice, a clearinghouse is used, and all contracts are marked to market every day. In a sense, the delivery day differs from other days in only one respect—all open positions are marked to market for the last time and then closed.

Cash settlement provides results similar to those associated with the delivery of all the securities in the index. It avoids the effort and transaction costs associated with (1) the purchase of securities by people who have taken short futures positions, (2) the delivery of these securities to people who have taken long futures positions, and (3) the subsequent sale of the securities by those who receive them.

Major Contracts

Toronto Futures Exchange
www.tse.com/investor/
futures.html

Several major stock market index futures are quoted in Figure 20.8, with the most popular one in terms of both trading volume and open interest based on the Standard & Poor's 500 (S&P 500). This contract, along with others on the Russell 2000 (small US stocks) and the Nikkei 225 (a major Japanese index), are traded on the Index and Option Market Division of the Chicago Mercantile Exchange (CME). The most recent addition is a contract on the Dow Jones Industrial Average, which began trading on October 6, 1997, at the Chicago Board of Trade. In Canada futures contracts on the TSE 35 and the TSE 100 are traded on the Toronto Futures Exchange (TFE), a subsidiary of the TSE. Trading in the TSE 100 contracts is extremely thin.

For many contracts, the multiplier is $500; for the Nikkei 225, it is $5, and for the S&P 500 it is $250. Thus, the purchase of an S&P 500 contract when the index is 800 would cost $200 000 ($250 × 800). The subsequent sale of this contract when the index is 840 would result in proceeds of $250 × 840 = $210 000 and a profit of $210 000 − $200 000 = $10 000.

Trading Volume

The volume of trading in futures contracts is very large. To assess its relative size, the number of contracts can be multiplied by the total dollar value represented by one contract. As shown in Figure 20.8, the estimated volume on October 8, 1998, for S&P 500 futures was 225 445 contracts. At a value of 969.30 for the lowest priced S&P 500 contract, the total dollar value is 225 445 × 969.30 × $250 = $55 billion. In comparison, the average daily dollar value of all trades of shares on the New York Stock Exchange during 1997 was about $23 billion per day—less than the dollar size of the S&P futures on October 8, 1998. This is not unusual. On many days the dollar value involved in trades of S&P 500 futures exceeds that of all trades of individual stocks.

Figure 20.8 | Quotations for index futures contracts.

— Lifetime —				— Daily —				Previous
High	Low	Month	Open	High	Low	Settle	Chg	open int.

Indexes

Commodity Research Bureau (NYFE)
500 x index points; 0.05 pt. = $25 per contract

High	Low	Month	Open	High	Low	Settle	Chg	open int.
234.75	199.60	Nov98	207.90	208.00	204.35	204.60	−1.90	852
224.15	203.00	Jan99	209.90	210.00	207.25	207.10	−1.85	806
Est. vol.	400		Prev. vol.	217		Prev. open int.		2,010

Dow Jones Indl Avg Index (CBOT)
10 x index points; 1 pt. = $10 per contract

9515.00	7415.00	Dec98	7785.00	7825.00	7500.00	7788.00	−2.00	16,732
9586.00	7550.00	Mar99	7655.00	7855.00	7560.00	7844.00	−1.00	1,348
				Prev. vol.	21,551	Prev. open int.		18,572

Goldman Sachs Cmmdty Index (CME)
250 x index points; 0.10 pt. = $25 per contract

175.10	139.90	Oct98	151.30	151.40	148.20	148.70	−3.10	18,711
169.90	142.70	Nov98	152.70	152.70	150.90	151.20	−2.90	7,923
Est. vol.	11,117		Prev. vol.	6,111		Prev. open int.		26,913

Municipal Bond Index (CBOT)
US$1,000 x index points; 1/32 pt. = $31.25 per contract

130-07	123-14	Dec98	128-10	128-21	126-20	127-00	−1-23	22,631
				Prev. vol.	6,649	Prev. open int.		22,657

NIKKEI 225 Index (CME)
$5 x index points; 5 pts. = $25 per contract

17330	12690	Dec98	12800	12820	12690	12750	−940	19,591
Est. vol.	2,191		Prev. vol.	3,928		Prev. open int.		19,709

NYSE Composite Index (NYFE)
250 x index points; 0.05 pt. = $12.50 per contract

611.15	465.00	Dec98	487.00	487.00	465.00	482.75	−5.15	5,607
617.50	485.75	Mar99	491.25	...	...	487.00	−5.15	2,159
623.85	490.55	June99	495.50	...	...	491.25	−5.15	1,100
Est. vol.	6,000		Prev. vol.	3,501		Prev. open int.		9,066

Russell 2000 Index (CME)
500 x index points; 0.05 pt. = $25 per contract

508.85	304.50	Dec98	317.00	317.00	304.50	315.50	−9.50	11,581
Est. vol.	802		Prev. vol.	1,094		Prev. open int.		11,582

S&P 500 Composite Index (CME)
250 x index points; 0.10 pt. = $25 per contract

1212.10	890.85	Dec98	982.00	985.10	929.00	969.30	−9.70	391,952
1225.00	902.85	Mar99	962.50	979.00	937.50	977.60	−9.90	6,810
1238.10	914.85	June99	...	...	947.50	985.30	−10.20	2,158
1263.90	960.70	Dec99	989.00	998.80	960.70	997.30	−11.40	658
Est. vol.	225,445		Prev. vol.	172,548		Prev. open int.		401,751

Toronto 35 (TFE)
500 x index points; 0.05 pt. = $25 per contract

344.00	291.30	Dec98	297.50	306.00	297.00	304.20	−4.30	21,726
Vol.	2,101		Prev. vol.	1,967		Open int.		21,728

Toronto 100 (TFE)
500 x index points; 0.05 pt. = $25 per contract

452.00	361.00	Dec98	...	...	...	332.50	...	1,673
Vol.	0		Prev. vol.	0		Open int.		1,673

Value Line Composite Index (KBOT)
500 x index points; 0.05 pt. = $25 per contract

				Prev. vol.	4	Prev. open int.		127

SOURCE: Reprinted with permission of *The Financial Post* (October 9, 1998).

The situation is quite different on the TFE, as interest in futures has not developed in Canada to the extent that it has in the US. On October 8, 1998, 2101 index futures traded, representing a total dollar volume of about $320 million or about 0.6% of the US trading value and 20% of the average daily value of TSE equity trades.

Hedging

What accounts for the popularity of market index futures in general and the S&P 500 in particular? Simply stated, they provide relatively inexpensive and highly liquid positions similar to those obtained with diversified stock portfolios.

For example, instead of purchasing 500 stocks in anticipation of a market advance, one can invest an equivalent amount of money in Treasury bills and take a long position in S&P 500 futures. Alternatively, instead of trying to take short positions in 500 stocks in anticipation of a market decline, one can take a short position in S&P 500 futures, using Treasury bills as margin.

Market index futures also allow broker-dealers to hedge the market risk associated with the temporary positions they often take in the course of their business.[20] This hedging ultimately benefits investors by providing them with greater liquidity than they would have otherwise. For example, consider an investor who wants to sell a large block of shares. In this situation a broker-dealer might agree to purchase the shares immediately at an agreed-upon price, and then spend time "lining up" buyers. In the interim, however, economic news might cause the market to fall, and with it the price of the shares. This would cause the broker-dealer to experience a loss, because the broker-dealer owns the shares during the period between purchasing them from the investor and lining up the ultimate buyers. One traditional way that broker-dealers protect themselves (at least partially) from this risk is to pay the investor a relatively low price for the stock. However, the broker-dealer can now hedge this risk (at least partially) by short selling S&P 500 futures at the time the stock is bought from the investor and reversing this position when the ultimate buyers are found.

Given competition among broker-dealers, the existence of S&P 500 futures will lead them to provide higher bid prices and lower ask prices. This reduced bid-ask spread means that the existence of S&P 500 futures has provided the associated spot market for stocks with greater liquidity.

It should be pointed out that the use of S&P 500 futures in such situations does not remove all risk from the position of the broker-dealer. All that it removes is market risk, because these futures contracts involve a broad market index, not an individual stock. Thus, it is possible for the broker-dealer to experience a loss even if an appropriate position has been taken in futures. Specifically, the individual stock with which the broker-dealer is involved may move up or down in price while the S&P 500 is stable, or the S&P 500 may move up or down while the individual stock is stable. In either case, the broker-dealer who has hedged with S&P 500 futures may still experience a loss. The possibility of this happening is substantial when the broker-dealer has little diversification, with the greatest possibility associated with a one-stock portfolio.

Index Arbitrage

When stock index futures were first proposed, a number of people predicted that at long last there would be an indicator of investors' expectations about the future course of the stock market. It was said that the market price of such a futures contract would indicate the consensus opinion of investors concerning the future level of the associated index. In times of optimism, the futures price might be much higher than the current level of the market, whereas in times of pessimism, the futures price might be much lower.

Such predictions have since been found to be quite off the mark. This is because the price of a futures contract on an asset will not diverge by more than the cost of carry from the spot price of the asset. Should a relatively large divergence occur, clever investors known as *arbitrageurs* will make trades designed to capture riskless (that is, "arbitrage") profits.

The presence of arbitrageurs has an effect on the pricing of stock index futures. Their actions will force the price of a stock index futures contract to stay close to an "appropriate" relationship with the current level of the associated index. To find out just what is meant by appropriate, consider a hypothetical example where today is a day in June when the TSE 35 is at 200 and a December TSE 35 futures contract is selling for 210. The following investment strategies can be compared:

1. Purchase the stocks in the TSE 35, hold them until December and then sell them on the delivery date of the December TSE 35 contract.

---

[20]Similarly, interest-rate futures are often used by financial institutions to hedge interest-rate risk to which they may be exposed—that is, when a large movement in interest rates would cause a large loss, these institutions will seek protection by either buying or selling interest-rate futures.

2. Purchase a December TSE 35 futures contract along with Treasury bills that mature in December. Hold the futures contract until the delivery date in December.

Strategy 1 would cost $200 (in "index terms") at the outset. In return, it would provide the investor with (1) an amount of money equal to the value of the TSE 35 on the delivery date and (2) dividends on those stocks that went ex-dividend prior to the delivery date. That is, by denoting the level the TSE 35 will have on the delivery date as P_d and assuming the dividend yield over the six-month time period from June to December is 3%, the investor following strategy 1 will receive in December an amount that is equal to $P_d + \$6$ [that is, $P_d + (.03 \times \$200)$].[21]

Assume that $200 is invested in Treasury bills in strategy 2. Since Treasury bills can be used as margin on futures, the total cost of strategy 2 is $200, which is the same as the cost of strategy 1. In return, strategy 2 would provide the investor with (1) an amount of money equal to the difference between the value of the TSE 35 and $210 on the delivery date and (2) the face value of the Treasury bills on the delivery date. That is, assuming that the six-month yield on the Treasury bills is 5%, the investor following strategy 2 will receive in December an amount that is equal to P_d [that is, $(P_d - \$210) + (1.05 \times \$200)$].

By design, both strategies require the same initial outlay. Furthermore, both strategies are subject to precisely the same uncertainty, the unknown level of the TSE 35 on the future delivery date, denoted by P_d. However, the inflows are not equal, indicating that an opportunity exists for **index arbitrage**.[22]

In this example, index arbitrage would cause an investor to go long on strategy 1 and short on strategy 2 because strategy 1 has a higher payoff than strategy 2 (note that $P_d + \$6 > P_d$). Going long on strategy 1 means that the investor is to do exactly what was indicated earlier—purchase the stocks in the TSE 35 and hold them until the December delivery date. Going short on strategy 2 means doing exactly the opposite. The investor shorts (that is, sells) a December TSE 35 futures contract and sells Treasury bills that mature in December. The net cash outflow of going long on strategy 1 and short on strategy 2 is zero—the $200 spent buying the stocks in going long on strategy 1 was obtained by selling $200 worth of December Treasury bills when going short on strategy 2. The margin necessary for being short on the future contract is met by having purchased the underlying stocks. Thus, no additional cash needs to be committed in order to engage in index arbitrage—owning Treasury bills that mature in December is sufficient.

Having gone long on strategy 1 and short on strategy 2, what is the investor's position on the delivery date in December? First, the investor bought the individual stocks in the TSE 35 at $200 and assured himself of a selling price of $210 by being short the TSE 35 futures contract. Thus, the investor has made $10 from being long on the individual stocks and short on the futures on the index. Second, the investor has received dividends totalling $.03 \times \$200 = \$6$ from owning the stocks from June to December. Third, by selling, in June, $200 of December Treasury bills the investor has forgone the $.05 \times \$200 = \$10$ on them. Overall, the investor has increased the dollar return by $\$10 + \$6 - \$10 = \$6$. Furthermore, this increase is certain, meaning it will be received regardless of what happens

---

[21]The 3% dividend yield is actually the accumulated December value of the dividends divided by the purchase price of the stocks. Hence, the dividends might be received in three months and amount to 2.93% of the purchase price of the index. Putting them in a risk-free asset that returns 2.47% for the last three months results in a yield of 3%, or $3, in December.

[22]Index arbitrage is one of two major forms of program trading. The other form, known as portfolio insurance, was discussed in the previous chapter. For a discussion and example of how futures can be used to procure portfolio insurance, see Stephen R. King and Eli M. Remolona, "The Pricing and Hedging of Market Index Deposits," Federal Reserve Bank of New York *Quarterly Review* 12, no. 2 (Summer 1987): 9–20; or Thomas J. O'Brien, *How Option Replicating Portfolio Insurance Works: Expanded Details*, Monograph Series in Finance and Economics no. 1988–4, New York University Salomon Center, Leonard N. Stern School of Business.

Index Arbitrage An investment strategy that involves buying a stock index futures contract and selling the individual stocks in the index or vice versa. The strategy is designed to take advantage of a mispricing between the stock index futures contract and the underlying stocks.

to the level of the TSE 35. Thus, by going long on strategy 1 and short on strategy 2, the investor will not have increased the risk of his portfolio but will have increased the dollar return.

Earlier, it was mentioned that an investor going long on strategy 1 would receive cash of $P_d + \$6$ in December, whereas an investor going long on strategy 2 would receive cash of P_d. From these figures it can be seen that going long on strategy 1 and short on strategy 2 will provide a net dollar return of $6 (that is, $(P_d + \$6) - P_d$). However, if enough investors do this, the opportunity for making the $6 riskless profit will disappear. This is because (1) going long on the individual stocks will push the prices of these stocks up, thereby raising the level of the TSE 35 above 200, and (2) going short on the TSE 35 futures will reduce the price of the futures below $210. These two adjustments will continue until it is no longer profitable to go long on strategy 1 and short on strategy 2.

What if the price of the TSE 35 December futures contract were $190 instead of $210? The dollar return from being long on strategy 1 is still equal to $P_d + \$6$. However, the dollar return from being long on strategy 2 will be different. Purchasing Treasury bills and the futures contract will provide the investor with a dollar return in December of $P_d + \$20$ [that is, $(P_d - \$190) + (1.05 \times \$200)$]. Since these two inflows are not equal, again there is an opportunity for index arbitrage. However, it would involve the investor going short on strategy 1 and long on strategy 2. This is because strategy 1 now has a lower payoff than strategy 2 (note that $P_d + \$6 < P_d + \$20$). By doing this, the investor will, without risk, earn $14 [that is, $(P_d + \$20) - (P_d + \$6)$]. Furthermore, being short the individual stocks and long the futures will reduce the level of the TSE 35 below 200 and raise the price of the futures above $190.

In equilibrium, because these two strategies cost the same to implement, prices will adjust so that their net cash inflows are equal. Letting y denote the dividend yield on the stocks in the index, P_f the current price of the futures contract on the index, and P_s the current spot price of the index (that is, P_s denotes the current level of the index), the net cash inflow from strategy 1 is

$$P_d + yP_s$$

Letting R denote the interest rate on Treasury bills, the net cash inflow from strategy 2 is

$$(P_d - P_f) + [(1 + R) \times P_s]$$

Setting these two inflows equal to each other results in

$$P_d + yP_s = (P_d - P_f) + [(1 + R) \times P_s] \tag{20.11}$$

Simplifying this equation results in

$$P_f - P_s = (R - y)P_s \tag{20.12}$$

or

$$P_f = P_s + RP_s - yP_s \tag{20.13}$$

Equation (20.12) indicates that the difference between the price of the futures contract and the current level of the index should depend only on (1) the current level of the index P_s, and (2) the difference between the interest rate on Treasury bills and the dividend yield on the index $R - y$. As the delivery date nears, the difference between the interest rate and the dividend yield diminishes, converging to zero on the delivery date. Thus as the delivery date approaches, the futures price, P_f, should converge to the current spot price P_s.

Equation (20.13) shows that index futures are priced according to the cost-of-carry model given earlier in equation (20.4), where the costs of ownership C are zero. Here the interest forgone by ownership I is equal to RP_s, whereas the benefit of ownership B is the dividend yield yP_s. Hence, the cost of carry is

$$\text{carry} = RP_s - yP_s \tag{20.14}$$

which will be positive as long as the risk-free interest rate, R, is greater than the dividend yield on the index, y,—a situation that exists nearly all the time.

In the example, the six-month interest rate was 5%, the six-month dividend yield was 3%, and the current level of the TSE 35 was 200. This means that the difference between the TSE 35 December futures contract and the current level of the TSE 35 should be $(.05 - .03) \times 200 = 4$. Equivalently, the equilibrium price of the futures contract when the TSE 35 is 200 would be 204. Note that when three of the six months have passed, the interest rate and dividend yield will be 5%/2 = 2.5% and 3%/2 = 1.5%, respectively. Thus, the difference should be about $(.025 - .015) \times 200 = 2$, assuming the TSE 35 is still at 200 at that time.

In practice, the situation is not this simple for a number of reasons. Positions in futures, stocks, and Treasury bills involve transaction costs.[23] This means that arbitrage will not take place unless the difference diverges far enough from the amount shown in equation (20.12) to warrant incurring such costs. The futures price, and hence the difference, can be expected to move within a band around the "theoretical value," with the width of the band determined by the costs of those who can engage in transactions most efficiently.

To add to the complexity, both the dividend yield and the relevant interest rate on Treasury bills are subject to some uncertainty. Neither the amounts of dividends to be declared nor their timing can be specified completely in advance. Furthermore, because futures positions must be marked to market daily, the amount of cash required for strategy 2 may have to be varied via additional borrowing (if short this strategy) or lending (if long this strategy). Also, on occasion market prices may be reported with a substantial time lag, making the current level and the futures price of the index appear to be out of line when they actually are not. (An extreme example of this situation occurred on Black Monday, October 19, 1987.) Thus, an investor may enter into the transactions necessary for index arbitrage when actual prices are in equilibrium, thereby incurring useless transaction costs. Nevertheless, index arbitrage is still actively pursued, most notably by brokerage firms.

Stock index futures are also used extensively by other professional money managers. As a result, prices of such contracts are likely to track their underlying indices very closely, taking into account both dividends and current interest rates. It is unlikely that a private investor will be able to exploit "mispricing" of such a contract by engaging in index arbitrage. Nevertheless, stock index futures can provide inexpensive ways to take positions in the stock market or to hedge portions of the risk associated with other positions. Furthermore, their use can lower transaction costs by reducing the size of the bid-ask spread in individual securities, thereby benefiting investors who may never take direct positions in futures contracts.

The 35 underlying stocks in the TSE 35, a "mutual" fund consisting of these stocks in the form of TIPs, options on TIPs, TSE 35 options, and TSE 35 futures contracts can all be traded and, therefore, it is possible to arbitrage freely between these securities. One therefore expects these securities to be fairly priced at most times.

The existence of index arbitrage permits the use of stock index futures as a substitute for holding the underlying stocks. The substitution of a futures position for a stock portfolio has led to the development of synthetic index funds. These allow a foreign investor to gain access to Canadian equity markets without hiring either research and portfolio management services or an investment counsellor, by creating a synthetic Toronto 35 index fund using futures contracts. The earlier example illustrated the equivalence of a TSE 35

---

[23]People involved in index arbitrage need to be able to quickly make a large number of transactions in individual stocks. In order to do this, they often have their computers send in their orders through CATS (discussed in Chapter 3). For a discussion of some of the complications involved in successfully executing index arbitrage strategies, see David M. Modest, "On the Pricing of Stock Index Futures," *Journal of Portfolio Management* 10, no. 4 (Summer 1984): 51–57.

stock position and a combination of TSE 35 futures contracts and Treasury bills; therefore, the investor can replicate the return on the index with minimal transactions costs and management fees.

Futures Versus Options

People occasionally make the mistake of confusing a futures contract with an options contract.[24] With an options contract there is the possibility that both parties involved will have nothing to do at the end of the life of the contract. In particular, if the option is "out of the money" on the expiration date, then the options contract will be worthless and can be thrown away. However, with a futures contract, both parties involved must do something at the end of the life of the contract. The parties are obligated to complete the transaction, either by a reversing trade or by actual delivery.

Figure 20.9 contrasts the situation faced by the buyer and the seller of a call option with the situation faced by the buyer and the seller of a futures contract. Specifically, terminal values for buyers and sellers are shown at the last possible moment—the expiration date for the option and the delivery date for the futures contract.

As shown in panel (a), no matter what the price of the underlying stock, an option buyer cannot lose and an option seller cannot gain on the expiration date. Option buyers compensate sellers for putting themselves in this position by paying them a premium when the contract is signed.

The situation is quite different with a futures contract. As shown in panel (b), the buyer may gain or lose, depending on the price of the asset in the delivery month. Whatever the buyer gains or loses, an exactly offsetting loss or gain will be registered by the seller. The higher the contract price (that is, the price of the futures contract when the buyer purchased it from the seller), the greater the likelihood that the buyer will lose and the seller will gain. The lower the contract price, the greater the likelihood that the seller will lose and the buyer will gain.

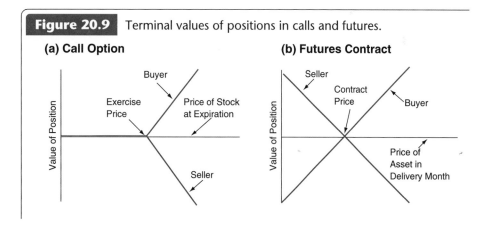

Figure 20.9 Terminal values of positions in calls and futures.

(a) Call Option

(b) Futures Contract

---

[24]Adding to the confusion is the existence of a contract known as a futures option, which is an option that has a futures contract instead of a stock as its underlying asset. Futures options are discussed in more detail in the Appendix.

Transportable Alpha

Years ago trustees of the $1 billion General Mills pension fund adopted a disciplined approach to allocating assets among various broad categories. This was accomplished by establishing specific long-run allocation targets: 60% to common stocks and 40% to fixed-income securities. The trustees believe that this *policy asset allocation* provides an optimal balance of expected return and risk, given their collective tolerance for possible adverse outcomes. The trustees expect the fund's staff, who handle the fund's day-to-day investment operations, to stick closely to this policy asset allocation. In turn, the staff follow a procedure of reducing exposure to the asset category that has appreciated in relative value and increasing exposure to the asset category that has depreciated in relative value.

To manage the pension fund's assets, the staff had retained what the trustees considered to be a superior group of domestic common stock managers. Over a 10-year period, those managers, in aggregate, had outperformed the S&P 500 by 1.5% annually (after all fees and expenses)—an exceptional amount by the standards of the investment management business. The trustees and staff expected such superior performance to continue in the future.

More recently, the trustees found themselves facing a dilemma: they would have liked to have assigned more than 60% of the fund's assets to the common stock managers. However, the trustees were also committed to the discipline of their asset allocation process. Could the trustees have their proverbial cake and eat it too? The answer was "yes," through a concept called *transportable alpha*.

Consider three strategies through which General Mills could have maintained its policy asset allocation, yet taken advantage of its common stock managers' skills. Each strategy involves allocating more than 60% of the pension fund's assets to the common stock managers, while simultaneously reducing the pension fund's common stock exposure and increasing its fixed-income exposure in order to comply with the fund's asset allocation targets.

1. *Long-short strategy.* The managers, in aggregate, purchase long positions in stocks as they typically would with their assigned assets. However, they also short sell stocks (see Chapter 2) equal in value to the pension fund's overweighting of domestic equity assets. The cash generated by these short sales is used to buy fixed-income securities that are held as margin, but nevertheless provide returns through interest income and price changes. The particular long-short transactions result from the managers' investment research, which identifies under- and overpriced securities.

2. *Futures strategy.* The managers purchase long stock positions with their assigned assets. At the same time the pension fund's staff sells futures contracts on a stock market index and buys futures contracts on Treasury bonds in sufficient amounts to compensate for the over- and underweighting of common stocks and fixed-income securities.

3. *Swap strategy.* The managers purchase long stock positions with their assigned assets. Through a financial intermediary (such as a bank or a broker) the pension fund "swaps" (exchanges) with another institutional investor the return on a common stock index in order to receive the return on a fixed-income index. These swaps (see Chapter 23) are based on dollar amounts equal to the over and underweightings of the common stocks and fixed-income securities.

In general, these strategies can be characterized as allowing the pension fund to earn (1) the total return generated by a 40% allocation to fixed-income securities, (2) the total return produced by a 60% allocation to common stocks (that is, the normal plus abnormal returns of the common stock managers), and (3) the abnormal returns earned by the common stock managers associated with the allocation in excess of 60% to common stocks. The common stock managers' abnormal returns (known as *alphas*) are effectively "transported" to the fixed-income asset category.

In the final analysis, General Mills chose to implement the second strategy. The pension fund's staff believed that listed futures contracts provided the cheapest and administratively least cumbersome means of carrying out its alpha transport program. Nevertheless, the ability to customize the other strategies to specific situations may make those strategies attractive at times to certain institutional investors.

These strategies highlight fundamental changes in the financial markets that began in the 1980s and have rapidly gathered momentum in the 1990s. Through the development of derivative financial instruments (options, futures, and swaps) and the technological advancements in communications and computing power, financial markets have become highly integrated and fungible. Investors are increasingly able to exploit perceived profit opportunities and simultaneously maintain desired risk positions.

Pacific Investment Management Company (PIMCO) provides another example of the transportable alpha concept. PIMCO is one of the largest fixed-income managers in the world, with assets under management exceeding $60 billion. Over the years, the firm has produced an enviable track record, earning positive risk-adjusted returns under a variety of fixed-income investment assignments.

Since 1986, PIMCO has transported its fixed-income management skills to the US stock market through a product called StocksPlus. PIMCO's process is simple. The firm purchases S&P 500 futures contracts equal to a specified *notional* principal. (A notional principal is the market exposure of the futures contracts—that is, the number of contracts purchased times the contracts' price times the contract multiplier.) At the same time PIMCO sets aside cash reserves equal to the notional principal. The cash reserves serve as collateral for the futures contracts.

As the text discusses, futures prices are set by investors predicated on the assumption that they can hold a combination of futures contracts and the risk-free asset. PIMCO uses its investment skills to create a short-term fixed-income portfolio that has substantially outperformed 90-day Treasury bills with little incremental risk. As a result, the firm's combination of S&P 500 futures contracts and short-term fixed-income investments has consistently exceeded the returns on the S&P 500.

PIMCO uses a variety of cash management strategies to add value relative to a portfolio of 90-day Treasury bills. The firm takes advantage of the most consistently upward portion of the yield curve—that is, maturities between zero days and one year. As the StocksPlus strategy needs liquidity from only a small portion of its fixed-income portfolio to meet margin requirements, PIMCO extends roughly one-half of its portfolio to maturities past 90 days. Further, the firm accepts some credit risk by purchasing non-government securities such as commercial paper. PIMCO also takes advantage of certain securities that offer little credit risk, but relatively high yields. At times these securities have included short-term tranches of collateralized mortgage obligations, floating-rate notes, and foreign government short-term securities (with currency risk fully hedged).

Transportable alpha involves investors capturing inefficiencies in certain markets, while maintaining desired exposure to markets beyond those in which the superior performance is earned. Transportable alpha is not a free lunch. Investors must pay commissions on their trades in stocks, options, futures, and swaps either directly or through bid-ask spreads. Real-world frictions such as collateral requirements and even custodial accounting difficulties still complicate the smooth implementation of the alpha transport strategies. Further, investors must take active management risk in order to earn their alphas.

For example, General Mills's common stock managers, in aggregate, may underperform the stock market, or PIMCO's short-term portfolio may underperform 90-day Treasury bills. However, institutional investors applying the transportable alpha concept believe that their active management investment strategies possess sufficiently positive expected returns to more than compensate for the additional risk assumed.

Synthetic Futures

For some assets, futures contracts are unavailable, but both put and call options are available. In such cases, an investor can create a **synthetic futures contract**.

The clearest example involves European options on common stocks. As shown in the previous chapter, the *purchase* of a European call option and the *sale* of a European put option at the same exercise price and with the same expiration date will provide a value at expiration that will be related, dollar for dollar, to the stock price at that time. This is shown in Figure 20.10.

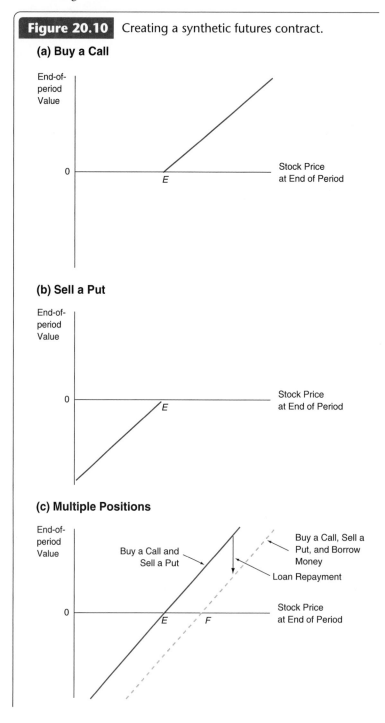

Figure 20.10 Creating a synthetic futures contract.

(a) Buy a Call

(b) Sell a Put

(c) Multiple Positions

Panel (a) shows the payoff associated with the purchase of a call at an exercise price E, whereas panel (b) shows the payoff associated with the sale of a put at the same exercise price. The results obtained by taking *both* positions are shown by the solid line in panel (c).

Depending on the prices (that is, premiums) of the call and the put, this strategy may initially either require a net outflow of cash or provide a net inflow. For comparability with the purchase of a futures contract, this cash flow may be offset with borrowing or lending as required to bring the net investment to zero. The dashed line in panel (c) shows a case in which the call option costs more than is provided by the sale of the put option. The difference is borrowed, requiring the loan repayment shown in the figure. The dashed line thus indicates the net end-of-period payoffs for a strategy requiring no initial outlay. Because these payoffs are equivalent to the payoffs from a futures contract with a contract price equal to F, a synthetic futures contract has been created.

In practice, the equivalence is not perfect. Most listed options are American, not European, raising the possibility that the buyer of the put will exercise it prior to maturity. Moreover, the synthetic future is not marked to market on a daily basis. Despite these differences, the existence of well-functioning markets for call and put options will enable investors to create arrangements similar to futures on the underlying asset synthetically.

Summary

1. A futures contract involves the delivery of a specific type of asset at a specific location at a given future date.
2. People who buy and sell futures can be classified as either hedgers or speculators. Hedgers transact in futures primarily to reduce risk, because these people either produce or use the asset in their ordinary course of business. Speculators transact in futures in pursuit of relatively short-term profits.
3. Futures are bought and sold on organized exchanges. Futures are standardized in terms of the type of asset, time of delivery, and place of delivery.
4. Each futures exchange has an associated clearinghouse that becomes the "seller's buyer" and the "buyer's seller" as soon as the trade is concluded.
5. A futures investor is required to deposit initial margin in order to guarantee fulfillment of her obligations.
6. A futures investor's account is marked to market daily, with the equity in the investor's account adjusted to reflect the change in the futures contract's settlement price.
7. A futures investor must maintain his account's equity equal to or greater than a certain percentage of the amount deposited as initial margin. If this requirement is not met, the investor will be requested to deposit variation margin in the account.
8. The basis for futures is the difference between the current spot price of the asset and the corresponding futures price.
9. There are three possible relationships between the current futures price and the expected spot price: the expectations hypothesis (futures price equal to expected spot price), normal backwardation (futures price less than expected spot price), and normal contango (futures price greater than expected spot price).
10. The current futures price should equal the current spot price plus the cost of carry. The cost of carry equals (1) the amount of interest that the owner forgoes by holding onto the asset, less (2) the benefits of owning the asset, plus (3) the costs of owning the asset.
11. If the price of a futures contract becomes too far removed from the current spot price of the asset plus the cost of carry, arbitrageurs will enter into transactions that generate riskless profits from the perceived price discrepancy. Their actions will cause prices to adjust until the opportunity to make such profits disappears.

FUTURES OPTIONS

Futures Options
(Alternatively, **Options on Futures**.) An option contract for which the deliverable asset is a specific futures contract.

The previous chapter described options, while this chapter has described futures. Interestingly, there are contracts currently in existence that are known as **futures options** (or options on futures). As might be expected, these contracts are, in a sense, combinations of futures and options contracts. In particular, a futures option is an option in which the underlying asset is a specific futures contract, with the expiration date on the option being shortly after the delivery date on the futures contract.[25] Figure 20.11 provides a set of quotations on some of the more frequently traded ones. As the figure shows, there are both put and call options on futures. Thus, an investor can be either a buyer or a writer of either a put or a call option on a futures contract.[26] Five futures options are traded on Canadian exchanges: commodity contracts (barley, canola, and flaxseed) trade on the WCE, and bond futures and bankers' acceptances contracts trade on the Montreal Exchange.

Call Options on Futures Contracts

If a call option on a futures contract is exercised, then the writer must deliver the appropriate futures contract to the buyer—that is, the writer must assume a short position in the futures contract while the buyer assumes the long position. For example, consider the buyer of a call option on May barley futures where the exercise price is 125 (that is, $125) per tonne. Because the futures contract is for 20 tonnes, the total exercise price is $20 \times 125 = \$2500$. If the buyer purchased this option at the settle price on October, 8, 1998, which is given in Figure 20.11, then the buyer would have paid the writer a premium of 9.80 (that is, $9.80) per tonne, or $20 \times 9.80 = \$196$ in total.

Now, if the buyer subsequently decides to exercise this option, then the writer of this option must deliver a May barley futures contract to the buyer. Furthermore, this futures contract will be fully marked to market at the time it is delivered. In the example, assume that the option is exercised in February when May barley futures are selling for $175 per tonne. The call writer must then provide the call buyer with a May barley futures contract that has a delivery price of $125, which has been marked to market. This can be accomplished in two steps. First, the writer must purchase a May barley futures contract and deliver it to the call buyer. Because the cost of the futures will be $175 per tonne (the current market price of May barley futures), this is costless to the call writer. Second, the futures contract that has been delivered must be marked to market, which is done by having the call writer pay the call buyer an amount of cash equal to $175 - 125 = \$50$ per tonne, or $50 \times 20 = \$1000$ in aggregate. Thus the call writer has lost $\$1000 - 196 = \$804$ while the call buyer has made an equivalent amount.

Triple Witching Hour
The date when options on individual stocks and market indices, futures on market indices, and options on market index futures expire simultaneously.

[25]The near-simultaneous quarterly expiration of (1) options on individual stocks and market indices, (2) futures on market indices, and (3) options on market index futures has been referred to as the **triple witching hour**. When it occurs, the stock market is allegedly roiled, particularly in the latter part of the day. See Hans R. Stoll and Robert E. Whaley, "Program Trading and Expiration Day Effects," *Financial Analysts Journal* 43, no. 2 (March–April 1987): 16–28; Arnold Kling, "How the Stock Market Can Learn to Live with Index Futures and Options," *Financial Analysts Journal* 43, no. 5 (September–October 1987): 33–39; and G. J. Santoni, "Has Programmed Trading Made Stock Prices More Volatile?" *Federal Reserve Bank of St. Louis Review* 69, no. 5 (May 1987): 18–29.

[26]For more on futures options, see Chapter 12 of the *Commodity Trading Manual*. For a computer program that can be used to determine the "true" value of these complex contracts, see Chapter 8 of Stuart M. Turnbull, *Option Valuation* (Holt, Rinehart and Winston of Canada, 1987).

Figure 20.11 Quotations for futures options contracts.

Futures Options Thurs., Oct. 8, 1998

Figures supplied by Star Data Systems Inc.

Currency

British Pound (CME)

62,500 pounds, US cents per Pound

Strike	Calls-Settle Oct	Calls-Settle Nov	Calls-Settle Dec	Puts-Settle Oct	Puts-Settle Nov	Puts-Settle Dec
1480	s	s	s	s	s	0.02
1500	s	s	s	s	s	0.06
1520	s	s	18.54	s	s	0.10
1540	s	s	s	s	s	0.14
1560	s	s	s	s	s	0.20
1580	s	s	s	r	s	0.26
1600	s	s	10.84	r	0.24	0.40
1610	9.52	s	s	r	r	0.50
1620	s	s	9.06	r	0.36	0.60
1630	7.54	s	s	0.02	0.48	0.76
1640	6.56	s	7.44	0.04	0.60	0.96
1650	5.60	r	6.76	0.08	0.76	1.28
1660	4.64	5.46	5.92	0.12	0.96	1.44
1670	3.68	4.70	5.24	0.16	1.20	1.74
1680	2.72	4.02	4.60	0.20	1.50	2.10
1690	1.84	3.40	4.02	0.32	1.88	2.50
1700	1.12	2.84	3.46	0.60	2.32	2.94
1710	0.62	2.36	3.00	1.10	2.84	3.48
1720	0.34	1.94	2.58	s	s	4.06
1730	0.22	1.58	2.22	s	s	s
1740	0.12	1.28	1.88	s	s	s
1750	r	1.04	1.58	s	s	s
1760	s	s	1.34	s	s	s
1780	s	r	0.94	s	s	s
1800	s	0.40	0.70	s	s	s

Est. call vol. 1,471 — Est. put vol. 549
Prev. open int. 16,873 — Prev. open int. 11,349

Canadian Dollar (CME)

C$100,000, US cents per C$

Strike	Calls-Settle Oct	Calls-Settle Nov	Calls-Settle Dec	Puts-Settle Oct	Puts-Settle Nov	Puts-Settle Dec
60	s	s	s	s	s	0.170
61	s	s	s	s	s	0.290
61.500	s	s	s	r	s	0.370
62	s	s	s	r	0.250	0.460
62.500	s	s	s	0.020	s	0.570
63	s	s	2.360	0.050	s	0.690
63.500	s	s	2.010	0.080	s	0.840
64	0.790	1.400	1.700	0.110	0.720	1.030
64.500	0.390	s	1.430	0.210	0.930	1.250
65	0.170	0.880	1.200	0.490	r	1.520
65.500	0.090	s	1.000	0.910	s	1.810
66	0.060	0.550	0.830	1.380	1.860	2.140
66.500	0.030	0.430	0.680	1.850	s	2.480
67	0.020	0.330	0.560	s	s	2.860
67.500	0.010	s	0.460	s	s	3.260
68	r	0.190	0.370	s	s	3.660
68.500	s	s	0.300	s	s	4.090
69	r	s	0.250	s	s	4.540
69.500	s	s	0.200	s	s	4.980
70	s	s	0.160	s	s	5.440
70.500	s	s	0.130	s	s	s
71	s	s	0.110	s	s	6.390
71.500	s	s	0.090	s	s	s
72	s	s	0.070	s	s	7.350
72.500	s	s	0.060	s	s	s
73	s	s	0.050	s	s	s
73.500	s	s	0.040	s	s	s
74	s	s	0.030	s	s	s
74.500	s	s	0.020	s	s	s
75	s	s	s	s	s	10.320

Est. call vol. 1,346 — Est. put vol. 341
Prev. open int. 25,272 — Prev. open int. 7,005

German Mark (CME)

125,000 marks, US cents per mark

Strike	Calls-Settle Oct	Calls-Settle Nov	Calls-Settle Dec	Puts-Settle Oct	Puts-Settle Nov	Puts-Settle Dec
51	s	s	10.300	s	s	r
53	s	s	8.300	r	0.010	0.010
54	s	s	7.300	r	s	0.020
55	6.300	s	6.300	r	0.020	0.030
55.500	5.800	s	s	r	0.030	0.050
56	5.300	s	5.340	r	r	0.070
56.500	4.800	s	s	r	r	0.090
57	4.300	s	4.410	r	0.070	0.140
57.500	3.800	3.900	3.980	r	0.120	0.210
58	3.300	3.450	3.550	r	0.160	0.280
58.500	2.800	3.030	3.160	r	0.240	0.380
59	2.300	2.610	2.800	r	0.320	0.520
59.500	1.810	2.220	2.450	0.010	0.430	0.670
60	1.330	1.850	2.120	0.030	0.560	0.830
60.500	0.890	1.530	1.790	0.090	0.730	1.000
61	0.530	1.260	1.520	0.230	0.960	1.220
61.500	0.280	1.020	1.270	0.480	1.220	1.470
62	0.140	0.840	1.070	0.840	1.540	1.760
62.500	0.070	0.660	0.920	1.270	1.850	2.110
63	0.040	0.540	0.800	1.740	2.230	2.490
63.500	s	0.440	0.680	s	s	s
64	s	0.360	0.560	s	s	3.240
64.500	s	0.290	s	s	s	s
65	s	s	0.400	s	s	s
65.500	s	0.180	s	s	s	s
66	s	0.140	0.260	s	s	s

Est. call vol. 3,077 — Est. put vol. 2,244
Prev. open int. 29,004 — Prev. open int. 21,451

Food and Fibre

Barley (WPG)

20 metric tons, C$ per metric ton

Strike	Calls-Settle Dec	Calls-Settle Mar	Calls-Settle May	Puts-Settle Dec	Puts-Settle Mar	Puts-Settle May
100	24.10	s	s	r	s	s
105	19.10	22.40	s	r	0.30	s
110	14.20	18.00	s	r	0.80	s
115	9.40	13.90	16.30	0.30	1.60	2.10
120	5.40	10.30	12.80	1.20	2.90	3.50
125	2.50	7.30	9.80	3.30	4.90	5.30
130	0.90	5.00	7.30	6.70	7.40	7.70
135	0.30	3.20	5.30	11.00	10.60	10.50
140	0.10	2.00	3.70	15.80	14.30	13.90
145	r	1.20	2.60	20.70	18.40	17.60
150	r	0.70	s	25.70	22.80	s
155	r	0.40	s	30.60	27.40	s
160	r	s	s	35.60	s	s
165	r	s	s	40.60	s	s

Prev. open int. 0 — Prev. open int. 390

Canola (WPG)

20 metric tons, C$ per metric ton

Strike	Calls-Settle Nov	Calls-Settle Jan	Calls-Settle Mar	Puts-Settle Nov	Puts-Settle Jan	Puts-Settle Mar
320	46.50	s	s	r	s	s
330	36.60	40.80	46.60	r	0.20	1.90
340	26.60	31.30	38.30	r	0.60	3.40
350	16.90	22.50	30.60	0.30	1.70	5.60
360	8.40	14.50	23.90	1.80	5.00	8.70
370	2.90	9.00	18.00	5.70	8.50	12.70
380	0.50	5.00	13.40	14.00	13.80	17.80
390	0.10	2.00	9.60	25.50	21.20	23.80
400	r	1.00	6.70	33.40	29.80	30.70
410	r	0.40	4.50	43.40	39.00	38.40
420	r	0.10	3.00	53.30	48.70	46.70
430	r	r	s	63.30	58.50	s
440	r	s	s	73.30	s	s

Prev. open int. 932 — Prev. open int. 1,836

Cattle - Feeder (CME)

50,000 lbs., US cents per lb.

Strike	Calls-Settle Oct	Calls-Settle Nov	Calls-Settle Jan	Puts-Settle Oct	Puts-Settle Nov	Puts-Settle Jan
60	s	s	s	s	r	0.075
62	s	s	s	s	r	0.150
63	s	s	s	r	0.025	s
64	s	s	s	r	0.050	0.350
65	s	s	s	0.025	0.075	s
66	3.250	s	s	0.050	0.100	0.600
67	2.275	s	s	0.075	r	s
68	1.450	4.175	5.975	0.250	0.225	0.800
68.500	s	s	s	0.375	s	s
69	0.800	3.325	s	0.600	0.400	s
69.500	0.550	s	s	s	s	s
70	0.300	2.550	4.450	1.100	0.600	1.250
70.500	0.200	s	s	s	s	s
71	0.100	s	s	s	1.000	s
72	0.025	1.250	3.225	2.825	1.300	2.000
74	r	0.450	2.100	4.800	2.475	2.850
75	s	0.250	s	s	s	s
76	r	0.100	1.425	6.800	4.125	4.125
78	r	0.050	0.900	8.800	6.075	s
80	r	0.025	0.500	s	s	s
84	r	r	0.175	s	s	s
86	r	s	0.100	s	s	s

Est. call vol. 290 — Est. put vol. 510
Prev. open int. 5,088 — Prev. open int. 5,594

Cattle - Live (CME)

40,000 lbs., US cents per lb.

Strike	Calls-Settle Dec	Calls-Settle Feb	Calls-Settle Apr	Puts-Settle Dec	Puts-Settle Feb	Puts-Settle Apr
52	s	s	s	0.075	0.125	s
54	s	s	s	0.125	0.225	0.300
55	s	s	s	0.150	s	s
56	s	s	s	0.200	0.400	0.500
57	s	s	s	0.250	r	s
58	s	s	s	0.325	0.725	0.725
59	s	s	s	0.425	0.925	s
60	4.525	5.250	s	0.575	1.150	1.025
61	3.750	s	s	0.800	1.400	s
62	3.000	3.800	s	1.050	1.650	1.425
63	2.375	r	s	1.400	r	s
64	1.825	2.500	4.175	1.850	2.325	2.100
65	1.325	s	s	2.350	r	s
66	0.900	1.350	2.725	2.900	3.150	2.600
67	0.600	r	s	s	s	s
68	0.375	0.625	1.400	4.375	4.400	3.225
69	0.200	s	s	s	s	s
70	0.100	0.300	0.650	6.075	6.050	s
72	0.050	0.150	0.350	s	s	s
74	r	0.075	0.200	10.025	s	s
76	r	0.050	0.125	s	s	s

Est. call vol. 894 — Est. put vol. 2,535
Prev. open int. 19,718 — Prev. open int. 27,357

Indexes

Goldman Sachs Cmmdty Index (CME)

250 x index points

Strike	Calls-Settle Oct	Puts-Settle Oct
149	s	1.70
150	s	2.10
154	0.10	s

Est. call vol. 0 — Est. put vol. 0
Prev. open int. 15 — Prev. open int. 15

Dow Jones Indl Avg Index (CBOT)

$10 x index points

Strike	Calls-Settle Oct	Calls-Settle Nov	Calls-Settle Dec	Puts-Settle Oct	Puts-Settle Nov	Puts-Settle Dec
5000	s	s	s	s	1.00	5.00
5400	s	s	s	s	s	7.40
5500	s	s	s	0.05	s	7.80
5600	s	s	s	s	s	8.25
5700	s	s	s	0.05	s	s
5800	s	s	s	s	s	10.00
6000	s	s	s	0.10	6.00	12.00
6200	r	s	r	0.40	r	r
6300	r	s	r	0.55	s	r
6400	139.10	r	r	0.70	11.00	18.00
6500	r	r	r	0.90	12.25	20.00
6600	r	r	r	1.15	13.75	22.00
6700	r	r	r	1.50	15.25	24.00
6800	r	r	r	1.90	17.00	26.00
6900	r	r	r	2.45	18.75	28.00
7000	81.60	r	r	3.15	20.85	30.50
7100	r	r	r	4.00	23.00	33.00
7200	r	84.00	r	5.10	25.50	36.00
7300	r	r	r	6.50	28.00	39.00
7400	46.75	r	80.00	8.25	31.00	42.00
7500	38.95	62.85	r	10.45	34.00	45.75
7600	31.65	56.40	68.00	13.15	37.50	50.25
7700	25.00	50.00	61.00	16.45	41.00	52.50
7800	19.00	44.05	55.00	20.45	45.00	56.50
7900	14.05	38.50	51.00	25.50	49.50	61.00
8000	9.95	33.00	45.00	31.25	54.00	66.00
8100	6.65	28.50	40.00	38.05	r	71.00
8200	4.20	24.00	35.00	45.60	65.00	76.00
8300	2.70	20.00	30.00	54.10	r	81.50
8400	1.90	16.50	26.00	63.25	r	87.50
8500	1.25	13.25	22.50	72.60	r	93.50
8600	0.85	11.00	18.50	82.25	91.95	100.50
8700	0.65	8.50	16.00	91.95	r	107.00
8800	0.50	r	13.50	101.90	r	114.00
8900	0.40	5.00	11.00	r	r	122.00
9000	0.30	4.00	9.10	121.65	r	130.20
9100	0.20	3.00	7.30	131.60	r	138.50
9200	0.10	2.00	6.00	141.55	r	147.00
9300	0.05	1.50	4.80	r	r	r
9400	0.05	r	3.90	r	r	r
9500	0.05	1.10	3.20	r	r	r
9600	0.05	s	2.70	s	r	r
9700	0.05	s	2.30	s	s	s
9800	s	s	2.00	s	s	s
9900	s	0.40	1.70	s	s	s
10000	s	0.30	1.50	s	s	s
10100	0.05	s	s	s	s	s
10200	0.05	s	1.20	s	s	s
10400	s	s	0.90	s	s	s
10500	s	0.05	0.50	s	s	s
10600	s	s	0.20	s	s	s

Prev. open int. 6,945 — Prev. open int. 10,963

S&P 500 Composite Index (CME)

250 x index points

Strike	Calls-Settle Oct	Calls-Settle Nov	Calls-Settle Dec	Puts-Settle Oct	Puts-Settle Nov	Puts-Settle Dec
650	319.30	s	s	r	2.30	5.30
675	s	s	s	0.10	3.00	7.50
700	s	s	s	0.15	4.00	9.80
725	s	s	s	0.20	5.50	11.50
750	219.50	s	s	0.40	7.30	15.50
775	s	s	s	0.60	9.80	19.20
800	170.00	s	190.80	0.85	12.40	23.20
810	160.10	s	182.50	0.95	13.80	s
820	150.20	s	s	1.10	15.30	26.50
825	s	s	s	1.20	16.00	27.40
830	140.40	s	s	1.30	16.80	s
840	s	s	s	1.70	18.40	30.20
850	s	s	s	2.20	20.20	32.20
860	s	s	s	2.80	22.10	34.50
870	s	s	s	3.50	24.10	37.00
875	s	s	s	4.00	25.20	38.30
880	s	s	128.10	4.40	26.30	39.70
885	s	s	s	4.90	s	s
890	s	s	s	5.40	28.50	42.50
900	75.90	99.80	113.90	6.70	31.00	45.30
910	s	s	s	8.20	33.70	48.30
920	s	s	100.20	10.00	36.60	51.40
925	s	s	96.80	11.00	38.10	53.00
930	51.30	s	93.60	12.10	39.70	54.70
935	s	s	s	13.40	41.30	56.40
940	44.10	s	87.10	14.80	43.00	58.10
945	s	s	s	16.20	s	59.80
950	37.10	65.80	80.70	17.80	46.60	61.60
955	s	s	s	19.50	s	63.60
960	30.60	59.60	74.50	21.30	50.40	65.30
965	s	s	s	23.30	s	67.20
970	24.70	53.70	68.50	25.40	54.40	69.20
975	22.00	50.80	65.60	27.70	56.50	71.20
980	19.40	48.10	62.80	30.10	58.70	73.40
985	17.00	s	60.10	32.70	s	75.60
990	14.70	42.90	57.40	35.40	63.50	77.90
995	12.60	s	54.70	38.30	65.90	80.10
1000	10.70	37.90	52.10	41.40	68.40	82.50
1005	9.10	s	49.60	44.70	71.00	84.90
1010	7.60	33.20	47.10	48.20	73.60	87.40
1015	6.30	s	44.60	51.90	76.40	89.80
1020	5.20	28.90	42.20	55.80	79.30	92.40
1025	4.20	26.80	39.90	59.80	82.10	95.00
1030	3.40	24.80	37.60	64.00	85.10	97.70
1035	2.70	22.90	35.40	68.30	88.20	100.40
1040	2.20	21.20	33.30	72.80	91.40	103.30
1045	1.75	s	31.30	77.30	s	106.20
1050	1.50	17.80	29.40	82.10	98.00	109.30
1055	1.25	s	27.60	86.80	s	112.40
1060	1.10	14.80	25.80	91.70	104.90	115.60
1065	0.95	s	24.10	96.50	108.60	118.80
1070	0.80	12.20	22.50	101.40	112.30	122.20
1075	0.70	10.80	20.90	106.30	s	125.50
1080	0.60	r	19.40	111.20	119.40	129.00
1085	0.50	8.90	17.90	116.10	s	132.50
1090	0.45	7.90	16.40	121.00	s	135.90
1095	0.40	s	s	s	s	s
1100	0.35	6.30	13.70	130.90	136.20	143.10
1105	0.30	s	12.50	s	s	s
1110	0.25	4.90	11.50	140.80	s	150.90

Petroleum

Crude Oil (NYME)

1,000 US barrels, US$ per barrel

Strike	Calls-Settle Nov	Calls-Settle Dec	Calls-Settle Jan	Puts-Settle Nov	Puts-Settle Dec	Puts-Settle Jan
10.50	r	r	s	0.01	r	s
11	r	r	s	0.01	0.02	s
11.50	r	r	s	0.01	0.04	s
12	r	r	2.90	0.01	0.07	0.12
12.50	r	2.21	s	0.02	0.11	0.18
13	1.46	1.78	r	0.04	0.18	0.27
13.50	1.02	1.39	1.68	0.10	0.28	0.39
14	0.61	1.05	1.34	0.19	0.44	0.55
14.50	0.33	0.76	1.05	0.41	0.65	0.75
15	0.15	0.55	0.82	0.73	0.94	1.02
15.50	0.07	0.39	0.63	1.15	1.28	1.33
16	0.03	0.26	0.48	1.61	1.64	1.67
16.50	0.02	0.17	0.36	2.10	2.05	2.05
17	0.01	0.12	0.27	2.59	2.50	2.45
17.50	0.01	0.08	0.20	3.09	2.96	2.88
18	0.01	0.06	0.15	3.59	3.44	3.33
18.50	0.01	0.05	0.11	4.09	3.93	3.79
19	0.01	0.04	0.10	4.59	4.42	s
19.50	0.01	0.03	0.07	r	4.91	s
20	0.01	0.02	0.06	r	5.40	r
20.50	0.01	0.01	s	6.09	r	s
21	0.01	0.01	0.04	r	6.39	s
21.50	r	0.01	s	r	r	s
22	0.01	0.01	0.02	r	7.39	s
23	0.01	0.01	0.01	r	r	s
23.50	r	r	0.01	r	r	s
24	0.01	0.01	0.01	r	r	r
25	r	0.01	s	r	r	r
26	r	0.01	s	r	11.39	r
27	r	0.01	s	r	r	s
30	r	0.01	s	r	r	s
35	r	0.01	r	r	r	s
40	r	0.01	r	r	r	s

Prev. open int. 236,323 — Prev. open int. 188,948

Natural Gas (NYME)

10,000 mm btus, US$ per mm btus

Strike	Calls-Settle Nov	Calls-Settle Dec	Calls-Settle Jan	Puts-Settle Nov	Puts-Settle Dec	Puts-Settle Jan
1.500	r	r	s	0.002	r	s
1.600	r	r	r	0.003	r	s
1.650	r	r	s	0.004	s	s
1.700	r	r	s	0.005	0.010	s
1.750	r	s	r	0.006	0.012	s
1.800	s	r	s	0.008	0.015	0.022
1.850	r	r	s	0.011	s	s
1.900	0.370	r	r	0.017	0.025	s
1.950	0.327	r	s	0.024	0.035	s
2	0.287	r	s	0.034	0.045	0.051
2.050	0.250	r	s	0.046	0.055	0.062
2.100	0.215	r	r	0.061	0.067	0.075
2.150	0.181	0.417	s	0.077	0.080	0.089
2.200	0.155	0.383	r	0.100	0.096	0.104
2.250	0.129	0.351	r	0.124	0.113	0.121
2.300	0.108	0.320	0.422	0.154	0.132	0.140
2.350	0.087	0.291	0.397	0.183	0.153	0.165
2.400	0.070	0.264	0.364	0.216	0.175	0.181
2.450	0.056	0.238	0.338	0.252	0.199	0.205
2.500	0.045	0.214	0.316	0.290	0.226	0.232
2.550	0.035	0.194	0.294	0.330	0.255	0.260
2.600	0.028	0.175	0.271	0.373	0.286	0.289
2.650	0.021	0.159	0.250	0.416	0.319	0.316
2.700	0.016	0.144	0.231	0.461	0.354	0.346
2.750	0.012	0.130	0.214	r	0.390	0.379
2.800	0.009	0.118	0.198	r	0.427	0.412
2.850	0.007	0.106	0.183	r	0.465	s
2.900	0.005	0.096	0.170	r	0.505	s
2.950	0.004	0.088	0.157	s	s	s
3	0.003	0.079	0.145	r	r	s
3.050	0.002	0.072	0.137	s	s	s
3.100	0.001	0.064	0.130	r	0.672	s
3.150	s	0.058	0.123	s	s	s
3.200	0.001	0.053	0.116	s	r	s
3.250	0.001	0.048	0.109	s	r	s
3.300	s	0.043	0.102	s	r	s
3.350	s	0.039	0.096	s	r	s
3.400	s	0.036	0.090	s	s	s
3.450	0.001	0.033	s	s	r	s
3.500	0.001	0.030	0.082	r	r	s
3.550	r	s	0.078	s	s	s
3.600	0.001	0.025	0.074	s	s	s
3.650	s	0.023	s	s	s	s
3.700	0.001	0.021	0.066	s	s	s
3.750	0.001	0.019	0.062	r	r	s
3.800	s	r	0.058	s	s	s
3.850	s	0.015	s	s	s	s
4	0.001	0.010	0.050	s	s	s
4.150	s	0.007	s	s	s	s
4.250	s	s	0.042	s	s	s
4.500	s	s	0.035	s	s	s

Prev. open int. 167,401 — Prev. open int. 131,639

SOURCE: Reprinted with permission of *The Financial Post* (October 9, 1998).

Whereas this example has shown what happens when the call is exercised, it should be noted that most futures options are not exercised. Instead, just as with most options and futures, buyers and writers of futures options typically make reversing trades before the expiration date.

Put Options on Futures Contracts

If a put option on a futures contract is exercised, then the writer must accept delivery of the appropriate futures contract from the buyer—that is, the writer must assume a long position in the futures contract while the buyer assumes the short position. For example, consider the buyer of a put option on May barley where the exercise price is 125, meaning $125 per tonne or $2500 in total because the futures contract is for 20 tonnes. If the buyer purchased this put at the settlement price on October 8, 1998, as shown in Figure 20.11, then the buyer would have paid the writer a premium of 5.30 per tonne, or $20 \times 5.30 = \$106$ in total.

Now, if the buyer subsequently decides to exercise this option, then the writer of this option must accept delivery of a May barley futures contract from the buyer. Furthermore, this futures contract must be fully marked to market at the time it is delivered. In the example, assume that the option is exercised in April when May barley futures are selling for 75 per tonne. What happens in April is that the put buyer will become the seller of a May barley futures contract where the purchase price is $75 per tonne. That is, when this contract is marked to market, the put writer must pay the put buyer an amount of cash equal to $125 - 75 = \$50$ per tonne, or $(50 \times 20) = \$1000$ in aggregate. Thus, the put writer has lost $894 ($1000 − $106), whereas the put buyer has made an equivalent amount.

Again, it should be kept in mind that most put options on futures are not exercised. Instead, these option buyers and writers typically enter reversing trades sometime before the expiration date.

In summary, the positions of futures options buyers and writers in the futures contracts upon exercise by the buyer are as follows:

	Buyer	Seller
Call	Long	Short
Put	Short	Long

As mentioned earlier, neither a writer nor a buyer needs to maintain his position. Both are free to enter into offsetting trades at any time, even after the buyer has exercised the option (but then the offsetting trade would be made in the futures market).

Comparision with Futures

At this point it is worthwhile to think about the distinctions between futures and futures options. In doing so, consider an investor who is contemplating *buying* a futures contract. If this contract is purchased, the investor can potentially make or lose a great deal of money. In particular, if the price of the asset rises substantially, then so will the price of the futures, and the investor will have made a sizeable profit. In contrast, if the price of the asset drops substantially, then the investor will have lost a sizeable amount of money.

In comparison, if the investor had bought a futures call option on the asset, then the investor would also make a sizeable profit if the price of the asset rose substantially. Unlike futures, however, if the price of the asset dropped, then the investor need not worry about incurring a sizeable loss. Instead, only the premium (the price paid to buy the futures option) would be lost. This does not mean that purchasing a futures call option is "better" than purchasing a futures contract. Why? Because the protection on the downside that an investor gets from buying a futures call option is paid for in the form of the premium. This premium would not be present if the investor had bought a futures contract instead.

Consider next an investor who is contemplating *selling* a futures contract. In doing so, the investor can potentially make a great deal of money if the price of the asset declines substantially. However, if the price of the asset rises substantially, then the investor will have lost a sizeable amount of money.

In comparison, the investor could buy a futures put option on the asset. The investor would make a sizeable profit if the price of the asset declined substantially. Unlike futures, however, if the price of the asset rose, then the investor need not worry about incurring a sizeable loss. Instead, only the premium would be lost. Again, this does not mean that purchasing a futures put option is "better" than selling a futures contract.

Comparison with Options

Having established that futures options can exist if futures already exist, one may wonder why futures options exist if options already exist. For example, there are futures options and options on Japanese yen (as well as futures on Japanese yen). The commonly given reason why futures options exist in such a situation is that it is easier to make or take delivery of a futures contract on the asset, as required by the futures options contract, than to make or take delivery in the asset itself, as required by the options contract. That is, the deliverable asset in the case of the Japanese yen futures option contract is a futures contract in Japanese yen, which is more easily delivered than Japanese yen, as required for the options contract.

In addition, there is sometimes more timely price information on the deliverable asset for the futures option contract (namely, price information on the futures contract) than on the deliverable asset for the options contract (namely, price information in the spot market).

For these reasons (although they are not compelling for certain contracts), futures, futures options, and options can exist simultaneously with the same underlying asset.

QUESTIONS AND PROBLEMS

1. Distinguish between a speculator and a hedger. Give an example of a short hedger and a long hedger.
2. Using the latest *Financial Post*, for the near futures contracts in corn, orange juice, and gasoline, calculate the percentage change in the settlement price from the previous day. Find the open interest in these contracts. Into how many units of the commodities do these open-interest figures translate?
3. How do organized futures exchanges ensure that the obligations incurred as various parties enter into futures contracts are ultimately satisfied?
4. What is the purpose of initial and maintenance margins? How does marking to market affect the amount of funds held in the futures investor's margin account?
5. Lloyd Wolf sells 10 June 5000-bushel corn futures at $2 per bushel. Lloyd deposits $5000 in performance margin. If the price of corn rises to $2.20 per bushel, how much equity is in Lloyd's margin account? What if corn falls to $1.80 per bushel?
6. Mai-Lin Chu has just bought four September 20 tonne canola futures contracts at $449 per tonne. The initial margin requirement is 3%. The maintenance margin requirement is 80% of the initial margin requirement.
   a. How many dollars in initial margin must Mai-Lin put up?
   b. If the September price of canola rises to $475, how much equity is in Mai-Lin's commodity account?
   c. If the September price of canola falls to $436, how much equity is in Mai-Lin's commodity account? Will Mai-Lin receive a margin call?

7. How does a futures contract differ from a forward contract?

8. Do exchange-imposed price limits protect futures traders from losses that would result in the absence of such limits? Explain.

9. Cora Withrow is long a stock market futures contract and short a diversified portfolio of stocks. Would Cora prefer the basis to widen or to narrow? Why?

10. A publication used by farmers such as Mordecai Brown provides diagrams of the typical annual patterns of cash prices for a number of seasonal commodities. Should Mordecai expect that the price of a futures contract will follow the same pattern? Why?

11. In the market for a particular agricultural or natural resource commodity, what kind of market forces might lead to normal backwardation or normal contango?

12. Consider a futures contract on mangoes that calls for the delivery of 2000 pounds of the fruit three months from now. The spot price of mangoes is $2 per pound. The three-month risk-free rate is 2%. It costs $.10 per pound to store mangoes for three months. What should be the price of this futures contract?

13. Barb Lynn owns a famous Renoir painting that has a current market value of $5 000 000. It costs Barb $200 000 annually to insure the painting, payable at the start of the year. Barb is able to loan the painting to a local art gallery for $300 000 per year, paid at the end of the year. Barb is considering selling the painting under a futures contract arrangement that calls for delivery one year from today. If the one-year risk-free rate is 5%, what is the fair value of the futures contract?

14. Tom Turner is planning a trip in six months to Germany, where he plans to purchase a BMW for 80 000 deutsche marks (DM). Using a recent *Globe and Mail*, calculate how much the purchase would cost in US dollars at the current exchange rate. Given the recent settlement price of a six-month DM futures contract, how much would Tom have to pay to hedge the cost of the BMW purchase?

15. Assume that the exchange rate between British pounds and US dollars is currently $1.80 per pound. If the six-month risk-free rate is 3% in the United States and 3.5% in Great Britain, what should the six-month futures price of US dollars in British pounds be? Why is the futures exchange rate greater or less than the current spot exchange rate?

16. The one-year futures price of the Utopian currency darmas is $2.03 per darma. The interest forgone by selling darmas in the futures market instead of the spot market is $.0591. The benefit of owning darmas instead of selling them is $.0788. If the Canadian one-year risk-free rate is 3%, according to interest-rate parity, what should be the Utopian one-year risk-free rate?

17. What should be the price of a three-month 90-day Treasury bill futures contract if the spot price of a six-month Treasury bill is currently $98 and the three-month risk-free rate is 1%?

18. Stella Paravano believes that the spread between long-term and short-term interest rates is going to narrow in the next few months but does not know in which direction interest rates in general will move. What financial futures position would permit Stella to profit from this forecast if it is correct?

19. Suzy Markotic bought five TSE 35 December futures contracts at 310. If the TSE 35 index rises to 318, what is Suzy's dollar profit?

20. Why does hedging a common stock portfolio using stock index futures work best if the portfolio being hedged is very similar to the underlying stock index of the futures contract?

20. Assume that the TSE 35 currently has a value of 200 (in "index" terms). The dividend yield on the underlying stocks in the index is expected to be 4% over the next six months. New-issue six-month Treasury bills now sell for a six-month yield of 6%.
    a. What is the theoretical value of a six-month futures contract on the TSE 35?
    b. What potential problems are inherent in this calculation?

22. In December 19X1 Jill Hamner bought a January 19X2 gold futures contract on the New York Commodity Exchange for $487.50 per ounce. Simultaneously, Jill sold an October 19X3 contract for $614.80. At the time, yields on Treasury notes with 1.75 years to maturity were 10.50%. Will this transaction be profitable for Jill? What factors are relevant to making this calculation?

23. In each of the following situations, discuss how Luc Sanio might use stock index futures to protect a well-diversified stock portfolio:

    a. Luc expects to receive a sizeable bonus cheque next month and would like to invest in stocks, believing that current stock market prices are extremely attractive (but realizing they may not remain so for long).

    b. Luc expects the stock market to decline dramatically very soon and realizes that selling a stock portfolio quickly would result in significant transaction costs.

    c. Luc has a large, unrealized gain and for tax purposes would like to defer the gain until the next tax year, which is several weeks away.

24. Does the fair value of a stock index futures contract depend on investors' expectations about the future value of the underlying stock index? Why?

25. Slava Swacina, a futures investor who has lost considerable sums in futures investments, said, "Even though I don't directly borrow to invest in futures, the performance of my investments acts as if I were highly leveraged." Is Slava correct? Why?

26. (Appendix Question) Distinguish between futures contracts and options on futures contracts.

27. (Appendix Question) Maya Swander buys a call option on a March 5000-bushel soybean futures contract. The call costs $.50 per bushel and has an exercise price of $5.25 per bushel. If Maya exercises the option in February at a price of $5.55 per bushel, what is Maya's return on investment in the option?

CFA Exam Questions

28. Robert Chen, CFA, is reviewing the characteristics of derivative securities and their use in portfolios.

    a. Chen is considering the addition of either a short position in stock index futures or a long position in stock index (put) options to an existing well-diversified portfolio of equity securities. Contrast the way in which each of these two alternatives would affect the risk and return of the resulting combined portfolios.

    b. Four factors affect the value of a futures contract on a stock index. Three of these factors are: the current price of the stock index, the time remaining until the contract maturity (delivery) date, and the dividends on the stock index. Identify the fourth factor and explain how and why changes in this factor affect the value of the futures contract.

    c. Six factors affect the value of call options on stocks. Three of these factors are: the current price of the stock, the time remaining until the option expires, and the dividend on the stock. Identify the other three factors and explain how and why changes in each of these three factors affect the value of call options.

29. The foundation's grant-making and investment policy issues have been finalized. Receipt of the expected $45 million Franklin cash gift will not occur for 90 days, yet the committee believes current stock and bond prices are unusually attractive and wishes to take advantage of this perceived opportunity.

    a. Briefly describe two strategies that utilize derivative financial instruments and could be implemented to take advantage of the committee's market expectations.

    b. Evaluate whether or not it is appropriate for the foundation to undertake a derivatives-based hedge to bridge the expected 90-day time gap, considering both positive and negative factors.

KEY TERMS

futures (p. 637)
speculators (p. 637)
hedgers (p. 637)
short hedger (p. 638)
long hedger (p. 638)
reversing trade (p. 638)
spot market (p. 638)
spot price (p. 638)
settle price (p. 639)
open interest (p. 639)
performance margin (p. 642)
marking to market (p. 642)

variation margin (p. 643)
basis (p. 646)
basis risk (p. 646)
expectations hypothesis (p. 648)
normal backwardation (p. 649)
normal contango (p. 650)
cost of carry (p. 654)
interest-rate parity (p. 656)
index arbitrage (p. 664)
synthetic futures contract (p. 670)
futures options (p. 672)
triple witching hour (p. 672)

REFERENCES

1. Many books either are devoted exclusively to futures or have futures as one of their primary subjects. Most cover everything discussed in this chapter in more detail and with a more complete list of citations. Here are a few:

Stephen Figlewski, *Hedging with Financial Futures for Institutional Investors* (Cambridge, MA: Ballinger, 1986).

Edward W. Schwarz, Joanne M. Hill, and Thomas Schneeweis, *Financial Futures* (Homewood, IL: Richard D. Irwin, 1986).

Commodity Trading Manual (Chicago: Chicago Board of Trade, 1989).

Darrell Duffie, *Futures Markets* (Englewood Cliffs, NJ: Prentice Hall, 1989).

Daniel R. Siegel and Diane F. Siegel, *Futures Markets* (Hinsdale, IL: Dryden Press, 1990).

Alan L. Tucker, *Financial Futures, Options, and Swaps* (St. Paul, MN: West, 1991).

David A. Dubofsky, *Options and Financial Futures* (New York: McGraw-Hill, 1992).

Hans R. Stoll and Robert E. Whaley, *Futures and Options* (Cincinnati, OH: South-Western, 1993).

Robert T. Daigler, *Financial Futures and Markets: Concepts and Strategies* (New York: HarperCollins, 1994).

Robert W. Kolb, *Understanding Futures Markets* (Miami, FL: Kolb, 1994).

Don M. Chance, *An Introduction to Derivatives* (Fort Worth, TX: The Dryden Press, 1995).

Fred D. Arditti, *Derivatives* (Boston: Harvard Business School Press, 1996).

Robert Jarrow and Stuart Turnbull, *Derivative Securities* (Cincinnati, OH: South-Western Publishing, 1996).

John C. Hull, *Options, Futures, and Other Derivative Securities* (Upper Saddle River, NJ: Prentice Hall, 1997).

2. For a discussion of the market structure of futures exchanges, see:

Sanford J. Grossman and Merton H. Miller, "Liquidity and Market Structure," *Journal of Finance* 43, no. 3 (July 1988): 617–633.

Michael J. Fishman and Francis A. Longstaff, "Dual Trading in Futures Markets," *Journal of Finance* 47, no. 2 (June 1992): 643–671.

3. For a more complete discussion of margin and marking to market, see:

Robert W. Kolb, Gerald D. Gay, and William C. Hunter, "Liquidity Requirements for Financial Futures Investments," *Financial Analysts Journal* 41, no. 3 (May–June 1985): 60–68.

Don M. Chance, *The Effect of Margins on the Volatility of Stock and Derivative Markets: A Review of the Evidence*, Monograph Series in Finance and Economics no. 1990–2, New York University Salomon Center, Leonard N. Stern School of Business.

Ann Kremer, "Clarifying Marking to Market," *Journal of Financial Education* 20 (November 1991): 17–25.

4. The concepts of spreads and basis are discussed in:

Martin L. Leibowitz, *The Analysis of Value and Volatility in Financial Futures*, Monograph Series in Finance and Economics no. 1981–3, New York University Salomon Center, Leonard N. Stern School of Business.

5. Foreign currency markets are discussed in:

J. Orlin Grabbe, *International Financial Markets* (Englewood Cliffs, NJ: Prentice Hall, 1996), Part II.

6. Interest-rate futures were shown to be useful in immunizing bond portfolios by:

Robert W. Kolb and Gerald D. Gay, "Immunizing Bond Portfolios with Interest Rate Futures," *Financial Management* 11, no. 2 (Summer 1982): 81–89.

Jess B. Yawitz and William J. Marshall, "The Use of Futures in Immunized Portfolios," *Journal of Portfolio Management* 11, no. 2 (Spring 1985): 51–58.

7. Using futures to hedge bond portfolios is discussed in:

Richard Bookstaber and David P. Jacob, "The Composite Hedge: Controlling the Credit Risk of High-yield Bonds," *Financial Analysts Journal* 42, no. 2 (March–April 1986): 25–35.

Robin Grieves, "Hedging Corporate Bond Portfolios," *Journal of Portfolio Management* 12, no. 4 (Summer 1986): 23–25.

8. Stock index futures and their relationship to the market crash in October 1987 have been heavily researched. Some of the papers are:

Paula A. Tosini, "Stock Index Futures and Stock Market Activity in October 1987," *Financial Analysts Journal* 44, no. 1 (January–February 1988): 28–37.

F. J. Gould, "Stock Index Futures: The Arbitrage Cycle and Portfolio Insurance," *Financial Analysts Journal* 44, no. 1 (January–February 1988): 48–62.

Lawrence Harris, "The October 1987 S&P 500 Stock-futures Basis," *Journal of Finance* 44, no. 1 (March 1989): 77–99.

Marshall E. Blume, A. Craig MacKinlay, and Bruce Terker, "Order Imbalances and Stock Price Movements on October 19 and 20, 1987," *Journal of Finance* 44, no. 4 (September 1989): 827–848.

Lawrence Harris, "S&P 500 Cash Stock Price Volatilities," *Journal of Finance* 44, no. 5 (December 1989): 1155–1175.

Hans R. Stoll and Robert E. Whaley, "The Dynamics of Stock Index and Stock Index Futures Returns," *Journal of Financial and Quantitative Analysis* 25, no. 4 (December 1990): 441–468.

Kalok Chan, K. C. Chan, and G. Andrew Karolyi, "Intraday Volatility in the Stock Index and Stock Index Futures Markets," *Review of Financial Studies* 4, no. 4 (1991): 657–684.

Avanidhar Subrahmanyam, "A Theory of Trading in Stock Index Futures," *Review of Financial Studies* 4, no. 1 (1991): 17–51.

Kalok Chan, "A Further Analysis of the Lead-lag Relationship Between the Cash Market and Stock Index Futures Market," *Review of Financial Studies* 5, no. 1 (1992): 123–152.

9. Papers on index arbitrage and program trading include:

A. Craig MacKinlay and Krishna Ramaswamy, "Index-futures Arbitrage and the Behavior of Stock Index Futures Prices," *Review of Financial Studies* 1, no. 2 (Summer 1988): 137–158.

Michael J. Brennan and Eduardo S. Schwartz, "Arbitrage in Stock Index Futures," *Journal of Business* 63, no. 1, part 2 (January 1990): S7–S31.

Hans R. Stoll and Robert E. Whaley, "Program Trading and Individual Stock Returns: Ingredients of the Triple-witching Brew," *Journal of Business* 63, no. 1, part 2 (January 1990): S165–S192.

Gary L. Gastineau, "A Short History of Program Trading," *Financial Analysts Journal* 47, no. 5 (September–October 1991): 4–7.

10. Forward and futures prices were shown to be equal when interest rates are constant over time in:

John C. Cox, Jonathan E. Ingersoll, and Stephen A. Ross, "The Relation Between Forward Prices and Futures Prices," *Journal of Financial Economics* 9, no. 4 (December 1981): 321–346.

11. The performance of commodity funds, which are investment companies that speculate in futures, has not been attractive, according to:

Edwin J. Elton, Martin J. Gruber, and Joel C. Rentzler, "Professionally Managed, Publicly Traded Commodity Funds," *Journal of Business* 60, no. 2 (April 1987): 175–199.

12. The relationships among futures, options, and futures options are discussed in:

Clifford W. Smith, Jr., Charles W. Smithson, and D. Sykes Wilford, "Managing Financial Risk," *Journal of Applied Corporate Finance* 1, no. 4 (Winter 1989): 27–48.

Charles W. Smithson, Clifford W. Smith, Jr., and D. Sykes Wilford, *Managing Financial Risk: A Guide to Derivative Products, Financial Engineering, and Value Maximization* (Homewood, IL: Irwin Professional Publishing, 1995).

13. The seminal paper on the pricing of futures options is:

Fischer Black, "The Pricing of Commodity Contracts," *Journal of Financial Economics* 3, nos. 1–2 (January–March 1976): 167–179.

14. For a thought-provoking book that covers futures markets, among other subjects, see:

Merton H. Miller, *Financial Innovations and Market Volatility* (Cambridge, MA: Blackwell, 1991).

15. For a Canadian perspective on the topics covered in this chapter, see:

J. E. Hore, *Trading on Canadian Futures Markets* (Toronto: The Canadian Securities Institute, 1989).

N. T. Khoury and P. Yourougou, "Price Discovery Performance and Maturity Effects in the Canadian Feed Wheat Market," *Review of Futures Markets* 8, no. 3 (1989): 402–419.

C. A. Carter and R. M. A. Lyons, *Hedging Canadian Grains and Oilseeds* (Winnipeg, MB: The Winnipeg Commodity Exchange, 1991).

N. T. Khoury and P. Yourougou, "The Informational Content of the Basis: Evidence from Canadian Barley, Oats, and Canola Futures Markets" *Journal of Futures Markets* 11, no. 1 (1991): 69–80.

S. Elfakhani, R. Wionzek, and M. Chaudhury, "A Close Examination of Profit Opportunities in the Canadian Canola and Feed Wheat Futures," *Proceedings, Administrative Sciences Association of Canada Conference,* Montreal, June 1996, pp. 62–70.

L. Gagnon and G. Lypny, "The Benefits of Dynamically Hedging the Toronto 35 Stock Index," *Canadian Journal of Administrative Sciences* 14, no. 1 (March 1997): 69–78.

M. C. Beaulieu and I. Morgan, "The Impact of the Reduction in Tick Size in TIPs," *Proceedings, Administrative Sciences Association of Canada Conference,* St. John's, June 1997, pp. 31–40.

T. Lappalainen and B. Goguen, "Benchmarking Synthetic Strategies," *Canadian Investment Review* X, no. 4 (Winter 1997–1998): 16–21.

Special Report, "International Derivatives," *Canadian Investment Review* XI, no. 3 (Fall 1998).

Investment Companies

Investment companies are a type of financial intermediary. They receive money from investors and use it to purchase financial assets such as stocks and bonds. In return, the investors receive certain rights regarding the financial assets the company has bought and any earnings that it may make. In the simplest and most common situation, the investment company has only one type of investor—shareholders. These shareholders directly own the investment company and thus indirectly own the financial assets that the company itself owns.

For an individual, there are two advantages to investing in such companies instead of investing directly in the financial assets these companies own. Specifically these advantages are the result of (1) economies of scale and (2) professional management. In describing these benefits, consider an individual with moderate financial resources who wishes to invest in the stock market.

In terms of economies of scale, the individual could buy stocks in odd lots and thus have a diversified portfolio. However, the brokerage commissions on odd-lot transactions are relatively high. Alternatively, the individual could purchase round lots, but would only be able to afford a few different securities. Unfortunately, the individual would then be giving up the benefits of owning a well-diversified portfolio, in which declines in some securities would more likely be offset by gains in others. In order to receive the benefits of diversification and substantially reduced brokerage commissions, the individual could invest in the shares of an investment company. Economies of scale make it possible for an investment company to provide diversification at a lower cost per dollar of investment than would be incurred by a small individual investor.

In terms of professional management, the individual investing directly in the stock market would have to go through all the details of investing, including making all buying and selling decisions and keeping records of all transactions for tax purposes. In doing so, the individual would have to be continually on the lookout for mispriced securities in an attempt to find undervalued ones for purchase, while selling any that were found to be overvalued. Simultaneously, the individual would have to keep track of the overall risk level of the portfolio so that it did not deviate from some desired level. However, by purchasing shares of an investment company, the individual can turn over all of these details to a professional money manager.

Many of these managers hope to identify areas of mispricing in the market, exploit them, and share the resultant abnormal gains with investors by charging them for a portion of the gains. However, it appears that they typically cannot find enough mispriced situations to recoup more than the additional costs they have incurred, costs that take the

Investment Company A type of financial intermediary that receives money from investors and uses that money to purchase financial assets. In return, the investors receive shares in the investment company, and thus indirectly own a proportion of the financial assets that the company itself owns.

form of increased management fees and transaction costs due to the continual buying and selling of securities. Nevertheless, other potential advantages to be gained from investing in an investment company may still outweigh any disadvantages, particularly for smaller investors.

Investment companies differ in many ways, and classification is difficult. Common practice will be followed here where the term is restricted to those financial intermediaries that do not obtain money from depositors. Thus, the traditional operations of trust companies and banks, for example, are excluded. However, the process of deregulation is rapidly breaking down previous barriers so that the future may very well bring even more competition for traditional investment companies.

Net Asset Value

Net Asset Value (NAV)
The market value of an investment company's assets, less any liabilities, divided by the number of shares outstanding.

An important concept in understanding how investment companies operate is **net asset value (NAV)**. Given that an investment company has assets consisting of various securities, it is generally quite easy to determine the market value of all the assets held by the investment company at the end of each business day. For example, an investment company that holds various common stocks traded on The Toronto Stock Exchange could easily find out what the closing prices of those stocks were at the end of the day and then simply multiply these prices by the number of shares that it owns. After adding up these figures, the investment company would subtract any liabilities that it had outstanding. Dividing the resulting difference by the number of outstanding shares of the investment company produces its net asset value.

Equivalently, an investment company's net asset value at the end of day t, NAV_t, can be determined by using the following equation:

$$NAV_t = \frac{MVA_t - LIAB_t}{NSO_t} \qquad (21.1)$$

where MVA_t, $LIAB_t$, and NSO_t denote the market value of the investment company's assets, the dollar amount of the investment company's liabilities, and the number of shares the investment company has outstanding, respectively, as of the end of day t.

As an example, consider an investment company with 4 000 000 shares outstanding whose assets consisted of common stocks with an aggregate market value of $102 000 000 and whose liabilities amounted to $2 000 000 as of November 15. This company would report a net asset value on that date of ($102 000 000 − $2 000 000)/4 000 000 = $25 per share. This amount will change every day, as the values of either MVA_t, $LIAB_t$, and NSO_t (or of some combination of the three) will typically change daily.

Investors should note that calculating NAV_t can be difficult if some of the assets do not trade frequently. In such situations, estimates of their fair market value must be used. Referring to the previous example, what if on August 15 there were 3 800 000 shares outstanding, the liabilities were $2 200 000, but the common shares had not been traded on any market since August 14? In this situation MVA_t is often calculated by using the last bid prices for the stocks on August 15, which in the example is assumed to result in a value for MVA_t of $101 000 000.[1] Hence, the net asset value on August 15 is ($101 000 000 − $2 200 000)/3 800 000 = $26.

---

[1] As mentioned in Chapter 3, dealers in securities generally quote both bid and asked prices. The bid price is the amount the dealer will pay for a security; the asked price is the amount an investor must pay to purchase the security from the dealer.

Major Types of Investment Companies

Managed Investment Company An investment company with a portfolio that may be altered at the discretion of the company's portfolio manager.

Investment Funds Institute of Canada
www.mutfunds.com/ific/home.html

Management Expense Ratio The percentage of an investment company's assets that were used to pay for management fees, administrative expenses, and other operating expenses in a given year.

Closed-end Investment Company (Alternatively, **Closed-end Mutual Fund**.) A managed investment company, with an unlimited life, that does not stand ready to purchase its own shares from its owners and rarely issues new shares beyond its initial offering.

The *Investment Funds Institute of Canada* (IFIC) classifies **managed investment companies** as either:

1. closed-end investment companies, or
2. open-end investment companies or investment funds.

Managed investment companies, whether incorporated or unincorporated, have a board of directors or a board of trustees to oversee the operation of the company. The board commonly hires a firm—the investment manager—to manage the company's assets for an annual fee that is typically based (at least in part) on the total market value of the assets.

These management companies may be independent firms, investment advisors, firms associated with brokerage firms, or insurance companies. Often the management company is the business entity (for example, a subsidiary of a brokerage firm) that started and promoted the investment company. One management company may have contracts to manage a number of investment companies, each of which is a separate entity with its own board of directors or board of trustees.

Annual management fees average about 1.5% (they range from about 0.3% to 3.0%) of the market value of the investment company's total assets, with the percentage decreasing as the value of the assets increase. Some funds provide "incentive compensation," where the better the fund's investment performance, the higher the fee paid to the management company.

In addition to the fee paid by an investment company to its management company, there are administrative and custodial expenses. These services are usually arranged by the investment manager, but the costs are charged to the investment company. For the typical investment company, such annual expenses are roughly 0.50% of the market value of its total assets. The term "management fees" tends to be used rather loosely; it includes administrative and custodial expenses in some cases and not in others. In order to compare costs on a uniform basis, the industry has defined the **management expense ratio** to be the total costs divided by the average net monthly assets for the year. The total costs include all fees paid by the fund (to the investment company and any third parties) except brokerage fees.

Closed-end Investment Companies

Closed-end investment companies (or closed-end funds) are not very popular in Canada, but the number offered has increased in recent years. These companies issue a specific number of shares at their inception. This number remains unchanged until such time as additional shares are issued. Their shares are traded either on an organized exchange or in the over-the-counter market. Thus, an investor who wants to buy or sell shares of a closed-end fund simply places an order with a broker, just as if he wanted to buy or sell shares of BCE.

Most closed-end funds have unlimited lives. Dividends and interest received and any net capital gains realized by a closed-end fund are paid out to its shareholders. However, most funds allow (and encourage) the reinvestment of such payments. The fund keeps the money and sends the investor additional shares based on the net asset value per share at that time. For example, consider a closed-end fund that has just declared a dividend of $1 per share. If its net asset value were $15 per share, a holder of 30 shares would have a choice of receiving either $30 × $1 = $30 or $30/15 = 2 shares.

Being a corporation, closed-end funds can issue new shares not only through reinvestment plans but also with public stock offerings. However, this is done infrequently, and the fund's capitalization is "closed" most of the time.

Although it is seldom done, most closed-end funds can repurchase their own shares in the open market. If a fund's market price falls substantially below net asset value, a repurchase will increase the fund's net asset value per share. For example, if net asset value were $20 per share at a time when the fund's shares could be purchased in the open market (say, on the Toronto Stock Exchange) for $16 per share, the managers of the fund could sell $20 worth of securities from the fund's portfolio, buy back one of the fund's outstanding shares, and have $4 left over. If the $4 were used to buy securities for the fund, the net asset value per share would increase, with the size of the increase depending on the number of shares repurchased, their repurchase price, and on the number of remaining shares.

In general, a closed-end fund's shares are initially offered to the public at a price that is nearly 10% above its net asset value due to investment banking fees charged to the fund. This suggests that the shares are overpriced because most funds' shares sell for a price below their net asset value in the aftermarket. US evidence indicates that there are no unusual movements in the price of a typical fund on the offering day, but that in the 100 days thereafter its price declines relative to the market to the point where it sells for roughly 10% below its net asset value. This is in sharp contrast to the price behaviour of non-fund initial public offerings, where the stocks, on average, experience a substantial price jump on the offering day of about 14% and no notable price movements in roughly the following 100 days.[2] Left unanswered is why an investor would want to be involved in the initial public offering of a closed-end fund.[3]

Quotations

Provided that the closed-end funds are listed on an exchange their market prices are published daily in the financial press. However, their net asset values are only published weekly, based on closing market prices for securities in their portfolios as of the previous Friday. Figure 21.1 provides an example. Both the net asset value and the market value based on either the closing or bid price at which the fund's shares traded on the day in question are shown. The final column indicates the percentage difference between each fund's share price and its net asset value. If this difference is positive (meaning the share price is greater than the NAV), the fund's shares are said to be selling at a premium. Conversely, if this difference is negative (meaning the share price is less than the NAV), the fund's shares are said to be selling at a discount. For example, Figure 21.1 indicates that the First Australia Prime Income fund was selling at a discount, while the Central Fund of Canada was selling for a premium.

◗ Open-end Investment Companies

Open-end Investment Company (Alternatively, **Open-end Mutual Fund**.)
A managed investment company, with an unlimited life, that stands ready at all times to purchase its shares from its owners and usually will continually offer new shares to the public.

An investment company that stands ready at all times to purchase its own shares at or near their net asset value is termed an **open-end investment company** (or open-end fund). These include both incorporated companies or unincorporated trusts.[4] Most of these companies, commonly known as *mutual funds*, also offer new shares or units to the public for a price at or near their net asset values on demand. When mutual fund shareholders want

---

[2]See Jay R. Ritter, "The Long-run Performance of Initial Public Offerings," *Journal of Finance* 46, no. 1 (March 1991): 3–27. It should be noted that over the three years following the initial offering date, non-fund initial public offerings underperformed a matching sample of firms by roughly 27%.

[3]Closed-end funds that have received permission from foreign governments to invest in their securities do not show the type of price behaviour described here, and hence may be initially attractive to investors. See John W. Peavey III, "Returns on Initial Public Offerings of Closed-end Funds." *Review of Financial Studies* 3, no. 4 (1990): 695–708. For more information about closed-end investment companies, see Albert J. Fredman and George Cole Scott, "Analyzing and Finding Data on Closed-end Funds." *AAII Journal* 13, no. 8 (September 1991): 15–19, and "Guidelines for Handling Closed-end Fund Transactions," *AAII Journal* 14, no. 5 (June 1992): 18–22.

[4]For practical purposes, except for some tax considerations that will be discussed subsequently, the differences between the two are negligible.

Figure 21.1 Listing of closed-end funds.

Closed-end funds

Fund	Ticker	NAVPS	Mkt. val. per sh.	Prm.(+) or disc. (−) %
ARC STRATEGIC	AEF.UN/TSE	9.75	8.50	-12.82
BGR Precious Mtls	BPT.A/TSE	14.49	10.75	-25.81
BioCapital Invstmts	BCK.IR/TSE	7.33	3.25	-55.66
Cda Trust Incm (Sep)	CNN.UN/TSE	9.95	10.00	0.50
Cdn General Invstmts	CGI/TSE	14.63	13.15	-10.12
Canadian World Fund	CWF/TSE	5.74	5.00	-12.89
Central Fund of Cda	CEF.A/TSE	5.87	6.30	7.33
China Opportunities	CHF.UN/TSE	12.01	10.10	-15.90
Citadel Diversified Inv	CTD.UN/TSE	7.86	7.00	-10.94
DDJ Cdn Hgh Yld Fd	HYB.UN/TSE	22.94	18.35	-20.01
Diversified Mthly Incm	XMI/TSE	25.62	23.25	-9.25
Economic Invstmt Tr	EVT/TSE	144.54	97.00	-32.89
First Asia Income Fd	FAI.UN/TSE	7.38	5.30	-28.18
First Australia Prime	FAP/TSE	12.60	10.35	-17.86
First Mercantile Curr	FMF.UN/TSE	15.48	14.00	-9.56
Health Care & Biotch	HCB.UN/TSE	6.49	4.75	-26.81
MINT	MID.UN/TSE	7.27	7.00	-3.71
NCE Diversified	NCD.UN/TSE	4.13	3.30	-20.10
New Altamira Value	NVL.UN/TSE	11.63	9.30	-20.03
Newcastle Mkt (Sep)	NMN.UN/TSE	16.08	11.25	-30.04
Old Cda Invtmt (Sep)	OCI/TSE	2.49	2.25	-9.64
Phoenix Hedge Fd	PHF.UN/TSE	18.00	11.85	-34.17
Polar Hedge Tr	PHT.UN/TSE	4.68	3.15	-32.69
SAGE	BBB.UN/TSE	12.96	11.40	-12.04
Templeton Emerg	TEM.UN/TSE	11.29	8.60	-23.83
Third Cdn Gen Inv	THD/TSE	19.74	17.00	-13.88
United Corps	UNC/TSE	63.79	45.05	-29.38

All funds valued weekly on November 5 except as noted.

SOURCE: Reprinted with permission of *The Financial Post* (November 7, 1998).

to sell their shares, they usually receive an amount equal to the fund's net asset value times the number of shares sold.

Some open-end companies, known as **no-load funds**, sell their shares at a price equal to net asset value. Others, known as **load funds**, offer shares through brokers or other selling organizations, thereby adding a percentage **load charge** to the net asset value. These funds charge either a front-end load, a back-end load or, in some cases, the investor can choose between the two. With the first type, a percentage of the money contributed to the fund is deducted before it is invested. With the second type, a percentage of the proceeds from redemption is deducted before the investor receives the money. For example, a fund that charges a 5% front-end load receives $1000 from an investor and will deduct $50 immediately leaving $950 to purchase the fund's units at the current net asset value. While this is described as a 5% load charge it is, in fact, equal to $50/950 = 5.3% of the amount ultimately invested. The same fund may give the investor the option to select a 6% back-end load instead of the front-end load. In this case, an investor who redeems $1000 worth of units will receive $940 in cash.

There have been dramatic changes in the structure of the industry in Canada over the last 15 years. In 1983, load funds represented 84% of all funds. By 1998 the distinction between load and no-load funds was becoming increasingly blurred. There are now load funds that are sold at zero load providing that the investor's purchase is of a given minimum size. On the other hand, no-load funds purchased through a regular broker may be subject to the brokerage firm's normal commission (about 2%) and those purchased through a discount broker often have a redemption fee of $35 to $50.

For load funds the normal front-end load in 1983 was about 9% whereas in 1998 the load for approximately 80% of these funds fell in the 2 to 3% range. For back-end load funds the normal deferred sales charge is 6% or somewhat less; however, the charge declines each year that the fund is held typically reaching zero after seven years.[5]

No-load Fund A mutual fund that does not have a load charge.

Load Fund A mutual fund that has a load charge.

Load Charge A sales charge levied by a mutual fund when an investor buys its shares.

---

[5]Information provided by IFIC.

Not surprisingly, the performance of no-load funds as a whole does not differ in any notable way from that of load funds. The load charge, which goes to the selling organization, represents the cost of education and persuasion. No-load funds do not employ sales people and are generally purchased directly from the financial institution that manages them.

Quotations

Figure 21.2 shows a portion of the quotations for mutual funds provided in the financial press daily.[6] Following the name is a brief description of the loading fees charged, the eligibility for RRSP investment, the method of distributing (i.e. selling) the fund and the net asset value, based on closing prices for the fund's securities on the day in question. The final column indicates the difference (in dollars) between the day's net asset value per share and that computed at the close of the previous trading day.

Figure 21.3 shows the daily quotations that appear for a special type of mutual fund known as a money market fund. Such funds invest in short-term, fixed-income securities such as Treasury bills, commercial paper, and bank term deposits. Next to the name of such a fund is shown a brief description of the way the fund is sold, the current annualized yield, and the compounded annual yield (known as the effective yield), with the final column showing the change in the yield from the previous day. Not shown, but an important factor in deciding in which money market fund to invest, is the degree of safety (that is, default risk) associated with the assets held by each fund.

An Example

In order to highlight the differences in purchasing shares of closed-end funds, no-load funds, and load funds, consider the following example. An investor has $1000 to use in purchasing shares of a fund and is considering the following funds, all of which have the same net asset value (NAV) of $10 per share.

Closed-end fund E is selling for a market price that equals its NAV, whereas closed-end fund D is selling at a 20% discount, or $10 \times .80 = $8. The broker charges a commission equal to 2% of the market price for each share purchased. Mutual fund N is a no-load fund, whereas mutual fund L charges a 3% load. How many shares does the investor end up with in each case?

Closed-end fund E: cost per share = $10 + $.20 commission = $10.20
         number of shares = $1000/$10.20 = 98.04

Closed-end fund D: cost per share = $8 + $.16 commission = $8.16
         number of shares = $1000/$8.16 = 122.55

Mutual fund N: cost per share = $10
         number of shares = $1000/$10 = 100

Mutual Fund L: cost per share = $10 + $.31 load = $10.31
         (note: 3% $\times$ $10.31 = $0.31)
         number of shares = $1000/$10.31 = 96.99

Thus the largest number of shares would be received when buying the shares of discounted closed-end fund D, while the lowest number of shares would be received when buying the shares of load fund L.

A number of institutions similar to investment companies exist. The next section describes some of the more important types of securities they offer.

---

[6]Funds are listed under a name in boldface type. This is the name of the common investment management company that is associated with those funds.

Figure 21.2 Listings of mutual funds (excerpts).

Recent prices of investment funds supplied by Fundata Canada Inc. at 6:00 p.m. Sep. 2. Prices reported by funds are the net asset value per share or unit last calculated and are for information purposes only. Confirmation of price should be obtained from the fund. Chg—$ change from last valuation; D—distributed by fund sponsor; G—redemption charge; I—distributed by independent dealers; L—sales charge; N—no sales charge; O—optional front—end or redemption charge;B—choice of front or back redemption charge;R—eligible for RRSPs; Z—not available for sale; m—minimum purchase of $150,000; u—U.S. currency; x—ex—dividend; (n)—not a member of IFIC; (Date following fund denotes last valuation).

Fund	Load	RSP	Dist	Val	Chg
ABAX					
uBrady Bonds 08/27	L		I	10.60	–
ABC FUNDS					
mAmer-Value 08/31	N		D	5.20	-.78
mFully-Mgd 08/31	N	R	D	6.53	-1.00
mFund-Value 08/31	N	R	D	8.69	-2.01
ACADIA INVESTMENT FUNDS					
Atlantic 09/01	G	R		9.74	+.06
Balanced 09/01	G	R		10.07	-.02
Bond 09/01	G	R		11.59	+.08
Cdn Equity 09/01	G	R		7.04	-.32
Diversified 09/01	G	R		9.84	+.09
Intl Equity 09/01	G			10.00	unch
Mortgage 09/01	G	R		9.95	unch
ACKER FINLEY					
OSA Cdn Equ	L	R	I	4.41	-.02
AGF GROUP OF FUNDS					
20/20 Aggr Gbl	O		I	6.72	+.07
20/20 Aggr Gth	O		I	15.49	+.33
20/20 Cdn Res	O	R	I	11.72	+.33
20/20 Emerg Mkt	O		I	2.35	+.04
20/20 India	O		I	2.01	+.01
20/20 Latin Am	O		I	3.79	-.03
20/20 Mgd Fut	O	R	Z	2.67	-.01
20/20 RSP Ag Eq	O	R	Z	6.00	+.20
20/20 RSP Ag Sm	O	R	I	5.01	+.09
AGF Amer Grth	O		I	25.55	-.17
AGF Amer TAA	O		I	20.79	-.16
AGF Asian Grth	O		I	6.78	+.13
AGF Cda Class	O		I	4.40	+.07
xAGF Cdn Bond	O	R	I	5.56	+.02
AGF Cdn Equity	O	R	I	10.84	+.15
AGF Cdn Growth	O	R	I	17.90	+.46
AGF Cdn TAA	O	R	I	5.20	+.07
AGF China Focus	O		I	4.29	+.06
AGF Dividend	O	R	I	20.11	+.46
AGF Euro AA	O		I	8.54	+.14
AGF Euro Growth	O		I	16.63	+.17
AGF Germany	O		I	38.40	+1.00
xAGF Glo GvtBnd	O		I	11.26	-.06
AGF Glo R/E Equ	O		I	5.96	unch
AGF Grth & Inc	O	R	I	16.09	+.21
AGF Grth Equity	O	R	I	22.43	+.46
xAGF High Income	O	R	I	10.04	+.05
AGF Intl ST Inc	O		I	11.35	-.04
AGF Intl Stock	O		I	6.32	+.09
AGF Intl Value	O		I	32.87	+.28
AGF Japan	O		I	4.94	-.02
xAGF RSP Gbl Bnd	O	R	I	5.32	-.03
AGF RSPIntlEqAl	O	R	I	5.31	+.05
AGF Special US	O		I	9.83	+.05
xAGF US Income	O		I	12.48	-.08
xAGF US ST HiYld	O		I	4.63	-.09
AGF World Bal	O		I	13.77	+.17
AGF World Equ	O		I	8.22	+.08
AGF GROUP OF FUNDS US$					
u20/20 Aggr Gbl	O		I	4.35	+.07
u20/20 Aggr Gth	O		I	10.03	+.27
u20/20 Emerg Mkt	O		I	1.52	+.03
u20/20 India	O		I	1.30	+.01
u20/20 Latin Am	O		I	2.46	unch
uAGF Amer Grth	O		I	16.55	-.01
uAGF Amer TAA	O		I	13.47	-.02
uAGF Asian Grth	O		I	4.39	+.11
uAGF Cda Class	O		I	2.85	+.06
uAGF China Focus	O		I	2.78	+.06
uAGF Euro AA	O		I	5.53	+.12
uAGF Euro Growth	O		I	10.78	+.19
uAGF Germany	O		I	24.88	+.80
xuAGF Glo GvtBnd	O		I	7.30	+.01
uAGF Glo R/E Equ	O	R	I	3.86	+.03
uAGF Intl ST Inc	O		I	7.35	+.02
uAGF Intl Stk	O		I	4.10	+.09
uAGF Intl Value	O		I	21.30	+.32
uAGF Japan	O		I	3.20	+.01
uAGF Special US	O		I	6.37	+.07
xuAGF US Income	O		I	8.09	unch
xuAGF US ST HiYld	O		I	3.00	-.04
uAGF World Bal	O		I	8.92	+.16
uAGF World Equ	O		I	5.33	+.09
AGF FUNDS INC.					
Germany C$ M	O		Z	41.01	+1.07
uGermany U$ M	O		Z	26.57	+.86
AIC ADVANTAGE FUND SERIES					
Advantage	O	R	I	60.50	+1.62
Advantage II	O	R	I	7.42	+.17
uAmer Advant U$	O		I	3.30	+.06
Amer Advantage	O		I	5.09	+.06
uWorld Advant U$	O		I	3.06	+.06
World Advantage	O		I	4.71	+.07
uAm Advantage U$	O		I	12.89	+.10
Am LrgCap Gr C$	O		I	33.23	-.42
uAm LrgCap Gr U$	O		I	21.63	-.04
Amer RSP Index	O	R	I	11.52	-.05
Cdn Balanced	O	R	I	14.72	+.03
xCdn Bond	O	R	I	10.93	+.02
xCdn Div Gro	O	R	I	11.22	+.07
Cdn EmergGrth	O	R	I	10.34	+.22
xCdn HiYldBnd	O	R	I	11.55	+.01
xCdn Income Tr	O	R		6.65	+.19
Cdn LrgCap Gth	O	R	I	18.27	+.28
Cdn LrgCap Val	O	R	I	12.07	+.23
Cdn Sml Cap Gro	O	R	I	9.05	+.04
Cdn Sml Cap Val	O	R	I	11.05	+.27
Euro Value	O		I	19.36	+.28
Glo Value	O		I	14.71	+.06
Inl Lrg Cap Gro	O		I	15.07	+.15
Intl Em Mk Gro	O		I	10.79	+.28
Intl RSP Index	O	R	I	11.57	+.22
Latin Amer	O		I	7.57	-.04
Pacific Basin	O		I	7.09	-.04
xWorld Bond	O	R	I	10.41	+.01
AZURA POOLED FUNDS					
Agg Growth RSP 09/01	O	R	I	8.22	-.07
Balanced 09/01	O		I	11.56	-.03
Balanced RRSP 09/01	O	R	I	11.01	-.01
Conservative 09/01	O	R	I	11.13	-.01
Growth 09/01	O		I	11.80	-.07
Growth RRSP 09/01	O	R	I	10.94	-.02
BANK OF MONTREAL					
FC Allocation	N	R	D	13.35	+.12
FC Bond	N	R	D	12.89	+.02
FC Div Income	N	R	D	16.93	+.32
FC Emerg Mkts	N		D	5.55	-.01
FC Equ Index	N	R	D	16.34	+.42
FC Euro Gth	N		D	17.57	+.24
FC Far East	N		D	6.00	+.05
FC Glo Sci&Tech	N		D	17.27	-.13
FC Growth	N	R	D	14.93	+.27
FC Intl Gth	N		D	17.68	+.18
FC Itl Bond	N		D	11.39	-.15
FC Jap Gth	N		D	5.34	-.08
FC Latin Amer	N		D	7.03	+.03
FC Mortgage	N	R	D	11.99	+.00
FC NAFTA Adv	N		D	12.35	+.17
FC Prec Metals	N	R	D	4.42	+.14
FC Resource	N	R	D	6.38	+.14
FC SpecGth	N	R	D	11.79	+.20
FC US Equ Index	N	R	D	11.37	-.11
FC US Gth	N		D	18.96	-.09
FC US Spec Gro	N		D	11.34	+.06
FC US Value	N		D	14.18	-.11
BARREAU DU QUEBEC(n)					
Balanced 08/28	N	R	D	12.00	–
Bond 08/28	N	R	D	10.84	–
BEUTEL GOODMAN(n)					
Amer Equity	L		I	9.24	-.03
Balanced	L	R	I	13.13	-.03
Cdn Equity	L	R	I	14.00	+.33
Income	L	R	I	11.27	+.02
Intl Equity	L		I	6.22	-.12
Small Cap	L	R	I	7.41	+.16
BISSETT					
Amer Equity	N			35.10	-.37
Bond	N	R		12.90	+.03
Cdn Equity	N	R		36.90	+.60
Dividend	N			17.74	+.19
Income Trust	N	R		10.45	+.26
Intl Equity	N			10.33	+.08
Microcap	N	R		9.23	+.04
Multinational	N			20.83	-.15
Retirement	N	R		17.94	+.10
Small Cap	N	R		29.03	+.12
BNP (CANADA) FUNDS					
Bond 09/01	N	R	D	10.95	+.08
Equity 08/28	N	R	D	31.21	–
BPI MUTUAL FUNDS					
Amer Equ Valu	O		I	9.08	-.10
Amer Small Co	O		I	25.52	+.15
Asia Pacific	O		I	5.55	+.02
xCdn Bond	O	R	I	4.96	+.01
Cdn Equ Value	O	R	I	7.82	+.07
Cdn Mid-Cap	O	R	I	8.18	+.18
Cdn Resource	O	R	I	9.20	+.29
Cdn Small Co	O	R	Z	7.34	unch
xCorp Bond	O	R	I	9.65	+.01
Div Equity	O	R	I	8.61	+.10
xDiv Income	O	R	I	12.04	+.14
Emer Markets	O		I	9.37	+.08
Glo Bal RSP	O	R	I	12.64	+.07
Glo Equity Val	O		I	23.68	+.04
xGlo RSP Bond	O	R	I	11.23	-.06
Glo Small Co	O		I	17.41	+.08
xHigh Income	O	R	I	9.30	+.11
xInc & Growth	O	R	I	11.81	-.02
Intl Equ Val	O		I	12.89	+.10
BPI MUTUAL FUNDS US$					
uAmer Equ Val U$	O		I	5.91	unch
uAmer Sml Co U$	O		I	16.61	+.28
uAsia Pacific U$	O		I	3.61	+.05
uEmer Markets U$	O		I	6.10	+.12
uGlo Equity U$	O		I	15.41	+.19
uGlo Small Co U$	O		I	11.33	+.17
uIntl Equ Val U$	O		I	8.39	+.16
CALDWELL					
Amer Equity	O			5.28	-.06
Associate	O	R		5.73	+.08
Cdn Equity	O	R		3.93	+.07
Cdn Income	O	R		4.95	+.03
International	O			5.02	-.04
CAMAF(n)					
Camaf 08/28	N	R	D	12.34	-.98
CANADA TRUST					
AmeriGrowth	N	R	D	11.54	-.13
Emerging Ecos	N			8.62	+.05
Energy 09/01	N	R		8.86	–
European Equ	N			14.83	+.13
Far East 09/01	N		D	6.85	–
Fin Companies	N	R	D	9.82	+.26
Glo Bond Index 09/01	N	R	D	10.87	–
Global Bond 09/01	N	R	D	11.41	–
Global Equ 09/01	N		D	19.84	–
Global Tech	N			13.51	-.02
Intl Index	N		D	10.29	+.06
Intl Index RRSP	N	R	D	11.09	+.02
Intl Sml Co	N		D	9.85	+.15
Japanese Equ	N			11.15	-.05
Latin American	N		D	7.44	-.07
Mortgage	N	R	D	11.79	+.00
NA Demo 09/01	N		D	15.23	+.28
Prec Metals 09/01	N	R		3.73	+.08
US Equity Index 09/01	N		D	20.39	–
US Index RRSP	N	R		13.53	-.13
US Small Co 09/01	N			9.03	–
CLARINGTON GROUP OF FUNDS					
Asia Pacific	O		I	5.34	+.10
Cdn Balanced	O	R	I	10.96	+.06
Cdn Equity	O	R	I	10.29	+.16
xCdn Income	O	R	I	9.24	+.04
Cdn Micro-Cap	O	R	I	8.42	+.13
Cdn Small Cap	O	R	I	8.66	+.19
Global Comm	O		I	16.03	+.04
Global Opps	O		I	13.01	+.09
US Equity	O		I	15.02	-.16
US Sml Co Gro	O		I	12.45	+.08
CLEAN ENVIRONMENT					
Balanced	O	R	I	9.81	+.13
Equity	O	R	I	10.92	+.34
Income	O	R	I	11.03	+.04
Intl Equity	O		I	8.36	+.17
CORMEL(n)					
Balanced 08/28	L	R		13.32	–
COTE 100(n)					
Amerique 08/31	N		I	19.21	–
EXP 08/31	N	R	I	17.69	–
Excel 08/31	N		I	8.75	–
REA 08/31	N		I	11.21	–
REER 08/31	N	R	I	24.45	–
uU.S. 08/31	N		I	9.00	–
CSA MGMT ENTERPRISES LTD(n)					
Goldfund	L		I	3.70	+.10
Goldtrust	L	R	I	4.38	+.05
CTI MUTUAL FUNDS INC(n)					
Cdn Bond 08/28	N	R		9.82	–
Cdn Equity 08/28	N	R		8.65	–
Cdn Growth Fund 08/28	N	R		9.00	–
CUNDILL GROUP SER A					
Security	L	R	Z	20.79	+.45
Value	L		Z	12.68	+.09
CUNDILL GROUP SER B					
Security	L	R	I	22.85	+.49
Value	L		I	13.74	+.10
DEACON CAPITAL CORP.					
Resolute Grth	O	R	D	13.23	+.03
DESJARDINS FUNDS					
American	N	R	D	12.04	+.47
Balanced	N	R	D	14.71	+.18
Bond	N	R	D	5.35	+.01
Divers Amb	N	R	D	10.10	+.13
Divers Aud	N	R	D	11.85	+.10
Divers Mod	N	R	D	11.21	+.05
Divers Sec	N	R	D	10.73	+.03
Dividend	N	R	D	13.10	+.18
Enviro	N	R	D	14.42	+.30
Equity	N	R	D	24.59	+.57
Growth	N	R	D	12.25	+.28
High Potential	N	R	D	7.99	+.15
Internat'l	N		D	36.88	+.54
Mortgage	N	R	D	4.52	unch
Quebec	N	R	D	10.83	+.14
World Balanced	N	R	D	10.81	+.07
DOMINION EQUITY					
Domequity	N	R	D	8.21	+.22
DUNDEE DYNAMIC FUNDS(n)					
Dyn $ Cost Avg	G	R	I	9.89	+.01
Dyn Amer C$	O		I	12.05	-.07
uDyn Amer U$	O		I	7.84	+.04
Dyn Cdn Gro	O	R	I	8.57	+.20
Dyn CdnRealEst	O	R	I	9.19	+.11
Dyn Div Gro	O	R	I	6.16	+.07
xDyn Dividend	O	R	I	6.32	+.03
Dyn Europe	O		I	21.47	+.17
Dyn Far East	O		I	8.09	+.06
Dyn Fund Cda	O	R	I	14.53	+.31
Dyn Glo Bond	O	R	I	5.39	-.04
xDyn Glo Inc&Gro	O		I	4.19	-.01
Dyn Glo Milna	O		I	4.82	+.07
Dyn Glo Partner	O		I	11.55	+.04
Dyn Glo Pre Met	O		I	2.88	+.10
Dyn Glo Resour	O		I	11.15	+.73
Dyn Govt Inc	L	R	I	9.91	+.01
xDyn Income	O	R	I	5.00	-.02
Dyn Intl	O		I	10.04	+.06
Dyn Israel GrC$	G		I	10.34	-.10
uDyn Israel GrU$	O		I	6.73	+.01
Dyn Lat Amer	O		I	3.63	-.06
Dyn Partners	O	R	I	8.39	+.05
Dyn Prec Met	O	R	I	1.02	+.05
Dyn Quebec Fund	O	R	I	9.58	+.13
Dyn RealEst	O		I	19.09	-.15
Dyn Sm Cap	O	R	I	4.46	+.08
Dyn Team	O	R	I	8.19	+.09
DUNDEE POWER FUNDS(n)					
Pwr American	O		I	4.57	-.04
Pwr Balanced	O	R	I	4.57	+.05
Pwr Bond	O	R	I	4.94	+.01
Pwr Canadian	O	R	I	4.17	+.10
ELLIOTT & PAGE					

SOURCE: Reprinted by permission of *The Globe and Mail: Report on Business* (September 3, 1998).

Figure 21.3 Listing of money market funds (excerpts).

MONEY MARKET FUNDS

Cur—current yield (actual return over past 7 days, annualized); Eff—effective yield. Effective yield includes compounding. Yields will vary; Chg—change from previous yield.

Fund	Dist	Cur	Eff	Chg
ACADIA INVESTMENT FUNDS				
MMF 09/01		3.76	3.83	unch
AGF FUNDS INC.				
xMMF	I	3.54	3.60	+.07
xuUS MMF	I	4.62	4.73	+.02
AIC INCOME FUND SERIES				
MMF	I	4.21	4.30	+.05
AIM FAMILY OF FUNDS C$				
Cash Prf	I	4.05	4.13	+.12
AIM GT FAMILY OF FUNDS C$				
MMF	I	3.88	3.95	+.07
ALLSTAR FUND GROUP LTD.				
xMoney Market	D	3.00	3.04	−.04
ALPHA FUNDS(n)				
MMF		3.87	3.94	−.01
ALTAMIRA				
T-Bill	I	4.16	4.25	+.03
ARGENTUM MANAGEMENT C$				
xST Asset Port	I	4.60	4.71	−.01
ATLAS MUTUAL FUNDS				
uAm MMF	I	4.47	4.57	−.05
MMF	I	4.03	4.11	+.04
T-Bill	I	3.51	3.57	+.02
BANK OF MONTREAL				
FC MMF	D	3.85	3.93	+.03
mFC Pr MMF		4.65	4.76	+.01
FC T-Bill	D	3.73	3.80	+.01
BEUTEL GOODMAN(n)				
MMF	I	4.49	4.59	+.16
BISSETT				
MMF		4.46	4.56	+.04
BNP (CANADA) FUNDS				
xMMF 08/28	D	3.67	3.74	—
BPI MUTUAL FUNDS				
T-Bill	I	4.34	4.43	+.01
uUS MMF		4.52	4.62	unch
CANADA TRUST				
xMMF	D	3.95	4.03	+.02
xPr MMF	D	4.32	4.41	unch
CAPSTONE GROUP(n)				
xCash	I	4.43	4.53	unch
CENTREPOST MUTUAL FUNDS				
Sh Term	D	4.37	4.46	+.02
CI MUTUAL FUNDS C$				
xMMF	I	4.13	4.21	+.04
CI MUTUAL FUNDS U$				
xuU$ MMF	I	4.51	4.61	unch
CIBC FUNDS				
Cdn TBill	D	3.88	3.95	+.05
MMF	D	4.08	4.16	+.01
mPrem TBill	D	4.54	4.64	+.06
uUS MMF	D	4.47	4.57	unch
CLARINGTON GROUP OF FUNDS				
MMF	I	4.24	4.33	+.01
DESJARDINS FUNDS				
MMF	D	3.81	3.88	+.29
DUNDEE DYNAMIC FUNDS(n)				
xDyn MMF	I	4.41	4.51	+.02
ELLIOTT & PAGE				
EP Mon	I	4.33	4.42	+.02
T-Bill	I	3.13	3.18	−.27
ETHICAL FUNDS				
MMF	I	3.52	3.58	+.01
FICADRE FUNDS				
xMMF 09/01	D	3.25	3.30	−.17
FIDELITY INVESTMENTS C$				
CdnST	I	3.97	4.05	+.03
FIDELITY INVESTMENTS U$				
uUS MMF	I	4.39	4.49	unch
GBC FUNDS(n)				
MMF 09/01	I	4.13	4.21	—
GLOBAL STRATEGY				

SOURCE: Reprinted by permission of the *Globe and Mail: Report on Business* (September 3, 1998).

Similar Types of Investments

Fixed and Deferred Annuities

Fixed Annuity A contract, usually sold by a life insurance company, that guarantees the beneficiary or annuitant a series of payments of a fixed and equal amount.

A **fixed annuity** is a contract in which a life insurance company promises to pay the investor a fixed dollar amount on a regular (generally monthly) basis. The size and number of these payments will depend on how much money the investor gives the insurance company and the size of an up-front fee (if any) that is charged. Also important are the investor's age and the annuity option that the investor chooses.

One option the investor may choose is a life annuity, where fixed dollar payments are provided regularly until the investor's death. Another option is a joint and last survivor annuity, where fixed dollar payments of a lesser amount continue on a regular basis until both the investor and spouse have died. A third option is a period certain annuity (or fixed period annuity), where fixed dollar payments are made on a regular basis for a prespecified number of years (perhaps 5, 10, 15, or 20); if the investor dies before then, subsequent payments are made to the investor's beneficiary. A fourth option, known as a life annuity with a period certain, is a combination of the first and third options. With this option, the investor receives regular fixed dollar payments until death. However, if death should occur before some prespecified number of years have elapsed, then payments will continue until that number of years has elapsed.

Variable Annuity An annuity contract that pays the annuitant a series of payments that depends on the performance of a specified investment portfolio

Some plan sponsors offer a **variable annuity** where the size of the regular payments is not prespecified but depends directly on the performance of an investment portfolio managed by the institution.

The previous discussion described an immediate annuity, where the investor purchases a fixed annuity with a single payment. However, the investor also has the option of making a single payment and acquiring a **deferred annuity** that starts making periodic payments on a specified future date based on the principal and accumulated investment returns. A variant on this is a **guaranteed investment annuity** which gives the investor the option of receiving either periodic payments or a lump sum at maturity.

Pooled Funds

Trust and insurance companies invest money for individuals and organizations. Trust companies manage personal trust funds; both trust and insurance companies manage individual retirement funds. Any such fund can be invested on an individual basis, with specific securities selected and held in a separate account. This is often done for large accounts. To capture economies of scale, small accounts are often pooled, allowing joint participation in one or more large pools of securities.

The vehicle utilized in this process is the **pooled fund**. In form (but not in law), it is similar to an open-end mutual fund. The securities in the fund are valued periodically, and total value divided by current number of units determines net asset value per unit. On any valuation date, money from an account may be used to purchase units at this value. Alternatively, units purchased at an earlier date may be redeemed at the current net asset value.

A trust or insurance company may offer several pooled funds. One fund may hold only short-term money market instruments, whereas another holds long-term bonds, and yet another holds common stocks. A pooled fund investing in mortgages may also be offered, as may one investing in real property.[7] When a menu of this sort is available, money from a given trust or retirement account can be invested in two or more pooled funds.

Segregated Funds

A **segregated fund** is the result of a "joint venture" between a life insurance company and an investment company in which the former offers the latter's family of mutual funds to individual investors. In practice, the insurance company can, and frequently does, offer the funds of more than one investment company. Segregated funds are similar to regular mutual funds, but with four important differences:

1. Maturity. The contract under which the mutual fund is purchased is subject to a maturity date, usually 10 years.
2. Guarantee of Principal. Segregated funds provide a guarantee of at least 75% of the invested capital at maturity or upon the death of the owner, whichever comes first, at which time the investor receives the larger of the market value or the guaranteed amount. Many of the segregated funds offered more recently offer a guarantee of 100% of the principal at death or maturity. Some segregated funds include a reset feature in the contract that allows the investor to reset the guarantee if the market value has increased. There are usually limitations on the frequency with which this can be done. If the value is reset then the guarantee period is also reset from that date.
3. Avoidance of Probate. Segregated funds are regarded as life insurance contracts; as a result the investor can name a beneficiary, thereby avoiding probate fees because ownership is transferred outside the owner's will. (This may also reduce the executor's fees and the legal fees.)

---

[7]Pooled funds are referred to as commingled funds in the US. Due to the illiquidity of the assets, the sponsor of real property commingled funds may reserve the right to limit the redemption of units, either temporarily or until sale of the underlying property. For an analysis of the performance of such funds, see Mike Miles and Arthur Esty, "How Well Do Commingled Real Estate Funds Perform?" *Journal of Portfolio Management* 8, no. 2 (Winter 1982): 62–68.

4. Creditor Protection. Segregated funds provide the investor with a measure of creditor protection in the event of suit or bankruptcy. This protection exists only if the beneficiary of the contract is a member of the investor's immediate family (spouse, child, grandchild, or parent).

The major disadvantage of segregated funds is that management expense ratios (MERs) are higher than those for the underlying mutual funds with the difference ranging from 0.15% to 1%, an amount that reflects the cost of the guarantee.

❯ Trust Units

Trust Units High-yield securities similar to closed-end mutual funds that hold revenue producing real assets.

Trust units are high-yield securities that are structured like unincorporated closed-end mutual funds. Instead of holding financial assets the trust has partial or full ownership of revenue-producing assets. Units are sold to individual investors in the same manner as common shares, i.e., they are listed on Canadian stock exchanges. The primary purpose of the trust is to generate attractive cash flows for the unit holders. In many cases these cash flows are partly or wholly tax sheltered either because the assets are covered under a tax incentive scheme such as Canadian Oil and Gas Property Expense, Canadian Development Expense, Canadian Exploration Expense, or because the benefits of the Capital Cost Allowances on the trust's assets are flowed through directly to the unitholder.

Trust units have been issued in a wide variety of industries including coal mining, iron ore production, propane distribution, oil and gas pipelines, forestry regeneration, electric power production, mutual fund commissions, natural gas wholesale distribution, public refrigerated warehousing, Northern Canadian retail store, business records storage, a Halifax cargo facility, air cargo space, and mattress manufacturing. Many of these industries are in the mature stage of their life cycle and, therefore, require a limited amount of capital for reinvestment. As a result the bulk of the generated cash flow can safely be paid out to the unitholders. Others are stable businesses with an established market with some growth potential.

Although many investors tend to classify trust units as fixed-income securities they should be regarded as equity because their cash distribution to unitholders is dependent on many other variables, such as general business conditions and commodity prices, besides interest rates.

Real Estate Investment Trust (REIT) An investment fund, similar to an investment company, whose investment objective is to hold primarily real-estate-related assets, either through mortgages, construction and development loans, or equity interests.

Real Estate Investment Trust (REIT) units are a special case where the underlying assets consist of real estate. Real estate investment trusts are plentiful in the US, but less so in Canada. These are a useful vehicle for the individual investor to use to invest in real estate. Although not classified as investment companies for legal purposes, REITs are similar to closed-end funds in that they serve as a conduit for earnings on certain types of investments, passing them on to their shareholders and avoiding corporate taxation.

REITs must invest primarily in real estate or loans secured by real estate. They can obtain funds by issuing shares, bonds, and even warrants. They can also borrow from banks, issue mortgages on some or all of their property, and issue commercial paper. Like other managed investment companies, REITs hire a management firm for a fee, usually about 1% per year of the value of the assets.

The shares of Canadian REITs are listed on the TSE; therefore, price and volume quotations are provided regularly in the financial press. Because the assets held by these trusts are generally quite illiquid, it is difficult to calculate NAVs on a regular basis. Consequently it is hard to tell whether they sell at a premium or at a discount from NAV.

Most REITs can be highly leveraged. A trust might have debt amounting to 70% of its total assets. Consequently, any decline in the value of the property held by such a trust will generally cause a greater percentage decline in the market value of its common stock. Furthermore, adverse changes in the relationship between the interest paid on a trust's short-term debt and that earned on the trust's assets will also result in declines in the market value of the trust's common stock—and may even lead to default and bankruptcy, as happened to many in the recession of 1973–1974 when all the existing Canadian REITs disappeared. The REITs that have been established since 1992 have followed more prudent financial structures by using less debt. REITs are a desirable investment for many individuals due to their unique investment policies and leverage. However, only a portion of an individual's portfolio should consist of such securities. The Institutional Issues box contains more information about Canadian REITs.

Labour-sponsored Investment Funds

Labour-sponsored Investment Funds
Vehicles similar to mutual funds, sponsored by labour organizations with a mandate to invest in small and medium-sized businesses.

Labour-sponsored investment funds are investment funds sponsored by a labour union with the objective of investing in small and startup businesses. Although sponsored by a labour union these funds are generally run by professional money managers (for a fee).[8] The attraction these funds hold for some investors is that a 15% federal tax credit is granted on a maximum yearly investment of $5000 that is matched by a corresponding tax credit in many provinces. The investor, however, must hold the units for at least eight years or return the tax credit. An unattractive feature is that these funds invest in extremely illiquid securities, so it is difficult to calculate NAVs and hence fund performance. Furthermore, the eight-year required holding period is a deterrent to some investors.

Unit Investment Trusts

Unit Investment Trust
An unmanaged investment company with a finite life that raises an initial sum of capital from investors and uses the proceeds to purchase a fixed portfolio of securities (typicaly bonds).

First Trust
www.firsttrust.com

Unit investment trusts are similar to traditional mutual funds in that they hold professionally managed portfolios whose units can readily be bought and sold by the investing public. These trusts differ from mutual funds in one important respect—the portfolio remains fixed for a predetermined period, usually five years. This offers the investor three advantages: first, there is no continuing portfolio management required and, therefore, management expenses are low; second, there is no turnover and, hence, no brokerage fees (other than at inception and liquidation)[9] and, third, the composition of the portfolio is known.

Typically, unit investment trusts are specialty funds that concentrate on an industry or an economic sector either locally or globally. As an example of units that are available in Canada, First Trust's North American Financial Institutions Trust '98 consists of a fixed portfolio with equal dollar amounts invested in each of 15 financial institutions. This trust was started in September 1997 and remained open for investment at its net asset value till the end of August 1998 at which point it closed and the units traded on the TSE thereafter. A new fund could then be initiated, which might be called North American Financial Institutions Trust '99 with the proceeds invested in a different group of financial institutions.

There is a negotiable front-end load that varies from 3.75% to 1.75% associated with the initial purchase of units. The management expense ratio for these units is of the order of 1.15%; that is substantially lower than the 2.35% charged by the median Canadian equity fund.

Any dividends received by the fund are reinvested and flow through to the investor as additional units, unless a cash distribution is specified. A zero turnover means that there are no realized capital gains until the fund is either sold or liquidated.

Figure 21.4 shows the quotations provided in the financial press for the above investments.

---

[8]The labour union also collects a fee for the use of its name.

[9]There may be some minor brokerage costs associated with the reinvestment of dividends.

Figure 21.4 Quotations for investments similar to mutual funds.[a]

TRUST UNITS

	10.30	8.30	APF Enr	AY.UN	1.73	8.45	8.40	8.40	+0.10	16	20.6	
	13.25	6.80	ARC Enr	AET.UN	1.28	7.50	7.00	7.30	+0.30	324	17.5	34.8
	10.50	**8.00**	**ARC Stra**	**AEF.UN**		**9.00**	**8.00**	**9.00**	**+1.00**	**6**		
	11.75	9.75	Algonq	APF.UN	0.18	10.50	10.30	10.40	+0.20	98	1.7	
	12.25	9.00	♣ AsscFrz	AFT.UN	0.99	9.35	9.35	9.35	-0.20	1	10.6	
	27.60	14.00	Athaba	AOS.UN	1.25	14.60	14.25	14.50		176	8.6	10.7
	8.05	4.40	Avista	AVS.UN	0.70	7.20	6.95	7.20	+0.25	285	9.8	
↓	9.20	3.75	BPI Cdn	BOI.UN		4.15	3.75	4.15	+0.05	123		
	24.10	18.25	CPL LT	CPL.UN	1.21	19.00	18.50	19.00		782	6.4	
	20.50	19.30	CRS II	CWO.UN		20.25	19.75	20.25	+0.50	474		
	10.80	8.75	Cda Tr	CNN.UN	0.66	9.65	9.50	9.50	+0.25	21	7.0	14.6
	10.50	7.70	CdnApt	CAR.UN	0.79	9.25	8.90	8.90	-0.35	44	8.9	
	14.00	8.25	Cdn Htl	HOT.UN	1.14	9.00	8.60	9.00	+0.40	108	12.7	17.6
	28.90	15.00	Cdn Oil	CO.UN	1.53	16.00	15.35	15.95	+0.05	293	9.6	9.2
	14.85	9.50	♣ CdRE	REF.UN	1.10	10.60	9.70	10.60	+0.45	214	10.4	11.0
	10.85	6.05	Cdn Rs	RTR.UN	0.94	6.45	6.20	6.35	+0.15	101	14.8	
	9.70	**4.75**	**Cdn Rs**	**RTU.UN**	**0.81**	**5.30**	**4.95**	**5.30**	**+0.35**	**413**	**15.2**	
	15.48	**9.60**	**Draytn**	**DVA.UN**	**0.27**	**10.40**	**9.85**	**10.40**	**+0.70**	**48**	**2.6**	
	7.45	3.25	♣ EnrMr	EIF.UN	0.84	3.85	3.62	3.75	+0.10	1102	22.3	15.6
	4.80	2.20	♣ Enerplu	ERF.G	0.51	2.50	2.30	2.45	+0.10	284	20.6	6.6
	9.70	**5.00**	**Enervest**	**EIT.UN**	**0.93**	**5.65**	**5.00**	**5.00**	**-0.65**	**623**	**18.6**	
	10.65	9.00	FACS	FXS.UN		9.20	9.20	9.20		32		
	16.75	10.80	1st Mrc	FMF.UN	0.11	16.00	15.50	16.00	-0.25	15	0.7	23.2
↓	30.50	22.80	1st Prem	FPI.UN	2.00	24.00	22.80	23.70	+0.55	113	8.4	4.9
	11.90	6.00	1st Prm	FPG.UN	0.75	6.30	6.30	6.30	+0.20	14	11.9	
	25.50	20.00	1st Prm	FPU.UN	2.00	23.45	22.00	23.45	-0.05	191	8.5	8.7
	11.85	**4.55**	**Freehol**	**FRU.UN**	**0.90**	**6.35**	**5.85**	**5.85**	**+0.90**	**425**	**15.4**	
	13.45	9.00	Gas Mn	GIF.UN	1.35	11.00	10.75	10.75	+0.50	61	12.6	
	12.30	9.00	H&R RE	HR.UN	0.82	10.00	9.25	9.55	+0.40	351	8.6	10.3
	10.20	7.55	Halterm	HAL.UN	0.97	7.70	7.70	7.70	-0.05	29	12.7	
	8.75	4.75	Hlthcar	HCB.UN	0.23	5.10	5.10	5.10		63	4.5	
	12.15	8.50	KMS	KMS.UN	1.07	9.00	8.80	9.00	+0.15	42	11.9	
	15.90	9.00	Labradr	LIF.UN	1.25	10.90	9.25	10.15	+0.40	378	12.3	7.5
↓	10.15	6.10	Legacy	LGY.UN	0.43	6.25	6.10	6.15	-0.10	216	7.1	
	12.35	**5.00**	**Luscar**	**LUS.UN**	**1.10**	**6.25**	**5.75**	**5.90**	**+0.40**	**3565**	**18.7**	
	10.10	3.10	♣ Maxi	MXT.UN	0.82	3.25	3.15	3.25	+0.10	136	25.2	36.1
	9.10	6.00	MINT	MID.UN	0.81	6.25	6.00	6.20	-0.30	92	13.1	
	11.70	4.25	MrsnFa	FND.UN	0.78	4.85	4.40	4.50	-0.05	551	17.3	40.9
↓	17.25	12.50	Multi-F	MFU.UN	0.91	13.00	12.50	12.50	-0.25	87	7.2	
	10.50	5.50	NAL Oil	NAE.UN	1.14	6.30	5.80	6.30	-0.05	244	18.1	
	5.45	2.80	NCE Di	NCD.UN	0.50	3.03	3.03	3.03	+0.02	19	16.3	
	7.50	3.00	NCE	NCA.UN	1.00	3.25	3.25	3.25		1	30.8	
	5.25	**2.10**	**NCE Ptr**	**NCF.UN**	**0.60**	**2.55**	**2.15**	**2.47**	**+0.32**	**2666**	**24.3**	**14.5**
	15.00	**7.10**	**♣ NwAlt**	**NVL.UN**	**1.52**	**8.00**	**7.80**	**8.00**	**+0.40**	**76**	**19.0**	**9.6**
↓	21.10	13.50	Newca	NMN.UN	1.60	13.55	13.50	13.50	-0.70	75	11.8	
	16.65	12.50	♣ NthW	NWF.UN	0.97	12.75	12.50	12.50	-0.50	29	7.8	18.9
	11.95	8.80	Nrthland	NPI.UN	0.92	9.65	9.05	9.40	+0.40	441	9.8	29.4
	21.75	14.50	Optus	OPT.UN	2.30	19.70	19.30	19.70	+0.45	210	11.7	
	6.20	4.25	Orion	OET.UN	1.13	4.65	4.40	4.65	-0.05	225	24.3	
	10.25	8.75	PRT Frs	PRT.UN		9.50	9.45	9.50		32		
	22.45	10.05	♣ Pengr	PGF.UN	1.62	10.75	10.35	10.75	+0.50	604	15.1	11.1
	9.75	5.10	PrimWs	PWI.UN	1.15	5.35	5.15	5.20	+0.05	668	22.1	
	16.05	**10.95**	**♣ Realf**	**RFN.UN**	**1.35**	**12.00**	**11.25**	**11.90**	**+0.85**	**179**	**11.3**	**9.4**
	11.35	**7.25**	**♣ RioCa**	**REI.UN**	**0.89**	**8.60**	**7.95**	**8.40**	**+0.45**	**969**	**10.6**	**10.8**
	10.30	7.75	Shining	SHN.UN	1.52	8.25	8.05	8.05		166	18.9	17.9
	13.15	**5.60**	**Starcor**	**STR.UN**	**1.17**	**6.50**	**5.90**	**6.50**	**+0.50**	**381**	**18.0**	**72.2**
	17.50	10.50	Summi	SMU.UN	1.47	11.55	11.15	11.20	+0.20	381	13.1	9.0
	15.25	11.90	Superio	SPF.UN	1.25	12.20	11.90	11.90	-0.25	10312	10.5	19.5
↓	15.40	5.80	Taylor	TAY.UN	0.96	6.35	5.80	6.30		346	15.2	8.3
	15.60	6.00	♣ Tmpl	TEM.UN	1.81	6.25	6.00	6.05	-0.05	158	29.9	11.9
	16.00	7.60	Timber	TBW.UN	1.06	7.90	7.60	7.80	+0.20	1024	13.6	
↓	**13.90**	**11.25**	**Triax Di**	**TRH.UN**	**0.95**	**12.35**	**11.25**	**12.35**	**+1.00**	**275**	**7.7**	**18.2**
↓	9.00	4.10	Viking	VKR.UN	1.03	4.35	4.10	4.35	+0.05	270	23.7	
	7.50	**4.05**	**♣ Wardl**	**WIT.UN**	**0.47**	**4.50**	**4.50**	**4.50**	**+0.25**	**10**	**10.4**	**48.4**
	6.50	3.75	Wstcstl	WCL.UN	0.94	5.65	5.50	5.65		346	16.6	
	11.10	6.00	♣ Wstr	WRE.UN	1.13	6.50	6.30	6.30	+0.05	32	17.9	7.4
	10.70	**6.20**	**♣ Wstrc**	**WRF.UN**	**1.07**	**6.75**	**6.55**	**6.75**	**+0.40**	**39**	**15.8**	**8.5**
	8.45	5.60	Wstshr	WTE.UN	0.91	5.95	5.75	5.95	+0.25	211	15.4	

OTHER FUNDS

Closed end, Variable annuity, Limited partnership, etc.

Fund	Load RSP Dist	Val	Chg
ALTAMIRA (CLOSED END)			
Value	N R Z	10.39	+.23
BPI MUTUAL FUNDS			
Cdn Opp RSP 08/28	O R Z	19.51	–
Glo Opp 08/28	O I	20.98	–
BPI MUTUAL FUNDS US			
uGlo Opp US 08/28	O I	13.38	–
BPI MUTUAL FUNDS (CE)			
Cdn Opp II	N R Z	6.88	-.03
CDN GENERAL (CLOSED END)(n)			
xCdn General Inv	N R I	13.22	+.33
CDN WORLD (CLOSED END)(n)			
Cdn World Fund 08/27	N I	5.61	–
C.I. FUNDS (CLOSED END)			
DDJ Cdn Hi Yld 08/31	N R I	11.01	–
CLA RRSP - BELL(n)			
Balanced 09/01	N R	13.10	-.03
Bond 09/01	N R	14.65	+.14
Equity 09/01	N R	10.75	+.06
CUNDILL GROUP			
McElvaine Inv 08/31	N RD	13.04	-1.07
FIRM CANADIAN GROWTH FUND(n)			
FIRM Cdn Gro 08/31	N R I	12.70	–
FIRST HORIZON CAPITAL(n)			
Multi-Asset 09/01	O I	10.17	-.10
RRSP Hedge 09/01	O R I	9.26	+.03
FIRST TRUST CDN(n)			
Fin Inst Trust	L R	14.49	+.38
Gl 15 Tar 97	L I	14.11	+.25
uGl 15 Tar Tr U$	L I	9.12	+.16
Pharmaceut96 C$	L I	31.88	+.13
uPharmaceut96 U$	L I	20.62	+.09
Pharmaceut97 C$	L I	22.22	+.12
uPharmaceut97 U$	L I	14.37	+.08
Pharmaceut98 C$	L I	13.93	+.09
uPharmaceut98 U$	L I	9.10	+.15
REIT & RE Tr 98	L R	11.28	+.34
Target 10 96 C$	L Z	21.96	-.07
uTarget 10 96 U$	L Z	14.20	-.04
Target 10 97 C$	L I	18.80	-.03
uTarget 10 97 U$	L I	12.15	-.03
Target 10 98 C$	L I	15.09	-.07
uTarget 10 98 U$	L I	9.76	-.04
Technology97 C$	L I	16.20	+.21
uTechnology97 U$	L I	10.48	+.14
Technology98 C$	L I	13.05	-.04
uTechnology98 U$	L I	8.44	-.02
Wealth Mgmt	L R	10.23	+.48
FRIEDBERG (LP)(n)			
Currency	N	24.97	+.60
uDiversified	N D	11.73	+.19
umEquity-Hedge	N D	9.80	+.05
uFutures	N	11.65	+.26
umIntl Sec	N	10.38	+.01
GLOBAL MGR (OFFSHORE) US(n)			
umGerman Bear	L I	3.49	-.11
umGerman Geared	L I	35.76	+3.91
umGerman Index	L I	20.27	+1.06
umHong Kong Bear	L I	8.77	-.09
umHong Kong Index	L I	7.45	+.11
umHongKong Geared	L I	2.88	+.06
umJapan Bear	L I	7.33	-.16
umJapan Geared	L I	2.76	+.02
umJapan Index	L I	5.02	-.03
umTactical Growth 08/26	L	10.80	–
umUK Bear Fund	L I	6.82	-.16
umUK Geared Fund	L I	27.19	+1.35
umUK Index Fund	L I	19.83	+.88
umUS Bear Fund	L I	5.19	-.21
umUS Bond Index	L Z	14.97	-.15
umUS Geared	L I	32.65	+2.75
umUS Index	L I	21.07	+.89
GOODWOOD FUND (PUCCETTI)(n)			
mGoodwood Fund 08/31	O	10.09	–
HILLSDALE INVESTMENT MGMT(n)			
umHillsdale LS	N D	11.23	-.00
MIDDLEFIELD GROUP(n)			
MINT	N R I	7.03	+.03
SAGE	N R I	5.92	-.12
MTC GROWTH			
MTC Growth 08/28	L R Z	8.84	–
NCE RESOURCES GROUP (LP)(n)			
NCE Res (97) 06/30	N R Z	17.01	–
PACIFIC FUNDS			
Total Return 08/31	L R I	8.70	
PHILLIPS, HAGER & NORTH			
Global Eq Tr	N	11.21	+.0
STRATEGIC VALUE FUNDS			
mStrategic Value	O I	9.11	+.0
TEMPLETON (CLOSED END)(n)			
Em Mkts App	N I	9.82	+.0
TRIAX CAPITAL (IR/NPV)(n)			
Div Hi-Yield	L I	13.96	+.03
Wld Strat Yld	L I	10.30	-.18
TRICAP STG MNGT(n)			
uFutures Fund 08/14	B D	14.85	–
VERTEX ONE (LP)(n)			
mBalanced 07/31	N R	10.13	–
mVertex LP 07/31	N	11.67	–
YIELD MANAGEMENT (IR/NPV)(n)			
High Inc Trust 08/31	L R	4.09	-.79
YMG CAPITAL MANAGEMENT			
mYMG Emerg Co	N R I	8.95	+.14

SEGREGATED FUNDS

Unitized funds managed by life insurance companies on behalf of policyholders

Fund	Load RSP Dist	Val	Chg
APEX FUNDS SEABOARD LIFE(n)			
Asian Pacific	O I	2.87	+.01
Balanced (AGF)	O R I	4.58	+.05
Balanced (Dyn)	O R I	4.41	+.06
Cdn Gro (AGF)	O R I	5.03	+.12
Cdn Stock	O R I	4.64	+.11
Cdn Value (Dyn)	O R I	4.11	+.09
Fixed Inc	O R I	5.04	+.01
Global Equity	O I	6.55	-.03
Growth & Income	O R I	4.89	+.06
Mortgage	O R I	4.99	+.01
U.S. Equity	O I	6.95	-.13
BPI LEGACY FUNDS(TRANSAM)(n)			
Am Eq Val Seg	O	11.37	-.12
Cdn Bond Seg	O R	10.13	+.02
Cdn Eq Val Seg	O R	8.25	+.08
Cdn Mid Cap Seg	O R	7.87	+.17
Div Inc Seg	O R	9.69	+.11
Glo Bal RSP Seg	O R	8.61	+.05
Glo Eq Val Seg	O	11.17	+.02
High Inc Seg	O R	8.56	+.10
Inc & Gro Seg	O R	9.38	-.01
Int Eq Val Seg	O	11.55	+.08
T-Bill Seg	O R	10.26	unch
C.U. SEGREGATED FUNDS(n)			
Asset Alloc	G R I	8.97	+.10
Cdn Bond Index	G R I	10.05	+.01
Cdn TSE 35 TRIF	G R I	9.07	+.23
Intl G7 Index	G I	10.88	-.11
U.S. Equ Ind	G I	10.70	-.19
CANADA LIFE(n)			
Asia Pacific 09/01	G	7.53	-.05
Cdn Equity 09/01	G RD	145.18	+.37
Enhanced Div 09/01	G R	9.03	-.01
European Equ 09/01	G	18.92	+.05
Fixed Income 09/01	G RD	97.64	+.68
Itl Bond 09/01	G RD	15.10	-.14
MM 09/01	G RD	66.39	+.02
Managed 09/01	G RD	39.37	+.22
US & Itl Equ 09/01	G D	71.19	+.94
CCPE RRSP FUNDS(n)			
Diversified 08/28	N R	79.88	–
Fixed Inc 08/28	N R	83.28	–
Global Equity 08/28	N	13.78	–
Growth 08/28	N R	101.15	–
MMF 08/28	N R	11.82	–
US Equity 08/28	N	22.11	–
CDA FUNDS(n)			
Aggressive (A) 08/28	N R	10.75	–
Balanced (K) 08/28	N R	6.19	–
Bond & Mort (C) 08/28	N R	15.82	–
Cdn Equity (T) 08/28	N R	8.91	–
Com Stock (A) 08/28	N R	26.56	–
Emer Mkts (K) 08/28	N	5.82	–
European (K) 08/28	N	19.93	–
Fixed Inc (MB) 08/28	N R	9.84	–
Glo Stock (TE) 08/28	N	10.33	–
Global (T) 08/28	N	11.13	–
Intl Equ (K) 08/28	N	13.78	–
MMF (C) 08/28	N R	8.16	–
Pacific Bas (K) 08/28	N	10.98	–
S&P 500 Ind(S) 08/28	N	15.11	–
Spec Equ (K) 08/28	N R	11.89	–
TSE 35 Index(S) 08/28	N R	9.14	–
U.S. Equ (K) 08/28	N	12.44	–
CI SEG FUNDS (TOR MUTUAL)			
American	O I	11.42	+.01
Global	O I	11.37	-.06
Harbour	O R I	9.03	+.06
Harbour Gth Inc	O R I	9.11	+.06
Hsbgr Value	O I	8.70	+.07
MMF	O R I	10.27	unch
COLONIA LIFE(n)			
Bond 08/31	G RD	16.09	–
Equity 08/31	G RD	15.75	–
MMF 08/31	N RD	12.99	–
Mortgage 08/31	G RD	14.17	–
Spec Growth 08/31	G RD	20.07	–
Strat Bal 08/31	G RD	13.03	–
COMMON SENSE FUNDS(n)			
AssetBuild I	G RD	15.22	+.06
AssetBuild II	G RD	16.46	+.12
AssetBuild III	G RD	16.82	+.16
AssetBuild IV	G RD	16.53	+.18
AssetBuild V	G RD	16.25	+.19
CO-OPERATORS LIFE(n)			
Balanced 08/25	N R	206.99	–
Cdn Equity 08/25	N R	190.96	–
Fixed Income 08/25	N R	183.26	–
MMF 08/25	N R	103.25	–
US Diversified 08/25	N	107.32	–
US Equity 08/25	N	289.57	–

POOLED FUNDS

Pooled funds are designed for pension plans, group RRSPs or large individual investors. Unit values shown are before the deduction of management fees., etc.

Fund	Load RSP Dist	Val	Chg
ACUITY POOLED			
mCanadian Equity 08/31	N R	10.40	–
mCdn Balanced 08/31	N R	11.50	–
mCons Asset All 08/31	N R	13.23	–
mEnv Sci & Tech 08/31	N	12.93	–
mFixed Income 08/31	N R	12.16	–
mGlo Balanced 08/31	N	13.82	–
mGlobal Equity 08/31	N	12.22	–
mHigh Income 08/31	N	12.46	–
mShort Term 08/31	N R	10.60	–
IMPERIAL LIFE FINANCIAL(n)			
Bal Growth 08/28	L R	18.53	–
Balanced (T) 08/28	L R	9.61	–
Cdn Bond 08/28	L R	11.37	–
Cdn Equity 08/28	L R	8.91	–
Cdn Growth 08/28	L R	9.43	–
Cons Divers 08/28	L R	129.50	–
Enhanced Mtg 08/28	L R	174.27	–
Equity 08/28	L R	282.48	–
Equity (T) 08/28	L R	8.98	–
Glo Equity (T) 08/28	L R	10.90	–
Glo Growth 08/28	L R	12.36	–
Intl Opport 08/28	L	12.11	–
MMF 08/28	L R	40.72	–
Strategic Bond 08/28	L R	254.23	–
U.S. Index Plus 08/28	L R	15.27	–
MARATHON PERFORM POOLED			
N.A. Long-Short 08/28	L I	10.55	–
SCEPTRE INVEST COUNSEL			
Balanced 09/01	N R	543.43	+1.22
Bond 09/01	N R	325.69	+2.33
Equity 09/01	N R	269.35	-.49
uForeign Equ 09/01	N	824.36	-1.85

VENTURE CAPITAL FUNDS

Labour sponsored venture capital funds qualifying for special income tax consideration

Fund	Load RSP Dist	Val	Chg
B.E.S.T. DISCOVERIES FUND			
B.E.S.T. Fund 08/28	G R I	9.24	–
CI MUTUAL FUNDS (n)			
Covington	G R I	12.14	unch
CAPITAL ALLIANCE (n)			
Cap All 08/28	G R I	10.86	–
CDN VENTURE OPP (n)			
Cdn Vent Opport 07/31	G R I	6.57	–
CENTERFIRE(n)			
Centerfire Grth	G R I	10.76	-.02
CROCUS INVESTMENT FUND(n)			
Crocus Fund 07/31	N R	13.43	–
DGC ENTERTAINMENT (n)			
DGC Ent Vent	G R I	11.58	+.06
ENSIS GROWTH FUND			
Growth Fund Inc 08/28	N R I	9.72	–
ENTERPRISE FUND (n)			
Enterprise 08/31	G R I	8.25	–
FIRST ONTARIO (n)			
1st Ontario 08/31	N RD	11.27	+.00
INNOVACAP CAPITAL CORP.(n)			
Innovacap 07/31	N R	8.70	–
MEDICAL DISCOVERY (n)			
CMDF	G R I	10.43	-.12
RETROCOM GROWTH (n)			
Retrocom Growth 08/31	G R	10.84	–
SPORTFUND MGMT (n)			
Sportfund 07/31	G R Z	11.72	–
TECHNOLOGY INVEST (n)			
CSTGF	G R I	10.11	-.06
TRIAX CAPITAL MANAGEMENT(n)			
Triax Growth	G R I	9.31	+.05
TRILLIUM GROWTH (n)			
Trillium 08/28	N R I	8.56	–
VENGROWTH FUND			
VenGrowth Inv 08/28	G R I	11.92	–
WORKERS INVEST (n)			
Workers Invest 07/31	N R	10.00	–
WORKING OPPORTUN (n)			
Working Opp 07/31	B R I	6.57	–
WORKING VENTURES (n)			
Working Vent 08/31	G R Z	13.79	–

[a]The table presents data for only a sample of the segregated funds offered.

SOURCE: Reprinted with permission of *The Globe and Mail: Report on Business* (September 3, 1998).

Real Estate Investment Trusts—Where Next?

REITs are now almost a $4 billion market, but what makes them tick?

By Stan Hamilton

It is now five years since the first real estate investment trust (REIT) vehicle[1] appeared in Canada. Time to pause and ask, what we have learned over this period of innovation? Has the initial Canadian experience been similar to that in the US? What, if anything, can we learn from the much longer US experience with REITs? Based on the short time period REITs have been available in Canada, what may we expect in the future?

In reviewing the past performance of real estate investment trusts in Canada, it is necessary to keep in mind that Canada still does not have specific legislation to provide for the type of REITs available in the US. Specifically, Canadians still do not enjoy the full limited liability protection afforded US investors. As a consequence, Canadian investors must still be mindful of the potential capital liability, although this does not appear to be a major impediment as all REITs in Canada have taken steps to minimize potential liability to unitholders.[2] Some income tax treatments differ between the Canadian and US REITs.[3]

In October, 1993 O'Reilly summarized the state of the REIT market in Canada, noting there were only two REIT type vehicles on the market (RealFund and CREIT). By year-end a third, Counsel REIT (subsequently RioCan), joined the group. By 1997 the market for REIT-type vehicles began to gain momentum. Seven new REITs appeared on the scene in 1997. The introduction of new REITs slowed considerably in 1998 as only two additional REITs appeared in the first half of 1998.[4]

The dollar value of the Canadian REITs followed a similar pattern: between the time the first REIT appeared in Canada in 1993 until June 1995, the market capitalization varied between $175 and $200 million (Figure 21.5). By the end of 1995, the market capitalization had increased to approximately $300 million and by the end of 1996 the market capitalization was approximately $1 billion. The significant growth of REITs in Canada continued in

1997 as approximately $1 billion in new equity capital[5] was attracted to the market, pushing the market capitalization to just under the $3 billion mark. By June 1998 the market capitalization of the 14 Canadian REITs exceeded $3.8 billion. The increase in the market capitalization is obviously a composite of market performance and the significant number of new and secondary issues.

Just how has the performance of the REIT industry in Canada compared with the stock market more generally? Since 1990, the TSE 300 index has enjoyed one of the strongest runs in recent memory. The total increase between 1993 and 1998 (May) for the TSE 300 is 76%. The TSE Real Estate and Construction sub-index has not performed at quite the same level. The sub-index suffered significant declines in 1991, 1994, and 1995, recovered strongly in 1996 and 1997, only to decline again in 1998.

REITs and Direct Real Estate

What has happened to direct real estate returns over this REIT life cycle? Generally the news is less favourable (Figure 21.6). The total returns for the Russell Canadian Property Index (RCPI) returns were generally negative from 1990 and 1993 and demonstrated steady, if modest, improvement from 1993 through 1998 (March). As in the case of the REIT market, the direct ownership returns were significantly higher in the 1997–1998 period. The income returns for the RCPI were consistently positive, but the capital changes remained negative through 1997. The market improved significantly in the first half of 1998, with both strong income and strong capital gains.

In many respects the Canadian REIT market performance appears to have been part of a more general trend. The Canadian REIT market began in 1993 as the TSE 300 began a strong six-year run. The Real Estate and Construction sub-index underperformed between 1993 and 1995, a slow period for REITs in Canada, but gained strength in 1996–1997 period (corresponding to the strong REIT market). The RCPI showed modest returns

---

Stan Hamilton is associate dean, faculty of commerce and business administration, University of British Columbia in Vancouver.

through 1996, but improved dramatically in 1997 and 1998.

The size of the existing REITs in Canada remains an issue. No Canadian REIT has a market capitalization in excess of $1 billion. This small scale of operation will continue to make REITs relatively less attractive to institutional investors. To put this in focus, the market capitulation of all REITs in Canada remains smaller than the top two real estate companies on the TSE. In this scene, REITs in Canada continue to play in the small capitalization arena, and until one or more of the Canadian vehicles break the $1 billion capitalization range, REITs in general are unlikely to attract significant institutional following.

One additional issue for Canadian REITs that must be factored into the market is the number of outstanding instalment payments.[6] These outstanding instalments coming due in the near term will compete with new issues for a limited pool of funds. Hence some of the instalment overhang for 1997 will impact 1998 market performance.

US Versus Canadian REITs

Alternative forms of REIT vehicles have been available in the US since the early 1960s. These early REITs were primarily highly levered construction and finance loan (debt) REITs. The 1986 Tax Reform Act set the stage for a renewed interest in REITs in the US. Between 1985 and 1997, the market capitalization of US REITs increased from $5 to over $130 billion while the number increased from 59 to over 250 publicly traded REITs. Between 1993 and 1997 (the period of the Canadian REIT) the market capitalization of US REITs increased from $32 billion to over $130 billion, a four-fold increase.[7] Both Canada and the US shared a strong financial market over the 1993–1998 (June) time period, yet REITs in the US enjoyed a significantly stronger growth.

While the US REITs have enjoyed a strong growth in the post–1985 period, the majority of the US REITs remain relatively small. Approximately 70% of all publicly traded US REITs have total assets of less than $500 million. Only 12% have total assets of over $1 billion. Hence even in the US with the strong growth, REITs continue to be relatively small ventures, a characteristic they share with Canadian REITs.

Operating on the basis that Canada should total 10% of the US, this would suggest a Canadian market capitalization of $13 billion, not the current approximately $4 billion. This is an unlikely event over the near term. Several factors help explain the lower levels of real estate securitization in Canada. In the first place, Canada does not (yet) have specific legislation for REITs while the US has enjoyed such status for many years. Moreover, it appears that the private and public pension plans in Canada are more active in real estate than in the US. This additional competition for prime real estate assets will help slow the growth of Canadian REITs.

What Can Be Learned?

Are there some lessons to be gained from the longer US experience? The US experience appears to give rise to more questions than answers as several unresolved questions persist. Are REITs real estate or stocks? Corgel summarizes the research literature and concludes (inconclusively) that "REIT returns and returns from unsecuritized markets share a strong common component(s) that reflects real estate fundamentals and REIT returns are noisy and the noise is different than that found in other real estate return series."

Advocates of the stock market data observe that REITs and shares of public companies trade in the same market, and that these public markets provide more timely and accurate information about real estate than do the appraisal based indexes (such as the Russell Property index). The counter view is that REIT performance have very different risk-return characteristics, and have low correlation with appraisal-based series. More recent research based on US data indicate that the relationship between equity REITs and appraisal-based return series are more closely related than previously thought. After allowing for lags in the appraisal-based series, Gyourko and Keim find that current changes in the returns for US equity REITs are reflected in future period appraisal based returns such as the Russell index. The limited evidence for Canada would appear to be equally inconclusive as REIT performance, albeit over a short period, appears to share elements with both the TSE 300 and the RCPI.

The US experience has also indicated pricing anomalies for new issues and secondary offerings. In particular it has indicated that unit prices do not appear to fully reflect the value of the underlying real estate assets.[8] However, the evidence is again inconclusive on this issue. Research in the US has also focused on the management of REITs, especially whether internal or external management results in preferred risk adjusted returns. This research addresses the "principal-agent" issues (Solt and Miller) associated with aligning the goals of the management and unitholders. Earlier research indicated that internal management was superior, but more recent research provides more mixed results. The evidence in Canada, albeit for a short time period, does not support a conclusion that internal management results in superior performance.[9]

Where to Now?

Looking forward, what might the market hold for REITs in Canada? As the market expanded, more analysts have followed this sector of the market, providing valuable insights to the individual investors. The size of the Canadian REIT market, both in aggregate and at the individual level, remains in the "small cap" domain and large institutional support remains unlikely.[10] However, the current scope of the market, both in size and in product mix, affords individual investors with an attractive addition to their portfolio. At the present time, exposure to all major property types and Canadian market areas are available through REITs, allowing investors to design a well-diversified portfolio that best suits their own needs. The level of debt employed by Canadian REITs is generally low, typically below 60%, hence avoiding the potential negative impact of high leverage.[11] At the same time, investors may elect to use their own personal leverage to try to enhance yields.

Since REITs must pay out the majority of their earnings, they typically pay a steady dividend. Prudent property management and acquisition strategies, coupled with low leverage, help maintain a steady income flow.

For individual investors seeking a component of real estate in their portfolios, without the risks associated with high leverage, the major management commitments, and with a low volatility dividend, REITs appear to have a major role to play. Moreover, the Canadian market is large enough to ensure reasonable liquidity, even under difficult market conditions. If REITs are to have a future in Canada, they must first serve the needs of the individual investors seeking low risk, steady dividend investments.

Endnotes

In the interests of full disclosure, the author notes he is a trustee for one of the Canadian REITs.

1. The introduction of the first REIT-type vehicles in Canada coincided with the liquidity difficulties facing several of the real estate open-ended mutual funds. In fact, several of these open-ended funds converted to REIT-type vehicles.
2. REITs in Canada use a low level of financial leverage and perform careful environmental investigations on their properties.
3. For a detailed review of the legal differences between the Canadian type REIT and the US counterpart, see Meretsky, 1995 and Brooks, 1996.
4. Several proposed REITs were withdrawn from the market in late 1997 and early 1998.
5. These data exclude debt capital attracted to the REIT market and exclude the rather significant new equity raised by corporate real estate.
6. Several REITs have issued new units with instalment payments, typically 60%+ of the unit price due on issue and the balance due in one year.
7. 1997 NAREIT Industry Statistics.
8. A characteristic observed in some closed-end mutual funds.
9. The risk adjusted returns for REITs in Canada appear to bear little relationship to the type of management, although the conclusions are weak since the asset mix varies considerably across management types.
10. Only one Canadian REIT has over $0.75 billion in market capitalization at this time.
11. However several REITS recently modified their Declarations of Trust to allow high debt ratios.

References

Brooks, Michael S. (1996). "Canadian Real Estate Investment Trusts: An Assessment of Risks," http://www.narer.com/rei96.htm

Corgel, John B., W. McIntosh, and S. H. Ott (1995). "Real Estate Investment Trusts: A Review of the Financial Economics Literature," *Journal of Real Estate Literature* 3, 13–43.

Gyourko, Joseph and Donald Keim (1992). "What Does the Stock Market Tell Us About Real Estate Returns," *AREUEA Journal* 20(3), 457–485.

Han, Jun and Youguo Liang (1995). "The Historical Performance of Real Estate Investment Trusts," *Journal of Real Estate Research* 10(3), 235–262.

Lee, Charles M. C., A. Shleifer, and R. Thaler (1990). "Anomalies: Closed-end Mutual Funds," *Journal of Economic Perspectives* 4(4), 153–164.

Meretsky, Jason (1995). "Real Estate Investment Trusts: An Analysis of the Investment Vehicle and Income Tax Implications," *University of Toronto Faculty of Law Review* 53 (Winter), 95–129.

National Association of REITs (1997). "1996 NAREIT Industry Statistics," National Association of Real Estate Investment Trusts, Washington, DC.

O'Reilly, Rossa (1993). "Real Estate Investment Trusts (REITS)," *Investment Research,* Wood Gundy, Toronto.

Solt, Michael E. and Norman Miller (1985). "Managerial Incentives: Implications for the Financial Performance of Real Estate Investment Trusts," *AREUEA Journal* 13(4) 404–423.

SOURCE: Stan Hamilton, "Real Estate Investment Trust—Where Next?" *Canadian Investment Review* (Fall 1998): 33–35.

Figure 21.5   The growth of REITs.

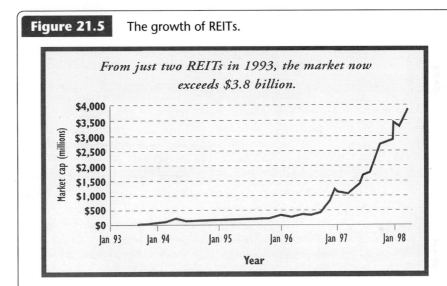

From just two REITs in 1993, the market now exceeds $3.8 billion.

SOURCE: Reprinted with permission of *The Globe and Mail: Report on Business* (September 3, 1998).

Regulation and Investment Policies

The regulation of mutual funds is currently in flux. A major report prepared for the Ontario Securities Commission (OSC) recommended sweeping changes to the way in which mutual funds should be regulated.[10] Many of the recommendations are controversial. During the summer of 1998 the Mutual Fund Dealers Association (MFDA) was established to be the Self Regulatory Organization (SRO) responsible for the regulation of the operations of mutual funds and the distribution practices of their sponsors. As a result of the establishment of the MFDA and a new Stromberg report, commissioned by the OSC

---

[10]Glorianne Stromberg, *Regulatory Strategies for the Mid-'90s: Recommendations for Regulating Mutual Funds in Canada* (Toronto: Ontario Securities Commission, January 1995). Some of the recommendations of this report are currently being implemented.

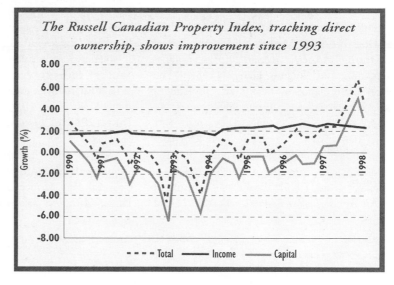

Figure 21.6 Direct ownership of real estate.

The Russell Canadian Property Index, tracking direct ownership, shows improvement since 1993

SOURCE: Reprinted with permission of *The Globe and Mail: Report on Business* (September 3, 1998).

to be released early in 1999, changes to the regulation and operation of mutual funds can be expected in the near future.

As of November 1998, investment funds are subject to provincial regulation under the appropriate Securities Act augmented by a number of national policies that have been agreed to by all provinces, but particularly National Policy No. 39, Mutual Funds.

Mutual funds can only be sold with a prospectus that describes (among other items) the fund's investment policies, discloses the fees and expenses, and particularly any incentive fees payable to the investment managers. Management expense ratios and financial statements for five prior years must also be included, all as specified in National Policy No. 39.

The regulations can influence a mutual fund's investment policy. For example, a mutual fund that wishes to become a qualified investment for registered retirement savings plans must limit the proportion of its funds that it invests in foreign securities to a maximum of 20%. It is important, therefore, to understand the constraints imposed by legislation.

Regulation of Mutual Funds

National Policy No. 39 imposes certain restrictions on both the investments that a mutual fund may undertake and the practices that it follows. The salient sections of National Policy No. 39 are: section 2.04 covering investment restrictions, section 2.05 describing investment practices, and section 2.07 outlining permitted transactions in derivatives. The following is a summary of the key points in these sections:

1. *Diversification:* no mutual fund may invest in such a manner that more than 10% of its portfolio consists of the securities of one issuer.
2. *Control:* a mutual fund may not own more than 10% of the shares of any other issuer, nor may a fund buy shares for the purpose of exercising control of a company.
3. *Illiquid assets:* assets that are not subject to regular arm's-length valuation (e.g., by being traded on an exchange) are generally not permitted or at least restricted. Examples include real estate, fine art, and commodities. Permissible illiquid assets are restricted to a maximum of 10% of the value of the portfolio (these include private placements,

mortgages (except a mortgage fund) and OTC options acquired for non-hedging purposes).[11]

4. *Derivatives:* trades in derivatives are not regulated as long as they are made in order to hedge a position. Funds may write covered calls and puts providing they either own the underlying asset or have a sufficient cash balance to cover the ensuing obligations.[12]

5. *Ownership of other funds:* investments in other funds are closely regulated and duplication of management fees and sales charges is prohibited.

6. *Borrowing:* funds may only borrow up to 5% of the portfolio value to meet unusually heavy redemption requests.

7. *Lending:* funds may not lend either cash or securities, except by buying debt obligations such as bonds.

8. *Margin transactions:* these are prohibited.

9. *Short sales:* these are prohibited.

10. *Guarantees:* funds may not guarantee another party's securities or obligations.

11. *Connected party dealings:* mutual funds owned by a brokerage house may not invest in securities underwritten or distributed by the owner for 60 days following the end of public distribution. (This rule is relaxed if the brokerage distributes no more than 5% of the shares.)

12. *Underwriting:* funds may not underwrite any securities.

National Policy No. 39 also provides for a 60-day "cooling off" period during which a buyer of mutual funds under a purchase plan is entitled to a full refund including 100% of any sales commission if she wishes to cancel the contract.

Investment Policies

Different investment companies follow different investment policies. Some companies are designed as substitutes for their shareholders' entire portfolio; others expect their shareholders to own other securities. Some restrict their domain or selection methods severely; others give their managers wide latitude. Many engage in highly active management, making substantial portfolio changes designed to exploit their perceived superior investment predictions. However, others are more passive, concentrating instead on tailoring a portfolio to serve the interests of a particular clientele.

The Investment Funds Institute of Canada identifies five generic types of funds that are distinguished by broad differences in their investment policies. These are:

1. Fixed income funds (bond funds)
2. Balanced funds
3. Common stock or growth funds
4. Specialty funds
5. Fixed trusts (or investment unit trusts).

Most funds fall into one of the first three categories. However, funds in the fourth category have become significant. Specialty funds include mortgage funds, money market funds, dividend funds, option income funds, real estate funds, and global funds.

Some mutual funds develop their own investment policies that complement the generic styles described above. For example, a family of ethical funds may include an ethical growth fund, an ethical balanced fund, or an ethical bond fund. International and

---

[11]An illiquid investment is defined as one that cannot be readily disposed of in its customary marketplace or where quotations are not regularly published. Examples of illiquid investments are limited partnership interests not traded on an exchange and securities of private companies.

[12]The use of currency forward and futures contracts is permitted, providing that these are used to hedge the portfolio against adverse foreign currency fluctuations.

global funds should probably be considered as a separate generic category, as there is an added element of risk (foreign exchange) associated with the investments. Asset allocation services are also investment vehicles that have their own investment objectives, management, and fees.

Categorization of a specific fund can be difficult, but broad classes can be identified. As mentioned earlier, money market funds hold short-term (typically less than one year) fixed-income instruments such as bank certificates of deposit, commercial paper, and Treasury bills. These open-end funds make it possible for small investors to move in and out of the short-term market. The fund manager will charge an annual fee for this service, usually between 0.25% and 1% of the average value of total assets. There are usually no load charges, and investors may add money to, or remove money from, their accounts at almost any time. Bond funds invest in fixed-income securities. Some go farther, specifying that particular types will be emphasized. There are corporate bond funds, government bond funds (Canadian and/or US), global bond funds, and so on. A few funds concentrate on holding preferred shares or both bonds and preferred shares in their portfolios. These funds aim to provide the investor with price stability and income.

Many funds consider themselves managers for the bulk of the investment assets of their clients. Those that hold both equity and fixed-income securities particularly fit this description and are referred to as balanced funds. These funds seek to "combine capital growth (gains) with income and price stability.[13] Some of these funds hold relatively constant mixes of bonds, preferred shares, convertible bonds, and equities; others alter the proportions periodically in attempts to "time the market." Option-income funds are a type of balanced fund that invests primarily in high-dividend-paying common stocks, while controlling risk by writing call options on these stocks. (Call options are discussed in Chapter 19.)

The largest group of investment funds are common stock or growth funds, of which a large variety exist. A diversified common stock fund invests most of its assets in common stocks, although some short-term money market instruments are often held to accommodate irregular cash flows or to engage in market timing. The majority of common stock funds have as their objective either growth or combined long-term growth and income.[14] Two factors appear to be involved in these objectives: the relative importance of dividend income versus capital gains and the overall level of risk to be taken. Since high-dividend portfolios are generally less risky than those with low dividends, relatively few major conflicts arise.

Some specialized investment companies concentrate on the securities of firms in a particular *industry* or *sector*. For example, there are resource funds, real estate funds, small capitalization stock funds, and gold funds. Others provide a convenient means for holding the securities of firms in a particular *country* or *region*, such as Global Strategy Japan or Latin American funds. There are also investment companies that invest even more widely internationally, purchasing stocks from a variety of different countries. International funds are those investing in non-Canadian securities, while global funds invest in both Canadian and non-Canadian securities.

An index fund attempts to provide results similar or identical to those computed for a specified market index. For example, the *Green Line Canadian Index Fund*, a no-load open-end investment fund, provides a vehicle for small investors who wish to obtain results similar to those of TSE 300 stock index. Despite continuing evidence that indexing outperforms most managers (after deducting fees) the number of index funds in Canada remains small.

---

[13]The Investment Funds Institute of Canada.

[14]The statement of a fund's objectives can be obtained from its prospectus, which must be available to all prospective buyers. Sometimes picturesque terminology, such as "maximum capital gain" or "aggressive growth," is used to describe the objectives, making the official statement of investment objectives less than lucid.

Taxation of Investment Funds

Investment funds can be either incorporated or unincorporated. The former are regulated by either the federal or provincial corporations act, depending on the jurisdiction in which it is chartered. The latter are subject to the appropriate provincial securities act and national policies agreed to by all provinces. They are taxed differently.

Incorporated Investment Funds

Incorporated funds are taxed as Canadian corporations at a 25% tax rate if they meet certain conditions. In order to qualify for this rate, 85% of their gross revenues must be derived from Canadian sources; interest may only account for 25% of their gross income; *and* at least 85% of taxable income must be distributed to shareholders as dividends. Failure to meet these three conditions results in tax being assessed at a regular corporate tax rate of about 45%. Dividends received by unitholders are treated as bona fide dividends from Canadian corporations and, therefore, are eligible for the dividend tax credit even though the fund's income may have been derived from interest income or dividends from foreign corporations. Furthermore, dividends received by the fund from tax-paying Canadian corporations are not subject to tax.

A fund that meets the necessary conditions and is largely invested in equities should not face a significant tax bill.

Unincorporated Investment Funds

These funds are not subject to tax. The fund's income, net of expenses, is flowed through to the individual unitholder and taxed in her hands. Thus, unitholders have to pay taxes on their proportionate share of the interest income, dividends, and realized capital gains received by the fund. Dividends from taxable Canadian corporations qualify for the dividend tax credit and capital gains are taxed at 75% of the regular rate. The fund's expenses are also flowed through to the investor and may be allocated to income in the most advantageous way. In general, expenses will first be allocated to foreign income, followed by interest income, then either dividends or capital gains depending on the investor's situation.

The total tax payable on income derived from an incorporated fund is very similar to that from an unincorporated fund. Incorporation is perhaps slightly advantageous in that it allows the fund a small measure of flexibility because it can retain for reinvestment up to 15% of its income.

Mutual Fund Performance

Mutual funds need to compute and publicize their net asset values daily. Since their income and capital gain distributions are also publicized, they are ideal candidates for studies of the performance of professionally managed portfolios. Thus, it is hardly surprising that mutual funds have frequently been the subject of extensive study in the US. Ironically, despite the importance of mutual funds in RRSP investments, only a limited number of Canadian studies (to be discussed in a later section) have been undertaken.

Calculating Returns

In studies of performance, the rate of return on a mutual fund for period t is calculated by adding the change in net asset value to the amount of income and capital gains distributions made during the period, denoted I_t and G_t, respectively, and dividing this total by the net asset value at the beginning of the period:

$$r_t = \frac{(\text{NAV}_t - \text{NAV}_{t-1}) + I_t + G_t}{\text{NAV}_{t-1}} \tag{21.2}$$

For example, a mutual fund that had a net asset value of $10 at the beginning of month t and made income and capital gain distributions of, respectively, $.05 and $.04 per share during the month, and then ended the month with a net asset value of $10.03 would have a monthly return of

$$r_t = \frac{(\$10.03 - \$10.00) + \$.05 + \$.04}{\$10.00}$$
$$= 1.20\%$$

It should be noted that returns calculated in this manner can be used to evaluate the performance of the portfolio manager of a mutual fund, since it indicates the results of the manager's investment decisions. However, it does not necessarily indicate the return earned by the shareholders in the fund, since there may have been a load charge involved. In the example, perhaps the investor paid $10.50 at the beginning of the month for one share of this fund, with $.50 being a front-end load. If this were the case, the investor's return for this month could be calculated using equation (21.2), where NAV_{t-1} would be $10.50, not $10.00:

$$r_t = \frac{(\$10.03 - \$10.50) + \$.05 + \$.04}{\$10.50}$$
$$= -3.62\%$$

Thus, the return for the investor who bought one share at the beginning of the month and paid a $.50 per share load charge at that time would be −3.62%. However, the portfolio manager was only given $10.00 per share to invest, since the load charge was given to those people who were responsible for getting the investor to buy the share. Accordingly, the portfolio manager should be evaluated on the basis of the return provided on the $10.00, which in this example was 1.20%.

Recently, data on professionally managed pension funds and bank commingled funds have become available. The performance of the managers of such funds appears to be similar to that of mutual fund managers: they do reasonably well tailoring portfolios to meet clients' objectives, but few seem to be able to consistently "beat the market." Although the following sections deal only with US mutual funds, many of the results apply to other investment companies, both in the United States and in other countries.[15] A more detailed discussion of certain risk-adjusted measures of performance and their application to mutual funds is deferred to Chapter 24.

---

[15]For evidence on funds outside the United States see, for example, Jess H. Chua and Richard S. Woodward, *Gains from Market Timing*, Monograph Series in Finance and Economics 1986–2, Salomon Brothers Center for the Study of Financial Institutions, Graduate School of Business Administration, New York University; Andre L. Farber, "Performance of Internationally Diversified Mutual Funds," in *International Capital Markets*, eds. Edwin J. Elton and Martin J. Gruber (Amsterdam: North-Holland Publishing Company, 1975), pp. 298–309; Michael A. Firth, "The Investment Performance of Unit Trusts in the Period 1965–75," *Journal of Money, Credit and Banking* 9, no. 4 (November 1977): 597–604; James R. F. Guy, "The Performance of the British Investment Trust Industry," *Journal of Finance* 33, no. 2 (May 1978): 443–455, and "An Examination of the Effects of International Diversification from the British Viewpoint on Both Hypothetical and Real Portfolios," *Journal of Finance* 33, no. 5 (December 1978): 1425–1438; John G. McDonald, "French Mutual Fund Performance: Evaluation of Internationally Diversified Portfolios," *Journal of Finance* 28, no. 5 (December 1973): 1161–1180; Juan A. Palacios, "The Stock Market in Spain: Tests of Efficiency and Capital Market Theory," in *International Capital Markets*, eds. Edwin J. Elton and Martin J. Gruber (Amsterdam: North-Holland Publishing Company, 1975), pp. 114–149; and R. S. Woodward, "The Performance of UK Investment Trusts as Internationally Diversified Portfolios Over the Period 1968 to 1977," *Journal of Banking and Finance* 7, no. 3 (September 1983): 417–426.

Average Return

Some US organizations have established two kinds of indices based on the net asset values of mutual funds that have similar investment objectives. One kind of index is based on nearly all of the US-based mutual funds, whereas the second kind is based on a much smaller sample. As shown in Figure 21.7, both types of indices are presented every week (and, more extensively, every quarter) in *Barron's*, where mutual fund indices that have been prepared by Lipper Analytical Services are published.

Many US studies have compared the performance of investment companies that invest primarily in common stocks with the performance of a **benchmark portfolio** that consisted of a combination of (1) a market index, such as Standard & Poor's 500-stock index, and (2) a risk-free asset, such as Treasury bills. Each particular combination was chosen so that the benchmark portfolio had a risk level that was equal to that of the investment company. Thus, an investment company that had a beta of 0.80 would be compared with a benchmark portfolio that had 80% invested in the market index and 20% invested in the risk-free asset.[16]

One way of determining whether or not a mutual fund has beaten the market is to subtract the average return on the benchmark portfolio from the average return of the mutual fund. This amount is known as the fund's *ex post* **alpha**, denoted α_p:

$$\alpha_p = ar_p - ar_{bp} \tag{21.3}$$

where ar_p is the average return on portfolio p and ar_{bp} is the average return on the benchmark portfolio associated with portfolio p. Note that if $\alpha_p > 0$, then the portfolio will have performed well because it will have had positive risk-adjusted returns. Conversely, if $\alpha_p < 0$, then the portfolio will have had inferior returns.

Data that allow Canadian investors to perform these comparisons is reported quarterly in *The Globe and Mail: Report on Canadian Mutual Funds*. A sample of the data provided is shown in Figure 21.8. Funds are grouped into categories according to the type of securities they predominantly invest in. As well as reporting one-month, three-month, six-month, and one-year total returns (including reinvestment of distributions) these tables provide 2-, 3-, 5-, and 10-year compound rates of return and a ranking of the one-month return volatility against other funds in the same category. Similar data are also provided for an extensive list of national and international benchmark portfolios. All mutual funds are placed in one of the following asset categories:

1. Canadian equity funds
2. Canadian small-to-mid cap equity funds
3. International equity funds
4. US equity funds
5. European equity funds
6. Asian and Pacific Rim funds
7. Latin American and emerging market funds
8. Precious metal and resource funds
9. Sector equity funds
10. Labour-sponsored investment funds
11. Canadian balanced funds
12. US and international balanced funds

---

[16]Alternatively, the benchmark portfolio may be based on the investment company's standard deviation relative to that of a market index, such as the S&P 500. For example, if the investment company's standard deviation has been 60% of the index's standard deviation, then the mix should consist of 60% invested in the market index and 40% invested in the risk-free asset. The results from evaluating mutual fund performance when using beta as the measure of risk seems to be very similar to the results when standard deviation is used. See, for example, Hany A. Shawky, "An Update on Mutual Funds: Better Grades," *Journal of Portfolio Management* 8, no. 2 (Winter 1982): 29–34.

Figure 21.7   Mutual fund indices.

LIPPER MUTUAL FUND PERFORMANCE AVERAGES

Weekly Summary Report: Thursday, March 19, 1998
Cumulative Performances With Dividends Reinvested

Net Asset	No. Funds		12/31/97-03/19/98	03/12/98-03/19/98	02/19/98-03/19/98	12/18/97-03/19/98	03/20/97-03/19/98
General Equity Funds:							
107,074.8	258	Capital Appreciation	+ 10.76%	+ 1.47%	+ 5.26%	+ 14.37%	+ 33.41%
609,120.4	979	Growth Funds	+ 11.77%	+ 1.51%	+ 5.37%	+ 14.59%	+ 36.60%
89,436.1	302	Mid Cap Funds	+ 10.94%	+ 1.46%	+ 5.73%	+ 15.68%	+ 36.51%
140,082.7	577	Small Cap Funds	+ 9.15%	+ 1.54%	+ 4.90%	+ 13.77%	+ 37.73%
3,270.7	45	Micro Cap Funds	+ 8.94%	+ 1.26%	+ 5.15%	+ 12.88%	+ 45.86%
549,876.0	721	Growth and Income	+ 10.80%	+ 1.52%	+ 5.46%	+ 12.87%	+ 35.19%
123,675.8	88	S&P 500 Objective	+ 12.54%	+ 1.83%	+ 6.04%	+ 14.34%	+ 40.77%
142,015.0	219	Equity Income	+ 9.38%	+ 1.40%	+ 5.33%	+ 11.30%	+ 33.76%
1,764,551.5	3,189	Gen. Equity Funds Avg.	+ 10.73%	+ 1.51%	+ 5.34%	+ 13.88%	+ 36.21%
Other Equity Funds:							
14,906.0	43	Health/Biotechnology	+ 11.43%	+ 0.69%	+ 4.25%	+ 14.71%	+ 32.04%
6,289.6	59	Natural Resources	+ 0.13%	− 0.05%	+ 2.54%	+ 3.03%	+ 0.52%
24,520.5	72	Science & Technol.	+ 15.25%	+ 1.30%	+ 3.07%	+ 21.15%	+ 35.13%
3,847.7	16	Telecommunication Funds	+ 20.47%	+ 3.60%	+ 11.17%	+ 23.20%	+ 55.88%
22,690.2	105	Utility Funds	+ 8.29%	+ 2.54%	+ 6.84%	+ 11.14%	+ 35.79%
20,648.2	45	Financial Services	+ 10.54%	+ 2.76%	+ 7.61%	+ 12.23%	+ 49.43%
12,893.5	87	Real Estate Fund	− 2.40%	− 0.16%	− 0.90%	+ 0.46%	+ 14.64%
3,130.1	63	Specialty/Misc.	+ 6.52%	+ 0.61%	+ 3.37%	+ 8.51%	+ 32.62%
2,785.2	44	Gold Oriented Funds	− 1.65%	− 2.98%	− 1.88%	+ 1.67%	− 42.71%
102,907.6	216	Global Funds	+ 11.69%	+ 1.73%	+ 5.98%	+ 13.02%	+ 25.08%
20,911.9	35	Global Small Cap Funds	+ 11.04%	+ 1.72%	+ 6.01%	+ 13.45%	+ 18.54%
162,712.1	515	International Funds	+ 12.50%	+ 1.96%	+ 6.29%	+ 12.51%	+ 19.99%
4,324.6	50	Int'l Small Cap Funds	+ 15.69%	+ 2.49%	+ 8.60%	+ 15.32%	+ 13.59%
14,621.4	92	European Region Fds	+ 17.45%	+ 2.63%	+ 9.16%	+ 17.54%	+ 35.76%
4,836.6	50	Pacific Region Funds	+ 2.32%	+ 1.47%	+ 0.43%	+ 1.03%	− 22.23%
1,694.4	35	Japanese Funds	+ 1.32%	− 0.98%	− 4.11%	− 1.02%	− 7.19%
4,496.1	82	Pacific Ex Japan Funds	+ 4.98%	+ 3.58%	+ 4.30%	+ 3.70%	− 31.12%
1,002.8	22	China Region Funds	+ 2.84%	+ 3.91%	+ 6.17%	+ 1.12%	− 18.99%
19,178.4	153	Emerging Markets Funds	+ 3.53%	+ 1.28%	+ 5.98%	+ 5.95%	− 8.28%
3,903.7	43	Latin American Funds	− 0.60%	+ 2.06%	+ 7.90%	+ 5.12%	+ 8.34%
113.4	5	Canadian Funds	+ 1.93%	− 2.34%	+ 3.19%	+ 8.72%	− 7.89%
343,488.2	1,342	World Equity Funds Avg.	+ 9.50%	+ 1.76%	+ 5.62%	+ 10.16%	+ 9.53%
2,216,965.5	5,021	All Equity Funds Avg.	+ 10.05%	+ 1.55%	+ 5.28%	+ 12.53%	+ 28.35%
Other Funds:							
62,767.8	218	Flexible Portfolio	+ 7.81%	+ 1.02%	+ 3.69%	+ 9.35%	+ 25.37%
24,039.7	92	Global Flex Port.	+ 7.68%	+ 1.14%	+ 3.87%	+ 8.69%	+ 18.83%
144,885.4	391	Balanced Funds	+ 7.19%	+ 0.91%	+ 3.36%	+ 8.61%	+ 24.98%
1,206.3	15	Balanced Target	+ 5.24%	+ 0.42%	+ 1.45%	+ 6.35%	+ 18.40%
7,586.7	57	Conv. Securities	+ 6.70%	+ 0.89%	+ 3.77%	+ 8.71%	+ 23.07%
26,767.5	74	Income Funds	+ 4.93%	+ 0.73%	+ 2.60%	+ 6.04%	+ 20.24%
22,745.6	266	World Income Funds	+ 2.43%	+ 0.24%	+ 0.84%	+ 2.62%	+ 8.09%
416,625.8	1,814	Fixed Income Funds	+ 1.84%	+ 0.07%	+ 0.25%	+ 2.05%	+ 10.32%
2,923,590.3	7,948	Long-Term Average	+ 7.61%	+ 1.10%	+ 3.79%	+ 9.38%	+ 22.87%
N/A		Long-Term Median	+ 8.23%	+ 1.17%	+ 4.37%	+ 10.37%	+ 24.48%
N/A		Funds with a % Change	+ 7,686	+ 7,381	+ 7,644	+ 7,650	+ 6,898

Securities Market Indexes

Value							
		U.S. Equities:					
474.30		Russell 2000 Index xd	+ 8.53%	+ 1.40%	+ 4.42%	+ 12.83%	+ 34.63%
567.38		NYSE Composite xd	+ 10.99%	+ 1.70%	+ 6.05%	+ 13.09%	+ 37.79%
1,260.82		S&P Industrials	+ 12.43%	+ 1.41%	+ 5.27%	+ 14.32%	+ 37.82%
1,089.74		S&P 500 xd	+ 12.29%	+ 1.85%	+ 5.98%	+ 14.07%	+ 39.24%
8,803.05		Dow Jones Ind. Avg. xd	+ 11.31%	+ 1.66%	+ 5.10%	+ 12.19%	+ 29.07%
Value		**International Equities:**					
1,667.90		Nikkei 225 Average xd	+ 9.31%	+ 0.63%	+ 0.38%	+ 3.20%	− 9.81%
5,997.90		FT S-E 100 Index	+ 16.79%	+ 3.50%	+ 4.89%	+ 16.05%	+ 40.86%
4,936.32		DAX Index	+ 16.16%	+ 2.00%	+ 7.72%	+ 18.48%	+ 51.20%

Fund Management Companies

Value:							
3,376.12		Stock-price Index	+ 15.91%	+ 1.22%	+ 6.62%	+ 16.72%	+ 52.52%

xd-Price only index. Calculated without reinvestment of dividends. The Nikkei index value is divided by 10 due to space limitation. Source: Lipper Analytical Services Inc., Summit, New Jersey 07901

SOURCE: Reprinted with permission of *Barron's, Dow Jones & Company, Inc.* (March 23, 1998), p. 92. All rights reserved worldwide.

13. Canadian bond funds
14. International bond funds
15. Mortgage funds
16. Money market funds
17. International money market funds

In October 1998 the Investment Fund Standards Committee, an independent committee representing newspapers and software providers, proposed a new list of 31 broad categories of mutual funds that should make fund comparisons more useful to investors. It is expected that these categories will be adopted shortly and start to be used early in 1999.

In addition to examining portfolio performance to see if some group of mutual funds has earned abnormally high (or low) returns, it also important to examine the persistence of funds' performances. That is, do the funds that have had the highest returns (or abnormal returns) over some time period continue to have the highest returns (or abnormal returns) over a succeeding time period? Do poor performers in one time period continue to be poor performers in the next time period? Alternatively, does a fund's performance in one time period provide any indication of how it will perform in the next time period? The next two sections examine portfolio performance and persistence of performance for first, US equity funds and second, US bond funds.

Equity Funds

A major study published in 1997 examined the performance of 1892 diversified equity funds over the 32-year period of 1962–1993.[17] This study first sorted funds on January 1 of each year by their returns the previous year and then put the top 10% into portfolio 1, the next 10% into portfolio 2, and so on through portfolio 10, which consisted of the 10% worst performers of the previous year. The portfolio's returns were then tracked over the next year. Thus, there is a series of monthly returns from 1963–1993 for each one of the 10 portfolios. In addition, the funds were similarly sorted into 10 portfolios on January 1 of each year based on their *abnormal* returns over the previous three years.

Figure 21.9 shows the average excess return (that is, the average monthly return over the monthly Treasury bill rate) on the 10 portfolios formed by sorting them on their previous year's returns. Note how the returns clearly decrease with the ranking, with portfolio 1 having the highest average excess return of .68% per month and portfolio 10, at .01%, having the lowest. Similarly, Figure 21.10 shows the average excess returns when the portfolios were sorted based on their abnormal returns over the previous three years. While again there is a clear relationship between return and portfolio rank, the difference in the average excess return between portfolios 1 and 10 is not as extreme in comparison with Figure 21.9.

Figures 21.9 and 21.10 also show the average monthly abnormal returns earned by the 10 portfolios subsequent to their formation. Three observations can be made. First, note that all of the abnormal returns are negative except one, portfolio 1 in Figure 21.10. Since the exception has an abnormal return that is not statistically significantly greater than zero, this would appear to be consistent with the argument that the typical mutual fund cannot "beat the market." Second, there is still dispersion in the returns, with portfolio 1 having the highest (or nearly the highest) and portfolio 10 having the lowest abnormal return. Third, the bottom decile portfolio stands out for having by far the lowest abnormal return.

---

[17]See Mark M. Carhart, "On Persistence in Mutual Fund Performance," *Journal of Finances* 51, no. 1 (March 1997): 57–82. Sector, balanced, and international equity funds were excluded from the sample.

BENCHMARKS

Index	97/98	96/97	95/96	94/95	93/94	92/93	91/92	90/91	89/90	88/89	87/88	86/87	85/86	84/85	83/84
CPI - All Items	0.9	1.6	1.5	2.3	0.2	1.9	1.3	5.4	4.2	5.3	4.1	4.5	4.1	4.1	3.8
Canada Savings Bonds Rate	2.8	2.9	5.3	6.6	5.1	6.1	7.7	10.9	10.7	10.2	8.9	7.8	9.2	11.2	9.8
FT-SE 100 Total Return Index	15.0	44.0	18.1	21.8	9.6	11.5	-	-	-	-	-	-	-	-	-
HANG SENG Total Return Index	-39.7	31.7	28.7	5.3	28.9	52.5	60.2	47.1	3.8	13.8	-39.8	84.3	43.2	65.3	56.8
MSCI EAFE	1.5	14.2	10.6	6.0	10.9	35.7	2.6	19.9	-28.8	18.6	-7.8	37.2	92.3	47.4	17.0
MSCI Emerging Markets Free	-42.4	8.2	6.4	-17.4	44.6	50.5	30.9	33.3	-2.0	49.6	-	-	-	-	-
MSCI Europe	19.9	38.1	16.0	19.7	12.3	19.9	14.7	16.7	-4.2	27.3	-20.4	30.2	68.4	50.6	11.6
MSCI Japan	-26.5	-14.4	1.6	-4.9	6.4	50.5	-9.7	22.4	-44.1	14.6	3.4	37.5	126.3	47.5	23.9
MSCI World	10.9	26.5	15.9	14.8	8.8	29.4	9.6	22.8	-22.6	21.7	-12.7	36.4	60.9	30.6	13.0
Mexico IPC (BOLSA) Price Index	-43.5	62.1	15.3	-53.3	37.4	42.4	19.0	123.1	7.6	83.5	-	-	-	-	-
Midland Walwyn Canadian Bond	4.9	11.7	10.6	12.9	-1.4	-	-	-	-	-	-	-	-	-	-
Midland Walwyn Canadian Equity	-21.8	28.9	14.3	2.6	9.0	-	-	-	-	-	-	-	-	-	-
Midland Walwyn Global Bond	10.0	5.2	6.9	9.6	-4.9	-	-	-	-	-	-	-	-	-	-
Midland Walwyn International Equity	-19.9	21.3	9.5	3.4	18.0	-	-	-	-	-	-	-	-	-	-
Midland Walwyn U.S. Equity	0.6	33.3	16.4	24.5	3.1	-	-	-	-	-	-	-	-	-	-
NIKKEI 225 Price Index	-26.6	-22.3	7.8	-7.8	4.8	39.8	-11.1	16.2	-41.8	18.7	9.2	44.7	100.2	40.6	16.2
Nesbitt Burns Cdn Small-Cap Index	-33.5	31.1	23.5	5.3	3.9	40.4	4.3	12.7	-21.0	19.9	-17.8	-	-	-	-
Russell 100 Growth Index	-19.2	30.0	17.5	2.6	8.3	23.9	-0.1	5.6	-14.4	26.0	-	-	-	-	-
Russell 100 Value Index	-14.1	36.9	20.3	9.0	18.3	19.8	0.1	18.7	-17.5	25.7	-	-	-	-	-
Russell 300 Growth Index	-21.7	32.6	18.7	4.1	5.1	26.3	0.3	7.2	-16.3	24.4	-	-	-	-	-
Russell 300 Value Index	-16.0	38.0	19.7	8.4	18.0	21.7	0.6	15.7	-18.0	23.5	-	-	-	-	-
S & P 500 Composite	20.4	42.5	22.0	29.4	4.4	21.0	22.2	28.5	-11.0	28.6	-18.7	35.5	33.0	19.4	11.9
SCM Universe Bond Total Return	8.8	13.5	12.7	14.4	0.7	14.0	14.6	22.8	4.0	11.1	14.9	1.7	18.8	22.4	8.0
Salomon World Gov't Bond	23.1	4.0	5.4	16.7	2.1	16.8	30.6	12.6	5.6	3.1	6.2	-0.3	30.5	-	-
TSE 300 Total Return	-19.0	35.4	19.4	6.5	11.7	24.6	0.7	11.6	-16.9	24.5	-12.9	34.5	16.7	14.0	-0.4
1-Year Average GIC Rate	3.6	2.7	4.3	6.6	5.3	5.3	6.4	9.7	12.2	11.2	9.4	8.3	8.9	10.0	10.8
5-Year Average GIC Rate	4.5	4.9	6.3	7.7	7.0	7.1	8.3	10.2	11.7	10.8	10.5	9.9	10.3	11.6	12.5
91 Day Treasury Bill	4.2	3.3	5.7	7.1	5.2	6.3	7.3	10.9	13.4	11.8	9.2	8.2	9.5	10.8	10.8

Note: All Benchmarks are expressed in Canadian Dollars
Source: Datastream, ScotiaMcLeod, Frank Russell Canada, Morgan Stanley Capital Int'l

CANADIAN EQUITY FUNDS

Funds in which the primary objective is long-term capital appreciation. These funds invest mainly in Canadian common shares but their investment content may vary given certain market conditions.

Fund Name	1997/98	1996/97	1995/96	1994/95	1993/94	1992/93	1991/92	1990/91	1989/90	1988/89	1987/88	1986/87	1985/86	1984/85	1983/84	MER	Telephone
ABC Fundamental Value(R)	-22.9	40.2	18.9	2.4	25.7	91.5	7.3	25.8	-2.2	-	-	-	-	-	-	2.00	888-673-6222
Acuity Pooled Canadian Equity(R)	-6.7	74.6	23.1	9.9	-13.0	-	-	-	-	-	-	-	-	-	-	1.00m	416-366-1737
AGF Canada Class	-38.6	-	-	-	-	-	-	-	-	-	-	-	-	-	-	2.63	800-268-8583
AGF Canada Class (US$)	-44.4	-	-	-	-	-	-	-	-	-	-	-	-	-	-	2.63	800-268-8583
AGF Canadian Stock	-21.3	37.9	7.8	8.1	10.6	17.5	-0.8	13.8	-9.0	-	-	-	-	-	-	2.46	800-268-8583
AGF Growth Equity	-30.1	36.5	24.1	3.3	1.1	63.2	15.7	11.0	-16.3	16.4	-24.6	28.4	27.2	18.0	-3.3	2.80	800-268-8583
AIC Diversified Canada	-3.2	57.6	50.6	-	-	-	-	-	-	-	-	-	-	-	-	2.39	800-263-2144
AIM Canadian Premier	-16.5	24.0	17.2	6.4	3.0	20.7	2.7	3.6	-	-	-	-	-	-	-	2.80	800-588-5684
AIM GT Canada Growth Class	-21.0	20.5	47.7	-	-	-	-	-	-	-	-	-	-	-	-	2.42	800-588-5684
AIM GT Canada Value Class	-13.1	-	-	-	-	-	-	-	-	-	-	-	-	-	-	2.89	800-588-5684
All-Canadian CapitalFund(R)	-7.9	6.4	5.0	7.9	20.9	15.8	5.2	-0.4	0.7	9.9	-10.7	23.7	15.2	10.3	5.0	2.00	905-648-2025
All-Canadian Compound(C)	-7.8	6.4	4.5	7.6	20.7	15.8	5.1	-0.3	0.6	9.9	-10.6	23.6	15.3	10.3	4.9	2.00m	905-648-2025
All-Canadian ConsumerFund(R)	-5.7	19.9	2.8	2.3	12.4	-	-	-	-	-	-	-	-	-	-	2.00	905-648-2025
Allstar AIG Canadian Equity(R)	-19.0	30.3	16.2	0.7	4.5	10.4	2.4	9.8	-16.4	19.4	-	-	-	-	-	2.68	800-822-6446
Altafund Investment Corp.	-35.0	20.2	34.9	-1.1	8.6	46.4	20.6	-	-	-	-	-	-	-	-	2.32	800-263-4769
Altamira Capital Growth	-17.8	24.5	3.5	3.5	18.1	19.5	19.8	7.6	-6.3	26.2	-8.4	16.3	8.0	9.8	-3.2	2.00	800-263-4769
Altamira Equity	-33.2	23.9	14.1	5.2	10.1	44.5	44.3	14.0	9.0	48.8	-	-	-	-	-	2.28	800-263-4769
Altamira North American Recovery	-23.7	49.0	14.5	-4.4	16.7	-	-	-	-	-	-	-	-	-	-	2.30	800-263-4769
APEX Canadian Growth (AGF)(R)	-29.5	28.0	19.1	6.6	-	-	-	-	-	-	-	-	-	-	-	3.00	800-363-2166
APEX Canadian Stock(R)	-17.2	-	-	-	-	-	-	-	-	-	-	-	-	-	-	2.55	800-363-2166
Associate Investors Ltd.(R)	1.9	40.8	19.9	7.7	2.5	17.3	1.0	12.0	-11.5	17.1	-1.2	16.9	12.2	20.5	4.0	1.83	416-864-1120
Atlas Canadian Large Cap Growth	-15.2	43.5	21.1	9.0	6.5	9.8	-2.4	14.8	-14.2	19.1	-11.4	20.4	-	-	-	2.44	800-463-2857
Atlas Canadian Large Cap Value	-18.9	30.7	7.0	6.2	-	-	-	-	-	-	-	-	-	-	-	2.55	800-463-2857
Azura Growth RSP Pooled(R)	-22.6	25.5	-	-	-	-	-	-	-	-	-	-	-	-	-	2.28	800-231-6539
Batirente - Section Actions(R)	-15.6	38.9	16.6	6.2	-	-	-	-	-	-	-	-	-	-	-	1.50m	514-288-7545
Beutel Goodman Canadian Equity	-10.6	29.2	13.5	1.4	20.4	12.7	-4.4	-	-	-	-	-	-	-	-	2.08	800-461-4551
Bissett Canadian Equity(R)	-15.0	50.6	26.5	12.7	3.7	31.0	7.9	14.9	-12.3	22.7	-9.8	22.2	18.4	15.6	2.2	1.33	888-247-7388
BNP (Canada) Equity	-18.5	36.3	17.4	6.5	7.4	14.0	3.9	-	-	-	-	-	-	-	-	2.39	514-285-2920
BPI Canadian Equity Value	-24.3	28.9	21.9	6.6	-1.8	28.5	6.7	13.2	-7.6	-	-	-	-	-	-	2.54	800-937-5146
BPI Canadian Opportunities RSP(C)	-49.4	11.3	87.9	-	-	-	-	-	-	-	-	-	-	-	-	2.48	800-937-5146
C.I. Canadian Growth	-24.6	23.6	11.0	3.8	14.1	-	-	-	-	-	-	-	-	-	-	2.36	800-563-5181
C.I. Canadian Sector Shares	-25.9	22.2	10.7	3.5	14.3	35.9	-3.1	-2.9	-19.5	15.9	-	-	-	-	-	2.41	800-563-5181
C.I. Canadian Sector Shares (US$)	-33.3	20.7	9.1	3.2	-	-	-	-	-	-	-	-	-	-	-	2.41	800-563-5181
Caldwell Canadian Equity(R)	-24.2	-	-	-	-	-	-	-	-	-	-	-	-	-	-	0.50	800-256-2441
CAMAF (Cdn-Anaesthetists)	-20.0	32.1	20.6	7.1	5.2	14.1	1.1	7.7	-11.9	19.8	-3.1	29.4	16.9	17.5	5.3	1.93	800-267-4713
Canada Life Canadian Equity S-9	-17.4	30.0	16.1	9.5	3.8	22.3	3.3	13.4	-19.7	25.0	-6.1	25.8	19.4	15.8	6.8	2.25	888-252-1847
Canada Trust Cdn. Equity Index	-19.5	-	-	-	-	-	-	-	-	-	-	-	-	-	-	0.76	800-668-8888
Canada Trust Stock	-24.4	43.8	11.8	4.5	2.6	32.3	8.3	8.7	-10.6	14.9	-	-	-	-	-	1.84	800-668-8888
Canadian Imperial Equity	-12.2	-	-	-	-	-	-	-	-	-	-	-	-	-	-	2.00	800-465-3863
Canadian Protected(R)	3.1	6.2	4.4	5.8	-2.1	22.2	5.7	7.3	7.0	5.5	5.3	15.7	14.1	-	-	2.40	416-960-4890
Canso Canadian Equity(R)	-1.3	-	-	-	-	-	-	-	-	-	-	-	-	-	-	2.00	888-601-2222
CCPE Growth(R)	-16.8	31.1	15.2	7.1	12.0	11.6	-2.7	12.6	-12.7	21.7	-5.0	21.5	-	-	-	1.35	800-265-7401
CDA Canadian Equity (Trimark)(R)	-15.1	-	-	-	-	-	-	-	-	-	-	-	-	-	-	1.45	800-561-9401
CDA Common Stock (Altamira)(R)	-17.2	20.2	6.3	2.8	9.8	22.9	5.1	13.1	-13.0	25.8	-9.9	30.8	23.3	19.7	4.9	0.96	800-561-9401
CentrePost Canadian Equity(R)	-25.0	19.9	22.9	2.4	-10.9	49.0	-	-	-	-	-	-	-	-	-	1.00	800-268-9597
Chou RRSP	15.5	56.9	10.9	10.0	-0.4	12.4	5.9	9.4	-15.0	16.4	3.9	-	-	-	-	2.02	416-299-6749
CIBC Canadian Index	-19.6	34.1	-	-	-	-	-	-	-	-	-	-	-	-	-	0.90	800-465-3863
CIBC Core Canadian Equity	-18.8	37.9	12.3	1.7	0.9	21.5	-2.9	2.1	-7.6	-	-	-	-	-	-	2.20	800-465-3863
Clarington Canadian Equity	-17.3	27.3	-	-	-	-	-	-	-	-	-	-	-	-	-	2.75	888-860-9888
Clean Environment Equity	-17.3	47.6	19.3	14.9	-2.8	47.0	-	-	-	-	-	-	-	-	-	2.60	800-461-4570
Co-operators Canadian Equity	-16.4	34.3	12.0	4.4	10.1	23.5	-	-	-	-	-	-	-	-	-	2.06	800-604-0050
Colonia Equity	-15.3	44.3	16.5	2.8	-1.4	13.3	-	-	-	-	-	-	-	-	-	2.27	800-463-9297

Figure 21.8 (Continued) Mutual fund performance data (excerpts).

How to use the tables

The Report on Business survey of mutual funds measures the performance of various types of funds for the period from Oct. 1 to Sept. 30 of each year. The results go back 15 years to Oct. 1, 1983.

Accompanying each table is a description of the funds that make up the category and their investment objectives. New funds launched in 1998 are not included.

The letter "C" after a fund name indicates a closed fund in which no new subscriptions are accepted.

The letter "R" indicates that the fund is restricted to certain investors (doctors, for example) or confined to sale in certain provinces.

Under the heading MER (for management expense ratio), all management fees and operating expenses (excluding goods and services tax) of the fund are shown as a percentage of the fund's average total net assets. An asterisk represents funds that arbitrarily do not include management fees in their management expense ratio.

The return figures show the percentage change in the value of the investment for a one-year period, reflecting a reinvestment of dividends, and subtracting management fees and expenses.

Sales fees, if any, and management fees charged directly to investors are not deducted from total returns.

In the final column, there is a long-distance or toll-free number for investors to call if they want more information about the fund.

The average return for the entire group, as well as the highest and lowest returns, are shown at the bottom of each table. This enables an investor to compare returns within the category, and average performance of the whole group with other groups.

Results are for the 12 months ended Sept. 30.

The next 15-year report, with results for the 12 months ending Dec. 31, will appear in February. The next monthly report will appear Thurs., Nov. 19.

SOURCE: Reprinted with permission of *The Globe and Mail* (November 5, 1998).

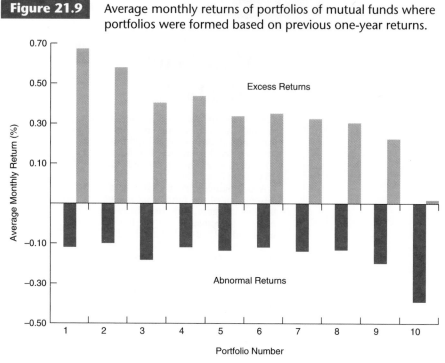

Figure 21.9 Average monthly returns of portfolios of mutual funds where portfolios were formed based on previous one-year returns.

SOURCE: Adapted from Mark M. Cathcart, "On Persistence in Mutual Fund Performance," *Journal of Finance* 52, no. 1 (March 1997): 77.

In order to see if an explanation can be found for the differing levels of abnormal returns, each fund's abnormal return was related to certain of the fund's characteristics. Measures of the following fund characteristics were used:

1. Operating expense ratio,
2. Portfolio turnover rate (a fund's portfolio turnover rate is the ratio of the smaller of purchases or sales during a time period divided by the average total asset value during the period, and hence is a measure of how much trading was done during that period),
3. Maximum load charge, and
4. Average total net assets.

The results indicated that there was a strong negative relationship between abnormal return and the first two of these characteristics. That is, funds with higher expense ratios and turnover had lower abnormal returns. While a negative relationship between load charges and abnormal returns was observed, it is likely due to the fact that load funds tend to have higher turnover rates, and thus the existence of higher loads does not, by itself, lead to lower performance. Larger funds tended to have slightly lower abnormal returns, but the relationship was not statistically significant. There is also evidence that transaction costs are inversely related to fund performance, as funds with lower abnormal returns tend to hold more illiquid stocks that cost more to trade.

Further analysis of the rankings of funds in the first year ("Subsequent Ranking") after they are sorted into portfolios ("Initial Ranking") used one year of *gross returns* for ranking purposes, where each fund's operating expense ratio was added back into its return.[18] If a

---

[18]By adding operating expenses to a fund's rate of return, it is possible to obtain an estimate of a fund's gross performance (that is, its performance based solely on what happened to the securities it bought and sold). This is done by adding to the numerator of equation (21.2) the per share values of such expenses. In the example shown earlier, perhaps the fund had paid expenses of this nature totalling $.02 per share during month *t*. In such a situation the net return of $.12/$10.00 = 1.20% corresponds to a gross return of ($.12 + $.02)/$10.00 = 1.40%.

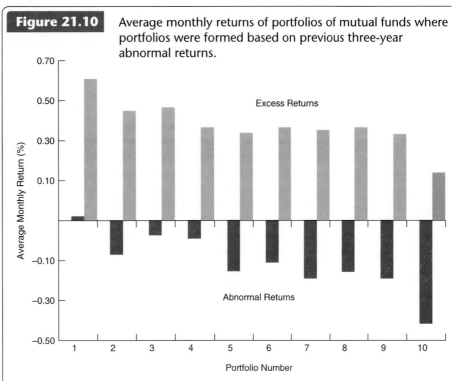

Figure 21.10 Average monthly returns of portfolios of mutual funds where portfolios were formed based on previous three-year abnormal returns.

SOURCE: Adapted from Mark M. Cathcart, " On Persistence in Mutual Fund Performance," *Journal of Finance* 52, no. 1 (March 1997): 64.

fund did not survive the year after it was assigned to a decile, it was put in a "dead fund" category. The results indicated that winners were a bit more likely to remain winners in the next year, and losers were a bit more likely to remain losers. In addition, the number of funds that become "dead" in the year after they were assigned to a portfolio increased monotonically with the fund's "Initial Ranking," meaning funds with lower gross returns were more likely to subsequently become "dead." Thus, for the most part the rankings of funds in the year after they are assigned to a portfolio decile appear to be random. Subsequent analysis of those top-decile funds that tended to remain in the top decile indicated that their high ranking was short-lived, since it disappeared in the second year after the "Initial Ranking" period.

Similar observations were made when the "Initial Ranking" was based on each fund's abnormal return over a three-year period. That is, relatively few funds remained in their portfolio decile in the "Subsequent Ranking" period, with only a few more than chance remaining in the top and bottom deciles.

Aside from concluding that the evidence suggests markets are efficient, the study provides three rules of thumb for the investor:

1. Do not purchase funds that have persistently poor performance,
2. Expect funds that had high returns in the last year to at most have high returns in only the next year, and
3. Expect high expense ratios, load fees, and transactions costs to hinder fund performance.

Another study reached similar conclusions.[19] Examining the returns from 1965 through 1984, 143 mutual funds were divided into two groups based on whether or not

---

[19]Edwin J. Elton, Martin J. Gruber, Sanjiv Das, and Matthew Hlavka, "Efficiency with Costly Information: A Reinterpretation of Evidence from Managed Portfolios," *Review of Financial Studies* 6, no. 1 (1993): 1–22.

they had a load charge. The average abnormal return of the load funds was (1.6%; for no-load funds it was −.8%. This suggests that funds with load charges do not on average earn sufficiently higher returns to justify investors' buying their shares.

The 143 funds were also divided into five groups based on the size of their operating expense ratios. Then the average abnormal return was calculated for each group. Going from the highest to the lowest expense group, these values were equal to −3.9%, −1.7%, −.7%, −1.2%, and −.6%. Note that with one exception there is a perfect ordering between performance and expenses—lower expenses are associated with better (but still negative) performance.

The mutual funds were again divided into five groups, but this time the division was based on the size of their turnover ratios. Again the average abnormal return was calculated for each group. Going from the highest to the lowest turnover group, these values were equal to −2.2%, −1.9%, −2.2%, −1.1%, and −.6%. Like the expense ratio results, there is a perfect ordering (again with one exception) between performance and turnover—lower turnover is associated with better performance.

One reasonable explanation for these observations is that in an efficient market, higher expense ratios and more frequent revisions will cause a fund to incur more costs, but without being able to consistently earn gains from the purchase of underpriced securities as an offset. Furthermore, whereas revisions in a fund's portfolio may be desirable so as to maintain a desired risk level or dividend yield, the evidence indicates that revisions intended to exploit supposed market inefficiencies generally prove unproductive because of the associated transaction costs.

These results suggest that the average equity mutual fund has not significantly outperformed an equal-risk passive alternative over any extended period.[20] This is not too surprising. After all, the market's performance is itself an average of the performance of all investors. If, on average, mutual funds had "beaten" the market, then some other group of investors would have "lost" to the market. With the substantial amount of professional management in today's stock market, it is difficult to think of a likely group of victims.

▶ Bond Mutual Funds

All of the results reported so far focus on mutual funds that have at least a large part of their assets invested in common stocks. This leaves open the question of bond mutual funds: Is their performance similar to that of stock funds? One study looked at a sample of 41 bond funds over the period from 1979 through 1988.[21]

Using a variety of models to produce benchmark returns, the average abnormal return ranged from −.023% to −.069% per month. Furthermore, regardless of the model, at least two-thirds of the funds had negative abnormal returns. Expanding the sample to cover 223 bond funds over the period of 1987 to 1991 produced similar results. It was determined that there was an inverse relationship between the size of a fund's expense ratio and its performance; that is, higher expenses tended to be associated with worse performance. In summary it appears that the results regarding stock funds are also applicable to bond funds.

A more recent study of 123 bond funds (excluding high-yield funds) over the six-year period of 1986 to 1991 revealed that no matter which one of four methods was used to estimate benchmark returns, the average bond fund had a negative abnormal return, and

[20]Similar conclusions can be drawn regarding pension and endowment funds. See Eugene F. Fama, "Efficient Capital Markets: II," *Journal of Finance* 46, no. 5 (December 1991): 1575–1617, particularly pp. 1605–1607, and Josef Lakonishok, Andrei Shleifer, and Robert W. Vishny, "The Structure and Performance of the Money Management Industry," *Brookings Papers on Economic Activity Microeconomics 1992* pp. 339–379. Also see T. Daniel Coggin, Frank J. Fabozzi, and Shafiqur Rahman, "The Investment Performance of U.S. Equity Pension Fund Managers: An Empirical Investigation," *Journal of Finance* 48, no. 3 (July 1993): 1039–1055.

[21]Christopher R. Blake, Edwin J. Elton, and Martin J.Gruber, "The Performance of Bond Mutual Funds," *Journal of Business*, 66, no. 3 (July 1993): 371–403.

in three of the cases it was significantly negative. Specifically, the four average abnormal returns were −.12%, −.06%, −.10%, and −.08% per month. Average abnormal returns calculated using gross returns were −.04%, .02%, −.02%, and .00% per month, with none of these values being significantly different from zero.[22] Thus, apparently the average fund approximately matches the returns on a similar-risk benchmark, but due to expenses, it underperforms its benchmark. This suggests that investors in bond mutual funds should choose low-expense funds, unless they are confident in the forecasting ability of a particular fund's manager.

Performance of Canadian Mutual Funds

Canadian studies of mutual fund performance are not plentiful. An early study, using Jensen's methodology, examined the performance of 19 Canadian mutual funds over the period 1960 to 1974.[23] The average beta for these funds was only 0.79 with a maximum of 0.99 and a minimum of 0.54, indicating that these funds are quite conservatively managed. The average R-squared was only 0.52 with a maximum of 0.69 and a minimum of 0.24, which suggests that these funds were not well diversified and had significant levels of unsystematic risk. None of the funds showed superior performance and, even after allowing for management and administration costs, underperformed the TSE index, which was used as a benchmark portfolio.

Dhingra attempted to determine whether *ex post* systematic risk levels of mutual funds were consistent with their stated investment objectives. Data on 88 mutual funds whose stated objectives could be identified were collected for the period 1966 to 1975. These funds fell into two categories—growth funds or income funds. In general, growth funds generated higher returns and exhibited higher betas than income funds suggesting that the funds are generally managed in a style consistent with their stated objectives. This conclusion is borne out by a later study of 71 mutual funds over the 1980 to 1989 time period which found that performance was not consistent from year to year but that management style was.[24]

Do mutual funds provide protection against inflation? This was the question addressed by Calvet and Lefoll. Using Jensen's measure of performance on a sample of 17 mutual funds from 1966 to 1979 they concluded that Canadian funds perform no better than the market after risk adjustment and provide no better inflation protection. The fund alphas and betas were remarkably similar in both real and nominal terms.[25]

Two studies examine the potential gains from market timing in Canada.[26] The first uses simulations to obtain estimates of the gains to be obtained from less than perfect forecasts of future market conditions. With perfect hindsight, after including modest transactions costs, a fund manager who switches between common stocks and T-bills can expect a return of about 4% more and a standard deviation of about 5% less than buying and hold-

---

[22]Edwin J. Elton, Martin J. Gruber, and Christopher R. Blake, "Fundamental Economic Variables, Expected Returns, and Bond Fund Performance," *Journal of Finance* 50, no. 4 (September 1995): 1229–1256, particularly pp. 1251–1252. It should be noted that all of these studies finding persistence have been challenged by others on methodological grounds.

[23]D. Grant, "Investment Performance of Canadian Mutual Funds: 1960–1974," *Journal of Business Administration* 8, no. 1 (Fall 1976): 1–9.

[24]H. L. Dhingra, "Portfolio Volatility Adjustment by Canadian Mutual Funds, *Journal of Business Finance and Accounting* 5, no.4 (Winter 1978): 305–333. J. McLaughlin and N. Bossen, "The Historical Performance of Canadian Investment Managers: Predictors of Future Performance?" *Canadian Investment Review* III, no.1 (Spring 1990): 87–91.

[25]A. L. Calvet and J. Lefoll, "Performance and Systematic Risk Stability of Canadian Mutual Funds Under Inflation," *Journal of Business Finance and Accounting* 8, no. 2 (Summer 1981): 279–289.

[26]J. H. Chua, R. S. Woodward, and E. C. To, "Potential Gains from Stock Market Timing in Canada," *Financial Analysts Journal* 43 (September–October 1987): 50–56; E. J. Weigel and J. H. Ilkiw, "Market Timing Skills in Canada: An Assessment," *Canadian Investment Review* IV, no. 1 (Spring 1991): 19–28.

Management Fees, Operating Expenses, and Brokerage Costs

If the old saw that you get exactly what you pay for were true in the mutual fund arena, costs might not matter. But the fact is that the reverse is true: the more you pay, the less you earn.[27]

—*John Bogle*

Over the past decade mutual funds have been the fastest growing segment of the financial services sector. At the end of 1985 there were 155 funds offered in Canada with a total of $10.2 billion under management. By the end of September 1998 these figures had grown to over 1300 funds with approximately $300 billion under management, representing impressive average compound growth rates of over 18% and 30% respectively. With an average management fee of 1.5%, the $300 billion would yield total fee revenues of about $4.5 billion, suggesting that mutual fund management had become big business in Canada. It is interesting, therefore, to examine the cost structure of mutual funds in more detail.

Funds typically incur two kinds of expenses: direct costs (i.e., management fees and operating expenses) are reported regularly in the financial press (see Figure 21.8, column marked MER, for Management Expense Ratio). Transactions costs,

Type of Fund	TD Green Line		Royal Bank	
	Fees	MERs	Fees	MERs
T-Bill	0.61%	0.84%	0.75%	0.92%
Premium Money Market	0.26	0.30	0.30	0.35
Canadian Money Market	0.62	0.84	0.75	0.95
US Money Market	1.00	1.22	1.00	1.12
Short-term Income	0.85	1.10	1.00	1.12
Mortgage	1.00	1.59	1.25	1.56
Canadian Bond	0.70	0.95	1.25	1.39
Canadian Index	0.80	1.08	1.25[a]	1.50
US Index	0.37	0.66	1.25[a]	1.50
Balanced Growth	1.70	1.95	1.75	2.23
Dividend	1.75	2.01	1.50	1.77
Canadian Equity	1.85	2.10	1.75	1.95
Small Cap Equity	2.00	2.40	1.75	2.23
US Blue Chip Equity	2.00	2.35	1.75	2.11
Energy	1.85	2.11	1.75	2.28
Precious Metal	1.85	2.12	1.75	2.41
Science and Technology	2.25	2.58	2.00	2.81
Global Government Bond	1.75	2.01	1.50	1.87
International Equity	2.00	2.34	2.00	2.68
European Growth	2.25	2.59	2.00	2.51
Japanese Growth	2.25	2.60	2.00	2.82
Asian Growth	2.25	2.59	2.00	2.97
Latin American Growth	2.25	2.60	2.25	2.99

[a]In October 1988 the Royal Bank introduced two new Canadian Index Funds and two US Index Funds with higher minimum investment requirements that have management fees ranging from 0.3 to 0.55%.

---

[27]John Bogle, *Bogle on Mutual Funds: New Perspectives for the Intelligent Investor* (New York: Dell Publishing, 1994), p. 208.

however, are only partly measurable. While brokerage costs can be identified, implicit costs such as the effect of bid-ask spreads and the price impacts of trading are hard to calculate and are rarely estimated. In Canada, brokerage costs are recorded only in the detailed annual financial statements of the fund and are not included in the calculation of the MER.

Management fees can vary quite dramatically even between funds that appear to have similar investment objectives. The table on p. 712 shows both management fees and MERs for comparable sets of no-load funds sponsored by two Canadian chartered banks. The data were taken from year-end financial reports for 1997.

Management Fees. There are six major reasons for differences in management fees between funds. We will look at each in turn.

1. **The asset mix.** Different asset mixes require different levels of management activity. In the case of money market and index funds, the assets and asset mix are predetermined. Therefore, little management effort is required for research, security analysis, and selection. As a result fees are generally low. Actively managed equity and international funds require constant monitoring and frequent analysis of markets and securities and, therefore, command higher fees.

2. **Investment practices.** Two funds that ostensibly invest primarily in the same type of assets may, in fact, differ noticeably in their investment practices. Whereas one fund will restrict its investments to the primary asset class (say mortgages), the other may include a 10 or 20% equity component to try to improve performance. This increases both research and brokerage costs. In the same vein, a global bond and equity fund may add investment in currency derivatives unrelated to any hedging strategy (in other words, a currency gamble). Such a move involves added expenses for derivative expertise that may have to be obtained from outside advisors—and thus, added management costs.

3. **Average unitholder account size.** When the average size of the unitholder accounts is small, the fund incurs more administrative costs to process statements, tax returns, and other unitholder communications. To control these costs many funds establish a minimum invest-

ment requirement. One of the fund groups with the lowest MERs has established an investment minimum of $25 000.

4. **Distribution system.** A fund that employs an in-house sales force and that charges a loading fee has a different management structure from a no-load fund that distributes its product through existing institutions like banks or trust companies. In general, load funds charge higher management fees than no-load funds because there is less sales administration involved in the latter. No-load funds, however, must sometimes pay minor trailer fees (commissions) to the institutions that distribute the units to the public.

The type of load can also affect the management fees of load funds. For example, the average fees for the Class A units (front-end load) of four typical load funds in 1994 were 1.70% while the fees for the Class B units (back-end load) of the same funds were 1.99%. This is because the load fee is not received by the fund from the investor until redemption occurs.

5. **Economies of scale.** There are economies of scale in the provision of management services to mutual funds, particularly in the case of money market and index funds. In these cases an increase in the size of the fund involves nothing more than purchasing more of the same assets. Even actively managed funds show a less than proportional increase in management costs with an increase in size as long as there is no change in asset mix. Economies of scale partially explain why management fees for US mutual funds are lower than those typically found in Canada. Earl Bederman, in "Competition and Change in the Individual Investment Market: A Study Conducted for The Investment Funds Institute of Canada" (Toronto: Investor Economics, Inc., October 1994), reports that, in 1993, average MERs for no-load international equity funds in Canada were 28.4% higher than those in the US (1.90% versus 1.48%) while the US funds were, on average, 278% larger than the corresponding Canadian ones. At the same time average Canadian MERs for deferred load international equity funds were 3% lower than those in the US, the average size of the funds being essentially equal. This suggests that management fees

should be calculated on a sliding scale such that they decrease as the fund size increases. The TD Green Line US Index Fund actually does this. The quoted management fees start at 0.5% for the first $25 million in assets and decline to 0.25% for asset values in excess of $100 million.

6. **Use of outside managers.** In most instances, the fund sponsor also acts as the investment manager, but in the case of specialized funds the sponsor may employ an outside specialist or an advisor to assist in the management of the investments. Outside managers/advisors are frequently associated with international and global funds and other specialized types such as science and technology or precious metal funds. This can result in a double set of management fees being paid to operate the fund.

The fact that management fees are based on a percentage of asset values should be a cause for unitholders to be concerned. Although such a scheme is intended to reward better performance—all other things being equal, the higher the fund value (i.e., the performance), the higher the fee—it can also encourage artificial inflation of the value of the fund. Valuation is based on continual recalculation of the fair market value of the assets held. Therefore, it is appropriate for mutual funds to invest only in assets that are themselves subject to continual revaluation in a liquid market. National Policy No. 39 recognizes the difficulties associated with thinly traded or illiquid assets and regulates the proportion of these that each fund can hold. For example, holdings of private placements or over-the-counter options are restricted to 10% of the value of the portfolio. Many mutual funds do hold some proportion of these assets in their portfolios, whose valuation, involving some degree of subjectivity, may be optimistic. Related party transactions, such as the negotiated purchase of an asset from a related company, can also involve a valuation of assets that differs from an objective market price.

Operating Expenses. Operating costs used in the calculation of MERs are defined as all costs associated with the operation of the fund (recordkeeping, custodial fees, audit, etc.) but excluding goods and services tax and brokerage commissions. The last two are costs an individual investor would have to incur when managing her own portfolio. The MER, then, reflects the additional costs an investor incurs by virtue of purchasing mutual fund units.

Brokerage Costs. It is clear that MERs do not tell the whole story. Brokerage costs can have a significant effect on a fund's performance. The following table shows an analysis of the total management costs (in millions of dollars and percent of average assets) incurred by the Altamira Equity Fund in 1996 and 1997, using data obtained from the 1997 annual report.

The table shows that although the MER changed little from year to year the change in the total cost is solely the result of changes in brokerage costs that are directly related to turnover. The two main factors that influence brokerage costs are portfolio turnover and soft-dollar transactions. A passively managed portfolio, like an index fund, will trade relatively

	1997		1996	
	$	%	$	%
Management fee	48.45	2.00	49.25	2.00
Operating expenses	6.65	0.28	6.80	0.28
MER-related expenses	55.10	2.28	56.05	2.28
Taxes	3.85	0.16	3.91	0.16
Brokerage costs	26.51	1.09	23.97	0.98
Non-MER costs	30.36	1.25	27.88	1.14
Total costs	85.46	3.53	83.93	3.42
Portfolio turnover rate	3.12×		2.34×	
Rate of return		4.1%		17.0%

infrequently and, therefore, incur lower transactions costs than an actively managed portfolio that is traded frequently in the expectation of exploiting undervalued (or disposing of overvalued) securities. The fund management can elect to execute their trades by using either a full-service broker or a discount broker. If they use the former the commission includes research and other services, including in some cases back-office operations (for example, recordkeeping, custodial, and even filing services). The effect of this is to remove a number of management expenses from the income statement where they are likely to be noticed and from the reported MER that an investor uses to assess fund performance. Furthermore, funds that are sponsored by brokerage houses may incur higher transactions costs through "churning" the portfolio to feed additional commission income back to the sponsor.

A recent Canadian study of simulated mutual fund after-tax performance concluded that, because of the unique nature of the Canadian personal tax structure, index funds produce returns that are superior to those of actively managed portfolios solely as a result of the difference in turnover. Differences in management fees and brokerage costs were much less important than the effect of the tax on realized capital gains resulting from the higher turnover.[28]

What does the investor get as a result of paying management fees, operating expenses and brokerage costs? Unfortunately, few Canadian studies address this question. A number of US studies, however,

shed some interesting light on the issue and lead to the following general conclusions. (References for these studies can be found at the end of the chapter.)

1. Large funds perform no better, other things being equal, than smaller funds, where size is measured by the dollar value of the fund's total assets.
2. Funds with load charges performed no better, other things being equal, than those with no load charges. Because of the load charge, investors in no-load funds did better than those in load funds.
3. Funds with higher **portfolio turnover rates** had lower levels of performance, other things being equal. (A fund's turnover rate is the ratio of the smaller of purchases or sales during a time period divided by the average total asset value during the period, and, therefore, is a measure of the amount of trading executed during the period.)

One reasonable explanation for these conclusions is that, in an efficient market, higher expense ratios and more frequent portfolio revisions will cause a fund to incur higher costs that cannot be consistently offset by the higher returns obtained by trading mispriced securities. Furthermore, whereas revisions to a fund's portfolio may be necessary in order to maintain a specified risk level or dividend yield, the evidence indicates that revisions intended to exploit supposed market inefficiencies generally prove to be unprofitable.

Portfolio Turnover Rate
A measure of how much buying and selling occurs in a portfolio over a given period of time.

Altamira
www.altamira.com

ing a market index. With less than perfect foresight the manager must achieve an accuracy of 80% in forecasting both bull and bear markets in order to outperform a buy and hold strategy. This is probably beyond the reach of most managers.

The second compares two different approaches to market timing. One, referred to as a *swing fund* (SW) approach, requires the manager to shift funds between asset classes in response to new forecasts about economic conditions. The other approach, referred to as *tactical asset allocation* (*TAA*), relies on the derivative securities market to implement shifts between asset classes. A comparison of eight TAA simulation models with six SF managers showed that six of the TAA models and three SF managers showed statistically significant market timing ability. On average the TAA "managers" outperformed the SF managers in market timing ability, although both added value to the portfolios.

---

[28]H. Thorfinson and J. Kiss, "The Overlooked Piranha," *Canadian Investment Review* IX, no. 3 (Fall 1996).

Evaluating Mutual Funds

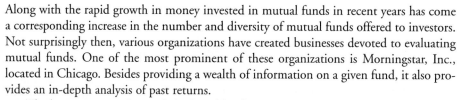

Morningstar Inc.
www.morningstar.net

Lehman Brothers
www.lehman.com

Along with the rapid growth in money invested in mutual funds in recent years has come a corresponding increase in the number and diversity of mutual funds offered to investors. Not surprisingly then, various organizations have created businesses devoted to evaluating mutual funds. One of the most prominent of these organizations is Morningstar, Inc., located in Chicago. Besides providing a wealth of information on a given fund, it also provides an in-depth analysis of past returns.

The best way to understand the breadth of Morningstar's mutual fund evaluations is to consider an analysis of a specific fund. An example involving the Fidelity Magellan Fund, an equity fund, is shown in Figure 21.11 and explained next. Where different, a description of the analysis is also given for a fixed-income fund.

• Performance

In the left-hand side of Figure 21.11 is a section with the heading *Performance.* Displayed here are first, the quarterly returns over the last five years, and second, the average returns earned by the fund over various time periods ending March 31, 1997, ranging from the past three months to the past 15 years. These returns are calculated net of operating expenses and fees, although load charges are ignored. Thus the average returns reflect what an investor would have earned after having bought the fund's shares.[29] Next to each average return is an indication of how it compares with the average return on the S&P 500 and Wilshire 750 indices over the same time period. For fixed-income funds these indices are replaced by the Lehman Brothers Aggregate Bond Index and another fixed-income bond index that best matches the fund's holdings.

In the fourth and fifth columns from the left are the percentile ranks of the fund's average return relative to all mutual funds and relative to those funds identified by Morningstar as having a similar stated investment objective. (For classification purposes, Morningstar refers to investment objectives as *categories.*)[30] Here a rank of 1 places a fund at the top and a rank of 100 places a fund at the bottom. The sixth column shows the amount a $10 000 dollar investment in the fund would have grown to over the applicable time period (ignoring taxes and load charges).

Over the three months ending March 31, 1997, Magellan had a return of −.56%, which was 3.24% lower than the S&P 500 and 2.44% lower than the Wilshire 750. This return caused the fund to be ranked at the 63rd percentile of all funds and the 88th percentile of those funds in the same category. Notably, over the past 15 years it can be seen that the Magellan Fund did substantially better than both indices, placing it in the first percentile overall and in its category. Note how a $10 000 investment in the Magellan Fund that was made on March 31, 1982, would have grown to $174 946 on March 31, 1997, 15 years later.

---

[29] Morningstar's average return referred to here and elsewhere is calculated using compounding. For example, the one-year return is calculated by compounding the four previous quarterly returns and subtracting one; the three-year average return is calculated by compounding the twelve previous quarterly returns, taking the cube root of the result, and then subtracting one.

[30] Morningstar determines a fund's investment objective based on a set of variables related to the composition of the fund's portfolio. For US common stock funds, these variables include the market value, the price-earnings and price-book ratios of the fund's holdings. For US bond funds, these variables include the maturity and issuer type of the fund's holdings. The Morningstar approach is complex but it allows an investor to more finely differentiate among funds.

Figure 21.11 — Performance and risk analysis of the Magellan Fund (excerpts).

Performance 03-31-97

	1st Qtr	2nd Qtr	3rd Qtr	4th Qtr	Total
1993	8.62	6.42	8.21	−0.34	24.66
1994	−1.59	−4.49	5.43	−0.90	−1.81
1995	8.44	15.77	10.60	−1.46	36.82
1996	1.79	1.00	1.67	6.85	11.69
1997	−0.56	—	—	—	—

Trailing	Total Return%	+/− S&P 500	+/−Wil Top 750	% Rank All	% Rank Cat	Growth of $10,000
3 Mo	−0.56	−3.24	−2.44	63	88	9,944
6 Mo	6.25	−4.99	−3.45	26	77	10,625
1 Yr	9.11	−10.71	−8.01	36	95	10,911
3 Yr Avg	14.88	−7.40	−6.43	23	89	15,163
5 Yr Avg	14.92	−1.49	−0.28	13	34	20,045
10 Yr Avg	13.79	0.42	0.98	7	6	36,391
15 Yr Avg	21.02	3.44	4.18	1	1	174,946

Historical Profile

Return	Above Avg
Risk	Average
Rating	★★★★ Above Avg

Risk Analysis

Time Period	Load-Adj Return %	Risk %Rank[1] All	Cat	Morningstar Return	Risk	Morningstar Risk-Adj Rating
1 Yr	5.84					
3 Yr	13.72	83	95	0.89	1.11	★★★
5 Yr	14.22	74	79	1.20	0.93	★★★
10 Yr	13.44	72	78	1.57	0.96	★★★★

Average Historical Rating (136 months) — 4.8★s

[1] 1=low, 100=high

Category Rating (3 Yr) ② ③ ④ ① ⑤ — Worst / Best

Return	Below Avg
Risk	High

Other Measures	Standard Index S&P 500	Best Fit index SPMid400
Alpha	−5.9	0.2
Beta	0.99	0.94
R-Squared	68	75
Standard Deviation	13.13	
Mean	14.61	
Sharpe Ratio	0.85	

Current Investment Style — Style Value Blnd Growth / Size Large Med Small

	Stock Port Avg	Relative S&P 500 Current	Hist	Rel Cat
Price/Earnings Ratio	22.7	0.96	1.1	0.97
Price/Book Ratio	3.8	0.72	0.9	0.77
4 Yr Earnings Gr%	23.9	1.33	1.6	1.25
Price/Cash Flow	12.7	0.90	1.1	0.92
Debt % Total Cap	32.6	1.03	1.0	1.04
Med Mkt Cap $mil	10,201	0.4	0.8	0.60
Foreign %	12.5	—	—	1.88

SOURCE: Excerpts from Morningstar Mutual Funds, Morningstar Inc., 225 W. Wacker Dr., Chicago, IL 60606, 312-696-6000 (September 25, 1997), p. 118.

Ratings

In the *Risk Analysis* section of Figure 21.11 are columns under *Load-Adj Return, Risk % Rank All,* and *Cat, Morningstar Return* and *Risk,* and *Morningstar Risk-Adj Rating.* The three columns labelled *Load-Adj Return, Morningstar Return,* and *Risk* need to be explained first. Here it is easiest to focus on the 10-year row, as the other rows are straightforward extensions of it. First, the average return for Magellan and all other portfolios in the same category are determined for the past 10 years. Here the actual net return is adjusted for any load charges that the fund levies on investors, producing a return of 13.44% in the *Load-Adj Return* column. Second, the average 10-year returns for all funds in the same category are averaged. Third, Magellan's average return is divided by this overall average. Hence a return measure of greater than 1 means that the fund did better than average, whereas a return measure of less than 1 indicates that the fund did worse than average. In Magellan's case the *Morningstar Return* measure of 1.57 indicates that its average return was 57% better than the overall average.

For the 10-year *Morningstar Risk* entry, the appropriate monthly Treasury bill return is subtracted from each of the previous 120 monthly net returns to calculate the fund's excess returns. Then only the negative excess returns are summed and the absolute value is divided by 120 to provide a measure of the fund's downside risk. (This risk measure is similar to the risk measure known as *mean shortfall,* which was discussed in Chapter 6's *Institutional Issues* section.)

For example, imagine that this risk measure is calculated over six months instead of 120 months, and that the following returns are observed:

Month	Fund Return	T-bill Return	Fund Return less T-bill Return
1	4.0%	.5%	3.5%
2	−2.0	.5	−2.5
3	.4	.6	−0.2
4	5.0	.6	4.4
5	−3.0	.6	−3.6
6	1.0	.7	.3

The three negative excess returns of −2.5%, −.2%, and −3.6% sum to −6.3%. Dividing this sum by 6, the total number of months, results in a downside risk measure of 6.3/6 = 1.05.

Downside risk measures are calculated by Morningstar for funds in the same category, and an overall average for these funds is determined. Then the fund's downside risk measure is divided by this overall measure; the resulting number is Morningstar's measure of the fund's relative risk. In the case of Magellan, it is .96, indicating that it had 4% less downside risk than the average similar fund over the 10-year period.

Under the heading *Risk % Rank* the percentile rankings are found for the fund's downside risk measure against all funds (*All*) and funds in the same category (*Cat*). Here a percentile rank of 1 indicates that the fund had the least risk, whereas a rank of 100 indicates that the fund had the most risk. In the case of Magellan, its ranks of 72 and 78 over 10 years indicate that it had more risk than 72% of all the other funds and 78% of the other funds in the same category.

Morningstar's rating system has five ranks, as follows:

Stars	Percentile	Return Rank	Risk Rank
★★★★★	1–10	Highest or High	Lowest or Low
★★★★	11–32.5	Above Average	Below Average
★★★	33.5–67.5	Average	Average
★★	68.5–90	Below Average	Above Average
★	91–100	Lowest or Low	Highest or High

Hence the percentile rank, based on the set of funds in the same category, determines how many stars the fund is given and the category in which it is placed.[31]

The *Morningstar Risk-Adj Rating* is determined by subtracting the fund's downside risk measure from its return measure. In the case of Magellan, its 10-year risk-adjusted measure is 1.57 − .98 = .59. This measure is also determined for all the other funds in the same category, and then percentile ranks are determined. In the case of Magellan, it ranked somewhere between 11 and 32.5, causing it to receive a four-star rating.[32]

---

[31]Similar ratings are provided in *The Individual Investor's Guide to No-load Mutual Funds* (Chicago: American Association of Individual Investors, 1997).

[32]For more on Morningstar's risk-adjusted ratings, see William F. Sharpe, "Morningstar's Risk-adjusted Ratings," unpublished paper. Graduate School of Business, Stanford University, 1998. This paper can be accessed on the Web at www.sharpe.stanford.edu/msrar.htm

Historical Profile

Summary performance measures are contained in the *Historical Profile* part of Figure 21.11. Consider the return measure first. Here the previously described return measures for 3, 5, and 10 years are averaged using weights of 20%, 30%, and 50% to arrive at a weighted-average return. After doing this for each of the other funds in the same category, the fund is given a percentile rank and then a rating, as indicated before. In the case of Magellan, its percentile rank was somewhere between 11 and 32.5, giving it an *above average* ranking. Similar weighted-average calculations are done for the fund's downside risk measure and risk-adjusted measure, resulting in Magellan's receiving an *average* risk rating and a four-star *above average* risk-adjusted rating.

Category Rating and Other Measures

In the bottom of the *Risk Analysis* section of the figure is a gauge that can point to one of five numbers based on the fund's returns over the last three years. This simply indicates the overall performance of the fund over the past three years but uses a gauge instead of the star-based system as described earlier. Thus, over the past three years Fidelity Magellan received a rating of "1," the lowest possible overall rating. This is undoubtedly due to its having received a rating of *Below Average* for its three-year return, and a rating of *High* for its level of risk over the past three years, as indicated directly below the gauge. These two ratings are the equivalent of two and one stars, respectively.

Next to the *Category Rating* in Figure 21.11 is the section that Morningstar refers to as *Other Measures*. The top part provides values for *Alpha*, *Beta*, and *R-Squared*. They correspond to the statistics related to a portfolio's *ex post* characteristic line, which is a regression model like the market model that was discussed in Chapter 7.[33] The only difference between the two is that the *ex post* characteristic line uses excess returns instead of returns. Hence Morningstar reports the results from regressing the previous 36 monthly excess returns of the mutual fund (that is, the fund's net returns less the corresponding Treasury bill rates) on the previous 36 monthly excess returns of the S&P 500 (that is, the index's returns less the corresponding Treasury bill rates). As a result the fund's *ex post* alpha (*Alpha*) and beta (*Beta*) are estimated. Similarly, *R-Squared* is the coefficient of determination (multiplied by 100) that is determined when the 36 excess returns of the fund are compared with those of the S&P 500. Morningstar also reports the regression results for the index that produced the highest *R-Squared* from a set of indices. For example, if the *R-Squared* of a fund is higher with the Russell 2000 than the S&P 500, this result would indicate that the fund follows an investment objective of investing in small companies.

It can be seen that Magellan had a beta of .99 and .94 when regressed against the S&P 500 and S&P MidCap 400 index, respectively. Its *ex post* alpha of −5.9% and .2% indicates that it did much worse than the S&P 500 but about the same as the S&P MidCap 400 index, respectively, over the last 36 months on a risk-adjusted basis. The *R-Squared* values of 68 and 75 mean that roughly 68% and 75% of the variation in the excess returns of the fund could be attributed to variations in the excess returns on the two S&P indices.

The second part of this section provides values for *Standard Deviation*, *Mean*, and *Sharpe Ratio*. These three values are also based on the previous 36 monthly rates of return on the fund. *Standard Deviation* and *Mean* are the standard deviation and the average return (annualized) for the portfolio, which for Magellan are 13.13% and 14.61%, respectively. The *Sharpe Ratio*, discussed more fully in Chapter 24, gives a risk-adjusted measure of performance. Here Morningstar takes the fund's average excess return over the previous 12 months and divides it by the fund's standard deviation over the previous 36 months. Hence it is the ratio of excess return to risk, which for Magellan equals .85.

---

[33]The *ex post* characteristic line is discussed more fully in Chapter 24.

Investment Style

This section appears in the lower right part of Figure 21.11. On the right are seven descriptive measures of the average stock held by the fund using the most recently available data. For example, the average *Price/Earnings Ratio* of the stocks held in the Magellan Fund was 22.7 as of March 31, 1997. This number is divided by the average price-earnings ratio of the stocks in the S&P 500, indicating a value of .96, or 4% less than the average ratio in the index. Furthermore, the average price-earnings ratio for the past three years for the stocks in the fund's portfolio was 1.1. Lastly, the current value of the ratio, when divided by the average for all funds in the same category, was .97, indicating the ratio was 3% less than the current average. The ratios shown here are weighted averages, where the weight for each security is based on the relative proportion of the fund that is invested in the security. In the case of a fund that invests in fixed-income securities, these seven measures are replaced by average measures such as effective duration, effective maturity, credit quality, coupon interest rate, and price.

Also in this part of Figure 21.11 is a 3 × 3 matrix, which Morningstar calls a *style box*. The two extreme columns represent the investment styles of value and growth, with the middle column representing a mixture of the two. A fund's style is determined by summing the fund's price-earnings ratio and price-book ratio, where both are expressed relative to the S&P 500. Note that this sum for the S&P 500 itself is 2.00 (since each ratio is, by definition, equal to 1.00). Morningstar has decided that if the sum for a fund is less than 1.75, then the fund follows a *value style*. This is because the fund has invested in stocks that collectively have relatively low valuation ratios and hence are viewed as value stocks. On the other hand, if the sum is greater than 2.25, then the fund is deemed to follow a *growth style* because it has invested in stocks with relatively high valuation ratios. Sums between 1.75 and 2.25 indicate that the fund follows a *blended style*, investing in stocks that in aggregate have no distinct style.

In the case of Magellan, its sum is .96 + .72 = 1.68, indicating that it currently follows a value style. As the value of this sum for the S&P 500 itself is 2.00, the Magellan Fund tends to purchase stocks that have price-earnings and price-book ratios that on average are lower than the two valuation ratios of stocks in the S&P 500.

The three rows of the style box are based on the size of the stocks held by the fund, where size is measured by the Median Market Capitalization figure for the fund. If this figure is less than $1 billion, the fund is deemed to be *small,* and if it is greater than $5 billion, then the fund is deemed to be *large*. A figure between $1 billion and $5 billion—as is the case with Magellan, as the median size of its holdings is $10.201 billion—results in the fund's being categorized as *large*.

In Chapter 16 it was mentioned that stocks can be classified along the two dimensions of value-growth and size. Now it can be seen that investment companies can be similarly classified. Morningstar does this by use of the style box, thereby allowing investors to quickly understand a fund's investment strategy. Nine combinations of the three levels of value-growth and size are possible. Morningstar indicates its classification of a fund by darkening one of the nine sections of the style box. In the case of Magellan the centre box is darkened, indicating that its investment strategy involves purchases of both value and growth stocks without concentrating on either large or small ones.

In the case of fixed-income funds, the columns of the style box are based on the average duration of the securities in the fund, and hence the style box focuses on the fund's interest rate sensitivity. The column headings are *Short Term* (if the average duration is between one and 3.5 years), *Intermediate Term* (if the average duration is between 3.5 and six years), and *Long Term* (if the average duration is greater than six years). The rows are based on the average credit quality of the securities in the fund, and hence measure default risk. The row headings are *High* (if the average bond rating is at least AA), *Average* (if the average is between BBB and AA), and *Low* (if the average is less than BBB); federal government securities are treated as being AAA.

In general, when Morningstar assigns a stock or bond fund to a category, it is based on where the fund is located in the style box. Hence, there are nine categories of stock funds and nine categories of bond funds for the two style boxes. In addition, there are special categories for sector and international stock funds as well as municipal and international bond funds.[34]

Caveats

Morningstar's performance measures are useful in giving an investor a quick reading of how a mutual fund has performed in the past relative to other funds. However, several things should be kept in mind.

1. Performance comparisons are made with the S&P 500 and Lehman Brothers Aggregate Bond Index for all equity and bond funds, respectively, but these indices may not be appropriate for certain funds. For example, a fund that invests primarily in securities listed on NASDAQ, might more appropriately be compared with an over-the-counter index. Morningstar attempts to overcome this problem by making performance comparisons within categories composed of funds with similar investment objectives.

2. As will be discussed in Chapter 23, portfolio managers can attempt to earn abnormal returns by trying to (1) buy underpriced securities and then profit from their subsequent abnormal price appreciation, or (2) if a stock fund, shift funds out of the stock market just before it goes down and then back into the stock market just before it rises or, if a bond fund, shift funds between long-term and short-term bonds depending on the forecast for interest rates, or (3) do both. Morningstar's performance measures do not indicate which approach the fund is using in its quest for abnormal returns.

3. The use of peer group comparisons to evaluate performance has several serious conceptual and practical shortcomings. For example, the set of similar funds may not be entirely appropriate (even though they may be the best match that Morningstar can provide), causing the ratings to be misleading. One fund may be restricted to buying just NYSE-listed common stock whereas another is free to purchase stocks that are listed on the NYSE, AMEX, or NASDAQ. Furthermore, similar funds may differ considerably in the amount of risk that they take on. Morningstar has attempted to minimize this problem by its use of more narrowly defined categories for comparison purposes, but such categorization is never perfect.

4. Finally, *survivorship bias* (the tendency for poorly performing funds to go out of business and hence leave the peer group) hampers comparisons with similar funds.

Canadian Mutual Fund Evaluation

BellCharts Inc. and Portfolio Analytics Ltd. provide investors with mutual fund evaluation data and software. Data is provided on disk to subscribers and the software allows the investor to process them in his own individual style. The information on disk is similar in both cases although the companies emphasize somewhat different aspects.

BellCharts™ Inc.

BellCharts Inc. has recently introduced its "five bells" ranking system that is the equivalent of Morningstar's five-star rating. The following is a description, provided by the company, of BellCharts' evaluation and ranking system:

---

[34]For more on mutual fund styles, see Stephen J. Brown and William N. Goetzmann, "Mutual Fund Styles," *Journal of Financial Economics* 43, no. 3 (March 1997): 373–399.

BellScore

BellScore measures mutual funds with performance histories of at least three years as at the most recently completed calendar quarter. The fund is assigned a rating ranging from one "BELL" at the low end to five "BELLS" for those funds achieving the highest score.

BellScores are not calculated for funds that are net of management fees, nor are they calculated for Pooled funds.

The BellCharts Rating System is an adaptation of an internationally recognized rating system developed by Asset Risk Consultants ("ARC") of Guernsey, Channel Islands. ARC is a wholly owned subsidiary of Bachmann Asset Management, also of Guernsey. Bachmann provides, through its subsidiaries, financial and administrative services including investment management, trust and company administration, insurance services, corporate ownership of property, and marine services worldwide. The Bachmann Group has over 2500 clients from more than 40 countries. Assets under management total $5.0 billion.

BellScores are based on the building blocks of
- Time-weighted rates of return
- Risk
- Correlation

BellScore

The formulae take into account time-weighted rates of return, excess risk, and correlation to create a resulting score by which individual funds are ranked within their respective categories. BellCharts then assigns a five Bell rating to those funds in the top 7% of each category list, four Bells to the next 25%, three Bells to the next 36%, two Bells to the next 25%, and one Bell to the last 7%. Funds with less than three years of history are not assigned a BellScore. A BellScore is also not assigned to money market funds as investors are generally not seeking excess returns from this investment and risk analysis is of marginal value.

Return

In standard performance tables each month's performance is equally weighted. Consequently, an exceptional performance in a single month will impact performance, for better or worse, equally throughout the period under review. BellScore uses a weighting system that evaluates monthly returns during a three-year period and assigns greater significance to the near-term results and less weight to the older monthly returns. This weighting lessens the potential distortion from exceptional monthly returns as time progresses. "Returns" refer to "Total returns" and make no distinction between income and capital gains. Tax efficiency is not a consideration.

Risk

BellScore also measures "excess returns," the extent to which one is rewarded for investing in a particular fund rather than investing in a benchmark. The BellScore methodology employs a proprietary variance risk analysis to evaluate the degree of risk associated with "excess returns." This step quantifies "excess risk," measuring the risk of the fund exclusive of the risk inherent in the market.

Correlation

Another component of the BellScore calculation is to consider the degree to which a fund's performance correlates to a relevant benchmark, i.e., how closely the performance of a fund follows the performance of its benchmark. The higher the correlation the greater the likelihood that the fund's future performance will follow those of its benchmark.

Figure 21.12 is typical of the information that can be derived from the BellCharts Inc. system, in this case about Ivy Canadian, a Canadian equity fund.

The chart shown in Figure 21.12 first gives some basic details of the fund such as the fund sponsor, the portfolio manager, any investment restrictions, the management fee and MER, the funds long-term objectives, the distribution of its holdings and the top 10 holdings as of October 31, 1991. The chart contains a wealth of information that deserves more explanation.

The box marked "Value of $1000.00" shows the terminal value of an investment of $1000 placed in the beginning of the given holding period. Note that this is net of any load charges.

The box marked "Risk versus Return (3 Years)" has the standard deviation of returns (the risk measure) along the horizontal axis and the returns along the vertical axis both calculated over the most recent three-year period. The horizontal line on the chart shows the return for the median fund and the vertical line, shows the risks of the median fund. The small rectangle shows the position of the Ivy Fund. This indicates that Ivy has considerably lower risk and a slightly higher return than the median fund.

The Fee Details box comes next. This tells the potential investor that he has a choice between a front-end load or a deferred fee. The information suggests that the front-end load is variable depending on the amount invested, but will not exceed 5%. The deferred fee declines through time reaching zero after seven years.

The Investment Style details show that this is an equity fund based on a Bottom-Up investment (see Chapter 22 for more details) and that the managers stock selection style is blend of Value, Growth and Sectoral approaches.

Historical details of the fund's distributions, average assets and NAVPS are provided next.

The final information on the left-hand side is the correlation of fund returns with those of the TSE 300 Total Return Index. The comparison of the three- and five-year results shows that the correlation coefficient is quite stable at about 0.84. This suggests that about 70% of Ivy's return can be "explained" by the TSE 300 Total Return.

The "What-if Chart" provides a comparison of the groawth of $1000 invested in the fund at its inception with the same investment over the same period in the TSE 300. This shows that over a six-year period the TSE 300 was consistently a superior investment, which suggests that an index fund would outperform Ivy. It should be remembered, however, that the TSE 300 results do not include the effect of the MER charged by an index fund, nor do the fund results reflect the effect of either a front-end load or a deferred fee.

The boxes in the "Annual Chart" show the range of returns for 90% of the funds in the Canadian equity class. The top and bottom 5% have been removed. The X shows the position of the Ivy fund in each year, the rectangle indicates the position of the TSE 300 Total Return Index and the bar, --, the location of the median fund. This chart shows that Ivy performed extremely poorly in its first year, the table below shows its rank at 126 out of 127, but is has improved significantly, being above the median in all years since 1993.

The "Compound Chart" shows data that are similar to the Annual Chart except that the returns are calculated over different time periods. In this case, the Ivy fund performs well, being in the top quartile for all periods (except one month).

The final chart labelled "All-time Period Analysis (1 Year Returns)" shows one-year returns for the fund calculated at the end of each month. The first bar covers the period from December 31, 1993, to December 31, 1994. The second bar covers the period from January 31, 1994, to January 31, 1995, and so on. The table below shows useful summary statistics derived from the chart. The last two columns of this table shows the frequency with which the fund showed a given return over the five-year period under investigation. For example, 98.4% of the time the return exceeded 0% and 75.4% of the time it exceeded 10%.

The rating of the fund based on the "bells" is shown at the top of the exhibit, in this case Ivy Canadian fund received the top rating of five bells.

Portfolio Analytics Limited

This company offers its PALTRAK™ that can be used to develop the following typical custom information, provided by the company, shown in Figure 21.13, panels A to F.

Portfolio Analytics Limited
www.pal.com

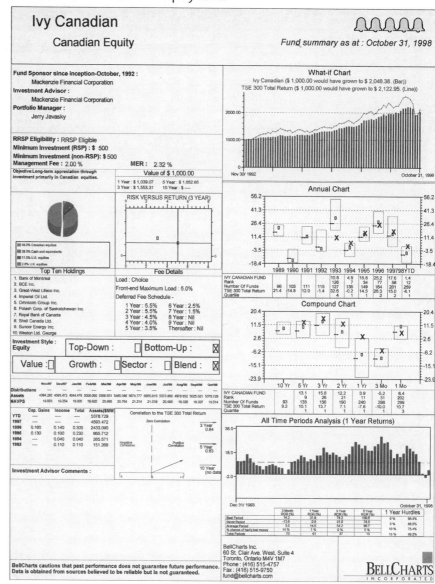

SOURCE: Charts reprinted with permission of BellCharts Incorporated (November 1998).

Panel A shows general information about the AGF Growth Equity fund including basic details of the fund such as the fund sponsor, the date of inception, the management fee and MER, the fund's long-term objectives, the distribution of its holdings compared with that of the average fund in the class, the top fifteen holdings as of October 31, 1998, some limited historical returns, and historical NAVPS. Panel B graphically shows the rolling 120-month annualized return for Templeton Growth fund together with useful summary information in the box below. This indicates, for example that this fund's worst 10-year compound rate of return was 11.63%—a respectable return indeed! Panel C graphically presents the risk-return characteristics of the AIC Advantage fund and compares it with the characteristics of a variety of other funds that can be chosen by the analyst. Panel D is a graphical comparative analysis of two similar funds (Salomon

Figure 21.13 Typical mutual fund information derived by the Paltrak system.

A. Summary Information about AGF Growth Equity Fund

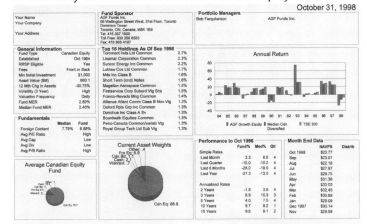

B. Rolling 120-Month Annualized Return for Templeton Growth

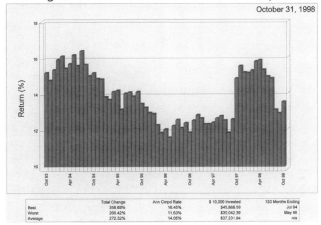

C. Three Year Risk/Return Report: User-Defined Peer Group

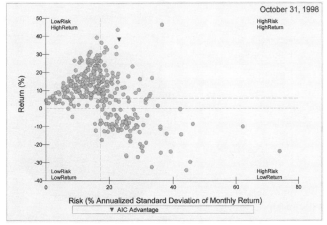

SOURCE: Charts reprinted with permission of Portfolio Analytics Limited (November 1998).

Figure 21.13 (Continued) Typical mutual fund information derived by the Paltrak system.

D. Comparative Monthly Returns over Five Years for Two Funds

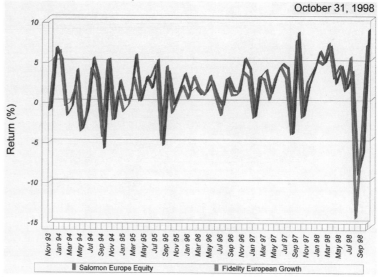

■ Salomon Europe Equity   ■ Fidelity European Growth

E. TSE Sectors Breakout for Trimark Canadian

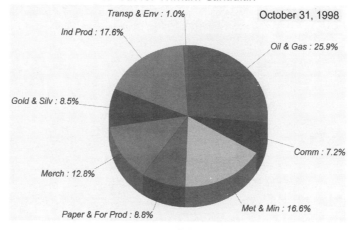

F. Geographic Breakout for C.I. Global

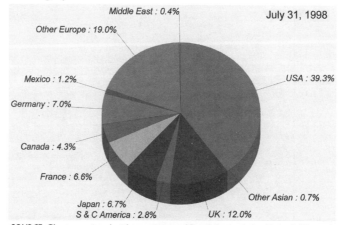

SOURCE: Charts reprinted with permission of Portfolio Analytics Limited (November 1998).

European Equity and Fidelity European Equity) over a five-year period. The investor can select the funds to be compared. Panel E shows the actual asset allocation amongst TSE Industrial sectors for Trimark Canadian equity fund as of October 31, 1998. Panel F indicates the geographical distribution of investments for CI Global fund.

In addition to the information shown here the company also provides detailed asset weights for a large number of funds, information that is published in *The Financial Post's* monthly Mutual Funds section.

Closed-end Fund Premiums and Discounts

Several studies have shown that the performance of diversified closed-end investment company managers in the United States is similar to that of open-end investment company managers.[35] When returns are measured by changes in net asset values (plus all distributions), closed-end investment companies appear to be neither better nor worse than open-end ones. Again, there is little evidence that portfolio managers can either select underpriced securities or time the market successfully.

Pricing of Shares

However, there is more to be said about closed-end funds. An investor can purchase an open-end fund's shares for their net asset value (plus any required load charge) and sell them later at the subsequent net asset value. Except for any load charges and fees, the performance of the *management* of such a fund, based on net asset values, corresponds exactly to the returns provided to the *shareholders*. This is not the case for closed-end investment companies, since investors buy and sell shares of investment companies at prices determined on the open (secondary) market. Although some companies have share prices that are above their net asset values (such shares are said to sell at a premium), many have share prices below their net asset values (such shares are said to sell at a discount). Canadian closed-end mutual funds exhibit the same divergence between net asset value and share price as shown in Figure 21.1.

This has resulted in several "puzzles" concerning the typical pricing of closed-end fund shares. Three of the most prominent are as follows. First, as mentioned earlier, the shares sell at a premium of roughly 10% of their net asset value when initially sold and then fall to a discount of roughly 10% of their net asset value shortly thereafter. Why would investors buy such shares when they are initially offered for sale, knowing that their price is going to fall substantially afterward? Second, the size of this discount fluctuates widely over time.[36] Figure 21.14 shows the price behaviour of a sample of 16 closed-end funds. Note how the average fund sells at a discount that ranged from roughly 3% to 12% over the previous four quarters. What causes these fluctuations? Third, it appears possible to earn abnormally high returns by purchasing funds with the biggest discounts. One study that examined closed-end funds from 1965 to 1985 found that buying a portfolio of

---

[35]See, for example, William F. Sharpe and Howard B. Sosin, "Closed-end Investment Companies in the United States: Risk and Return," *Proceedings*, 1974 Meeting of the European Finance Association, ed. B. Jacquillat (Amsterdam: North-Holland Publishing Co., 1975); Antonio Vives, "Analysis of Forecasting Ability of Closed-End Fund's Management," (working paper, Carnegie-Mellon University, September 1975) and "Discounts and Premiums on Closed-end Funds: A Theoretical and Empirical Analysis," Ph.D. diss., Carnegie-Mellon University, 1975.

[36]These two puzzles are presented and investigated in Charles M. C. Lee, Andrei Shleifer, and Richard H. Thaler, "Investor Sentiment and the Closed-end Fund Puzzle," *Journal of Finance* 46, no. 1 (March 1991): 75–109. In the June 1991 issue of *Journal of Finance* there is a contentious debate about their findings. For a comparison of the volatility of closed-end fund share prices and the volatility of the underlying securities in their portfolios, see Jeffrey Pontiff, "Excess Volatility and Closed-end Funds," *American Economic Review* 87, no. 1 (March 1987): 155–169.

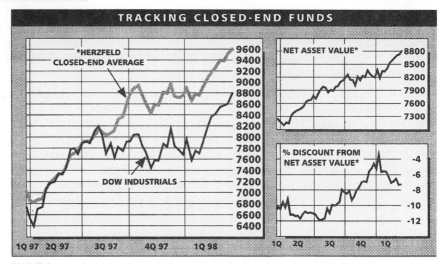

Figure 21.14 Closed-end fund performance.

TRACKING CLOSED-END FUNDS

SOURCE: Reprinted with permission of *Barron's*, Dow Jones & Company, Inc. (March 23, 1998): p. mw91. All rights reserved worldwide.

roughly seven or eight funds with the biggest discounts and holding them until their discounts shrank so that there were about 15 funds with larger discounts resulted in an inexplicable average abnormal monthly return of .8% (or about 10% per year).[37] How can such a simple investment strategy exist in an efficient market?

Investing in Fund Shares

The fact that the price of a closed-end investment company differs from its net asset value, with the magnitude of the difference varying from time to time, introduces an added source of risk and potential return to investors. By purchasing shares at a discount, an investor may be able to earn more than just the change in the company's net asset value. Even if the company's discount remains constant, the effective dividend yield will be greater than that of an otherwise similar no-load, open-end investment company, since the purchase price will be less. If the discount is substantial when the shares are purchased, it may subsequently narrow, and the return will be even greater.[38] On the other hand, if the discount increases, the investor's overall return may be less than that of an otherwise comparable open-end investment company.

Consider a closed-end fund that at the beginning of the year has a net asset value of $10 per share but is selling at a 10% discount for $9 per share. Over the year it receives cash dividends amounting to $.50 per share, which it distributes to its shareholders. Hence

---

[37]See Jeffrey Pontiff, "Closed-end Fund Premia and Returns: Implications for Financial Market Equilibrium," *Journal of Financial Economics* 37, no. 3 (March 1995): 341–370, especially the appendix. Also see Rex Thompson, "The Information Content of Discounts and Premiums on Closed-end Fund Shares," *Journal of Financial Economics* 6, no. 2/3 (June–September 1978): 151–186.

[38]There is evidence that this is what happens to those funds with the greatest discounts; see Pontiff, "Closed-end Fund Premia and Returns." There is also some evidence that discounts narrow during "down markets" and widen during "up markets," and that the size of discounts and premiums increase as interest rates increase. See R. Malcolm Richards, Donald R. Fraser, and John C. Groth, "Premiums, Discounts, and the Volatility of Closed-end Mutual Funds," *Finance Review* (Fall 1979): 26–33; "The Attractions of Closed-end Bond Funds," *Journal of Portfolio Management* 78, no. 2 (Winter 1982): 56–61; and Jeffrey Pontiff, "Costly Arbitrage: Evidence from Closed-end Funds," *Quarterly Journal of Economics* 111, no. 4 (November 1996): 1135–1151.

its dividend yield is $.50/$9.00 = 5.6%$, which is larger than the $.50/$10 = 5%$ yield that it would pay if it were an open-end fund. Furthermore, its net asset value at year-end remains at $10 per share but its discount shrinks to 4% so that it is selling at $9.60 per share, then its annual return $(.60 + $.50)/$9 = 12.2%$ would be notably larger than the 5% return of its open-end counterpart. Of course, if its discount widened to 20% so that it was selling at $8 per share, then its annual return of $(-$1 + $.50)/$9 = -5.6%$ would be notably lower than the counterpart's 5% return.

Some of the risk associated with varying discounts can be reduced by holding a portfolio of shares in several closed-end investment companies. Discounts on different companies move together, but not perfectly. For example, past data suggest that the standard deviation of the percentage change in the ratio of market price to net asset value for a portfolio of 10 to 12 closed-end investment companies is likely to be approximately half that of a typical investment in the shares of a single closed-end investment company.[39]

Open-ending Closed-end Funds

Explaining the puzzling behaviour of prices of closed-end investment companies is a challenge for anyone who believes that capital markets are highly efficient. For anyone not firmly committed to such a view, the purchase of shares of closed-end investment companies at prices sufficiently below net asset values may provide an opportunity for superior returns.[40] One way of realizing superior returns is for the closed-end investment company to convert to an open-end one.[41] By doing so, the discount on the shares would have to disappear because conversion would result in the investment company's offering its shareholders the right to redeem their shares for their net asset value.

In one study, a sample of 138 closed-end funds was examined from 1979 to 1989 by determining the amount of concentrated ownership in each fund. Shareholdings of officers and directors as well as others who owned 5% or more of a fund's shares were determined and aggregated for each fund in the sample. After discarding eight funds where at least some shareholders were actively involved in attempting to open up the fund, the remaining funds were examined. It was observed that those with blockholdings sold at an average discount of 14.2% while those without blockholdings sold at a discount of only 4.1%. Subsequent analysis revealed that the larger the size of the blockholdings, the larger the discount. An explanation put forth is that the funds with blockholdings were less likely to be opened up, since it was determined that large investors in such funds were receiving a variety of private benefits (for example, being involved with firms that execute the fund's trades, being involved with the management firm that receives the fund's management fees, being able to find employment at the fund for close friends and relatives) that were not available to small investors. Given their voting power, these large investors apparently gain more from these benefits than they would gain from opening up the fund, and hence vote against any effort to do so.[42] Needless to say, this leaves open the question of why small investors hold shares in such funds.

---

[39]Sharpe and Sosin, "Closed-end Investment Companies in the United States."

[40]Burton G. Malkiel advocated such an investment strategy in the 1973, 1975, and 1981 editions of *A Random Walk Down Wall Street* (New York: W. W. Norton), but not in the 1985 and 1990 editions. The basis for his initial advocacy can be found in two studies: Burton Malkiel, "The Valuation of Closed-end Investment Company Shares," *Journal of Finance* 32, no. 3 (June 1977): 847–859; and Rex Thompson, "The Information Content of Discounts and Premiums on Closed-end Fund Shares," *Journal of Financial Economics*, 6, no. 2–3 (June–September 1978): 151–186. Pontiff's more recent study supports these two earlier studies; see Pontiff, "Closed-end Premia and Returns."

[41]For an analysis of the "open-ending" of closed-end investment companies, see Greggory A. Brauer, "'Open-Ending' Closed-end Funds," *Journal of Financial Economics*, 13 no. 4 (December 1984): 491–507.

[42]See Michael Barclay, Clifford Holderness, and Jeffrey Pontiff, "Concentrated Ownership and Discounts on Closed-end Funds," *Journal of Applied Corporate Finance* 8, no. 1 (Spring 1995): 32–42 (an expanded version of this paper appears in the June 1993 issue of the *Journal of Financial Economics*).

Summary

1. Investment companies are financial intermediaries that receive money from investors and use it to purchase financial assets.
2. Investment companies offer investors the advantages of economics of scale and professional management.
3. The net asset value of an investment company is the difference between the market value of its assets and its liabilities divided by the number of outstanding shares.
4. The management expense ratio of an investment company represents the annual percentage of total assets that are spent in operating the fund. Typically these expenses consist of fees paid to the management company as well as administrative and other operating expenses.
5. The two major types of investment companies are closed-end investment companies and open-end investment companies.
6. Closed-end investment companies issue an initial number of shares to capitalize the fund. After that, new shares are rarely issued (or repurchased). Closed-end investment company shares trade on organized exchanges or on the over-the-counter market at prices determined by the market.
7. Open-end investment companies have a variable capitalization, standing ready to issue new shares or repurchase existing shares at prices based on their net asset values.
8. Different investment companies follow different investment policies. These polices determine such characteristics as the asset classes in which the investment companies invest, the degree of active management (if any), and the emphasis on income as opposed to capital appreciation.
9. Owing to data availability, mutual funds have been the subject of many performance studies. The results show that the typical fund has not been able to produce superior rates of return consistently.
10. There is weak evidence that the superior results of top performing and inferior results of the bottom performing mutual funds persist over time. However, this evidence is not strong, indicating that many top performers subsequently become middle of the pack performers.
11. Closed-end investment companies typically sell at premiums to their net asset values at their initial offerings. Later they typically sell at discounts to their net asset values, which vary over time. Explaining why investors buy initial public offerings of closed-end investment companies, why the discounts of these companies vary over time, and why a strategy that involves buying a portfolio of seven or eight funds with the deepest discounts produces abnormally high returns, are puzzles for efficient market proponents.

QUESTIONS AND PROBLEMS

1. The Neptune Value Fund has sold 15 000 shares to investors. Currently the fund has accrued investment management fee obligations of $50 000. The fund's portfolio is shown below. Calculate the fund's net asset value.

Stock	Shares	Price/Share
A	50 000	$ 10
B	20 000	7
C	35 000	30
D	10 000	100

2. Bill Schulter, a veteran mutual fund investor, argued: "I can compute the monthly rate of return on a mutual fund by calculating the percentage change in the fund's NAV from the beginning to the end of the month (assuming no distributions to shareholders)." Is Bill correct? Why?

3. The X Fund, a closed-end investment company, has a portfolio of assets worth $500 million. It has liabilities of $2 million. It also has 40 million shares outstanding.
   a. What is the fund's NAV?
   b. If the fund trades at an 8% discount from its NAV, what is the market price of the fund's shares?

4. Distinguish between closed-end and open-end investment companies.

5. Why do some mutual funds have load charges whereas others do not? Why are investors willing to pay load charges?

6. Assume that you placed a $1000 investment with a mutual fund that charged an 8.5% load. Management and other fees charged by the fund total 1.10% per annum. Ignoring other costs, over five years, what annual return would the fund have to produce to equal the value that your initial investment would have earned in a savings account paying 5% interest? (Assume annual compounding of income and no taxes.)

7. In recent years so-called "families of funds" that offer a wide range of investment policies through narrowly focused mutual funds have become popular. Discuss why these funds have achieved such popularity.

8. There are literally thousands of mutual funds available for purchase. Describe what criteria you might use in selecting from among these many funds.

9. At the beginning of the year, the Saturn Fund's NAV was $18.50. At the end of the year its NAV was $16.90. At year-end the fund paid out $1.25 in income and capital gains. What was the return to an investor in the Saturn Fund during the year?

10. Over the last three years, the Pluto Fund produced the following per-share financial results. Calculate the annual returns on an investment in the Pluto Fund over this period.

	Year 1	Year 2	Year 3
NAV at Beginning of Year	$13.89	$14.40	$15.95
NAV at End of Year	14.40	15.95	15.20
Income Distribution	0.29	0.33	0.36
Capital Gains Distribution	0.12	0.25	0.05

11. Analysis of mutual fund performance has been extensive. What does the evidence indicate about the ability of mutual fund managers, as a group, to produce positive abnormal returns consistently?

12. Lesley Pike is attempting to select a superior-performing mutual fund. Based on the evidence presented in the text, discuss how much importance Lesley should attach to the past performance of mutual funds in making decisions.

13. Why do the stated percentage load charges of mutual funds not fully reflect the percentage costs of these sales fees?

14. Distinguish between a common stock fund and a balanced fund. In particular, compare their expected return and risk characteristics.

15. If most investment managers appear unable to "beat the market" on a risk-adjusted basis, should an investor still consider investing in investment companies? Why?

16. Consider three individuals: a young, well-educated woman just beginning a career with high expected future earnings; a middle-aged man with a young family who has a secure job but modest expected future earnings growth; a widow in her seventies, living comfortably but not richly off a pension. Referring to *The Globe and Mail: Report*

on Mutual Funds, prescribe and explain an investment strategy for these persons involving investments in the various funds listed. (Feel free to introduce other assumptions regarding such things as the individuals' risk tolerances and consumption preferences.)

17. Assuming that certain conditions are satisfied, an investment company does not have to pay federal tax on the income it earns. Why?

18. Why do the market prices of closed-end investment company shares represent a "mystery" to proponents of market efficiency?

KEY TERMS

investment company (p. 682)

net asset value (NAV) (p. 683)

managed investment company (p. 684)

management expense ratio (p. 684)

closed-end investment company (p. 684)

open-end investment company (p. 685)

no-load fund (p. 686)

load fund (p. 686)

load charge (p. 686)

fixed annuity (p. 689)

variable annuity (p. 689)

deferred annuity (p. 690)

guaranteed investment annuity (p. 690)

pooled fund (p. 690)

segregated fund (p. 690)

trust unit (p. 691)

Real Estate Investment Trust (REIT) (p. 691)

labour-sponsored investment fund (p. 692)

unit investment trust (p. 692)

benchmark portfolio (p. 703)

ex post alpha (p. 703)

portfolio turnover rate (p. 715)

REFERENCES

1. Good reference sources for information on investment companies are:

William J. Baumol, Stephen M. Goldfeld, Lilli A. Gordon, and Michael F. Koehn, *The Economics of Mutual Fund Markets: Competition Versus Regulation* (Boston: Kluwer Academic Publishers, 1990).

Investment Companies Yearbook 1993 (to order, write: CDA Investment Technologies, Inc., 1355 Piccard Drive, Rockville, MD 20850).

1997 Mutual Fund Fact Book (to order, write: Investment Company Institute, P.O. Box 66140, Washington, DC 20035-6140). See also the website: www.ici.org.

John C. Bogle, *Bogle on Mutual Funds* (Burr Ridge, IL: Richard D. Irwin, 1994).

The Individual Investor's Guide to No-Load Mutual Funds (to order, write: American Association of Individual Investors, 625 North Michigan Avenue, Research Department, Chicago, IL 60611).

Morningstar Mutual Funds (to order this biweekly publication, write: Morningstar, Inc., 225 West Wacker Drive, Chicago, IL 60606).

Peter Fortune, "Mutual Funds, Part 1: Reshaping the American Financial System," *New England Economic Review*, Federal Reserve Bank of Boston, July–August 1997, 45–72.

2. Although annual management fees of investment companies are usually a given percentage of the market value of the assets under management, performance-based fees are allowed. In addition to the January–February 1987 issue of the *Financial Analysts Journal*, which is devoted to this topic, see:

Laura T. Starks, "Performance Incentive Fees: An Agency Theoretic Approach," *Journal of Financial and Quantitative Analysis* 22, no. 1 (March 1987): 17–32.

Mark Grinblatt and Sheridan Titman, "How Clients Can Win the Gaming Game," *Journal of Portfolio Management* 13, no. 4 (Summer 1987): 14–23.

Joseph H. Golec, "Do Mutual Fund Managers Who Use Incentive Compensation Outperform Those Who Don't?" *Financial Analysts Journal* 44, no. 6 (November–December 1988): 75–78.

Mark Grinblatt and Sheridan Titman, "Adverse Risk Incentives and the Design of Performance-based Contracts," *Management Science* 35, no. 7 (July 1989): 807–822.

Jeffery V. Bailey, "Some Thoughts on Performance-based Fees," *Financial Analysts Journal* 46, no. 4 (July–August 1990): 31–40.

Philip Halpern and Isabelle I. Fowler, "Investment Management Fees and Determinants of Pricing Structure in the Industry," *Journal of Portfolio Management* 17, no. 2 (Winter 1991): 74–79.

Keith C. Brown, W. V. Harlow, and Laura T. Starks, "Of Tournaments and Temptations: An Analysis of Managerial Incentives in the Mutual Fund Industry," *Journal of Finance* 51, no. 1 (March 1996): 85–110.

Tarun Chordia, "The Structure of Mutual Fund Charges," *Journal of Financial Economics* 41, no. 1 (May 1996): 3–39.

Robert Ferguson and Dean Leistikow, "Investment Management Fees: Long-run Incentives," *Journal of Financial Engineering* 6, no. 1 (March 1997): 1–30.

Peter Tufano and Matthew Sevick, "Board Structure and Fee-setting in the U.S. Mutual Fund Industry," *Journal of Financial Economics* 46, no. 3 (December 1997): 321–355.

3. Closed-end investment companies known as "country funds" have been examined by:

Catherine Bonser-Neal, Greggory Brauer, Robert Neal, and Simon Wheatley, "International Investment Restrictions and Closed-end Country Fund Prices," *Journal of Finance* 45, no. 2 (June 1990): 523–547.

Gordon Johnson, Thomas Schneeweis, and William Dinning, "Closed-end Country Funds: Exchange Rate and Investment Risk," *Financial Analysts Journal* 49, no. 6 (November–December 1993): 74–82.

4. Real estate investment trusts (REITs) are discussed in:

William L. Burns and Donald R. Epley, "The Performance of Portfolios of REITS Stocks," *Journal of Portfolio Management* 8, no. 3 (Spring 1982): 37–42.

Robert H. Zerbst and Barbara R. Cambon, "Real Estate: Historical Returns and Risks," *Journal of Portfolio Management* 10, no. 3 (Spring 1984): 5–20.

Paul M. Firstenburg, Stephen A. Ross, and Randall C. Zisler, "Real Estate: The Whole Story," *Journal of Portfolio Management* 14, no. 3 (Spring 1988): 22–34.

Stephen E. Roulac, "How to Value Real Estate Securities," *Journal of Portfolio Management* 14, no. 3 (Spring 1988): 35–39.

Steven D. Kapplin and Arthur L. Schwartz, Jr., "Investing in REITS: Are They All They're Cracked Up to Be?" *AAII Journal* 13, no. 5 (May 1991): 7–11.

Joseph Gyourko and Donald B. Keim, "Risk and Return in Real Estate: Evidence from a Real Estate Stock Portfolio," *Financial Analysts Journal* 49, no. 5 (September–October 1993): 39–46.

5. For evidence on the performance of funds outside of North America, see:

André L. Farber, "Performance of Internationally Diversified Mutual Funds," in *International Capital Markets*, eds. Edwin J. Elton and Martin J. Gruber (Amsterdam: North-Holland Publishing, 1975): 298–309.

R. S. Woodward, "The Performance of UK Investment Trusts as Internationally Diversified Portfolios Over the Period 1968 to 1977," *Journal of Banking and Finance* 7, no. 3 (September 1983): 417–426.

Jess H. Chua and Richard S. Woodward, *Gains from Market Timing*, Monograph Series in Finance and Economics 1986–2, New York University Salomon Center, Leonard N. Stern School of Business.

Robert E. Cumby and Jack D. Glen, "Evaluating the Performance of International Mutual Funds," *Journal of Finance* 45, no. 2 (June 1990): 497–521.

Cheol S. Eun, Richard Kolodny, and Bruce G. Resnick, "US-Based International Mutual Funds: A Performance Evaluation," *Journal of Portfolio Management* 17, no. 3 (Spring 1991): 88–94.

6. Studies of mutual fund performance are discussed and cited in:

Gordon J. Alexander and Jack Clark Francis, *Portfolio Analysis* (Englewood Cliffs, NJ: Prentice Hall, 1986), Chapter 13.

Bruce N. Lehmann and David M. Modest, "Mutual Fund Performance Evaluation: A Comparison of Benchmarks and Benchmark Comparisons," *Journal of Finance* 42, No. 2 (June 1987): 233–265.

Richard A. Ippolito, "Efficiency with Costly Information: A Study of Mutual Fund Performance," *Quarterly Journal of Economics* 104, no. 1 (February 1989): 1–23.

Mark Grinblatt and Sheridan Titman, "Mutual Fund Performance: An Analysis of Quarterly Portfolio Holdings," *Journal of Business* 62, no. 3 (July 1989): 393–416.

Cheng-few Lee and Shafiqur Rahman, "Market Timing, Selectivity, and Mutual Fund Performance: An Empirical Investigation," *Journal of Business* 63, no. 2 (April 1990): 261–278.

Cheng F. Lee and Shafiqur Rahman, "New Evidence on Timing and Security Selection Skill of Mutual Fund Managers," *Journal of Portfolio Management* 17, no. 2 (Winter 1991): 80–83.

John C. Bogle, "Selecting Equity Mutual Funds," *Journal of Portfolio Management* 18, no. 2 (Winter 1992): 94–100.

Ravi Shukla and Charles Trzcinka, "Performance Measurement of Managed Portfolios," *Financial Markets, Institutions & Instruments* 1, no. 4 (1992).

Mark Grinblatt and Sheridan Titman, "The Persistence of Mutual Fund Performance," *Journal of Finance* 47, no. 5 (December 1991): 1977–1984.

Mark Grinblatt and Sheridan Titman, "Performance Measurement Without Benchmarks: An Examination of Mutual Fund Returns," *Journal of Business* 66, no. 1 (January 1993): 47–68.

Edwin J. Elton, Martin J. Gruber, Sanjiv Das, and Matthew Hlavka, "Efficiency with Costly Information: A Reinterpretation of Evidence from Managed Portfolios," *Review of Financial Studies* 6, no. 1 (1993): 1–22.

Richard A. Ippolito, "On Studies of Mutual Fund Performance," *Financial Analysts Journal* 49, no. 1 (January–February 1993): 42–50.

Darryll Hendricks, Jayendu Patel, and Richard Zeckhauser, "Hot Hands in Mutual Funds: Short-run Persistence of Relative Performance, 1974–1988," *Journal of Finance* 48, no. 1 (March 1993): 93–130.

Mark Grinblatt, Sheridan Titman, and Russ Wermers, "Momentum Strategies, Portfolio Performance, and Herding: A Study of Mutual Fund Behavior," *American Economic Review* 85, no. 5 (December 1995): 1088–1105.

Christopher R. Blake, Edwin J. Elton, and Martin J. Gruber, "The Performance of Bond Mutual Funds," *Journal of Business* 66, no. 3 (July 1993): 371–403.

John Bogle, *Bogle on Mutual Funds* (Burr Ridge, IL: Richard D. Irwin, 1994), Chapter 4.

Mark Grinblatt and Sheridan Titman, "A Study of Monthly Mutual Fund Returns and Performance Evaluation Techniques," *Journal of Financial and Quantitative Analysts* 29, no. 3 (September 1993): 419–444.

William N. Goetzmann and Roger G. Ibbotson, "Do Winners Repeat?" *Journal of Portfolio Management* 20, no. 2 (Winter 1994): 9–18.

Edwin J. Elton and Martin J. Gruber, *Modern Portfolio Theory and Investment Analysis* (New York: John Wiley & Sons, 1995), Chapter 24.

Burton G. Malkiel, "Returns from Investing in Equity Mutual Funds," *Journal of Finance* 50, no. 2 (June 1995): 549–572.

Stephen J. Brown and William N. Goetzmann, "Performance Persistence," *Journal of Finance* 50, no. 2 (June 1995): 679–698.

Edwin J. Elton, Martin J. Gruber, and Christopher R. Blake, "Fundamental Economic Variables, Expected Returns, and Bond Fund Performance," *Journal of Finance* 50, no. 4 (September 1995): 1229–1256.

Ronald N. Kahn and Andrew Rudd, "Does Historical Performance Predict Future Performance?" *Financial Analysts Journal* 51, no. 6 (November–December 1995): 43–52.

Edwin J. Elton, Martin J. Gruber, and Christopher R. Blake, "The Persistence of Risk-adjusted Mutual Fund Performance," *Journal of Business* 69, no. 2 (April 1996): 133–157.

Wayne E. Ferson and Rudi W. Schadt, "Measuring Fund Strategy and Performance in Changing Economic Conditions," *Journal of Finance* 51, no. 2 (June 1996): 425–461.

Mark M. Carhart, "On Persistence in Mutual Fund Performance," *Journal of Finance* 51, no. 1 (March 1997): 57–82.

7. *Survivorship bias* refers to the problems incurred in mutual fund studies due to the fact that either unskilled portfolio managers are usually fired while the skilled ones stay around, or poor performing funds are shut down or merged into better-performing ones. These problems are examined in:

Stephen J. Brown, William Goetzmann, Roger G. Ibbotson, and Stephen A. Ross, "Survivorship Bias in Performance Studies," *Review of Financial Studies* 5, no. 4 (1992): 553–580.

Edwin J. Elton, Martin J. Gruber, and Christopher R. Blake, "Survivorship Bias and Mutual Fund Performance," *Review of Financial Studies* 9, no. 4 (Winter 1996): 1097–1120.

8. For a discussion and extensive set of references regarding closed-end funds, see, along with the citations given in the chapter, the following papers:

Rex Thompson, "The Information Content of Discounts and Premiums on Closed-end Fund Shares," *Journal of Financial Economics* 6, no. 2–3 (June–September 1978): 151–186.

Greggory A. Brauer, "Closed-end Fund Shares' Abnormal Returns and the Information Content of Discounts and Premiums," *Journal of Finance* 43, no. 1 (March 1988): 113–127.

Kathleen Weiss, "The Post-offering Price Performance of Closed-end Funds," *Financial Management* 18, no. 3 (Autumn 1989): 57–67.

Charles M. C. Lee, Andrei Shleifer, and Richard H. Thaler, "Anomalies: Closed-end Mutual Funds," *Journal of Economic Perspectives* 4, no. 4 (Fall 1990): 153–164.

John W. Peavey III, "Returns of Initial Public Offerings of Closed-end Funds," *Review of Financial Studies* 3, no. 4 (1990): 695–708.

Charles M. C. Lee, Andrew Shleifer, and Richard H. Thaler, "Investor Sentiment and the Closed-end Fund Puzzle," *Journal of Finance* 46, no. 1 (March 1991): 75–109.

Albert J. Fredman and George Cole Scott, "An Investor's Guide to Closed-end Fund Discounts," *AAll Journal* 13, no. 5 (May 1991): 12–16.

James Brickley, Steven Manaster, and James Schallheim, "The Tax-timing Option and Discounts on Closed-end Investment Companies," *Journal of Business* 64, no. 3 (July 1991): 287–312.

J. Bradford DeLong and Andrei Shleifer, "Closed-end Fund Discounts," *Journal of Portfolio Management* 18, no. 2 (Winter 1992): 46–53.

Nai-fu Chen, Raymond Kan, and Merton H. Miller, "Are the Discounts on Closed-end Funds a Sentiment Index?" and "A Rejoinder," *Journal of Finance* 48, no. 2 (June 1993): 795–800 and 809–810.

Navin Chopra, Charles M. C. Lee, Andrei Shleifer, and Richard H. Thaler, "Yes, Discounts on Closed-end Funds are a Sentiment Index," and "Summing Up," *Journal of Finance* 48, no. 2 (June 1993): 801–808 and 811–812.

Jeffrey Pontiff, "Closed-end Fund Premia and Returns: Implications for Financial Market Equilibrium," *Journal of Financial Economics* 37, no. 3 (March 1995): 341–370.

Michael Barclay, Clifford Holderness, and Jeffrey Pontiff, "Concentrated Ownership and Discounts on Closed-end Funds," *Journal of Applied Corporate Finance* 8, no. 1 (Spring 1995): 32–42.

Jeffrey Pontiff, "Excess Volatility and Closed-end Funds," *American Economic Review*, 87, no. 1 (March 1997): 155–169.

9. Open-ending of closed-end investment companies is discussed in:

Greggory A. Brauer, "'Open-ending' Closed-end Funds," *Journal of Financial Economics* 13, no. 4 (December 1984): 491–507.

James A. Brickley and James S. Schallheim, "Lifting the Lid on Closed-end Investment Companies: A Case of Abnormal Returns," *Journal of Financial and Quantitative Analysis* 20, no. 1 (March 1985): 107–117.

Jeffrey Pontiff, "Costly Arbitrage: Evidence From Closed-end Funds," *Quarterly Journal of Economics*, 111, no. 4 (November 1996): 1135–1151.

10. In addition to the references in the footnotes to the chapter, the following article provides a Canadian perspective on the issues raised:

John Rae Sayer and Lucy Ackert, "Win Some, Lose Some," *Canadian Investment Review* IX, no. 3 (Fall 1996).

Financial Analysis

I n a broad sense, financial analysis involves determining the levels of risk and expected return of individual financial assets as well as groups of financial assets. For example, financial analysis involves both individual common stocks, such as Stelco; groups of common stocks, such as the steel industry; or, on an even larger basis, the stock market itself. In this case, financial analysis would result in a decision regarding how to split the investor's money between the stock and bond markets as well as a decision regarding whether to buy or sell steel stocks in general and Stelco in particular.

An alternative definition of financial analysis is more pragmatic: Financial analysis is what financial analysts do. The *Financial Analyst's Handbook*[1] defines the term **financial analyst** as synonymous with security analyst or investment analyst—"one who analyzes securities and makes recommendations thereon."[2] Using this definition, financial analysis can be viewed as the activity of providing inputs to the portfolio management process. This chapter (as well as Chapters 17 and 18) take such a view in discussing the financial analysis of common stocks. Chapter 23 subsequently discusses how financial analysis can be used by **portfolio managers**, also known as investment managers.

Financial Analyst (Alternatively, **Security Analyst or Investment Analyst**.) An individual who analyzes financial assets in order to determine the investment characteristics of those assets and to identify mispricings among those assets.

Portfolio Manager An individual who utilizes the information provided by financial analysts to construct a portfolio of financial assets.

Professional Organizations

Stelco
www.stelco.com

Association for Investment Management and Research
www.aimr.org

In Canada and the United States, those who belong to a local society of financial analysts automatically belong to an umbrella organization known as the Association for Investment Management and Research (AIMR). The local societies offer members the opportunity to meet as a group with corporate managements, consultants, money managers, and academics to discuss issues of relevance to the investment management business.

The AIMR organization acts as an advocate for the financial analyst profession, presenting unified positions before regulators and governments. It also hosts conferences and workshops designed to enhance the investment knowledge of its members. In addition, AIMR publishes the *Financial Analysts Journal*, a major source of information on basic research conducted by other analysts and by members of the academic community. In 1996 there were almost 28 000 members of AIMR.

[1]Sumner N. Levine, ed., *Financial Analyst's Handbook I* (Homewood, IL.: Dow Jones-Irwin, 1975).

[2]William C. Norby, "Overview of Financial Analysis," in Levine, *Financial Analyst's Handbook I*, 3.

In 1962 the Institute of Chartered Financial Analysts (ICFA) was formed by the Financial Analysts Federation (the precursor to the AIMR) to award the professional designation of Chartered Financial Analyst (CFA). In 1996 over 21 000 analysts held the CFA designation. The CFA program is designed to establish a common set of investment knowledge and ethical standards for the various types of investment professionals. The ICFA attempts to accomplish the first objective by requiring that prospective CFAs pass a series of three exams and attain several years of investment experience. It attempts to achieve the second objective by disseminating and enforcing a set of professional conduct guidelines. (The CFA program is discussed further in this chapter's *Institutional Issues* section.)[3]

Societies of financial analysts have been formed around the world. For example, the European Federation of Financial Analysts draws its membership from ten European countries. Other societies are located in countries such as Australia, Japan, and Brazil.

The Canadian Securities Institute (CSI) is another important educational institution that provides not only a basic course for those who whish to enter the financial services industry but also advanced courses for professionals already in the industry. The Canadian Securities Course (CSC) provides a complete overview of the industry and is virtually a requirement for entry into it. Successful completion of this course allows individuals to apply for mutual fund licensing, thereby permitting them to sell mutual funds. Those seeking a career in Canada's brokerage sector must continue to complete the Conduct and Practices Handbook Course.

Other professional courses offered by the CSI that follow on from the CSC include the following:

- Professional Financial Planning course, a requirement to practise financial planning and a prerequisite for the Investment Management Techniques and Portfolio Management Techniques courses for portfolio managers.
- Derivatives Fundamentals course, which is a prerequisite for the:
  (1) Options Licensing course and the Registered Options Principals Qualifying Examination for options traders and their supervisors, and
  (2 Futures Licensing Course and the Canadian Commodity Supervisors Examination for futures traders and their supervisors.

The CSI also offers shorter programs in Management training and specialty learning related specifically to the financial services industry. note.[4]

Reasons for Financial Analysis

There are two primary reasons for engaging in financial analysis. The first reason is to try to determine certain characteristics of securities; the second reason is to attempt to identify mispriced securities.[5]

These reasons are discussed next.

---

[3]To obtain more information about becoming a CFA, contact the Toronto Society of Financial Analysts, 390 Bay Street, Toronto, ON M5H 9Z9; the telephone number is (416) 366-5755. A useful annual publication of the Institute is *The CFA Candidate Study and Examination Program Review.*

[4]Further information about the CSC and other courses can be obtained from the Canadian Securities Institute, 121 King Street West, Suite 1550, Toronto, ON M5H 3T9 [the telephone number is (416) 364-9130, the fax number is (416) 359-0486] or from their Web site: www.csi.ca.

[5]Some would add a third reason for conducting financial analysis: monitoring the firm's management in order to prevent managers from consuming an excessive amount of perquisites and failing to make appropriate decisions to the detriment of the firm's shareholders. See Michael C. Jensen and William H. Meckling, "Theory of the Firm: Managerial Behavior, Agency Costs and Ownership Structure," *Journal of Financial Economics* 3, no. 4 (October 1976): 305–360.

Determining Security Characteristics

According to modern portfolio theory, a financial analyst will want to estimate a security's future beta and unique risk, since these are needed to determine the risk (measured by standard deviation) of a portfolio. Perhaps the analyst may also want to estimate the dividend yield of a security over the next year in order to determine its suitability for portfolios in which dividend yield is relevant (owing to, for instance, legal restrictions). Careful analysis of such things as a company's dividend policy and likely future cash flows may lead to better estimates than can be obtained by simply extrapolating last year's dividend yield.

In many cases it may be desirable to know something about the sources of a security's risk and return. If a portfolio is being managed for a person who is in the oil business, one might want to minimize the sensitivity of the portfolio's return to changes in oil prices. This is because it is likely that if oil prices are in a decline, then the person's income from the oil business will also be in a decline. If the portfolio were sensitive to oil prices (which would be the case if it contained a substantial investment in oil stocks), then it too would be in a decline in value, thereby reinforcing the deterioration of the person's financial position.[6]

Attempting to Identify Mispriced Securities

Fundamental Analysis A form of security analysis that seeks to determine the intrinsic value of securities based on underlying economic factors. These intrinsic values are compared to current market prices to estimate current levels of mispricing.

A search for a mispriced security typically involves the use of **fundamental analysis**. In essence, this entails searching for a security in which the financial analyst's estimates of such things as the firm's future earnings and dividends:

1. differ substantially from consensus (that is, average) estimates of others,
2. are viewed as being closer to the correct values than the consensus estimates, and
3. are not currently reflected in the security's market price.

Two rather different approaches may be taken in the search for mispriced securities using fundamental analysis. The first approach involves valuation, where an attempt is made to determine the appropriate "intrinsic" or "true" value for a security. After making this determination, the intrinsic value is compared with the security's current market price. If the market price is substantially greater than the intrinsic value, the security is said to be overpriced, or overvalued. If the market price is substantially less than the intrinsic value, the security is said to be underpriced, or undervalued. Instead of comparing price with value, the analyst sometimes estimates a security's expected return over a specified period, given its current market price and intrinsic value. This estimate is then compared with the "appropriate" return for securities with similar attributes.

Determining a security's intrinsic value may be done in great detail, using estimates of all major factors (for example, gross national product of the economy, industry sales, firm sales and expenses, and capitalization rates). Alternatively, a shortcut may be taken where, for example, an estimate of earnings per share may be multiplied by a "justified," or "normal," price-earnings ratio to determine the intrinsic value of a share of common stock. (To avoid complications arising when seeking the intrinsic value of a share that has negative earnings per share, some analysts estimate sales per share and multiply this figure by a "normal" price-sales ratio).

A second approach has the analyst estimate only one or two financial variables and then compare these estimates directly with consensus estimates. For example, next year's earnings per share for a stock may be estimated. If the analyst's estimate substantially exceeds the consensus of other analysts' estimates, the stock may be considered an attractive invest-

---

[6]For a discussion regarding portfolio selection by an investor who has earned income (for example, from wages or from running a business), see Edward M. Miller, "Portfolio Selection in a Fluctuating Economy," *Financial Analysts Journal* 34, no. 3 (May–June 1978): 77–83.

The Chartered Financial Analyst Program

The investment profession encompasses a wide range of activities. Investment bankers, brokers, portfolio managers, traders, security analysts, salespeople, consultants, and pension fund administrators all fall under the rubric of investment professionals. These individuals, and the organizations for which they work, directly or indirectly affect the financial well-being of millions of people.

The Chartered Financial Analyst (CFA) program was born of a need to bring a common set of investment management concepts and standards of professional conduct to the diverse membership of the investment industry. From its modest beginnings in 1963, when 268 professionals were effectively "grandfathered" as chartered members, the CFA program has grown to a worldwide organization, with approximately 21 000 CFA charters awarded and more than 30 000 candidates currently enrolled. Although the CFA charter is far from a prerequisite for employment in the investment industry, many organizations are encouraging or even requiring new employees to participate in the CFA program.

From its inception, the Institute of Chartered Financial Analysts (ICFA), which administers the CFA program, has pursued three explicit objectives:

1. To compile a comprehensive set of currently accepted concepts and techniques relevant to the investment decision-making process (the CFA "Body of Knowledge").
2. To establish a uniform set of ethical standards to guide the activities of investment professionals.
3. To ensure that CFA charterholders have demonstrated satisfactory understanding of the Body of Knowledge and that they adhere to the established ethical standards.

Of course, like any other professional certification organization, the ICFA has multiple motives for promoting the CFA designation. By setting difficult hurdles for prospective members to clear, the CFA certification process enhances the monetary value of the charter to existing holders. Further, by demonstrating a responsible and comprehensive education and ethics program, the ICFA helps the investment industry ward off onerous government regulation and provides the industry with wider latitude to police itself.

To enroll in the CFA program, an individual must hold a bachelor's degree (or equivalent work experience), provide three acceptable character references, and pay the required registration fee. Once accepted into the program, to earn the CFA designation a candidate must pass three exams, possess three years of investment-related work experience, be a member of (or have applied to) a constituent financial analyst society, demonstrate a high level of professional conduct, and abide by the Code of Ethics and Standards of Practice of the Association for Investment Management and Research.

The CFA course of study and examinations are the cornerstone of the CFA certification process. Candidates must pass three six-hour exams. The ICFA administers these exams once a year in June at 140 locations, primarily in the United States and Canada. As candidates may take only one exam per year, a minimum of three years is required to complete the examination sequence.

The ICFA specifies a set of review materials and assigned readings for candidates to use in preparation for the exams. The study program has evolved over the years as new concepts have been introduced into the exams. The ICFA estimates that candidates average 200 hours per exam in individual study time. Many candidates also participate in independently sponsored study groups.

The CFA examinations were designed in a progressive format. The exam levels became increasingly comprehensive, building on previous levels. The CFA curriculum underwent a major change in 1993, which was phased in over three years. When it was fully implemented in 1995, the exams were divided into four major subject areas and several subtopics within each major subject:

1. Ethical and professional standards:
   a. Applicable laws and regulations
   b. Professional standards of practice
   c. Ethical conduct and professional obligations
   d. International ethical and professional considerations

2. Tools for inputs for investment valuation and management:
   a. Quantitative methods and statistics
   b. Macroeconomics
   c. Microeconomics
   d. Financial statements and accounting
3. Investment (asset) evaluation:
   a. Overview of the valuation process
   b. Applying economic analysis in investment valuation
   c. Applying industry analysis in investment valuation
   d. Applying company analysis in investment valuation
   e. Equity securities
   f. Fixed-income securities
   g. Other investments
   h. Derivative securities
4. Portfolio management:
   a. Capital market theory
   b. Portfolio policies
   c. Expectational factors
   d. Asset allocation
   e. Fixed-income portfolio management
   f. Equity portfolio management
   g. Real estate portfolio management
   h. Specialized asset portfolio management
   i. Implementing the investment process
   j. Performance measurement

The CFA exams are rigorous and difficult. A high number of the candidates fail at least one exam, although exams can be retaken. In 1997, a total of 30 627 candidates sat for the exams. Only 53%, 59%, and 59% of the candidates taking the first, second, and third exams, respectively, passed.

The CFA program experienced tremendous growth in the 1980s and 1990s. The number of candidates sitting for the exams has increased over fifteen-fold since 1980. Given this past success, where does the CFA program go from here?

Clearly, the ICFA desires to continue to enhance the prestige and uniqueness of its CFA certification. In recent years, however, the ICFA has also begun to strongly emphasize the continuing education aspect of its mission. Technological obsolescence is a serious problem in the rapidly changing investment industry. (For example, organized financial futures markets—see Chapter 20—did not even exist in 1980). Many professionals who received the CFA designation just a decade ago might find it difficult to pass an exam now. Current charterholders are encouraged (although not yet required) to participate in a self-administered continuing education program.

The ICFA also sees a role for itself globally. With the investment industry becoming increasingly international in scope, the ICFA has moved to administer its program abroad. It has also begun to join forces with analyst societies in other countries to develop means of jointly recognizing one another's certification programs.

ment. This is because the analyst expects the actual earnings to provide a happy surprise for the market when announced. In turn, there will be an increase in the share's price at that time, resulting in the investor receiving a greater-than-normal return. Conversely, when an analyst's estimate of earnings per share is substantially below that of the other analysts, then the analyst expects the market will receive an unhappy surprise. The resulting decrease in the share's price will lead to a smaller-than-normal return.

At an aggregate level, an analyst may be more optimistic about the economy than the consensus of other analysts. This would suggest that a larger-than-normal investment in stocks be taken, offset perhaps by a smaller-than-normal investment in fixed-income securities. Conversely, a relatively pessimistic view would suggest a smaller-than-normal investment in stocks, offset perhaps by a larger-than-normal investment in fixed-income securities.

Alternatively, the analyst might agree with the consensus view on both the economy and the individual characteristics of specific securities but feel that the consensus view of the prospects for a certain group of securities in a particular industry is in error. In such a case, a larger-than-normal investment may be made in stocks from an industry having prospects about which the analyst feels relatively optimistic. Conversely, a smaller-than-normal investment would be made in stocks from an industry about which the analyst feels relatively pessimistic.

The use of fundamental analysis to identify mispriced common stocks and fixed-income securities was discussed in previous chapters. This chapter will introduce the method of technical analysis and compare it to fundamental analysis.

Beating the Market

Many books and articles have been written that allegedly show how financial analysis can be used to beat the market, meaning they purport to show how to make abnormally high returns by investing in the stock market. In order to evaluate such systems, an understanding of what "the market" is and how to measure its performance is in order.

Conveying Advice on Beating the Market

It is interesting to ponder whether or not advice on how to beat the market will remain useful after becoming public. It seems logical that any such prescription that has been in print for long is not likely to allow the investor to beat the market without fail. Even if an approach has worked in the past (and because someone asserts it has worked does not mean that it has), as more and more investors apply it, prices will be driven to levels at which the approach will not work in the future. Any system designed to beat the market, once known to more than a few people, carries the seeds of its own destruction.

There are two reasons for not including advice on "guaranteed" ways to beat the market in this book. First, to do so would make a successful system public and hence unsuccessful. Second, the authors know of no such system. Some apparent anomalies and possible inefficiencies have been described previously. But any book that purports to open the door to the *certainty* of making abnormally high returns for those who follow its advice should be regarded with the greatest skepticism.

This does not mean that financial analysis is useless. Although individuals should be skeptical when others tell them how to use financial analysis to beat the market, individuals can try to *understand* the market with the use of financial analysis.

Financial Analysis and Market Efficiency

The concept of an efficient market (discussed in Chapter 4) may appear to be based on a paradox. Financial analysts carefully analyze the prospects for companies, industries, and the economy in the search for mispriced securities. If an undervalued security is found, for example, then it will be purchased. However, the act of purchasing the security will tend to push its price upward towards its intrinsic value, thereby making it no longer undervalued. That is, financial analysis tends to result in security prices that reflect intrinsic values, which is equivalent to saying that financial analysis tends to make markets efficient. But if this is the case, why would anyone perform financial analysis in an attempt to identify mispriced securities?

There are two responses to this question. First, there are costs associated with performing financial analysis. This means that financial analysis may not be conducted on all securities all the time. As a result, the prices of all securities will not reflect intrinsic values all the time. Pockets of opportunity may occasionally arise, thereby opening the possibility for added benefits from financial analysis. This suggests that people should engage in financial analysis only to the point at which the added benefits cover the added costs.[7] Ultimately, in a highly competitive market, prices would be close enough to intrinsic values to make it worthwhile for only the most skillful analysts to search for mispriced securities. Thus, the market would be nearly, but not perfectly, efficient. Skilled investors will be able to earn abnormally high gross returns, but after the costs of gathering and processing information and then making the requisite trades are taken into consideration, they will end up with a net return that is not abnormal.[8]

The other response to the question focuses on the first reason given earlier for engaging in financial analysis: to determine certain characteristics of securities. This reason is appropriate even in a perfectly efficient market. Since investors differ in their circumstances (consider the person in the oil business, discussed earlier), portfolios should be "tailored" to accommodate such differences. Successful performance of this task generally requires estimation of certain characteristics of securities, thereby justifying the use of financial analysis.

Needed Skills

To understand and estimate the risk and return of individual securities as well as groups of securities (such as industries), financial markets and the principles of valuation must be understood. Much of the material required for such an understanding can be found in this book. However, even more is required. Future prospects must be estimated and interrelationships assessed. This requires the skills of an economist and an understanding of industrial organization. To process relevant historical data, some command of quantitative methods is needed, along with an understanding of the nuances of accounting.

This book cannot provide all the material necessary to becoming a successful financial analyst. Books on accounting, economics, industrial organization, and quantitative methods are required. Instead, some techniques used by financial analysts are discussed, along with some of the pitfalls involved. In addition, sources of investment information are presented.

Technical Analysis

Technical Analysis A form of security analysis that attempts to forecast the movement in the prices of securities based primarily on historical price and volume trends in those securities.

One of the major divisions in the ranks of financial analysts is between those using fundamental analysis (known as fundamental analysts, or fundamentalists) and those using **technical analysis** (known as technical analysts, or technicians). The fundamentalist tends to look forward; the technician, backward. The fundamentalist is concerned with such things as future earnings and dividends, whereas the technician thinks little (if at all) about such things.

> Technical analysis is the study of the internal stock exchange information as such. The word "technical" implies a study of the market itself and not of those external factors which are reflected in the market ... [A]ll the relevant factors, whatever they may be, can be reduced to the

---

[7]If the added benefits exceeded the added costs, then it would be profitable to perform more financial analysis because the incremental benefits from doing so would cover the associated costs. If, on the other hand, the added costs exceeded the added benefits, then it would be profitable to cut back on the amount of financial analysis because costs would be reduced by an amount greater than benefits.

[8]For an interesting argument on why the existence of trading costs results in some investors' performing financial analysis in an efficient market, see Sanford J. Grossman, "On the Efficiency of Competitive Stock Markets Where Traders Have Diverse Information," *Journal of Finance* 31, no. 2 (May 1976): 573–585; Sanford J. Grossman and Joseph E. Stiglitz, "On the Impossibility of Informationally Efficient Markets," *American Economic Review* 70, no. 3 (June 1980): 393–408; and Bradford Cornell and Richard Roll, "Strategies for Pairwise Competitions in Markets and Organizations," *Bell Journal of Economics* 12, no. 1 (Spring 1981): 201–213.

volume of the stock exchange transactions and the level of share prices; or more generally, to the sum of the statistical information produced by the market.[9]

The technician usually attempts to predict short-term price movements and thus makes recommendations concerning the *timing* of purchases and sales of specific stocks, groups of stocks (such as industries) or of stocks in general. It is sometimes said that fundamental analysis is designed to answer the question What? and technical analysis to answer the question When?

The concept of technical analysis is completely at odds with the notion of efficient markets:

> ... the methodology of technical analysis ... rests upon the assumption that history tends to repeat itself in the stock exchange. If a certain pattern of activity has in the past produced certain results nine times out of ten, one can assume a strong likelihood of the same outcome whenever this pattern appears in the future. *It should be emphasized, however, that a large part of the methodology of technical analysis lacks a strictly logical explanation.*[10] (Emphasis added.)

Thus, technicians assert that the study of past patterns of things such as prices and volumes allows the investor to identify accurately times when certain specific stocks (or groups of stocks, or the market in general) are either overpriced or underpriced. Most (but not all) technical analysts rely on charts of stock prices and trading volumes. The appendix describes some of the more frequently used ones.

Early studies found little evidence showing technical analysis to be useful in enabling investors to "beat the market."[11] Many "proofs" of this ability were offered, but most committed at least one of the errors described earlier. However, several recent studies have indicated that technical analysis may be useful to investors.[12] The evidence presented in these studies can be divided into two groups based on the strategies involved. The first group, consisting of momentum and contrarian strategies, simply examines the returns on stocks over a time period that just ended in order to identify candidates for purchase and sale. The second group, consisting of moving average and trading range breakout strategies, makes such an identification based on the relationship of a security's price over a relatively short time period that just ended to its price over a relatively longer time period.

Momentum and Contrarian Strategies

Consider ranking a group of stocks based on the size of their returns over some time period that just ended. *Momentum investors* seek out for purchase those stocks that have recently risen significantly in price on the belief that they will continue to rise due to an upward shift in their demand curves. Conversely, those stocks that have recently fallen significantly in price are sold on the belief that their demand curves have shifted downward.

Investors who call themselves *contrarians* do just the opposite of what most other investors are doing in the market: they buy stocks that other have shunned and think of as

---

[9]Felix Rosenfeld, ed., *The Evaluation of Ordinary Shares,* a summary of the proceedings of the Eighth Congress of the European Federation of Financial Analysts Societies (Paris: Dunod, 1975): 297.

[10]Rosenfeld, *The Evaluation of Ordinary Shares,* pp. 297–298. For an argument that technical analysis can be of value in an efficient market, see David P. Brown and Robert H. Jennings, "On Technical Analysis," *Review of Financial Studies* 2, no. 4 (1989): 527–551. Also see Jack L. Treynor and Robert Ferguson, "In Defense of Technical Analysis," *Journal of Finance* 40, no. 3 (July 1985): 757–773; and Lawrence Blume, David Easley, and Maureen O'Hara, "Market Statistics and Technical Analysis: The Role of Volume," *Journal of Finance* 49, no. 1 (March 1994): 153–181.

[11]See, for example, Eugene F. Fama, "Efficient Capital Markets: A Review of Theory and Empirical Work," *Journal of Finance* 25, no. 2 (May 1970): 383–417.

[12]See, for example, Eugene F. Fama, "Efficient Capital Markets: II," *Journal of Finance* 46, no. 5 (December 1991): 1575–1617.

losers and they sell stocks that others have feverishly pursued and think of as winners. They do so in the belief that investors tend to overreact to news. That is, stocks that have plunged in price because of some recent piece of bad news (such as recently announced weak earnings) are thought to have fallen too far in price. Such stocks are viewed as being ready for a price rebound, as investors realize that they have overreacted to the bad news associated with the stock and subsequently drive the price upward toward the stock's fundamental value.

Similarly, stocks that have risen rapidly in price due to some recent piece of good news (such as recently announced strong earnings) are thought to have risen too far in price. These stocks are viewed as being ready for a price drop, as investors realize that they have overreacted to the good news associated with the stock and subsequently drive the price downward toward the stock's fundamental value. Researchers have tested strategies of this type. Their overall test design is discussed first, followed by the results.

The Test Design

Consider the following investment strategy:

1. Identify those stocks that have been listed on either the NYSE or AMEX (or just the NYSE). This focuses the technician's attention on established stocks.
2. Rank these stocks based on the size of their returns over a just-ending time period, referred to as the portfolio "formation period."
3. Assign some of those stocks that have the lowest average return in the formation period to the "loser" portfolio and some of those stocks that have the highest average return in this period to the "winner" portfolio.
4. Determine the returns on the winner and loser portfolios over a just-starting subsequent time period, referred to as the portfolio "test period."
5. Repeat the analysis all over again, starting with step 1, but moving forward one time period. Stop after several repetitions.
6. Determine the abnormal returns on the winner portfolio by subtracting the returns on a benchmark portfolio having a comparable level of risk (see Chapter 21); calculate the average of these abnormal returns. Similarly, determine the average abnormal returns on the loser portfolio.

If a momentum strategy works, then the winner portfolio should have a positive average abnormal return and the loser portfolio a negative one. Furthermore, the difference in their abnormal returns should be significantly positive. Conversely, if a contrarian strategy works, then the loser portfolio should have a positive abnormal return and the winner portfolio a negative one. and the difference should be significantly negative.

However, if stocks are priced efficiently, then their past price behaviour is useless in terms of its predictive value. Neither momentum nor contrarian strategies should "work"— winner portfolios should perform no differently from loser portfolios. Both portfolios should have average abnormal returns of approximately zero.

Test Results

Table 22.1 presents the test results. In part A, portfolios were formed based on their returns during the past week. All stocks with an above-average return were put into a winner portfolio and those with a below-average return were put into a loser portfolio. Then the returns on these two portfolios were tracked for the next week. When this was done repeatedly week by week from 1962 through 1986, it was found that there were marked differences in the annualized average abnormal returns on the two portfolios. Specifically, the returns were nearly −25% for the winner and 90% for the losers, with both returns being (as well as the other returns in the table) statistically significantly different from zero. Note

Table 22.1 Returns from Momentum and Contrarian Strategies.

Length of Portfolio Formation and Test Periods	Annualized Abnormal Returns		
	Winner Portfolio	Loser Portfolio	Winner Return less Loser Return
A. Weekly, 1962–1986: Top 50% and bottom 50% of NYSE and AMEX stocks	−24.9%	89.8%	−114.7%
B. Monthly, 1929–1982: Top 10% and bottom 10% of all NYSE and AMEX stocks	−11.6%	12.1%	−23.7%
C. Semiannually, 1962–1989: Top 10% and bottom 10% of all NYSE and AMEX stocks	8.7%	−3.5%	12.2%
D. Annually, 1929–1982: Top 10% and bottom 10% of all NYSE and AMEX stocks[a]	5.0%	−6.1%	11.1%
E. Three years, 1926–1982: Top 35 and bottom 35 NYSE stocks	−1.7%	6.5%	−8.2%
F. Five years, 1926–1982: Top 50 and bottom 50 NYSE stocks	−2.4%	7.2%	−9.6%

[a]Abnormal returns were measured over one month subsequent to the portfolio formation date.

SOURCE: Adapted from: A. Bruce N. Lehmann, "Fads, Martingales, and Market Efficiency," *Quarterly Journal of Economics* 105, no. 1 (February 1990): 16. B. Narasimhan Jegadeesh, "Evidence of Predictable Behavior of Security Returns," *Journal of Finance* 45, no. 3 (July 1990): 890–891. C. Narasimhan Jegadeesh and Sheridan Titman, "Returns to Buying Winners and Selling Losers: Implications for Stock Market Efficiency," *Journal of Finance* 48, no. 1 (March 1993): 79. D. Narasimhan Jegadeesh, "Evidence of Predictable Behavior of Security Returns," *Journal of Finance* 45, no. 3 (July 1990): 890–891. E. Werner F. M. De Bondt and Richard Thaler, "Does the Stock Market Overreact?" *Journal of Finance* 40, no. 3 (July 1985): 799. F. Werner F. M. De Bondt and Richard Thaler, "Further Evidence on Investor Overreaction and Stock Market Seasonality," *Journal of Finance* 42, no. 3 (July 1987): 561.

that a similar but not as extreme observation is apparent in part B, where the time frame is one month instead of a week.[13] Overall, this evidence indicates that contrarian strategies hold promise. Interestingly, the correction for the overreaction is asymmetric in part A because the losers rebound by a much larger percentage than the winners fall. This suggests that contrarians should concentrate more on identifying losers than on winners if they are going to focus on weekly returns.

In part C of Table 22.1, portfolios were formed based on their returns over the past six months. The 10% of stocks with the highest returns were put in the winner portfolio whereas the 10% with the lowest returns were put in the loser portfolio. Tracking their returns over the next six months revealed significant differences. In complete contrast to parts A and B, now the winners have a much higher average abnormal return than the

---

[13]There are other studies that present evidence that is consistent with these results. See Barr Rosenberg, Kenneth Reid, and Ronald Lanstein, "Persuasive Evidence of Market Inefficiency," *Journal of Portfolio Management* 11, no. 3 (Spring 1985): 9–16; John S. Howe, "Evidence on Stock Market Overreaction," *Financial Analysts Journal* 42, no. 4 (July–August 1986): 74–77; and Andrew W. Lo and A. Craig MacKinlay, "When Are Contrarian Profits Due to Stock Market Overreaction?" *Review of Financial Studies* 3, no. 2 (1990): 175–205.

losers, suggesting that momentum strategies have promise. Stocks that shot up in price over six months continued to go up during the next six months, whereas those that plunged over six months continued their plunge. Although not quite as strong, similar results were observed when the top 10% and bottom 10% were identified based on a full year's returns, as shown in part D.[14]

Oddly, parts E and F show that the momentum strategy would not have worked if the winner and loser portfolios were formed based on three-year or five-year stock returns. (It should be noted that there are subtle differences in how the portfolios in parts E and F were formed.) Instead, the contrarian strategy appears to have worked once again. Note that the average annual abnormal return in part E on the loser portfolio was +6.5%. Conversely, the average annual abnormal return on the winner portfolio was −1.7%, resulting in a significant difference of 8.2%. Part F shows that similar results were obtained when portfolios were formed based on returns over the previous five years.[15] As in part A, the correction for the overreaction is asymmetric in that losers rebound by a much larger percentage than the winners fall.

In summary, there does appear to be some merit to the contrarian strategy for both very short (a week or month) and very long (three to five years) time periods.[16] Surprisingly, for intermediate periods such as six months and one year, an exact opposite strategy—momentum—seems to have merit. Unfortunately, both strategies involve a high degree of turnover, as portfolios are reconstituted frequently—particularly for the weekly

---

[14]One explanation for these results that has been offered is that investors underreact to quarterly earnings announcements. See Chapter 18, and Victor L. Bernard, Jacob K. Thomas, and Jeffrey S. Abarbanell, "How Sophisticated Is the Market in Interpreting Earnings News?" *Journal of Applied Corporate Finance* 6, no. 2 (Summer 1993): 54–63. Another related observation involved buying the 10 highest dividend-yielding stocks in the Dow Jones Industrial Average (DJIA) and holding them for one year, at which point the portfolio was revised accordingly for another year. From 1973 through 1992 this strategy outperformed the DJIA by 5.15% per year, on average. See Dale L. Domian, David A. Louton, and Irene M. Seahawk, "The Dow Dividend Strategy: How it Works—and Why," *AAII Journal* 16, no. 4 (May 1994): 7–10.

[15]A puzzling observation associated with part F was that 5% of the 7.2% abnormal return for the loser portfolio was earned during the Januaries that occurred during the test period. Conversely, −.8% of the −2.4% abnormal return for the winners was earned during Januaries. Hence, the January anomaly (discussed in the appendix to Chapter 16) appears to somehow be intertwined with the long-term contrarian strategy.

[16]It should be noted that other studies have examined contrarian strategies and have been unable to confirm the usefulness of such strategies. In two of these studies it was argued that the benchmark portfolio returns were incorrectly determined. This means that the abnormal returns were not calculated correctly because by definition they are equal to the difference between the returns on the portfolio and its benchmark. In a third study, the alleged cause of the overreaction—security analysis underpredicting earnings on losers and overpredicting earnings on winners—was contested. As fourth study suggested that the size effect (discussed in the appendix to Chapter 16) was largely responsible for the results because losers tend to be smaller than winners. Lastly, a fifth study argued that incorrect prices were used when the costs of buying and selling stocks were determined in arriving at the results reflected in parts E and F of Table 22.1. However, these studies have, in turn, been contested in a sixth study. Specifically, after taking the objections into consideration it was found that losers outperform winners by 5% to 10% per year, with the difference being the largest when only small firms were classified into winners and losers.

The six studies are, respectively, K. C. Chan, "On Contrarian Investment Strategy," *Journal of Business* 61, no. 2 (April 1988): 147–163; Ray Ball and S. P. Kothari, "Nonstationary Expected Returns: Implications for Tests of Market Efficiency and Serial Correlations in Returns," *Journal of Financial Economics* 25, no. 1 (November 1989): 51–74; April Klein, "A Direct Test of the Cognitive Bias Theory of Share Price Reversals," *Journal of Accounting and Economics* 13, no. 2 (July 1990): 155–166; Paul Zarowin, "Size, Seasonality, and Stock Market Overreaction," *Journal of Quantitative Analysis* 25, no. 1 (March 1990): 113–125; Jennifer Conrad and Gautam Kaul, "Long-term Overreaction or Biases in Computed Returns?" *Journal of Finance* 48, no. 1 (March 1993): 39–63; and Navin Chopra, Josef Lakonishok, and Jay R. Ritter, "Measuring Abnormal Performance: Do Stocks Overreact?" *Journal of Financial Economics* 31, no. 2 (April 1992): 235–268.

contrarian strategy. As the strategies would incur substantial transaction costs, it remains to be seen whether they are profitable after such costs are fully accounted for.[17]

Adding to the puzzle is the behaviour of Canadian stocks. For one-year test periods the results were similar to those in the United States in that a momentum strategy seemed to work (as in part D of Table 22.1). For three-year and five-year test periods, neither a momentum nor a contrarian strategy worked (unlike parts E and F of Table 22.1).[18]

Moving Average and Trading Range Breakout Strategies

Consider the following investment strategy:

1. Calculate the average closing price of a given stock over the last 200 trading days.
2. Take today's closing price and divide it by the 200-day average to form a short-to-long price ratio.
3. If the ratio is greater than one, this is a buy signal that indicates that the stock is to be bought tomorrow. If the ratio is less than one, this is a sell signal that indicates that the stock is to be sold tomorrow.
4. Tomorrow after closing, repeat the above process.
5. At the end of a test period, calculate the average daily return during both the "buy" days and the "sell" days.

If the stock market is efficient, the average return during the buy days should be approximately the same as the average return during the sell days. That is, *the difference in their returns should be approximately zero*. However, technical analysis might have merit if they are significantly different.

A study examined this strategy using daily data from 1897 to 1986, a total of over 25 000 trading days. However, the daily closing level of the Dow Jones Industrial Average (DJIA) was used instead of daily closing prices for individual stocks. As shown in part A of Table 22.2, this strategy resulted in markedly different returns on buy and sell days. In particular, the annualized average return on buy days was 10.7%, whereas the return on sell days was −6.1%. *The difference of 16.8% was statistically significantly different from zero (as were the differences in the other parts of the table).*

Because this strategy classifies every day as either a buy day or a sell day, thereby allowing a given stock to be bought on consecutive days, it is referred to as a variable-length moving average strategy. However, it can result in many trades over the course of a year, as an investor using it could be "whipsawed" into buying and selling repeatedly. In order to reduce the frequency of changing positions from buying to selling, or selling to buying, the strategy can be modified as follows to become a fixed-length moving average strategy. Buy signals are now generated only when the ratio *changes* from less than one to greater than one, and sell signals are generated only when the ratio *changes* from greater than one to less than one. Furthermore, when a buy signal is generated, the stock is bought the next day and then held for 10 days. Similarly, when a sell signal is generated, the stock is sold and not bought for 10 days. In either case, when the 10 days are over, the investor starts looking again for a buy or sell signal. Whereas the variable-length strategy classified every day

---

[17]Apparently significant returns can be earned from the weekly strategy if transaction costs are small (such as for large institutional investors). However, larger transaction costs result in negative net returns. See Bruce N. Lehmann, "Fads, Martingales, and Market Efficiency," *Quarterly Journal of Economics* 105, no. 1 (February 1990): 1–28. For an argument that Lehmann has underestimated the size of transaction costs, see Jennifer Conrad, Mustafa N. Gultekin, and Gautam Kaul, "Profitability of Short-term Contrarian Portfolio Strategies," unpublished paper, The University of Michigan, 1991.

[18]See Lawrence Kryzanowski and Hao Zhang, "The Contrarian Investment Strategy Does Not Work in Canadian Markets," *Journal of Financial and Quantitative Analysis* 27, no. 3 (September 1992): 383–395.

as either a buy or sell day, there can be days that are not classified as either buy or sell with the fixed-length strategy.

Part A of Table 22.2 shows that the fixed-length moving average strategy performed similarly to the variable length one. The annualized average return on buy days was 13.8% and on sell days was −4.8%, resulting in a significant difference of 18.6%. On average there were about 1.3 and 1.7 buy and sell signals per year, respectively.

The trading range breakout strategy is similar to the fixed-length moving average strategy. Here the high and low prices over the past 200 trading days are noted. A buy signal is generated on a given day only when that day's closing price is greater than the high, provided that the previous day's closing price was less than the high. Conversely, a sell signal arises when the closing price moves from being above the low on one day to being below the low on the next day. When a buy signal is generated, the stock is bought the next day and then held for 10 days. Similarly, when a sell signal is generated, the stock is sold and not bought for 10 days. In either case, when the 10 days are over, the investor starts looking again for a buy or sell signal.

Part B of Table 22.2 shows that the trading range breakout strategy performed similarly to the two moving average strategies. The annualized average returns on buy days was 11.8% and on sell days was −5.8%, with a significant difference of 17.6%. On average there were about 5.2 and 2.0 buy and sell signals per year, respectively.

The Bottom Line

The four strategies reported in Tables 22.1 and 22.2 have been rigorously tested, avoiding the pitfalls mentioned earlier. Furthermore, although not reported, slight variations among the strategies had only a minor effect on their results. However, the usefulness of such technical strategies remains an open question subject to much debate. Despite appearing to be profitable, even after considering transaction costs, it is quite possible that a more complete consideration of these costs (including such things as the impact of bid-ask spreads) will reveal that they are incapable of generating abnormal profits. Hence, evaluating investment systems will not always provide unambiguous answers on their potential usefulness. Furthermore, it has been speculated that the commonplace usage of computerized trading programs designed to implement technical strategies will ultimately eliminate any potential such strategies have for generating abnormal profits.[19] Nevertheless, the apparent success of these strategies offers a challenge to those who contend that the stock market is highly efficient.

Table 22.2	Returns from Moving Average and Trading Range Breakout Strategies.		
	Annualized Average Returns		
	Buy Signal	Sell Signal	Buy Return Less Sell Return
A. Moving average tests:			
Variable length	10.7%	−6.1%	16.8%
Fixed length	13.8	−4.8	18.6
B. Trading range breakout tests:	11.8%	−5.8%	17.6%

SOURCE: Adapted from William Brock, Josef Lakonishok, and Blake LeBaron, "Simple Technical Trading Rules and the Stochastic Properties of Stock Returns," *Journal of Finance* 47, no. 5 (December 1992): 1739, 1741, 1742. Based on one-day short and 200-day long periods during 1897 to 1986 with no filter, annualized assuming that there are 260 trading days in a year and 26 ten-day trading periods in a year.

[19]Lehmann, "Fads, Martingales, and Market Efficiency," p. 26.

Fundamental Analysis

The rest of this chapter is concerned with the principles of fundamental analysis of common stocks. Although technical analysis is used by many investors, fundamental analysis is far more prevalent. Furthermore, unlike technical analysis, it is an essential activity if capital markets are to be efficient.

Top-down Versus Bottom-up Forecasting

Fundamental analysts forecast, among other things, future levels of the economy's gross domestic product, future sales and earnings for a number of industries, and future sales and earnings for an even larger number of firms. Eventually such forecasts are converted to estimates of expected returns of specific stocks and, perhaps, certain industries and the stock market itself. In some cases the conversion is made explicitly. For example, an estimate of next year's earnings per share for a firm may be multiplied by a projected price-earnings ratio in order to estimate the expected price of the firm's shares a year hence, thereby allowing a forecast of the expected return to be made. In other cases the conversion is implicit. For example, stocks with projected earnings exceeding consensus estimates may be placed on an "approved" list.

Some investment organizations that employ financial analysts follow a sequential **top-down approach** to forecasting. With this approach, the financial analysts first make forecasts for the economy, then for industries, and finally for companies. The industry forecasts are based on the forecasts for the economy and, in turn, the company forecasts are based on the forecasts for both its industry and the economy.

Other investment organizations begin with estimates of the prospects for companies and then build to estimates of the prospects for industries and ultimately the economy. Such a **bottom-up approach** may unknowingly involve inconsistent assumptions. For example, one analyst may use one forecast of foreign exchange rates in projecting the foreign sales of company A, whereas another analyst may use a different forecast in projecting the foreign sales of company B. Top-down systems are less susceptible to this danger, since all the analysts in the organization would use the same forecast of exchange rates.

In practice, a combination of the two approaches is often employed. For example, forecasts are made for the economy in a top-down manner. These forecasts then provide a setting within which financial analysts make bottom-up forecasts for individual companies. The sum of the individual forecasts should be consistent with the original economy-wide forecast.[20] If not, the process is repeated (perhaps with additional controls) to ensure consistency.

Probabilistic Forecasting

Explicit **probabilistic forecasting** often focuses on economy-wide forecasts, since uncertainty at this level is of the greatest importance in determining the risk and expected return of a well-diversified portfolio. A few alternative economic scenarios may be forecast, along with their respective probability of occurrence. Then accompanying projections are made of the prospects for industries, companies, and share prices. Such an exercise provides an idea of the likely sensitivities of different stocks to surprises concerning the economy. By assigning probabilities to the different scenarios, risks may also be estimated.

Top-down Forecasting A sequential approach to security analysis that entails first making forecasts for the economy, then for industries, and finally for individual companies. Each level of forecast is conditional on the previous level of forecast made.

Bottom-up Forecasting A sequential approach to security analysis that entails first making forecasts for individual companies, then for industries, and finally for the economy. Each level of forecast is conditional on the previous level of forecast made.

Probabilistic Forecasting A form of security analysis that begins with a series of economic scenarios, along with their respective probabilities of occurrence. Under each of these scenarios, accompanying projections are made as to the prospects for various industries, companies, and stock prices.

---

[20]Input-output analysis is sometimes used to ensure consistency between various industries and the economy in aggregate. This type of analysis is based on the notion that the output of certain industries (for example, the steel industry) is the input for certain other industries (for example, the household appliance industry).

Econometric Models

An **econometric model** is a statistical model that provides a means of forecasting the levels of certain variables, known as **endogenous variables**. In order to make these forecasts, the model relies on assumptions that have been made in regard to the levels of certain other variables, known as **exogenous variables**. For example, the level of next year's car sales may be specified by an econometric model to be related to next year's level of gross domestic product and interest rates. The values of next year's gross domestic product and interest rates, the exogenous variables, must be provided in order to forecast next year's car sales, the endogenous variable. The model may be extremely complex or it may be a simple formula that can be used with a desk calculator. In any event, it should involve a blend of economics and statistics, where economics is used to suggest the forms of relevant relationships and statistical procedures are applied to historical data to estimate the exact nature of the relationships involved.

Some investment organizations utilize large-scale econometric models to translate predictions about such factors as the federal budget, expected consumer spending, and planned business investment into predictions of future levels of gross domestic product, inflation, and unemployment. Several firms and non-profit organizations maintain such models, selling either the forecasts or the computer program itself to investment organizations, corporate planners, public agencies, and others.

The developers of large-scale models usually provide several "standard" predictions, based on different sets of assumptions about the exogenous variables; some also assign probabilities to the alternative predictions. In some cases, users can substitute their own sets of assumptions and subsequently examine the resulting predictions.

Large-scale econometric models of this type employ many equations that describe many important relationships. Although estimates of the magnitudes of such relationships are obtained from historical data, these estimates may or may not enable the model to work well in the future. When predictions turn out to be poor, it is sometimes said that there have been structural changes in the underlying economic relationships. However, the failure may be due to the influence of factors omitted from the model. In any event, inaccurate predictions require changes in either the size of the estimates or the basic form of the econometric model, or even both. Rare indeed is the user who does not "fine-tune" (or completely overhaul) such a model, from time to time in light of further experience.

Financial Statement Analysis

For some, the image of a typical financial analyst is that of a gnome, fully equipped with green eyeshade, poring over financial statements in a back room. Though the physical description is rarely accurate, it is true that many analysts do study financial statements in an attempt to predict the future.

A company's financial statements can be regarded as the output of a model of the firm—a model designed by management, the company's accountants, and (indirectly) the tax authorities. Different companies use different models, meaning they treat similar events in different ways. One reason this is possible is because generally accepted accounting principles (GAAP), as established by the Canadian Institute of Chartered Accountants (CICA), allow a certain degree of latitude in how to account for various events. Examples include the method of depreciating assets (straight-line or accelerated) and the method of valuing inventory.

To understand a company fully and to compare it with others that use different accounting procedures, the financial analyst must be a financial detective, looking for clues in footnotes and the accompanying text that discuss how the financial statements were prepared. Those who take bottom-line figures such as earnings per share on faith may be more surprised by future developments than those who try to look behind the accounting veil.

The ultimate goal of the fundamental analyst is to determine the values of the outstanding claims on a firm's income (claimants include the firm's bondholders and shareholders). The firm's income must first be projected; then the possible distributions of that income among the claimants must be considered, with relevant probabilities assessed.

In practice, shortcut procedures are often used. Many analysts focus on reported accounting figures, even though such numbers may not adequately reflect true economic values. In addition, simple measures are often used to assess complex relationships. For example, some analysts attempt to estimate the probability that short-term creditors will be paid in full and on time by examining the ratio of liquid assets to the amount of short-term debt (known as the *quick ratio*). Similarly, the probability that interest will be paid to bondholders in a timely fashion is often estimated by examining the ratio of earnings before interest and taxes to the periodic amount of such interest payments (known as *times interest earned*). Often the prospects for a firm's common shares are estimated by examining the ratio of earnings after taxes to the book value of equity (known as *return on equity*).

Financial statement analysis can help an analyst understand a company's current situation, where it may be going, what factors affect it, and how these factors affect it. If others are doing such analysis and doing it well, it will be difficult to find mispriced securities in this manner. However, it should be possible to more accurately identify firms likely to go bankrupt, firms with higher or lower betas, and firms with greater or lesser sensitivities to major factors. Increased understanding of such aspects may well provide ample rewards.

Analysts who regularly work with financial statements develop a keen sense of what items are important to their research. Those items will vary depending on the type of security being examined (for example, the common stock of a company as opposed to its debt securities). Furthermore, the list of critical items may vary from industry to industry and from company to company. Moreover, one analyst may approach the analysis of a particular company's financial statements differently from another analyst. Despite these differences, certain standard techniques are commonly applied and are discussed next. Understanding the analysis of financial statements is facilitated by applying the process to a specific example. In the discussion below, general steps and observations are presented along with reference to the Dayton Hudson Corporation, a large retailing company whose stock is both listed on the New York Stock Exchange and is a constituent of the Standard and Poor's 500 index.[21]

Dayton Hudson Corporation
www.dhc.com

Company Background

The analysis of a company's financial statements in a security analyst's research report typically begins with an overview of the company. While the reporting analyst presumably knows the company well, the purpose of the overview is to acquaint readers with the research about the company. Among other topics that this discussion may include are a short corporate history, a description of the company's lines of business, a listing of its primary competitors, a description of the key business challenges facing the company, and a summary of basic financial information.

---

[21]The issues discussed below are equally applicable to Canadian firms and their analysis.

Background Information

Dayton Hudson Corporation is one of the largest general merchandise retailers in the United States. The company has its roots in the department store business, even though today the vast majority of its sales and profits are derived from discount retailing. The J.L. Hudson Company was founded in Detroit in 1881 and the Dayton Department Store Company was established in 1902 in Minneapolis. Both companies were predominately department stores with long and storied traditions in their Midwestern markets when they merged in 1969 to form the Dayton Hudson Corporation. In 1963 the Dayton Company opened its first Target store, an initial entrance into the low-margin merchandising business. In 1978, the Dayton Hudson Corporation acquired Mervyn's, a West Coast moderate-priced promotional department store chain. In 1990, the company purchased Chicago-based Marshall Field & Company, thereby establishing its dominance in the department store business in the Upper Midwest.

Today, Dayton Hudson Corporation operates three lines of retailing business: Target, Mervyn's, and the Department Stores Division. Target is an upscale discount store business with a high-volume, low-margin orientation. Target offers high-quality merchandise, convenience, and competitive prices. Mervyn's is a moderate-priced family department store, specializing in national brand and private-label clothing and other soft goods. The Department Stores Division operates stores that emphasize fashion leadership and quality merchandise in the moderate to high-price range supported by superior customer service.

Due to its multiline business, Dayton Hudson Corporation encounters a number of different retail competitors. Its Target stores compete primarily against Walmart and Kmart on a national level. Mervyn's competes against J.C. Penney and Sears, Roebuck and Company, and to a lesser extent against Kohl's, a rapidly growing regional chain. Finally, in the Midwest, the Department Stores Division faces Federated Department Stores, May Department Stores Company, and Nordstrom.

Dayton Hudson confronts a number of imposing business challenges, including:

- Can the company sustain the rebound in earnings that occurred in 1996 following a poor year in 1995? Further, can it meet its goal of 15% long-run annual earnings growth in a highly competitive industry?
- Can it maintain the extraordinary growth of its Target stores?
- Can stagnant sales growth at its Mervyn's and Department Stores be reversed?
- Can the multidivision corporation become better organized to take advantage of synergies between its operations and achieve increased economies of scale?

Review of Accounting Statements

From an investment perspective, the analysis of a company's accounting statements is not an end in itself. Rather it is a means to identify financial aspects of a company that may have direct relevance to understanding the intrinsic values and risks of the company's securities. The analyst will want to obtain access to a wide range of financial information about the company under review. Much of that information is found in three primary accounting statements issued by the company in its annual report: the balance sheet, the income statement, and the statement of cash flows.

Statistical Abstract			
Ticker/Exchange	DH/NYSE	Dividend	$0.64
Price (31-Aug-97)	$57.000	Dividend Yield	1.05%
52-week Price Range	$30.750 – $64.625	Book Value per Share	$17.33
Earnings per Share (1996) (Fully diluted)	$1.95	Market Capitalization	$13.1 billion
Sales (1996)	$25.4 billion	Net income (1996)	$463 million

Balance Sheet

The balance sheet (also called the statement of financial position) presents a snapshot of the company's financial position at a point in time. The statement describes amounts or levels of various items. In particular, the balance sheet presents a listing of the company's *assets*, *liabilities*, and *shareholders' equity*.

Assets represent the company's economic resources. An asset is an item that has the potential to generate economic benefits (that is, cash inflows) for the company in the future. For example, plant and equipment can produce goods or services that can be sold to customers for cash. Liabilities are claims on the company's economic resources. These claims are usually of a specified amount and must be satisfied as of a certain date in the future. Both assets and liabilities are classified on the balance sheet as either current or long-term. Current assets consist of cash or other assets, such as marketable securities, inventory, and accounts receivable, that are expected to be turned into cash in the near future. Current liabilities are expected to be (or are at risk of being) discharged shortly, usually within one year. Long-term assets are held and used for several years while long-term liabilities are due more than a year in the future. Shareholders' equity (or *net worth*) is a residual claim of the owners of the company on the company's assets, after all liabilities have been extinguished.

The balance sheet does not show all of a company's assets and liabilities. For example, the capabilities of a management team are often the company's most valuable asset, yet the value of those capabilities is nowhere to be found on the balance sheet. On the liability side, the value of operating leases signed by the company may be large, yet are relegated to footnotes in the company's annual report.

Because the balance sheet represents the resources of the company and the claims on those resources, it must be the case that assets equal liabilities plus shareholders' equity. In this sense, the components of the balance sheet must balance. In fact, a balance sheet is often presented with assets and their values listed on the left-hand side and liabilities and shareholders' equity and their values listed on the right-hand side. Balance sheet items are generally reported at their unadjusted or adjusted acquisition costs. For example, a building will be carried on the balance sheet at its purchase price plus the value of any physical improvements less accumulated depreciation. Accounts receivable will be reported as the actual amount of the account less an allowance for doubtful accounts.

Dayton Hudson Corporation

Table 22.3 presents the fiscal year-end consolidated balance sheets of the Dayton Hudson Corporation over the period 1990 to 1996.

A look at the company's balance sheets confirms that Dayton Hudson Corporation is a large company and is growing at a fairly rapid pace. The company's assets now total over $12 billion and have grown at almost an 8% annual rate since 1990. Property and equipment, composed primarily of the company's stores and fixtures, represents the largest asset, making up 56% of 1996 total assets. Inventories, at 23% of 1996 total assets, are also a prominent asset. Somewhat surprisingly, accounts receivable, at 13% of 1996 total assets, have grown much more slowly than total assets. This is due in part to the company's policy of selling off a portion of its receivables to investors through a securitization process similar to that used to create mortgage-backed securities. (Asset-backed securities are discussed in Chapter 13.) It is also due to the increasing importance of Target in the company's total financial picture; as a discount retailer, Target tends to carry relatively low levels of receivables.

On the liability side, the company's long-term debt relative to total assets is almost 36% in 1996. That debt has been declining as a proportion of total assets after reaching a high of 45% following the 1990 acquisition of Marshall Field & Company. Shareholders' equity now represents about 28% of total assets. Net working capital (current assets less current liabilities) is almost 10% of total assets, down from over 14% in 1990. Again, this decline is again due to the growth of Target, which has a higher asset turnover than the other two operating divisions.

Income Statement

The income statement (also called the statement of earnings) indicates the *earnings* (or *profits* or *net income*) of the company (see Table 22.4). Instead of presenting levels at a point in time, the income

Table 22.3 Dayton Hudson Corporation Consolidated Balance Sheets ($ millions).

	1990	1991	1992	1993	1994	1995	1996
Assets							
Cash & equivalents	$92	$96	$117	$321	$147	$175	$201
Receivables	1 407	1 430	1 514	1 536	1 810	1 510	1 720
Inventories	2 016	2 381	2 618	2 497	2 777	3 018	3 031
Other	143	125	165	157	225	252	488
Total Current Assets	$3 658	$4 032	$4 414	$4 511	$4 959	$4 955	$5 440
Property & equipment (net)	4 525	5 102	5 563	5 947	6 385	7 294	7 467
Other assets	341	351	360	320	353	321	482
Total Assets	$8 524	$9 485	$10 337	$10 778	$11 697	$12 570	$13 389
Liabilities and							
Shareholder's Equity	$357	$453	$394	$373	$209	$182	$233
Short-term debt	1 267	1 324	1 596	1 654	1 961	2 247	2 528
Accounts payable	638	705	849	903	1 045	957	1 168
Accrued liabilities	160	98	125	145	175	137	182
Taxes payable	$2 422	$2 580	$2 964	$3 075	$3 390	$3 523	$4 111
Total Current Liabilities	3 682	4 227	4 330	4 279	4 488	4 959	4 808
Long-term debt	372	447	557	687	626	685	608
Deferred taxes and other	$6 476	$7 254	$7 851	$8 041	$8 504	$9 167	$9 599
Total Liabilities	$2 048	$2 231	$2 486	$2 737	$3 193	$3 403	$3 790
Shareholder's Equity							
Total Liabilities and **Shareholder's Equity**	$8 524	$9 485	$10 337	$10 778	$11 967	$12 570	$13 389

statement reports flows that occur over a period of time. A company's net income is the difference between its sales (or revenues) and expenses. Sales measure the inflow of assets from selling goods and services to the company's customers. Expenses measure the outflow of assets (or the increase in liabilities) associated with generating sales. Ultimately, the success of a company is directly related to producing a sufficient surplus of sales over expenses.

The income statement provides a breakdown of the sources of sales and expenses for the company. Sales are reported net of returns and allowances. Expenses are divided into two groups. The first group are those expenses, such as costs of goods sold, selling, general, and administrative (S, G, & A) expenses, and depreciation and amortization, that are directly associated with producing and selling the company's goods and services. These are called *operating expenses*. The second group are costs associated with financing and taxes on the company's income. These are called *non-operating expenses*. Thus, the income statement has the following general format:

Sales – Operating expenses

= Operating income (or earnings before interest and taxes, *EBIT*) – Interest expense

= Pre-tax income (or earnings before taxes, *EBT*) – Taxes

= Net income (or earnings after taxes, *EAT*)

The income statement is related to the beginning and end-of-period balance sheets. Net income that is not distributed to shareholders in the form of dividends increases retained earnings. On the balance sheet it increases the end-of-period shareholders' equity and reflects an increase in one or more asset items and (or) decrease of one or more liability items.

Earnings are often presented on a "per share" basis. As Chapter 17 discussed, analysts commonly use the ratio of a stock's market price to the company's earnings per share as a measure of the stock's relative valuation. To calculate earnings per share, net income is divided by the average number of common shares outstanding over the period. To make comparisons with current numbers relevant, historical earnings per share must be adjusted for any stock splits or stock dividends that may have occurred after the earnings were originally reported. For example, if last year's income statement shows earnings per share of $6 and this year's of $4, it would be tempting to believe that the firm was less profitable this year. However, suppose that a two-for-one stock split took place right after the last year's earnings were announced. Consequently, in this year's financial statements, last year's earnings per share would be reported as $6/2 = $3, thereby revealing the firm has actually been more, not less, profitable this year.

A company may issue securities, such as convertible bonds, convertible preferred stock, stock options, and warrants, that at some future date can be converted into common stock at the discretion of the company or the security holder, or sometimes both. Companies that issue these convertible securities must calculate per share earnings on a primary and fully diluted basis. The primary basis assumes no conversion of the securities into common shares, while the fully diluted basis assumes full conversion. Because the existence of additional common shares "dilutes" or reduces the net income available to existing common shareholders, fully diluted earnings per share will generally be less than or equal to primary earnings per share, with the difference depending on the existence and the terms of the dilutive securities.[22]

Sometimes a company will report non-recurring (or one-time) expenses or income. While these transactions may be intended to enhance the future operating profitability of the company, they are not expect to appear again on the company's income statement. The analyst generally will want to exclude these transactions in evaluating the company's operating performance.

Confusingly, some non-recurring transactions are categorized as extraordinary items. Companies that incur these transactions must report them separately. The result is two sets of net income and earnings per share calculations: both before and after consideration of the extraordinary items. However, all non-recurring transactions are not deemed extraordinary items. In those cases, the transactions enter the income statement as operating items and consequently only one set of net income and earnings per share will be reported. To summarize:

Non-recurring Items

Extraordinary	Not Extraordinary
1. reported separately	1. not reported separately
2. two sets of income figures	2. one set of income figures

Certain companies regularly report large transactions identified as non-recurring. For example, from 1985 to 1994, AT&T reported four non-recurring restructuring charges totalling $14.2 billion. The company's total reported net income over this period was only $10.3 billion. The high frequency of non-recurring transactions at some companies has led analysts to question the reporting companies' motives and to wonder just how "non-recurring" the transactions truly are.

Dayton Hudson Corporation

Table 22.4 shows the annual consolidated income statements for Dayton Hudson Corporation from 1990 to 1996.

Dayton Hudson Corporation's revenues have grown at a 9.5% annual rate over the last six years. Earnings, on the other hand, have not kept pace, increasing only 2.5% per year on average. In the mid-1990s, the company's net income stagnated. In fact, in 1995 it was lower than in 1990. The primary explanation for the slow growth in earnings was the company's lack of pricing power to expand revenues relative to operating expenses, as well insufficiently tight controls over S, G, & A expenses. As a result,

---

[22]In 1997, the Financial Accounting Standards Board proposed rule no. 128 that would affect how earnings per share are reported. The rule would replace *primary earnings per share,* which factors in some dilution for certain common-stock equivalents, with an entirely undiluted measure of earnings per share called *basic earnings per share. Fully diluted earnings per share* would remain calculated in almost the same manner as before, but would now be called *diluted earnings per share.* Financial analysts will have two distinct measures of earnings per share, one with no dilution and one with full dilution. For many companies, the change will be insignificant. For some companies however, the change will highlight the large impact that dilutive securities, such as warrants and employee stock options, potentially can have on earnings per share. The same general rules apply in Canada.

| Table 22.4 | Dayton Hudson Corporation Consolidated Income Statements ($ millions). |

	1990	1991	1992	1993	1994	1995	1996
Revenue (Sales)	$14 739	$16 115	$17 927	$19 233	$21 311	$23 516	$25 371
Expenses							
Cost of goods sold	$10 652	$11 751	$13 129	$14 164	$15 636	$17 527	$18 628
S, G, & A expenses	2 478	2 801	2 978	3 175	3 614	4 043	4 289
Depreciation and amortization	369	410	459	498	548	594	650
Other taxes	256	283	313	343	373	409	445
Non-recurring operating expenses	0	0	0	0	0	0	134
Total Operating Expenses	$13 755	$15 245	$16 879	$18 180	$20 171	$22 573	$24 146
Operating Income (EBIT)	$984	$870	$1 048	$1 053	$1 140	$943	$1 225
Interest expense	325	398	437	446	426	442	442
Pre-tax Income (EBT)	$659	$472	$611	$607	$714	$501	$783
Taxes	249	171	228	232	280	190	309
Net Income (EAT)	410	301	383	375	434	311	$474
Extraordinary items	0	0	0	23	0	0	11
Net Income after Extraordinary Items	$410	$301	$383	$352	$434	$311	$463
Earnings per Share (Fully diluted)	$1.72	$1.24	$1.61	$1.59	$1.84	$1.30	$2.00
Extraordinary charges	0.00	0.00	0.00	(0.18)	0.00	0.00	(0.05)
Earnings per Share (Fully diluted)	$1.72	$1.24	$1.61	$1.41	$1.84	$1.30	$1.95

operating expenses grew from 93% of sales in 1990 to 96% of sales in 1995. Note, however, that in 1996 the company experienced a significant rebound in net income, in part due to a concerted cost control campaign. In addition, note that in both 1993 and 1996, Dayton Hudson reported charges to earnings related to earthquake damage and an early redemption of long-term debt, respectively. Hence, in both years extraordinary charges were reported, resulting in two sets of net income and earnings per share figures. In addition, in 1996 the company reported a large non-recurring, operating expense related to the closing of stores in several states. This expense, however, was not classified as an extraordinary item.

Statement of Cash Flows

Analysts are concerned with the amount of cash that a company generates. In the long-run, a company can only afford to make payments to its security-holders if it produces surplus cash flow from its operations. Even profitable companies may find themselves facing cash shortages that, in the extreme, can lead to bankruptcy. In the short-run, dwindling cash balances may be augmented by bor-

rowing or through the sales of assets. However, those strategies may adversely affect the company's future profitability.

The statement of cash flows shows how a company's cash balance changed from one year to the next. It assists the analyst in evaluating the ability of the company to meet its obligations for cash, its needs for future external financing, and the effectiveness of its financing and investing strategies. The statement of cash flows is divided into three parts:

1. cash flow from operating activities,
2. cash flow from investing activities, and
3. cash flow from financing activities.

Construction of the statement of cash flows begins with a comparison of balance sheets from one period to another. Each activity of the corporation is classified into either operating, investing, or financing categories and identified as either inflows or outflows. For example, an increase in inventory constitutes an operating outflow of cash while an increase in long-term debt represents an inflow of financing cash.

To obtain cash flows from operating activities, the company's operating cash inflows are added to, and the operating cash outflows are subtracted from net income. Cash from investing activities are primarily calculated from changes in the property, plant, and equipment accounts. Cash flows from financing are associated with raising or reducing capital through debt or equity offerings or refinancings and the payment of dividends.

Closely related to these measures of cash flows is a company's *free cash flow*, which takes two forms. First of all, there is *free cash flow to the firm*, determined as:

After-tax operating income
+ Depreciation, amortization, and deferred taxes
− Increase in working capital
− Investment in fixed assets
= Free cash flow to the firm

Here after-tax operating income is equal to operating earnings times one minus the tax rate, that is, $EBIT(1 − t)$, or equivalently $EAT + tI$. Investment in fixed assets involves spending on items such as property, plant, and equipment. Thus, free cash flow to the firm is the cash generated by the company's operations that is available to all of the company's debt- and equityholders. Note that it is equivalent to the sum of cash flow from operating activities, cash flow from investing activities, and the after-tax cost of any interest and preferred stock dividend payments.

The second type of free cash flow is *free cash flow to equity*, defined as:

Net income
+ Depreciation, amortization, and deferred taxes
− Increase in working capital
− Investment in fixed assets
− Principal repayments
+ New debt issued
= Free cash flow to equity

Thus, free cash flow to equity represents cash flow generated by the company's operations that is left after the company has covered all its financial obligations, working capital needs, and fixed asset needs. Accordingly, it is what is left for the company to pay

out as dividends, although most companies do not use the entire amount for this purpose. Note that it is equal to the sum of cash flow from operations, cash flow from investing, cash flow from financing, and dividends.[23]

Dayton Hudson Corporation

Table 22.5 shows the annual consolidated statements of cash flows for Dayton Hudson Corporation from 1990 to 1996.

Dayton Hudson Corporation has a large need for cash to finance its capital expenditures program, a need that is primarily related to the rapid growth of its Target stores and is indicated by its reported total investing cash flow figures. The company meets much of these cash requirements through its net income and non-cash expenses (principally depreciation), as indicated by its total operating cash flow figures. Since 1992, cash from financing sources has generally been negative as indicated by its total financing cash flow figures, as the company has reduced its long-term debt outstanding as a proportion of total assets. Also interesting is the steadily increasing pattern in aggregate dividends paid while free cash flow to equity has been much more volatile, being sometimes above and sometimes below the amount of dividends paid.

Additional Financial Statement Information

The balance sheet, income statement, and statement of cash flows contain much of the financial statement information required by the analyst. However, considerable detail about the financial performance of the company also can be found in other parts of a company's annual report. Thus, as part of her research, the analyst will want to examine:

• Notes to the financial statements
• Management discussion and analysis
• Auditor's report

The notes to the financial statements contain supplemental information regarding particular accounts, such as the company's method of valuing

---

[23]For more on free cash flow and how it can be used to value a firm and its equity, see Aswath Damodaran, *Corporate Finance: Theory and Practice* (New York: John Wiley, 1997), pp. 170–171, 634–646.

Table 22.5 Dayton Hudson Corporation Consolidated Statements of Cash Flows ($ millions).

	1990	1991	1992	1993	1994	1995	1996
Cash from Operating Activities							
Net income	$410	$301	$383	$375	$434	$311	$474
Depreciation and amortization	372	410	459	498	548	594	650
Deferred taxes and other	(18)	60	59	89	(3)	46	(96)
Changes in Working Capital							
Receivables	(116)	(23)	(84)	(22)	(274)	300	(210)
Inventories	(36)	(365)	(237)	121	(280)	(241)	(13)
Accounts payable	8	57	272	58	307	286	281
Accrued liabilities	(15)	59	142	63	147	(88)	275
Income taxes payable	(13)	(62)	27	20	30	(38)	55
Other	33	0	(37)	17	(17)	(9)	42
Total Operating Cash Flow	$625	$437	$984	$1 219	$892	$1 161	$1 458
Cash from Investing Activities							
Capital expenditures	$(1 732)	$(1 009)	$(918)	$(969)	$(1 095)	$(1 522)	$(1 301)
Proceeds from disposals, etc.	2	19	10	79	89	17	103
Total Investing Cash Flow	$(1 730)	$(990)	$(908)	$(890)	$(1 006)	$(1 505)	$(1 198)
Cash from Financing Activities							
Change in notes payable	$(130)	$161	$(242)	$(23)	$247	$501	$416
Change in long-term debt	1 337	476	260	(53)	(199)	(60)	(286)
Equity issuance	0	0	0	0	0	0	0
Dividends	(116)	(128)	(133)	(138)	(144)	(148)	(155)
Other	3	48	60	89	36	79	51
Total Financing Cash Flow	$1 094	$557	$(55)	$(125)	$(60)	$372	$(234)
Change in Cash	$(11)	$4	$21	$204	$(174)	$28	$(26)
Beginning Cash	$103	$92	$96	$117	$321	$147	$175
Ending Cash	$92	$96	$117	$321	$147	$175	$201
Free Cash Flow Analysis							
Total operating cash flow	$625	$437	$984	$1 219	$892	$1 161	$1 458
Total investing cash flow	(1 730)	(990)	(908)	(890)	(1 006)	(1 505)	(1 198)
After-tax interest expense	123	144	163	170	167	168	174
Free Cash Flow to the Firm	$(982)	$(409)	$239	$499	$53	$(176)	$434
Total operating cash flow	$625	$437	$984	$1 219	$892	$1 161	$1 458
Total investing cash flow	(1 730)	(990)	(908)	(890)	(1 006)	(1 505)	(1 198)
Total financing cash flow	1 094	557	(55)	(125)	(60)	372	(234)
Dividends	116	128	133	138	144	148	155
Free Cash Flow to Equity	$105	$132	$154	$342	$(30)	$176	$181

inventory and a listing of its long-term debt outstanding. Furthermore, the notes will present information regarding major acquisitions or divestitures, officer and employee retirement and stock option plans, leasing arrangements, legal proceedings, and changes in accounting procedures, among other issues.

Management discussion and analysis provide an interpretation by the company's senior officers of financial trends and significant events affecting the company, particularly as they affect the company's liquidity, financial resources, and results of operations. In preparing this report, some corporate managements are more forthcoming than others. Consequently, the value of the report to the analyst varies widely among companies.

The auditor's report presents the opinion of the company's independent auditor regarding the "fairness" of the company's financial statements. In the vast majority of cases, the auditor issues an unqualified opinion, stating that over the accounting period the company's financial statements fairly present, in all material respects, the financial position, results of operations, and the cash flows in conformance with generally accepted accounting principles (GAAP). A qualified opinion, indicating material departures from GAAP, is a rarity and may signal serious problems with the company's disclosures. The mere threat that the auditor might issue a qualified opinion is usually sufficient to prevent a company from releasing intentionally incorrect reports. Note, however, that an unqualified opinion merely relates to the fairness of the disclosures; it does not imply any endorsement on the part of the auditor as to the quality of the company's business operations or the value of the company's securities.

Ratio Analysis

Ratio analysis is a technique commonly employed by analysts examining a company's financial statements. Standing alone, the values of various financial statement items are difficult to interpret. They display more meaning when they are considered relative to one another. For example, a growing firm will generally increase the amount of its debt outstanding. Such increases are expected and appropriate. However, when that debt relative to total assets or shareholders' equity increases significantly, a red flag is raised for analysts. They will want to know the reasons for, and ramifications of, such an increase in leverage.

Ratios may be used in several ways. Some analysts apply absolute standards, on the grounds that a substandard ratio indicates a potential weakness that merits further analysis. Other analysts compare a company's ratios to those of the "average" firm in the same industry in order to detect differences that may need further consideration. Others analyze trends in a company's ratios over time, perhaps in comparison to industry trends, hoping that these trends will help them predict future changes. Still others combine ratios with technical analysis (discussed in this chapter's Appendix) in order to arrive at investment decisions.

Ratio analysis can be very sophisticated, but it can also be overly simplistic. Routine extrapolation of a present ratio (or its recent trend) may produce a poor estimate of its future value. (For example, there is no reason for a firm to maintain a constant ratio of inventory to sales.) Moreover, a series of simple projections may produce inconsistent financial statements. For example, projections of ratios imply predictions of the levels of various balance sheet items. However, it may be that when these levels are looked at altogether, the resulting balance sheet does not balance. Furthermore, comparisons of one company's ratios with those of its competitors can be fraught with problems. In many industries, competitors' lines of business do not precisely match up. Even very similar companies may use different accounting procedures. The result is often an apples and oranges situation that diminishes the value of peer comparisons.

The types of ratios considered depends on the purpose of the analysis. Generally, analysts concerned with a company's equity securities will look at ratios relating to the firm's return on equity. Analysts viewing the company from a creditor's perspective will focus on measures of debt capacity and liquidity.

Equity Ratio Analysis

Share prices are ultimately determined by expected growth in corporate earnings. Analysts, therefore, are naturally concerned with identifying the elements that cause a company's long-run earnings growth rate to increase or decrease. Equation (17.51b) demonstrated that the long-run (or *sustainable*) growth rate of a company's earnings depends on (1) the proportion of earnings that is retained $(1 - p)$, and (2) the average return on equity for the earnings that are retained (r). That is:

$$g = r(1 - p) \qquad (17.51b)$$

Ratio analysis is used to plumb the past return on equity for clues as to improvements or deterioration in the return on equity in the future. Ratio analysis breaks down the return on equity into its various components, which in turn are examined for trends and relative position versus competing companies. The simplest expression for return on equity (ROE) is to view it as the product of profit margin (net income divided by sales) and equity turnover (sales divided by shareholders' equity).[24] That is:

$$ROE = \frac{Net\ income}{Shareholders'\ equity}$$
$$= \frac{Net\ income}{Sales} \times \frac{Sales}{Shareholders'\ equity}$$

While it is a useful starting point, this expression aggregates considerable detail concerning the company's financial performance. A better understanding is gained by recognizing that the profit margin reflects not only the operating results of the company, but non-operating factors as well. Disaggregating those two elements allows for a more intensive analysis. Similarly, equity turnover reflects not only the company's operating efficiency, but how it finances its operations.

Operating Results

Operating results measure the performance of the company's underlying business. That is, how profitable and efficient has the company been in producing (or acquiring) and selling its goods and services to its customers? A company's (pre-tax) return on operating assets (ROA) is expressed in a manner similar to its return on equity. That is, it is a function of operating margin (operating income divided by sales) and asset turnover (sales divided by total assets). However, in defining operating margin, operating income replaces sales and total assets replaces shareholders' equity. That is:

$$ROA = \frac{Operating\ income}{Total\ assets}$$
$$= \frac{Operating\ income}{Sales} \times \frac{Sales}{Total\ assets}$$

Operating margin can be further disaggregated. Operating expenses in turn are composed of three primary components: cost of goods sold (primarily labour and materials), selling, general, and administrative (S, G, & A), and depreciation. The difference between sales and costs of goods sold is called gross income, while the ratio of the two items is known as gross margin. Subtracting the other operating expenses from gross income yields operating income. An analyst will consider the extent to which changes in operating margin have been related to changes in the company's control over pricing (as reflected in gross margin) and its management of operating expenses.[25]

Asset turnover can likewise be further disaggregated. The analyst will explore how the use of those assets relative to sales has changed over time and thus increased or lowered the return on assets. Furthermore, the analyst will examine how the company's use of its assets compares to that of other similar companies.

Non-operating Factors

Operating results translate into total financial performance through the interaction of two non-operating factors: leverage and taxes. While operating results are a measure of how effective management has been in producing and selling the goods and services of the company, another critical aspect of management policy is how the company finances its business

---

[24] Analysts typically calculate an average value for balance sheet items used in financial ratios. This facilitates comparisons of point-in-time levels on the balance sheet with period flows on the income statement. In the Dayton Hudson example, the financial ratios were computed using an average of beginning-of-year and year-end values for balance sheet items.

[25] In recent years analysts have increasingly come to view earnings before interest, taxes, depreciation, and amortization (EBITDA) relative to the total market value of the firm (its equity and debt) as a more effective measure of operating performance than pre-tax ROA. EBITDA is essentially a measure of the company's pre-tax cash flow.

activities. Common shares and long-term debt are the principal sources of financing for most businesses. Although leverage causes the return on equity to become more variable, effective use of debt financing can enhance shareholder returns. Return on equity (pre-tax) can be expressed as:

$$\text{Pre-tax ROE} = \frac{\text{Pre-tax income}}{\text{Shareholders' equity}}$$
$$= \frac{\text{Operating income}}{\text{Total assets}}$$
$$\times \frac{\text{Total assets}}{\text{Shareholders' equity}} - \frac{\text{Interest}}{\text{Shareholders' equity}}$$

Finally, taxes reduce the return to shareholders. Multiplying the pre-tax return on equity by one minus the tax rate yields the after-tax return on equity, ROE:

$$\text{After-tax ROE} = \frac{\text{Net income}}{\text{Shareholders' equity}}$$
$$= \frac{\text{Pre-tax income}}{\text{Shareholders' equity}}$$
$$\times (1 - \text{tax rate})$$

Summarizing the relationship between the various financial ratios yields the expression for ROE:

$$\text{After-tax ROE} = \frac{\text{Net income}}{\text{Shareholders' equity}}$$
$$= \left[\frac{\text{Operating income}}{\text{Sales}} \right.$$
$$\times \frac{\text{Sales}}{\text{Total assets}} \times \frac{\text{Total assets}}{\text{Shareholders' equity}}$$
$$\left. - \frac{\text{Interest}}{\text{Shareholders' equity}} \right] \times (1 - \text{tax rate})$$

Effectively, the company can influence its after-tax return on equity through three primary factors: (1) expenses relative to sales (operating margin); (2) sales relative to assets (asset turnover); and, (3) the cost of debt used to support the company's capital structure (interest divided by shareholders' equity). The effect of these factors is magnified by financial leverage (total assets divided by shareholders' equity) and reduced by taxes. The interaction of the various ratios to derive the after-tax return on equity is shown in Figure 22.1.

Dayton Hudson Corporation

Table 22.6 contains various relevant financial ratios for the Dayton Hudson Corporation over the period 1990 through 1996. From the company's income statement, the variability in the earnings per share is readily apparent. That variability is even more noticeable looking at the company's return on equity. Return on equity reached a high of 21.6% in 1990, declining to 9.4% in 1995 and rebounding to 13.2% in 1996. Examining the principal components of Dayton Hudson's return on equity reveals two observations. The first observation is that throughout the period the company's equity turnover (sales divided by shareholders' equity) has steadily declined, from 7.8 times in 1990 to 7.1 times in 1996. This trend largely represents a deliberate effort by the company to reduce its debt-to-shareholders' equity ratio. The resulting relative increase in equity in its capital structure has had the effect of reducing equity turnover. That this decline is not caused by a less efficient use of company resources is confirmed by noting that the company's asset turnover shows a fairly constant value of roughly 1.9 times over the period, and has actually increased slightly in recent years. Presumably then, the equity turnover ratio will flatten out as the company approaches its desired debt level.

The second observation is that the profit margin (net income divided by sales) has mirrored the up and down nature of the company's financial results. In 1990, Dayton Hudson's profit margin was 2.8%. In 1995, the profit margin fell to 1.3%, but improved to 1.9% in 1996.

Dayton Hudson's operating margin (operating income divided by total assets) has displayed less variability than the profit margin, as leverage tends to magnify the effects of variations in operating results on bottom line financial performance. However, despite some interim fluctuations, the company's operating margin was lower in 1996 than it was in 1990. In part, this decline is due to the fact that 1990 was an exceptional year for the company. Further, the decline is also a result of the growing importance of the Target division in Dayton Hudson's overall financial picture. In 1990, Target's sales represented 56% of the company's total sales. By 1996, that figure had increased to 70%. Because Target's discount retailing operations involve lower

Figure 22.1 Interaction of financial ratios to derive after-tax return on equity.

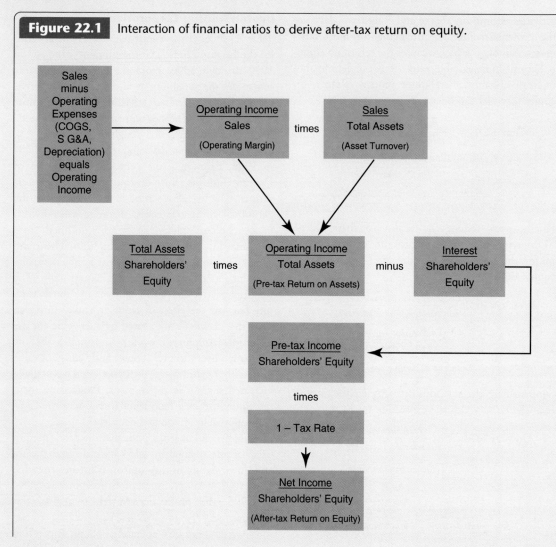

operating margins than either Mervyn's or particularly the Department Stores Division, the increasing prominence of Target reduces the company's total operating margin.

Breaking down the operating margin further, the ratio of both costs of goods sold and S, G, & A expenses relative to sales had been on an upward trend, in combination peaking in 1995. Some of that increase is again related to the lower margin business of Target. However, the company still can act to control costs, which it did in 1996. In total, operating expenses as a percent of sales declined from 94.3% in 1995 to 92.9% in 1996—a 1.4 percentage point improvement—which was a critical component of

Dayton Hudson's improved financial performance. This improvement was due both to a more favourable experience in terms of the company's gross margin (cost of goods sold divided by sales) and to lower S, G, & A and interest expenses as a percent of sales. In terms of asset turnover, the key items of accounts receivable and inventories both have demonstrated improved operating efficiency (higher sales to asset ratios), while the ratio of sales to net plant and equipment has changed little.

Examining non-operating factors, as discussed, the company has made a concerted effort to decrease leverage on its balance sheet. This is evidenced by the decline in the company's debt-to-shareholders'

Table 22.6 Dayton Hudson Corporation Selected Financial Ratios.

	1990	1991	1992	1993	1994	1995	1996
Profit margin	2.8%	1.9%	2.1%	2.0%	2.0%	1.3%	1.9%
Equity turnover	7.8	7.5	7.6	7.4	7.2	7.1	7.1
Return on equity	21.6%	14.1%	16.2%	14.4%	14.6%	9.4%	13.2%
Operating margin	6.7%	5.4%	5.9%	5.5%	5.4%	4.0%	5.4%
Asset turnover	1.9	1.8	1.8	1.8	1.9	1.9	2.0
Return on operating assets	12.9%	9.7%	10.6%	10.0%	10.1%	7.8%	10.5%
Cost of goods sold/sales	72.3%	72.9%	73.2%	73.6%	73.4%	74.5%	73.4%
S, G, & A/sales	16.8%	17.4%	16.6%	16.5%	17.0%	17.2%	16.9%
Depreciation/sales	2.5%	2.5%	2.6%	2.6%	2.6%	2.5%	2.6%
Interest expense/sales	2.2%	2.5%	2.4%	2.3%	2.0%	1.9%	1.7%
Sales/cash	151.2	171.4	168.3	87.8	91.1	146.1	135.0
Sales/accounts receivable	11.6	11.4	12.2	12.6	12.7	14.2	15.7
Sales/inventories	7.7	7.3	7.2	7.5	8.1	8.1	8.4
Sales/current assets	4.4	4.2	4.3	4.3	4.5	4.7	4.9
Sales/net plant & equipment	3.7	3.4	3.4	3.3	3.5	3.4	3.4
Total assets/shareholders' equity	4.0	4.2	4.2	4.0	3.8	3.7	3.6
Interest/shareholders' equity	17.1%	18.6%	18.5%	17.1%	14.4%	13.4%	12.3%
Pre-tax income/shareholders' equity	34.5%	22.1%	25.9%	23.2%	24.1%	15.2%	25.5%
Tax rate	37.8%	36.2%	37.3%	38.2%	39.2%	37.9%	39.5%
Total debt/shareholders' equity	3.00	3.21	3.20	3.04	2.79	2.68	2.61
Current assets/current liabilities	1.47	1.54	1.52	1.48	1.46	1.43	1.36
Operating income/interest expense	3.03	2.19	2.40	2.36	2.68	2.13	3.07

equity ratio from 3.21 in 1991 to 2.61 in 1996. This reduced debt load has decreased the company's relative interest expense. Interest payments relative to sales fell from 2.5% in 1991 to 1.7% in 1996. The reduction in leverage will ultimately lower the variability of the company's return on equity. However, it will also give less of a boost to net income in periods of high operating margins. In terms of taxes, the company's tax rate has remained fairly constant over the period at approximately 38%.

Being a national multiline retailer, Dayton Hudson faces a wide range of competitors. The diversity of its competition tends to limit the validity of comparing its financial ratios to those of its competitors. Nevertheless, Table 22.7 lists various year-end 1996 ratios for five of the company's competitors: Wal-Mart, Kmart, Sears, J.C. Penney, and Federated Department Stores.

Wal-Mart and Sears are the largest US retailers and both have earned returns on equity much higher than their competitors including Dayton Hudson, as shown in Table 22.7. Walmart accomplishes this result with low amounts of leverage, while Sears with its large and profitable credit card business, carries more debt relative to its equity. Comparing Dayton Hudson's financial ratios to the five-company average shows a slightly below-average profit margin more than offset by efficient use of shareholders' equity to produce an above-average return on equity. At the operating level, Dayton Hudson's operating margin and asset turnover interact to produce a comparatively strong return on assets. Operating expense relative to sales and sales relative to current assets both indicate superior performance by Dayton Hudson. Further, the company has accomplished these results

Table 22.7 Large US Retailers Versus Dayton Hudson 1996 Selected Financial Ratios.

	Wal-Mart	Kmart	Sears	JC Penney	Federated	Average	Dayton Hudson
Profit margin	2.9%	0.7%	3.3%	2.4%	1.8%	2.2%	1.9%
Equity turnover	5.8	5.2	6.1	3.9	3.3	4.8	7.1
Return on equity	16.8%	3.8%	20.2%	9.4%	5.7%	11.2%	13.2%
Operating margin	4.2%	2.5%	9.0%	6.6%	7.9%	6.0%	5.4%
Asset turnover	2.7	2.2	1.1	1.1	1.1	1.6	2.0
Return on assets	11.1%	5.4%	9.5%	7.1%	8.4%	8.3%	10.5%
Cost of goods sold/sales	79.8%	77.6%	65.2%	71.2%	61.0%	71.0%	73.4%
S, G, & A/sales	16.0%	20.0%	25.8%	22.2%	31.1%	23.0%	16.9%
Interest expense/sales	0.8%	1.4%	3.6%	1.5%	3.3%	2.1%	1.7%
Sales/current assets	5.8	4.1	1.3	2.0	2.4	3.1	4.9
Sales/net plant & equipment	5.2	5.5	6.5	3.6	2.3	4.6	3.4
Total assets/shareholders' equity	2.2	2.4	5.7	3.7	3.1	3.4	3.6
Interest/shareholders' equity	4.7%	7.5%	21.7%	6.0%	10.7%	10.1%	12.3%
Pre-tax income/shareholders' equity	19.3%	5.3%	33.0%	20.0%	15.0%	18.5%	25.5%
Tax rate	37.0%	n.a.	39.6%	37.8%	39.8%	38.6%	39.5%
Total debt/shareholders' equity	1.18	1.35	4.74	2.66	2.05	2.40	2.61
Current assets/current liabilities	1.64	2.14	1.90	1.47	1.79	1.79	1.36
Operating income/interest expense	5.22	1.71	2.53	4.36	2.41	3.25	3.07

while at the same time bringing its debt to total assets ratio down very near that of its competitors.

In summary, through its improved gross margin and its cost cutting efforts in 1996, Dayton Hudson managed to increase its profit margin and continued to make efficient use of company assets. It also was able to continue its reduction in balance sheet leverage. These accomplishments put it in a strong financial position relative to its competitors. In turn, those improvements were associated with a 57.0% surge in the company's stock price in 1996 as compared to a 18.7% average increase for its competitors. Dayton Hudson's challenge and the question confronting investors in its common shares is whether the company can continue its rapid revenue growth while maintaining and even building on the 1996 profit margin expansion.

Fixed-income Ratio Analysis

Holders of a company's debt are primarily concerned with being paid their interest and principal in a full

and timely manner. Some lenders want to know about the company's short-run ability to service its debt. For example, a banker making a short-term loan will want to examine financial ratios that indicate the company's liquidity. Holders of the company's long-term debt, on the other hand, will place more emphasis on the company's long-run earnings power, somewhat akin to an equity analyst.

Liquidity ratios measure the company's ability to quickly discharge its near-term obligations. The most commonly used liquidity ratios are the *current ratio* (current assets divided by current liabilities) and the *quick ratio* (current assets less inventory, divided by current liabilities). The greater are these liquidity ratios, the greater is the company's capacity to generate cash that can be used to pay off its short-term obligations.

Leverage ratios indicate the extent to which the company's capital was financed through debt as opposed to equity. Higher leverage ratios indicate that more financing came from debt sources. As a result, more risk of the business is placed on creditors. Moreover, the higher is the company's leverage, the more variable will be the company's earnings, as a larger fixed expense (that is, interest payments) must be paid before earnings can flow through to the company's owners. The most widely recognized leverage ratio is the ratio of *total-debt-to-shareholders' equity*. Coverage ratios, such as *times interest earned* (operating income divided by interest expense), measure the extent to which interest expense is covered by the company's operating income.

Dayton Hudson Corporation

As shown in Table 22.7, Dayton Hudson's current ratio has remained fairly constant over the last six years and is somewhat lower than its peers due in part to the company's previously mentioned program of selling off its accounts receivables to investors.

While this has the effect of lowering its available liquidity, the company apparently believes that it can make more efficient use of those assets through investments in its capital projects and paying down debt. In fact, the company's current asset turnover (sales divided by current assets) has increased in recent years and is far above most of its competitors. Again, the increasing importance of Target, which has exceptionally high inventory turnover, is largely responsible for this result.

Dayton Hudson appears to be managing its debt effectively. As noted, it has managed to bring down its total debt-to-shareholders' equity ratio considerably over the last several years and is now near the average of its competitors. Furthermore, the company's times interest earned ratio (operating income divided by interest expense) has also improved in recent years and it too is very close that of its competitors.

....

Analysts' Recommendations and Stock Prices

When a security analyst decides that a stock is mispriced and informs certain clients of this, some of the clients may act on the information. As they do so, the price of the security may be affected. As news of the analyst's recommendation spreads, more investors may act, and the price may react even more. At some point, the analyst's information will be "fully reflected" in the stock price.

Target
www.targetstores.com

Sears Canada
www.sears.ca

If the analyst decides that the shares of a company are underpriced and clients subsequently purchase them, the shares' price will tend to rise. Conversely, if the analyst decides that the shares are overpriced and clients subsequently sell them, the shares' price will tend to decline. If the analyst's views were well founded, no subsequent counterreaction in the shares' price would be expected. Otherwise, the price is likely to return to its pre-recommendation level at some later time.

Table 22.8 summarizes six studies of publicly available analysts recommendations. Two of the studies deal with recommendations that appeared in *First Call* and *Zach's Investment Research*, which are large computer databases that keep up-to-date records of analysts' recommendations from a number of different brokerage firms for a large number of securities.[26] The third study deals with recommendations that appeared annually in *Barron's*, a weekly

---

[26]Similar observations have been made in regard to other studies of the recommendations made by major brokerage houses. See Hohn C. Groth, Wilbur G. Lewellen, Gary G. Schlarbaum, and Ronald C. Lease, "An Analysis of Brokerage House Securities Recommendations," *Financial Analysts Journal* 35, no 1 (January–February 1979): 32–40; James H. Bjerring, Josef Lakonishok, and Theo Vermaelen, "Stock Prices and Financial Analysts' Recommendations," *Journal of Finance* 38, no. 1 (March 1983): 187–204; and Philip Heitner, "Isn't it Time to Measure Analysts' Track Records?" *Financial Analysts Journal* 47, no. 3 (May–June 1991): 5–6. For a comment on the first study, see the Letter to the Editor in the May–June 1980 issue by Clinton M. Bidwell, with a responding Letter to the Editor in the July–August 1980 issue by Wilbur G. Lewellen. Also see footnote 1 in Chapter 23. Also, note that the Appendix to Chapter 18 discussed a study of the recommendations made by Value Line analysts.

Table 22.8 A Summary of Studies That Have Evaluated the Performance of Security Analysts.

	Before Announcement		Around Announcement		After Announcement	
Source	Time Period	Abnormal Return	Time Period	Abnormal Return	Time Period	Abnormal Return
A. Buy Recommendations						
First Call[1]	6 months	1.2%	−1 to +1	3.0%*	1 month	2.4%*
Zach's[2]	10 days	.7*	0 to +10	.9*	20 days	.6*
Barron's Roundtable[3]	25 days	2.7†	0	1.0*	25 days	.3
Dartboard[4]	25 days	.6	0 to +1	4.1*	24 days	−2.1
Heard on the Street[5]	28 days	.4	−2 to +1	2.1*	29 days	−.5
Value Line[6]	50 days	8.7*	0 to +2	2.4*	48 days	.7
B. Sell Recommendations						
First Call[1]	6 months	−2.1%	−1 to +1	−4.7%*	6 months	−9.2%*
Zach's[2]	10 days	−1.1*	0 to +10	−.8*	20 days	−.3
Barron's Roundtable[3]	25 days	−1.8†	0	−1.2*	25 days	.1
Heard on the Street[5]	28 days	.4	−2 to +1	−3.6*	29 days	1.3
Value Line[6]	50 days	−7.0*	0 to +2	−.3*	48 days	−1.3*

*denotes that the number was found to be statistically significantly different than zero at the 5% level.

†denotes that a test of statistical significance was neither presented in the study nor could be conducted by an outside reader from the data provided.

SOURCES: The data in the table are adapted from the following sources: (1) Kent L. Womack, "Do Brokerage Analysts' Recommendations Have Investment Value?" *Journal of Finance* 51, no. 1 (March 1996): pp. 148–149. (2) Scott E. Stickel, "The Anatomy of the Performance of Buy and Sell Recommendations," *Financial Analysts Journal* 51, no. 5 (September – October 1995): p. 28. (3) Hemang Desai and Prem C. Jain, "An Analysis of the Recommendations of the 'Superstar' Money Managers at *Barron's* Annual Roundtable," *Journal of Finance* 50, no. 4 (September): pp. 1264, 1270. (4) Brad M. Barber and Douglas Loeffler, "The 'Dartboard' Column: Second-hand Information and Price Pressure," *Journal of Financial and Quantitative Analysis* 28, no. 2 (June 1993): p. 276. (5) Messod D. Beneish, "Stock Prices and the Dissemination of Analysts' Recommendations," *Journal of Business* 64, no. 3 (July 1991): pp. 403, 406–407. (6) Scott E. Stickel, "The Effect of Value Line Investment Survey Rank Changes on Common Stock Prices," *Journal of Financial Economics* 14, no. 1 (March 1985): pp. 130–131.

Wall Street Journal
www.wsj.com

publication, and involves 8 to 12 prominent money managers who had been invited to participate in their "Roundtable," referring to them as "Wall Street Superstars." The next two studies deal with recommendations that appeared in columns in *The Wall Street Journal.* One of these columns, "Heard on the Street," appears daily and involves a changing group of a variable number of analysts who discuss a variety of stocks.[27] The "Dartboard" is the second column; it appears monthly and presents "Pros Picks" provided by a changing panel of four analysts who each recommend one stock. The last study involves recommendations made by Value Line analysts that appeared weekly in the *Value Line Investment Survey,* reputed to be the largest stock investment advisory service in the United States.[28]

[27]Two other studies of "Heard on the Street" recommendations reached similar conclusions to those shown here. See Peter Lloyd-Davies and Michael Canes, "Stock Prices and the Publication of Second-hand Information," *Journal of Business* 51, no. 1 (January 1978): 43–56 and Lu Piu, Stanley D. Smith, and Azmat A. Syed, "Stock Price Reactions to *The Wall Street Journal's* Securities Recommendations," *Journal of Financial and Quantitative Analysis* 25, no. 3 (September 1990): 399–410. Interestingly, a former author of the "Heard on the Street" column, R. Foster Winans, was convicted of fraud and theft in 1985 for leaking the contents of his column to four brokers and subsequently sharing in the associated trading profits.

[28]Value Line also has a service called *VALUE/SCREEN III* (formerly called *VALUE/SCREEN Plus*) that investors can subscribe to that involves software and periodic updates of their rankings as well as other data. Besides its stock recommendations, Value Line also provides a measure of the risk of individual securites that is known as Safety Rank. This risk measure was found to be more highly correlated with subsequent returns than either beta or standard deviation, suggesting that it is a more useful measure of risk. See Russel J. Fuller and G. Wenchi Wong, "Traditional Versus Theoretical Risk Measures," *Financial Analysts Journal* 44, no. 2 (March–April 1988): 52–57, 67.

First Call Corporation
www.firstcall.com

Barron's Online
www.barrons.com

In terms of how soon the analysts' recommendations appear publicly, *First Call* is the quickest since the brokerage firms generally send them in promptly. *Barron's* and *The Wall Street Journal* are probably the slowest, as these analysts may have disclosed their recommendations to their clients at some point before publication (in the case of *Barron's*, the Roundtable meets on average about two weeks before publication). Zach's and Value Line are probably somewhere in the middle.

While the recommendations in *The Wall Street Journal* and *Barron's* are simple recommendations to buy or sell, those in *First Call*, Zach's, and Value Line are more complicated. Usually an analyst following a stock gives it a rating on a five-point scale where 1 = strong buy, 2 = buy, 3 = hold, 4 = sell, and 5 = strong sell, or some similar metric. Thereafter, the rating will be either changed or confirmed at irregular intervals. In the *First Call* study, buy recommendations were defined as those recommendations that represented a rating upgrade to a "1" and sell recommendations were defined as a rating downgrade to a "5." In contrast, the Zach's study defined "buys" as those recommendations that were upgraded to a "1" or "2." Similarly, "sells" were those recommendations that were downgraded to a "3," "4," or "5." In the Value Line study, the results shown in Table 22.8 focus on those shares that were upgraded to a "1" and those that were downgraded to a "5."

Overall, the table reveals the following about analysts' recommendations:

1. It appears that the buy recommendations are associated with a slight abnormal price rise in the period before the recommendations are widely published, perhaps due to the recommendations being released early to certain special clients or perhaps due to analysts changing their recommendations after a notable upward price movement by the shares under analysis. Neither of these situations seem to apply for sell recommendations since there was no unusual movement in their prices before publication.

2. Around the time the announcement (that is, day 0, with −1 and +1 referring to the day before and after the announcement) the "buys" jumped up in price and the "sells" slumped in price. This indicates that investors immediately acted on the recommendations when they were published.

3. There is mixed evidence regarding what happened after the announcement. The evidence that recommended buys keep rising for a month after *First Call* publishes a buy recommendation, and that their recommended sells keep falling for six months after publication is compelling since *First Call* has the "freshest" recommendations. These results appear to be inconsistent with the notion of efficient markets, because it suggests that an investor might be able to earn abnormal returns by reacting promptly to *First Call* recommendations (note that as transaction costs have not been accounted for, it is entirely possible that these post-announcement abnormal returns are illusory). Nevertheless, at a minimum the absence of a subsequent correction to the announcement day's abnormal stock price movement for the other studies suggests that the recommendations in all of the studies contained information of value.[29]

4. While not shown in the table, most of the recommendations were "buys" of large firms. One reason given for the predominance of "buys" is that there are several costs associated with "sells," perhaps the biggest one being possible lost investment banking opportunities. That is, an analyst who issues a "sell" recommendation about a firm's stock may be fearful of annoying management of the firm to such an extent that they will not use the analyst's firm for any investment banking activities in the future.

[29]One study of Value Line recommendations found that most rank changes occur shortly after earnings announcements are made. Subsequent investigation revealed that Value Line's superior performance was attributable to the "post-earnings-announcement drift" (this phenomenon was discussed in Chapter 18). Hence the two anomalies appear to be related. See John Affleck-Graves and Richard R. Mendenhall, "The Relation Between the Value Line Enigma and Post-earnings-announcement Drift," *Journal of Financial Economics* 31, no. 1 (February 1992): 75–96.

Hence, there is an incentive to not say anything negative about a firm's stock unless it is particularly obvious.

5. Also not shown in the table is the observation that analysts recommendations are often made public around the same time that earnings forecasts are released. Hence it is possible that one of these two pieces of information dominates the other by making the other valueless when both are provided to the investor. For example, a significant upward revision in the earnings forecast of a firm by a prominent analyst might cause the firm's share price to jump up, while the issuance of a buy recommendation two days later might not result in any notable price change. However, a study found that this is not the case, since both announcements were found to be associated with notable share price movements. [30] Furthermore, share recommendations were found to be more valuable when they represent a change of position instead of a reiteration of a position. Most interesting, it appears that earnings forecast revisions are of more value when the analyst's report contains a buy recommendation rather than a sell recommendation. Apparently, this is because the known bias for analysts to issue buy recommendations means that investors tend to look at other things in the analyst's report when such a recommendation is made.

A study of the recommendations made by a regional Canadian investment service company obtained similar results.[31] This company published lists of *recommended, speculative*, and *representative* stocks. The recommended lists consisted of stocks the firm's investment committee recommended for purchase, the speculative list contained stocks regarded as risky and the representative list consisted of stocks that either had been recently dropped from the recommended list or had been evaluated by a new analyst for the first time. The stocks on the representative list were interpreted to be those an investor should hold if they were already owned, but were not encouraged to buy. The firm provided these lists for both Canadian and US stocks. Figure 22.2 presents a comparison of the cumulative abnormal returns for the combined Canadian and US stocks on the recommended and representative lists over the period September 1977 through February 1981 and covered 221 recommendations. This shows that substantial returns could be achieved by following the buy recommendations. The firm was successful in outperforming both the TSE 300 in a bull market with their Canadian recommendations and the S&P 500 with their US recommendations. Stocks on the speculative list showed negative, but not statistically significant, abnormal returns. Representative stocks showed no abnormal returns.

Analyst Following and Stock Returns

An interesting issue involves the relationship between the amount of attention devoted by analysts to individual stocks and the price behaviour of those stocks. Do stocks that are intensively followed have significantly different returns from those stocks that are relatively neglected by analysts? One study examined all stocks in the S&P 500 for the period from 1970 to 1979 in order to answer such a question. Table 22.9 summarizes the results.

---

[30] Jennifer Francis and Leonard Soffer, "The Relative Informativeness of Analysts' Stock Recommendations and Earnings Forecast Revisions," *Journal of Accounting Research* 35, no. 2 (Autumn 1997): 193–211. Chapter 18 contains discussion of analysts' forecasts of earnings.

[31] J. Bjerring, J. Lakonishok, and T. Vermaelen, "Stock Prices and Analysts' Recommendations," *Journal of Finance* 38, no. 1 (March 1983):187–204. A similar study over a later time period (March 1983 through December 1985) found that following Canadian analysts' recommendations provided substantial gains; see L. Brown, G. Richardson, and C. Trzcinka, "Strong-form Efficiency on the Toronto Stock Exchange: An Examination of Analyst Price Forecasts," *Contemporary Accounting Research* 7, no. 2 (Spring 1991): 323–46.

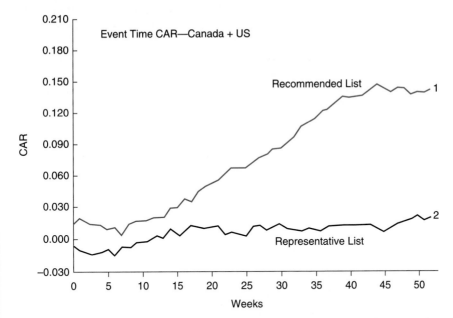

Figure 22.2 Cumulative abnormal returns from a broker's recommended list compared with the representative list, US and Canadian stocks.

SOURCE: J.B. Jerring, J. Lakonishok, and T. Vermaelen, "Stock Prices and Financial Analysts' Recommendations," *Journal of Finance* 38, no. 1 (March 1983): 198.

Table 22.9 Analyst Following and Stock Returns.

Amount of Following	All Stocks (1)	Small Firms (2)	Medium Firms (3)	Large Firms (4)
High	7.5%	5.0%	7.4%	8.4%
Moderate	11.8%	13.2%	11.0	10.2%
Low	15.4	15.8	13.9%	15.3
Low-high	7.9%	10.8%	6.5%	6.9%
Average return	11.0	13.5	10.7	9.8

SOURCE: Adapted from Avner Arbel and Paul Strebel, "Pay Attention to Neglected Firms!" *Journal of Portfolio Management* 9, no. 2 (Winter 1983): 39.

Neglected Firm Effect

An empirical observation that firms followed by relatively few security analysts have had abnormally high returns.

Column (1) shows that the stocks followed by the largest number of analysts had the lowest average returns. However, the stocks followed by the fewest analysts had the highest average returns, thereby suggesting the presence of a **neglected firm effect**.

It is possible that this effect is simply a reflection of the size effect, as the average return on small-sized firms has been shown to be larger than the average return on larger firms.[32] The reason for this possibility is that the number of analysts following a stock is generally

---

[32]See the appendix to Chapter 16 for a discussion of the size effect.

related to the size of the underlying firm. However, columns (2), (3), and (4) show that this is not simply another manifestation of the size effect.[33] It can be seen that the neglected firm effect exists for all firm sizes. Furthermore, it is most pronounced for small firms—note that the difference between the high and low categories is largest in column (2).

What are the implications of the neglected firm effect? First, it could be that the higher average return associated with neglected firms is a reward for investing in securities that have less available information. Second, because the neglected firm effect exists across all sizes of firms, large institutional investors that are prohibited from investing in small firms can still take advantage of this effect, as it also exists from medium and large firms (although it is notably less significant). Finally, whether or not such a simple rule will be useful in the future is open to debate. Why? If investors increase their purchases of neglected firms, then such firms will no longer be neglected and hence will no longer provide abnormally high returns.

Insider Trading

Insider Narrowly defined, insiders are shareholders, officers, and directors of a corporation who own a "significant" proportion of a corporation's stock. More broadly defined, anyone who has access to information that is both "materially" related to the value of a corporation's securities and is unavailable to the general public.

The Ontario Securities Commission requires the officers and directors of a corporation whose securities are traded on an organized exchange in Ontario to report any transactions they have made in the firm's shares within 10 days after the end of the month in which the transaction(s) occurred. Shareholders who own 10% or more of the firm's shares, known as *beneficial owners*, must also report their trading activities. Such shareholders, officers, and directors are often referred to as **insiders**. The information they provide about their trading activity is subsequently reported in the Ontario Securities Commission's weekly *Ontario Securities Commission Bulletin.*[34] Almost two months may elapse before knowledge of these trades becomes widespread. For example, the information about trades made in January must be reported by early February and will appear in the late February issue of the OSC Bulletin. When a person first acquires 10% of a firm's shares he is subject to the OSC's *early warning disclosure*. This requires them to make an immediate public announcement and report the transaction to the OSC within one day.

The business press reports information about insider trading obtained from the *OSC Bulletin*. In addition, some investment dealers use insider trading activity as part of the information employed to develop buy and sell recommendations.

It is illegal for anyone to enter into a security transaction if they have taken advantage of "inside" information about the corporation that is unavailable to other people involved in the transaction. This proscription includes not only insiders but also those to whom they give such secret information (the recipient of such a tip is termed the *tippee*).

Legal issues aside, two questions of relevance to outside investors may be posed: (1) Do insiders make unusual profits on transactions in their own stocks? (2) If they do, can others profit by following their example as soon as it becomes public knowledge?

Insiders trade their shares for many reasons. For example, some purchases result from the exercise of options and some sales result from the need for cash. Moreover, it is not unusual to find some insiders purchasing shares during a month in which other insiders are selling. However, when a major piece of inside information suggests that a stock's value differs significantly from its current market price, it would be reasonable to expect a preponderance of insider trades on one side of the market (that is, either purchases or sales). This

---

[33]The presence of the size effect can be seen by noting that the average return for small firms of 13.5% is much larger than the average return for medium and large firms of 10.7% and 9.8%, respectively.

[34]In some provinces, notably Quebec and Alberta, insiders are required to report their activity within 10 days of executing a trade.

is a situation where there is *asymmetric information* in the marketplace, as insiders know more than others and are trading on the basis of this information.

One way to search for such situations is to examine the *OSC Bulletin* and count the number of times during a month that insiders traded their firm's shares (excluding the exercise of options). If the number of purchases exceeds the number of sales, it might be inferred that favourable inside information motivated the insider trades during the month. If the number of sales exceeds the number of purchases, this can be regarded as an unfavourable signal.

Different cutoff levels could be used in this process to reflect the intensity of insider trading. A cutoff of 1 would require a simple majority of trades of one type, whereas a cutoff of 5 would require a "supermajority" of trades of one type.

Such a procedure was used in a detailed US study of insider transactions during the 1950s and 1960s.[35] Table 22.10 summarizes the key results. The two columns on the right-hand side of the table indicate the abnormal returns over an eight-month period on securities that exceeded the cutoff level for insider trading. For example, during the 1960s, if an investor purchased every stock in the sample for which there were three or more net purchasers and sold every stock for which there were three or more more net sellers during a month, more or less coincident with the transactions of the insiders themselves, then the investor would have earned, on average, an abnormal return of 5.07% over the subsequent eight months. If the transactions had been made instead at roughly the time the information was published in the SEC's *Official Summary*, an average abnormal return of 4.94% would have been earned over the next eight months.

Table 22.10	Abnormal Returns Associated with Insider Trading.			
			Average Abnormal Return over Eight Months Following	
Sample				
Cutoff (No. of Net Purchasers or Sellers)	No. of Cases	Period	Month of Transaction	Month Information Became Publicly Available
1	362	1960s	1.36%	.70%
3	861	1960s	5.07	4.94
4	293	1950s	5.14	4.12
5	157	1950s	4.48	4.08

SOURCE: Jeffrey F. Jaffe, "Special Information and Insider Trading," *Journal of Business* 47, no. 3 (July 1974): 421, 426.

As the first row in the table shows, a bare majority of insider trades does not appear to isolate possible effects of insider information. But a majority of three, four, or five does seem to do so. The figures shown are gross of any transaction costs, but even so it appears that insiders can and do make money from their special knowledge of their companies. This is not surprising, since if anyone can know the true value of a firm, it should be the insiders. Since the information these insiders presumably are using is nonpublic in nature, these findings suggest that markets are not strong-form efficient. On the other hand, the abnormal returns associated with transactions that could have been made by outsiders,

---

[35]Jeffrey F. Jaffe, "Special Information and Insider Trading," *Journal of Business* 47, no. 3 (July 1974): 410–428. Also see Joseph E. Finnerty, "Insiders and Market Efficiency," *Journal of Finance* 31, no. 4 (September 1976): 1141–1148; and Aaron B. Feigen, "Information Opportunities from Insider Trading Laws," *AAII Journal* 11, no. 8 (September 1989): 12–15.

using only publicly available information on insider trading, are quite surprising. Moreover, those associated with cutoffs of three, four, or five pass statistical tests designed to see if they might be simply due to chance. After transaction costs, trades designed to capitalize on such information would still appear to produce abnormal returns (although not highly so), suggesting that markets are not even semistrong-form efficient. However, more recent studies have found that outsiders cannot use the publicly available information about insider trading to make abnormal profits; these studies thus support the notion that markets are semistrong-form efficient.[36] Whether or not insider trading information can be profitably used by outsiders is an open question given the conflicting evidence. It is also possible that the inefficiency has disappeared as a result of the publicity it has received.

The Canadian situation is less contradictory. Figure 22.3 shows the cumulative abnormal returns (CAR), based on monthly data, for both buy and sell signals derived from an examination of some 17 000 insider trades executed between 1967 and 1977. Period 0 on the graph represents the publication date of the *OSC Bulletin* and, therefore, indicates the time when outsiders would become aware of inside trading activity. The CARs for month minus one (when the insiders traded) indicate that insiders, on average, are able to buy low and sell high, that outsiders can profit from observing the actions of insiders, and that abnormal returns persist for about 12 months after the original signal. None of these conclusions are consistent with semistrong-form market efficiency. These results have been confirmed by a number of other studies. Some of these also find that not all insiders are

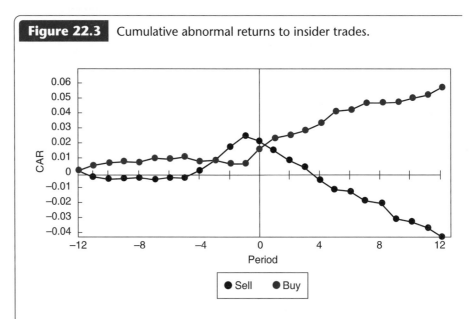

Figure 22.3 Cumulative abnormal returns to insider trades.

SOURCE: D. Fowler and H. Rorke, "Insider Trading Profits on the Toronto Stock Exchange: 1967–1977," *Canadian Journal of Administrative Sciences* 5, no. 1 (March 1988): 20.

---

[36]See Herbert S. Kerr, "The Battle of Insider Trading and Market Efficiency," *Journal of Portfolio Management* 6, no. 4 (Summer 1980): 47–58; Wayne Y. Lee and Michael E. Solt, "Insider Trading: A Poor Guide to Market Timing," *Journal of Portfolio Management* 12, no. 4 (Summer 1986): 65–71; H. Nejat Seyhun, "Insiders' Profits, Costs of Trading, and Market Efficiency," *Journal of Financial Economics* 16, no. 2 (June 1986): 189–212; Michael S. Rozeff and Mir A. Zaman, "Market Efficiency and Insider Trading: New Evidence," *Journal of Business* 61, no. 1 (January 1988): 25–44; and Ji-Chai Lin and John S. Howe, "Insider Trading in the OTC Market," *Journal of Finance* 45, no. 4 (September 1990): 1273–1284.

Inside Information

In 1990, Michael Milken pleaded guilty to six felony charges. He was fined an astounding $600 million and sentenced to 10 years in prison. Milken's conviction brought to a close a saga involving criminal behaviour by a number of highly influential individuals and organizations on Wall Street. The common thread tying together all of the defendants: rampant trading on inside information.

Insider trading has always been a controversial subject. The concept itself is rife with paradox. At the heart of our prosperous capital markets is the proposition that certain participants should not possess significant, unfair advantages over others. If you believe that the game is rigged against you, that the people with whom you trade consistently have ready access to valuable inside information, then you will soon take your investments to a fairer playing field.

Conversely, without inside information, there would be little rationale for trading to occur. Unless you believe that you know something many others do not, why trade? (This question ignores the occasional portfolio adjustments necessitated by changing financial situations or rebalancing holdings back to target positions.) Further, how would information relevant to security values be transmitted to stock prices unless someone who knew more than others traded on that information?

Thus an overdose or a dearth of inside information trading would seem detrimental to security markets. But how much inside information trading is optimal? While no one knows the answer, to better understand the issues involved we have to be more specific about what we mean by "inside information."

US Supreme Court Justice Potter Stewart once wrote about pornography: "I can't define it. But I know what it is when I see it." A similar attitude must be taken in defining, inside information. The Association for Investment Management and Research, the representative organization for investment professionals, defines inside information (or more formally, material non-public information) as:

> ...any information about a company or the market for the company's securities, that has not been generally disclosed to the marketplace, the dissemination of which is likely to affect significantly the market price of the company's securities or is likely to be considered important by reasonable investors in determining whether to trade in such securities. (*AIMR Standards of Practice Handbook,* 5th ed.)

While this definition provides a useful starting point, it involves several vague concepts. Does "generally disclosed" mean that everyone know the information or that it is available simply by contacting the company? Similarly, how large a price impact is implied by the term "affect significantly"? Further, who are the "reasonable investors" who determine the importance of the information? Unfortunately, neither the Securities Exchange Commission nor the Ontario Securities Commission has been able or willing to operationally define inside information. The issue has been handled on a case-by-case basis, à la Justice Stewart.

If defining inside information has proved troublesome, enforcing the laws against trading on inside information has been much more difficult, even in some flagrant cases. As the concept has evolved in the courts, for an "insider" to have violated insider trading laws through the disclosure of inside information, that person must:

1. Be in possession of inside information.
2. Be in a position of trust and confidence.
3. Stand to gain from the disclosure, for example, monetarily or through an exchange with someone or as a "gift" to another person.

An individual receiving and trading on inside information (the "tippee") may also violate the law if: (1) the "tipper" had a fiduciary duty to the client, (2) the tipper breached that duty through the disclosure, and (3) the tippee had knowledge of that breach. Proving all three points makes it difficult to prosecute may tippees, especially those who have received inside information third- or fourth-hand.

Security analysts are placed in a precarious position with respect to inside information. One can view their jobs as the creation of inside information, Security analysts examine the prospects for companies and their securities, attempting to identify mispriced securities. If they are successful, their information is unique, nonpublic, and material—clearly inside information. The courts have generally recognized the legality of trading on inside information derived in this manner. But security analysts maintain frequent contact with corporate insiders as part of their jobs. This contact potentially exposes them to inside information of the illegal, if unintentional, kind. Most investment firms and the AIMR have Guidelines for dealing with these situations. Nevertheless, the ambiguity of the situation can cause confusion and may be difficult to control.

The interrelated nature of many large investment firms makes the dissemination of inside information a potentially serious problem. For example, investment banking firms typically operate divisions

that trade for the firms's own accounts. Investment bankers have access to valuable inside information concerning corporate mergers and acquisitions. If traders at an investment banking firm acquired this information, they would be in a position to profit handsomely. To prevent such conflicts, investment firms establish "Chinese Walls"; that is, regulations against information transfers, rules against trading on inside information, and policies against personnel serving in multiple capacities in various departments. Unfortunately, these precautions are not always effective. The insider trading scandals of the 1980s in the US were largely a result of the ample opportunities for inside information abuse existing at investment banking firms.

equal. Directors of firms who are also bank directors appear to have access to better inside information than other insiders.[37]

Sources of Investment Information

Since information affects the values of investments, the serious financial analyst must be well informed. There is a staggering array of such investment information, some of it published on paper (hard copy) and some of it appearing in computer-readable form.

Publications

Financial Post
www.canoe.com/FP/home.html

Financial Times
www.ft.com

Space precludes a detailed listing of publications relating to investing; however, a selected bibliography of general sources of investment information is presented below. Nothing can substitute for a careful perusal of these (and other) publications, and no attempt is made here to describe each one. A serious investor should, at the very least, read *The Globe and Mail: Report on Business* or *The Financial Post* plus *The Wall Street Journal* and *The Financial Times* (London). These provide extensive statistical data, financial news, analysis, and even

---

[37]D. J. Fowler and C. H. Rorke, "Insider Trading Profits on the Toronto Stock Exchange, 1967–1977," *Canadian Journal of Administrative Sciences* 5, no. 1 (March 1988): 13–24. This study also found that the abnormal returns were higher for thinner stocks than for those more frequently traded. See also J. Baesel and G. Stein, "The Value of Information: Inferences from the Profitability of Insider Trading," *Journal of Financial and Quantitative Analysis* 14 (September 1979): 553–569; M. H. Lee and H. Bishara, "Recent Canadian Experiences on the Profitability of Insider Trades," *Financial Review* 24, no. 2 (May 1989): 235–249; J-M. Suret and E. Cormier, "Insiders and the Stock Market," *Canadian Investment Review* III, no. 2 (Fall 1990): 87–90. This study finds that abnormal returns persist after insider trading information has been distributed to a brokerage firm's clients. R. Heinkel and A. Kraus, "The Effect of Insider Trading on Average Rates of Return," *Canadian Journal of Economics* 20, no. 3 (August 1987): 588–611 examined insider trades on the Vancouver Stock Exchange and found weak evidence of superior insider profits.

a bit of humour. Other daily newspapers contain financial information, but much less than those listed above.

A useful source of daily stock price and volume figures is the *Toronto Stock Exchange Daily Record.* Historical data and analyses for a number of Canadian and foreign stocks can be found in the *Value Line Investment Survey: Canadian Edition.* Adjusted betas are also shown for the individual stocks in the *Survey.*[38] *The Toronto Stock Exchange Monthly Review* also contains a wealth of historical information.

In addition to providing bond quality ratings, the bond rating service companies produce other useful information. For example, *Canadian Bond Rating Service* provides ratings, on a quarterly basis, for bonds and debentures, commercial paper, asset-backed securities, mortgage-backed securities, provincial and municipal government bonds, crown corporations, Eurobonds, preferred shares and investment funds as well as industry and individual company financial analyses.

Publications of major security analysts' societies include the *Financial Analysts Journal* (US); *Analyse Financière* (France); and *The Investment Analyst* (United Kingdom). Academic journals that emphasize various aspects of investing include the *Journal of Business,* the *Journal of Finance,* the *Journal of Financial and Quantitative Analysis,* the *Journal of Financial Economics,* the *Review of Financial Studies,* the *Canadian Journal of Administrative Sciences, Finéco,* and the proceedings of the *Administrative Sciences Association of Canada: Finance Division.*

Anyone interested in the management of money for institutional or corporate investors (especially pension funds) should read the *Canadian Investment Review* and the *Journal of Portfolio Management,* which publish the views of both practitioners and academicians. Periodicals aimed at institutional investors and money managers are *Benefits Canada, Canadian Business* and the *Investor's Digest.* A company's annual report provides useful information, which can be supplemented by information filed with the *Ontario Securities Commission* and published in their weekly *Bulletin.*

Sources of macroeconomic data such as monetary aggregates (like the money supply) and other monetary items are the monthly *Bank of Canada Review* and the *Bank of Canada Weekly Financial Statistics.* The C. D. Howe Institute and the Economic Council of Canada provide analysis of economic conditions and forecasts on a periodic basis.

The Conference Board of Canada and Data Resources of Canada publish quarterly macroeconomic forecasts based on economic indicators. **Leading indicators** have been found to signal future changes in the economy, whereas **lagging indicators** change after the economy has done so; **coincident indicators** change simultaneously with the economy. Data on national income and production along with industry information is published regularly by Statistics Canada.

Computer-readable Data

The rapid increase in the use of microcomputers by those who invest money for others as well as by those who invest for themselves has led to a major expansion in the availability of computer-readable investment data.

Large amounts of financial and economic data, such as common stock prices and financial statements, are made available to investors for a fee by Standard & Poor's Canadian Compustat Services, Infoglobe, *The Financial Post* Corporate Database, Micromedia, and Value Line, Inc. These databases are also available online and on disks for use in microcomputers.

Dial-up services are also provided by *Telerate, Bloomberg, Interactive Data Corporation,* and others. Each service is designed so that users of microcomputers can download prices

Canadian Business
www.canbus.com

C.D. Howe Institute
www.cdhowe.org

Conference Board of Canada
www.conferenceboard.ca

Leading Indicators
Economic variables that have been found to signal future changes in the economy.

Lagging Indicators
Economic variables that have been found to follow movements in the economy.

Coincident Indicators
Economic variables that have been found to change at the same time that the economy is changing.

---

[38]These estimates for common stocks appear to be useful in helping the US investor beat the market. See the appendix to Chapter 18.

and other data into their own machines easily and inexpensively. Often the data are in spreadsheet format, readily available for analysis using programs such as Excel.

Databases containing prices, fundamental information, and predictions made by brokerage houses and others are provided on disks by Standard and Poor's Corporation.

The Internet has the potential to revolutionize the delivery of investment information. Virtually every organization involved in investment management maintains a Web site. In many cases, information that just a few years ago would have cost thousands of dollars to access is now available for free on demand over the Internet. The Internet simply is too dynamic to make it possible to list all attractive Web sites here. Nevertheless, students are encouraged to use this text's Weblinks as a starting-point to explore for themselves the immense investment resources now available to them on the Internet. [39]

Summary

1. Financial analysts are investment professionals who evaluate securities and then make investment recommendations. Those recommendations may be used by professional money managers (portfolio managers) or by certain clients of the analysts.

2. There are two primary reasons for engaging in financial analysis: to determine certain characteristics of securities and to attempt to identify mispriced securities.

3. To understand and estimate the risks and returns of individual securities as well as groups of securities, both financial markets and the principles of security valuation must be understood.

4. Technical analysis involves short-term predictions of security price movements based on past patterns of prices and trading volumes. Fundamental analysis concerns estimates of the basic determinants of security values, such as future sales, expenses, and earnings for firms.

5. Many financial analysts focus their research efforts on analyzing company financial statements. Such research permits an analyst to better understand a company's business operations, its plans for future growth, what factors affect its profitability, and how those factors affect its profitability.

6. When prominent analyst publish favourable reports on a stock, its price tends to immediately rise by an abnormal amount. Conversely, when they publish unfavourable reports on stock, its price tends to immediately fall. Neither of these price movemnets are subsequently reversed.

7. Stocks that are neglected by analysts tend to have abnormally high returns.

8. In North America, trading on inside information is illegal in public security markets. However, defining inside information is difficult.

9. There are many printed sources of information about investing in general and firms in particulat that are available to the public. However, currently the fastest growing source is an electronic one—the Internet.

---

[39]While such information can become quickly outdated, a comprehensive list of useful investment-related Web sites is found in Jean Henrich, "The Individual Investor's Guide to Investment Web Sites," *AAII Journal* 19, no. 8 (September 1997): 15–23. Also see the following three articles in the Fall–Winter issue (vol. 6, no. 6) of *Financial Practice and Education*: "An Introduction to Finance on the Internet" by Russ Ray; "A Guide to Locating Financial Information on the Internet" by James B. Pettijohn; and "The Ways in Which the Financial Engineer Can Use the Internet" by Anthony F. Herbst. Finally, Canadian resources are detailed in Jim Carroll and Rick Broadhead, *Canadian Money Management Online* (Scarborough, ON: Prentice Hall Canada, 1996).

TECHNICAL ANALYSIS

As mentioned earlier, most (but not all) technical analysts rely on charts of stock prices and trading volumes. Virtually all employ colourful, and sometimes even mystical, terminology. For example, a significant price rise on relatively large trading volume might be described as an *accumulation*, where the stock is allegedly moving from "weak hands" to "strong hands." This is because a rising stock price on large trading volume is viewed as a situation where demand is stronger than supply. In contrast, a significant price decline on relatively large trading volume may be described as a *distribution*, where the stock is allegedly moving from "strong hands" to "weak hands." This is because a declining stock price on large trading volume is viewed as a situation where supply is stronger than demand. In both situations, relatively large trading volume might be considered a sign of sustainable change in the stock's price, while relatively small trading volume indicates a transitory change.

What if there is a period when a stock's price does not move significantly? If the stock's price movements are within a narrow band, the stock is said to be in a *consolidation phase*. A price level that a stock has difficulty rising above is known as a *resistance level*, and a price level that a stock does not seem to fall below is known as a *support level*.

Such statements may sound meaningful, but an efficient market proponent would argue that they fail to pass the test of simple logic. First, changes in a stock's price occur when the consensus opinion concerning its value changes. This means that large volume associated with a price change only reflects a substantial difference of opinion concerning the impact of new information on the stock's value; small volume reflects smaller differences of opinion. Second, if price or volume data could be used to predict future short-term price movements, investors would rush to exploit such information, moving prices rapidly enough to make the information useless. However, as shown in Tables 22.1 and 22.2, some evidence suggests that there may be some technical trading rules that have merit. Whether they will be useful after transaction costs are fully taken into account is difficult to determine. Even if they do pass muster with respect to transaction costs, it is uncertain whether they will be useful in the future.

Charts

Chartist A technical analyst who primarily relies on stock price and volume charts when evaluating securities.

Chartists (technicians who rely on chart formations) nonetheless believe that certain patterns carry great significance, although they often disagree among themselves on the significance of a pattern or even on the existence of a pattern. Before displaying some hypothetical examples of patterns, it should be noted that there are three basic types of charts used. They are known as bar charts, line charts, and point and figure charts.

For a *bar chart* the horizontal axis is a time line, with the vertical axis measuring a particular stock's price. Corresponding to a given day on the horizontal axis will be a vertical line, the top and bottom of which represent the high and low price for that stock on that day. Somewhere on this vertical line will be a small horizontal line representing the closing price for that day. As an example, consider the following hypothetical stock, whose trading background over the last five days is as follows:

Day	High Price	Low Price	Closing Price	Volume
$t-5$	11	9	10	200
$t-4$	12	9	11	300
$t-3$	13	12	12	400
$t-2$	11	10	11	200
$t-1$	14	11	12	500

Panel (a) of Figure 22.4 presents a bar chart for this stock, whereas panel (b) indicates how such a bar chart of prices can be augmented by adding trading volume at the bottom. Figure 22.5 (a) shows a bar chart exhibiting a pattern that is known as "head and shoulders." As time passed, the stock's price initially rose, hit a peak at A, and then fell to a bottom at B. Recovering from this fall, it went up to an even higher peak at C but then fell again to a bottom at D. Next it rose to a peak at E that was not as high as the previous peak, C, and then started to fall. As soon as the price went down past its previous low, D,

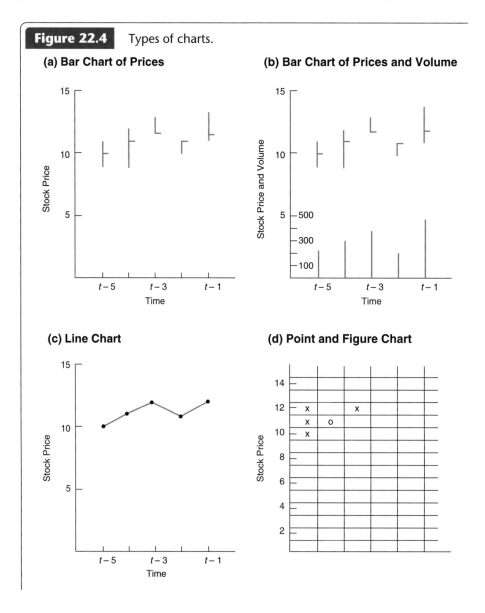

Figure 22.4 Types of charts.

(a) Bar Chart of Prices

(b) Bar Chart of Prices and Volume

(c) Line Chart

(d) Point and Figure Chart

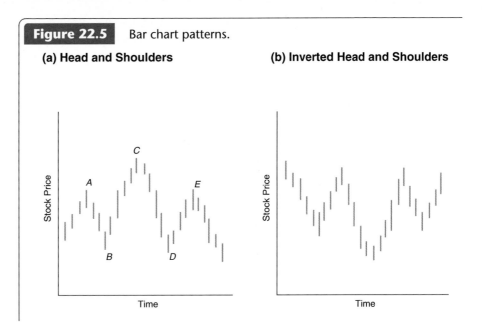

Figure 22.5 Bar chart patterns.

(a) Head and Shoulders

(b) Inverted Head and Shoulders

immediately a forecast was made that the stock was going to plunge much lower (if the stock had not reached a level equal to *D*, no such forecast would have been made).

Figure 22.5(b) shows a bar chart pattern known as "inverted head and shoulders," which results in a forecast that the stock is going to quickly rise by a substantial amount.[40]

For a *line chart*, the axes are the same as with a bar chart. However, only closing prices are presented, and they are connected to each other successively with straight lines, as illustrated in panel (c) of Figure 22.4. Although it is not shown, line charts are also frequently augmented with volume data in a manner identical to bar charts.

Details for construction of *point and figure charts* vary, but the idea is to plot closing prices that form a trend in a single column, moving to the next column only when the trend is reversed. For example, closing prices might be rounded to the nearest dollar and the chart begun by plotting a beginning rounded price on a certain day. As long as the (rounded) price does not change, nothing is done. When a different price is recorded, it is plotted on the chart. A price higher than the initial price is indicated with an *X*, with any gaps between the prices also marked with an *X*. A price below the initial price is marked with an *O* in a similar fashion. Then when a price that is different from the last one is recorded, it is plotted in the same column only if it is in the same direction.

For example, if the first different price is above the beginning price, this price is plotted above the beginning one. Then, if a price is recorded that is above the second one, it is plotted in the same column, but if it is below the second one, then it is plotted in a new column to the right of the first column. Continuing, as long as new prices are in the same direction, they are plotted in the same column. Whenever there is a reversal, a new column is started. Panel (d) of Figure 22.4 presents a point and figure chart for the same hypothetical stock used in the other panels.

---

[40]For details on many kinds of patterns, see Alan R. Shaw, "Technical Analysis," in Levine, *Financial Analyst's Handbook I,* pp. 944–988; Chapter 8 in Jerome B. Cohen, Edward D. Zinbarg, and Arthur Zeikel, *Investment Analysis and Portfolio Management* (Homewood, IL: Richard D. Irwin, 1987); and Richard L. Evans, "Chart Basics Using Bars, Point & Figure, and Candlesticks," *AAII Journal* 15, no. 4 (April 1993): 24–28.

Point and figure enthusiasts look for all sorts of patterns in their charts. As with all chartist techniques, the idea is to recognize a pattern early enough to profit from one's ability to foresee the future course of prices—a neat trick, if one can do it.

Moving Averages

Many other procedures are used by technicians. Some construct moving averages to try to detect "intermediate" and "long-term" trends. Here a set number of the most recent closing prices on a security are averaged each day. (For example, daily closing prices over the previous 200 days may be used.) This means that each day, the oldest price is replaced with the most recent price in the set of closing prices that will be averaged. Frequently a line chart of these moving averages is plotted, along with a line chart of daily closing prices. Each day the charts are updated and then examined for trends to see if there is a buy or sell signal present somewhere.

Alternatively, a long-term moving average may be compared with a short-term moving average (the distinction between the two averages is that the long-term average uses a substantially larger set of closing prices in its calculations than the short-term average). When the short-term average crosses the long-term average, a "signal" is said to have been given. The action recommended will depend on such things as whether the averages have been rising or falling, as well as the direction from which the short-term average crossed the long-term average (it may have been below and now is above, or it may have been above and now is below). A moving average trading rule was used to generate the returns shown in part A of Table 22.2.

Relative Strength Measures

Another procedure used by technicians involves measuring what they call relative strength. For example, a stock's price may be divided by a price index of its industry each day to indicate the stock's movement relative to its industry. Similarly, an industry index may be divided by a market index to indicate the industry's movement relative to the market, or a stock's price may be divided by a market index to indicate a stock's movement relative to the market. The idea here is to examine changes in these relative strength measures with the hope of finding a pattern that can be used to accurately predict the future.

The momentum trading rules used in preparing Table 22.1 were based on the notion of relative strength in its simplest form. Stock returns over a just-ended holding period were calculated and then portfolios of winners and losers were formed. When this was done using semi-annual or annual returns, the momentum trading rules seemed to have merit.

Some procedures of technical analysts focus on relationships among different indexes. For example, the Dow Theory requires that a pattern in the Dow Jones Industrial Average be "confirmed" by a certain movement in the Dow Jones Railroad (now Transportation) Average before action be taken.[41] Another example involves computing the difference between the number of issues advancing and the number declining each day. A chart of the differences cumulated over time, known as the *advance-decline line*, may then be compared with a market index such as the Dow Jones Industrial Average.

---

[41]For more on the Dow Theory, see Richard L. Evans, "Dow's Theory and the Averages: Relevant ... or Relics?" *AAII Journal* 15, no. 1 (January 1993): 27–29.

Contrary Opinion

Many technical procedures are based on the idea of contrary opinion. The idea here is to determine the consensus opinion and then do the opposite. Two examples that were discussed earlier involved (1) buying stocks that had recently dropped in price and selling stocks that had recently risen in price, and (2) buying stocks with low P/E ratios and selling stocks with high P/E ratios. For a third example, one might see whether the "odd-lotters" (those with trade orders involving less than 100 shares) are buying, and then sell any holdings of these stocks. If "the little investor is usually wrong," this will be a procedure that is usually right. However, the basic premise about the little investor has yet to be factually established.

The widespread availability of personal computers and online services with data on stock prices and volumes has made it possible for individual investors to engage in technical analysis in the privacy of their own homes. Producers of software have been quick to provide programs to perform such analysis, complete with multicoloured graphs. Nevertheless, the number of investors using fundamental analysis is much larger than the number using technical analysis.

QUESTIONS AND PROBLEMS

1. If security markets are highly efficient, what role is there for financial analysts?
2. If an analyst can correctly forecast a company's next year earnings, does that necessarily imply the the analyst can correctly forecast how the company's stock will perform? Why?
3. Compare the price reaction to the purchase of stocks that have been identified with a system that previously has been able to "beat the market" with the reactions to (a) the accurate prediction of rainfall and (b) the accurate prediction of the locations of enemy submarines.
4. Despite the arguments and evidence of efficient markets proponents, many investors pay attention to technical analysis in some form. Speculate as to why these investors use this kind of investment research.
5. Describe the types of behaviour that must be exhibited by investors as a group if momentum and contrarian investment strategies are to be successful. In what ways do those behaviours run counter to how the efficient markets hypothesis assumes investor will act?
6. Distinguish between "top-down" and "bottom-up" approaches to financial forecasting. What are the primary advantages and disadvantages of each approach?
7. Last year both Hudson Homes and Baldwin Construction earned $1 million in net income. Both companies have assets of $10 million. However, Hudson generated a return on equity of 11.1% whereas Baldwin produced a return on equity of 20.0%. What can explain the differences in return on equity between the two companies?
8. Last fiscal year, Afton Machinery had the following financial statement data:

Sales/Assets	2.10
Profits/EBIT	0.65
EBIT/Sales	0.10
Assets/Equity	3.00

Calculate Afton's return on assets and return on equity.
9. Augusta Ironworks reported the following fiscal year-end financial data (stated in 000's).

Assets	$1500
Liabilities	$900
Shareholders' equity	$600
Net income	$200
Dividends per share	$0.50
Stock price	$30
Shares outstanding	100

Given this information, calculate Augusta's:

a. Price-earnings ratio

b. Book value per share

c. Price-book ratio

d. Dividend yield

e. Payout ratio

10. Is it true that, when comparing the reported earnings of corporations, "a dollar is a dollar"?

11. Obtain an annual report for a corporation of your choosing. Using the financial statements contained in the report, compute the company's most recent year's return on equity by first calculating:

a. operation margin

b. asset turnover

c. total assets-to-shareholders' equity

d. interest-to-to-shareholders' equity

e. tax rate

12. If Company A has a higher return on equity than Company B, does that necessarily mean that Company A's earnings should grow faster than Company B's earnings? Why?

13. Why does financial statement analysis typically rely heavily on examining financial ratios as opposed to absolute numbers (for example, net income-to-sales as opposed to just net income)?

14. What are some of the drawbacks of comparing a company's financial ratios to those of other companies within the same industry?

15. From the perspective of an efficient market proponent, why is it surprising that trades based on insider trading data found in the OSC's *Monthly Bulletin* appear to produce significant abnormal profits?

16. (Appendix Question) Technical analysis is predicated on stock prices moving in repetitive patterns. What would one have to believe about the timing of the receipt of information by financial markets' participants in order to believe in the existence of such patterns?

17. (Appendix Question) The closing, high, and low prices for Fort McCoy Packaging stock over a 10-day interval are shown below. Construct a bar chart for Fort McCoy Packaging stock over this period of time.

	Fort McCoy Packaging		
Day	Closing Price	High	Low
1	20	21	19
2	20.10	20.10	18
3	21	22	20.50
4	21.05	22.90	21.05
5	21	23.10	20
6	21.75	22	20.75
7	22	23.50	20.05
8	20.05	22	19.10
9	19.05	21.50	19
10	18.10	21.90	17.05

18. (Appendix Question) Calculate the relative strength of Fort McCoy Packaging stock versus the TSE 35 over the 10-day period referred to in Problem 17, given the following closing prices for the TSE 35.

	Day									
	1	2	3	4	5	6	7	8	9	10
TSE 35 Closing Price	300	302	306	310	320	315	330	325	325	330

CFA Exam Question

19. The duPont formula defines the net return on shareholders' equity as a function of the following components:
- operating margin,
- asset turnover,
- interest burden,
- financial leverage, and
- income tax rate.

Using only the data in the table shown below:
  a. Calculate each of the five components listed above for 1985 and 1989, and calculate the return on equity (ROE) for 1985 and 1989, using all of the five components. Show calculations.
  b. Briefly discuss the impact of the changes in asset turnover and financial leverage on the change in ROE from 1985 to 1989.

	1985	1989
Income Statement Data		
Revenues	$542	$979
Operating income	38	76
Depreciation and amortization	3	9
Interest expense	3	0
Pre-tax income	32	67
Income taxes	13	37
Net income after tax	19	30
Balance Sheet Data		
Fixed assets	$41	$70
Total assets	245	291
Working capital	123	157
Total debt	16	0
Total shareholders' equity	159	220

KEY TERMS

financial analyst (p. 738)
portfolio manager (p. 738)
fundamental analysis (p. 740)
technical analysis (p. 744)
top-down forecasting (p. 751)
bottom-up forecasting (p. 751)
probabilistic forecasting (p. 751)
econometric model (p. 752)

endogenous variable (p. 752)
exogenous variable (p. 752)
neglected firm effect (p. 771)
insiders (p. 772)
leading indicator (p. 777)
lagging indicator (p. 777)
coincident indicators (p. 777)
chartists (p. 779)

REFERENCES

1. For a discussion of contrarian investment strategies, see the references in Table 22.1 and in footnote 35 and:

David Dreman, *Contrarian Investment Strategies* (New York: Random House, 1979).

Paul Zarowin, "Short-run Market Overreaction: Size and Seasonality Effects," *Journal of Portfolio Management* 15, no. 3 (Spring 1989): 26–29.

Paul Zarowin, "Does the Stock Market Overreact to Corporate Earnings Information?" *Journal of Finance* 44, no. 5 (December 1989): 1385–1399.

Jennifer Conrad, Mustafa N. Gultekin, and Gautam Kaul, "Profitability of Short-term Contrarian Portfolio Strategies," unpublished paper, The University of Michigan, 1991.

Victor L. Bernard, Jacob K. Thomas, and Jeffrey S. Abarbanell, "How Sophisticated Is the Market in Interpreting Earnings News?" *Journal of Applied Corporate Finance* 6, no. 2 (Summer 1993): 54–63.

Joseph Lakonishok, Andrei Shleifer, and Robert W. Vishny, "Contrarian Investment, Extrapolation, and Risk," *Journal of Finance* 49, no. 5 (December 1994): 1541–1578.

Ray Ball, S. P. Kothari, and Charles E. Wasley, "Can We Implement Research on Stock Trading Rules?" *Journal of Portfolio Management* 21, no. 2 (Winter 1995): 54–63.

Ray Ball, S. P. Kothari, and Jay Shanken, "Problems in Measuring Portfolio Performane: An Application to Contrarian Investment Strategies," *Journal of Financial Economics* 38, no. 1 (May 1995): 79–107.

Tim Loughran and Jay Ritter, "Long-term Market Overreaction: The Effect of Low-priced Stocks," *Journal of Finance* 51, no. 5 (December 1996): 1959–1970.

S. P. Kothari and Jerold Warner, Measuring Long-horizon Security Price Performance," *Journal of Financial Economics* 43, no. 3 (March 1997): 301–339.

2. Closely related to the issue of contrarian investment strategies is the issue of how stock price levels in one period are related to stock price levels in a subsequent period. This issue, like the usefulness of contrarian strategies, has been open to debate. Two of the earliest papers and two recent ones that contradict them are:

Eugene F. Fama and Kenneth R. French, "Permanent and Temporary Components of Stock Prices," *Journal of Political Economy* 96, no. 2 (April 1988): 246–273.

James M. Poterba and Lawrence H. Summers, "Mean Reversion in Stock Prices: Evidence and Implications," *Journal of Financial Economics* 22, no. 1 (October 1988): 27–59.

Myung Jig Kim, Charles R. Nelson, and Richard Startz, "Mean Reversion in Stock Prices? A Reappraisal of the Empirical Evidence," *Review of Economic Studies* 58, no. 3 (May 1991): 515–528.

Grant McQueen, "Long-horizon Mean-reverting Stock Prices Revisited," *Journal of Financial and Quantitative Analysis* 27, no. 1 (March 1992): 1–18.

3. Momentum strategies are discussed in:

Narasimhan Jegadeesh and Sheridan Titman, "Returns to Buying Winners and Selling Losers: Implications for Stock Market Efficiency," *Journal of Finance* 48, no. 1 (March 1993): 65–91.

4. Moving average and trading range breakout strategies are discussed in:

William Brock, Joseph Lakonishok, and Blake LeBaron, "Simple Technical Trading Rules and the Stochastic Properties of Stock Returns," *Journal of Finance* 47, no. 5 (December 1992): 1731–1764.

5. The reaction of stock prices to the publication of analysts' recommendations is discussed in the sources shown in Table 22.8 and in:

Peter Lloyd-Davies and Michael Canes, "Stock Prices and the Publication of Second-hand Information," *Journal of Business* 51, no. 1 (January 1978): 43–56.

John C. Groth, Wilbur G. Lewellen, Gary G. Schlarbaum, and Ronald C. Lease, "An Analysis of Brokerage House Securities Recommendations," *Financial Analysts Journal* 35, no. 1 (January–February 1979): 32–40.

Clark Holloway, "A Note on Testing an Aggressive Investment Strategy Using Value Line Ranks," *Journal of Finance* 36, no. 2 (June 1981): 711–719.

Thomas E. Copeland and David Mayers, "The Value Line Enigma (1965–1978): A Case Study of Performance Evaluation Issues," *Journal of Financial Economics* 10, no. 3 (November 1982): 289–321.

James H. Bjerring, Josef Lakonishok, and Theo Vermaelen, "Stock Prices and Financial Analysts' Recommendations," *Journal of Finance* 38, no. 1 (March 1983): 187–204.

Gur Huberman and Shmuel Kande, "Value Line Rank and Firm Size," *Journal of Business* 60, no. 4 (October 1987): 577–589.

Gur Huberman and Shmuel Kande, "Market Efficiency and Value Line's Record," *Journal of Business* 63, no. 2 (April 1990): 187–216.

Pu Liu, Stanley D. Smith, and Azmat A. Syed, "Stock Price Reactions to *The Wall Street Journal's* Securities Recommendations," *Journal of Financial and Quantitative Analysis* 25, no. 3 (September 1990): 399–410.

Messod Beneish, "Stock Prices and the Dissemination of Analysts' Recommendations," *Journal of Business* 64, no. 3 (July 1991): 393–416.

Philip Heitner, "Isn't It Time to Measure Analysts' Track Records?" *Financial Analysts Journal* 47, no. 3 (May–June 1991): 5–6.

Donna R. Philbrick and William E. Ricks, "Using Value Line and IBES Analyst Forecast in Accounting Research," *Journal of Accounting Research* 29, no. 2 (Autumn 1991): 397–417.

John Affleck-Graves and Richard R. Mendenhall, "The Relation Between the Value Line Enigma and Post-earnings-announcement Drift," *Journal of Financial Economics* 31, no. 1 (February 1992): 75–96.

John Markese, "The Role of Earnings Forecasts in Stock Behavior," *AAII Journal* 14, no. 4 (April 1992): 30–32.

Rajiv Sant and Mir A. Zaman, "Market Reaction to *Business Week* "Inside Wall Street" Column: A Self-fulfilling Prophecy," *Journal of Banking and Finance* 20, no. 4 (May 1996): 617–643.

Jennifer Francis and Leonard Soffer, "The Relative Informativeness of Analysts' Stock Recommendations and Earnings Forecast Revisions," Journal of *Accounting Research* 35, no. 2 (Autumn 1997): 193–211.

6. The "Heard on the Street" column also sometimes discusses takeover rumours. For an analysis of the effects these rumours have on stock prices, see John Pound and Richard Zeckhauser, "Clearly Heard on the Street: The Effect of Takeover Rumors on Stock Prices," *Journal of Business* 63, no. 3 (July 1990): 291–308.

7. For a discussion of the neglected firm effect, see:

   Avner Arbel and Paul Strebel, "Pay Attention to Neglected Firms!" *Journal of Portfolio Management* 9, no. 2 (Winter 1983): 37–42.

   Avner Arbel, Steven Carvel, and Paul Strebel, "Giraffes, Institutions, and Neglected Firms," *Financial Analysts Journal* 39, no. 3 (May–June 1983): 57–63.

   Craig G. Beard and Richard W. Sias, "Is There a Neglected-firm Effect?" *Financial Analysts Journal* 53 no. 5 (September–Obtober 1997): 19–23.

8. Insider trading has been examined in a number of studies. Some of the major ones are:

   Jeffrey F. Jaffe, "Special Information and Insider Trading," *Journal of Business* 47, no. 3 (July 1974): 410–428.

   Joseph E. Finnerty, "Insiders and Market Efficiency," *Journal of Finance* 31, no. 4 (September 1976): 1141–1148.

   Herbert S. Kerr, "The Battle of Insider Trading and Market Efficiency," *Journal of Portfolio Management* 6, no. 4 (Summer1980): 47–58.

Wayne Y. Lee and Michael Solt, "Insider Trading: A Poor Guide to Market Timing," *Journal of Portfolio Management* 12, no. 4 (Summer 1986): 65–71.

H. Nejat Seyhun, "Insiders' Profits, Costs of Trading, and Market Efficiency," *Journal of Financial Economics* 16 no. 2 (June 1986): 189–212.

H. Nejat Seyhun, "The Information Content Of Aggregate Insider Trading," *Journal of Business* 61, no. 1 (January 1988): 1–24.

Michael S. Rozeff and Mir A. Zaman, "Market Efficiency and Insider Trading: New Evidence," *Journal of Business* 61, no. 1 (January 1988): 25–44.

Ji-Chai Lin and JohnS. Howe, "Insider Trading in the OTC Market," *Journal of Finance* 45, no. 4 (September 1990): 1273–1284.

Lisa K. Meulbroek, "An Empirical Analysis of Illegal Insider Trading," *Journal of Finance* 47, no. 5 (December 1992): 1661–1699.

Mustafa Chowdhury, John S. Howe, and Ji-Chai Lin, "The Relation Between Aggragate Insider Transactions and Stock Market Returns," *Journal of Financial and Quantitive Analysis* 28, no. 3 (September 1993): 431–437.

9. Leading books on technical analysis, financial statement analysis, and fundamental analysis are, respectively:

Robert D. Edwards and John Magee, *Technical Analysis of Stock Trends* (Boston: John Magee, 1966).

George Foster, *Financial Statement Analysis* (Englewood Cliffs, NJ: Prentice Hall, 1986).

Sidney Cottle, Roger Murray, and Frank Block, *Graham and Dodd's Security Analysis* (New York: McGraw-Hill, 1988).

10. Information sources for investing are described in:

Maria Crawford Scott and John Bajkowski, "Sources of Information for the Simplified Approach to Valuation," *AAII Journal* 16, no. 3 (April 1994): 29–32.

John Markese, "Picking Common Stocks: What Seems to Work, At Least Sometimes," *AAII Journal* 16, no. 5 (June 1994): 24–27.

11. For a Canadian perspective on the topics covered in this chapter, see:

S. Foerster, A. Prihar and J. Schmitz, "Price Momentum Models and How They Beat the Canadian Equity Markets," *Canadian Investment Review* VII, no. 4 (Winter 1994–95).

P. Brockman, C. Mossman and D. Olson, "What's the Value of Fundamental Analysis?" *Canadian Investment Review* X, no. 3 (Fall 1997).

Investment Management

Investment management, also known as portfolio management, is the process by which money is managed. It may (1) be active or passive, (2) use explicit or implicit procedures, and (3) be relatively controlled or uncontrolled. The trend is toward highly controlled operations consistent with the notion that capital markets are relatively efficient. However, approaches vary, and many different investment styles can be found. This chapter will discuss investment management, and in doing so it will present various types of investment styles.

Traditional Investment Management Organizations

Few people or organizations like to be called "traditional." However, some investment management organizations follow procedures that have changed little from those that were popular decades ago, and thus deserve the title. Figure 23.1 shows the major characteristics of a traditional investment management organization.

Projections concerning the economy and the money and capital markets are made by economists, technicians, fundamentalists, or other market experts within or outside the organization. The projected economic environment is communicated via briefings and written reports—usually in a rather implicit and qualitative manner—to the organization's **security analysts**. Each analyst is responsible for a group of securities, often those in one or more industries (in some organizations, analysts are called industry specialists). Often a group of analysts report to a senior analyst responsible for a sector of the economy or market.

The analysts, often drawing heavily on reports of others (for example, "street analysts" in brokerage houses), make predictions about the securities for which they are responsible. In a sense, such predictions are conditional on the assumed economic and market environments, although the relationship is typically quite loose.

Analysts' predictions seldom specify an expected rate of return or the time over which predicted performance will take place. Instead, an analyst's feelings about a security may be summarized by assigning it one of five codes, where a 1 represents a buy and a 5 represents a sell, as indicated in Figure 23.1.[1] In many organizations, a simple buy-hold-sell designation is given.

Security Analyst
(Alternatively, **Financial Analyst** or **Investment Analyst**.) An individual who analyzes financial assets to determine the investment characteristics of those assets and to identify mispricings among those assets.

---

[1]One study found that a firm's share price tended to move upward when analysts upgraded its coding, and downward when analysts downgraded its coding. See Edwin J. Elton, Martin J. Gruber, and Seth Grossman, "Discrete Expectational Data and Portfolio Performance," *Journal of Finance* 41, no. 3 (July 1986): 699–713.

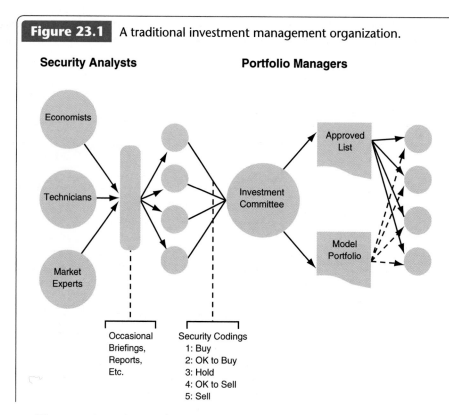

Figure 23.1 A traditional investment management organization.

Security Analysts

Portfolio Managers

Economists

Technicians

Market
Experts

Investment
Committee

Approved
List

Model
Portfolio

Occasional
Briefings,
Reports,
Etc.

Security Codings
1: Buy
2: OK to Buy
3: Hold
4: OK to Sell
5: Sell

These security codings and various written reports constitute the information formally transmitted to an **investment committee**, which typically includes the senior management of the organization. In addition, analysts occasionally brief the investment committee on their feelings about various securities. The investment committee's primary formal output is often an **approved** (or authorized) **list**, which consists of the securities deemed worthy of accumulation in a given portfolio. The rules of the organization typically specify that any security on the list may be bought, whereas those not on the list should be either held or sold, barring special circumstances.

The presence or absence of a security on the approved list constitutes the major information transmitted explicitly from the investment committee to a **portfolio manager**. In some organizations, senior management supervises a "model portfolio" (for example, a bank's major commingled equity fund), the composition of which indicates to portfolio managers the relative intensity of senior management's feelings regarding different securities.

In many ways, this description is a caricature of an investment organization—even one run along traditional lines. Nevertheless, most of these attributes can be observed in practice in one form or another.

In recent years, specialty investment firms have gained considerable popularity. As opposed to traditional investment firms that invest in a broad spectrum of securities, these organizations concentrate their investment efforts on a particular asset class, such as stocks or bonds. They often specialize even further, focusing on a narrow segment of a particular asset class, such as the shares of small start-up companies.

Although these specialty investment firms may follow many of the security analysis procedures of the traditional investment organizations, they usually employ few security analysts. Often the portfolio managers serve as analysts. Furthermore, their decision-making processes are typically more streamlined, often avoiding investment committee structures entirely, thereby permitting portfolio managers considerable discretion to research securities and construct portfolios. Whether this less hierarchical approach to investing actually produces superior results is open to question.

Investment Committee
Within a traditional investment organization, a group of senior management responsible for establishing the organization's broad investment strategy.

Approved List A list of securities that an investment organization deems worthy of inclusion in a given portfolio.

Portfolio Manager An individual who utilizes the information provided by financial analysts to construct a portfolio of financial assets.

Investment Management Functions

In Chapter 1 a five-step procedure was outlined for making investment decisions. These steps can all be viewed as functions of investment management, and they must be undertaken for each client whose money is being managed. They are as follows:

1. *Set investment policy*—identify the client's investment objectives, particularly as regards her attitude toward the trade-off between expected return and risk.
2. *Perform security analysis*—scrutinize individual securities or groups of securities in order to identify mispriced situations.
3. *Construct a portfolio*—identify specific securities in which to invest, along with the proportion of investable wealth to be put into each security.
4. *Revise the portfolio*—determine which securities in the current portfolio are to be sold and which securities are to be purchased to replace them.
5. *Evaluate the performance of the portfolio*—determine the actual performance of a portfolio in terms of risk and return, and compare the performance with that of an appropriate "benchmark" portfolio.

The remainder of this chapter deals with how an investment management organization could perform the first four functions; the next chapter deals with the fifth function.

Setting Investment Policy

An investment manager who is in charge of a client's entire portfolio must be concerned with the client's risk-return preferences. Investors who use more than one manager can select one to help in this important phase, or they may employ the services of a consultant or financial planner. In any event, one of the key characteristics that differentiates clients from one another concerns their investment objectives. According to modern portfolio theory, these objectives are reflected in the client's attitude toward risk and expected return. As mentioned in Chapter 6, specifying indifference curves is one method of describing these objectives. However, determining a client's indifference curves is not a simple task. In practice, it is often done in an indirect and approximate fashion by estimating the client's level of **risk tolerance**, defined as the largest amount of risk that the client is willing to accept for a given increase in expected return.

Risk Tolerance The trade-off between risk and expected return demanded by a particular investor.

Estimating Risk Tolerance

The starting point in making such an estimation is to provide the client with a set of risks and expected returns for different combinations of two hypothetical portfolios. For example, imagine that the client is told that the expected return on a stock portfolio is 12%, while the return on a risk-free portfolio consisting of Treasury bills is 7.5% (that is, $\bar{r}_S = 12\%$ and $r_F = 7.5\%$). Similarly, the client is told that the standard deviation on the stock portfolio is 15%, while the standard deviation on the risk-free portfolio is, by definition, 0.0% (that is, $\sigma_S = 15\%$ and $\sigma_F = 0.0\%$).[2] Additionally, the client is told that all combinations of these two portfolios lie on a straight line that connects them. (This is because the covariance between these two portfolios is 0.0, meaning that $\sigma_{SF} = 0.0$.) Some combinations of these two portfolios are shown in Table 23.1.

---

[2]This example is taken from William F. Sharpe, *Asset Allocation Tools* (Redwood City, CA: Scientific Press, 1987), p. 38.

Table 23.1 Combinations of Stock and Risk-free Treasury Bill Portfolios.

Proportion In		Expected Return	Standard Deviation	Implied Level of Risk Tolerance
Stocks	Bills			
0%	100%	7.50%	0.0%	0
10	90	7.95	1.5	10
20	80	8.40	3.0	20
30	70	8.85	4.5	30
40	60	9.30	6.0	40
50	50	9.75	7.5	50
60	40	10.20	9.0	60
70	30	10.65	10.5	70
80	20	11.10	12.0	80
90	10	11.55	13.5	90
100	0	12.00	15.0	100
110	−10	12.45	16.5	110
120	−20	12.90	18.0	120
130	−30	13.35	19.5	130
140	−40	13.80	21.0	140
150	−50	14.25	22.5	150
.	.	.	.	.
.	.	.	.	.
.	.	.	.	.

Note that the investor is being presented with the efficient set that arises when there is a set of stocks and a risk-free borrowing and lending rate. As shown in Chapter 8, this efficient set is linear, meaning that it is a straight line that emanates at the risk-free rate and goes through a tangency portfolio that consists of a certain combination of securities. (In this case those securities are common stocks.) Hence, negative percentages in Treasury bills (shown at the bottom of Table 23.1) represent risk-free borrowing in order to purchase greater amounts of stocks.

At this point, the client is asked to identify the combination that appears to be most desirable, in terms of expected return and standard deviation. Asking the investor to identify the most desirable combination is equivalent to asking the investor to locate where one of her indifference curves is tangent to the linear efficient set, as this point will represent the most desirable portfolio.[3]

After the client has selected the best stock/Treasury bill mix, what can be said about her risk tolerance? One would, of course, like to identify all the indifference curves that represent a client's attitude toward risk and expected return. However, in practice a more modest goal is usually adopted—to obtain a reasonable representation of the shape of such curves in the region of risk and expected return within which the client's optimal choices will most likely fall.

---

[3]If such a decision is made on behalf of the client (for example, by a trustee for one or more beneficiaries), the task is much more difficult, but a decision is still required.

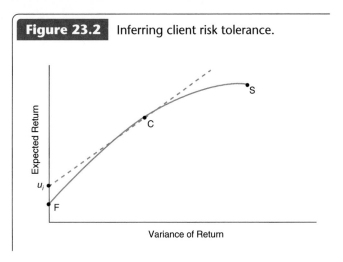

Figure 23.2 Inferring client risk tolerance.

The points in Figure 23.2 plot the alternative mixes presented to the client that were given in Table 23.1. Curve *FCS* shows the risk-return characteristics of all possible mixes, and point *C* identifies the attributes of the mix chosen by the client. In this figure expected return is measured on the vertical axis and *variance* on the horizontal axis. Although the combinations available to the client plot on a straight line when standard deviation is measured on the horizontal axis, the combinations plot on a concave curve when variance is used (as in this figure).

Assuming that all the possible mixes had been presented to the client and point *C* had been chosen, it could be inferred that the slope of the client's indifference curve going through *C* is precisely equal to that of curve *FCS* at this point. As mentioned earlier, this follows from the observation that the portfolio on the efficient set that a client identifies as being the "best" corresponds to the one where the client's indifference curves are just tangent to the efficient set.

Constant Risk Tolerance

In principle, the choice of a mix provides information about the slope of an indifference curve at only one point. To go beyond this, an assumption must be made about the general shape of the client's indifference curves. An assumption commonly made is that the client has constant risk tolerance over a range of alternative portfolios in the neighbourhood of the point originally chosen. Figure 23.3 shows the nature of this assumption. As indicated in panel (a), indifference curves in a diagram with *variance* on the horizontal axis are *linear* when it is assumed that the client has constant risk tolerance. This means that the equation for an indifference curve of such an investor is equivalent to the equation for a straight line where the variable on the horizontal axis is variance (σ_P^2) and the variable on the vertical axis is expected return ($\bar{r}_P$). Given that the equation of a straight line takes the form of $Y = a + bX$, where a is the vertical intercept and b is the slope, the equation for an indifference curve can be written as

$$\bar{r}_P = a + b\sigma_P^2$$

or

$$\bar{r}_P = u_i + \frac{1}{\tau}\sigma_P^2 \tag{23.1}$$

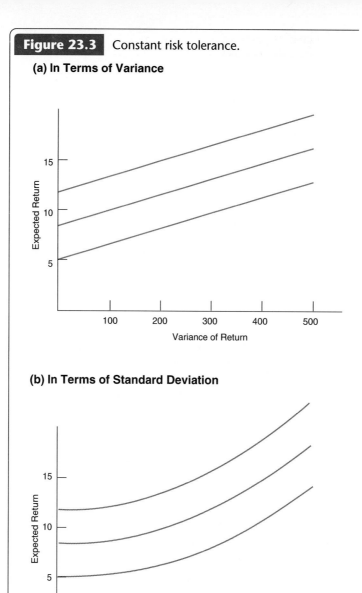

Figure 23.3 Constant risk tolerance.

(a) In Terms of Variance

Expected Return

Variance of Return

(b) In Terms of Standard Deviation

Expected Return

Standard Deviation of Return

where u_i is the vertical intercept for indifference curve i and the slope of the indifference curve is $1/\tau$.[4] Note how any two indifference curves for a client differ from one another by only the value of the vertical intercept. This is because the indifference curves are parallel, meaning that they have the same slope, $1/\tau$.

Figure 23.3(b) plots the same indifference curves in a more familiar manner—with *standard deviation* on the horizontal axis. Note that the curves have the conventional shape—they indicate that the investor requires more return to compensate for an addi-

---

[4]Normally risk tolerance τ is expressed as units of variance per unit of expected return. However, the reciprocal of risk tolerance $1/\tau$ appears in equation (23.1). This is necessitated by having risk on the horizontal axis in Figure 23.3.

tional unit of standard deviation as the risk of the portfolio increases. That is, the curves are *convex* when standard deviation is measured on the horizontal axis.

In order to estimate the client's level of risk tolerance τ, it was mentioned that the slope of the indifference curves, $1/\tau$, would be set equal to the slope of the efficient set at the location of the portfolio that was selected, denoted portfolio C. Doing so results in the following formula for estimating τ:

$$\tau = \frac{2[(\bar{r}_C - r_F)\sigma_S^2]}{(\bar{r}_S - r_F)^2} \tag{23.2}$$

where $\bar{r}_C$ denotes the expected return of the portfolio that the client selected, $\bar{r}_S$ and r_F denote the expected return of the stock portfolio and risk-free rate, respectively, and σ_S^2 denotes the variance of the stock portfolio. (A detailed presentation of how this formula was derived is presented in the appendix.)

In the example, the client was given a choice between S, F, and various combinations of S and F where $\bar{r}_S = 12\%$, $r_F = 7.5\%$, and $\sigma_S^2 = 15^2 = 225$. Now, by using equation (23.2), the level of risk tolerance τ inferred from the choice of portfolio C can be determined to equal

$$\tau = \frac{2[(\bar{r}_C - 7.5)225]}{(12 - 7.5)^2} \tag{23.3}$$

$$= 22.22\bar{r}_C - 166.67$$

Assuming the choice of a portfolio consisting of a 50% investment in stocks and a 50% investment in risk-free Treasury bills, the client in this example has chosen a portfolio C with an expected return of 9.75%. Accordingly, equation (23.3) can be used to determine the value of τ for this client, resulting in an estimated level of τ equal to $(22.22 \times 9.75) - 166.67 = 50$. This means that the client will accept up to an additional 50 units of variance in order to receive an extra 1% in expected return. Thus, the client's indifference curves are estimated to have the form of

$$\bar{r}_P = u_i + \frac{1}{50}\sigma_P^2 \tag{23.4}$$

Table 23.1 shows the inferred level of risk tolerance τ if a different portfolio had been chosen by the client. These levels were determined by substituting the appropriate values for $\bar{r}_C$ into the right-hand side of equation (23.3) and then solving for τ. First, note that the level of risk tolerance is the same as the percentage invested in the stock portfolio associated with C. That is, equation (23.3) can be rewritten as $\tau = 100X_S$, where X_S is the proportion invested in the stock portfolio associated with C. It can be shown that this will always be the case when $\bar{r}_S - r_F = 4.5\%$ and $\sigma_S = 15\%$. Other estimates would give different expressions for τ, but the relationship between X_S and τ would still be linear.

Second, note how the level of risk tolerance is lower if the selected portfolio is more conservative (that is, when the selected level of expected return and standard deviation is lower). Thus, more conservative risk-averse clients will have lower levels of risk tolerance (and thus steeper indifference curves) than less conservative risk-averse clients.

Having estimated the client's indifference curves, recall from Chapter 6 that the objective of investment management is to identify the portfolio that lies on the indifference curve furthest to the northwest because such a portfolio will offer the investor the level of expected return and risk that is preferable to all the other portfolios. This is equivalent to identifying the portfolio that lies on the indifference curve that has the highest vertical intercept, u_i. This can be seen graphically in Figures 23.3(a) and 23.3(b), where the indifference curves have been extended to the vertical axis.

Certainty Equivalent Return

Certainty Equivalent Return For a particular risky investment, the return on a risk-free investment that makes the investor indifferent between the risky and risk-free investments.

The term u_i can be thought of as the **certainty equivalent return** for any portfolio that lies on indifference curve i.[5] Thus portfolio C in Figure 23.2 is as desirable for this particular client as a hypothetical portfolio with an expected return of u_i and no risk—that is, one providing a return of u_i with certainty. When viewed in this manner, the job of the portfolio manager is to identify the portfolio with the highest certainty equivalent return.

Equation (23.1) can be rewritten so that the certainty equivalent return u_i appears on the left-hand side. Doing so results in

$$u_i = \bar{r}_P - \frac{1}{\tau}\sigma_P^2 \tag{23.5}$$

This equation shows that the certainty equivalent return can be thought of as a risk-adjusted expected return because a risk penalty that depends on both the portfolio's variance and the client's risk tolerance must be subtracted from the portfolio's expected return in determining u_i.

In the example, the investor selected the portfolio with $\bar{r}_P = 9.75\%$ and $\sigma_P^2 = 56.25$ ($= 7.5^2$). Thus, the certainty equivalent return for this portfolio is $9.75 - (56.25/50)$ $= 8.625\%$. Equivalently, the risk penalty for the portfolio that was selected was $56.25/50 = 1.125\%$. If the certainty equivalent return for any other portfolio shown in Table 23.1 is calculated, it will have a lower value. For example, the 80/20 portfolio has a certainty equivalent return of $11.1 - (144/50) = 8.22\%$. Thus, the goal of investment management can be thought of as identifying the portfolio that has the maximum value of $\bar{r}_P - (\sigma_P^2/\tau)$, because it will provide the client with the maximum certainty equivalent return.

Security Analysis and Portfolio Construction

Passive and Active Management

Passive Management The process of buying and holding a well-diversified portfolio.

Active Management A form of investment management that involves buying and selling financial assets with the objective of earning positive risk-adjusted returns.

Index Fund A passively managed investment in a diversified portfolio of financial assets designed to mimic the investment performance of a specific market index.

Within the investment industry, a distinction is often made between **passive management**—holding securities for relatively long periods with small and infrequent changes—and **active management**. Passive managers generally act as if the security markets are relatively efficient. Put somewhat differently, their decisions are consistent with the acceptance of consensus estimates of risk and return. The portfolios they hold may be surrogates for the market portfolio that are known as **index funds**, or they may be portfolios that are tailored to suit clients with preferences and circumstances that differ from those of the average investor.[6] In either case, passive portfolio managers do not try to outperform their designated benchmark.

For example, a passive manager might only have to choose the appropriate mixture of Treasury bills and an index fund that is a surrogate for the market portfolio. The best mixture would depend on the shape and location of the client's indifference curves. Figure 23.4 provides an illustration.

---

[5]The term u_i is also known as the expected utility of indifference curve i. It represents the level of satisfaction associated with all portfolios plotting on indifference curve i. For more about utility theory, indifference curves, and certainty equivalent returns, see Mark Kritzman, "… About Utility," *Financial Analysts Journal* 48, no. 3 (May–June 1992): 17–20. In considering an investor's utility of wealth function, Chapter 6 discussed a closely related concept, the certainty equivalent of wealth.

[6]An example of a tailored portfolio would be one consisting of shares with high dividend yields. Such a portfolio might be purchased for a corporate investor because 100% of all dividends received by a corporate investor are exempt from corporate income tax.

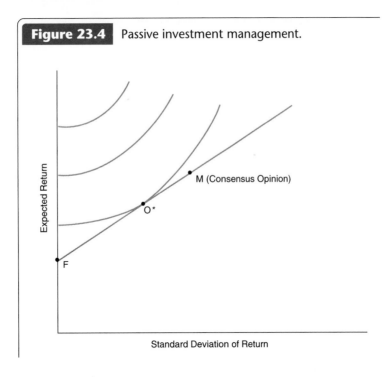

Figure 23.4 Passive investment management.

Point *F* plots the risk-free return offered by Treasury bills, and point *M* plots the risk and expected return of the surrogate market portfolio, using consensus forecasts. Mixtures of the two investments plot along line *FM*. The client's attitude toward risk and return is shown by the set of indifference curves, and the optimal mixture lies at the point *O** where an indifference curve is tangent to line *FM*. In this example, the best mixture uses both Treasury bills and the surrogate market portfolio. In other situations, the surrogate market portfolio might be "levered up" by borrowing (that is, money might be borrowed and added to the client's own investable funds, with the total being used to purchase the surrogate market portfolio).

When management is passive, the overall mixture is altered only when (1) the client's preferences change; (2) the risk-free rate changes; or (3) the consensus forecast about the risk and return of the benchmark portfolio changes. The manager must continue to monitor the last two variables and keep in touch with the client concerning the first one. No additional activity is required.

Active managers believe that from time to time there are mispriced securities or groups of securities. They do not act as if they believe that security markets are efficient. Put somewhat differently, they use deviant predictions: their forecasts of risks and expected returns differ from consensus opinions. Whereas some managers may be more bullish than average about a security, others may be more bearish. The former will hold "more-than-normal" proportions of the security, while the latter will hold "less-than-normal" proportions.

Assuming that there is no tailoring, it is useful to think of a portfolio as having two components: (1) a benchmark portfolio and (2) deviations designed to take advantage of security mispricing. For example, a portfolio can be broken down as follows:

Name of Security (Col. 1)	Proportion in Actual Portfolio (Col. 2)	Proportion in Market Portfolio (Col. 3)	Active Position (Col. 4)
S1	.30	.45	−.15
S2	.20	.25	−.05
S3	.50	.30	+.20
	1.00	1.00	.00

The second column shows the actual proportions in the actively managed portfolio. The third column indicates the percentages in a benchmark portfolio, which in this case is represented by a surrogate market portfolio—the holdings that might be best for an average client in a perfectly efficient market. The **active positions** can be represented by the differences between the proportions in the actual and benchmark portfolios. Such differences arise because active managers disagree with the consensus forecast about expected returns or risks. When expressed as differences of this sort, the actual portfolio can be viewed as an investment in the benchmark portfolio with a series of *bets* being placed on certain securities (such as S3) and against certain other securities (such as S1 and S2). Note how the bets are "balanced" in that the amount of the negative bets exactly counters the amount of the positive bets.

Active Position The difference between the percentage of an investor's portfolio invested in a particular financial asset and the percentage of a benchmark portfolio invested in that same asset.

Security Selection, Asset Allocation, and Market Timing

Security Selection

In principle, the investment manager should make forecasts of expected returns, standard deviations, and covariances for all available securities. This will allow an efficient set to be generated, upon which the indifference curves of the client can be plotted. Having done this, the investment manager should invest in those securities that form the optimal portfolio (that is, the portfolio indicated by the point where an indifference curve is tangent to the efficient set) for the client in question. Such a one-stage **security selection** process is illustrated in Figure 23.5(a).

Security Selection (Alternatively, **Portfolio Construction**.) A component of the investment process that involves identifying which assets to invest in and determining the proportion of funds to invest in each of the assets.

In practice, this is rarely (if ever) done. Excessive costs would be incurred to obtain detailed forecasts of the expected returns, standard deviations, and covariances for all the individual securities under consideration. Instead, the decision on which securities to purchase is made in two or more stages.

Figure 23.5(b) illustrates a two-stage procedure where the investment manager has decided to consider investing in common stocks and corporate bonds for a client. In this case, the expected returns, standard deviations, and covariances are forecast for all common stocks under consideration. Then, based on just these common stocks, the efficient set is formed and the optimal stock portfolio identified. Next, the same analysis is performed for all corporate bonds under consideration, resulting in the identification of the optimal bond portfolio. The security selection process used in each of these two **asset classes** can be described as being myopic. That is, covariances between the individual common stocks and corporate bonds have not been considered in the identification of the two optimal portfolios.

Asset Class A broadly defined generic group of financial assets, such as stocks or bonds.

Although this example has only two asset classes—stocks and bonds—it should be noted that the number of asset classes can be relatively large. Other asset classes that are often used are money market securities ("cash"), foreign stocks, foreign bonds, and real estate.

Figure 23.5 Investment styles.

(a) Security Selection

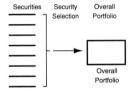

(b) Security Selection and Asset Allocation

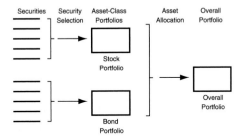

(c) Security Selection, Group Selection, Asset Allocation

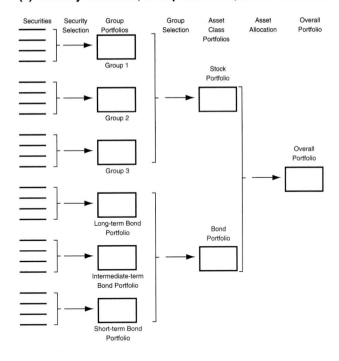

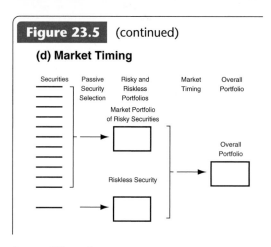

Figure 23.5 (continued)

(d) Market Timing

Asset Allocation

Asset Allocation The process of determining the optimal division of an investor's portfolio among available asset classes.

The second stage of the process divides the client's funds among two (or more) asset class portfolios, and is known as **asset allocation**.[7] In this stage, forecasts of the expected return and standard deviation are needed for both the optimal stock portfolio and the optimal bond portfolio, along with the covariance between the two portfolios. This will allow the expected return and standard deviation to be determined for all combinations of these two portfolios. Finally, after generating the efficient set from these combinations, the indifference curves of the client can be used to determine which portfolio should be chosen.[8]

Some people refer to two types of asset allocation. *Strategic asset allocation* refers to how a portfolio's funds would be divided, given the portfolio manager's long-term forecasts of expected returns, variances, and covariances, whereas *tactical asset allocation* refers to how these funds are to be divided at any particular moment, given the investor's short-term forecasts. Hence, the former reflects what the portfolio manager would do for the long term and the latter reflects what he would do under current market conditions.

For example, the first stage might have indicated that the investor should hold the proportions of stocks S1, S2, and S3 given earlier (that is, the optimal stock portfolio has proportions of .30, .20, and .50, respectively). Similarly, the first stage might have indicated that the investor should hold a proportion of .35 in bond B1 and .65 in bond B2. Then, under tactical asset allocation, the second stage might indicate that the client's funds should be split so that 60% goes into stocks and 40% into bonds because of current market conditions (whereas under strategic asset allocation these percentages might have been 70% and 30%, respectively). This translates into individual investments of the following magnitudes:

[7] For evidence suggesting that asset allocation is the most important decision an investor has to make, see Gary P. Brinson, L. Randolph Hood, and Gilbert L. Beebower, "Determinants of Portfolio Performance," *Financial Analysts Journal* 42, no. 4 (July–August 1986): 39–44; and Gary P. Brinson, Brian D. Singer, and Gilbert L. Beebower, "Determinants of Portfolio Performance II: An Update," *Financial Analysts Journal* 47, no. 3 (May–June 1991): 40–48.

[8] One study examined four prominent sources who provided recommendations for how investors should allocate their money and found that all of them recommended that the ratio of bonds to stocks should be higher for conservative investors relative to more aggressive investors. According to the separation theorem (see Chapter 9), this ratio should not change. This is because capital market theory says that investors should purchase the market portfolio, which is a fixed blend of stocks and bonds, and then either invest or borrow money at the risk-free rate. Consequently, they refer to this as the "asset allocation puzzle." See Niko Canner, N. Gregory Mankiw, and David N. Weil, "An Asset Allocation Puzzle," *American Economic Review* 87, no. 1 (March 1997): 181–191.

$$
\begin{array}{lll}
\text{Stocks:} & & \\
\quad \text{S1} & .60 \times .30 = & .18 \\
\quad \text{S2} & .60 \times .20 = & .12 \\
\quad \text{S3} & .60 \times .50 = & .30 \\
\text{Bonds:} & & \\
\quad \text{B1} & .40 \times .35 = & .14 \\
\quad \text{B2} & .40 \times .65 = & \underline{.26} \\
& & 1.00
\end{array}
$$

The two-stage process just discussed can be extended by introducing groups (sometimes referred to as sectors). Figure 23.5(c) illustrates a three-stage process. In the first stage, known as security selection, the investment manager would exercise discretion in identifying groups of securities in each asset class. Then having identified the groups, the investment manager would determine the optimal portfolio for each one. For example, within the asset class of common stocks, it could be that the investment manager has identified all industrial stocks as the first group, all utility stocks as the second group, and all transportation stocks as the third group. Within the asset class of bonds, groups of long-term, intermediate-term, and short-term bonds have been identified. Then, the investment manager would proceed to identify six optimal portfolios, one for each group of securities.

Group Selection A component of the security selection process involving the identification of desirable combinations of groups within an asset class.

In the second stage, known as **group selection** (or group rotation), the investment manager determines the appropriate combination of the groups within each asset class. For example, the manager may have decided that the appropriate combination is 70% industrials, 10% utilities, and 20% transportation stocks. Similarly, the manager may have decided that the appropriate combination of bonds is 100% in long-term, with nothing in either intermediate-term or short-term bonds. Thus, in this stage the manager will determine the composition of an optimal stock portfolio and an optimal bond portfolio but will not know how much to allocate to each one.

The third and final stage makes this allocation and, as noted previously, is referred to as asset allocation. It is performed in a manner that is identical to the second stage of the two-stage procedure illustrated in Figure 23.5(b).

Active or passive management may be used in any stage. For example, *active bets* might be placed on individual securities, but with funds allocated across asset classes based on consensus long-term forecasts of expected returns for such classes. That is, the investment manager may decide to stick to a long-term mix of 75% stocks and 25% bonds. However, the choice of individual stocks and bonds in which to invest will change with time, based on the manager's forecasts.

Alternatively, passive portfolios of individual securities might be constructed, with deviant predictions of asset class returns used to allocate funds actively among the asset classes. For example, the investment manager may decide to always hold common stocks in the same relative proportions they have in the TSE 300, which is often used as a surrogate for the Canadian stock market portfolio. However, the proportion of funds invested in the TSE 300 will change at the start of every period, based on the overall prognosis for the stock and bond markets. Thus, during one period the manager may have as much as 100% of the client's funds in stocks, on the strong belief that the stock market is going to rise rapidly in the near future. Conversely, during another period the manager may have as much as 100% of the client's funds in bonds, in the strong belief that the stock market will soon decline sharply.

Market Timing A form of active management that entails shifting an investor's funds between a surrogate market portfolio and a risk-free asset, depending on the investor's perception of their near-term prospects.

Market Timing

Figure 23.5(d) portrays a manager following an investment style that is known as **market timing**. The only active decision concerns the appropriate allocation of funds between a surrogate market portfolio (usually consisting of either stocks or long-term bonds) and a risk-free asset, such as Treasury bills. An investment organization following this style

Evaluating Investment Systems

Institutional investors are constantly in search of the holy grail: an investment system that can produce high returns with low risk and without the expense of retaining a team of skilled analysts. This search has led down many and varied paths. Over the years, numerous individuals and organizations have claimed to have developed mechanical investment systems that use only available historical data and a set of objective analytical procedures to produce results superior to passive management. Some mechanical systems simply provide predictions of how "the market" will behave; others prescribe a complete set of instructions for investing in individual securities. Almost all of them present impressive statistics based on tests using data from some past evaluation period.

Advocates of such mechanical investment systems may sincerely believe that they have found the path to instant affluence. However, their proofs often rest on shaky ground. When evaluating any system, it is imperative that several possible errors be avoided.

Failure to Adjust for Risk. Any investment system that results in the selection of high-beta stocks is likely to produce above-average returns in bull markets and below-average returns in bear markets. Because the stock market over the long term has trended upward, on balance such a system will tend to produce above-average returns over the long run (as will systems that involve purchasing either small capitalization stocks or stocks with high book-to-market ratios—see Chapter 16). Therefore, an evaluation of the performance of any investment system should involve not only measuring the resulting average return but also determining the amount of risk incurred. Then the average return from a passive management benchmark of similar risk can be computed for comparison. Techniques for making such comparisons are presented in Chapter 24.

Failure to Consider Transaction Costs. Systems that rely on frequent, high-volume trading may produce *gross* returns that exceed those of a similar risk passive management benchmark. However, if transaction costs have not been included in the analysis, the results may be invalid. *Net* returns are calculated by adding transaction costs to the purchase price of an investment, and deducting them from the investment's selling price. After inclusion of realistic transaction costs, most high-turnover investment systems produce negative risk-adjusted performance.

Failure to Consider Dividends. When the performance of a mechanical system is compared with that of a passive management benchmark, dividends (and interest payments) are often ignored. This may seriously bias the results. For example, a system may be advocated that, in effect, selects low-yield stocks. The prices of such stocks should increase at a faster rate than those of high-yield stocks with the same amount of risk. This is because a stock's return consists of both dividends and capital appreciation. Two stocks with the same risk should have the same return, meaning that the stock with a smaller yield will have a larger capital appreciation. Thus if just capital appreciation is examined, a system that selects low-yield stocks would tend to show a more rapid rate of capital appreciation than a passive management benchmark involving a well-diversified portfolio consisting of both low- and high-yield stocks. Consequently, when yields of systems differ significantly from average yields, it is important to examine *total* returns, not just the rate of capital appreciation.

Non-operational Systems. Although obvious, it still must be mentioned: to be useful, a system must not require knowledge about the future. For example, many systems require action after some time series of values (such as a stock's price) has reached a "peak" or "trough." But it is rarely apparent until well afterward that in fact a peak or trough has been reached. Hence such a system is non-operational. Similarly, an investigator might use a database prepared in 1998 with stock price data relating to the period from 1987 through 1997. The stocks included in the database may have been chosen because they existed and were important in 1998 (for example, they may have been considered important because they were listed on the TSE in 1998). A superior investment system based on an analysis of this database is a type of non-operational system involving *ex post* **selection bias** (or survivorship bias). That is, the system discovered in 1998 was based on an analysis of those stocks that were certain to be alive and important in 1998. Accordingly, it should have done well over the period of 1987 to 1997. However, these systems require some information not available in advance. In particular, they require knowledge before 1998 of which stocks will be around in 1998.

Spurious Fits. Using a set of data from a past period, it is not difficult to discover a investment system that works quite well when tested on the same data. One simply has to test enough systems. However, this does not mean that it would be useful to the investor. If 100 seemingly irrelevant systems are tried with a set of data, due to the laws of probability one of them is likely to give results that are "statistically significant at the 1% level." This should not cause undue excitement because it would not necessarily have any notable predictive power in the future. For example, stock prices in the United States have been shown to be correlated with both sunspot activity and with the length of skirts. However, these correlations are unlikely to demonstrate actual causal relationships. Instead, they are likely to have been "spurious," meaning that they probably were coincidental. Without solid reasons to believe that a relationship is due to underlying forces, it would be unwise to predict its continuation in the future.

Reliance on Misleading Visual Comparisons. Occasionally the proponent of a system will produce a graph that plots both the level of an indicator intended to predict market moves and the levels of the market itself. Visual comparison of the two curves may suggest that the indicator does indeed predict changes in the market. However, the eye can-

not easily differentiate between a situation in which changes in a market "predictor" *lead* the market and one in which the changes *lag* behind the market. This is a crucial distinction because only a leading indicator can bring superior investment performance.

Failure to Use Out-of-sample Data. Can any evidence concerning a system's ability to beat the market be persuasive? Probably not to those who believe absolutely in market efficiency. But there are appropriate tests that can be undertaken. The search for a system should be conducted using one set of data, and the test of the system's predictive ability should be performed using an entirely different set of data. The latter set of data is sometimes known as **out-of-sample data** or a holdout sample. To be complete, such a test should involve the (simulated) management of a portfolio and be designed so that each investment decision is based solely on information available at the time the decision is made. Finally, the performance of the system should be measured in the way one would measure the performance of any investment manager (to be discussed in Chapter 24). This involves, among other things, attempting to determine the probability that the investment results were due to chance rather than skill.

Despite the increasing popularity of passive management, the search for successful investment systems will continue. As always the most useful advice to investors considering such systems is *caveat emptor* (buyer beware). Checking for the errors described above will make for more intelligent evaluations of prospective investment systems.

Investment Style The method an investor uses to take active positions in certain types of securities.

Ex Post Selection Bias In the context of constructing a security valuation model, the use of securities that have performed well and the avoidance of securities that have performed poorly, thus making the model appear more effective than it truly is.

changes its mixture of risky and risk-free assets based on its own forecasts of the risk and expected return of "the market" relative to the risk-free rate, even if there is no change in consensus forecasts or the client's attitude toward risk and return.

Investment organizations that engage in the type of management where active bets are placed on individual securities are said to have a *security selection style*. Those that engage in the type of management where active bets are placed on asset classes are said to have an *asset allocation style*, with market timing being one specific example. Lastly, investment organizations that place active bets on certain groups of securities are said to employ a *group rotation style*. Some organizations use relatively pure **investment styles**, meaning that they use basically just one of the three styles previously mentioned. Others employ various combinations, making it difficult to classify them into neat categories.

Out-of-sample Data
(Alternatively, **Holdout Sample**.) In the context of constructing a security valuation model, information that is obtained from periods different from those used to estimate the valuation model.

Although these styles have been described in terms of modern portfolio theory, it should be pointed out that other procedures could be used to implement them. For example, with modern portfolio theory an optimal stock portfolio [as in Figure 23.5(b)] is identified by use of forecast expected returns, standard deviations, and covariances in conjunction with indifference curves. Once it is identified, the portfolio manager will have determined the appropriate relative investments in individual common stocks. However, such an identification could be made using some other procedure. Often it is done on a much less formal and more qualitative basis.

International Investing

An interesting extension of the previous discussion of investment styles involves international investing (which is the subject of Chapter 25). Consider security selection first. This style, when applied internationally, would involve determining the efficient set associated with a number of stocks found around the world. Alternatively, a security selection style could be combined with an asset allocation style. Here, for example, the portfolio manager could first determine the optimal portfolios associated with just Japanese stocks, just Canadian stocks, and just German stocks. Then, using these optimal portfolios, the manager would decide how much to allocate to each one of the three countries.

Imagine that the optimal Japanese portfolio consisted of two stocks, J_1 and J_2, in proportions of 70% and 30%, respectively, and half of the portfolio's funds were to be devoted to Japanese stocks. As a result, $.50 \times 70\% = 35\%$ and $.50 \times 30\% = 15\%$ of the portfolio would be invested in J_1 and J_2, respectively. Similar calculations could be done for the sets of Canadian and German stocks.

Procedures analogous to those previously described could be followed for the security selection, group rotation, asset allocation, and market timing styles in an international setting. However, the issue of foreign currency risk adds a complicating element to this comparison.[9]

Portfolio Revision

With the passage of time, a previously purchased portfolio that is currently held will often be viewed as suboptimal by the investment manager, meaning that the portfolio is no longer viewed as the best one for the client. This is because either the client's attitude toward risk and return is thought to have changed or, more likely, the manager's forecasts have changed. In response, the manager could identify a new optimal portfolio and then make the necessary revisions to the current portfolio so that subsequently the new optimal portfolio will be held. However, this is not as straightforward as it might seem at first because transaction costs will have to be paid when any revisions are made. Such costs must be compared with the perceived benefits associated with the revision in order to determine what course of action to take.

Cost-benefit Analysis

Transaction costs were discussed in Chapter 3. They include brokerage commissions, price impacts, and bid-ask spreads. Because of these costs, a security would have to increase in

---

[9]An intriguing description of how to use equilibrium models (like the CAPM, discussed in Chapter 9) and portfolio optimizers (see the *Institutional Issues* section in Chapter 7) to make asset allocation decisions in a global setting is presented in Fischer Black and Robert Litterman, "Global Portfolio Optimization," *Financial Analysts Journal* 48, no. 5 (September–October 1992): 28–43. Black and Litterman's model includes foreign currencies as one of the assets; see Chapter 25 for a discussion of foreign currencies and their risks.

value by a certain amount just to pay these costs and leave the investor neither better nor worse off. This necessary increase in value may exceed 1% for many securities and can range as high as 5% to 10% or more for others, particularly small-size stocks.

The existence of transaction costs greatly complicates the life of any investment manager, and the more active the manager, the greater the complications. The hoped-for advantage of any revision must be weighed against the cost of making that revision. That is, a revision can be viewed as bringing certain kinds of benefits—either it will increase the expected return of the portfolio, or it will reduce the standard deviation of the portfolio, or it will do both. To be weighed against these benefits are the transaction costs that will be incurred if the revision is made. As a result, some of the revisions in the holdings of individual securities that the manager may initially want to make will be dropped from consideration because of the transaction costs involved. The goal of the manager is to identify the set of individual revisions that collectively maximizes the improvement, after transaction costs, in the risk-return characteristics of the current portfolio.

In order to identify the appropriate set of individual revisions, sophisticated procedures (for example, quadratic programming) are required to compare the relevant costs and benefits. Fortunately, improvements in procedures and dramatic decreases in computing costs have made such approaches economically feasible for many investment managers.

In some situations investors may find it economically more attractive to revise their portfolios by transacting in entire asset classes instead of individual securities. Buying or selling futures contracts (see Chapter 20) on stock market indices or government bonds is one such approach. A potentially more flexible strategy makes use of the swaps market.

Swaps

Consider a situation where a portfolio manager wants to make major changes in the proportions of funds that are invested in different asset classes. He recognizes that substantial transaction costs will be incurred if the traditional method of selling certain securities and replacing them with others is used to make these changes. Indeed, these costs can be so large that most of the changes, if conducted in this manner, should not be made. One relatively new method that has become very popular in allowing such changes to be made at relatively low transaction costs involves the use of swaps.[10]

While the unique features of swaps can become quite complicated, their general nature is quite simple. Such "plain-vanilla" swaps are contracts that typically involve two parties (in the language of swaps they are referred to as *counterparties*) exchanging sets of cash flows over a predetermined period of time.[11] Two types of swaps—equity and interest rate—are considered here.

Equity Swaps

Equity Swap A contract between two counterparties in which one pays the other a fixed stream of cash flows and in return receives a varying stream whose cash flows are regularly reset based on the performance of a given stock market index.

With an **equity swap**, one counterparty agrees to pay a second counterparty a stream of variable cash payments that is based on the rate of return of an agreed-upon stock market index. In return, the second counterparty agrees to pay the first counterparty a stream of fixed cash payments that is based on current interest rates. Both sets of payments are to be

---

[10]The discussion of swaps here should not be confused with the discussion of bond swaps in Chapter 15.

[11]For a discussion of many of the complicating features present in swaps, see Robert H. Litzenberger, "Swaps: Plain and Fanciful," *Journal of Finance* 47, no. 3 (July 1992): 831–850. He reports that at that time the amount of outstanding interest rate and currency swaps was estimated to be about $3 trillion, with over two-thirds of them being of the "plain vanilla" variety, and that the first major swap took place in 1981. The International Swaps and Derivatives Association (an industry association for participants in swaps and other privately negotiated derivatives transactions) reports on its Web site that at June 30, 1997, the notional amount of interest rate and currency swaps outstanding was $22.1 trillion and $1.6 trillion, respectively.

made for a given time period and are based on a certain percentage (the percentage is variable for one counterparty and fixed for the other) of an underlying *notional principal*. Through an equity swap the first counterparty has, in essence, sold stocks and bought bonds while the second counterparty has sold bonds and bought stocks. Both of them have effectively restructured their portfolios without having to pay any transaction costs, other than a relatively small fee to a **swap bank** (usually a commercial or investment bank) that set up the contract.

Swap Bank Typically a chartered or investment bank that sets up equity, interest rate, and other kinds of swaps between interested counterparties.

Consider the example that is shown in Figure 23.6(a). Ms. Bright, a pension fund manager, thinks that the stock market is going to move upward sharply in the next three years. In contrast, Mr. Gloom, who also runs a pension fund, thinks that the stock market is likely to move downward in the next three years. Ms. Bright is considering selling $100 million of bonds and investing the proceeds in common stocks whereas Mr. Gloom is thinking of selling $100 million of common stocks and using the proceeds to purchase bonds. However, both portfolio managers realize that such changes will involve the payment of substantial transaction costs. Consequently, both of them contact a swap bank.

The swap bank sets up the following contract for Ms. Bright and Mr. Gloom. Shortly after the end of each quarter Mr. Gloom is to pay Ms. Bright an amount that is equal to the rate of return on the TSE 300 for the quarter times the notional principal. At the same time, Ms. Bright is to pay Mr. Gloom an amount that is equal to 2% of the notional principal. Both Ms. Bright and Mr. Gloom agree that the notional principal will be equal to $100 million, and that the contract will last for three years. Each pay the swap bank a fee for setting up the contract.[12]

Imagine that the quarterly rates of return on the TSE 300 during the first year of the swap contract are equal to 3%, −4%, 1%, and 5%, as shown in Figure 23.6(b). While Ms. Bright must pay $2 million (.02 × $100 million) to Mr. Gloom each quarter, in return Mr. Gloom must pay Ms. Bright the following amounts:

First quarter:	.03 × $100 million =	$3 million
Second quarter:	−.04 × $100 million =	−4 million
Third quarter:	.01 × $100 million =	1 million
Fourth quarter:	.05 × $100 million =	5 million

Hence, it appears that in the first quarter Ms. Bright pays $2 million to Mr. Gloom and in return Mr. Gloom pays $3 million to Ms. Bright. However, the way the contract is structured, only the net amount is paid—in this case, Mr. Gloom will pay $1 million ($3 million − $2 million) to Ms. Bright. In the second quarter it appears that Mr. Gloom must pay −$4 million to Ms. Bright. The minus sign means that Ms. Bright must pay Mr. Gloom $4 million plus the fixed payment of $2 million, for a total payment of $6 million. In the third period, Ms. Bright must pay Mr. Gloom $1 million ($2 million − $1 million), and in the fourth quarter Mr. Gloom must pay Ms. Bright $3 million ($5 million − $2 million). In summary, the net payments are

---

[12]Swaps can be compared to a series of forward contracts (forward contracts were discussed in Chapter 5). In this case, Ms. Bright has a swap position equivalent to having long positions in a series of equity forward contracts, whereas Mr. Gloom has short positions in these contracts. Consider the swap contract's first quarterly payment. Imagine that instead of the swap contract Ms. Bright had taken a long position in a forward contract. In general, forward contracts involve the exchange of a stated amount of cash for a given asset at a specified future date. Here Ms. Bright has agreed to pay $2 million one quarter later for delivery of an asset that can be thought of as shares in a TSE 300 index fund (the number of shares will be determined on the delivery date, and will be equal to $100 million times the quarterly return on the TSE 300, divided by the fund's net asset value at the end of the quarter).

Figure 23.6 Equity swap.

(a) The Contract

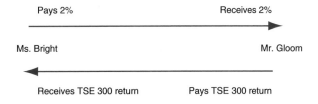

Pays 2% → Receives 2%

Ms. Bright   Mr. Gloom

Receives TSE 300 return ← Pays TSE 300 return

(b) The Cash Flows

		Ms. Bright's Cash Flows*			Mr. Gloom's Cash Flows*		
Quarter	TSE 300 Return	Payment from Gloom	Payment to Gloom	Net	Payment from Bright	Payment to Bright	Net
First	3%	$3	$2	$1	$2	$3	−$1
Second	−4	−4	2	−6	2	−4	6
Third	1	1	2	−1	2	1	1
Fourth	5	5	2	3	2	5	−3

*All cash flows are in millions as the notional principal is $100 million.

First quarter:	Mr. Gloom pays $1 million to Ms. Bright
Second quarter:	Ms. Bright pays $6 million to Mr. Gloom
Third quarter:	Ms. Bright pays $1 million to Mr. Gloom
Fourth quarter:	Mr. Gloom pays $3 million to Ms. Bright

These amounts reflect what would have happened (roughly) if Mr. Gloom had sold stocks and bought bonds and Ms. Bright had sold bonds and bought stocks, and both incurred relatively low transaction costs. Consider the first quarter. If Mr. Gloom had sold the stocks and replaced them with 2% bonds, he would have earned $2 million. Instead, he kept the stocks and earned $3 million on them (remember that the TSE 300 went up 3%) but had to pay Ms. Bright a net amount of $1 million, leaving him with $2 million, the same amount.

There are many ways that equity swaps can be modified. For example, a foreign stock market index such as the Nikkei 225 could be used instead of the TSE 300. This would allow one counterparty to achieve the benefits of international diversification more cheaply. Alternatively, the swap could involve two stock market indices, such as a large stock index like the TSE 300 and a small stock index like *The Financial Post* All-Canadian Junior Index. There are many other variations, limited only by investors' imaginations and their ability to periodically determine the value of the swaps.

Interest Rate Swaps

Interest Rate Swap A contract between two counterparties in which one pays the other a fixed stream of cash flows and in return receives a varying stream whose cash flows are regularly reset based on the level of a given interest rate.

With an **interest rate swap**, one counterparty agrees to pay a second party a stream of cash payments whose size is reset regularly based on the current level of a highly visible interest rate. A popular one is the London Interbank Offered Rate (LIBOR), which is an interest rate set daily in London that applies to loans made among large international banks. In return, the second counterparty agrees to pay the first counterparty a stream of fixed-size cash payments that is based on the level of interest rates in existence at the time the contract is signed. Like equity swaps, both sets of payments are to be made for a certain number of years and are based on a certain percentage of an underlying notional principal. (The percentage is variable—or "floating"—for one counterparty and fixed for the other.)

Through the interest rate swap the first counterparty has, in essence, sold short-term fixed-income securities and bought long-term bonds while the second counterparty has sold these bonds and bought the short-term fixed-income securities. Like equity swaps, both of them have effectively restructured their portfolios without having to pay any transaction costs other than a relatively small fee to a swap bank that set up the contract.

Consider the example that is shown in Figure 23.7(a). Ms. Uppe, a fixed-income mutual fund manager, thinks that interest rates are going to move upward in the near future. In contrast, Mr. Downe, who also runs a fixed-income mutual fund, thinks that interest rates are likely to move downward. Consequently, Ms. Uppe is considering selling $100 million of long-term bonds and investing the proceeds in money market securities, whereas Mr. Downe is thinking of selling $100 million of money market securities and using the proceeds to purchase long-term bonds.[13] As with the case of an equity swap, both of them contact a swap bank to help them make such changes without the payment of substantial transaction costs.

The swap bank sets up the following contract for the two of them. Shortly after the end of each quarter Mr. Downe is to pay Ms. Uppe an amount that is equal to the end-of-quarter three-month LIBOR times the notional principal. At the same time, Ms. Uppe is to pay Mr. Downe an amount that is equal to 2% of the notional principal. Both Ms. Uppe and Mr. Downe agree that the notional principal will be equal to $100 million, and that the contract will last for five years. Each pays the swap bank a fee for setting up the contract.

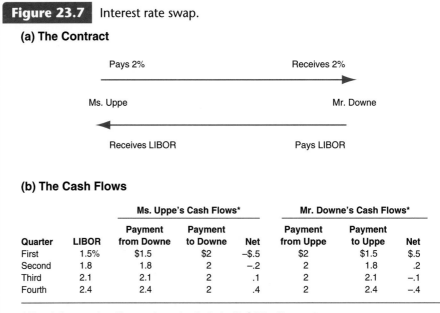

Figure 23.7 Interest rate swap.

(a) The Contract

Pays 2% → Receives 2%

Ms. Uppe   Mr. Downe

← Receives LIBOR   Pays LIBOR

(b) The Cash Flows

Quarter	LIBOR	Ms. Uppe's Cash Flows*			Mr. Downe's Cash Flows*		
		Payment from Downe	Payment to Downe	Net	Payment from Uppe	Payment to Uppe	Net
First	1.5%	$1.5	$2	−$.5	$2	$1.5	$.5
Second	1.8	1.8	2	−.2	2	1.8	.2
Third	2.1	2.1	2	.1	2	2.1	−.1
Fourth	2.4	2.4	2	.4	2	2.4	−.4

*All cash flows are in millions as the notional principal is $100 million.

Imagine that the three-month LIBOR at the beginning of each of the next four quarters equals, successively, 1.5%, 1.8%, 2.1%, and 2.4%. This means that the following amounts are to be paid by Mr. Downe to Ms. Uppe:

---

[13]By convention, the counterparty that makes the fixed payments (Ms. Uppe) is known as the *swap buyer,* and the counterparty that makes the variable payments (Mr. Downe) is known as the *swap seller.* Hence, the swap buyer "pays fixed and receives floating," and the swap seller "pays floating and receives fixed."

First quarter: $.015 \times \$100$ million $= \$1.5$ million
Second quarter: $.018 \times \$100$ million $=$ 1.8 million
Third quarter: $.021 \times \$100$ million $=$ 2.1 million
Fourth quarter: $.024 \times \$100$ million $=$ 2.4 million

In return, Ms. Uppe must pay $.02 \times \$100$ million $= \$2$ million to Mr. Downe each quarter. Since the payments from Ms. Uppe and Mr. Downe are netted against each other, the net payments are

First quarter: Ms. Uppe pays $.5 million to Mr. Downe
Second quarter: Ms. Uppe pays $.2 million to Mr. Downe
Third quarter: Mr. Downe pays $.1 million to Ms. Uppe
Fourth quarter: Mr. Downe pays $.4 million to Ms. Uppe

These amounts reflect what would have happened (roughly) if Ms. Uppe had sold bonds and bought money market securities and Mr. Downe had sold money market securities and bought bonds, and both incurred relatively low transaction costs. Consider the first quarter. If Ms. Uppe had sold the bonds and replaced them with money market securities yielding roughly LIBOR, she would have earned $1.5 million in interest. Instead, she kept the bonds and earned $2 million on them but had to pay Mr. Downe a net amount of $.5 million, leaving her with $1.5 million, the same amount.[14]

As with equity swaps, there are many variations on this plain-vanilla type of interest rate swap. For example, the notional principal could change over time, or one variable-rate stream of cash flows based on one interest rate (such as LIBOR) could be swapped for a variable rate stream of cash flows based on another interest rate (such as Treasury bills). In addition, there can be caps or floors or collars on the size of the variable payments.

Swaps Market

The swaps market is an unregulated market in that no governmental agency has oversight responsibilities. As a consequence, there has been a high degree of innovation in the types of swap contracts that have been created.[15] Furthermore, there is privacy for all parties involved, as no reporting requirements exist other than those imposed by accountants. In addition, it means that anyone involved in a swap must be concerned with counterparty risk. That is, each counterparty to a swap must pay close attention to the creditworthiness of the other counterparty in order to reduce the risk that the other counterparty will default in making his required payments under the terms of the contract.

At the heart of the swaps market are swap banks, which facilitate the creation of swaps for their clients, and will often take the other side of the contract if another counterparty is not available at the moment. In such situations they are acting as swap dealers, and they

---

[14]In this case, Ms. Uppe has a swap position equivalent to having long positions in a series of money market forward contracts, whereas Mr. Downe has short positions in these contracts. For example, the first quarterly payment is identical to what would happen if Ms. Uppe signed a forward contract agreeing to pay $2 million in exchange for the delivery of shares in a money market mutual fund (the number of shares will be determined on the delivery date, and will be equal to $100 million times the LIBOR, divided by the fund's net asset value at the end of the quarter). See footnote 12.

[15]One interesting innovation is the *swaption,* a contract that combines an option (usually European) with an interest rate swap (or some other kind of swap). Call swaptions involve the right to "pay fixed and receive floating" and put swaptions involve the right to "pay floating and receive fixed." The notional principal, fixed rate, source of the floating rate, and swap life are all set when the swaption is created, as is the life of the swaption itself. If the owner of either type of swaption decides to exercise the option, then the writer (usually a swap bank) must become the other counterparty to the swap. In return for this right, the owner pays the writer a premium. Owners of calls will exercise their options if interest rates rise because then the fixed payment cash outflows will be less than the floating rate cash inflows. Conversely, put owners will exercise their options if interest rates fall. See David R. Smith, "A Simple Method for Pricing Interest Rate Swaptions," *Financial Analysts Journal* 47, no. 3 (May–June 1991): 72–76.

will use various kinds of techniques (such as taking positions in futures or contacting other swap banks) to hedge their exposure to financial risk. In such a situation no fee is typically charged to the counterparty. Instead, the terms of the swap are set in the swap dealer's favour, thereby allowing the dealer to make a profit after hedging his or her position.

What happens if at some point during the life of the swap one counterparty wants to get out of the contract? In such a situation the counterparty has a choice of contacting either the other counterparty or a swap bank. In the first case, it is possible that the swap contract can be cancelled if a mutually acceptable cash payment is made from one counterparty to the other. In the interest rate swap example, if interest rates have risen high enough (as in the third and fourth quarter), then Ms. Uppe will be in a favourable position because the swap's net cash flows will be going from Mr. Downe to her. Hence, regardless of who wants to get out of the swap, Ms. Uppe would want to be compensated for the loss of the anticipated future cash flows. This means that Mr. Downe would give her a lump sum payment when the contract is cancelled.

Similarly, if a swap bank is contacted, then either it will assume the counterparty's position in the contract or it will search for someone else to do so. (Note that the counterparty that wants to get out of the contract can conduct such a search without using a swap bank.) In the previous example, if Ms. Uppe wants to get out of the contract, then the swap bank will pay her a lump sum. Conversely, if Mr. Downe wants to get out, then he will have to pay a lump sum to the swap bank. In either case, the contract remains in force afterward for the other counterparty.

It is also possible that the swap bank will arrange for the party that wants to get out to agree to a second swap contract that effectively cancels the first one. For example, if after one year Ms. Uppe wants to get out of the contract where she "pays fixed and receives floating," then the swap bank could construct a four-year swap where she "pays floating and receives fixed" for the same amount of notional principal. With the first contract she pays 2% and receives LIBOR, and with the second contract she will pay LIBOR and receive 2.3%. Note that the fixed rate is higher with the second contract (2.3% > 2%) as interest rates have risen since the first contract was signed. Now Ms. Uppe both receives and pays LIBOR, so those two cash streams effectively cancel each other out. She also pays 2% and receives 2.3%, meaning that, on balance, she receives .3%, or $.003 \times \$100$ million $= \$300\ 000$. Thus, for the next four years she will receive $\$300\ 000$ quarterly.

Manager-client Relations

The larger the amount of money managed, the more communication there is likely to be between investment manager and client. Not surprisingly, corporate, union, and government officials responsible for pension funds spend a great deal of time with those who manage their money. Such officials also concern themselves with a number of questions: who should manage the money, how should it be managed, and how should the managers be instructed and constrained?

Many aspects of manager-client relations can be characterized as responses to a difference of opinion concerning the manager's ability to make "good bets." Often clients will divide their funds among two or more managers. This type of **split-funding** is used by most pension funds. Two reasons are given. First, it allows the employment of managers with different skills or different styles. Second, the impact of erroneous "bets" can be reduced by diversifying across different managers because the managers are the "bettors." However, if a client were to broadly diversify across managers without regard to the managers' investment abilities, the overall portfolio would likely produce results similar to those of the market portfolio. Thus, excessive use of split-funding is like explicitly investing in a passive fund, but at considerably greater cost to the client, owing to the expenses associated with transaction costs and fees charged by the investment managers.

Split-funding A situation in which an institutional investor divides its funds among two or more professional money managers.

Manager Structuring

Administrators of pension and endowment funds might be surprised to find themselves referred to as investment engineers. Yet these particular institutional investors (who are often called "plan sponsors") face the complex problem of efficiently allocating their assets among various investment managers so as to best achieve their stated investment objectives. The disciplined process through which this manager "structuring" problem can best be resolved is analogous to an engineer designing a building or a machine.

When plan sponsors choose to invest in a particular asset class, especially a well-defined and liquid one such as the common stock market, they typically choose a market index to characterize the expected return and risk opportunities of the asset class and to serve as a benchmark against which to evaluate the subsequent performance of their investments. In this context, the selected market index is called an *asset class target*. For example, a plan sponsor might specify the TSE 300 and the ScotiaMcLeod Index as the asset class targets for its Canadian common stock and fixed-income investments, respectively. In a sense these market indices represent the portfolios that the plan sponsors would own if all of their investments in these asset classes were passively managed.

Plan sponsors rarely opt to conduct all of their investments in an asset class on a strictly passive basis. Instead, they typically hire a number of active investment managers (possibly in addition to using an index fund). In aggregate, these active managers are expected to exceed the performance of the asset class target on a risk-adjusted basis.

For various reasons most active investment managers pursue distinct investment styles, focusing their efforts in particular niches of the marketplace. For example, some common stock managers concentrate on small capitalization growth stocks, whereas some bond managers invest only in mortgage-backed securities.

Just as an investment manager will diversify within a portfolio to avoid unintended risks, a plan sponsor will diversify across investment managers. (The text refers to this as *split-funding*.) This manager diversification reduces the possibility that one manager's mistakes will seriously harm the plan sponsor's total portfolio. Further, it avoids the risk that the total portfolio will be excessively exposed to the results of a specific investment style. In particular, it is this "diversification of style" that underlies the plan sponsor's investment engineering problem.

The goal of efficient style diversification is to be *style neutral* relative to the asset class target. That is, in aggregate, the investment styles of a plan sponsor's managers should exhibit exposures to factors of risk and return (see Chapter 10) similar to those of the asset class target.

Suppose that a plan sponsor decision maker, who had selected the TSE 300 as the asset class target for his Canadian common stock investments, were to hire only investment managers that invested in large capitalization, high-dividend-yield stocks. The aggregate of the managers' investment styles would display investment characteristics quite different from those of the TSE 300. For example, relative to the TSE 300, the aggregate manager style would heavily emphasize utility stocks, which pay high dividends, and deemphasize technology stocks, which pay small dividends or none.

In some periods, such as during an economic downturn, these large high-yield stocks would perform well relative to the TSE 300. In other periods, they might perform relatively poorly. This relative performance difference would occur regardless of whether the large capitalization, high-yield managers were good or bad stock pickers within their area of expertise. The aggregate style of these managers does not "fit" with the asset class target. Therefore the risk that the aggregate manager style will perform differently from the asset class target is known as *style bias* or *misfit risk*. Style diversification seeks to limit misfit risk.

Unfortunately, simply hiring many active managers with differing investment styles is not a cost-effective means of controlling misfit risk. Investment skill is a rare commodity. A plan sponsor decision maker may not be able to identify what he believes to be skillful managers in sufficient quantity to provide a diverse group of investment styles. As the costs of active management are much higher than those of passive management, a strategy of hiring a large number of active managers with different investment styles within an asset category is likely to produce nothing more than an expensive index fund.

Plan sponsors would prefer to allocate their assets only to those managers whom they believe can perform best relative to the managers' investment styles, without concern for how those investment styles in aggregate compare to the asset class target. How can plan sponsors accommodate this preference and at the same time control misfit risk? That is the essence of the investment engineering problem.

Consider a plan sponsor who has identified certain managers that he believes will be the strongest risk-adjusted performers. Upon examining the managers' aggregate investment style, the plan sponsor finds that it heavily emphasizes smaller companies and companies expected to produce high relative earnings growth. The plan sponsor has selected the TSE 300 as the asset class target, which tends to be dominated by large, mature companies. Thus, considerable misfit risk exists.

The plan sponsor could reduce this misfit risk by also investing in a specially designed, passively managed portfolio. This portfolio, called a *completeness fund*, would hold long positions in securities underrepresented by the managers' aggregate investment style relative to the asset class target. Conversely, it would contain short positions in overrepresented securities. In our example, the completeness fund would purchase large capitalization, low-growth stocks and sell short smaller, high-growth stocks.

Properly constructed, the completeness fund will eliminate misfit risk and create a style-neutral total portfolio. If the active managers exceed the performance of their respective investment style benchmarks, then the total portfolio will outperform the asset class target.

Complicating the issue is the fact that the active managers' investment styles may have non-zero covariances with one another. If so, various allocations among them will produce different levels of misfit risk. Moreover, the plan sponsor may have more confidence in some managers than in others, and therefore wish to allocate more funds to the former than to the latter. These active manager allocation decisions directly affect the aggregate manager investment style and thus the composition of the completeness fund.

Determining desired allocations to the active managers and the composition of the resulting completeness fund requires a disciplined, quantitative approach. Further, the problem is dynamic, with the appropriate solution shifting over time as the investment characteristics of securities evolve and plan sponsors' estimates of the relative skills of their current and prospective managers change. Each plan sponsor faces a unique misfit problem. Effective solutions typically require specialized risk control computer software and experience in manipulating the inputs to and understanding the output from that software. The task of manager structuring is truly one of investment engineering.

Whether or not split-funding is used, a client who feels that a manager is "betting" too much would like to simply reduce the size of the "bets." For example, the client might ask a manager to diverge only half as much as he normally would from passive proportions of individual securities. Thus, if the manager decides that the optimal proportion in stock S1 is 30% and the market proportion is 45%, this would mean that the manager would ultimately invest only a proportion equal to (30% + 45%)/2 = 37.5%. However, there is no simple way to monitor compliance. In the example, the manager could buy 30% of S1 and state that he originally wanted to invest 45% in it but settled for 30%, even though truthfully he originally wanted 30%. Instead, a simpler approach is often employed: limits are placed on the holdings in any single security.[16]

---

[16]There are other kinds of limits frequently imposed on the manager, such as limits on the holdings of bonds versus stocks, or on the amount invested in a single industry.

Institutional investors (for example, pension and endowment funds) often use more than one investment manager and provide each with a set of objectives and a set of constraints on allowed divergences from specified target positions.[17] Individual investors who employ investment managers tend to give such instructions implicitly, if at all. This may reflect less sophistication, a less formal relationship with the manager, or the fact that the management fee for a small account is not large enough to cover the cost of dealing with a series of client-specific objectives and constraints.

Summary

1. Investment decisions are made through a five-step procedure: (1) set investment policy; (2) perform security analysis; (3) construct a portfolio; (4) revise the portfolio; and (5) evaluate the performance of the portfolio.
2. To set investment policy, an investor should specify his risk tolerance—that is, the maximum amount of additional risk that the investor will accept for a given increase in expected return.
3. One means of establishing an investor's risk tolerance is for the investor to identify the most desirable portfolio from a set of portfolios. Once this identification has been made, the slope of the investor's indifference curve, and hence the investor's attitude toward risk and expected return, can be established.
4. Passive management rests on the belief that markets are efficient and typically involves investing in an index fund. Active management, conversely, involves a belief that mispriced situations occur and can be identified with reasonable consistency.
5. There are many forms of active management. They can involve security selection, group selection, asset allocation, and market timing.
6. Portfolio revision involves both realizing that the currently held portfolio is not optimal and specifying another portfolio to hold with superior risk-return characteristics. The investor must balance the costs of moving to the new portfolio against the benefits of the revision.
7. Swaps often provide a low-cost method of restructuring a portfolio's funds across various asset classes.

APPENDIX A

DETERMINING THE RISK TOLERANCE OF AN INVESTOR

The purpose of this appendix is to derive in some detail the formula for determining the risk tolerance τ of an investor. As mentioned earlier, the equation for an indifference curve of an investor having constant risk tolerance is of the form:

$$\bar{r}_P = u_i + \frac{1}{\tau}\sigma_P^2 \qquad (23.1)$$

where u_i and $1/\tau$ are the vertical intercept and slope for indifference curve i when variance is measured on the horizontal axis. As the equation shows, an indifference curve will be a straight line because u_i and $1/\tau$ are constants (thus the equation is of the general form $Y = a + bX$, which is a straight line). Furthermore, any two indifference curves for an investor will have the same slope $(1/\tau)$ but will have different vertical intercepts (u_i).

---

[17]Sometimes these objectives and constraints are stated vaguely; in other cases they are specified precisely.

In order to estimate the investor's level of risk tolerance τ, it was mentioned that the slope of the indifference curve, $1/\tau$, would be set equal to the slope of the efficient set at the location of the portfolio that was selected, denoted portfolio C. This is because the indifference curve is tangent to the efficient set at this point, so the two must have the same slope. Thus the slope of the efficient set at point C must be determined in order to estimate τ.

Let X_S denote the proportion invested in the stock portfolio S and $(1 - X_S)$ denote the proportion invested in a risk-free Treasury bill portfolio F. Now the expected return of any portfolio consisting of S and F is simply

$$\bar{r}_P = X_S\bar{r}_S + (1 - X_S)r_F \tag{23.6}$$

where $\bar{r}_S$ and r_F are the expected return of the stock portfolio and the risk-free rate, respectively. This equation can be solved for X_S, resulting in

$$X_S = \frac{\bar{r}_P - r_F}{\bar{r}_S - r_F} \tag{23.7}$$

The equation for the variance of portfolio P is equal to

$$\sigma_P^2 = X_S^2\sigma_S^2 + (1 - X_S)^2\sigma_F^2 + 2X_S(1 - X_S)\sigma_{SF} \tag{23.8}$$

where σ_S^2 and σ_F^2 are the variances of the stock and risk-free portfolios, respectively, and σ_{SF} is the covariance between these two portfolios. However, because F is the risk-free portfolio, by definition, σ_F^2 and σ_{SF} are equal to zero. Thus, equation (23.8) reduces to

$$\sigma_P^2 = X_S^2\sigma_S^2 \tag{23.9}$$

Next, the right-hand side of equation (23.7) can be substituted for X_S in equation (23.9), resulting in

$$\sigma_P^2 = \frac{(\bar{r}_P - r_F)^2}{(\bar{r}_S - r_F)^2}\sigma_S^2 \tag{23.10}$$

This equation can be viewed as describing the functional relationship between the expected return and variance of any portfolio P that can be formed by combining the stock portfolio S and the risk-free portfolio F. That is, for a particular S and F, it gives the variance for a portfolio consisting of S and F with expected return $\bar{r}_P$. Equivalently, it represents the slope of the curved line in Figure 23.2 that connects S and F. Using calculus, the slope of this line can be shown to be equal to[18]

$$\text{Slope} = \frac{(\bar{r}_S - r_F)^2}{2[(\bar{r}_P - r_F)\sigma_S^2]} \tag{23.11}$$

The next step in estimating the slope of the client's indifference curves is to note that the portfolio on the curve connecting S and F that is of concern is the tangency portfolio C. Thus, the slope of the curve at C is determined by substituting $\bar{r}_C$ for $\bar{r}_P$ in equation (23.11) and equating this value with the slope of the indifference curves, $1/\tau$. Doing this results in the following equation:

$$\frac{1}{\tau} = \frac{(\bar{r}_S - r_F)^2}{2[(\bar{r}_C - r_F)\sigma_S^2]} \tag{23.12}$$

Finally, equation (23.12) can be solved for τ:

$$\tau = \frac{2[(\bar{r}_C - r_F)\sigma_S^2]}{(\bar{r}_S - r_F)^2} \tag{23.13}$$

---

[18]Note that the slope of this line, $d\bar{r}_P/d\sigma_P^2$, is equal to $1/(d\sigma_P^2/d\bar{r}_P)$. Thus the slope can be determined by taking the derivative of σ_P^2 with respect to $\bar{r}_P$ in equation (23.10) and then inverting the resulting expression.

Note that this is the same formula that was given earlier in equation (23.2) for estimating τ, given the client's choice of portfolio C.[19]

After substituting $\bar{r}_C$ for $\bar{r}_P$, equation (23.7) can be rewritten as

$$(\bar{r}_S - r_F)X_S = \bar{r}_C - r_F \tag{23.14}$$

Thus, $(\bar{r}_S - r_F)X_S$ can be substituted for $\bar{r}_C - r_F$ in the numerator of equation (23.13). Doing so and simplifying results in

$$\tau = \frac{2[X_S\sigma_S^2]}{(\bar{r}_S - r_F)} \tag{23.15}$$

In the example given earlier in the chapter, $\sigma_S = 15\%$ and $\bar{r}_S - r_F = 4.5\%$. Substituting these values into equation (23.15) and simplifying results in

$$\tau = \frac{2[X_S \times 15^2]}{4.5} \tag{23.16}$$
$$= 100X_S$$

as was previously mentioned and illustrated in Table 23.1.

QUESTIONS AND PROBLEMS

1. Describe the functioning of a "traditional" investment management organization. Much of the decision making in these organizations is "qualitative" in nature. What types of "quantitative" decision-making techniques might be introduced?
2. Technological changes have decreased the cost and increased the speed of information dissemination in security markets. Why might one suspect that firms following a "traditional" approach to investment management would find it increasingly difficult to generate "positive alphas" (that is, to identify and acquire underpriced securities) in this environment?
3. Consider Table 23.1. If your investment advisor presented you with this data, which stock/Treasury bill combination would you choose? Describe your thought process in making this choice.
4. Why is it difficult to specify the risk-return preferences of investment management clients? Why are these problems particularly acute in the case of institutional investor clients (for example, pension and endowment funds)?
5. Consider a portfolio whose asset mix can vary between stocks and Treasury bills. Given the historical returns on these two assets that is provided in Chapter 1, describe the distribution of possible portfolio returns as the proportion of the portfolio invested in stocks increases and that invested in Treasury bills decreases. What causes the distribution to change as the asset mix changes?
6. Explain the meaning of the slope of an investor's indifference curve at any particular point. For a "typical" risk-averse investor, describe how the investor's risk-return trade-off changes at different points along one of his indifference curves.
7. Assume that the expected return on stocks is 12%, the standard deviation of stocks is 18%, and the risk-free rate is 5%. Given this information, an investor selects a portfolio comprised of a 70% allocation to stocks and a 30% allocation to the risk-free asset. According to the derivation of risk tolerance found in equation (23.2), what risk tolerance is indicated by this choice?

---

[19]Risk tolerance, along with a procedure for estimating the value of τ, is presented in William F. Sharpe, *Asset Allocation Tools* (Redwood City, CA: Scientific Press, 1987), pp. 33–39.

8. Buzz Arlett, a portfolio manager for an investment management firm, has estimated the following risk-return characteristics for the stock and bond markets.

	Expected Return	Standard Deviation
Stocks	18.0%	22.0%
Bonds	10.0	5.0

The correlation between stocks and bonds is estimated to be 0.50.

Using these estimates, Buzz ran a number of simulations, tracing out the implications of different bond/stock mixes for the financial situation of Arnold Beck, a client. After much thought, Arnold indicated that, of the mixes considered, the most desirable was the allocation of 60% to stocks and 40% to bonds. Given this information, calculate Arnold's risk tolerance. [Hint: To solve this problem algebraically, write equation (23.5) using the 60/40 stock/bond allocation. Do the same for a 61/39 allocation. Finally, set these two formulas equal to each other and solve for the risk tolerance.] Is this answer likely to represent Arnold's risk tolerance over all possible stock/bond allocations?

9. Should an "overpriced" stock definitely be excluded from an investor's portfolio? Why?

10. Studies that simulate the value of an investment portfolio under alternative mixes of stocks and bonds invariably demonstrate that higher stock allocations produce higher returns, particularly as the holding period increases. If you as an investor have a time horizon that is reasonably long, say over 10 years, and you have no current income needs, could you justify holding any bonds in your portfolio?

11. Assume a risk-free return of 7%, an expected stock return of 18%, and a standard deviation of 21%. Under these conditions, if Maria Gomez chooses a 40% stock, 60% risk-free portfolio, what is Maria's risk tolerance? In words, describe what this value means.

12. Louise Cousineau can earn a risk-free return of 6%. Louise expects the stock market to return 15% and exhibit a standard deviation of 20%. If Louise chooses a portfolio of 60% stocks and 40% risk-free asset, calculate Louise's certainty equivalent return.

13. The portfolio manager's job can be defined as identifying the portfolio with the highest certainty equivalent return. Explain.

14. Despite its obvious simplicity and potential benefits, common stock passive management is a relatively "new" investment tool. Yet in the last 20 years, assets under passive management have grown from essentially zero to hundreds of billions of dollars. What are some possible reasons for the tremendous growth in passive management?

15. It is often argued (especially by active managers) that passive management implies settling for "mediocre" performance. Is this statement necessarily true? Why?

16. Gavin Crowther, an astute investor, once commented, "With the stock market composed of about 6000 actively traded securities, I view my portfolio as about 5950 short positions and 50 long positions." Explain what Gavin means.

17. Why is the "one-stage" approach to security selection theoretically superior to the "two-stage" approach? Why is the "two-stage" approach preferred by most investment managers?

18. Why should investment portfolios, even those that are passively managed, be periodically revised? What factors weigh against making such revisions?

19. A typical money management firm, particularly one specializing in stocks or bonds, invests in essentially the same portfolio for all of its clients, regardless of the clients' individual risk-return preferences. Speculate as to why money managers often operate in this manner. What can clients do to ensure that their portfolios reflect their own specific risk-return preferences?

20. Many investment management clients split their assets among a number of managers. Two rationales for this approach have been described as "diversification of judgment" and "diversification of style." Explain the meaning of these two terms.

CFA Exam Questions

21. Advisor 1: "Long-term asset allocation should be determined using an efficient frontier. Returns, risks (standard deviations), and correlations can be determined for each asset class from historical data. After calculating the efficient frontier for various allocations, you should select the asset mix on the efficient frontier that best meets your fund's risk tolerance."

Advisor 2: "History gives no guide to the future. For example, everybody agrees that bond risk has increased above historical levels as a result of financial deregulation. A far better approach to long-term asset allocation is to use your best judgment about expected returns on the various asset classes, based on current market conditions. You should rely on your experience to determine the best asset mix and avoid being influenced by computer printouts."

Advisor 1 Rebuttal: "Current market conditions are not likely to persist into the future and are not appropriate for long-term asset allocation decisions. Moreover, your use of judgment and experience can be influenced by biases and emotions and is not as rigorous a method as my efficient frontier approach."

Evaluate the strengths and weaknesses of each of the two approaches presented above. Recommend and justify an alternative process for asset allocation that draws from the strengths of each approach and corrects their weaknesses.

22. Colinos Associates is an investment management firm utilizing a very rigorous and disciplined asset allocation methodology as a key element of its investment approach. Twice a year, three or four economic scenarios are developed, based on the judgment of Colinos' most senior people. Probabilities are then assigned to the scenarios; return forecasts for stocks, bonds, and cash equivalents (the only asset types used by the firm) are generated; and expected values are computed for each asset category. These expected values are then combined with historical standard deviations and covariances to produce forecasts of results from various combinations of the three asset classes.

From this range of possible outcomes, senior staff selects what it regards as the best asset combinations, defined as those combinations promising the highest three-year returns with a 90% probability of achieving a preset minimum annual return requirement. These optimal allocations (sample output in the following table) are then presented to all clients for discussion and implementation. The process is repeated in roughly six months' time, when new allocations are developed.

Minimum Annual Required Return (90%) Probability	Anticipated Three-year Compound Annual Return	Recommended Asset Allocation		
		Cash	Bonds	Stocks
–6%	12.0%	10%	30%	60%
–4	11.0	20	40	40
–2	10.0	30	40	30
0	9.0	50	30	20
2	8.5	60	30	10
4	8.0	70	20	10
6	7.5	80	15	5

a. Discuss the strengths and weaknesses of Colinos' asset allocation approach.

b. Recommend and justify an alternative asset allocation approach for wealthy individuals.

KEY TERMS

security analyst (p. 791)
investment committee (p. 792)
approved list (p. 792)
portfolio manager (p. 792)
risk tolerance (p. 793)
certainty equivalent return (p. 798)
passive management (p. 798)
active management (p. 798)
index fund (p. 798)
active position (p. 800)
security selection (p. 800)

asset classes (p. 800)
asset allocation (p. 802)
group selection (p. 803)
market timing (p. 803)
investment styles (p. 805)
ex post selection bias (p. 805)
out-of-sample data (p. 806)
equity swap (p. 807)
swap bank (p. 808)
interest rate swap (p. 809)
split-funding (p. 812)

REFERENCES

1. Investment management is discussed in:

William F. Sharpe, "Decentralized Investment Management," *Journal of Finance* 36, no. 2 (May 1981): 217–234.

Jeffery V. Bailey and Robert D. Arnott, "Cluster Analysis and Manager Selection," *Financial Analysts Journal* 42, no. 6 (November–December 1986): 20–28.

Richard A. Brealey, "Portfolio Theory Versus Portfolio Practice," *Journal of Portfolio Management* 16, no. 4 (Summer 1990): 6–10.

William F. Sharpe, "The Arithmetic of Active Management," *Financial Analysts Journal* 47, no. 1 (January–February 1991): 7–9.

Robert H. Jeffrey, "Do Clients Need so Many Portfolio Managers?" *Journal of Portfolio Management* 18, no. 1 (Fall 1991): 13–19.

C. B. Garcia and F. J. Gould, "Some Observations on Active Manager Performance and Passive Indexing," *Financial Analysts Journal* 47, no. 6 (November–December 1991): 11–13.

Richard C. Grinold and Ronald N. Kahn, *Active Portfolio Management* (Chicago: Probus Publishing, 1995).

2. Investment management for an individual investor is discussed in:

Burton G. Malkiel, *A Random Walk Down Wall Street* (New York: W. W. Norton, 1996), particularly Chapter 11.

3. Assessment of investor risk tolerance is discussed in:

Gail Farrelly and Dean LeBaron, "Assessing Risk Tolerance Levels: A Prerequisite for Personalizing and Managing Portfolios," *Financial Analysts Journal* 45, no. 1 (January–February 1989): 14–16.

W. V. Harlow and Keith C. Brown, "Understanding and Assessing Financial Risk Tolerance: A Biological Perspective," *Financial Analysts Journal* 46, no. 6

(November–December 1990): 50–62.

William B. Riley, Jr., and K. Victor Chow, "Asset Allocation and Individual Risk Aversion," *Financial Analysts Journal* 48, no. 6 (November–December 1992): 32–37.

Karen Hube, "Time for Investing's Four-letter Word," *The Wall Street Journal*, January 23, 1998, pp. C1, C17.

4. An extensive discussion of risk tolerance is included in:

William F. Sharpe, *Asset Allocation Tools* (Redwood City, CA: Scientific Press, 1987), Chapter 2.

William F. Sharpe, "Integrated Asset Allocation," *Financial Analysts Journal* 43, no. 5 (September–October 1987): 25–32.

5. Market timing, asset allocation, and investment styles are discussed in the previous article and in:

Keith P. Ambachtsheer, "Portfolio Theory and the Security Analyst," *Financial Analysts Journal* 28, no. 6 (November–December 1972): 53–57.

Jack L. Treynor and Fischer Black, "How to Use Security Analysis to Improve Portfolio Selection," *Journal of Business* 46, no. 1 (January 1973): 66–86.

William F. Sharpe, "Likely Gains From Market Timing," *Financial Analysts Journal* 31, no. 2 (March–April 1975): 60–69.

———"Major Investment Styles," *Journal of Portfolio Management* 4, no. 2 (Winter 1978): 68–74.

Keith P. Ambachtsheer and James L. Farrell, Jr., "Can Active Management Add Value?" *Financial Analysts Journal* 35, no. 6 (November–December 1979): 39–47.

Robert D. Arnott and James N. von Germeten, "Systematic Asset Allocation," *Financial Analysts Journal* 39, no. 6 (November–December 1983): 31–38.

Jess H. Chua and Richard S. Woodard, *Gains From Market Timing*, Monograph Series in Finance and Economics #1986–2, New York University Salomon Center, Leonard N. Stern School of Business.

Richard A. Brealey, "How to Combine Active Management with Index Funds," *Journal of Portfolio Management* 12, no. 2 (Winter 1986): 4–10.

André F. Perold and William F. Sharpe, "Dynamic Strategies for Asset Allocation," *Financial Analysts Journal* 44, no. 1 (January–February 1988): 16–27.

William F. Sharpe, "Asset Allocation," in John L. Maginn and Donald L. Tuttle (eds.), *Managing Investment Portfolios: A Dynamic Process* (Boston, MA: Warren, Gorham & Lamont, 1990), Chapter 7.

David E. Tierney and Kenneth Winston, "Defining and Using Dynamic Completeness Funds to Enhance Total Fund Efficiency," *Financial Analysts Journal* 46, no. 4 (July–August 1990): 49–54.

Craig B. Wainscott, "The Stock-bond Correlation and its Implications for Asset Allocation," *Financial Analysts Journal* 46, no. 4 (July–August 1990): 55–60, 79.

John Markese, "All Eggs in One Basket, or A Basket for Each Egg?" *AAII Journal* 12, no. 7 (August 1990): 31–33.

David E. Tierney and Kenneth Winston, "Using Generic Benchmarks to Present Manager Styles," *Journal of Portfolio Management* 17, no. 4 (Summer 1991): 33–36.

P. R. Chandy and William Reichenstein, "Timing Strategies and the Risk of Missing Bull Markets," *AAII Journal* 13, no. 7 (August 1991): 17–19.

William F. Sharpe, "Asset Allocation: Management Style and Performance Measurement," *Journal of Portfolio Management* 18, no. 2 (Winter 1992): 7–19.

P. R. Chandy and William Reichenstein, "Stock Market Timing: A Modest Proposal," *AAII Journal* 14, no. 4 (April 1992): 7–10.

Mark Hulbert, "Market Timing Strategies: Taxes are a Drag," *AAII Journal* 14, no. 7 (August 1992): 18–20.

Maria Crawford Scott, "Asset Allocation Among the Three Major Categories," *AAII Journal* 15, no. 4 (April 1993): 13–16.

Mark Hulbert, "Bond Market Timing: Even More Tough Than Timing the Stock Market," *AAII Journal* 16, no. 3 (April 1994): 11–13.

Joseph B. Ludwig, "The Market Timing Approach: A Guide to the Various Strategies," *AAII Journal* 16, no. 4 (May 1994): 11–14.

Richard Bernstein, *Style Investing* (New York: John Wiley, 1995).

T. Daniel Coggin, Frank J. Fabozzi, and Robert Arnott, eds., *The Handbook of Equity Style Management* (New Hope, PA: Frank J. Fabozzi Associates, 1997).

6. Investing in an international context is discussed in Chapter 25 (see the references listed there) and in:

Robert D. Arnott and Roy D. Henriksson, "A Disciplined Approach to Global Asset Allocation," *Financial Analysts Journal* 45, no. 2 (March–April 1989): 17–28.

Bruno Solnik, *International Investments* (Reading, MA: Addison-Wesley, 1991), particularly Chapter 5.

Fischer Black and Robert Litterman, "Global Portfolio Optimization," *Financial Analysts Journal* 48, no. 5 (September–October 1992): 28–43.

Carlo Capaul, Ian Rowley, and William F. Sharpe, "International Value and Growth Stock Returns," *Financial Analysts Journal* 49, no. 1 (January–February 1993): 27–36.

Jess Lederman and Robert A. Klein, eds., *Global Asset Allocation: Techniques for Optimizing Portfolio Management* (New York: John Wiley & Sons, 1994).

Claude B. Erb, Campbell R. Harvey, and Tadas E. Viskanta, "Expected Returns and Volatility in 135 Countries," *Journal of Portfolio Management* 22, no. 3 (Spring 1996): 46–58.

Lucie Chaumeton, Gregory Connor, and Ross Curds, "A Global Stock and Bond Model," *Financial Analysts Journal* 52, no. 6 (November–December 1996): 65–74.

7. For a discussion of portfolio revision procedures, see:

Gordon J. Alexander and Jack Clark Francis, *Portfolio Analysis* (Englewood Cliffs, NJ: Prentice Hall, 1986), 221–228.

William F. Sharpe, *Asset Allocation Tools* (Redwood City, CA: Scientific Press, 1987), 65–68.

8. Swaps are discussed in many of the textbooks on options and futures listed in the references for Chapters 19 and 20. Also see the following and their lists of references:

Robert H. Litzenberger, "Swaps: Plain and Fanciful," *Journal of Finance* 47, no. 3 (July 1992): 831–850.

Charles W. Smithson, Clifford W. Smith, Jr., and D. Sykes Wilford, *Managing Financial Risk: A Guide to Derivative Products, Financial Engineering, and Value Maximization* (Burr Ridge, IL: Irwin Professional Publishing, 1995).

John F. Marshall and Vipul K. Bansal, *Financial Engineering* (Boston: Blackwell Pulishing, 1995).

Robert W. Kolb, *Futures, Options, and Swaps* (Boston: Blackwell Publishing, 1998).

Frank J. Fabozzi, Franco Modigliani, and Michael G. Ferri, *Foundations of Financial Markets and Institutions* (Upper Saddle River, NJ: Prentice Hall, 1998).

Also see the Web site for the International Swaps and Derivatives Association, an industry association for the participants in swaps and other privately negotiated deriatives transactions, at www.isda.org

9. For a Canadian perspective on the topics covered in this chapter, see:

J. A. Knowles and W. R. Waters, "Professional Portfolio Management: Is 'Style' Substance?" *Canadian Investment Review* II, no. 2 (Fall 1989): 87–94.

R. Auger and D. Parisien, "Understanding Asset Allocation," *Canadian Investment Review* IV, no. 1 (Spring 1991).

P. Potvin, "Passive Management, the TSE 300 and the Toronto 35 Stock Indexes," *Canadian Investment Review* V, no. 1 (Spring 1992).

H. Marmer, "Investment Style and Its Impact on Canadian Equity Returns," *Canadian Investment Review* VIII, no. 1 (Spring 1995): 17–21.

P. Williams, "Special Report: The CIR Roundtable, Shaking Down the Devil: Meeting the Derivatives Challenge Head On," *Canadian Investment Review* VIII no. 2 (Summer 1995): 26–31.

P. Brodeur and S. Wiseman, "A Style Allocation Is a Powerful Tool for Managing Risk," *Canadian Investment Review* VIII, no. 3 (Fall 1995): 15–20.

J. Schmitz and R. Wirick, "Right On Time," *Canadian Investment Review* IX, no. 1 (Spring 1996): 29–35.

M. Rouillard and M. Rhéaume, "Sticking to the Index," *Canadian Investment Review* XI, no. 1 (Spring 1998): 17–20.

L. Ackert and G. Athanassakos, "The Seasonal Impact of Institutional Investors," *Canadian Investment Review* XI, no. 3 (Fall 1998): 28–31.

Harry Marmer, "Investment Management's Future," *Canadian Investment Review* XI, no. 3 (Fall 1998): 20–23.

CHAPTER 24

Portfolio Performance Evaluation

An investor who has been paying someone to actively manage his portfolio has every right to insist on knowing what sort of performance was obtained. Such information can be used to alter either the constraints placed on the manager, the investment objectives given to the manager, or the amount of money allocated to the manager. Perhaps more importantly, by evaluating performance in specified ways, a client can forcefully communicate his interests to the investment manager and, in all likelihood, affect the way in which his portfolio is managed. Moreover, an investment manager, by evaluating her own performance, can identify sources of strength or weakness. Thus, although the previous chapter indicated portfolio performance evaluation was the last stage of the investment management process, it can also be viewed as simply part of a continuing operation. More specifically, it can be viewed as a feedback and control mechanism that can make the investment management process more effective.

Superior performance in the past may have been due to good luck, in which case such performance should not be expected to continue in the future. On the other hand, superior performance in the past may have been due to the actions of a highly skilled investment manager (and support staff). Conversely, inferior performance in the past may have been the result of bad luck, but it may also have been due to excessive turnover, high management fees, or other costs associated with an unskilled investment manager. This suggests that the first task in performance evaluation is to try to determine whether past performance was superior or inferior. Once this task is done, the second task is to try to determine whether such performance was due to skill or luck. Unfortunately, there are difficulties associated with carrying out both of these tasks. Accordingly, this chapter presents not only certain methods that have been advocated and used for evaluating portfolio performance but also a discussion of the difficulties encountered with their use.

Measures of Return

Frequently portfolio performance is evaluated over a time interval of at least four years, with returns measured for a number of periods within the interval—typically monthly or quarterly. This provides a fairly adequate sample size for statistical evaluation (for example, if returns are measured quarterly for four years, there will be 16 observations). Sometimes, however, a shorter time interval must be used in order to avoid examining returns earned under a different investment manager. The examples to follow will involve 16 quarterly observations for tractability. In practice, one would prefer monthly observations if only four years were to be analyzed.

In the simplest situation, where the client neither deposits nor withdraws money from the portfolio during a time period, calculation of the portfolio's return is straightforward. All that is required is that the market value of the portfolio be known at two points in time—the beginning and the end of the period.

In general, the market value of a portfolio at a point in time is determined by adding the market values of all the securities held at that particular time. For example, the value of a common stock portfolio at the beginning of a period is calculated by (1) noting the market price per share of each stock held in the portfolio at that time, (2) multiplying each of these share prices by the corresponding number of shares held, and (3) adding the resulting products. This sum will equal the market value of the portfolio at the beginning of the period. The market value of the portfolio at the end of the period is calculated in the same way, only using end-of-period prices and shares.

With the beginning and ending portfolio values in hand, the return on the portfolio can be calculated by subtracting the beginning value (V_b) from the ending value (V_e) and then dividing the difference by the beginning value:

$$r_p = \frac{V_e - V_b}{V_b} \tag{24.1}$$

For example, if a portfolio has a market value of $40 million at the beginning of a quarter and a market value of $46 million at the end of the quarter, then the return on this portfolio for the quarter is ($46 million − $40 million)/$40 million = 15%.

Measurement of portfolio returns is complicated by the fact that the client may either add or withdraw money from the portfolio. This means that the percentage change in the market value of the portfolio during a period may not be an accurate measurement of the portfolio's return during that period.

For example, consider a portfolio that at the beginning of a quarter has a market value of $100 million. Just before the end of the quarter the client deposits $5 million with the investment manager, and, subsequently, at the end of the quarter the market value of the portfolio is $103 million. If the quarterly return was measured without consideration of the $5 million deposit, the reported return would be ($103 million − $100 million)/$100 million = 3%. However, this would be incorrect, since $5 million of the ending $103 million market value was not due to the investment actions of the manager. Consideration of the deposit would suggest that a more accurate measure of the quarterly return would be [($103 million − $5 million) − $100 million]/$100 million = −2%.

Identification of exactly *when* any deposits or withdrawals occur is important in accurately measuring portfolio returns. If a deposit or withdrawal occurs just *before* the end of the period, then the return on the portfolio should be calculated by adjusting the ending market value of the portfolio. In the case of a deposit, the ending value should be reduced by the dollar amount (as was done in the previous example); in the case of a withdrawal, the ending value should be increased by the dollar amount.

If a deposit or withdrawal occurs just *after* the start of the period, then the return on the portfolio should be calculated by adjusting the beginning market value of the portfolio. In the case of a deposit, the beginning value should be increased by the dollar amount; in the case of a withdrawal, the beginning value should be decreased by the dollar amount. For example, if the $5 million deposit in the earlier example had been received just after the start of the quarter, the return for the quarter should be calculated as [$103 million − ($100 million + $5 million)]/($100 million + $5 million) = −1.90%.

Dollar-weighted Returns

Difficulties are encountered when deposits or withdrawals occur sometime *between* the beginning and end of the period. One method that has been used for calculating a portfolio's return in this situation results in the portfolio's **dollar-weighted return** (or internal rate

Dollar-weighted Return
A method of measuring the performance of a portfolio over a particular period of time. It is the discount rate that makes the present value of cash flows into and out of the portfolio, as well as the portfolio's ending value, equal to the portfolio's beginning value.

of return). For example, if the $5 million deposit in the earlier example was made in the middle of the quarter, the dollar-weighted return would be calculated by solving the following equation for r:

$$\$100 \text{ million} = \frac{-\$5 \text{ million}}{(1 + r)} + \frac{\$103 \text{ million}}{(1 + r)^2} \tag{24.2}$$

The solution to this equation, $r = -.98\%$, is a semiquarterly rate of return. It can be converted into a quarterly rate of return by adding 1 to it, squaring this value, and then subtracting 1 from the square, resulting in a quarterly return of $[1 + (-.0098)]^2 - 1 = -1.95\%$.[1]

Time-weighted Returns

Time-weighted Return
A method of measuring the performance of a portfolio over a particular period of time. It is the cumulative compounded rate of return of the portfolio, calculated on each date that a cash flow moves into or out of the portfolio over the performance measurement period.

Alternatively, the **time-weighted return** on a portfolio can be calculated when there are cash flows occurring between the beginning and end of the period. This method involves using the market value of the portfolio just before each cash flow occurs. In the earlier example, assume that in the middle of the quarter the portfolio had a market value of $96 million, so that right after the $5 million deposit the market value was $96 million + $5 million = $101 million. In this case, the return for the first half of the quarter would be ($96 million − $100 million)/$100 million = −4%; the return for the second half of the quarter would be ($103 million − $101 million)/$101 million = 1.98%. Next, these two semiquarterly returns can be combined to give a quarterly return by adding 1 to each return, multiplying the sums, and then subtracting 1 from the product. In the example, this procedure results in a quarterly return of $[(1 - .04)(1 + .0198)] - 1 = -2.1\%$.

Comparing Dollar-weighted and Time-weighted Returns

Which method is preferable for calculating the return on a portfolio? In the example given here, the dollar-weighted return was −1.95%, whereas the time-weighted return was −2.1%, suggesting the difference between the two methods may not be very important. Although this may be true in certain situations, examples can be given to show that such differences can be quite large and that the time-weighted return method is preferable.

Consider a hypothetical portfolio that starts a quarter with a market value of $50 million. In the middle of the quarter, it has fallen to a market value of $25 million, at which point the client deposits $25 million with the investment manager. At the end of the quarter the portfolio has a market value of $100 million. The semiquarterly dollar-weighted return for this portfolio is equal to the value of r in the following equation:

$$\$50 \text{ million} = \frac{-\$25 \text{ million}}{(1 + r)} + \frac{\$100 \text{ million}}{(1 + r)^2} \tag{24.3}$$

Solving this equation for r results in a value of 18.6%, which in turn equals a quarterly dollar-weighted return of $(1.186)^2 - 1 = 40.66\%$. However, its quarterly time-weighted return is 0%, since its return for the first half of the quarter was −50% and its return for the second half of the quarter was 100% (note that $(1 - .5)(1 + 1) - 1 = 0\%$).

Comparing these two returns—40.66% and 0%—indicates a sizeable difference exists. However, the time-weighted return figure of 0% is more meaningful for performance evaluation than the dollar-weighted return figure of 40.66%. To understand why, consider the return over the entire quarter on each dollar that was in the portfolio at the start of the quarter. Each dollar lost half of its value over the first half of the quarter, but then the remaining half-dollar doubled its value over the second half. Consequently, a dollar at the

---

[1]This procedure provides a quarterly return with "quarterly compounding." Alternatively, the semiquarterly return could be doubled, resulting in a quarterly return with "semiquarterly compounding" of $-.98\% \times 2 = -1.96\%$.

beginning was worth a dollar at the end, suggesting a return of 0% on the portfolio is a more accurate measure of the investment manager's performance than the 40.66% figure.

In general, the dollar-weighted return method of measuring a portfolio's return for purposes of evaluation is regarded as inappropriate. The reason behind this view is that the return is strongly influenced by the size and timing of the cash flows (namely, deposits and withdrawals) over which the investment manager has no control. In the example, the dollar-weighted return was 40.66% because the client fortuitously made a big deposit just before the portfolio appreciated rapidly in value. Thus, the 40.66% return figure is due at least partly to the actions of the client, not the manager.

Annualizing Returns

The previous discussion has focused on calculating quarterly returns. Such returns may be added or multiplied to obtain an annual measure of return. For example, if the return in the first, second, third, and fourth quarters of a given year are denoted by r_1, r_2, r_3, and r_4, respectively, then the annual return could be calculated by adding the four figures:

$$\text{Annual return} = r_1 + r_2 + r_3 + r_4 \tag{24.4}$$

Alternatively, the annual return could be calculated by adding 1 to each quarterly return, then multiplying the four figures, and finally subtracting 1 from the resulting product:

$$\text{Annual return} = [(1 + r_1)(1 + r_2)(1 + r_3)(1 + r_4)] - 1 \tag{24.5}$$

The latter return is more accurate because it reflects the value that $1 would have at the end of the year if it were invested at the beginning of the year and grew *with compounding* at the rate of r_1 for the first quarter, r_2 for the second quarter, r_3 for the third quarter, and r_4 for the fourth quarter. That is, it assumes reinvestment of both the dollar and any earnings at the end of each quarter.

Making Relevant Comparisons

The essential idea behind performance evaluation is to compare the returns obtained by the investment manager through active management with the returns that could have been obtained for the client if one or more appropriate alternative portfolios had been chosen for investment. The reason for this comparison is straightforward—performance should be evaluated on a relative basis, not on an absolute basis.

As an example, consider a client who is told that his portfolio, invested in common stocks and of average risk, had a return of 20% last year. Does this suggest superior or inferior performance? If the stock market went up by 10% last year, then it suggests superior performance and is good news. However, if the stock market went up by 30% last year, then it suggests inferior performance and is bad news. In order to infer whether the manager's performance is superior or inferior, the returns on similar portfolios that are either actively or passively managed are needed for comparison.

Such comparison portfolios are often referred to as **benchmark portfolios**. In selecting them, the client should be certain they are relevant, feasible, and known in advance, meaning they should represent alternative portfolios that could have been chosen for investment instead of the portfolio being evaluated. That is, the benchmark should reflect the objectives of the client. Hence, if the objective is to earn superior returns by investing in small stocks, then the TSE 35 would be an inappropriate benchmark. Instead, an index like the *Financial Post* All-Canadian Junior Index may be more suitable. *Return* is a key aspect of performance, of course, but some way must be found to account for the portfolio's exposure to *risk*. The choice of benchmark portfolios may be restricted to portfolios perceived to have similar levels of risk, thereby permitting a direct comparison of returns.

Benchmark Portfolio A portfolio, of equivalent risk, against which the performance of an investor's holdings can be compared for the purpose of determining investment skill. A benchmark portfolio represents a relevant and feasible alternative to the investor's actual portfolio and, in particular, is similar in terms of risk exposure.

Figure 24.1 illustrates such a comparison for a hypothetical common stock (or "equity") portfolio referred to as Fund 07632. In this figure, Fund 07632's performance for each year is represented by a diamond. The hypothetical comparison portfolios are other common stock portfolios that are represented by the box surrounding the diamond (such a representation is known as a *box plot* or a *floating bar chart*). The top and bottom lines of the box indicate the returns of the 5th and 95th percentile comparison portfolios, respectively. Similarly, the top and bottom dashed lines represent the 25th and 75th percentiles, respectively. The solid line in the middle represents the median (that is, the 50th percentile) portfolio. Note that this particular evaluation technique presumes that the comparison portfolios exhibit risk similar to Fund 07632 and that they represent feasible alternatives for Fund 07632's owner. Failing to meet these conditions (as is often the case in such peer group comparisons) will generally invalidate the performance evaluation.

Alternatively, risk may be explicitly measured so that a single measure of performance taking both return and risk into account can be employed. This will allow benchmark portfolios of varying degrees of risk to be compared with the portfolio being evaluated. One way to do this is by comparing the portfolio to a market index that is constructed from the same set of securities that the portfolio manager evaluates in making investments. It is useful, therefore, to understand how market indices are constructed.

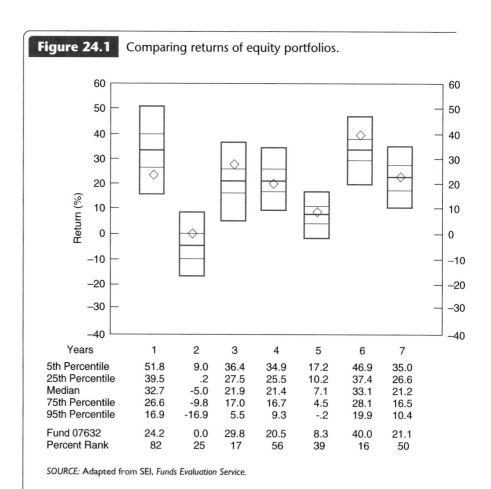

Figure 24.1 Comparing returns of equity portfolios.

Years	1	2	3	4	5	6	7
5th Percentile	51.8	9.0	36.4	34.9	17.2	46.9	35.0
25th Percentile	39.5	.2	27.5	25.5	10.2	37.4	26.6
Median	32.7	-5.0	21.9	21.4	7.1	33.1	21.2
75th Percentile	26.6	-9.8	17.0	16.7	4.5	28.1	16.5
95th Percentile	16.9	-16.9	5.5	9.3	-.2	19.9	10.4
Fund 07632	24.2	0.0	29.8	20.5	8.3	40.0	21.1
Percent Rank	82	25	17	56	39	16	50

SOURCE: Adapted from SEI, *Funds Evaluation Service.*

Custom Benchmark Portfolios

I nvestment management has become increasingly specialized in recent years. Managers have chosen not only to concentrate on specific asset classes (for example, stocks or bonds), but within those asset classes they have further focused their efforts on certain types of securities. This specialization has been particularly prevalent among domestic common stock managers. For example, some managers specialize in small, emerging growth stocks. Others select only from certain industries, such as health care. These specializations have come to be known as "investment styles." Investment styles have significant ramifications for the evaluation of investment manager performance.

Investment management can be viewed as a fishing contest. Each angler has her own fishing hole (investment style). No one fishing hole is assumed to be any better than another, although from year to year the sizes and quantity of fish fluctuate independently in each hole. The anglers attempt to catch the largest fish from their fishing holes. How should institutional investor clients evaluate the proficiency of these anglers based on their catches? It would make little sense to directly compare the anglers' respective catches. If Angler A's fishing hole was extremely well-stocked this year and Angler B's was not, Angler B would be at a tremendous disadvantage. More appropriately, clients would like to compare what each angler caught against the opportunities available in their respective fishing holes. In other words, the clients should want to take into account the impact of managers' investment styles on their performance.

Investment styles tend to dominate the performance of investment managers within a particular asset class. For example, suppose that the domestic common stock market was split along two dimensions similar to those discussed in Chapter 16: market capitalization (share price times shares outstanding) and growth prospects. In 1997, for example, the best-performing US group was small value stocks, which returned 32%. Conversely, small growth stocks returned 13%, a difference of 19 percentage points. Differences among investment styles of similar magnitudes can be found in other years.

These differences are typically large enough so that no investment manager can hope to consistently overcome the performance effect of her investment style. Therefore, to evaluate a manager's investment skill, how the manager has performed relative to her investment style should be considered explicitly.

One means of dealing with this issue is to develop a comparison portfolio that specifically represents the manager's investment style. This comparison portfolio is referred to as a *custom benchmark portfolio*. The custom benchmark contains the types of securities from which the manager typically selects. Further, these securities are weighted in the custom benchmark in a manner similar to weights typically assigned by the manager. Moreover, the custom benchmark displays portfolio characteristics (for example, price-earnings ratios, earnings growth rates, and market capitalizations) consistent with the manager's actual portfolio.

Consider a manager whose investment style entails investing in large-capitalization, high-dividend-yield stocks. In building portfolios, the manager follows certain rules, some explicitly, others implicitly. For example, the manager does not buy stocks with less than $500 million in market capitalization. All stocks in the manager's portfolio must display at least a 5% dividend yield. The manager assigns each stock an equal weight in the portfolio. Further, to avoid overconcentrations, no industry may constitute more than 10% of the portfolio's market value.

A custom benchmark can be designed to reflect these characteristics of the manager's investment style. The custom benchmark might be composed of 300 stocks, as opposed to the manager's portfolio, which might contain only 30 stocks. The manager, in effect, has selected the 30 stocks that she thinks will perform the best. An evaluation of the manager's performance over time will be based on how these 30 stocks perform relative to the 300 stocks.

This performance evaluation process takes advantage of a powerful paired-comparison test. Given a group of stocks, can the manager consistently identify the best-performing issues? The question is simple and the results easy to interpret. No special risk-adjusted performance measures are required. If the custom benchmark has been properly constructed, it exhibits a risk level consistent with that exhibited on average by the manager.

The primary drawback of custom benchmarks is the effort required to design them. Each manager's investment style has unique aspects, and not all of them are as explicit as those of the large-capitalization, high-yield manager discussed above. Typically, identifying those unique aspects involves examining past portfolios and engaging in lengthy discussions with the manager.

Recently a number of analysts have adopted a method in which a benchmark made up of combinations of standard indices is constructed based on statistical analysis of a manager's past returns. The

use of this procedure, known as *style analysis*, can in many cases provide some of the advantages of custom benchmark portfolios at a fraction of the cost, time, and effort. (For details on this approach, see the references listed at the end of the chapter.)

Custom benchmarks, whether derived via detailed analyses or using style analysis, can provide effective performance evaluations. Moreover, they have uses outside of performance evaluation. For example, as discussed in Chapter 23's *Institutional Issues* section, clients who hire more than one investment manager can use custom benchmarks to examine how various investment styles fit together into an aggregate portfolio. This type of analysis permits a client to better understand and control the investment risks present in the client's total portfolio.

Market Indices

Market Index A collection of securities whose prices are averaged to reflect the overall investment performance of a particular market for financial assets.

What did the market do yesterday? How much would an unmanaged common stock portfolio have returned last year? Such questions are often answered by examining the performance of a **market index**. Figure 24.2 displays many indices that are commonly discussed. These indices differ from one another with respect to (1) the securities included in the index and (2) the method employed in calculating the value of the index.[2]

In order to understand how some of the most popular indices are computed, consider a simple example where the market index is based on two stocks, referred to as A and B. At the end of day 0, their closing prices are, respectively, $10 and $20 per share. Furthermore, at this time A has 1500 shares outstanding and B has 2000 shares outstanding.

▶ Price Weighting

Price-weighted Market Index A market index in which the contribution of a security to the value of the index is a function of the security's current market price.

There are three weighting methods that are often used in computing a market index. The first method, involving **price weighting**, begins by summing the prices of the shares that are included in the index and ends by dividing this sum by a constant (the divisor). If the index includes only stocks A and B and was started on day 0, the divisor would be equal to the number of stocks in the average, 2. Thus, on day 0 the index would have a value of $(10 + 20)/2 = 15$. The divisor is adjusted thereafter whenever there is a stock split in order to avoid giving misleading indications of the market's direction. The divisor is also adjusted whenever the composition of the stocks in the index changes (meaning whenever one stock is substituted for another).

---

[2]For more on the construction of market indices, see Mary M. Cutler, "Market Indices: A Learning Exercise Using Warsaw Stock Exchange Prices," *Financial Practice and Education* 5. no. 2 (Fall–Winter 1995): 99–106.

North American Indexes

52W high	52W low	Index	% Yield	P/E	Vol 00s	High	Low	Close	Net change	% change
Toronto Stock Exchange										
7835.75	6066.69	TSE 300	1.63	28.83	604755	6741.46	6647.31	6730.98	+26.65	+0.4
5485.41	3096.47	Metals & Minerals	2.33	28.24	29067	3161.47	3096.47	3147.29	+39.06	+1.3
5619.84	3239.30	Integrated Mines	2.44	17.92	9980	3301.72	3239.30	3288.26	+36.51	+1.1
3012.57	1553.84	Mining	1.86	n.a.	19088	1597.95	1553.84	1588.00	+28.58	+1.8
9257.80	5185.18	Gold & Precious Mnrl	0.83	n.a.	59211	5450.81	5375.55	5441.16	+45.57	+0.8
8094.31	5320.74	Oil & Gas	0.81	35.95	82509	5401.15	5320.74	5363.22	-49.50	-0.9
9729.68	7683.29	Integrated Oils	1.91	21.06	15179	7955.43	7749.83	7955.43	+15.88	+0.2
7461.88	4671.09	Oil & Gas Producers	0.30	93.48	59181	4774.68	4671.09	4700.26	-71.70	-1.5
4353.30	1790.97	Oil & Gas Services	0.85	9.51	8148	1815.68	1790.97	1805.13	-2.55	-0.1
5527.46	3722.68	Paper & Forest Prods	1.64	23.42	25618	4025.49	3980.65	4025.49	+3.54	+0.1
12537.10	9728.88	Consumer Products	1.49	23.21	21879	11083.38	10878.15	11010.30	+42.36	+0.4
11191.03	8613.39	Food Processing	1.35	21.20	657	9158.61	8929.69	9158.61	+130.12	+1.4
31803.59	20423.22	Tobacco	2.43	22.73	12348	30172.53	29364.81	29718.19	+125.35	+0.4
16741.39	10820.96	Distilleries	1.88	17.27	2535	13233.90	12811.02	13184.15	+310.95	+2.4
7261.62	5397.12	Breweries, Beverages	2.30	21.74	2973	5896.92	5789.64	5789.64	-85.10	-1.4
2016.33	1446.35	Household Goods	0.57	21.74	263	1838.13	1762.67	1782.35	-67.87	-3.7
1885.79	1321.47	Biotchnlg Phrmctcls	0.06	61.50	3102	1569.59	1541.79	1551.10	-19.60	-1.2
5896.20	4432.72	Industrial Products	0.80	26.55	111395	4997.13	4916.00	4965.36	-15.06	-0.3
1750.59	1245.52	Steels	2.66	9.99	4518	1267.02	1245.52	1267.02	+18.26	+1.5
6311.11	4928.16	Fabricating & Engr	0.73	18.59	1942	5021.18	4928.16	4928.16	-109.70	-2.2
75165.97	45488.06	Transportation Equip	0.85	30.77	22565	67821.80	65296.62	67280.92	+673.83	+1.0
19155.23	13104.26	Technology Hardware	0.47	65.85	57388	15950.69	15510.23	15744.03	-66.08	-0.4
8228.46	6122.61	Building Materials	0.83	21.50	1971	6762.78	6709.86	6716.70	-28.47	-0.4
6928.79	5210.34	Chemicals & Fertlzrs	1.27	15.85	13496	5800.04	5723.35	5775.86	+6.69	+0.1
2726.45	1749.43	Technology Software	n.a.	77.15	5199	2037.34	1981.55	2025.84	-33.50	-1.6
24797.59	16488.84	Autos & Parts	0.92	17.30	4316	19895.89	19598.22	19888.82	-114.10	-0.6
3015.08	2447.11	Real Estate	0.72	24.96	6994	2476.08	2447.11	2455.46	-27.57	-1.1
9374.31	6390.94	Transn & Envrnmtl	1.30	11.31	47068	6557.44	6416.35	6557.44	+140.21	+2.2
7252.80	5461.25	Pipelines	4.78	14.68	29445	6181.33	6093.63	6175.60	+85.22	+1.4
8413.15	5185.39	Utilities	2.37	n.a.	56223	7462.36	7245.27	7462.36	+97.64	+1.3
8560.13	5062.48	Telephone Utilities	2.11	n.a.	51389	7564.82	7330.65	7564.82	+105.73	+1.4
6668.91	4946.50	Gas & Electric Utls	4.09	16.74	4835	5966.65	5858.47	5966.65	+43.43	+0.7
16216.83	11659.37	Communs & Media	1.27	43.91	17110	15123.65	14970.34	15110.96	+84.30	+0.6
13660.01	9897.34	Broadcasting	0.71	24.69	1046	12216.72	12112.51	12112.51	-93.99	-0.8
28078.09	15317.98	Cable & Entmt	0.15	n.a.	6486	25692.26	25469.62	25544.23	+53.75	+0.2
17214.13	13213.64	Publishing & Prtg	1.97	17.08	9578	16094.76	15825.89	16094.76	+168.04	+1.1
6792.47	5338.98	Merchandising	0.98	25.47	23950	6031.51	5982.03	6023.44	+1.39	nil
10413.66	7506.89	Wholesale Distrs	0.78	14.01	649	7663.42	7506.89	7663.42	+36.16	+0.5
18166.40	10970.69	Food Stores	0.88	20.27	7314	17104.70	16772.18	17013.01	+103.83	+0.6
2031.55	1481.27	Department Stores	1.92	n.a.	8509	1739.87	1698.59	1718.79	-37.35	-2.1
2611.34	1784.54	Specialty Stores	0.82	20.32	5053	2306.86	2265.22	2306.86	+26.98	+1.2
82868.32	50651.88	Hospitality	0.62	27.41	2426	51742.92	50651.88	51020.36	-307.17	-0.6
10881.08	6892.22	Financial Services	2.02	14.61	86526	9100.15	8903.01	9063.14	+45.38	+0.5
11901.14	7411.93	Banks & Trusts	2.46	13.24	67890	9521.95	9210.77	9458.44	+92.53	+1.0
18008.64	11699.24	Investment Companies	1.00	20.22	13614	16538.22	15277.80	15511.19	-118.19	-0.8
16509.56	9503.92	Insurance	0.34	20.92	965	15728.92	14984.38	15363.47	-439.63	-2.8
5422.33	2701.27	Financial Mgmt Cos	0.72	24.07	4057	4830.97	4771.73	4824.67	+11.92	+0.2
11030.92	7851.75	Conglomerates	1.96	11.73	7760	9019.21	8776.82	9019.21	+89.05	+1.0
164.07	128.83	TSE 300 Unweighted	1.18	24.42	604755			129.25	-0.84	-0.6
473.29	365.62	TSE 200	0.78	n.a.	202482	391.49	385.69	387.25	-4.55	-1.2
477.64	367.51	TSE 100	1.82	25.00	402274	413.34	405.47	412.80	+3.01	+0.7
324.56	225.24	Resource	1.48	53.49	81616	233.80	229.81	233.18	+0.88	+0.4
566.93	433.28	Industrial	1.12	18.70	131250	475.20	465.85	474.42	+2.38	+0.5
715.72	470.05	Interest Sensitive	2.40	24.26	149010	621.32	605.63	619.97	+6.10	+1.0
428.17	328.85	Consumer	1.55	23.85	40398	387.69	381.48	386.41	+3.10	+0.8
427.10	325.71	Toronto 35	1.97	29.59	282431	370.12	359.70	369.43	+4.74	+1.3
Financial Post										
1498.14	1246.92	FPX Growth						1410.33	+12.98	+0.9
1445.72	1239.11	FPX Balanced						1384.02	+8.48	+0.6
1383.43	1227.54	FPX Income						1344.17	+3.02	+0.2
Montreal Exchange										
3971.66	3111.54	Market Portfolio	1.85	27.05	250143	3416.87	3333.04	3413.25	+46.11	+1.4
8233.99	5156.03	Banking	2.46	13.53	79290	6650.32	6432.44	6600.37	+55.27	+0.8
3167.43	2120.95	Forest Products	2.38	38.33	15635	2281.62	2247.41	2281.62	+4.56	+0.2
4335.17	3072.08	Industrial Products	1.11	18.93	59840	3881.79	3804.46	3851.96	-9.74	-0.3
3137.49	1818.34	Mining & Minerals	1.98	92.80	30647	1860.46	1818.34	1860.46	+36.23	+2.0
3084.42	2221.82	Oil & Gas	1.30	30.78	40273	2303.78	2269.83	2295.82	-7.55	-0.3
4543.14	2968.18	Utilities	3.51	33.47	85518	4006.18	3944.51	4003.42	+28.84	+0.7
Vancouver Stock Exchange										
848.42	473.79	Composite			125123	477.54	473.79	474.30	-4.06	-0.8
765.29	332.96	Mining			84501	338.80	332.96	334.45	-4.35	-1.3
Alberta Stock Exchange										
2611.40	1950.44	Combined Value			72060	1980.71	1950.44	1951.92	-28.79	-1.5
Dow Jones										
9412.64	6936.45	Industrials			988991	8641.79	8316.10	8546.78	+59.47	+0.7
3735.38	2829.52	Transportation			109772	3151.17	3031.07	3095.58	+8.30	+0.3
296.78	226.94	Utilities			112405	277.18	268.94	273.92	+0.18	+0.1
2994.23	2287.46	Composite			1211168	2721.85	2622.42	2686.84	+13.00	+0.5
New York Stock Exchange										
601.76	450.91	Composite				546.06	534.01	544.01	+2.65	+0.5
737.66	561.74	Industrials				669.33	654.57	667.08	+3.07	+0.5
540.47	426.32	Transportation				455.13	445.31	451.92	-0.37	-0.1
399.69	278.93	Utilities				371.46	364.50	371.45	+1.62	+0.4
599.87	432.88	Financial				534.39	520.60	530.06	+3.40	+0.6
American Stock Exchange										
753.75	631.65	Composite				678.80	665.31	672.07	-6.69	-1.0
980.77	720.46	Major Market				916.71	895.16	913.42	+10.34	+1.1
Nasdaq Stock Market										
2028.18	1465.61	Composite				1804.60	1750.81	1788.20	+2.56	+0.1
1417.92	1133.77	Industrials				1202.82	1173.89	1190.23	-9.08	-0.8
1949.62	1615.71	Insurance				1634.69	1615.71	1620.49	-7.76	-0.5
2306.75	1685.99	Banks				1954.28	1917.12	1933.28	-17.47	-0.9
2746.06	2007.77	Financial				2436.90	2396.76	2414.12	-11.27	-0.5
1254.06	985.45	Transportation				1002.70	985.45	993.26	-2.46	-0.2
464.81	254.51	Telecomms				406.04	394.35	403.10	+4.10	+1.0
1485.97	925.92	100 Index				1343.12	1289.91	1329.90	+12.66	+1.0
Russell										
492.28	394.03	2000				402.30	394.03	398.69	-2.94	-0.7
Standard & Poor's										
1190.58	855.27	500 Composite				1084.80	1057.35	1081.43	+9.31	+0.9
1385.95	993.87	Industrials				1268.22	1236.90	1265.58	+10.38	+0.8
769.69	629.81	Transportation				644.95	630.02	641.88	+4.49	+0.7
147.93	102.28	Financials				130.77	126.78	129.72	+1.55	+1.2
249.74	180.46	Utilities				231.77	227.28	230.33	+0.15	+0.1
582.27	407.51	100 Stocks				533.48	518.68	531.63	+5.99	+1.1
Value Line										
999.91	446.03	Arithmetic				862.92	848.06	858.26	-1.45	-0.2

SOURCE: Reprinted by permission of *The Financial Post* (August 6, 1998).

For example, assume that on day 1, B splits 2-for-1 and closes at $11 per share, while A closes at $13. In this situation, it is clear that the market has risen, since both stocks have a higher price than on day 0 after adjusting B for the split. If nothing were done in computing the index, its value on day 1 would be $(13 + 11)/2 = 12$, a drop of $20\% = (12 - 15)/15$ from day 0 that falsely suggests the market went down on day 1. In reality, the market went up to $[13 + (11 \times 2)]/2 = 17.5$, a gain of $16.67\% = (17.5 - 15)/15$.

A stock split is accounted for in a price-weighted index by adjusting the divisor whenever a split takes place. In the example, the divisor is adjusted by examining the index on day 1, the day of the split. More specifically, the following equation would be solved for the unknown divisor d:

$$\frac{13 + 11}{d} = 17.5 \tag{24.6}$$

The value of d that solves this equation is 1.37. The new divisor will continue in use after day 1 until there is another split, when it will again be recalculated.

If the index begins at a given level, such as 100 on day 0, then updating it is straightforward. First, the percentage change in average price is calculated. In the example, this was determined to be 16.67%. Second, this percentage is multiplied by the previous day's index value in order to determine the change in the index. Continuing with the example, the index level on day 0 was 100, so the change from day 0 to day 1 would be $16.67\% \times 100 = 16.67$, resulting in a level on day 1 of 116.67. This is equivalent to dividing the average price on day 1 (17.5) by the average price on the beginning date (15) and then multiplying the result by the index's level on the beginning day (100). Mathematically the formula is

$$I_t = I_0 \times \frac{AP_t}{AP_0} \tag{24.7}$$

where AP_t denotes the average price on day t and I_t denotes the index level on day t.

The *Dow Jones Industrial Average*, one of the most widely followed US indices, is this type of index. It involves the prices of 30 stocks that generally represent large-size firms.[3] Other Dow Jones Averages, for example one involving 20 transportation stocks and another involving 15 utility stocks, are similarly calculated. Furthermore, Dow Jones calculates stock market indices for each of several countries as well as an Asia/Pacific index and two World Indices, one with and one without the United States. Levels of several of these Dow Jones Averages are reported in many US daily newspapers. Historical data on the Averages, including quarterly dividends and earnings figures, are published from time to time in *Barron's* and other periodicals. Some bond market indices are also calculated in this manner. For example, the *Dow Jones 20-Bond Index* is computed by averaging the price of 10 utility and 10 industrial bonds. More on bond indices is discussed later in this chapter.

● Value Weighting

Value-weighted Market Index (Alternatively, **Capitalization-weighted Market Index**.) A market index in which the contribution of a security to the value of the index is a function of the security's market capitalization.

A second weighting method is known as **value weighting** (or capitalization weighting). With this method, the prices of the shares of the stocks in the index are multiplied by their respective numbers of shares outstanding and then added up in order to arrive at a figure equal to the aggregate market value for that day. This figure is then divided by the corresponding figure for the day the index was started, with the resulting value being multiplied by an arbitrarily set beginning index value.

---

[3]The Montreal Exchange index is calculated in this manner. The Montreal *Market Portfolio Index* consists of 25 of the largest publicly held corporations in Canada.

Continuing with the example, assume that the start-up day for the index is day 0 and that the index is assigned a beginning value of 100. First, note that the aggregate market value on day 0 is equal to ($10 × 1500) + ($20 × 2000) = $55000. Next, note that the aggregate market value on day 1 is equal to ($13 × 1500) + ($11 × 4000) = $63500. Dividing $63 500 by $55 000 and then multiplying the result by 100 gives the index value for day 1 of ($63500/$55000) × 100 = 115.45. Thus, the market would be reported as having risen by 15.45% = (115.45 − 100)/100 from day 0 to day 1.

Note how no special procedures are needed to handle stock splits, since the resulting increased number of shares for a company is automatically used after a split in calculating its market value. In general, the total market value of the securities in the index on day t (MVP_t) is divided by the total market value on the beginning date (MVP_0) and then multiplied by the index's level on the beginning day in order to get its value on day t. Mathematically the formula is:

$$I_t = I_0 \times \frac{MVP_t}{MVP_0} \qquad (24.8)$$

The Standard & Poor's 500, widely used by institutional investors, is a value-weighted average of 500 large-sized stocks. Standard & Poor's also computes value-weighted indices for industrial, transportation, utility, and financial stocks. Furthermore, a variety of industry indices are also calculated. Values for all indices, along with quarterly data on dividends, earnings, and sales, may be found in Standard & Poor's *Analysts' Handbook* (annual), *Trade and Securities Statistics* (annual), and *Analysts' Handbook Supplement* (monthly). The Vancouver Stock Exchange index is a value-weighted index of those companies that trade at least 50% of their volume on the VSE.

More comprehensive value-weighted indices for US stocks are also computed. The New York Stock Exchange publishes a composite index of all stocks listed on that exchange, as well as four subindices (industrials, utilities, transportation, and finance). The American Stock Exchange computes an index of its stocks. The National Association of Securities Dealers (NASD), using its automated quotation service (NASDAQ), computes indices based on the market value of approximately 5000 over-the-counter stocks; in addition to a composite index, NASD calculates indices for six categories representing industrials, banks, insurance, other finance, transportation, and utilities. NASD also publishes four indices that are based on just those stocks in their National Market System (the previously mentioned NASD indices are based on both NMS and non-NMS stocks).

The broadest value-weighted index is calculated by Wilshire Associates. Their index, known as the Wilshire 5000 Equity Index, is based on all stocks listed on the New York and American Stock exchanges plus those "actively traded over-the-counter." The Russell 1000, 2000, and 3000 are also broad value-weighted indices, covering roughly the largest 1000 stocks; the next 2000; and the sum of the two. Various value-weighted US stock indices are also produced to represent certain investment styles, as were discussed in Chapter 16. For example, the S&P 500 is split into a value stock index and a growth stock index. Stocks in the S&P 500 are first ordered by their book-value-to-market-value (BV/MV) ratios. Then the index is divided into two segments with equal aggregate market value. The half with the low BV/MV stocks is called the S&P/BARRA 500 Growth Index while the high BV/MV stocks constitute the S&P/BARRA 500 Value Index. A similar procedure is used to construct growth and value indices for Standard & Poor's middle-capitalization stocks (the S&P 400) and small capitalization stocks (the S&P 600).

In terms of international indices, *Morgan Stanley Capital International Perspective* publishes value-weighted indices using various combinations of over 1000 stocks from 19 different countries, resulting in a "world market index." These and other international indices are discussed in Chapter 25 (see Figure 25.2).

The TSE 300 is a modified value-weighted index. The number of shares in all control blocks (representing more than 20% of outstanding shares) is subtracted from the number

National Association of Securities Dealers
www.nasd.com

Wilshire Associates
www.wilshire.com

of shares outstanding to determine an adjusted market value. The following are the criteria for inclusion in the TSE 300: an annual trading volume of at least 100 000 shares, and trading value greater than $1 million per year. The 300 stocks with the largest adjusted market value that meet the above criteria are included in the index. The TSE 35 is also a modified value-weighted index that includes 35 of Canada's larger publicly listed corporations that are among the more heavily traded issues on the TSE. In order to prevent one stock from dominating this index the maximum weight assigned to any stock is 10%. The TSE 100 is constructed in a similar manner and consists of the largest 100 companies.

The values of the TSE 300 (and its associated subindices), the TSE 35, the Montreal Exchange, Vancouver Stock Exchange and various US indices are published daily in *The Financial Post* (as shown in Figure 24.1) and *The Globe and Mail: Report on Business.*

Both the TSE 300 and the TSE 35 are calculated in two forms—a price index and a total return index. The former follows the procedure described above and represents aggregate price movements. The total return index includes reinvested dividend payments on each of the stocks as well as capital gains.

Equal Weighting

Equal-weighted Market Index A market index in which all the component securities contribute equally to the value of the index, regardless of the various attributes of those securities.

Price Relative The price of a security in one period divided by the price of that same security in a previous period.

The third method of weighting in known as **equal weighting**. This index is computed daily by multiplying the level of the index on the previous day by the arithmetic mean of the daily **price relatives** (today's price divided by yesterday's price) of the relevant stocks in the index. For example, the value of the index consisting of *A* and *B* on day 1 would be calculated by first determining the price relatives to be equal to $13/10 = 1.3$ for *A* and $(11 \times 2)/20 = 1.1$ for *B*. Note how an adjustment was made in calculating the price relative for *B* due to its stock split. All that was required was to multiply the post-split price of 11 by 2, the split ratio.

Once the price relatives have been determined, then their arithmetic mean would be calculated as

$$(1.3 + 1.1)/2 = 1.20$$

If the value of the index on day 0 was 100, then the value on day 1 would be reported as $100 \times 1.20 = 120$, an increase of 20% $(1.20 - 1)$. (When the index is created, its value on that day can be set at any arbitrary starting value, such as 100.) The Value Line Composite (Arithmetic) Index, based on over 1500 stocks, is prepared in this manner.

Geometric Mean

One popular index that does not involve price weighting, value weighting, or equal weighting is the *Value Line Composite (Geometric) Index.* This index is computed daily by multiplying the previous day's index by the geometric mean of the daily price relatives (today's price divided by yesterday's price) of the relevant stocks in the index. For example, the value of the index consisting of stocks A and B on day 1 would be calculated by first determining the price relatives to be equal to $(13/10) = 1.3$ for A and $(11 \times 2)/20 = 1.1$ for B. Then the geometric mean would be calculated as[4]

$$(1.3 \times 1.1)^{1/2} = 1.1958$$

If the value of the index on day 0 was 100, then the value on day 1 would be reported as $100 \times 1.1958 = 119.58$, an increase of $1.1958 - 1 = 19.58\%$. In the case of the Value

---

[4]In order to determine the geometric mean for *N* stocks, multiply their price relatives and then take the *N*th root of the resulting product.

Line index, the initial value was set at 100 on June 30, 1961, and has been updated ever since then in this manner.[5]

In summary, four types of indices have been presented; various people use these indices when they refer to how the market has done. However, the indices can give notably different answers. In the example shown here, the market was calculated to have risen by either 16.67%, 15.45%, 20%, or 19.58%, depending on the index used. In practice, most professional money managers use either the TSE 300 or the S&P 500 as the barometer (depending on the market in which they are trading) since they have a fairly wide base and weight larger companies more heavily than smaller companies, thereby representing more closely the performance of the average dollar invested in the market.

....

Risk-adjusted Measures of Performance for Equity Portfolios

Having measured the periodic returns for a portfolio during an evaluation interval (for example, quarterly returns for a four-year evaluation interval), the next step is to determine if these returns represent superior or inferior performance. In order to do this, an estimate of the portfolio's risk level during the evaluation interval is needed. For equity portfolios, two kinds of risk can be estimated—the portfolio's market (or systematic) risk, measured by its beta, and the portfolio's total risk, measured by its standard deviation.

It is important to analyze risk appropriately. The key issue here is determining the impact of the portfolio on the client's overall level of risk. If the client has many other assets, then the market risk of the portfolio provides the relevant measure of the portfolio's impact on the client's overall level of risk. If, however, the portfolio provides the client's sole support, then its total risk is the relevant measure of risk. Risk-adjusted performance evaluation is generally based on one of these two viewpoints, taking either market risk or total risk into consideration.

Assume there are T time periods in the evaluation interval (for example, $T = 16$ when there are four years of quarterly data) and let r_{pt} denote the return on the portfolio during period t. The average return on the portfolio, denoted by ar_p, is simply

$$ar_p = \frac{\sum\limits_{t=1}^{T} r_{pt}}{T} \tag{24.9}$$

Having calculated ar_p, the *ex post* (that is, after the fact) standard deviation can be calculated as

$$\sigma_p = \left[\frac{\sum\limits_{t=1}^{T} (r_{pt} - ar_p)^2}{T - 1} \right]^{1/2} \tag{24.10}$$

This estimate of the portfolio's standard deviation can be used as an indication of the amount of total risk that the portfolio had during the evaluation interval.[6] It can be com-

---

[5]Value Line also has indices for industrials, rails, and utilities that are similarly computed and updated. Before March 1986 the Montreal Exchange index was also a geometric index.

[6]Sometimes the excess return for a portfolio, which is equal to its return minus the risk-free rate $(r_{pt} - r_{ft})$, is used instead of r_{pt} in equation (24.9) to determine the average excess return (denoted by aer_p). Then, the summation in the numerator of equation (24.10) is carried out using $[(r_{pt} - r_{ft}) - aer_p]^2$ instead of $(r_{pt} - ar_p)^2$. The resulting number is the standard deviation of excess returns, which is sometimes used as an estimate of the total risk of the portfolio. Typically, the two standard deviations are quite similar in numerical value.

pared directly with the standard deviations of other portfolios, as illustrated in Figure 24.3. (This figure is to be interpreted in the same manner as Figure 24.1.)

The returns of a portfolio may also be compared with those of a substitute for the market portfolio, such as the TSE 300, in order to determine the portfolio's *ex post* beta during the evaluation interval. Denoting the *excess return* on the portfolio during period t by $er_{pt} = r_{pt} - r_{ft}$, the return on the TSE 300 (or some other market substitute) during period t by r_{Mt}, and the excess return on the TSE 300 during period t by $er_{Mt} = r_{Mt} - r_{ft}$, this beta can be estimated as follows:

$$\beta_p = \frac{\left(T\sum_{t=1}^{T} er_{Mt}er_{pt}\right) - \left(\sum_{t=1}^{T} er_{pt}\sum_{t=1}^{T} er_{Mt}\right)}{\left(T\sum_{t=1}^{T} er_{Mt}^2\right) - \left(\sum_{t=1}^{T} er_{Mt}\right)^2} \tag{24.11}$$

This estimate of the portfolio's beta can be used as an indication of the amount of market risk that the portfolio had during the evaluation interval.[7] It can be compared directly with the betas of other portfolios, as illustrated in Figure 24.4.

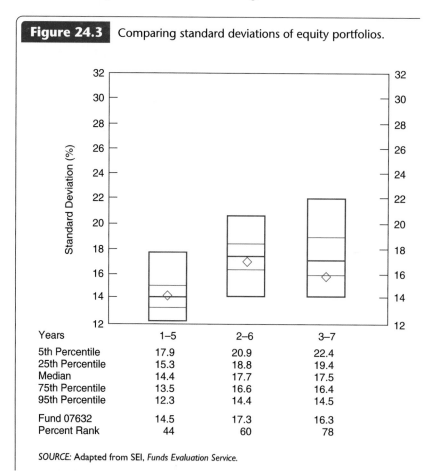

Figure 24.3 Comparing standard deviations of equity portfolios.

Years	1–5	2–6	3–7
5th Percentile	17.9	20.9	22.4
25th Percentile	15.3	18.8	19.4
Median	14.4	17.7	17.5
75th Percentile	13.5	16.6	16.4
95th Percentile	12.3	14.4	14.5
Fund 07632	14.5	17.3	16.3
Percent Rank	44	60	78

SOURCE: Adapted from SEI, *Funds Evaluation Service.*

---

[7]Equation (24.11) corresponds to the formula for estimating the slope term in a simple regression model where the independent variable is er_{Mt} and the dependent variable is er_{pt}. Sometimes returns are used in equation (24.11), where er_{Mt} is replaced by r_{Mt} and er_{pt} is replaced by r_{pt}. In this situation, the beta corresponds to the slope term in the *market model* for the portfolio. Typically, the two betas are quite similar in numerical value.

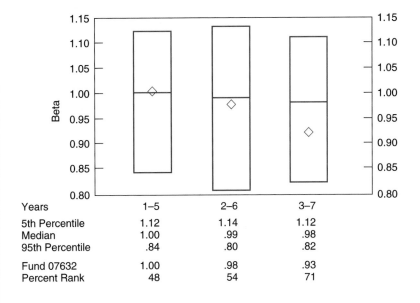

Figure 24.4 Comparing betas of equity portfolios.

Years	1–5	2–6	3–7
5th Percentile	1.12	1.14	1.12
Median	1.00	.99	.98
95th Percentile	.84	.80	.82
Fund 07632	1.00	.98	.93
Percent Rank	48	54	71

SOURCE: Adapted from SEI, *Funds Evaluation Service.*

Although a portfolio's return and a measure of its risk can be compared individually with those of other portfolios, as in Figures 24.1, 24.3, and 24.4, it is often not clear how the portfolio performed on a risk-adjusted basis relative to these other portfolios. For the fund shown in the figures, the average percent rank for the portfolio's return over the five years ending in year 7 is $(17 + 56 + 39 + 16 + 50)/5 = 36\%$. Over the same period, its standard deviation put it in the 78th percentile rank. Assuming the client is concerned with total risk, how does he interpret these percent ranks? In the case of the return, the portfolio was slightly above average; in terms of standard deviation, it was less risky than approximately three-fourths of the other portfolios. Overall, this suggests that the portfolio did better on a risk-adjusted basis than the others, but it does not give the client a clear and precise sense of how much better.

Such a sense can be conveyed by certain CAPM-based measures of portfolio performance. Each one of these measures provides an estimate of a portfolio's risk-adjusted performance, thereby allowing the client to see how the portfolio performed relative to other portfolios as well as the market. They are presented next.

Ex Post Characteristic Lines

Over an evaluation interval, an *ex post security market line* (SML) can be estimated by determining the average risk-free rate and market return:

$$ar_f = \frac{\sum_{t=1}^{T} r_{ft}}{T} \tag{24.12}$$

$$ar_M = \frac{\sum_{t=1}^{T} r_{Mt}}{T} \tag{24.13}$$

Once these averages have been calculated, the *ex post* SML is simply the equation of the line going through the points $(0, ar_f)$ and $(1, ar_M)$:

$$ar_p^e = ar_f + (ar_M - ar_f)\beta_p \tag{24.14}$$

Equivalently, the equilibrium average return during this interval of time for a portfolio with a beta of β_p would simply be equal to $ar_f + (ar_M - ar_f)\beta_p$. Accordingly, ar_p^e can be used as the benchmark return for a portfolio with a beta of β_p.

Panel (a) of Table 24.1 presents an example by using the quarterly returns for the TSE 300 over a 16-quarter time interval, along with corresponding returns on 91-day Treasury bills. Using equations (24.12) and (24.13), the average risk-free return and market return were, respectively, 2.39% and 3.05%. Inserting these values into equation (24.14), the *ex post* SML for this time interval was

$$ar_p^e = 2.39\% + (3.05\% - 2.39\%)\beta_p$$
$$= 2.39\% + 0.66\%\beta_p \tag{24.15}$$

Table 24.1 The *Ex Post* Characteristic Line for the First Fund.

a. Return Data

Quarter	Treasury Bill Return	First Fund		TSE 300	
		Return	Excess Return	Return	Excess Return
1	2.64%	3.94%	1.30%	5.84%	3.20%
2	2.20	1.27	−0.93	2.02	−0.18
3	2.07	−4.89	−6.96	−2.74	−4.81
4	2.08	7.01	4.93	3.74	1.66
5	1.82	16.59	14.77	22.70	20.88
6	2.00	−0.57	−2.57	0.68	−1.32
7	2.26	8.78	6.52	4.94	2.68
8	1.95	−29.44	−31.39	−18.33	−20.28
9	2.09	10.13	8.04	5.65	3.56
10	2.21	1.50	−0.71	4.72	2.51
11	2.32	−3.91	6.23	−3.64	−5.96
12	2.60	7.90	5.30	4.20	1.60
13	2.80	12.03	9.23	6.47	3.67
14	3.09	3.53	0.44	6.15	3.06
15	3.02	10.80	7.78	5.72	2.70
16	3.04	1.89	−1.15	1.58	−1.46

Table 24.1 (continued)

b. Calculations[a]

Quarter	First Fund Excess Returns = Y (1)	TSE 300 Excess Returns = X (2)	Y² (3)	X² (4)	Y × X (5)
1	1.30	3.2	10.24	1.695204	4.1664
2	−0.93	−0.18	0.0324	0.871235	0.168012
3	−6.96	−4.81	23.1361	48.40402	33.46461
4	4.93	1.66	2.7556	24.30292	8.183468
5	14.77	20.88	435.9744	218.1056	308.3641
6	−2.57	−1.32	1.7424	6.623416	3.397152
7	6.52	2.68	7.1824	42.54170	17.48003
8	−31.39	−20.28	411.2784	985.3572	636.5973
9	8.04	3.56	12.6736	64.71880	28.63948
10	−0.71	2.51	6.3001	0.503674	−1.78134
11	−6.23	−5.96	35.5216	38.84779	37.14748
12	5.30	1.6	2.56	28.11120	8.4832
13	9.23	3.67	13.4689	85.10247	33.85611
14	0.44	3.06	9.3636	0.193424	1.345788
15	7.78	2.7	7.29	60.48172	20.9979
16	−1.15	−1.46	2.1316	1.317444	1.675788
	$\Sigma Y = 8.37$	$\Sigma X = 11.51$	$\Sigma Y^2 = 981.65$	$\Sigma X^2 = 1607.2$	$\Sigma XY = 1142.2$

1. Beta:

$$\frac{(T \times \Sigma XY) - (\Sigma Y \times \Sigma X)}{(T \times \Sigma X^2) - (\Sigma X)^2} = \frac{(16 \times 1142.19) - (11.51 \times 8.37)}{(16 \times 981.65) - (11.51)^2} = 1.16$$

2. Alpha:

$$\frac{\Sigma Y}{T} - \left(\text{Beta} \times \frac{\Sigma X}{T}\right) = \frac{8.37}{16} - \left(1.16 \times \frac{11.51}{16}\right) = -0.31\%$$

3. Standard deviation of random error term:

$$\left[\frac{\Sigma Y^2 - (\text{alpha} \times \Sigma Y) - (\text{Beta} \times \Sigma XY)}{T - 2}\right]^{1/2}$$

$$= \left[\frac{1607.18 - (-0.31 \times 8.37) - (1.16 \times 1142.19)}{16 - 2}\right]^{1/2} = 4.49\%$$

4. Standard error of beta:

$$\frac{\text{Standard deviation of random error term}}{[\Sigma X^2 - (\Sigma X)^2 / T]^{1/2}} = \frac{4.49}{[981.65 - (11.51)^2/16]^{1/2}} = .14$$

5. Standard error of alpha:

$$\frac{\text{Standard deviation of random error term}}{[T - (\Sigma X)^2 / \Sigma X^2]^{1/2}} = \frac{4.49}{[16 - (11.51)^2/981.65]^{1/2}} = 1.12$$

6. Correlation coefficient:

$$\frac{(T \times \Sigma XY) - (\Sigma Y \times \Sigma X)}{[(T \times \Sigma Y^2) - (\Sigma Y)^2] \times [(T \times \Sigma X^2) - (\Sigma X)^2]^{1/2}}$$
$$= \frac{(16 \times 1142.19) - (11.51 \times 8.37)}{[(16 \times 1607.18) - (8.37)^2] \times [(16 \times 981.65) - (11.51)^2]^{1/2}} = .91$$

7. Coefficient of determination:

$$(\text{Correlation coefficient})^2 = (.91)^2 = .83$$

8. Coefficient of nondetermination:

$$1 - \text{coefficient of determination} = 1 - .83 = .17$$

---

[a]All summations are to be carried out over t, where t goes from 1 to T (in this example, $t = 1, \ldots, 16$).

Thus, after estimating a portfolio's *ex post* beta and entering this value on the right-hand side of equation (24.15), a benchmark return for the portfolio can be determined. For example, a portfolio with a beta of .8 would have a benchmark return of $2.39\% + (0.66\% \times .8) = 2.92\%$. Figure 24.5 presents a graph of the *ex post* SML given by equation (24.15).

If the average return on a portfolio was ar_p, calculated as shown in equation (24.9), then one measure of its risk-adjusted performance would be the difference between its average return and the return on its corresponding benchmark. This difference is generally referred to as the portfolio's **ex post alpha** (or differential return) and is denoted by α_p (see Chapter 21):

Ex Post Alpha A portfolio's alpha calculated on an *ex post* basis. Mathematically, over an evaluation interval, it is the difference between the average return on the portfolio and the average return on the benchmark portfolio.

$$\alpha_p = ar_p - ar_{bp} \tag{21.3}$$

A positive value of α_p for a portfolio would indicate that the portfolio had an average return greater than the benchmark return, suggesting its performance was superior. On the other hand, a negative value of α_p would indicate that the portfolio had an average return less than the benchmark return, suggesting its performance was inferior.[8]

By substituting the right-hand side of equation (24.14) for ar_{bp} in equation (21.3), it can be seen that a portfolio's *ex post* alpha based on the *ex post* SML is equal to:

$$\alpha_p = ar_p - [ar_f + (ar_M - ar_f)\beta_p] \tag{24.16}$$

Characteristic Line A simple linear regression model expressing the relationship between the excess return on a security and the excess return on the market portfolio.

After determining the values for α_p and β_p for a portfolio, the **ex post characteristic line** for the portfolio can be written as

$$r_p - r_f = \alpha_p + \beta_p(r_M - r_f) \tag{24.17}$$

The characteristic line is similar to the market model except that the portfolio's returns and the market index's returns are expressed as the excess over the risk-free return. Graphically, this is the equation of a straight line, where $r_M - r_f$ is measured on the horizontal axis and $r_p - r_f$ is measured on the vertical axis. Furthermore, the line has a vertical intercept of α_p and a slope of β_p.

As an example, consider the performance of the hypothetical portfolio "First Fund," indicated in panel (a) of Table 24.1 for the evaluation interval. During this interval, the First Fund had an average quarterly return of 2.85%. Using equation (24.11), it can be shown that First Fund had a beta of 1.16. Having an average beta over the 16 quarters that

---

[8]This measure of performance is sometimes known as the *Jensen coefficient* because it was developed by Michael C. Jensen in "The Performance of Mutual Funds in the Period 1945-1964," *Journal of Finance* 23, no. 2 (May 1968): 389–416.

Figure 24.5 Performance evaluation using the ex post SML.

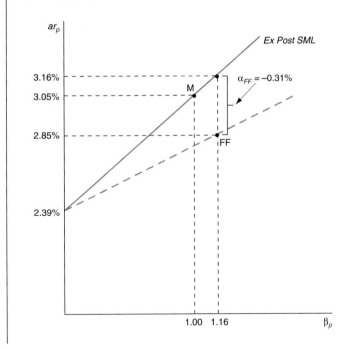

is greater than the market portfolio's beta of 1 indicates that First Fund was relatively aggressive (if it were less than 1, it would have been defensive).

Given these values for its beta and average return, the location of First Fund in Figure 24.5 is represented by the point having coordinates of (1.16, 2.85%), denoted by *FF*. The exact vertical distance from *FF* to the *ex post* SML can be calculated by using equation (24.16):

$$\alpha_p = ar_p - [ar_f + (ar_M - ar_f)\beta_p]$$
$$= 2.85\% - [2.39\% + (3.05\% - 2.39\%)1.16]$$
$$= -0.31\%$$

Since *FF* lies below the *ex post* SML, its *ex post* alpha is negative, and its performance would be viewed as inferior.[9] Using equation (24.17), the *ex post* characteristic line for First Fund would be

$$r_p - r_f = -0.31\% + 1.16(r_M - r_f)$$

Figure 24.5 provides an illustration of this line.[10]

---

[9]Alternatively, if *FF*'s average return had been 4%, then its coordinates would have been (1.16, 4.00%), placing it above the *ex post* SML. In this situation, *FF*'s *ex post* alpha would have been 0.84%, and its performance would have been viewed as superior.

[10]An alternative measure of performance involves dividing the ex post alpha by an estimate of the ex post unique (or unsystematic) risk of the portfolio. This measure, known as the *appraisal ratio*, would be equal to −0.31%/4.48% = −0.07 for First Fund. Comparisons can be made with the value of the appraisal ratio for the market portfolio (its value is defined to be 0) and other portfolios. Note that a positive value indicates superior performance and that the larger the value, the better the performance. See Jack L. Treynor and Fischer Black, "How to Use Security Analysis to Improve Portfolio Selection," *Journal of Business* 46, no. 1 (January 1973): 66–86.

The method of determining a portfolio's *ex post* alpha, beta, and characteristic line suggests the use of a five-step procedure:

1. Determine the periodic rates of return for the portfolio and market index over the time interval, as well as the corresponding risk-free rates.
2. Determine the average market return and risk-free rate by using the formulas in equations (24.12) and (24.13).
3. Determine the portfolio's *ex post* beta by using the formula in equation (24.11).
4. Determine the portfolio's *ex post* alpha by using the formula given in equation (24.16).
5. Insert these values for alpha and beta in equation (24.17) in order to determine the portfolio's *ex post* characteristic line.

However, there is a simpler method for determining a portfolio's *ex post* alpha, beta, and characteristic line that also provides a number of other pieces of information relating to the portfolio's performance. This method involves the use of **simple linear regression** and corresponds to the method presented in Chapters 7 and 16 for estimating the market model line for an individual security.

With this method, the excess return on portfolio p in a given period t is viewed as having three components. The first component is the portfolio's alpha, the second component is a risk premium equal to the excess return on the market times the portfolio's beta, and the third component is a random error term.[11] These three components can be seen on the right-hand side of the following equation:

$$r_{pt} - r_{ft} = \alpha_p + \beta_p(r_{Mt} - r_{ft}) + \epsilon_{pt} \qquad (24.18)$$

Since α_p and β_p are assumed to be constant during the evaluation interval, equation (24.18) can be viewed as a regression equation. Accordingly, there are certain standard formulas for estimating α_p, β_p, and a number of other statistical parameters associated with the regression equation.

Panel (b) of Table 24.1 presents these formulas, with First Fund being used as an example. As can be seen, the formulas indicate that First Fund's *ex post* alpha and beta were equal to −0.31% and 1.16, respectively. These values are the same as those arising when equations (24.11) and (24.16) were used earlier. Indeed, they will always result in the same values.

Figure 24.6 presents a scatter diagram of the excess returns on First Fund and the TSE 300. Based on equation (24.18), the regression equation for First Fund is

$$r_{FF} - r_f = -0.31\% + 1.16(r_M - r_f) + \epsilon_{FF} \qquad (24.19)$$

where −0.31% and 1.16 are the estimated *ex post* alpha and beta for First Fund. As mentioned earlier, also shown in the figure is the *ex post* characteristic line for First Fund, a line that is derived by the use of simple linear regression:

$$r_{FF} - r_f = -0.31\% + 1.16(r_M - r_f) \qquad (24.20)$$

The vertical distance between each point in the scatter diagram and the regression line represents an estimate of the size of the random error term for the corresponding quarter. The exact distance can be found by rewriting equation (24.19) as

$$\epsilon_{FF} = (r_{FF} - r_f) - [-0.31\% + 1.16(r_M - r_f)] \qquad (24.21)$$

For example, in the twelfth quarter, the excess return on First Fund and the TSE 300 were 5.30% and 1.60%, respectively. The value of ϵ_{FF} for that quarter can be calculated by using equation (24.21) as follows:

---

[11]The random error term can be viewed as a number that arises from a spin of a roulette wheel, where the numbers on the wheel are symmetrically distributed around zero. That is, the expected outcome from a spin of the roulette wheel is zero; the standard deviation associated with the wheel is denoted by σ_{ϵ_p}.

Simple Linear Regression
(Alternatively, **Ordinary Least Squares**.) A statistical model of the relationship between two random variables in which one variable is hypothesized to be linearly related to the other. This relationship is depicted by a regression line which is a straight line, "fitted" to pairs of values of the two variables, so that the sum of the squared random error terms is minimized.

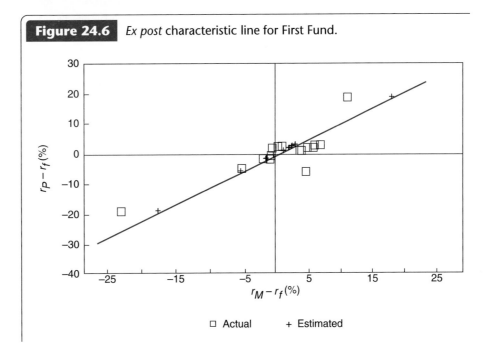

Figure 24.6 *Ex post* characteristic line for First Fund.

$$\epsilon_{FF} = 5.30 - (-0.31 = 1.16 \times 1.60)$$
$$= 3.75\%$$

The values of ϵ_{FF} can be calculated similarly for the other 15 quarters of the evaluation interval. The standard deviation of the resulting set of 16 numbers is an estimate of the standard deviation of the random error term (also known as the residual standard deviation), and is shown in panel (b) of Table 24.1 to be equal to 4.48%. This number can be viewed as an estimate of the *ex post* unique (or unsystematic or nonmarket) risk of First Fund.

The regression line for First Fund that is shown in Figure 24.6 is the line of best fit for the scatter diagram. What is meant by "best fit?" Given that a straight line is defined by its intercept and slope, there are no other values for alpha and beta that will define a straight line that fits the scatter diagram any better than this one. In simple regression, best fit means that there is no line that could be drawn such that the resulting standard deviation of the random error term is smaller than the one of best fit.

It should be pointed out that a portfolio's "true" *ex post* beta cannot be observed. All that can be done is to estimate its value. Thus, even if a portfolio's true beta remained the same forever, its estimated value, obtained in the manner illustrated in Table 24.1 and Figure 24.6, would still change from time to time because of errors (known as sampling errors) in estimating it. For example, if a different set of 16 quarters were examined, the resulting estimated beta for First Fund would almost certainly be different from 1.16.

The standard error of beta shown in Table 24.1 indicates the extent of such estimation errors. Given a number of necessary assumptions (for example, the true beta did not change during the estimation period), the chances are roughly two out of three that the true beta is within one standard error, plus or minus, of the estimated beta. Thus, First Fund's true beta is likely to be between the values of $1.16 - 0.14 = 1.02$ and $1.16 + 0.14 = 1.30$. Similarly, the value for standard error of alpha provides an indication of the magnitude of the possible sampling error that has been made in estimating it.

The value for the correlation coefficient provides an indication of how closely the excess returns on First Fund were associated with the excess returns on the TSE 300. Since its range is between -1 and $+1$, the value for First Fund of 0.91 indicates a strong positive relationship between First Fund and the TSE 300. That is, larger excess returns for First Fund seem to have been closely associated with larger excess returns on the TSE 300.

The coefficient of determination represents the proportion of variation in the excess return on First Fund that is related to the variation in the excess return on the TSE 300. That is, it shows how much of the movement in First Fund's excess returns can be explained by movements in the excess returns on the TSE 300. With a value of 0.83, it can be seen that 83% of the movement in the excess return on First Fund over the 16 quarters can be attributed to movement in the excess return on the TSE 300.

Since the coefficient of nondetermination is 1 minus the coefficient of determination, it represents the proportion of movement in the excess return on First Fund that is not due to movement in the excess return on the TSE 300. Thus, 17% of the movement in First Fund cannot be attributed to movement in the TSE 300.

Although Table 24.1 shows the formulas for calculating all these values, it should be pointed out that there are many different software packages that can carry out all these calculations in a fraction of a second. The only substantive effort involves gathering all the return data shown in panel (a) of Table 24.1 and then entering the information into a computer.

The Reward-to-volatility Ratio

Reward-to-volatility Ratio (Treynor Ratio) An *ex post* risk-adjusted measure of portfolio performance in which risk is defined as the market risk of the portfolio. Mathematically, over an evaluation interval it is the excess return of portfolio divided by the beta of the portfolio.

Closely related to the differential return measure of portfolio performance is a measure known as the **reward-to-volatility ratio**.[12] This measure, denoted RVOL_p, also uses the *ex post* security market line to form a benchmark for performance evaluation. The calculation of the reward-to-volatility ratio for a portfolio involves dividing its average excess return by its market risk:

$$\text{RVOL}_p = \frac{ar_p - ar_f}{\beta_p} \tag{24.22}$$

Here, the beta of the portfolio can be determined using the formula in equation (24.11).

Continuing with the example of First Fund, it was noted earlier that its average return for the evaluation interval was 2.851% and the average Treasury bill rate was 2.39%. Thus, the average excess return for First Fund was 2.85% − 2.39% = 0.46% and, given a beta of 1.16, its reward-to-volatility ratio was 0.46%/1.16 = 0.40%.

The reward-to-volatility ratio corresponds to the slope of a line originating at the average risk-free rate and going through the point (β_p, ar_p). This can be seen by noting that the slope of a line is easily determined if two points on the line are known—it is simply the vertical distance between the two points (rise) divided by the horizontal distance between the two points (run). In this case, the vertical distance is $ar_p - ar_f$ and the horizontal distance is $\beta_p - 0 = \beta_p$, so the slope is $(ar_p - ar_f)/\beta_p$; this corresponds to the formula for RVOL_p given in equation (24.22). Note that the value being measured on the horizontal axis is β_p and the value being measured on the vertical axis is ar_p, suggesting that the line can be drawn on the same diagram as the *ex post* SML.

In the First Fund example, remember that the *ex post* SML was shown by the solid line in Figure 24.5. Also appearing in this figure was the point denoted by *FF*, corresponding to $(\beta_p, ar_p) = (1.16, 2.85\%)$ for First Fund. The dashed line in this figure dashed originates from the point $(0, ar_f) = (0, 2.39\%)$, goes through *FF*, and has a slope of $(2.85\% - 2.39\%)/1.16 = 0.40\%$, which corresponds to the value noted earlier for RVOL_p.

---

[12]This measure of performance is sometimes known as the *Treynor ratio* because it was developed by Jack L. Treynor in "How to Rate Management of Investment Funds," *Harvard Business Review* 43, no. 1 (January–February 1965): 63–75.

The benchmark for comparison with this measure of performance is the slope of the *ex post* SML. Since this line goes through the points $(0, ar_f)$ and $(1, ar_M)$, its slope is simply $(ar_M - ar_f)/(1 - 0) = (ar_M - ar_f)$. If $RVOL_p$ is greater than this value, the portfolio lies above the *ex post* SML, indicating it has outperformed the market. Alternatively, if $RVOL_p$ is less than this value, the portfolio lies below the *ex post* SML, indicating it has not performed as well as the market.

In the case of First Fund, the benchmark is $(ar_M - ar_f) = (3.05\% - 2.39\%) = 0.66\%$. Since $RVOL_p$ for First Fund is less than the benchmark $(0.40\% < 0.66\%)$, according to this measure of portfolio performance, First Fund did not perform as well as the market.

In comparing the two measures of performance that are based on the *ex post* SML, α_p and $RVOL_p$, it should be noted that they *always* give the same assessment of a portfolio's performance relative to the market portfolio. That is, if one measure indicates the portfolio outperformed the market, so will the other. Similarly, if one measure indicates the portfolio did not perform as well as the market, the other measure will show the same thing. This can be seen by noting that any portfolio with a positive *ex post* alpha (an indication of superior performance) lies *above* the *ex post* SML and thus must have a slope *greater* than the slope of the *ex post* SML (also an indication of superior performance). Similarly, any portfolio with a negative *ex post* alpha (an indication of inferior performance) lies *below* the *ex post* SML and thus must have a slope *less* than the slope of the *ex post* SML (also an indication of inferior performance).

However, it should be noted that it is possible for the two measures to *rank* portfolios differently on the basis of performance simply because the calculations are different. For example, if Second Fund had a beta of 1.5 and an average return of 3.00%, its *ex post* alpha would be $3.00\% - [2.39\% + (3.05\% - 2.39\%)1.5] = -0.38\%$. Thus, its performance appears to be worse than First Fund, since it has a smaller *ex post* alpha $(-0.38\% < -0.31\%)$. However, its reward-to-volatility ratio of $0.41\% = (3.00\% - 2.39\%)/1.5$ is larger than the reward-to-volatility of 0.40% for First Fund, suggesting its performance was better than that of First Fund.

The Sharpe Ratio

Reward-to-variability Ratio (Sharpe Ratio) An *ex post* risk-adjusted measure of portfolio performance in which risk is defined as the standard deviation of the portfolio's returns. Mathematically, over an evaluation interval, it is the excess return of a portfolio divided by the standard deviation of the portfolio's returns.

Both measures of risk-adjusted performance described so far, *ex post* alpha (that is, differential return) and the reward-to-volatility ratio, use benchmarks that are based on the *ex post* SML. Accordingly, they measure returns relative to the market risk of the portfolio. In contrast, the **Sharpe ratio** (or reward-to-variability ratio) is a measure of risk-adjusted performance that uses a benchmark based on the *ex post* Capital Market Line (CML).[13] This means that it measures returns relative to the total risk of the portfolio, where total risk is the standard deviation of portfolio returns.

In order to use the Sharpe ratio (SR_p), the location of the *ex post* CML must be determined. This line goes through two points on a graph where average return is measured on the vertical axis and standard deviation is measured on the horizontal axis. The first point is the vertical intercept of the line and corresponds to the average risk-free rate during the evaluation interval. The second point corresponds to the location of the market portfolio, meaning its coordinates are the average return and standard deviation of return for the market portfolio during the evaluation interval, or (σ_M, ar_M). Since the *ex post* CML goes through these two points, its slope can readily be calculated as the vertical distance between the two points divided by the horizontal distance between the two points, or

---

[13]This measure of performance is known as the *Sharpe ratio* because it was developed by William F. Sharpe in "Mutual Fund Performance," *Journal of Business* 39, no. 1 (January 1966): 119–38. Morningstar Inc. in the US uses this means in its evaluation of mutual fund performance.

$(ar_M - ar_f)/(\sigma_M - 0) = (ar_M - ar_f)/\sigma_M$. Given a vertical intercept of ar_f, the equation of this line is

$$ar_p^e = ar_f + \frac{ar_M - ar_f}{\sigma_M}\sigma_p \tag{24.23}$$

In the example shown in Table 24.1, the average return and standard deviation for the TSE 300, calculated using equations (24.9) and (24.10), were 3.05% and 7.83%, respectively. Since the average return on Treasury bills was 2.39%, the *ex post* CML during these 16 quarters was

$$\begin{aligned} ar_p^e &= 2.39\% + \frac{3.05\% - 2.39\%}{7.83\%}\sigma_p \\ &= 2.39\% + 0.084\sigma_p \end{aligned} \tag{24.24}$$

Figure 24.7 presents a graph of this line.

Having determined the location of the *ex post* CML, the average return and standard deviation of the portfolio being evaluated can be determined next by using equations (24.9) and (24.10). With these values in hand, the portfolio can be located on the same graph as the *ex post* CML. In the case of First Fund, its average return and standard deviation were 2.85% and 10.10%, respectively. Thus, in Figure 24.7 its location corresponds to the point having coordinates (10.1%, 2.85%), which is denoted by *FF*.

The calculation of the Sharpe ratio (SR_p) is analogous to the calculation of the reward-to-volatility ratio ($RVOL_p$) described earlier. Specifically, $RVOL_p$ involves dividing the portfolio's average excess return by its beta, whereas SR_p involves dividing the portfolio's average excess return by its standard deviation:

$$SR_p = \frac{ar_p - ar_f}{\sigma_p} \tag{24.25}$$

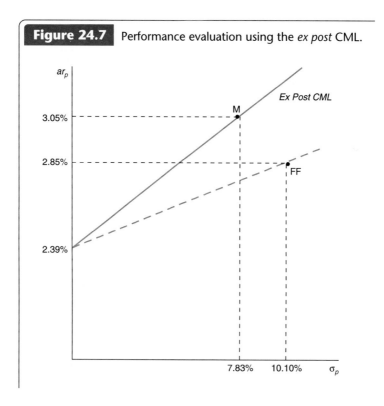

Figure 24.7 Performance evaluation using the *ex post* CML.

Note that SR_p corresponds to the slope of a line originating at the average risk-free rate and going through a point having coordinates of (σ_p, ar_p). This can be seen by noting that the slope of this line is simply the vertical distance between the two points divided by the horizontal distance between the two points, or $(ar_p - ar_f)/(\sigma_p - 0) = (ar_p - ar_f)/\sigma_p$, which corresponds to the formula for SR_p given in equation (24.25). Since the value being measured on the horizontal axis is σ_p and the value being measured on the vertical axis is ar_p, the line can be drawn on the same diagram as the *ex post* CML.

In the First Fund example, recall that the *ex post* CML was shown by the solid line in Figure 24.7. Also appearing in this figure was the point denoted by *FF*, corresponding to $(\sigma_p, ar_p) = (10.1\%, 2.85\%)$ for First Fund. The dashed line in this figure originates from the point $(0, ar_f) = (0, 2.39\%)$ and goes through *FF*; the slope of this line is simply $(2.85\% - 2.39\%)/10.1\% = 0.046$.

Since the *ex post* CML represents various combinations of risk-free lending or borrowing with investing in the market portfolio, it can be used to provide a benchmark for the reward-to-variability ratio in a manner similar to the SML-based benchmark for the reward-to-volatility ratio. As noted earlier, the slope of the *ex post* CML is $(ar_M - ar_f)/\sigma_M$. If SR_p is greater than this value, the portfolio lies above the *ex post* CML, indicating it has outperformed the market. Alternatively, if SR_p is less than this value, the portfolio lies below the *ex post* CML, indicating it has not performed as well as the market.

In the case of First Fund, the benchmark is $(3.05\% - 2.39\%)/7.83\% = 0.084$. Since SR_p is less than the benchmark $(0.046 < 0.084)$, First Fund did not perform as well as the market, according to this risk-adjusted measure of portfolio performance.

▸ M^2

The measure M^2 uses standard deviation as the relevant measure of risk. [14] Thus, like the reward-to-variability ratio, it is based on the *ex post* CML. This measure simply takes a portfolio's average return and determines what it would have been if the portfolio had the same degree of total risk as the market portfolio, usually represented by the TSE 300. Consider a line that goes through the average risk-free rate and the average return on the portfolio where standard deviation is being used as the measure of risk, such as the line going through the average risk-free rate of 2.39% and First Fund (FF) in Figure 24.7. The following equation describes such a line:

$$ar_i = ar_f + \left(\frac{ar_p - ar_f}{\sigma_p} \right) \sigma_i \qquad (24.26)$$

since the line has a vertical intercept of ar_f and a slope of $(ar_p - ar_f)/\sigma_p$. This equation indicates the average return, ar_i, that would have been earned by investing in portfolio p and either investing or borrowing at the risk-free rate to such a degree that the resulting standard deviation was σ_i. M_p^2 is the average return that would have been earned if the amount of risk-free investing or lending resulted in the standard deviation being equal to that of the market portfolio. Hence, setting σ_i equal to σ_M in equation (24.26) results in the value of M_p^2 for portfolio p:

$$M_p^2 = ar_f + \left(\frac{ar_p - ar_f}{\sigma_p} \right) \sigma_M \qquad (24.27)$$

Accordingly, M_p^2 measures the return an investor would have earned if the portfolio had been altered by use of the risk-free rate through borrowing or lending in order to match

---

[14]The popular use of M^2 to refer to this measure of performance can be attributed to the fact that the measure was put forth by Nobel laureate Franco Modigliani and his granddaughter, Leah Modigliani, in "Risk-Adjusted Performance," *Journal of Portfolio Management* 23, no. 2 (Winter 1997): 45–54.

the market portfolio's risk level as measured by standard deviation.

For example, First Fund had on a quarterly basis an average return of 3.05% and a standard deviation of 10.10%. Since the average risk-free rate was 2.39%, the equation describing the dashed line in Figure 24.7 can be determined by using Equation (24.26) to be:

$$ar_i = 2.39 + \left(\frac{3.05 - 2.39}{10.1}\right)\sigma_i$$
$$= 2.39 + .0653\sigma_i \qquad (24.28)$$

Since the standard deviation of the market portfolio (estimated by using the TSE 300) is 7.83%, it follows that M_p^2 for the First Fund is 2.90%. That is, by investing 7.83/10.1 = 77.5% in First Fund and 22.5% in the risk-free rate, the investor would have had a portfolio that had the same standard deviation as the market portfolio. In this example, M^2 effectively "de-levers" First Fund's return to bring its risk level down to that of the market portfolio and then proportionately reduces First Fund's return by the degree of deleveraging. If the market portfolio's standard deviation had been greater than that of First Fund, then M^2 would have leveraged First Fund's return by borrowing at the risk-free rate to increase its standard deviation to that of the market portfolio. This would have proportionately increased First Fund's return by the degree of leveraging.

M_p^2 can be compared directly with the average return on the market portfolio ar_M in order to see if the portfolio outperformed or underperformed the market portfolio on a risk-adjusted basis. In the case of First Fund, the market portfolio had an average return of 3.05%, suggesting underperformance on the fund's part since $M_{FF}^2 = 2.90\% < 3.05\% = ar_M$.

In comparing the two measures of risk-adjusted performance that are based on the *ex post* CML, SR_p and M_p^2, it should be noted that they will always give the same assessment of a portfolio's performance relative to the market portfolio.[15] Hence, it is impossible for one measure to indicate that a portfolio performed better than the market and the other to indicate that it performed worse. This can be seen by noting that if a portfolio plots below the *ex post* CML, then: (1) the slope of the line going through the portfolio (SR_p) will be less than the slope of the *ex post* CML and (2) M_p^2 will lie on the line going through the portfolio at a point that is directly below the location of the market portfolio on the *ex post* CML. The converse is also true if the portfolio plots above the *ex post* CML.

Furthermore, the two measures will rank a set of portfolios exactly the same, since comparing slopes of lines that all go through the average risk-free rate will rank portfolios exactly the same as comparing the average returns (that is, the Y values) on all of these lines at a given level of standard deviation (that is, at a given X value). Equivalently, equations (24.25) and (24.27) can be combined to show that:

$$M_p^2 = ar_f + SR_p\sigma_M \qquad (24.29)$$

Thus, the value of M_p^2 for any portfolio is simply equal to a positive constant plus the portfolio's reward-to-variability ratio multiplied by a positive constant. Since these two constants are the same for all portfolios, the ranking for M_p^2 will be exactly the same as the ranking for SR_p.

---

[15]There is a third measure of portfolio performance that is based on the *ex post* CML. This measure, called the *ex post total risk alpha*, is simply the vertical distance the portfolio lies above or below the *ex post* CML. It is similar to the measure referred to earlier as *ex post* alpha, expect that it is based on a different risk measure (total risk instead of market risk) and uses a different benchmark (the *ex post* CML instead of the *ex post* SML). It also gives the same assessment of a portfolio's performance relative to the market as the Sharpe Ratio and M^2, but can lead to a different ranking for the portfolio.

Comparing the Risk-adjusted Measures of Performance

The measures of performance that are based on the *ex post* SML, SR_p, and $RVOL_p$, can be compared with the measure of performance that is based on the *ex post* CML, SR_p.[16] Focusing on $RVOL_p$ (the comparison also applies to α_p), it should be noted that in certain situations, $RVOL_p$ and SR_p can give different assessments of a portfolio's performance relative to the market portfolio.

In particular, if $RVOL_p$ indicates the portfolio outperformed the market, it is possible for SR_p to indicate the portfolio did not perform as well as the market. The reason for this is that the portfolio may have a relatively large amount of unique risk. Such risk would not be a factor in determining the value of $RVOL_p$ for the portfolio, since only *market risk* is in the denominator. However, such risk would be included in the denominator of SR_p for the portfolio, since this measure is based on *total risk* (that is, both market and unique risk). Thus, a portfolio with a low amount of market risk could have a high amount of total risk, resulting in a relatively high $RVOL_p$ (due to the low amount of market risk) and a low SR_p (due to the high amount of total risk). Accordingly, $RVOL_p$ could indicate the portfolio outperformed the market, while at the same time SR_p may indicate it did not perform as well as the market.[17]

As an example, consider Third Fund, which had an average return of 3.0%, a beta of .8, and a standard deviation of 18%. Accordingly, $RVOL_{TF} = (3.0\% - 2.39\%)/.8 = 0.76\%$, indicating that Third Fund outperformed the market portfolio, since the benchmark is $(3.05\% - 2.39\%)/1.0 = 0.66\%$. However, $SR_{TF} = (3.0\% - 2.39\%)/18\% = 0.034$, indicating that Third Fund did not perform as well as the market portfolio, since the benchmark is $(3.05\% - 2.39\%)/7.83\% = 0.084$. The reason for the difference can be seen by noting Third Fund's low beta relative to the market ($.8 < 1.0$) but high standard deviation relative to the market ($18\% > 7.83\%$). This suggests that Third Fund had a relatively high level of unique risk.

It also follows that it is possible for $RVOL_p$ and SR_p to rank two or more portfolios differently on the basis of their performance. This is because these two measures of risk-adjusted performance use different types of risk.

Continuing the example, First Fund had an average return of 1.85%, a beta of 1.16, and a standard deviation of 10.1%. Thus, $RVOL_{FF} = (2.85\% - 2.39\%)/1.16 = 0.40\%$, which is less than $RVOL_{TF} = (3.0\% - 2.39\%)/0.8 = 0.76\%$, thereby indicating that First Fund ranked lower than Third Fund. However, $SR_{FF} = (2.85\% - 2.39\%)/10.1\% = 0.046$, which is greater than $SR_{TF} = 0.034$, thereby indicating that First Fund ranked higher than Third Fund.

Did Third Fund do better or worse than the market on a risk-adjusted basis? And did Third Fund perform better or worse than First Fund? The answer to these two questions lies in identifying the appropriate measure of risk for the client. If the client has many other assets, then beta is the relevant measure of risk, and performance should be based on $RVOL_p$. To such a client, Third Fund should be viewed as a superior performer relative to both the market and First Fund. However, if the client has few other assets, then standard deviation is the relevant measure of risk, and performance should be based on SR_p. To such a client, Third Fund should be viewed as an inferior performer relative to both the market and First Fund.

---

[16]As the other *ex-post* CML based measure, M_p^2, yields the same portfolio evaluation as SR_p there is no need to compare α_p and $RVOL_p$ with it.

[17]Since the market portfolio does not have any unique risk, it can be shown that if $RVOL_p$ indicates a portfolio did not perform as well as the market, then SR_p must also indicate that the portfolio did not perform as well as the market. This is because a portfolio with a relatively high amount of market risk will also have a relatively high amount of total risk.

Market Timing

A successful market timer positions a portfolio to have a relatively high beta during a market rise and a relatively low beta during a market decline. This is because, as noted earlier, the expected return on a portfolio is a linear function of its beta:

$$\bar{r}_p = \alpha_p + r_f + (\bar{r}_M - r_f)\beta_p \qquad (24.30)$$

This means that the market timer will want to have a high-beta portfolio when he expects the market to have a higher return than the risk-free rate because such a portfolio will have a higher expected return than a low-beta portfolio. Conversely, the market timer will want to have a low-beta portfolio when he expects the market to have a lower return than the risk-free rate, as it will have a higher expected return than a high-beta portfolio. Simply put, the market timer will want to:

1. Hold a high-beta portfolio when $\bar{r}_M > r_f$, and
2. Hold a low-beta portfolio when $\bar{r}_M < r_f$.

If the timer is accurate in his forecasts of the expected return on the market, then his portfolio will outperform a benchmark portfolio that has a constant beta equal to the average beta of the timer's portfolio.

For example, if the market timer successfully set the portfolio beta at 0 when $\bar{r}_M < r_f$ and at 2 when $\bar{r}_M > r_f$, the return on the portfolio would be higher than the return on a portfolio having a beta constantly equal to 1. Unfortunately, if the market timer alters the portfolio's beta in ways unrelated to subsequent market moves (for example, sometimes setting the beta equal to zero when $\bar{r}_M > r_f$ and equal to two when $\bar{r}_M < r_f$), then the timer's portfolio will not perform as well as a constant beta portfolio.

To "time the market," either the average beta of the stocks held in the portfolio can be changed or the relative amounts invested in the risk-free asset and stocks can be altered. For example, to increase the beta of a portfolio, low-beta stocks could be sold, with the proceeds used to purchase high-beta stocks. Alternatively, Treasury bills in the portfolio could be sold (or the amount of borrowing increased), with the resulting proceeds invested in stocks or stock index futures. Because of the ease of trading stock index futures, most investment organizations specializing in market times prefer this approach.

In Figure 24.8, the excess returns of two hypothetical portfolios are measured on the vertical axis, while those of a market index are on the horizontal axis. Straight lines, fit via standard regression methods, reveal positive *ex post* alpha values in each case. However, the scatter diagrams tell a different story. Panel (a) seems to indicate that the relationship between the portfolio's excess returns and the market's excess returns was linear, since the points cluster close to the regression line. This suggests that the portfolio consisted of securities in a manner such that the beta of the portfolio was roughly the same at all times. Since the *ex post* alpha was positive, it appears that the investment manager successfully identified and invested in some underpriced securities.

The scatter diagram for the portfolio shown in panel (b) seems to indicate the relationship between this portfolio's excess returns and the market's excess returns was not linear, since the points in the middle lie below the regression line and those at the ends lie above the regression line. This suggests that the portfolio consisted of high-beta securities during periods when the market return was high and low-beta securities during periods when the market return was low. Upon examination, it appears that the portfolio has a positive *ex post* alpha due to successful market timing by the investment manager.

Quadratic Regression

To measure the ability of an investment manager to time the market successfully, something more complex than a straight line can be fit to scatter diagrams such as those shown

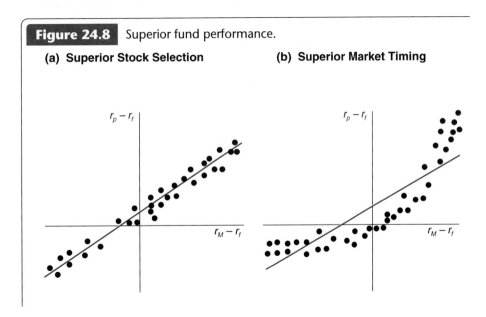

Figure 24.8 Superior fund performance.

(a) Superior Stock Selection **(b) Superior Market Timing**

in Figure 24.8. One procedure fits a curve, where statistical methods are used to estimate the parameters a, b, and c in the following *quadratic regression equation*:

$$r_{pt} - r_{ft} = a + b(r_{Mt} - r_{ft}) + c[(r_{Mt} - r_{ft})^2] + \epsilon_{pt} \qquad (24.31)$$

where ϵ_{pt} is the random error term.

The *ex post characteristic curve* shown in Figure 24.9(a) is simply the following quadratic function, where the values of a, b, and c for the portfolio have been estimated by standard regression methods:

$$r_{pt} - r_{ft} = a + b(r_{Mt} - r_{ft}) + c[(r_{Mt} - r_{ft})^2] \qquad (24.32)$$

If the estimated value of c is positive [as it is for the portfolio depicted in Figure 24.9(a)], the curve would become less steep as one moves to the left. This would indicate that the portfolio manager successfully timed the market. Note that this equation corresponds to the equation for the *ex post* characteristic line if c is equal to zero; in such a situation, a and b would correspond to the portfolio's *ex post* alpha and beta, respectively.[18]

Dummy Variable Regression

An alternative procedure fits two *ex post* characteristic lines to the scatter diagram, as shown in Figure 24.9(b). Periods when risky securities outperform risk-free securities (that is, when $r_{Mt} > r_{ft}$) can be termed *up markets*. Periods when risky securities do not perform as well as risk-free securities (that is, when $r_{Mt} < r_{ft}$) can be termed *down markets*. A successful market timer would select a high up-market beta and a low down-market beta. Graphically, the slope of the *ex post* characteristic line for positive excess market returns is greater than the slope of the *ex post* characteristic line for negative excess market returns.

---

[18]The quadratic regression equation (24.31), originally suggested by Treynor and Mazuy, has been refined by Sudipto Bhattacharya and Paul Pfleiderer in a 1983 Stanford University unpublished paper (Technical Report 714) whose principal results are described on pp. 1040–1043 of T. Daniel Coggin, Frank J. Fabozzi, and Shafiqur Rahman, "The Investment Performance of U.S. Equity Pension Fund Managers: An Empirical Investigation," *Journal of Finance* 48, no. 3 (July 1993).

Figure 24.9 *Ex post* characteristic curve and lines.

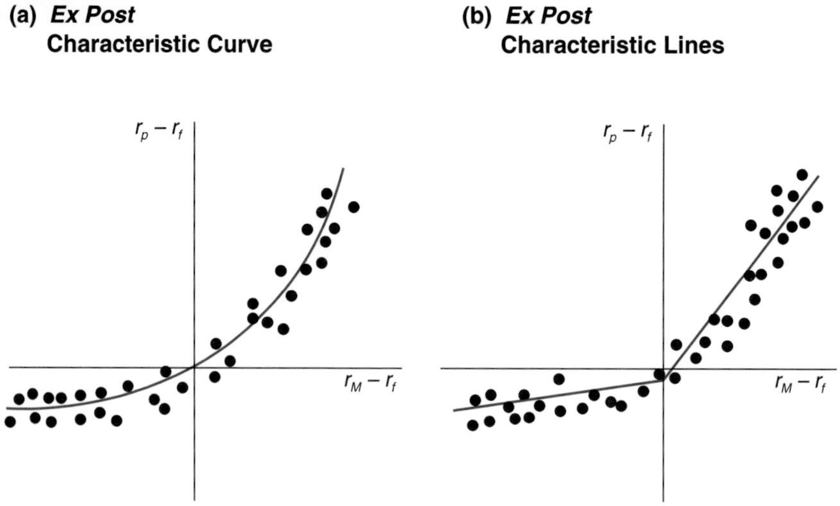

**(a) *Ex Post*
Characteristic Curve**

**(b) *Ex Post*
Characteristic Lines**

To estimate such a relationship, standard regression methods can be used to estimate the parameters a, b, and c in the following *dummy variable regression equation*:

$$r_{pt} - r_{ft} = a + b(r_{Mt} - r_{ft}) + c[D_t(r_{Mt} - r_{ft})] + \epsilon_{pt} \qquad (24.33)$$

Here, ϵ_{pt} is the random error term and D_t is a dummy variable that is assigned a value of 0 for any time period t when $r_{Mt} > r_{ft}$ and a value of -1 for any time period t when $r_{Mt} < r_{ft}$. To see how this works, consider the effective equations for different values of $r_{Mt} - r_{ft}$:

Value of $r_{Mt} - r_{ft}$	Equation
> 0	$r_{pt} - r_{ft} = a + b(r_{Mt} - r_{ft}) + \epsilon_{pt}$
$= 0$	$r_{pt} - r_{ft} = a + \epsilon_{pt}$
< 0	$r_{pt} - r_{ft} = a + (b - c)(r_{Mt} - r_{ft}) + \epsilon_{pt}$

Note that the parameter b corresponds to the portfolio's up-market beta, whereas $(b - c)$ corresponds to the portfolio's down-market beta. Thus, the parameter c indicates the difference between the two betas and is positive for the successful market timer.

For the portfolio shown in Figure 24.9(b), the *ex post* characteristic line on the right side of the graph corresponds to the equation

$$r_{pt} - r_{ft} = a + b(r_{Mt} - r_{ft}) \qquad (24.34a)$$

whereas the *ex post* characteristic line shown on the left side of the graph corresponds to the equation

$$r_{pt} - r_{ft} = a + (b - c)(r_{Mt} - r_{ft}) \qquad (24.34b)$$

In this example, the investment manager has successfully engaged in market timing, since the slope of the line on the right side (that is, b) is greater than the slope of the line on the left side (that is, $b - c$).

In either regression equation (24.31) or (24.33), the value of the parameter a provides an estimate of the investment manager's ability to identify mispriced securities (that is, security selection), and the value of the parameter c provides an estimate of the manager's ability at market timing. The difference between the two equations is that the quadratic equation indicates the portfolio's beta fluctuated over many values, depending on the size of the market's excess returns. This can be seen graphically by noting that the slope of the quadratic curve is continually increasing when moving from left to right in Figure 24.9(a). On the other hand, the dummy variable equation indicates the portfolio's beta fluctuates between just two values, depending on whether r_M is less or greater than r_f. This can be seen graphically by noting that the slope of the equation increases from one value (that is, $b - c$) to a second value (that is, b) when moving from left to right in Figure 24.9(b).

As an example, consider again the First Fund. Table 24.2 presents the results from applying regression equations (24.31) and (24.33) to this portfolio for the 16 quarters along with the *ex post* characteristic line results. The results in the table provide evidence of some positive selectivity, but negative market timing ability by the portfolio manager. This can be seen by noting that the parameter a is negative in the simple regression but becomes positive when the effect of market timing is taken into account. The parameter c, however, is negative in both cases indicating that the manager tends to increase beta in down-markets and decrease it in up-markets.[19] The correlation is higher for both multiple regressions than for the *ex post* characteristic line. This is further evidence that negative market timing ability is present. Care should be taken in drawing conclusions from these regressions. An examination of Figure 24.6 suggests that three large outliers may be producing the results obtained.

Criticisms of Risk-adjusted Performance Measures

The previously mentioned risk-adjusted measures of portfolio performance have been criticized on several grounds. Some of the major criticisms are described in this section.

Table 24.2	Market Timing Test Results for First Fund.		
Parameter Being Estimated[a]	Ex Post Characteristic Line	Quadratic Equation	Dummy Variable Equation
a	−0.31%	1.10%	2.20%
	(1.13)	(0.82)	(1.01)
b	1.16	1.16	1.66
	(.14)	(0.096)	(0.16)
c	—	−0.02	−1.01
	—	(.005)	(0.26)
Correlation[b]	0.91	0.96	0.95

[a] Standard errors are shown in parentheses below the respective parameters.
[b] The correlation coefficient for the quadratic and dummy variable equations has been adjusted for the number of independent variables.

[19]The size of parameter c (as well as the parameters a and b) should be judged relative to its standard error. In both equations shown here, it is quite large relative to the corresponding standard error. Most standard statistical textbooks have an introductory discussion of the regression procedures that are used here. See, for example, David Levine, Mark Berenson, and David Stephan, *Statistic for Managers Using Microsoft Excel, Second Edition* (Upper Saddle River, NJ: Prentice Hall, 1999).

Use of a Market Surrogate

All the measures other than the reward-to-variability ratio require the identification of a market portfolio. This means that whatever surrogate is used, it can be criticized as being inadequate. Indeed, it has been shown that by making slight changes in the surrogate, the performance rankings of a set of portfolios can be completely reversed (that is, the top-ranked portfolio with one surrogate could be the bottom-ranked portfolio if a slightly different surrogate was used). However, it has been noted that when commonly used NYSE-based surrogates are involved, such as the Dow Jones Industrial Average, the S&P 500, and an index comparable to the New York Stock Exchange Composite, the performance rankings of common stock portfolios appear to be quite similar.[20]

A related criticism of using a market index such as the S&P 500 or TSE 300 to determine the benchmark portfolio's return is that it is nearly impossible for an investor to form a portfolio whose returns replicate those on such an index over time. This is because transaction costs will be encountered in initially forming the portfolio, in restructuring the portfolio when stocks are replaced in the index, and in purchasing more shares of stocks when cash dividends are received.[21] Hence it has been argued that the returns on an index overstate the returns that a passive investor could earn, meaning that the returns on the benchmark portfolio are too high.[22]

Distinguishing Skill from Luck

A very long evaluation interval is needed in order to be able to obtain a measure of performance that can distinguish skill from luck on the part of the investment manager. That is, it would be useful to know if an apparently successful manager was skilled or just lucky, since skill can be expected to have a favourable impact on the portfolio's performance in the future, whereas luck cannot be expected to continue. Unfortunately, too many years' worth of experience is generally needed to make such a determination.[23]

Measuring the Risk-free Rate

The use of Treasury bills for measuring the risk-free rate in determining benchmark portfolios based on either the *ex post* SML or CML can be criticized. Consider a benchmark portfolio that involves an investment in both Treasury bills and the market portfolio. Such a benchmark portfolio can be criticized for having too low a rate of return, making it easy for a portfolio to show superior performance. This is because Treasury bills may provide excessively low returns to compensate for their high degree of liquidity. If a higher risk-free rate (such as the commercial paper rate) is used, then any benchmark portfolio that lies between this risk-free rate and the market portfolio on either the *ex post* SML or CML will have a higher rate of return and thus represent a higher but more appropriate standard.

---

[20]See Richard Roll, "Ambiguity When Performance Is Measured by the Security Market Line," *Journal of Finance* 33, no. 4 (September 1978): 1051–1069; and David Peterson and Michael L. Rice, "A Note on Ambiguity in Portfolio Performance Measures," *Journal of Finance* 35, no. 5 (December 1980): 1251–1256; and Heinz Zimmermann and Claudia Zogg-Wetter, "On Detecting Selection and Timing Ability: The Case of Stock Market Indexes," *Financial Analysts Journal* 48, no. 1 (January–February 1992): 80–83.

[21]The problem is much more severe when the index is equal-weighted, because periodically part of the holdings of those stocks that had risen the most would have to be sold and the proceeds invested in additional shares of those stocks that had risen the least in order to keep equal weights in each stock.

[22]With the existence of index funds and index futures (discussed in Chapters 20 and 23), this criticism has lost much of its validity.

[23]See Dan W. French and Glenn V. Henderson, Jr., "How Well Does Performance Evaluation Perform?" *Journal of Portfolio Management* 11, no. 2 (Winter 1985): 15–18.

Assessing Manager Skill

Perhaps no issue elicits more frustration among institutional investors than the evaluation of manager investment skill. The problem stems from the inherent uncertainty of manager investment performance. Even the most talented managers can underperform their benchmarks during any given quarter, year, or even multiyear period. Conversely, ineffective managers at times may make correct decisions and outperform their benchmarks simply by good fortune.

The odds that a "skillful" manager will underperform her benchmark over what most observers would consider to be acceptably long evaluation intervals are surprisingly high (under reasonable assumptions about expected return and return volatilty, roughly 1 out of 4 over a three-year evaluation period). The chances that an "unskillful" manager will outperform his benchmark are likewise considerable (roughly 1 out of 3 over a three-year evaluation period). Even when we extend the evaluation period out to five years (an eternity in the investment management business), the possibility of confusing skillful with unskillful managers decreases only slightly.

Let us step back for a moment and define the term "investment skill." It as the ability to outperform a passive risk-adjusted benchmark consistently over time. In other words, the skillful manager is capable of generating a statistically significant "alpha." Because no manager is omniscient, every manager's alpha, regardless of skill, will be positive in some periods and negative in others. Nevertheless, a skillful manager will produce a larger alpha more frequently than her less talented peers.

Note that a skillful manager may produce a small alpha very frequently or a larger alpha less frequently. It is the magnitude of the alpha relative to the volatility around that alpha value that determines a manager's skill (the ratio of these two variables is a form of the Sharpe ratio discussed in the text). Yet when plan sponsors evaluate their managers, most focus solely on the level of alpha produced, while ignoring volatility around the alpha. As a consequence, superior managers may be terminated (or not hired) and inferior managers may be retained (or hired), on the basis of statistically questionable performance data.

Attempting to evaluate manager skill strictly by consulting past performance data is a problem in statistical inference. Essentially, we want to test whether the manager's alpha is positive enough to be considered unlikely a result of mere chance. To undertake this analysis, we must make three key assumptions concerning the shape and dispersion of the manager's returns around her benchmark. Somewhat paradoxically, we first assume that the manager has no investment skill. That is, we begin with a *null hypothesis* that the manager's alpha is zero on average over time. It is actually this assumption of no skill that we want to test. Second, we assume that the manager's alpha is normally distributed around the average (or mean) value of zero (that is, the alpha distribution is in the form of the familiar bell-shaped curve, with zero as its centre). Third, we assume that the volatility of the manager's returns around the benchmark in the future will be the same as that that occurred in the past. That is, we will assume that the standard deviation of the manager's alpha is constant over time. (Recall that a normally distributed random variable will have two-thirds of its outcomes fall within plus/minus one standard deviation from the mean.)

Statistical inference by its nature can be a baffling exercise in double negatives. For example, we do not accept the null hypothesis. Rather, we fail to reject it. Conversely, although we may reject the null hypothesis, that does not necessarily mean that we accept an alternative hypothesis. Nevertheless, the equivocal nature of this type of analysis is well-suited to the world of investments where luck often masquerades as skill, and skill is frequently overwhelmed by random events.

Consider a manager whose alpha exhibits an annual standard deviation of 4.0%. Assuming a normal distribution and a mean alpha of 0.0, the expected distribution of the manager's alpha over a three-year period should appear as in the accompanying graph. (Note that as time passes the normal distribution will become tighter around the mean of zero. This is because the longer the evaluation period, the more likely that the manager's random positive and negative alphas will offset one another, gradually converging on the mean value. Specifically, the three-year annualized standard deviation is 2.3% or $1/\sqrt{3}$ times the one-year standard deviation of 4.0%.) Now suppose, based on monthly observations, that the manager actually produced an alpha of 3% per year over the three years. What are we to make of that outcome? If our null hypothesis of no skill is correct, then there is only a 10-in-100 chance that this result would have occurred by luck. It is up to us to decide whether we want to believe that luck was the cause of this outcome or whether we should reject the null hypothesis. That is, do we believe that the manager actually does have skill and that her true expected alpha is not zero but some positive number? This would make the 3% realized alpha seem much more plausible.

Unfortunately, it is the rare manager who demonstrates sufficiently strong results to allow us to comfortably reject the null hypothesis. Most man-agers live in a statistical netherworld, producing neither sufficiently large positive or negative alphas to warrant definitive conclusions. For example, few US common stock managers can hope to outperform their benchmarks by more than 1% per year on average after accounting for all fees and expenses. With an alpha standard deviation of 4%, it would take over 40 years before our statistical test would indicate that there is less than a 5 in 100 chance that such an outcome was due to luck.

As a result of these nebulous statistical answers, it should not be surprising that institutional investors turn to various qualitative decision rules to help them identify manager skill. For example, they will intensively examine the manager's process for selecting securities and want to understand the pedigree of the firm's portfolio managers. Whether such investigations actually help to uncover skillful managers is a highly debatable proposition.

Figure 24.13 Manager's expected alpha distribution over three years.

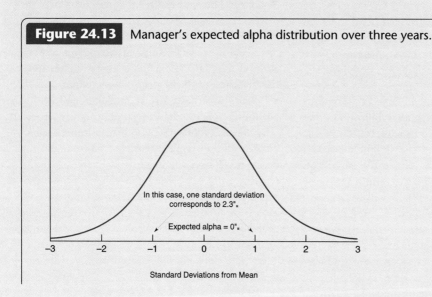

In this case, one standard deviation corresponds to 2.3".

Expected alpha = 0".

Standard Deviations from Mean

Next, consider a benchmark portfolio that involves levering a positive investment in the market portfolio by borrowing at the risk-free rate. Use of the Treasury bill rate can be criticized because realistic borrowing alternatives typically involve a higher rate and are thus less attractive. Accordingly, benchmarks that involve borrowing at the Treasury bill rate have too high a rate of return, making it difficult for a portfolio to show superior performance. If a higher risk-free borrowing rate (such as the call money rate plus a small premium) is used, then any benchmark portfolio involving risk-free borrowing will have a lower rate of return and thus represent a lower but more appropriate standard.

In summary, measures of portfolio performance based on either the *ex post* SML or CML and using Treasury bills to determine the risk-free rate are alleged to discriminate in favour of conservative portfolios and against aggressive ones.

Validity of the CAPM

The measures of portfolio performance that involve beta (namely, the *ex post* alpha and reward-to-volatility measures) are based on the CAPM, yet the CAPM may not be the correct asset pricing model. That is, perhaps assets are priced according to some other model. If so, the use of beta-based performance measures will be inappropriate.

Interestingly, a measure analogous to *ex post* alpha has been shown to be a meaningful gauge of performance if the arbitrage pricing theory's (APT) model of asset pricing is believed to be more appropriate.[24] In such a situation, the APT is used to estimate the benchmark portfolio's return ar_{bp} that is used in equation (21.3) to calculate α_p. Furthermore, the reward-to-variability ratio is immune to this criticism, since it uses standard deviation as a measure of risk and does not rely on the validity of the CAPM or the APT or on the identification of a market portfolio.

Performance Attribution

Performance Attribution
The identification of sources of returns for a portfolio or security over a particular evaluation interval of time.

The previously mentioned risk-adjusted measures of performance concentrate on the question of *how* a portfolio did relative to both a benchmark and a set of other portfolios. The use of quadratic and dummy variable regression is an attempt to evaluate separately the manager's ability at selectivity and timing. However, the client might want to know more about *why* the portfolio had a certain return over a particular time period. **Performance attribution** using a *factor model* is one method that has been used to try to make such a determination; an example is presented in the appendix.

Bond Portfolio Performance Evaluation

The performance of portfolios consisting of bonds (and other types of fixed-income securities) is often evaluated by comparing their total returns (consisting of coupon payments plus capital gains or losses) with those of an index representing a comparable class of securities over some evaluation interval. Hence a portfolio that is invested in investment-grade long-term corporate bonds would be compared with an investment-grade long-term cor-

---

[24]Under APT (discussed in Chapter 11), there is another measure of portfolio performance that has even more theoretical justification than the APT-based *ex post* alpha. This measure is analogous to the CAPM-based "appraisal ratio" and involves dividing the APT-based *ex post* alpha by the *ex post* standard deviation of the APT-based random error term. For details, see Gregory Connor and Robert A. Korajczyk, "Performance Measurement with the Arbitrage Pricing Theory: A New Framework for Analysis," *Journal of Financial Economics* 15, no. 3 (March 1986): 373–394; and Bruce N. Lehmann and David M. Modest, "Mutual Fund Performance Evaluation: A Comparison of Benchmarks and Benchmark Comparisons," *Journal of Finance* 42, no. 2 (June 1987): 233–265.

porate bond index, a portfolio invested in mortgage-backed securities would be compared with a mortgage-backed security index and a junk bond fund would be compared with a "high-yield" index.

Bond Indices

Bond indices typically represent either the average yield-to-maturity or the average price on a portfolio of bonds that have certain similar characteristics. Figure 24.10 presents various bond indices that are published monthly by ScotiaMcLeod Inc. Average yield as well as price and total return indices are reported. This bulletin also includes information (not shown) about residential mortgages, mortgage-backed securities, money market instruments, Euro-Canadian bonds and Canadian Yankee bonds. Historical information is provided in ScotiaMcLeod's *Handbook of Canadian Debt Market Indices*, published annually.

Time Series and Cross-sectional Comparisons

Figure 24.11 illustrates two ways of comparing the returns on a bond portfolio with those on a bond index over an evaluation interval. In panel (a), a time-series comparison is made, where the bond portfolio's quarterly returns over time during the evaluation interval are graphed along with those of the bond index. In panel (b), a cross-sectional comparison is made in a manner similar to the equity performance measures that were based on the *ex post* CML. Here, the bond portfolio's average return and standard deviation are graphed and compared with a line that goes through the average risk-free rate and the average return and standard deviation of the bond index (instead of an equity index), based on quarterly returns during the evaluation interval.

A variation of this procedure involves estimating the bond portfolio's *ex post* alpha by using the *ex post* characteristic line approach described earlier. That is, a figure similar to Figure 24.6 would be prepared, but now the excess returns on a bond portfolio would be measured on the vertical axis and the excess returns on a bond index would be measured on the horizontal axis.[25] The returns on the Scotia-McLeod overall total return bond index, which is an index of government and corporate investment-grade bonds can be used as the market index. Alternatively, the returns on a bond index that most closely fits with the investment objectives and policies of the portfolio under scrutiny should be used. In either case, an *ex post* alpha would be calculated and used as a measure of portfolio performance.

Bond Market Line

A different approach involves the use of a *bond market line*.[26] Assume that the performance of a bond portfolio is to be evaluated over a given quarter (or year, as this approach can be used for a longer period). There are five steps to this approach:

1. Calculate the quarterly return for the portfolio, along with its average duration for the quarter (this could be calculated by averaging the portfolio's duration at the beginning

---

[25]In the US, this method is used by Morningstar, Inc. in evaluating bond mutual fund performance. It is also used by Christopher R. Blake, Edwin J. Elton, and Martin J. Gruber in "The Performance of Bond Mutual Funds," *Journal of Business* 66, no. 3 (July 1993): 371–403. These authors also used multiple regression where the excess returns on more that one bond index were the explanatory variables.

[26]See Wayne H. Wagner and Dennis A. Tito, "Definitive New Measures of Bond Performance and Risk," *Pension World* 13, no. 5 (May 1977): 10–12; and "Is Your Bond Manager Skillful?" *Pension World* 13, no. 6 (June 1977): 9–13. Bond portfolio performance evaluation is also discussed in Peter O. Dietz and Jeannette R. Kirschman, "Evaluating Portfolio Performance," Chapter 14 in *Managing Investment Portfolios: A Dynamic Process,* eds. John L. Maginn and Donald L. Tuttle (Boston: Warren, Gorham & Lamont, 1990).

Figure 24.10 Bond indices published monthly by ScotiaMcLeod Inc.

Canadian Bond Market Sector Performance

July 31, 1998

	Avg. Yield	Price Index	Total Return Index	Last Month	Last 3 Months	Last 6 Months	Year to Date	Last 1 Year	Last 3 Years	Last 5 Years	Last 10 Years	Sector Weight	Macaulay Duration	Modified Duration	Value of 01	Average Coupon	Average Term	Con-vexity	Yld & Price	Yld & T.R.
SHORT-TERM BOND INDEX (1-5 YEARS)																				
Canadas	5.41	98.65	305.56	0.16	0.73	2.02	2.87	4.16	8.43	7.29	9.27	70.00	2.26	2.20	2.38	7.68	2.50	0.07	25026	26026
Provincials	5.55	99.86	324.61	0.08	0.64	1.99	2.92	4.28	8.68	7.68	9.92	15.90	2.89	2.81	3.12	8.84	3.40	0.11	25027	26027
Municipals	5.64	96.57	340.34	0.13	0.67	2.11	3.04	4.34	9.13	8.01	10.36	0.70	2.51	2.44	2.81	10.37	2.90	0.08	25028	26028
All Governments	5.44	99.18	311.21	0.15	0.72	2.01	2.88	4.18	8.48	7.38	9.46	86.60	2.38	2.32	2.52	7.91	2.70	0.08	25034	26034
AA	5.68	103.08	319.26	0.06	0.61	2.21	3.11	4.33	8.84	7.85	9.85	6.10	2.97	2.89	3.04	7.06	3.40	0.11	25031	26031
A	5.78	103.55	328.25	0.12	0.73	2.41	3.31	4.57	8.85	8.16	10.07	6.10	2.85	2.77	2.98	7.79	3.30	0.11	25032	26032
BBB	6.20	111.29	377.35	0.24	0.87	2.65	3.41	4.48	10.27	10.36	11.32	1.20	2.60	2.52	2.66	7.99	2.90	0.09	25033	26033
All Corporates	5.77	104.36	329.07	0.10	0.69	2.34	3.23	4.45	9.03	8.22	10.05	13.40	2.88	2.80	2.98	7.48	3.30	0.11	25029	26029
Overall	5.48	99.51	312.64	0.14	0.71	2.05	2.92	4.21	8.53	7.46	9.52	100.00	2.45	2.38	2.58	7.85	2.80	0.08	25035	26035
MID-TERM BOND INDEX (5-10 YEARS)																				
Canadas	5.46	118.75	365.19	-0.23	0.55	1.92	3.74	6.50	12.41	9.40	11.23	62.90	5.71	5.56	6.49	7.99	7.40	0.40	25011	26011
Provincials	5.67	119.48	380.77	-0.27	0.48	2.11	3.67	6.02	12.27	9.83	11.74	19.10	5.59	5.43	6.11	7.88	7.50	0.40	25012	26012
Municipals	5.69	120.26	402.45	-0.29	0.59	2.28	4.08	6.93	13.06	10.52	12.23	1.20	5.99	5.82	6.64	7.86	8.00	0.44	25013	26013
All Governments	5.51	119.14	371.64	-0.24	0.53	1.98	3.73	6.38	12.39	9.57	11.44	83.30	5.69	5.54	6.40	7.97	7.40	0.40	25014	26014
AA	5.82	121.62	384.50	-0.33	0.42	2.35	3.97	6.18	12.86	10.27	11.91	6.30	5.82	5.66	6.18	7.25	7.60	0.41	25016	26016
A	6.05	117.95	380.19	-0.16	0.75	2.66	4.13	5.91	12.49	10.57	11.74	7.80	5.69	5.52	6.05	7.69	7.90	0.41	25017	26017
BBB	6.70	131.68	441.72	-0.30	-0.16	2.38	3.41	5.19	13.18	12.80	13.52	2.70	6.30	6.09	6.34	7.19	8.40	0.48	25018	26018
All Corporates	6.07	120.74	385.20	-0.24	0.50	2.49	3.97	5.92	12.61	10.41	11.93	16.70	5.84	5.67	6.15	7.45	7.90	0.43	25019	26019
Overall	5.61	119.30	373.41	-0.24	0.53	2.06	3.77	6.32	12.41	9.67	11.50	100.00	5.71	5.56	6.36	7.88	7.50	0.41	25020	26020
LONG-TERM BOND INDEX (10+ YEARS)																				
Canadas	5.55	145.45	450.06	-0.26	2.14	4.02	7.25	13.34	18.32	12.53	13.50	47.70	11.46	11.15	15.51	8.75	22.30	1.94	25001	26001
Provincials	5.91	144.96	480.00	-0.43	1.78	4.38	6.99	12.01	19.17	13.56	14.26	34.70	11.09	10.77	14.15	8.68	22.30	1.87	25002	26002
Municipals	5.86	141.70	481.94	-0.46	1.50	3.49	5.98	11.44	18.15	13.33	14.35	1.70	9.17	8.91	11.93	9.18	15.10	1.13	25003	26003
All Governments	5.71	145.22	460.15	-0.34	1.97	4.12	7.12	12.83	18.55	12.87	13.76	84.10	11.26	10.95	14.87	8.73	22.20	1.90	25004	26004
AA	5.95	145.25	472.64	-0.52	1.76	4.78	7.44	12.27	18.70	13.56	14.13	3.00	10.47	10.17	13.95	9.15	21.50	1.59	25006	26006
A	6.12	146.19	484.14	-0.46	1.84	4.94	7.19	11.63	18.40	13.55	14.39	12.50	10.41	10.10	13.59	9.35	21.30	1.67	25007	26007
BBB	7.35	140.79	502.13	-0.73	-1.15	0.82	2.40	7.06	18.75	17.02	14.88	0.30	8.07	7.79	10.03	10.41	13.90	0.88	25008	26008
All Corporates	6.11	141.80	467.54	-0.48	1.75	4.81	7.12	11.64	18.43	13.56	14.07	15.90	10.37	10.07	13.58	9.33	21.20	1.63	25009	26009
Overall	5.77	144.99	461.50	-0.36	1.94	4.22	7.11	12.64	18.53	12.95	13.80	100.00	11.12	10.81	14.66	8.83	22.00	1.85	25010	26010
HIGH-YIELD BOND INDEX (COMPOSITE)																				
Real Estate	6.74	121.20	168.50	-0.18	0.35	2.68	3.82	5.86	15.03	N/A	N/A	30.20	4.94	4.77	5.29	8.08	4.80	0.35	25146	26146
Industrial	6.46	127.54	172.58	-0.45	-0.40	1.90	3.22	6.50	15.83	N/A	N/A	5.10	6.34	6.14	7.36	9.10	9.00	0.51	25147	26147
Resources	6.74	118.30	148.10	-0.13	0.39	2.90	3.80	7.00	13.67	N/A	N/A	17.10	5.80	5.61	6.51	9.47	9.30	0.53	25148	26148
Retail	6.44	108.21	148.02	-0.22	0.41	2.50	3.50	4.83	10.29	N/A	N/A	24.90	4.71	4.56	4.78	7.58	6.00	0.31	25149	26149
Other	7.41	131.77	182.40	0.52	1.08	3.91	5.64	8.00	18.17	N/A	N/A	22.70	5.84	5.62	6.06	8.67	9.30	0.44	25150	26150
Overall	6.80	119.20	164.65	-0.05	0.48	2.91	4.13	6.45	14.05	N/A	N/A	100.00	5.30	5.13	5.64	8.38	7.10	0.40	25151	26151

SOURCE: Melanie Moore, *Debt Market Indices*, ScotiaMcLeod Inc. (July 31, 1998).

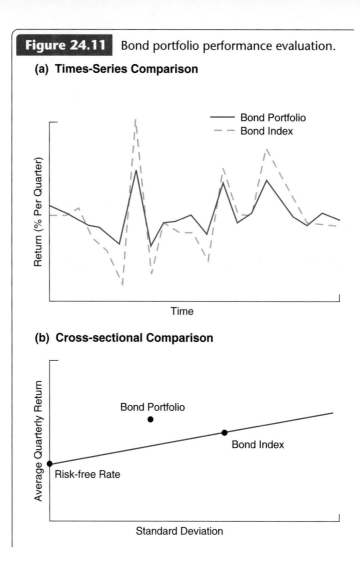

Figure 24.11 Bond portfolio performance evaluation.

(a) Times-Series Comparison

— Bond Portfolio
-- Bond Index

Return (% Per Quarter)

Time

(b) Cross-sectional Comparison

Average Quarterly Return

Bond Portfolio

Bond Index

Risk-free Rate

Standard Deviation

and end of the quarter), and plot the portfolio on a graph that measures return on the vertical axis and duration on the horizontal axis. (Duration is discussed in Chapter 15.)

2. Calculate the return and average duration for a broadly representative bond index for the same quarter, and plot the index on the same graph.

3. Determine the 90-day Treasury bill rate at the beginning of the quarter, and plot it on the same graph (because the Treasury bill is a pure discount security, its duration is the same as its term-to-maturity—90 days, or roughly .25 years).

4. Construct the bond market line by drawing a straight line connecting the Treasury bill and bond index.

5. Determine whether the portfolio plots above or below this line, and measure its performance by its distance from this line.

With this approach the bond market line is used to determine the benchmark in evaluating the performance of the bond portfolio. If the portfolio lies above the bond market line, as in Figure 24.12, it outperformed the benchmark (the benchmark portfolio lies on the bond market line directly below the portfolio) and its performance would be viewed as superior. Conversely, if the portfolio lies below the bond market line, it underperformed the benchmark (the benchmark portfolio lies on the bond market line directly above the

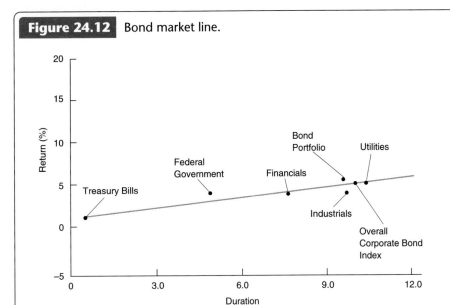

Figure 24.12 Bond market line.

SOURCE: Adapted from Wayne H. Wagner and Dennis A Tito, "Definitive New Measures of Bond Performance and Risk," *Pension World* 13, no. 5 (May 1977): 12.

portfolio) and its performance is viewed as inferior. Hence, equation (21.3) is being used to calculate the bond portfolio's *ex post* alpha, with the bond market line being used to determine the return on the benchmark portfolio, ar_{bp}.[27]

Other bond portfolios and indices can also be shown on the graph to give more information on the relative performance of the portfolio being evaluated. In Figure 24.12, one federal government bond index and three corporate bond indices are shown, in addition to the overall bond index published by Merrill Lynch. Their *ex post* alphas can be compared to the bond portfolio's *ex post* alpha. Furthermore, the bond portfolio's *ex post* alpha can be used to determine its rank among a group of bond portfolios.

Summary

1. Performance measurement is an integral part of the investment management process. It is a feedback and control mechanism that can make the investment management process more effective.
2. In evaluating performance, there are two major tasks: determining whether the performance is superior or inferior, and determining whether the performance is due to luck or skill.
3. Without intra-period contributions or withdrawals, measurement of periodic portfolio returns is simple: the difference between ending and beginning portfolio values divided by beginning portfolio value.

---

[27]Using the bond market line as a benchmark in this manner is similar to using the SML as a benchmark in evaluating the performance of stock portfolios.

4. Intra-period cash flows complicate the calculation of periodic portfolio returns. Two methods have been developed to calculate returns when these cash flows occur: dollar-weighted and time-weighted returns.

5. The dollar-weighted return is influenced by the size and timing of cash flows, whereas the time-weighted return is not. As a result, the time-weighted return is generally the preferred method when evaluating portfolio performance.

6. The essential idea behind performance evaluation is to compare an actively managed portfolio's returns against the returns of an alternative benchmark portfolio. An appropriate benchmark should be relevant and feasible, and it should exhibit risk similar to that of the actively managed portfolio.

7. Risk-adjusted performance measures involve both a portfolio's *ex post* return and its *ex post* risk.

8. *Ex post* alpha (differential return) and the reward-to-volatility ratio compare a portfolio's excess return to the portfolio's systematic risk. The Sharpe ratio and M^2 involve analysis of a portfolio's excess return and total risk.

9. Successful market timers will hold portfolios with relatively high betas during market rises and relatively low betas during market declines. Quadratic regression and dummy variable regression are two methods designed to measure market timing performance.

10. Risk-adjusted measures of performance have been criticized for using a market surrogate instead of the "true" market portfolio; being unable to statistically distinguish luck from skill except over very long periods of time; using an inappropriate risk-free rate; and relying on the validity of the CAPM.

APPENDIX A

PERFORMANCE ATTRIBUTION

With performance attribution, an attempt is made to ascertain why an equity portfolio had a given return over a particular time period. One procedure for making such a determination involves assuming security returns are related to a number of pre-specified factors as well as to sector-factors.[28] For example, there may be a beta factor, a size factor, and two sector-factors that indicate whether or not a stock is an industrial. With such a model, the returns for a set of stocks during a given time period are related to these factors and sector-factors in the following manner:

$$r_i = \beta_i F_1 + s_i F_2 + c_{i1} SF_1 + c_{i2} SF_2 + \epsilon_i \qquad (24.35)$$

Here, each stock has four attributes—β_i, s_i, c_{i1}, and c_{i2}. The attributes β_i and s_i are, respectively, the beta and firm size of stock i in a given time period, and c_{i1} and c_{i2} are sector-factor attributes that have values of 1 and 0, respectively, if stock i is an industrial firm and values of 0 and 1 if stock i is not an industrial firm. (For example, it may be a utility or transportation company such as Canadian Utilities or Air Canada.)

The factors and sector-factors F_1, F_2, SF_1, and SF_2 are parameters that can be estimated using a statistical technique known as multiple regression. For example, the returns for 500 firms for 1999 could be calculated. Then, the betas for each stock could be estimated using 16 quarters of returns ending with the last quarter of 1998 (by using the *ex-post* characteristic line equation given earlier). The firm size for each stock could be measured by taking the market price per share as of December 31, 1998, multiplying it by the number of shares

---

[28]For a discussion of factor models, see Chapter 10 and William F. Sharpe, "Factors in New York Stock Exchange Security Returns, 1931–1979," *Journal of Portfolio Management* 8, no. 4 (Summer 1982): 5–18.

outstanding at that time, and then taking the logarithm of the product (expressed in billions). Lastly, each firm can be classified as either an industrial or nonindustrial, resulting in a value of 0 or 1 assigned to c_{i1} and c_{i2}. This will give four columns of 500 numbers representing security attributes—one column with the betas for each stock, one column for the firm sizes of each stock, and two columns of 0s and 1s corresponding to whether the firms are industrials or nonindustrials—upon which will be "regressed" the column of returns for the 500 stocks during 1999.

Suppose the resulting regression resulted in estimated values for F_1, F_2, SF_1, and SF_2 of 1.20, −.40, 10.00, and 9.00, respectively. Then, equation (24.35) for 1999 would be

$$r_i = 1.20\beta_i - .40s_i + 10.00c_{i1} + 9.00c_{i2} + \epsilon_i \qquad (24.36)$$

Since the estimated value of F_1 (1.20) is positive, 1999 was a year where high beta stocks tended to outperform low beta stocks. Furthermore, since the estimated value of F_2 (−.40) is negative, the year 1999 was one where the stocks of small firms tended to outperform the stocks of large firms. With an estimated value for SF_1 that is greater than the estimated value for SF_2 (10.00 > 9.00), 1999 also appears to have been a year when industrials tended to outperform nonindustrials.

Equation (24.36) can be used to analyze the 1999 return on a stock. Consider, for example, a hypothetical industrial stock that had a return of 12.13%, a beta of .8, and size of 4.00 (its market value was \$54.6 billion, so s_i = natural logarithm of 54.6 = ln(54.6) = 4.00). According to equation (24.36), the "normal" return on such a stock is $(1.20 \times .8) - (.40 \times 4.00) + (10.00 \times 1) + (9.00 \times 0) = 9.36\%$. Thus, for this stock, its "nonfactor return" (ϵ_i) for 1994 was 12.13% − 9.36% = 2.77%, suggesting this particular stock did relatively well in comparison with other stocks having comparable attributes.

Similar analysis can be conducted on a portfolio's return for 1999. Consider a hypothetical portfolio that had a return of 10.03% in 1999. Upon close examination, it has been determined that this portfolio had an average beta of 1.3 and an average size of 3.2 (that is, the average value of s_i for all the stocks held was 3.2). Furthermore, 67% of the stocks in the portfolio were industrials and 33% were nonindustrials. According to equation (24.36), the normal return on such a portfolio is $(1.20 \times 1.30) - (.40 \times 3.20) + (10.00 \times .67) + (9.00 \times .33) = 9.95\%$. Since the nonfactor return on this portfolio was 10.03% − 9.95% = .08%, this portfolio shows little evidence of successful security selection.

Such absolute performance evaluation with a factor model is interesting, but in many cases comparative performance is more relevant. A manager may do poorly in a bad market. But if he provides a higher return than would have been obtained otherwise, the client is clearly better off. With comparative performance, the overall return of a portfolio is compared with that of one or more other portfolios or market indices in order to determine the *differences* in the returns. Then the sources of the differences can be determined with **comparative performance attribution**.

Assume that the i in equation (24.35) refers to the portfolio under evaluation. Letting j refer to the return on a portfolio (or market index) to which it is to be compared, the difference in their returns is simply $r_i - r_j$. Using equation (24.35), this difference can be expressed as

$$\begin{aligned} r_i - r_j = &(\beta_i F_1 + s_i F_2 + c_{i1}SF_1 + c_{i2}SF_2 + \epsilon_i) \\ &- (\beta_j F_1 + s_j F_2 + c_{j1}SF_1 + c_{j2}SF_2 + \epsilon_j) \end{aligned} \qquad (24.37)$$

Gathering similar terms, this equation can be rewritten as

$$\begin{aligned} r_i - r_j = &F_1(\beta_i - \beta_j) + F_2(s_i - s_j) \\ &+ SF_1(c_{i1} - c_{j1}) + SF_2(c_{i2} - c_{j2}) + (\epsilon_i - \epsilon_j) \end{aligned} \qquad (24.38)$$

Each of the first four terms represents a differential effect equal to the product of (1) the difference in the attributes of the two portfolios and (2) the actual value of the related

Table 24.3 Comparative Performance Attribution.

| | Attribute | | | | Differential |
	Portfolio i (a)	Portfolio j (b)	Difference (c) = (a) − (b)	Factor (d)	Effect (e) = (c) × (d)
a. Factors:					
Common factors					
Beta	1.30	1.50	−.20	1.20	− .24%
Size	3.20	1.40	1.80	−.40	− .72%
Sector-factors					
Industrials	.67	.80	−.13	10.00	−1.30%
Non-industrials	.33	.20	.13	9.00	1.17%
					−1.09%

| | Returns | | |
	Portfolio i (a)	Portfolio j (b)	Difference (c) = (a) − (b)
b. Returns:			
Factor return	9.95%	11.04%	−1.09%
Nonfactor return	.08%	.17%	− .09%
Total return	10.03%	11.21%	−1.18%

factor. The last term in the equation indicates the difference in the nonfactor returns of the two portfolios.

Table 24.3 provides an example where portfolio i is the one mentioned earlier that had a return in 1999 of 10.03%. It is being compared with a benchmark portfolio that had a return in 1999 of 11.21%. This benchmark portfolio had a beta of 1.50, and the average size of the firms whose stocks it held was 1.40. Furthermore, 80% of the portfolio's funds were invested in industrials, with the remaining 20% being invested in non-industrials. Using equation (24.36), the normal return on such a portfolio in 1999 was $(1.20 \times 1.50) - (.40 \times 1.40) + (10.00 \times .80) + (9.00 \times .20) = 11.04\%$, indicating the portfolio had a nonfactor return of 11.21% − 11.04% = .17%.

A direct comparison of the two portfolios reveals a difference in returns of $r_i - r_j = 10.03\% - 11.21\% = -1.18\%$. That is, portfolio i performed worse than the benchmark by 1.18%. Security selection played a small role, since the nonfactor returns were both quite low (.08% for portfolio i and .17% for the benchmark). On balance, sector selection lowered returns for portfolio i relative to the benchmark slightly—the sum of the values in the last column for the two sector-factors was −0.13%. In portfolio i, industrials were underweighted relative to the benchmark, while non-industrials were overweighted. A successful "sector picker" would have placed bets on (that is, overweighted) the sector with a relatively high factor value (industrials) and placed bets against (that is, underweighted) the sector with a relatively low factor value (non-industrials), leading to a net positive *sector bet effect*. In 1994, the investment manager for portfolio i was not as successful a sector picker relative to the benchmark.

The major sources of the relatively lower performance of portfolio i were those associated with common factors. The manager had lower-beta stocks than those in the benchmark during a period when high-beta stocks tended to do better than low-beta stocks. That is, the manager placed a bet against high-beta stocks in favour of low-beta stocks and lost.

He also had invested in stocks that were larger than those in the benchmark during a period when larger stocks tended to do poorly. That is, the manager placed a bet against smaller firms in favour of larger firms and lost. Both differences lowered returns relative to the benchmark, with the size bet being more detrimental than the beta bet.

QUESTIONS AND PROBLEMS

1. Craig Patrick owns a portfolio of three stocks. Craig's holdings and the prices of the stocks at the end of Year 1 and Year 2 are shown below. Assuming no contributions, withdrawals, or dividends paid, what is the return on Craig's portfolio in Year 2?

Stock	Shares Owned	Year 1 Price	Year 2 Price
A	100	$10	$15
B	300	5	4
C	250	12	14

2. Why do cash inflows and outflows between the beginning and end of a performance evaluation period complicate the measurement of portfolio returns?
3. At the beginning of the year, Lorne Grossman's portfolio was worth $39 000. At year-end, Lorne received a gift of $4000, which was invested in the portfolio. The portfolio's value at year-end was $42 000. What was the return on Lorne's portfolio during the year?
4. New Lisbon Laundry's pension fund was worth $30 million at the end of Year 1. On the first day of Year 2 the firm made a $2 million contribution to the fund. At the end of Year 2, the pension fund was valued at $38 million. What was the return on the New Lisbon pension fund during Year 2?
5. At the beginning of the year, Connie Daily's portfolio was worth $9000. At the end of each of the next four quarters, Connie received a gift of $500, which was invested in the portfolio. At the end of each quarter, Connie's portfolio was worth, respectively, $9800, $10 800, $11 200, and $12 000. What was the time-weighted rate of return on Connie's portfolio during the year?
6. Dave Das's portfolio is worth $12 000 at the beginning of a 30-day month. On day 10 of the month, Dave received a contribution to the portfolio of $800. At the end of the month, Dave's portfolio is worth $13 977.71. What was the dollar-weighted return on Dave's portfolio for the month?
7. Ginger Beaumont began the year with a portfolio valued at $10 000 and made a contribution to and a withdrawal from this portfolio over the next three months. Information regarding amounts and dates of these cash flows and the portfolio's market value at various dates is shown below.

Date	Contribution (+) or Withdrawal (−)	Portfolio Value
12/31	$ 0	$10 000
1/31	+956	9 000
2/28	−659	12 000
3/31	0	13 000

a. Calculate the dollar-weighted return for the three-month period. (Hint: Unless you have a suitable calculator, you will have to use trial and error to find the dollar-weighted return. To begin, the monthly dollar-weighted return is less than 10%.)

b. Calculate the time-weighted return for the three-month period.

c. Why is the time-weighted return of the quarter less than the dollar-weighted return in this particular period?

8. Distinguish between time-weighted and dollar-weighted rates of return. Under what performance measurement circumstances might the dollar-weighted return be preferred to the time-weighted?

9. Oscar DeMaestri's portfolio is valued at $22 000 at the beginning of a 31-day month. During the month, Oscar withdrew $1500 from the portfolio on day 12 and contributed $600 on day 21. At month-end, the portfolio was worth $21 769.60. What was Oscar's dollar-weighted return for the month?

10. At the beginning of a 30-day month, Lindsay Dickerson owned a portfolio valued at $5000. On day 10, Lindsay's portfolio was worth $7300 after a $2000 contribution had been made on that day. At the end of the month, the portfolio was worth $9690.18. Calculate both the time-weighted and dollar-weighted returns on Lindsay's portfolio for the month. Why do the two returns differ so substantially?

11. Why does performance evaluation require an appropriate benchmark in order to be meaningful? How would you define the term *appropriate* in this context?

12. It is common practice for performance evaluation services to compare the returns on a common stock portfolio to a distribution of returns obtained from a large sample of other common stock portfolios. What potential problems are involved in this sort of analysis?

13. Consider a price-weighted market index composed of two securities, A and B, with prices of $16 and $30, respectively. The index divisor is currently 2.0. Calculate the value of the divisor when:

a. Stock A issues a 5% stock dividend.

b. Stock B undergoes a 3-for-1 stock split.

c. Stock A undergoes a 4-for-1 stock split.

14. It is often argued that the S&P 500 is a better indicator than the Dow Jones Industrial Average of the performance of the entire US stock market. Explain the reasoning behind this contention.

15. Assume that the market is composed of the following three securities:

Security	Current Price	Shares Outstanding
A	$20	$20 000
B	35	40 000
C	30	40 000

a. What is the aggregate value of the market?

b. If security C's price increases by 20%, what is the percentage change in the market's aggregate value?

c. If security B splits 2-for-1, what is the percentage change in the market's aggregate value?

16. Consider three stocks, X, Y, and Z, with the following closing prices on two particular dates:

Stock	Date 1	Date 2
X	$16	$22
Y	5	4
Z	24	30

On date 1 there are 100 shares of stock X, 200 shares of stock Y, and 100 shares of stock Z outstanding.

    a. Construct a price-weighted market index using the three stocks, X, Y, and Z. What is the index's value on date 1?

    b. What is the price-weighted index's value on date 2?

    c. Assume that, on date 2, stock X splits 4-for-1. What is the price-weighted index's value on that date?

    d. Construct a value-weighted index using the three stocks. Assign the value-weighted index a value of 100 on date 1. What is the index's value on date 2?

17. According to Phillip Fain, "The success of a stock market index depends on its ability to measure the performance of stocks not included in the index." Explain what Phillip means.

18. Consider an equal-weighted market index composed of three securities. The market prices of those securities on three dates are shown below.

	Market Prices		
Security	Date 1	Date 2	Date 3
A	$50	$55	$60
B	30	28	30
C	70	75	73

    a. What is the return on the index from date 1 to date 2?

    b. What is the return on the index from date 2 to date 3?

19. Consider a market index based on three securities and their associated prices on three dates.

	Market Prices		
Security	Date 1	Date 2	Date 3
L	$20	$23	$30
M	27	30	31
N	40	35	29

If the index's value is 200 on date 1, calculate its value on date 2 and date 3 if the index return is computed on a geometric mean basis.

20. Janice Dillhoefer owns a portfolio that over the last five years has produced a 16.8% annual return. During that time the portfolio produced a 1.10 beta. Further, the risk-free return and market return averaged 7.4% and 15.2% per year, respectively. What was the *ex post* alpha on Janice's portfolio over this time period? Draw the *ex post* SML and the position of Janice's portfolio.

21. The performance of the Venus Fund, a common stock mutual fund, compared with that of the TSE 300 over a 10-year period, is as follows:

	Venus Fund	TSE 300
Average quarterly excess return	0.6%	0.5%
Standard deviation of quarterly excess returns	9.9%	6.6%
Beta	1.10	1.00

John Vance is considering investing in either the Venus Fund or another mutual fund whose objective is to track the performance of the TSE 300. Which fund would you recommend that John select, assuming that your decision is based solely on past performance? Justify your answer using various measures of risk-adjusted performance.

22. Why is the Sharpe ratio a more appropriate measure of performance than the *ex post* alpha if the portfolio being assessed represents the entire wealth of the portfolio's owner?

23. Can the *ex post* alpha, the reward-to-volatility ratio, and the Sharpe ratio give conflicting answers to the question of whether a particular portfolio has outperformed a market index on a risk-adjusted basis? If so, which of these measures can conflict with the others, and why can this conflict occur?

24. Does a portfolio's *ex post* alpha measure gains and losses due to security selection, market timing, or both? Explain.

25. Assume that broad stock market indices, such as the TSE 300, are not good surrogates for the "true" market portfolio. What potential problems does this cause for performance evaluation using the *ex post* alpha measure?

26. You are given the following historical performance information on the capital markets and the Jupiter Fund, a common stock mutual fund.

Year	Jupiter Fund Beta	Return on Jupiter Fund	Return on Market Index	Return on Treasury Bills
1	0.90	-2.99%	-8.50%	6.58%
2	0.95	0.63	4.01	6.53
3	0.95	22.01	14.30	4.39
4	1.00	24.08	18.98	3.84
5	1.00	-22.46	-14.66	6.93
6	0.90	-25.12	-26.47	8.00
7	0.80	29.72	37.20	5.80
8	0.75	22.15	23.84	5.08
9	0.80	0.48	-7.18	5.12
10	0.85	6.85	6.56	7.18

a. Compute the Jupiter Fund's average beta over the 10-year period. What investment percentages in the market index and Treasury bills are required in order to produce a beta equal to the fund's average beta?

b. Compute the year-by-year returns that would have been earned on a portfolio invested in the market index and Treasury bills in the proportions calculated in part (a).

c. Compute the year-by-year returns that would have been earned on a portfolio invested in the market index and Treasury bills in the proportions needed to match Jupiter's beta year by year. (Note: These proportions will change yearly as the fund's beta changes yearly.)

d. One measure of a fund's market timing ability is the average difference between (1) what the fund would have earned annually by investing in the market index and Treasury bills so that the year-by-year beta equals the fund's actual year-by-year beta, and (2) what the fund would have earned annually by investing in the market index and Treasury bills so that the year-by-year beta equals the fund's average beta. Given your previous calculations, evaluate the market timing ability of Jupiter's manager.

e. One measure of a fund's security selection ability is the average difference between (1) the fund's annual returns and (2) what the fund would have earned annually by investing in the market index and Treasury bills so that the year-by-year beta equals the fund's actual year-by-year beta. Calculate Jupiter's average return and then, using your previous calculations, evaluate the security selection ability of Jupiter's manager.

27. Consider the following annual returns produced by a MiniFund, a mutual fund investing in small stocks:

1971	16.50%	1976	57.38%	1981	13.88%	1986	6.85%
1972	4.43	1977	25.38	1982	28.01	1987	−9.30
1973	−30.90	1978	23.46	1983	39.67	1988	22.87
1974	−19.95	1979	43.46	1984	−6.67	1989	10.18
1975	52.82	1980	39.88	1985	24.66	1990	−21.56

Referring to Table 1.1, use the Treasury bill returns as the risk-free return and the common stock returns as the market return, and calculate the following risk-adjusted return measures for the small stock mutual fund:

a. *ex post* alpha

b. reward-to-volatility ratio

c. Sharpe ratio.

Comment on the mutual fund's risk-adjusted performance. What problems are associated with using a large capitalization index such as the TSE 300 (the source of the common stock returns) as the benchmark in evaluating this small company mutual fund?

28. In an article in *Journal of Finance* (March 1983), Jess Chua and Richard Woodward investigated the investment skill of the legendary economist John Maynard Keynes. A portfolio managed by Keynes had the returns shown at the top of the following page. Chua and Woodward concluded that Keynes demonstrated superior investment abilities. They did not, however, distinguish between his market timing and security selection skills. Using the quadratic regression and dummy variable techniques, evaluate Keynes's market timing skills. (Hint: Use of a regression package found in a standard personal computer spreadsheet program is highly recommended.)

	Keynes's Return	Market Return	Risk-free Return
1928	−3.4%	7.9%	4.2
1929	0.8	6.6	5.3
1930	−32.4	−20.3	2.5
1931	−24.6	−25.0	3.6
1932	44.8	−5.8	1.6
1933	35.1	21.5	0.6
1934	33.1	−0.7	0.7
1935	44.3	5.3	0.6
1936	56.0	10.2	0.6
1937	8.5	−0.5	0.6
1938	−40.1	−16.1	0.6
1939	12.9	−7.2	1.3
1940	−15.6	−12.9	1.0
1941	33.5	12.5	1.0
1942	−0.9	0.8	1.0
1943	53.9	15.6	1.0
1944	14.5	5.4	1.0
1945	14.6	0.8	1.0

29. Discuss the potential drawbacks of evaluating bond portfolio performance by using a bond market line.

30. (Appendix Question) What is the purpose of performance attribution? What types of problems can hinder performance attribution?

31. (Appendix Question) Assume that security returns are explained by a sector-factor model. Eugene Stephens has been asked to develop a performance attribution report analyzing the returns on portfolio A versus those of a market index for the latest year, and he has collected the following information:

	Portfolio A	Market Index	Sector-Factor Values
Return	12.50%	5.50%	—
Beta	1.10	1.00	−0.50
Size	1.30	6.00	−0.60
% Industrial	40%	80%	8.00
% Non-industrial	60%	20%	16.00

Unfortunately, Eugene is confused by the subject of performance attribution. Carry out the analysis for him.

CFA Exam Question

32. As a corporate treasurer, you are responsible for evaluating prospective investment managers for your company's pension fund. You have interviewed three managers, examined their reported investment performances, and identified clear-cut differences in their investment approaches.

Manager A has developed a very appealing and apparently successful investment process based on extensive research and back-testing but she has not yet managed money using this process.

Manager B has been investing relatively small amounts of money over only the past two years, producing what appears to be extraordinary investment performance. His process is based on exploiting what he believes to be a market inefficiency (or anomaly) to produce superior returns.

Manager C is a global investment counsellor who emphasizes active selection of stocks and bonds across the major world markets. He has a long track record and uses a well-established and widely accepted process for selecting securities.

a. Discuss the usefulness of historical investment performance in evaluating investment managers.

b. For each of the three managers, identify and discuss the two most important factors that you would consider in assessing the manager's performance.

KEY TERMS

dollar-weighted return (p. 825)
time-weighted return (p. 826)
benchmark portfolio (p. 827)
market index (p. 830)
price weighting (p. 830)
value weighting (p. 832)
equal weighting (p. 834)
price relatives (p. 834)

characteristic line (p. 840)
ex post alpha (p. 840)
simple linear regression (p. 842)
reward-to-volatility ratio (p. 844)
Sharpe ratio (p. 845)
performance attribution (p. 857)
comparative performance attribution (p. 863)

REFERENCES

1. The use of portfolio benchmarks for performance evaluation is discussed in:

Richard Roll, "Performance Evaluation and Benchmark Errors (I)," *Journal of Portfolio Management* 6, no. 4 (Summer 1980): 5–12.

Richard Roll, "Performance Evaluation and Benchmark Errors (II)," *Journal of Portfolio Management* 7, no. 2 (Winter 1981): 17–22.

Gary P. Brinson, Jeffrey J. Diermeier, and Gary G. Schlarbaum, "A Composite Portfolio Benchmark for Pension Plans," *Financial Analysts Journal* 42, no. 2 (March–April 1986): 15–24.

Mark P. Kritzman, "How to Build a Normal Portfolio in Three Easy Steps," *Journal of Portfolio Management* 13, no. 4 (Summer 1987): 21–23.

Jeffery V. Bailey, Thomas M. Richards, and David E. Tierney, "Benchmark Portfolios and the Manager/Plan Sponsor Relationship," *Journal of Corporate Finance* 4, no. 4 (Winter 1988): 25–32.

Arjun Divecha and Richard C. Grinold, "Normal Portfolios: Issues for Sponsors, Managers, and Consultants," *Financial Analysts Journal* 45, no. 2 (March–April 1989): 7–13.

Edward P. Rennie and Thomas J. Cowhey, "The Successful Use of Benchmark Portfolios: A Case Study," *Financial Analysts Journal* 46, no. 5 (September–October 1990): 18–26.

Jeffery V. Bailey, "Are Manager Universes Acceptable Performance Benchmarks?" *Journal of Portfolio Management* 18, no. 3 (Spring 1992): 9–13.

Jeffery V. Bailey, "Evaluating Benchmark Quality," *Financial Analysts Journal* 48, no. 3 (May–June 1992): 33–39.

Martin L. Leibowitz, Lawrence N. Bader, Stanley Koegelman, and Ajay R. Dravid, "Benchmark Departures and Total Fund Risk: A Second Dimension of Diversification," *Financial Analysts Journal* 51, no. 5 (September–October 1995): 40–48.

2. The four measures of risk-adjusted performance were initially developed in:

Jack L. Treynor, "How to Rate Management of Investment Funds," *Harvard Business Review* 43, no. 1 (January–February 1965): 63–75.

William F. Sharpe, "Mutual Fund Performance," *Journal of Business* 39, no. 1 (January 1966): 119–138.

Michael C. Jensen, "The Performance of Mutual Funds in the Period 1945–1964," *Journal of Finance* 23, no. 2 (May 1968): 389–416.

Michael C. Jensen, "Risk, the Pricing of Capital Assets, and the Evaluation of Investment Portfolios," *Journal of Business* 42, no. 2 (April 1969): 167–185.

Franco Modigliani and Leah Modigliani, "Risk-adjusted Performance," *Journal of Portfolio Management* 23, no. 2 (Winter 1997): 45–54.

3. More sophisticated measures of portfolio performance that also measure market timing ability were initially developed by:

Jack L. Treynor and Kay K. Mazuy, "Can Mutual Funds Outguess the Market?" *Harvard Business Review* 44, no. 4 (July–August 1966): 131–136.

Robert C. Merton, "On Market Timing and Investment Performance I: An Equilibrium Theory of Value for Market Forecasts," *Journal of Business* 54, no. 3 (July 1981): 363–406.

Roy D. Henriksson and Robert C. Merton, "On Market Timing and Investment Performance II: Statistical Procedures for Evaluating Forecasting Skill," *Journal of Business* 54, no. 4 (October 1981): 513–533.

4. There have been many criticisms leveled at the various measures of portfolio performance that are presented in this chapter. One of the most formidable critiques was:

Richard Roll, "Ambiguity When Performance Is Measured by the Security Market Line," *Journal of Finance* 33, no. 4 (September 1978): 1051–1069.

5. APT-based measures of portfolio performance have been developed by:

Gregory Connor and Robert Korajczyk, "Performance Measurement with the Arbitrage Pricing Theory: A New Framework for Analysis," *Journal of Financial Economics* 15, no. 3 (March 1986): 373–394.

Bruce N. Lehmann and David M. Modest, "Mutual Fund Performance Evaluation: A Comparison of Benchmarks and Benchmark Comparisons," *Journal of Finance* 42, no. 2 (June 1987): 233–265.

Nai-Fu Chen, Thomas E. Copeland, and David Mayers, "A Comparison of Single and Multifactor Portfolio Performance Methodologies," *Journal of Financial and Quantitative Analysis* 22, no. 4 (December 1987): 401–417.

Edwin J. Elton, Martin J. Gruber, and Christopher R. Blake, "Fundamental Economic Variables, Expected Returns, and Bond Fund Performance," *Journal of Finance* 50, no. 4 (September 1995): 1229–1256.

6. Some recent developments in measuring portfolio performance are discussed in:

Stanley J. Kon, "The Market-timing Performance of Mutual Fund Managers," *Journal of Business* 56, no. 3 (July 1983): 323–347.

Anat R. Admati and Stephen A. Ross, "Measuring Investment Performance in a Rational Expectations Equilibrium Model," *Journal of Business* 58, no. 1 (January 1985): 1–26.

Philip H. Dybvig and Stephen A. Ross, "Differential Information and Performance Measurement Using a Security Market Line," *Journal of Finance* 40, no. 2 (June 1985): 383–399.

Philip H. Dybvig and Stephen A. Ross, "The Analytics of Performance Measurement Using a Security Market Line," *Journal of Finance* 40, no. 2 (June 1985): 401–416.

Mark Kritzman, "How to Detect Skill in Management Performance," *Journal of Portfolio Management* 12, no. 2 (Winter 1986): 16–20.

Ravi Jagannathan and Robert A. Korajczyk, "Assessing the Market Timing Performance of Managed Portfolios," *Journal of Business* 59, no. 2, pt. 1 (April 1986): 217–235.

Anat R. Admati, Sudipto Bhattacharya, Paul Pfleiderer, and Stephen A. Ross, "On Timing and Selectivity," *Journal of Finance* 41, no. 3 (July 1986): 715–730.

Gary P. Brinson, L. Randolph Hood, and Gilbert L. Beebower, "Determinants of Portfolio Performance," *Financial Analysts Journal* 42, no. 4 (July–August 1986): 39–44.

William Breen, Ravi Jagannathan, and Aharon R. Ofer, "Correcting for Heteroscedasticity in Tests for Market Timing Ability," *Journal of Business* 59, no. 4, pt. 1 (October 1986): 585–598.

Robert E. Cumby and David M. Modest, "Testing for Market Timing Ability: A Framework for Forecast Evaluation," *Journal of Financial Economics* 19, no. 1 (September 1987): 169–189.

Larry J. Lockwood and K. Rao Kadiyala, "Measuring Investment Performance with a Stochastic Parameter Regression Model," *Journal of Banking and Finance* 12, no. 3 (September 1988): 457–467.

Alex Kane and Gary Marks, "Performance Evaluation of Market Timers: Theory and Evidence," *Journal of Financial and Quantitative Analysis* 23, no. 4 (December 1988): 425–435.

Mark Grinblatt and Sheridan Titman, "Portfolio Performance Evaluation: Old Issues and New Insights," *Review of Financial Studies* 2, no. 3 (1989): 393–421.

Cheng-few Lee and Shafiqur Rahman, "Market Timing, Selectivity, and Mutual Fund Performance: An Empirical Investigation," *Journal of Business* 63, no. 2 (April 1990): 261–278.

Michel Gendron and Christian Genest, "Performance Measurement Under Asymmetric Information and Investment Constraints," *Journal of Finance* 45, no. 5 (December 1990): 1655–1661.

Cheng-few Lee and Shafiqur Rahman, "New Evidence of Timing and Security Selection Skill of Mutual Fund Managers," *Journal of Portfolio Management* 17, no. 2 (Winter 1991): 80–83.

Gary P. Brinson, Brian D. Singer, and Gilbert L. Beebower, "Determinants of Portfolio Performance II: An Update," *Financial Analysts Journal* 47, no. 3 (May–June 1991): 40–48.

Chris R. Hensel, D. Don Ezra, and John H. Ilkiw, "The Importance of the Asset Allocation Decision," *Financial Analysts Journal* 47, no. 4 (July–August 1991): 65–72.

Eric J. Weigel, "The Performance of Tactical Asset Allocation," *Financial Analysts Journal* 47, no. 5 (September–October 1991): 63–70.

G. L. Beebower and A. P. Varikooty, "Measuring Market Timing Strategies," *Financial Analysts Journal* 47, no. 6 (November–December 1991): 78–84, 92.

L. R. Glosten and R. Jagannathan, "A Contingent Claim Approach to Performance Evaluation," *Journal of Empirical Finance* 1, no. 2 (January 1994): 133–160.

Wayne E. Ferson and Rudi Schadt, "Measuring Fund Strategy and Performance in Changing Economic Conditions," *Journal of Finance* 51, no. 2 (June 1996): 425–461.

Zhiwu Chen and Peter Knez, "Portfolio Performance Measurement: Theory and Applications," *Review of Financial Studies* 9, no. 2 (Summer 1996): 511–555.

Jeffery V. Bailey, "Evaluating Investment Skill with a VAM Graph," *Journal of Investing* 5, no. 2 (Summer 1996): 64–71.

7. An alternative approach to portfolio performance evaluation that is called style analysis is described in:

William F. Sharpe, "Major Investment Styles," *Journal of Portfolio Management* 4, no. 2 (Winter 1978): 68–74.

William F. Sharpe, "Determining a Fund's Effective Asset Mix," *Investment Management Review* (December 1988): 59–69.

William F. Sharpe, "Asset Allocation," in *Managing Investment Portfolio: A Dynamic Process*, eds. John L. Maginn and Donald L. Tuttle (Boston: Warren, Gorham & Lamont, 1990), Chapter 7.

William F. Sharpe, "Asset Allocation: Management Style and Performance Measurement," *Journal of Portfolio Management* 18, no. 2 (Winter 1992): 7–19.

Richard Bernstein, *Style Investing* (New York: John Wiley, 1995).

T. Daniel Coggin, Frank J. Fabozzi, and Robert Arnott, eds., *The Handbook of Equity Style Management* (New Hope, PA: Frank Fabozzi Associates, 1997).

Dan diBartolomeo and Erik Witkowski, "Mutual Fund Misclassification:Evidence Based on Style Analysis," *Financial Analysts Journal* 53, no. 5 (September–October 1997):32–43.

8. Bond portfolio performance evaluation is discussed in:

Wayne H. Wagner and Dennis A. Tito, "Definitive New Measures of Bond Performance and Risk," *Pension World* 13, no. 5 (May 1977): 10–12.

Wayne H. Wagner and Dennis A. Tito, "Is Your Bond Manager Skillful?" *Pension World* 13, no. 6 (June 1977): 9–13.

Peter O. Dietz, H. Russell Fogler, and Donald J. Hardy, "The Challenge of Analyzing Bond Portfolio Returns," *Journal of Portfolio Management* 6, no. 3 (Spring 1980): 53–58.

Mark Kritzman, "Can Bond Managers Perform Consistently?" *Journal of Portfolio Management* 9, no. 4 (Summer 1983): 54–56.

Robert N. Anthony, "How to Measure Fixed-Income Performance Correctly," *Journal of Portfolio Management* 11, no. 2 (Winter 1985): 61–65.

Peter O. Dietz and Jeannette R. Kirschman, "Evaluation Portfolio Performance," Chapter 14 in *Managing Investment Portfolios: A Dynamic Process*, eds. John L. Maginn and Donald L. Tuttle (Boston: Warren, Gorham & Lamont, 1990).

Ronald N. Kahn, "Bond Performance Analysis: A Multi-Factor Approach," *Journal of Portfolio Management* 18, no. 1 (Fall 1991): 40–47.

Christopher R. Blake, Edwin J. Elton, and Martin J. Gruber in "The Performance of Bond Mutual Funds," *Journal of Business* 66, no. 3 (July 1993): 371–403.

Edwin J. Elton, Martin J. Gruber, and Christopher R. Blake "Fundamental Economic Variables, Expected Returns, and Bond Fund Performance," *Journal of Finance* 50, no. 4 (September 1995): 1229–1256.

9. Performance attribution was initially developed and then expanded in:

Eugene F. Fama, "Components of Investment Performance," *Journal of Finance* 27, no. 3 (June 1972): 551–567.

H. Russel Fogler, "Common Stock Management in the 1990s," *Journal of Portfolio Management* 16, no. 2 (Winter 1990): 26–35.

Ernest M. Ankrim, "Risk-adjusted Performance Attribution," *Financial Analysts Journal* 48, no. 2 (March–April 1991): 74–82.

Peter J. Higgs and Stephen Goode, "Target Active Returns and Attribution Analysis," *Financial Analysts Journal* 49, no. 3 (May–June 1993): 77–80.

Brian D. Singer and Denis S. Karnosky, "The General Framework for Global Investment Management and Performance Attribution," *Journal of Portfolio Management* 21, no. 2 (Winter 1995): 84–92.

10. For a Canadian perspective on the topics covered in this chapter, see:

J. McLaughlin and N. Bossen, "The Historical Performance of Canadian Investment Managers: Predictor of Future Performance," *Canadian Investment Review* III, no. 1 (Spring 1990).

T. Appelt, "Active Management: What Is the Right Performance Benchmark?" *Canadian Investment Review* V, no. 1 (Spring 1992).

B. Curwood, "Solving the Mysteries of Performance Measurement," *Canadian Investment Review* VII, no. 1 (Spring 1994).

P. Brodeur, "The Changing Face of Money Management and Risk," *Canadian Investment Review* XI, no. 3 (Fall 1998).

International Investing

O ne of the major themes of modern portfolio theory concerns the merits of diversification: in an efficient capital market, sensible investment strategies will include holdings of many different assets. Previous chapters have considered traditional securities, such as stocks and bonds, and some less traditional ones, such as options and futures. However, an investor should also consider holding foreign securities, thereby diversifying his portfolio internationally. (Some people also believe that investing in tangible assets brings additional diversification benefits; see the Appendix to this chapter for a discussion.)

If the world were under one political jurisdiction, with one currency and complete freedom of trade, then "the market portfolio" could be thought of as including all securities in the world, each in proportion to its market value. In such a situation, limiting one's investments to securities representing firms located in only one part of the world would most likely result in a relatively low rate of return per unit of risk. After all, few people would advocate that Albertans own only securities issued by Alberta firms. And in a world without political boundaries, few people would advocate that Canadians own only securities issued by Canadian firms.

Unfortunately, there are political boundaries, different currencies, and restrictions on trade and currency exchange. Such irritants diminish, but do not destroy, the advantages to be gained from international investment.

⚬ The Total Investable Capital Market Portfolio

Figure 25.1 provides a 1997 year-end estimate of the size of the total investable capital market portfolio in the world, which can be thought of as representing the set of investments that are available to Canadian portfolio managers. Many problems are encountered in the construction of such a portfolio. It is almost impossible to adequately represent *all* security markets, as undoubtedly certain classes of assets have been omitted (such as foreign real estate) and double counting is involved in that some firms own parts of other firms.[1]

The figure indicates that non-US bond and equity markets amount to 7.4 + 2.3 + 0.7 + 8.7 + 1.0 + 3.8 + 1.0 = $24.9 trillion, and comprise about one-half the value of the entire $49.1 trillion portfolio (there are seven foreign categories—*Japan Equity, Other Equity, Emerging Markets Equity, Other Bonds, Emerging Market Debt, Japan Bonds,* and *Dollar*

---

[1]For a discussion of the difficulties in measuring the size of the world portfolio along with an estimate of its size at year-end 1984, see Roger G. Ibbotson, Laurence B. Siegel, and Kathryn S. Love, "World Wealth: Market Values and Returns," *Journal of Portfolio Management* 12, no. 1 (Fall 1985): 4–23.

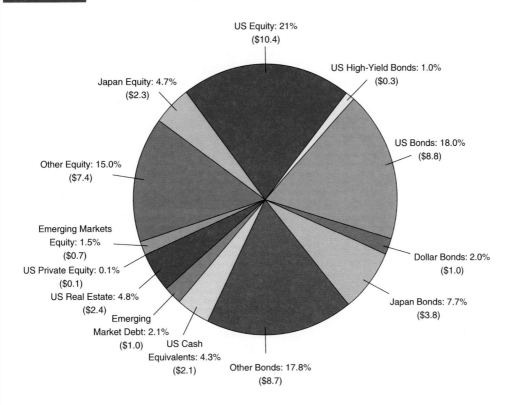

Figure 25.1 Total investable capital market portfolio, year-end 1997.[a]

US Equity: 21%
($10.4)

US High-Yield Bonds: 1.0%
($0.3)

Japan Equity: 4.7%
($2.3)

US Bonds: 18.0%
($8.8)

Other Equity: 15.0%
($7.4)

Emerging Markets
Equity: 1.5%
($0.7)

Dollar Bonds: 2.0%
($1.0)

US Private Equity: 0.1%
($0.1)

US Real Estate: 4.8%
($2.4)

Japan Bonds: 7.7%
($3.8)

Emerging
Market Debt: 2.1%
($1.0)

US Cash
Equivalents: 4.3%
($2.1)

Other Bonds: 17.8%
($8.7)

[a] Preliminary, figures measured in trillions of US dollars.
SOURCE: Brinson Partners, Inc. (Chicago, 1998).

Bonds; the latter are foreign and Eurobonds denominated in US dollars). Also of interest is the observation that fixed-income securities amount to 8.8 + 0.5 + 2.1 + 8.7 + 1.0 + 3.8 = 25.9 trillion, and make up slightly more than 50% of the portfolio's value.[2] About one-half of this total is non-US fixed-income securities. Similarly, about 50% of the $20.8 trillion (7.4 + 10.4 + 0.7 + 2.3) equity market consists of non-US stocks.

A more detailed breakdown of the stock market capitalization at the end of January 1998 in the countries followed by *Morgan Stanley Capital International* is provided in column (2) of Table 25.1. The largest market for common stocks is the United States, followed by Japan. These two countries make up 63.4% of the total. A distant third is the United Kingdom, and then notably behind the United Kingdom come Germany and France. These five countries represent 82.9% of the total. It will be shown next how Morgan Stanley calculates international stock market indices involving these countries.

[2]A more detailed study of bonds estimated their global value to be $11 trillion at the end of 1989. Of this total, $6.3 trillion was government debt, $2.4 trillion was local corporate debt, $1 trillion was "crossborder" debt (that is, foreign bonds and Eurobonds), and $1.3 trillion was "other domestic" debt. See Roger G. Ibbotson and Laurence B. Siegel, "The World Bond Market: Market Values, Yields, and Returns," *Journal of Fixed Income* 1, no. 1 (June 1991): 90–99.

Table 25.1 World Stock Market Capitalization, January 1998.

Country (1)	Market Capitalization Dollars* (2)	Market Capitalization Percentage (3)
Austria	$23.8	.2%
Belgium	78.2	.6
Denmark	63.3	.5
Finland	48.0	.4
France	490.9	3.8
Germany	602.5	4.7
Ireland	24.7	.2
Italy	262.1	2.0
Netherlands	339.6	2.7
Norway	29.2	.2
Portugal	36.4	.3
Spain	170.9	1.3
Sweden	158.3	1.2
Switzerland	483.0	3.8
UK	1,343.7	10.5
Total Europe	$4 154.6	32.1%
Australia	$174.9	1.4
Hong Kong	143.1	1.1
Japan	1 631.5	12.8
Malaysia	43.4	0.3
New Zealand	17.7	.1
Singapore	44.6	.3
Total Pacific	$2 055.2	16.0%
Canada	$299.8	2.3
US	6 283.6	49.1
Total North America	$6 583.4	51.4%
Total World	$12 493.4	

*Measured in billions of US dollars
SOURCE: Adapted from *Morgan Stanley Capital International Global Investment Monitor*, January 30, 1998, p. 3.

International Equity Indices

In most countries, there are indices of overall stock values and of the values of stocks within various industry or economic sectors. Such indices can be used for assessing "market moves" within the country and, more importantly, for comparative performance measurement. Important indices include the Financial Times-Stock Exchange 100 Index (often referred to as FT-SE, or the "footsie") for the London Stock Exchange; the Nikkei 225 Average for the Tokyo Stock Exchange; the Paris Bourse's CAC 40 and the DAX Index for the Frankfurt Stock Exchange.

These and other indices from both developed and emerging markets are reported daily in *The Globe and Mail: Report on Business* as shown in Figure 25.2(a). Figure 25.2(b) shows the extensive daily coverage given to US indices in the *Report on Business*. With the advent of 24-hour trading across different exchanges worldwide and greater international broker-

Figure 25.2 International equity indices and benchmarks.

(a)

Overseas indexes

	Yesterday	Previous	1998 high	1998 low
Amsterdam AEX	851.11	827.67	1315.63	827.67
Brussels	2816.29	2762.91	3632.07	2404.95
Frankfurt DAX	3983.64	3896.08	6212.80	3896.08
Hong Kong	8506.79	7939.51	11810.63	6779.95
London FT 250	4289.0	4251.2	5966.6	4251.2
FT-SE 100	4823.4	4698.9	6179.0	4648.7
Mexico City	3444.06	3387.46	5204.00	2856.10
Milan	16761	16812	26377	16761
Paris CAC-40	3092.90	2959.97	4388.48	2862.54
Sydney All ord	2491.3	2503.3	2987.9	2458.2
Tokyo	12879.97	13026.06	17264.34	12879.97
Zurich SMI	5419.0	5293.7	8412.0	5124.7

Emerging markets

	Close	Chg		Close	Chg
Athens	1772.09	−57.46	**Kuala Lumpur**	372.22	−0.77
Bangkok	292.50	+7.28	**Madrid**	657.73	+14.24
Bombay	2916.66	+20.52	**Manila**	1301.36	+50.95
Buenos Aires	385.45	+21.63	**Santiago**	3125.99	+33.07
Caracas	3624.84	+129.92	**Sao Paulo**	527.54	+352.33
China World	511.74	+30.52	**Seoul**	327.96	+22.74
Jakarta	304.84	+16.29	**Singapore**	976.65	+25.69
Johannesburg	5061.80	+58.80	**Taipei**	944.17	−26.06
Karachi	941.82	−20.65	**Turkey**	1946.05	+93.77

(b)

U.S. INDEXES

New York Stock Exchange

52-week high	low	Index	Open	High	Low	Close	Chg	% Chg	Vol (100s)
9337.97	7161.15	DJ Industrials-T	7806.57	7976.76	7628.15	7899.52			16448
3686.02	2319.80	DJ Transport-T	2375.75	2469.55	2319.80	2429.52			129849
320.51	237.44	DJ Utilities-T	319.73	320.45	308.25	311.46			159111
2960.79	2358.51	DJ 65 Compos-T	2469.73	2521.90	2406.20	2484.70			305408
9337.97	7161.15	DJ Industrials-A	7734.74	7917.28	7666.51	7899.52	+167.61	+2.2	1000000
3686.02	2344.04	DJ Transport-A	2348.14	2436.03	2344.04	2429.52	+84.52	+3.6	129849
320.51	237.44	DJ Utilities-A	320.51	320.57	310.59	311.46	−9.05	−2.8	159111
2960.79	2358.51	DJ 65 Compos-A	2451.35	2488.48	2426.16	2484.70	+33.98	+1.4	1000000
107.02	103.89	Dow Jones Bon	106.11	106.19	106.11	106.19	−0.13	−0.1	
933.14	439.51	S&P 100	471.90	483.78	468.86	483.72	+11.88	+2.5	
380.67	275.93	S&P 400 MidCap	275.93	283.64	275.93	283.63	+7.70	+2.8	
1186.75	696.02	S&P 500	959.49	984.39	952.84	984.39	+24.95	+2.6	
147.69	95.45	S&P Financial	95.81	102.04	95.45	102.04	+6.24	+6.5	
1380.57	1024.17	S&P Industrials	1153.16	1178.24	1144.20	1177.84	+24.76	+2.1	
964.61	539.98	S&P Transport	540.20	560.39	539.98	559.93	+19.73	+3.6	
267.44	122.22	S&P Utilities	267.38	267.43	258.79	259.08	−8.30	−3.1	

New York

Index	High	Low	Close	Chg	% Chg
NYSE Composit	486.88	473.47	486.70	+9.50	+2.0
NYSE Financial	418.81	398.65	418.75	+19.56	+4.9
NYSE Industrial	605.79	589.00	605.58	+12.09	+2.0
NYSE Transport	365.48	351.13	365.29	+14.16	+4.0
NYSE Utilities	393.22	383.25	383.70	−9.46	−2.4

Nasdaq

Index	High	Low	Close	Chg	% Chg
Nasdaq comp	1493.54	1419.11	1492.49	+73.37	+5.2
NNM Composite	676.78	642.74	676.31	+33.56	+5.2
NNM Industrial	374.18	362.37	374.18	+13.00	+3.6

American

Index	High	Low	Close	Chg	% Chg
Amer Biotech	132.45	123.86	132.42	+8.56	+6.9
Amex Composi	574.86	563.18	574.73	+10.98	+1.9
Institutional	563.00	543.96	562.93	+14.04	+2.6
Japan Index	132.90	132.90	132.90	−1.77	−1.3
Major market	871.23	846.64	870.19	+13.86	+1.6
Oil and gas	439.81	429.85	438.53	+4.39	+1.0

Figure 25.2 (continued)

(c)

THIS WEEK IN NUMBERS

	This week	Last week	Change in a week	Change in a year
TSE 300	5481.84	5517.13	–0.6%	–22.9%
Best group: Mines & minerals	3072.32	2909.85	+5.6%	–33.2%
Worst group: Merchandising	4657.63	4920.56	–5.3%	–23.0%
Toronto 35	308.44	302.65	+1.9%	–15.8%
TSE 100	336.42	336.43	–0.0%	–20.3%
TSE 200	314.30	326.32	–3.7%	–32.6%
Dow Jones industrial average	7899.52	7784.69	+1.5%	–1.8%
Standard & Poor's 500	984.39	1002.60	–1.8%	+1.8%
Morgan Stanley world index ($U.S.)	914.03*	922.99†	–1.0%	–5.7%
–World ex U.S. and Canada (EAFE)	1147.86*	1114.62†	+3.0%	–10.6%
–Emerging Markets	244.06*	243.49†	+0.2%	–51.7%
DS Barra bond market index	316.36*	319.65†	–1.0%	+7.9%
Gold ($U.S. an ounce)	296.30	300.50	–1.4%	–9.9%

* preliminary numbers; † revised numbers

SOURCE: Reprinted with permission of *The Globe and Mail* (October 10, 1998).

age representation for investors, the financial press also reports prices for a selected sample of individual companies traded on 14 different overseas markets.[3]

On the international level, the indices produced by *Morgan Stanley Capital International* are also widely used for such purposes.[4] Each index is based on a valued-weighted portfolio of stocks (using total shares outstanding) in a particular country. Nearly all of these stocks can be purchased by foreigners. Values for each of the national indices (plus various industry indices for each country) are given in both the local currency and in US dollars based on exchange rates at the time. The stocks selected for each index are designed to represent about 60% of the aggregate market value of the particular country's equity markets.[5] A listing of the countries with the largest and most mature stock markets is presented in Table 25.1.

The individual country indices are combined into various regional indices. Furthermore, all of these indices are also used to compute a "World" index based on 23 countries with well-developed capital markets (see Table 25.1), an "Emerging Markets" index based on 26 countries, and an "All-Country World" index based on the combined 48 countries (Malaysia is in both the World and Emerging Markets indexes). These indices are formed using weights that are based on market capitalization, thus producing value-weighted indices. In addition, alternative versions of these indexes are calculated using gross domestic product (GDP) to form weights. Some countries with well-established stock markets but relatively small economies (such as the United Kingdom) have less weight in a GDP-weighted index than in a market capitalization-weighted index compared to countries with large economies but relatively smaller stock markets (such as Germany).

---

[3]For a discussion of European stock markets, see Gabriel Hawawini, *European Equity Markets: Price Behavior and Efficiency*, Monograph Series in Finance and Economics #1984–4/5, New York University Salomon Center, Leonard N. Stern School of Business. Also see Victor A. Canto, "Everything You Always Wanted to Know About the European Monetary System, the ECU and ERM, But Didn't Know Who to Ask," *Financial Analysts Journal* 47, no. 6 (November–December 1991): 22–25.

[4]For a discussion of the Morgan Stanley indices, see Campbell R. Harvey, "The World Price of Covariance Risk," *Journal of Finance* 46, no. 1 (March 1991): 111–157.

[5]For more on these and other indices, see Chapter 5 in Bruno Solnik, *International Investments* (Reading, MA: Addison-Wesley, 1991); and John Markese, "An Investor's Guide to the International Marketplace," *AAII Journal* 14, no. 7 (August 1992): 29–32.

Morgan Stanley also calculates the "Europe, Australia, Far East: (EAFE) index, which is widely used as a benchmark when evaluating the performance of international portfolio managers. The index excludes the United States, Canada, and South Africa and is currently based on the stock performance in the remaining 21 countries listed in Table 25.1. Three of the Morgan Stanley composite indices published weekly in *The Globe and Mail*, and shown in panel (c) of Figure 25.2, are The World Index, the EAFE, and the Emerging Markets Index.

Emerging Markets

In recent years several countries have instituted organized stock exchanges or highly active over-the-counter stock markets. In general, these countries have in common a relatively low (compared to Western countries) level of per capita gross domestic product, improved political and economic stability, a currency convertible into Western countries' currencies (or at least some means for foreigners to repatriate income and capital gains), and most important, securities available for investment by foreigners. Such countries have what are referred to as **emerging markets**.

Investments in emerging market stocks have proven attractive to a number of institutional investors, who in many cases have invested directly in those securities, or when that is not possible, through regional funds (such as a Latin American Fund; see Chapter 21). Because many emerging market economies are undergoing rapid growth, and because their stock markets are not highly developed and therefore are less efficient, there is considerable opportunity for relatively high returns from emerging market investments. However, there is also a relatively high level of risk involved.

Morgan Stanley Capital International defines 26 countries as emerging markets, and publishes stock market indices for each of these countries as well as various regional stock market indices and an overall emerging markets index.[6] Also popular are the International Financial Corporation (IFC) Emerging Market Indexes and the IFC Investable Indexes. The latter are based on stocks that can be held by foreigners, and hence are often the indices of choice for international investors.

Risk and Return from Foreign Investing

Investing in a foreign security involves all the risks associated with investing in a domestic security plus some additional ones. The investor expects to receive cash flows in the future from the foreign security. However, these cash flows will be in a foreign currency and thus will be of relatively little use to the investor if they cannot be converted into the investor's domestic currency. The additional risks associated with foreign investing result from uncertainties associated with converting these foreign cash flows into domestic currency. They are known as **political risk** and **exchange** (or currency) **risk**.[7]

Political risk refers to uncertainty about the *ability* of an investor to convert the foreign currency into domestic currency. Specifically, a foreign government might restrict, tax, or completely prohibit the exchange of one currency for another. Because such policies change from time to time, the ability of an investor to repatriate foreign cash flows may be subject

[6]For more on emerging markets, see Vihang Errunza, "Emerging Markets: A New Opportunity for Improving Global Portfolio Performance," *Financial Analysts Journal* 39, no. 5 (September–October 1983): 51–58; Vihang Errunza and Etienne Losq, "How Risky are Emerging Markets? Myths and Perceptions Versus Theory and Evidence," *Journal of Portfolio Management* 14, no. 1 (Fall 1987): 62–67; and Vihang Errunza and Prasad Padmanabhan, "Further Evidence on the Benefits of Portfolio Investments in Emerging Markets," *Financial Analysts Journal* 44, no. 4 (July–August 1988): 76–78.

[7]The effects these types of risk have on asset pricing has been considered by a number of people. For a discussion and list of references, see Chapter 1 and 5 in Solnik, *International Investments*.

Emerging Markets
Financial markets in countries that have a relatively low level of per capita gross domestic product, improved political and economic stability, a currency that is convertible into Western countries' currencies, and securities available for investment by foreigners.

Political Risk The uncertainty in the return on a foreign financial asset due to the possibility that the foreign government might take actions that are detrimental to the investor's financial interests.

Exchange Risk (Alternatively, **Currency Risk**.) The uncertainty in the return on a foreign financial asset due to unpredictability regarding the rate at which the foreign currency can be exchanged into the investor's own currency.

to some uncertainty. There may even be a possibility of complete expropriation, making political risk very large.

Exchange risk refers to uncertainty about the *rate* at which a foreign currency can be exchanged for the investor's domestic currency in the future. That is, at the time a foreign security is bought, the rate at which future foreign cash flows can be converted into domestic currency is uncertain, and it is this uncertainty that is known as exchange risk.

Managing Exchange Risk

To an extent, exchange risk can be reduced by hedging in the forward (or futures) market for foreign currency. In the case of default-free fixed-income securities, it may be possible to completely eliminate such risk in this way. For example, assume that a one-year pure discount bond paying 1000 British pounds at maturity can be purchased for 925 British pounds. Furthermore, assume that a forward contract can be signed where the investor will receive $2609.80 for delivering 1000 British pounds a year from now. In this situation, the rate of return *in British pounds* on this security is $(1000 - 925)/925 = 8.11\%$.

If the current (that is, spot) exchange rate were $2.6564 per pound, then the cost of this bond to a Canadian investor would be $925 \times \$2.6564 = \$2457.17$. Thus, the rate of return *in Canadian dollars* on this British security would be $(\$2609.8 - \$2457.17)/\$2457.17 = 6.21\%$. Except for political risk, this is a certain return, since exchange risk has been completely removed by hedging with a forward contract.

Unfortunately, it is not possible to hedge completely the exchange risk associated with risky investments. Forward contracts can be made to cover expected cash flows, but if the actual cash flows are larger or smaller than expected, then some of the foreign currency may have to be exchanged at the spot rate prevailing at the time that the cash is received. Since future spot rates usually cannot be predicted with complete certainty, this will affect overall risk. As a practical matter, this "unhedgeable" risk is likely to be small in cases involving fixed-income investments, but mat be large in the case of equities. Nevertheless, the cost of hedging foreign investments may exceed the benefit (see the *Institutional Issues* section, "Currency Risk: To Hedge or Not to Hedge").

It is important to differentiate between two very different approaches to managing exchange risk. The first approach is *passive currency management,* which involves a strategy of permanently controlling a portfolio's exposure to currency risk. For example, a foreign-stock manager may choose to use forward contracts to consistently remove half of the portfolio's currency exposure. While an attempt might be made initially to examine the effect such a strategy has on the portfolio's level of risk, afterwards all decisions with respect to currency management are mechanical. The second approach is *active currency management,* which involves a strategy of frequently changing currency exposures to take advantage of perceived short-run mispricings among currencies. In doing so, the effect of such a strategy on the portfolio's level of risk is constantly being taken into consideration.

Passive currency management requires the investor to set a policy concerning the desired level of exchange risk. This acceptable risk level is predicated on the investor's risk tolerance as well as the investor's assumptions about the long-run levels of volatilities and correlations of the currencies in the portfolio. Active currency management, on the other hand, involves moving away from the investor's normally desired levels of currency exposures. It assumes that currency markets are at times in disequilibrium. Further, it assumes that the investor can add value by appropriately altering the portfolio's currency exposures as the disequilibrium corrects or shifts.

Unfortunately, both currency management approaches have come to be know as "hedging." Yet only passive currency management is truly hedging in the sense of attempting to eliminate or reduce unwanted risk. Active currency management, like any other active management strategy, might very well add risk to a portfolio, not reduce it.

If an investor chooses to actively manage the currency exposure of diversified foreign portfolio, there are several ways of doing so. First, the investor could manage the currency exposures directly or hire a *currency specialist* to perform that function. Second, after deciding who is to manage these exposures, the investor must determine how integrated the currency management and security selection decisions are to be. At one extreme, the currency management and security selection decisions are made independently. In that case, if a currency specialist is used, that manager is often referred to as a *currency overlay* manager (that is, the currency management is *overlaid* on top of the foreign security portfolio). Here judgments on the amount and types of currency exposures to put in place are made without any consideration of which foreign securities are in the portfolio. It is this type of currency management that is not likely to result in reducing the risk of a portfolio. At the other extreme, the currency management and security selection decisions are made jointly, and hence do not involve the use of a currency manager. That is, decisions of which securities to purchase and how to manage the resulting currency exposures are made at the same time by one manager, keeping in mind how the two decisions impact each other. This type of currency management is likely to reduce the risk of a portfolio. A middle course involves making such decisions sequentially, where the foreign investor selects the portfolio of securities first and then a currency specialist chooses the make-up of the portfolio's currency exposures based on the securities selected. Not surprisingly, one study found that the best approach was the joint-decision approach, and that the least desirable one was where the decisions were made independently.[8]

Foreign and Domestic Returns

Changes in exchange rates can cause major differences between the returns obtained by domestic investors and the returns obtained by unhedged foreign investors.

Consider a Canadian investor and a Swiss investor, both of whom purchase shares of a Swiss company whose shares are traded only in Switzerland. Let the price of the shares in Swiss francs be P_0 at the beginning of a period and P_1 at the end of the period. The **domestic return**, denoted by r_d, is

Domestic Return The return on an investment in a foreign financial asset, excluding the impact of exchange rate changes.

$$r_d = \frac{P_1 - P_0}{P_0} \tag{25.1}$$

For example, if $P_0 = 10$ Swiss francs and $P_1 = 12$ Swiss francs, then $r_d = (12 - 10)/10 = 20\%$.

For the Swiss investor, r_d is the shares' return. Not so for the Canadian investor. Assume that at the beginning of the period the price (in dollars) of one Swiss franc is $1.1910. Denoting this exchange rate (that is, the exchange rate at the beginning of the period) by X_0, the cost of a share to the Canadian investor will be $X_0 P_0$. In the example, this cost will be $1.191 \times 10 = \$11.91$.

Now, assume that the exchange rate falls to $1.1701 per Swiss franc at the end of the period. Denoting this by X_1, the ending value of a share for the Canadian investor will be $X_1 P_1$. In the example, this value will be $1.1701 \times 12 = \$14.04$.

The **foreign return** (that is, the return to a foreign investor), denoted by r_f, is

Foreign Return The return on an investment in a foreign financial asset, including the impact of exchange rate changes.

$$r_f = \frac{X_1 P_1 - X_0 P_0}{X_0 P_0} \tag{25.2}$$

In the example, the foreign investor (a Canadian) would have earned a return of $r_f = (\$14.04 - \$11.91)/\$11.91 = 17.88\%$ on an investment in the Swiss firm's stock.

---

[8]See Philippe Jorion, "Mean/Variance Analysis of Currency Overlays," *Financial Analysts Journal* 50, no. 3 (May–June 1994): 48–56. The integration issue of managing a foreign portfolio's currency exposures and security holdings is essentially the same as the integration of security selection, asset allocation, and market timing decisions discussed in Chapter 23.

In effect, the Canadian has made *two* investments: (1) an investment in Swiss shares and (2) an investment in the Swiss franc. Accordingly, the overall return to the Canadian can be decomposed into a return on the investment in the Swiss shares and a return on an investment in the Swiss franc. This can be illustrated by considering a Canadian who had purchased a Swiss franc at the beginning of the period. If the Canadian subsequently sold the franc at the end of the period, the return on foreign currency, denoted by r_c, would be

$$r_c = \frac{X_1 - X_0}{X_0} \tag{25.3}$$

In the example, $r_c = (\$1.1701 - \$1.1910)/\$1.1910 = -1.75\%$.

From equations (25.1), (25.2), and (25.3), it can be shown that

$$1 + r_f = (1 + r_d)(1 + r_c) \tag{25.4}$$

which can be rewritten as

$$r_f = r_d + r_c + r_d r_c \tag{25.5}$$

In the example, equation (25.5) reveals that $r_f = .20 - .0175 + (.20 \times -.0175) = 17.9\%$.

The last term in this equation ($r_d r_c$) will generally be smaller than the two preceding ones, since it equals their product and both are generally less than 1.0. Thus, equation (25.5) can be restated as an approximation:

$$r_f \approx r_d + r_c \tag{25.6}$$

It can now be seen that the return on a foreign security (r_f) can be decomposed into two parts, representing the domestic return on the security (r_d) and the return on foreign currency (r_c). In the example, the precise value for r_f was shown earlier to be 17.88%; use of the approximation indicates its value to be equal to $.20 - .0175 = 18.25\%$. Thus, the approximation is in error by 0.37%, a relatively small amount.

Expected Returns

Equation (25.6) leads directly to the proposition that the expected return on a foreign security will approximately equal the expected domestic return plus the expected return on foreign currency:

$$\bar{r}_f \approx \bar{r}_d + \bar{r}_c \tag{25.7}$$

It might be tempting for an investor to purchase a foreign security that has a high expected return in its host country, $\bar{r}_d$, on the belief that this means the security will have a high expected return to the foreign investor, $\bar{r}_f$. However, equation (25.7) reveals this logic to be flawed. Just because a foreign security has a high value for $\bar{r}_d$ does not mean that it has a high value for $\bar{r}_f$, since $\bar{r}_c$ can be negative. This can be shown by considering the case of bonds.

The expected domestic returns of bonds in countries with high expected inflation rates will typically be high. However, a foreign investor in a country with a lower expected inflation rate should expect a *negative* return on foreign currency, as her currency can be expected to *appreciate* relative to that of the country with the higher expected inflation rate. Hence, in evaluating the expected return on the foreign security, there is good news (a high expected domestic return, $\bar{r}_d$) and bad news (a negative expected return on foreign currency, $\bar{r}_c$). On balance, the expected foreign return $\bar{r}_f$ might not be as exceptional as first thought when just $\bar{r}_d$ was considered. Indeed, if markets were completely integrated, it would be reasonable to expect the values of $\bar{r}_d$ and $\bar{r}_c$ to sum to an amount $\bar{r}_f$ that is equal to the expected return on an equivalent bond in the investor's own country. When government securities are involved, this is known as the **interest rate parity** (Chapter 20 also discussed interest rate parity).

As an example, assume an investor can buy either one-year Government of Canada

Interest Rate Parity An explanation for why spot and futures exchange rates differ. It asserts that such differences result from different interest rates in the two countries.

bonds that have a yield of 5% or similar one-year German government bonds that are at 7%, where both securities have no coupons before they mature. Both securities are free from default risk, call risk, and political risk. Interest rate parity states that the expected return from owning either security is the same. This is because, in the market's view, the German mark is expected to depreciate against the dollar so that at the end of the year, the 2% extra return a Canadian investor would earn from holding the German security will be exactly offset by a currency loss when it is exchanged for dollars. Applying equation (25.5) to this situation results in the following equation:

$$.05 = .07 + \bar{r}_C + 0.7\bar{r}_C$$

which has the solution: $\bar{r}_C = -1.87\%$ [or, using equation (25.6) as an approximation, -2%]. Accordingly, interest rate parity would say that the reason the German security has a 2% higher yield is because the mark is expected to fall by roughly 2%. Indeed, the one-year dollar-mark forward rate should be roughly 2% lower than the spot rate, meaning if the spot rate is \$0.96 per mark, then the one-year forward rate should be about \$.9420[$= .96 \times (1 - .0187)$] per mark. In sum, an investor should not expect to make more by investing in fixed-income securities of a country that has higher interest rates than in the investor's home country.

Columns (2) and (3) of Table 25.2 indicate what average excess returns (that is, returns over the London Interbank Offered Rate, an estimate of the risk-free rate) were for the stocks and bonds of six countries as well as the United States for the 200-month period ending August 1991. These averages were measured from the perspective of a US investor, and hence represent the historical average value of r_f. The table indicates that while the stock and bond averages for the six countries are very similar to the US averages, there are some notable differences among individual countries. For both stocks and bonds, the Canadian market had an average return that was much lower than the US average, while the UK and Japanese averages were notably higher.[9]

Foreign and Domestic Risks

Having seen in equation (25.7) that the expected return on a foreign security consists of two components, it is appropriate that the risk of the foreign security be evaluated next. As before, consider a Canadian investor and a Swiss investor who have purchased shares of a Swiss company. The domestic variance, denoted by σ_d^2, is the risk that the Swiss investor faces with respect to the Swiss shares. Correspondingly, the foreign variance, denoted by σ_f^2, is the risk that the Canadian investor faces with respect to the Swiss shares. Based on equation (25.6), it can be shown that the foreign variance consists of three components:

$$\sigma_f^2 = \sigma_d^2 + \sigma_c^2 + 2\rho_{dc}\sigma_d\sigma_c \tag{25.8}$$

where σ_c^2 is the variance associated with the currency return to a Canadian from investing in Swiss francs and later exchanging them for Canadian dollars, and ρ_{dc} is the correlation coefficient between the returns on the Swiss stock and the return on Swiss francs.

For example, assume that the domestic variance is 225 (meaning that the domestic standard deviation, σ_d, is $\sqrt{225} = 15\%$) and the currency variance is 25 (meaning the currency standard deviation, σ_c, is $\sqrt{25} = 5\%$). If $\rho_{dc} = 0$, then equation (25.8) indicates that the foreign variance is $225 + 25 = 250$. Accordingly, the foreign standard deviation is $\sqrt{250} = 15.8\%$, which is only slightly greater than the domestic standard deviation of 15%.

---

[9] In a study of monthly stock returns from February 1970 through May 1989 using the Morgan Stanley indices, it was found that the return on Japanese stocks was inexplicably high. See Harvey, "The World Price of Covariance Risk."

Table 25.2 Security Returns, January 1975–August 1991.*

(a) Excess Returns and Standard Deviations

Country (1)	Average Excess Returns		Standard Deviation	
	Stocks (2)	Bonds (3)	Stocks (4)	Bonds (5)
Australia	4.5%	−.8%	21.9%	5.5%
Canada	.9	−1.5	18.3	7.8
France	4.8	−.1	22.2	4.5
Germany	4.7	.9	18.3	4.5
Japan	7.3	2.1	17.8	6.5
UK	8.6	1.2	24.7	9.9
US	5.2	−.3	16.1	6.8
Average (ex. US)	5.1%	.3%	20.5%	6.4%
Average	5.1	.2	19.9	6.5

(b) Correlations with US Stocks and Bonds**

Country (1)	US Stocks with Foreign		US Bonds with Foreign	
	Stocks (2)	Bonds (3)	Stocks (4)	Bonds (5)
Australia	.48%	.24%	1.05%	.20%
Canada	.74	.31	.18	.82
France	.50	.21	.20	.31
Germany	.43	.23	.17	.50
Japan	.41	.12	.11	.28
UK	.58	.23	.12	.28
Average	.52%	.22%	.12%	.40%

*Results are given from US investor perspective and are in excess of the London Interbank Offered Rate (LIBOR).
**Correlation of US stocks with US bonds was .32.

SOURCE: Adapted from Fischer Black and Robert Litterman, "Global Portfolio Optimization," *Financial Analysts Journal* 48, no. 5 (September–October 1992): 30–31.

Equation (25.8) reveals that the smaller the correlation between returns on a foreign currency and returns on a foreign investment, the smaller will be the foreign variance.[10] One study that used data from 17 countries over the period from January 1971 through December 1980 found an average correlation of .034, which is effectively, zero.[11] Thus, it appears that the correlation is sufficiently small that the foreign variance typically will be near, but not less than, the sum of the domestic and currency variances.[12] However, it should be remembered that this is an *average figure*, and that there can be individual situ-

---

[10]The importance of accurately estimating the correlations between asset and currency returns in determining whether or not to hedge a portfolio is stressed in Victor S. Filatov and Peter Rappoport, "Is Complete Hedging Optimal for International Bond Portfolios?" *Financial Analysts Journal* 48, no. 4 (July–August 1992): 37–47.

[11]Bruno Solnik and Eric Nemeth, "Asset Returns and Currency Fluctuations: A Time Series Analysis," paper presented at the second tagung, Geld Banken und Versicherungen, Universitat Karlsruhe, December 1982.

[12]Since standard deviation is the square root of variance, this means that the foreign standard deviation will typically be substantially less than the sum of the domestic and currency standard deviations.

ations where the correlation is not approximately zero (such as the United States and Canada).

Columns (4) and (5) of Table 25.2 provide the standard deviations of the excess returns for six foreign countries along with the United States from the perspective of a US investor. Hence, it provides estimates of the value of σ_f for the 200-month period ending in August 1991. The six-country average standard deviation for both stocks and bonds is similar to the respective US values, with the United Kingdom having notably larger values for both stocks and bonds.

Table 25.3 provides evidence on the relative magnitudes of the three types of risk. Standard deviations of monthly values over the period from December 1970 through December 1980 are shown for domestic risk (corresponding to σ_d), currency risk (corresponding to σ_c), and foreign risk (corresponding to σ_f), where the latter two types of risk have been measured from the perspective of a US investor. The last column represents the ratio of foreign risk to domestic risk. Thus, a ratio greater than 1 can be taken as an indication that the risk to a US investor is greater than the risk to a domestic investor. Indeed,

Table 25.3	Risks for Domestic and US Investors Based on Historic Values, December 1970–December 1980.			
	Domestic Risk (1)	Currency Risk (2)	Foreign Risk (3)	Foreign Domestic Risk (4)
Stocks				
Australia	24.62%	9.15%	27.15%	1.10
Belgium	13.28	11.02	18.76	1.41
Canada	18.92	4.16	20.29	1.07
Denmark	15.41	10.28	17.65	1.15
France	22.00	10.24	25.81	1.17
Germany	13.87	11.87	18.39	1.33
Hong Kong	47.95	5.63	45.80	.96
Italy	24.21	8.58	26.15	1.08
Japan	16.39	10.42	19.55	1.19
Netherlands	16.37	10.97	18.91	1.16
Norway	28.61	8.89	29.92	1.05
Singapore	35.82	6.52	36.03	1.01
Spain	16.71	9.10	20.26	1.21
Sweden	15.05	8.89	18.06	1.20
Switzerland	16.80	14.67	21.40	1.27
United Kingdom	28.94	8.84	31.61	1.09
United States	16.00	.00	16.00	1.00
Bonds				
Canada	6.16	4.16	7.93	1.29
France	4.39	10.24	11.80	2.69
Germany	6.91	11.87	14.35	2.08
Japan	6.53	10.42	14.36	2.20
Netherlands	7.16	10.97	13.61	1.90
Switzerland	4.33	14.67	15.33	3.54
United Kingdom	12.30	8.84	16.29	1.32
United States	8.96	.00	8.96	1.00

SOURCE: Adapted from Bruno Solnik and Bernard Noetzlin, "Optimal International Asset Allocation," *Journal of Portfolio Management* 9, no. 1 (Fall 1982): 13.

Currency Risk: To Hedge or Not to Hedge

Investors in securities denominated in currencies other than those of their home country incur a risk not borne by their domestic investor counterparts: currency risk. For investors in foreign assets, currency risk is the variability in portfolio returns caused by fluctuations in the rate at which foreign currencies can be converted into their home currency. Whether investors in foreign securities should attempt to minimize currency risk in their portfolios has become a topic of considerable controversy in recent years. Among institutional investors, the issue has taken on increased importance as these investors have expanded their foreign investments.

As the text describes, the return on an investor's foreign portfolio can be divided into two components: a domestic (also called local) return and a currency (also called foreign exchange) return. Likewise, foreign portfolio risk can be decomposed into domestic risk, currency risk, and any possible interaction between the two. Most studies indicate that currency risk can increase total portfolio risk by anywhere from 15% to 100% of the underlying domestic risk.

Investors have a choice of whether to bear currency risk. Through a variety of techniques, currency risk can be "hedged" and almost eliminated. The most popular means of hedging currency risk is to purchase units of the investor's home currency in the forward market equal to the value of the foreign investment. For example, consider an investor holding 1000 shares of a Japanese company selling for 4000 yen per share. She can purchase dollars for delivery six months from today at a rate of 125 yen per dollar. The forward market is quite similar to the futures market—see Chapter 20. Both forward and futures contracts involve a promise to deliver something of value on a specified future date at a currently agreed-upon price. The forward market, however, does not involve a standardized contract traded on an organized exchange with a third-party clearinghouse that ensures that contracts are honoured. Moreover, forward contracts, unlike futures contracts, are not "marked to market" daily. By purchasing $32 000 for delivery six months from today to be paid for with 4 million yen, the investor insulates

herself from changes in the exchange rate between the yen and the dollar over the next six months.

Despite the availability of effective hedging tools, why do many investors in foreign securities choose not to hedge their currency risks and instead remain exposed to exchange rate fluctuations? Considered next are the primary arguments in support of and in opposition to currency risk hedging.

Proponents of hedging currency risk contend that a no-hedge policy violates one of the basic laws of modern portfolio theory: only accept risks for which adequate compensation is expected to be earned. They view currencies as having zero expected returns. That is, in a world in which capital is free to flow across borders, there is no reason to expect the value of foreign currencies to move systematically in one direction relative to an investor's home currency. However, exchange rates do fluctuate, generating additional risk for an investor in foreign securities. Proponents view currency risk as uncompensated and believe that risk-averse investors should seek to minimize it. Investors who do not hedge would seem to be passing up an opportunity to reduce portfolio risk while not diminishing portfolio returns. Proponents point out that the reduction in portfolio variability gained by hedging currency risk can be substantial.

Opponents of currency hedging generally concede that forgoing hedging means accepting additional uncompensated risks. (However, there is a school of thought that contends that currency risk should be systematically rewarded by the market.) Nevertheless, they believe that market "frictions" cause the costs of currency hedging to outweigh the risk reduction benefits. That is, significant expenses are likely to be incurred by an investor managing currency risk. Currency dealers must be compensated for facilitating hedging transactions. Custodian banks must be paid for recordkeeping. Investment managers charge fees for maintaining the hedge. Estimates of the total cost of hedging typically range from .25% to .50% per year of the value of the hedged assets, enough to convince opponents that currency risk hedging may not be cost-effective.

In addition, some hedging opponents have questioned the wisdom of hedging for an investor who spends a high percentage of her income on goods produced abroad. Suppose the value of foreign currencies declines relative to the investor's home currency (thereby negatively affecting the investor's foreign portfolio returns, other things being equal). The declining relative value of the foreign currencies also reduces the effective cost of foreign-produced goods to the investor. In a sense the investor's own consumption basket serves as a hedge against currency risk in her portfolio.

In the final analysis, an investor's optimal currency hedge will depend on a number of factors, including the following:

1. correlations between currencies,
2. correlations between domestic returns and currency returns,
3. the cost of hedging,
4. the portions of the investor's portfolio allocated to foreign securities,
5. the variability of foreign asset returns,
6. the variability of currency returns,
7. the investor's consumption basket,
8. the investor's level of risk aversion, and
9. the premium earned (if any) for holding foreign currencies.

These factors are difficult to quantify, making it hard to build a strong case for or against currency hedging. Moreover, as investors differ in both their financial circumstances and their beliefs about the characteristics of currencies and security markets, it is not surprising that everything from zero hedges to fully hedged positions is observed.

with the exception of Hong Kong stocks, all the ratios are greater than 1, suggesting that fluctuations in currency exchange rates increased the risk a US investor would have faced in buying foreign securities. While the exact values of these ratios have undoubtedly changed since the study was conducted, it still is likely that the conclusion—that exchange risk in general increases the risk to US investors from buying foreign securities—remains valid today.

The importance of currency risk can easily be exaggerated. Calculations such as those in Table 25.3 assume that investors purchase only domestic goods and services and thus convert all proceeds from foreign investments into their own currency before engaging in any spending for consumption purposes. But most people buy foreign goods and many buy foreign services as well (for example, as tourists). The cheaper another country's currency relative to one's own, the more attractive purchases of its goods and services will be. Other things being equal, it may make sense to invest more in countries whose products and scenery are admired, for the effective currency risk is likely to be smaller there than elsewhere.

The Implications for Canadian Investors

In a global perspective, Canadian markets are small (the equity market represents about 2.5% of global equity capitalization) and heavily concentrated in cyclical resource industries. International investment, therefore, offers Canadian investors an opportunity to increase return and reduce risk through extended diversification. A revealing study demonstrates the advantages of global diversification by examining the effects of adding foreign stocks to a diversified Canadian portfolio.[13] The S&P 500 and EAFE indices were used as

---

[13]Robert Auger and Denis Parisien, "The Risks and Rewards of Global Investing," *Canadian Investment Review* II, no. 1 (Spring 1989): 25–30.

proxies for two different kinds of diversified foreign portfolios. The study looked at the addition of these foreign portfolios (both hedged and unhedged) to a domestic portfolio. Hedging was accomplished by buying the appropriate forward contracts. Table 25.4 shows the correlation coefficients between the foreign portfolios (hedged and unhedged) and three classes of Canadian securities.

The correlations between the EAFE portfolios and the Canadian securities are much lower than the correlations between the S&P 500 and the Canadian securities, indicating that the EAFE provides useful diversification opportunities. Table 25.5 shows the risk and return relationships for all the investments considered.

The differences between the columns listed as unhedged and local in this table provide an indication of the degree of foreign exchange risk present. As can be seen, foreign exchange risk varies significantly in different time periods. The hedged EAFE portfolio provides the most attractive risk-return combination of any investment considered. Table 25.6 shows the results of implementing three optimal investment strategies based on different levels of risk tolerance.

All three of these portfolios outperform a portfolio consisting of 100% Canadian stocks. These optimal portfolios exclude US stocks as these do not provide as attractive diversification as does the EAFE index. A prospective investment strategy was also investigated in which an expected return was assigned to each asset class and the optimal portfolios reconstructed. The results were similar to those shown in Table 25.6. The authors report that, for a large institutional investor, hedging can be accomplished at a cost of 0.1 to 0.15% per annum of the value of the portfolio. They conclude that "Foreign investments have a natural place in Canadian investment portfolios, even in conservative ones. They permit an increase in stock exposure without any increase in risk."

Auger and Parisien's results suggest that there is a substantial degree of integration of Canadian and US stock markets. The empirical evidence is mixed. Jorion and Schwartz, using data from 1968 to 1982, concluded that there were sufficient rigidities in the financial system that the two markets were effectively segmented, even for interlisted stocks. A more recent study finds that the two markets show evidence of segmentation in the five-year period 1977 to 1982, but that there is strong evidence of integration in a later period, 1982 to 1986.[14]

Table 25.4	Correlation Coefficients for Domestic and Foreign Returns, 1973–1987.						
	TSE 300	Cdn. Paper	Cdn. Bonds	Hedged S&P 500	Unhedged S&P 500	Hedged EAFE	Unhedged EAFE
TSE 300	1.0	−0.2	0.2	0.7	0.7	0.5	0.4
Cdn. Paper		1.0	0.0	0.0	0.0	−0.1	−0.3
Cdn. Bonds			1.0	0.5	0.5	0.3	0.3
Hedged S&P 500				1.0	1.0	0.8	0.6
Unhedged S&P 500					1.0	0.8	0.6
Hedged EAFE						1.0	0.8
Unhedged EAFE							1.0

SOURCE: Robert Auger and Denis Parisien, "The Risks and Rewards of Global Investing," *Canadian Investment Review* II, no. 1 (Spring 1989): 27.

---

[14]P. Jorion and E. S. Schwartz, "Integration versus Segmentation in the Canadian Stock Market," *Journal of Finance* 41, no. 4 (Sept 1988): 897–914; U. R. Mittoo, "Additional Evidence on the Integration of the Canadian and US Stock Markets," Department of Accounting and Finance Working Paper, University of Manitoba, October 1991. Further evidence of the benefits of international diversification for Canadian investors is provided in Harry S. Marmer, "International Investing: A New Canadian Perspective," *Canadian Investment Review* IV, no. 1 (Spring 1991): 47–53.

Table 25.5 Domestic and Foreign Investments: Annualized Average Returns and Standard Deviations, 1973–1987.

Period	TSE 300	Unhedged EAFE	Local EAFE	Hedged EAFE	Unhedged S&P 500	Local S&P 500	Hedged S&P 500	Cdn. Paper	Cdn. Bonds
1973–1987									
Return	11.0	17.7	12.0	16.0	11.8	9.8	10.7	10.8	9.7
Std dev.	22.2	27.2	17.3	19.3	17.8	18.0	18.5	1.2	14.5
1973–1987									
Return	1.6	4.6	−0.2	0.2	1.7	−0.2	0.8	8.6	7.2
Std.dev.	12.4	21.6	18.0	19.5	18.8	18.2	19.2	1.7	8.5
1978–1982									
Return	18.3	14.5	13.8	20.8	16.8	14.0	14.5	14.0	8.1
Std. dev.	26.1	18.6	7.9	7.6	12.4	12.8	12.3	4.1	13.9
1983–1987									
Return	13.8	36.2	23.7	29.0	17.5	16.4	17.7	9.9	13.9
Std. dev.	20.4	27.1	11.6	12.4	14.4	15.5	16.0	1.5	14.9

SOURCE: Robert Auger and Denis Parisien, "The Risks and Rewards of Global Investing," *Canadian Investment Review* II, no. 1 (Spring 1989): 26.

International Listings

The common stocks of many firms are traded not only on the major stock exchange in their home country but also on an exchange in at least one foreign country. Therefore, foreign investors no longer have to engage in foreign currency transactions when buying and selling the firm's shares. It is also possible that foreign investors can escape certain taxes and regulations to which they would be subject if the security had been bought in the firm's home country.

As mentioned in Chapter 3, there are two ways in which foreign securities can be traded in the United States. Either shares are interlisted on two (or more) exchanges, one in the US and the other in the home market, or American depository receipts are used.

Table 25.6 Optimal Investment Strategies, 1973–1987.

Level of risk tolerance:	Lower	⟶	Higher
Portfolio weightings (%):			
Canadian paper	15	15	5
Bonds	45	35	35
TSE 300	25	25	25
Hedged S&P 500	0	0	0
Unhedged S&P 500	0	0	0
Hedged EAFE	15	25	18
Unhedged EAFE	0	0	17
Average rate of return (%)	11.2	11.8	12.6
Standard deviation	11.2	11.6	13.9

SOURCE: Robert Auger and Denis Parisien, "The Risks and Rewards of Global Investing," *Canadian Investment Review* II, no. 1 (Spring 1989): 28.

As of December 31, 1998 there were 228 Canadian issues representing 210 companies interlisted on US exchanges reported in the *TSE Monthly Review*. Of the 228 issues, 74 traded on the NYSE, 35 on the AMEX, 101 on NASDAQ, and 18 on unidentified exchanges. These stocks provide US investors with a direct and easy means of participating in the Canadian market, thereby achieving a degree of additional diversification. There are also 61 foreign firms listed on the TSE. Table 25.7 shows the number of firms listed from each country of origin. Access to international diversification through interlisted companies is, somewhat, limited for Canadian investors. A number of Canadian brokers, however, are represented on foreign exchanges and can trade there on their customers' behalf. For smaller investors a number of regional, international, and global funds are available from various financial institutions (see Chapter 21).

American Depository Receipts (ADRs) Financial assets issued by US banks that represent indirect ownership of a certain number of shares of a non-US firm. ADRs are held on deposit in a bank in the firm's home country.

Foreign securities can also be traded in the United States through **American depository receipts** (ADRs).[15] ADRs are financial assets that are issued by US banks and represent indirect ownership of a certain number of shares of a specific foreign firm that are held on deposit in a bank in the firm's home country. The advantage of ADRs over direct ownership is that the investor need not worry about the delivery of the share certificates or converting dividend payments from a foreign currency into dollars. The depository bank automatically does the conversion for the investor and also forwards all financial reports from the firm; the investor pays the bank a relatively small fee for these services. Typically non-Canadian firms utilize ADRs. For example, Mexican firms are traded in this manner in the United States—at year-end 1996, all 25 Mexican firms with their stock listed on the NYSE utilized ADRs.

Table 25.8 displays the extent of foreign stock listings in the United States at year-end 1996. As the table shows, about 900 foreign issues were listed on either the NYSE, AMEX, or NASDAQ, and nearly 45% of them were in the form of ADRs. Interestingly, the NYSE has nearly 70% of its foreign issues in the form of ADRs, whereas for NASDAQ the per-

Table 25.7	Foreign Issues Listed on the Toronto Stock Exchange, 1997.
Country of Origin	*Number of Listings*
Australia	5
Bahamas	3
Barbados	1
Bermuda	5
British Virgin Islands	3
British West Indies	5
French Guiana	1
Ghana	1
Greenland	1
Hong Kong	1
Japan	1
United Kingdom	4
United States	29
Venezuela	1
Total	61

---

[15]The London Stock Exchange began trading many of these ADRs simultaneously in August 1987, with prices being quoted in US dollars.

Table 25.8	Foreign Company Listings in the United States, Year-end 1996.		
	Number of	ADR Issuers	
	Issues	Number	Percent
NYSE	365	247	67.7%
AMEX	65	7	10.8
NASDAQ	460	142	30.9
Total	890	396	44.5

SOURCE: *The NASDAQ Stock Market 1997 Fact Book & Company Directory* (Washington, DC: National Association of Security Dealers, 1997): p. 28.

centage is about half of this amount, due in large part to the 101 Canadian firms that are traded on NASDAQ without the use of ADRs.

One study examined the diversification implications of investing in ADRs and found that such securities were of notable benefit to US investors.[16] Specifically, a sample of 45 ADRs was examined and compared with a sample of 45 US securities over the period from 1973 to 1983. Using an index based on all NYSE-listed stocks, the betas of the ADRs had an average value of .26, which was much lower than the average beta of 1.01 for the US securities. Furthermore, the correlation of the ADRs' returns with those of the NYSE market portfolio averaged .33, whereas US securities had a notably higher average correlation of .53.

Given these two observations, it is not surprising that portfolios formed from US securities and ADRs had much lower standard deviations than portfolios consisting of just US securities. For example, portfolios consisting of 10 US securities had an average monthly standard deviation of 5.50%, whereas a 10-security portfolio split evenly between US securities and ADRs had an average monthly standard deviation of 4.41%. Thus, in contrast to investing in multinationals, it seems that investing in ADRs brings significant risk reduction. ADRs offer Canadian investors a viable method for investing the shares of foreign companies since few of these are listed on Canadian exchanges.

The SEC currently requires that foreign firms prepare their financial statements using US generally accepted accounting principles (GAAP) if they want their shares or ADRs to be listed on a US exchange or on NASDAQ. There are two consequences of this requirement. First, many foreign firms have their shares and ADRs traded in the segment of the over-the-counter market that does not involve NASDAQ.[17] Second, many large and actively traded foreign firms have decided against listing their shares in the United States. This has caused US exchanges to fear that certain foreign exchanges that do not have such reporting requirements (particularly London) will become the financial centres of the world in the future. In response to the complaints of the exchanges, the SEC argues that this requirement is necessary to protect US investors and that it would be patently unfair to US firms if they had to meet such requirements but their foreign competitors did not

---

[16]Dennis T. Officer and J. Ronald Hoffmeister, "ADRs: A Substitute for the Real Thing?" *Journal of Portfolio Management* 13, no. 2 (Winter 1987): 61–65. See also Leonard Rosenthal, "An Empirical Test of the Efficiency of the ADR Market," *Journal of Banking and Finance* 7, no. 1 (March 1983): 17–29.

[17]An article published in 1993 stated that at that time there were 722 ADRs listed in the US over-the-counter market. (Large bid-ask spreads are commonplace for these thinly traded ADRs, thereby limiting the ability to invest profitably in them.) In comparison, at year-end 1993, there were 536 foreign companies (with 213 of them being ADRs) that had their shares listed on a US exchange. See Franklin R. Edwards, "Listing of Foreign Securities on US Exchanges," *Journal of Applied Corporate Finance* 5, no. 4 (Winter 1993): 28–36.

have to do so. One thing is certain—this conflict between the exchanges and the SEC will not go away.[18]

Correlations Between Markets

If all economies were tied together completely, stock markets in different countries would move together, and little advantage could be gained through international diversification. However this is not the case. Table 25.9 shows the correlations of returns on diversified portfolios of equities and bonds of various countries with the returns on indexes of Canadian equities and bonds. Two general conclusions can be drawn:

1. With the exception of the United States and Hong Kong, the correlations of foreign equities with Canadian equities are less than 0.7 and only four others are greater than 0.5.[19] These figures, taken along with the results shown in Table 25.5 that indicate that foreign equities can outperform the TSE 300, suggest that there are potential diversification advantages for Canadian equity investors.

2. With the exception of the United States, the correlations of foreign bonds with Canadian bonds are less than 0.3 and in five cases they are negative. These figures, taken along with the results shown in Table 25.2 that indicate that foreign bonds can outperform the Canadian bonds, suggest that there are potential diversification advantages for Canadian bond investors.

Further evidence of the potential advantages of international diversification for Canadian investors is given by the data presented in Table 25.10, which shows the correlation between the TSE 300 index and its major subindices with five important international equity markets. With the possible exception of the UK, all countries' correlations are extremely low.

The bottom line is that international diversification is beneficial. Earlier, Figure 7.10 in Chapter 7 showed how diversification in general reduces the total risk of a portfolio. Similarly, Figure 25.3 shows that internationally well-diversified portfolios will have lower levels of risk than those that are diversified just among domestic securities. Investors can either increase their expected return without increasing their risk or decrease their risk without decreasing their expected return by judiciously adding foreign securities to their portfolios.[20] Consequently, the efficient set of domestic securities, denoted *DD* in Figure 25.4, is dominated by the efficient set constructed from both domestic and foreign securities, denoted *FF*.

---

[18]Rule 144A (see Chapter 3), which permits the issuance of unregistered securities on a private placement basis, was intended in part to accommodate foreign issuers of stock that did not want to meet the SEC's financial reporting requirements. For more on the reporting requirements for foreign firms that want to have their securities traded in the US, see Frederick D. S. Choi, "Financial Reporting Requirements for Non-US Registrants: International Market Perspectives," *Financial Markets, Institutions & Instruments* 6, no. 5 (December 1997): 23–44.

[19]Another study of 349 stocks in 11 countries revealed an average intercountry correlation coefficient of .234 for the period from January 1973 to December 1983. See D. Chinhyung Cho, Cheol S. Eun, and Lemma W. Senbet, "International Arbitrage Pricing Theory: An Empirical Investigation," *Journal of Finance* 41, no. 2 (June 1986): 313–329. In addition, the correlations between emerging markets and the United States have historically been near zero; see the references given in footnote 6. For a multiperiod approach that indicates the benefits from international diversification, particularly for highly risk-averse investors, see Robert R. Grauer and Nils H. Hakansson, "Gains from International Diversification: 1968–85 Returns on Portfolios of Stocks and Bonds," *Journal of Finance* 42, no. 3 (July 1987): 721–739. Although the correlation between Canadian and foreign stock markets is frequently much less than one, the actual values are highly dependent on the time period studied.

[20]Unfortunately, a recent study has found that the benefits from international diversification are lessened just when these benefits are most needed by investors. Specifically, the low correlations between market returns appear to increase when markets become more volatile. See Patrick Odier and Bruno Solnik, "Lessons for International Asset Allocation," *Financial Analysts Journal* 49, no. 2 (March–April 1993): 63–77. Another study found that the diversification benefits from international investing were due more to the fact that different countries have unique sources causing their returns to vary than that they have different industrial structures. Hence, international diversification efforts should be aimed more at investing in different countries than in different industries. See Steven L. Heston and K. Geert Rouwenhorst, "Does Industrial Structure Explain the Benefits of International Diversification?" *Journal of Financial Economics* 36, no. 1 (August 1994): 3–27.

Table 25.9 — Correlations of Returns on Foreign Equity and Bond Portfolios with Returns on Canadian Equity and Bond Indices, 1960–1980.[a]

Country	Equities	Bonds
Austria	0.239	0.244
Belgium	0.623	0.159
Denmark	0.341	−0.010
France	0.441	0.010
Germany	−0.037	0.179
Italy	0.269	−0.225
Netherlands	0.554	0.211
Norway	0.469	n/a
Spain	0.260	−0.102
Sweden	0.312	0.264
Switzerland	0.350	0.037
Hong Kong	0.791	n/a
Japan	0.231	−0.172
Singapore	0.598	n/a
Australia	0.577	n/a
United States	0.710	0.632

[a]All figures are US dollar adjusted total returns.

SOURCE: Roger G. Ibbotson, Richard C. Carr and Anthony W. Robinson, "International Bond and Equity Portfolios," *Financial Analysis Journal* 38, no. 4 (July–August 1982): 61–83.

Table 25.10 — Co-movement of TSE Sub-indices and Foreign Markets. (R-Squared between returns, all in CDN$.)

	United Kingdom	Hong Kong	West Germany	Japan	France
Metals	0.25	0.13	0.00	0.11	0.23
Gold and precious metals	0.19	0.14	0.01	0.08	0.09
Oil and gas	0.18	0.19	0.00	0.02	0.03
Forest Products	0.51	0.10	0.01	0.28	0.42
Consumer	0.51	0.12	0.14	0.15	0.44
Steel	0.36	0.04	0.00	0.11	0.16
Real Estate	0.14	0.05	0.03	0.19	0.20
Transportation	0.28	0.17	0.00	0.12	0.16
Pipelines	0.01	0.07	0.05	0.04	0.00
Utilities	0.04	0.03	0.01	0.00	0.02
Communications	0.22	0.05	0.08	0.09	0.36
Retail	0.30	0.03	0.18	0.05	0.28
Banks	0.01	0.07	0.12	0.07	0.13
Financial	0.07	0.08	0.14	0.01	0.19
Management	0.20	0.19	0.04	0.20	0.32
TSE 300	0.44	0.20	0.05	0.08	0.28

SOURCE: Evan Schulman, "The 'Global Village' Securities Market: Will Canada be a Participant... or a Bystander?" *Canadian Investment Review* II, no. 2 (Fall 1989): 63.

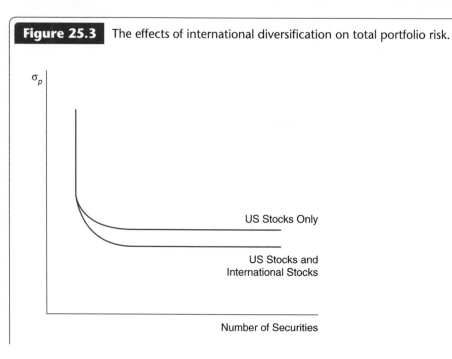

Figure 25.3 The effects of international diversification on total portfolio risk.

US Stocks Only

US Stocks and
International Stocks

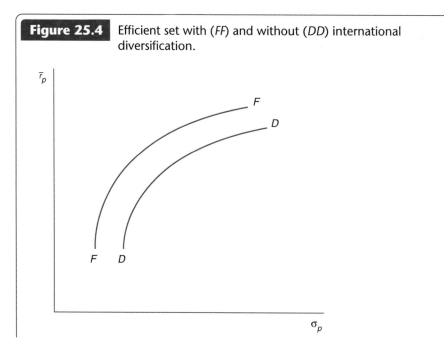

Figure 25.4 Efficient set with (*FF*) and without (*DD*) international diversification.

How Firms in the People's Republic of China Raise Funds

By Ann E. Sherman

Companies in the communist People's Republic of China (PRC) are very different from those of capitalist countries. Most large firms are State Owned Enterprises (SOEs), which traditionally had to return all reported "profits" to the government each year. On the other hand, any losses could be covered by "loans" from the state-owned banks. The loans did not have to be repaid, and were counted as profits by the firm. Accounting methods varied by industry, and the accounting records were prepared by the firm itself, without the help of an independent auditor. Any revenue shortfall for the enterprise would be offset by "loans," so that managers and employees would not lose anything because of low output, and they were not allowed to keep any of the profit from high output.

Reforming SOEs has been a top goal of the Chinese Communist Party since 1976. Many attempts have been made. In the early 1980s, managers were allowed some discretion and were allowed to keep part of any cost savings from greater efficiency. The cost savings could be used, for instance, to pay bonuses or to build better worker housing. In the mid-1980s, there was an attempt to make corporate taxes uniform across firms (at a rate of 55%). However, since managers had so much discretion in preparing accounting statements, they were easily able to avoid any taxable "profits." Beginning in 1987 target profit levels were set for each firm. Managers were allowed to keep any profits above the target. Managers were given much more discretion than before and can now do almost anything except fire workers or raise outside funds (except with permission, which was hard to obtain).

China has chosen to go very slowly in its reforms of SOEs, "groping for stones to cross the river." Although the government has resisted following outside examples, viewing its problems as uniquely Chinese, these problems were easily predictable by anyone with a basic knowledge of managerial incentives. In spite of the many reforms, managers of SOEs simply do not have an incentive to make companies profitable and efficient. They typically have no ownership stake, and their pay does not increase as corporate profits increase. One might guess that managing more efficiently would help them to keep their jobs, but in fact the truth is often the opposite. If a company is very profitable, then a Communist Party official may consider it easy to run and put a relative or a crony in charge. The manager of a troubled firm is less likely to lose his job, because it is less likely that someone else will want it.

Changes continue to be made, however. In 1992, the Communist Party adopted the goal of a "socialist market economy," although it insisted that state ownership was still the backbone of the economy and that the market system was a temporary stage in its communist evolution. In 1993, a new business model was established that should allow greater separation of ownership and control. It became possible to privatize some companies, giving the state limited liability (as a shareholder), although the state usually maintains majority control of the shares. In 1997, the move towards markets was continued. It was announced that roughly half (in terms of assets) of all state owned firms would be privatized. By the number of firms, most SOEs should be privatized in the next few years. However, the largest firms will remain untouched, at least for now. The reasons for privatization are: to raise funds for new investment; and to transform management by using markets both to allocate capital efficiently and to give companies the right incentives.

There are already several ways in which a PRC firm can raise funds. Joint ventures have become common, although they usually involve forming a new corporation. Thus joint ventures allow an SOE to raise funds through a subsidiary to take on a new project, but they are not methods for transforming existing SOEs. Another popular method has been a "back door listing" on the Hong Kong market. PRC firms have bought controlling interests in shell companies already listed on the Stock Exchange of Hong Kong (SEHK). The companies picked are usually small and thinly traded (and thus cheap to purchase). The PRC parent can then issue new shares or debt through the subsidiary in order to raise funds. Funds are transferred through the sale of assets from parent to subsidiary or vice-versa.

Back door listings are a relatively painless method of raising capital, since they do not require greater disclosure, reorganization or the translation of the parent firm's accounting into international or Hong Kong standards. For that reason, however, they also do not improve the efficiency of the corporation, plus they enable firms to transfer assets out of the PRC. Back door listings are known as red chips (a play on the term "blue chips," since the companies are from "red" or communist China). They typically sell at extremely low price/earnings ratios compared to other companies listed in Hong Kong, since investors are always hoping for future asset injections from the parent company.

Another way in which a PRC company can raise funds is through an A or B share listing on one of the country's two exchanges, in Shanghai or Shenzhen. For a PRC company to be listed on any exchange (local or foreign), it must first become a stock company, which is defined as an enterprise with legal person status that divides its capital into equal shares. Enterprises in areas such as national defense or strategic resources are not allowed to organize as stock companies, while enterprises in priority industries such as energy, transportation and communication can only become stock companies if the state still owns a majority of the shares. Equity in a stock company must be divided into four categories: state shares (purchased with state assets by government departments), legal person shares (held by a PRC "legal person," or corporation), individual shares (purchased by a PRC citizen) and foreign investment shares (purchased by foreigners). The first two categories are known as C shares and usually are not tradable. Shares held by PRC citizens and purchased in Reminbi (the Chinese currency) are called A shares, while shares held by foreign parties and denominated in US dollars are known as B shares.

The fact that each type of share has a separate legal status means that there is a potential for discrimination; state shares may be treated better than individual shares, or A shareholders may be favoured over B shareholders. Prices vary widely across the different share types, but it is virtually always true that B shares sell at a substantial discount to A shares. This reflects the fact that foreign investors have many choices, while PRC citizens have very few

investment choices. The stock markets are still small relative to the amount of savings of PRC investors, but the government is trying to speed up listings. As a result of the huge excess demand for investments in the PRC, prices of A shares have been bid well above the prices of B shares in the same firms. With B shares selling at a substantial discount, PRC investors found ways to purchase them, in spite of the fact that they are not legally allowed to do so. This bid the prices up above levels that foreign investors were comfortable with, and now the B share market is primarily dominated by PRC investors. Occasionally, PRC officials threaten to crack down on the holding of B shares by PRC citizens. When the market takes these threats seriously, the prices of B shares fall dramatically, which frightens regulators into backing off.

Listing standards for A or B shares on the Shanghai or Shenzhen exchanges are noticeably lower than for reputable foreign exchanges. For instance, B share firms have disclosed financial performance figures to analysts before revealing them to shareholders, failed to comply with disclosure obligations, failed to give adequate notice of shareholders' meetings, and failed to use funds in the manner specified in the prospectus. In direct contradiction to the plans outlined in prospectuses, a large portion of the funds raised so far have been used for property speculation.

A more prestigious funding choice for eligible firms is a foreign listing, for instance an H (Hong Kong) or N (New York) listing. H and N shares are Reminbi-denominated shares that may be purchased and traded in a foreign currency only by non-PRC residents. By June 1996, there were 226 A shares listed on the Shanghai Exchange and 155 A's listed on the Shenzhen Exchange, 40 B listings, 50 H listings, and 2 listings of N shares. Firms are also seeking to list on the Singapore, Taiwan, and Vancouver exchanges. However, there are many adjustments for PRC firms wanting to list on an outside exchange. One problem is that many SOEs have several operating units, and it is difficult to decide which should be included in the public company. For instance, PRC firms in the past have been responsible for providing housing, medical care, education and pensions to workers and their families. Thus they often provide and run hospitals, schools, dormitories, child care centres, and even recreational facilities, which do not generate revenues and are not normally part of, say, a steel-making company. Changing accounting standards is another major adjustment. For example, PRC accounting methods do not recognize "prudence concepts" such as making provisions for bad debt or writing off obsolescent inventory.

Finally, one of the biggest adjustments is in the attitude of managers towards shareholders. It is very difficult to convince PRC managers that they have obligations to shareholders, such as deploying funds in the way that they have promised. Of the first batch of H shares listed in Hong Kong in 1993, the most-respected was Tsingtao Brewery. In its prospectus, Tsingtao stated that it would use the proceeds of its offering to build new breweries and update equipment. When investors read the first annual report,

more than a year after the listing, they were shocked to learn that Tsingtao had simply lent out most of the proceeds to other PRC firms. Tsingtao calmly announced that it was planning a rights issue to raise even more funds from shareholders, since it still wanted to expand and update its breweries at some point. From the standpoint of the company managers, they were simply responding to profitable investment opportunities as they arose. The fact that investors wanted to invest in a brewery, rather than a bank, was of no concern to them. Although it was upsetting to investors to learn how their funds had been used, at least holders of H shares were able to find out where their money went. Issuers of A and B shares in the PRC are not required to tell investors how their funds have been used, and most firms choose not to make such disclosures.

Finding Trouble in the Footnotes

by Pauline Loong

Investing in Chinese securities is nor for the faint-hearted. Almost every year since H-shares started reporting, sharp-eyed analysts have found worrying pieces of news tucked away in footnotes to company announcements. Last year the problem was housing reform. This year, it would appear to be bank deposits.

Two H-shares—mainland Chinese firms that are listed but not based in Hong Kong—have had trouble retrieving fixed-term deposits from well-known Chinese banks and non-bank financial institutions. One H-share, Dongfang Electrical Machinery, was taking legal steps to recover its money while the other H-share, Maanshan Iron and Steel (Magang), was able to secure agreement for repayment from its financiers only after the central bank intervened.

The fact that Dongfang and Magang were unable to retrieve funds placed with mainland banks and financial institutions appeared in small print in the final results published by the two companies in late April. Dongfang is owed Rmb 156 million

($19 million) by the Chongqing branch of the Construction Bank. Interest income of Rmb 13 million on these deposits was booked to profits for 1997. In the case of Magang, which is owed Rmb 339 million, interest was not booked on the amount in its 1997 profit and loss statement but the company has made provisions for costs associated with getting the money back.

The big question for investors is whether this is the tip of the iceberg or whether Dongfang and Magang are isolated problems, Graham Ormerod, head of China research at Jardine Fleming, says: "It would be a big leap to assume from what may be an isolated incident that the whole system is shot through. Investors should not overreact."

As is so often the case with China's serious problems, the gap between on and off-the-record accounts is enormous. On the record, everyone is in denial mode. The Chinese central bank, the People's Bank of China, would say only that an investigation is being carried out. A spokeswoman told *Euromoney*: "We are looking into the situation. Chinese banks and financial institutions have no

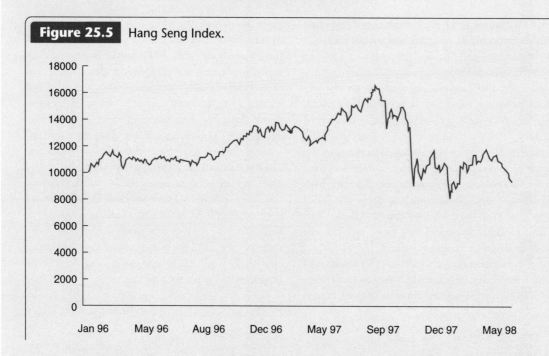

Figure 25.5 Hang Seng Index.

problems with repayment abilities. Speak to the Construction Bank."

The Construction Bank, which is being sued by Dongfang, declined to comment except to say: "There is no problem with our ability to repay." Earlier, the bank's Hong Kong branch had informed the Hong Kong Monetary Authority of its financial viability after an inquiry from the authority. The head of branch corporate affairs, Yao Li, said: "We are a large state-owned commercial bank with a sound track record. It is impossible for us to have repayment difficulties."

Dongfang, in turn, describes the pending court case with the Construction Bank as "a perfectly normal procedure for commercial disputes." It adds that it has no doubts about the Construction Bank's ability to repay as it is a state-owned bank. By suing, it is simply "exploring all avenues." A company spokesman based in the Chinese province of Sichuan says: "We do not rule out getting our money back soon." The other H-share, Magang, feels that it is inappropriate to talk to media as it also expects to be repaid soon. A Magang spokesman says: "We expect to be fully repaid in two or three months. As long as we get our money, we do not care to speculate why

the funds were not available earlier as stipulated in our agreement."

The message from on-the-record comments is that the incidents are just a storm in a teacup. But the impression from off-the-record briefings is that the authorities are concerned that the Chinese banking system may be perceived as being unpredictable. It is likely that the two creditors, who repeatedly affirm their faith in the system, will soon get their money back because Beijing does not want further adverse publicity.

But the story does not end there. What is particularly worrying is not only that the banks involved are local branches of well-known names, such as the Construction Bank. nor that some of the unnamed non-bank financial institutions involved are accredited by the central bank. Setting the alarm bells ringing is the practice of some H-share companies of lending money to banks on a fiduciary basis for high-risk high-return investments.

These deposits, known as trust deposits, offer a higher rate of return than ordinary fixed deposits. To get these returns, the bank and finance companies invest in riskier projects. It is a grey area whether the financial institutions are legally bound to repay the trust deposit if the third party fails to pay. Although it is illegal to offer rates above those sanctioned by the central bank, many financial institutions fight for deposits by ignoring Beiiing's directives and offering depositors higher interest rates. A mainland Chinese banker says that some institutions offer rates which are two to three percentage points higher than those for ordinary bank deposits. Others offer rates of as much as 15%.

The good news is that the exposure of H-shares to unreliable deposits is probably limited. A BNP Prime Peregrine survey showed that just four out of 41 H-share firms had deposited money with non-bank financial institutions held by parent companies. But it is not known how many firms had exposure to other financial institutions.

Expect the unexpected

H-shares have a habit of springing unpleasant surprises on investors. Tsingtao Brewery, the first H-share to list back in 1993, used the proceeds of its listing to lend to other companies in China at a high rate of interest. Its prospectus had indicated that funds would be used to develop Tsingtao's business. When the lending was made public, the beer com-

pany was pilloried by the financial press. Investors fled the counter as the price of its Hong Kong shares withered to around their offering price. Tsingtao executives were surprised at the change in investor sentiment. Their attitude was: why should investors care about how we use the funds as long as profit is booked at the end of the day?

In 1996, Shanghai Hai Xing Shipping Company reported a 90% drop in net profit for the previous year. Fund managers were not forewarned. Many complained that the company had given no inkling of the tough operating environment that led to the drop in profits.

That same year, another H-share provided a nasty shock to investors in its earnings statement. Chengdu Telecommunications Cable Co had led the market to believe that it would be able to secure a contract estimated to be worth $1.87 million. It was not until its earnings statement was made public that investors realized that the company did not get the deal.

On top of that, it sold staff quarters to workers at favourable prices. This was in response to the government's housing reform program. Again, investors first heard of the development in the company's earnings statement. The company recorded a short-

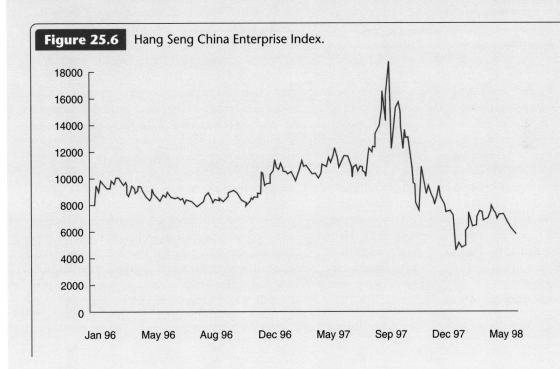

Figure 25.6 Hang Seng China Enterprise Index.

fall of Rmb 49 million, which it classified as other assets pending clarification by the authorities. The shortfall was the difference between sales proceeds and the property's book value.

Chengdu Cable turned out to be the first to report its involvement in housing reform. It was not until two years down the road that other H-shares confirmed that they too were affected. Analysts say that the extent of the disclosure varied greatly and so did the accounting treatment so that it was difficult to ascertain how much the reforms affected the companies concerned. For example, eight H-shares confirmed that they were transferring quarters to employees during the reorganization. But it was unclear whether they were building new quarters and, if so, whether these would be sold with losses. Some had written off the losses immediately upon disposal. Some had deferred and would amortize the losses over the average remaining service lives of relevant employees. Still others planned to sell the quarters in the future but failed to mention any intended accounting treatment.

Alden Leung, a technical principal at the accounting firm Ernst & Young, says: "Significant losses must be announced as soon as they are known, not left until the year-end result announcements." When the scandal first broke, he urged the accounting profession and the regulators to seek a consensus on accounting treatment for staff quarter disposal and, in particular, the different criteria for writing off and deferring the losses. He said: "[There should be] disclosure requirements which, at a minimum, include the book value of the companies' staff quarters, the cost of quarters now being built, policy on disposal, amount of losses and potential losses, and accounting treatments thereon."

One analyst points out that top executives in H-share companies tend to be government officials and are used to reporting to the Chinese government but are unused to making disclosures to shareholders. But he adds that things are getting better. He estimates that about 70% of H-share companies now talk regularly to analysts. Shanghai Petrochemical, for example, has a Hong Kong office to take care of investor relations.

Alex Tang, research director at brokerage Core Pacific-Yamaichi, says: "H-shares require regular monitoring. But we need access to the top management who know what is going on in the company. All too often, analysts are able only to see public relations executives or middle management. They can't alert us to problems."

Tang advises investors to focus on power plant projects, such as Beijing Datang and Huaneng Power. He says that they are more transparent than other firms and it's easier for analysts to access top management. He also believes that expressway projects—such as Anhui Expressway, Jiangsu Expressway, Shenzhen Expressway, and Sichuan Expressway are good stock picks as they have high-quality earnings.

H-shares account for only 4% of the Hong Kong stockmarket. It is a small and illiquid part of the market, say analysts, and it doesn't take too much money to set share prices moving. Moreover, H-shares are high beta stocks. This means that when the market is on the upswing, H-shares do better than other counters. But equally, when the market is down, these shares fall substantially. In the middle of last year, H-shares had a fantastic run on the back of rumours of mergers and acquisitions. The H-share index soared more than 50% in the six weeks following the handover of Hong Kong to Chinese rule in July. Turnover touched a high of HK$4.2 billion (US$540 million) in August last year.

But the fervour was not sustained. As Hong Kong came under the onslaught of the Asian financial crisis, prices of H-shares tumbled. Turnover shrank to a low of HK$211 million in January this year. The National People's Congress, China's legislature, met in March amid the market's hope that there would be positive news on the restructuring of state-owned enterprises to boost flagging H-share prices. But the reforms that were announced, while positive in the long term, did not help sentiment in the short term. Investors worried about potential social unrest resulting from an expected increase in unemployment as well as the overall health of the Chinese financial system which has to cope with the non-performing loans of state-owned enterprises.

Jardine Fleming's Ormerod says: "We have a neutral weighting on the H-shares." The next reporting season for H-shares is in August but the market is not expecting much in the way of good news then. All eyes are on the June visit to China by US president Bill Clinton. The signs are that China will try to wrestle some concessions from the US for not devaluating the renminbi. Devaluation will come back on the agenda if the concessions do not open the door to a sufficient expansion of Chinese exports to make up for the trade lost to Asian rivals who have devalued. Although premier Zhu Rongji has promised there will not be a devaluation, it is not an open-ended commitment. Investors will be watching the summit closely for the impact on H-shares.

Source: Pauline Loong, "Finding Trouble in the Footnotes," *Euromoney* (June 1998): 227–228.

Summary

Ernst and Young
www.ey.com

1. Investing in a foreign security involves all the risks associated with investing in a domestic security, plus political and exchange (currency) risks associated with converting foreign cash flows into domestic currency.
2. The return on a foreign security can be decomposed into a domestic return and a return on the currency in which the security is denominated.
3. Passive currency management refers to the process of controlling a portfolio's exposure to exchange risk on a long-term policy basis. Active currency management refers to the process of altering a portfolio's exposure to foreign currencies based on a near-term forecast of relative valuations among currencies.
4. Due to interest rate parity, the expected return from owning government securities of either one of two countries is the same, provided they are both free from political risk.
5. The standard deviation of return on a foreign security is a function of the security's domestic return standard deviation, the foreign currency return standard deviation, and the correlation between the two returns.
6. Exchange risk can be reduced by hedging in the forward or futures market for foreign currency.
7. Interlisted securities and ADRs offer significant diversification opportunities for Canadian investors.
8. Purchasing domestic and foreign securities typically results in an efficient frontier whose portfolios have more favourable risks and returns that those associated with the efficient frontier resulting from purchasing just domestic securities.

APPENDIX A

TANGIBLE ASSETS

In the first half of the 1970s, marketable securities such as stocks and bonds provided returns that were relatively disappointing, especially after adjusting for inflation. And, as shown in Chapter 12, neither bonds nor stocks have served as good hedges against unanticipated inflation in recent years. Overall, tangible assets have been better hedges against inflation. One example, real estate, was shown in Chapter 12 to have been an attractive inflation hedge in some years.[21] Other examples, such as collectible assets and precious metals (like gold and silver), provide various degrees of protection against inflation.

Collectible Assets

Not surprisingly, disenchantment with returns on marketable securities has led some investors to examine a host of tangible assets that are normally considered only by collectors. Table 25.11 shows the average returns over three five-year periods for several different kinds of collectible assets (often simply referred to as *collectibles*).

Some of the returns shown in the table are quite high. However, none of the collectible assets provided consistently high results over all three periods. This is not surprising because if one (or more) had provided consistently high returns, many investors would have been attracted to it and bid its price up to a level where high returns would no longer have been possible. Indeed, more recent studies of prints and paintings have concluded that their risk and return characteristics make them relatively unattractive investments for risk-averse investors.[22]

In a sense, a collectible asset often provides income to the owner in the form of consumption. For example, an investor can admire a Rembrandt, sit on a Chippendale, play a Stradivarius, and drive a Morgan. Value received in this manner is not subject to income taxation and is thus likely to be especially attractive for those in high tax brackets. However, the value of such consumption depends strongly on one's preferences.

If markets are efficient, collectible assets will be priced so those who enjoy them most will find it desirable to hold them in greater-than-market-value proportions, whereas those who enjoy them least will find it desirable to hold them in less-than-market-value proportions (and, in many cases, not at all).

Institutional funds and investment pools have been organized to hold paintings, stamps, coins, and other collectible assets. Such arrangements are subject to serious question if they involve locking such objects in vaults where they cannot be seen by those who derive pleasure from this sort of consumption. On the other hand, if the items are rented to others, the only loss may be that associated with the transfer of a portion of the consumption value to the government in the form of a tax on income.

Table 25.11	Annual Returns on Collectible Assets, Five-year Periods Ending June 1.		
	1969–1974	*1974–1979*	*1979–1984*
Chinese ceramics	31.1%	−3.1%	15.7%
Coins	9.5	32.4	11.3
Diamonds	11.6	13.6	6.1
Old masters	7.3	17.3	1.5
US stamps	14.1	24.9	9.8

SOURCE: Based on data in R. S. Salomon, Jr., and Mallory J. Lennox, "Financial Assets—A Temporary Setback," *Stock Research Investment Policy*, Salomon Brothers, Inc., June 8, 1984.

---

[21]While not a tangible asset, commodity futures were shown in Chapter 20 to have also been an attractive inflation hedge.

[22]See James E. Pesando, "Art as an Investment: The Market for Modern Prints," *American Economic Review* 83, no. 5 (December 1993): 1075–1089. See also William N. Goetzmann, "Accounting for Taste: Art and the Financial Markets Over Three Centuries," *American Economic Review* 83, no. 5 (December 1993): 1370–1376.

Investors in collectibles should be aware of two types of risk that are especially notable. The first is that the bid-ask spread is often very large. Thus, an investor must see a large price increase just to recoup the spread and break even. The second is that collectibles are subject to fads. (This risk has been referred to as stylistic risk.)[23] For example, Chinese ceramics may be actively sought by many investors today, leading to high prices and big returns for earlier purchasers. However, they may fall out of favour later on and plunge in value. Unlike financial assets, there is no such thing as a fair value for collectibles that can act as a kind of anchor for the market price.

Gold

In the United States, private holdings of gold bullion were illegal before the 1970s. There have been no Canadian restrictions on private holdings of gold since the end of World War II. In other countries, investment in gold has long been a tradition. According to one estimate, at the end of 1984 gold represented over 6% of the world market wealth portfolio.[24]

Table 25.12 contrasts a US investor's returns from gold with the returns from US equities over the period from 1960 through 1984. Gold is clearly a risky investment, but in this period, at least, it also provided high average returns. For any single investment, risk and return are only parts of the story: correlations of an asset's return with the returns on other assets are also relevant. In the period covered in Table 25.12, gold price changes were slightly negatively correlated with stock returns. Similar results have been obtained for other periods. Gold thus appears to be an effective diversifying asset for an equity investor. Table 25.12 also shows that gold prices were highly correlated with the rate of inflation in the United States, as measured by changes in the Consumer Price Index.

This is consistent with gold's traditional role as a hedge against inflation, since higher inflation generally brings higher gold prices. It should be noted, however, that an international study that examined the inflation hedging properties of gold for investors in six countries—Canada, Germany, Japan, Switzerland, UK, and US—demonstrated that only for US investors was it an effective vehicle.[25]

Investors interested in gold need not restrict themselves to bullion. Other possibilities range from stocks of gold mining companies to gold futures to gold coins and commemoratives. Furthermore, there are other types of precious metals, such as silver and platinum, that investors may want to consider.

Table 25.12	Characteristics of Gold and US Equity Returns, 1960–1984.	
	Average Annual Return	Standard Deviation of Annual Return
US equities	10.20%	16.89%
Gold	12.62	29.87
Correlation: Gold and US equities	−.09	
Gold and inflation	.63	

SOURCE: Adapted from Roger G. Ibbotson, Laurence B. Siegel, and Kathryn S. Love, "World Wealth: Market Values and Returns," *Journal of Portfolio Management* 12, no. 1 (Fall 1985): 17, 21.

---

[23]The term *stylistic risk* was coined by William N. Goetzmann in "Accounting for Taste," p. 1371.

[24]Ibbotson, Siegel, and Love, "World Wealth: Market Values and Returns," p. 9.

[25]J. Chua and R. S. Woodward, "Gold as an Inflation Hedge: A Comparative Study of Six Major Industrial Countries," *Journal of Business Finance and Accounting* 9, no. 2 (March 1982): 191–197. For a view against investing in gold, see James B. Cloonan, "Goodbye Gold: It's Now Just Another Commodity," *AAII Journal* 14, no. 9 (October 1992): 25–25.

Alternative Investments

Institutional investors have long acknowledged the wisdom of holding well-diversified portfolios. For many years, however, they focused their investments almost exclusively on Canadian common stocks, bonds, and short-term securities. The spectrum of investable asset categories extends well beyond these three (for example, see the discussion of the world capital market portfolio in this chapter). Thus, for a considerable time institutional investors overlooked fertile opportunities to reduce their portfolios' risks and perhaps even enhance returns as well.

That myopia receded in the 1980s. Institutional investors began to take significant positions in international stocks and bonds. Furthermore, they made sizeable commitments to a variety of asset categories commonly grouped under the rubric *alternative investments*.

Although there is no precise definition of the term, in practice institutional investors consider alternative investments to be virtually any type of asset not actively traded in the public markets. In terms of their relative importance in institutional investors' portfolios, the most prominent types of alternative investments are:

- *Venture capital*, which involves investments in young companies, ranging from start-up firms to developed businesses preparing to initially offer their stock in the public market.
- *Resource investments*, which involve primarily holdings of properties producing or expected to produce crude oil and natural gas. In recent years, timber properties have gained in relative importance as a resource investment.
- *Leveraged buy-outs*, which involve acquisitions of existing companies using large amounts of debt and little equity to finance the deal. Typically, these companies are restructured, with various divisions sold off to retire debt and other divisions consolidated or otherwise altered to improve efficiency for later reissuance of equity in the public market.
- *Real estate*, which involves investments in income-producing physical structures, including retail shopping centres, office buildings, apartments, and commercial warehouses.

Each type of alternative investment exhibits its own distinct risk and return characteristics. As a result, treating them as one monolithic category leads to faulty analysis. Yet each of these asset types has several similar features:

- Illiquidity
- Difficulty in determining current market values
- Limited historical return and risk data
- Extensive investment analysis required.

The primary distinguishing characteristic of alternative investments is their illiquidity. Institutional investors typically participate in alternative investments through a limited partnership structure (although sometimes direct investments are made with the issuing entity). In a limited partnership, a general partner (or partners) negotiates a deal with the issuing entity. The general partner then solicits limited partners to provide the financing for the deal. The general partners exercise complete control over the investment, while limited partners absorb the risk of failure and share any profits with the general partners.

With rare exceptions, limited partnerships are not registered with the Ontario Securities Commission. Thus, the limited partners cannot freely trade their ownership interests in the public market. Some secondary markets for limited partnership exist but trading is thin. Essentially, institutional investors participating in alternative investments must be prepared to hold those investments until they expire.

For similar reasons, little pricing data is available for alternative investments. General partners periodically (at most quarterly, often annually) supply estimates for a partnership's current market value. Limited partners, however, have few practical means of independently verifying those prices.

Because of the relative newness of alternative investments and the paucity of market prices, virtually no historical return and risk data on these investments is available. Such questions as, "How can the standard deviation of my existing portfolio be expected to change if I place 10% of my funds in venture capital?" are essentially unanswerable. Thus, when making portfolio allocation decisions, institutional investors must rely on highly subjective estimates of alternative investments' expected returns, standard deviations, and correlations with other asset categories.

Finally, alternative investments require considerable analysis on the part of institutional investors. Information on potential investments is not readily available. Investors must carefully study partnership agreements, consider the management fees and other operating costs, and investigate the capabilities of the general partners. Unlike common stocks and bonds, investors cannot rely on the market to provide efficient pricing. Although these less efficient markets present many potential pitfalls, conversely they offer the opportunity for relatively high returns.

Each of the alternative investment categories described previously has seen dramatic highs and lows over the last 20 years. For all these categories, the high-water marks of performance were attained in the late 1970s and early 1980s, followed soon after by disappointing results. Venture capital returns declined in the poor market for small capitalization stocks in the mid and late 1980s. Real estate suffered staggering losses in the late 1980s. Oil and gas prices plummeted in the mid-1980s and have yet to rebound significantly. By the early 1990s, leveraged buy-out deals had fallen in terms of the volume and profitability after the most obvious targets were purchased in the 1980s. The mid- and late 1990s, on the other hand, have been much kinder to alternatives investments of all types. For venture capital and leveraged buy-out deals, returns have attained or surpassed their 1980s high-water marks. Real estate returns have been more subdued, but have rebounded to double-digit levels. Resource investment returns have at least stabilized.

What the near future holds for alternative investment returns as always is unclear. Nevertheless, the diversification argument seems to have remained intact. Bearing in mind the questionable quality of much alternative investment pricing data, over the last two decades, returns have apparently exhibited low or even negative correlations with those of the stock and bond markets. Those features combined with seemingly attractive long-run return prospects would argue for the inclusion of alternative investments in most institutional investor's portfolios.

QUESTIONS AND PROBLEMS

1. What types of political risks are relevant only for foreign investors? What types are relevant for both foreign and domestic investors? To what extent and in what manner would you expect the current prices of securities in a particular country to reflect these types of political risk?

2. Using a recent *Globe and Mail*, find the exchange rate between German marks, British pounds, and Canadian dollars. Lloyd Luttrell, a British citizen, is planning a trip to Germany and has budgeted expenses of 30 pounds per day. At current exchange rates, into how many dollars and marks does 30 pounds translate?

3. Why would an investor wish to hedge the currency risk in a portfolio of foreign securities? What considerations are relevant to making the decision whether to hedge?

4. Andrew Jolly is a Canadian investor who has the opportunity to convert $1 into 76 Japanese yen and 1.07 German deutchmarks. Given this information, into how may yen should Andrew be able to convert one deutschmark?

5. How might a US citizen or company use currency futures to hedge against exchange-rate risk? How would a Canadian citizen proceed in the same situation?

6. Willy McAvoy, a Canadian citizen, holds a portfolio of French common stocks. Last year the portfolio produced an 8% return, denominated in French francs. Over that year the franc appreciated 20% against the Canadian dollar. What was Willy's return measure in Canadian dollars?

7. Terry Speaker bought a Japanese stock one year ago when it sold for 280 yen per share and the exchange rate was $0.008 per yen. The stock now sells for 350 yen and the exchange rate is $0.010 per yen. The stock paid no dividends over the year. What was Terry's rate of return on this stock? What would be the rate of return on the stock to a Japanese investor?

8. John Stewart, a Canadian investor, owns a portfolio of Argentine securities that earned a return of 14.0% last year, measured in Canadian dollars. If the portfolio also earned 19.7% measured in Argentine pesos, what must have been the currency return in John's portfolio?

9. Why is international diversification attractive to an investor who already has a well-diversified portfolio?

10. Owen Carroll owns a portfolio composed of Canadian stocks and bonds. Interested in further diversifying the portfolio, Owen decides to add investments in US common stocks. Owen's broker, Dick Castleman, voices the opinion that the US securities would not be particularly effective risk-reducing investments. Discuss the logic behind Dick's opinion.

11. Patsy Veach, a Canadian citizen, estimates that a diversified portfolio of German common stocks has a standard deviation of 24%. Patsy also estimates that the standard deviation of the Canadian and German currency return is 7%. Finally, Patsy estimates the correlation between the dollar-mark currency return and the German stock market return to be 0.20. Given this information, what should Patsy conclude is the standard deviation for a Canadian investor investing solely in the German stock market?

12. When a Canadian citizen is attempting to estimate the expected return and standard deviation for a foreign security, what factors, in addition to those recognized in domestic security analysis, should he consider?

13. Why is it the case that a foreign security with a high expected *domestic* return relative to what an investor could earn in his home country does not necessarily have a high expected *foreign* return for that inveator?

14. Assume that the one-year Canadian risk-free rate is 6%. Mike Gibson, an investor knowledgable concerning the implications of interest rate parity, expects the UK pound to appreciate by 3% next year relative to the Canadian dollar. What does that expectation imply about the current one-year UK risk-free rate?

15. Lin Liu, a Canadian citizen, is considering investing in both Canadian and Zanistan common stock index funds. Lin estimates the following market characteristics:

Cdn. market expected return	20%
Cdn. market standard deviation	18%
Zanistan market expected return	30%
Zanistan market standard deviation	30%
Cdn.-Zanistan expected currency return	0%
Cdn.-Zanistan currency return standard deviation	10%
Zanistan domestic return and Cdn.-Zanistan currency return correlation	0.15

Further, Lin estimates that the Canadian and Zanistan markets are uncorrelated, as is the Canadian market return (or the Zanistan market return) and the Canadian-Zanistan currency exchange rate. Given that Lin is planning to hold a portfolio 60% invested in the Canadian index fund and 40% invested in the Zanistan index fund, what is the expected return and standard deviation of Lin's portfolio?

16. Eva Langevin wants the diversification benefits of international investments but does not want to own foreign securities directly. Would investing in domestically headquartered multinational corporations and ADRs be effective substitutes for Eva? Explain.

17. Discuss why mutual funds are a particularly cost-effective means for small investors to own foreign securities.

18. Is a low correlation between the price movements of two countries' market indices a sufficient condition to ensure that a portfolio containing securities of both countries dominates a portfolio containing only domestic securities?

19. What practical difficulties prevent collectible assets from playing a major role in most investors' portfolios?

CFA Exam Questions

20. Robert Devlin and Neil Parish are portfolio managers at the Broward Investment Group. At their regular Monday strategy meeting, the topic of adding international bonds to one of their portfolios came up. The portfolio, a pension account for a US client, was currently 90% invested in US Treasury bonds, and 10% invested in 10-year Canadian government bonds. Devlin suggested buying a position in 10-year German government bonds, while Parish argued for a position in 10-year Australian government bonds.

    a. Briefly discuss the three major issues that Devlin and Parish should address in their analysis of the return prospects for German and Australian bonds relative to those of US bonds.

    Having made no changes to the original portfolio, Devlin and Parish hold a subsequent strategy meeting and decide to add positions in the government bonds of Japan, United Kingdom, France, Germany, and Australia.

    b. Identify and discuss two reasons for adding a broader mix of international bonds to the pension portfolio.

21. Advisor 1: "A currency cannot consistently appreciate or depreciate relative to an investor's local currency, since some local or global economic adjustment must eventually redress the currency change. Therefore, having currency exposure in a portfolio increases risk but does not increase long-term expected returns. Since you are not compensated for taking currency risk, you should always hedge a portfolio's currency exposure back to your local currency."

    Advisor 2: "I completely disagree, except as to the implication that economic changes are related to currency changes. Because economic changes affect international stocks, bonds, and currencies, as well as domestic stocks and bonds in ways that often offset each other, currency exposure improves diversification in a portfolio. Portfolios should never hedge their currency exposures; otherwise, they would be less diversified."

    Advisor 1 Rebuttal: "I have evidence which would appear to refute your claim of improved diversification resulting from currency exposure. My studies of hedged and unhedged international bond portfolios show very little difference between either their risks or returns over the past 10 years."

    Evaluate the strengths and weaknesses of each of the two approaches presented above. Recommend and justify an alternative currency strategy that draws from the strengths of each approach and corrects their weaknesses.

emerging markets (p. 881)
political risk (p. 881)
exchange risk (p. 881)
domestic return (p. 883)

foreign return (p. 883)
interest rate parity (p. 884)
American depository receipts (ADRs)
(p. 892)

REFERENCES
· ·

1. Two books devoted to understanding international financial markets and investing are:

Bruno Solnik, *International Investments* (Reading, MA: Addison-Wesley, 1991).

Roger G. Ibbotson and Gary P. Brinson, *Global Investing* (New York: McGraw-Hill, 1993).

Piet Sercu and Raman Uppal, *International Financial Markets and the Firm* (Cincinnati: Southwestern, 1995).

J. Orlin Grabbe, *International Financial Markets* (New York: Elsevier Science, 1996).

2. Foreign stock market indices are studied in:

Campbell R. Harvey, "The World Price of Covariance Risk," *Journal of Finance* 46, no. 1 (March 1991): 111–157.

Richard Roll, "Industrial Structure and the Comparative Behavior of International Stock Market Indices," *Journal of Finance* 47, no. 1 (March 1992): 3–41.

3. Investing internationally in bonds has been recently studied by:

Kenneth Cholerton, Pierre Pieraerts, and Bruno Solnik, "Why Invest in Foreign Currency Bonds?" *Journal of Portfolio Management* 12, no. 4 (Summer 1986): 4–8.

Haim Levy and Zvi Lerman, "The Benefits of International Diversification of Bonds," *Financial Analysts Journal* 44, no. 5 (September–October 1988): 56–64.

Paul Burik and Richard M. Ennis, "Foreign Bonds in Diversified Portfolios: A Limited Advantage," *Financial Analysts Journal* 46, no. 2 (March–April 1990): 31–40.

Roger G. Ibbotson and Laurence B. Siegel, "The World Bond Market: Market Values, Yields, and Returns," *Journal of Fixed Income* 1, no. 1 (June 1991): 90–99.

Victor S. Filatov, Kevin M. Murphy, Peter M. Rappoport, and Russell Church, "Foreign Bonds in Diversified Portfolios: A Significant Advantage," *Financial Analysts Journal* 47, no. 4 (July–August 1991): 26–32.

Mark Fox, "Different Ways to Slice the Optimization Cake," *Financial Analysts Journal* 47, no. 4 (July–August 1991): 32–36.

Richard M. Ennis and Paul Burik, "A Response from Burik and Ennis," *Financial Analysts Journal* 47, no. 4 (July–August 1991): 37.

Fischer Black and Robert Litterman, "Asset Allocation: Combining Investors Views with Market Equilibrium," *Journal of Fixed Income* 1, no. 2 (September 1991): 7–19.

Shmuel Hauser and Azriel Levy, "Effect of Exchange Rate and Interest Rate Risk on International Fixed-Income Portfolios," *Journal of Economics and Business* 43, no. 4 (November 1991): 375–388.

Mark R. Eaker and Dwight M. Grant, "Currency Risk Management in International Fixed-Income Portfolios," *Journal of Fixed Income* 1, no. 3 (December 1991): 31–37.

Steven Dym, "Global and Local Components of Foreign Bond Risk," *Financial Analysts Journal* 48, no. 2 (March–April 1992): 83–91.

John Markese, "Foreign Bond Funds: What Are You Buying Into?" *AAII Journal* 14, no. 10 (November 1992): 28–31.

Kent G. Becker, Joseph E. Finnerty, and Kenneth J. Kopecky, "Economic News and Intraday Volatility in International Bond Markets," *Financial Analysts Journal* 49, no. 3 (May–June 1993): 81–86, 65.

Richard M. Levich and Lee R. Thomas, "The Merits of Active Currency Risk Management: Evidence from International Bond Portfolios," *Financial Analysts Journal* 49, no. 5 (September–October 1993): 63–70.

Claude B. Erb, Campbell R. Harvey, and Tadas E. Viskanta, "Naional Risk in Global Fixed-income Allocation," *Journal of Fixed Income* 4, no. 2 (September 1994): 17–26.

Antti Ilmanen, "Time-varying Expected Returns in International Bond Markets," *Journal of Finance* 50 no. 2 (June 1995): 481–506.

Claude B. Erb, Campbell R. Harvey, and Tadas E. Viskanta, "The Influence of Political, Economic, and Financial Risk on Expected Fixed-income Returns," *Journal of Fixed Income* 6, no. 2 (June 1996): 7–30.

Kenneth J. Winston and Jeffery V. Bailey, "Investment Policy Implications of Currency Hedging," *Journal of Portfolio Mangement* 22, no. 4 (Summer 1996): 50–57.

Richard Cantor and Frank Packer, "Determinants and Impacts of Sovereign Ratings," *Journal of Fixed Income* 6, no. 3 (December 1996): 76–91.

4. Investing internationally in stocks has also been studied recently by:

Jeff Madura and Wallace Reiff, "A Hedge Strategy for International Portfolios," *Journal of Portfolio Management* 12, no. 1 (Fall 1985): 70–74.

Lee R. Thomas III, "Currency Risks in International Equity Portfolios," *Financial Analysts Journal* 44, no. 2 (March–April 1988): 68–71.

Fischer Black, "Universal Hedging: Optimizing Currency Risk and Reward in International Equity Portfolios," *Financial Analysts Journal* 45, no. 4 (July–August 1989): 16–22.

Warren Bailey and Rene M. Stulz, "Benefits of International Diversification: The Case of Pacific Basin Stock Markets," *Journal of Portfolio Management* 16, no. 4 (Summer 1990): 57–61.

Mark R. Eaker and Dwight Grant, "Currency Hedging Strategies for Internationally Diversified Equity Portfolios," *Journal of Portfolio Management* 17, no. 1 (Fall 1990): 30–32.

John E. Hunter and T. Daniel Coggin, "An Analysis of the Diversification Benefit from International Equity Investment," *Journal of Portfolio Management* 17, no. 1 (Fall 1990): 33–36.

Martin L. Leibowitz and Stanley Kogelman, "Return Enhancement from 'Foreign' Assets: A New Approach to the Risk Return Trade-off," *Journal of Portfolio Management* 17, no. 4 (Summer 1991): 5–13.

Mark Eaker, Dwight Grant, and Nelson Woodard, "International Diversification and Hedging: A Japanese and US Perspective," *Journal of Economics and Business* 43, no. 4 (November 1991): 363–374.

Wayne E. Ferson and Campbell R. Harvey, "The Risk and Predictability of International Equity Returns," *Review of Financial Studies* 6, no. 3 (1993): 527–566.

Steven L. Heston and K. Geert Rouwenhorst, "Does Industrial Structure Explain the Benefits of International Diversification?" *Journal of Financial Economics* 36, no. 1 (August 1994): 3–27.

Wayne E. Ferson and Campbell R. Harvey, "Sources of Risk and Expected Returns in Global Equity Markets," *Journal of Banking and Finance* 18, no. 4 (September 1994): 775–803.

Claude B. Erb, Campbell R. Harvey, and Tadas E. Viskanta, "Inflation and World Equity Selection," *Financial Analysts Journal* 51, no. 6 (November–December 1995): 28–42.

Claude B. Erb, Campbell R. Harvey, and Tadas E. Viskanta, "Political Risk, Economic Risk, and Financial Risk," *Financial Analysts Journal* 52, no. 6 (November–December 1996): 29–46.

Claude B. Erb, Campbell R. Harvey, and Tadas E. Viskanta, "Expected Returns and Volatility in 135 Countries," *Journal of Portfolio Management* 22, no. 3 (Spring 1996): 46–59.

5. Many of the previously cited papers include a discussion of hedging foreign exchange risk. For a description, see:

Andre F. Perold and Evan C. Schulman, "The Free Lunch in Currency Hedging: Implications for Investment Policy and Performance Standards," *Financial Analysts Journal* 44, no. 3 (May–June 1988): 45–50.

Fischer Black, "Equilibrium Exchange Rate Hedging," *Journal of Finance* 45, no. 3 (July 1990): 899–907.

Stephen L. Nesbitt, "Currency Hedging Rules for Plan Sponsors," *Financial Analysts Journal* 47, no. 2 (March–April 1991): 73–81.

Ira G. Kawaller, "Managing the Currency Risk of Non-Dollar Portfolios," *Financial Analysts Journal* 47, no. 3 (May–June 1991): 62–64.

Evi Kaplanis and Stephen M. Schaefer, "Exchange Risk and International Diversification in Bond and Equity Portfolios," *Journal of Economics and Business* 43, no. 4 (November 1991): 287–307.

Michael Adler and Bhaskar Prasad, "On Universal Currency Hedges," *Journal of Financial and Quantitative Analysis* 27, no. 1 (March 1992): 19–38.

Mark Kritzman, "… About Currencies," *Financial Analysts Journal* 48, no. 2 (March–April 1992): 27–30.

Mark Kritzman, "The Minimum-risk Currency Hedge Ratio and Foreign Asset Exposure," *Financial Analysts Journal* 49, no. 5 (September–October 1993): 77–79.

Ira G. Kawaller, "Foreign Exchange Hedge Management Tools: A Way to Enhance Performance," *Financial Analysts Journal* 49, no. 5 (September–October 1993): 79–80.

Jack Glen and Philippe Jorion, "Currency Hedging for International Portfolios," *Journal of Finance* 48, no. 5 (December 1993): 1865–1886.

John Markese, "How Currency Exchange Rates Can Affect Your International Returns," *AAII Journal* 16, no. 2 (February 1994): 29–31.

Bernard Dumas and Bruno Solnik, "The World Price of Foreign Exchange Risk," *Journal of Finance* 50, no. 2 (June 1995): 445–479.

Gary L. Gastineau, "The Currency Hedging Decision: A Search for Synthesis in Asset Allocation," *Financial Analysts Journal* 51, no. 3 (May–June 1995): 8–17.

6. International asset allocation has been studied by:

Philippe Jorion, "Asset Allocation with Hedged and Unhedged Foreign Stocks and Bonds," *Journal of Portfolio Management* 15, no. 4 (Summer 1989): 49–54.

Fischer Black and Robert Litterman, "Global Portfolio Optimization," *Financial Analysts Journal* 48, no. 5 (September–October 1992): 28–43.

Patrick Odier and Bruno Solnik, "Lessons for International Asset Allocation," *Financial Analysts Journal* 49, no. 2 (March–April 1993): 63–77.

Bruno Solnik, "The Performance of International Asset Allocation Strategies Using Conditional Information," *Journal of Empirical Finance* 1, no. 1 (June 1993): 33–55.

Philippe Jorion, "Mean/Variance Analysis of Currency Overlays," *Financial Analysts Journal* 50. no. 3 (May–June 1994): 48–56.

7. For an interesting paper that examines the market crash of October 1987 from a worldwide perspective, and three subsequent related papers, see:

Richard Roll, "The International Crash of October 1987," *Financial Analysts Journal* 44, no. 5 (September–October 1988): 19–35.

Mervyn A. King and Sushil Wadhwani, "Transmission of Volatility Between Stock Markets," *Review of Financial Studies* 3, no. 1 (1990): 5–33.

Yasushi Hamao, Ronald W. Masulis, and Victor Ng, "Correlations in Price Changes and Volatility Across International Stock Markets," *Review of Financial Studies* 3, no. 2 (1990): 281–307.

C. Sherman Cheung and Clarence C. Y. Kwan, "A Note on the Transmission of Public Information Across International Stock Markets," *Journal of Banking and Finance* 16, no. 4 (August 1992): 831–837.

(The following paper attempts to find an explanation for the crash in the US: Jeremy J. Siegel, "Equity Risk Premia, Corporate Profit Forecasts, and Investor Sentiment Around the Stock Market Crash of October 1987," *Journal of Business* 65, no. 4 (October 1992): 557–570.

8. In addition to the references provided in footnote 6, emerging markets are also discussed in:

W. Scott Bauman, "Investment Research Analysis in an Emerging Market: Singapore and Malaysia," *Financial Analysts Journal* 45, no. 12 (November–December 1989): 60–67.

Jarrod W. Wilcox, "Global Investing in Emerging Markets," *Financial Analysts Journal* 48, no. 1 (January–February 1992): 15–19.

Warren Bailey and Joseph Lim, "Evaluating the Diversification Benefits of the New Country Funds," *Journal of Portfolio Management* 18, no. 3 (Spring 1992): 74–80.

Arjun B. Divecha, Jamie Drach, and Dan Stefek, "Emerging Markets: A Quantitative Perspective," *Journal of Portfolio Management* 18, no. 1 (Fall 1992): 41–50.

Mark Mobius, *The Investor's Guide to Emerging Markets* (Burr Ridge, IL: Irwin, 1995).

Christopher B. Barry and Larry J. Lockwood, "New Directions in Research on Emerging Capital Markets," *Financial Markets, Institutions & Instruments* 4, no. 5 (1995): 15–36.

Campbell R. Harvey, "Predictable Risk and Returns in Emerging Markets," *Review of Financial Studies* 8, no. 3 (Fall 1995): 773–816.

9. Discussions of international and global factor models can be found in:

Richard Grinold, Andrew Rudd, and Dan Stefek, "Global Factors: Fact or Fiction?" *Journal of Portfolio Management* 15, no. 1 (Fall 1989): 79–88.

Martin Drummen and Heinz Zimmerman, "The Structure of European Stock Returns," *Financial Analysts Journal* 48, no. 7 (July–August 1992): 15–25.

Claude B. Erb, Campbell R. Harvey, and Tadas E. Viskanta, "Country Risk and Global Equity Selection," *Journal of Portfolio Management* 21, no. 2 (Winter 1995): 74–83.

10. For some general thoughts on investing in collectibles and three studies of collectibles (stamps, prints, and paintings), see:

Burton G. Malkiel, *A Random Walk Down Wall Street* (New York: W. W. Norton, 1990), pp. 304–309.

William M. Taylor, "The Estimation of Quality-Adjusted Auction Returns with Varying Transaction Intervals," *Journal of Financial and Quantitative Analysis* 27, no. 1 (March 1992): 131–142.

James E. Pesando, "Art as an Investment: The Market for Modern Prints," *American Economic Review* 83, no. 5 (December 1993): 1075–1089.

William N. Goetzmann, "Accounting for Taste: Art and the Financial Markets Over Three Centuries," *American Economic Review* 83, no. 5 (December 1993): 1370–1376.

11. For a Canadian perspective on the topics covered in this chapter, see:

T. Zouikin, "Is International Investing Losing its Lustre?" *Canadian Investment Review* V, no. 2 (Winter 1992).

H. Chrisman, J-M Suret et K. Belkacem, "Avantages et Limites de la Diversification Internationale: Le Point de Vue Canadien," *Finéco* 2, no. 2 (2ᵉ semestre 1992).

K. P. Ambachtscheer, "Foreign's Outer Limits," *Canadian Investment Review* VII, no. 1 (Spring 1994).

V. Lacroix, "Risk and Reward in Emerging Markets," *Canadian Investment Review* VII, no. 2 (Summer 1994).

J. McDonald and M. Cheung, "Optimizing Exposure to Foreign Securities," *Canadian Investment Review* VII, no. 2 (Summer 1994).

M. Gilroy, "Is There a Role for Foreign Bonds in the Canadian Investment Portfolio?" *Canadian Investment Review* VIII, no. 2 (Summer 1995).

E. Peters, B. Clarke and P. Rathjens, "Taking a Portfolio Global on the Wings of Tactical Asset Allocation," *Canadian Investment Review* VIII, no. 3 (Fall 1995).

K. Ho, M. Milevsky and C. Robinson, "International Diversification and Shortfall Risk," *Proceedings, Administrative Sciences Association of Canada Conference,* St. John's, June 1997.

L. Booth, "The Case Against Foreign Bonds," *Canadian Investment Review* XI, no. 2 (Summer 1998).

Special Report, "The 1998 Global Investment Conference," *Canadian Investment Review* XI, no. 2 (Summer 1998).

Usha Mittoo, "The Winners and Losers of Listing in the US," *Canadian Investment Review* XI, no. 2 (Fall 1998).

Solutions

Selected Solutions to End-of-chapter Questions and Problems

Chapter 1

3. 18.2%

4. a. 30.0%　　**b.** −13.3%　　**c.** 4.0%

8. Small stock average return: 21.23%
Small stock standard deviation: 19.94%
Common stock average return: 15.37%
Common stock standard deviation: 13.65%

Chapter 2

2. Five board lots and one 11-share odd lot

5. Total assets: $15 000
Total liabilities: $6750

6. a. 62.5%　　**b.** 75.0%　　**c.** 57.1%

8. $9.23

9. $30 000

10. 17.1%

11. 74.0%, −26.0%

12. a. 56.0%　　**b.** −65.2%　　**c.** 36.7%, −30.0%

14. Total assets: $18 750
Total liabilities: $12 500

15. a. 25.0%　　**b.** 72.6%

16. Actual margin: 39.5%

17. $53.57

19. −20.0%

20. a. −27.6%　　**b.** 43.6%

22. a. $5400　　**b.** $5500

23. Total assets: $12 750
Total liabilities: $7600

Chapter 3

11. Asked price: $45.19
Bid price: $42.66

Chapter 5

1. a. 7.0%　　**b.** 9.0%

2. $939.26, $1066.23

4. a. 10.0%　　**b.** 9.8%

5. One-year spot rate: 7.5%
Two-year spot rate: 4.0%
Three-year spot rate: 2.8%

6. Three-year discount factor: .810
Four-year discount factor: .731
Five-year discount factor: .650

8. Forward rate from year one to year two: 6.0%
Forward rate from year two to year three: 8.5%
Forward rate from year three to year four: 8.5%

9. One-year spot rate: 10.0%
Two-year spot rate: 9.8%
Three-year spot rate: 9.5%
Four-year spot rate: 9.2%

10. $994.45

11. a. One-year discount rate: .909
Two-year discount rate: .819
Three-year discount rate: .749

b. Forward rate from today to one year. 10.0%
Forward rate from year one to year two: 11.0%
Forward rate from year two to year three: 9.4%

c. $1470.20

12. a. 6.1%　　**b.** 6.2%

13. a. $39 916.80　**b.** $40 195.58

20. Yield on one-year pure-discount bond: 10.0%
Yield on two-year pure-discount bond: 12.0%

Chapter 6

12. 18.3%

13. 35.0%

14. Expected return: 8.5%
Standard deviation: 10.1%

15. Expected return: 17.0%
Standard deviation: 15.4%

18. Covariance: −52.1
Correlation: −.98

19. Covariance: (A, B): .53
Correlation: (A, C): .71
Correlation: (B, C): .21

20. 11.6%

21. Expected return: 5.3%
Standard deviation: 4.7%

24. a. 34.1%   **b.** 25.0%   **c.** 9.2%

25. a. 8.8%   **b.** 4.7%
c. Weight in security A: .556
Weight in security B: .444

Chapter 7

7. Minimum standard deviation: 9.2%
Maximum standard deviation: 23.3%

9. 12.3%

15. 1.03%

17. 19.7%

18. Portfolio 1 standard deviation: 25.0%
Portfolio 2 standard deviation: 22.1%

21. 0.80

22. a. 1325   **b.** 152

Chapter 8

4. a. 17.0%   **b.** 14.0%   **c.** 12.5%

5. Risky portfolio weight: 1.46

6. a. 26.0%   **b.** 18.0%   **c.** 14.0%

7. 11.0%

14. b. Expected return: 9.0%
Standard deviation: 10.2%
c. Expected return: 8.0%
Standard deviation: 7.7%

Chapter 9

10. $\bar{r}_p = 5.0\% + .39\sigma_p$

12. 15.8%

20. 1.03

21. 25.2%

22. c. Security A expected return: 9.4%
Security B expected return: 10.8%

23. b. $\beta_1 = 1.50$
$\beta_2 = 0.60$

25. $\beta_A = 0.74$
$\beta_B = 1.17$

Chapter 10

6. 82% factor related, 18% nonfactor related

7. a. 1069.3   **b.** 43.8   **c.** 33.4%

8. a. 866.1   **b.** 35.5   **c.** 30.0%

9. 22.4%

10. Standard deviation of security A: 28.9%
Standard deviation of security B: 26.3%

11. 22.5, 2.25, 0.225

13. 220, 20

15. Sensitivity to factor 1: 0.28
Sensitivity to factor 2: 4.60
Sensitivity to factor 3: 0.24

17. Expected return: 15.5%
Standard deviation: 15.8%

19. Earnings yield factor value: .243%
Book-price factor value: 4.286%

22. Security A standard deviation: 64.8%
Security B standard deviation: 30.2%
Covariance (A, B): 1936.5

Chapter 11

6. Weight of security B: −.10
Weight of security C: −.10

10. 26.0%

12. $r_f = 5.0\%$

14. 13.6%

15. a. $b_{p1} = 0.0$
$b_{p2} = 0.5$
b. $b_{p1} = 0.0$
$b_{p2} = 1.0$
c. 17.0%
d. 7.0%

16. a. Weight of security A: −.043
Weight of security B: −.019
Weight of security C: .012
b. 0.3%

21. a. $\beta_A = 0.65$
$\beta_B = 1.02$
b. Security A expected return: 9.9%
Security B expected return: 12.1%

22. $\beta_A = 2.08$
$\beta_B = 1.56$

Chapter 12

8. 5.26%, 5.55%

9. a. 6.90%   **b.** 6.82%   **c.** 6.74%

11. a. 15.6%   **b.** 27.3%   **c.** 42.9%

15. 8.1%

22. Nominal value triples in 12.8 years.
Real value triples in 29.5 years.

Chapter 13

1. 16.9%
2. **a.** 13.0%   **b.** 13.6%
10. 12.8%

Chapter 14

1. Bond's intrinsic value: $937.82
2. Bond's intrinsic value: $9358.16
3. **a.** $9366.03   **b.** 12.0%
4. Change in five-year bond's price: −7.6%
   Change in ten-year bond's price: −12.3%
6. 107 basis points
7. **a.** 9.0%   **b.** 12.5%
8. 12.9%
9. Actual yield with 15% reinvestment: 9.7%
   Actual yield with 0% reinvestment: 8.0%
14. 7.6%

Chapter 15

1. $10 000.00, $8770.68, $12 316.36
2. Price of bond A: $10 912.50
   Price of bond B: $10 388.70
3. 5-year bond's price: $713.00
   10-year bond's price: $508.30
   20-year bond's price: $258.40
4. 4-year bond's price change: −11.7%
   15-year bond's price change: −24.6%
5. −7.2%, 8.0%
6. Proportion of 5-year bond's price increase due to change in present value of principal: 79.1%
   Proportion of 20-year bond's price increase due to change in present value of principal: 42.4%
7. 10% coupon bond's price increase: 14.1%
   8% coupon bond's price increase: 14.7%
8. Duration: 2.8 years
   Modified duration: 2.6 years
9. 2.7 years
11. 3.4 years
14. −.98%
23. Overall rate of return: 50.9%

Chapter 16

2. **a.** 750 001   **b.** 500 001   **c.** 1
8. **a.** 1 380 000, $34.78
   b. 1 600 000, $30.00
   c. 400 000, $120.00
9. **a.** 0.05   **b.** $0.476   **c.** $74.00
10. **a.** $6.00   **b.** $35 310.00
    c. $34 050.70   **d.** $34 050.70
12. 0.67
13. 0.84

14. **a.** 1.18   **b.** −0.05
    c. 1.45   **d.** 0.91
23. $308 million
24. **a.** 1.07   **b.** 1.39
25. 0.69

Chapter 17

1. $25.82
2. $1978.10
3. 7.0%
4. **a.** $6.52   **b.** 8.0%
5. $80.00
6. $52.00
7. 12.0%
10. $106.83
11. $70.44
12. **a.** $35.00   **b.** $46.34   **c.** 3.13
13. $73.03
15. $44.00
16. 10.60
17. 27.8%
18. 14.53

Chapter 18

2. **a.** Purchase $400 000 of new equity
   b. Sell $400 000 of existing equity
   c. No action
7. D_1 = $13.0 million
   D_2 = $15.7 million
   D_3 = $15.3 million
   D_4 = $13.6 million
   D_5 = $14.4 million
8. 0.60
17. $4.88
18. SUE_6 = −0.03
    SUE_7 = +1.14
    SUE_8 = +0.77
    SUE_9 = −0.91

Chapter 19

9. $4.87
10. $3.28
11. $5.08
14. .41
15. .40
16. 216 contracts
17. **a.** 5.4%   **b.** 5.94
18. $3.13
19. $12.40
21. **a.** $2.19
25. **a.** $750.00   **b.** $240.00   **c.** $900.66

Chapter 20

5. $0.00, $15 000.00
6. **a.** $1050.00   **b.** $3050.00   **c.** $50.00
12. $4280
13. $5 164 286.00
15. $1.79
16. 4.0%
17. $98.98
19. $20 000.00
21. **a.** 204
27. −40.0%

Chapter 21

1. $17.60
3. **a.** $12.45   **b.** $11.45
6. 8.0%
9. −1.9%
10. Year 1: 6.6%
    Year 2: 14.8%
    Year 3: −2.1%

Chapter 22

8. ROA = 13.7%
   ROA = 41.1%
9. **a.** 15.0   **b.** $6.00   **c.** 5.0
   d. 1.7%   **e.** 25.0%

Chapter 23

7. 64.8
8. 54.0
11. 32.1
12. 8.7%

Chapter 24

1. 12.7%
3. −2.6%
4. 18.8%
5. 10.5%
6. 9.4%
7. **a.** 26.0%   **b.** 22.6%
9. 3.1%
10. 40.7%, 43.0%
20. 0.8%
26. **d.** −0.51%   **e.** 1.11%
27. 3.50, 8.24, 0.35

Chapter 25

6. 29.6%
7. 56.3%
11. 26.3%
15. 17.0%

Index

The page on which the key term is defined is printed in boldface.